Services marketing

A European perspective

To the memory of

Eric Langeard

A European pioneer in services marketing

Services marketing

A European perspective

Christopher Lovelock

Sandra Vandermerwe

Barbara Lewis

FINANCIAL TIMES

Prentice Hall

An imprint of Pearson Education

Harlow, England · London · New York · Reading, Massachusetts · San Francisco · Toronto · Don Mills, Ontario · Sydney
Tokyo · Singapore · Hong Kong · Seoul · Taipei · Cape Town · Madrid · Mexico City · Amsterdam · Munich · Paris · Milan

Pearson Education Limited
Edinburgh Gate
Harlow
Essex CM20 2JE
England

and Associated Companies throughout the world

Visit us on the World Wide Web at:
http://www.pearsoneduc.com

Original third edition entitled *Services Marketing*
published by Prentice Hall Inc.
Copyright © 1996 by Christopher H. Lovelock

This edition published by Prentice Hall Europe © 1999
Authorized for sale only in Europe, the Middle East and Africa

Typeset in 9.5pt Meridien
by Pantek Arts, Maidstone, Kent

Printed and bound in Great Britain
by Ashford Colour Press Ltd, Hampshire

British Library Cataloguing in Publication Data

A catalogue record for this book is available from
the British Library

ISBN: 0-13-095991-X

10 9 8 7 6 5 4 3
05 04 03 02 01

Contents

v

Cases

Preface

The publication of *Services Marketing: A European Perspective* is very timely. Marketing practice in the service sector continues to evolve rapidly and more and more business schools in Europe are offering courses in services marketing. At the same time, a growing number of service industries now find themselves competing in a pan-European environment. With greater academic commitment to the field has come increased student interest in understanding management issues in services. This is not surprising since, following graduation, most of these individuals will be going to work in service industries. Managers already working in those industries report that manufacturing-based models of business practice are not always useful and relevant to them in their work.

Services marketing first emerged as an academic field during the 1970s. It was distinguished from the start by the contributions and collaboration of both European and North American researchers, as well as by active participation from research-oriented business practitioners. Bilingual seminars on services were held in France as early as 1975 under the sponsorship of the Institut d'Administration des Entreprises (Université d'Aix-Marseille). Other service marketing conferences on both sides of the Atlantic brought together Europeans, including members of the Nordic School (representing Finnish and Scandinavian researchers) and North Americans. In recent years, international conferences in locations such as Dublin, La Londe les Maures and Stockholm have drawn participants from around the world.

As defined by government statistics, services account for a major share of the gross domestic product (GDP) in all member nations of the European Union, as well as being responsible for most new jobs created in recent years. Even in developing economies, the contribution made by services to both the GDP and employment is growing rapidly.

The service sector of the economy can best be characterized by its diversity. Service organizations range in size from huge international corporations in such fields as airlines, banking, insurance, telecommunications, hotel chains and freight transport to a vast array of locally owned and operated small businesses, including restaurants, dry cleaners, hairdressers, opticians, repair services, taxis and numerous business-to-business services. Franchised service outlets in a wide array of fields combine the marketing characteristics of a large chain offering a standardized product with the benefits of local ownership and operation of a specific store or office.

Many services are concerned with the distribution, installation and upkeep of physical objects; they include such diverse operations as retailing and warehousing, computer installation and car repair, office cleaning and landscape maintenance. Increasingly, firms that create a time-sensitive physical output, such as printing and photographic processing, describe themselves as being service businesses. Governments and nonprofit organizations are also in the business of providing services, although the extent of such involvement may vary widely from one country to another, reflecting both traditions and political values. In many countries, universities, hospitals and museums are in public ownership or operate on a not-for-profit basis, but for-profit versions of each type of institution also exist.

In Europe – as throughout the world – service industries continue to face dramatic changes in their environment, ranging from developments in computerization and telecommunications (including the internet) to the emergence of pan-European and even global markets for their output. Perhaps the most significant trend – representing both a threat and an opportunity – is the increasingly competitive nature of service markets. The European Commission is vigorously pursuing policies of opening up formerly protected national markets to competition.

Established ways of doing business are no longer adequate. Across Europe and around the world, innovative newcomers offering new standards of service are succeeding in markets where established competitors have failed to please today's demanding customers. In particular, customers now expect higher standards of service quality and greater speed. On the other hand, investments in quality must be made with reference to the returns that can be expected in terms of improved revenues and stronger customer loyalty. To a growing degree, forward-looking firms seek to couple improvements in quality with improvements in productivity. In fact, innovative applications of technology are often the best way to achieve such dual gains.

The first edition of *Services Marketing* (published in 1984, with subsequent editions in 1991 and 1996) was based on the MBA course, Marketing of Services, which Christopher Lovelock developed and taught at Harvard Business School. This European edition represents another substantial revision and update (it anticipates many of the enhancements planned for the fourth American edition to be published in 2000). Prepared by Lovelock as the lead author, in collaboration with Sandra Vandermerwe and Barbara Lewis, it is designed to incorporate European perspectives and examples into each chapter of the text. Many new readings and cases have also been selected with similar objectives in mind.

The theme of this book is that service organizations differ in many important respects from manufacturing businesses, requiring a distinctive approach to planning and implementing marketing strategy. By this, we don't mean to imply that services marketing is uniquely different from goods marketing. If that were true, it would undermine the whole notion of marketing as a coherent management function. Rather, we stress the importance of understanding service organizations on their own terms and then tailoring marketing goals and strategies accordingly. Within this group we include the service divisions of manufacturing firms.

The structure and content of the text has been significantly revised and now comprises 16 chapters. The 14 readings, reprinted from leading international journals and other sources, collectively embrace important insights and research by leading academics and thoughtful practitioners on both sides of the Atlantic. Finally, there are 19 cases, half of which are quite short, prepared in response to professors' and lecturers' requests for a combination of both simple and complex case materials. These cases cover a wide array of industries and service marketing situations, with the great majority having European settings. Both cases and readings were selected for their ability to complement or reinforce issues raised in the chapters (and most are cross-referenced within those chapters). Researchers will find many useful references at the end of each chapter and in several of the articles. There is also a detailed index (covering not only the text but also the readings and cases) at the end of the book.

Recognizing that this book will be used in many different countries, we have anticipated the introduction of the euro (€) by employing it in the text chapters as the unit of value for examples relating to cost and pricing. Throughout the chapters, wherever monetary amounts are given in a specific currency, such as dollars, pounds or francs, we have added the euro equivalent, using the exchange rates prevailing against the ECU (European Currency Unit) in mid-October 1998. We also use both metric and imperial measures in the chapters. Finally, please note that the term 'billion' denotes 1,000 million.

Acknowledgements

Over the years, many colleagues in both the academic and business worlds have provided us with valuable insights into the management and marketing of services, through their writings or in conference and seminar discussions. They include John Bateson of Gemini Consulting, Leonard Berry of Texas A&M University, David Bowen of Thunderbird Graduate School of Management, Steven Brown and Mary Jo Bitner of Arizona State University, Pierre Eiglier of Université d'Aix-Marseille III, Ray Fisk of the University of New Orleans, Jean-Paul Flipo of ESC Lyon, Mark Gabbott of Monash University, Christian Grönroos of the Swedish School of Economics (in Finland), Gillian Hogg of the University of Stirling, Robert Johnston of the University of Warwick, Jean-Claude Larréché of INSEAD, Theodore Levitt, James Heskett, Earl Sasser and Leonard Schlesinger of Harvard Business School, David Maister of Maister Associates, 'Parsu' Parasuraman of the University of Miami, Paul Patterson of the University of New South Wales, Frederick Reichheld of Bain & Co., Roland Rust of Vanderbilt University, Benjamin Schneider of the University of Maryland, Rhett Walker of the University of Tasmania, Charles Weinberg of the University of British Columbia, Lauren Wright of California State University at Chico, and Valarie Zeithaml of the University of North Carolina.

Among those to whom we are grateful for having made specific suggestions or contributions to this book are Liam Glynn of University College Dublin, Denis Lapert of Groupe ESC Reims, Marika Taishoff of Imperial College, London, and Jochen Wirtz of the National University of Singapore. We are especially appreciative of the many helpful comments and suggestions offered by our reviewers, Gary Akehurst of the University of Portsmouth, UK, Klaes Eringa of the Christelijke Hogeschool Noord-Nederland, Leeuwarden, the Netherlands, Evert Gummesson of Stockholm University, Sweden, Jan Moorhouse of Thames Valley University, London, UK, and Tiure Ylikoski, of the Helsinki School of Economics and Business Administration, Finland.

We are also grateful to the authors of the readings and cases, who are listed in the section 'About the authors and contributors', as well as to the copyright holders of these materials for their permission to republish them here.

Our thanks go, too, to our editor at Prentice Hall Europe, Julia Helmsley, and to members of the production team: Alison Stanford, production editor, and Jill Birch, project editor.

Finally, we would like to pay a special tribute to the late Eric Langeard, who died on 27 November 1998, shortly before this book went to press. Energetic, insightful and creative, Eric was truly one of the European pioneers of services marketing. He taught for many years at IAE, Université d'Aix-Marseille III, working closely with his colleague Pierre Eiglier, with whom he developed the concept of the 'servuction' system to represent customer involvement in the visible elements of service operations and delivery. Eric played a very important role in building early but highly durable bridges between European and North American service researchers. In addition to holding visiting appointments overseas, he was actively involved in a collaborative research programme at the Marketing Science Institute in Cambridge, Massachusetts from 1977 to 1981. Eric will be remembered by his numerous friends not only for his research contributions but also for his lively presence at IAE's biennial services seminar, which he co-founded and which drew researchers to France from around the world. We dedicate this book to his memory.

Christopher Lovelock
Sandra Vandermerwe
Barbara Lewis

Permissions acknowledgements

Grateful acknowledgement is made for permission to reproduce material in this book previously published elsewhere. Every effort has been made to trace the correct copyright holder, but if any have been inadvertently overlooked the publisher will be pleased to make the necessary arrangement at the first opportunity.

About the authors and contributors

∙∙

Christopher Lovelock, one of the pioneers of services marketing, is a British citizen but based in the United States. An author, teacher and consultant, he gives seminars around the world. His past academic career has included 11 years on the faculty of the Harvard Business School, two years as a visiting professor at the International Institute for Management Development (IMD) in Switzerland, and short-term appointments at MIT, Stanford and Berkeley. A frequent visitor to Europe, Dr Lovelock can present in both English and French and has taught on many occasions at INSEAD and the Theseus Institute in France and at Euroforum in Spain. He serves on the editorial board of professional journals published in Britain, Singapore and the United States. Early in his career he worked in marketing jobs in both London and Montreal. Christopher Lovelock is author of 60 articles, over 100 teaching cases, and 20 books, including *Services Marketing*, 3rd edition (Prentice-Hall, 1996) and *Product Plus* (McGraw-Hill, 1994). He is a recipient of the *Journal of Marketing*'s Alpha Kappa Psi Award, the American Marketing Association's Award for Career Contributions to the Services Discipline, and many awards for outstanding cases. He holds MA and BCom degrees from the University of Edinburgh, an MBA from Harvard, and a PhD from Stanford.

Sandra Vandermerwe holds the Chair of Management at The Management School, Imperial College, University of London, where she is Professor of International Marketing and Services. She also teaches in executive development programmes at Vrije University, London Business School and Manchester Business School. Previously she spent 10 years as Professor of Marketing and Services at IMD in Switzerland and was Professor of Marketing at Witwatersrand University in South Africa. She also held managerial and executive positions in retailing and marketing research. Her teaching, research and consulting interests emphasize the transformations needed to achieve customer-focused strategies in today's global environment. An Irish citizen, Professor Vandermerwe has won many international awards for her case studies. She is a Fellow of the Royal Society of Arts, Manufactures & Commerce (RSA) and serves on several editorial boards. She has published numerous articles and many books, including *Customer Capitalism* (Nicholas Bradley, 1999) and *From Tin Soldiers to Russian Dolls: Creating Added Value through Service* (Butterworth-Heinemann, 1993). She holds BA and MBA degrees from the University of Cape Town and a DBA in marketing from Stellenbosch University.

Barbara Lewis is Senior Lecturer in Marketing at the Manchester School of Management at UMIST. Her teaching and research has long focused on marketing in the service sector, with recent research emphasizing customer care and service quality. Dr Lewis has published over 100 journal articles and conference papers and recently edited the *Encyclopaedic Dictionary of Marketing* (Blackwell, 1997). She was founder editor of the *International Journal of Bank Marketing*, has edited special issues for a number of marketing journals and currently serves on the editorial board of several prominent journals. An active participant and presenter at conferences in both Europe and the United States, she was responsible for organizing the UK Services Marketing Conference for a number of years. Currently, she is Director of the Customer Research Academy at UMIST. A British citizen, she obtained a BSc from Manchester University, an SM degree from the Sloan School of Management at MIT, and her PhD from Manchester.

Contributors of readings and cases

Kimberley Bechler was formerly a research associate at IMD

Leonard Berry is a professor at Texas A&M University

Mary Jo Bitner is an associate professor at Arizona State University

Martin Bless was formerly a research associate at IMD

Bernard Booms is a professor at Washington State University

Jacques Bouvard is a professor at IMD

Bo Edvardsson is an associate professor at the University of Karlstad

Mark Gabbott is a professor at Monash University

Gard Gabrielsen was formerly at the Manchester School of Management, UMIST

Shikhar Ghosh is chairman of Open Markets

Christian Grönroos is a professor at the Swedish School of Economics, Helsinki

James Heskett is an emeritus professor at the Harvard Business School

Thomas Jones is a professor at the Harvard Business School

Gillian Hogg is a senior lecturer at the University of Stirling

Jean-Claude Larréché is a professor at INSEAD

Gary Loveman is executive vice president, Harrah's Entertainment Inc.

David H. Maister is president of Maister Associates Inc.

Tim Mason is Marketing Director, Tesco plc

Ivor Morgan is a professor at Babson College

Rhys Morgan is a software and IT consultant

Lois A. Mohr is an associate professor at Georgia State University

Jan Olsson is an internal consultant at Swedish Telecom

A. ('Parsu') Parasuraman is a professor at the University of Miami

Delphine Parmenter was formerly a research associate at INSEAD

Earl Sasser is a professor at the Harvard Business School

Leonard Schlesinger is a professor and vice president of development at Brown University

Lynn Shostack is managing director of Joyce International, Inc.

Marika Taishoff is a senior research fellow at Imperial College Management School

Dominique Turpin is a professor at IMD

André Vandermerwe was formerly a professor at IMD

PART i

Understanding services

CHAPTER 1

Distinctive aspects of service management

Learning objectives

After reading and reflecting on this chapter, you should be able to:

1. Describe what kinds of organizations provide services.

2. Recognize the major changes occurring in the service sector.

3. Identify the characteristics that make services different from goods.

4. Understand the 8Ps of integrated services management.

5. Explain why service businesses need to integrate the marketing, operations and human resource functions.

The service revolution

Across Europe – and, indeed, around the world – the service sector of the economy is going through a period of almost revolutionary change in which established ways of doing business continue to be shunted aside. At the turn of a new millennium, all of us are seeing the way we live and work being transformed by new developments in services. Innovators continually launch new ways to satisfy our existing needs and to meet needs that we did not even know we had. (How many of us, ten years ago, ever thought we would need electronic mail?) The same is true of services directed at corporate users.

Although many new service ventures fail, a few succeed. Many long-established firms are also failing – or being merged out of existence; but others are making spectacular progress by continually rethinking the way they do business, looking for innovative ways to serve customers better and taking advantage of new developments in technology.

Consider the following examples:

The Conrad International Dublin, a 5-star hotel in Ireland's capital, has won a significant quality-related award every year since it opened in 1989. The hotel was purpose-built as a luxury hotel and has, of course, all the physical trappings that might be expected of Hilton Hotel Corporation's luxury international brand. But great hotels are made (or broken) by the quality of the personal service provided. The Conrad encourages its guests to expect the highest standards of service, and management equips its employees with the skills needed to meet these expectations. A highly structured approach to staff recruitment, training and development is the natural starting point. 'It all starts with getting the right people,' says the general manager. 'You can teach skills, but what really comes across, especially to business people, is attitude.' Pursuing a strategy of continuous improvement, each department has a detailed training plan and each employee's development needs are assessed regularly in consultation with line managers. A recent 'listening' initiative from the personnel department has led to the creation of a formal channel for staff to communicate ideas for service improvement based on their interactions with guests. In short, a strategy of investing in employee development (and listening to employee feedback) results in better service for customers, making them willing to pay a higher price, more likely to return, and more likely to recommend the hotel to other people.

Albert Heijn BV is the largest supermarket chain in the Netherlands, with 650 branches, an annual turnover of some Fl 12 billion (€5.4 billion), and a 28 per cent market share. To extend its reach (and offer greater convenience for customers) it is working in partnership with other organizations to create mini-stores. It signed an agreement with Shell to set up Miniwinkels stores in 500 filling stations throughout the country. These mini-shops sell about 1,500 different products, including fruit, vegetables and meat. In 1997 it began testing a convenience store in the Academic Hospital in Groningen. Although most patronage comes from hospital staff, some patients shop there too. Other innovations by the chain include home delivery throughout the Netherlands, an on-line home shopping service and experimental store designs.

British Airways, now one of the world's largest and most profitable airlines, was formed in 1972 through the merger of two smaller, government-owned carriers. For many years, it had a reputation for inefficiency and incompetence; in fact, people joked that the initials BA stood for 'bloody awful'. Following major efforts to reduce costs, the airline was privatized, with shares being offered to private investors. Through a series of transformations, every aspect of the airline's operation and the passengers' experience has been improved, with particular attention being paid to recruitment and staff training. BA offers a variety of different service categories, from supersonic Concorde service to the Shuttle, which operates between major British cities. Each class of service is managed as a 'sub-brand', with distinctive, clearly defined features and standards. The airline's reach has been extended through investments in French, German and Australian airlines and partnerships with Canadian, Hong Kong and US carriers. It has also pioneered the use of franchising by licensing several smaller airlines to operate certain European routes in its name, featuring aircraft painted in BA colours and cabin crew trained to offer BA standards of service. In 1997, *Fortune* magazine named British Airways as the world's most admired airline. In 1998, the company launched a new subsidiary airline named GO to compete with the growing number of low-fare airlines in Europe.

Amazon.com likes to describe itself as 'Earth's Biggest Bookstore', yet it has no physical bookshops. Instead, it's a virtual bookshop doing business on the Web and accessible 24 hours a day to anyone in the world who has a computer capable of connecting to the internet. The company opened its 'virtual doors' in the United States in July 1995, and has grown at an extraordinary rate. By mid-1998, Amazon.com stated that it had made sales to more than three million customers in 160 countries, claiming that it was now the leading on-line shopping site. In addition to books, the company offers 125,000 music titles, ten times the number offered by the average music store. Through its web site, customers can search for books by author, title, subject or keyword – or browse for books in 28 subject areas. The software at Amazon.com's user-friendly web site simulates a knowledgeable bookshop assistant. By indicating your mood, preferences and other authors or artists you like, you can get recommendations for new books or music that you might enjoy. Customers are invited to send in their own reviews of books, which visitors to the web site can then compare to those written by professional reviewers. When a customer places an order through the web site, the company arranges for the book, CD or other item to be shipped directly from a warehouse.

Services in the modern economy

As consumers, we use services every day. Turning on a light, watching TV, talking on the telephone, catching a bus, visiting the dentist, posting a letter, getting a haircut, refuelling a car, writing a cheque or sending clothes to the cleaners are all examples of service consumption at the individual level. The institution at which you are studying is itself a complex service organization. In addition to educational services, the facilities at today's colleges and universities usually comprise libraries and cafeterias, counselling services, a bookshop and careers offices, copy services, telephones and internet connections, and maybe even a bank. If you are registered at a residential university, additional services are likely to include halls of residence, health care, indoor and outdoor sports and athletic facilities, a theatre and, perhaps, a post office.

Unfortunately, customers are not always happy with the quality and value of the services they receive. People complain about late deliveries, rude or incompetent personnel, inconvenient service hours, poor performance, needlessly complicated procedures and a host of other problems. They grumble about the difficulty of finding sales assistants to help them in shops, express frustration about mistakes on their credit card bills or bank statements, shake their heads over the complexity of new self-service equipment, mutter about poor value and sigh as they are forced to wait for service or stand in queues almost everywhere they go.

Suppliers of services often seem to have a very different set of concerns. Many complain about how difficult it is to make a profit, how hard it is to find skilled and motivated employees, or how difficult to please customers have become. Some firms seem to believe that the surest route to financial success lies in cutting costs and eliminating 'unnecessary frills'. A few even give the impression that they could run a much more efficient operation if it weren't for all the stupid customers who keep making unreasonable demands and messing things up!

Happily, in almost every field of endeavour there are service suppliers who know how to please their customers while also running a productive, profitable operation, staffed by pleasant and competent employees. By studying organizations such as Conrad International, Albert Heijn, British Airways, Amazon.com and the many others featured in this book, we can draw important insights about the most effective ways to manage the different types of services found in today's economy.

What is a service?

Services have traditionally been difficult to define. Complicating matters further is the fact that the way in which services are created and delivered to customers is often hard to grasp, since many inputs and outputs are intangible. Most people have little difficulty creating simple definitions of manufacturing (physical inputs are processed or assembled in a factory to create goods) or agriculture (live plants are grown and then harvested for use as food or other purposes), but defining *service* can elude them. Here are two approaches that capture the essence.[1]

■ A service is an act or performance offered by one party to another. Although the process may be tied to a physical product, the performance is essentially intangible and does not normally result in ownership of any of the factors of production.

■ Services are economic activities that create value and provide benefits for customers at specific times and places, as a result of bringing about a desired change in – or on behalf of – the recipient of the service.

More amusingly, services have also been described as 'something which can be bought and sold, but which you cannot drop on your foot'.[2]

Understanding the service sector

Services make up the bulk of today's economy across Europe and in developed economies around the world. Changes in the composition of the economy in some European nations have been dramatic over the past three decades (see Table 1.1). These changes reflect a combination of economic growth (in which most of the new value added has come from services) and in some nations a relative or even absolute decline in traditional economic activities such as agriculture, mining and certain types of manufacturing. Some of the changes in manufacturing output can be explained by productivity gains obtained through automation – a substitution of technology for labour – resulting in both fewer workers and lower costs. In other instances, the decline is absolute as certain industries contract.

Not everyone is comfortable with the notion of turning agricultural land into shopping centres and office parks, or of seeing the shrinkage in many European nations of traditionally important industries such as shipbuilding and coal mining. Some people worry about the political implications of being dependent on foreign nations for the supply of strategically important products. However, relaxation of international trade barriers and increasing competition has resulted in significant shifts in economic activity both within Europe and around the world.

As suggested in the footnote to Table 1.1, there are difficulties in measuring economic activity within services, so that comparisons between different European countries should be approached with caution. Based on the data available, Ireland shows the strongest growth in the value added by services as a percentage of GDP, thanks to such factors as a remarkable economic growth rate which has given people more spending power, increased tourism (embracing a variety of service-based industries) and development of such areas as financial services, telecommunications, and customer call centres.

Across Europe, services account for most of the growth in new jobs. Unless you are already predestined for a career in a family manufacturing or agricultural business, the probability is high that you will spend most of your working life in companies (or public agencies and nonprofit organizations) that create and deliver services.

As a national economy develops, the relative share of employment between agriculture, industry (including manufacturing and mining) and services changes dramatically. Figure 1.1 shows how the evolution to a service-dominated employment base is likely to take place over time as per capita income rises. In most countries, the service sector of the economy is very diverse, comprising a wide array of different industries that sell to individual consumers, business customers and to numerous government agencies.

It comes as a surprise to most people to learn that the dominance of the service sector is not limited to highly developed nations. For instance, World Bank statistics show that the service sector accounts for more than half the GNP and employs more than half the labour force in many Latin American and Caribbean nations, too.[3] In many of these countries, there is a large 'underground economy' which is not

Table 1.1 ■ Share of GDP and employment accounted for by services in different European countries

Value added by services as a percentage of Gross Domestic Product in 1994, 1980 and 1960[a]

	1994	1980	1960
Ireland	83	n.a.	52
France	70	62	50
Netherlands	70	n.a.	45
Denmark	69	65	58
Sweden	68	62	53
United Kingdom	66	55	54
Austria	64	56	42
Finland	63	51	48
Hungary	60	n.a.	n.a.
Italy	60	55	47
Czech Republic	55	30[b]	n.a

Source: The Economist Pocket Europe in Figures, 1997.

a. Caution should be used in interpreting these data since they are based on national government statistics whose collection procedures and classification criteria may not be consistent across countries, or even across time within the same country.
b. Data for Czechoslovakia before partition.

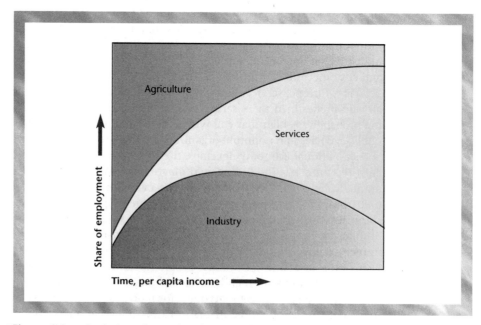

Figure 1.1 ■ Evolution of a service-dominated employment base

captured in official statistics. In Mexico, it has been estimated that as much as 40 per cent of trade and commerce is 'informal'.[4] Significant service output is created by undocumented work in domestic jobs (e.g., cook, housekeeper, gardener) or small, cash-based enterprises such as restaurants, laundries, boarding houses and taxis.

Studies suggest that parallel situations prevail to varying degrees in many European countries. Technology and specialized skills enable many people to earn their living (or to supplement it) through service-based self-employment from their homes; the resulting income is relatively easy to conceal. *The Economist* reports that the underground (or shadow) economy is believed to range from about 14 per cent in Germany to as much as 25 per cent of GDP in Italy (which even adjusts its official statistics upwards to take account of missing output).[5] In Russia, it is thought that the underground economy may be as large as the official one.

Service organizations range in size from huge international corporations like airlines, banking, insurance, telecommunications, hotel chains and freight transportation to a vast array of locally owned and operated small businesses, including restaurants, laundries, taxis, opticians and numerous business-to-business services. Franchised service outlets – in fields ranging from fast foods to bookkeeping – combine the marketing characteristics of a large chain that offers a standardized product with local ownership and operation of a specific facility. Some firms that create a time-sensitive physical product, such as printing or photographic processing, are now describing themselves as service businesses, because much of the value added is created by speed, customization and convenient locations. Regis McKenna has written, 'Companies best equipped for the twenty-first century will consider investment in real time systems as essential to maintaining their competitive edge and keeping their customers.'[6]

There's a hidden service sector, too, within many large corporations, classified by government statisticians as being in manufacturing, agricultural or natural resources industries. So-called *internal services* cover a wide array of activities, potentially including recruitment, publications, legal and accounting services, payroll administration, office cleaning, landscape maintenance, freight transport and many other tasks. To a growing extent, organizations are choosing to outsource those internal services that can be performed more efficiently by a specialist subcontractor. Internal services are also being spun out as separate service operations offered in the wider marketplace. For instance, Ciba-Geigy, the Swiss-based pharmaceutical company, did this successfully with both their advertising department and their information unit.[7]

As such tasks are outsourced, they become part of the competitive marketplace and are therefore more likely to be categorized as contributing to the services component of the economy. Even when such services are not outsourced, however, managers of the departments that supply them would do well to think in terms of providing good service to their internal customers.

Governments and nonprofit organizations are also in the business of providing services, although the extent of such involvement may vary widely from one country to another, reflecting both tradition and political values. In many countries, colleges, hospitals and museums are in public ownership or operate on a not-for-profit basis, but for-profit versions of each type of institution also exist.

Service customers are not limited to individual consumers and households. Organizations of all types buy services, too. An important group of services consists of what are known as advanced producer services, whose principal function is to provide intermediate inputs into the production processes of client firms. They include advertising and market research; architectural and property-related services; banking, legal, computer and financial services; insurance; consultancy; and secretarial services. It used to be thought that most such services were consumed by manufacturing firms, but research in Leeds and Sheffield showed that the service sector (including government agencies) was more important as a source of clients for suppliers of advanced producer services.[8] In other words, the growth of the service sector is itself a stimulus for additional business-to-business services.

The evolving environment of services

Around the world, innovative newcomers offering new standards of service have succeeded in markets where established competitors have failed to please today's demanding customers. Many barriers to competition are being swept away, allowing the entry of eager newcomers, ranging from tiny start-up operations like garden maintenance or baby-sitting services to well-financed multinational firms importing service concepts previously developed and tested in other countries. Established businesses often find it hard to maintain customer loyalty in the face of competition from innovative firms offering new product features, improved performance, price-cutting, clever promotions and the introduction of more convenient, technology-driven delivery systems.

Depending on the industry and the country in which the service firm does business, the underlying causes of such changes may include any of the twelve forces listed in Table 1.2. Like the factors underlying any revolution, some of the origins of today's service sector revolution go back a number of years, whereas others reflect a chain of relatively recent events that continues to unfold.

Let's look at each of these dynamics in more detail.

Table 1.2 ■ Forces for change in service management

- Changing patterns of government regulation.
- Relaxation of professional association restrictions on marketing.
- Privatization of some public and nonprofit services.
- Technological innovations.
- Growth of service chain and franchise networks.
- Internationalization and globalization.
- Pressures to improve productivity.
- The service quality movement.
- Expansion of leasing and rental businesses.
- Manufacturers as service providers.
- Need for public and nonprofit organizations to find new income.
- Hiring and promotion of innovative managers.

Changing patterns of government ownership and regulation

Traditionally, many service industries were highly regulated. Government agencies set price levels, placed geographic constraints on distribution strategies and, in some instances, even defined the product attributes. Since the late 1970s, there has been a trend in the USA and Europe towards partial or complete deregulation in a number of major service industries. Further relaxation of regulations on trade in services between members of the European Union has already started to reshape the economic landscape of Europe. Meanwhile, in Latin America, democratization and new political initiatives are creating economies that are much less regulated than in the past. Reduced government regulation has already eliminated or minimized many constraints on competitive activity in such industries as airfreight, airlines, railways, road transport, banking, securities, insurance and telecommunications. Barriers to entry by new firms have been dropped in many instances, geographic restrictions on service delivery have been reduced, there is more freedom to compete on price and existing firms have been able to expand into new markets or new lines of business.

But reduced regulation is not an unmixed blessing. Fears have been expressed that if successful firms become too large – through a combination of internal growth and acquisitions – there may eventually be a decline in the level of competition. Conversely, lifting restrictions on pricing may benefit customers in the short run as competition cuts prices, but may leave insufficient profits for needed future investments. For instance, fierce price competition among American domestic airlines led to huge financial losses within the industry, bankrupting several airlines. This made it difficult for unprofitable carriers to invest in new aircraft and raised worrying questions about service quality and safety. Profitable foreign airlines, such as British Airways and Singapore Airlines, gained market share by offering better service than American carriers on international routes. Of course, not all regulatory changes represent a relaxation of government rules. In many countries, steps continue to be taken to strengthen consumer protection laws, to safeguard employees, to improve health and safety, and to protect the environment.

Privatization

The term 'privatization' was coined in Great Britain to describe the policy of transforming government organizations into investor-owned companies. Led by Britain, privatization of public corporations has been moving rapidly ahead in a number of countries across Europe, as well as in Canada, Australia, New Zealand and, more recently, in some Asian and Latin American states. The transformation of such service operations as national airlines, telecommunication services and utilities such as gas, electricity and water into private enterprise services has led to restructuring, cost-cutting and a more market-focused posture. When privatization is combined with a relaxing of regulatory barriers to allow entry of new competitors, as in the British telecommunications or water industries, the marketing implications can be dramatic. The privatization of utilities has led to a trend towards international ownership, which many authorities see as irreversible.[9]

Privatization can also apply to regional or local government departments. At the local level, for instance, services such as refuse collection and cleaning have been shifted from the public sector to private firms. Not everyone is convinced, however, that such changes are beneficial to all sectors of the population. When services are provided by public agencies, there are often cross-subsidies, designed to achieve broader social goals. With privatization, there are fears that the search for efficiency and profits will lead to cuts in service and price increases. The result may be to deny less affluent segments the services they need at prices they can afford. Hence the argument for continued regulation of prices and terms of service in key industries such as healthcare, telecommunications, water, electricity and passenger rail transportation.

Technological innovations

New technologies are radically altering the ways in which many service organizations do business with their customers – as well as what goes on behind the scenes. Perhaps the most powerful force for change today comes from the integration of computers and telecommunications. Companies operating information-based services, such as financial service firms, are seeing the nature and scope of their businesses totally transformed by the advent of national (or even global) electronic delivery systems, including the internet and its best-known component, the World Wide Web. For instance, Amazon.com delivers the same product to customers as a traditional bookshop, but in a very different context. Although booklovers may complain that it cannot offer the chance to browse the shelves of a friendly bookshop and leaf through a book, Amazon.com offers far more choice and convenience, global access and often lower prices.

Technological change affects many other types of services, too, from airfreight to hotels to retail stores. Express courier firms such as TNT, DHL, FedEx and UPS, for instance, recognize that the ability to provide real-time information about customers' packages has become as important to success as the physical movement of those packages. Technology does more than enable the creation of new or improved services. It may also facilitate re-engineering of such activities as delivery of information, order-taking and payment, enhance a firm's ability to maintain more consistent service standards, permit the creation of centralized customer service departments, allow replacement of personnel by machines for repetitive tasks and lead to greater involvement of customers in operations through self-service technology.

Growth of service chains and franchise networks

More and more services are being delivered through national or even global chains. Respected brand names such as Burger King, Body Shop, Crédit Suisse, Hertz, Ibis, Lufthansa and Mandarin Oriental Hotels have spread far from their original roots. In some instances, such chains are entirely company-owned; in others, the creator of the original concept has entered into partnerships with outside investors. *Franchising* involves the licensing of independent entrepreneurs to produce and sell a branded service according to tightly specified procedures. It is an increasingly popular way to finance the expansion of multi-site service chains that deliver a consistent service concept. Large franchise chains are replacing (or absorbing) a wide array of small, independent service businesses in fields as diverse as bookkeeping, car hire, dry-cleaning, hairdressing, photocopying, plumbing, fast-food restaurants and estate agency services. Among the requirements for success are the creation of mass media advertising campaigns to promote brand names nationwide (and even worldwide), standardization of service operations, formalized training programmes, a never-ending search for new products, continued emphasis on improving efficiency and dual marketing programmes directed at customers and franchisees, respectively.

Internationalization and globalization

The internationalization of service companies is readily apparent to any tourist or business executive travelling abroad. Airlines and airfreight companies that were formerly just domestic in scope today have extensive foreign route networks. Numerous financial service firms, advertising agencies, hotel chains, fast-food restaurants, car hire agencies and accounting firms now operate on several continents. This strategy may reflect a desire to serve existing customers better, to penetrate new markets, or both. The net effect is to increase competition and encourage the transfer of innovation in both products and processes from country to country. Many well-known service companies in Europe are foreign-owned; examples include Citicorp, McDonald's, Andersen Consulting, TNT, Harrods and Four Seasons Hotels. In turn, Americans are often surprised to learn that Burger King and Holiday Inn are both owned by British companies. A walk round many of the world's major cities quickly reveals numerous famous service names that originated in other parts of the globe. Franchising allows a service concept developed in one country to be delivered around the world through distribution systems owned by local investors.

Internationalization of service businesses is being facilitated by free trade agreements – such as those between Canada, Mexico and the United States (NAFTA), between the South American countries comprising Mercosur or Pacto Andino, and, of course, between the 15 current member states of the European Union. However, there are fears that barriers will be erected to impede trade in services between free trade blocs and other nations, as well as between the blocs themselves. Developing a strategy for competing effectively across numerous different countries is becoming a major marketing priority for many service firms.

Pressures to improve productivity

With increasing competition, often price-based, has come greater pressure to improve productivity. Demands by investors for better returns on their investments have also fuelled the search for new ways to increase profits by reducing the costs of service delivery. Historically, the service sector has lagged behind the manufacturing sector in productivity improvement, although there are encouraging signs that some services are beginning to catch up, especially when allowance is made for simultaneous improvements in quality. Using technology to replace labour (or to permit customer self-service) is one cost-cutting route that has been followed in many industries. Re-engineering of processes often results in speeding up operations by cutting out unnecessary steps. However, managers need to be aware of the risk that cost-cutting measures driven by finance and operations personnel without regard for customer needs may lead to a perceived deterioration in quality and convenience.

The service quality movement

The 1980s were marked by growing customer discontent with the quality of both goods and services. Many of the problems with manufactured products concerned poor service at the retail point-of-purchase and with difficulties in solving problems, obtaining refunds or getting repairs made after the sale. Service industries such as banks, hotels, car hire firms, restaurants and telephone companies were as much criticized for human failings on the part of their employees as for failures on the technical aspects of service.

With the growing realization that improving quality was good for business and necessary for effective competition, a radical change in thinking took place. Traditional notions of quality (based on conformance to standards defined by operations managers) were replaced by the new imperative of letting quality be customer-driven, which had enormous implications for the importance of service marketing and the role of customer research in both the service and manufacturing sectors.[10] Numerous firms have invested in research to determine what their customers want on every dimension of service, in quality improvement programmes designed to deliver what customers want, and in regular measurement of how satisfied their customers are with the quality of service received.[11]

Expansion of leasing and rental businesses

Leasing and rental businesses represent a marriage between service and manufacturing businesses. Increasingly, both corporate and individual customers find that they can enjoy the use of a physical product without actually owning it. Long-term leases may involve use of the product alone – such as a lorry – or provision of a host of related services at the same time. In road transport, for instance, full-service leasing provides almost everything, including painting, washing, maintenance, tyres, fuel, licence fees, road service, substitute vehicles and even drivers. In the UK, as the home improvement and the do-it-yourself markets have grown, many entrepreneurs have gone into business to rent electrical and mechanical equipment ranging from carpet cleaners and hedge trimmers to power tools, wallpaper strippers and cement mixers.

Personnel, too, can be hired for short periods rather than employed full-time, as evidenced by the growth of firms supplying temporary workers, from secretaries to security guards (whom Americans sometimes refer to jokingly as 'rent-a-cops'). Europe is following practices that have long prevailed in Canada and the United States, with more students becoming part-time workers.

Manufacturers as service providers

Service profit centres within manufacturing firms are transforming many well-known companies in fields such as computers, motor vehicles and electrical and mechanical equipment. Supplementary services once designed to help sell equipment – including consultation, credit, transportation and delivery, installation, training and maintenance – are now offered as profit-seeking services in their own right, even to customers who have chosen to purchase competing equipment.

Several large manufacturers (including General Electric, Ford and Mercedes) have become important players in the global financial services industry as a result of developing credit financing and leasing divisions. Similarly, numerous manufacturing firms now seek to base much of their competitive appeal on the capabilities of their worldwide consultation, maintenance, repair and problem-solving services. In fact, service profit centres often contribute a substantial proportion of the revenues earned by such well-known 'manufacturers' as IBM, Hewlett-Packard and Rank Xerox.

Pressures on public and nonprofit organizations to find new income sources

The financial pressures confronting public and nonprofit organizations are forcing them not only to cut costs and develop more efficient operations, but also to pay more attention to customer needs and competitive activities. In their search for new sources of income, many 'nonbusiness' organizations are developing a stronger marketing orientation, which often involves rethinking their product lines, adding profit-seeking services such as shops, retail catalogues, restaurants and consultancy, becoming more selective about the market segments they target and adopting more realistic pricing policies.[12]

As the costs of staging soccer matches has risen (not least because of the sharp rise in players' salaries), many football clubs across Europe have become highly marketing-oriented. A growing number engage in significant merchandising activities, with shops selling goods from replica football strips to babywear. New or renovated stadia now feature restaurants and special spectator boxes that can be sold or rented to companies.

Hiring and promotion of innovative managers

Traditionally, many service industries were very inbred. Managers tended to spend their entire careers working within a single industry, even within a single organization. Each industry was seen as unique and outsiders were suspect. Relatively few managers possessed graduate degrees in business, such as an MBA, although they might have held an industry-specific diploma in a field such as hotel management or healthcare administration. In recent years, however, competition and enlightened self-interest have led companies to recruit better qualified managers who are willing to question traditional ways of doing business and able to bring new ideas from previous work experience in another industry. In retail banking, for instance, senior managers in fields such as marketing are sometimes recruited from fast-moving consumer goods companies. And within many firms, intensive training programmes are now exposing employees at all levels to new tools and concepts.

None of the industries in the service sector find themselves untouched by some of the factors described above. In many industries, notably transportation and financial services, several elements are converging – like a gale, a new moon and heavy rains – to produce a flood tide that will wreck organizations whose management seeks to maintain the status quo. Other managers with more foresight recognize, like Shakespeare's Brutus, that a tide taken at the flood can lead to fortune. But where does this tide lead and what does it imply for the role of marketing in the service sector? We've described some of the challenges facing service managers, but these changes also bring opportunities.

Marketing services versus physical goods

The dynamic environment of services today places a premium on effective marketing. Although it's still very important to run an efficient operation, that no longer guarantees success. The service product must be tailored to customer needs, priced realistically, distributed through convenient channels and actively promoted to customers. New market entrants are positioning their services to appeal to specific market segments through their pricing, communication efforts and service delivery, rather than trying to be all things to all people. But are the marketing skills that have been developed in manufacturing companies directly transferable to service organizations? The answer is often no, because marketing management tasks in the service sector tend to differ from those in the manufacturing sector in several important respects.

Basic differences between goods and services

Every *product* – a term that we use in this book to describe the core output of any type of industry – delivers benefits to the customers who purchase and use them. *Goods* can be described as physical objects or devices, while *services* are actions or performances.[13] Early research into services sought to differentiate them from goods, focusing particularly on four generic differences, referred to as intangibility, heterogeneity (or variability), perishability of output and simultaneity of production and consumption.[14] Although these characteristics are still cited, researchers such as Grönroos qualify these descriptions and admit that they do not apply in all circumstances.[15] More practical insights are provided in Table 1.3, which lists nine basic differences that can help us to distinguish the tasks associated with marketing and managing services from those involved with physical goods.

It's important to note that in identifying these differences we're still dealing with generalizations that do not apply equally to all services. (In Chapter 2, we classify services into distinct categories, each of which presents somewhat different challenges for marketers and other managers.) Let's examine each characteristic in more detail.

Customers do not obtain ownership of services

Perhaps the key distinction between goods and services lies in the fact that customers usually derive value from services without obtaining permanent ownership of any tangible elements. In many instances, service marketers offer customers the opportunity to rent the use of a physical object like a car or hotel room, or to hire for a short period of time the labour and expertise of people whose skills range from brain surgery to knowing how to check customers into a hotel. As a purchaser of services yourself, you know that while your main interest is in the final output, the way in which you are treated during service delivery can also have an important impact on your satisfaction.

Table 1.3 ■ Basic differences between goods and services

- Customers do not obtain ownership of services.
- Service products are intangible performances.
- There is greater involvement of customers in the production process.
- Other people may form part of the product.
- There is greater variability in operational inputs and outputs.
- Many services are difficult for customers to evaluate.
- There is typically an absence of inventories.
- The time factor is relatively more important.
- Delivery systems may involve both electronic and physical channels.

Service products as intangible performances

Although services often include tangible elements – such as sitting in an airline seat, eating a meal or getting damaged equipment repaired – the service performance itself is basically an intangible. The benefits of owning and using a manufactured product come from its physical characteristics (although brand image may convey benefits, too). In services, the benefits come from the nature of the performance. The notion of service as a performance that cannot be touched or wrapped up and taken away leads to the use of a theatrical metaphor for service management, visualizing service delivery as like the staging of a play, with service personnel as the actors and customers as the audience. (We'll discuss the managerial implications of this metaphor in Chapter 10.)

Rental services include a physical object like a car or a power tool. But marketing a car hire performance is very different from attempting to market the sale (or long-term lease) of the physical object on its own. For instance, when hiring a car for a short period which might range from just one day to a couple of weeks, customers usually reserve a particular category of vehicle, rather than a specific brand and model. Instead of worrying about colours and upholstery, customers focus on such elements as price, the location and appearance of pickup and delivery facilities, extent of insurance coverage, cleanliness and maintenance of vehicles, provision of free shuttle buses at airports, availability of 24-hour reservations service; hours when rental offices are staffed, and quality of service provided by customer-contact personnel. By contrast, the core benefit derived from owning a physical good normally comes specifically from its tangible elements, even though it may also provide intangible benefits, too. An interesting way to distinguish between goods and services is to place them on a scale from tangible dominant to intangible dominant (illustrated in Figure 1.2).[16]

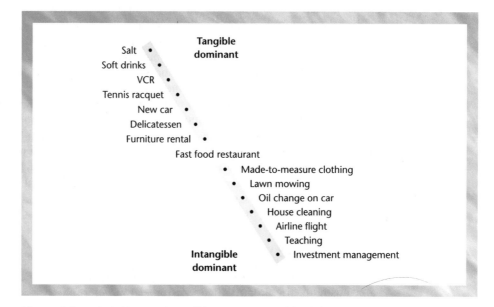

Figure 1.2 ■ Dominance of tangible versus intangible elements

Customer involvement in the production process

Performing a service involves assembling and delivering the output of a mix of physical facilities and mental or physical labour. Often customers are actively involved in helping to create the service product – either by serving themselves (as in using a launderette or withdrawing money from an automated cash machine (ATM)) or by cooperating with service personnel in settings such as hairdressers, hotels, colleges or hospitals. Under such circumstances, service firms have much to gain from trying to educate their customers so as to make them more competent.[17] As we shall see in Chapter 2, services can be categorized according to the extent of contact that the customer has with the service organization. Changing the nature of the production process often affects the role that customers are asked to play in that process.

People as part of the product

In high-contact services, customers not only come into contact with service personnel, but they may also rub shoulders with other customers (literally so, if they travel by bus or train during the rush hour). The difference between service businesses often lies in the quality of employees serving customers. It can be a challenging task to manage service encounters between customers and service personnel in ways that will create a satisfactory experience. Similarly, the type of customers who patronize a particular service business helps to define the nature of the service experience. If you go to a soccer match, the behaviour of the fans can be a big bonus and add to the excitement of the game if they are enthusiastic but well-behaved. But if some of them become rowdy and abusive, it can detract from the enjoyment of other spectators at the stadium. For good or ill, other customers become part of the product in many services.

Greater variability in operational inputs and outputs

The presence of personnel and other customers in the operational system makes it difficult to standardize and control *variability* in both service inputs and outputs. Manufactured goods can be produced under controlled conditions, designed to optimize both productivity and quality, and then checked for conformance with quality standards long before they reach the customer. (Of course, their subsequent use by customers will vary widely, reflecting customer needs and skills, as well as the nature of the usage occasion.) But when services are consumed as they are produced, final 'assembly' must take place under real-time conditions, which may vary from customer to customer and even from one time of the day to another. As a result, mistakes and shortcomings are both more likely and harder to conceal. These factors make it difficult for service organizations to improve productivity, control quality and offer a consistent product.

However, not all variations in service delivery are necessarily negative and modern service businesses are coming to recognize the value of customizing at least some aspects of the service offering to the needs and expectations of individual customers. In fields such as healthcare, it's essential.[18]

Harder for customers to evaluate

Most physical goods tend to be relatively high in 'search properties'; these are characteristics of the product that a customer can determine prior to purchasing it, such as colour, style, shape, price, fit, feel, hardness or smell. Other goods and some services, by contrast, may emphasize 'experience properties' which can be discerned only after purchase or during consumption; as with taste, wearability, ease of handling, quietness and personal treatment. Finally, there are 'credence properties' – characteristics that customers find hard to evaluate even after consumption. Examples include surgery, professional services such as accountancy, and technical repairs that are not readily apparent.[19]

No stocks for service performances

Because a service is a deed or performance, rather than a tangible item that the customer keeps, it is 'perishable' and cannot be stocked for sale later. Of course, the necessary facilities, equipment and labour can be held in readiness to create the service, but these simply represent productive capacity, not the product itself. Thus an ATM at a bank has the potential to deliver service 24 hours a day, but it cannot create the desired performance of delivering a specified amount of cash from a designated account or accepting a deposit or making a transfer until a customer instructs it to do so. Similarly, the accident and emergency department at a hospital can be staffed with talented medical personnel and equipment, but it can't provide medical care unless patients arrive who need treatment.

Having unused capacity in a service business is rather like running water into a sink without a plug. The flow is wasted unless customers (or possessions requiring service) are present to receive it. On the other hand, when demand exceeds capacity, customers may be kept waiting (unless they leave, feeling disappointed, in search of another provider). An important task for service marketers, therefore, is to find ways of smoothing demand levels to match capacity.

Importance of the time factor

Many services are delivered in real time. Customers have to be physically present to receive service from organizations such as airlines, hospitals, hairdressers and restaurants. There are limits as to how long customers are willing to be kept waiting; further, service must be delivered quickly so that customers do not waste time receiving service. Even when service takes place in the back office, customers have expectations about how long a particular task should take to complete – whether it is repairing a machine, completing a research report, cleaning a suit or preparing a legal document. Today's customers are increasingly time-sensitive and speed is often a key element in good service.

Different distribution channels

Unlike manufacturers, which require physical distribution channels to move goods from factory to customers, many service businesses either use electronic channels (as in broadcasting or electronic funds transfer) or combine the service factory, retail outlet and point of consumption at a single location. In the latter instance, service firms are responsible for managing customer-contact personnel. They may also have to manage the behaviour of customers in the service factory to ensure smoothly running operations and to avoid situations in which one person's behaviour irritates other customers who are present at the same time.

An integrated approach to service management

This book is not just about services marketing. Throughout the chapters, you'll also find continuing reference to two other important functions: service operations and human resource management. Imagine you are the manager of a small travel agency; or think big, say you are the chief executive of a major airline. In both instances, you need to be concerned on a day-to-day basis that your customers are satisfied, that your operational systems are running smoothly and efficiently, and that your employees are not only working productively but are also doing a good job either of serving customers directly or of helping other employees to deliver good service. Even if you see yourself as a middle manager, with specific responsibilities in either marketing, operations or human resources, your success in the job will often involve understanding these other functions and periodic meetings with colleagues working in these areas. In short, integration of activities between functions is the name of the game. If there are problems in any one of these three areas, it may signal financial problems ahead.

The notion of cross-functional collaboration is developed by Christian Grönroos in his article 'From scientific management to service management' (reprinted on pages 66–77). Grönroos and other Nordic researchers have long argued that marketing in a service economy cannot be divorced from other functions and needs to be incorporated in an overall, customer-focused management perspective.

The eight components of integrated service management

When discussing strategies to market manufactured goods, marketers usually address four basic strategic elements: product, price, place (or distribution) and promotion (or communication). Collectively, these four categories are often referred to as the '4Ps' of the marketing mix.[20] However, the distinctive nature of service performances, especially such aspects as customer involvement in production and the importance of the time factor, requires that other strategic elements be included. To capture the nature of this challenge, we will be using the '8Ps' model of *integrated service management*, which highlights eight decision variables facing managers of service organizations (Table 1.4).[21]

Table 1.4 ■ The eight components of integrated service management

- Product elements.
- Place and time.
- Process.
- Productivity and quality.
- People.
- Promotion and education.
- Physical evidence.
- Price and other costs of service.

Product elements

Managers must select the features of both the core product (either a good or service) and the bundle of supplementary service elements surrounding it, with reference to the benefits desired by customers and how well competing products perform.

In short, we need to be attentive to all aspects of the service performance that have the potential to create value for customers.

Place and time

Delivering product elements to customers involves decisions on the place and time of delivery, as well as the methods and channels employed. Delivery may involve physical or electronic distribution channels (or both), depending on the nature of the service being provided. Firms may deliver service directly to customers or through intermediary organizations, such as retail outlets owned by other companies, which receive a fee or percentage of the selling price to perform certain tasks associated with sales, service and customer-contact. Speed and convenience of place and time for the customer are becoming important determinants in service delivery strategy.

Process

Creating and delivering product elements to customers requires the design and implementation of effective processes. A process describes the method and sequence of actions in which service operating systems work. Badly designed processes are likely to annoy customers when the latter experience slow, bureaucratic and ineffective service delivery. Similarly, poor processes make it difficult for front-line staff to do their jobs well, result in low productivity and increase the likelihood of service failures.

Productivity and quality

These elements, often treated separately, should be seen as two sides of the same coin. No service firm can afford to address either element in isolation. Productivity relates to how inputs are transformed into outputs that are valued by customers, while quality refers to the degree to which a service satisfies customers by meeting their needs, wants and expectations. Improving productivity is essential to keep costs under control, but managers must beware of making inappropriate cuts in service levels that are resented by customers (and perhaps by employees, too). Service quality, as defined by customers, is essential for product differentiation and for building customer loyalty. However, investing in quality improvement without understanding the trade-off between incremental costs and incremental revenues may place the profitability of the firm at risk.

People

Many services depend on direct, personal interaction between customers and a firm's employees (like getting a haircut or eating at a restaurant.) The nature of these interactions strongly influences the customer's perceptions of service quality.[22] Customers will often judge the quality of the service they receive largely on their assessment of the people providing the service. Successful service firms devote significant effort to recruiting, training and motivating their personnel, especially – but not exclusively – those who are in direct contact with customers.

Promotion and education

No marketing programme can succeed without effective communications. This component plays three vital roles: providing needed information and advice, persuading target customers of the merits of a specific product, and encouraging them to take action at specific times. In services marketing, much communication is educational in nature, especially for new customers. Companies may need to teach these customers about the benefits of the service, where and when to obtain it, and provide instructions on how to participate in service processes. Communications can be delivered by individuals, such as salespeople and trainers, or through such media as TV, radio, newspapers, magazines, posters, brochures and web sites. Promotional activities may serve to marshal arguments in favour of selecting a particular brand or use incentives to catch customers' attention and motivate them to act.

Physical evidence

The appearance of buildings, landscaping, vehicles, interior furnishing, equipment, staff members, signs, printed materials and other visible cues all provide tangible evidence of a firm's service quality. Service firms need to manage physical evidence carefully, since it can have a profound impact on customers' impressions. In services with few tangible elements, such as insurance, advertising is often employed to create meaningful symbols. For instance, an umbrella may symbolize protection, and a fortress, security.

Price and other costs of service

This component addresses management of the *costs* incurred by customers in obtaining benefits from the service product. Responsibilities are not limited to the traditional pricing tasks of establishing the selling price to customers, setting trade margins and establishing credit terms. Service managers also recognize and, where practical, seek to minimize other costs that customers may bear in purchasing and using a service, including time, mental and physical effort, and unpleasant sensory experiences such as noises and smells.

Linking services marketing, operations and human resources

As shown by the component elements of the 8Ps model, marketing cannot operate in isolation from other functional areas in a successful service organization. Three management functions play central and interrelated roles in meeting customer needs: marketing, operations and human resources. Figure 1.3 illustrates this interdependency. In future chapters, we will be raising the question of how marketers should relate to and involve their colleagues from other functional areas in planning and implementing marketing strategies.

Service firms must understand the implications of the eight components of integrated service management, as described above, in order to develop effective strategies. Firms whose managers succeed in developing integrated strategies will

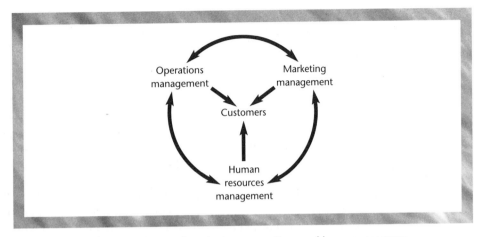

Figure 1.3 ■ Interdependence of marketing, operations and human resources

have a better chance of surviving and prospering. Those that fail to grasp these implications, by contrast, are likely to be outmanoeuvred by competitors who are more adept at responding to the dramatic changes affecting the service economy.

You can expect to see the 8Ps framework used throughout this book. Although any given chapter is likely to emphasize just one (or a few) of the eight components, you should always keep in mind the importance of integrating the component(s) under discussion with each of the others when formulating an overall strategy.

Creating value in a context of values

Managers need to be concerned about giving good value to customers and treating them fairly in decisions involving all elements of the 8Ps. Value can be defined as the worth of a specific action or object relative to an individual's (or organization's) needs at a particular point in time.

Firms create value by offering the types of services that customers need, accurately presenting their capabilities, and delivering them in a pleasing and convenient fashion at a fair price. In return, firms receive value from their customers, primarily in the form of the money paid by the latter to purchase and use the services in question. Such transfers of value illustrate one of the most fundamental concepts in marketing, that of *exchange*, which takes place when one party obtains value from another in return for something else of value. These exchanges aren't limited to buying and selling. An exchange of value also takes place when employees go to work for an organization. The employer gets the benefit of the worker's efforts; in turn, the employee receives wages, benefits and possibly such valued experiences as training, on-the-job experience and working with friendly colleagues.

As a customer yourself, you regularly make decisions about whether or not to invest time, money and effort to obtain a service that promises the specific benefits you seek. Perhaps the service in question solves an immediate need, such as getting a haircut, eating a pizza, repairing your bike or car, or spending a couple of hours at a cinema or another entertainment facility. Alternatively, as with getting an education, you may be prepared to take a long-term perspective before the payoff is realized. But if, after the fact, you find you've had to pay more than you expected or received fewer benefits than anticipated, you're likely to feel cheated. At a minimum, you'll be muttering darkly about 'poor value' (more likely, your discontent will be loudly and colourfully expressed!). If you feel you were badly treated during service delivery, although the service itself provided the desired benefits, you may conclude that this treatment diminished the value received. Alternatively, perhaps you, or people you know, have worked for a company that treated its employees poorly, even to the extent of not computing wages fairly or failing to deliver promised job-related benefits. That's not the best way for management to build employees' commitment to the firm or dedication to serving customers, is it? In fact, customers are quick to pick up on bad vibes from unhappy service workers.

No firm that seeks long-term relationships with either customers or employees can afford to mistreat them or to provide poor value on an ongoing basis. At a minimum, it's bad business; at worst, it's unethical. Sooner or later, shortchanging or mistreating customers and employees is likely to rebound to the firm's disadvantage. Unfortunately, not all firms, employees or even customers have the other parties' best interests at heart. The potential for abusive behaviour is perhaps higher in services than in manufacturing, reflecting the difficulty of evaluating many services in advance (and even after the fact), the need to involve customers in service production and delivery in many instances, and the face-to-face encounters that customers often have with service personnel and other customers.[23]

Hence companies need a set of morally and legally defensible values to guide their actions and to shape their dealings with both employees and customers. A useful way of thinking about 'values' is as underlying beliefs about how life should be lived, how people should be treated (and behave) and how business should be conducted. To the extent possible, managers would be wise to use their firm's values as a reference point when recruiting and motivating employees. They should also clarify the firm's values and expectations in dealing with prospective customers, as well as making an effort to attract and retain customers who share and appreciate those same values.

Businesses and business schools are devoting more attention today to discussions of what constitutes ethical behaviour. However, there's nothing new in the notion of ethical conduct of business affairs, nor in the recognition of the merit of good values. More than 30 years ago, Siegmund Warburg of the investment banking house of S.G. Warburg (now SBC Warburg) remarked that the reputation of a firm for 'integrity, generosity, and thorough service is its most important asset, more important than any financial item. However, the reputation of a firm is like a very delicate living organism which can easily be damaged and which has to be taken care of incessantly, being mainly a matter of human behaviour and human standards.'[24]

What's new today is the greater scrutiny given to a firm's business ethics and the presence of tougher legislation designed to protect both customers and employees from abusive treatment. In this book, we will periodically raise ethical issues as they relate to different aspects of service management. Don't be surprised to find occasional questions relating to ethical practice, as well as some examples and case studies. We'll also look at the responsibility of customers to behave in considerate ways towards suppliers and other customers. In particular, in Chapter 6 we discuss how managers should deal with customers who behave in unethical or abusive ways.

Conclusion

Why study services? Because modern economies are driven by service businesses, both large and small. Services are responsible for the creation of a substantial majority of new jobs, both skilled and unskilled, around the world. The service sector includes a tremendous variety of different industries, including many activities provided by public and nonprofit organizations. It accounts for over half the economy in most developing countries and for around 70 per cent in many highly developed economies.

As we've shown in this chapter, services differ from manufacturing organizations in many important respects and require a distinctive approach to marketing and other management functions. As a result, managers who want their enterprises to succeed cannot continue to rely solely on tools and concepts developed in the manufacturing sector. In the remainder of this book, we'll discuss in more detail the unique challenges and opportunities faced by service businesses. It's our hope that you'll use the material from this text to enhance your future experiences not only as a service employee or manager, but also as a customer of many different types of service businesses!

Study questions

1. Review the definitions of service on pp. 6–7. Do you agree that services are necessarily 'economic activities'?

2. Business schools have traditionally placed more emphasis on manufacturing industries than on service industries in their courses. Why do you think this is so? Does it matter?

3. Why is time so important in services?

4. What are the implications of freer competition for managers in service industries that used to be heavily regulated?

5. Give examples of how, during the past ten years, computer and telecommunications technology has changed some of the services that you use.

6. Choose a service company with which you are familiar and show how each of the eight elements (8Ps) of integrated service management applies.

7. Is the risk of unethical business practices greater or lesser in service businesses than in manufacturing firms. Why (or why not)?

8. Why do marketing, operations and human resources have to be more closely linked in services than in manufacturing? Give examples.

Notes

1. These two definitions are derivatives of a collection of definitions from various sources collected by Christian Grönroos, *Service Management and Marketing*, Lexington, MA: Lexington Books, 1990, pp. 26–7.

2. Evert Gummesson, 'Lip Service – A Neglected Area in Services Marketing', *Journal of Services Marketing*, No. 1, 1987, p. 22 (referring to an unidentified source).

3. World Bank, *El Mundo del Trabajo en una Economia Integrada*, Washington DC 1995.
4. Javier Reynoso, 'The Evolution of Services Management in Developing Countries: Insights from Latin America', in Tony Meenaghan (ed.), *New and Evolving Paradigms: The Emerging Future of Marketing*, Dublin: American Marketing Association and University College Dublin, 1997, pp. 112–21 (published on CD-ROM).
5. 'Light in the Shadows: So Nothing is Uncertain except Death and Taxes? Look at the Growth of the Underground Economy and Think Again about Taxes', *The Economist*, 3 May 1997.
6. Regis McKenna, *Real Time*, Boston: Harvard Business School Press, 1997.
7. Sandra Vandermerwe, 'Making Internal Services More Market Driven', *Business Horizons*, Vol. 32, No. 6, November–December 1989, pp. 83–9; 'Ciba-Geigy Allcomm (A), (B)', Lausanne: IMD, 1992.
8. L.E. Juleff-Tranter, 'Advanced Producer Services: Just a Service to Manufacturing?', *The Service Industries Journal*, Vol. 16, July 1996, pp. 389–400.
9. Simon Holberton, 'Utilities: Privatisation is an Irreversible Trend', *Financial Times*, 19 September 1997.
10. See, for example, Valarie A. Zeithaml, A. Parasuraman and Leonard L. Berry, *Delivering Quality Service*, New York: The Free Press, 1990; Sandra Vandermerwe, 'The Market Power is in the Services Because the Value is in the Results', *European Management Journal*, Vol. 8, No. 4.
11. See, for example, Barbara R. Lewis, 'Customer Care in Services', in W.J. Glynn and J.G. Barnes, *Understanding Services Management*, Chichester: John Wiley & Sons, 1995.
12. Christopher H. Lovelock and Charles B. Weinberg, *Public and Nonprofit Marketing*, 2nd edition, Redwood City, CA.: The Scientific Press/Boyd and Davis, 1989; and Philip Kotler and Alan Andreasen, *Strategic Marketing for Nonprofit Organizations*, 5th edition, Upper Saddle River, NJ: Prentice-Hall, 1996.
13. Leonard L. Berry, 'Services Marketing is Different', *Business*, May–June 1980.
14. W. Earl Sasser, R. Paul Olsen and D. Daryl Wyckoff, *Management of Service Operations: Text, Cases, and Readings*, Boston: Allyn & Bacon, 1978.
15. Grönroos, *op.cit.*, p. 29.
16. G. Lynn Shostack, 'Breaking Free from Product Marketing', *Journal of Marketing*, April 1977.
17. Bonnie Farber Canziani, 'Leveraging Customer Competency in Service Firms,' *International Journal of Service Industry Management*, Vol. 8, No. 1, 1997, pp. 5–25.
18. Curtis P. McLaughlin, 'Why Variation Reduction is Not Everything: A New Paradigm for Service Operations', *International Journal of Service Industry Management*, Vol. 7, No. 3, 1996, pp. 17–31.
19. This section is based on Valarie A. Zeithaml, 'How Consumer Evaluation Processes Differ between Goods and Services', in J.A. Donnelly and W.R. George, *Marketing of Services*, Chicago: American Marketing Association, 1981, pp. 186–90.
20. The 4Ps classification of marketing decision variables was created by E. Jerome McCarthy, *Basic Marketing: A Managerial Approach*, Homewood, IL: Richard D. Irwin, Inc., 1960.
21. The 8Ps model of integrated service management was introduced in Christopher Lovelock and Lauren Wright, *Principles of Service Marketing and Management* (Upper Saddle River: Prentice Hall, 1999). It represents an extension and enhancement of the 7Ps model created by Bernard H. Booms and Mary Jo Bitner, 'Marketing Strategies and Organizational Structures for Service Firms', in *Marketing of Services* (eds), J.H. Donnelly and W.R. George (Chicago: American Marketing Association, 1981), pp. 47–51.
22. For a review of the literature on this topic, see Michael D. Hartline and O.C. Ferrell, 'The Management of Customer Contact Service Employees', *Journal of Marketing*, Vol. 60, No. 4, October 1996, pp. 52–70.
23. K. Douglas Hoffman and John E.G. Bateson, 'Ethical Issues in Services Marketing', Chapter 6 in *Essentials of Services Marketing*, New York: The Dryden Press, 1997, pp. 100–20.
24. Cited in a presentation by Derek Higgs, London, September 1997.

CHAPTER **2**

Customer involvement in service processes

Learning objectives

After reading and reflecting on this chapter, you should be able to:

1. Appreciate the value of classification in services marketing.

2. Understand useful ways of classifying differences between various types of services.

3. Define a service process.

4. Describe four different types of service processes and their implications for management strategy.

5. Recognize that the nature of a customer's contact with a service varies according to the underlying process.

A busy day for Anna Claes

Anna Claes, a business student, had breakfast and then turned on the TV to watch the weather forecast. It forecast rain, so she grabbed an umbrella before leaving the flat that she shared with three fellow students and walking to the bus stop for her daily journey to the university. On the way, she posted a letter. The bus arrived on time. It was the usual driver, who recognized her and gave a cheerful greeting as she showed her monthly pass. The bus was quite full, carrying a mix of students and office workers, so she had to stand.

Arriving at her destination, Anna left the bus and walked to the business school. Joining a throng of other students, she took a seat in the large classroom where her finance class was held. The professor lectured in a near-monotone for 75 minutes, occasionally projecting charts on the large screen to illustrate certain calculations. Anna reflected that it would be just as effective – and far more convenient – if the course were transmitted by TV or recorded on videotapes that students could watch at their leisure. She much preferred the marketing course which followed, since this professor was a very dynamic individual who believed in having an active dialogue with students. Anna made several contributions to the discussion and felt that she learned a lot from listening to others' analyses and viewpoints.

For lunch, she and three friends went to eat at the recently modernized Student Union. The old cafeteria, a gloomy place that served unappetizing food at high prices, had been replaced by a well-lit and colourfully decorated new food hall, featuring a variety of small kiosks. These included both local suppliers and brand-name fast-food chains, which offered choices ranging from burgers to sandwiches as well as health foods and a variety of desserts. Although she had wanted a sandwich, the queue of waiting customers at the sandwich shop was rather long, so Anna joined her friends at Burger King and then splurged on a caffé latte from the adjacent coffee stand. The food court was unusually crowded today, perhaps because of the rain now pouring down outside. When they finally found a table, however, they had to clear off the dirty trays. 'Lazy slobs!' commented her friend Marc, referring to the previous customers.

After lunch, Anna stopped at the cash machine, inserted her bank card and withdrew some money. Remembering that she had a job interview at the end of the week, she telephoned her hairdresser from a payphone and counted herself lucky to be able to make an appointment for later in the day, thanks to a cancellation by another client. Leaving the union, she ran across the rain-soaked plaza to the Language Department. In preparation for her next class, Commercial German, she spent an hour in the language lab, watching an engaging videotape of customers making purchases at different types of store, then repeating key phrases and listening to her own, recorded voice. 'My accent's definitely getting better!' she said to herself.

The class over, it was time for her haircut and shampoo. The hair salon was within walking distance. She liked the interior, which had bright, trendy decor and well-groomed, friendly staff. Unfortunately, her hairdresser was running late and so Anna had to wait 20 minutes, which she used to review a chapter for tomorrow's human relations course. Some of the other waiting customers were reading magazines provided by the salon. Eventually, it was time for a shampoo, after which the hairdresser suggested a slightly different cut from her usual one, to which Anna agreed; but she drew the line at the suggestion that she have a colour tint. She sat very still, watching the process in the mirror and turning her head when requested. She was pleased with the result and complimented the hairdresser on her work. Including the shampoo, the process had lasted about 40 minutes. She tipped the woman and paid at the reception desk.

The rain had stopped and the sun was shining as Anna left the hair salon, so she walked home, stopping on the way to pick up some clothes from the cleaners. This shop was rather gloomy, smelled of cleaning solvents and badly needed repainting. She was annoyed to find that although her silk blouse was ready as promised, the suit she would need for her interview was not. The assistant, who had dirty fingernails, mumbled an apology in an insincere tone without making eye-contact. Although the shop was conveniently located and the quality of work quite good, Anna considered the employees to be unfriendly and not very helpful. Back at the block of flats where she lived, she opened the letter box in the entrance hallway and collected the mail for herself and her flatmates. Her own mail, which was rather dull, included a quarterly bill from her insurance company, which required no action since she had signed an agreement to deduct the funds automatically from her bank account. There was also a postcard from her optician, reminding her that it was time to make an appointment to have her eyes tested. Anna made a mental note to call for an appointment, anticipating that she might need a revised prescription for her contact lenses. Among the other letters was a flyer promoting a new dry cleaning store and including a coupon for a discount. She decided to try the new firm and pocketed the coupon.

Since it was her turn to cook dinner, Anna wandered into the kitchen and started looking in the kitchen cupboards and then the refrigerator to see what was available. Hmm . . . not much. Maybe she should make a salad and telephone for home delivery of a large pizza.

How do services differ from one another?

The service sector is amazingly varied, and the array of transactions made by Anna Claes represents only a small sample of all the services directed at individual consumers. As a review of the listings in your local Yellow Pages (or commercial telephone directory) will show, there are also vast numbers of business services directed at corporate purchasers. It's surprising how many managers in service businesses consider their industries to be unique – or at least distinctively different. Certainly, there are distinctions to be drawn, but it would be a mistake to assume that any one service used by Anna has nothing in common with any of the others she might use.

In Chapter 1, we looked at some of the ways in which services might differ from goods. In this chapter, our focus will be on developing useful ways of grouping services into categories that share managerially relevant characteristics, particularly as these relate to marketing strategy. We'll find that important insights can be gained by looking for similarities between 'different' service industries. The more service managers can identify meaningful parallels to their own firm's situations, the better their chances of beating the competition by taking good ideas from other businesses and applying them to their own. One hallmark of innovative service firms is that their managers have been willing to look outside their own industries for useful ideas that they can try in their own organizations. We'll start our search for useful categorization schemes by examining how goods have traditionally been classified.

The value of classification schemes

Marketing practitioners have long recognized the value of developing distinctive strategies for different types of goods. One of the most famous classification schemes divides goods into convenience, shopping and speciality categories, according to how frequently consumers buy them and how much effort they are prepared to put into comparing alternatives and locating the right product to match their needs.[1] This scheme helps managers obtain a better understanding of consumer expectations and behaviour and provides insights into the management of retail distribution systems. This same classification can also be applied to retail service institutions. For instance, a bank ATM is a convenience service, a package holiday is a shopping service and obtaining a skilled barrister to defend or prosecute a complex legal case is an example of a speciality service. In each instance, the task of finding the desired service has been made somewhat easier by the internet, which enables customers to use search engines and web sites to identify and evaluate alternative suppliers.

Another major classification is between durable and nondurable goods. Durability is closely associated with purchase frequency, which has important implications for development of both distribution and communications strategy. Although service performances are intangible, the durability of benefits is relevant to repurchase frequency. For example, you will probably purchase a haircut less often than you buy a caffé latte (at least if you are a typical student or a coffee connoisseur!).

Yet another classification is consumer goods (those purchased for personal or household use) versus industrial goods (those purchased by companies and other organizations). This classification relates not only to the types of goods purchased – although there is some overlap – but also to methods for evaluating competing alternatives, purchasing procedures, the size of purchase orders and actual usage behaviour. Once again, this classification is transferable to services. For example, you may be the only one involved in a decision about which internet provider to select for use with your own computer. But a corporate decision about choice of online services for use by employees may involve managers and technical specialists from several departments. Business-to-business services, as the name suggests, comprise a large group of services targeted at corporate customers and may range from executive recruiting to security and from payroll management to sandblasting.

While these goods-based classification schemes are helpful, they don't go far enough in highlighting the key strategic issues facing service managers. We need to classify services into marketing-relevant groups, looking for points of similarity between different industries. We can use the insights from these classifications to help us focus on marketing strategies that are relevant to specific service situations.

How might services be classified?

The traditional way of grouping services is by industry. Service managers may say: 'We're in the transportation (or hospitality, or banking, or telecommunications or repair and maintenance) business.' These groupings help us to define the core products offered by the firm and to understand both customer needs and competition. However, they may not capture the true nature of each business within the industry, since service delivery can differ widely even within a single category. For example, food can be provided to customers in settings ranging from a McDonald's at Heathrow Airport to an exclusive Paris restaurant bearing the coveted Michelin 3-star rating. Various proposals have been made for classifying services.[2] Among the meaningful ways in which services can be grouped or classified are those listed in Table 2.1 and discussed below.

The degree of tangibility or intangibility of service processes

Does the service do something physical and *tangible* (like food services or dry cleaning), or do its processes involve a greater amount of *intangibility* (like teaching or telephoning)? Different service processes not only shape the nature of the service delivery system but also affect the role of employees and the experience of customers.

Who or what is the direct recipient of the service process?

Some services, like hairdressing or public transport, are directed at customers themselves. In other situations, customers seek services (like dry cleaning) to restore or improve objects that belong to them, but remain uninvolved themselves in the process of service delivery and do not consume the benefits until later. The nature of the service encounter between service suppliers and their customers varies widely according to the extent to which customers themselves are integrally involved in the service process. Contrast Anna's extended interactions with the hairdresser and her brief encounter with the letter box to post a letter on her way to the university.

The place and time of service delivery

When designing delivery systems, service marketers must ask themselves whether customers need to visit the service organization at its own sites (as Anna did with

---

Table 2.1 ■ Selected ways of classifying services

- Degree of tangibility of service processes.
- Who or what is the direct recipient of the service process?
- The place and time of service delivery.
- Customization versus standardization.
- Nature of the relationship with customers.
- Extent to which demand and supply are in balance.
- Extent to which facilities, equipment and people are part of the service experience.

the university, the hairdresser and the cleaners) or whether service should come to the customer (like the pizza delivery to her flat). Or perhaps the interaction can occur through physical channels like postal delivery (as with her insurance) or electronic channels (as with her banking transaction). These managerial decisions involve consideration of the nature of the service itself, where customers are located (both home and workplace may be relevant), their preferences relating to time of purchase and use, and the relative costs of different alternatives.

Customization versus standardization

Services can be classified according to the degree of *customization* or *standardization* involved in service delivery. An important marketing decision is whether all customers should receive the same service or whether service features (and the underlying processes) should be adapted to meet individual requirements. Anna's insurance policy is probably one of several standard options. The bus service is standardized with a fixed route and timetable (unlike a taxi), but passengers can choose when to ride and where to get on and off. By encouraging student discussion and debate, Anna's marketing professor is offering a more customized course than her finance professor. Her haircut is customized (although other young women may wear the same style) and her future eye test will follow standardized procedures but must come up with a customized diagnosis if the prescription for her new contact lenses is to be accurate.

Nature of the relationship with customers

Some services involve a formal relationship, in which each customer is known to the organization and all transactions are individually recorded and attributed (like Anna's bank or optician). But in other services, unidentified customers undertake fleeting transactions and then disappear from the organization's sight (for instance, the phone company has no record of her call from the union pay-phone, nor the TV station of her watching the weather forecast). As we shall see in Chapter 6, some services lend themselves naturally to a 'membership' relationship in which customers must apply to join the 'club' and their subsequent performance is monitored over time (as in insurance or college enrolment). Other services, like buses, hairdressers, dry cleaners and restaurants need to undertake proactive efforts to create an ongoing relationship. Although the bus company does not record her rides, it can keep records of all monthly pass holders so that it can post passes every month; it could include a newsletter describing service improvements or route and timetable changes. Sometimes companies create special club membership or frequent-user programmes to reward loyal users. For instance, both the hairdresser and the cleaner could record customers' names and addresses and periodically make them special offers.

Extent to which demand and supply are in balance

Some service industries face steady demand for their services while others encounter significant fluctuations. In Chapter 13, we address the problem faced by marketers when the demand for service fluctuates widely over time. In such situations, either capacity must be adjusted to accommodate the level of demand or marketing strategies must be implemented to predict, manage and smooth demand levels to bring them into balance with capacity. On a wet day, more students are eating lunch at the union at Anna's university and so there are queues at the sandwich bar and tables are hard to find.

Extent to which facilities, equipment and people are part of the service experience

Customers' service experiences are shaped, in part, by the extent to which they are exposed to tangible elements in the service delivery system (the bus that Anna rides is very tangible, as are her classrooms, the table and chairs in the food hall, and the videorecorder in the language lab). By contrast, the physical evidence of her insurance company may be limited to occasional letters and she may see little more of her bank than monthly statements and the cash machine that she uses at the union.

The cheerful bus driver humanizes Anna's bus ride. She appears to think better of her dynamic marketing professor than her dull finance professor. She likes her trendy hair salon and the friendly woman who cuts her hair, but not the smelly dry-cleaning shop and its surly employees, even though the quality of cleaning is good; when the cleaner fails to deliver her suit on time and, coincidentally, she receives a discount coupon in the post from a competitor, she's ready to switch.

The service classification strategies we've just discussed can help managers better answer the following questions: 'What does our service operation actually do? What sorts of processes are involved in creating the core product that we offer to customers? And speaking of customers, where do they fit in our operation?' The answers will differ depending on the nature of the underlying service process required to create and deliver a particular service. So now we turn to the most fundamental of the 8Ps of integrated service management: the *processes* by which service products are created and delivered.

Service as a process

Marketers don't usually need to know the specifics of how physical goods are manufactured – that's the responsibility of the people who run the factory. However, the situation is different in services. Because customers are often involved in service production, marketers do need to understand the nature of the processes to which their customers may be exposed. A process is a particular method of operation or a series of actions, typically involving multiple steps that often need to take place in a defined sequence. Think about the steps that Anna went through at the hair salon: phoning in advance to make an appointment, arriving at the salon, waiting, having a shampoo, discussing options with the hairdresser, having her hair cut and styled, tipping, paying and finally leaving.

Service processes range from relatively simple procedures involving only a few steps – such as filling a car's tank with petrol – to highly complex activities like transporting passengers on an international flight. In later chapters, we show how these processes can be represented in diagrams known as flowcharts that help us to understand what is going on (and perhaps how a specific process might be improved).

Categorizing service processes[3]

A process implies taking an input and transforming it into output. But if that's the case, then what is each service organization actually processing and how does it perform this task? Two broad categories of things get processed in services: people and objects. In many cases, ranging from passenger transportation to education, customers themselves are the principal input to the service process (as in Anna's haircut); in other instances, the key input is an object like a malfunctioning computer or a piece of financial data. In some services, as in all manufacturing, the process is physical: something tangible takes place. But in information-based services, the process can be intangible.

By looking at services from a purely operational perspective, we see that they can be categorized into four broad groups. Table 2.2 shows a four-way classification scheme based on tangible actions either to people's bodies or to customers' physical possessions and intangible actions to people's minds or to their intangible assets. Each of these four categories involves fundamentally different forms of processes,

Table 2.2 ■ Understanding the nature of the service act

What is the nature of the service act?	Who or what is the direct recipient of the service?	
	People	Possessions
Tangible actions	*(People processing)*	*(Possession processing)*
	Services directed at people's bodies:	*Services directed at physical possessions:*
	Passenger transportation	Freight transportation
	Healthcare	Repair and maintenance
	Lodging	Warehousing/storage
	Beauty salons	Office cleaning services
	Physical therapy	Retail distribution
	Fitness centres	Laundry and dry cleaning
	Restaurants/bars	Refuelling
	Hairdressers	Landscaping/gardening
	Funeral services	Disposal/recycling
Intangible actions	*(Mental stimulus processing)*	*(Information processing)*
	Services directed at people's minds:	*Services directed at intangible assets:*
	Advertising/PR	Accounting
	Arts and entertainment	Banking
	Broadcasting/cable	Data processing
	Management consulting	Data transmission
	Education	Insurance
	Information services	Legal services
	Music concerts	Programming
	Psychotherapy	Research
	Religion	Securities investment
	Voice telephone	Software consulting

with vital implications for marketing, operations and human resource managers. We will refer to the categories as: people processing; possession processing; mental stimulus processing; and information processing. Although the industries within each category may appear, at first sight, to be very different, analysis will show that they do, in fact, share important, process-related characteristics. As a result, managers in one industry may be able to obtain useful insights from studying another one and then create valued innovations for their own organization.

1. People processing involves tangible actions to people's bodies

Examples of people processing services include passenger transportation, hairdressing and dentistry. Customers need to be physically present throughout service delivery in order to receive the desired benefits of such services.

2. Possession processing includes tangible actions to goods and other physical possessions belonging to the customer

Examples of possession processing include airfreight, lawn mowing and cleaning services. In these instances the object requiring processing must be present, but the customer need not be.

3. Mental stimulus processing refers to intangible actions directed at people's minds

Services in the mental stimulus processing category include entertainment, spectator sports events, theatrical performances and education. In such instances, customers must be present mentally but can be located either in a specific service facility or in a remote location connected by broadcast signals or telecommunication linkages.

4. Information processing describes intangible actions directed at a customer's assets

Examples of information processing services include insurance, banking and consulting. In this category, little direct involvement with the customer may be needed once the request for service has been initiated.

Let's examine why these four different types of processes often have distinctive implications for marketing, operations and human resource strategies.

People processing

From ancient times, people have sought services directed at themselves (for example, being transported, fed, lodged, restored to health or made more beautiful). To receive these types of services, customers must physically enter the service system. Since they are an integral part of the process, they cannot obtain the benefits they desire by dealing at arm's length with service suppliers. They must enter the 'service factory', which is a physical location (sometimes mobile like Anna's bus) where people or machines (or both) create and deliver service benefits to customers. Sometimes, of course, service providers are willing to come to customers, bringing the necessary tools of their trade with them to create the desired benefits in the customers' choice of locations. Examples include doctors who are willing to make house calls and hairdressing or beauty services for infirm residents of nursing homes.

If customers want the benefits that a people-processing service has to offer, they must be prepared to spend time actively cooperating with the service operation. The level of involvement required of customers may entail anything from boarding a city bus for a five-minute journey to undergoing a lengthy course of unpleasant treatments at a hospital. In between these extremes are activities such as ordering and eating a meal, having one's hair washed, cut and styled, and spending a couple of nights in a hotel room. The output from these services (after a period of time that can vary from minutes to months) is a customer who has reached her destination, or satisfied his hunger, or is now sporting clean and stylishly cut hair, or has had a couple of good nights' sleep away from home, or is now in physically better health. Anna cooperates with her stylist by sitting still and turning her head as requested: it's actually her hair that is being processed. She will also have to be part of the process when she visits the optician to have her eyes tested (this time it's her eyes that are being processed).

It's important for managers to think about process and output in terms of what happens to the customer (or other object being processed), because it helps them to identify what benefits are being created. Reflecting on the service process itself helps to identify some of the non-financial costs – time, mental and physical effort, even fear and pain – that customers incur in obtaining these benefits.

Possession processing

Often, customers ask a service organization to provide treatment to some physical possession – this could be anything from a house to a hedge, a car to a computer, or a dress to a dog. Many such activities are quasi-manufacturing operations and don't always involve simultaneous production and consumption. Examples include cleaning, maintaining, storing, improving or repairing physical objects – both live and inanimate – that belong to the customer in order to extend their usefulness. Additional possession-processing services include transport and storage of goods, wholesale and retail distribution, and installation, removal and disposal of equipment – in short, the entire value-adding chain of activities that may take place during the lifetime of the object in question.

Customers are less physically involved with this type of service than with people-processing services. Consider the difference between passenger and parcel transportation. In the first instance, you have to go along for the ride in order to obtain the benefit of getting from one location to another. But with parcel service, you hand the package to a clerk at a post office counter (or request that a courier collect it from your home or office) and simply wait for it to be delivered. In most possession-processing services, the customer's involvement is usually limited to dropping off the item that needs treatment, requesting the service, explaining the problem and later returning to pick up the item and pay the bill (like Anna's visit to the dry cleaners to pick up her blouse and suit). If the object to be processed is something that is difficult or impossible to move, like landscaping, installed software, heavy equipment or part of a building, then the 'service factory' must come to the customer, with service personnel bringing the tools and materials necessary to complete the job on-site. If a pipe bursts in Anna's flat, a plumber will have to come and fix it (and the sooner the better!).

In other instances, the service process might involve applying insecticide in a house to get rid of woodworm, trimming a hedge at an office park, repairing a car, installing software in a computer, cleaning a jacket or giving an injection to the family dog. The output in each instance should be a satisfactory solution to a customer's problem or some tangible enhancement of the item in question. In Anna's case, the cleaners let her down because her suit was not ready at the promised time.

Mental stimulus processing

Services that interact with people's minds include education, news and information, professional advice, psychotherapy, entertainment and certain religious activities. Anything touching people's minds has the power to shape attitudes and influence behaviour. So, when customers are in a position of dependency or there is potential for manipulation, strong ethical standards and careful oversight are required.

Receiving these services requires an investment of time on the customer's part. However, recipients don't necessarily have to be physically present in a service factory – just mentally in communication with the information being presented. There's an interesting contrast here with people-processing services. Although passengers can sleep through a flight and still obtain the benefit of arriving at their desired destination, if Anna falls asleep in class or during an educational TV broadcast, she will not be any wiser at the end than at the beginning!

Services such as entertainment and education are often created in one place and transmitted by TV or radio to individual customers in distant locations. However, they can also be delivered to groups of customers at the originating location in a facility such as a theatre or lecture hall. (Anna would prefer the broadcast approach for her finance class.) We need to recognize that watching a live concert on TV in one's home is not the same experience as watching it in a concert hall in the company of hundreds or even thousands of other people. In the latter instance, managers of concert halls find themselves facing many of the same challenges as their colleagues in people-processing services. Similarly, the experience of participating in a discussion-based class through interactive cable TV lacks the intimacy of people debating with each other in the same room.

Since the core content of all services in this category is information-based (whether it's music, voice or visual images), they can easily be converted to digital bits or analogue signals, recorded for posterity, and transformed into a manufactured product, such as a compact disc, videotape or audio-cassette, which may then be packaged and marketed much like any other physical good. These services can thus be 'stocked', since they can be consumed at a later date than they were produced. For instance, Anna's German videotape can be used over and over again by students visiting the language lab.

Information processing

Information processing, one of the buzzwords of our age, has been revolutionized by computers. But not all information is processed by machines: professionals in a wide variety of fields use their brains, too. Information is the most intangible form of service output, but it may be transformed into more enduring, tangible forms as letters, reports, books, tapes or discs. Among the services that are highly dependent on effective collection and processing of information are financial services and professional services like accounting, law, marketing research, management consulting and medical diagnosis.

The extent of customer involvement in both information and mental stimulus processing services is often determined more by tradition and a personal desire to meet the supplier face-to-face than by the needs of the operational process. Strictly speaking, personal contact is quite unnecessary in industries like banking or insurance. Why should managers subject their firm to all the complexities of managing a people-processing service when they could deliver the same core product at arm's length? As a customer, why go to the service factory when there's no compelling need to do so? Anna appears comfortable dealing at arm's length with both her bank and her insurance company, using a self-service cash machine for her banking transactions and receiving communications by post from her insurance company.

Habit and tradition often lie at the root of existing service delivery systems and service usage patterns. Professionals and their clients may say they prefer to meet face-to-face because they feel they learn more about each other's needs, capabilities and personalities that way. However, experience shows that successful personal relationships, built on trust, can be created and maintained purely through telephone or e-mail contact.

Different processes pose distinctive management challenges

The challenges and tasks facing managers who work in each of the four different service categories that we've just described are likely vary to some extent. The classification scheme displayed in Table 2.1 is central to understanding these differences and developing effective service strategies. Not only does it offer insights into the nature of service benefits in each instance, but it also provides an understanding of the behaviour that is required of the customer. There are also implications for developing channel strategy, designing and locating the service delivery system, and using information technology to best advantage.

Identifying service benefits

Managers need to recognize that operational processes, however important, are basically just a means to an end. The key is to understand the specific benefits that a service provides for its users. Many firms bundle together lots of different activities as part of their effort to provide good service. But innovation in service delivery requires that a constant spotlight be focused on the processes underlying delivery of the core product – a bed for the night in the hotel industry, fast transportation of people in the airline industry, or cleaning and pressing clothes in the laundry industry. New technology often allows service organizations to deliver the same (or improved) benefits to customers via distinctly different processes. Sometimes customers are delighted to receive service through faster, simpler, more convenient procedures. However, operations managers need to beware of imposing new processes, in the name of efficiency, on customers who prefer the existing approach (particularly when the new approach relies on technology and equipment to replace personal service by employees). By working with marketing personnel, operations specialists will improve their chances of designing new processes that deliver the benefits desired by customers in user-friendly ways.

Design of the service factory

Every service has customers (or hopes to find some), but not every service interacts with them in the same way. Customer involvement in the core activity may vary sharply for each of the four categories of service process. Nothing can alter the fact that people-processing services require the customer to be physically present within the service factory. If you're currently in Amsterdam and want to be in Toronto tomorrow, you simply can't avoid boarding an international flight and spending time in a jet high above the Atlantic. If you want your hair cut, you can't delegate this activity to somebody else's head – you have to sit in the hairdresser's chair yourself. If you have the misfortune to break your leg, you will personally have to submit to the unpleasantness of having the bone X-rayed, reset by an orthopaedic surgeon and then encased in a protective cast for several weeks.

When customers visit a service factory, their satisfaction will be influenced by such factors as:

- encounters with service personnel,
- appearance and features of service facilities – both exterior and interior,
- interactions with self-service equipment,
- characteristics and behaviour of other customers.

Where customers are required to be physically present throughout service delivery, then the process must be designed around them from the moment they arrive at the service factory. Customers may initially need a parking space (or other assistance in travelling to and from the service facility). The longer they remain on site, the more they are likely to need other services, including hospitality basics like food, beverages and toilets. In many instances, they will have to play active roles in creation and delivery of the service. Well-managed service firms teach their customers how to participate effectively in service operations.

Service delivery sites that customers need to visit must be located and designed with their convenience in mind. If the service factory is noisy, smelly, confusingly laid out and sited in an inconvenient location, then customers are likely to be turned off. Marketing managers need to work closely with their counterparts in operations in order to design facilities that are both pleasing to customers and efficient to operate. The redesigned food hall at the student union replaces a cafeteria that provided a less attractive experience (as well as worse food). The exterior of a building creates important first impressions, while the interior can be thought of as the 'stage' on which the service performance is delivered. The longer customers remain in the factory, and the more they expect to spend, the more important it is to offer facilities that are comfortable and attractive. The interior of Anna's hair salon appeals to her, but that of the dry cleaner does not.

Marketers need to work with human resource managers, too. Here the task is to ensure that those employees who are in contact with customers present an acceptable appearance and have both the personal and technical skills needed to perform well. The staff at the dry cleaners appear to lack such skills. If service delivery requires customers to interact with employees, then both parties may need some basic training or guidance on how to work together cooperatively to achieve the best results. If customers are expected to do some of the work themselves – as in self-service – then facilities and equipment must be user-friendly.

Alternative channels for service delivery

Unlike the situation in people-processing services, managers responsible for possession-processing, mental stimulus-processing, and information-processing services need not oblige their customers to visit a service factory. Instead, they may be able to offer a choice between one of several alternative delivery channels. Possibilities include: (1) letting customers come to a user-friendly factory, (2) limiting contact to a small retail office that is separate from the main factory (or 'back office'), (3) coming to the customer's home or office, and (4) conducting business at arm's length.

Let's take cleaning and pressing of clothes – a possession-processing service – as an example. One approach is to do your laundry at home. If you lack the necessary machines, then you can pay to use a launderette, which is essentially a self-service cleaning factory. If you prefer to leave the task of laundry and dry cleaning to professionals, as Anna does with her best clothes, then you can go to a retail outlet that serves as a drop-off location for dirty clothes and pick-up point for newly cleaned items. Sometimes, cleaning is conducted in the store, at other times, the clothing is transported to an industrial operation some distance away. Home pick-up and delivery is available in some cities, but this service tends to be expensive because of the extra costs involved. Some people will pay a housekeeper or maid to come to their home and do their laundry and ironing (usually in conjunction with other household tasks).

Both physical and electronic channels allow customers and suppliers to conduct service transactions at arm's length. For instance, instead of shopping at a shopping centre, you can study a printed catalogue and order by telephone for parcel delivery, or you can try shopping on the internet, entering your orders electronically after reviewing your choices on a web site display. Information-based items, like software or research reports, can even be downloaded immediately to your own computer.

Today's managers need to be creative, since the combination of information technology and modern package transportation services like those of FedEx offers many opportunities to rethink the *place and time* of service delivery. Some manufacturers of small pieces of equipment allow customers to bypass retail dealers when a product needs repair. Instead, a courier will pick up the faulty item (suitably packaged, of course), ship it to a repair site and return it a few days later when the problem has been fixed. Electronic distribution channels offer even more convenience, since transportation time can be eliminated. For instance, using telecommunication links, engineers in a central facility (which could even be on the other side of the world) may be able to diagnose problems in defective computers and software at distant customer locations and send signals to correct the defects.

As we noted in Chapter 1, advances in telecommunications and in the design of user-friendly terminals have played an important role in creating new services and new delivery channels for existing services. Later in the book, we describe in more detail some of the key developments that are changing the traditional face of retail banking.

Rethinking service delivery procedures for all but people-processing services may allow a firm to get customers out of the factory and transform a 'high-contact' service into a 'low-contact' one. When the nature of the process makes it possible to deliver service at arm's length, then the design and location of the factory can focus on purely operational priorities. Some industry observers are predicting that by early in the twenty-first century the traditional bank branch will cease to exist and we will be conducting most of our banking transactions via ATMs, telephones or PCs and modems (not everybody agrees with this prediction!). The chances of success in such an endeavour will be enhanced when the new procedures are user-friendly and offer customers greater convenience.

Balancing supply and demand

Sharp fluctuations in demand are a bane in the lives of many managers. But manufacturing firms can stock supplies of their product as a hedge against fluctuations in demand. This enables them to enjoy the economies derived from operating factories at steady production levels. Few service businesses can do this easily. For example, the potential income from an empty seat on an airliner is lost for ever once that flight takes off. Hotel room-nights are equally 'perishable'. And the productive capacity of a car repair garage is wasted if no cars come in for servicing on a day when the garage is open. Conversely, when demand for service exceeds supply, the excess business may be lost. If someone can't get a seat on one flight, another carrier gets the business or the trip is cancelled. In other situations, customers may be forced to wait in a queue until sufficient productive capacity is available to serve them.

In general, services that process people and physical objects are more likely to face capacity limitations than those that are information based. Radio and television transmissions, for instance, can reach any number of homes within their receiving area or cable distribution network. In recent years, information processing and transmission capacity has been vastly increased by greater computer power, digital switching and the replacement of coaxial cables by fibreoptic ones. Although the surge in demand for internet services is now causing capacity problems on many telecommunication lines, this problem will eventually be resolved through installation of broadband communication capability. Early 1998 saw the introduction of the first transatlantic cable network to cater principally to internet service. The next generation of cables, due to be deployed in 2000–5, is expected to increase transmission capacity tenfold.[4]

However, technology has not found similar ways to increase the capacity of those service operations that process people and their physical possessions without big jumps in costs. So managing demand becomes essential to improving productivity in those types of services that involve tangible actions. Either customers must be given incentives to use the service outside peak periods, or capacity must be allocated in advance through reservations. For example, a golf course may employ both of these strategies by discounting greens fees during off-peak hours and requiring reservations for the busier tee times.

The problem in people-processing services is that there are limits to how long customers will wait in a queue. They have other things to do and become bored, tired, impatient and even hungry. Anna wasn't prepared to wait for a sandwich at the food hall, so opted for a burger instead. One strategy for reducing or eliminating the need for waiting is to institute a reservation system, but the times offered should be realistic. (Note that Anna's hair salon offered appointments but was not running on schedule the day that she visited it.) By contrast, physical possessions rarely suffer if they have to wait (unless they are highly perishable). More relevant to customers is the cost and inconvenience associated with such delays. (How will Anna cope if her suit is not returned from cleaning in time for her job interview?) The issue of demand and capacity management is so central to productive use of assets (and thus profitability) that we'll devote significant coverage to the topic in Chapter 13.

People as part of the product

The more involved customers become in the service delivery process, the more they tend to see of service personnel (the *people* element of the 8Ps). In many people-processing services, customers meet lots of employees and often interact with them for extended periods of time. They are also more likely to run into other customers – after all, many service facilities achieve their operating economies by serving large numbers of customers simultaneously. Anna's bus ride, classes, meal and haircut all involved other customers. When other people become a part of the service experience, they can enhance it or detract from it. Anna enjoyed the comments made by other students in her marketing class. In the food hall, lazy customers had failed to clear their table; so even though they had already left, their behaviour still detracted in a small way from the experience of Anna and her friends. The poor attitude and appearance of the employee at the cleaners compounded the problem of delays in cleaning Anna's suit and may lead to the loss of her custom in the future.

Direct involvement in service production means that customers evaluate the quality of employees' appearance and social skills as well as their technical skills. And since customers also make judgements about other customers, managers find themselves trying to manage customer behaviour, too. Service businesses of this type tend to be harder to manage because of the human element. As a manager, how would you get everyone to clear their table after eating in the food hall? How would you make the staff at the cleaners more friendly? How would you ensure that all bus drivers give a pleasant greeting to passengers boarding their vehicles?

Making the most of information technology

It's clear that *information-based services* (a term that covers both mental stimulus-processing and information-processing services) have the most to gain from advances in information technology, since they allow the operation to be physically separate from customers. Many examples of using *technology* to transform the nature of the core product and its delivery system are based on radio and television. From studio symphony performances to electronic churches to call-in gardening advice programmes, broadcasting – and now interactive cable – have created new ways to bring advice, entertainment, culture and spiritual enlightenment to widely scattered audiences. In many countries, education is offered through electronic channels as an alternative to the traditional mode of face-to-face presentations in a physical class-room. One of the largest efforts of this nature is the Open University (OU) in Great Britain. The OU has been offering degree programmes to students nationwide through the electronic campus of BBC television and radio for over 30 years. Anyone can watch or hear the programmes, of course, but registered students also receive printed course material and communicate with tutors by mail, e-mail or telephone. Distance learning is not confined to degree programmes. In 1998, Plymouth University began a year-long pilot course transmitted by digital satellite TV to train doctors studying for membership of the Royal College of Surgeons.[5] Among the objectives are exposing young doctors to leading surgeons, physicians and radiologists while minimizing the need for travel.

Modern telecommunications and computer technologies allow customers to connect their own computers (or other input–output devices) with the service provider's system in another location. For example, a growing number of web sites allow customers to access information on goods and services and to place orders or reservations. As banks build their internet capability, customers will be able to access their accounts and conduct certain transactions from their home or office computers.

Conclusion

We've shown you in this chapter that while not all services are the same, many do share important characteristics. Rather than focusing on broad distinctions between goods and services, it's more useful to identify different categories of services and to study the marketing, operations and human resource challenges that they raise.

The four-way classification scheme in this chapter focuses on different types of service processes. Some services require direct physical contact with customers (hair-dressing and passenger transport); others centre on contact with people's minds (education and entertainment). Some involve processing of physical objects (cleaning and freight transport); others process information (accounting and insurance). As you can now appreciate, the processes that underlie the creation and delivery of any service have a major impact on marketing and human resources. Process design (or redesign) is not just a task for the operations department. Both managers and employees must understand underlying processes (particularly those in which customers are actively involved), in order to run a service business that is both efficient and user friendly.

Study questions

1. Consider each of the services used by Anna Claes.
   - What needs is she attempting to satisfy in each instance?
   - What alternative product or self-service could solve her need in each instance?
   - What similarities and differences are there between the dry-cleaning store and the hair salon? What could each learn from the other?
2. Make a list of all the services that you have used during the past week. Then categorize them by type of process.
3. Note down the different types of 'service factory' that you visit in the course of a typical month and how many times you visit each type.
4. Review each of the different ways in which services can be classified. How would you explain the usefulness of this framework to managers?
5. Give examples of durable and non-durable benefits in services and describe the implications
6. In what ways does design of the service factory affect (a) customer satisfaction with the service, and (b) employee productivity?
7. Identify what strategies are used by a telephone company, an airline or a restaurant to manage demand.
8. What do you see as the major ethical issues facing those responsible for creating and delivering mental stimulus-processing services?
9. How have other customers affected your own service experiences – either positively or negatively?

Notes

1. Melvin T. Copeland, 'The Relation of Consumers' Buying Habits to Marketing Methods', *Harvard Business Review*, Vol. 1, April 1923, pp. 282–9.

2. See, for example, Christopher H. Lovelock, 'Classifying Services to Gain Strategic Marketing Insights', *Journal of Marketing*, Vol. 47, Summer 1983, pp. 9–20; Christian Grönroos, *Service Management and Marketing*, Lexington, MA: Lexington Books, 1990, pp. 31–4; and Rhian Silvestro, Lyn Fitzgerald, Robert Johnston and Christopher Voss, 'Towards a Classification of Service Processes', *International Journal of Service Industry Management*, Vol. 3, No. 3, 1992, pp. 62–75.

3. These classifications are derived from Lovelock (1983) and represent an extension and adaption of a framework in T.P. Hill, 'On Goods and Services', *Review of Income and Wealth*, Vol. 23, December 1977, pp. 315–38.

4. Alan Cane, 'Transatlantic Internet Cable Goes into Service', *Financial Times*, 5 March 1998, p. 4.

5. Tom Linton, 'Surgical Studies Across the Miles', *Financial Times*, 27 February 1998, p. 13.

Managing service encounters

Learning objectives

After reading and reflecting on this chapter, you should be able to:

1. Recall that the extent of customer contact with a service varies according to the nature of the underlying processes.

2. Recognize that there are significant differences in managing service businesses according to the level of customer contact.

3. Distinguish between backstage and frontstage operations.

4. Understand service encounters, especially in situations where other people are part of the service product.

5. Understand the nature of critical incidents and recognize their significance for customer satisfaction and dissatisfaction.

6. Appreciate the potential role of customers as 'co-producers' of services.

The bank with no branches

'Hello, First Direct. How may I help you?' says a friendly voice to a customer who has telephoned in the middle of the night to conduct some banking transactions. First Direct, a division of Britain's Midland Bank (now a subsidiary of HSBC), has no branches. It serves customers throughout the United Kingdom and abroad from several customer-service call centres located far from the financial power-houses of London.[1]

Many banks now offer telephone service, but it's usually just a supplement to traditional branch operations. But there is a trend in larger banks to offering person-to-person contact by phone 24 hours a day, every day of the year. Bankers from all over the globe come to study First Direct to see what they can learn from the world's first all-telephone bank.

The idea for what became First Direct grew out of research undertaken by Midland Bank in 1988. A national survey of British bank customers revealed some surprising findings:

- 51 per cent of account holders said they would rather visit their branch as little as possible,
- 20 per cent had not visited their branch in the past month,
- 38 per cent said banking hours were inconvenient,
- 27 per cent wished they could conduct more business by telephone (but with a real person).

In response, Midland decided to create a brand new bank without branches. To serve customers entirely by telephone required new processes that would be user-friendly for both staff and customers. As one operations manager remarked, 'We had to be able to respond in seconds, not minutes – normal banking procedures simply did not apply. We had to create a workable system that would be the servant, not the master, of those using it.' Planners travelled widely to find existing computer and telecommunication systems that could deliver service with the speed, productivity and quality needed to attract customers and make the new bank profitable. Access to cash was a simple matter – customers would use a national ATM network.

In recruiting what it called 'banking representatives', First Direct did not look for traditional bank clerks. Instead, it sought people with strong communication abilities to create trust and confidence among customers, who would never meet employees face-to-face and would almost certainly deal with a different staff member every time they called. Another important criterion was excellent listening skills. Intensive training honed these skills and added knowledge of banking products and procedures.

Despite gloomy predictions by traditional bankers and other sceptics that the new venture would soon fail, First Direct has become profitable and successful. Its staffing and transaction costs are sharply below those of conventional banks with branches. A high proportion of its new customers are attracted by recommendations from existing, satisfied customers. The bank anticipates more than one million customers by 2000. More significantly, First Direct has stimulated an industry-wide shift from high-contact bank branches to low-contact banking by telephone plus ATMs. The next step is home-banking by web site.

Summing up the bank's philosophy, a marketing manager remarked: 'People do not see banks as a fundamental part of their lives. We're trying to market First Direct as a background activity. The whole idea . . . is that it's efficient, easy and available when you want it. You simply tap into it and then you go away and do something more interesting.'

Customers and the service operation

Where does the customer fit within a service organization? Addressing this question has important implications for marketers seeking to build profitable relationships with customers, for operations managers seeking to create efficient, convenient, responsive delivery systems, and for human resource managers responsible for selecting, training and motivating service personnel who interact with customers.

This chapter builds on our earlier discussion of processes in Chapter 2 and introduces the notion of a spectrum of customer contact with the service organization that ranges from high to low. We'll show how the extent of customer contact affects the nature of the service encounter as well as strategies for achieving productivity and quality improvements. As you review the contents of the chapter, including its examples, you should be asking yourself how a strategy of reducing (or increasing) the level of customer contact may impact decisions relating to product elements, place and time, people, and physical evidence.

Clearly, First Direct's customers have a different type of relationship with their bank from those who continue to visit a traditional retail bank branch. The former benefit from place and time convenience: they deal with bank personnel at arm's length by using a telephone (which could be anywhere), and are thus saved the time and effort involved in travelling to a service factory. Their only physical contact is with ATMs, which can be found in numerous convenient locations. Customers' impressions of First Direct's operation, therefore, reflect how fast the phone is answered (standards require 75 per cent of all calls to be answered in 20 seconds or less), the courtesy and professionalism of the employee's voice, and the speed with which the desired transactions can be completed.

Visiting a branch involves different and more time-consuming contacts. Customers can only visit a branch during opening hours and may have to travel some distance to get there. They are exposed to the exterior and interior of the building, may have to spend time waiting in a queue with other customers, and deal face-to-face with an employee who, in many banks, will be sitting behind a security grill or glass screen. Many people enjoy the social interaction of visiting a retail outlet, especially if they know the staff members who serve them, and don't trust machines. A recent US study found that 73 per cent of respondents preferred to bank in a staffed branch and 64 per cent said that they would rather not use technology at all for certain types of transactions. On the other hand, this still means that there are tens of millions of people who prefer banking by phone and through automated technology. That's a large market and traditional banks ignore it at their peril.

An important theme in this chapter is that 'high-contact' encounters between customers and service organizations differ sharply from 'low-contact' ones. The four process-based service categories described in Chapter 2 prescribe the minimum level of customer contact needed to obtain service in each instance. However, many service organizations currently provide far higher levels of contact than is theoretically necessary to deliver the service in question. Sometimes these high-contact levels reflect customer preferences for person-to-person service with customer contact personnel. However, in many instances they result from a management decision to continue relying on traditional approaches, instead of re-engineering existing service processes to create innovative, lower-contact approaches. Most banks, for instance, continue to build their strategy around the delivery of people-processing services rather than information-processing services.

Variability is a fact of life in situations where customers differ widely and service personnel interact with those customers on a one-to-one basis.[2] The longer and more actively that customers are involved in the process of service delivery, the greater the likelihood that each customer's experience will be somewhat different from that of other customers (and from previous experiences by the same customer). Not all variations are bad; in fact many customers seek a tailored approach that recognizes them as individuals with distinctive needs. The challenge is for employees to be flexible, treating each person as an individual rather than as a clone of the last customer.[3]

Many service problems revolve around unsatisfactory incidents between customers and service personnel. In an effort to simplify service delivery, improve productivity and reduce some of the threats to service quality, some firms are using technology to minimize or even eliminate contact between customers and employees. Thus, face-to-face encounters are giving way to telephone encounters. Meanwhile, personal service is being replaced by self-service, often through the medium of computers or easy-to-use machines. And web sites are beginning to replace voice telephone contacts for some types of service transactions.

Service encounters: three levels of customer contact

A *service encounter* is a period of time during which customers interact directly with a service.[4] In some instances, the entire service experience can be reduced to a single encounter, involving ordering, payment and execution of service delivery on the spot. In other cases, the customer's experience comprises a sequence of encounters, which may be spread out over a period of time, involve a variety of employees, and even take place in different locations (think about flying on a passenger airline). Although some researchers use the term 'encounter' simply to describe personal interactions between customers and employees,[5] realistically we also need to think about encounters involving interactions between customers and the seller's systems, machinery and routines.[6] Interacting with self-service equipment, voice mail systems, or web sites is an increasingly common form of service encounter. As the level of customer contact with the service operation increases, there are likely to be more and longer service encounters. So we've grouped services into three *levels of customer contact*, representing the extent of interaction with service personnel, physical service elements, or both (see Figure 3.1). Notice the different locations on the chart of traditional retail banking, telephone banking and home banking by web site.

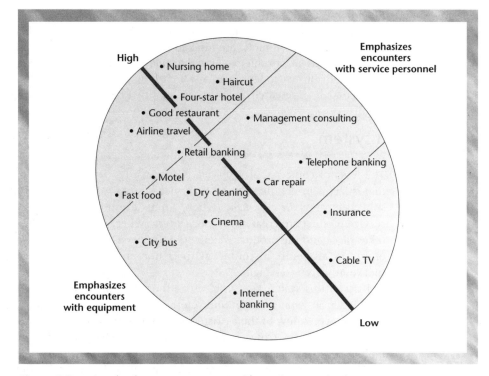

Figure 3.1 ■ Levels of customer contact with service organizations

High-contact services tend to be those in which customers visit the service facility in person. Customers are actively involved with the service organization and its personnel throughout service delivery (e.g., hairdressing or medical services). All people-processing services (other than those delivered at home) are high-contact. Services from the other three processing categories may also involve high levels of customer contact when, for reasons of tradition, preference or lack of other alternatives, customers go to the service site and remain there until service delivery is completed. Examples of services which have traditionally been high-contact but which technology allows to be lower contact today include retail banking, purchase of retail goods and higher education.

Medium-contact services entail less involvement with service providers. They involve situations in which customers visit the service provider's facilities (or are visited at home or at a third-party location by that provider) but either do not remain throughout service delivery or else have only modest contact with service personnel. The purpose of such contacts is often limited to: (1) establishing a relationship and defining a service need (e.g., management consulting or personal financial advising, where clients make an initial visit to the firm's office but then have relatively limited interactions with the provider during service production); (2) dropping off and picking up a physical possession that is being serviced; or (3) trying to resolve a problem.

Low-contact services involve very little, if any, physical contact between customers and service providers. Instead, contact takes place at arm's length through the medium of electronic or physical distribution channels – a fast-growing trend in today's convenience-oriented society. Both mental stimulus-processing (e.g., radio, television) and information-processing services (e.g., insurance) fall naturally into this category. Also included are possession-processing services in which the item requiring service can be shipped to the service site or subjected to 'remote fixes' delivered electronically to the customers' premises from a distant location (increasingly common for resolving software problems). Finally, many high-contact services are being transformed into *low-contact services* as customers engage in home shopping, do their banking by telephone, or research and purchase products through the World Wide Web.

Service as a system

The level of contact that a service business intends to have with its customers is a major factor in defining the total service system, which includes three overlapping sub-systems: *service operations* (where inputs are processed and the elements of the service product are created), *service delivery* (where final 'assembly' of these elements takes place and the product is delivered to the customer), and *service marketing* which embraces all points of contact with customers, including advertising, billing and market research (see Figure 3.2).

Parts of this system are visible (or otherwise apparent) to customers; other parts are hidden in what is sometimes referred to as the technical core, and the customer may not even know of their existence.[7] Some writers use the terms 'front office' and 'back office' in referring to the visible and invisible parts of the operation. Others talk about 'frontstage' and 'backstage', using the analogy of theatre to dramatize the notion that service is a performance.[8] We like this analogy and will be using it throughout the book.

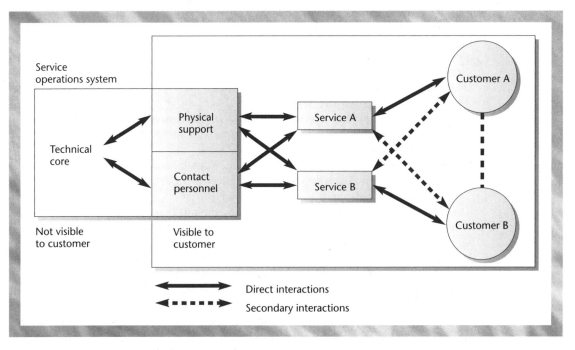

Figure 3.2 ■ The service business as a system

Source: Adapted from Langeard *et al.*[9]

Service operations system

Like a play in a theatre, the visible components of service operations can be divided into those relating to the actors (or service personnel) and those relating to the stage set (or physical facilities, equipment and other tangibles). What goes on backstage is of little interest to customers. Like any audience, they evaluate the production on those elements they actually experience during service delivery and, of course, on the perceived service outcome. Naturally, if the backstage personnel and systems (e.g., billing, ordering, account-keeping) fail to perform their support tasks properly in ways that affect the quality of frontstage activities, customers will notice. For instance, restaurant patrons will be disappointed if they order fish from the menu but are told it is unavailable (in reality, someone forgot to go to the fish market that morning), or find that their food is overcooked (actually caused by improperly set oven controls). Other examples of backstage failures include receiving an incorrect hotel bill due to a keying error, not receiving your course grades because of a computer failure in the college registrar's office, or being unable to bury a loved one because of a strike by gravediggers (sadly, such strikes have actually occurred).

The proportion of the overall service operation that is visible to customers varies according to the level of customer contact. Since high-contact services directly involve the physical person of the customer, either customers must enter the service 'factory' (although there may still be many backstage activities that they don't see), or service workers and their tools must leave their backstage and come to the customer's chosen location. Examples include roadside car repair by automobile clubs like the RAC or Green Flag, or physical fitness trainers who work with clients at their homes or offices. Medium-contact services, by contrast, require a less substantial involvement of the customer in service delivery. Consequently, the visible component of the service operations system is smaller. Low-contact services usually have a strategy of minimizing customer contact with the service provider, so most of the service operations system is confined to a remotely located backstage (sometimes referred to as a technical core); frontstage elements are normally limited to post and telecommunications contacts. Think for a moment about the telephone company that you use. Do you have any idea where its exchange is located? If you have a credit card, it's likely that your transactions are processed far from where you live.

Service delivery system

Service delivery is concerned with where, when and how the service product is delivered to the customer. As seen in Figure 3.2, this sub-system embraces not only the visible elements of the service operating system – buildings, equipment and personnel – but may also entail exposure to other customers.

Traditionally, service providers had direct interactions with their customers. But to achieve goals ranging from cost-reduction and productivity improvement to greater customer convenience, many services that don't need the customers to be physically present in the factory now seek to reduce direct contact. Midland Bank's creation of First Direct is a prime example of this trend. As a result, the visible component of the service operations system is shrinking in many industries as electronic technology or redesigned physical flows are used to drive service delivery from higher to lower levels of contact.

Self-service delivery often offers customers greater convenience than face-to-face contact. Machines such as automated petrol pumps, ATMs, or coin-operated food and drink dispensers can be installed in numerous locations and made accessible 24 hours a day, seven days a week. Cafeteria service allows customers to see menu items before making their selection. Self-guided museum tours allow visitors to enjoy an exhibition at their own pace. But there are potential disadvantages, too. The shift from personal service (sometimes referred to as 'high touch') to self-service ('high tech') sometimes disturbs customers. So a strategy of replacing employees by machines or other self-service procedures may require an information campaign to educate customers and promote the benefits of the new approach. It also helps to design user-friendly equipment, including free telephone access to an employee who can answer questions and solve problems. Of course, not all self-service is installed in remote locations. Cafeterias and self-guided museum tours are examples of customers taking on tasks that would otherwise have to be assigned to service personnel. Later in this chapter, we'll discuss the role of the customer as a co-producer of service in collaboration with the service provider.

Using the theatrical analogy, the distinction between high-contact and low-contact can be likened to the differences between live theatre on a stage and a drama created for radio. That's because customers of low-contact services normally never see the 'factory' where the work is performed; at most, they will talk with a service provider (or problem-solver) by telephone. Without buildings and furnishings or even the appearance of employees to provide tangible clues, customers must make judgements about service quality based on ease of telephone access, followed by the voice and responsiveness of a telephone-based customer service representative.

When service is delivered through impersonal electronic channels, such as self-service machines, automated telephone calls to a central computer, or via the

What options do you use for delivery of bank services?

Not everyone is comfortable with the trend towards lower-contact services, which is why some firms give their customers a choice. For instance, some retail banks now offer an array of service delivery options. Consider this spectrum of alternatives. Which options do you currently use at your bank? Which would you like to use in the future? And which are currently available?

1. Visit the bank in person and conduct transactions with a bank clerk.
2. Use postal service to send deposits or request new chequebooks.
3. Use an automated teller machine (ATM).
4. Conduct transactions by telephone with a customer service representative.
5. Use the keys on a telephone to interact with the bank in response to voice commands (or a telephone screen display).
6. Conduct home banking through your own computer, using a modem and special software.
7. Conduct transactions by computer through the World Wide Web.

In each instance, what factors explain your preference? Do they relate to the type of transactions you need to conduct or a situational element like the weather or time of day? Are you influenced by your feelings of liking (or disliking) human contact in a banking context? Or is there some other explanation?

customer's own computer, there is very little traditional 'theatre' left to the performance. Some firms compensate for this by giving their machines names, playing recorded music or installing moving colour graphics on video screens, adding sounds and creating computer-based interactive capabilities to give the experience a more human feeling. Many web sites are designed to look like displays in shop windows.

Responsibility for designing and managing service delivery systems has traditionally fallen to operations managers. But marketing needs to be involved, too, because understanding customer needs and concerns is important to ensure that the delivery system works well. What's more, if we're dealing with a service facility where customers may interact with each other – such as a hotel, aircraft or post office – their behaviour has to be managed discreetly so that they will act in ways that are compatible with the firm's strategy, including the comfort and safety of other customers.

Service marketing system

Other elements, too, may contribute to the customer's overall view of a service business. These include communication efforts by the advertising and sales departments, telephone calls and letters from service personnel, billings from the accounts department, random exposures to service personnel and facilities, news stories and editorials in the mass media, word-of-mouth comments from current or former customers, and even participation in market research studies.

Collectively, the components just cited – plus those in the service delivery subsystem – add up to what we term the service marketing system. In essence, this represents all the different ways in which the customer may encounter or learn about the organization in question. Since services are experiential, each of these elements offers clues about the nature and quality of the service product. Inconsistency between different elements may weaken the organization's credibility in the customers' eyes. Figure 3.3 depicts the service marketing system for a high-contact service.

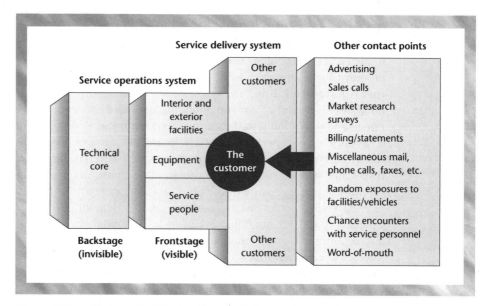

Figure 3.3 ■ High contact: the service marketing system

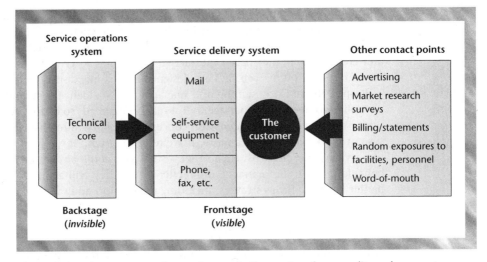

Figure 3.4 ■ Low contact: the service marketing system for a credit card account

As you know from your own experience, the scope and structure of the service marketing system often vary sharply from one type of organization to another. Figure 3.4 shows how the picture changes when we are dealing with a low-contact service, such as a credit card account. The significance of this approach to conceptualizing service creation and delivery is that it represents a customer's view, looking at the service business from the outside, as opposed to an internally focused operations perspective.

Physical evidence

Since many service performances are inherently intangible, they are often hard to evaluate. As a result, customers often look for tangible clues as to the nature of the service. Sometimes, encounters are random rather than planned. For instance, what impression would it create on you to see a damaged vehicle belonging to an express delivery service broken down by the side of the road? Or to observe a poorly groomed flight attendant travelling to (or from) the airport and wearing a uniform that is frayed and dirty? Or to visit a friend in a hospital where the grounds and buildings are beautifully maintained, the interior decor cheerful rather than institutional, and the friendly staff wearing smart, immaculate uniforms?

Because service performances are intangible, physical evidence gives clues as to the quality of service, and in some cases will strongly influence how customers (especially inexperienced ones) evaluate the service. Hence managers need to think carefully about the nature of the physical evidence provided to customers by the service marketing system. We'll be addressing this element of the 8Ps in more depth in Chapters 9 and 12, but Table 3.1 provides an initial checklist of the main tangible and communication elements to which customers might be exposed. Of course, the number of elements that are visible will vary depending on whether service delivery involves high or low customer contact. In low-contact services, additional physical evidence may be communicated through advertising, using video footage on TV or printed illustrations in newspapers, magazines or brochures.

Table 3.1 ■ Tangible elements and communication components in the service marketing system

1. Service personnel

Contacts with customers may be face-to-face, by telecommunications (telephone, fax, telegram, telex, electronic mail) or by mail and express delivery services.

These personnel may include:

- Sales representatives
- Customer service staff

- Accounting/billing staff
- Operations staff who do not normally provide direct service to customers (e.g., engineers, caretakers)
- Designated intermediaries whom customers perceive as directly representing the service firm

2. Service facilities and equipment

- Building exteriors, parking areas, landscaping
- Building interiors and furnishings
- Vehicles

- Self-service equipment operated by customers
- Other equipment

3. Nonpersonal communications

- Circulars
- Brochures/catalogues/instruction manuals
- Advertising

- Signage
- News stories/editorials in the mass media

4. Other people

- Fellow customers encountered during service delivery

- Word-of-mouth comments from friends, acquaintances or even strangers

Managing service encounters

Many services (especially those classified as high-contact) involve numerous encounters between customers and service employees, either in person or by phone. Service encounters may also take place between customers and physical facilities or equipment. In low-contact services, customers are having more and more encounters with automated systems that are designed to replace human personnel. Consider your own service experiences: how have they changed during the last few years as a result of the internet and automated equipment?

To highlight the risks and opportunities associated with service encounters, Richard Normann, a Paris-based Swedish consultant, borrowed the metaphor 'moment of truth' from bullfighting. Normann writes: .

> We could say that the perceived quality is realized at the moment of truth, when the service provider and the service customer confront one another in the arena. At that moment they are very much on their own. . . . It is the skill, the motivation, and the tools employed by the firm's representative and the expectations and behavior of the client which together will create the service delivery process.[10]

In bullfighting, what is at stake is the life of either the bull or the matador (or possibly both). The moment of truth is the instant at which the latter deftly slays the bull with his sword – hardly a very comfortable analogy for a service organization intent on building long-term relationships with its customers! Normann's point, of course, is that it's the life of the relationship which is at stake. Contrary to bullfighting, the goal of relationship marketing – which is discussed in depth in Chapter 6 – is to prevent one unfortunate (mis)encounter from destroying what is already, or has the potential to become, a mutually valued, long-term relationship.

Jan Carlzon, the former chief executive of Scandinavian Airlines System, used the 'moment of truth' metaphor as a reference point for transforming SAS from an operations-driven business into a customer-driven airline. Carlzon made the following comments about his airline:

> Last year, each of our 10 million customers came into contact with approximately five SAS employees, and this contact lasted an average of 15 seconds each time. Thus, SAS is 'created' 50 million times a year, 15 seconds at a time. These 50 million 'moments of truth' are the moments that ultimately determine whether SAS will succeed or fail as a company. They are the moments when we must prove to our customers that SAS is their best alternative.[11]

Managing people in service encounters

The above quote immediately makes apparent the link between marketing and human resource management in service organizations. With its own people as part of the product, no service business can afford to divorce its customer contact employees from the firm's marketing strategy. Increasingly, high-contact employees in what have traditionally been service delivery jobs with no sales content are now expected to play a selling role, too. This role shift requires them to be both producers and marketers of a service. As a result, waiters, bank clerks and even auditors in accountancy firms are being asked to promote new services, encourage customers to purchase additional items or refer them to sales specialists.

Making matters even more complex for managers is the fact that primary responsibility for their organization's success often rests with relatively junior personnel in such customer contact positions as bus driver, shop assistant, telephone-based customer service representative, receptionist in a professional service firm (e.g., architects, lawyers or management consultants) or car rental agent. These individuals, who are often young and inexperienced, and less well educated than their customers, need both technical and interpersonal skills to succeed. Not only must they be able to perform the technical aspects of the job quickly and accurately, but to do so while relating well to customers. In Chapter 14, we consider how careful recruitment, training and ongoing mentoring of employees can contribute to improvements in both productivity and quality.

To cope effectively with all these challenges, managers should brief employees on what the firm is trying to achieve in the marketplace. However, there are limits to the ability of policy manuals and other control procedures to ensure that employees consistently deliver good service. Service employees also need training, authority and management support to ensure that their important but often brief encounters with customers result in satisfactory outcomes. The case is often made for flattening the organization chart and turning it upside down, thereby placing customer contact personnel on the upper level of an inverted pyramid.[12] This implies that instead of striving to control employee behaviour, managers should be acting as coaches and role models to help the latter provide better service to customers.

Critical incidents in service encounters

Critical incidents are specific encounters between customers and service employees that are especially satisfying or dissatisfying for one or both parties. The critical incident technique (CIT) is a methodology for collecting and categorizing such incidents in service encounters. Conducting such an analysis offers an opportunity to determine what types of incidents during service delivery are likely to be particularly significant in determining whether or not customers are satisfied.

The customer's perspective

Findings from a CIT study can be very helpful in pinpointing opportunities for future improvements in service delivery processes. Determining the most likely 'failure points' in service encounters, where there is a risk of significantly upsetting customers, is the first step in taking corrective action to avoid such incidents. Similarly, CIT findings concerning the nature of incidents that customers seem to find very satisfying may enable managers to train their employees to replicate such positive experiences in the future.

Studying critical incidents in the airline, hotel and restaurant businesses

In a study of critical incidents, a sample of customers was asked:

■ Think of a time when, as a customer, you had a particularly *satisfying (dissatisfying)* interaction with an employee of an airline, hotel, or restaurant.

■ When did the incident happen?

■ What specific circumstances led up to this situation?

■ Exactly what did the employee say or do?

■ What resulted that made you feel the interaction was *satisfying (dissatisfying)*?

A total of 699 incidents were recorded, split roughly equally between satisfying and dissatisfying incidents. They were then categorized into three groups: (1) employee response to service failures, (2) employee responses to requests for customized service, and (3) unprompted and unsolicited employee actions.

When employees responded to critical incidents involving a service failure, analysis showed that the outcomes were twice as likely to be unsatisfactory for customers as satisfactory. The reverse was true when customers asked employees to adapt the service in some way to meet a special need or request. In the third grouping, relating to unexpected events and employee behaviour, satisfactory and unsatisfactory outcomes were equally matched. (What do you think explains these findings?) Table 3.2 displays reports on specific incidents, as described in the customers' own words.

Studying critical incidents in the airline, hotel and restaurant businesses (*continued*)

Table 3.2 ■ Customer reports on critical incidents involving service employees

Group 1 Sample incidents: employee response to service delivery failures

Incident	
Satisfactory	**Dissatisfactory**
A. Response to unavailable service	
They lost my room reservation but the manager gave me the V.I.P. suite for the same price.	We had made advance reservations at the hotel. When we arrived we found we had no room – no explanation, no apologies and no assistance in finding another hotel.
B. Response to unreasonably slow service	
Even though I didn't make any complaint about the hour and a half wait, the waitress kept apologizing and said that the bill was on the house.	The airline employees continually gave us erroneous information; a one-hour delay turned into a six-hour wait.
C. Response to other core service failures	
My prawn cocktail was half frozen. The waitress apologized and didn't charge me for any of my dinner.	One of my suitcases was all dented and looked as though it had been dropped from 30,000 feet. When I tried to make a claim for my damaged luggage, the employee insinuated that I was lying and trying to rip them off.

Group 2 Sample incidents: employee response to customer needs and requests

A. Response to 'special needs' customers	
The flight attendant helped me calm and care for my airsick child.	My young son, flying alone, was to be assisted by the stewardess form start to finish. At the Albany airport she left him alone in the airport with no one to escort him to his connecting flight.
B. Response to customer preferences	
The front desk telephoned around and found me tickets to the Mariners' opening game.	The waitress refused to move me from a window table on a hot day, because there was nothing left in her section.
It was snowing outside – car broke down. I checked 10 hotels and there were no rooms. Finally one understood my situation and offered to rent me a bed and set it up in one of their small banquet rooms.	The airline wouldn't let me bring my scuba gear on board coming back from Hawaii even though I brought it over as carry-on luggage.
C. Response to admitted customer error	
I lost my glasses on the plane; the stewardess found them and they were delivered to my hotel free of charge.	We missed our flight because of car trouble. The service clerk wouldn't help us find a flight on an alternative airline.

Studying critical incidents in the airline, hotel and restaurant businesses (*continued*)

Table 3.2 ■ Customer reports on critical incidents involving service employees (*continued*)

Incident	
Satisfactory	Dissatisfactory

D. Response to potentially disruptive others

The manager kept his eye on an obnoxious person at the bar, to make sure that he didn't bother us.	The hotel staff wouldn't deal with the noisy people partying in the hall at 3 a.m.

Group 3 Sample incidents: unprompted and unsolicited employee actions

A. Attention paid to customer

The waiter treated me like royalty. He really showed he cared about me.	The lady at the front desk acted as if we were bothering her. She was watching TV and paying more attention to the TV than to the hotel guests.

B. Truly out-of-the-ordinary employee behaviour

We always travel with our teddy bears. When we got back to our room at the hotel we saw that the maid had arranged our bears very comfortably in the chair. The bears were holding hands.	I needed a few more minutes to decide on a dinner. The waitress said, 'If you would read the menu and not the road map you would know what you want to order.'

C. Employee behaviours in the context of cultural norms

The waitress ran after us to return a £20 note my boyfriend had dropped under the table.	The waiter at this expensive restaurant treated us like dirt because we were only high school kids on a prom date.

D. Gestalt evaluation

The whole experience was so pleasant . . . everything went smoothly and perfectly.	The flight was a nightmare. A one-hour layover went to $3^1/_2$ hours. The air conditioning didn't work. The pilots and stewardesses were fighting because of an impending flight attendant strike. The landing was extremely rough. To top it all off, when the plane stopped, the pilots and stewardesses were the first ones off.

E. Performance under adverse circumstances

The counter agent was obviously under stress, but kept his cool and acted very professionally.	

Source: Adapted from Bitner *et al*.[13]

Negative critical incidents that are satisfactorily resolved have great potential for enhancing loyalty, because they demonstrate to customers that the organization really cares about them. But the reverse is also true. In a study of 838 critical incidents that led customers to switch to a competitor, dissatisfactory service encounters (cited by 34 per cent of respondents) ranked second to core service failures (cited by 44 per cent) as a reason for switching. Other key reasons were high, deceptive or unfair pricing (30 per cent), inconvenience in terms of time, location or delays (21 per cent), and poor response to service failures (17 per cent). Many respondents described a decision to switch suppliers as resulting from interrelated incidents, such as a service failure followed by an unsatisfactory response to resolving the problem.[14] These findings underscore the importance of the dictum: 'Service is everybody's business', regardless of their job or departmental affiliation.

The employee's perspective

As you reflect on service encounters, you need to recognize that customer–employee contact is a two-way street. Understanding the employee's view of the situation is really important, because thoughtless or poorly behaved customers can often cause needless problems for service personnel who are trying hard to serve them well. Continuing dissatisfaction with a succession of negative incidents can even drive good employees to leave their jobs.

Another CIT study (by the same researchers who conducted the study described in the boxed insert), examined hundreds of critical incidents from an employee perspective.[15] This research is described in detail in the reading 'Critical service encounters: the employee's viewpoint' by Mary Jo Bitner, Bernard Booms and Lois Mohr, which appears on pages 78–94. The results showed that more than 20 per cent of all incidents that employees found unsatisfactory could be attributed to problem customers, whose bad behaviour included drunkenness, verbal and physical abuse, breaking laws or company policies, and failing to cooperate with service personnel. It's simply not true that 'the customer is always right'. We'll return to the issue of problem customers and how to deal with them in Chapter 6.

The customer as co-producer

In some service environments, customers play a relatively passive role, waiting to be served. So long as you can state your needs clearly and pay promptly when billed, you play a minimal role in the process of service delivery (think about leaving clothes at a laundry). In other instances, however, you are expected to be actively involved in the production process – one of the distinctive features of service management that we noted in Chapter 1. This involvement may take two forms. Sometimes, you are given the tools and equipment to serve yourself (as when you take your clothes to a launderette); in others, such as health improvement, you work jointly with health professionals as 'co-producers' of the service from which you wish to benefit. Table 3.3 illustrates the differing levels of participation required of customers across an array of service businesses.

Table 3.3 ■ Levels of customer participation across different services

Low: Customer presence required during service delivery	Moderate: Customer inputs required for service creation	High: Customer co-produces the service product
Products are standardized	Client inputs customize a standard service	Active client participation guides the customized service
Service is provided regardless of any individual purchase	Provision of service requires customer purchase	Service cannot be created apart from the customer's purchase and active participation
Payment may be the only required customer input	Customer inputs (information, materials) are necessary for an adequate outcome, but the service firm provides the service	Customer inputs are mandatory and co-produce the outcome
Examples:		
End-consumer		
Airline travel	Hair cut	Marriage counselling
Motel stay	Annual health check-up	Personal training
Fast-food restaurant	Full-service restaurant	Weight-reduction programme
Business-to-business customer		
Uniform cleaning service	Agency-created advertising campaign	Management consulting
Pest control	Payroll service	Executive management seminar
Interior plant maintenance service	Independent freight transportation	Install wide area network (WAN)

Source: Adapted from Bitner *et al.*[16]

Service firms as teachers

The more work that customers are expected to do, the greater their need for information about how to perform for best results. In such situations, the firm should take responsibility for educating inexperienced customers. Lack of knowledge can lead to frustration with the process, unsatisfactory results and even put the customer at risk – think about the unpleasant things that might happen to a customer who smokes a cigarette and spills petrol while refuelling a car at a self-service pump! Now you can see why we believe that both promotion and education are important activities in marketing communications strategy for service businesses.

The necessary education can be provided in many different ways. Brochures and posted instructions are two widely-used approaches. Automated machines often contain detailed operating instructions and diagrams (unfortunately, these are sometimes only intelligible to the engineers who wrote them). Thoughtful banks place a telephone beside their ATMs so that customers can call a real person for help and advice at any time if they are confused about the on-screen instructions. Advertising for new services often contains significant educational content. In many businesses, customers look to employees for advice and assistance and are frustrated if they can't obtain it. Service providers, ranging from sales assistants and customer service representatives to flight attendants and nurses, must themselves be trained in teaching skills. As a last resort, people may turn to other customers and ask for help.

Schneider and Bowen suggest giving customers a realistic *service preview* in advance of service delivery to provide them with a clear picture of the role they will play in service co-production.[17] For example, a company might show a video presentation to help customers understand their role in the service encounter. This technique is used by some dentists to help patients understand the surgical processes they are about to experience and indicate how they should cooperate to help make things go as smoothly as possible – certainly a sensible goal for all parties involved.

Increasing productivity and quality when customers are co-producers

The greater customers' involvement in service production, the greater their potential to influence the processes in which they are engaged. From an operational perspective, one way to view customers is as 'partial employees', who can influence the productivity and quality of service processes and outputs.[18] This perspective requires a change in management mindset, as Schneider and Bowen make clear:

> If you think of customers as partial employees, you begin to think very differently about what you hope customers will bring to the service encounter. Now they must bring not only expectations and needs but also relevant service production competencies that will enable them to fill the role of partial employees. The service management challenge deepens accordingly.[19]

They go on to suggest that customers who are offered an opportunity to participate at an active level are more likely to be satisfied – regardless of whether or not they actually choose the more active role – because it is gratifying to be offered a choice. Managing customers as partial employees, requires using the same human resource logic as in managing a firm's paid employees and should follow these four steps:

1. Conduct a 'job analysis' of customers' present roles in the business and compare it against the roles that the firm would like them to play.

2. Determine if customers possess an awareness of how they are expected to perform and have the skills needed to perform as required.

3. Motivate customers by ensuring that they will be rewarded for performing well (for instance: satisfaction from better quality and more customized output; enjoyment of participating in the actual process; a belief that their own productivity speeds the process; and keeps costs down).

4. Regularly appraise customers' performance. If this is unsatisfactory, seek to change their role and the procedures in which they are involved. Alternatively, consider 'terminating' these customers (nicely, of course!) and look for new ones.

Effective human resource management starts with recruitment and selection. The same approach should hold true for 'partial employees'. So, if co-production requires specific skills, firms should target their marketing efforts to recruit new customers who have the competency to perform the necessary tasks.[20] After all, many colleges and universities do the same in their student selection process!

Conclusion

Service businesses can be divided into three, overlapping systems. The operations system consists of the personnel, facilities and equipment required to run the service operation and create the service product; only part of this system, described here as 'frontstage', is visible to the customer. The delivery system incorporates the visible operations elements and the customers who, in self-service operations, take an active role in helping create the service product – as opposed to being passively waited on. Finally, the marketing system includes not only the delivery system, which is essentially composed of the product and distribution elements of the traditional marketing mix, but also additional components such as billing and payment systems, exposure to advertising and sales people, and word-of-mouth comments from other people.

In all types of services, understanding and managing service encounters between customers and service personnel is central to creating satisfied customers who are willing to enter into long-term relationships with the service provider. There are wide variations, however, in the nature of such encounters. In high-contact services, for example, customers are exposed to many more tangible clues and experiences than they are in medium-contact and low-contact situations. Critical incidents occur when some aspect of the service encounter is either highly satisfactory or dissatisfactory. In some instances, including self-service, customers participate in the process of creating and delivering services, effectively working as 'partial employees' whose performance will affect the productivity and quality of output. Under these circumstances, service managers must be sure to educate and train customers so that they have the skills needed to perform well.

Study questions

1. As a senior bank executive, what actions would you take to encourage more customers to bank by phone, post, internet or through ATMs rather than visiting a branch?

2. What are the backstage elements of (a) an insurance company, (b) a car repair facility, (c) a hotel, (d) an airline, (e) a university, (f) a funeral parlour, (g) a consulting firm, (h) a television station? Under what circumstances would it be appropriate to allow customers to see some of these backstage elements and how would you do it?

3. What roles are played by frontstage service personnel in low-contact organizations? Are these roles more or less important to customer satisfaction than in high-contact services?

4. Why is it valuable for service operations managers to try to see their business through the eyes of their customers?

5. Use the list in Table 3.1 to develop a profile of the service marketing system for a variety of services – hospital, airline, consulting engineer or legal service, college, hotel, dry cleaner, credit union, automobile service centre, or post office. (You can base your profiles on your own experience or interview other customers.)

6. What is the difference between a moment of truth, a service encounter and a critical incident?

7. Review Table 3.2. As a manager, how would you try to prevent future recurrence of each of the 12 unsatisfactory incidents? (Hint: consider the underlying cause of the problem and possible reasons for the inappropriate response that upset the customer.)

8. Define the term 'partial employee' and give examples.

9. Are customers playing 'partial employee' roles more or less likely to be taken advantage of by unscrupulous service providers? Why? (or why not?)

Notes

1. Based on material in: Delphine Parmenter, Jean-Claude Larréché and Christopher Lovelock, *First Direct Branchless Banking'*, Fontainebleau, France: INSEAD, 1997; Saul Hansell, '500,000 Clients, No Branches', *New York Times*, 3 September 1995, Section 3, p. 1; and Christopher Lovelock, *Product Plus*, New York: McGraw-Hill, 1994.

2. Curtis P. McLaughlin, 'Why Variation Reduction Is Not Everything: A New Paradigm for Service Operations', *International Journal of Service Industry Management*, Vol. 7, No. 3, 1996, pp. 17–39.

3. Lance A. Bettencourt and Kevin Gwinner, 'Customization of the Service Experience: The Role of the Frontline Employee', *International Journal of Service Industry Management*, Vol. 7, No. 2, 1996, pp. 2–21.

4. Lynn Shostack, 'Planning the Service Encounter', in J.A. Czepiel, M.R. Solomon and C.F. Surprenant (eds), *The Service Encounter*, Lexington, MA: Lexington Books, 1985, pp. 243–54.

5. Carole F. Surprenant and Michael R. Solomon, 'Predictability and Personalization in the Service Encounter', *Journal of Marketing*, Vol. 51, Winter 1987, pp. 73–80.

6. William J. Glynn and Uolevi Lehtinen, 'The Concept of Exchange: Interactive Approaches in Services Marketing', in W.J. Glynn and J.G. Barnes (eds), *Understanding Services Management*, Chichester: John Wiley & Sons, 1995, pp. 89–118.

7. Richard B. Chase, 'Where Does the Customer Fit in a Service Organization?', *Harvard Business Review*, Vol. 56, November–December 1978, pp. 137–42.

8. Stephen J. Grove, Raymond P. Fisk and Mary Jo Bitner, 'Dramatizing the Service Experience: A Managerial Approach', in T.A. Schwartz, D.E. Bowen and S.W. Brown, *Advances in Services Marketing and Management*, Vol. I, Greenwich, CT: JAI Press, 1992, pp. 91–122.

9. Eric Langeard, John E.G. Bateson, Christopher H. Lovelock and Pierre Eiglier, *Services Marketing: New Insights from Consumers and Managers*, Cambridge, MA: Marketing Science Institute, 1981.

10. Normann first used the term 'moments of truth' in a Swedish study in 1978; subsequently it appeared in English in Richard Normann, *Service Management: Strategy and Leadership in Service Businesses*, Chichester: John Wiley & Sons, 2nd edition, 1991, pp. 16–17.

11. Jan Carlzon, *Moments of Truth*, Cambridge, MA: Ballinger Publishing Co., 1987, 2nd edition, p. 3.

12. Sandra Vandermerwe, *From Tin Soldiers to Russian Dolls: Creating Added Value through Service*, Oxford: Butterworth-Heinemann, 1993, p. 81.

13. Mary Jo Bitner, Bernard H. Booms and Mary Stanfield Tetreault, 'The Service Encounter: Diagnosing Favorable and Unfavorable Incidents', *Journal of Marketing*, Vol. 54, January 1990, pp. 71–84.

14. Susan M. Keaveney, 'Customer Switching Behaviour in Service Industries: An Exploratory Study', *Journal of Marketing*, Vol. 59, April 1995, pp. 71–82.

15. Mary Jo Bitner, Bernard Booms and Lois A. Mohr, 'Critical Service Encounters: The Employee's Viewpoint', *Journal of Marketing*, Vol. 58, October 1994, pp. 95–106.
16. Mary Jo Bitner, William T. Faranda, Amy R. Hubbert and Valarie A. Zeithaml, 'Customer Contributions and Roles in Service Delivery', *International Journal of Service Industry Management*, Vol. 8., No. 3, 1997, pp. 193–205.
17. Benjamin Schneider and David E. Bowen, *Winning the Service Game*, Boston: Harvard Business School Press, 1995, p. 92.
18. David E. Bowen, 'Managing Customers as Human Resources in Service Organizations', *Human Resources Management*, Vol. 25, No. 3, 1986, pp. 371–83; Roland van Dierdonck, 'Success Strategies in a Service Economy', *European Management Journal*, 10 September 1992, pp. 365–73.
19. Schneider and Bowen, *op. cit.* p. 85.
20. Bonnie Farber Canziani, 'Leveraging Customer Competency in Service Firms', *International Journal of Service Industry Management*, Vol. 8, No. 1, 1997, pp. 5–25.

From scientific management to service management

A management perspective for the age of service competition

Christian Grönroos

Service management draws insights from business practice and from marketing, operations, human resources, service quality management, organizational theory and economics. Its five key facets are an overall perspective that guides decisions in all areas of management, customer focus, a holistic approach to cross-functional collaboration, an emphasis on quality and internal development of personnel.

Introduction

Service management is not a well-delineated concept. It is, however, used more and more by academics as well as by practitioners. Conferences on service management are arranged, books with the phrase service management as part of the title are published and academic courses called service management are developed. Service management is inevitably establishing itself as a recognized field. However, it is understandable that an outside observer easily feels confused when confronted with the concept. The purpose of this article is to discuss how service management emerged, what it is and what contributions it offers to management research and practice.

Today, service management is more a perspective than one discipline or one coherent area of its own. It is a perspective that gives firms that face service competition (i.e. that have to understand and manage service elements in their customer relationships in order to achieve a sustainable competitive advantage), more or less similar guidelines to the development of such separate areas as management, marketing, operations, organizational theory and human resources management as well as quality management including service quality management and TQM. This perspective is described very well by the observation by Schneider and Rentch (1987) that firms that apply service management principles consider 'service as *the* organizational imperative'.

The service management perspective includes some more or less general shifts in the focus of management (Grönroos, 1990a, p. 118):

1. From the product-based utility to total utility in the customer relationship.
2. From short-term transactions to long-term relationships.
3. From core product (goods or services) quality or the mere technical quality of the outcome to total customer-perceived quality in enduring customer relationships.
4. From production of the technical quality of products (goods or services) as the key process in the organization to developing and managing total utility and total quality as the key process.

In addition to this, a number of principles of service management that seem to be fairly commonly accepted are discussed in the lead article of the first volume of the *Journal of Services Industry Management* from 1990 (Grönroos, 1990c).

Facets of service management

The service management perspective has emerged within several disciplines with a number of somewhat different and yet interrelated angles. One can say that

International Journal of Service Industry Management, Vol. 5, No. 2, 1994, pp. 5–20. © MCG University Press.

major impacts on this perspective come from at least six different areas: marketing, operations management, organizational theory and human resources management, management/and service quality management, and finally as a sixth area business executives and consultants. The approach by executives and consultants was originally heavily influenced by the Scandinavian experience in turning around and managing service firms, particularly by SAS Scandinavian Airlines System (see Albrecht and Zemke, 1985; Carlzon, 1987). In addition to these areas, there are scattered contributions from other disciplines as well (e.g. economics).

As service management has emerged from so many points of view and not yet merged into one management theory, there is no definition of it that would have been commonly accepted. In fact, most authors seem to avoid in-depth discussion of the definition issue. However, Grönroos (1990a, see also Grönroos, 1988) offers a fairly exhaustive definition of service management:

Service management is:

1. To understand the utility customers receive by consuming or using the offerings of the organization and how services alone or together with physical goods or other kinds of tangibles contribute to this utility, that is, to understand how total quality is perceived in customer relationships, and how it changes over time;
2. To understand how the organization (personnel, technology and physical resources, systems and customers) will be able to produce and deliver this utility or quality;
3. To understand how the organization should be developed and managed so that the intended utility or quality is achieved; and
4. To make the organization function so that this utility or quality is achieved and the objectives of the parties involved (the organization, the customers, other parties, the society, etc.) are met. (Grönroos, 1990a, p. 117)

Albrecht (1988) presents a shorter definition. Some of the information content of the above mentioned definition is of course lost, but it clearly demonstrates some of the key facets of service management:

Service management is a total organizational approach that makes quality of service, as perceived by the customer, the number one driving force for the operations of the business. (p. 20)

The shift of focus and the definitions presented above demonstrate the major meaning and significance of service management. Five key facets of the service management perspective can be recognized, *viz.*, overall management perspective, customer focus, holistic approach, quality focus, and internal development and reinforcement:

1. It is an *overall management perspective* which should guide decisions in all areas of management (not only provide management principles for a separate function such as customer service);
2. It is *customer-driven* or market-driven (not driven by internal efficiency criteria);
3. It is a *holistic perspective* which emphasizes the importance of intraorganizational, cross-functional collaboration (not specialization and the division of labour);
4. Managing *quality is an integral part* of service management (not a separate issue); and
5. *Internal development* of the personnel and reinforcement of its commitment to company goals and strategies are strategic prerequisites for success (not only administrative tasks).

In the major part of this article these five facets of service management will be discussed. However, today the mainstream management focus is still on economies of scale and a striving to decrease the cost of production and of administering the business, in order to minimize the unit cost of the products, accompanied by aggressive traditional marketing and sales campaigns and continuous product development efforts. While there is no contradiction between service management and product development efforts, the overemphasis on cost reduction and economies of scale as well as on traditional marketing activities is challenged as obsolete and even potentially dangerous as general management principles.

From 'scientific management' to service management

The mainstream management principles of today are based on a perspective that emerged during the industrial revolution. They can be traced back to Adam Smith's analysis of the pin factory. In *The Wealth of Nations* (1950/1776) Smith advocated that one should pursue specialization and the division of labour. Later in *Scientific Management* (Taylor, 1947) principles along the same lines were formulated, although Taylor did take into account the wellbeing of the workforce. Mass production and economies of scale were considered fundamental parts of this management philosophy.

Long-lasting and well-established structures are not easily changed from within. Environmental changes may put enough pressure on the establishment so that marginal corrections of problems are made, but the structure itself lasts. This is what seems to have happened with today's management principles based on the scientific management perspective. The educational level and standard of living of the workforce has increased tremendously and made people much more sophisticated and demanding as employees and consumers; the magnitude of competition has increased and its nature changed which, for example, has made firms much more vulnerable to international competition and has made the competitive edge provided by excellent core products much less effective; the exploding development of information technology has made customers and competitors much more aware of available options; and the nature of the new technology makes it possible to achieve results totally different from mass production and standardization which have been the traditional gains of new technology. In spite of all these trends, the grip of the traditional management principles has remained steady.

However, all these trends make old management principles less appropriate and effective. The work environment becomes less encouraging for the employees, technology is not used to create as much job satisfaction for employees and value for customers as possible, enduring customer relationships are not developed and competitive advantages are not achieved. Service firms were among the first to observe the problems created by the old management structure. An interest in studying service-specific issues emerged first among marketing researchers.[1] The development of new models, concepts and tools based on the characteristics of services and of their production and delivery processes started during the 1970s. Following a few earlier doctoral dissertations and articles, the doctoral dissertations by Judd (1965), Johnson (1969) and George (1972) offered a thorough description of the nature of services and of specific problems in services marketing. Wilson's (1972) and Rathmell's (1974) books on professional services and the service sector in general respectively were the first ones exploring marketing problems in service firms. Even if research into services took off at approximately the same time in North America (resulting in, for example, two widely used texts and readings by Lovelock from 1984 and 1988), much of the dominance of services marketing progress shifted to Europe (e.g., Bateson, 1989 in English; Grönroos, 1979 and Gummesson, 1977 in Swedish; Langeard and Eiglier, 1987 in French; Lehtinen, 1983 in Finnish; and in addition, a number of books published in, at least, Austria, Belgium, Denmark, Germany, Italy, the Netherlands, Norway and Spain (see Grönroos, 1990a)).

Among other things, the nature of the customer relationships and of operations and the production and delivery processes were considered different for services by the pioneering researchers, and the quality of services was found to be formed and perceived in such a way that traditional models from manufacturing did not apply. However, researchers interested in services did not predominantly attempt to change old management models and concepts in a marginal fashion in order to fit services. This is especially true for the so-called Nordic School of services with its roots in the mid-1970s (e.g. Grönroos and Gummesson, 1985), where, for example, marketing was viewed as an area that cannot be separated from overall management. Instead a totally new approach to the problem of how to manage various aspects of service organizations was taken. This was the beginning of what later, by Richard Normann (1982/1984), was labelled 'service management'.[2]

The overall management perspective

Normann (1982/1984) and Grönroos (1982) have shown how a traditional management focus overemphasizing cost reduction efforts and scale economies may become a management trap for service firms and lead to a vicious circle where the quality of the service is damaged, internal workforce environment deteriorates, customer relationships suffer, and eventually profitability problems occur. Growing marketing and sales budgets may slow down the negative trend for some time, but as this normally only means increased persuasion and overpromising, in the long run it only leads to unsatisfied and defecting customers. In the tradition of Adam Smith and scientific management, the traditional management principles are largely based on specialization and the division of labour. From this has frequently followed a short-term, manipulative and transaction-oriented view of market relationships and an adversary relationship between functions within the firm and between the firm and its external partners, such as customers, suppliers and middlemen. Service management is based on a different assumption of how the intraorganizational and interorganizational relationships should be viewed and developed. Teamwork, interfunctional collaboration and inter-organizational partnership, and a long-term perspective are, generally speaking, inherent values in service management.

Originally, Normann and Grönroos discussed service firms only, but as it has gradually become evident that services are growing in importance for manufacturers as well, the arguments for a management trap and vicious circles become more generally valid. Grönroos's definition of service management and the notion of service competition clearly imply that not only service firms but all types of organizations may be included.

Service management as an overall management perspective gives high priority to the external efficiency of the firm, how customers perceive the quality of the core products and the total performance of a firm, instead of overemphasizing internal efficiency, economies of scale and cost reduction. This combines the overall management perspective of service management with its customer-driven and quality-oriented facets, employee-oriented concerns and its long-term perspective.

Customer orientation

As a general lesson from service management, Heskett (1986 and 1987) argues for a focus on 'market economies' instead of emphasizing scale economies too much. By this he means that a competitive edge and profitability are accomplished by a closer market orientation rather than by a focus on large-scale production of more or less standardized products in order to keep unit production costs down. More recently, Sasser and Reichheld have stressed this point in their studies of the economic effects of retaining customers as compared to cost reduction efforts without diminishing customer defection rates (Reichheld, 1993; Reichheld and Sasser, 1990). Their studies show that the decrease of the defection rate by a comparatively small percentage has an impact on profits that would be difficult to achieve by cost reduction efforts. The figures differ greatly from industry to industry but the trend is the same. Additional studies will most probably support these findings. For services businesses where the service outcome and the production and delivery processes can be highly standardized, economies of scale based on a production-line approach as suggested by Levitt (1972) may be possible. McDonald's would be an example of such a case, but as Schlesinger and Heskett (1991) more recently have argued, when facing more pressure from new competitors even firms like McDonald's may have less support from technology-driven standardization of the production and delivery of their services. This does not, of course, mean that economies of scale and cost reduction efforts would be a thing of the past; on the contrary. It means, however, that the major focus cannot be on such efforts any more. 'Market economies' and a genuine interest in the customer become imperative.

Customer loyalty is the cornerstone of successful service management (Heskett et al., 1991). However, a word of warning is needed here. Even if customer retention is important, the firm should strive to keep the right customers from defecting. The recently emerging interest in what we in another context (Grönroos, 1993b) have labelled 'customer relationship economics' has shown that 'customer relationship profitability', to use an expression coined by Storbacka (1993), is not only a function of a stable customer base. As he points out, the firm must not retain the wrong customers, i.e., customers that are not and cannot be expected to become profitable (Storbacka, 1993; see also Barnes and Cumby, 1993). Doing a thorough customer relationship profitability analysis is equally important as efforts directed towards creating a loyal customer base and retaining customers.

Voices have been raised that service management overemphasizes the importance of customer satisfaction and efforts to improve customer perceived quality. Productivity and profitability issues may suffer from this alleged myopic view of the importance of service quality and customer satisfaction (Storbacka, 1993). If the service management perspective is applied so that the firm loses track of the importance of productivity and profitability, this criticism is of course valid. In this sense, the critical voices are important, because in the service management literature, productivity and profitability are far too often given only marginal attention. And without proper segmentation and a customer relationship profitability analysis done for each segment of customers, mistakes may easily be made. Large groups of unprofitable customer relationships may easily be tolerated and not even recognized, if total profitability is good enough. This does not, however, decrease the importance of service management in today's competitive situation. Any model or concept can be implemented in a less than satisfactory way.

Research into service management has shown that, contrary to common belief, quality improvement and productivity gains are not necessarily mutually exclusive (e.g., Haywood and Pickworth, 1988). This view is partly due to the fact that most frequently productivity is measured in an unsophisticated way (Steedle, 1988). The influence of scientific management can be seen here as well. Productivity is treated as an internal efficiency issue only, where the impact on perceived

quality and customer satisfaction is neglected. Productivity measurement models have also always been developed within a manufacturing context, and there the customer's impact on operations and on quality formation has been ignored. Still, today, how to measure productivity in a service organization is more or less an unsolved problem. Manufacturing models, which inevitably become unsophisticated in service contexts, give wrong signals to management. They are internally oriented, they are short term in nature, they do not give information about long-term productivity, and they seldom measure the productivity of the whole operation. As noted by Pickworth (1987), who uses a restaurant example,

> . . . the issue is whether food-service managers should think of their outputs *as meals produced or customers satisfied*. If customer satisfaction is the measure, *a quality dimension* is also needed in productivity measurement. (p. 43, emphasis added)

The same efforts may, correctly implemented, improve service quality and at the same time have a favourable impact on productivity (e.g., Cowell, 1984). For example, training employees makes them more knowledgeable of the services and the production and delivery processes, and, therefore, they make fewer mistakes and can answer questions asked by customers more quickly. The customer gets faster service and more accurate information. A new technology may remove bottlenecks in operations and speed up the service production and delivery process, a fact that the customers perceive as improved quality.

As far as profitability is concerned, the slowly growing number of studies of customer relationship economics demonstrate, as has been noted previously, that customer retention has a positive effect on profitability. Customer retention again is among other things depending on how well the firm can provide its customers with services. Of course, the core product and price issues are important here, too.

Customer perceived quality orientation

Quality is another area where research into the various areas of service management has had a decisive impact. As noted by Gummesson (1993a), quality has been a black box in management and marketing theories. And in operations and production management quality has been treated as a production problem from an internal efficiency point of view. Especially, research into the marketing of services (e.g., Grönroos, 1982, 1984, 1993a; Gummesson, 1993; Parasuraman et al., 1985) has demonstrated the need for including quality management as an integral part of service management theory.[3] The perceived service quality model (Grönroos 1982, 1993a), the gap analysis model (Parasuraman et al., 1985), the SERVQUAL instrument (Parasuraman et al., 1986, 1994), the Meyer-Mattmuller model (Meyer and Mattmuller, 1987), Lindqvist's index (Lindqvist, 1988), and other quality management models and instruments (e.g., Andersson, 1992; Edvardsson and Gustavsson, 1988; Lemmink and Behara, 1992; Liljander and Strandvik, 1993, and 1994; Stauss, 1993) are examples of what has been developed within the marketing-oriented approach to services. In service operations research quality has been studied as well (cf. Haywood-Farmer and Stuart, 1988; Johnston, 1987).[4] The literature on services by consultants also includes service quality books (e.g., Davidow and Uttal, 1989).

The customer focus of the research into services has had a decisive impact on the general approach to quality management. Service researchers very strongly put forward the view that it is the customer who decides what quality is and, that it is customer perceived quality that has to be studied. Subsequently, this view has been supported by, for example, the findings of the PIMS project (Buzzell and Gale, 1987) and by the total quality management (TQM) movement. Customer orientation is a central aspect of TQM programmes. Nevertheless, many such programmes seem to fail.[5] One reason for this may be the fact that marketing is often missing. As Kordupleski et al. (1993) observe,

> there is a considerable participation by quality control engineers, manufacturing people, operations managers, human resource people, and organizational behaviour experts. A group notable by its absence is the function closest to the customers – namely, marketing. . . . Why are marketing people not more involved in quality improvement? (p. 83)

Here is a big difference between TQM and service management. TQM has been developed by non-marketing people who only recently have observed that customers are important to the success of the business. The customer-perceived quality focus and quality management models inherent in service management have been developed by marketing and operations as part of the interface between those two areas. Marketing and quality are seen as two sides of the same coin. Hence, the contact with marketing is more natural in service management than in TQM.

Long-term perspective

The long-term perspective inherent in service management has had an important impact on marketing. Services marketing research has demonstrated the importance of long-term relationships instead of short-term deals and campaigns (cf. Grönroos, 1982 and Gummesson, 1987). The emerging interest in customer relationship economics (Storbacka, 1993) and recently published studies of the economic impact of customer retention (Reichheld and Sasser, 1990) support this view. Relationship marketing (cf. Christopher et al., 1991; Grönroos, 1994 and Gummesson, 1993b; see also Berry, 1983) is a new approach to marketing which is quickly growing in importance.

The long-term orientation is clearly in line with current trends in business (cf. Kotler, 1992). Partnerships and networks as well as strategic alliances are formed in international business and in many industries are becoming increasingly important on domestic markets as well. As Frederick Webster (1992) concludes in an analysis of current trends in business,

> there has been a shift from a transactions to a relationship focus (p. 14) . . . and . . . from an academic or theoretical perspective, the relatively narrow conceptualization of marketing as a profit-maximization problem, focused on market transactions, seems increasingly out of touch with an emphasis on long-term customer relationships and the formation and management of strategic alliances. . . . The focus shifts from products and firms as units of analysis to people, organizations, and the social processes that bind actors together in ongoing relationships. (p. 10)

In service management, marketing efforts are often considered investments in customers more than marketing expenses. This view is nothing entirely new in marketing. In the network approach to industrial marketing the concepts of market and marketing investments have been introduced (Johanson and Mattsson, 1985). More recently, Slywotzky and Shapiro (1993) also argue for a new attitude towards marketing, where marketing is treated as investments instead of short-term expenses.

> In 1992, US companies spent more than $700 billion on activities such as selling, advertising, and sales promotion. For many companies, sales and marketing expenditures represent 15 per cent to 20 per cent of each revenue dollar. From that same dollar, about 4 per cent to 10 per cent is devoted to capital budgeting projects. While capital budgeting expenditures are carefully examined and analysed – and treated as investments – the much larger marketing piece is viewed as an annual expense. (p. 98)

Holistic approach to management

Service management's holistic approach to management has had several effects. In marketing it has clearly demonstrated the need for expanding the notion of who the marketers in a firm are. Gummesson (1991) has introduced the breakthrough concept 'part-time marketers' for the employees outside a traditional marketing department, who normally are not trained as marketers or even appointed as marketers, but who nevertheless take care of customer contacts and thus make an impact on the future purchasing behaviour of the firm's customers. He emphasizes the importance of the part-time marketers by stating that:

> marketing and sales departments (the full-time marketers) are not able to handle more than a limited portion of the marketing *as its staff cannot be at the right place at the right time with the right customer contacts.* (p. 72)

It has, thus, been concluded that everyone is a marketer, one way or the other (Grönroos, 1982 and Gummesson, 1990; see also Webster, 1988).

Even more important is the influence that the holistic view of the service management perspective has had as a means of crossing traditional business functions and corresponding academic disciplines. In service marketing research the importance of operations as part of marketing has been observed. The concept 'interactive marketing function' (Grönroos, 1982) has been developed to point out the marketing impact of the service production and delivery process. Langeard and Eiglier (1987) introduced the *servuction* concept which treats service operations in the context of marketing. In his services marketing system, Lovelock (1988) has integrated marketing, operations and human resources management. In operations a similar trend can be observed. The service management perspective has made researchers within the area of production and operations interested in the impact of the operations systems on customers (e.g., Bowen *et al.*, 1990; Chase, 1978, 1991; Collier, 1987; Voss *et al.*, 1985). The textbook on service operations by Sasser *et al.* (1978) was a first major step in this direction, which at Harvard Business School led to an experiment with an academic course combining service operations and services marketing. However, apparently this experiment was not allowed to last very long.

In organizational theory and human resources management a similar trend can be seen. The service management perspective has, for example, created such concepts as the service management system (Normann, 1982) incorporating a marketing and operations view in an organizational theory context, and empowerment (Bowen and Lawler, 1992) which relates human resources management to marketing. Other contributions from this field include publications by Schneider (1980) and Mills (1986).[6]

Focus on internal development

Service management also has an internal focus where the development of the personnel and the creation of employee commitment to the goals and strategies of the firm are key issues. In service marketing research the need for internal marketing has been observed (Grönroos 1982; see also, for example, Barnes, 1989;

Berry, 1981; George, 1984, 1990). In 1982 Grönroos formulated the internal marketing concept, according to which the internal market of employees is best motivated for service mindedness and customer-oriented performance by an active, marketing-like approach, where a variety of activities are used internally in an active, marketing-like and co-ordinated way.

Without active and continuous internal marketing efforts the interactive marketing impact on customers will deteriorate, service quality will suffer and customers will start to defect with negative effects on profitability as a result. In this sense internal marketing is a prerequisite for successful external marketing. Internal marketing includes both an attitude management aspect and a communications management aspect (Grönroos, 1990a). In organizational theory and human resources management the same issues have been addressed and for example the above mentioned concept of empowerment has emerged as an element of internal marketing. Generally speaking, internal marketing and HRM represent an interface between marketing and organizational theory that has been emphasized by the service management perspective (cf. Grönroos, 1990b).

Internal marketing is not, of course, anything entirely new in a firm. Internal programmes to make employees committed to various goals have always existed. What is new is the active, market-oriented approach as suggested by the internal marketing concept. Some marketing activities from traditional external marketing may be used together with training and other traditional personnel development activities. At best, internal marketing offers an umbrella for all these and other activities which make the development of personnel a strategic issue.[7]

In conclusion: What is service management?

As the discussion of service management and its five key facets above demonstrates, service management is not a well-defined area or a single theory of management. Rather it is a management perspective that fits today's competitive situation. Cost reductions and core product quality are still important to success, but to achieve customer satisfaction and a competitive advantage through differentiation of the market offer (cf. Quinn et al., 1990) more value has to be added to the core product. This is done through a variety of services and by turning activities such as deliveries, technical service, claims handling, telephone exchange, invoicing, etc. into customer-oriented, value-adding services.

The service management perspective has had a novel impact on cross-disciplinary research. Volumes including research from various fields are published (Swartz et al., 1992, 1993). International conferences have been arranged, mostly in Europe, on service management (Proceedings from the 1st and 2nd International Research Seminars in Service Management 1990 and 1992) and on service quality management (e.g. Kunst and Lemmink, 1992; Brown et al., 1991; Scheuing et al., 1992),[8] where researchers representing marketing, operations, organizational theory, psychology, finance, economics and other disciplines together discuss various aspects of management from a service perspective. In these areas research has taken new directions guided by this common perspective.

The term service management was introduced in Swedish in 1982 and in English in 1984. Since then it has slowly become a term used to indicate a common perspective. But this perspective started to evolve long before this term came into use within disciplines such as marketing, organizational theory and human resources management, and operations. Various disciplines have brought contributions of their own to service management, e.g., service competition, the long-term relationship marketing notion, interactive and internal marketing, the part-time marketer concept and the perceived service quality model (marketing), the service management system, the high-contact/low-contact personnel distinction, empowerment and the notion of people as the major resource of a firm (organizational theory and human resources management), the customer-oriented and outward looking approach to operations, and the front-office/back-office notion (operations management), and service guarantees, the market economics focus and customer retention analysis (management), to mention just a few. However, true cross-disciplinary research is still rare. In the future such research projects will broaden and deepen the service management perspective even more.

Notes

1. Berry and Parasuraman provide an interesting analysis of the development of services marketing thought in their article 'Building a New Academic Field – Case of Services Marketing' (Berry and Parasuraman, 1993). See also the article on the evolution of the English language services marketing literature by Fisk *et al.* (1993).

2. Subsequently, among other things, building on the notion that customer participation in the production and delivery process is a central characteristic of services and service management, Normann has developed this further into an interactive strategy model for any type of business, according to which successful firms not only create value but reinvent it together with their customers (see Normann and Ramirez, 1993).

3. There have been earlier attempts to treat quality in a more explicit way in the microeconomic and marketing literature. In the 1950s researchers such as Abbott (1955), who wanted to add more realism to microeconomic price theory, included quality in their models. Abbott, for example, had an astonishingly modern view of quality: 'The term "quality" will be used . . . in its broadest sense, to include all qualitative elements in the competitive exchange process – materials, design, service provided, location, and so forth', (p. 4). These models influenced parameter theory (Mickwitz, 1959), a marketing theory which was somewhat similar to but much more developed than the marketing mix approach which since the 1960s has dominated marketing. In this theory quality was an integral element. With parameter theory, quality as anything other than a black box disappeared from the literature.

4. Specific contributions from the area of operations management are not discussed in detail here, as the role of that area in service management is the topic of Robert Johnston's article 'Operations: From Factory to Service Management' (1994).

5. Compare, for example, the disappointing findings in two studies by the consulting firms A.T. Kearney and Arthur D. Little (*The Economist*, 1992). In a study of more than 100 firms in the UK, 80 per cent reported that no significant impact could be observed as a result of TQM, and in a study of 500 US firms, almost two-thirds said that they had achieved no competitive gains.

6. The integration of marketing and operations management with human resources management is further elaborated on in Benjamin Schneider's article 'HRM – A Service Perspective: Towards a Customer-focused HRM' (1994).

7. However, even this umbrella notion of internal marketing is not entirely new. Major changes in management perspectives always require extensive internal attention. It is interesting to notice that Frederick Taylor in his testimony about scientific management before the American congress in 1912 explicitly states that '. . . in its essence, scientific management involves a complete *mental revolution* on the part of the working men engaged in any particular establishment or industry. . . . And it involves the equally complete mental revolution on the part of those on the management's side. . . . And without this complete mental revolution on both sides scientific management does not exist' (Taylor, 1947, testimony part, p. 27; emphasis added). Taylor stressed the importance of this internal focus, which, however, seems to have been neglected by his followers. Service management, equally, requires such a mental revolution or, to use a modern metaphor, cultural change. The similarity between Taylor's mental revolution and the attitude management aspect of internal marketing is obvious.

8. Two international service management conferences were arranged in France in 1990 and 1992 by IAE at the University-d'Aix-Marseille. In service quality management three QUIS (Quality in Services) conferences initiated by the Service Research Center at the University of Karlstad have so far been arranged bi-annually since 1988, two in Sweden by the Service Research Center and one in the US by St John's University, and furthermore three international workshops devoted to quality management in services co-sponsored by the European Institute for Advanced Studies in Management have been arranged annually since 1991, in Brussels, Maastricht and Helsinki respectively.

References

Abbott, L. (1955), *Quality and Competition*, Columbia University Press, New York.

Albrecht, K. (1988), *At America's Service*, Dow Jones-Irwin, Homewood, IL.

Albrecht, K. and Zemke, R. (1985), *Service America!*, Dow Jones-Irwin, Homewood, IL.

Andersson, T.D. (1992), 'Another Model of Service Quality: A Model of Causes and Effects of Service Quality tested on a Case within the Restaurant Industry', in Kunst, P and Lemmink, J. (eds), *Quality Management in Services*, Van Gorcum, Assen, Maastricht, pp. 41–58.

Barnes, J.G. (1989), 'The Role of Internal Marketing: If the Staff Won't Buy It, Why Should the Customer?', *Irish Marketing Review*, Vol. 4, No. 2, pp. 11–21.

Barnes, J.G. and Cumby, J.A. (1993), 'The Cost of Quality in Service-Oriented Companies: Making Better Customer Service Decisions Through Improved Cost Information', Research Paper, *ASB Conference 1993*, University of New Brunswick, Canada.

Bateson, J. (1989), *Managing Services Marketing: Text and Readings*, Dryden Press, Hinsdale, IL.

Berry, L.L. (1981), 'The Employee as Customer', *Journal of Retail Banking*, Vol. 3, No. 1, pp. 33–40.

Berry, L.L. (1983), 'Relationship Marketing', in Berry, L.L., Shostack G.L. and Upah, G.D. (eds), *Emerging Perspectives of Services Marketing*, American Marketing Association. Chicago, IL, pp. 25–8.

Berry, L.L and Parasuraman, A. (1991), *Marketing Services. Competing Through Quality*, Free Press/Lexington Books, Lexington, MA.

Berry, L.L. and Parasuraman, A. (1993), 'Building a New Academic Field – The Case of Services Marketing', *Journal of Retailing*, Vol. 69, Spring, pp. 13–60.

Bowen, D.E., Chase, R.B. and Cummings, T.G. (eds) (1990), *Service Management Effectiveness*, Jossey-Bass, San Francisco, CA.

Bowen, D.E. and Lawler III, E.E. (1992), 'The Empowerment of Service Workers: What, Why, How and When', *Sloan Management Review*, Vol. 33, No. 3, pp. 31–9.

Brown, S.W., Gummesson, E., Edvardsson, B. and Gustavsson, B.O. (eds) (1991), *Quality in Services. Multidisciplinary and Multinational Perspectives*, Lexington Books, Lexington, MA.

Buzzell, R.D. and Gale, B.T. (1987), *The PIMS Principles. Linking Strategy to Performance*, Free Press. New York.

Carlzon, J. (1987), *Moments of Truth*, Ballinger, Cambridge, MA.

Chase, R.B. (1978), 'Where Does the Customer Fit in a Service Operation', *Harvard Business Review*, Vol. 56, November–December, pp. 137–42.

Chase, R.B. (1991), 'The Service Factory: A Future Vision', *International Journal of Service Industry Management*, Vol. 2, No. 3, pp. 60–70.

Christopher, M., Payne, A. and Ballantyne, D. (1991), *Relationship Marketing Bringing Quality, Customer Service and Marketing Together*, Butterworth-Heinemann, Oxford.

Collier, D.A. (1987), *Service Management. The Automation of Services*, Prentice-Hall, Englewood Cliffs, NJ.

Cowell, D. (1984), *The Marketing of Services*, Heinemann, London.

Davidow, W.H. and Uttal, B. (1989), *Total Customer Service. The Utimate Service*, Harper & Row, New York.

Edvardsson, B. and Gustavsson, B.O. (1988), *Quality in Services and Quality in Service Organizations – A Model of Quality Assessment*, Center for Service Research, Karlstad, Sweden.

Fisk, R.P., Brown, S.W. and Bitner, M.J. (1993), 'The Evolution of the Services Marketing Literature', *Journal of Retailing*, Vol. 69, Spring, pp. 61–103.

George, W.R. (1972), 'Marketing in the Service Industries', Unpublished dissertation, University of Georgia.

George, W.R. (1984), 'Internal Marketing for Retailers. The Junior Executive Employee', in Lindqvist, J.D. (ed.), *Developments in Marketing Science*, Academy of Marketing Science.

George, W.R. (1990), 'Internal Marketing and Organizational Behavior: A Partnership in Developing Customer-Conscious Employees at Every Level', *Journal of Business Research*, Vol. 20, No. 1, pp. 63–70.

Grönroos, C. (1979), *Marknadsföring av tjänster. En studie av marknadsfunktionen i tjänsteföretag* (Marketing of services. A study of the marketing function of service firms), with English summary, Akademilitteratur/Marknadstekniskt Centrum, Stockholm, Sweden.

Grönroos, C. (1982), *Strategic Management and Marketing in the Service Sector*, Swedish School of Economics and Business Administration, Helsingfors, Finland (published in 1983 in the US by Marketing Science Institute and in the UK by Studentlitteratur/Chartwell-Bratt).

Grönroos, C. (1984), 'A Service Quality Model and Its Marketing Implications', *European Journal of Marketing*, Vol. 18, No. 4, pp. 36–44.

Grönroos, C. (1988), 'New Competition in the Service Economy: The Five Rules of Service', *International Journal of Operations and Product Management*, Vol. 8, No. 3, pp. 9–18.

Grönroos, C. (1990a), 'Service Management and Marketing. Managing the Moments of Truth in Service Competition', Free Press/Lexington Books, Lexington, MA.

Grönroos. C. (1990b), 'Relationship Approach to the Marketing Function in Service Contexts: The Marketing and Organizational Behavior Interface', *Journal of Business Research*, Vol. 20, No. 1, pp. 3–12.

Grönroos, C. (1990c), 'Service Management: A Management Focus for Service Competition', *International Journal of Service Industry Management*, Vol. 1, No. 1, pp. 6–14.

Grönroos, C. (1993a), 'Toward a Third Phase in Service Quality Research: Challenges and Future Directions', in Swartz, T.A., Bowen, D.E. and Brown, S.W. (eds), *Advances in Services Marketing and Management*, Vol. 2, JAI Press, Greenwich, CT, pp. 49–64.

Grönroos, C. (1993b), 'From Marketing Mix to Relationship Marketing: Toward a Paradigm Shift in Marketing', Working Paper, No. 263. Swedish School of Economics and Business Administration, Helsingfors, Finland.

Grönroos, C. (1994), 'Quo Vadis, Marketing? Toward a Relationship Marketing Paradigm', *Journal of Marketing Management*, Vol. 10, No. 4.

Grönroos, C. and Gummesson, E. (1985), 'The Nordic School of Service Marketing', in Grönroos, C. and Gummesson, E. (eds), *Service Marketing – Nordic School Perspectives*, Stockholm University, Sweden, pp. 6–11.

Gummesson, E. (1977), *Marknadsföring och inköp av konsulttjänster* (Marketing and purchasing of professional services), Akademilitteratur, Stockholm, Sweden.

Gummesson, E. (1987), 'The New Marketing – Developing Long-term interactive Relationships', *Long Range Planning*, Vol. 20, pp. 10–20.

Gummesson, E. (1991), 'Marketing-orientation Revisited: The Crucial Role of The Part-time Marketer', *European Journal of Marketing*, Vol. 25, No. 2, pp. 60–75.

Gummesson, E. (1993a), *Quality Management in Service Organizations*, ISQA, International Service Quality Association, New York.

Gummesson, E. (1993b), *Relationsmarknadsföring Frön 4 P till 30 R* (Relationship marketing. From 4 Ps to 30 Rs), Stockholm University, Sweden.

Haywood, K.M. and Pickworth, J.R. (1988), 'Connecting Productivity with Quality through the Design of Service Delivery Systems', in Thomas, E.G. and Rao, S.R. (eds), *Proceedings from an International Conference on Services Marketing*, Special Conference Series, Vol. V, Academy of Marketing Science/Cleveland State University, pp. 261–73.

Haywood-Farmer, K.M. and Stuart, F.I. (1988), 'Measuring the Quality of Professional Services', in Johnston, R. (ed.), *The Management of Service Operations*, IFS Publications, Kempston, pp. 207–20.

Heskett, J.L. (1986), *Managing in the Service Economy*, Harvard Business School Press, Boston, MA.

Heskett, J.L. (1987), 'Lessons in the Service Sector', *Harvard Business Review*, Vol. 65, March–April, pp. 118–26.

Heskett, J.L., Sasser, W.E. and Hart, C.W.L. (1991), *Service Breakthroughs: Changing the Rules of the Game*, Free Press, New York.

Johanson, J. and Mattsson, L.G. (1985), 'Marketing Investments and Market Investments in Industrial Networks', *International Journal of Research in Marketing*, Vol. 2, No. 3, pp. 185–95.

Johnson, E.M. (1969), 'Are Goods and Services Different? An Exercise in Marketing Theory', unpublished dissertation, Washington University.

Johnston, R. (1987), 'A Framework for Developing a Quality Strategy in a Customer Process Processing Operation', *International Journal of Quality & Reliability Management*, Vol. 4, No. 4, pp. 35–44.

Johnston, R. (1994), 'Operations: From Factory to Service Management', *International Journal of Service Industry Management*, Vol. 5, No. 1.

Judd, R.C. (1965), *The Structure and Classification of the Service Market*, Dissertation, University Microfilms, Ann Arbor, MI.

Kordupleski, R.E., Rust, R.T. and Zahorik, A.J. (1993), 'Why Improving Quality Doesn't Improve Quality, (Or Whatever Happened to Marketing?)', *California Management Review*, Vol. 35, No. 3, pp. 82–95.

Kotler, P. (1992), 'It's Time for Total Marketing', *Business Week ADVANCE Executive Brief*, Vol. 2.

Kunst, P. and Lemmink, J. (1992), *Quality Management in Services*, Van Gorcum, Assen, Maastricht.

Langeard, E. and Eiglier, P. (1987), *Servuction. Le marketing des services*. Wiley, Paris.

Lehtinen, J. (1983), *Asiakasohjautuva palveluyritys* (Customer-oriented service firm), Weilin+Göös, Espoo, Finland.

Lemmink, J. and Behara, R.S. (1992), 'Q-Matrix: A Multi-Dimensional Approach to Using Service Quality Measurements', in Kunst, P. and Lemmink, J. (eds), *Quality Management in Services*, Van Gorcum, Assen, Maastricht, The Netherlands, pp. 79–88.

Levitt, T. (1972), 'Production-line Approach to Service', *Harvard Business Review*, Vol. 50, September–October, pp. 41–52.

Liljander, V. and Strandvik, T. (1993), 'Estimating Zones of Tolerance in Perceived Service Quality and Perceived Service Value', *International Journal of Service Industry Management*, Vol. 4, No. 2, pp. 6–28.

Liljander, V. and Strandvik, T. (1994), 'Different Comparison Standards as Determinants of Service Quality', *Journal of Consumer Satisfaction, Dissatisfaction and Complaining Behavior*, Vol. 7.

Lindqvist, L.J. (1988), *Kundernas kvalitesupplevelse i konsumtionsfasen* (The quality perception of customers in the consumption phase), Swedish School of Economics and Business Administration, Heisingfors, Finland.

Lovelock, C.H. (1984), *Services Marketing*, Prentice-Hall, Englewood Cliffs, NJ.

Lovelock, C.H. (1988), *Managing Services. Marketing, Operations, and Human Resources*, Prentice-Hall, Englewood Cliffs, NJ.

Meyer, A. and Mattmuller, R. (1987), 'Qualität von Dienstleistungen. Entwurf eines praxisorientierten Qualitätsmodells' (The quality of services. Outline of a practice-oriented quality model), *Marketing*, ZPF, Vol. 3.

Mickwitz, G. (1959), *Marketing and Competition*, Societas Scientarium Fennica, Helsingfors, Finland (available from University Microfilms, Ann Arbor, MI).

Mills, P.K. (1986), *Managing Service Industries: Organizational Practices in a Post-Industrial Economy*, Ballinger, Cambridge, MA.

Normann, R. (1982), *Service Management*, Liber, Malmö, Sweden (published in English in 1984 by John Wiley and Sons, New York).

Normann, R. and Ramirez, R. (1993), 'From, Value Chain to Value Constellation: Designing Interactive Strategy', *Harvard Business Review*, Vol. 71, July–August, pp. 65–77.

Parasuraman, A., Zeithaml, V.A. and Berry, L.L. (1985), 'A Conceptual Model of Service Quality and its Implications for Future Research', *Journal of Marketing*, Vol. 49, Fall, pp. 41–50.

Parasuraman, A., Zeithaml, V.A. and Berry, L.L. (1986), 'SERVQUAL: A Multiple-Item Scale for Measuring Customer Perceptions of Service Quality', *Journal of Retailing*, Vol. 64, Spring, pp. 12–40.

Parasuraman, A., Zeithaml, V.A. and Berry, L.L. (1994), 'Reassessment of Expectations as a Comparison Standard in Measuring Service Quality: Implications for Future Research', *Journal of Marketing*, Vol. 58, Winter.

Pickworth, J.P. (1987), 'Minding the Ps and Qs: Linking Quality and Productivity', *The Cornell Hotel and Restaurant Administration Quarterly*, Vol. 28, No 1, pp. 40–7.

Proceedings from the 1st International Research Seminar in Service Management, Marketing, Operations, Human Resources Insights Into Services, IAE, Aix-en-Provence, France, June 1990.

Proceedings from the 2nd International Research Seminar in Service Management, Marketing, Operations, Human Resources Insights Into Services, IAE, Aix-en-Provence, France, June 1992.

Quinn, J.B., Dorley, T.L. and Paquette, P.C. (1990), 'Beyond Products: Service-Based Strategy', *Harvard Business Review*, Vol. 68, March–April, pp. 58–67.

Rathmell, J.M. (1974), *Marketing in the Service Sector*, Winthrop Publishers, Cambridge, MA.

Reichheld, F.E. and Sasser, Jr, W.E. (1990), 'Zero Defections: Quality Comes To Service', *Harvard Business Review*, Vol. 68, September–October, pp. 105–11.

Reichheld, F.E. (1993), 'Loyalty-Based Management', *Harvard Business Review*, Vol. 71, March–April, pp. 64–73.

Sasser, W.E., Olsen R.P. and Wyckoff, D.D. (1978), *Management of Service Operations*, Allyn and Bacon, Boston, MA.

Scheuing, E.E., Gummesson, E. and Little. C.H. (eds) (1992), *Quality in Services (QUIS 2) Conference. Selected Papers*, St. John's University, New York.

Schlesinger, L.A. and Heskett, J.L. (1991), 'The Service-Driven Service Company', *Harvard Business Review*, Vol. 69, September–October, pp. 71–81.

Schneider, B. (1980), 'The Service Organization: Climate is Crucial', *Organizational Dynamics*, Vol. 9, No. 2, pp. 52–65.

Schneider, B. (1994), 'HRM – A Service Perspective: Towards a Customer-focused HRM', *International Journal of Service Industry Management*, Vol. 5, No. 1, pp. 64–76.

Schneider, B. and Rentsch, J. (1987), 'The Management of Climate and Culture: A Futures Perspective', in Hage, J. (ed.), *Futures of Organizations*, Lexington Books, Lexington, MA.

Slywotzky, A.J. and Shapiro, B.P. (1993), 'Leveraging to Beat the Odds: The New Marketing Mind-Set', *Harvard Business Review*, Vol. 71, September–October, pp. 97–107.

Smith, A. (1950/1776), *The Wealth of Nations. An Inquiry into the Nature and Cause of the Wealth of Nations*, Methuen, London (the original published 1776).

Stauss, B. (1993), 'Service Deployment: Transformation of Problem Information into Problem Prevention Activities', *International Journal of Service Industry Management*, Vol. 4, No. 3, pp. 41–62.

Steedle, L.F. (1988), 'Has Productivity Measurement Outgrown Infancy?', *Management Accounting*, Vol. 70, No. 2, p. 15.

Storbacka, K. (1993), *Customer Relationship Profitability in Retail Banking*, Research Report, Swedish School of Economics and Business Administration, Helsinki, Finland.

Swartz, T.A., Bowen, D.E. and Brown, S.W. (eds) (1992), *Advances in Services Marketing and Management*, Vol. 1, JAI Press, Greenwich, CT.

Swartz, TA., Bowen, D.E. and Brown, S.W. (eds) (1993), *Advances in Services Marketing and Management*, Vol. 2, JAI Press, Greenwich, CT.

Taylor, F.W. (1947), *Scientific Management*, Harper & Row, London (a volume of two papers originally published in 1903 and 1911 and a written testimony for a Special House Committee in the US in 1912).

Voss, C.A., Armistead, C.G., Johnston, R. and Morris, B. (1985), *Operations Management in Service Industries and the Public Sector*, Wiley, Chichester, UK.

Webster, F.E. (1988), 'The Rediscovery of the Marketing Concept', *Business Horizons*, Vol. 31, May–June, pp. 29–39.

Webster, Jr. F.E. (1992), 'The Changing Role of Marketing in the Corporation', *Journal of Marketing*, Vol. 56, October, pp. 1–17.

Wilson, A. (1972), *The Marketing of Professional Services*, McGraw-Hill, London.

Critical service encounters: the employee's viewpoint

Mary Jo Bitner ■ *Bernard H. Booms* ■ *Lois A. Mohr*

In service settings, customer satisfaction is often influenced by interactions with contact employees. Previous research identified the sources of satisfaction and dissatisfaction in service encounters from the customer's point of view; this study explores these sources in service encounters from the contact employee's point of view. Drawing on insights from the role, script and attribution theories, 774 critical service encounters reported by hotel, restaurant and airline employees are analyzed. The findings have implications for business practice in managing service encounters, employee empowerment and training and managing customers.

The worldwide quality movement that has swept the manufacturing sector over the last decade is beginning to take shape in the service sector (*Business Week*, 1991; Crosby, 1991). According to some, the shift to a quality focus is essential to the competitive survival of service businesses, just as it has become essential in manufacturing (Heskett *et al.* 1994; Schlesinger and Heskett, 1991).

Service quality researchers have suggested that 'the proof of service [quality] is in its flawless performance' (Berry and Parasuraman, 1991, p. 15), a concept akin to the notion of 'zero defects' in manufacturing. Others have noted that 'breakthrough' service managers pursue the goal of 100 per cent defect-free service (Heskett, Sasser and Hart, 1990). From the customer's point of view, the most immediate evidence of service occurs in the service encounter or the 'moment of truth' when the customer interacts with the firm. Thus, one central goal in the pursuit of 'zero defects' in service is to work toward 100 per cent flawless performance in service encounters. Here, flawless performance is not meant to imply rigid standardization, but rather 100 per cent satisfying performance from the customer's point of view. The cost of not achieving flawless performance is the 'cost of quality', which includes the costs associated with redoing the service or compensating for poor service, lost customers, negative word of mouth and decreased employee morale.

Although more firms are realizing the importance of service quality and customer satisfaction, it is not always clear how to achieve these goals. Situations arise in which quality is low and the problem is recognized by both the firm (i.e., employees) and the customer, but there may be disagreement on the causes of the problem and the appropriate solutions. In service encounters such disagreements, sure to diminish customer satisfaction, underscore the importance of understanding the types of events and behaviours that cause customers to be satisfied or dissatisfied. Because the service encounter involves at least two people, it is important to understand the encounter from multiple perspectives. Armed with such understanding, firms are better able to design processes and educate both employees and customers to achieve quality in service encounters.

Previous research in the context of the restaurant, hotel and airline industries identified categories of events and behaviours that underlie critical service encounters from the customer's point of view (Bitner, Booms and Tetreault, 1990; hereafter BBT). The primary purpose of this study is to examine the contact employee's perspective of critical service encounters and to understand, in the context of the same three industries, the kinds of events and behaviours that employees believe underlie customer satisfaction. The employee perspective is then compared with BBT to gain insight into any disparities in perspectives. A second purpose of the study is to evaluate the usefulness of the classification scheme developed by BBT (1990). If the scheme is conceptually robust, it should hold for different respondent groups.

The research is guided by the following questions:

■ From the contact employee's point of view, what kinds of events lead to satisfying service encounters for the customer? What causes these events to be remembered favourably?
■ From the contact employee's point of view, what kinds of events lead to dissatisfying service encounters for the customer? What causes these events to be remembered with distaste?
■ Do customers and employees report the same kinds of events and behaviours leading to satisfaction and dissatisfaction in service encounters?

Before presenting the empirical study, we discuss relevant research and theory.

Customer and contact employee viewpoints

Frontline personnel are a critical source of information about customers. There are two basic ways that customer knowledge obtained by contact employees is used to improve service: (1) such knowledge is used by the contact employees themselves to facilitate their interactions with customers; and (2) it is used by the firm for making decisions. First, employees often modify their behaviour from moment to moment on the basis of feedback they receive while serving customers. Schneider (1980) argues that people who choose to work in service occupations generally have a strong desire to give good service. To the extent that this is true, contact personnel can be expected to look frequently for cues that tell them how their service is received by customers. The more accurate their perceptions are, the more likely their behavioural adjustments are to improve customer satisfaction.

Second, because contact personnel have frequent contact with customers, they serve a boundary-spanning role in the firm. As a result, they often have better understanding of customer needs and problems than others in the firm. Researchers have theorized and found some evidence that open communication between frontline personnel and managers is important for achieving service quality (Parasuraman, Berry and Zeithaml, 1990; Zeithaml, Berry and Parasuraman, 1988). Schneider and Bowen (1984) argue that firms should use information gathered from contact personnel in making strategic decisions, especially decisions regarding new service development and service modifications.

It seems reasonable to conclude that accurate employee understanding of customers enables both the employee and the firm to adjust appropriately to customer needs. However, previous research correlating customer and employee views of service is sparse and offers mixed conclusions. Schneider and Bowen (1985) and Schneider, Parkington and Buxton (1980) found high correlations (r = .63 and r = .67, respectively) between employee and customer attitudes about overall service quality in a bank setting. Their results are contradicted, however, in a study by Brown and Swartz (1989). These researchers gathered data on patient experiences with their physicians and compared them with the physicians' perceptions of their patients' experiences. The differences they found were rather large and inversely related to overall patient satisfaction.

Another study of 1,300 customers and 900 customer service professionals conducted by Development Dimensions International found differences in perceptions between the two groups (*Services Marketing Newsletter 1989*). Customer service professionals in that study consistently rated the importance of particular service skills and competencies and their actual performance higher than customers rated the same skills and competencies. Similarly, Langeard and colleagues (1981) found that field managers at two banks tended to overestimate (compared with customer ratings) the importance of six broad service delivery dimensions. Other studies have found differences when comparing customer and employee evaluations of business situations using scenarios and role playing in product failure contexts (Folkes and

Kotsos, 1986), a complaint context (Resnik and Harmon, 1983), and the context of retailer responses to customer problems (Dornoff and Dwyer, 1981).

We would therefore expect, on the basis of these studies, to find similarities in employee and customer views of the service encounter, but we would expect significant differences as well. Role, script and attribution theories provide conceptual bases for these expectations.

Theoretical explanations

Role and script theories

Similarities in how customers and employees view service encounters are most likely when the two parties share common *role* expectations and the service script is well defined (Mohr and Bitner, 1991; Solomon *et al.*, 1985). A *role* is the behaviour associated with a socially defined position (Solomon *et al.*, 1985), and *role expectations* are the standards for role behaviour (Biddle, 1986). In many routine service encounters, particularly for experienced employees and customers, the roles are well defined and both the customer and employee know what to expect from each other.

In addition, many types of service encounters, such as seating customers in a restaurant, are repeated frequently throughout a person's life, resulting in strong, standardized and well-rehearsed scripts (i.e., structures that describe appropriate sequences of role behaviours) (Schank and Abelson, 1977). When service encounters have strong scripts, the employee and customer are likely to share expectations about the events that will occur and the order of occurrence. They are less likely to share ideas about subscripts, which are prescriptions for handling what Schank and Abelson describe as 'obstacles and errors', two types of interferences that may occur in otherwise predictable scripts.

Role and script theory, combined with the routine nature of many service encounters, suggests that customers and employees are likely to share a common perspective on service experiences. It is also clear that differences in perspective may arise when roles are less defined, a participant is unfamiliar with expected behaviours, or interferences require the enactment of complex or less routine subscripts.

Attribution theory

Dissimilarities in viewpoint may arise when service encounter partners have conflicting views of the underlying causes behind the events, that is, when their attributions differ. Research shows that there are many biases in the attribution process (Fiske and Taylor, 1984). Most clearly relevant for the perceptions of service providers and customers is the self-serving attribution bias. This is the tendency for people to take credit for success (i.e., to give internal attributions for their successes, a self-enhancing bias) and deny responsibility for failure (i.e., to blame failure on external causes, a self-protecting bias). Given these biases we would expect employees to blame the system or the customer for service failures, whereas the customer would be more likely to blame the system or the employee. The result would be different views of the causes of service dissatisfaction. It is less clear that this bias would operate in the case of a service encounter success. Although the desire for self-enhancement might lead both the employee and customer to give themselves credit for the success, the fact that the customer is paying the firm for a service would probably preclude the bias on the customer's side. Overall, then, the self-serving attribution bias leads to the expectation that the perspectives of the employee and customer will differ more in service success situations.

Both empirical research and theory suggest that similarities as well as differences in perspective are likely to occur between service encounter participants. Role and script theories suggest that in relatively routine situations such as the ones studied, there will be strong similarities in perspective. However, attribution biases suggest that there will also be significant differences in viewpoint. We explore to what extent the perspectives of contact personnel and those of customers are different. And, to the degree that they are different, the data provide insight into the nature of these disparities.

Method and analysis

Data collection

Data were collected using the critical incident technique (CIT), a systematic procedure for recording events and behaviours that are observed to lead to success or failure on a specific task (Ronan and Latham, 1974), in this case, satisfying the customer. (For more detailed discussions of the method, see BBT; Flanagan, 1954; Wilson-Pessano, 1988). Using the CIT, data are collected through structured, open-ended questions, and the results are content analyzed. Respondents are asked to report specific events from the recent past (within 6 to 12 months). These accounts provide rich details of firsthand experiences in which customers have been satisfied or dissatisfied. Because respondents are asked about specific events rather than generalities, interpretation or conclusions, this procedure meets criteria established by Ericsson and Simon (1980) for providing valuable, reliable information about cognitive processes. Researchers have concluded that when used appropriately (Flanagan, 1954; Wilson-Pessano, 1988), the critical incident method is reliable in terms of stability of the categories identified across judges, valid with respect to the content identified, and relevant in that the behaviours illuminated have proven to be important to the success or failure of the task in question (Ronan and Latham, 1974; White and Locke, 1981).

Hotel, restaurant and airline employees were interviewed and asked to recall critical service encounters that caused satisfaction or dissatisfaction for customers of their firms. Thirty-seven trained student interviewers collected the data – 781 total incidents. Each one recruited a minimum of ten employees from among the same three industries studied in BBT, asking each employee to describe one incident that was satisfactory and one that was dissatisfactory from the customer's point of view.

Because all the interviewers were employed in the hospitality sector, they recruited fellow employees and employees of establishments with which they were familiar. They were instructed not to interview fellow students. The refusal rate was negligible. The incident sample represented 58 hotels, 152 restaurants and 4 airlines. On average, the employees providing the incidents had 5.5 years of working experience in their respective industries. The employees ranged in age from 16 to 65 (mean age 27) and were 55 per cent female and 45 per cent male. The instructions to the employees being interviewed were as follows:

Put yourself in the shoes of customers of your firm. In other words, try to see your firm through your customer's eyes.

Think of a recent time when a customer of your firm had a particularly satisfying (dissatisfying) interaction with yourself or a fellow employee. Describe the situation and exactly what happened.

They were then asked the following questions:

1. When did the incident happen?
2. What specific circumstances led up to this situation?
3. Exactly what did you or your fellow employee say or do?
4. What resulted that made you feel the interaction was satisfying (dissatisfying) from the customer's point of view?
5. What should you or your fellow employee have said or done? (for dissatisfying incident only)

To be used in the analysis, an incident was required to (1) involve employee–customer interaction, (2) be very satisfying or dissatisfying from the customer's point of view, (3) be a discrete episode, and (4) have sufficient detail to be visualized by the interviewer. Seven incidents failed to meet these criteria, leaving 774 incidents (397 satisfactory and 377 dissatisfactory).

Classification of incidents

The incident classification system developed by BBT was used as a starting point for sorting the data with the assumption that, to the degree that customers and employees remember satisfying and dissatisfying encounters in the same way, the same classification system should be appropriate. Incidents that could not be classified within the original scheme would then provide evidence for differences in perspective.

One researcher trained in the classification scheme coded the incidents. Any that did not fit into the scheme were put aside. This researcher and a second then worked together on categorizing this group of 86 incidents (11 per cent of the total). These incidents were read and sorted, combined and resorted until a consistent coding scheme was developed that combined similar incidents into distinct, meaningful categories. When the new categories were labelled and the two researchers achieved consensus on assignment of the incidents, the new categories (one major group with four subcategories) were added to the original classification system.

A set of complete coding instructions was then written (see Appendix A). They included general instructions for coders, operational definitions of each category and decision rules for assigning incidents to categories. These are procedures recommended by Perreault and Leigh (1989) for improving the reliability of judgement-based data. The coding instructions were used to train a third researcher who had not participated in the categorization decisions. This researcher then coded the 774 employee incidents, providing an inter-judge reliability check on the classification system. Discrepancies between the first and third researchers' assignments were resolved by the second researcher.

The inter-judge agreement between the first and third researchers was 84 per cent for the satisfying incidents and 85 per cent for the dissatisfying incidents. These figures are respectably high, especially considering that the classification system in this study contains 16 categories. The percentage agreement statistic probably underestimates inter-judge reliability in this case because this statistic is influenced by the number of coding categories (i.e., the more categories, the lower the percentage agreement is likely to be) (Perreault and Leigh, 1989). For this reason, two other measures of inter-judge reliability were calculated. Cohen's κ, which corrects for the likelihood of chance agreement between judges, was found to be .816 for the satisfying and .823 for the dissatisfying incidents. Perreault and Leigh (1989) argue, however, that κ is an overly conservative measure of reliability because it assumes an a priori knowledge of the likely distribution of responses across categories.

To correct for this they designed an alternative index of reliability, I_r appropriate for marketing data. Rather than contrasting inter-judge agreement with an estimate of chance agreement, I_r is based on a model of the level of agreement that might be expected given a true (population) level of reliability. Furthermore, the index focuses on the reliability of the whole coding process, not just on the agreement between judges. I_r was found to be .911 and .914 for the satisfying and dissatisfying incidents, respectively.

Results and discussion

The categories of events and behaviours that employees believe underlie their customers' satisfaction and dissatisfaction in service encounters are identified and discussed first. Then the results are compared with customer perceptions using the BBT data.

Classification of employee-reported incidents

The critical incident classification system based on incidents gathered from customers (BBT) consists of three major groups of employee behaviours that account for all satisfactory and dissatisfactory incidents: (1) employee response to service delivery system failures, (2) employee response to customer needs and requests, and (3) unprompted and unsolicited employee actions. Of the 774 employee incidents, 668 were classified into one of these three groups and the 12 categories within them. The incidents were very similar in detail to those provided by customers. (See BBT for detailed descriptions of the groups and categories and sample incidents.)

Eighty-six encounters (11 per cent of the total) did not fit any of the predetermined groups. These incidents were categorized into one major group labelled 'problem customer behaviour', and they were added to the categorization scheme as 'Group 4'. In these cases, the coders could not attribute the satisfaction and dissatisfaction to an action or attitude of the employee – instead, the root cause was the customer. Such customers were basically uncooperative, that is, unwilling to cooperate with the service provider, other customers, industry regulations, and/or laws. These situations created problems for the employees, and rarely were they able to deal with them in such a way as to bring about customer satisfaction; only 3 of these incidents were satisfactory.

Within the problem customer behaviour group, four categories emerged (Table 1 provides examples of incidents from the four new categories):

Table 1 ■ Group 4 sample incidents: problem customers

Incident	
Dissatisfactory	Satisfactory
A. Drunkeness	
An intoxicated man began pinching the female flight attendants. One attendant told him to stop, but he continued and then hit another passenger. The co-pilot was called and asked the man to sit down and leave the others alone, but the passenger refused. The co-pilot then 'decked' the man, knocking him into his seat.	A person who became intoxicated on a flight started speaking loudly, annoying the other passengers. The flight attendant asked the passenger if he would be driving when the plane landed and offered him coffee. He accepted the coffee and became quieter and friendlier.
B. Verbal and physical abuse	
While a family of three was waiting to order dinner, the father began hitting his child. Another customer complained about this to the manager who then, in a friendly and sympathetic way, asked the family to leave. The father knocked all the plates and glasses off the table before leaving.	None
C. Breaking company policies or laws	
Five guests were in a hotel room two hours past checkout time. Because they would not answer the phone calls or let the staff into the room, hotel security staff finally broke in. They found the guests using drugs and called the police.	None
D. Uncooperative customer	
When a man was shown to his table in the non-view dining area of the restaurant, he became extremely angry and demanded a window table. The restaurant was very busy, but the hostess told him he could get a window seat in half an hour. He refused to wait and took his previously reserved table, but he complained all the way through dinner and left without tipping.	None

1. *Drunkenness* – The employee perceives the customer to be clearly intoxicated and creating problems such as harassing other customers nearby, giving the employee a hard time or disrupting the atmosphere of the establishment;

2. *Verbal and physical abuse* – The customer verbally and/or physically abuses either the employee or other customers;

3. *Breaking company policies or laws* – The customer refuses to comply with policies or laws, and the employee attempts to enforce compliance; and

4. *Uncooperative customers* – The customer is generally rude and uncooperative or unreasonably demanding. From the employee's perspective, the customer is unwilling to be satisfied, no matter what is done for him or her.

The employee's view of satisfactory versus dissatisfactory encounters

Here we examine the frequencies and proportions of employee accounts in the four groups and 16 categories as shown in Table 2. It should be noted that the frequencies and proportions shown in the table reflect numbers of reported events. The actual frequency of occurrence of the type of event represented by a particular group or category cannot be inferred from the data. Nor can greater importance be inferred by greater frequencies in a particular category (Wilson-Pessano, 1988). The data are shown in full in Table 2; however, our discussion focuses on the four major groups. To facilitate understanding, the employee-reported incidents are summarized and ranked according to the percentage of incidents in the four major incident groups:

Distribution of dissatisfactory incidents

Rank order	Group	Percentage
1	Group 1 – Response to failures	51.7
2	Group 4 – Problem customers	22.0
3	Group 2 – Response to requests	16.4
4	Group 3 – Unprompted action	9.8

Distribution of satisfactory incidents

Rank order	Group	Percentage
1	Group 2 – Response to requests	49.4
2	Group 1 – Response to failures	27.5
3	Group 3 – Unprompted action	22.4
4	Group 4 – Problem customers	.8

When employees were asked to report incidents resulting in customer dissatisfaction, they tended to describe problems with external causes such as the delivery system or inappropriate customer behaviours. By far the largest number of dissatisfactory incidents were categorized in Group 1 (response to delivery system failures), with the next largest proportion falling into Group 4 (problem customers). These results are not unexpected given what attribution theory suggests. When things go wrong, people are more likely to blame external, situational factors than to attribute the failure to their own shortcomings. A modest number of dissatisfactory incidents were found in Group 2. In many of these cases, the employees implied that they were unable to satisfy customer needs due to constraints placed on them by laws or their own organization's rules and procedures, again placing the blame on an external source. The smallest percentage of dissatisfactory incidents were classified in Group 3, which reflects spontaneous negative employee behaviours (e.g., rudeness, lack of attention). Again, this is consistent with the bias toward not blaming oneself for failures.

The largest proportion of satisfactory incidents, from the employee's point of view, occurred in response to customer needs and requests (Group 2). Almost half of particularly satisfying customer encounters reported by employees resulted from their ability to adjust the system to accommodate customer needs and requests. Success is attributed in these cases to the employee's own ability and willingness to adjust. The next largest proportion of satisfactory incidents were categorized in Group 1. This is an interesting set of incidents, because each one began as a failure but ended as a success because of the ability of the

Table 2 ■ Group and category classification by the type of incident outcome (employees only)

Group and category	Satisfactory No.	Satisfactory %	Dissatisfactory No.	Dissatisfactory %	Row total No.	Row total %
Type of incident outcome						
Group 1. Employee response to service delivery system failures						
A. To unavailable service	31	7.8	37	9.8	68	8.8
B. To unreasonably slow service	23	6.0	48	12.7	71	9.2
C. To other core service failures	55	13.9	110	29.2	165	21.3
Subtotal, Group 1	109	27.5	195	51.7	304	39.3
Group 2. Employee response to customer needs and requests						
A. To 'special needs' customers	80	20.2	14	3.7	94	12.1
B. To customer preferences	99	24.9	43	11.4	142	18.3
C. To admitted customer error	11	2.8	0	0.0	11	1.4
D. To potentially disruptive others	6	1.5	5	1.3	11	1.4
Subtotal, Group 2	196	49.4	62	16.4	258	33.3
Group 3. Unprompted and unsolicited employee actions						
A. Attention paid to customer	43	10.8	6	1.6	49	6.3
B. Truly out of the ordinary employee behaviour	25	6.3	28	7.4	53	6.8
C. Employee behaviours in the context of cultural norms	7	1.8	3	0.8	10	1.3
D. Gestalt evaluation	0	0.0	0	0.0	0	0.0
E. Performance under adverse circumstances	14	3.5	0	0.0	14	1.8
Subtotal, Group 3	89	22.4	37	9.8	126	16.3
Group 4. Problematic customer behaviour						
A. Drunkenness	3	0.8	16	4.2	19	2.5
B. Verbal and physical abuse	0	0.0	9	2.4	9	1.2
C. Breaking company policies or laws	0	0.0	16	4.2	16	2.1
D. Uncooperative customer	0	0.0	42	11.1	42	5.4
Subtotal, Group 4	3	0.8	83	22.0	86	11.1
Column Total	397	51.3	377	48.7	774	100.0

employee to recover. Employees clearly remember their ability to recover in failure situations as a significant cause for ultimate customer satisfaction. A relatively modest (when compared with the customer view) number of satisfactory incidents were categorized as unprompted and unsolicited employee actions (Group 3). Perhaps employees do not view their own behaviours as 'spontaneous', but they instead remember them in association with a specific external cause (e.g., a customer need, a service failure). Finally, there were virtually no satisfactory incidents categorized in the problem customer group (Group 4). This makes sense, because it is difficult to imagine a very problematic customer leaving the encounter feeling satisfied except under highly unusual circumstances.

Comparing customer and employee views

Table 3 combines data from the current study with the original BBT data for purposes of comparison. Because the employees and customers in these two studies all described different incidents, conclusions from employee–customer comparisons are exploratory, and the explanations are somewhat speculative. Although we rely on role and attribution theories to explain the differences we observed, it is possible that these differences could be due to sampling variations or differences in the incident pool from which the two groups drew. However, given the care taken in collecting the data to avoid systematic biases, that both studies were conducted in the same city using the same three industries, and that many of the same firms were the source of incidents in both studies, we have confidence in our theoretical explanations of the results.

A large majority of the employee incidents from the current study could be categorized in the original three groups and 12 categories, suggesting strong similarities in the way employees and customers report the sources of satisfaction and dissatisfaction in service encounters. Recall that these are relatively routine service encounters and in both studies the respondents were experienced service participants. Even so, the addition of a fourth group and the significant differences in frequencies and proportions of incidents found in the groups suggest that there are dissimilarities in what they report as well. Hierarchical log-linear analysis of Table 3 shows a significant

Table 3 ■ Comparison of employee and customer responses: incident classification by type of incident outcome

| Group and category | Type of incident outcome | | | | | |
| | Satisfactory | | Dissatisfactory | | Row total | |
	No.	%	No.	%	No.	%
Group 1. Employee response to service delivery system failures						
Employee data	109	27.5	195	51.7	304	39.3
Customer data	81	23.3	151	42.9	232	33.2
Group 2. Employee response to customer needs and requests						
Employee data	196	49.4	62	16.4	258	33.3
Customer data	114	32.9	55	15.6	169	24.2
Group 3. Unprompted and unsolicited employee actions						
Employee data	89	22.4	37	9.8	126	16.3
Customer data	152	43.8	146	41.5	298	42.6
Group 4. Problematic customer behaviour						
Employee data	3	0.8	83	22.0	86	11.1
Customer data	0	0.0	0	0.0	0	0.0
Column total						
Employee data	397	51.3	377	48.7	774	100.0
Customer data	347	49.6	352	50.4	699	100.0

three-way interaction between group (1, 2, 3 or 4), type of outcome (satisfactory or dissatisfactory), and incident source (employee or customer) (L.R. χ^2 change = 8.17; p = .04). There is also a significant two-way interaction between group and incident source (L.R. χ^2 change = 263.31; $p < .0001$). Because of the significant three-way interaction, the results are discussed separately for satisfactory and dissatisfactory incidents.

Within the dissatisfactory incident classifications, customers and employees have relatively similar proportions in Groups 1 and 2. The significant interaction is caused by Group 3, which is dominated by customer incidents, and Group 4, which contains incidents reported by employees only. These results are very consistent with expectations based on attribution biases. Employees are highly unlikely to describe customer dissatisfaction as being caused by their own predispositions, attitudes, or spontaneous behaviours. Customers, on the other hand, will be likely to blame the employee rather than anything they themselves might have contributed. This is clearly reflected in the observation that customers report no dissatisfactory incidents caused by their own problem behaviours (Group 4).

The differences in how customers and employees report satisfactory encounters are provocative as well, albeit less extreme. Again, this is consistent with attribution theory, which predicts larger differences in perceptions in failure than in success situations. Within the satisfactory incidents, Groups 1 and 4 are equally represented for both customers and employees. The significant interaction is the result of Group 2 being dominated by employee incidents and Group 3 being dominated by customer incidents.

Implications for researchers

Generalizability of the service encounter classification scheme

The importance and usefulness of robust classification schemes for theory development and practical application have been discussed by social scientists (e.g., McKelvey, 1982) and marketing scholars (e.g.,

Hunt, 1991; Lovelock, 1983). Yet we have few such frameworks in marketing, primarily because the classification schemes that have been proposed have rarely been subjected to empirical validation across times and contexts.

This study represents one contribution in a programme of research designed to test the validity and generalizability of a scheme for categorizing sources of service encounter satisfaction and dissatisfaction (BBT). If the scheme holds in different settings (e.g., different industry contexts, or in internal as well as external encounters) and across different respondents (e.g., customers versus providers, customers in different cultures), then the scheme can be viewed as more robust and of greater theoretical as well as practical value. Other studies have reported that the three major groups of behaviours identified by BBT are also found in a retail context (Kelley, Hoffman and Davis, 1993) and a study of 16 consumer services (Gremler and Bitner, 1992). Through replication, the framework becomes more valuable in identifying generalizable 'service behaviours'.

The results of our research indicate that all the categories found in the original customer-prospective study were also found when employees were asked to report except 'problem customers'. The addition of this new group provides a more complete classification system that can be further examined in other contexts.

Problem customers

A primary contribution of this research effort is the empirically based finding that unsatisfactory service encounters may be due to inappropriate customer behaviours – the notion that sometimes customers are wrong. Others have suggested the existence of problem customers (e.g., Lovelock, 1994; Schrage, 1992; Zemke and Anderson, 1990). Lovelock, for example, suggests the term 'jaycustomers' to label customers who 'misconsume' in a manner similar to jaywalkers who cross streets in unauthorized places. Our research provides empirical evidence that these difficult customer types do exist and in fact can be the source of their own dissatisfaction.

Although no one really believes customers are always right, firms have policies that pretend this is so, and managers urge and demand that customer-contact employees treat customers as if they are always right. Needless to say, such avoidance leads to stresses and strains for managers and frontline personnel alike and potentially bigger problems for firms. (See Hochschild, 1983, for a discussion of personal and organizational impacts of nonauthentic ways of dealing with customers.) With a better understanding of problem customers can come better methods of eliminating or dealing with the underlying causes of the problems.

This area is ripe with important research questions, such as the following: What types of problems do customers cause? What are the most frequent problems? What types of customers tend to be problem customers? Under what circumstances do customers create either more or fewer problems? And, from a management viewpoint, what can be done to identify problem customers, and how can and should employees deal with them?

This initial research represents a start at addressing some of these questions and the beginnings of a typology of problem customer behaviours. The categories of behaviours discovered are not surprising given the nature of the industries studied. Each service involves the possible serving of food and drink – including alcoholic beverages. In each service the customers are in close physical proximity for extended periods of time. Restaurant, airline and hotel customers are many times in tight public spaces that put them cheek to jowl with other customers. Personal social interactions are carried out in front of other customers who are most often strangers. And, as mentioned previously, the types of encounters studied here are all relatively routine and commonly experienced. Finally, customers frequently have transaction-based encounters with the service personnel rather than long-term relationship-based encounters. It is assumed that these circumstances influenced the nature of the subcategories of problems identified in Group 4. Thus, although we believe that the major problem customer group will surface whenever employees are asked to relate instances of dissatisfactory encounters, further research is needed to identify other subcategories within the group and

relate problem types to serve industry conditions, circumstances and customer segments.

Although we have identified problem customers by exploring the sources of customer dissatisfaction, there may be other types of 'wrong customers'. For example, even when customers do not misbehave, they may not be good relationship customers for the organization because they do not meet the target market profile, they are not profitable in the long term, or in some cases they may not be compatible with the service provider in terms of personality or work style (Lovelock, 1994; Zeithaml and Bitner, 1995). It is beyond the scope of this article to discuss the full conceptualization of wrong customers, but it may be fruitful for researchers in the future to incorporate the misbehaving customers we have identified into this more extensive conceptual scheme.

Theory implications

Role and script theories suggest that customers and employees in routine, well-understood service transactions will share parallel views of their roles and the expected sequence of events and behaviours. The types of service encounters studied here and in the original study do represent frequently encountered and routine services. Shared views of the encounter should result in common notions of the sources of customer satisfaction and dissatisfaction. The fact that 89 per cent of the employee incidents could be classified in the original classification scheme suggests that customers and employees do indeed report incidents with most of the same sources of satisfaction and dissatisfaction.

An interesting issue for further research is whether the overall strong similarity of views between customers and employees would result if the industries studied were ones in which the scripts were less routine and well practised.

Results of the study indicate that though employees and customers do report many of the same sources of customer satisfaction and dissatisfaction, there are also significant differences. These disparities show up in the distribution of incidents across the major groups, and the differences were most dramatic for the dissatisfactory service encounters. The self-serving attribution bias suggests explanations for why some of these differences were observed.

Managerial implications

Using the classification scheme

One purpose of this study was to evaluate the soundness of the classification scheme developed by BBT in a distinctive context. Through the addition of the problem customer grouping, the framework is now more complete, and the scheme itself can provide a starting point for a company or industry to begin identifying with greater specificity the events and behaviours peculiar to its own setting. For example, the framework has been used for proprietary purposes in medical and travel agent contexts. In these cases, the companies began with the existing groups in the classification scheme and fleshed out the categories with useful specifics that could be employed in service training or service redesign.

The customer is not always right

In the industries studied here, problem customers were the source of 22 per cent of the dissatisfactory incidents. This group may be even larger in industries in which the customer has greater input into the service delivery process (e.g., healthcare, education, legal services).

Several implications are suggested by the problem customer group. First, managers must acknowledge that the customer is not always right, nor will he or she always behave in acceptable ways. Contact employees who have been on the job any period of time know this, but frequently they are being told that the 'customer is king' and are not given the appropriate training and tools to deal with problem customers. Employees need appropriate coping and problem-solving skills to handle customers as well as their own personal feelings in these situations. Employees can also be taught to recognize characteristics of situations (e.g., unexpected peaks in demand, inordinate delays) and anticipate the moods of their customers so that some potential problem situations can be avoided completely or alleviated before they accelerate.

To provide employees with the appropriate training and skills for working with problem customers, the organization must clarify its position regarding such customers. A basic problem customer strategy might be conceptualized as ranging along a continuum from 'refuse to serve them' to 'satisfy them at all costs'. For example, some car rental companies have attempted to refuse customers with bad driving histories by checking records in advance and rejecting bad-risk drivers (Dahl, 1992). In a different context, some Madison Avenue ad agencies say that 'some accounts are so difficult to work with that they simply cannot – or will not – service them' (Bird, 1993). Although organizations have intuitively recognized that not all customer segments are right for the firm and that each individual customer is not right all the time, some are beginning to acknowledge these facts more explicitly and are attempting to quantify the impact of problem or 'wrong' customers on profitability and organizational stress.

Beyond the need to develop employee skills, there is the need for 'training' customers so that they will know what to expect and appropriate behaviours in given situations. For example, some upscale resorts that offer highly discounted rates in nonpeak seasons find that their discount customers, who may not be accustomed to the 'rules of behaviour', appreciate information on what to wear and other expected behaviours while at the resort. In other more complex and less familiar service situations (e.g., professional services), customers may truly appreciate knowing more about their role in the service process and the behaviours and information that are needed from them to make the service succeed (Bloom, 1984). It has been suggested that by treating customers as 'partial employees' they can learn to contribute to the service in ways that will enhance their own satisfaction (Bowen, 1986).

Employees as sources of customer data

Previous research has suggested that contact employees are good sources of information on customer attitudes (Schneider and Bowen, 1985; Schneider,

Parkington and Buxton, 1980). Our study confirms these findings in so far as employees of hotels, restaurants, and airlines report all the same categories of customer satisfaction and dissatisfaction reported by customers in the same industries. However, we would caution against relying too much on contact employee interpretations of customer satisfaction for two reasons. First, although they report the same basic categories, the proportions of incidents found in the categories are significantly different from those reported by customers. Second, in some industries in which service encounters are less routine, contact employees may not be as accurate in their assessment of customer expectations and satisfaction (see Brown and Swartz, 1989).

Employee desire for knowledge and control

It is apparent in reading the incidents that contact employees *want* to provide good service and are very proud of their abilities to do so. This pride comes through in the large percentage of satisfactory incidents found in Group 2, in which employees' own skills, abilities and willingness to accommodate customer needs were the sources of customer satisfaction. Balancing out this sense of pride are a large number of frustrating incidents in which employees believe they cannot for some reason recover from a service failure or adjust the system to accommodate a customer need. These reasons usually stem from lack of basic knowledge of the system and its constraints, inability to provide a logical explanation to the customer, cumbersome bureaucratic procedures, poorly designed systems or procedures, or the lack of authority to do anything.

Reliability is critical

The data show that a majority of the dissatisfactory incidents reported by employees resulted from inadequate responses to service delivery system failures. This result, together with other research reporting service reliability as the single most important dimension used by consumers to judge service quality (Parasuraman, Zeithaml and Berry, 1988, 1990), implies a need for service process and system analysis

to determine the root causes of system failures (Kingman-Brundage, 1989; Shostack, 1984, 1987). Systems can then be redesigned and processes implemented to ensure higher reliability from the customer's point of view. The best way to ensure satisfaction, however, is not to have a failure in the first place.

Conclusion

The research suggests that many frontline employees do have a true customer orientation and do identify with and understand customer needs in service encounter situations. They have respect for customers and a desire to deliver excellent service. Oftentimes the inability to do so is governed by inadequate or poorly designed systems, poor or nonexistent recovery strategies, or lack of knowledge. When employees have the skills and tools to deliver high-quality service, they are proud of their ability to do so.

We also learned from employees that customers can be the source of their own dissatisfaction through inappropriate behaviour or being unreasonably demanding. We suspect that this new group of dissatisfactory incidents caused by problem customers would surface in any service industry and that its existence represents a strategic challenge for the organization as well as an operational, real-time challenge for service employees. In a time when 'customer is king' is the stated philosophy of most forward-thinking organizations, acknowledgement that wrong customers exist, coupled with creative thinking about customer roles and management of customer expectations, may considerably deepen understanding of and ability to cultivate customer relationships.

Appendix A Instructions for coders

Overview

1. You will be provided with a set of written critical service encounter events. Each 'story' or 'event' is recorded on a standardized questionnaire. Two types of questionnaires were used, one for satisfying interactions and one for dissatisfying interactions.
2. Each service encounter questionnaire reflects the events and behaviours associated with an

encounter that is memorable because it is either particularly satisfying or particularly dissatisfying. The respondents were employees of restaurants, airlines and hotels. However, they were asked to take the customer's point of view in responding to the questions. Thus, the data reflect employees' remembrances of times when customers had particularly dis/satisfying encounters with their firms.

3. You will be asked to categorize each incident into one of 16 categories, based on the key factor that triggered the dis/satisfactory incident. Sorting rules and definitions of categories are detailed below.

4. It is suggested that you read through each entire service encounter before you attempt to categorize it. If an incident does not appear to fit within any of the 16 categories, put it aside. In addition, do not attempt to categorize incidents that do not meet the basic criteria. An incident must: (A) include employee–customer interaction (B) be very satisfying or dissatisfying from the customer's point of view, (C) be a discrete episode, and (D) have sufficient detail to be visualized by the interviewer.

Coding rules

Each incident should be categorized within one category only. Once you have read the incident, you should begin asking the following questions in order to determine the appropriate category. Definitions of the categories are attached.

1. Is there a service delivery system failure? That is, is there an initial failure of the core service that causes the employee to respond in some way? Is it the employee's response that causes the event to be remembered as highly satisfactory or dissatisfactory?

If the answer is *yes*, place the incident in Group 1. Then ask, what type of failure? (A) unavailable service; (B) unreasonably slow service; (C) other core service failures.

If the answer is *no*, go on to question 2.

2. Is there an explicit or implicit request or need for accommodation or extra service(s)? That is, is the customer asking (either explicitly or implicitly) that the system be somehow adjusted to accommo-

date him/her? Is it the employee's response that causes the event to be remembered as highly satisfactory or dissatisfactory?

If the answer is *yes*, place the incident in Group 2. Then ask what type of need/request is triggering the incident: (A) 'special needs' customer; (B) customer preferences; (C) admitted customer error; (D) potentially disruptive other customers.

If the answer is *no*, go on to question 3.

3. Is there an unprompted and unsolicited action on the part of the employee that causes the dis/satisfaction? (Since this follows rules 1 and 2, it obviously implies that there is no service failure and no explicit/implicit request.)

If the answer is *yes*, place the incident in Group 3. Then, ask what type of unprompted and unsolicited action took place: (A) attention paid to customer; (B) truly out-of-the-ordinary action; (C) employee behaviours in the context of cultural norms; (D) gestalt evaluation; (E) exemplary performance under adverse circumstances.

If the answer is *no*, go to question 4.

4. Does the dis/satisfaction stem from the actions/ attitudes/behaviours of a 'problem customer'? That is, rather than the dis/satisfaction being attributable to an action or attitude of the employee, is the root cause actually the customer?

If the answer is *yes*, place the incident in Group 4. Then, ask what type of behaviour is causing the problem: (A) drunkenness; (B) verbal/physical abuse; (C) breaking/resisting company policies or laws; (D) uncooperative customer.

If the answer is *no*, put the incident aside.

CIT classification system – definitions
Group 1

Employee response to service delivery system failure (failure in the core service, e.g., the hotel room, the restaurant meal service, the flight, system failures).

A. Response to unavailable service (services that should be available are lacking or absent, e.g., lost hotel room reservation, overbooked airplane, unavailable reserved window table).

B. Response to unreasonably slow service (services or employee performances are perceived as inordinately slow). (Note: When service is both slow and unavailable, use the *triggering* event.)

C. Response to other core service failures (e.g., hotel room not clean, restaurant meal cold or improperly cooked, damaged baggage).

Group 2

Employee response to customer needs and requests (when the customer requires the employee to adapt the service delivery system to suit his/her unique needs; contains either an explicit or inferred request for customized [from the customer's point of view] service).

A. Response to 'special needs' customers (customers with medical, dietary, psychological, language or sociological difficulties; children; elderly customers).

B. Response to customer preferences (when the customer makes 'special' requests due to personal preferences; this includes times when the customer requests a level of service customization clearly beyond the scope of or in violation of policies or norms).

C. Response to admitted customer error (triggering event is a customer error that strains the service encounter, e.g., lost tickets, incorrect order, missed reservations).

D. Response to potentially disruptive others (when other customers exhibit behaviours that potentially strain the encounter, e.g., intoxication, rudeness, deviance).

Group 3

Unprompted and unsolicited employee actions (events and behaviours that are truly unexpected from the customer's point of view, not triggered by a service failure, and show no evidence of the customer having a special need or making a special request).

A. Attention paid to customer (e.g., making the customer feel special or pampered, ignoring or being impatient with the customer).

B. Truly out-of-the-ordinary employee behaviour (particularly extraordinary actions or expressions of courtesy, or profanity, inappropriate touching, violations of basic etiquette, rudeness).

C. Employee behaviours in the context of cultural norms (norms such as equality, honesty, fairness, discrimination, theft, lying or refraining from the above when such behaviour was expected).

D. Gestalt evaluation (no single feature stands out, instead 'everything went right' or 'everything went wrong').

E. Exemplary performance under adverse circumstances (when the customer is particularly impressed or displeased with the way an employee handles a stressful situation).

Group 4

Problematic customer behaviour (customer is unwilling to cooperate with laws, regulations or the service provider; this includes rudeness, abusiveness, or a general unwillingness to indicate satisfaction with the service regardless of the employees' efforts).

A. Drunkenness (in the employee's perception, the customer is clearly intoxicated and creating problems, and the employee has to handle the situation).

B. Verbal and physical abuse (the customer verbally and/or physically abuses either the employee or other customers, and the employee has to handle the situation).

C. Breaking/resisting company policies or laws (the customer refuses to comply with policies [e.g., showing airplane ticket to the flight attendant before boarding] or laws [e.g., use of illegal drugs in the hotel room], and the employee has to enforce compliance).

D. Uncooperative customer (customer is generally rude and uncooperative or extremely demanding; any efforts to compensate for a perceived service failure are rejected; customer may appear unwilling to be satisfied; and the employee has to handle the situation).

References

Berry, Leonard L. and A. Parasuraman (1991), *Marketing Services*, New York: The Free Press.

Biddle, B.J. (1986), 'Recent Developments in Role Theory', *Annual Review of Sociology*, 12, 67–92.

Bird, Laura (1993), 'The Clients That Exasperate Madison Avenue', *Wall Street Journal* (2 November), B1.

Bitner, Mary Jo, Bernard H. Booms and Mary Stanfield Tetreault (1990), 'The Service Encounter: Diagnosing Favorable and Unfavorable Incidents', *Journal of Marketing*, 54 (January), 71–84.

Bloom, Paul N. (1984), 'Effective Marketing for Professional Services', *Harvard Business Review* (September/October), 102–10.

Bowen, David E. (1986), 'Managing Customers as Human Resources in Service Organizations', *Human Resource Management*, 25 (3), 371–83.

Brown, Stephen W. and Teresa A. Swartz, (1989) 'A Gap Analysis of Professional Service Quality', *Journal of Marketing*, 53 (April), 92–8.

Business Week (1991), Special Issue on Quality.

Crosby, Lawrence A. (1991), 'Expanding the Role of CSM in Total Quality', *International Journal of Service Industry Management*, 2 (2), 5–19.

Dahl, Jonathan (1992), 'Rental Counters Reject Drivers Without Good Records', *Wall Street Journal* (October 23), B1.

Dornoff, Ronald J. and F. Robert Dwyer (1981), 'Perceptual Differences in Market Transactions Revisited: A Waning Source of Consumer Frustration', *The Journal of Consumer Affairs*, 15 (Summer), 146–57.

Ericsson, K. Anders and Herbert A. Simon (1980), 'Verbal Reports as Data', *Psychological Review*, 87 (May), 215–50.

Fiske, Susan T. and Shelley E. Taylor (1984), *Social Cognition*, Reading, MA: Addison-Wesley.

Flanagan, John C. (1954), 'The Critical Incident Technique', *Psychological Bulletin*, 51 (July), 327–58.

Folkes, Valerie S. and Barbara Kotsos (1986), 'Buyers' and Sellers' Explanations for Product Failure: Who Done It?' *Journal of Marketing*, 50 (April), 74–80.

Gremler, Dwayne and Mary Jo Bitner (1992), 'Classifying Service Encounter Satisfaction Across Industries', in *Marketing Theory and Applications*, Chris T. Allen *et al.*, eds. Chicago: American Marketing Association, 111–18.

Heskett, James L., Thomas O. Jones, Gary W. Loveman, W. Earl Sasser, Jr. and Leonard A. Schlesinger (1994), 'Putting the Service-Profit Chain to Work', *Harvard Business Review* (March/April), 164–72.

Heskett, James L., W. Earl Sasser, Jr., and Christopher W.L. Hart (1990), *Service Breakthroughs*, New York: The Free Press.

Hochschild, Arlie Russell (1983), *The Managed Heart*, Berkeley, CA: University of California Press.

Hunt, Shelby (1991), *Modern Marketing Theory*, Cincinnati, OH: South-Western Publishing Company.

Kelley, Scott W., K. Douglas Hoffman and Mark A. Davis (1993), 'A Typology of Retail Failures and Recoveries', *Journal of Retailing*, 69 (4), 429–52.

Kingman-Brundage, Jane (1989), 'The ABC's of Service System Blueprinting', in *Designing a Winning Service Strategy*, Mary Jo Bitner and Lawrence A. Crosby, eds., Chicago: American Marketing Association, 30–33.

Langeard, Eric, John E.G. Bateson, Christopher H. Lovelock and Pierre Eiglier (1981), *Services Marketing: New Insights from Consumers and Managers*, Cambridge, MA: Marketing Science Institute.

Lovelock, Christopher (1983), 'Classifying Services to Gain Strategic Marketing Insights', *Journal of Marketing*, 47 (Summer), 9–20.

Lovelock, Christopher (1994), *Product Plus*, New York: McGraw-Hill.

McKelvey, Bill (1982), *Organizational Systematics: Taxonomy, Evolution, Classification*, Berkeley, CA: University of California Press.

Mohr, Lois A. and Mary Jo Bitner (1991), 'Mutual Understanding Between Customers and Employees in Service Encounters', in *Advances in Consumer Research*, Vol. 18, Rebecca H. Holman and Michael R. Solomon, eds., Provo, UT: Association for Consumer Research, 611–17.

Parasuraman, A., Leonard L. Berry and Valarie A. Zeithaml (1991), 'Refinement and Reassessment of the SERVQUAL Scale', *Journal of Retailing*, 67 (4), 420–50.

Parasuraman, A., Valarie Zeithaml and Leonard L. Berry (1988), 'SERVQUAL: A Multiple-Item Scale for Measuring Consumer Perceptions of Service Quality', *Journal of Retailing*, 64 (Spring), 12–40.

Parasuraman, A., Valarie Zeithaml and Leonard L. Berry (1990), 'An Empirical Examination of Relationships in an Extended Service Quality Model', Report No. 90-122. Cambridge, MA: Marketing Science Institute.

Perreault, William D., Jr. and Laurence E. Leigh (1989), 'Reliability of Nominal Data Based on Qualitative Judgments', *Journal of Marketing Research*, 26 (May), 135–48.

Resnik, Alan J. and Robert R. Harmon (1983), 'Consumer Complaints and Managerial Response: A Holistic Approach', *Journal of Marketing*, 47 (Winter), 86–97.

Ronan, William W. and Gary P. Latham (1974), 'The Reliability and Validity of the Critical Incident Technique: A Closer Look', *Studies in Personnel Psychology*, 6 (Spring), 53–64.

Schank, Roger C. and Robert P. Abelson (1977), *Scripts, Plans, Goals and Understanding*, New York: John Wiley and Sons, Inc.

Schlesinger, Leonard A. and James L. Heskett (1991), 'The Service-Driven Service Company', *Harvard Business Review* (September/October), 71–81.

Schneider, Benjamin (1980), 'The Service Organization: Climate Is Crucial', *Organizational Dynamics* (Autumn), 52–65.

Schneider, Benjamin and David E. Bowen (1984), 'New Services Design, Development and Implementation and the Employee', in *Developing New Services*, William R. George and Claudia Marshall, eds., Chicago: American Marketing Association, 82–101.

Schneider, Benjamin and David E. Bowen (1985), 'Employee and Customer Perceptions of Service in Banks: Replication and Extension', *Journal of Applied Psychology*, 70 (3), 423–33.

Schneider, Benjamin, John J. Parkington and Virginia M. Buxton (1980), 'Employee and Customer Perceptions of Service in Banks', *Administrative Science Quarterly*, 25 (June), 252–67.

Schrage, Michael (1992), 'Fire Your Customers', *Wall Street Journal* (March 16), A8.

Services Marketing Newsletter (1989), 'Recent Study Shows Gap Between Customers and Service Employees on Customer Service Perceptions', 5 (Summer), 1.

Shostack, G. Lynn (1984), 'Designing Services That Deliver', *Harvard Business Review* (January/ February), 133–39.

Shostack, G. Lynn (1987), 'Service Positioning Through Structural Change', *Journal of Marketing*, 51 (January), 34–43.

Solomon, Michael R., Carol Surprenant, John A. Czepiel and Evelyn G. Gutman (1985), 'A Role Theory Perspective on Dyadic Interactions: The Service Encounter', *Journal of Marketing*, 49 (Winter), 99–111.

White, Frank M. and Edwin A. Locke (1981), 'Perceived Determinants of High and Low Productivity in Three Occupational Groups: A Critical Incident Study', *Journal of Management Studies*, 18 (4), 375–87.

Wilson-Pessano, Sandra R. (1988), 'Defining Professional Competence: The Critical Incident Technique 40 Years Later', American Institutes for Research, invited address to the Annual Meeting of the American Educational Research Association, New Orleans.

Zeithaml, Valarie A., Leonard L. Berry and A. Parasuraman (1988), 'Communication and Control Processes in the Delivery of Service Quality', *Journal of Marketing*, 52 (April), 35–48.

Zeithaml, Valarie A. and Mary Jo Bitner (1995), *Services Marketing*, New York: McGraw-Hill.

Zemke, Ron and Kristin Anderson (1990), 'Customers From Hell', *Training* (February), 25–33.

Publicis Technology: advertising services in cyberspace

Sandra Vandermerwe ■ *Rhys Morgan*

A full-service advertising agency, which targets companies marketing high-tech products around the world, seeks to offer its clients the convenience of doing business by internet through offices in cyberspace.

Publicis Technology was created in September 1997, when Paris-based Publicis Group, the second largest advertising agency in Europe, acquired London's SMI Group for a rumoured £8 million (€11 million). As a separate division from the French network, Publicis Technology was based in London, with Alex Letts, founder of SMI, as its chief executive.

Letts had been determined for some time to build an internet-based advertising agency for clients such as IBM, Oracle, Olivetti and Adobe, which needed to market high-tech products through a single message distributed worldwide and communicated cost-effectively at top speed. A client would typically come in with a brief already prepared, or simply a request, such as 'I need to sell more PCs'. Recent technological advancements had enabled Letts to turn his vision into reality.

The agency offered a full range of services, including marketing consultancy, creative advertising input and media space buying. To position the new company as a highly specialized operation, Letts knew that he and his team would have to adopt a completely different approach to creating and executing global communications campaigns from that of traditional advertising agencies.

Creating a supranational, internet-based organization

The positioning strategy adopted by Letts represented a deliberate attempt to differentiate Publicis Technology from traditional advertising agencies, which managed global clients through a large, multinational network, typically involving some physical presence in each country. Not surprisingly, the nature of the communications produced (such as advertising, direct mail, media buying, interactive media, etc.) tended to reflect the culture of the country in which the creative work originated, rather than constituting a truly global message. This was fine, Publicis Technology believed, for clients who sought communications campaigns that would be implemented on a market-by-market basis; however, it was not appropriate for customers in high-tech products who sought to manage their brand and messages globally and in real time. The very nature of the IT business, after all, meant that marketing efforts had to be accomplished ever more speedily.

Publicis Technology's structure needed to reflect this requirement of the high-tech, global market client segment. In particular, Letts and his team recognized that the agency had to minimize the number of regional locations employed. 'One job from one location' is how Letts described his vision for a supranational organization. Publicis would be one of the first agencies in the world to use the open standards of the internet for marketing, making offices available to clients in cyberspace, so that they could work with the agency on a day-to-day basis to increase collaboration and efficiency.

The firm's Web interface, combined with other communications techniques – such as desk-to-desk videoconferencing, group videoconferencing, e-mail and normal telecommunications – created an alternative distribution channel to the traditional advertising industry norm of almost daily face-to-face meetings. Letts hoped that Publicis Technology's new value proposition would give it the edge in its market segment, removing national bias, guaranteeing centralized control over multi-country campaigns and speeding contact between the agency and its clients.

In general, big multinational agencies had been slow to adopt new technologies; they were constrained by 'mature cultures' which made them very different from the kind of agency Publicis Technology wanted to be. Size was also a factor. Said Letts:

> It was difficult to bring a new way of working to a large network of say 5,000 people. The people who run big agencies were not smitten by technology, and very few really understood its strategic importance to their clients.

The predecessor company, SMI, had been an early adopter of Lotus Notes, a collaborative workgroup application software.[1] SMI had used Notes since 1991, initially as an e-mail platform that could centralize names and addresses within the service organization. Over the years, Notes itself became progressively more sophisticated. Publicis Technology upgraded its system to include such applications as a shared diary database, a company-wide, open, free discussion database, a news feed internal database and a document library/knowledge base offering employees insights on how to do business with each client. Subsequent enhancements allowed Publicis to create a fully-fledged advertising service workflow system, creating the basis for transforming itself into an innovative cyber-agency.

Building the supranet technology

Originally Publicis Technology supplied its customers with the equipment and software they needed to connect to the Notes server and talk to their advertising agency. But this strategy was rarely successful – customers were neither ready for the new way of working with the agency nor educated enough to take advantage of the opportunities that it presented. Then in 1995 Lotus produced InterNotes, a tool that enabled Notes databases to be securely and privately published on the Web. But still it only allowed 'static' publishing, since users could only view the documents in a database. Consequently, it was not possible for the agency personnel to capture customer-generated content and revise the advertising based on their clients' input or feedback.

Further innovations in 1997 not only enabled Notes databases to be published on the Web, but also allowed customers to create forms, edit documents and add their responses. This was what Alex Letts and his management team had been waiting for – the technology that could truly change the way an agency worked with global clients by converting static documents into what he called a 'dynamic total publishing solution'. The agency could now interact simultaneously with all countries involved in a global campaign – for instance all thirteen Olivetti offices could get feedback on a proposed advertisement and give approval simultaneously to a single Publicis Technology site. Publicis Technology used what they call 'Client FORUM' on their Web database. This database supported the total workflow within the agency and between the agency and its clients. One example was 'Action Required' forms which could be forwarded for the attention of the relevant people and time flagged as they moved back and forth.

To publish a document on the Web, all the customer had to do was click a button, see the document and respond to it instantly. For a client to participate in the discussion, it was necessary to enter a password in order to view an access page which displayed all the forums in which that particular client was allowed to participate. Some clients were involved in more than one project and access in each instance was therefore limited to certain employees. In order to preserve a permanent and auditable record of the relationship, the system did not allow subsequent editing of previously submitted documents. For instance, once the client had approved a budget proposal, this document was stored in the form in which it had been approved.

Other multimedia files – such as television clips, radio messages or press images – could also be put into the system. In this way, a client could watch a TV commercial, listen to the audio or view a print advert, and then subsequently discuss it, make alterations and finally approve the end-product. As soon as the client responded, the relevant account executive at Publicis Technology was automatically notified, thus ensuring immediate responsiveness.

Group decision-making

The 'SupraNet' allowed Publicis Technology to match the working cycles of a client's offices all over the world in different time zones. Previously, when a new advertisement needed approval, a colour proof of the advert had to be couriered to each client site, resulting in delays. Now, when the electronic file was published from the Notes database, the client could see it immediately and comment on it interactively.

There were significant cost and time savings to be gained through this new way of working. Traditionally, hard copies of each advertisement had to be dispatched to the client, typically followed by an agency representative to discuss it. Now, while there still had to be a final proof check, the prior movement of physical objects had been considerably reduced through the use of the technology. Group decision making, central to the agencies service offering, was possible in real time. And the SupraNet enabled work and therefore 'applied knowledge' to flow across the boundaries of Publicis Technology into the 'customer's space' in various forms like comments, responses and annotated multimedia files. Each person involved was able to participate in this workflow and the total cycle from start to finish was made considerably faster.

By the spring of 1998 Publicis Technology was enjoying successful relations with a growing number of geographically dispersed, time-sensitive, high workload clients. It employed 80 staff, consisting of account handling teams, creative teams and a media-buying department; the agency also used freelancers and subcontractors. Turnaround times on certain tasks had been cut from three days to as little as half a day, leading to sharp increases in productivity. And the magazine *Going International* had named the agency as the winner of the Arthur Andersen Enterprise Award for Best Practice in reaching new markets abroad. Customers were getting used to the technology and use of the internet was expanding rapidly worldwide. Publicis Technology itself was expanding into the US and Asian markets, where it was looking for acquisitions.

Note

1. A workgroup is a collection of individuals working together on a task. Workgroup computing occurs when all the individuals have computers connected to a network that allows them to send e-mail to one another, share data files, schedule meetings, and so on. Sophisticated workgroup systems allow users to define workflows so that data are automatically forwarded to appropriate people at each stage of a process. Lotus Notes is a 'groupware' (software for workgroups) application developed by Lotus Corporation, (now part of IBM). By 1998, Notes had 20 million users world-wide and more than 18,000 third-party developers. Its sophisticated replication features enabled users to work with local copies of documents and have their modifications propagated throughout an entire Notes network. For many years, Notes was the only full-featured groupware solution. With the sudden popularity of the World Wide Web, and intranets (secure, internal networks employing website-like features), new groupware solutions were emerging, such as Novell GroupWise and Microsoft Exchange.

Sullivan's Motor World

Christopher H. Lovelock

A young manager working in the travel industry unexpectedly finds herself responsible for running a family-owned car dealership that is in trouble. She is very concerned about the poor performance of the service department and wonders if a turnaround is possible.

Viewed from Wilson Avenue, the dealership presented a festive sight. Strings of triangular pennants in red, white and blue fluttered in the late afternoon breeze. Rows of new model cars gleamed and winked in the sunlight. Geraniums graced the flowerbeds outside the showroom entrance. A huge rotating sign at the corner of Wilson Avenue and Victoria Street sported the Ford logo and identified the business as Sullivan's Motor World. Banners below urged 'Let's Make a Deal!'.

Inside the handsome, high-ceilinged showroom, three of the new model Fords were on display – a dark-blue minivan, a red sports car and a white Mondeo. Each car was polished to a high sheen. Two groups of customers were chatting with salespeople, and a middle-aged man sat in the driver's seat of the Mondeo, studying the controls.

Upstairs in the comfortably furnished general manager's office, Carol Sullivan-Brown finished running another spreadsheet analysis on her laptop computer. She felt tired and depressed. Her father, Walter Sullivan, had died four weeks earlier at the age of 56 of a sudden heart attack. As executor of his estate, the bank had asked her temporarily to assume the position of general manager of the dealership. The only visible changes that she had made to her father's office were installing a fax machine and laser printer, but she had been very busy analyzing the current position of the business.

Carol did not like the look of the numbers on the printout. Sullivan's financial situation had been deteriorating for 18 months, and it had been running at a loss for the first half of the current year. New car sales had declined, reflecting a turndown in the regional economy. Margins had been squeezed by promotions and other efforts to move new cars off the forecourt. Industry forecasts of future sales were discouraging, and so were her own financial projections for Sullivan's sales department. Service revenues, which were below average for a dealership of this size, had also declined, although the service department still made a small surplus.

Had she made a mistake last week, Carol wondered, in turning down Peter Turner's offer to buy the business? It was true that the price offered had been substantially below the offer from Turner that her father had rejected two years earlier, but the business had been more profitable then.

The Sullivan family

Walter Sullivan had purchased a small Ford dealership in 1977, renaming it Sullivan's Motor World, and had built it up to become one of the best known in the district. Six years ago, he had borrowed heavily to purchase the current site at a major suburban crossroads, in an area of town with many new housing developments.

There had been a dealership on the site, but the buildings were 30 years old. Sullivan had retained the service and repair bays, but demolished the showroom in front of them, and replaced it by an attractive modern facility. On moving to the new location, which was substantially larger than the old one, he had renamed his business Sullivan's Motor World.

Everybody had seemed to know Walter Sullivan. He had been a consummate showman and entrepreneur, appearing in his own radio commercials and active in community affairs. His approach to car sales had emphasized promotions, discounts and deals in order to maintain volume. He was never happier than when making a sale.

Carol Sullivan-Brown, aged 28, was the eldest of Walter and Mary Sullivan's three daughters. After obtaining a BSc in economics, she had gone on to take an MBA degree and had then embarked on a career in the travel industry. She was married to Dr Robert Brown, a surgeon at St Luke's Hospital. Her 20-year-old twin sisters, Gail and Joanne, who were students at the local university, lived with their mother.

In her own student days, Carol had worked part-time in her father's business on secretarial and bookkeeping tasks, and also as a receptionist in the service department; so she was quite familiar with the operations of the dealership. At business school, she had been attracted to a career in the fast-growing travel industry. After graduation, she had been recruited to work in the marketing department of a major airline. Three years later, she joined one of the country's largest package tour operators as assistant director of customer relations, a position she had now held for almost two years. Her responsibilities included complaint handling, market research and customer retention programmes.

Carol's employer had given her a six-week leave of absence to put her father's affairs in order. She doubted that she could extend that leave much beyond the two weeks still remaining. Neither she nor other family members were interested in making a career of running the dealership. However, she was prepared to take time out from her travel industry career to work on a turnaround if that seemed a viable proposition. She had been successful in her present job and believed it would not be difficult to find another position in the future.

The dealership

Like other car dealerships, Sullivan's Motor World operated both sales and service departments, often referred to in the trade as 'front end' and 'back end', respectively. However, Sullivan's did not have a body shop for repairing damaged bodywork. Both new and used vehicles were sold, since a high proportion of new car and van purchases involved part exchange with the purchaser's existing vehicle. Sullivan's would also buy well-maintained used cars at auction for resale. Purchasers who decided that they could not afford a new car would often buy a 'pre-owned' vehicle instead, while shoppers who came in looking for a used car could sometimes be persuaded to buy a new one.

The front end of the dealership employed a sales manager, four salespeople, an office manager and a secretary. One of the salespeople had given notice and would be leaving at the end of the following week. The service department, when fully staffed, consisted of a service manager, a parts supervisor, six mechanics, and two receptionists. The Sullivan twins often worked part-time as receptionists, filling in at busy periods, when one of the other staff was sick or on holiday, or when – as currently – there was an unfilled vacancy. The job entailed scheduling appointments for repairs and maintenance, writing up each work order, calling customers with repair estimates, assisting customers when they returned to pick up the cars and pay for the work that had been done, and making post-purchase phone calls to customers – which constituted a brief, informal, survey of customer satisfaction.

Carol knew from her experience as a receptionist that it could be a stressful job. Few people liked to be without their car, even for a day. When a car broke down or was having problems, the owner was often nervous about how long it would take to get it fixed and, if the warranty had expired, how much the labour and parts would cost. Customers were quite unforgiving when a problem was not fixed completely on the first attempt and they had to return their vehicle for further work.

Major mechanical failures were not usually difficult to repair, although the parts replacement costs might be expensive. It was often the 'little' things like water leaks and wiring problems that were the hardest to diagnose and correct, and it might be necessary for the customer to return two or three times before such a problem was resolved. In these situations, parts and materials costs were relatively low, but labour costs mounted up quickly, being charged out at £30 per hour, plus VAT. Customers could often be quite abusive, shouting at receptionists over the phone or arguing with receptionists, mechanics and the service manager in person.

Turnover in the receptionist job was high, which was one reason why Carol – and more recently her sisters – had often been pressed into service by their father to 'hold the fort', as he described it. More than once, she had seen an exasperated receptionist respond sharply to a complaining customer or hang up on one who was being abusive over the telephone. Gail and Joanne were currently taking turns to cover the vacant position, but there were times when both of them had classes and the dealership had only one receptionist on duty.

By national standards, Sullivan's Motor World was a medium-sized dealership, selling around 700 cars a year, divided between new and used vehicles in the ratio of 2:1. In the most recent year, its revenues totalled £8.9 million (€12.5 million) from new and used car sales and £1.8 million from service and parts – down from £10.2 million and £2.2 million, respectively, in the previous year. Although the unit value of car sales was high, the margins were quite low. The reverse was true for service. Industry guidelines suggested that the contribution margin (known as the departmental selling gross) from car sales should be about 5.5 per cent of sales revenues, and from service, around 25 per cent of revenues. In a typical dealership, 60 per cent of the selling gross came from sales and 40 per cent from service. The selling gross was then applied to fixed expenses, such as administrative salaries, rent or mortgage payments and utilities.

For the most recent 12 months at Sullivan's, Carol had determined that the selling gross figures were 4.6 per cent and 24 per cent, respectively, both of them lower than in the previous year and insufficient to cover the dealership's fixed expenses. Her father had made no mention of financial difficulties and she had been shocked to learn from the bank after his death that Sullivan's had been two months behind in mortgage payments on the property. Further analysis also showed that accounts payable had also risen sharply in the previous six months. Fortunately, the dealership held a large insurance policy on Sullivan's life, and the proceeds from this had been more than sufficient to bring mortgage payments up to date, pay all overdue accounts and leave some funds for future contingencies.

The opportunities for expanding new car sales did not appear promising, given the state of the economy. However, recent promotional incentives had reduced the stock to manageable levels. From discussions with Frank Broadbent, Sullivan's sales manager, Carol had concluded that costs could be reduced by not replacing the departing salesperson, maintaining stock at somewhat lower levels, and trying to make more efficient use of advertising and promotion. Although Broadbent did not have Walter's exuberant personality, he had been Sullivan's leading salesperson before being promoted, and had shown strong managerial capabilities in his current position.

As she reviewed the figures for the service department, Sullivan-Brown wondered what potential might exist for improving its sales volume and selling gross. Her father had never been very interested in the parts and service business, seeing it simply as a necessary adjunct of the dealership. 'Customers always seem to be miserable back there,' he had once remarked to her. 'But here in the front end, everybody's happy when someone buys a new car.' The service department was not easily visible from the main road, being hidden behind the showroom. The building was old and greasy, although the equipment was modern and well maintained.

Customers were required to bring cars in for servicing before 08:30. After parking their cars, customers entered the service building by a side door and waited their turn to see the service receptionists, who occupied a cramped room with peeling paint and an interior window overlooking the service bays. Customers stood while work orders for their cars were written up by hand on large sheets. Ringing telephones frequently interrupted the process. Filing cabinets containing customer records and other documents lined the far wall of the room.

If the work were of a routine nature, such as an oil change or tune up, the customer was given an estimate immediately. For more complex jobs, they would be called with an estimate later in the morning once the car had been examined. Customers were required to pick up their cars by 18:00 on the day the work was completed. On several occasions, Carol had urged her father to computerize the service work order process, but he had never acted on her suggestions.

The service manager, David Barton, who was in his late forties, had held the position since Sullivan's opened at its current location. The Sullivan family considered him to be technically skilled, and he managed the mechanics effectively. However, his manner with customers could be gruff and argumentative.

Customer survey results

Another set of data that Sullivan-Brown had studied carefully were the results of the customer satisfaction surveys that were mailed to the dealership monthly by a research firm retained by the Ford Motor Company.

Purchasers of all new Ford cars were sent a questionnaire by mail within 30 days of making the purchase and asked to use a ten-point scale to rate their satisfaction with the dealership sales department, vehicle preparation and the characteristics of the vehicle itself. The questionnaire asked how likely the purchaser would be to recommend the dealership, the salesperson and the manufacturer to someone else. Other questions asked if the customers had been introduced to the dealer's service department and been given explanations on what to do if their cars needed service. Finally, there were some classification questions relating to customer demographics.

A second survey was sent to new car purchasers nine months after they had bought their cars. This questionnaire began by asking about satisfaction with the vehicle and then asked customers if they had taken their vehicles to the selling dealer for service of any kind. If so, respondents were then asked to rate the service department on a number of different attributes – ranging from the attitudes of service personnel to the quality of the work performed – and then to rate their overall satisfaction with service from the dealer.

Customers were also asked about where they would go in the future for maintenance service, minor mechanical and electrical repairs, major repairs in those same categories, and bodywork. The options listed for service were selling dealer, another Ford dealer, 'some other place' or 'do-it-yourself'. Finally, there were questions about overall satisfaction with the dealer sales department and the dealership in general, as well as the likelihood of their purchasing another Ford Motor Company product and buying it from the same dealership.

Dealers received monthly reports summarizing customer ratings of their dealership for the most recent month and for several previous months. To provide a comparison with how other Ford dealerships performed, the reports also included regional and national rating averages. After analysis, completed questionnaires were returned to the dealership; since these included each customer's name, a dealer could see which customers were satisfied and which were not.

In the 30-day survey of new purchasers, Sullivan's achieved better than average ratings on most dimensions. One finding which puzzled Carol was that almost 90 per cent of respondents answered 'yes' when asked if someone from Sullivan's had explained what to do if they needed service, but less than a third said that they had been introduced to someone in the service department. She resolved to ask Frank Broadbent about this discrepancy.

The nine-month survey findings disturbed her. Although vehicle ratings were in line with national averages, the overall level of satisfaction with service at Sullivan's was consistently low, placing it in the bottom 25 per cent of all Ford dealerships.

The worst ratings for service concerned promptness of writing up orders, convenience of scheduling the work, convenience of service hours and appearance of the service department. On length of time to complete the work, availability of needed parts and quality of work done (was it fixed right?), Sullivan's rating was close to the average. For interpersonal variables such as attitude of service department personnel, politeness, understanding of customer problems and explanation of work performed its ratings were relatively poor.

When Carol reviewed the individual questionnaires, she found that there was a wide degree of variation between customers' responses on these interpersonal variables, ranging all the way across the scale from 'completely satisfied' to 'very dissatisfied'. Curious, she had gone to the service files and examined the records for several dozen customers who had recently completed the nine-month surveys. At least part of the ratings could be explained by which receptionist the customer had dealt with. Those who had been served two or more times by her sisters, for instance, gave much better ratings than those who had dealt primarily with Jim Duffy, the service receptionist who had recently left.

Perhaps the most worrying responses were those relating to customers' likely use of Sullivan's service department in the future. More than half indicated that they would use another Ford dealer or 'some other place' for maintenance service (such as oil change, lubrication or tune up) or for minor mechanical and electrical repairs. About 30 per cent would use another source for major repairs. The rating for overall satisfaction with the selling dealer after nine months was below average and the customer's likelihood of purchasing from the same dealership again was significantly below that of buying another Ford product.

An unwelcome disturbance

Sullivan-Brown pushed aside the spreadsheets she had printed out and shut down her laptop. It was time to go home for dinner. She saw the options for the dealership as basically twofold: either prepare the business for an early sale at what would amount to a distress price, or take a year or two to try to turn it round financially. In the latter instance, if the turn-around succeeded, the business could subsequently be sold at a higher price than it presently commanded, or the family could install a general manager to run the dealership for them.

Peter Turner, owner of another nearby dealership, had offered to buy Sullivan's for a price that represented a fair valuation of the net assets, according to Sullivan's accountants, plus a valuation of goodwill.

As Carol left her office, she spotted the sales manager coming up the stairs leading from the showroom floor. 'Frank,' she said, 'I've got a question for you.'

'Fire away!' replied the sales manager.

'I've been looking at the customer satisfaction surveys. Why aren't our salesmen introducing new customers to the people in the Service Department? It's supposedly part of our sales protocol, but it only seems to be happening about one third of the time!'

Frank Broadbent shuffled his feet. 'Well, Carol, basically I leave it to their discretion. We tell them about service, of course, but some of the people on the floor feel a bit uncomfortable taking customers over to the service bays after they've been in here. It's quite a contrast, if you know what I mean.'

Suddenly, the sound of shouting arose from the floor below. A man of about 40, wearing an anorak and jeans, was standing in the doorway yelling at one of the salespeople. The two managers could catch snatches of what he was saying, in between various obscenities:

'. . . three visits . . . still not fixed right . . . service stinks . . . who's in charge here?' Everybody else in the showroom had stopped what they were doing and had turned to look at the newcomer.

Broadbent looked at his young employer and rolled his eyes. 'If there was something your father couldn't stand, it was people like that, shouting and screaming in the showroom and asking for the boss. Walter would hide in his office! Don't worry, Tom'll take care of that fellow and get him out of here. What an idiot!'

'No,' said Sullivan-Brown, 'I'll deal with him! One thing I learned when I worked at the airline was that you don't let people shout about their problems in front of everybody else. You take them off somewhere, calm them down, and find out what the problem is.'

She stepped quickly down the stairs, wondering to herself, 'What else have I learned from the travel industry that I can apply to this business?'

Euro Disney: an American in Paris

Christopher H. Lovelock ■ Ivor P. Morgan

The new Disney theme park and resort near Paris has not met its attendance and revenue projections. Management is evaluating the situation and seeking a turnaround strategy.

'Last call for the Euro-Disneyland Express . . .' The recorded American voice boomed out loud and clear even as the Express disappeared from view down the tracks. The crowds still waiting behind the station barriers muttered to themselves in a variety of languages, complaining that station employees had failed yet again to fill all the empty seats on the train. One visitor remarked to a companion that, although they had passed the 'Maximum 30 Minutes Wait' sign at the station entrance over 45 minutes earlier, they had at their present rate of progress at least that long to wait again. 'Let's try something else!' he said to his friend.

It was a cool autumn Saturday at Euro Disneyland, near Paris, and raining hard. Main Street, USA, flanked principally by stores selling Disney paraphernalia, was almost deserted. Only a few individuals wearing bright yellow rain capes with a Mickey Mouse insignia lit up the street. The absence of people outside the station suggested, at least, quick access to the rest of the park's attractions and restaurants.

This was not a promising start to a day at the Walt Disney Co.'s newest theme park, the fourth in a series, each of which had previously seemed a guaranteed success no matter where located. The company's ventures in California and Florida had become a staple 'must visit' for many American families and also a draw for visitors from other parts of the world, including Europe and Asia. Tokyo Disneyland, opened in 1983, had been successful, too, even though Japanese culture was widely accepted as being very different from that of the United States. But more than two years after its April 1992 opening, managers of the Euro Disney resort (which comprised both the Euro Disneyland theme park and an adjoining cluster of six hotels) were struggling to boost park attendance and hotel occupancy to help it turn around its continuing financial problems.

Background

Walt Disney dreamed in the 1950s of a new type of entertainment, which came to be known as the theme park. Seeing the amusement parks of that time as dirty, phony places run by tough-looking people, he envisioned something better. Disneyland opened in 1955 on an 80-acre (32 hectare) site in the suburban town of Anaheim, easily accessible from both Los Angeles and San Diego. The park featured many of Walt's famous cartoon figures, including Mickey Mouse, Goofy and other characters from Disney movies.

Walt Disney died in 1966 but his company continued to prosper. In 1971, it opened a second theme park in central Florida, named Walt Disney World. The new park, which most people called simply 'Disney World', was located within the company's huge landholdings outside Orlando. The development included on-site hotels and, subsequently, the futuristic Epcot Center. Stimulated by the success of Disney World, Orlando became a boom area boasting numerous other attractions and hotels. The third park followed in 1983 with the opening of Tokyo Disneyland on a relatively small site just outside the Japanese capital. Despite some initial difficulties, this park, too, became highly popular and a significant financial success for both Disney and the Japanese owners, the Oriental Land Co. However, the Walt Disney Co. had no equity stake, being limited to royalties of 10 per cent on admission revenues and 5 per cent on food and souvenir sales.

This case was developed from published sources and the personal experiences of individual Euro Disney visitors.

Exchange rates for the French franc (FFr) against other currencies varied widely during the early 1990s. Representative rates were FFr 1.00 = £0.12 or US$0.19.

In the mid-1980s the company turned its attention to Europe, from which numerous visitors to its California and (especially) Florida parks were drawn. Disney executives evaluated a variety of locations for what was to become Euro Disney, but eventually the choice narrowed to two sites: one outside Paris (population 8 million) in northern France, and the second near Barcelona (population 2.5 million) in eastern Spain.

Barcelona, site of the 1992 Summer Olympics and located on the Mediterranean coast, offered a warmer, drier climate. (See Exhibit 1 for comparative weather statistics in Paris, Barcelona, Tokyo, Central Florida and Los Angeles.) However, Paris had the advantage of offering easier access to potential visitors from densely populated areas of Northern Europe (see map in Exhibit 2), in addition to being one of the most popular tourist cities in Europe.

Disney executives were also influenced by the French government's offer of generous subsidies, tax allowances, and rail and highway improvements, designed to attract some 12,000 jobs to what was then a depressed agricultural region. The French inducements were successful and Disney purchased a site encompassing almost 20 square kilometres (5,000 acres), located 32 km (20 miles) southeast of the French capital.

Theme parks in Europe

The size and scope of Euro Disneyland far exceeded that of any existing European theme park. Some parks were relatively compact and urban, such as Copenhagen's famous Tivoli Gardens. Others, like Britain's popular Alton Towers, had been built as

Exhibit 1 ■ Comparative rainfall and temperature statistics

	Monthly rainfall by frequency and volume									
	Los Angeles, California		Orlando, Florida		Tokyo, Japan		Paris, France		Barcelona, Spain	
	days	inches	days	inches	days	inches	days	inches	days	inches
Jan.	6	2.7	6	2.1	5	2.2	17	1.5	5	1.4
Feb.	6	3.0	7	2.8	6	2.8	14	1.2	5	1.3
Mar.	6	2.2	8	3.2	10	4.4	12	1.6	8	2.7
Apr.	4	0.5	5	2.2	10	4.9	13	1.7	9	2.0
May	2	0.2	9	4.0	10	5.7	12	2.1	8	1.4
Jun.	1	0.1	14	7.4	12	6.5	12	2.3	6	1.3
Jul.	–	–	17	7.8	10	5.3	12	2.2	4	1.1
Aug.	–	–	16	6.3	9	5.7	13	2.2	6	1.4
Sep.	1	0.3	14	5.6	12	8.7	13	2.0	7	3.0
Oct.	2	0.7	8	2.8	11	7.4	13	2.3	9	3.0
Nov.	3	1.0	6	1.8	7	4.2	15	1.8	6	1.8
Dec.	6	2.3	6	1.8	5	2.1	16	1.7	6	1.7

Note: 'Days' refers to average number of days per month during which rain falls; 'inches' refers to average rainfall volume during that month (1 inch = 25 mm). Florida's rainfall is usually concentrated in short but extremely heavy showers, whereas in Paris rain may fall steadily for many hours.

Exhibit 1 ■ Comparative rainfall and temperature statistics *(continued)*

	Average daily temperatures: high and low for each month (in degrees Celsius)									
	Los Angeles, California		Orlando, Florida		Tokyo, Japan		Paris, France		Barcelona, Spain	
	high	low	high	low	high	low	high	low	high	low
Jan.	18°	8°	22°	10°	8°	–2°	6°	1°	13°	6°
Feb.	19	8	23	10	9	–1	7	1	14	7
Mar.	19	9	26	13	12	2	12	4	16	9
Apr.	21	10	29	16	17	8	16	6	18	11
May	22	12	31	19	22	12	20	10	21	14
Jun.	24	13	33	22	24	17	23	13	25	18
Jul.	27	16	33	23	28	21	25	15	28	21
Aug.	28	16	33	23	30	22	24	14	28	21
Sep.	27	14	32	23	26	19	21	12	25	19
Oct.	24	12	29	19	21	13	16	8	21	15
Nov.	23	10	26	14	16	6	10	5	16	11
Dec.	19	8	23	11	11	1	7	2	13	8

Note: Conversion: 0°C = 32°F, 10°C = 50°F, 20°C = 68°F, 30°C = 86°F. Data are based on averages for 24-hour periods, not highest and lowest temperatures within a 24-hour period

adjuncts to an existing attraction (in this case an English stately home). Many amusement parks lacked a coherent theme beyond the appeal of fairground rides promising increasing degrees of stomach-churning thrills. However, Legoland in Denmark was created out of giant versions of the successful children's construction toy. Several European parks promoted the Schtroumpfs (better known as 'Smurfs' in English). But these little blue cartoon characters, a big hit on children's television during the early 1980s, had largely disappeared from toy stores, comic books, and the mass media a decade later.

France boasted some 25 theme and entertainment parks, including Parc Asterix, Walibi-Schtroumpf, and Futuroscope (for details, see the Appendix). However, two major French parks, Mirapolis and Zygofolies, opened (like Futuroscope) in 1987, had both subsequently closed. Observers ascribed these failures to competition from other entertainment options, including numerous small amusement parks.

Euro Disney

With an investment totalling 21 billion francs, characters drawn from Disney cartoon movies, a site equivalent in area to one fifth the city of Paris, a projected 12,000 'cast members' (employees) on opening day, and a forecast of 11 million visitors in its first year, the Euro Disney project exemplified to its many French critics all that was wrong with American culture – namely size, money and Hollywood.

As opening day approached, many French intellectuals denounced the park; one described it as 'this new beachhead of American Imperialism.' Alain Finkelkraut, a philosopher, portrayed it as a 'terrifying giant's step towards world homogenization.'

Exhibit 2 ■ West and central Europe

Jean-Marie Rouart, a novelist, argued that Euro Disney symbolized the transformation of craft into industry. 'If we do not resist it,' he warned, 'the kingdom of profit will create a world that will have all the appearance of civilization and all the savage reality of barbarism.'[1]

On the other hand, there was plenty of evidence to suggest that large numbers of French people, especially younger ones, enjoyed watching American movies and TV shows – including those produced by Disney – as well as listening to American rock bands, eating American-style fast food and wearing American-inspired clothing.

The first phase of the project covered about one third of the available land area and included the Euro Disneyland park, six hotels with a total of 5,200 rooms, the Festival Disney entertainment and retail area (located between the park and the hotel complex), Camp Davy Crockett with 414 rental cabins and 181 campsites, and Golf Euro Disney, an 18-hole championship golf course. An average occupancy of 70 per cent was anticipated for the hotels. The original plans called for a proposed Phase II to be built in stages and were to include the Disney-MGM Studios Europe (comprising a second theme park plus movie and TV production facilities), initially scheduled to open in 1995. Once completed, these new attractions were projected to attract 5 million guests in its first year of operation and 8 million in the second year, encouraging Euro Disneyland guests to extend their stays. Subsequent stages would eventually add another 13,000 hotel rooms, a major convention centre, a water park, a second golf course and additional campsites.

The design of Euro Disneyland followed the same basic approach as other Disney parks, with some adaptations for northern European weather conditions. Advance press releases described the park as 'a giant outdoor stage where guests leave behind their ordinary world and enter lands of memory, imagination, and fantasy.' Facing the main entrance lay the complex known as Main Street, USA, flanked by shopping arcades offering weather-protected connections to several other attractions. Looping around the boundaries of the park was the Euro Disneyland

Express, with stations at Main Street, Frontierland, and Fantasyland. The other two groups of attractions were Adventureland and Discoveryland.

Dominating the park's Central Plaza were the spires of the fairy castle, taller and more lavishly finished than its counterparts in other Disney parks. There was no Matterhorn, but a substantially higher Big Thunder Mountain made up for the former's absence.

Financial arrangements

To defray the financial risk of this enormous project, of which Phase I alone took several years to complete, the Walt Disney Co. established a separate company, Euro Disney SCA, in which it held 49 per cent of the stock; the balance was sold to investors through public offerings. Though Euro Disney was responsible for operating the Euro Disneyland theme park, it would not own it fully until the end of the 20-year lease period. The Walt Disney Co. provided management for the company through a wholly-owned subsidiary.

In return for use of the Disney name and logistical support, Euro Disney paid Walt Disney Co. a number of royalties and fees, including a brand name royalty of 10 per cent on all revenues from admissions, sponsorship payments and parking, plus 5 per cent on food, drink and merchandise sales. There was also a base management fee of 5 per cent of all revenues through 1996, after which the rate increased to 6 per cent. Finally, there was an incentive management fee, levied at a progressive rate on operating income less the expenses needed to maintain the park's existing attractions. Critics felt that the arrangements left the Walt Disney Co. with the upside potential and the European investors with the downside risk.[2]

But Euro Disney had not attempted to avoid all risk. Having seen other real estate developers profit mightily from investments in land for hotels and other purposes in the area surrounding Disney World in Florida, Disney executives hoped that the opening of Euro Disney would lead to soaring values for their huge land investment near Paris. The Phase II plans for a big increase in hotel rooms assumed that visitors would stay longer at the resort. Consequently, to maximize the profit potential of the project, the company decided to own and operate the hotels and other resort facilities rather than lease them to third parties. Also on the drawing board were plans for enormous office developments, shopping malls, golf courses, apartment complexes and vacation homes. The idea was that Euro Disney would control the design, build nearly everything itself, and, at the right moment, sell off completed properties at a big profit.[3]

Catering to a multinational audience[4]

For Disney officials, their new European venture represented even more of a challenge than their first foreign theme park, Tokyo Disneyland. Visitors were expected to come from all over Europe (and beyond). At any one time, there might be as many as 50,000 guests in the park. Unlike the California, Florida, or Tokyo parks, no one nationality was expected to dominate at Euro Disney; so handling languages required careful planning.

An early decision, responding to concerns of 'American cultural imperialism', was that French would be the first official language at Euro Disney. Some of the attractions would be named in French, others would retain the names used in the American original. Most other signage would be in both English and French (in addition to use of international symbols), and knowledge of two or more languages would be an important criterion in hiring front-line employees.

Recruitment centres were set up in France and also in London, Amsterdam and Frankfurt. During 1992, approximately two-thirds of those hired were French nationals; the balance comprised another 75 nationalities, principally British, Dutch, German and Irish. Some knowledge of French was required of all employees; in the park's opening year, about 75 per cent of them spoke this language fluently, another 75 per cent spoke English, roughly 25 per cent spoke Spanish, and 25 per cent could speak German.

Although Euro Disney retained the basic orientation of other Disney theme parks, some adaptation was made to European culture and languages. The popular 'Pirates of the Caribbean' attraction, for instance, acknowledged that it wasn't only English-speaking pirates who enjoyed themselves attacking shipping and coastal ports in a jolly frenzy of looting, burning and drinking, but also their equally colourful French and Dutch counterparts. So pirate songs were played in three languages. Similarly, 'Sleeping Beauty's Castle' recognized the European origins of the popular fairy story and was known instead as *Le Château de la Belle au Bois Dormant*. But 'Main Street, USA' remained just that – no one really expected it to be renamed *Rue Principale, États-Unis*.

Many attractions and rides required little explanation, but guests could replace the French commentary in the Visionarium (a 360-degree film theatre) by using audio receivers that offered a choice of English, Spanish, German and Italian. The reservations centre catered to people of many tongues, with separate phone lines for each of 12 different languages. The main information centre in the park, City Hall, was staffed by cast members speaking a broad cross-section of languages.

Special procedures were instituted at the park's medical centre to handle emergencies involving guests speaking less commonly encountered languages. With over 70 nationalities represented among employees, there was a high probability that a cast member could be found to interpret in such a situation. Euro Disney could access the language capabilities of every employee by computer (who do we have on duty who speaks Turkish?) and could page them immediately by beeper or walkie-talkie.

Early operating experience

The park and resort opened to great fanfare on 12 April 1992. Visitors familiar with other Disney theme parks noted that everything at Euro Disneyland seemed to be larger and more ornate; the hotels, too, were enormous. At FFr 225 for adults and FFr 150 for children, admission prices were not only high by European standards but also higher than at Disney's two American parks.

Despite massive publicity, the first season was not a success. Ignoring much of the glitter and the excitement, the mass media highlighted difficulties and accentuated negative stories, including labour problems. The fiscal year ending 30 September 1992 concluded with an operating loss of FFr 682 million (reduced by other income and exceptional items to a net loss of FFr 188 million). The situation did not improve the following year. Attendance figures were particularly low during the cold, wet winter months, even though many of the rides were weather-protected and Disney had organized various seasonal events, including one for Halloween (a popular American children's celebration at the end of October, featuring ghosts, witches and lanterns made from carved pumpkins).

Among the problems were that attendance at Euro Disneyland had failed to reach target levels, particularly among the local French population which had been expected to form a substantial share of the early market.[5] Average expenditures per visitor, including food and souvenir purchases, were below projections, too. There was also a major seasonality problem, with the lowest levels of attendance a mere one-tenth of those on peak days – a ratio greatly exceeding that of the three sister parks. Finally, occupancy rates in the resort's hotels had proved to be far below projections; for instance, many guests visiting the park for two days would only spend one night in a Euro Disney hotel.

Complicating Euro Disney's financial situation was the company's inability to capitalize on its enormous landholdings. Reflecting falling demand for new commercial developments, land prices fell sharply during the recession that hit France and other European countries in the early 1990s. Worse, interest rates on the billions of dollars in loans and other debt proved to be higher than expected.

Management and training

In April 1993, a French chairman, Philippe Bourguignon, had replaced Robert Fitzpatrick, the American executive responsible for planning and building Euro Disney. Fitzpatrick, who spoke French and was married to a Frenchwoman, was seen by observers as having spared no expense in constructing the park but had experienced problems in managing day-to-day operations. Bourguignon, president of the park since September 1992, had previously operated the US subsidiary of the French hotel group Accor before taking charge of Disney's property operations in 1988. As chairman, Bourguignon's objective was to ensure that the park adapted itself to European conditions without losing the American feel that he saw as its main draw.[6]

Disney's policy was to have American managers train Europeans who would eventually replace them. However, turnover had been higher than expected. Bourguignon's team was composed of one-third French nationals and one-third Americans, with the balance coming mainly from the United Kingdom, Ireland and the Netherlands. Under Bourguignon, Euro Disney was striving to develop its own managerial culture, neither just a reflection of its American parent nor typically French either.

A key issue involved employee training. Disney had always been known for its strict guidelines. 'The Look Book', for example, dictated that female employees should wear only clear nail polish, very little – if any – make-up, and flesh-coloured stockings. Men could not wear beards or moustaches and had to keep their hair short and tapered. Guests should be greeted within 60 seconds of entering a facility and helped as needed. The company's 1990 Annual Report announced that 'a leading priority was to indoctrinate all employees in the Disney service philosophy, in addition to training them in operational policies and procedures.' Euro Disney's goal was to convert the employees, 60 per cent of whom were French, into clean-cut, customer-friendly, American-style service providers. 'The French are not known for their hospitality,' declared Margot Creviaux, the park's manager of training and development for Disney University. 'But Disney is.'[7]

However, during the first four months, more than 1,000 employees left. According to management, half quit, and the rest were asked to leave. The women's grooming guidelines were modified because 'what is considered a classic beauty in Europe is not considered a classic beauty in America.' At Euro Disney, the rules were changed to allow female cast members to wear pink or red nail polish, red lipstick and different coloured stockings as long as they 'complement [the] outfit and are in dark, subdued colours.' Another Disney trademark was to smile a lot. But those familiar with French culture noted that if asked to smile the French were likely to respond, 'I'll smile if I want to. Convince me.' So Creviaux had to adapt the training to suit Euro Disney's work force. Although Disney stressed total customer satisfaction, in the eyes of some employees the company had imposed controls making that goal impossible to deliver.

To end the labour disputes that had plagued the park, Bourguignon recognized standard French job classifications, set a maximum work week, and annualized hourly work schedules. In doing so, he obtained greater flexibility from his work force. But in response to the poor financial results, 950 jobs were cut from the 11,000-person work force.[8] A Euro Disney spokesperson said the cuts were necessary as the company shifted from start-up to its operating phase.[9] Roger Dupont, a local representative of the CGT union responded, 'It isn't the jobs cutting that will improve the image of Euro Disney.'

Marketing concerns

Euro Disney management planned to attract half of the park's visitors from France and the balance from other European countries. The off season particularly depended on the local population because of reduced travel across Europe in winter. The other Europeans came as expected, but the French comprised only 29 per cent of the attendance. Different reasons were advanced for this shortfall, including the American orientation, the high prices, the weather, and the location. Unlike Americans, Europeans had proved reluctant to take their children out of school for a vacation trip made at the parents' convenience.

Bourguignon blamed the poor financial results in part on Euro Disney's strongly American orientation. 'Although most of our visitors come to enjoy an authentically American atmosphere,' he noted, 'it was just a little too much for them to have to celebrate Halloween.'[10] Management therefore decided to place the accent more on events familiar to Europeans. And the American-inspired advertising was changed to a more descriptive campaign explaining what visitors could do at the park.

New policies were introduced to make the park more attractive to Europeans. In June 1993, Disney finally agreed to relax its prohibition on serving alcohol at Euro Disneyland. Four restaurants received permission to serve wine and beer. According to Yves Boulanger, the introduction of alcohol was primarily for non-French visitors from Germany and Britain who wanted wine because it was part of the French experience.[11]

Problems had also occurred with waiting queues, which were noticeably less orderly than in Disney's other parks. 'The most often-heard complaint is how unruly and even chaotic the queues seemed to be,' reported a *New York Times* correspondent, 'even though the lines are not particularly long.' Whole families sneaked under ropes and pushed ahead. No Disney employees appeared to be detailed to police the queues, and when guests complained to the offenders, everyone appeared to be speaking a different language and either did not – or pretended that they could not – understand what they had done wrong.

Complaints about high prices for admission and the hotels, combined with substantial seasonal variations in demand, led Bourguignon to break another Disney taboo by introducing cut-rate entry and room rates for the off-season. A lower priced evening ticket, available after 5 pm, was aimed at Parisians.[12] Price reductions were also introduced for school groups, as well as for individuals under 25 years of age or over 60.

Financial analysts continued to blame high prices for many of Euro Disney's difficulties. Disney had forecast that each visitor would buy $33 in food and souvenirs but actual expenditures were averaging 12 per cent lower. Despite the distances involved, many Europeans found that it was actually cheaper to visit Disney World in Florida. The marketing manager of a British travel agency described how, thanks to cheaper accommodations and an Atlantic airfare war, she was able to offer her clients a package price of $115 a day for travel, hotel and park entry, compared to $200 a day for a similar Euro Disney package.[13]

Financial results for 1993

The full impact of the company's crushing FFr 21 billion debt load became evident with publication of the financial results for the 1993 fiscal year (ending 30 September). On 10 November 1993, Euro Disney SCA announced an operating loss of FFr 1.8 billion and a net loss after exceptional items of FFr 5.3 billion (US$930 million).

Reflecting a full 12 months of operation, revenues from the theme park and resorts rose from FFr 3.8 billion francs in the previous year to almost FFr 4.9 billion. Although a large loss had been predicted by financial analysts, who had been tracking the company's fortunes closely, the magnitude of the loss was a surprise to many. Euro Disney's financial condition caused the Walt Disney Co. to defer the payment of royalties.[14]

The company changed its accounting policies to charge start-up costs directly to the income statement rather then capitalizing them on the balance sheet. Negotiations were begun with the company's banks to restructure the debt, but rumours began to fly that Euro Disney might have to shut down the park altogether.

The Walt Disney Co. agreed to help fund Euro Disney for a limited period in order to give the latter time to attempt its capital restructuring. Observers believed that while the Walt Disney Co. was anxious to protect its own investors, it could not afford to allow a company bearing the Disney brand name to go under.

Plans were temporarily frozen for the proposed FFr 15 billion Phase II Disney-MGM Studios Park, which was to be a separate operation from Euro Disneyland.[15] Meantime, Euro Disney was attempting to scale down its plan for a 3,400 room hotel and accompanying office complex and to replace it with a commercial complex on the proposed site.[16] This would bring fewer jobs to the region but could reduce Euro Disney's financial burden. The French government, however, might not favour changes of this type.

A visit to the park

It was a Saturday morning at the end of the first week of September. The weather had been forecast as overcast and cool, with showers developing in the afternoon, followed by bright periods. Two foreign visitors, who were familiar with both Disneyland and Walt Disney World, decided to see for themselves what Euro Disneyland was like. Noting a poster that promoted sale of Euro Disney tickets at his hotel, one of the visitors went to the reception desk to buy an entrance ticket for the park with his credit card. The following conversation ensued (in French):

Hotel employee: 'Sorry, sir, you must pay cash for a ticket here.'

Visitor: 'Why?'

Employee: 'It's a special promotion.'

Visitor: 'Does that mean tickets here are cheaper than at the gate?'

Employee: 'No, but you won't have to wait in line.'

The visitor decided to buy his ticket later, remembering a bargain price promotion for a combined RER (regional express metro) train ticket and entry to Euro Disney that he had seen advertised in Paris Metro (subway) stations. At the Châtelet station, bilingual French and English posters advertised the offer, but a clerk in the ticket office declared that the special offer was not available.

The station for Euro Disney was located at the end of the RER line, on a specially constructed extension. Set amid farmland, the new station was named 'Marne La Vallée-Chessy' after two nearby towns. Apart from a Mickey Mouse silhouette on the glass exit doors, nothing acknowledged Euro Disney's presence right outside. A left turn from the station and a short walk brought visitors to the entrance to Euro Disneyland. A right turn would have taken them past an entertainment mall offering a variety of souvenir stores and food stands and on to the six hotels of the Euro Disney Resort (see Exhibit 3).

It was now around 11:45 a.m. and starting to rain. There were no queues at the entrance booths. One of the visitors asked the ticket seller if he spoke German. The latter said that he did, but subsequently proved unable to carry on a simple conversation in that language. From the entrance, the park appeared to be almost deserted. Main

Disneyland Hotel

500 rooms, very luxurious Victorian theme. Daily room rate, FFr 1,990.

Hotel New York

575 rooms, luxury convention hotel. 'Big Apple' theme evoking New York City skyscrapers and terraced houses. Includes ice-skating rink, convention centre, tennis. Daily room rate, FFr 1,025.

Newport Bay Club

1,098 rooms. Elegant theme evoking New England yacht and beach club resort. Includes lighthouse and lakeside verandah with rocking chairs. Daily room rate. FFr 875.

Sequoia Lodge

1,011 rooms, Yosemite/Yellowstone theme based on rustic lodges at US national parks. Fireplaces, year-round outdoor pool. Daily rook rate, FFr 775.

Hotel-Cheyenne

1,000 rooms, American West theme. Log fort with lookout tower, corral, covered wagons. Room included double bed and bunk beds, no air-conditioning. Daily room rate, FFr 675.

Hotel Santa Fe

1,000 rooms, American Southwest theme, including American Indian cliff dwellings, adobe style pueblos. No air-conditioning. Daily room rate, FFr 550.

Old West Camp Davy Crockett

414 cabins in family-style 'wilderness' setting with Old West theme featuring miners, settlers and tavern (plus swimming pool). Daily rate, FFr 770.

All Euro Disney accommodation offered rooms set up for a family of four. Competition was limited within a radius of 4–5 miles (6–8 km) of the park. Offerings in 1994 included Novotel and Days Inn, both of which offered substantially cheaper rates than available at Euro Disney. Other hotel chains, including Accor and Comfort Inn, were constructing inexpensive hotels near the park, due to open in 1995. Visitors to Euro Disneyland could also stay at hotels in the centre of Paris or its suburbs.

Exhibit 3 ■ Euro Disney hotel and cabins: proposed peak season rates, 1994–95

Street, USA, was built to a larger scale than the Disneyland original in California and its theme had been updated from the late ninetheenth century to include reproduction antique cars.

With the rain now falling steadily, the Euro Disneyland Express seemed an attractive option, since the station was weather protected. The line of prospective passengers started well short of the sign which said '30 minutes wait beyond this point' so the two visitors joined the queue with optimism. 'It can't take more than 15 minutes from here,' said one. However, their optimism proved ill-founded, because the trains were arriving full and only a handful of people were getting off. To compound the problem, the few conductors were failing to fill all the empty seats on the train. Finally, the two visitors decided to wait no longer and headed up Main Street in search of Mickey Mouse.

But there was not a mouse (or other Disney character) to be seen. An earlier discussion with French friends living in a neighbouring town had suggested this was an ongoing omission. 'It's particularly irritating for my teenage granddaughters to see the TV advertisements full of Mickey Mouse and other Disney characters,' the friend had said, 'only to go to the park and not to be able to find them. I know they do appear in the parade but that is just for a very limited time in the evening. Another problem for me,' the grandfather continued, 'is the distance involved in getting around the park. The walk from the car park to the gates is bad enough, but when you get inside, the distances are so great that I can only get to a couple of attractions before I am tired out.'

Not only were there no Disney characters to be seen on this particular day, there seemed to be an almost total absence of Disney employees, except cleaners. Undeterred, the two visitors set themselves another target: to count the number of Disney paraphernalia – funny hats or other memorabilia – that they encountered. Fantasyland seemed to be a likely place but this proved to be very sparsely populated. So, with the rain getting harder, the search moved on to Frontierland.

Frontierland proved to be the first location with crowds of visitors. Without any success in adding to the number of Disney souvenirs, apart from the yellow Mickey Mouse rain garb, the visitors entered Phantom Manor. 'At least it will be dry there,' one declared. This haunted house proved to be much more high tech than its California counterpart, containing some dramatic, although not very scary, holograms.

Next it was on to Big Thunder Mountain for the mine train ride. There was a long queue, but patrons could wait under cover. Since there was no entertainment or other distraction to pass the time, the two visitors struck up conversations with other people in the queue. 'How has Euro Disneyland met your expectations?' was the question posed to a number of students from southern Germany. 'Great!' they said, enthusias-

tically. 'This is much bigger than we had expected.' The mine train ride was too fast for umbrellas, so passengers got quite wet (the benefits of the yellow Disney rain gear were becoming clear!). However, everyone gave the ride high marks. On leaving the train, one of the two friends, looking for a men's toilet, accidentally entered one for females; the relevant gender signs were posted low on the exterior wall and were blocked from view by people seeking shelter from the rain.

Lunch was the next order of the day. But in Frontierland the queues were horrendous as guests tried to keep dry. So it was back to Main Street, still relatively deserted, for a pleasant lunch at a Nestlé restaurant. 'Let's try the Pirates of the Caribbean next,' one of the visitors declared. Unlike *La Cabane des Robinson* or *Indiana Jones et le Temple du Péril*, Euro Disney had chosen to retain the original English as the title for this attraction. 'Which way is the Pirates of the Caribbean?' a friendly-looking cleaner was asked. This question received a blank response, even when repeated very slowly. But asking in French for *'Les Pirates des Caraïbes'* brought a warm smile and immediate directions.

There was no queue for the Pirates (which was prominently advertised by a large sign in English). On the boat, instructions were in English and French, but a careful listener could hear strains of sea shanties in English, French and Dutch. It was now over four hours into the visit and still no sign of Mickey Mouse or any other Disney character. Only two funny hats had been spotted, worn by a boy and a girl of about ten years of age.

The next stop was at Star Tours, where professional entertainment helped pass the time while waiting. The two visitors got into conversation with a Belgian family living in Paris. 'What do you think of Euro Disney?' they asked. 'The cleanliness is extraordinary,' one of them responded. 'You just don't expect to see that in Europe.' Added another, 'Overall it's too American, especially the food. It's hard to get an alcoholic drink here. We expect to be able to drink wine and beer with a meal.' Afterwards, everyone pronounced The Star Tours ride immensely enjoyable.

Around 6 p.m. the rain stopped and the sun came out, creating a dramatic change in atmosphere. Almost immediately, it seemed, the crowds became thicker, smiles broke out, and people became jolly. The flowers and other plantings became more noticeable and the park was suddenly awash with colour. During a ride on the *Molly Brown* riverboat, the visitors chatted with a couple from Barcelona; the latter were astounded to learn that the tall trees growing lushly around the lakeshore had only been planted a few years earlier. But they didn't like the climate. 'We wanted to have Euro Disney in Barcelona,' the man said, shaking his head. 'It would have been better there.'

With only a short wait required, it was time for a trip on the Euro Disneyland Express. Unfortunately, the recorded announcements were out of synch and the wrong stations announced. Passengers were being told in German, English and French to admire the marvels of the 'Grand Canyon' as they passed through totally different scenery.

At 6.35 p.m. came the first sighting of a Disney character: Alice and the White Rabbit were spotted shaking hands with visitors! Ten minutes later, *Blanche-Neige et les Sept Nains* (alias Snow White and the Seven Dwarfs) could be seen dancing together on stage, but Mickey and Minnie Mouse were never sighted. On returning to Frontierland for a meal, the short queues at the take-out 'Cowboy Cookout Barbecue' promised quick service. However, members of the extended family group at the head of the queue were unable to work out what they could and could not get for their prepaid food coupons, so purchasing food actually proved to be a very slow process. A request for a beer was turned down – it could only be satisfied at another restaurant – but no one knew which.

Finally, it was time to leave. By 8 p.m., the atmosphere was really beginning to feel festive, like that of Disneyland and Disney World. Returning to Paris on the RER, a British couple with a baby in a stroller was asked what they thought of the park. 'It was all right. We've already been to the one in Florida', the husband answered. 'How did Euro Disney compare?' 'Much the same, I guess.' Had they seen Mickey Mouse? 'Yes, he was greeting visitors when we arrived at 10 a.m. But I expect they sent him inside so that the rain wouldn't spoil his costume.'

Planning for the 1995 season

Euro Disney's financial performance continued to cause alarm during the 1994 fiscal year, which began with 60 creditor banks rejecting a proposed 11 billion franc restructuring of the outstanding debt. Rumors began to circulate that Disney would be forced to close the park. Some months later, however, agreement was reached on restructuring a substantial portion of the debt. A senior French banker familiar with the company described Euro Disney as 'a good theme park married to a bankrupt real estate development – and the two can't be divorced.'[17]

Philippe Bourguignon had succeeded in achieving some FFr 500 million in cost savings, including laying off 900 staff and placing some 2,000 of the park's remaining 10,000 employees on part-time contracts. Some of the hotels had shut down over the winter months. There were concerns, however, that further cost cutting would lead to a decline in service quality. On the positive side, wait times for many rides had been reduced.

The fiscal 1994 results told a mixed story.[18] After extraordinary items, the net loss fell to FFr 1.8 billion. But revenues were down by 15 per cent to FFr 4.5 billion, including FFr 2.2 billion from the park, FFr 1.6 billion from the hotels, and FFr 0.3 billion from sources such as corporate sponsorship programmes. Exhibit 4 reproduces the financial statements of Euro Disney SCA in US dollars, with the results restated in accordance with US-standard generally accepted accounting principles (GAAP).

Despite some price promotions in the off-season, attendance was down substantially over the previous year:

Period	Fiscal year 1993	Fiscal year 1994
October–March	3.4 million	3.1 million
April–June	3.1 million	2.6 million
July–September	3.3 million	3.1 million

Disney executives blamed these results on public concerns that the park was going to fail. Still, Euro

Exhibit 4 ■ Financial statements of Euro Disney SCA

In US$ millions in accordance with generally accepted accounting practices (GAAP) in the US

Balance sheet	1994	1993	1992	
Cash & investments	289	211	479	
Receivables	227	269	459	
Fixed assets	3,791	3,704	4,346	
Other assets	137	214	873	
Total assets	4,444	4,397	6,157	
Accounts payable and other liabilities	560	647	797	
Borrowing	3,051	3,683	3,960	
Common stock		1,042	1,042	
Retained earnings (deficit)	833*	(975)	358	
Total liabilities + stockholders' equity	4,444	4,397	6,157	
Statement of operations	1994	1993	1992	1991
Revenues	751	873	738	–
Costs and expenses	(1,198)	(1,114)	(808)	–
Operating loss	(447)	(241)	(70)	–
Net interest income (Expense)	(280)	(287)	(95)	76
Income (loss) before income taxes and cumulative effect of accounting change	(727)	(528)	(165)	76
Income taxes	–	–	30	28
Income (loss) before cumulative effect of accounting change	(727)	(528)	(135)	48
Cumulative effect of change in accounting – for pre-opening costs		(578)	–	–
Net income (loss)	(727)	(1,106)	(135)	48
Proforma amount assuming the change in accounting method is applied retroactively		(528)	(418)	(87)

Note: Under French GAAP, Euro Disney incurred a 1993 net loss of FFr 5.3 billion (FFr 2.1 billion before the cumulative effect of accounting change), a net loss of FFr 1.8 million in 1992 and net income of FFr 249 million in 1991. During 1993, Euro Disney changed its method of accounting for project-related pre-opening costs. Under the new method, such costs are expensed as incurred. The cumulative effect of the change in method on prior years was a charge against income of FFr 3.2 billion. The effect of the change on the year ended 30 September 1993 was to decrease the loss before the cumulative effect of accounting change by FFr 338 million.

Source: The Walt Disney Company 1993 & 1994 Annual Reports .

Disneyland remained Europe's biggest paid tourist attraction. Thanks in part to reduced off-season rates, hotel occupancy rose during the October to March period from 37 per cent in 1993 to 48 per cent in 1994; but between April and September it fell slightly from 72 per cent in 1993 to 71 per cent in the latest year.

Senior management was working to develop a turn-around marketing strategy for 1995. Competition was intensifying, with many European parks, including nearby Parc Astérix, adding dramatic new rides or other attractions. A huge new amusement park, Port Aventura, was scheduled to open near Barcelona, Spain, in March 1995.

Bourguignon told reporters that the company was still undecided on whether to raise or cut admission prices to the park for the coming year. However, he conceded that many French visitors still regarded the park as expensive. Executives anticipated that improvements in European economies would stimulate spending on tourism and entertainment. They looked forward to the much delayed opening of the Channel Tunnel, linking the French and British rail systems under the English Channel. This link would enhance access to the park via a new Euro Disney station on the TGV high-speed rail line, which also connected to many other cities in France and neighbouring countries.

New advertising was under development, and a new ride, Space Mountain, was due to open in June. Based on a book by the nineteenth-century French science fiction writer, Jules Verne, this indoor roller coaster would give visitors the impression of being fired to the moon from a giant cannon. Even so, Euro Disney would still have about ten fewer attractions than Disney World. And contentious issues remained. Attendance by French visitors remained disappointing, leading some experts to recommend closing the park during the off-season – November through March. There was also a proposal to relaunch the park, changing the name from 'Euro Disneyland' to 'Disneyland Paris.'

Appendix
Details of three other major French amusement parks
Parc Astérix

Parc Astérix, located just north of Paris and opened in 1989, was based on a famous French comic book character. Astérix and his fellow characters had their mythical home in a small village in Brittany during Roman times. Many of their stories concerned their triumphs over the Romans. The history of France played an integral role in the park, and its cuisine was essentially French. Robert Fitzpatrick, formerly CEO of Euro Disney had declared 'Astérix has a better image than any other French park in the minds of kids.' Initially costing FFr 900 million, the park attracted 1.35 million visitors in its first year, well below its forecast. The first-year deficit of FFr 60 million was also very disappointing.

Unlike Euro Disney, Parc Astérix was open only from April to October; however maintaining the park during the winter months still required considerable operational expense. Visitors were attracted to Astérix by its lower prices and the possibility of taking their own food into the park rather than buying it inside. The park was easily accessible by car or bus, being located just off a major autoroute.

Attendance had dropped by 30 per cent following the opening of Euro Disney, but numbers had recovered to 1.3 million in 1993, reflecting a new competitive strategy. Prices were cut, the park design improved, waiting lines reduced, and more signs posted within the park. An 800-seat self-service restaurant and a large new playground were opened, and a children's parade became a daily summer feature. Additionally, a shuttle bus service was introduced to link the park to the nearest RER express metro station.

Many of the attractions at Parc Astérix emphasized French culture and history. Thrills included some traditional fairground rides, such as a giant carousel, as well as 'National 7' (the designation of France's most famous highway) which consisted of a tour in antique automobiles through scenes reminiscent of the French countryside and the streets of Paris. There were also several exciting flume rides and the park was constructing Europe's largest roller coaster, featuring five loops and a double corkscrew, due to open in 1995. With a sharp increase in the promotional budget, the park's CEO organized a 'Tour of Gaul' (the name given to France in Roman times), involving promotional activities in many French cities.

Big Bang Schtroumpfs

Opened in Moselle, by the French–German border, in 1988 at a cost of FFr 720 million, this park drew only 800,000 visitors in its first year, compared to projections based on US data of 1.8 million. Although the park had a 90 per cent satisfaction rating, only 25 per cent of its visitors were returnees. In 1991, the park was sold to Walibi (Belgium) for FFr 50 million.

Walibi management already operated eight amusement parks in Europe and achieved a combined total of some 4.3 million visitors each year in its parks. At FFr 90, the Walibi Schtroumpfs ticket price was only 40 per cent that of Euro Disneyland. Walibi-Schtroumpfs was the third Walibi park in France and the firm had plans to open a fourth park in 1994. By Euro Disney standards, the Walibi operation was a modest one with profits of FFr 30 million in 1990. Its new parks reinvested 100 per cent of their revenues and even its established parks reinvested 30 per cent. Every three years, a major new attraction was introduced at each park, for example, in 1993 a 'Colorado train' opened at Walibi's park in Brussels, the Belgian capital. Promotion costs were set at about 10 per cent of revenues. Labour costs were minimized: the Walibi takeover of the Schtroumpf park led to labour costs falling from FFr 38 million to FFr 13 million.

Futuroscope

Futuroscope, the only large new amusement park seen as a financial success, was situated on the outskirts of Poitiers, 380 km (240 miles) southwest of Paris. Focusing on cinema and technology, Futuroscope also served as a laboratory for new experimental tech-

niques. Among the attractions were several theatres with huge screens. In one, the screen extended through a continuous 360-degree circle, while another simulated a 'flying carpet' experience through screens at both eye-level and below one's feet; in a third theatre, visitors sat in mechanical chairs that moved in synchonization with the film being showed, and in a fourth they watched three-dimensional films. There was also an interactive media theatre and other activities related to media imaging. The orientation was fact, not fiction. With its unusual modern architecture, Futuroscope formed an activity pole for small high-tech companies, a high school, a college, and a research institute for physics and mathematics. The overall concept promoted education through leisure and attendance was expected to reach 3 million visitors in 1994.

Observers believed that Futuroscope's success lay in its high-technology appeal to parents and children alike. The park had been relatively cheap to build. Its hotels were inexpensive and operated by experienced companies. Marketing efforts for the park had emphasized carefully targeted mailings to schools and colleges, social-events committees, and retirement clubs, thereby avoiding the expenses of a mass media blitz.

Notes

1. 'Only the French Elite Scorn Mickey's Debut', *New York Times*, 13 April 1992.
2. 'The Not So Magic Kingdom', *The Economist*, 26 September 1992, p. 87.
3. 'Mouse Trap: Fans Like Euro Disney, But its Parent's Goofs Weight the Park Down', *Wall Street Journal*, 10 March 1994, p. 1.
4. This section is based on material in Christopher Lovelock, *Product Plus*, New York: McGraw-Hill, 1994, pp. 308–9.
5. 'Euro Disney Draws Over 1.5 million in First 7 Weeks', *Wall Street Journal*, 10 June 1992.
6. 'Disney's Bungle Book', *International Management*, July/August 1993, p. 26.
7. 'Mickey Mouse's Source of Manners', *The Washington Post*, 11 August 1992, p. B1.
8. 'Euro Disney Giving Investors a Rough Ride', *Boston Globe*, 27 November 1993, p. 94.
9. 'Euro Disney Plans', *The Wall Street Journal*, 19 October 1993, p. A1.
10. 'Disney goes European', *Marketing*, 15 April 1993, p. 3.
11. 'Euro Disney Adding Alcohol', *New York Times*, 12 June 1993, p. A42.

12. 'Euro Disney's Off-Season Success Depends on Attracting French', *The Washington Post*, 13 October 1993.

13. 'The Mouse Isn't Roaring', *Business Week*, 24 August 1993, p. 28.

14. 'Euro Disney SCA Company Report', *Dean Witter Reynolds*, 31 December 1992.

15. 'Playing Disney in the Parisian Fields', New York Times, 17 February 1991.

16. Ridding, *op. cit.*

17. 'Mouse Trap: Fans Like Euro Disney', op. cit.

18. 'Fears of Closure Haunt Paris Amusement Park', Financial Times, 4 November 1994.

PART ii

Understanding customers and managing relationships

CHAPTER 4

Customer behaviour in service settings

Learning objectives

After reading and reflecting on this chapter, you should be able to:

1. Distinguish between search, experience and credence properties as they relate to the ease of evaluating goods and services before or after consumption.

2. Discuss how service characteristics like the intangibility of service performances and variability in service inputs and outputs affect consumer evaluation processes.

3. Explain the purchase process for services.

4. Differentiate between core and supplementary service elements, as well as between hygiene factors and enhancing factors.

5. Construct a simple flowchart showing a service process from the customer's perspective.

Club Med seeks to keep up with changing tastes and life styles[1]

When Gilbert Trigano launched 'Club Med' in the 1950s, the concept of all-inclusive holiday villages, with limitless food and innumerable sporting activities provided at a single price in splendid natural surroundings, was not only unique, but also reflected a significant change in consumer behaviour in France and across Europe at that time. While French and European society in the 1950s was still very traditional and formal, a new, younger segment of consumers was emerging who were influenced by growing affluence and American values. Trigano's strength was his ability to sense this new trend in consumer behaviour, and to cater to it through the Club Med concept. As the *Financial Times* put it:

> At a time when France was dominated by rigid social norms, Club Med provided an attractive form of escapism with its informality – including compulsory use of first names and the familiar French 'tu' form of address. In a country not renowned for its emphasis on friendly customer service, Club Med resorts established a reputation thanks to their pioneering emphasis on *gentils organisateurs* (GOs) and highly trained and plentiful staff present at all times to help their *gentils membres* (GMs), or guests, to enjoy themselves.

From its very beginnings, the atmosphere at Club Med attracted a crowd which was primarily young, well-off financially, educated and single. These people enjoyed sports, travel and exotic locations. It was a burgeoning market, and by the late 1960s, Club Med, with its communal life style – which included shared huts, group activities and large dining tables designed to break down any remaining social barriers between guests – captured the spirit of the times. In the 1970s and 1980s, as European standards of living and status seeking behaviour continued to grow, leisure (in all its aspects) became a much more important part of people's lives. Club Med epitomized the ultimate leisure experience: a relatively expensive holiday, characterized by sea, sports, sun, fun and sex.

Yet ten years later, problems emerged. The group's financial situation began to weaken and there was widespread criticism that the 'Club concept' was now out-moded and had outlived its time. Younger people, critics claimed, were now more individualistic, and no longer keen on the kinds of sybaritic, group activities for which Club Med was renowned. Finding young, new customers was becoming harder and harder. As for the Club's most loyal customers – those who kept returning every year for their holidays – they were now older, and had a whole new set of criteria when it came to vacations: rather than seeking ways to have fun as 'swinging singles', these guests were now more concerned about what to do with their kids on holiday and with achieving an all-round healthy life style. Nutritious food, together with low-impact exercises, massage and other methods of maintaining physical and emotional well-being were more important than a rollicking time on the beach.

At the same time, by the 1990s, as the recession took hold in Europe, the conspicuous consumption of the 1980s – which had fuelled Club Med's growth, given the status associated with going on a Club Med vacation – had given way to more emphasis on value for money. The emergence of low-price, all-inclusive holiday package tours thus began to erode Club Med's traditional customer base. Club Med, however, had not lowered its prices.

After losses of FFr 743 million (€111 million) in 1996 – the largest ever – the Trigano family was ousted from the daily running of the company, and Philippe Bourguignon – who had turned Disneyland Paris around – was brought in to revive Club Med. In his words, 'Club Med has tried to be everything for everyone. But you have to make choices . . .'

The problem was that whereas Club Med had initially been successful by understanding consumer behaviour, their existing customers' needs had changed as they grew older, while the new generation wanted something different. Bourguignon's plan was to try to enhance value for money, attract a younger clientele, and extend the holiday season by providing services such as entertainment, sports and cafés throughout the year rather than simply during an annual holiday. He adopted a two-pronged approach aimed at meeting the requirements of two very different kinds of segments – the younger, value-conscious market which Club Med had not yet succeeded in winning over; and the longstanding, but now mature group of customers who had been the backbone of Club Med's success from the 1960s to the 1980s, but who were now looking elsewhere when it came to their holiday plans.

To meet the needs of younger, value-conscious consumers, Bourguignon immediately closed several loss-making villages, and converted a number of others into lower priced 'Club Aquarius' camps. Similarly, plans were also afoot to transform the traditional Club Med concept by catering more to the 'creature comfort' requirements of its older, existing customers.

Understanding customer needs and expectations

Customers buy goods and services to meet specific needs, and they evaluate the outcomes of their purchases based on what they expect to receive. Needs are deeply rooted in people's unconscious and concern long-term existence and identity issues. When people feel a need, they are motivated to take action to fulfil it. Abraham. Maslow identified five categories of human needs – physiological, safety, love, esteem and self-actualization – and proposed that basic needs like food and shelter must be met before others were fulfilled.[2] Although poverty, malnutrition and lack of housing remain pressing issues around the world, including parts of Europe, physiological needs have long ceased to be the sole issue for many Europeans. Greater prosperity means that increasing numbers of individuals are seeking to satisfy social and self-actualization needs. These needs, which are more complex, create demand for more sophisticated goods and services.

It was Serge Trigano's ability to understand changing needs and values in 1950s Europe that led to the creation of Club Med and propelled the success of this new style of holiday. On the other hand, Club Med failed to realize not only that its customers' needs were changing as they grew older and had families, but also that the new generation of young adults in the 1990s had a different set of values and expectations. It took the appointment of a new chief executive, Philippe Bourguignon, to redirect the Club's emphasis.

Providing a company can get its focus right, the holiday market is a good one to be in. In Europe, as in other highly developed regions, there is evidence that many consumers are reaching the point where they have all the physical goods they want and are now turning to services to fill unmet needs. More elaborate holidays are only one element. In the United States, for instance, shoppers reported that they planned to spend more money overall during the 1997 Christmas season than they did in 1996, but they didn't intend to buy as many goods as before, reporting that they would rather give or receive services instead. So they planned to spend 2 per cent less on tangible gifts and 45–55 per cent more on entertainment and travel expenditures. According to Daniel Bethamy of American Express, consumers want 'memorable experiences, not gadgets'.[3] This shift in consumer behaviour and attitudes provides opportunities for those service companies that can not only understand and meet changing needs, but can also remain flexible and continue to adapt their offerings over time as needs evolve. As Pine and Gilmore point out, the notion of service experiences can also extend to business and industrial situations; they cite the example of modern trade shows where exhibitors, including manufacturers, set out to engage the customer's interest through interactive presentations and even entertainment.[4]

Customers' expectations about what constitutes good service are likely to vary from one situation to another. For example, although accounting and veterinary surgery are both professional services, you would expect a visit to an accountant to talk about your tax returns to be a very different experience from a visit to a vet to get treatment for your sick pet. Your expectations are also likely to vary concerning differently positioned service providers in the same industry. While travellers expect no-frills service for a short intra-European flight on EasyJet, they would undoubtedly be very dissatisfied with that same level of service on a Swissair flight from Zurich to Singapore, even in economy class. Consequently, it's very important for marketers to understand customers' expectations of their own firm's service offerings.

How are expectations formed?

When individual customers or corporate purchasing departments evaluate the quality of a service, they are judging it against some internal standard that existed prior to the service experience.[5] Perceived service quality results from customers comparing the service they perceive they have received against that which they expected to receive. People's expectations about services are most influenced by their own prior experience as customers – with a particular service provider, with competing services in the same industry, or with related services in different industries. If they have no relevant prior experience, customers may base their pre-purchase expectations on factors like word-of-mouth comments, advertising or sales presentations.

Over time, certain norms develop for what customers can expect from various service providers within a given industry. These norms are reinforced by both customer experience and supplier-controlled factors such as advertising, pricing and the physical appearance of the service facility and employees. For example, French customers don't expect to be greeted by a doorman and a valet at a Formule 1 budget hotel, but they certainly do at the Ritz in Paris. Different industries may also have their own norms for quality which affect customers' expectations. In many countries, people have lower expectations of government service providers than they do of private companies. Expectations may even vary within different demographic groups (for example, between men and women, older and younger consumers, or blue- versus white-collar workers). To make things more complicated, expectations also differ from country to country. For instance, while it may be acceptable for a train to arrive several hours late in Greece, rail schedules are so precise in Switzerland that the margin for error is measured in seconds.

German and American expectations of banking services[6]

A recent cross-cultural study tested the conventional wisdom that the US is a more customer-centred and service-oriented society than Germany. Researchers from both countries worked together to design a self-administered questionnaire that asked respondents to rate 26 different expectations about excellent service quality and to evaluate their own banks on these factors. Overall, Americans had higher expectations for banking services than did Germans. One of the biggest differences between the two groups was that Americans expected significantly more access to technologically-based services like telephone banking. (This difference might be partly explained by the high price of telephone service in Germany, where local calls are still relatively expensive, whereas they are free in the United States, being included in the monthly subscription charge.)

US customers ranked trust and friendliness as the two most important attributes of high-quality banking services, while Germans wanted competent investment advice and timely service delivery. Still, the two groups did agree on some things. Four of the five top-ranked expectations were the same for both countries, and both groups agreed that bank size, receiving promotional information by mail and corporate social responsibility were low in importance.

Almost all customers, regardless of nationality, had higher expectations for service quality than their banks actually delivered. And in both countries, women had slightly higher expectations than men. However, the gap between expectations and performance was generally greater for Americans than for Germans. Even though Americans expected and received better banking service than their German counterparts, they reported a higher level of dissatisfaction. In this case, better service performance did not lead to increased perceptions of service quality – perhaps because it created even higher expectations!

The components of customer expectations

Customer expectations involve several different elements, including desired service, adequate service, predicted service and a zone of tolerance which falls between the desired and adequate service level.[7] The model shown in Figure 4.1 shows how expectations for desired service and adequate service are formed.

Desired and adequate service levels

Desired service is the type of service customers hope to receive. It is a 'wished for' level of service – a combination of what customers believe can and should be delivered in the context of their personal needs. Although they would prefer to receive 'ideal' service, customers do not usually have extravagant or unreasonable expectations. They understand that companies can't always deliver the best possible service.

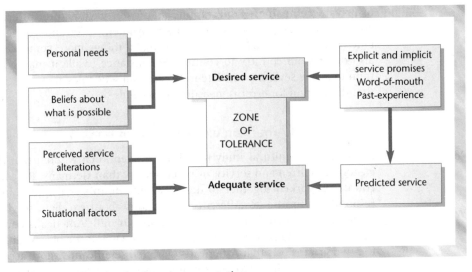

Figure 4.1 ■ Two levels of service expectation

Source: Adapted from Valarie Zeithaml and Mary Jo Bitner, *Services Marketing*, New York: McGraw-Hill, 1996, pp. 77–91.

For this reason, argue Zeithaml, Berry and Parasuraman, they also have a lower level of expectations, termed *adequate service*, which is defined as the minimum level of service customers will accept without being dissatisfied. Among the factors that help to set this expectation are the anticipated performance of perceived service alternatives and situational factors related to use of the service on this occasion. The levels of both desired and adequate service expectations may reflect both explicit and implicit service promises made by the provider, what the customer has heard through word of mouth, and past experience (if any) with this organization.[8]

Customers have different desired levels of expectations *across* subcategories of services in an industry. For example, within the restaurant industry, customers expect different things from expensive restaurants than from fast-food establishments. Taco Bell discovered from its customer surveys that customers desired accurate orders prepared quickly and served at the right temperature in a clean environment. While customers of a more upmarket restaurant chain like Mövenpick might value some of the same basic attributes, they will probably have additional expectations about the atmosphere, the behaviour of service employees and the way food is presented. The adequate service level is likely to vary for businesses even *within* the same subcategory. Thus customers may expect a higher level of adequate service from a McDonalds than from a small independently-owned restaurant if they've experienced more consistent service from McDonalds over time.

Predicted service

The level of service customers actually anticipate receiving from the service provider during a particular service encounter is known as *predicted service*; it directly affects how customers define 'adequate service' in that situation. If good service is predicted, the adequate level will be higher than if poorer service is predicted. For example, if you visit the student health centre in winter, you probably anticipate a long queue to see a doctor because you expect lots of people to be ill at that time of the year. So a wait of 45 minutes may not fall below your adequate service level. However, on a warm spring afternoon you might be quite impatient if the wait is 20 minutes, because your prediction was that the health centre would be uncrowded.

Zone of tolerance

As we discussed in Chapter 1, the inherent nature of services makes consistent service delivery difficult across employees in the same company and even within the same service employee from day to day. The extent to which customers are willing to accept this variation is called the *zone of tolerance*. As you can see from Figure 4.1 adequate service is the minimum level that is acceptable to customers. Service below this level will cause frustration and dissatisfaction. Service that falls above the desired service level will both please and surprise customers, creating what is sometimes referred to as 'customer delight'. Another way of looking at the zone of tolerance is to think of it as the range of service within which customers don't pay explicit attention to service performance.[9] When service falls outside the range, customers will definitely react in either a positive or a negative way.

The zone of tolerance can increase or decrease for individual customers depending on factors including competition, price or importance of specific service attributes. These factors most often affect adequate service levels (which move up and down due to situational factors), while desired service levels tend to move up very slowly in response to accumulated customer experiences. For example, an airline passenger's ideal level of service may include being booked on the most direct flight possible to her destination. Now suppose she is travelling on a ticket that has been 'purchased' with frequent flyer miles. Her ideal service level probably won't change, but her zone of tolerance for travel time and changes of flight at intermediate airports may increase since she is travelling 'free'. Airlines know that passengers in these situations have lower adequate service thresholds and tend to book them accordingly.

How customers evaluate service performances

Service performances – especially those that contain few tangible clues – can be very complex for consumers to evaluate. Unlike goods, their attributes can't be as easily determined before, or sometimes even after, a purchase is made. And the consequences of making a mistake by choosing the wrong service are often more personally felt, especially when customers are directly involved in service production.

Customers who have purchased a physical good that subsequently proves to be a poor choice can often recover easily from their mistake (e.g., they can return a defective CD player, exchange clothing that is the wrong size or take a car in for repairs under warranty). However, these options are not as readily available with services. Possession-processing services are most similar to goods in this respect, since the customer's possessions can often be re-serviced if the work is not performed adequately the first time. For example, a cleaning service can clean an office again if a customer complains about the quality of the job. By contrast, people-processing services that are performed on people's bodies may be hard to reverse. After all, a bad haircut must be grown out, and the consequences of a faulty surgical operation or a poorly done tattoo may last for ever!

Mental stimulus-processing services like education and live entertainment (such as theatre performances or soccer games) can also be difficult to 'replace' if quality does not meet customers' expectations. Theatre goers cannot realistically ask for their money back if actors perform their roles poorly or the script is bad; nor can sports fans expect refunds if their favourite team plays badly (instead, they use other methods to let the players know of their dissatisfaction!). Similarly, universities don't usually compensate students for poor quality classroom experiences. Even if a college was willing to let students repeat classes free of charge with a different lecturer, the latter would still incur significant time and psychological costs (such costs are discussed in depth in Chapter 10).

Finally, information-based services can present challenges for customers when service quality is unsatisfactory. Unhappy customers of insurance, banking or accounting services may be reluctant even to switch providers because of the potential time, psychological and financial costs involved. If people want to change insurance companies, they will have to spend time providing required application materials. Drivers who switch from an insurance company that they have used for a long time will lose the 'good customer' discounts offered as a reward for their loyalty to the firm.

A continuum of product attributes

In Chapter 1, we pointed out that one of the basic differences between goods and services is that services are harder for customers to evaluate. We also briefly mentioned that product characteristics could be divided into search, experience and credence properties.[10] We'll expand on the concept of these three categories here, since they provide a useful framework for understanding how consumers evaluate different types of market offerings.

All products can be placed on a continuum ranging from 'easy to evaluate' to 'difficult to evaluate'. As you can see from Figure 4.2, most physical goods are towards the left of the spectrum, since they are high in *search properties* – those attributes that allow customers to evaluate a product before purchasing it. Features like style, colour, texture, taste, sound and price allow prospective consumers to try out, taste test or 'test drive' the product prior to purchase. This helps customers understand and evaluate what they will get in exchange for their money and reduces the sense of uncertainty or risk associated with the purchase occasion. Goods such as clothing, furniture, cars, electronic equipment and foods are high in search properties.

Experience properties can't be evaluated prior to purchase. Customers must 'experience' these features to know what they are getting. Holidays, live entertainment performances, sporting events and restaurants fall into this category. Although people can examine colourful and informative brochures explaining the features of a holiday destination, view travel films or read reviews by travel experts, they can't really evaluate (or feel) the dramatic beauty associated with hiking in the Swiss Alps or the magic of scuba diving in the Mediterranean until they actually experience these activities. Nor can customers always rely on information from friends, family or other personal sources when evaluating these or other types of services. Think about how often friends have urged you to see a film they really liked. Although you probably walked into the cinema with high expectations, after 'experiencing' the film yourself, you may sometimes have been disappointed.

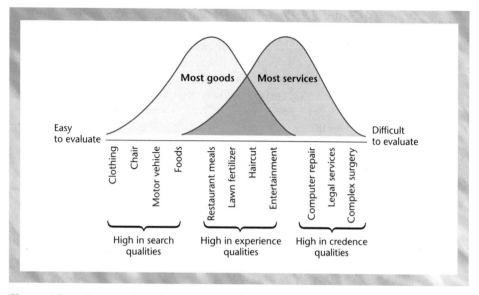

Figure 4.2 ■ How product characteristics affect ease of evaluation

Source: Adapted from Valarie A. Zeithaml, 'How Consumer Evaluation Processes Differ Between Goods and Services', in J.H. Donnelly and W.R. George (eds), *Marketing of Services*, Chicago: American Marketing Association, 1981.

Credence properties refer to characteristics that customers may find impossible to evaluate confidently even after purchase and consumption. For example, relatively few people possess enough knowledge about financial markets to assess whether or not their stockbroker obtained the best possible returns on their invested funds. Patients can't usually evaluate how well their dentists have performed complex dental procedures. And most college students must simply have faith that their professors are providing them with a worthwhile educational experience!

Most goods fall to the left of the continuum in Figure 4.1, since they are high in search properties. Most services, however, tend to be located from the centre to the right of the continuum, reflecting two of the eight basic differences between goods and services that we discussed in Chapter 1: intangibility of service performances; and variability of inputs and outputs (which often leads to quality control problems). These characteristics present special challenges for service marketers, who need to find ways to reassure their customers and reduce the perceived risks associated with buying and using services whose performance and value cannot easily be predicted.

Strategic responses to the intangibility of service performances

Marketers whose products are high in experience characteristics often try to provide more search attributes for their customers. One way to do this is by providing a free trial of the service. Providers of online computer services are good examples of this strategy. For example, the internet service provider AOL offers potential users a free software diskette and the chance to try its services without charge for a limited number of hours. This reduces customers' concerns about entering into a formal membership relationship without first being able to test the service. Of course, AOL is gambling that consumers will be 'hooked' on its web services after the free trial is over.

Companies also use advertising to help customers visualize service benefits when there are few inherent search attributes. For instance, the only tangible thing holders of a Eurocard or Mastercard get directly from the company is a small plastic card, followed at monthly intervals by an account statement. But that is obviously not the essence of the service provided. Think about the credit card advertisements you've seen recently. It's likely that they've featured exciting products you could purchase or exotic places to which you could travel by using your card. These advertisements are designed to help us get excited about the tangible benefits of using our credit cards.

Providers of services that are high in credence characteristics have an even greater challenge. Their benefits may be so intangible that customers can't evaluate what they've received even *after* the service has been purchased and consumed. In this case, marketers often try to provide tangible cues to customers about their services. For example, high-contact services may carefully design and maintain their facilities to provide customers with physical evidence of service quality. Professional service providers like doctors, architects and lawyers often display their degrees and other certifications for the same reason – they want customers to 'see' the credentials that underlie the services they provide.

Since industry standards have changed to allow advertising for most professional services (see Chapter 1), many professionals have turned to new marketing arenas to help make their offerings tangible to customers. For example, in some countries, solicitors and other lawyers use the Yellow Pages, and even print and broadcast adverts to promote their services.

Although we've focused on services that fall in the experience and credence areas of the continuum in Figure 4.1, companies that are dominated by search attributes also face an interesting challenge. Marketers of physical goods often choose to play up the intangible characteristics of their products to increase their appeal to customers. A commonly used strategy is to emphasize the prestige associated with wearing an expensive watch like a Rolex or driving a luxury car.

Variability and quality control problems

The continuum of product attributes in Figure 4.2 also has implications for another distinguishing service characteristic – the degree of customer involvement in the production process. The products that are highest in search properties are most likely to be physical goods that are manufactured in a factory with no customer involvement. Quality is much easier to control in this situation since the elements of production can be more closely monitored and failures spotted before the product is sold to the customer and then consumed. However, quality control for services that fall in the experience and credence ranges is more difficult because production often involves customer involvement.

Customers' evaluations of such services often involve clues provided by the physical setting of the business, employees and even other customers. For example, your experience in purchasing a haircut combines the following factors: your impression of the barbershop or hair salon; how well you can describe what you want to the barber or hair stylist; this individual's ability to understand and deliver what you've requested; and the appearance of other customers and workers in the shop. Barbers and hairdressers will tell you, if asked, that it is difficult for them to do a good job if customers don't cooperate during service delivery.

For products with lots of credence characteristics, the situation can be very complex. Many of these are 'pure services' that have few tangible characteristics and rely on the expertise of a professional service provider to provide a quality offering. In this case, providers must be able to interact with customers effectively to produce a satisfactory product. Problems can occur when this interaction doesn't produce an outcome that meets customers' expectations, even though the service provider may not be at fault.

For example, an architectural firm may design a building that it believes closely matches the features desired by a client. However, the latter may be disappointed when the structure is completed and feel that the architect has delivered a poor quality product. Alternative explanations may include the clients' inability to describe their needs accurately or to interpret from the plans what the architect was proposing. Alternatively, the builder may not have executed the plans accurately or may have cut costs in places that affected the building's appearance and structural integrity. What should an architect do to prevent such situations from occurring? A first step is to work very hard to ensure that communication with customers is effective and to help them articulate their needs. Computer technology is extremely useful to architects, not only for design purposes but also to create simulations for clients. For instance, virtual reality enables a client to 'walk round' both the interior and exterior of a proposed building and to experience visually the impact of changes in dimensions, layout, building materials and design.

Service providers must also work hard to keep the quality of their products consistent over time. This is more difficult when production involves direct interaction with service employees, whose performances are likely to vary from one day to another. But customers don't want variations in service quality, as Michael Flatley, the Irish founder, director and lead dancer of *Lord of the Dance* knows. As he said in a recent television interview, 'The people who drive hundreds of miles to see this show . . . they don't want to know I'm almost 39 . . . they don't want to know my legs are sore . . . they don't want to know I go home and put my feet in ice. They just want to know that what they're seeing is the best show ever – tonight, not tomorrow night!'[11] Flatley's insistence on providing the best performance possible every time has produced results – his company achieves sell-out performances around the world, and audiences often show their appreciation by giving the dancers a standing ovation.

The purchase process for services

When customers decide to buy a service to meet an unfilled need, they go through what is often a complex purchase process. This process has three separate stages – the pre-purchase stage, the service encounter stage and the post-purchase stage, each containing two or more steps (see Figure 4.3). We now describe each of these stages.

The pre-purchase stage

The decision to buy and use a service is made in the pre-purchase stage. Individual needs and expectations are very important here, because they influence what alternatives customers will consider. In some instances, customers may move quickly to selecting and using a specific service provider, particularly if the purchase is routine

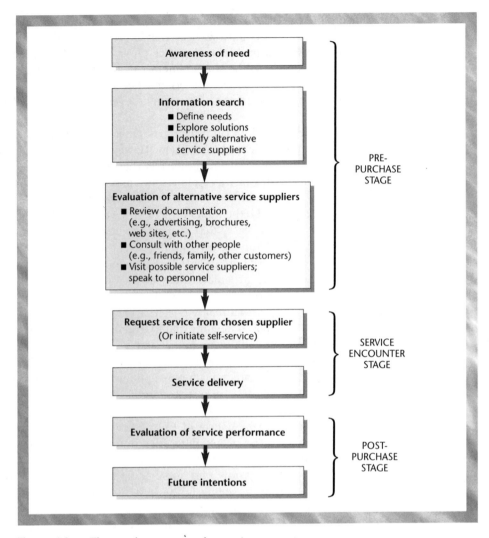

Figure 4.3 ■ The purchase process for services

and relatively low-risk. But when more is at stake or customers are first-time users of a service, they may conduct an intensive information search (contrast how you approached the process of applying to university versus buying a pizza or a hamburger!). After a customer has conducted an information search, which can range from brief and casual to extended and thorough, he or she may identify several alternative suppliers and then weigh the benefits and risks of each option before making a purchase decision.

This element of perceived risk is especially relevant for services that are high in experience or credence attributes and thus difficult to evaluate prior to purchase and consumption. First-time users are especially likely to face greater uncertainty. Risk perceptions are based on customers' judgements of the likelihood that negative outcomes will occur. The worse the possible outcome and the more likely it is to occur, the higher the risk. Different types of perceived risks are outlined in Table 4.1.

Table 4.1 ■ Perceived risks in purchasing services

Type of risk	Examples of customer concerns
Functional risk (unsatisfactory performance outcomes)	■ Will this training course give me the skills I need to get a better job? ■ Will this credit card be accepted wherever and whenever I want to make a purchase? ■ Will the dry cleaner be able to remove the stains from this jacket?
Financial risk (monetary loss, unexpected costs)	■ Will I lose money if I make the investment recommended by my stockbroker? ■ Will I incur lots of unanticipated expenses if I go on this holiday? ■ Will repairing my car cost more than the original estimate?
Temporal risk (wasting time, consequences of delays)	■ Will I have to wait in a queue before entering the exhibition? ■ Will the service at this restaurant be so slow that I will be late for my afternoon meeting? ■ Will the renovations to our bathroom be completed before our friends come to stay with us?
Physical risk (personal injury or damage to possessions)	■ Will I get hurt if I go skiing at this resort? ■ Will the contents of this package get damaged in the mail? ■ Will I fall ill if I travel abroad on holiday?
Psychological risk (personal fears and emotions)	■ How can I be sure this aircraft won't crash? ■ Will the consultant make me feel stupid? ■ Will the doctor's diagnosis upset me?
Social risk (how others think and react)	■ What will my friends think of me if they learn I stayed at this cheap motel? ■ Will my relatives approve of the restaurant I have chosen for the family reunion dinner? ■ Will my business colleagues disapprove of my selection of an unknown law firm?
Sensory risk (unwanted impacts on any of the five senses)	■ Will I get a view of the car park from my room, rather than the beach? ■ Will the bed be uncomfortable? ■ Will I be kept awake by noise from the guests in the room next door? ■ Will my room smell of stale cigarette smoke? ■ Will the coffee at breakfast taste disgusting?

When customers feel uncomfortable with risks, they can use a variety of methods to reduce them during the pre-purchase stage. In fact, you've probably tried some of the following risk-reduction strategies yourself before deciding to purchase a service:

■ seeking information from respected personal sources (friends, respected peers),

■ relying on the reputation of the firm,

■ looking for guarantees and warranties,

■ looking for opportunities to try the service before purchasing,

■ asking knowledgeable employees about competing services,

■ examining tangible cues or other physical evidence as a means,

■ using the World Wide Web to compare service offerings.

Service encounter stage

After deciding to purchase a specific service, customers experience one or more encounters with their chosen service provider. These service encounters often begin with submitting an application, requesting a reservation, or placing an order. As we saw in Chapter 3, they may take the form of personal exchanges between customers and service employees, or impersonal interactions with machines or computers. In high-contact services, such as restaurants, health care, hotels and public transportation, customers may experience a variety of service encounters during service delivery. They evaluate service quality based on such factors as the nature of service environments, customer-contact personnel, support services and other customers.

Service environments include all of the tangible characteristics of the environment where service delivery takes place. The appearance of the building exterior and interior, the nature of furnishings and equipment, the presence or absence of dirt, odour or noise, and the appearance and behaviour of other customers can all serve to shape expectations and perceptions of service quality. We discuss these topics in more depth in Chapters 9 and 12.

Service personnel are the most important factor in most high-contact service encounters, where they have direct, face-to-face interactions with customers, but they can also affect service delivery in low-contact situations, as in telephone-based service delivery. Knowledgeable customers expect employees to follow specific scripts during the service encounter; excessive deviations from these scripts can lead to dissatisfaction. Handling service encounters effectively on the part of the employee usually combines learned skills with the right type of personality. Careful recruitment, training, compensation and motivation are essential inputs. We discuss the necessary human resource strategies in Chapter 14.

Support services are made up of the materials and equipment plus all of the back-stage processes that allow frontstage employees to do their work properly. This element is critical, because many customer-contact employees can't perform their jobs well without receiving internal services from support personnel. As an old service firm axiom goes: 'If you aren't servicing the customer, you are servicing someone who is.'[12]

Other customers. When customers use a people-processing service, they often find themselves in close proximity to other customers. Waiting rooms at a clinic may be filled with other patients; trains, buses or aircraft are usually carrying many passengers at once, requiring travellers to sit next to strangers. Similarly, restaurants serve many patrons simultaneously, and a successful play or film will attract a large audience (in fact, the absence of an audience is a bad sign!). Unfortunately, some of these other customers occasionally behave badly, thus detracting from the service experience. We discuss the challenge of managing badly behaved customers later in this chapter.

Post-purchase stage

During the *post-purchase stage*, customers continue a process they began in the service encounter stage – evaluating service quality and their satisfaction/dissatisfaction with the service experience. The outcome of this process will affect their future intentions, such as whether or not to remain loyal to the provider that delivered service and whether to pass on positive or negative recommendations to family members and other associates.

Customers evaluate service quality by comparing what they expected with what they perceive they received. If their expectations are met or exceeded, they believe they have received high-quality service. These satisfied customers are more likely to be repeat purchasers or loyal customers. However, if the service experience does not meet customers' expectations, they will feel that service quality is poor. They may complain, suffer in silence or switch providers in the future.

The pivotal role of satisfaction

Customer satisfaction is not an end in itself. It is the means to achieving a number of key business goals and a competitive advantage (Figure 4.4). First, as already mentioned, satisfaction is inextricably linked to customer loyalty and relationship commitment. Second, highly satisfied (delighted) customers spread positive word-of-mouth, and in effect become a walking, talking advertisement for an organization whose service has pleased them, thus lowering the cost of attracting new customers. First Direct, the all-telephone bank introduced in Chapter 3, has gained huge numbers of new-customers from recommendations by its existing account holders. Recommendations are particularly important for professional service firms (lawyers, accountants, consultants, engineers, etc.), since the quality of their services is hard to evaluate in advance of purchase and positive comments by a satisfied client reduce the risk for a new purchaser.

Highly satisfied, long-term customers are also more forgiving. Having enjoyed good service delivery many times in the past, they are more likely to believe that a service failure is a deviation from the norm, so it generally takes more than one unsatisfactory incident for loyal customers to change their perceptions and think about switching. One way to look at this situation is to see high satisfaction as like an insurance policy against something going wrong. On the other hand, as we discuss in Chapter 6, it is only those customers who are delighted with a particular service who are likely to act as 'apostles' who actively promote that service to prospective users. Finally, delighted customers are less susceptible to competitive

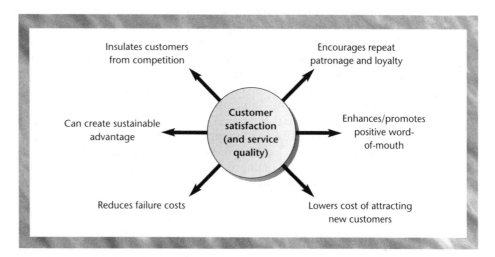

Figure 4.4 ■ Benefits of customer satisfaction and service quality

Source: Christopher H. Lovelock, Paul G. Patterson and Rhett H. Walker, *Services Marketing – Australia and New Zealand*, Sydney: Prentice Hall Austrialia, 1998, p. 119.

offerings. It is in these ways, that achieving satisfaction helps provide a key competitive advantage. Hence, service managers must find effective ways to address customer expectations and perceptions to enhance service satisfaction. We return to this topic in Chapter 12, where we take a closer look at service quality issues.

Keeping customers satisfied is no simple task. It requires detailed research to determine what customers want, creative thinking to identify those small but important things that may delight them, and a long-term strategy to implement new, customer-satisfying strategies. In the article, 'The best shopping trip? How Tesco keeps the customer satisfied' (reprinted on pages 213–18), Tim Mason describes how management of the British supermarket chain Tesco attempted to turn the business around by focusing on what its customers wanted.

The service offering

Because the consumer evaluation and purchase processes are more complex for services, it's especially important that service managers understand how customers view the totality of the service offering (sometimes referred to as the 'service package'). One of the best and most customer-oriented definitions of a service offering comes from FedEx. Early in the company's history, its senior managers decided to define service very simply as '*All Actions and Reactions that Customers Perceive They Have Purchased*' (see the case, 'Federal Express: quality improvement programme' on pages 686–700). This statement can be applied to any business and clarifies what customers have known all along, namely that 'service' is a bundle consisting of the core product plus a cluster of supplementary services.

Core and supplementary product elements

Whatever the business, companies have to think in terms of performing well on all actions and reactions that customers perceive they are purchasing. And they need to be clear about which of these various interactions constitutes the core product and which represent supplementary service elements. The core product provides the central benefit that addresses specific customer needs. It defines the fundamental nature of a company's business. Supplementary service elements supply additional benefits to enhance the core product and differentiate it from competitors' offerings.

In most businesses – both service and manufacturing – the core product tends to become a commodity as competition increases and the industry matures. In natural resources, such as oil, minerals or agricultural produce, the product begins life as a commodity. It's very difficult to protect innovative products from imitation by competitors (brand names and proprietary software are among the few aspects of service design that can be legally protected). Even in manufacturing, where inventions can be patented, it's becoming increasingly difficult to sustain product leadership. Just think how quickly innovative new high-tech products are cloned and protective patents circumvented!

Competing on supplementary service elements

Every business that aspires to market leadership should be working to enhance existing products and to develop new ones. But achieving significant innovation in the core product is nearly always time-consuming and expensive, sometimes requiring enormous research investments. In mature product categories, such innovation only occurs infrequently. Think for a moment: What was the most recent successful *major* innovation in airline travel, hotels, dry cleaning services or package holidays? And when did each take place?

Since significant innovation in core products seems to be an infrequent event in many industries, much of the action takes place among supplementary service elements. That's where most companies in mature industries should focus their strategic thinking for the short and medium term since supplementary services offer the best opportunity for increasing customers' perceptions of value. This idea is not a new one by any means. Twenty years ago, Ted Levitt observed, 'We live in an age in which our thinking about what a product or service is must be quite different from what it was before. It is not so much the basic, generic, central thing we are thinking about that counts, but the whole cluster of satisfactions with which we surround it.'[13] After all, customers expect companies to do a decent job on the core product – whether it's a manufactured good like a microwave oven or a service like cleaning a company's offices at the end of the business day. If they can't perform effectively on the core task, sooner or later they'll go out of business.

Where's the leverage?

For customers of a mature industry, meaningful differentiation and added value usually come from a whole bundle of supplementary service elements. Performing on the core product is a matter of 'do or die'. Banks that lose their customers' money, airlines whose aircraft never arrive at their intended destinations, and architectural firms which design buildings so flawed that they subsequently collapse will soon go out of business. But there are some differences in the relative role and importance of the various supplementary services that surround (or might surround) the core product (Figure 4.5). These supplementary services can usefully be portrayed in terms of what are called hygiene and enhancing factors.[14] The latter can be further divided into parity and superiority elements.

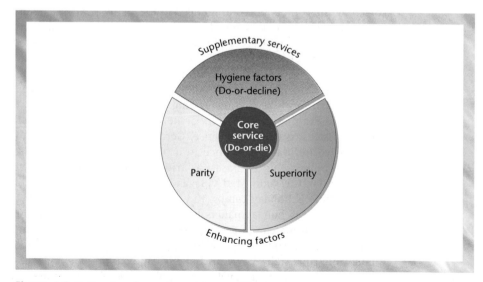

Figure 4.5 ■ Service elements and competitive leverage

Hygiene factors

At the top of Figure 4.5 are those supplementary services that may be described as hygiene factors. These factors are service elements that customers take for granted. If they are absent or present but performed below a certain threshold level of accept-ability, customers are dissatisfied. From a strategic standpoint, they can be viewed as 'do-or-decline factors'. For instance, managers are starting to find that customers expect firms to provide needed information (by phone or otherwise), take orders promptly and accurately, provide intelligible bills and accept responsibility for prob-lem-solving as a matter of course. (Inevitably, there are some variations by industry and by country in this respect.) If an organization can't perform well on these tasks – which are generic to almost all service industries – it will appear incompetent and uncaring to its customers and the stage will be set for a steady decline. Hygiene fac-tors for service businesses vary from industry to industry. But companies must provide these elements at a certain threshold level just to stay in business.

Enhancing factors

Other supplementary services can be seen as optional service 'extras', whose presence will create satisfaction but whose absence will not necessarily cause dissatisfaction. Enhancing factors can be divided into parity and superiority elements, depending on whether the organization seeks just to match the average service level on each ele-ment provided by those competing suppliers who also offer it, or whether the firm will try to offer enhancing service elements that are distinctively superior (or even unique) relative to competing offerings. Service marketers must decide what the basis for their organization's competitive strategy will be. When targeting a specific market segment, managers need to determine through research which elements of superior performance will yield a meaningful competitive edge and for which others it will suffice simply to offer the industry standard of performance. In a highly competitive environment, innovation often centres on creating new enhancing factors that can help distinguish the firm's service from its competitors.

An important issue here is how long it will take before a new enhancing factor is copied by the competition and reduced to the status of a hygiene factor. For instance, once it became clear that telephone banking was here to stay, other British banks sought, with varying degrees of success, to compete with First Direct by adding tele-phone-based delivery systems of their own and trying to match the level of service established by the original innovator. Meanwhile, forward-looking banks in many other European countries monitored the British experience and soon began to develop their own versions of telephone banking.

Another example comes from Center Parc, the Rotterdam-based company with holiday villages in Belgium, France, Germany, the Netherlands and Britain. It offers an inclusive holiday experience in a purpose-built complex targeted at middle-income families. Center Parc has tried to position itself differently from such alternatives as the Club Med villages described earlier or the more 'downmarket' chain of Butlin's holiday camps. Key features include: a dome-covered leisure com-plex that protects holidaymakers from bad weather – an enhancing factor that few competitors can match; an aesthetically pleasing physical environment that contrasts sharply with the sometimes garish appearance of traditional holiday camps; and friendly, informal staff. As we discuss in Chapter 14, good employees who enjoy their jobs and perform at high levels – especially in service encounters with customers – offer a competitive advantage that other providers are likely to find hard to duplicate.

Managers must decide where the opportunities lie for adding distinctive extras and when the focus should be on improving basic performance. While some supplementary elements are industry-specific, many others are not (e.g., telephone information and order-taking, statements and billing, and food and beverage service). We cover the topic of supplementary service elements in more detail in Chapter 8, where we examine their role in providing additional value for customers.

Understanding customer behaviour at different points in the service experience

In order to design a service that meets or exceeds the expectations of its customers, service providers must have an idea of what those customers actually experience during their service encounters. In the high-contact service environments typified by most people-processing services, most customers arrive at a service site with certain expectations. Their subsequent behaviour, however, may be shaped by the nature of the physical environment, the employees they encounter, the sequence in which different activities take place and by the roles that they are expected to play.

Managers and service employees are often unaware of the full extent of a typical customer's service experience. One of the most effective ways to gain insights into customer behaviour during service delivery is to create a description of the steps that customers and employees must go through in a given service environment. These steps can be shown visually using a tool called a *flowchart*. By depicting each of the service encounters, or occasions when contact takes place between customers and a service provider, flowcharts can highlight problems and opportunities in the service delivery process as it affects customers themselves – what we call frontstage activities. Flowcharts can be used by both high-contact and low-contact services to gain a better understanding of how the service is created and delivered from the customer's point of view, since they include all interactions between customers and the firm's employees, physical facilities and equipment.

Developing a flowchart

Flowcharting can usefully be applied to any type of service when management needs to gain a better understanding of how the service is currently being created and delivered. An alternative term, *service blueprinting*, is often used when planning a new or revised process and prescribes in often minute detail how it ought to function. The objective of this exercise is to relate an understanding of customers' behaviour and experience to the backstage activities that must take place behind the scenes in order that customers may be served effectively and in timely fashion front stage.[15]

Developing a flowchart begins by identifying each interaction that a particular type of customer has when using a specific service. Managers need to distinguish between the core product and the supplementary service elements; in fact, flowcharting is a very useful way of figuring out what the supplementary elements actually are.

The next step is to put all these interactions linearly into the sequence in which they occur. The service delivery process is like a river: some activities take place upstream as it were, others downstream. At each step, management needs to ask:

What does the customer really want (perhaps the customer would like to speed up this step or even avoid it altogether)? Where is the potential for failure at this step?

Let's illustrate flowcharting with a simplified model of a service to which most readers can relate fairly easily: a stay at a hotel. As with many services, the customer's first encounter with a hotel involves a supplementary service rather than the core product (which is basically rental of a bedroom for a night's sleep). The initial step, for most travellers, is to make a reservation. This action may be taken some time before the visit actually takes place.

On arrival, guests travelling by car will need to park the vehicle in the hotel's garage or car park (perhaps a staff member will do it for them). The next step is to check in at reception, after which guests may be escorted to their rooms by a porter who carries the bags. Already, four supplementary services have been delivered before a guest even reaches the room. Before retiring for the night – the core service – a guest may choose to use several more services, such as a drink in the cocktail lounge, dinner at one of the hotel restaurants and watching a pay-TV movie. After rising, the guest may request that breakfast be sent up by room service, then make some phone calls, before checking out at the cashier's desk and asking a valet or porter to retrieve the car from the garage car park.

Figure 4.6 depicts the customer's experience, in simplified form, as a series of boxes on the frontstage portion of the flowchart. Note that the core product – a bed for the night – is surrounded by a variety of supplementary services. But a variety of backstage activities are taking place, behind the scenes. We've captured a few of these backstage steps on the chart for illustrative purposes (to show every detail of the backstage service processes would require a substantially larger page format than used in this book!). In fact, each step in the frontstage process is supported by a series of backstage activities, including assignment of staff, maintenance of facilities and equipment, and capture, storage and transfer of information – shown here by the flashes to and from the database. As you review this flowchart, ask yourself: at what points might the behaviour of staff members and even other customers spoil a guest's experience? And as the manager, what strategy would you plan for anticipating and handling such problems?

In summary, flowcharting provides a means for managers to gain understanding of customer behaviour in relation to underlying service processes; it is thus a necessary first step in exercising control over such procedures. Marketers find this technique particularly useful for defining the point(s) in the process at which the customer uses the core service and identifying the different supplementary services that make up the overall service package. Suggestions for how to undertake flowcharting in order to obtain the best value from this technique are shown in Table 4.2. Managers must recognize that unless they fully understand the customer's own exposure to and involvement in a service environment, it is difficult to improve service quality and productivity.[16] Speeding up processes and weeding out unnecessary steps to avoid wasted time and effort are often important ways to improve the perceived value of a service.

Managers must recognize that unless they fully understand the service experience from the customer's perspective, it is difficult to improve service quality and productivity. Improving delivery processes and weeding out unnecessary steps to avoid wasted time and effort are often important ways to improve the customer's evaluation of service quality.

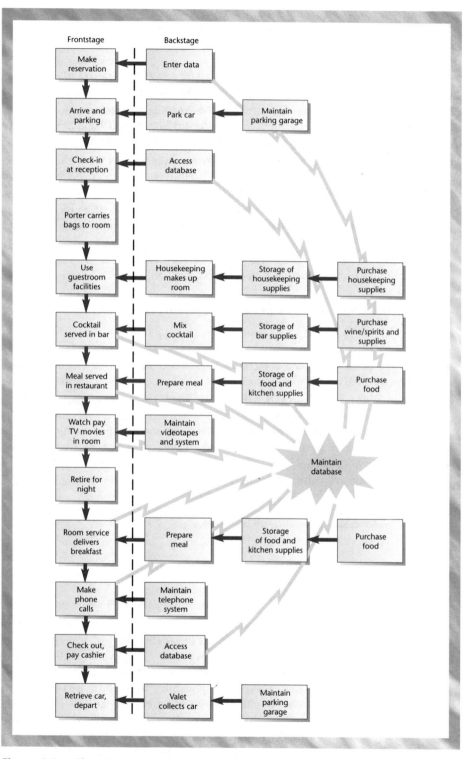

Figure 4.6 ■ Flowcharting a hotel visit

Table 4.2 ■ Basic advice on flowcharting the customer experience

Key steps

1. Define the *purpose* of the flowchart clearly: What do you wish to learn (and why) about what type of service, involving what sorts of customers and under what types of usage conditions?

2. Compile a list of the activities that constitute the experience of relevant customers. Initially, keep those activities aggregated (e.g., do not decompose 'board aircraft' into 'hand boarding pass to agent, walk down gangway, enter aircraft, find seat, stow carry-on bag, sit down').

3. Chart each step in the customer's experience in the sequence in which it is normally encountered (alternative charts may be needed if sharply different sequences are encountered – there may be evidence of segments with differing needs or of alternative versions of the service).

4. For every frontstage activity, chart backstage supporting activities. (This task is of particular value in examining service quality problems and in developing internal marketing programmes designed to reach backstage personnel.)

5. Validate your description – solicit inputs from customers and be sure to involve relevant service personnel. (Each may have his/her understanding of the process – an open discussion may help to achieve consensus.)

6. Supplement the flowchart by a brief narrative describing the activities and their interrelationships. Be sure to identify the different players clearly.

General advice

■ Remember that there is no one, correct way to do a flowchart: two differently structured descriptions may serve your purpose equally well.

■ Note complaints by customers and personnel concerning problems at specific points in the process, because such problems provide good clues as to where you should go into greater detail and disaggregate broad steps like 'board aircraft' into more specific components. (The term 'granularity' is often used to describe level of detail; the desired level is achieved when all questions have been answered.)

■ If informational processes are an important issue, you may wish to show a parallel flow indicating points at which information is collected and records/databases are created, accessed or updated.

Source: Adapted from Table 10.1 in Christopher Lovelock, *Product Plus:
How Product + Service = Competitive Advantage*, New York: McGraw-Hill, 1994, p. 155.

Conclusion

Gaining a better understanding of how customers evaluate, select, use (and occasionally abuse) services should lie at the heart of strategies for service design and delivery. In this chapter we discovered that several of the distinctive characteristics of services (especially intangibility and quality control problems) mean that customer evaluation processes often differ from those involved in evaluating physical goods and thus present unique challenges for services management, as do each of the other stages that customers go through in the purchase decision process.

Because the consumer evaluation and purchase processes for many services are often complex, it's especially important that service managers understand how customers view the service offering. We briefly examined the concept of core and supplementary elements, noting that the latter can be divided into hygiene factors (those that must be provided) and enhancing factors (optional extras). Achieving competitive advantage in the marketplace often centres on choosing which enhancing factors to offer and whether to match or exceed competitive performance on these optional supplementary elements.

Finally, the chapter demonstrated how to create a visual picture of the service delivery process from the customer's perspective. This diagram, called a flowchart, provides a step-by-step analysis of a typical customer's service encounters, indicating how a customer's experience of each step of 'frontstage' service delivery relates to the many operational tasks performed back stage.

The field of consumer behaviour is a huge one. You will find additional coverage and detailed references to past research in the reading, 'Consumer behaviour and services: a review' by Mark Gabbott and Gillian Hogg, reproduced on pages 219–28.

Study questions

1. Describe search, experience and credence attributes and give examples of each.
2. Explain why services are often harder for customers to evaluate than physical goods.
3. How are customers' expectations formed? Explain the distinction between desired service and adequate service with reference to a recent service experience of your own.
4. What role do needs play in consumer purchase behaviour?
5. Define the three stages in the purchase process for services.
6. Distinguish between the core product and supplementary service elements. Which of these provides the most opportunities for competitive advantage? Why?
7. Clarify the difference between hygiene factors and enhancing factors. What is the implication of each for competitive strategy?
8. Choose a service that you are familiar with and create a simple flowchart for it. Explain what is meant by 'frontstage' and 'backstage' activities.

Notes

1. Based in part on articles in the *Financial Times*, 24 February 1997 and 7 October 1997.
2. Abraham H. Maslow, *Motivation and Personality*, New York: Harper and Brothers, 1954.
3. Stephanie Anderson Forest, Katie Kerwin and Susan Jackson, 'Presents That Won't Fit under the Christmas Tree', *Business Week*, 1 December 1997, p. 42.
4. B. Joseph Pine and James H. Gilmore, 'Welcome to the Experience Economy', *Harvard Business Review*, Vol. 76, July–August 1998, pp. 97–108.
5. See Benjamin Schneider and David E. Bowen, *Winning the Service Game*, Boston, MA: Harvard Business School Press, 1995; and Valarie A. Zeithaml, Leonard L. Berry and A. Parasuraman, 'The Nature and Determinants of Customer Expectations of Services', *Journal of the Academy of Marketing Science*, Vol. 21, 1993.
6. Excerpted from Terrence Witkowski and Joachim Kellner, 'How Germans and Americans Rate Their Banking Services', *Marketing News*, 7 October 1996, p. 7. Also Allyson L. Stewart-Allen, 'Customer Care: European Marketers Try to Catch Up with Service, Not Servitude, as a Strategic Option', *Marketing News*, 18 November 1996, p. 17.
7. Valarie A. Zeithaml, Leonard L. Berry and A. Parasuraman, 'The Behavioral Consequences of Service Quality', *Journal of Marketing*, Vol. 60, 1996, p. 35.

8. Cathy Johnson and Brian P. Mathews, 'The Influence of Experience on Service Expectations', *International Journal of Service Industry Management*, Vol. 8, No. 4, 1997, pp. 46–61.

9. Robert Johnston, 'The Zone of Tolerance: Exploring the Relationship between Service Transactions and Satisfaction with the Overall Service', *International Journal of Service Industry Management*, Vol. 6, No. 5, 1995, pp. 46–61.

10. Valarie A. Zeithaml, 'How Consumer Evaluation Processes Differ Between Goods and Services', in J.H. Donnelly and W.R. George, *Marketing of Services*, Chicago: American Marketing Association, 1981.

11. Quoted from a television interview with Michael Flatley on the news magazine *Dateline NBC*, 13 October 1997.

12. Bill Fromm and Len Schlesinger, *The Real Heroes of Business*, New York: Currency Doubleday, 1993, p. 241.

13. Theodore Levitt, 'What's Your Product and What's Your Business?', Chapter 2 in *Marketing for Business Growth*, New York: McGraw-Hill, 1973, p. 7.

14. See, for example, Barbara R. Lewis, 'Service Quality: An Investigation of Customer Care in Major UK Organisations', *International Journal of Service Industry Management*, Vol. 1, No. 2, 1990, pp. 33–44; Robert Johnston, 'The Determinants of Service Quality: Satisfiers and Dissatisfiers', *The International Journal of Service Industry Management*, Vol. 6, No. 5, 1995, pp. 53–71; and Barbara R. Lewis, 'Customer Care in Services', in W.J. Glynn and J.G. Barnes, *Understanding Services Management* (Chichester: John Wiley & Sons, 1995), pp. 57–88.

15. For more details of this technique see G. Lynn Shostack, 'Understanding Services through Blueprinting', in T.A. Schwartz, D.E. Bowen and S.W. Brown, *Advances in Services Marketing and Management*, Vol. I, Greenwich, CT: JAI Press, 1992, pp. 75–90. For alternative approaches, see Christian Grönroos's description of 'The Customer Relationship Life Cycle', in *Service Management and Marketing*, Lexington, MA: Lexington Books, 1990, pp. 129–33; and Sandra Vandermerwe, 'Jumping into the Customer's Activity Cycle', Chapter 4 in *From Tin Soldiers to Russian Dolls*, Oxford: Butterworth Heinemann, 1993, pp. 48–71.

16. A related tool for gaining understanding of service processes is SADT (structured analysis and design technique), which allows a service modeller to decompose a service process into successively more detailed levels in order to answer specific questions. For more details, see Carole Congram and Michael Epelman, 'How to describe your service: an invitation to the structured analysis and design technique', *International Journal of Service Industry Management*, Vol. 6, No. 2, 1995, pp. 6–23.

CHAPTER 5

Positioning a service in the marketplace

Learning objectives

After reading and reflecting on this chapter, you should be able to:

1. Describe the four different focus approaches.

2. Understand the principle of target market segmentation.

3. Distinguish between important and determinant attributes in consumer choice decisions.

4. Explain the elements of a service strategy.

5. Define the concepts of competitive positioning and repositioning.

6. Know how to design and interpret positioning maps.

Repositioning a Swedish car-hire firm[1]

The car rental industry has grown rapidly in Europe. In most countries, the players range from the big franchise agencies of global firms such as Hertz and Avis, with hundreds or even thousands of cars at their disposal, to local garages that may have just one or two older vehicles available for hire. It's a very competitive industry, serving market segments that include business travellers, holiday-makers and people needing a car while their own is being repaired after an accident. Business travellers are a particularly desirable market segment, since they tend to need a hire car with a high degree of frequency. Car rental firms market their services not only through mass media advertising, but also through sales forces that call on travel agents and corporate travel departments.

InterRent (now merged with Europcar) was the largest car hire firm in Sweden, but it faced increasing competition. Travel agents and individual customers considered the offerings of all major firms on the market more or less undifferentiated – in other words, none had a truly distinctive position. The firm's sales representatives complained that they had no really good answers to such questions as: 'Why should we rent a car from you?' or 'What can you offer that our present service provider cannot?' So the firm's long-time chief executive, Hans Åke Sand decided that he needed to create a unique position for InterRent, so that it could replace generic promises such as 'we do it with a smile' or 'we try harder' with distinctive benefits built around trustworthiness and reliability. The firm would offer terms of service that would respond to customer needs yet which many competitors (especially smaller ones) would presumably find time-consuming, difficult or even impossible to match.

The firm's core product was defined as an 'immediately accessible solution to temporarily occurring transportation problems'. Completing the basic service package were supplementary services that comprised information about terms, reservation, delivery of the car to the customer, return of the car, pricing, billing and payment, and handling complaints.

The next step was to design each of these service elements so that the basic package functioned in a service-oriented way. Traditionally, car rental firms had seen themselves in the business of providing a vehicle at a particular location and leaving customers with responsibility for any difficulties they might encounter, just as they would be when driving their own cars. But Sand concluded that this philosophy would not do. 'We'll have to take more responsibility for our customers', he declared. Three specific features were therefore built into the new offering: (1) a 'get to the destination' guarantee; (2) a 'lowest price' guarantee; and (3) a 'trouble-free service' guarantee.

The 'get to the destination' feature involved provision of alternative transportation services for the customer within 45 minutes in the unlikely event that the hired car broke down. Operationalizing this goal required not only maintaining the highest standards of maintenance (to minimize the chance of breakdowns in the first place) but also implementation of a 24-hour telephone service and procedures for sending an alternative car or taxi to the stranded customer.

The 'lowest price' goal related to transparency in pricing – as opposed to being the cheapest provider of car-hire services – and was designed to save customers the need to calculate which of the various pricing alternatives available (e.g., flat-rate versus kilometre-based, daily versus weekend rate) would result in the lowest charge for them. The national computer network was programmed to allow agents to inform the customer in advance of the most economical rate and also to ensure that the most advantageous rate was charged when the car was returned.

Finally, 'trouble-free service' was based on the premise that customers who had reserved a car should always receive the category of vehicle they had booked or an upgrade without extra charge. Further, to simplify their lives, they should be able to pick up and drop off cars as conveniently as possible. InterRent decided to allow customers to choose between pickups at car-hire offices and delivery of a car to company addresses, railway stations or hotels. It also guaranteed on-time delivery, with a free day if the car was delivered more than five minutes late. Avoiding such delays required staff to think ahead and take into account the risk of traffic jams. Finally, customers could drop off a car at any location.

Implementation of the new market position required not only changes to existing internal systems, acquisition of new resources (some involving subcontractors) and employee training, but also education of customers so that they knew what to expect and what action to take if anything went wrong. This education was accomplished through marketing communications, printed documentation and instructions from employees at the time of hiring a vehicle.

When all was ready, the new service was launched through an advertising campaign focusing on the three service guarantees and a campaign directed at travel agents, who often influenced a customer's choice of car-hire firm. InterRent sought to create an image of trustworthiness and reliability leading to real value and comfort for its customers. The results were immediately apparent: sales through travel agents, which had been declining, promptly rose sharply and overall sales during the following year rose by 23 per cent.

The search for competitive advantage

Ask a group of managers from different service businesses how they compete, and the chances are high that many will say simply, 'on service'. Press them a little further, and they may add words and phrases like 'value for money', 'our people are the key' or 'convenience'.

None of this is particularly informative to a marketing specialist who is trying to develop strategies to help an organization compete more effectively in the marketplace. At issue is what makes consumers or institutional buyers select – and remain loyal to – one service supplier over another. Terms such as 'service' typically subsume a variety of specific characteristics, ranging from the speed with which a service is delivered to the quality of interactions between customers and service personnel; and from avoiding errors to providing desirable 'extras' to supplement the core service. Likewise, 'convenience' could refer to a service that's delivered at a convenient location, available at convenient times or easy to use. Without knowing which product features are of specific interest to customers, it's hard for managers to develop an appropriate competitive strategy for their firm and its products, and harder still to evaluate a product's subsequent performance in the marketplace.

The InterRent example demonstrates the power of thinking systematically about all facets of the service package and making specific improvements that will be valued by customers. It also demonstrates that repositioning a more or less undifferentiated service may require substantial internal changes within the organization in addition to external marketing communications.

As competition intensifies in the service sector, it's becoming progressively more important for service organizations to differentiate their products in ways that are meaningful to customers, just as InterRent did. In highly developed economies, growth is slowing in such mature consumer service industries as banking, insurance, hospitality and education. So corporate growth will have to be based on taking share from domestic competitors – or by expanding into international markets – which is one reason why so many service firms that once limited their activities to their home country are now expanding across Europe or even further afield. In each instance, firms should be selective in targeting customers and seek to be distinctive in the way they present themselves. A market niche that may seem too narrow to offer sufficient sales within one country may represent a substantial market when viewed from a pan-European perspective.

Competitive strategy can take many different routes. George Day observes:

> The diversity of ways a business can achieve a competitive advantage quickly defeats any generalizations or facile prescriptions . . . First and foremost, a business must set itself apart from its competition. To be successful, it must identify and promote itself as the best provider of attributes that are important to target customers.[2]

Four focus strategies

It's not usually realistic for a firm to try to appeal to all actual or potential buyers in a market, because customers are too numerous, too widely scattered and too varied in their needs, purchasing behaviour and consumption patterns. Different service firms also vary widely in their abilities to serve different types of customers. So rather than attempt to compete in an entire market, each company needs to focus its efforts on those customers it can serve best. In marketing terms, focus means providing a relatively narrow product mix for a particular market segment – a group of buyers who share common characteristics, needs, purchasing behaviour, or consumption patterns. This concept is at the heart of virtually all successful service firms, who have identified the strategically important elements in their service operations and have concentrated their resources on them.

The extent of a company's focus can be described on two different dimensions – market focus and service focus.[3] *Market focus* is the extent to which a firm serves few or many markets, while *service focus* describes the extent to which a firm offers few or many services. These two dimensions define the four basic focus strategies shown in Figure 5.1.

A fully-focused organization provides a very limited range of services (perhaps just a single core product) to a narrow and specific market segment. A market-focused company concentrates on a narrow market segment but has a wide range of services. Service-focused firms offer a narrow range of services to a fairly broad market.

Finally, many service providers fall into the *unfocused* category because they try to serve broad markets and provide a wide range of services.

As you can see from Figure 5.1, focusing requires a company to identify the market segments that it can serve best with the services it offers. Marketers define a market as the set of all actual or potential buyers of a particular core product. However, it is usually unrealistic for a firm to try to appeal to all buyers in that market – or at least not to buyers in the same way. For in most instances, buyers, whether they be individuals or corporations, are too numerous, too widely scattered and too varied in their needs, purchasing behaviour and consumption patterns. Furthermore, different service firms vary widely in their abilities to serve different types of customers. Hence, rather than trying to compete in an entire market, perhaps against superior competitors, each firm should adopt a strategy of market segmentation, identifying those parts, or segments, of the market that it can serve best. In InterRent's case, there was little perceived differentiation between car hire firms. So the company decided to employ a needs-based segmentation approach, focusing on those customers who would value trustworthiness, reliability and ease of accessibility; in pursuit of this focus it created a service concept of 'providing immediately accessible transportation solutions to temporarily occurring transportation problems' and then developed a revised service offering and marketing strategy based around this concept. It's also worth noting that by targeting travel agents in its sales efforts, the company was seeking to reach travellers whose purchasing decisions were based on using an expert intermediary to solve their travel problems.

Because each person or corporate purchaser has distinctive (even unique) characteristics and needs, any prospective buyer is potentially a separate target segment. Some personal and professional services are, indeed, customized to the needs of individual buyers. A dentist treats the needs of each patient on the basis of their specific dental condition; an architect may design a unique house for a wealthy client; and a bank may develop a sophisticated loan package tailored to the requirements of a large corporate customer. However, the majority of service businesses do not find

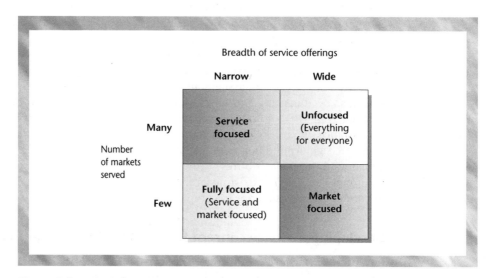

Figure 5.1 ■ Basic focus strategies for services

Source: Robert Johnston, 'Achieving Focus in Service Organizations', *The Service Industries Journal*, Vol. 16, January 1996, pp. 10–20.

such *micro-segmentation* worthwhile in their industries. Instead, they look to achieve economies of scale by marketing to all customers within a specific market segment and serving each in a similar fashion. A strategy of *mass customization* – offering a service with some individualized product elements to a large number of customers at a relatively low price – may be achieved by offering a standardized core product but tailoring supplementary service elements to fit the requirements of individual buyers.[4] We will have more to say about opportunities for customization of supplementary services in Chapter 8.

Identifying and selecting target segments

As we saw in Chapter 4, a *market segment* is composed of a group of buyers who share common characteristics, needs, purchasing behaviour or consumption patterns. Effective segmentation should group buyers into segments in ways that result in as much similarity as possible on the relevant characteristics within each segment but dissimilarity on those same characteristics between each segment.

A *target segment* is one that a firm has selected from among those in the broader market. Frequently, target segments are defined on the basis of several variables. For instance, a department store in a particular city might target residents of the metropolitan area (geographic segmentation) who had incomes within a certain range (demographic segmentation), valued personal service from a knowledgeable staff and were not highly price-sensitive (both reflecting segmentation according to expressed attitudes and behavioural intentions). Because competing retailers in the city would probably be targeting the same customers, the department store would have to position itself in ways that created a distinctive appeal (appropriate characteristics to highlight might include a wide array of merchandise categories, breadth of selection within each product category, and the availability of such supplementary services as advice and home delivery). Service firms that are developing strategies based on use of technology recognize that customers can also be segmented according to their degree of competence and comfort in using technology-based delivery systems.

An important marketing issue for any business is to accept that some market segments offer better opportunities than others. Target segments should be selected not only on the basis of their sales and profit potential but also with reference to the firm's ability to match or exceed competing offerings directed at the same segment.

In order to select target segments and to design effective positioning strategies, managers need insights into how the various components (or attributes) of a service are valued by current and prospective customers within different market segments. For instance, what level of quality and performance is required for each attribute? Are there significant differences between segments in the importance that customers attach to different attributes? How well do competing products meet customer requirements? Can an existing product be redesigned so that it better meets customer needs and is superior to competing offerings?

Developing a service concept for customers in a target segment

How can a firm develop the right service concept for a particular target segment? Formal research is often needed to identify what attributes of a given service are important to specific market segments and how well prospective customers perceive competing organizations as performing against these attributes. But it's dangerous to overgeneralize. Strategists should recognize that the same individuals may set different priorities for attributes according to:

- The purpose of using the service,
- Who makes the decision,
- The timing of use (time of day/week/season),
- Whether the individual is using the service alone or with a group,
- The composition of that group.

Consider the criteria that you might use when choosing a restaurant for lunch while on a holiday with friends or family, versus selecting a restaurant for an expense account business lunch at which you were meeting with a prospective client, versus choosing somewhere to eat for a quick lunchtime meal with a co-worker. Given a reasonable selection of alternatives, it's unlikely that you would choose the same type of restaurant in each instance, let alone the same one. It's also possible that if you left the decision to another person in the party, he or she would make a different choice.

It's also important to identify who is making the decision to select a specific service. In the case of a hospital, the decision-maker might be the end-user (e.g., a patient) or some intermediary (e.g., a doctor). In the latter situation, a two-step model prevails. The marketer needs to determine, first, what attributes are important to the customer in choosing the intermediary and, second, what attributes are important to the intermediary in selecting the service provider.

Research of this nature often begins with focus group interviews, in which customers from specific segments are brought together in small groups for a semi-structured discussion under the guidance of a professional group leader. Insights from these discussions can then be used to construct formal survey instruments, which might be administered to scientifically selected samples by mail, telephone or other means.

Importance versus determinance

Consumers usually make their choices between alternative service offerings on the basis of perceived differences between them. But the attributes that distinguish competing services from one another are not always the most important ones. For instance, many travellers rank 'safety' as their primary consideration in air travel. They may avoid travelling by unknown carriers or on an airline that has a poor safety reputation, but after eliminating such alternatives from consideration, a traveller flying on major routes within the EU is still likely to have several choices of carrier available that are perceived as equally safe. Hence, safety is not usually an attribute that influences the customer's choice at this point. Determinant attributes (i.e., those that actually determine buyers' choices between competing alternatives) are often some way down the list of service characteristics that are important to purchasers, but they are the attributes on which customers see significant differences between competing alternatives. For example, convenience of departure and arrival times, availability of frequent flyer miles and related loyalty privileges, quality of food and drinks service on board the aircraft, or the ease of making reservations, might be examples of determinant characteristics for business travellers when selecting an airline. For budget-conscious holiday-makers, on the other hand, price might assume primary importance.

You may find it helpful to take a moment to think about your own selection criteria for different types of services. For instance, what are the most important considerations for you in choosing a restaurant or food-service outlet for an evening meal with friends of your own age? Make a note of the different criteria that you use and how important each one is to you. Now, apply these criteria to one or more recent restaurant visits in a situation where you had a choice of several competing alternatives and consider which attributes were determinant in making your selection between these different restaurants.

The marketing researchers' task, of course, is to survey customers in the target segment, identify the relative importance of different attributes and then ask which ones have been determinant during recent decisions involving a choice of service suppliers. Researchers also need to be aware how well each competing service is perceived by customers as performing on these attributes. Findings from such research form the necessary basis for developing a positioning (or repositioning) campaign.[5]

One further issue in evaluating service characteristics and establishing a positioning strategy is that some attributes are easily quantified whereas others are qualitative and highly judgemental. Price, for instance, is a straightforward quantitative measure. Punctuality of transport services can be expressed in terms of the percentage of trains, buses or flights arriving within a specified number of minutes from the scheduled time. Both of these measures are easy to understand and therefore generalizable. But characteristics such as the quality of personal service or a hotel's degree of luxury are more qualitative and therefore subject to individual interpretation – although in the case of hotels, travellers may be prepared to trust the evaluations of independent rating services such as the *Michelin Guide*, an automobile association or (in many parts of the world) a government authority.

Creating a competitive position

Positioning is the process of establishing and maintaining a distinctive place in the market for an organization and/or its individual product offerings. Heskett frames the issue nicely:

> The most successful service firms separate themselves from 'the pack' to achieve a distinctive position in relation to their competition. They differentiate themselves . . . by altering typical characteristics of their respective industries to their competitive advantage.[6]

Understanding the concept of product positioning is key to developing an effective competitive posture. This concept is certainly not limited to services – indeed, it had its origins in packaged goods marketing – but it offers valuable insights by forcing service managers to analyze their firm's existing offerings and to provide specific answers to the following questions:

■ What does our firm currently stand for in the minds of current and prospective customers?

■ What customers do we now serve and which ones would we like to target for the future?

■ What are the characteristics of our current service offerings (core products and their accompanying supplementary service elements)?

■ In each instance, how do our service offerings differ from those of the competition?

■ How well do customers in different market segments perceive each of our service offerings as meeting their needs?

■ What changes do we need to make to our offerings in order to strengthen our competitive position within the market segment(s) of interest to our firm?

Trout distills the essence of positioning into the following four principles:[7]

1. A company must establish a position in the minds of its targeted customers.
2. The position should be singular, providing one simple and consistent message.
3. The position must set a company apart from its competitors.
4. A company cannot be all things to all people – it must focus its efforts.

Domino's Pizza is an example of a company that took these four principles to heart. In an industry where the core product is a commodity, competition is often based on value-added dimensions. While pizza is the basic product that customers are purchasing, they also want service attributes like convenience (home delivery) and speed. For years, Domino's has stressed speed with the line '30 Minutes or It's On Us' in its adverts. As a result, the company 'owns' the distinctive attribute of speed in the pizza delivery business. When people think of fast, reliable service, Domino's comes to mind. According to Tom Monaghan, the company's president, the secret of its success is: 'A fanatical *focus* on doing *one* thing well'.

The principles of positioning apply equally well to any public and nonprofit organization that must compete for customers. Thus national postal services compete with private courier firms, public and nonprofit hospitals compete vigorously with each other and with private healthcare providers, and museums compete not only with other museums but also, at a generic level, with alternative forms of education, entertainment and recreation. The marketplace for adult education courses is extremely competitive, consisting of both nonprofit and for-profit operations; to succeed, an institution needs a clear sense of mission and a distinctive position that sets it apart from the competition in ways that appeal to prospective students.

Repositioning

Sometimes firms have to make a significant change in an existing position. Such a strategy, known as repositioning, could mean revising service characteristics (as in InterRent's case) or redefining target market segments. At the firm level, repositioning may entail abandoning certain products and withdrawing completely from some market segments.

Copy positioning versus product positioning

In a competitive marketplace, a 'position' reflects how consumers perceive the product's (or organization's) performance on specific attributes relative to that of one or more competitors. Customers' brand choices reflect which brands are even known and remembered and then, how each of these brands is positioned within each customer's mind. These positions are, of course, simply perceptual, but we need to remember that people make their decisions based on their individual perceptions of reality, rather than on an expert's definition of that reality. It is worth noting that staff members who are close to customers and have been trained to listen and to be observant may be able to infer customer perceptions with reasonable accuracy.

Many marketers associate positioning primarily with the communication elements of the marketing mix, notably advertising, promotions and publicity. This view reflects the widespread use of advertising in packaged goods marketing to create images and associations for broadly similar branded products so as to give them a special distinction in the customer's mind – an approach sometimes known as *copy positioning*. A classic example is the visual imagery of the rugged Western cowboy created for a major cigarette brand by the Marlboro man. Note, however, that this imagery has nothing to do with the physical qualities of the tobacco; it is just a means of differentiating and adding glamour to what is essentially a commodity. Examples of how imagery may be used for positioning purposes in the service sector are found in the different colour schemes and styles of consumer advertising employed by major oil companies, the distinctive 'bullish' theme used by Merrill Lynch (whose symbol is a bull), and the imagery associated with a specific brand name. For instance, research has shown that Virgin, one of Britain's best known international brand names, is associated with fun, quality, trust and innovation.[8] Some slogans promise a specific benefit, designed to make the company stand out from its competitors, such as British Airways' 'Arrive in Better Shape', CU Assurance's 'We Won't Make a Drama Out of a Crisis', or Credit Suisse First Boston's 'Global Vision. Euro Knowhow'. However, as Dibb and Simkin point out:

> Evidence of strong branding in the service sector does not end with such catch phrases. Companies as diverse as Vidal Sassoon, BUPA, The Royal Shakespeare Company, and even Harvard Business School already have a strong brand image in the sense that customers generally know exactly what they stand for. They are, already, clearly positioned in the customers' minds.[9]

Our primary concern in this chapter is the role of positioning in guiding marketing strategy development for services that compete on more than just imagery or vague promises. This entails decisions on substantive attributes that are known from research to be important to customers, relating to product performance, price and service availability. To improve a product's appeal to a specific target segment, it may be necessary to change its performance on certain attributes, to reduce its price, or to alter the times and locations when it is available or the forms of delivery that are offered. In such instances, the primary task of communication – advertising, personal selling and public relations – is to ensure that prospective customers accurately perceive the position of the service on dimensions that are important to them in making choice decisions. Additional excitement and interest may be created by evoking certain images and associations in the advertising, but these are likely to play only a secondary role in customer choice decisions unless competing services are perceived as virtually identical on performance, price and availability.

Positioning's role in marketing strategy

Positioning plays a pivotal role in marketing strategy, because it links market analysis and competitive analysis to internal corporate analysis. From these three, a position statement can be developed that enables the service organization to answer the questions, 'What is our product (or service concept), what do we want it to become, and what actions must we take to get there? Table 5.1 summarizes the principal uses of positioning analysis as a diagnostic tool, providing input to decisions relating to product development, service delivery, pricing and communication strategy.

Table 5.1 ■ Principal uses of positioning analysis as a diagnostic tool

---

1. Provide a useful diagnostic tool for defining and understanding the relationships between products and markets:

■ How does the product compare with competitive offerings on specific attributes?

■ How well does product performance meet consumer needs and expectations on specific performance criteria?

■ What is the predicted consumption level for a product with a given set of performance characteristics offered at a given price?

2. Identify market opportunities for:

a. *Introducing new products*
   ■ What segments to target?
   ■ What attributes to offer relative to the competition?

b. *Redesigning (repositioning) existing products*
   ■ Appeal to the same segments or to new ones?
   ■ What attributes to add, drop or change?
   ■ What attributes to emphasize in advertising?

c. *Eliminate products that*
   ■ Do not satisfy consumer needs
   ■ Face excessive competition

3. Making other marketing mix decisions to pre-empt, or respond to, competitive moves:

a. *Distribution strategies*
   ■ Where to offer the product (locations, types of outlet)?
   ■ When to make the product available?

b. *Pricing strategies*
   ■ How much to charge?
   ■ What billing and payment procedures to employ?

c. *Communication strategies*
   ■ What target audience(s) are most easily convinced that the product offers a competitive advantage on attributes that are important to them?
   ■ What message(s)? Which attributes should be emphasized and which competitors – if any – should be mentioned as the basis for comparison on these attributes?
   ■ Which communication channels – personal selling versus different advertising media? (Selected not only for their ability to convey the chosen message(s) to the target audience(s), but also for their ability to reinforce the desired image of the product.)

Developing a positioning strategy can take place at several different levels, depending on the nature of the business in question. Among multi-site, multi-product, service businesses, a position might be established for the entire organization, for a given service outlet, or for a specific service offered at that outlet. It's particularly important that there be some consistency between the positions held by different services offered at the same location, since the image of one may spill over onto the others. For instance, if a hospital has an excellent reputation for obstetrical services, this may enhance perceptions of its services in gynaecology, paediatrics, surgery, and so forth.

Because of the intangible, experiential nature of many services, an explicit positioning strategy is valuable in helping prospective customers to get a mental 'fix' on a product that would otherwise be rather amorphous. Failure to select a desired position in the marketplace – and to develop a marketing action plan designed to achieve and hold this position – may result in one of several possible outcomes, all undesirable:

1. The organization (or one of its products) is pushed into a position where it faces head-on competition from stronger competitors.

2. The organization (product) is pushed into a position which nobody else wants because there is little customer demand there.

3. The organization's (product's) position is so blurred that nobody knows what its distinctive competence really is.

4. The organization (product) has no position at all in the marketplace because nobody has ever heard of it.

Steps in developing a positioning strategy

Competitive strategy is often narrowly focused at direct competitors – firms that market products that offer customers a similar way of achieving the same benefits (e.g., in the case of education, another college offering similar classes). However, there may also be a serious threat from generic competitors, which offer customers a different way of achieving similar benefits (for instance, distance learning via broadcast programmes or self-study through use of books, CDs and videotapes both offer generic competition to conventional university classes).

The research and analysis that underlie development of an effective positioning strategy are designed to highlight both opportunities and threats to the firm in the competitive marketplace, including the presence of generic competitors. Figure 5.2 identifies the basic steps involved in identifying a suitable market position and developing a strategy to reach it.

Market analysis is needed to determine such factors as the overall level and trend of demand, and the geographic location of this demand. Is demand increasing or decreasing for the benefits offered by this type of service? Are there regional or international variations in the level of demand? Alternative ways of segmenting the market should be considered and an appraisal made of the size and potential of different market segments. Research may be needed to gain a better understanding not only of customer needs and preferences within each of the different segments, but also of how each perceives the competition.

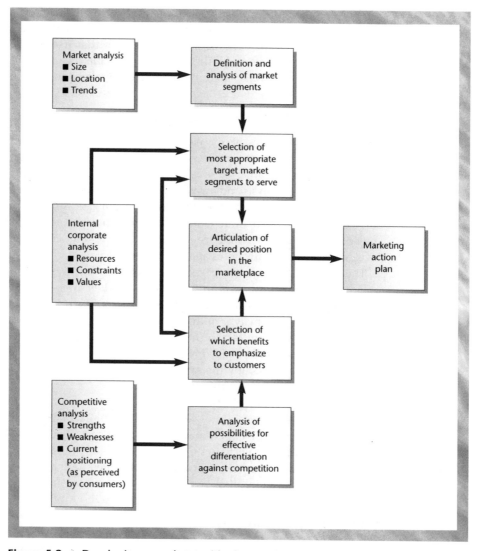

Figure 5.2 ■ Developing a market positioning strategy

Source: Developed from an earlier schematic by Michael R. Pearce.

Internal corporate analysis requires the organization to identify its resources (financial, human labour and know-how, and physical assets), any limitations or constraints, and the values and goals (profitability, growth, professional preferences, etc.) of its management. Using insights from this analysis, the organization should be able to select a limited number of target market segments which it is willing and able to serve with either new or existing services.

Competitive analysis. Identification and analysis of competitors can provide a marketing strategist with a sense of their strengths and weaknesses, which, in turn, may suggest opportunities for differentiation. Relating these insights back to the internal corporate analysis should suggest which benefits should be offered to which target market segments. This analysis should consider both direct and indirect competition.

The outcome of integrating these three forms of analysis is a *position statement* that articulates the desired position of the organization in the marketplace (and, if desired, that of each of the component services that it offers). Armed with this understanding, marketers should be able to develop a specific plan of action. The cost of implementing this plan must, of course, be related to the expected payoff.

Anticipating competitive response

Before embarking on a specific plan of action, however, management should consider the possibility that one or more competitors might pursue the same market position. Perhaps another service organization has independently conducted the same positioning analysis and arrived at similar conclusions? Or an existing competitor may feel threatened by the new strategy and take steps to reposition its own service so as to compete more effectively. Alternatively, a new entrant to the market may decide to play 'follow the leader', yet be able to offer customers a higher service level on one or more attributes and/or a lower price.

The best way to anticipate possible competitive responses is to identify all current or potential competitors and to put oneself in their own management's shoes by conducting an internal corporate analysis for each of these competitors.[10] Coupling the insights from the analysis with data from existing market and competitive analysis (with one's own firm cast in the role of competitor) should provide a good sense of how competitors might be likely to act. If chances seem high that a stronger competitor will move to occupy the same niche with a superior service concept, then it would be wise to reconsider the situation.

Some firms develop sophisticated computer models to analyze the impact of alternative competitive moves. How would a price-cut affect demand, market share and profits? Based on past experience, how might customers in different segments respond to increases or decreases in the level of quality on specific service attributes? How long would it take before customers responded to a new advertising campaign designed to change perceptions?

Evolutionary positioning

Positions are rarely static: they need to evolve over time in response to changing market structures, technology, competitive activity and the evolution of the firm itself. Many types of business lend themselves to evolutionary repositioning by adding or deleting services and target segments. Some companies have shrunk their offerings and divested certain lines of business in order to be more focused. Others have expanded their offerings in the expectation of increasing sales to existing customers and attracting new ones. Thus petrol stations have added small retail stores offering extended hours of service, while supermarkets and other retail stores have added banking services. New developments in technology provide many opportunities for introducing not only new services but also new delivery systems for existing products. You will find that the reading by Lynn Shostack, 'Service positioning through structural change' (reproduced on pages 229–40), offers a number of useful strategic insights for narrowing or broadening the firm's existing product line and for deciding whether to make specific types of services more standardized or more customized.

Rentokil Initial has evolved over a period of almost 80 years from its origins as a manufacturer of rat poison and a pesticide for killing wood-destroying deathwatch beetles. Through organic growth and acquisition of over 200 companies, it has grown to become the world's largest business services company. It sees its core competence as 'the ability to carry out high quality services on other people's premises through a well-recruited, well-trained, and motivated staff'. Cross-selling its existing customers – promoting the use of an additional service to a customer who is already using the company for one or more services – is an important aspect of its strategy.

The company, which has been highly profitable, operates in more than 40 countries, providing a range of services within each of the following categories: hygiene and cleaning, pest control, distribution and plant services, personnel services, and property services and security. According to its chief executive, Sir Clive Thompson,

> We see ourselves very much as an industrial and commercial service company, with markets driven by outsourcing of blue-collar activities on the one hand, and on the other by the demand by employers for an improved and/or sustained environment for their employees.
>
> Our objective has been to create a virtuous circle. We provide a quality service in industrial and commercial activities under the same brand-name, so that a customer satisfied with one Rentokil Initial Service is potentially a satisfied customer for another . . . Although it was considered somewhat odd at the time, one of the reasons we moved into [providing and maintaining] tropical plants [for building interiors] was in fact to put the brand in front of decision makers. Our service people maintaining the plants go in through the front door and are visible to the customer. This contrasts with pest control where no one really notices unless we fail . . . The brand stands for honesty, reliability, consistency, integrity and technical leadership.[11]

The essence of Rentokil Initial's success lies in its ability to position each of its many business and commercial services in terms of the company's core brand values, which are highly relevant to the nature and quality of service that is delivered. In the case of acquisitions, improving results often requires repositioning the attributes of the newly acquired service to reflect these brand values in addition to taking advantage of economies of scale, technical and people-management skills, and cross-selling possibilities. The brand image is reinforced through physical evidence in terms of distinctive uniforms, vehicle liveries and use of the corporate logo on all correspondence.

Developing positioning maps

Developing a positioning 'map' – a task sometimes referred to as perceptual mapping – is a useful way of representing consumers' perceptions of alternative products graphically. A map is usually confined to two attributes (although three-dimensional models can be used to portray three of these attributes). When more than three dimensions are needed to describe product performance in a given market, then a series of separate charts need to be drawn for visual presentation purposes. A computer model, of course, can handle as many attributes as are relevant.[12]

Information about a product (or company's position relative to any one attribute) can be inferred from market data, derived from ratings by representative consumers, or both. If consumer perceptions of service characteristics differ sharply from 'reality' as defined by management, then marketing efforts may be needed to change these perceptions.

As a generalization, graphic representations of product positions are much easier to grasp than tables of quantitative data or paragraphs of prose. They enable management to understand the nature of competitive threats and opportunities, they can highlight gaps between how customers (or prospects) see the organization and how management sees it, and they can help confirm or dispel beliefs that a service – or its parent organization – occupies a unique niche in the marketplace.

Using positioning maps to plot strategy: an example from the hotel industry

The hotel business is highly competitive, especially during seasons when the supply of rooms exceeds demand. A famous hotelier once declared that the three most important things for the success of a hotel were location, location and location. Certainly, location is an important choice criterion among each of the principal market segments served by the industry: business travellers, tourists and holiday-makers, and conference delegates. The preferred location will, of course, depend on guests' intended destinations in the local area. Some, for instance, may be visiting business clients in the financial district, others attending a congress at the conference centre, while tourists may be intent on sightseeing, shopping and museum visits.

But both research and management experience show that location is not the only attribute that customers in each segment consider when selecting a hotel. Let's focus on the needs of the business traveller. Unlike tourists who must pay their own way, he or she is probably travelling on an expense account, which may determine the level of hotel price that can be afforded. The attribute of price may serve to define different market segments, ranging from (say) chief executives whose firms may be willing to pay for them to stay in a five-star hotel, to business executives and senior professionals who are entitled to stay in a four-star hotel, to junior sales representatives whose expense accounts limit them to less luxurious types of accommodation. In short, there are different classes of hotel based on ability and willingness to pay for increasing levels of luxury and service, as well as for factors such as a more desirable location.

Within each class of hotels, customers visiting a large city may find that they have several alternatives from among which to select a place to stay. The degree of luxury and comfort in physical amenities will be one choice criterion; research shows that business travellers are concerned not only with the comfort and facilities offered by their rooms (where they may wish to work as well as sleep), but also with other physical spaces, ranging from the reception area to restaurants to meeting rooms to swimming pools and exercise facilities. The quality and range of services offered by hotel staff is another key criterion: Can a guest get 24-hour room service? Can clothes be laundered and pressed? Is there a knowledgeable concierge on duty? Are staff available to offer professional business services? There are other choice criteria, too, perhaps relating to the ambience of the hotel (modern architecture and decor are favoured by some customers, others may prefer old-world charm and antique furniture). Additional attributes include factors such as quietness, safety, cleanliness and special rewards programmes for frequent guests.

Let's look at an example, based on a real-world situation, of how developing a positioning map of their own and competing hotels helped managers of the Palace, a successful four-star hotel, develop a better understanding of future threats to their established market position in a large city that we will call Belleville.

Located on the edge of the booming financial district, the Palace was an elegant old hotel that had been extensively renovated and modernized a few years earlier. Its competitors included eight 4-star establishments, and the Grand, one of the city's oldest hotels, which had a 5-star rating. The Palace had been very profitable for its owners in recent years and boasted an above-average occupancy rate. For many months of the year, it was sold out on weekdays, reflecting its strong appeal to business travellers, who were very attractive to the hotel because of their willingness to pay a higher room rate than tourists or congress delegates. But the general manager and his staff saw problems on the horizon. Planning permission had recently been granted for four large new hotels in the city and the Grand had just started a major renovation and expansion project, which included construction of a new wing. There was a risk that customers might see the Palace as falling behind.

To understand better the nature of the competitive threat, the hotel's management team worked with a consultant to prepare charts that displayed the Palace's position in the business traveller market both before and after the advent of new competition. Four attributes were selected for study: room price, level of physical luxury, level of personal service and location. In this instance, management did not conduct new consumer research; instead they inferred customer perceptions based on published information, data from past surveys, and reports from travel agents and knowledgeable hotel staff members who interacted frequently with customers. Information on competing hotels was not difficult to obtain, since the locations were known, the physical structures were relatively easy to visit and evaluate, and the sales staff kept themselves informed on pricing policies and discounts. A convenient surrogate measure for service level was the ratio of rooms per employee, easily calculated from the published number of rooms and employment data provided to the city authorities. Data from surveys of travel agents conducted by the Palace provided additional insights on the quality of personal service at each competitor.

Scales were then created for each attribute. Price was simple, since the average price charged to business travellers for a standard single room at each hotel was already quantified. The rooms per employee ratio formed the basis for a service level scale, with low ratios being equated with high service. This scale was then modified slightly in the light of what was known about the quality of service actually delivered by each major competitor. Level of physical luxury was more subjective. The management team identified the hotel that members agreed was the most luxurious (the Grand) and then the 4-star hotel that they viewed as having the least luxurious physical facilities (the Airport Plaza). All other 4-star hotels were then rated on this attribute relative to these two benchmarks. Location was defined with reference to the stock exchange building in the heart of the financial district, since past research had shown that a majority of the Palace's business guests were visiting destinations in this area. The location scale plotted each hotel in terms of its distance from the stock exchange. The competitive set of ten hotels lay within a four-mile, fan-shaped radius, extending from the exchange through the city's principal retail area (where the conference centre was also located) to the inner suburbs and the nearby airport. Two positioning maps were created to portray the existing competitive situation. The first (Figure 5.3) showed the ten hotels on the dimensions of price and service level; the second (Figure 5.4) displayed them on location and degree of physical luxury.

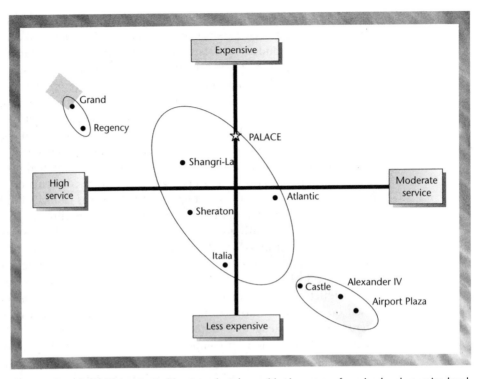

Figure 5.3 ■ Belleville's principal business hotels: positioning map of service level vs. price level

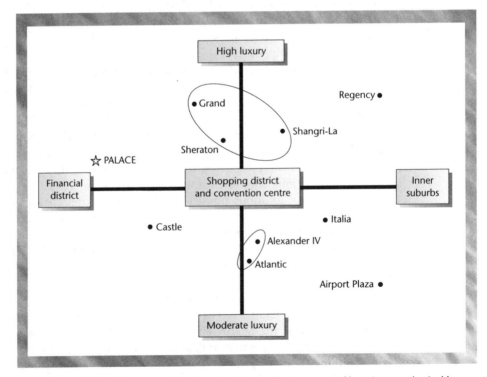

Figure 5.4 ■ Belleville's principal business hotels: positioning map of location vs. physical luxury

A quick glance at Figure 5.3 shows a clear correlation between the attributes of price and service: hotels offering higher levels of service are relatively more expensive. The shaded bar running from upper left to lower right highlights this relationship, which is not a surprising one (and can be expected to continue diagonally downwards for 3-star and lesser-rated establishments). Further analysis shows that there appear to be three clusters of hotels within what is already an upscale market category. At the top end, the 4-star Regency is close to the 5-star Grand; in the middle, the Palace is clustered with four other hotels, and at the lower end, there is another cluster of three hotels. One surprising insight from this map is that the Palace appears to be charging significantly more (on a relative basis) than its service level would seem to justify. Since its occupancy rate is very high, guests are evidently willing to pay the going rate.

In Figure 5.4 we see how the Palace is positioned relative to the competition on location and degree of luxury. We would not expect these two variables to be related and they do not appear to be so. A key insight here is that the Palace occupies a relatively empty portion of the map. It is the only hotel in the financial district – a fact that probably explains its ability to charge more than its service level (or degree of physical luxury) would seem to justify. There are two clusters of hotels in the vicinity of the shopping district and conference centre: a relatively luxurious group of three, led by the Grand, and a second group of two offering a moderate level of luxury.

What of the future? The Palace's management team next sought to anticipate the positions of the four new hotels being constructed in Belleville, as well as the probable repositioning of the Grand (see Figures 5.5 and 5.6). The construction sites were already known; two would be in the financial district and two in the vicinity of the conference centre, itself under expansion. Press releases distributed by the Grand had already declared its management's intentions: The 'New Grand' would not only be larger, but the renovations would also be designed to make it even more luxurious, and there were plans to add new service features.

Predicting the positions of the four new hotels was not difficult for experts in the field, whereas customers might have had more difficulty in predicting each hotel's level of performance on different attributes, especially if they were unfamiliar with the chain that would be operating the hotel in question. Preliminary details of the new hotels had already been released to city planners and the business community. The owners of two of the hotels had declared their intentions to seek 5-star status, although this might take a few years to achieve. Three of the newcomers would be affiliated with international chains and their strategies could be anticipated by examining recent hotels opened in other cities by these same chains.

Pricing was also easy to project. New hotels use a formula for setting posted room prices (the prices typically charged to individuals staying on a week-night in high season). This price is linked to the average construction cost per room at the rate of 1 euro per night for every 1,000 euros of construction costs. Thus, a 200-room hotel that costs €30 million to build (including land costs) would have an average room cost of €150,000 and would need to set a price of €150 per room night. Using this formula, Palace managers concluded that the four new hotels would have to charge significantly more than the Grand or Regency, in effect establishing what marketers call a *price umbrella* above existing price levels and thereby giving competitors the option of raising their own prices. To justify their high prices, the new hotels would have to offer customers very high standards of service and luxury. At the same time, the New Grand would need to raise its own prices to recover the costs of renovations, new construction and enhanced service offerings (see Figure 5.5).

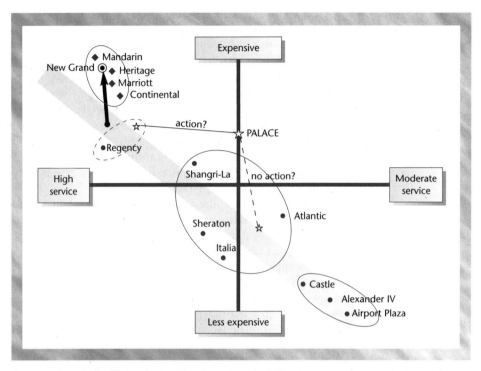

Figure 5.5 ■ Belleville's principal business hotels, following new construction: positioning map of service level vs. price level

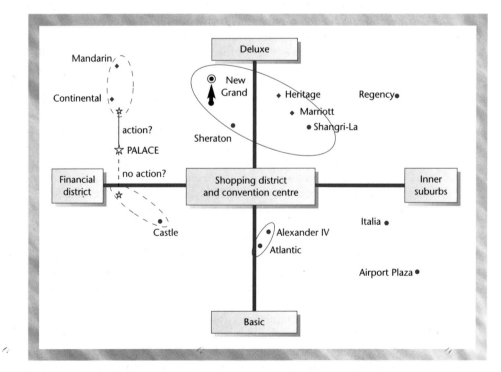

Figure 5.6 ■ Belleville's principal business hotels after new construction: positioning map of location vs. physical luxury

Assuming no changes by either the Palace or other existing hotels, the impact of the new competition in the market clearly posed a significant threat to the Palace, which would lose its unique locational advantage and in future be one of three hotels in the immediate vicinity of the financial district (Figure 5.6). The sales staff believed that many of the Palace's existing business customers would be attracted to the Continental and the Mandarin and willing to pay their higher rates in order to obtain the superior benefits offered. The other two newcomers were seen as more of a threat to the Shangri-La, Sheraton and New Grand in the shopping district/conference centre cluster. Meantime, the New Grand and the newcomers would create a high price/high service (and high luxury) cluster at the top end of the market, leaving the Regency in what might prove to be a distinctive – and therefore defensible – space of its own.

What action should the Palace take in these circumstances? Imagine for a moment that you are the consultant. One option is to do nothing in terms of service enhancements or physical improvements. But loss of its unique locational advantage would destroy the hotel's ability to charge a price premium, leading to lower prices, lower revenues and profits, and less ability to maintain the physical fabric to high standards. Some of the best staff might be enticed away by the newcomers, leading to a decline in service quality. And without renovations, there would be a gradual decline in physical luxury, too. The net result over time might be to shift the Palace into a new cluster with the Castle, serving guests who wanted to visit destinations in the financial district, but were unable (or unwilling) to pay the high prices charged at the Mandarin and Continental. In summary, doing nothing does have strategic implications! If other, existing hotels decide to upgrade and the Palace continues to do nothing, it will eventually slide even further down the scales on luxury and service, risking reclassification as a 3-star hotel.

An alternative strategy is to recommend that management take action, implementing an immediate round of renovations and service improvements, plus programmes to reinforce the loyalty of frequent guests, before the new hotels are completed. The price umbrella these hotels create will allow the Palace to raise its own prices. The net result may be that on the dimensions of price and service the hotel will move to a new position in which it is clustered with the Regency (located several miles away in the inner suburbs), while on the dimensions of luxury and location it will be clustered with the Mandarin and Continental, but slightly less expensive than either.

So what did the Palace actually do? Management selected the second of the two options presented above, concluding that the future profitability of the hotel lay in competing with the Continental and, to a lesser extent, with the Mandarin for the growing number of business travellers visiting the financial district. Attention was also paid to retaining the loyalty of frequent guests by recording their preferences and special needs on the hotel database, so that staff could give them a more personalized level of service. Advertising and selling efforts promoted these improvements, with frequent guests targeted by personal letters from the general manager. In subsequent years, occupancy levels and profits held up very well.

Changing perceptions through advertising

Improving product features and correcting weaknesses can be expensive. Sometimes, however, weaknesses are perceptual rather than real. Advertising campaigns can help to reframe the terms of reference for customers when choosing from among competing suppliers. If potential customers can be persuaded that one attribute (on which the firm excels) can be made a significant choice criterion, then perceived strength on this one attribute may have a positive, 'halo' effect on all other attributes.

In a broader context, researchers note that the presence of such halo effects – either positive or negative – can make it more difficult to assess the specific strengths and weaknesses of competing services.[13] For instance, reported customer dissatisfaction with attribute A of a particular service may be real (and thus need corrective action). Alternatively, it could be the result of a negative halo effect caused by high dissatisfaction with attribute B or even by a high overall dissatisfaction with the brand. One of the problems in consumer satisfaction research is that respondents often complete survey questionnaires quickly, without thoughtful consideration of each of the different dimensions on which they are rating a service firm's performance. In-depth personal interviews may offer a more reliable way to probe customers' evaluations but are, of course, considerably more expensive to administer.

A positioning strategy is only as good as the quality of the information used in constructing it. As conditions change, research needs to be repeated and positioning maps redrawn to reflect the dynamic nature of the marketplace. New market entrants and repositioning of existing competitors, together with evolving customer beliefs about what is important, may mean that a formerly distinctive position has ceased to be so. In some instances, different maps may need to be drawn for different market segments, if research shows that there are sharp variations in perceptions or priorities between segments. In the case of hotels, for instance, tourists and conference delegates may have somewhat different priorities from business travellers and are probably less likely to be frequent guests of the same hotel.

Conclusion

Most service businesses face active competition. Marketers need to find ways of creating meaningful competitive advantages for their products. Ideally, they should be targeting segments that they can serve better than other providers.

The concept of positioning is valuable because it forces explicit recognition of the different attributes comprising the overall service concept and emphasizes the need for marketers to understand which attributes determine customer choice behaviour. Positioning maps provide a visual way of summarizing research data and display how different firms are perceived as performing relative to each other on key attributes. When combined with information on the preferences of different segments, including the level of demand that might be anticipated from such segments, positioning maps may suggest opportunities for creating new services or repositioning existing ones to take advantage of unserved market needs. If offering such a service is seen as compatible with the organization's resources and values, then the firm may be able to develop a profitable niche for itself in the market.

Study questions

1. Why should service firms focus their efforts? What options do they have for doing so?

2. Describe what is meant by *positioning*. Choose an industry you are familiar with (like fast food restaurants or supermarkets) and create a perceptual map showing the competitive positions of different companies in the industry.

3. What is the connection between positioning, market segmentation and customer choice behaviour?

4. Explain the distinction between importance and determinance.

5. Review advertisements for retail financial service firms (e.g. banks and insurance companies in the area where you live (or go to university). To what extent is each firm trying to differentiate itself from its competitors through the use of copy positioning? Which imagery do you see as the most effective, and why?

6. What are the consequences for a company of not having a clear position in the market?

7. Review the discussion of the Palace Hotel in the chapter. As a marketing consultant, what advice would you give to a private hotel company (not a chain) that is considering building a new hotel in Belleville, but has not yet decided on location or positioning?

Notes

1. Based on information in Christian Grönroos and Hans Åke Sand, 'A Winning Service Offer in Car Rental', *Management Decision*, Vol. 21, No. 1, 1993, pp. 45–51.
2. George S. Day, *Market Driven Strategy*, New York: The Free Press, 1990, p. 164.
3. Robert Johnston, 'Achieving Focus in Service Organizations', *The Service Industries Journal*, Vol. 16, January 1996, pp. 10–20.
4. Christopher W.L. Hart, 'Mass Customization: Conceptual Underpinnings, Opportunities, and Limits', *International Journal of Service Industry Management*, Vol. 6, No. 2, 1995, pp. 36–45.
5. For further insights into multiattribute modelling, see William D. Wells and David Prensky, *Consumer Behaviour*, New York: John Wiley & Sons, 1996, pp. 321–5.
6. James L. Heskett, *Managing in the Service Economy*, Boston: Harvard Business School Press, 1984, p. 45.
7. Jack Trout, *The New Positioning: The Latest on the World's #1 Business Strategy*, New York: McGraw-Hill, 1997.
8. Richard Branson, 'Why We Stretch the Virgin Brand', *Evening Standard* (London), 4 August 1997.
9. Sally Dibb and Lyndon Simkin, 'The Strength of Branding and Positioning in Services', *International Journal of Service Industry Management*, Vol. 4, No. 1, 1993, pp. 25–35.
10. For a detailed approach, see Michael E. Porter, *Competitive Strategy*, Chapter 3, 'A Framework for Competitor Analysis', New York: The Free Press, 1980, pp. 47–74.
11. Sir Clive Thompson, Rentokil Initial: Building a Strong Corporate Brand for Growth and Diversity', in F. Gilmore (ed.), *Brand Warriors*, London: HarperCollins Business, 1997, pp. 123–4.
12. For examples of developing research data for perpetual mapping purposes, see Glen L. Urban and John M. Hauser, *Design and Marketing of New Products*, 2nd edition, Englewood Cliffs, NJ: Prentice Hall, 1993.
13. Jochen Wirtz and John E.G. Bateson, 'An Experimental Investigation of Halo Effects in Satisfaction Measures of Service Attributes', *International Journal of Service Industry Management*, Vol. 6, No. 3, 1995, pp. 84–102.

CHAPTER 6

Targeting customers, managing relationships and building loyalty

Learning objectives

After reading and reflecting on this chapter, you should be able to:

1. Recall the principles of segmentation, particularly as they relate to customer behaviour.

2. Understand the bases by which firms can set priorities for targeting specific segments.

3. Understand why capacity-constrained firms need to target multiple market segments.

4. Recognize that not all customers are attractive for a firm and consider strategies for dealing with abusive behaviour.

5. Calculate the value of a customer who remains loyal to a firm and recognize the role that loyalty plays in determining financial success.

6. Develop ideas for creating customer loyalty programmes.

Creating customer loyalty at Superquinn[1]

'The most successful way to have customers come back is to make them feel guilty if they don't', says Feargal Quinn, managing director of the 16-store Superquinn chain in Ireland. The small, family-owned supermarket chain has gained a remarkable reputation for customer service, inspiring a degree of loyalty among its customers that is the envy of retailers across Europe. Quinn himself is renowned for his philosophy of keeping close to the customer and is the author of a well-received book, *Crowning the Customer*, originally written as a training manual for new staff.[2] The chain's customer focus comes from Quinn's belief that customer service is the best way his company can distinguish itself from the competition.

Quinn explained to a visitor how, in 1993, he came to relaunch Superclub, the chain's innovative loyalty scheme which, within four years, had signed up some 300,000 cardholders, representing one in four of all Irish households. Chatting with a customer one day, he was surprised when she told him: 'I went to your competitor one time but I felt guilty about it.' Intrigued by this confession, he probed for more details, expecting that paying high prices at the other store was the source of the woman's guilty feelings. However, it turned out that on one shopping expedition to Superquinns, she discovered that she had forgotten her purse and had no money to pay the fairly substantial amount due. So she asked the checkout operator if the store would be willing to put her frozen food purchases in the freezer until she returned with money in about 45 minutes. But instead, the manager came over and told her, 'No, no take it away and pay me next week.' Ever since, confessed the customer, she had felt guilty about doing her grocery shopping anywhere else. Quinn asked when the incident had occurred and was amazed to discover that it had taken place 14 years earlier. 'It's worth almost anything to achieve that sort of guilt – and loyalty!' he declared.

Superclub allows customers to earn points based on the total amount of their purchase (points can also be earned by purchasing petrol from Texaco stations). Certain products qualify for bonus points, and customers get double points on Wednesdays, traditionally a relatively quiet day, to help divert traffic from busy Fridays. The points can be redeemed for merchandise and for very low-priced airline tickets. About 80 per cent of purchases are paid for with customer cards. The store has two display units on each cash register, the one facing the checkout operator displays the cardholder's name, enabling the operator to thank the customer personally. The system is programmed to identify regular customers, allowing the store to offer special privileges to make them even more loyal, such as cheque-cashing privileges and birthday cakes featuring their name.

To encourage customers to act as quality controllers, Superquinn stores hand out 'goof cards' printed with a list of 15 potential quality failures (which change monthly) that the customer is asked to look for and report. One month, for instance, the card might list such problems as a supermarket trolley with shaky wheels, poor packing of supermarket bags (e.g., soft things on the bottom underneath heavier items), an outdated product or a sausage on display with burst skin. Finding and reporting such a goof entitles a customer to 200 Superclub points.

A big point of difference at his stores, says Quinn, is that they are run on what he calls 'The Boomerang Principle', persuading people to come back again and again. Every decision is examined from the perspective of 'Will this help to bring the customer back next week and the week after?' If the answer is 'No, but it will make us a fast buck now', then 'we don't want to know', declares Quinn, adding:

It's the long-term income stream that we concentrate on winning. And that's the framework that all the things we're known for slot into. That gives direction and focus to how we listen to customers, how we seek to serve them, how we try to meet and even anticipate their needs.

But in the fiercely competitive environment we operate in, we also have to make sure we stay in business long enough for the customers to come back to us. It doesn't mean that we can take our eye off this week's bottom line.

Quinn is adamant about the importance of listening to customers. Listening systems include the manager and all team members at each store, market research and customer panels whose sessions Quinn himself attends. 'Listening is more important than price competition', he argues. 'We must stay closer to our customers.'

Targeting the right customers

Grocery shops such as Superquinn tend to serve a geographically compact market area, which is a good first step in segmenting a retail market where customers must come to the service provider. By defining service and customer loyalty as its corporate goals, Superquinn is appealing to a market segment that values good service and extended relationships, rather than the cheapest price available that day; this shows that the firm understands the principle of benefit segmentation.

The term 'mass marketing' is used less and less these days. Instead, as we suggested in Chapter 5, today's marketers are concerned with 'focus' or 'targeting' or 'mass customization'.[3] Underlying such terms is the notion of market segmentation. More and more firms are trying to decide which types of customers they can serve well and thus maintain as loyal users, rather than trying to be all things to all people. Managers in innovative firms constantly debate what improvements in *product elements* – or entirely new services – they need to offer to attract and retain customers in specific segments that are believed to present good opportunities for growth and profits. (Market segmentation is a central topic in most introductory marketing courses, so if you have not previously taken such a course, please take a moment to review key aspects of segmentation in the boxed review on pages 172–3.)

Few service businesses can survive by serving just a single segment, especially if they have a lot of productive capacity to fill over the course of the business year. In this chapter, we emphasize the importance of choosing to serve a mix – or portfolio – of several carefully chosen target segments and taking pains to build and maintain their loyalty. We also note that not all segments are worth serving and it may not be realistic to try to retain all customers. One researcher makes this point nicely in a discussion of banking:

A bank's population of customers undoubtedly contains individuals who either cannot be satisfied, given the service levels and pricing the bank is capable of offering, or will never be profitable, given their banking activity (their use of resources relative to the revenue they supply). Any bank would be wise to target and serve only those customers whose needs it can meet better than its competitors in a profitable manner. These are the customers who are most likely to remain with that bank for long periods, who will purchase multiple products and services, who will recommend that bank to their friends and relations, and who may be the source of superior returns to the bank's shareholders.[4]

Even when customers fit the desired profile, a few of them – usually a very tiny proportion – may prove, through their undesirable behaviour, to be candidates for prompt termination rather than retention. Although slogans claim that the customer is always right, unfortunately that's not true in every instance. When customers behave badly in a service context – particularly people-processing services where customers come to the service factory and interact with employees and other customers – it can have a damaging effect on productivity, employee morale and service quality. We'll address this issue in more depth later in the chapter.

Searching for value, not just numbers

Too many service firms still focus on the *number* of customers they serve – an important issue for operations and human resource planning – without giving sufficient attention to the *value* of each customer. Generally speaking, heavy users, who buy more frequently and in larger volumes, are more profitable than occasional users. Think about the activities that you do on a regular basis. Do you have a favourite restaurant or pizza parlour where you often eat with friends or family? Is there a cinema that you patronize regularly? Do you travel by bus or train to work or college every weekday? Are you often to be seen at your local launderette?

If you answered 'yes' to any of these questions, then you are potentially a lot more interesting to the management of the organizations in question than a one-time visitor who is just passing through town. The revenue stream from your purchases – and those of others like you – may amount to quite a considerable sum over the course of the year (go ahead, figure it out!). Sometimes your value as a frequent user is openly recognized and appreciated: you sense that the business is tailoring its service features, including service hours and prices, to attract people like you and doing its best to make you loyal. In other instances, however, you may feel that nobody knows or cares who you are. Your purchases may make you a valuable customer, but you certainly don't feel valued.

Matching customers to the firm's capabilities is vital. Managers must think carefully about how customer needs relate to such operational elements as speed and quality, the times when service is available, the firm's capacity to serve many customers simultaneously, and the physical features and appearance of service facilities. They also need to consider how well their service personnel can meet the expectations of specific types of customers in terms of both personal style and technical competence. Finally, they need to ask themselves: Can my company match or exceed competing services that are directed at the same types of customers?

Relationship marketing

Traditionally, marketing has overemphasized attraction of new customers. But well-managed firms work hard to retain and grow their existing customers. A widely circulated statement is that on average it costs a firm five to six times as much to attract a new customer as it does to implement retention strategies to hold on to an existing one.[5]

Review of basic marketing principles:
identifying and selecting target segments

Market segmentation is central to almost any professionally planned and executed marketing programme. The concept of segmentation recognizes that customers and prospects within a market vary across a variety of dimensions and that not every segment constitutes a desirable target for the firm's marketing efforts.

Market segments: A segment is composed of a group of current and potential customers who share common characteristics, needs, purchasing behaviour or consumption patterns. Effective segmentation should group buyers into segments in ways that result in as much similarity as possible on the relevant characteristics *within* each segment but dissimilarity on those same characteristics *between* each segment.

Two broad categories of variables are useful in describing the differences between segments. The first have to do with user characteristics, the second with usage behaviour.

User characteristics may vary from one person to another, reflecting *demographic* characteristics (for instance, age, income and education), *geographic* location, and *psychographics* (the attitudes, values, life styles and opinions of decision-makers and users). More recently, marketers have begun to speak of *technographics* – the extent to which customers are willing and able to use the latest technology – a variable that is especially relevant in the context of new service delivery systems. Another important segmentation variable is the specific benefits that individuals and corporate purchasers seek from consuming a particular good or service.

Usage behaviour relates to how customers purchase, obtain and use a product. Among such variables are when and where purchase and consumption take place, the quantities consumed ('heavy users' are always of particular interest to marketers), frequency and purpose of use, the occasions under which consumption takes place (sometimes referred to as 'occasion segmentation'), and sensitivity to such marketing variables as advertising, pricing, speed and other service features, and the value of customers' relationships with the firm.

Finally, there are customers whose abusive behaviour makes them very undesirable.

Target segment: After evaluating different segments in the market, a firm should focus its marketing efforts by targeting one or more segments that fit well with the firm's capabilities and goals. Target segments are often defined on the basis of several variables. For instance, a hotel in a particular city might target prospective guests who shared such user characteristics as (1) travelling on business (demographic segmentation), (2) visiting clients within a defined area around the hotel (geographic segmentation), and (3) willing to pay a certain daily room rate (user response).

When researching the marketplace, service marketers should be looking for answers to such questions as:

■ In what useful ways can the market for our firm's service be segmented?

■ What are the needs of the specific segments that we have identified?

■ Which of these segments best fits our institutional mission and our current operational capabilities?

■ What do customers in each segment see as our firm's competitive advantages and disadvantages? Are the latter correctable?

■ In the light of this analysis, which specific segment(s) should we target?

■ How should we differentiate our marketing efforts from those of the competition to attract and retain the types of customers that we want?

Review of basic marketing principles: identifying and selecting target segments (*continued*)

- What is the long-term financial value to us of a loyal customer in each of the segments that we currently serve (and those that we would like to serve)?

- How should our firm build long-term relationships with customers from the target segments? And what strategies are needed to create long-term loyalty?

In contrast to transaction marketing, which refers to an occasional deal, relationship marketing aims to create a long-term, interactive relationship between providers and customers. As emphasized by Gummesson, relationship marketing is more often focused on one-to-one relationships and less on impersonal mass marketing. He argues that 'Its core is mutually beneficial and voluntary relationships where both supplier and customer remain satisfied. Both parties should be free to leave, but their incentives to break the relationship should be reduced.'[6]

Relationship marketing strategies include activities aimed at developing long-term, cost-effective links between an organization and its customers for the mutual benefit of both parties. Service firms use a variety of strategies to maintain and enhance relationships, including such basics as treating customers fairly, offering service augmentations and treating each customer as though he or she were a segment of one – the essence of mass customization. Superquinn achieves this, in part, through its Superclub programme. Service enhancements play a key role in building and sustaining relationships between vendors and purchasers of industrial goods and services, which is the arena in which relationship marketing initially developed on a widespread basis. And Levitt has this to say about relationship management in professional firms:

> It is not surprising that in professional partnerships, such as law, medicine, architecture, consulting, investment banking, and advertising, individuals are rated and rewarded by the client relationships they control. These relationships, like other assets, can appreciate or depreciate . . . Relationship management requires company wide programs for maintenance, investment, improvement, and even for replacement.[7]

Not all existing customer relationships are worth keeping. Some customers no longer fit the firm's strategy, either because that strategy has changed or because the nature of the customer's behaviour and needs has changed. Careful analysis may show that many relationships are no longer profitable for the firm, since they cost more to maintain than the revenues they generate. Just as investors need to dispose of poor investments and banks may have to write off bad loans, each service firm needs to regularly evaluate its customer portfolio and consider terminating unsuccessful relationships. Legal and ethical considerations, of course, will determine whether or not it is proper to take such actions.

At a minimum, a firm should focus its advertising and promotional strategy to reach prospects from desired segments and to avoid attracting customers who do not fit the desired profile. Professional firms, such as accounting or legal partnerships, provide a good example of the importance of considering the mix of business held by the firm. Marketing is about getting *better* business, not just *more* business. The calibre of a professional firm is measured by the type of clients it serves and the nature of the tasks on which it works. Volume alone is no measure of excellence, sustainability or profitability.[8] For additional coverage of this issue, see the reading by David Maister, 'Measuring your marketing success', which appears on pages 611–15.

Selecting the appropriate customer portfolio

Artists and writers often prepare a portfolio of their work to show to prospective purchasers or employers. The term also describes the collection of financial instruments held by an investor or the array of loans advanced by a bank. In financial services, the goal of portfolio analysis is to determine the mix of investments (or loans) that is appropriate to one's needs, resources and risk preference. In an investment portfolio, the contents should change over time in response to the performance of individual portfolio elements, as well as reflecting changes in the customer's situation or preferences.

Creating a portfolio of market segments

We can apply the concept of portfolio to service businesses with an established base of customers. If managers know the annual value of each category of customers (revenues received minus the associated costs of serving them) as well as the proportions represented by each category within the customer base, they can project the ongoing value of all these customers in terms of future revenue streams. Models exist for projecting the future value of the *customer portfolio*, based on historical data of customer acquisitions, classes of service purchased, service upgrades and downgrades, and terminations. These historical data can be adapted to reflect pricing and cost changes, promotional efforts and market-related risks (including the anticipated impact of competitive actions or changes in market dynamics). A good example is subscriptions to cable or satellite TV. Another is financial services, both corporate and retail.

Segmentation strategies for effective capacity utilization

One reason for serving multiple segments is to fill capacity at all times that the service is available for use. Capacity-constrained service businesses need to make the best use of their productive capacity, but finding enough customers to use their service at any given time and place often requires appealing to a broad market base. Managers should recognize the risks involved in trying to fill capacity with just any warm body. Instead, they should be asking themselves whether they have attracted the right sorts of customers at the right places, times and prices. In people-processing services, where customers themselves become part of the product, conflicts may arise when people from distinctively different segments come together simultaneously in the same facility. Imagine the dismay among patrons at a bar that prides itself on providing a quiet and romantic environment when a group of rowdy sports fans arrive to celebrate their team's victory in a big match!

Most businesses face fluctuations in demand over time, with predictable peak and off-peak periods. When customers from a firm's principal target segment are absent, marketers often seek to attract customers from other segments to fill capacity during periods of low demand. In general, there's less risk of customer conflicts when different segments patronize a facility at different times. In principle, if the off-peak business is financially profitable, can be handled effectively and is not going to hurt the organization's image, then it's worth accepting. Little harm is probably done to an airline's positioning strategy if it uses its aircraft for charter flights when business demand is low. But if a hotel or restaurant gains a reputation for attracting a totally different type of customer in the off-season, there is a risk that this may negate its desired high-season image, particularly if a few high-season customers happen to visit during another season expecting to find the same types of customers and service levels as before. One solution is to be quite explicit about the different positioning strategies. We address this issue in more depth in Chapter 13.

Customers as part of the service experience

When service users share a common facility – such as a hotel, restaurant, retail store or transport vehicle – other customers become part of the product. As a result, the size and composition of the customer base has important implications for both the image of the service organization and the nature of the service experience. If you are a customer of a high-contact, shared service, you can quickly determine whether it is well or poorly patronized. You can also see what sorts of people are using the service – their appearance, age range, apparent income bracket, dress (formal or casual) and whether they appear to have come alone, in couples or in groups. Also apparent (sometimes obtrusively so!) is how these other customers are behaving: Are they quiet or noisy, slow or active in their movements? Do they appear cheerful or glum, considerate towards others or rude?

Since customers contribute strongly to the atmosphere of many high-contact services, a firm should seek to attract (and retain) customers from the most appropriate market segments. Managers also need to ensure that prospective customers are aware of what constitutes appropriate dress and behaviour. For instance, if you are the owner of a restaurant that thrives on business from casually dressed students, it would probably be unwise to try to attract middle-aged people in business suits. In contrast, a hotel that has succeeded in building up a clientele of business travellers should consider how they might react to the presence in the lobby or dining room of a large group of tourists on a packaged vacation. Some establishments, such as coffee houses, thrive on attracting a diverse mix of customers. This diversity becomes part of their culture and works well as long as no one's behaviour actively disturbs other people.

A uniform customer base is not always possible or even desirable for many service businesses. Two or more distinct market segments may each contribute importantly to the organization's success, yet they may not mix well. Ideally, potentially conflicting segments should be separated in place and time. Examples of place separation include seating airline passengers in first class, business class and economy class cabins (based upon how much they are willing to pay for enhanced service features), placing congress delegates on a different floor of a hotel from other guests, and assigning bank customers with substantial accounts a separate entrance and transaction area – even a special branch of their own – to offer more privacy. Separation of customers in time can be achieved through sequential rather than joint use of the same service facility by customers from different market segments: in that way neither group encounters the other.

As you know from your own experience, the way in which other customers behave can affect your own enjoyment of a service. If you like classical music and attend symphony concerts, you expect audience members to keep quiet during the performance, rather than spoiling the music by talking or coughing loudly. By contrast, a silent audience would be pretty deadly during a rock concert or team sports event, where active audience participation usually adds to the excitement. There is a fine line, however, between spectator enthusiasm and abusive behaviour by hooligan supporters of rival soccer teams, as seen at some European games (including the UK!).

Abusive customers and how to deal with them

One issue of greater concern to service marketers than to goods marketers relates to customers who behave in abusive ways. Such customers are a problem for any company, but they have more potential for mischief in service businesses, particularly those in which the customer comes to the service factory. When badly behaved customers come face-to-face with service personnel and other customers, their behaviour can put employees at risk and spoil other people's service experiences. Unfortunately, the presence of customers in the service factory offers potential for theft and vandalism. And customers who act inappropriately can interfere with a firm's efforts to improve productivity and quality.

Addressing the challenge of jaycustomers[9]

Visitors to North America are often puzzled by the term 'jaywalker', that distinctively American word used to describe people who cross streets at unauthorized places or in a dangerous manner. The prefix 'jay' comes from a nineteenth-century slang term for a stupid person. We can create a whole vocabulary of derogatory terms by adding the prefix 'jay' to existing nouns and verbs. How about 'jaycustomer', for example, to denote someone who 'jayuses' a service or 'jayconsumes' a product (and then 'jaydisposes' of it afterwards)? Or 'jayemployees' who deliver poor service and abuse customers? Or even 'jaymanagers'?

We define a jaycustomer as one who acts in a thoughtless or abusive way, causing problems for the organization, its employees and other customers. Every service encounters its share of jaycustomers. But management opinions on this topic seem to polarize around two opposing views of the situation. One is denial: 'the customer can do no wrong'. The other view sees the marketplace of customers as positively overpopulated with nasty people (and even nastier corporate purchasers) who simply cannot be trusted to behave in ways that self-respecting suppliers should expect and require.

The first viewpoint finds expression in the phrase 'the customer is always right' and has received wide publicity in gung-ho management books and in motivational presentations to captive groups of employees. But the second, highly distrustful view may be widely held among cynical managers who have been burned at some point in their professional lives. As with so many opposing viewpoints in life, there are important grains of truth in both perspectives.

Service marketers must be very careful not to fall into the trap of distrusting all customers, since that can lead to situations in which everyone is regarded with suspicion. This viewpoint often leads to introduction of elaborate and rigid procedures designed to prevent fraud and abuse. The end-result is that each customer's service experience is degraded when using that firm's services. On the other hand, no manager can afford to be naïve about the existence of what we call jaycustomers. The challenge is to understand the potential for abuse and respond in ways that avoid resorting to draconian measures that could upset the vast majority of honest and decent users of the organization's services. At worst, a firm needs to control or deter abusive behaviour. At best, it should try to avoid attracting the attention of potential jaycustomers in the first place.

Five types of jaycustomers

Since defining the problem is the first step in resolving it, let's start by considering the different types (or segments) of jaycustomers who prey upon suppliers of both goods and services. We've identified five broad categories and given them generic names, but many customer contact personnel have come up with their own special terms of endearment for these charming people. As you reflect on these categories, you may, perhaps, be stimulated to add a few more of your own.

The thief

This jaycustomer has no intention of paying and sets out to steal goods and services (or to pay less than full price by such devices as switching price tickets, or contesting bills on baseless grounds). Shoplifting is a major problem in retail stores. What retailers euphemistically call 'shrinkage' is estimated to cost enormous amounts of money each year, which simply gets passed back to honest customers through slightly higher prices. Certain services lend themselves to clever schemes for avoiding payment. For those with a technical bent, it is sometimes possible to bypass electricity meters, access telephone lines free of charge, or circumvent normal cable TV feeds. Customers who succeed in travelling free on public transportation, sneaking into cinemas or not paying for restaurant meals are a constant problem for managers in those industries. Both individual and corporate buyers have been known to use fraudulent forms of payment such as stolen credit cards or to issue cheques that are intended to bounce. Managers need to devise procedures for protecting themselves against thieves, while avoiding the risk of harassing or inconveniencing the overwhelming percentage of honest customers.

One of us, while studying as a graduate student in California, was asked by the regional manager of Greyhound Bus Lines in San Francisco where he could obtain a book that described how to steal a wide variety of goods and services without getting caught. Wittily – if unwisely – titled *Steal This Book*, the volume included a whole chapter on how to travel free on long-distance buses.[10] We found the book invitingly displayed at the Stanford University bookstore. Sure enough, it included a veritable encyclopaedia of tips on how to rip off 'capitalist-pig' enterprises (this was in the 1970s). Greyhound was indeed featured, complete with a host of ideas for travelling free and avoiding detection. Feeling a little foolish at ignoring the invitation on the cover, we took the priceless volume to the young woman at the cash register, wondering if this was the first time that anyone had actually paid for it. Today, its updated contents are probably somewhere on the internet.

The man from Greyhound had the right idea. Determining how dishonest people steal your product is the first step in taking preventive measures to stop thieves or corrective measures to catch them and, where appropriate, to prosecute. But managers shouldn't risk alienating their honest customers by degrading the latter's own service experiences. And provision must be made for honest but absentminded customers who forget to pay. Many retailers now attach electronic tags to their merchandise, which can only be removed at a cashier's desk. If the customer passes a point near the exit doors with merchandise that still bears a tag, it sets off an alarm, thus offering the customer a clear choice between returning to the register or making a break for it. The bottom line on theft is that in most environments it is committed by only a very small proportion of customers. The example from Superquinn supermarkets suggests that displaying a willingness to trust customers helps to generate long-term loyalty.

The rulebreaker

Just as highways need safety regulations (including 'Don't Jaywalk'), many service businesses find it necessary to establish rules of behaviour for employees and customers. Some of these rules are imposed by government departments for reasons of health and safety. Air travel is perhaps the best example; there can be few other environments outside prison where healthy, mentally competent, adult customers are quite so constrained (albeit with good reason). In addition to enforcing government regulations, suppliers often lay down their own set of rules to facilitate the smooth functioning of the operation, avoid unreasonable demands being placed on employees, prevent misuse of products and facilities, protect themselves legally and discourage individual customers from behaving in ways that would detract from the quality of other people's service experiences.

There are risks attached to making lots of rules. They can make an organization appear bureaucratic and overbearing. And they can transform employees, whose orientation should be service to customers, into police officers who see (or are told to see) their most important task as enforcing all the rules. A third problem is that there will always be some customers who break the rules anyway – either inadvertantly or deliberately.

How should a firm deal with rulebreakers? Much depends on which rules have been broken. In the case of legally enforceable ones – theft, bad debts, trying to take guns on aircraft – the courses of action need to be laid down explicitly, as much to protect employees as to punish or discourage wrongdoing. Company rules are a little more ambiguous. Are they really necessary in the first place? If not, get rid of them. Do they deal with health and safety? If so, advance education and reminders will reduce the need for taking corrective action. The same is true for rules designed to protect the comfort and enjoyment of all customers using the same facility. And then there are unwritten social norms such as 'thou shalt not jump the queue' (although this is a much stronger cultural expectation in Britain than in many other countries, as any visitor to Paris Disneyland can attest!). Other customers can often be relied upon to help service personnel to enforce rules that affect everybody else, or even take the initiative to do so themselves. The fewer the rules, the more explicit the important ones can be.

The belligerent

You've probably seen him (or her) in a store, at the airport, in a hotel or restaurant. Red in the face and shouting angrily, or perhaps icily calm and voicing insults, threats and obscenities. Things don't always work as they should: machines break down, service is clumsy, customers are ignored, a flight is delayed, an order is delivered incorrectly, staff are unhelpful, a promise is broken. Or perhaps the customer in question is going through a difficult period in his or her personal life. Service personnel are often abused, even when they are not to blame. If an employee lacks authority to resolve the problem, that may make the belligerent madder still, even to the point of physical attack. Drunkenness and drug abuse add extra layers of complication. Organizations that care about their employees go to great efforts to develop skills in dealing with these difficult situations. Training exercises that involve role-playing help employees to develop the self-confidence and assertiveness that they need to stand up to upset customers. Employees also need to learn how to defuse anger, calm anxiety and comfort distress (particularly when there is good reason for the customer to be upset with the organization's performance).

But what is an employee to do when an aggressive customer brushes off attempts to defuse the situation? In a public environment, one priority should be to move the person away from other customers. Sometimes supervisors may have to arbitrate disputes between customers and staff members; at other times, they need to stand behind the employee's actions. If an employee has been physically assaulted by a customer, then it may be necessary to summon security officers or the police. Some firms try to conceal such events, fearing bad publicity, but others feel obliged to make a public stand on behalf of their employees, such as the Body Shop manager who ordered a viciously ill-tempered customer out of the store, telling her: 'I won't stand for your rudeness to my staff!'

Telephone rudeness poses a different challenge. Service personnel have been known to hang up on angry customers, but that action doesn't resolve the problem. Bank customers, for instance, tend to get upset when learning that cheques have been returned because they are overdrawn (they've broken the rules) or that a request for a loan has been denied. One approach suggested by First Direct for handling customers who continue to berate a telephone-based employee is to say firmly: 'This conversation isn't getting us anywhere. Why don't I call you back in a few minutes when you've had time to digest the information?' In many cases, a breathing space for reflection is exactly what's needed. Where necessary, service managers need to be prepared to think on their feet and act fast.

The vandal

It's astonishing the level of physical abuse to which service facilities and equipment can be subjected. Soft drinks are poured into a bank's cash machines; graffiti are scrawled on both interior and exterior surfaces; cigarettes burn holes in carpets, tablecloths and bedcovers; bus seats are slashed and hotel furniture broken; telephone handsets are ripped off; customers' cars are vandalized; glass is smashed and fabrics torn. The list is endless. Not all of the damage is done by customers, of course. Much exterior vandalism is done by bored youths. And disgruntled employees have been known to commit sabotage. But much of the problem does originate with wrongly behaved, paying customers. Alcohol and drugs are sometimes the cause, psychological problems may contribute and plain carelessness plays a role. And there are occasions when unhappy customers, feeling mistreated by the service provider, try to get their own back. Finally, there are those charming people with a constant urge to carve their name on something, so that posterity may remember their visit.

The best cure is prevention. Improved security can discourage some vandals. Good lighting helps, as does open design of public areas. Consultants can suggest pleasing yet vandal-resistant surfaces, protective coverings for equipment and rugged furnishings. Better education of customers on how to use equipment properly (rather than fighting with it) and warnings about fragile objects can reduce the likelihood of careless handling. And then there are economic sanctions: security deposits or signed agreements in which customers agree to pay for any damage that they cause.

And what should managers do if prevention fails and damage is done? If the perpetrator is caught, they should first clarify whether or not there are any extenuating circumstances (accidents do happen). Sanctions for deliberate damage can range from a warning to prosecution. As far as the physical damage itself is concerned, the priority should be to repair it quickly (within any constraints imposed by legal or insurance considerations). The general manager of a bus company had the right idea when he said:

> If one of our buses is vandalized, whether it's a broken window, a slashed seat, or graffiti on the ceiling, we take it out of service immediately, so nobody sees it. Otherwise you just give the same idea to five other characters who were too dumb to think of it in the first place!

The deadbeat

Leaving aside those who never intended to pay in the first place (our term for them is 'thief'), there are many reasons why customers end up as delinquent accounts who fail to pay what is due for the service they have received. But once again, prevention is better than cure. A growing number of service businesses insist on pre-payment, any form of ticket sale being a good example. Direct marketing organizations ask for your credit card number as they take your order. The next best thing is to present the customer with a bill immediately on completion of service. If the bill is to be sent by mail, it's a good idea to send it quickly, while the service is still fresh in the customer's mind.

Not every apparent delinquent is a hopeless deadbeat. Perhaps there's good reason for the delay, perhaps acceptable payment arrangements can be worked out. A key question is whether or not such a personalized approach can be cost justified, relative to the results obtained by purchasing the services of a collection agency. There may be other considerations, too. If the client's problems are only temporary ones, what is the long-term value of maintaining the relationship? Will it create positive goodwill and word-of-mouth to help the customer work things out? These decisions are judgement calls, but if creating and maintaining long-term relationships is the firm's goal, they bear exploration.

Can firms restrict service to target customers only?

Many marketers would probably like to be able to decline requests for service from prospective customers who do not fit the market position sought by their firm. There are ways to discourage unwanted persons from requesting services – for instance, by insisting on certain standards of dress – but outright refusal to admit someone to a service facility may be viewed as illegal or unethical if that person has the ability to pay and is not behaving in a disorderly manner.

One of marketing's roles is to educate prospective customers in advance about the specific nature of a service, so they know what to expect and whether or not the service in question will meet their needs. This increases the chances of a satisfactory 'fit' between customers and organization. Sometimes, however, friction develops between customers and staff – or between different customers – and employees may have to play police officer and either resolve the problem or ask the offending individuals to leave the premises. In fact, some businesses have employees assigned specifically to this role, like bouncers at a bar. However, well-managed bars try to select people for this role who will be cheerful and helpful in their dealings with customers and only resort to a stern, security role with difficult customers when friendly persuasion has failed to solve the problem.

Creating and maintaining valued relationships

What is a valued relationship? It's one in which the customer finds value because the benefits received from service delivery significantly exceed the associated costs of obtaining them. For the firm, it's a relationship that is financially profitable over time and in which the benefits of serving a customer may extend beyond revenues to include such intangibles as the knowledge and pleasure obtained from working with that customer. Having a good working relationship between two parties implies that they relate positively to one another, as opposed to just conducting a series of almost anonymous transactions. In a healthy and mutually profitable relationship, both parties have an incentive to ensure that it extends for many years. And the seller, in particular, recognizes that it pays to take an investment perspective, justifying the initial costs of acquiring new customers and learning about their needs – which may even make the account unprofitable in its first year – by an expectation of future profits.

Relationships versus transactions

A *transaction* is an event during which an exchange of value takes place between two parties. One transaction – or even a series of transactions – does not necessarily constitute a relationship, since relationships require mutual recognition and knowledge between the parties. When each transaction between a customer and a supplier is essentially anonymous, with no long-term record kept of a customer's purchasing history and little or no mutual recognition between the customer and the firm's employees, then no meaningful marketing relationship can be said to exist.

With very few exceptions, consumers buying manufactured goods for household use do so at discrete intervals, paying for each purchase separately and rarely entering into a formal relationship with the original manufacturer – although they may have a relationship with the dealer or retail intermediary that sells them. The same is true for many services, ranging from passenger transport to food service or visits to a cinema, where each purchase and use is a discrete event. However, in other instances, purchasers receive certain services – or the right to those services – on a continuing basis. The different nature of these situations offer an opportunity for categorizing services as shown in Table 6.1.

Table 6.1 ■ Relationships with customers

Nature of service delivery	Type of relationship between the service organization and its customers	
	'Membership' relationship	No formal relationship
Continuous delivery of service	Insurance Cable TV subscription College enrolment Banking	Radio station Police protection Lighthouse Public highway

Discrete transactions	Long-distance calls from
	    subscriber phone
	Theatre series subscription
	Travel on season ticket
	Repair under warranty
	Health treatment for
	    HMO member
		Car rental
		Postal service
		Toll road
		Pay phone
		Cinema
		Public transport
		Restaurant

First, we can ask: Does the supplier enter into a *membership relationship* with customers, as with telephone subscriptions, banking and the family doctor? Or is there no formal relationship? And second: Is the service delivered on a continuous basis, as in insurance, broadcasting and police protection? Or is each transaction recorded and charged separately? The table shows the matrix resulting from this categorization, with examples in each category.

A *membership relationship* can be defined as a formal relationship between the firm and an identifiable customer which offers special benefits to both parties. The advantage to the service organization of such a relationship is that it knows who its current customers are and, usually, what use they make of the services offered (Superquinn stores, for instance, know how much each Superclub member spends on each visit and also the frequency of shopping at one of the chain's supermarkets). This information can be valuable, too, for segmentation purposes if good records are kept and the data are readily accessible in a format that lends itself to computerized analysis. Knowing the identities and addresses of current customers enables the organization to make effective use of direct mail, telephone selling and personal sales calls – all highly targeted methods of marketing communication.

The nature of service relationships also has important implications for pricing. Whenever service is offered on an ongoing basis, there is usually just a single periodic charge covering all contracted services. Most insurance policies fall in this category, as do tuition and residential fees at a college. The big advantage of this package approach is its simplicity. Some memberships, however, entail a series of separate and identifiable transactions with the price paid being tied explicitly to the number and type of such transactions. While more complex to administer, such an approach is fairer to customers (whose usage patterns may vary widely) and may discourage wasteful use of what are perceived as 'free' services. In such instances, 'members' may be offered advantages over casual users – for instance, discount rates (telephone subscribers pay less for long-distance calls made from their own phones than do pay phone users) or advance notification and priority reservations (theatre subscriptions). Some memberships offer certain services (such as rental of equipment or connection to a public utility system) for a base fee and then make incremental charges for each separate transaction above a defined minimum.

When no formal relationship exists between supplier and customer, continuous delivery of the product is normally found only among those free services that economists term 'public goods' – for instance, broadcasting, police protection, lighthouse services, and public roads – which are continuously available to all comers and financed from tax revenues.

Membership relationships usually result in customer loyalty to a particular service supplier. (Sometimes, however, there is no choice, because the supplier has a monopoly.) As a marketing strategy, many service businesses seek ways to develop formal, on-going relations with customers in order to ensure repeat business and/or ongoing financial support. Airlines create clubs for frequent fliers and hotels develop 'frequent guest programmes' offering priority reservations, upgraded rooms and other rewards for frequent guests. Many nonprofit organizations, such as museums, are creating membership programmes in order to reinforce the links with some of their most active supporters. The marketing task here is to determine how to build sales and revenues through such 'memberships', while avoiding the risk of freezing out a large volume of desirable casual business.

Discrete transactions – when each usage involves a payment to the service supplier by an essentially 'anonymous' consumer – are typical of services like transport, restaurants, cinemas and shoe repairs. The problem for marketers of such services is that they tend to be less informed about who their customers are and what use each customer makes of the service than their counterparts in membership-type organizations.

Managers in businesses that sell discrete transactions have to work a little harder to establish relationships. In small businesses such as hairdressers, frequent customers are (or should be) welcomed as 'regulars' whose needs and preferences are remembered. Keeping formal records of customers' needs, preferences and purchasing behaviour is useful even in small firms, since it helps employees avoid having to ask repetitive questions on each service occasion, allows them to personalize the service given to each customer, and also enables the firm to anticipate future needs.

In large companies with substantial customer bases, transactions can still be transformed into relationships by opening accounts, maintaining computerized customer records and instituting account management programmes that may involve a telephone number to call for assistance or even a designated account representative. Long-term contracts between suppliers and their customers take the nature of relationships to a higher level, transforming them into partnerships and strategic alliances.

The loyalty effect

Loyalty is an old-fashioned word which has traditionally been used to describe fidelity and enthusiastic devotion to a country, cause or individual. More recently, in a business context, it has been used to describe a customer's willingness to continue patronizing a firm over the long term, purchasing and using its goods and services on a repeated and preferably exclusive basis, and voluntarily recommending the firm's products to friends and associates. 'Few companies think of customers as annuities', says Frederick Reichheld.[11] And yet that is precisely what a loyal customer can mean to a firm: a consistent source of revenues over a period of many years. However, as Feargal Quinn recognizes, this loyalty cannot be taken for granted and his firm's 'boomerang principle' focuses management on the actions needed to keep customers coming back. Loyalty will only continue as long as the customer feels that he or she is receiving better value (including superior quality relative to price) than could be obtained by switching to another supplier. If the original firm does something to disappoint the customer – or if a competitor starts to offer significantly better value – then there is a risk that the customer will defect.

'Defector' was a nasty word during the Cold War. It described disloyal people who sold out their own side and went over to the enemy. Even when they defected towards 'our' side, rather than away from it, they were still suspect. Today, the term *defection* is being used to describe customers who drop off a company's radar screen and transfer their brand loyalty to another supplier. Reichheld and Sasser popularized the term 'zero defections', which they describe as keeping every customer the company can profitably serve (as we've already said, there are always some customers a firm is not sorry to lose!).[12] Not only does a rising defection rate indicate that something is already wrong with quality (or that competitors offer better value), it may also signal the risk of a coming fall in profits. Large customers don't necessarily disappear overnight; they may signal their mounting disaffection by steadily reducing their purchases. Observant firms record customer purchase trends carefully and are quick to respond with service recovery strategies – the topic of Chapter 7 – in the event of customer complaints or other service failures.

There are many possible ways to disappoint customers through service quality failures (see Chapter 12). A major source of disappointment, especially in high-contact service situations, is poor performance by service employees. Reichheld and other researchers believe that there is an explicit link between customers' satisfaction with service on the one hand, and employees' satisfaction with their jobs on the other. To the extent that service workers are capable, enjoy their jobs and perceive themselves as well treated by their employer, they will be motivated to remain loyal to that firm for an extended period of time rather than constantly switching jobs. Competent and loyal workers tend to be more productive than new recruits, to know their customers well, and to be better able to deliver high quality service. In short, employee loyalty can contribute to customer loyalty through a series of links that Heskett *et al.* refer to as the 'service-profit chain'.[13] This topic is discussed in more depth in Chapter 15, as well as in the Heskett *et al.* reading on pages 638–48.

Realizing the full profit potential of a customer relationship

How much is a loyal customer worth in terms of profits? In 1990, Reichheld and Sasser analyzed the profit per customer in different service businesses, categorized by the number of years that a customer had been with the firm.[14] They found that the longer customers remained with a firm in each of these industries, the more profitable they became to serve. Annual profits per customer, which have been indexed over a five-year period for easier comparison, are summarized in Figure 6.1. The industries studied (with average profits from a first-year customer shown in parentheses) were: credit cards ($30), industrial laundry ($144), industrial distribution ($45) and automobile servicing ($25).

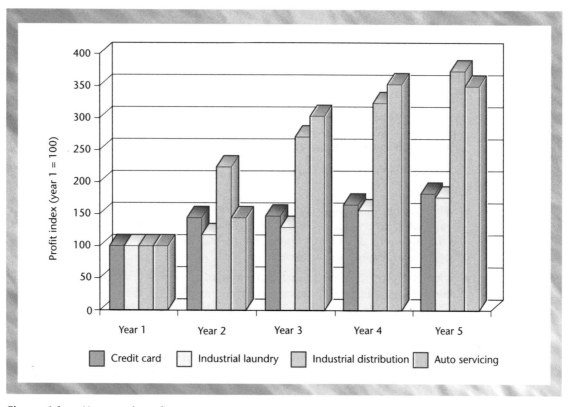

Figure 6.1 ■ How much profit a customer generates over time

Source: Based on data in Fredrick F. Reichheld and W. Earl Sasser, Jr, 'Zero Defections: Quality Comes to Services', *Harvard Business Review*, October 1990.

Underlying this profit growth, say the two researchers, are four factors working to the supplier's advantage to create incremental profits. In order of magnitude at the end of seven years, these factors are:

1. *Profit derived from increased purchases* (or, in a credit card or banking environment, higher account balances). Over time, business customers often grow larger and so need to purchase in greater quantities. Individuals may purchase more as their families grow or as they become more affluent. Both types of customers may decide to consolidate their purchases with a single supplier who provides high quality service.

2. *Profit from reduced operating costs.* As customers become more experienced, they make fewer demands on the supplier (for instance, less need for information and assistance); they may also make fewer mistakes when involved in operational processes, thus contributing to greater productivity.

3. *Profit from referrals to other customers.* Positive word-of-mouth recommendations are like free sales and advertising, saving the firm from having to invest as much money in these activities.

4. *Profit from price premium.* New customers often benefit from introductory promotional discounts whereas long-term customers are more likely to pay regular prices. Moreover, when customers trust a supplier they may be more willing to pay higher prices at peak periods or for express work.

Reichheld argues that the economic benefits of customer loyalty noted above often explain why one firm is more profitable than a competitor. Further, the start-up costs of attracting these buyers can be amortized over many years. For insights on how to calculate customer value in any given business, see the worksheet in Table 6.2.

For profit-seeking firms, the potential profitability of a customer should be a key driver in marketing strategy. Grant and Schlesinger declare:

> Achieving the full profit potential of each customer relationship should be the fundamental goal of every business . . . Even using conservative estimates, the gap between most companies' current and full potential performance is enormous.[15]

They suggest analysis of the following three gaps between actual and potential performance:

■ What percentage of its target customers does a firm currently have – market share – and what percentage could it potentially obtain? (If there is a large gap between a firm's current share and its potential, then it may make sense to develop strategies to attract these new customers.)

■ What is the current purchasing behaviour of customers in each target segment? And what would be the impact on sales and profits if they exhibited the ideal behaviour profile of (1) buying all services offered by the firm, (2) using these to the exclusion of any purchases from competitors, and (3) paying full price? (In many instances, firms need to examine opportunities to cross-sell new services to existing customers. Meanwhile, frequent user programmes that are designed to reward loyalty can help to cement relationships more tightly. Getting customers to

Table 6.2 ■ Worksheet for calculating customer value

Acquisition		Year 1	Year 2	Year 3	Year n
Initial revenue	**Annual revenues**				
Application fee[a]	Annual account fee[a]	___	___	___	___
Initial purchase[a]	Sales	___	___	___	___
	Service fees[a]	___	___	___	___
	Value of referrals[b]	___	___	___	___
Total revenues		___	___	___	___
Initial costs	**Annual costs**				
Marketing	Account management	___	___	___	___
Credit check[a]	Cost of sales	___	___	___	___
Account set up[a]	Write-offs (e.g., bad debts)	___	___	___	___
Less total costs		___	___	___	___
Net profit (Loss)		___	___	___	___

a If applicable.
b Anticipated profits from each new customer referred (could be limited to the first year or expressed as the net present value of the estimated future stream of profits through year *n*); this value could be negative if an unhappy customer starts to spread negative word of mouth that leads existing customers to defect.

pay higher prices than they have been used to, however, may be more difficult unless competitors are also trying to reduce the availability of discount promotions.)

■ How long, on average, do customers remain with the firm? What impact would it have if they remained customers for life? (As we showed earlier, the profitability of a customer often increases over time. Management's task is to identify the reasons why customers defect and then take corrective action.)

Many elements are involved in gaining market share, cross-selling other products and services to existing customers, and creating long-term loyalty. The process starts, as we suggested earlier, by identifying and targeting the right customers, then learning everything possible about their needs, including their preferences for different forms of service delivery. Consistently doing an outstanding job of satisfying these needs should lie at the heart of any service quality programme, as described in Chapter 12. The big challenge for service marketers lies not only in giving prospective customers a reason to do business with their firms, but also in offering them incentives to remain as customers and even increase their purchase – yet without the firm having to give away all the potential profits in the process!

Reinforcing loyalty by rewarding repeat users

Retail clubs such as the Superclub discussed at the beginning of the chapter are one of many different loyalty schemes offered today. Perhaps the best-known programmes for rewarding repeat users are those offered by most passenger airlines. The original 'frequent flyer' programme was established by American Airlines in 1983. Targeted at business travellers (the individuals who fly the most), this promotion enabled passengers to claim travel awards based on the accumulated distance they had travelled on the airline. Miles flown became the scoring system that entitled customers to claim from a menu of free tickets in different classes of service. American was taken by surprise at the enormous popularity of this programme. Other major airlines soon felt obliged to follow and implemented similar schemes of their own. Each airline hoped that its own frequent flyer programme, branded with a distinctive name such as 'AAdvantage' (American) or 'Mileage Plus' (United), would induce a traveller to remain brand-loyal, even to the extent of some inconvenience in scheduling. However, many business travellers enrolled in several programmes, thereby limiting the effectiveness of these promotions for individual carriers.

To make their programmes more appealing, the airlines signed cooperative agreements with regional and international carriers, as well as with 'partner' hotels and car rental firms, allowing customers to be credited with mileage accrued through a variety of travel-related activities. What had begun as a one-year promotion by American Airlines was soon transformed into a permanent – and quite expensive – part of the industry's marketing structure.

As time passed, airlines in the US started to use double and triple mileage bonus awards as a tool for demand management (the topic of Chapter 13), seeking to encourage travel on less popular routes. A common strategy was to award bonus miles for changing flights at an intermediate hub rather than taking a nonstop flight or for flying during the low season when many empty seats were available. To avoid giving away too many free seats at peak times, some airlines offered more generous redemption terms during off-peak periods; some even blocked key vacation periods like Christmas and New Year, making them ineligible for free flight tickets.

Competitive strategies often involved bonus miles, too. Bonus wars broke out on certain routes. At the height of its mid-1980s battle with New York Air on the lucrative 370 km (230 mile) New York–Boston shuttle service, PanAm offered passengers 2,000 miles for a one-way trip and 5,000 miles for a return journey completed within a single day. Bonus miles also came to be awarded for travel in first or business class. And bonuses might also be awarded to encourage passengers to sample new services or to complete market research surveys. In due course, many international airlines felt obliged to introduce their own frequent flyer programmes, offering miles (or kilometres) to compete with American carriers and then with each other.

To record the mileage points earned by passengers enrolled in their frequent flyer programmes, the airlines had to install elaborate tracking systems that captured details of each flight. They also had to create systems for recording and maintaining each member's current account status and to devise procedures for redeeming miles for free travel (some of these activities were often outsourced to independent contractors).

American Airlines was probably the first carrier to realize the value of its frequent flyer database for learning more about the travel behaviour of its best customers, enabling it to create highly targeted direct mail lists, such as travellers who flew regularly between a certain pair of cities. The airline was also able to examine bookings for individual flights to see what percentage of seats was filled by frequent flyers, most of whom were probably travelling on business and therefore not as price-sensitive as people travelling on holiday or pleasure trips. This information proved to have great value when countering competition from low-cost discount airlines, whose primary target segment was price-conscious pleasure travellers. Rather than reducing all fares on all flights between a pair of cities, American realized that it only needed to offer a limited number of discount fares, primarily on those flights known to be carrying significant numbers of non-business passengers. Even on such flights, the airline would seek to limit availability of discount fares by such means as requiring an advance purchase or an extended stay in the destination city, so that it would be difficult for business travellers to trade down from full fare to a discount ticket.

A number of other service businesses have sought to copy the airlines with loyalty programmes of their own. Hotels, car rental firms, telephone companies, retailers and even credit card issuers have been among those that seek to identify and reward their best customers. Although some provide their own rewards – such as free merchandise, class of vehicle upgrades or free hotel rooms in holiday resorts – many firms denominate their awards in miles that can be credited to a selected frequent-flyer progmmme. In short, air miles have become a form of promotional currency in the service sector.

Rewarding value of use, not just frequency, at British Airways

Many international carriers initially resisted creating frequent flyer programmes of their own. They were concerned not only about the expense, but also that these programmes required the airline to give award claimants free seats that could have been sold, during periods of high demand, to paying passengers. However, the competitive threat, especially on routes served by North American carriers, eventually became too strong to resist. Progressive airlines, such as British Airways, also recognized the potential of frequent flyer programmes for helping a carrier learn more about its best customers and for building brand loyalty.

British Airways (BA) created its own programme, known as Executive Club, in 1992. Unlike many programmes, in which customer usage is measured simply in miles, Executive Club members receive both *air miles* towards redemption of air travel awards and *points* towards silver- or gold-tier status for travel on BA and its partner airlines, including Deutsche BA, Air Liberté and Qantas (in each of which it holds a share). Travel on American Airlines also qualifies, but only on specified routes.

As shown in Table 6.3, silver and gold cardholders are entitled to special benefits while they are actually travelling, such as priority reservations and a superior level of on-the-ground service. For instance, even if a gold cardholder is only travelling in economy class, he or she will be entitled to first-class standards of treatment at check-in and in the airport lounges. But whereas miles can be accumulated for up to five years (after which they expire), tier status is only valid for 15 months beyond the calendar year in which it was earned. In short, the right to special privileges must be re-earned every year. The objective of awarding tier status (which is not unique to BA) is to encourage passengers who have a choice of airline to concentrate their travel on British Airways, rather than belonging to several frequent flyer programmes and collecting mileage awards from all of them. Few passengers

Table 6.3 ■ Benefits offered by British Airways to its most valued customers

Benefit	Silver cardholders	Gold cardholders
Travel insurance	Competitively priced	Complimentary in some countries
Lounge access	Club departure lounges	First class departure lounges and (if in economy) arrivals lounges in London
Immunization (UK only)	25 per cent discount at any of BA's 40 travel clinics in the UK	Same
Check in desk	Club (for economy travellers)	First (for economy or Club)
Reservations	Dedicated phone line, priority booking and waiting list	Dedicated phone line, priority reservations in Club, First and Concorde; top priority waiting list in all classes (see note)
Advance notification of delays	–	When flight delays exceed four hours and customer has provided contact number
48-hour ticket dispatch (UK only)	–	If purchased through dedicated phone line
Special services assistance	–	Problem-solving (beyond that accorded to other BA travellers)
Bonus air miles (US only)	25 per cent	100 per cent

Note: British Airways has branded its economy class as World Traveller on intercontinental routes and as Euro-Traveller in Europe. Similarly, business class is known as Club World and Club Europe.

travel with such frequency that they will be able to obtain the benefits of gold-tier status (or its equivalent) on more than one airline.

The assignment of points also varies according to class of service: BA seeks to recognize higher ticket expenditures with proportionately higher awards. Longer trips earn more points than shorter ones (a domestic trip in economy class generates 15 points, a transatlantic trip 60 points, and a trip from the UK to Australia or New Zealand, 100 points). To reward purchase of higher-priced tickets, passengers earn points at double the economy rate if they travel in Club (business class), at triple the rate in First, and more than four times the economy rate if flying Concorde supersonic service between London and New York. Likewise, passengers get class-of-service mileage bonuses for both Club (+25 per cent) and First (+50 per cent). In contrast, certain deeply discounted fares do not qualify for points at all.

To encourage gold and silver cardholders to remain loyal, BA offers incentives for Executive Club members to retain their current tier status (or to move up from silver to gold). Silver cardholders receive a 25 per cent bonus on all air miles, regardless of class of service; while gold cardholders receive a 100 per cent bonus; in other words, it doesn't pay to spread the miles among several frequent-flyer programmes! The airline also makes it slightly easier to retain existing tier status once this has been achieved. For instance, it takes an annual total of 700 points to qualify for silver-tier status and 1,700 points for gold-tier status, but once a traveller has reached that level, requalification requires only 500 points for silver or 1,200 points for gold.

Although the airline makes no promises on complimentary upgrades, members of BA's Executive Club are more likely to receive such an invitation than other passengers, with tier status being an important consideration. For obvious reasons, however, BA does not wish its most frequent travellers to feel that they can plan on buying a less expensive ticket and then receive an upgrade!

Of course, rewards alone will not suffice to retain a firm's most desirable customers. If customers are dissatisfied with the quality of service they receive, or believe that they can obtain better value from a less expensive service, they may quickly become disloyal. Neither BA nor any other service business which has instituted an awards programme for frequent users can ever afford to lose sight of its broader goals of offering high service quality and good value relative to the price and other costs incurred by customers.

Conclusion

All marketers need to be concerned about who their customers are, but this concern takes on added dimensions for certain types of services. When customers have a high level of contact with the service organization and with one another, the customer portfolio helps to define the character of the organization, because customers themselves become a part of the product. Too diverse a portfolio may result in an ill-defined image, especially if all segments are present at the same time. Abusive customers may spoil the experience for others and hurt profitability in other ways, too. So marketers must be selective in targeting the desired customer segments, and guidelines must be established for customers' behaviour while they are using the service.

For services that are capacity-constrained, the marketer's task is not only to balance supply and demand, but also to obtain the most desirable types of customers at a particular point in time. This may require targeting different segments at different times. For profit-seeking businesses, a key issue is which segments will yield the greatest net revenues. Public and nonprofit organizations, while not ignoring financial issues, need to consider which segments will help them best fulfil their nonfinancial objectives. In all instances, accurate market analysis and forecasting assume great importance in guiding marketing strategy.

Finally, marketers need to pay special attention to those customers who offer the firm the greatest value since they purchase its products with the greatest frequency and spend the most on premium services. Programmes to reward frequent users – of which the most highly developed are the frequent flyer clubs created by the airlines – not only serve to identify and provide rewards for high-value customers but also enable marketers to track the former's behaviour in terms of where and when they use the service, what service classes or types of product they buy, and how much they spend. The greatest success is likely to go to organizations which can give their best customers incentives to remain loyal, rather than playing the field and spreading their patronage among many other suppliers.

Study questions

1. What criteria should a marketing manager use to decide which of several possible segments should be targeted by the firm?

2. Identify some of the measures that can be used to encourage long-term relationships with customers.

3. What does segmentation have to do with capacity utilization? For what types of services is this a relevant issue?

4. Make a case both for and against the statement that 'the customer is always right'.

5. Select a people-processing service business, then pick two types of jaycustomer and develop strategies designed (a) to discourage these people from using your service in the first place, (b) if they have already begun to cause problems, to prevent them from causing distress to other customers and/or to employees, and (c) to minimize financial loss to your organization.

6. Explain what is meant by a customer portfolio. How should a firm decide what is the most appropriate mix of customers to have?

7. What are the arguments for spending money to keep existing customers loyal?

8. Evaluate the strengths and weaknesses of frequent user programmes in different service industries.

9. Review the methods used by Superquinn to keep customers loyal. Which of these might be adapted for use in other types of service business?

Notes

1. Based on information in 'Superquinn's Feargal Quinn', *Decision*, September 1997, pp. 16–19; Neil Raphel and Murray Raphel, 'Make Your Customers Feel Guilty', *Progressive Grocer*, June 1994, pp. 15–16; Larry Schaeffer, 'Boomerang Principle Brings Customers Back Again and Again', *Grocer*, 27 August 1994, p. 16; 'Where the Customer is King', *Progressive Grocer*, June 1995, pp. 73–4; and Des Crowley, 'Family Man', *Business Plus*, March 1998, pp. 12,14.

2. Feargal Quinn, *Crowning the Customer – How to Become Customer Driven*, Dublin: The O'Brien Press, 1990.

3. Christopher W.L. Hart, 'Mass Customization: Conceptual Underpinnings, Opportunities, and Limits', *International Journal of Service Industry Management*, Vol. 6, No. 2, 1995, pp. 36–45.

4. Roger Hallowell, 'The Relationships of Customer Satisfaction, Customer Loyalty, and Profitability: An Empirical Study', *International Journal of Service Industry Management*, Vol. 7, No. 4, 1996, pp. 27–42.

5. According to Paul S. Bender, *Design and Operation of Customer Service Systems* (New York: AMACOM, 1976), a lost customer reduces profits by $118 compared with a $20 cost to keep a customer satisfied.

6. Evert Gummeson, 'Relationship Marketing: Its Role in the Service Economy', in W.J. Glynn and James G. Barnes (eds), *Understanding Services Management*, Wiley: Chichester, 1995, pp. 244–68.

7. Theodore Levitt, *The Marketing Imagination*, new expanded edition, New York: The Free Press, 1986, p. 121.

8. David Maister, *True Professionalism*, New York: The Free Press, 1997, pp. 178–84.

9. This section is adapted from Christopher Lovelock, *Product Plus*, New York: McGraw-Hill, 1994, Chapter 15.

10. Abbie Hoffman, *Steal This Book*, San Francisco: Grove Press, 1972.

11. Frederick F. Reichheld, *The Loyalty Effect*, Boston: Harvard Business School Press, 1996.

12. Frederick F. Reichheld and W. Earl Sasser, Jr, 'Zero Defections: Quality Comes to Services', *Harvard Business Review*, October 1990.

13. James L. Heskett, W. Earl Sasser, Jr, and Leonard A. Schlesinger, *The Service Profit Chain*, New York: The Free Press, 1997.

14. Reichheld and Sasser, *op. cit.*

15. Alan W.H. Grant and Leonard H. Schlesinger, 'Realize Your Customer's Full Profit Potential', *Harvard Business Review*, Vol. 73, September–October 1995, pp. 59–75.

CHAPTER 7

Complaint handling and service recovery

Learning objectives

After reading and reflecting on this chapter, you should be able to:

1. Identify the extent of consumer complaining behaviour and the effectiveness of current service recovery practices.

2. Outline the courses of action open to a dissatisfied consumer.

3. Explain the factors influencing complaining behaviour.

4. Identify the principles of an effective service recovery system.

5. Demonstrate the value of a well-planned unconditional guarantee.

Why did the hotel guests turn down a free breakfast?[1]

An alert hostess at a Hampton Inn in California noticed that two guests from an Australian tour group were not taking her hotel's popular complimentary breakfast. On the second morning, she asked if anything was wrong. 'To be honest, the food is just not what we're used to at home,' they replied, describing a typical Australian breakfast.

When they came down the next morning, the hostess greeted them cheerfully. 'I think we might be able to give you some breakfast this morning,' she smiled, laying out items they had mentioned the previous day. She had made a quick trip to a nearby supermarket and added items from her own kitchen at home. The guests were thrilled, 'So this is what 100 per cent satisfaction means?' they asked. '*We* get to define satisfaction?' They were so impressed that they arranged to have the other members of their tour group, who were staying at another hotel, moved to the Hampton Inn. The two weeks worth of unexpected revenue from the tour group certainly was a more than adequate return on the extra time and money spent by the hostess to satisfy her guests!

Promus Hotel Corporation offers a unique proposition to guests staying at its more than 700 Hampton Inns: an *unconditional* guarantee of their satisfaction. Guests define satisfaction on their own terms and the hotel guarantees the customer-defined satisfaction – without negotiation. These two elements make the Promus guarantee extraordinary and provide Hampton Inn with a competitive advantage in its chosen market position. Since then, only a few competitors have imitated the Promus 100 per cent Satisfaction Guarantee. More importantly, mere imitation has not produced the results achieved by Promus, since they lack the supporting infrastructure, culture and, above all, the *attitude* that makes the guarantee more than a slogan.

Initially, the Hampton Inn guarantee was viewed as a proactive approach to what Ray Schultz, now president of Promus Hotel Corporation, referred to as 'the heartbreak of franchising'. Schultz was determined that Hampton Inn would not fall prey to the all-too-familiar deterioration of a hotel chain that had traditionally plagued the industry. He recognized how easily quality and service standards could slip as properties aged. And he knew how often investments in properties, either hard dollars put into capital improvements or so called 'soft dollars' put into employee training, for example, were compromised to support short-term earnings.

Further, Schultz recognized the inherent difficulty of maintaining quality standards across a large and diverse multi-site franchise system. He knew that the challenge would only intensify given the company's aggressive growth strategy to increase the number of Hampton Inns to over 700 in 1997. 'We cannot compromise the quality of Hampton Inn as we grow, because ultimately that would constrain our growth,' asserted Schultz in 1989, at a time when there were only 200 Hampton Inns. 'Deteriorating quality inevitably will result in declining guest satisfaction, lower guest loyalty and negative word-of-mouth. That's a recipe for further deterioration in revenue and operating cash flow. It is easy to lower service standards. But once lowered, it is very difficult to raise them.'

The guarantee has been so successful that Promus has extended it to other chains that it owns, including Embassy Suites and Homewood Suites.

Consumer complaining behaviour

'Thank Heavens for Complainers' was the provocative title of an article about customer complaining behaviour, which also featured a successful manager exclaiming 'Thank goodness I've got a dissatisfied customer on the phone! The ones I worry about are the ones I never hear from.'[2] Customers who complain give a firm the chance to correct problems, restore relationships with the complainer and improve service quality for all.

Although the first law of service productivity and quality might be 'Do it right the first time', we can't ignore the fact that failures continue to occur, sometimes for reasons outside the organization's control. You've probably noticed from your own experience that the various 'moments of truth' in service encounters are especially vulnerable to breakdowns. Such distinctive service characteristics as real-time performance, customer involvement, people as part of the product, and difficulty of evaluation greatly increase the chance of perceived service failures. How well a firm handles complaints and resolves problems may determine whether it retains or loses its customers' patronage.

The chances are that you're not entirely satisfied with the quality of at least some of the services that you use. How do you respond when you have been disappointed? Do you complain informally to an employee, ask to speak to the manager, file a complaint with the head office of the firm that let you down, write to some regulatory authority or telephone a consumer advocacy group? Or do you just grumble to your friends and family, mutter darkly to yourself and take your business elsewhere next time you need that type of service?

If you don't normally tell a company (or outside agency) of your displeasure with unsatisfactory service or faulty goods, then you're not alone. Research around the world has exposed the sad fact that most people do not complain, especially if they don't think it will do any good. And even when they do communicate their dissatisfaction, managers may not hear about complaints made to customer-contact personnel.[3]

Customer response to service failures

What options are open to customers when they experience a service failure? Figure 7.1 depicts the courses of action available. This model suggests at least four major courses of action:

- Do nothing.
- Complain in some form to the service firm.
- Take action through a third party (consumer advocacy group, consumer affairs or regulatory agencies, civil or criminal courts).
- Abandon this supplier and discourage other people from using the service (negative word-of-mouth).

Following through the sequence of possible reactions, we can see a variety of end-results, leaving the customer anything from furious to delighted. The risk of defection is high, especially when there are a variety of competing alternatives

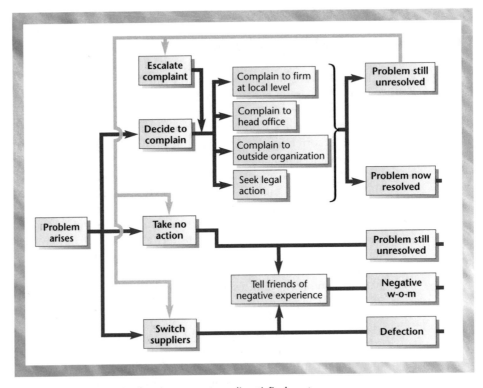

Figure 7.1 ■ Courses of action open to a dissatisfied customer

available. One study of customer-switching behaviour in service industries found that close to 60 per cent of all respondents who reported changing suppliers did so because of a perceived failure: 25 per cent cited failures in the core service, 19 per cent reported an unsatisfactory encounter with an employee, 10 per cent reported an unsatisfactory response to a prior service failure, and 4 per cent described unethical behaviour on the part of the provider.[4]

Managers need to be aware that the impact of a defection can go far beyond the loss of that person's future revenue stream. Angry customers often tell many other people about their problems. The Web has made life more difficult for companies that provide poor service, since unhappy customers can now reach thousands of people by posting complaints on bulletin boards or setting up web sites to publicize their bad experiences with specific organizations.[5]

The TARP study of consumer complaint handling

TARP is a research organization that has studied consumer complaint handling in many countries. In 1986, it published a landmark research study based on its own research and a detailed review of other studies from around the world. Its findings, which were widely publicized, prompted many managers to consider the impact of dissatisfied customers – especially those who never complained but simply defected to a competitor. Let's take a closer look at some specific findings.

What percentage of problems are reported?

From its own research and detailed literature studies, TARP found that when American customers experienced problems concerning manufactured consumer products, only 25–30 per cent of them actually complained. For grocery products or their packaging, the market research firm of A.C. Nielsen found a complaint rate of 30 per cent. Even for problems with high-priced durables, TARP determined that the complaint rate among dissatisfied customers was only 40 per cent. Similar findings come from other countries. A Norwegian study found that the percentage of dissatisfied consumers who complained ranged from 9 per cent for coffee to 68 per cent for cars. A German study showed that only a small fraction of customers expressed dissatisfaction, but among this group the complaint rates ranged from 29 per cent to 81 per cent. And finally, a Japanese study found complaint rates of 17 per cent among those experiencing a problem with services and 36 per cent for those experiencing a problem with goods.

Where do people complain?

Studies show that the majority of complaints are made at the place where the product was bought or the service received. Very few dissatisfied consumers complain directly to the manufacturers or to the head office. In fact, industry-specific studies conducted by TARP suggest that fewer than 5 per cent of complaints about high-priced durable goods or services ever reach corporate headquarters, presumably because retail intermediaries fail to pass them on.

Who is most likely to complain?

In general, research findings suggest that consumers from high income households are more likely to complain than those from lower income ones, and younger people are more likely to complain than older ones. People who complain also tend to be more knowledgeable about the products in question and the procedures for complaining. Other factors that increase the likelihood of a complaint include problem severity, importance of the product to the customer and whether or not financial loss is involved.

Why don't unhappy customers complain?

TARP found three primary reasons why dissatisfied customers don't complain. In order of frequency, customers stated:

■ They didn't think it was worth the time or effort.
■ They decided no one would be concerned about their problem or resolving it.
■ They did not know where to go or what to do.

Unfortunately, this pessimism seems justified since a large percentage of people (40–60 per cent in two studies) reported dissatisfaction with the outcome of their complaints. Another reason why people don't complain reflects culture or context. A study in Japan found that 21 per cent of dissatisfied customers felt awkward or embarrassed about complaining. In some European countries, there is a strong guest–host relationship between service providers and customers (especially in the restaurant industry) and it's considered bad manners to tell customer-contact personnel that you are dissatisfied in any way with the service or the meal. It probably never even occurred to the two Australians in our opening story to complain about the absence of an Australian-style breakfast in an American hotel. Think about a couple of occasions when you were dissatisfied but did not complain. What were the reasons?

Impact on repurchase intentions

When complaints are satisfactorily resolved, there's a much better chance that the customers involved will remain brand-loyal and continue to repurchase the items in question. TARP found that intentions to repurchase different types of products ranged from 69 per cent to 80 per cent among those complainers who were completely satisfied with the outcome of the complaint. This figure dropped to 17–32 per cent (depending on the type of product) for complainers who felt that their complaint had not been settled to their satisfaction.

Variations in dissatisfaction by industry

Although significant improvements in complaint-handling practices occurred during the 1980s and early 1990s in some industries, many customers remain dissatisfied with the way in which their problems are resolved.

Many service industries are still a long way from meeting their customers' expectations on service. (Of course, there can be considerable variation on performance between firms within the same industry.) Consumers in some countries, however, may be getting smarter and more aggressive about seeking satisfactory outcomes for their complaints. Recent findings from a large-scale study of consumer complaining behaviour in Australia showed that, among the industries studied, a majority of customers who had a serious problem did make the effort to complain.[6] The data in Table 7.1 show considerable disparity from one service industry to another in both the incidence of unsatisfactory service as well as in customers' likeliness to complain. As you review this table, ask yourself: Why are more Australians willing to complain about telephone service and other utilities than about restaurants and health services?

Other key findings from this study were that:

■ 57 per cent of respondents had experienced at least one problem with products or services within the past 12 months.

■ On average, 73 per cent of those respondents who had a serious problem took some action to have it corrected.

■ Only 34 per cent who took action were satisfied with the way the problem was resolved.

■ Among those who were not happy with their complaint outcome, 89 per cent reported they would not deal with the same firm again.

■ Complaining households made an average of 3.4 contacts each in an effort to have their most serious problems resolved.

■ The further up the management hierarchy customers had to go to get the problem resolved, the more their satisfaction declined.

■ On average a dissatisfied Australian customer told nine other people while a satisfied customer told only half that number.

Table 7.1 ■ Service problems and complaining behaviour in Australia

Service type	Percentage of respondents experiencing a problem in past year	Percentage taking action about a serious problem
Computers	27	83
Government (e.g. social services)	26	76
Car and motorbike repairs, service	24	75
Tradespeople	21	81
Investment advice	18	80
Housing (purchase and rental)	18	69
Banking	17	75
Public transport	15	52
Telephone	13	93
Restaurant/cafés	13	54
Health (medical/dental, etc.)	12	56
Professional services	11	68
Airlines and coaches	10	79
Accommodation	9	63
Insurance	9	74
Utilities (gas, water, electricity)	9	84
Entertainment and sport	6	59

Source: SOCAP-TARP Study of Consumer Complaining Behaviour in Australia, 1995.

Factors influencing complaining behaviour

When consumers have an unsatisfactory service encounter, their initial (often unconscious) reaction is to assess what is at stake. In general, studies of consumer complaining behaviour have identified two main purposes for complaining. First, consumers will complain to recover some economic loss, seeking either to get a refund or to have the service performed again (e.g., car repairs, dry cleaning services). They may take legal action if the problem remains unresolved. A second reason for complaining is to rebuild self-esteem. When service employees are rude, aggressive, deliberately intimidating or apparently uncaring (such as when a sales assistant is discussing the weekend social activities with colleagues and pointedly ignores waiting customers), the customers' self-esteem, self-worth or sense of fairness may be negatively affected. They may feel that they should be treated with more respect and become angry or emotional.

There are perceived *costs* to complaining. These may include the monetary cost of a stamp or phone call, time and effort in writing a detailed letter or making a verbal complaint, and the psychological cost of risking an unpleasant personal confrontation with a service provider – especially if this involves someone whom the customer knows and may have to deal with again. Such costs may well deter a dissatisfied customer from complaining. Often, it is simply less stressful to defect to an alternative service supplier – especially when the switching costs are low or non-existent. If you are unhappy with the service you receive from your travel agent, for example, what is there to prevent you from switching to a different agent next time? However, if you decide to switch doctors or dentists, you may have to ask to have all of your medical records transferred. This requires more effort and might make you feel uncomfortable.

Complaining represents a form of social interaction and therefore is likely to be influenced by role perceptions and social norms. One study found that for services where customers have 'low power' (defined as the perceived ability to influence or control the transaction), they are less likely to voice complaints.[7] Professional service providers, such as doctors, dentists, lawyers and architects, are a good example. Social norms tend to discourage customer criticism of such individuals, who are seen as 'experts' on the service being offered. A clear implication is that professionals need to develop comfortable ways for customers to express legitimate complaints.

Complaints as market research data

Responsive service organizations look at complaints as a stream of information that can be used to help monitor productivity and quality and highlight improvements needed to improve service design and execution. Complaints about slow service or bureaucratic procedures, for instance, may provide useful documentation of inefficient and unproductive processes. For complaints to be useful as research input, they should be funnelled into a central collection point, recorded, categorized and analyzed. Compiling this documentation requires a system for capturing complaints wherever they are made – without hindering timely resolution of each specific problem – and transmitting them to a central location where they can be recorded in a company-wide complaint log (a detailed record of all customer complaints received by a service provider). Coordinating such activities is not a simple matter, because there are many different entry points, including:

■ The firm's own employees at the front line, who may be in contact with customers face-to-face or by telecommunications.

■ Intermediary organizations acting on behalf of the original supplier.

■ Managers who normally work backstage but who are contacted by a customer seeking higher authority.

■ Suggestion or complaint cards mailed or placed in a special box.

■ Complaints to third parties – consumer advocate groups, legislative agencies, trade organizations and other customers.

The most useful roles for centralized complaint logs are: (1) to provide a basis for follow-up and tracking all complaints to see that they have in fact been resolved; (2) to serve as an early warning indicator of perceived deterioration in one or more aspects of service; and (3) to indicate topics and issues that may require more detailed research. Firms that find ways of centralizing complaint data often discover that this information provides a valuable foundation for additional market research, using sample designs targeted at a broad cross-section of customers including those who – for cultural or other reasons – might be reluctant to initiate a complaint. Personal or telephone interviews also offer much better opportunities than mail or in-store surveys to dig deeper and probe for what lies behind certain responses. A skilled interviewer can solicit valuable information by asking customers questions like: 'Can you tell me why you feel this way? Who (or what) caused this situation? How did customer contact employees respond? What action would you like to see the firm take to prevent a recurrence of such a situation?'

The Marks & Spencer retail chain enters details of all complaints on a database to allow relevant staff to see if problems are recurring. The company deals with all complaints on the assumption that they're genuine, and it periodically contacts a random sample of complainers to check on residual satisfaction levels.[8]

In their article, 'Listening to the customer: the concept of a service quality information system' (reprinted on pages 241–53), Leonard Berry and A. Parasuraman describe how to create ongoing 'listening systems' using multiple methods among different customer groups to find out what current, former and prospective customers are thinking, saying and doing.

Making it easier for customers to complain

How can managers make it easier for unhappy customers to complain about service failures? Many companies have improved their complaint collection procedures by adding special free phone lines, prominently displayed customer comment cards and video or computer terminals for recording complaints. Some go even further, training their staff to ask customers if everything is satisfactory and to intervene if a customer is obviously discontented.[9] The hostess at Hampton Inn was clearly very observant: she noticed that the two Australian guests missed breakfast two mornings in a row and sensed their disappointment.

Of course, just collecting complaints doesn't necessarily help resolve them. In fact, accepting complaints and then ignoring them may make matters worse! Although friendly sympathy from an employee is a lot better than an irritable shrug, the challenge is to have a well-designed service recovery strategy that empowers employees to resolve problems quickly and satisfactorily. At Hampton Inn, the hostess asked the two guests what they would normally eat for breakfast in Australia and then took the initiative during her free time to obtain the preferred items and bring them to the hotel.

Impact of service recovery efforts on customer loyalty

TARP argues that complaint handling should be seen as a profit centre not a cost centre, and has even created a formula to help companies relate the value of retaining a profitable customer to the overall costs of running an effective complaint-handling unit. Putting American industry data into this formula yielded some impressive returns on investment: from 50 to 170 per cent for banking, 20 to 150 per cent for gas utilities, over 100 per cent for automobile service, and from 35 per cent to an astonishing 400 per cent for retailing.[10]

Underlying these return rates is a simple fact. When a dissatisfied customer defects, the firm loses more than just the value of the next transaction. It may also lose a long-term stream of profits from that customer and from anyone else who switches suppliers because of negative comments from an unhappy friend. So it pays to invest in service recovery efforts designed to protect those long-term profits.

Efforts to design service recovery procedures must take into account a firm's specific environment and the types of problems that customers are likely to encounter. Figure 7.2 displays the components of an effective service recovery system.

Service recovery following customer complaints

Service recovery is an umbrella term for systematic efforts by a firm to correct a problem following a service failure and retain a customer's goodwill. Service recovery efforts play a crucial role in achieving (or restoring) customer satisfaction. In every organization, things may occur that have a negative impact on its relationships with customers. The true test of a firm's commitment to satisfaction and service *quality* isn't in the advertising promises or the decor and ambience of its offices, but in the way it responds when things go wrong for the customer. (Unfortunately, firms don't always react in ways that match their advertised promises.) Effective service recovery requires thoughtful procedures for resolving problems and handling disgruntled customers. It is critical for firms to have effective recovery strategies, because even a single service problem can destroy a customer's confidence in a firm under the following conditions:

■ The failure is totally outrageous (for instance, blatant dishonesty on the part of the supplier).

■ The problem fits a pattern of failure rather than being an isolated incident.

■ The recovery efforts are weak, serving to compound the original problem rather than correct it.[11]

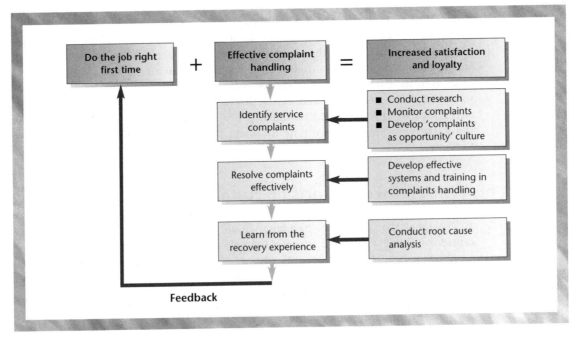

Figure 7.2 ■ Components of an effective service recovery system

Source: Christopher H. Lovelock, Paul G. Patterson and Rhett H. Walker, *Services Marketing – Australia and New Zealand*, Sydney: Prentice Hall Australia, 1998, p. 455.

Some complaints are made while service delivery is still taking place, while others are made after the fact. In both instances, how the complaint is handled may determine whether the customer remains with the firm or seeks new suppliers in the future. The advantage of getting 'real-time' complaints is that there may still be a chance to correct the situation before service delivery is completed. The drawback of real-time complaints (from an employee perspective) is that they can be demotivating. Dealing with them in real time can also interfere with service delivery. The real difficulty for employees is that they often lack the authority and the tools to resolve customer problems, especially when it comes to arranging alternatives at the company's expense or authorizing compensation on the spot. When complaints are made after the fact, the options for recovery are more limited. In this case, the firm can apologize, repeat the service to achieve the desired solution or offer some other form of compensation.

Principles of effective problem resolution

Recovering from service failures takes more than just pious expressions of determination to resolve any problems that may occur. It requires commitment, planning and clear guidelines. Both managers and front-line employees must be prepared to deal with angry customers who are confrontational and sometimes behave in insulting ways towards service personnel who aren't at fault in any way. Service recovery efforts should be flexible and employees should be empowered to use their judgement and communication skills to develop solutions that will satisfy complaining customers.[12]

The following guidelines for effective problem resolution are based on discussions with executives in many different industries. Of course, the service recovery process for a particular firm must take into account its specific environment and the types of problems that its customers are likely to encounter.

Guidelines for effective problem resolution

1. *Act fast.* If the complaint is made during service delivery, then time is of the essence to achieve a full recovery. When complaints are made after the fact, many companies have established policies of responding within 24 hours, or sooner. Even when full resolution is likely to take longer, fast acknowledgement remains very important.

2. *Admit mistakes but don't be defensive.* Acting defensively may suggest that the organization has something to hide or is reluctant to explore the situation fully.

3. *Show that you understand the problem from each customer's point of view.* Seeing situations through the customer's eyes is the only way to understand what he or she thinks has gone wrong and why he or she is upset. Service personnel should avoid jumping to conclusions with their own interpretations.

4. *Don't argue with customers.* The goal should be to gather facts to reach a mutually acceptable solution, not to win a debate or prove that the customer is an idiot. Arguing gets in the way of listening and seldom diffuses anger.

Guidelines for effective problem resolution (*continued*)

5. *Acknowledge the customer's feelings*, either tacitly or explicitly (for example, 'I can understand why you're upset'). This action helps to build rapport, the first step in rebuilding a bruised relationship.

6. *Give customers the benefit of the doubt.* Not all customers are truthful and not all complaints justified. But customers should be treated as though they have a valid complaint until clear evidence to the contrary emerges. If a lot of money is at stake (as in insurance claims or potential lawsuits) careful investigation is warranted; if the amount involved is small, it may not be worth haggling over a refund or other compensation. But it's still a good idea to check records to see if there is a past history of dubious complaints by the same customer.

7. *Clarify the steps needed to solve the problem.* When instant solutions aren't possible, telling customers how the organization plans to proceed shows that corrective action is being taken. It also sets expectations about the time involved (so firms should be careful not to promise too much!)

8. *Keep customers informed of progress.* Nobody likes being left in the dark. Uncertainty breeds anxiety and stress. People tend to be more accepting of disruptions if they know what is going on and receive periodic progress reports.

9. *Consider compensation.* When customers do not receive the service outcomes that they paid for or have suffered serious inconvenience and/or loss of time and money because the service failed, either a monetary payment or an offer of equivalent service in kind is appropriate. This type of recovery strategy may also reduce the risk of legal action by an angry customer. Service guarantees often lay out in advance what such compensation will be, and the firm should ensure that all guarantees are met.

10. *Persevering to regain customer goodwill.* When customers have been disappointed, one of the biggest challenges is to restore their confidence and preserve the relationship for the future. Perseverance may be required to defuse customers' anger and to convince them that actions are being taken to avoid a recurrence of the problem. Truly exceptional recovery efforts can be extremely effective in building loyalty and referrals.

Well-managed companies seek to act quickly and perform well on each of the ten guidelines discussed above. Research suggests that the slower the resolution of a service problem, the greater the compensation (or 'atonement') needed to make customers satisfied with the outcome of the service recovery process.[13] Treating complaints with suspicion is likely to alienate customers. There's a real danger in assuming that all complainers are what we called 'jaycustomers' in Chapter 6. The president of TARP (the company that undertook the studies of complaining behaviour described earlier) notes:

> Our research has found premeditated rip-offs represent 1 to 2 percent of the customer base in most organizations. However, most organizations defend themselves against unscrupulous customers by … treating the 98 percent of honest customers like crooks to catch the 2 percent who *are* crooks.[14]

Service guarantees

A small but growing number of organizations offers customers an unconditional guarantee of satisfaction, promising that if service delivery fails to meet pre-defined standards, the customer is entitled to one or more forms of compensation – such as an easy-to-claim replacement, refund or credit. Christopher Hart argues that these service guarantees are powerful tools for both promoting and achieving service quality for the following reasons:

1. Guarantees force firms to focus on what their customers want and expect in each element of the service.
2. Guarantees set clear standards, telling customers and employees alike what the company stands for. Payouts to compensate customers for poor service cause managers to take guarantees seriously, because they highlight the financial costs of quality failures.
3. Guarantees require the development of systems for generating meaningful customer feedback and acting on it.
4. Guarantees force service organizations to understand why they fail and encourage them to identify and overcome potential failure points.
5. Guarantees build 'marketing muscle' by reducing the risk of the purchase decision and building long-term loyalty.[15]

Many firms have enthusiastically leapt on the service guarantees bandwagon without carefully thinking through what is implied in making and keeping the promises of an unconditional service guarantee. Compare the following two examples of service guarantees and ask yourself whether you would like to be a customer of either organization.

Examples of two service guarantees

(1) Excerpt from the 'Quality Standard Guarantees' from an office services company
We guarantee 6-hour turnaround on documents of two pages or less . . . (does not include client subsequent changes or equipment failures). We guarantee that there will be a receptionist to greet you and your visitors during normal business hours . . . (short breaks of less than five minutes are not subject to this guarantee). You will not be obligated to pay rent for any day on which there is not a manager on site to assist you (lunch and reasonable breaks are expected and not subject to this guarantee).

Source: Reproduced in Eileen C. Shapiro, *Fad Surfing in the Boardroom*.[16]

(2) Example of L.L. Bean's guarantee
Our Guarantee. Our products are guaranteed to give 100 per cent satisfaction in every way. Return anything purchased from us at any time if it proves otherwise. We will replace it, refund your purchase price or credit your credit card, as you wish. We do not want you to have anything from L.L. Bean that is not completely satisfactory.

Source: L.L. Bean mail order catalogue.

Building company strategy around the service guarantee at Promus[17]

In general, North American service providers are well ahead of most of their European counterparts in their procedures for handling customer complaints and in developing service guarantees (there are, of course, exceptions to this general rule on both sides of the Atlantic). So it's helpful to study examples of best practices in the United States with a view to learning from their experiences. Promus Hotel Corporation – introduced in the example at the beginning of this chapter – has now instituted its 100 per cent Satisfaction Guarantee (see Figure 7.3) throughout its entire hotel system, including Hampton Inn, Hampton Inn & Suites, Embassy Suites and Homewood Suites, uniting all of the Promus brands with a single, common commitment to guest satisfaction.

As a business-building programme, Promus views the 100 per cent Satisfaction Guarantee as a great success. Its strategy of offering to refund the cost of the room for the day on which the guest expressed dissatisfaction has attracted new customers and also served as a powerful guest-retention device. People choose to stay at a Hampton Inn because they are confident they will be satisfied. At least as important, the guarantee has become a vital tool to help managers to identify new opportunities for quality improvement and creating the impetus to make those improvements. In this regard, the 100 per cent Satisfaction Guarantee 'turned up the pressure in the

Figure 7.3 ■ The Hampton Inn 100 per cent satisfaction guarantee

hose', as one manager put it, showing where 'leaks' existed, and providing the incentive to plug them. As a result, the guarantee has had an important impact on product consistency and service delivery across the Hampton Inn chain. Finally, studies of the 100 per cent Satisfaction Guarantee's impact have shown a dramatically positive effect on financial performance.

However, fully implementing a 100 per cent Satisfaction Guarantee is no easy task, as some of Promus's competitors who have tried to imitate its guarantee can attest. The boxed story is a pointed example.

How unconditional is your guarantee?

Christopher Hart tells this story of an incident at a hotel in a well-known chain during the summer of 1997, while accompanying his two cousins. Jeff and Roxy Hart were nearing the end of an extended holiday weekend. They needed to find an inexpensive place to stay. It was late in the day and their flight left early the following morning. Jeff called Hampton Inn and found nothing available in the area. So he called (name deleted) Inn, which had rooms available and booked one for $62 (€52).

We found the hotel [said Chris], noticing a huge banner draped from the bottom of the sign, advertising, 'Rooms for $55.95, including breakfast.' We went inside. After giving the front-desk clerk the basic information, Jeff was told that his room would be $69. 'But the reservation agent I just booked the room with quoted me $62. What's the story? And, by the way, what about the $55.95 price advertised on your sign? Can I get a room for that price?'

'Oh,' replied the front-desk clerk. 'That was a special promotion for the Spring. It's over now.' (It was late June.)

Jeff replied, 'But you're still advertising the price. It's illegal to advertise one price and charge another one.'

'Let me get my manager,' came the nervous response. Out came the manager. In the middle of the conversation in which Jeff was arguing the same points that he made with the front-desk clerk, Chris interjected, 'By the way, I understand you offer a satisfaction guarantee. Right?'

'Not on the $55.95 rooms,' came the reply from the manager.

'Well, what rooms is it on?'

'Only the good rooms.'

'You mean you have bad rooms?'

'Well, we have some rooms that have not been renovated. Those are the ones we sell for $55.95. But we're sold out of them tonight.'

Chris said, 'Well, Jeff, you'd better get one of the more expensive rooms, because I'm not sure how satisfied you're going to be tomorrow.'

The manager quickly added, 'Did I mention that the guarantee doesn't apply on weekends?'

'No,' barked Jeff, who had worked for fifteen years conducting cost-benefit and compliance studies for the US Government, 'and that's illegal too!'

'Wait just a minute,' said the manager, getting a puzzled look like something had just popped into his head. 'Let me see something.' He then buried his head into the computer, clicking away madly at the keyboard, creating the impression that he was working on our behalf. After an appropriate time, up popped his head, now with a big smile.

'One of the guests who originally reserved a $55.95 room, called and upgraded – but the upgrade wasn't recorded in the computer. I could let you have that room – but I can't guarantee your satisfaction.'

'We'll take it,' said Roxy, exhausted.

Successful implementation of the 100 per cent Satisfaction Guarantee requires that its underlying philosophy of guest satisfaction be embraced by every employee, from senior management to hourly workers. The challenge is to create a corporate culture based on a proactive commitment to consistently meet guests' expectations of 100 per cent satisfaction. However, despite its proven benefits, the guarantee has faced both resistance and scepticism among hotel managers, not only at Hampton Inn but also as it was extended to Embassy Suites and Homewood Suites.

Designing the guarantee

The first step in designing the guarantee at Hampton Inn was to answer a key question: 'What would guests want in a guarantee?' Research revealed that they were most interested in the quality and cleanliness of their accommodation, friendly and efficient service, and a moderate price. They also wanted a guarantee that was simple and easy to invoke if warranted. In-depth guest interviews yielded an 'ideal customer-interaction flow' and a map of 53 'moments of truth' critical to guests' satisfaction with their Hampton Inn stays. These moments of truth translated into concrete and controllable aspects of Hampton Inn's product and service delivery. Throughout the guarantee design process, an important new mindset was reinforced: listen to the guests, who knew best what satisfied them. Only the guests make the decision to return to a particular hotel or positively recommend a Promus hotel to others.

The vice-president – marketing, stated, 'Designing the guarantee made us understand what made guests satisfied, rather than what *we thought* made them satisfied.' It became imperative that everyone from reservations staff and front-line employees, to general managers and personnel at corporate headquarters, listen carefully to guests, anticipate their needs to the greatest extent possible and remedy problems quickly so that guests were satisfied with the solution. Viewing a hotel's function in this customer-centric way had a profound impact on the way Promus conducted business.

Concurrent with its guest-based qualitative research, Promus interviewed its most progressive and customer-oriented franchisees and hotel managers to understand their perceptions of the proposed guarantee. Even among those who fully supported the guarantee concept in principle, pressing concerns remained:

- 'Will guests try to cheat and rip us off?'
- 'Will our employees give away all our revenues?'
- 'What will be the return on our efforts to increase the satisfaction of our customers?'

To prepare for the launch of the guarantee, a pilot test was conducted in 30 hotels that already had high customer satisfaction. Training was seen as critical. First, general managers were trained in the fundamentals of the guarantee – what it was and how it worked. Then the general managers trained their employees. Managers were taught to take a leadership role by actively demonstrating their support for the guarantee and helping their employees gain the confidence to handle guest concerns and problems. Finally, the guarantee was explained and promoted to guests.

Even at hotels that already had a high-satisfaction culture, Promus found that front-line employees were not always *fully empowered* to do whatever was needed to make a guest 100 per cent satisfied. Further, employees did not always feel they were charged with explicit responsibility for guest satisfaction. They needed to understand that their job responsibilities would now extend beyond the functional roles they were initially hired for (i.e., property maintenance, breakfast staff, front desk).

Managers and employees learned that the guarantee was not about giving money away – it was about making guests satisfied. They learned that satisfying guests by correcting problems had to be a priority. Employees were encouraged to creatively fix problems 'on the spot', and rely on the guarantee as a 'safety net' to catch guests who were still dissatisfied.

After learning the basic guarantee concepts, and seeing the Hampton Inn 100 per cent Satisfaction Guarantee, general managers were asked to form groups of 10 to 12. Their charge was to list the positive and negative aspects of the guarantee on a flipchart. Few groups could come up with more than one or two pages of positives, but had little difficulty creating lists of negatives; one such list ran to 26 pages! Senior corporate managers went through each negative issue, addressing managers' concerns, one by one. The concerns remained relatively consistent and centred on management control. There were also concerns about guests abusing the guarantee and cheating (what we nicknamed 'jaycustomers' in Chapter 6).

As part of the feedback loop for all Promus brands, the company provides reports every quarter, showing the top five reasons for guarantee invocations. Managers are helped to develop clear action plans for eliminating the sources of guarantee payouts at their hotels. Coupled with an employee-awards programme for employees who had undertaken exceptional acts of customer service, guest satisfaction has increased substantially at those hotels where the guarantee has been most strongly embraced. Further, once the sources of problems were systematically eliminated, payouts became

Tracking down guests who cheat

As part of its guarantee tracking system, Promus has developed ways to identify guests who appeared to be cheating – using aliases or different satisfaction problems to invoke the guarantee repeatedly in order to get the cost of their room refunded. Guests showing high invocation trends receive personalized attention and follow-up from the Promus Guest Assistance Team. Wherever possible, senior managers will telephone these guests to ask about their recent stays. The conversation might go as follows:

Hello, Mr Jones. I'm the director of guest assistance at Promus Hotel corporation, and I see that you've had some difficulty with the last four properties you've visited. Since we take our guarantee very seriously, I thought I'd give you a call and find out what the problems were.

The typical response is dead silence! Sometimes the silence is followed with questions of how headquarters could possibly know about their problems. These calls have their humorous moments as well. One individual, who had invoked the guarantee seventeen times in what appeared to be a trip that took him across the US and back, was asked, innocuously, 'Where do you like to stay when you travel?' 'Hampton Inn', came the enthusiastic response. 'But', said the Promus executive making the call, 'our records show that the last seventeen times you have stayed at a Hampton Inn, you have invoked the 100 per cent Satisfaction Guarantee.' 'That's why I like them!' proclaimed the guest (who turned out to be a long-distance lorry driver).

less frequent. When this 'cycle of success' occurred at a specific hotel, its staff became 'guarantee advocates' who spread word of their success throughout the chain.

Over time, hotel managers have come to recognize two things. First, the number of people invoking the guarantee represents only a small percentage of all guests. Second, the percentage of cheaters in this group amounts to a ridiculously small number. As one manager admitted, 'It occurred to me that I was managing my entire operation to accommodate the half of one per cent of guests who actually invoke the guarantee. And out of that number, maybe only 5 per cent were cheating. Viewed this way, I was focused on managing my business to only 0.025 per cent of total revenues.'

Experience has shown that guests are not typically looking for a refund – they just want to be satisfied with what they pay for. And because Promus's 100 per cent Satisfaction Guarantee promises that they will be satisfied, it is a powerful vehicle for attracting and retaining guests. A 1996 survey found that:

- 54 per cent of guests interviewed said they were more likely to consider Promus hotels because of the guarantee.
- 77 per cent of guests interviewed said they would stay again at the same Promus hotel.
- 93 per cent of guests interviewed said they would stay at another Promus hotel.
- 59 per cent of guests interviewed have already returned.

Learning from the Promus experience

Among the reasons for Promus's success with its service guarantee are careful planning, listening to employee and manager concerns, an emphasis on training and a willingness to delegate more authority to employees. The company has evaluated the possibility that customers would abuse its service guarantee – making fraudulent claims so as to obtain a free night in a hotel – and determined that the incidence of such fraud is confined to a tiny fraction of its customers. Hence, customers are trusted when they register a complaint and a refund is cheerfully given on the spot. However, the firm's management is not naïve: there is careful tracking *after the fact* of all claims against the guarantee and any suspicious-looking pattern of repeated claims is followed up.

Guarantees need to be clear, so that customers and employees can understand them easily. Some services are more complex than hotels, so that the guarantee may be related to satisfaction with a specific activity rather than an overall performance. For instance, the Irish Electricity Supply Board (ESB) offers 12 clearly stated service guarantees in its 'Customer Charter', relating to such elements as network repair, the main fuse, meter connection and accuracy, and scheduled appointments (when an employee visits the customer's premises). In each instance, the ESB has established a service standard, such as a promised speed of response, stating the payment that will be made to the customer if the company fails to meet its promised standards. The charter is written in simple language and tells customers what to do if they encounter any of the problems covered by the 12 guarantees. Compensation payments range from IR£20–100 (€25–125) depending on the problem and whether the customer is a household or a business.

Taking care of the customers requires that management first takes care of its employees.[18] A sufficient number of well-trained and motivated employees is essential to providing good service in the first place and to undertaking effective service recovery efforts when things go wrong. Companies with a good reputation for customer care cannot afford to be complacent, especially in a time of rapid change. 'Downsizing' (a policy of reducing the number of employees to reduce costs) often results in replacing employees by automated equipment and taking a calculated gamble on the firm's ability to respond to customer problems.

Good reputations can be lost very quickly. In 1993, British Gas received an award from the prime minister for the excellence of its service, yet three years later the company was in crisis, with one manager admitting, 'We have now become a national joke'.[19] Following the government's decision to open the gas supply industry to competition, British Gas had undertaken an extensive reorganization, sharply reduced the number of its employees, and introduced new computer and telephone systems. Unfortunately, bugs in a new computerized billing system resulted in thousands of new customers receiving letters threatening them with disconnection before they had even received their first bill. Even worse, other customers paying by direct debit found that huge sums of money had been deducted from their bank accounts. Phone lines were jammed by angry customers trying to reach the company, but there were too few staff to take the calls, due to the fact that more than 3,000 experienced employees in customer service and support had been dismissed in recent years as part of a cost-saving campaign. Seeking to recover, the company announced it would spend £70 million (€98 million) to recruit 700 extra staff and open two new telephone answering centres. However, it lost significant market share to competitors as a result of the crisis.

Conclusion

Collecting customer feedback via complaints, suggestions and compliments provides a means of increasing customer satisfaction. It's a terrific opportunity to get into the hearts and minds of customers. In all but the worst instances, complaining customers are indicating that they want to continue their relationship with the service firm. But they are also signalling that all is not well, and that they expect the company to make things right.

Service firms need to develop effective strategies for recovering from service failures so that they can maintain customer goodwill. This is vital for the long-term success of the company. However, service personnel must also learn from their mistakes and try to ensure that problems are eliminated. After all, even the best recovery strategy isn't as good in the customer's eyes as being treated right the first time! Well-designed unconditional service guarantees have proved to be a powerful vehicle for identifying and justifying needed improvements, as well as creating a culture in which staff members take proactive steps to ensure that guests will be satisfied.

Study questions

1. Explain the courses of action open to a dissatisfied consumer.
2. Describe the factors that may inhibit a dissatisfied consumer from complaining.
3. Concerning the TARP study results described in this chapter, what are the implications for managers?

4. Think about the last time you experienced a less than satisfactory service experience. Did you complain? Why? If you did not complain, explain why not.

5. To whom would you feel most and least uncomfortable complaining? Why? How could the service providers in question reduce your discomfort in order to be sure of receiving important feedback from you and other customers?

6. When was the last time you were delighted with an organization's response to your complaint. Describe in detail what happened. Why do you think you were delighted?

7. Apply the four principles of service recovery at the managerial level to a service organization with which you are familiar. Describe how this organization follows/does not follow these guidelines. What impact do you see this as having on their customers' loyalty?

8. Evaluate the service guarantee introduced by Promus Hotels. What do you see as its main advantages and disadvantages?

Notes

1. This material is based on information in Christopher W. Hart with Elizabeth Long, *Extraordinary Guarantees*, New York: AMACOM, 1997.
2. Oren Harari, 'Thank Heavens for Complainers', *Management Review*, March 1997, pp. 25–9.
3. Technical Assistance Research Programs Institute (TARP), *Consumer Complaint Handling in America; An Update Study, Part II*, Washington DC: TARP and US Office of Consumer Affairs, April 1986.
4. Susan M. Keveaney, 'Customer Switching Behavior in Service Industries: An Exploratory Study', *Journal of Marketing*, Vol. 59, April 1995, pp. 71–82.
5. Bernd Stauss, 'Global Word of Mouth', *Marketing Management*, Fall 1997, pp. 28–30.
6. Society of Consumer Affairs Professionals (SOCAP), *Study of Consumer Complaint Behaviour in Australia*, 1995.
7. Cathy Goodwin and B.J. Verhage, 'Role Perceptions of Services: A Cross-Cultural Comparison with Behavioral Implications', *Journal of Economic Psychology*, Vol. 10, 1990, pp. 543–58.
8. Rhymer Rigby, 'The Alchemy of Complaint Handling', *Management Today*, April 1998, pp. 90–2.
9. Christopher W.L. Hart, James L. Heskett and W. Earl Sasser Jr., 'The Profitable Art of Service Recovery', *Harvard Business Review*, July–August 1990, pp. 148–56.
10. TARP, *op. cit.*
11. Leonard L. Berry, *On Great Service: A Framework for Action*, New York: The Free Press, 1995, p. 94.
12. Barbara R. Lewis, 'Customer Care in Services', in W.J. Glynn and J.G. Barnes (eds), *Understanding Services Management*, Chichester: Wiley, 1995, pp. 57–89.
13. Christo Boshoff, 'An Experimental Study of Service Recovery Options', *International Journal of Service Industry Management*, Vol. 8, No. 2, 1997, pp. 110–30.
14. John Goodman, quoted in 'Improving Service Doesn't Always Require Big Investment', *The Service Edge*, July–August, 1990, p. 3.
15. Christopher W.L Hart, 'The Power of Unconditional Service Guarantees', *Havard Business Review*, July–August 1990, pp. 54–62.
16. Eileen C. Shapiro, *Fad Surfing in the Boardroom*, Reading, MA: Addison-Wesley, 1995, p. 180.
17. Hart, *op. cit.*
18. Barbara R. Lewis, 'Managing the Service Encounter: A Focus on the Employee', *International Journal of Service Industry Management*, Vol. 1, No. 3, 1990, pp. 110–30.
19. Michael Streeter, 'How British Gas Became a National Joke', *The Independent on Sunday*, 29 September 1996.

The best shopping trip? How Tesco keeps the customer satisfied

Tim Mason

Using the findings from ongoing marketing research, a large British supermarket chain seeks to become more customer focused. Initiatives include offering greater value, improvements to store design and facilities, efforts to delight customers in small ways, creating a new culture of customer service, and introduction of a clubcard.

This paper describes a number of things that Tesco has done over the past years. It tries to put them into context and illustrate the threads that knit them together, and hopefully, to explain the sort of business that we are trying to be.

It stems back to 1993 when I was working in Retail Operations and was summoned back at short notice, to work for Terry Leahy, who was then Marketing Director. He was in the process of conducting research to understand why things were not quite as bright as we hoped they might be. We had been through a couple of years of rather bleak trading and we had to try and understand why, and then decide what we were going to do about it.

The extraordinary thing about our business is that we ended up deciding that we were actually in pursuit of a loss of 3 per cent of customers, which sounds tiny, but is in fact highly significant.

In 1993 Terry and I wrote a plan on the basis of a lot of research that had been carried out previously, to try and turn around the performance of the business.

An extract from the plan states our aim, which was that:

> In overall terms, we should aim to be positively classless, the best value, offering the best shopping trip. This will be achieved by having a contemporary business and therefore one that remains relevant by responding to changing needs. We should aim to be the natural choice of the middle market by being relevant to their current needs and serving them better, i.e. customer-focused.

The bits that we felt were really important were first that we should be customer-focused. We had done a lot of things in the preceding period to become more productive, more efficient, to squeeze more out of what we have got, and quite frankly we had got it wrong. So we said, from now on, every time we do anything, the final question that we will ask is *'what is in it for the customer?'* If we could not answer that question easily, then we would not do whatever we intended to do and we would go away and do something that *did* have something in it for the customer.

The second important phrase is *'responding to changing needs'*. One of the things that the customers said to us in our research, is that they like businesses that are innovative. And so we set about being innovative with determination. Another important phrase is *'the best value'*. It was pretty clear that whilst our offer was broadly acceptable, it was not as attractive as some, and we were asking people to pay, in their view, too much for it. So we were faced with the uncomfortable position of needing to get better and cheaper at the same time.

We were aiming to deliver the best shopping trip! Some of our competitors aimed to deliver the best prices, others aimed to deliver the best food, but we decided that the reason that people come to Tesco is that they come to shop, and shopping is an amalgam of a lot of different things. When I came into the business it was

This paper is based on a talk presented to The Marketing Society, 11 September 1996. Reprinted from *Journal of the Market Research Society*, Vol. 40, No. 1, January 1998, pp. 5–12.

a price/quality trade-off and price plus quality equals value. But consumers are actually a lot more sophisticated than that and roll a lot more things from the shopping trip into their calculation of value.

So we aimed to offer the best shopping trip. In broad terms that is made up of the prices that we charge; the promotions we run; the quality of products we stock; the types of stores and the way we lay them out; how accessible they are; how good their car parks are; etc. Essentially it is about where we actually locate the stores and the service that we offer.

We were looking to manage that amalgam of attributes in what became known as 'every little helps': Tesco's version of 'we try harder'; we wanted people to say 'Tesco is the best place for me to do my shopping'.

We embarked upon a number of initiatives. I am going to concentrate on some of the attributes more than others, starting with price. I am then going to move on to talk a little bit about stores, customer service and Clubcard.

Value

In 1995 I was on summer holiday, and I walked into our store in Barnstaple. The manager, true to form, had done a really good Tesco job and the place was full of blue and white packaged products. This was a direct response to customers saying you have got to get cheaper. We had looked across the core commodity markets and got to about 110 so that we could say to our customers, 'you do not need to cross-shop with the discounters'.

The Tesco shopper is a value-oriented shopper and the effect of launching those products started the turn-around. From almost the week that we launched them, the trade started to edge forward. We followed that up about a year later with 'new deal pricing', a phrase that never exactly took fire but we thought it was quite good at the time. That was saying that there are certain commodity products and major branded products which, with the best will in the world, we do not actually add any value to. So if you can buy that product at a competing store at a lower price, you are going to say this does not feel quite right.

We reduced the prices of quite a number of major branded items and brought them down to the lowest price in the marketplace. We then followed that up in 1995 with certain key lines on fruit and vegetables, notably bananas, when the share price in the retail sector seemed to have more to do with the banana price than anything else that was going on in the world and we went from 49p to 19p in the space of a few weeks. Slowly but surely we all saw reason and got back to a level of equilibrium, but we were all at the same price. That was the only time in my career that bananas were actually cheaper in England than they were in the States.

We then moved on from there, about a year later, to in-store bakery. A number of us in the trade had allowed Morrison's and as a result Asda, to sell in-store bakery products at much cheaper prices than ourselves. Morrison's had done it for years, it was a real feature of their business. We always managed to find an excuse not to match it – 'too expensive, throwing money away, we shall never make the profit', and so on and so forth. Eventually we just got sick of customers saying to us, 'well it's a nice store but your bread is too dear', so we reduced the prices of all our in-store bakeries which resulted in some very busy and tired bakers. But it had a very significant volume effect.

We then launched what we called 'Unbeatable Value'. We reduced the price on about 600 basic lines across a number of markets and said that we will not be beaten on the price of those products. If we are, we shall refund twice the difference to the customer. In addition to that, we said that our promotion is unbeatable value. But the important move is on the 600 core products.

It is about trying to get cheaper, as well as getting better and it is a measured and steady investment in the competitiveness of one's product. Unbeatable Value serves, we believe, to wrap up existing initiatives that exist. 'New deal pricing' can be consigned to the dustbin and this is the way of communicating this and our price position.

I think the situation is still competitive and will remain so. Ours has always been a competitive industry. I think it is likely to be so for quite a while to come.

Stores

We have tried very hard to improve our stores. According to our research, customers said 'well they're sort of nice but they are a bit sterile and a bit grey'. They *were* very grey, stainless steel, motorway signage; product location signage which you could not read, and did not tell you where anything was. The other problem was that not only were they grey, they were the most expensive supermarkets in the world to build.

We were faced with an interesting challenge of getting better and cheaper at the same time, and we managed to do it. We were able to simplify a number of things and we have reduced the cost of building our stores by about 30 per cent in the five years. Our research also tells us that they are significantly nicer to shop in.

We have developed a number of new formats. The first thing we developed is what we know as 'a Compact'. When Mr Gummer came along and said that one of the economic phenomena of the 1980s, the superstore, was no longer going to be given planning permission, it was a bit of a blow to those of us who made our living out of building superstores. The analysts felt it saved us from ourselves and it stopped multiples from building stores on smaller and smaller plots of land, until eventually we shared the same car park and slugged it out, pistols at dawn.

It was a bit of a shock to us. Fortunately we saw it coming and set about developing new strategies. 'Compacts' are a bit smaller than the standard superstore which sits on a main intersection on a main road on the edge of a large conurbation. These stores are capable of going into smaller market towns.

It also meant that we had to be able to build them for less. We have about 26 'Compacts' now. They are very popular stores and have enabled us to access new markets.

The second concept, 'Metro', is more familiar, particularly to people who work in London. This is going back into the high street. There are a lot of problems associated with serving the high street, which is probably why we left in the first place, but nevertheless, they are very popular stores. People like them, they have been very good for our image; they are busy and very popular and I am sure that we shall see more of these stores over the next few years.

A third concept is 'Express', which is a petrol station and convenience store and has also proved to be extremely popular What these different formats have enabled us to do is get into different markets, and they have enabled us, throughout the problems of managing the new planning environment, to open profitably and successfully, 600,000 square feet or so of new selling space a year, so that the new store element of our business has been able to be sustained.

It has been about flexible concepts: understanding how you can tune your brand to fit different elements of the marketplace.

The next thing we have done with stores is largely as a result of the planning environment. If you have got the best store in the best location in the town, and your competitors are not able to open against you, what you need to do is to make a more attractive asset. We are spending about £130 million this year improving and extending existing stores so that they dominate their marketplace more than they do today.

The crucial lesson is that you can spend millions of pounds making these places look nicer, but you have to return to the question 'what's in it for the customer?'. You have to put in more range and more service. So whether it is meat counters, hot chickens, pharmacies, leisure world, textiles – whatever it may be – you have to improve the offer so that people find the stores more attractive. Otherwise you spend millions, you open the doors, and nothing happens!

Service

We have a programme which runs in the business which we call 'Listening to customers'. We have as many ways as we can think of listening to customers, hearing what they have got to say and pulling it into some sort of shape so that we can actually do something about it. We use market research and I think we have got some quite good techniques for understanding what is happening.

We have Customer Panels. They started about three years ago. People are recruited as they come through the checkouts. They are then invited to come back. We organize the day so that we have a customer panel after lunch where we get the afternoon shopper. We then have some staff in to run a tea-time panel, followed by a panel with evening shoppers who come in at around 19:00. Basically the management team of the store, with one or two visitors from head office, sit at the front like Aunt Sally and just let their customers and indeed their staff 'throw things' at them. The outcome is a long list of things to do. This list is then put into two heaps: those things that can be done in the store and by the store – and hopefully they go away with great vim and vigour and sort those things out – and a list of corporate things, like trolleys that do not steer straight, and we go away and find some aerospace engineer to solve that problem.

The critical issue is to respond. You can listen, but are you actually going to do anything about it? That, for all of us, is the critical issue: when customers speak, do you hear, do you understand and do you do something about it? We find all the time that we have to drive ourselves to keep responding, particularly when more and more of the ideas customers are knocking are our own ideas, rather than somebody else's.

Our customer service strategy breaks down into three parts. The first part is *facilities*. Right at the beginning we launched 'The New Look'. What we said was, if we want to demonstrate to people that we are a customer-facing organization, one of the ways to do that is to put tangible things into the store that they can kick and touch, or remove them, so that they do not kick and touch them. The first thing we did was take the gates out, so customers walked straight into the store, instead of having those metal barriers that let you in and out. That is a big issue for the retailer, because the manager is concerned that stock is going to start walking out of the front door: it is not a small decision.

We put more checkouts into the stores where we needed them, we changed the signage to blue and white and we put in customer service desks. We actually had a suite of 100 facilities and we pulled one of our regional directors off the road and he went around the country, worked with the local people and then he decided what part of this package they needed. We spent anything from £20,000 to £500,000 giving a store 'The New Look'.

The aim was that customers would reach a point in a shopping trip and suddenly say *'Wasn't that thoughtful of them'*, *'That was just what I needed at the moment'*. The classic thing was the towel in the meat aisle. You pick up a pack of meat, your hand is sticky and you think *'I don't really want to wipe it on my trousers'*. Then suddenly at the end of the aisle, there is a towel and you can wipe your hand, and just think that somebody has thought of you, somebody understands shopping.

The next element of customer service strategy after facilities, is about setting measurable standards of operation and managing them around the store. The most obvious one for our industry was that people do not like queuing very much. We discovered, through research, that as far as the customer was concerned, as long as there was only ever one person in front of them, and they could start getting on with unloading, and they were busy, it was not a queue. So we coined this phrase *'One In Front'* which we launched in the autumn of 1994 and spent about £15 million, to try and be able to deliver the service.

That again was a remarkably successful initiative. One of the reasons we took so long to launch it was because it was very difficult to measure whether there was any benefit.

Service culture

Service culture is probably the most difficult and intangible of all, because people's ideas about what constitutes 'good service' differ so much.

In 1992 we launched an initiative which we called *'First Class Service'*, the elements of the customer-focused amalgam.

When you have 130,000 staff it is no mean challenge allowing people to look after their customers how *they* want to took after them. This was a remarkable initiative. It was launched by a colleague who made a speech to staff saying 'imagine, if you will, the best customer service in the world. What would it look like? If you want to be part of this, just give me a ring.' There was no launch date, there was no training manual, he just said '*if you want to be part of this give me a ring*'.

By the next day he had been phoned by 150 general managers, one of whom was selected. His was the first store that implemented '*First Class Service*' and it went from there. It is about a very different style from the command and control style and historically the way that certainly this retailer used to operate. It is about changing the way you manage your people, recognizing their achievements, and treating them as individuals, so that they feel encouraged to treat their customers as individuals.

It has been quite remarkable. The stories of what has happened have been extraordinary. If you have got a customer standing in your store, the relationship is quite close. It is easy to respond to that person as an individual. For those of us who work in our offices, or those people who work in manufacturing, the further and further you move away from direct customer contact, the harder it gets.

There was the story of the customer who came into the store and said 'I have lost my wedding ring in your recycling bin!' Dutifully three general assistants went out and they emptied the entire recycling bin all over the car park until they found this woman's wedding ring. You can understand she was fairly impressed.

There was somebody who got hold of one of our assistant managers in one of our stores on a Sunday, and said 'You've got the *Sunday Times* but you haven't got the Customer Service supplement.' They went through all the *Sunday Times* and there was no Customer Service supplement. So they said, 'no problem we'll get hold of one and get it to you'. She said 'Well I don't live that nearby and I am going out.' They took her name and address and promised to sort it out.

They rang around a few stores and eventually found one. Sure enough, when this person came in that night, there were two *Sunday Times* sitting on her

doormat. She wrote to the chairman and said this was fantastic service!

There are lots of things going on in Tesco like that every day. If that is what you want, somehow or another I will sort it out. How you get there, how you can do it can be very difficult,

The next thing we did was to launch Customer Assistants.

We spent £20 million purely to give service. Everybody else in our business has a function and this was a role that is something other than filling shelves, serving ham, checking out goods: these people are there simply to help customers. It is a philosophical development that is going on.

Clubcard

What Clubcard enabled us to do was to try corporately to see if we could not harness some of that individual relationship-building approach from the centre as well as from the branches.

We launched it as the 'Thank you Card'. One of our advertisements said 'Thank you Mrs Jarvis'. Mrs Jarvis wrote to me and said 'I couldn't believe that you had made an advert about me!' Clubcard has enabled us to do a number of things. It has enabled us to know who our customers are. Some of them spend £3000, £5000, £7000 a year with us. We ought at least to be able to say thank you.

We have issued about 8 million cards and we have about 6.5 million that are used in a six-week period.

It enabled us to thank people for their custom. They did not expect to be thanked. We gave away about £60 million in reward last year, and we were able to do so at slightly better than break-even.

It has enabled us to promote and indeed defend stores. It has enabled us to write and say to customers 'we are very sorry you have stopped shopping with us during this awful period of building. We can quite understand why you thought it was bad. But it's all over now I can promise you, so why don't you come back'. We did 130 variations of that last year, all based upon the fact that we knew who our customers were.

It has enabled us to form links with brands with other companies. We have been in partnership with B&Q on Clubcard. B&Q did a remarkable thing in suppressing their brand pride to work with Tesco in a loyalty scheme.

The next thing it enabled us to do remarkably successfully was to defend lost petrol volume as a result of the Price Watch campaign. The irony was that the loyalty systems were going out of the door that way, and coming in the door this way, and it just happened that it worked extremely well for us.

It enabled us to develop new promotional techniques, putting points on products. That has been quite good for us. It worked quite well and was very cost-effective. It enabled us to segment our customer base: we now have five different customer mailings, which are quite subtly targeted.

Clubcard makes us think about customers as individuals, and where we are incapable of thinking of them as individuals, at least we think of them in smaller segments. There is no such thing as an average customer.

We have now launched Clubcard Plus.

We found that we were able to put together a deal which was unbeatable. Five per cent on deposit, 9 per cent on borrowing and no minimum amount.

The reason why we were first with Clubcard is probably threefold. The first is back to the point about being innovative: we do aim to be the first whenever and wherever we possibly can, and the reason for that is that in our view the scenery only changes for the lead dog.

Customers realize that the person who does it first does it for customers, and the people who follow do it to neutralize competitive advantage.

So whilst they are very happy to receive the product or service from the followers, you never quite get the same image benefit you get by being the innovator and being first.

The second reason is because we know who our customers are and the third is because we have spent two and a half years thinking of customers as individuals and not as a mass.

I believe that that is the key to the future, which is going to be about an individual response to individual customers. It is no good talking about 'the best shopping trip'. You have got to deliver the best shopping trip for each and every individual customer. That is an enormously tall order and it has huge systems ramifications for a business like ours that is centrally controlled, and it impinges on the area of centralization versus decentralization. But that is where the customer will be won and lost in the next five or so years.

Our industry is extremely fortunate, because of its dynamics, to have data which are constantly refreshed. I think the challenge for us is genuinely to give the best service; not the best service in retail, but the best service, and that again is a challenge that we set ourselves and hope that we shall be able to meet.

For marketers, we are talking about better understanding and better response. This actually means better marketing, and that, at the end of the day, will lead to more loyalty, more custom and a better future.

Consumer behaviour and services: a review

Mark Gabbott ■ *Gillian Hogg*

A distinctive approach is needed for studying consumer behaviour as it relates to the consumption of services. This article reviews the literature to clarify the main issues for consumers in obtaining information about services, comparing alternative service offerings, and evaluating service encounters.

Introduction

Since the early work of Judd (1964), Rathwell (1966) and Levitt (1972) there has been increasing attention paid to the marketing of services. This interest has been motivated by a recognition of the importance of the 'services sector' and a need to understand the problems of marketing services more explicitly. Early work by Sasser *et al.* (1978) provided a clear articulation of the characteristics of services which distinguished them from goods and these provided an agenda for considering how the nature of services marketing differed from that of goods, as well as highlighting some of the problems associated with adopting goods marketing terminology and concepts.

The dominant feature of the existing literature on the marketing of services is its implicit management orientation, a concentration on how services are, or should be, marketed. This approach makes a fundamental assumption which this article seeks to challenge, specifically that consumer behaviour is unaffected by the nature of the product. While research into the consumption of services is sparse, this literature has already established a number of areas where the characteristics of services make accepted forms of consumer behaviour problematic. This article reviews the current services and consumer behaviour literature in order to clarify the main issues for consumers in obtaining information about services, comparing alternative service provision and evaluating the service encounter. Until the mid-1980s the dominant theoretical paradigm in consumer behaviour was the information-processing approach. More recently, experiential and behavioural perspectives have been recognized as providing realistic alternatives to the information-processing approach. While these perspectives may provide a means to amplify our understanding of consumer behaviour and services, the discussion in this article will take place using the information processing model in order to provide a means to synthesize service marketing and consumer behaviour literatures. This analysis highlights a number of aspects of consumer behaviour which need to be considered by service marketers.

Products, goods and services

As a first stage it is necessary to make a distinction between, products, goods and services. Marketing theory has been dominated by concepts and terminology derived from the marketing of goods. This orientation has endured despite a recognition that services have a number of unique characteristics. In as much as goods and services both provide benefits and customer satisfaction, they have both been described as products in the widest sense of the word (Cowell, 1991; Enis and Reoring, 1981) which has allowed services literature to develop based upon a sound marketing literature. However there has also been a tendency to use the terms 'good' and 'products' interchangeably with little attention paid to the service dimension which may have far-reaching implications for marketers. If it is accepted that services do have distinguishing characteristics, such as those identified by Lovelock (1981) and Booms and Bitner (1981) for example, then it is necessary to restate and understand the differences between a product, which can include both a good and service element, and a good which is defined purely in terms of its physical properties.

Most definitions of services are still framed in terms of differences with goods. The distinction is provided on the basis of a comparison of the dominant characteristics of each (Schifiman and Kanuk, 1991; Regan, 1963; and Blois, 1974). However, as Foxall (1985) points out, if services are seen not as a separate entity but only as a different type of product, the differences identified between goods and services are not fundamental but merely classification. What is needed is an appreciation of the dimensions of services which place different demands on both the purchaser and the provider.

As a way of highlighting the inadequacy of discriminating between goods and services Levitt (1972) argues that there is no such thing as a service industry, only industries where service components are greater. The distinction is between suppliers where the core of what they are selling is a service and suppliers that use a service element associated with a goods element as a competitive advantage, a theme developed by Grönroos (1978). The corollary of this argument is that all purchases of goods involve an element of service. Shostack (1977) argues that there are very few 'pure' products or services and describes a product continuum from tangible dominant goods to intangible dominant services. However, even within this approach there is a service element which is still indistinct from the good. Kotler (1991) provides structure to the continuum by identifying four distinct categories of offer: purely tangible goods, tangible goods with accompanying services, a major service with accompanying goods and services and pure services. A common feature of these approaches is a recognition that services have a number of distinguishing characteristics. These characteristics have been identified as: intangibility, inseparability, heterogeneity, perishability and ownership (Sasser et al., 1978; Shostack, 1977; Grönroos, 1978).

Service characteristics

Intangibility is one of the most important characteristics of services, they do not have a physical dimension. Often services are described using tangible nouns but this obscures the fundamental nature of the service which remains intangible. Shostack (1987) for instance points out that 'airline' means air transportation, 'hotel' means lodging rental. Berry (1980) argues that even although the performance of most services is supported by tangibles the essence of what is purchased is a performance, therefore as McLuhan (1964) points out, it is the process of delivering a service which comprises the product. The implication of this argument is that consumers cannot see, touch, hear, taste or smell a service; they can only experience the performance of it (Carman and Uhl, 1973; Sasser et al., 1978). The second characteristic of services is the inseparability of the production and consumption aspects of the transaction. The service is a performance, in real time, in which the consumer cooperates with the provider (Bell, 1981). According to Thomas (1978) the degree of this involvement is dependent upon the extent to which the service is people-based or equipment-based. The inference of this distinction is that people-based services tend to be less standardized than equipment-based services or goods producing activities. Goods are produced, sold and then consumed, whereas services are sold and then produced and consumed simultaneously (Regan, 1963; Cowell, 1984). The inseparability of the role of service provider and consumer also refers to the lack of standardization since the consumer can alter both the way in which the service is delivered, as well as what is delivered, which has important implications for the process of evaluation.

The heterogeneity of services is also a function of human involvement in the delivery and consumption process. It refers to the fact that services are delivered by individuals to individuals and therefore each service encounter will be different by virtue of the participants or time of performance. As a consequence each consumer is likely to receive a different service experience. The perishability of services describes the real time nature of the product. Services cannot be stored unlike goods and the absence of the ability to build and maintain stocks of the product means that fluctuations in demand cannot be accommodated in the same way as goods, i.e. in periods of excess demand more product cannot be utilized. For the consumer of services the time at which the consumer chooses to use the service may be critical to its performance and therefore the consumer's experience. Kelley *et al.* (1990) make the observation that consumption is inextricably linked to the presence of other consumers and their presence can influence the service outcome.

To the above characteristics of services, Judd (1964), Wyckham *et al.* (1975) and Kotler (1982) have identified the concept of ownership as a distinguishing feature of services. With the sale of a good the purchaser generally obtains ownership of it. By contrast in the case of a service the purchaser only has temporary access or use of it: what is owned is the benefit of the service, not the service itself, i.e. in terms of a holiday the consumer has the benefit of the flight, hotel and beach but does not own them. The absence of ownership stresses the finite nature of services for consumers, there is no enduring involvement in the product only in the benefit.

These separate characteristics which distinguish a service from a good have formed the basis of most analyses of services marketing. However, very few attempts have been made to consider these characteristics together in order to investigate their joint effect upon consumers' behaviour. Simply, we know that intangibility creates a problem for consumers in evaluation and choice, we also know that heterogeneity presents an impediment to learning and routinizing behaviour but the combined effect of service characteristics are still not clearly understood.

Consumer behaviour and services

With the developing interest in services and services marketing it might be expected that the consumer behaviour literature would include references to the evaluation and consumption of intangibles. However, there are very few examples of published work which refer explicitly to the consumption characteristics of services. There would appear to be an assumption, consistent with the interchangeability of terminology, that consumer behaviour related to goods is the same

as that related to products, i.e. the difference between goods and services is insignificant. In the case of products where the 'good' element is dominant this may be a valid assumption, but for products where the dominant characteristic is the service intangibility this assumption denies the significant impact upon consumption behaviour of the characteristics identified above.

As a vehicle for examining likely differences in consumer behaviour and services, a simple process model of consumer behaviour will be used, drawn from the dominant information processing perspective. This view implies that consumers first search for information about possible alternatives and attributes, selected alternatives are then compared on the basis of these attributes and once consumption has occurred the product is re-evaluated. Under each of these three process headings the services and consumer behaviour literature will be reviewed in order to provide some indication of the likely consumer responses to the problems presented by services.

Information search

The literature on consumer information activity in relation to goods is large and concentrates upon classifying the various sources of information (e.g. Beales *et al.*, 1981; Engel *et al.*, 1986; Westbrook and Fornell, 1979; Fletcher, 1987), the ability to assimilate information from these sources (e.g., Jacoby *et al.*, 1974; Miller, 1956; Keller and Staelin, 1987; Summers, 1974; Wilkie, 1974; Jacoby, 1984; Muller, 1984); the motivation for external search behaviour and the extent of that behaviour (e.g., Johnson and Russo, 1984; Urbany *et al.*, 1989; Bucklin, 1966; Moore and Lehlann, 1980). The characteristics of services which we believe place an additional information burden on consumers are associated with information sources used, the nature of information available from each source and the consumer's response to that information.

Commonly two types of consumer information sources are referred to: internal and external sources. The search of internal sources of information is characterized by Bettman (1979b) as a scan of memory. When faced with a purchase decision consumers first examine memory for information which may be relevant to the decision (Jacoby *et al.*, 1978). This information may be the result of previous experiences, which constitute a body of knowledge about, or an attitude toward, a product or a product class. If previous service experience is available this is an extremely credible source even if it is recognized that the experiences which comprise this information are event-specific and may not provide any clear indication as to future performance. The work carried out by Murray (1991) provided some support for this and pointed to a preference for internal sources of information in evaluating services.

Where information gained from previous experience is not available to consumers, or the information already held is considered insufficient to discriminate between different offerings, then the consumer may be motivated to search for information externally. This external information search implies a conscious recognition of the need for more decision-relevant information. The extent of external search is said to be dependent upon a number of factors, such as product category experience, product complexity or the degree of buyer uncertainty. On each of these dimensions, services are likely to prompt significant external search effort. In itself, this does not indicate any specific differences in the consumption behaviour related to services with that of goods. An alternative approach suggested by Murray (1991) is that in considering the degree of external information search it is inadequate to merely analyze the absolute number of sources used but more productive to assess source effectiveness.

The effectiveness of information available from external sources is related to the nature of services. Nelson (1970) identifies experience and search qualities of products where search qualities are those product attributes which can be almost completely determined and evaluated prior to purchase, for example, colour, size, price, etc. Experience qualities are those attributes which cannot be known or assessed prior to purchase but are determined during or after consumption. The more tangible the product the more dominant are the search qualities and the more intangible the less information is available before consumption. Services are therefore high in experience qualities and low in search qualities.

The implication for the consumer is that experiential information is perhaps the most difficult to obtain pre-purchase. The only sources of this type of information are pre-purchase trial, observation or reliance upon the experiences of others (Locander and Hermann, 1979). Pre-purchase trial is not an option in the case of services since they are produced as they are consumed and they therefore have to be experienced in total before they can be assessed, for instance it is not possible to try a haircut before purchase. Observation is equally unreliable as a source of information since the service is intangible and the participation of any other individual gives no guarantee of a repeated performance. As a consequence a number of authors (e.g., Murray, 1991) suggest that consumers look towards personal sources of information. This position is supported by Zeithaml (1981) who suggests that the need for experience information of the service prompts a reliance upon word-of-mouth sources as they are perceived to be more credible and less biased. This is also consistent with the work of Robertson (1970), Eiglier *et al.*, (1977) and Urbany and Weilbacker (1987) who indicate that word-of-mouth sources are pivotal in relation to services. As a consequence we can say that where service is a dominant element of a product, consumers face a number of problems, primarily in acquiring and using their own knowledge and also that the external environment cannot provide appropriate objective information. The likely response is an increased reliance on personal sources of information.

Comparison

The process of information search leads the consumer to an evoked set of alternatives that will form the basis of comparison and choice. The difficulties of obtaining effective pre-purchase information about services is likely to result in a smaller evoked set in services than goods. Zeithaml (1981) suggests that because of the nature of services and the difficulties in obtaining effective information consumers tend to be more loyal once they have found an acceptable alternative, for instance in the case of professional services like solicitors; indeed, if the consumer has previous experience of a service the evoked set may be as small as one (see Johnston and Bonama, 1981). However if the internal information is negative or the consumer does not have experience on which to base the choice then the size of evoked set will be dependent upon the effectiveness of the external information that was available. There are various models of how consumers choose between available alternatives in different situations, such as Bettman (1979a), Grether and Wilde (1984), Wright (1975) and Fletcher and Hastings (1983). The common component of these models is a set of attributes. There are two identifiable problems for consumers in defining attribute sets in relation to services, problems of identifying attributes and problems of making comparisons on the basis of these attributes.

All products have attributes or defining characteristics, in the case of goods these attributes are tangible, can be determined in advance of purchase and common to all consumers purchasing the product. By contrast in the case of services the attributes of provision are intangible, cannot be determined in advance of purchase and are not common to all consumers, i.e. the individual consumers' needs are accommodated by their involvement in the service delivery, for example, in the case of hairdressing where the consumer is involved in describing and modifying the service outcome. In the absence of any tangible indications of what the service will be like consumers must use other means of comparing services in the pre-purchase phase. Shostack (1977) and Berry (1980) point to the subsequent reliance upon peripheral tangible cues to predict quality. The more intangible dominant the service the fewer clues are likely to be available. Levitt (1981) suggests that in these circumstances it is necessary for consumers to establish metaphors for tangibility or cues that help them to 'tangibilize the intangible', in order that they may create a credible expectation. Various authors have pointed to the role of the environment in which the consumption of the service takes place in providing these metaphors or cues such as Bitner (1992) or Lewis (1991). These would include corporate wear, decor, appearance of

service providers, standard of equipment or furnishing and all may be used to approximate the missing tangible product information (Gabbott, 1991). The key problem for the consumer is identifying the cues which will most accurately predict the nature of the service experience.

The second issue for consumers is in comparing service alternatives on the basis of common attributes. Services cannot be compared simultaneously, but can only be compared in series, not parallel, i.e. a consumer cannot put two services side by side at any one time. Added to this time dimension is the problem of heterogeneity. The absence of truly common attributes implies that services are non-comparable products. Johnson (1984) suggests that faced with non-comparable product alternatives the consumer will search for the basis of a comparison by moving to more abstract product attributes, e.g. necessity, social status or entertainment value. In the case of services non-comparability is likely to evoke a reverse form of abstraction where services are compared on increasingly material or tangible criteria until there is little left to compare other than the service provider as the ultimate physical embodiment of the service.

Another characteristic of service dominant products is that some attributes are bargainable in the sense that they are determined between provider and consumer. Brucks and Shurr (1990) define bargaining as a process whereby two or more parties mutually define one or more attribute values for a product. For instance, in the case of insurance services the terms of the offering are negotiated before delivery. The bargainable nature of some service attributes serves to emphasize the uncertainty of the comparison process. This factor also has implications for the number of alternatives compared where bargainability reduces the number of alternatives as well as significantly reducing the number of attributes used in the comparison process.

Evaluation

A critical stage in the consumption process is the evaluation of the product after consumption as a means of building experience and knowledge as well as learning about the product class. Any product is evaluated on the basis of whether it fulfils the predetermined need and whether the outcome meets the consumer's expectations about how the need should have been fulfiled. In this sense there is a predetermined standard against which to compare the outcome. Several researchers have made a distinction between objective and perceived quality in evaluating products, e.g. Zeithaml (1988). Objective quality refers to the technical superiority or excellence of a product against measurable and verifiable standards. Garvin (1983) describes this as evaluation based upon amounts of specific attributes or ingredients, for example, weight, colour or size. Perceived quality can be defined as the consumers' judgement about a product's overall excellence or superiority. Quality is defined solely in terms of the consumer's perception which is a much more use-oriented approach to evaluation and is closer to the definition of service quality proposed by Zeithaml et al. (1990) as 'meeting or exceeding customer expectations'. The determination of satisfaction or dissatisfaction is therefore on the basis of a comparison between perceived quality and expected quality of the service experience.

Parasuraman et al. (1991) suggest that there is a fundamental expectation of a service; which is that it provides what it promises, i.e. accountants produce accurate accounts and dry cleaners produce clean clothes. This fundamental expectation has been described as a reliability dimension of service by Parasuraman et al. (1991) and by Grönroos (1991) as the technical quality dimension. This basic expectation generally relates to the more tangible elements of a product and as such it can be measured by the consumer in a reasonably objective manner. Swan and Comb (1976) make a similar point using the term instrumental performance to describe a minimum level of quality.

In the case of goods, what has been received is evident before its performance is evaluated. By comparison services are produced as they are consumed therefore the difference between goods and service elements of a product is that the consumer of a service evaluates how a service is received before it is clear what has been received. Once the service perfor-

mance is complete it is conceivable that satisfaction with how the service was delivered will be reviewed. This makes the process of evaluating performance, i.e. determining satisfaction or dissatisfaction much more complex in the case of services.

The problem with this approach comes when consumers do not have the knowledge or experience to evaluate what they have received or that their expectations of what they wanted from the service are not clear. Darby and Karni (1973) refer to these as the credence qualities, these are characteristics of a product that the consumer finds difficult to evaluate even after purchase and consumption. In these circumstances how a service was delivered may be used to evaluate what was delivered, this is referred to by Grönroos as the functional quality, or by Swan and Comb (1976) as expressive performance. Parasuraman et al. (1991) refer to both as process dimensions and argue that these dimensions are usually evaluated as the service is delivered. Process dimensions have been described as service responsiveness (willingness to help), assurance (knowledge and courtesy of providers), and empathy (the caring individualized relationship between provider and consumer) and the signs, symbols and artefacts of delivery (signposting, decor, personal presentation) (Zeithaml, 1981; Bitner, 1992). These dimensions added to the reliability of the delivered service and form five dimensions of service quality identified by Zeithaml et al. (1990). This research suggests that although reliability ('the what') is important in meeting customer expectations the process dimensions ('the how') are the most important in exceeding customer expectations. The 'how' dimensions are almost invariably associated with the individual service provider.

In terms of satisfaction, the way in which the consumer participates in the service will influence his evaluation of the service received. Customers may be required to participate in the definition and production of the service and may therefore feel personally involved in the success or failure of the outcome (Zeithaml, 1981). If a consumer cannot or does not clearly articulate or understand their own requirements, or has formed unrealistic expectations of the service then they may feel that some responsibility for the failure was their own. Therefore the process of evaluating services in terms of satisfaction and dissatisfaction is a shared responsibility between provider and consumer.

Discussion

This article has suggested that acquiring information, choice and the evaluation of services present a number of problems for consumers. These problems are derived from the nature of services in particular their intangibility and their heterogeneity. In the first stage of the simple process model, information is difficult to obtain since the service is intangible and there is no objective information that the consumer can obtain other than relying upon personal experience. However, since service experiences vary across consumers and across time so experience information either from self or others can only be a guide to future performance rather than a predictor. Other information gained from search has to be tempered by the evaluation of the source of the information. As such information effectiveness for the consumer of services is questionable.

The second problem for consumers is in comparing service alternatives. Again intangibility and heterogeneity present the main impediments to the effective assessment of future performance. What is being assessed in the case of a service is the perceived benefit from the service rather than the service itself. The consumer is choosing between their own subjective assessments of the likely service outcome. Comparison is hampered further by the heterogeneity of service provision and the difficulties in identifying or generating attributes upon which to base a choice. Finally, once the service has been initiated either by purchase, by acceptance or instruction there are problems in evaluating what is being, or what has been provided. In this context the role of expectations are pivotal. It has been argued that failure to achieve satisfaction from a service is as much the responsibility of the consumer as the provider in not identifying precise needs, yet it must also be recognized that consumers may not have a precise set of needs to communicate and this is central to the delivery of satisfaction and benefit.

The description of services as problematic for consumers is a theme which is common across a broad range of literature. Most suggestions propose marketing responses tackling some of the fundamental characteristics of services. These include making services appear less intangible by focusing upon physical dimensions, or less heterogeneous through standardized delivery or by recognizing the importance of word-of-mouth information sources using such techniques as personal endorsement. However, little attention has been paid to the likely consumer responses to the problems presented by services.

Responses

It is generally accepted that consumers are ultimately seeking to simplify or routinize their purchase decisions at the same time as minimizing the level of risk attached to the outcome. In relation to goods two key responses have been identified: first, the reliance upon product cues which are used to approximate missing information or predict likely outcomes and second, the reliance upon inertia or loyalty built upon satisfaction in order to routinize the consumption decision. However, both these responses need to be examined in the light of the characteristics of services.

Existing work on product cues associated with goods has tended to concentrate upon the identification of cues used by the consumer. A number of studies have identified brand name, origin or price as active cues. The basis of this analysis is that goods have a finite number of available attributes which can serve as prepurchase clues for the consumer. In the case of services the range of cues is much wider since they are present in all tangible accompaniments to the service, i.e. provider, artefacts, premises or goods components. If the range of cues available prepurchase is wider than that associated with goods and the cues are also uniquely associated with each service. The presence of variable cues both within service products and across service products do not provide support for the simplification function of cues for the consumer. A second implicit assumption associated with product cues is the ability to justify or prove their worth. Since tangible cues vary from provider to provider and form a small part of the service experience, the effectiveness of individual cues is likely to vary from provider to provider. Finally, product cues in relation to goods are used pre-purchase and their value assessed post-purchase. Where services are concerned the delivery may take place at a different time, with a different provider, with different tangibles or in a different place to the purchase transaction. As a result cues used to evaluate a service pre-purchase may be different to those used to evaluate during delivery or even after delivery has taken place.

The second response of consumers in relation to goods is brand or product loyalty which is one form of routinizing purchase behaviour. In the case of services loyalty can only be placed with the provider of the service rather than the service itself, i.e. it is theoretically impossible to obtain the same service from a different provider. Loyalty is built up from a series of successful service encounters with the same provider and the number of consumers with successful encounters builds reputation. An aspect of loyalty in relation to services which is different to that of goods is the potential to cement a relationship between customer and provider. We have identified above the inability in some circumstances of the consumer to accurately vocalize or identify needs and expectations. Subsequent service encounters allow needs and expectations of the consumer to be synchronized with the abilities and performance of the provider. This process of repeat purchasing is likely to result in the continued and increment strengthening of service relationships where the consumer is able to take full advantage of the potential benefits offered. In the case of goods the relationship is likely to plateau once all benefits have been experienced and may in some circumstances start to decline. It is evident that this continued relationship also produces a sense of ownership over the service with consumers referring to 'my accountant', 'my hairdresser', or 'my mechanic'. Equally this may have an impact upon attribution in the case of failure. The amount of investment in the relationship may lead consumers to rationalize failures on the basis of 'just a bad day', since they have experienced better or that it is their own fault in not correctly communicating needs. Either way relationships are likely to be more stable in the case of services than goods.

Conclusion

This article has investigated the implications for consumer behaviour presented by services as opposed to goods. It has concluded that services present a number of problems for consumers and also that suggested consumer responses in relation to goods may not be applicable to services. Specifically that there is a body of knowledge which explains consumer behaviour in relation to goods and that this body of knowledge suggests problems for consumers in choosing and evaluating services. It also suggests a number of responses to these problems which are again derived from this goods perspective. The final consideration is that the whole argument is being framed within the rational information processing perspective of consumer behaviour. Either consumer problems in relation to services need to be more fully explored within this framework or research will need to move outside this perspective perhaps towards examining the personal relationship between provider and consumer such as the degree of empathy or sympathy or explore the alternative behavioural perspectives. These may provide a means to integrate service design, service encounter and service consumption which emerge as crucial to service marketing. This article has endeavoured to concentrate upon consumer behaviour rather than reiterate the managerial implications of service characteristics which form the basis of a substantial part of the services literature. It is our contention that unless consumer behaviour and in particular consumer responses to the problems associated with service are clarified, service marketing may be in danger of pursuing provider-oriented solutions to the problems perceived to be faced by consumers rather than truly understanding the nature of consumer decision processes or the reality of consumer behaviour.

References

Beales, H., Mazis M., Salop S. and Staelin, R. (1981) 'Consumer Search and Public Policy', *Journal Of Consumer Research* **8** (June): 11–22.

Bell, M. L. (1981) 'A Matrix Approach to the Classification of Marketing Goods and Services', In *Marketing of Services* (J. H. Donnelly and W. R. George, eds). Chicago: AMA.

Berry, L. L. (1980) 'Services Marketing is Different', *Business* (May–June): 24–9.

Bettman, J. R. (1979a) *An Information Processing Theory of Consumer Choice*, Massachusetts, Addison-Wesley.

Bettman, J. R. (1979b) 'Memory Factors in Consumer Choice: A Review', *Journal of Marketing* 43: 37–53.

Bitner, M. J. (1992) 'Servicescapes: The Impact of Physical Surroundings on Customers and Employees', *Journal of Marketing* 56 57–71.

Blois, K. J. (1974) 'The Marketing of Services: An Approach'. *European Journal of Marketing* 8 (Summer): 137–45.

Booms, B. H. and Bitner, M. J. (1981) 'Marketing Strategies and Organizational Structures for Service Firms', in *Marketing of Services* (J. H. Donnelly and W. R. George, eds). Chicago: AMA.

Brucks, M. and Schurr, P. (1990) 'The Effects of Bargainable Attributes and Attribute Range Knowledge on Consumer Choice Processes', *Journal of Consumer Research* 16 (March): 409–19.

Bucklin, L. (1966) 'Testing Propensities to Shop', *Journal of Marketing* (January): 22–7.

Carman, J. and Uhl, K. (1973) *Marketing Principles and Methods*, Homewood, IL: Irwin.

Cowell, D. (1984) *The Marketing of Services*, London: Heinemann.

Cowell, D. W. (1991) 'Marketing Services', in *The Marketing Book* (M. J. Baker, ed.). Oxford, Butterworth Heinemann.

Darby, M. R. and Karni, E. (1973) 'Free Competition and the Optimal Amount of Fraud', *Journal of Law and Economics* 16 (April): 67–86.

Eiglier, P., Langeard, E., Lovelock, C., Bateson, J. and Young, R. (1977) *Marketing Consumer Services: New Insights*. Cambridge, MA: Marketing Science Institute.

Engel, J., Blackwell, R. and Miniard, P. (1986) *Consumer Behaviour*. New York: Dryden.

Enis, B. M. and Roering, K. (1981) 'Services Marketing: Different Products, Similar Strategies', in *Marketing of Services* (J. H. Donnelly and W. R. George, eds). Chicago: AMA.

Fletcher, K. and Hastings, W. (1983) 'The Relevance of the Fishbein Model to Insurance Buying', *Service Industries Journal* 3 (No. 3): 296–307.

Fletcher, K. (1987) 'Consumers' Use and Perceptions of Retailer Controlled Information Sources', *International Journal of Retailing* 2 (No. 3): 59–66.

Foxall, G. (1985) 'Marketing is Service Marketing', in *Marketing in the Service Industries*. London: Frank Cass.

Gabbott, M. (1991) 'The Role of Product Cues in Assessing Risk in Second Hand Markets', *European Journal of Marketing* 25 (No. 9): 38–50.

Garvin, D. (1983) 'Quality on the Line', *Harvard Business Review* 61 (Sept–Oct): 65–73.

Grether, D. and Wilde, L. (1984) 'An Analysis of Conjunctive Choice: Theory and Experiments', *Journal of Consumer Research* 10 (March): 373–85.

Grönroos, C. (1978) 'A Service Orientated Approach to Marketing Services', *European Journal of Marketing* 12 (No. 8): 589.

Grönroos, C. (1991) *Strategic Management and Marketing in the Services Sector*. Studentlitteratur: Lund, Sweden.

Jacoby, J. (1984) 'Perspectives on Information Overload', *Journal of Consumer Research* 10 (March).

Jacoby, J., Chestnut, R. and Fisher, W. (1978) 'A Behavioural Process Approach to Information Acquisition in Nondurable Purchasing', *Journal of Marketing Research* 15 (No. 3, August): 532–44.

Jacoby, J., Speller, D. and Berning, C. (1974) 'Brand Choice Behaviour as a Function of Information Load: Replication and Extension', *Journal of Consumer Research* 1: 33–42.

Johnson, E. and Russo, J. E. (1984) 'Product Familiarity and Learning New Information', *Journal of Consumer Research* 11 (June): 542–50.

Johnson, M. (1984) 'Consumer Choice Strategies for Comparing Noncomparable Alternatives', *Journal of Consumer Research* 11 (December): 741–53.

Johnston, W. and Bonoma T. (1981) 'Purchase Process for Capital Equipment and Services', *Industrial Marketing* 4: 253–64.

Judd, R. C. (1964) 'The Case for Redefining Services', *Journal of Marketing* 28: 59–73.

Keller, K. and Staelin, R. (1987) 'Effects of Quality and Quantity of Information on Decision Effectiveness', *Journal of Consumer Research* 14 (September): 200–13.

Kelley, S. W., Donnelly, J. H. and Skinner, S. J. (1990) 'Customer Participation in Service Production and Delivery', *Journal of Retailing* 66 (No. 3): 315–35.

Kotler, P. (1982) *Principles of Marketing*. New Jersey: Prentice-Hall.

Kotler, P. (1991) *Marketing Management*. New Jersey: Prentice-Hall.

Levitt, T. (1972) 'Production-line Approach to Service', *Harvard Business Review* (Sept–Oct): 41–52.

Levitt, T. (1981) 'Marketing Intangible Products and Product Intangibles', *Harvard Business Review* 59 (May–June): 94–102.

Lewis, B. (1991) 'Service Quality: An International Comparison of Bank Customers' Expectations and Perceptions', *Journal of Marketing Management* 7: 47–62.

Locander, W. and Hermann, P. (1979) 'The Effect of Self-confidence and Anxiety on Information Seeking in Consumer Risk Reduction', *Journal of Marketing Research* 19: 268–74.

Lovelock, C. (1981) 'Why Marketing Management Needs to be Different for Services', in *Marketing of Services* (J. H. Donnelly and W. R. George, eds). Chicago: AMA.

McLuhan, M. (1964) *Understanding Media*. New York: McGraw-Hill.

Miller, G. (1956) 'The Magical Number Seven Plus or Minus Two, Some limitations on our Capacity for Processing Information', *Phychological Review* 63 (No. 2).

Moore, W. L. and Lehmann, D. (1980) 'Individual Differences in Search Behaviour for a Nondurable', *Journal of Consumer Research* 7 (December): 296–307.

Muller, T. (1984) 'Buyer Response to Variation in Product Information Load', *Journal of Applied Psychology* 69 (No. 2, May).

Murray, K. (1991) 'A Test of Services Marketing Theory: Consumer Information Acquisition Activities', *Journal of Marketing* 55 (January): 10–25.

Nelson, P. (1974) 'Advertising as Information', *Journal of Political Economy* **81** (July–August): 729–54.

Parasuraman, A., Berry, L. and Ziethaml, V. (1991) 'Understanding Customer Expectations of Service', *Sloan Management Review* (Spring): 39–48.

Rathwell, J. M. (1966) 'What is Meant by Services?', *Journal of Marketing* **30**: 32–6.

Rathwell, J. M. (1974) *Marketing in the Services Sector.* Cambridge, MA: Winthrop.

Regan, W.J. (1963) 'The Service Revolution', *Journal of Marketing* **27** (July): 57–62.

Robertson, T. S. (1970) *Innovative Behaviour and Communication.* New York: Holt, Rheinhart and Winston.

Sasser, W. E., Olsen, R. P. and Wyckoff, D. D. (1978) *The Management of Service Operations.* Boston, MA: Allyn & Bacon.

Schiffman, L. and Kanuk, L. (1991) *Consumer Behaviour,* 4th Edition. New Jersey: Prentice Hall.

Shostack, G. L. (1977) 'Breaking Free From Product Marketing', *Journal of Marketing* **41**: 73–80.

Shostack, G. L. (1987) 'Service Positioning Through Structural Change', *Journal of Marketing* **51**: 34–43.

Summers, J. (1974) 'Less Information is Better', *Journal of Marketing Research* **XI** (November): 467–68.

Swan, J. and Comb, L. (1976) 'Product Performance and Consumer Satisfaction: A New Concept', *Journal of Marketing* **40** (April): 25–33.

Thomas, D. R. E. (1978) 'Strategy is Different in Service Businesses', *Harvard Business Review* (July–August): 158–65.

Urbany, J. and Weilbacker, D. (1987) 'A Critical Examination of Nelson's Theory of Inflation and Consumer Behaviour', in *AMA Educators Conference Proceedings* (S. Douglas *et al.,* eds). Chicago: AMA.

Urbany, J., Dickson, P. and Wilkie, W. (1989) 'Buyer Uncertainty and Information Search', *Journal of Consumer Research* **16** (September): 208–15.

Westbrook, R. A. and Fornell, C. (1979) 'Patterns of Information Source Usage Among Durable Goods Buyers', *Journal of Marketing Research* **16** (August): 303–12.

Wilkie, W. L. (1974) 'Analysis of Effects of Information Load', *Journal of Marketing Research* **XI** (November): 462–6.

Wright, P. (1975) 'Consumer Choice Strategies: Simplifying or Optimising', *Journal of Marketing Research* **12** (February): 60–7.

Wyckham, R., Fitzroy, P. and Mandry, G. (1975) 'Marketing of Services: An Evaluation of Theory', *European Journal of Marketing* **9** (No. 1): 59–67.

Zeithaml, V. (1988) 'Consumer Perceptions of Price, Quality and Value: A Means–End Model and Synthesis', *Journal of Marketing* **52** (July): 2–22.

Zeithaml, V. (1981) 'How Consumer Evaluation Processes Differ Between Goods and Services', in *Marketing of Services* (J. H. Donnelly and W. R. George, eds). Chicago: AMA.

Zeithaml, V., Parasuraman, A. and Berry, L. (1990) *Delivering Quality Service.* New York: Collier Macmillan.

Service positioning through structural change

G. Lynn Shostack

The basis of any service positioning strategy is the service itself, but marketing offers little guidance on how to craft service processes for positioning purposes. A new approach suggests that within service systems, structural process design can be used to 'engineer' services on a more scientific, rational basis.

When a firm or provider establishes and maintains a distinctive place for itself and its offerings in the market, it is said to be successfully positioned. In the increasingly competitive service sector, effective positioning is one of marketing's most critical tasks.

For some marketers (e.g., Ries and Trout, 1981), positioning is strictly a communications issue. The product or service is a given and the objective is to manipulate consumer perceptions of reality. As Lovelock (1984) rightly points out, however, positioning is more than just advertising and promotion. Market position can be affected by pricing, distribution and, of course, the product itself, which is the core around which all positioning strategies revolve.

Apart from promotion, pricing and distribution, the product is indeed a critical, manageable factor in positioning. Products often are engineered explicitly to reach certain markets, as the original Mustang was designed to reach the youth market and light beer was created to tap the calorie-conscious consumer. Sometimes products are invented first and positioned afterwards. The Xerox copier and the Polaroid camera are examples of products that were first created, then positioned to various markets. Finally, an existing product may be changed in order to change its market position, as the Jeep was altered physically from a military vehicle to a vehicle for the family market.

Services are not things, however. McLuhan (1964) perhaps put it best and most succinctly more than 20 years ago when he declared that the *process* is the product. We say 'airline' when we mean 'air transportation'. We say 'movie', but mean 'entertainment services'. We say 'hotel' when we mean 'lodging rental'. The use of nouns obscures the fundamental nature of services, which are processes, not objects.

As processes, services have many intriguing characteristics. Judd (1964), Rathmell (1974), Shostack (1977) Bateson (1977) and Sasser, Olsen and Wyckoff (1978) were among the first to ponder the implications of service intangibility, service perishability, production/consumption simultaneity and consumer participation in service processes. They found that traditional marketing, with its goods-bound approaches, was not helpful in process design, process modification or process control.

If processes are the service equivalent of a product's 'raw materials', can processes be designed, managed and changed for positioning purposes the way physical goods are? The purpose of this article is to take a closer look at processes as structural elements and suggest some ways in which they can be 'engineered' for strategic service positioning purposes.

Process characteristics

Processes have been studied for some time in disciplines other than marketing. Systematic, quantified methods for describing processes have been developed in industrial engineering (Deming, 1982), computer programming (Fox, 1982), decision theory (Holloway, 1979) and operations management (Schroeder, 1981), to name a few examples and well-known authors in each field. Though their techniques and nomenclatures may differ, process-oriented disciplines share certain basic concepts. First, each of them provides a way of breaking any process down

Reprinted with permission from *Journal of Marketing*, Vol. 51 (January 1987), 34–43, published by the American Marketing Association, Chicago, IL 60606.

into logical steps and sequences to facilitate its control and analysis. Second, each includes ways to accommodate more variable processes in which outcomes may differ because of the effects of judgement, chance or choice on a sequence. Finally, each system includes the concept of deviation or tolerance standards in recognition that processes are 'real-time' phenomena that do not conform perfectly to any model or description, but rather function within a band or 'norm' of some sort.

Little process description can be found in marketing literature. However, several writers on services have drawn upon manufacturing sources in using the words 'standardized' and 'customized' to define the poles of a process continuum (see Levitt, 1976; Lovelock, 1984). 'Standardized' usually implies a non-varying sequential process, similar to the mass production of goods, in which each step is laid out in order and all outcomes are uniform. 'Customized' usually refers to some level of adaptation or tailoring of the process to the individual consumer. The concept of deviation usually is treated as a quality issue, in reference to services that do not perform as they should.

Complexity and divergence

Extracting from various approaches, we can suggest two ways to describe processes. One way is according to the steps and sequences that constitute the process; the other is according to the executional latitude or variability of those steps and sequences. Let us call the first factor the complexity of the process and the second its divergence. Deviation, a real-time operating factor, can then be thought of as an inadvertent departure from whatever process model and standards have been established for the first two factors.

We can define a service's complexity by analyzing the number and intricacy of the steps required to perform it. Accounting, for example, is more complex than bookkeeping because accounting is a more elaborated process, involving more functions and more steps. Architecture is more complex than plumbing. Plumbing is more complex than lawn mowing.

Apart from complexity, however, some processes include a high level of executional latitude and others do not. The degree of freedom allowed or inherent in a process step or sequence can be thought of as its divergence. A highly divergent service thus would be one in which virtually every performance of the process is unique. A service of low divergence would be one that is largely standardized.

Every service can be analyzed according to its overall complexity and divergence. A physician's services, for example, are highly complex. They are also highly divergent. As the service is being performed, a doctor constantly alters and shapes it by assimilating new data, weighing probabilities, reaching conclusions and then taking action. Every case may be handled differently, yet all performances may be satisfactory from the consumer point of view. Architecture, law, consulting and most other 'professional' services have similarly high divergence (as well as high complexity), because they involve a considerable amount of judgement, discretion and situational adaptation.

However, a process can be high in complexity and low in divergence. Hotel services, for example, are a complex aggregation of processes, but hotels standardize these processes through documentation and establishment of executional rules for every sequence from room cleaning to checkout. Telephone services are also highly complex, yet telephone companies have standardized and automated them to ensure uniformity and achieve economies of scale.

Services also can be low in complexity but high in divergence. In process terms, a singer renders the service of entertainment in one step: singing. This service is infinitely divergent, however, because each execution is unique and unlike that of any other provider. A painter 'merely' paints, a teacher simply 'transmits knowledge', a minister 'spreads the gospel'. These services do not consist of orderly, mechanical procedures, but of unique performances. Services that involve interpretational skills, artistic crafting, or highly individualized execution often appear simple in process terms, yet are highly divergent in operation. In fact, for such services, defining 'what' is done in process terms is often easier than describing 'how' it is done.

Blueprinting complexity and divergence in service systems

Though processes can be reduced to steps and sequences, services must be viewed as interdependent, interactive systems, not as disconnected pieces and parts. One approach for visualizing service systems is a mapping technique called 'blueprinting' (Shostack, 1984a, 1984b). Blueprinting is a holistic method of seeing in snapshot form what is essentially a dynamic, living phenomenon.

For process design purposes, a blueprint should document all process steps and points of divergence in a specific service. This documentation must be carried to whatever level of detail is needed to distinguish between any two competing services. In other words, specific blueprints of real services are more productive than generic or generalized visualizations in working out position strategies based on process.

Figure 1 shows how one Park Avenue florist's service appears in blueprint form. The 'fan' is borrowed from decision theory (see Holloway, 1979) in which a fan attached to a circle is used to show a range of poten-

tial events that may occur, whereas a fan attached to a square denotes a range of potential actions that may be taken. This is a useful symbol for divergence and is used throughout the following illustrations. The florist provides a service of low complexity that is highly divergent. Though the process steps are few, the fans indicate broad executional latitude stemming from the judgement and decisions of the individual performing the service.

For comparison, Figure 2 illustrates a complex but standardized service – consumer instalment lending at a large commercial bank. Here, the process has many more specific steps, but the steps are executed in a strict and unvarying manner. As Levitt would say, the service has been 'industrialized' (1976). There is one and only one permissible manner and order in which the service is provided. Parts of the process have been automated for further conformity, and the bank's design for this service does not allow employees who are part of the service system to modify or change the service in any way. Such a service may not function perfectly at all times. However, as noted before, such quality failures represent deviation from

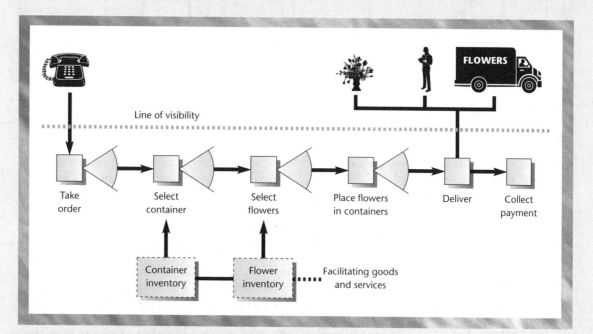

Figure 1 ■ Park Avenue florist

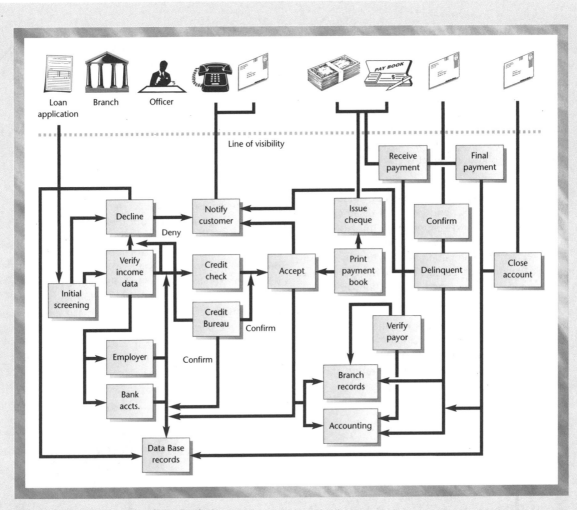

Figure 2 ■ Instalment lending: Bank X

a design standard, whereas true divergence is an integral part of the process.

Figure 3 shows yet another structure – the highly complex and highly divergent service of a general medical practitioner. Here, not only is the process complex, but virtually every step involves variable execution.

Blueprints as a tool in consumer research

It may be noted that this analytical approach is a useful and natural companion to market research. Lovelock (1984) noted the difficulty of researching service 'attributes' for positioning purposes, which is caused at least partly by the inherent ambiguity and subjectivity of verbal descriptions. Blueprints provide visible portraits to which consumers can react, and which can facilitate exploration of more parts of the service system than just its processes. Blueprints can be used to educate consumers, focus their evaluative input on various aspects of the service system, elicit comparative or competitive assessments, and generate specific responses to contemplated changes or new service concepts. As Schneider and Bowen (1984) pointed out, regardless of whether consumers

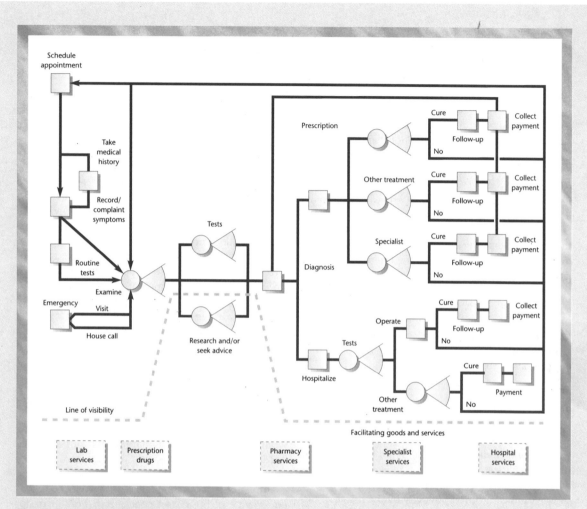

Figure 3 ■ General practitioner services

are privy to or even aware of all parts of the process, their awareness of its results and evidence makes them potentially valuable participants in the design of the entire system, not just those parts they see.

Changing the process

Complexity and divergence are not fixed and immutable. They are factors that can be changed. Once a service has been documented accurately, it can be analyzed for opportunities either to increase or decrease one or both variables.

Alternative directions for structural change

A change in overall complexity or divergence generally indicates one of four overall strategic directions. Each one has management consequences as well as certain market risks.

Reduced divergence

Reducing divergence leads to uniformity which tends to reduce costs, improve productivity, and make distribution easier. It usually indicates a shift to a volume-oriented positioning strategy based on economies of scale. The positive market effects of such a move can include perceived increases in reliability – more uniform service quality and greater service availability. However, reducing divergence also can have negative market effects. It dictates conformity as well as inflexibility in operating procedures. Customers may perceive the shift as one that lowers customization and limits their options, and may reject a highly standardized service even if it costs less.

Increased divergence

Raising divergence is the service equivalent of creating a 'job shop'. Greater customization and flexibility tend to command higher prices. Increased divergence usually indicates a niche positioning strategy, dependent less on volume and more on margins. The market can respond positively to such a shift if the service taps a desire for prestige, customization, or personalization. Here, too, however, care is needed in making such a shift. A divergent service is more difficult to manage, control, and distribute. Moreover, customers may not be willing to pay the price that customization demands.

Reduced complexity

Reduced complexity usually indicates a specialization strategy. As steps or functions are dropped from the system, resources can be focused on a narrower service offering (radiology, for example, versus general medical services). Narrowing the service offering usually makes distribution and control easier. Such a service can be perceived positively by the market if the provider stands out as an expert. However, reduced complexity also can cause a service to be perceived as 'stripped down' or so limited that its specialized quality is not enough to overcome the inconvenience or price of obtaining it. Reducing complexity can be competitively risky if other providers continue to offer a broader, more extensive full-service alternative.

Increased complexity

Higher complexity usually indicates a strategy to gain greater penetration in a market by adding more services or enhancing current ones. Supermarkets, banks and retailers have expanded their service lines with this strategic goal in mind. Increasing complexity can increase efficiency by maximizing the revenue generated from each customer. In contrast, too much complexity can be confusing to customers and can cause overall service quality to fall. Thus, a highly complex service system may be vulnerable to inroads by competitors who specialize.

Marketing strategy and structural change

Service industries offer numerous examples of changes in complexity and divergence and how they affect market position. Barbering, for example, is a relatively simple service, but beginning in the 1970s some providers began to reposition it. They added processes borrowed from women's beauty salons, such as tinting, body perms and backcombing, redefined their mission, and transformed 'hair cutting' into 'hair styling' – a more complex, divergent service structure. Hair styling tapped or created a new market segment of men willing to pay substantially higher prices for a more elaborated process and carved a niche in the market through structural differentiation.

In retailing, there are many examples of adding to the complexity of service systems. Supermarkets began as specialty food stores and have added banking services, pharmacist services, flowers, books and magazines, and even food preparation to their basic food retailing structure. In the fast-food industry, what were once simple hamburger outlets have become providers of breakfast, dining room services and even entertainment. Retailing also affords many examples of reducing complexity, as evidenced by the emergence of businesses specializing only in pasta, only in cookies, and only in ice cream.

For examples of lowered divergence, we need only to look at professional services. Legal services, for instance, have historically had both high complexity and high divergence. A consumer needing legal assistance first had to seek out and select a lawyer, and was then dependent upon the variable performance of that individual. Over the past few years, however, this service has been repositioned through the actions of business-minded entrepreneurs who perceived a market need for less complex, less divergent alternatives. The result has been the creation of legal 'clinics' and chains that offer a limited menu of services executed uniformly at published rates. This repositioning not only has opened a new market for legal services, but also has had and will continue to have a profound effect on the positioning strategies of traditional law firms.

A similar downshifting and repositioning of traditional personal accountant services was effected by the innovations of H & R Block, which tapped a vast market of consumers who did not require the variable and costly services of a personal accountant, but who were willing to pay someone else to prepare their tax returns.

Most of these examples are based on entrepreneurial response to the perception of an unmet market need. What is perhaps less clearly recognized is that such changes need not be intuitive or accidental. They can be made deliberately to support explicit positioning or competitive strategies.

Implications of service system changes

Let us assume that Figure 1 is an accurate representation of a specific florist's service. Assume further that in an analysis of competitors, very similar structures were found. One strategic option to reposition and differentiate the service would be to reengineer it as a less divergent system. Figure 4 illustrates a redesigned blueprint that accomplishes this objective. The number of container choices has been limited to two; there are only two groups of flowers and only two

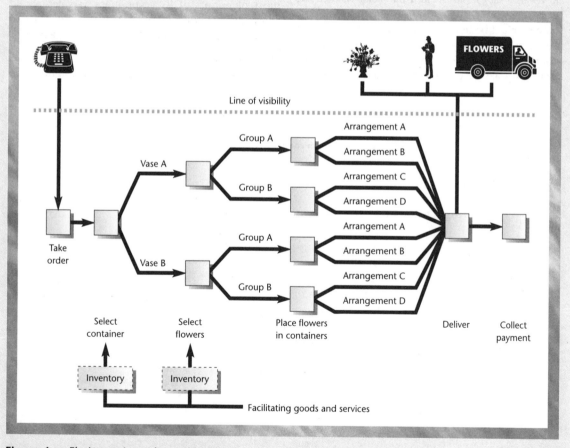

Figure 4 ■ Florist services: alternative design

choices of arrangements for each group. Thus, only eight combinations are possible.

Obviously, the new design has implications for inventory management as well as productivity. Inventory can be ordered in larger, more economic quantities. More arrangements can be produced by the florist because the process is more standardized. These two effects will lower prices and potentially allow the service to be repositioned to a broader market. The new structure also will allow wider service distribution, because simpler blueprints are easier to replicate. FTD (Florists' Transworld Delivery) arrived at a similar conclusion and expanded florist services from a local craft into a national service industry.

However, if all the florists in a particular market had structures similar to Figure 4, a logical positioning strategy might be to move towards the design shown in Figure 1 – a highly artistic, high-priced structure. Alternatively, a marketer might choose to increase complexity alone, through retailing a selection of plants and supplies, or to increase both complexity and divergence by offering flower arranging classes.

Identifying and evaluating strategic choices

Services can be structurally evaluated on a stand-alone basis and also as members of service families. Within a service family, a marketer can consider positioning strategies based on structural complementarity, structural diversity, and overall developmental direction.

In Figure 2, a bank's consumer instalment lending service is diagrammed. This service, of course, is only one of a constellation of services that constitute consumer banking. Though consumer banking, in its totality, is an extraordinary complex service system, most blueprints of its component services would show low divergence stemming from 20 years of effort to standardize and automate the service system.

One strategy for a bank with this structure is to continue increasing complexity by adding more

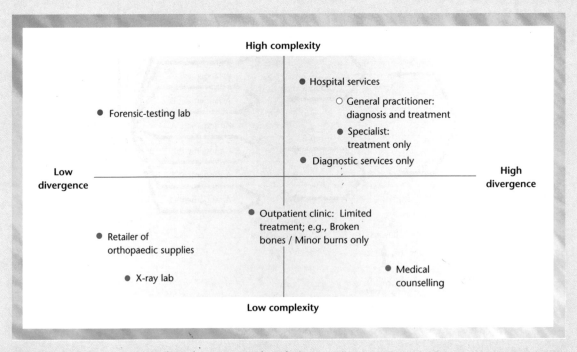

Figure 5 ■ Relative positions based on structural analysis

subservices while continuing to minimize divergence through standardization and automation. For a competitor, an equally valid strategy would be to adopt the counterposition, which would call for increasing the customization of services. The latter strategy is evident in banks offering 'private' banking, an integrated package of services for the upscale market that includes such divergent services as customized lending, portfolio management, and financial planning.

The general practitioner previously described also has numerous strategic choices. Figure 5 illustrates the relative structural positions held by a number of medical service providers, including the general practitioner analyzed in Figure 3. From the present position, he or she can move in any direction on the scale by adding or deleting service functions to create a new family. Depending on the complexity and divergence of these functions, the overall service system's complexity divergence will change, thus altering its relative position.

For example (Figure 6), retailing orthopaedic supplies would add complexity to the doctor's overall service system, but little divergence. Adding counselling, in contrast, would add considerable divergence, but little operational complexity. Conversely, if minor surgical procedures that have been performed in the office were eliminated, the service system would be reduced in both complexity and divergence and move closer to the position held by diagnosticians, who perform no treatment themselves. At the extreme position, complexity and divergence could be lowered to the point where only the simple service, such as X-rays, is provided in a completely standardized way. Consumer research can be instrumental in facilitating this strategic process, and blueprints are a useful tool for focusing consumer input and response to new structural concepts.

In simplified terms, Figure 7 shows some changes that a mid-priced family restaurant might consider to alter complexity and divergence for competitive purposes. Any prospective change or mix of changes can be compared with competitors' offerings to determine which mix is most likely to provide the maximum competitive differentiation.

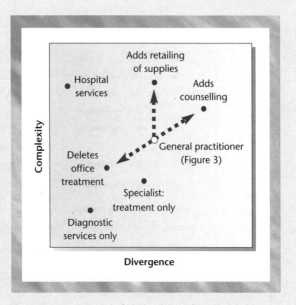

Figure 6 ■ Positional shifts through structural change

Positioning charts are a useful tool for market analysts wishing to compare the perceived performance of competing services on two or three attributes simultaneously. Examples of such charts (also known as perceptual maps) are given by Tybout and Hauser (1981) and Lovelock (1984). Blueprinting works well in tandem with this technique by serving as a focal point for determining which parts of the service system or process components are important to the market, and in evaluating change across many elements of the system.

Implementing change

Though processes are intangible, the means by which services are rendered are very real. There are only two, people (both providers and consumers) and facilitating goods. Any shift in overall complexity or divergence, or the introduction of any new process design, must be implemented with a clear understanding of the potential impact on these 'producers' of the process.

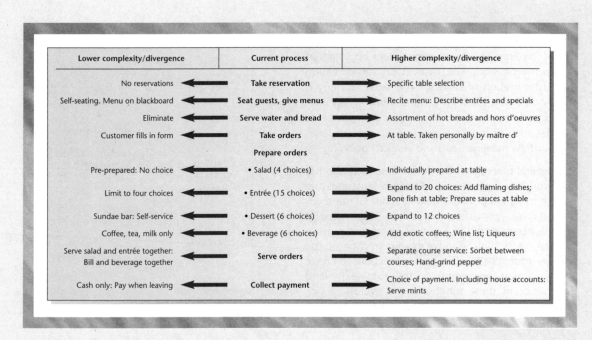

Lower complexity/divergence	Current process	Higher complexity/divergence
No reservations	Take reservation	Specific table selection
Self-seating. Menu on blackboard	Seat guests, give menus	Recite menu: Describe entrées and specials
Eliminate	Serve water and bread	Assortment of hot breads and hors d'oeuvres
Customer fills in form	Take orders	At table. Taken personally by maître d'
	Prepare orders	
Pre-prepared: No choice	• Salad (4 choices)	Individually prepared at table
Limit to four choices	• Entrée (15 choices)	Expand to 20 choices: Add flaming dishes; Bone fish at table; Prepare sauces at table
Sundae bar: Self-service	• Dessert (6 choices)	Expand to 12 choices
Coffee, tea, milk only	• Beverage (6 choices)	Add exotic coffees; Wine list; Liqueurs
Serve salad and entrée together: Bill and beverage together	Serve orders	Separate course service: Sorbet between courses; Hand-grind pepper
Cash only: Pay when leaving	Collect payment	Choice of payment. Including house accounts: Serve mints

Figure 7 ■ Structural alternatives

Role of service employees and customers

Considerable attention has been paid to people in the service system. Whether they are providers or consumers, the management and control of human behaviour is a critical factor in process design, change, and operating quality. Mills (1985) suggests that management controls over service employees should depend on the structure of the service system. For low-contact, standardized services, behaviour can be controlled through mechanistic means, such as rules and regulations. However, for high-contact, divergent services, Mills suggests that employee self-management and peer-reference techniques are more effective. Smith and Houston (1983), in contrast, propose that a script-based approach to managing customer and employee behaviour can help to control expectations as well as process compliance. Bowen and Schneider (1985) speak of 'boundary spanners', that is, employees with high customer interaction, as a valuable source of design information and as change agents whose acceptance and commitment are critical to success in altering any process. Schneider and Bowen (1984) as well as others (Berry, 1983; Heskett, 1986) stress that employee involvement and 'internal' marketing to employees are important factors in ensuring successful service operations. Deming (1982), however, argues that both behaviour and motivation are controlled by the design of the process itself and that if the process is properly designed, high motivation and effectiveness will be the natural results.

In terms of consumer participation, Lovelock and Young (1979), Chase (1978), Bateson (1985), and others have discussed whether and how to involve consumers in the service process, and the management of their involvement. Chase argues that consumer participation should be kept to a minimum in the interests of greater process efficiency. However, as we have seen, process design offers many routes to market success. A service (self-service petrol stations, for example) can be designed for maximum consumer participation and still be profitable. In fact, Bateson's (1985) work suggests that consumers can be segmented on the basis of control needs, resulting in services that are designed to capitalize profitably on the consumer's own desire for participation.

These brief descriptions illustrate the richness and diversity of current thought about the human side of service systems. Our purpose here is not to choose one approach over another, but to underscore the fact that people are just as important as structural design. If people issues are not addressed effectively, even the best design will fail.

Role of facilitating goods

Facilitating goods are also important in structural planning. Educational services, for example, can be rendered by a human being who lectures in a traditional classroom setting. Education also can be rendered via videotape, television, computer and book, to name just a few alternative facilitating goods. For the designer of a new or different educational service, any of these choices will yield a different service structure. These structures will differ in complexity and divergence, as well as in cost dynamics, distribution constraints, and market position.

Sometimes facilitating goods are used as a replacement for human performance to reduce divergence. Computers are the prime example of a good that has been used in this way to standardize service systems. However, simplification is not the only use for technology. Technology also can be used to increase complexity and divergence. When bank automated teller machines first were introduced, for example, they could deliver only simple cash dispensing and deposit services. Now, technology has allowed the addition of funds transfer and investment services to the system, increasing its overall complexity. Tomorrow, what are called 'smart' cards will make possible the delivery of a wide range of credit, payment, and information services. Ultimately, technology may even make possible a degree of customization (i.e., divergence) that only human providers can now deliver.

For all these reasons, the consideration of changes to any service structure demands an appreciation of the interrelatedness and intricacy of service systems. Unlike a product, a service cannot be engineered and then made in a factory. 'Producing' a service is a dynamic, continuous event.

Conclusion

Though our discussion focuses on process design, other elements of the service system can and do affect market position. Advertising and promotion are, of course, powerful forces in the positioning process. American Express, for example, has repositioned its credit services to women solely through advertising.

Distribution channels also affect market position. Marketing stock brokerage through Sears stores is one example of positioning a service to a new, broader consumer base through a change in distribution channels. Moreover, as Shostack (1985), Blackman (1985) and others have noted, various forms of physical service evidence, from the environment in which a service is rendered to the correspondence, brochures, signage, and even people to which a customer is exposed, can affect position. Facilitating goods also can affect position, even without process change. A provider who substitutes limousines for taxicabs, for example, may succeed in charging higher prices and tapping a different market for exactly the same transportation service.

In short, the issues involved in service positioning are numerous, and this discussion by no means encompasses all of the subjects relevant to the positioning process. In a structural sense, however, processes themselves appear to have characteristics that not only affect market position, but also can be deliberately and strategically managed for positioning purposes. By manipulating complexity and divergence, a service marketer can approximate some of the product analysis and design functions that are traditional in product marketing. Moreover, the use of blueprints provides a mechanism through which services can be 'engineered' at the drawing board, as well as a tool for identifying gaps, analyzing competitors, aiding in market research and controlling implementation.

The marketplace affords evidence that both complexity and divergence are concepts that are understood and employed in service industries. Though the practice is not formalized, it works. How much more powerful the result might be if marketers brought a professional discipline, capable of crafting service systems on a rational basis, to bear on the service positioning task!

For managers in service industries, taking a structural approach can help increase their control over some of the most critical elements of service system management. For marketers, process design may be a tool that can substantially increase their impact and role in the service sector and help service marketing come of age.

References

Bateson, John E. G. (1977) 'Do We Need Service Marketing?', *Marketing Consumer Services: New Insights*, Report #77–115, Cambridge, MA: Marketing Science Institute.

Bateson, John E.G. (1985) 'Perceived Control and the Service Encounter', in *The Service Encounter*, John A. Czepiel *et al.*, eds, Lexington, MA: Lexington Books.

Berry, Leonard L. (1983) 'Relationship Marketing', in *Emerging Perspectives on Services Marketing*, Leonard L. Berry *et al.*, eds, Chicago: American Marketing Association, 25–8.

Blackman, Barry (1985) 'Making a Service More Tangible Can Make It More Manageable', in *The Service Encounter*, John A. Czepiel *et al.*, eds, Lexington, MA: Lexington Books.

Bowen, David E. and Benjamin Schneider (1985) 'Boundary-Spanning-Role Employees and the Service Encounter', in *The Service Encounter*, John A. Czepiel *et al.*, eds, Lexington, MA: Lexington Books.

Chase, Richard B. (1978, November–December) 'Where Does the Consumer Fit in a Service Operation?', *Harvard Business Review*, 56, 137–42.

Deming, W. Edwards (1982) *Quality, Productivity and Competitive Position*. Cambridge: Massachusetts Institute of Technology, Center for Advanced Engineering Study.

Fox, Joseph M. (1982) *Software and Its Development*, Englewood Cliffs, NJ: Prentice Hall.

Heskett, James L. (1986) *Managing in the Service Economy*, Boston: Harvard Business School Press, pp. 45–74, 117–34.

Holloway, Charles A. (1979) *Decision Making Under Uncertainty: Models and Choices*, Englewood Cliffs, NJ: Prentice Hall.

Judd, Robert C. (1964, January) 'The Case for Redefining Services', *Journal of Marketing*, 28, 58–9.

Levitt, Theodore (1976, September–October). 'The Industrialization of Service', *Harvard Business Review*, 54, 63–74.

Lovelock, Christopher H. (1984) *Services Marketing, Text, Cases & Readings*, Englewood Cliffs, NJ: Prentice Hall, pp. 55–6, 133–9.

Lovelock, Christopher H. and Robert F. Young (1979, May–June) 'Look to Consumers to Increase Productivity', *Harvard Business Review*, 57, 168–78.

McLuhan, Marshall (1964) *Understanding Media*, New York: McGraw-Hill.

Mills, Peter K. (1985) 'The Control Mechanisms of Employees at the Encounter of Service Organizations', in *The Service Encounter*, John A. Czepiel *et al.*, eds, Lexington, MA: Lexington Books.

Rathmell, John M. (1974) *Marketing in the Service Sector*, Cambridge, MA: Winthrop Publishers.

Ries, Al and Jack Trout (1981) *Positioning*, New York: McGraw-Hill.

Sasser, W. Earl, Jr, R. Paul Olsen and D. Daryl Wyckoff (1978) *Management of Service Operations: Text, Cases, and Readings*, Boston: Allyn & Bacon.

Schneider, Benjamin and David E. Bowen (1984) 'New Service Design, Development and Implementation', in *Developing New Services*, William R. George and Claudia Marshall, eds, Chicago: American Marketing Association, Proceedings Series, pp. 82–102.

Schroeder, Roger G. (1981) *Operations Management*, New York: McGraw-Hill.

Shostack, G. Lynn (1977, April) 'Breaking Free from Product Marketing', *Journal of Marketing*, 41, 73–80.

Shostack, G. Lynn (1984a) 'A Framework for Service Marketing', in *Marketing Theory, Distinguished Contributions*, Stephen W. Brown and Raymond P. Fisk, eds, New York: John Wiley, p. 250.

Shostack, G. Lynn (1984b, January–February) 'Designing Services That Deliver', *Harvard Business Review*, 62, 133–9.

Shostack, G. Lynn (1985) 'Planning the Service Encounter', in *The Service Encounter*, John A. Czepiel *et al.*, eds, Lexington, MA: Lexington Books, pp. 243–53.

Smith, Ruth A. and Michael J. Houston. (1983) 'Script-Based Evaluation of Satisfaction with Services', in *Emerging Perspectives on Services Marketing*, Leonard Berry *et al.*, eds, Chicago: American Marketing Association.

Tybout, Alice M. and John R. Hauser (1981, Summer) 'A Marketing Audit Using a Conceptual Model of Consumer Behavior: Application and Evaluation', *Journal of Marketing*, 45, 82–101.

Listening to the customer: the concept of a service-quality information system

Leonard L. Berry ■ *A. Parasuraman*

To improve service, companies must use multiple research approaches among different customer groups to ensure that they are hearing what customers are saying and responding to their suggestions.

The quality of listening has an impact on the quality of service. Firms intent on improving service need to listen continuously to three types of customers: external customers who have experienced the firm's service; competitors' customers who the firm would like to make its own; and internal customers (employees) who depend on internal services to provide their own services. Without the voices of these groups guiding investment in service improvement, all companies can hope for are marginal gains.

In this paper, we discuss the concept of a service-quality information system. We argue that companies need to establish ongoing listening systems using multiple methods among different customer groups. A single service-quality study is a snapshot taken at a point in time and from a particular angle. Deeper insight and more informed decision-making come from a continuing series of snapshots taken from various angles and through different lenses, which form the essence of systematic listening.

Systematic listening

A service-quality information system uses multiple research approaches to systematically capture, organize, and disseminate service-quality information to support decision-making. Continuously generated data flow into databases that decision-makers can use on both a regular scheduled and as needed basis.

The use of multiple research approaches is necessary because each approach has limitations as well as strengths. Combining approaches enables a firm to tap the strengths of each and compensate for weaknesses. Continuous data collection and dissemination informs and educates decision-makers about the *patterns* of change – for example, customers' shifting service priorities and declining or improving performance in the company's or the competitors' service.

An effective service-quality information system offers a company's executives a larger view of service quality along with a composite of many smaller pictures. It teaches decision-makers which service attributes are important to customers and prospects, what parts of the firm's service system are working well or breaking down, and which service investments are paying off. A service-quality information system helps to focus service improvement planning and resource allocation. It can help sustain managers' motivation for service improvement by comparing the service performance of various units in the organization and linking compensation to these results. And it can be the basis for an effective first-line employee reward system by identifying the most effective service providers. (See Figure 1 for the principal benefits of a service-quality information system.)

The task of improving service in organizations is complex. It involves knowing what to do on multiple fronts, such as technology, service systems, employee selection, training and education, and reward systems. It involves knowing how to implement these actions and how to transform activity into sustainable improvement. Genuine service improvement requires an integrated strategy based on systematic listening. Unrelated, incomplete studies, outdated research, and findings about customers that are not shared provide insufficient support for improving service.

Reprinted with permission from *Sloan Management Reveiw*, Spring 1997.

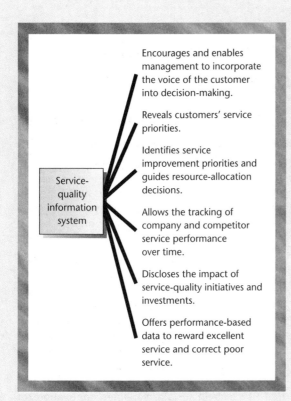

Encourages and enables management to incorporate the voice of the customer into decision-making.

Reveals customers' service priorities.

Identifies service improvement priorities and guides resource-allocation decisions.

Allows the tracking of company and competitor service performance over time.

Discloses the impact of service-quality initiatives and investments.

Offers performance-based data to reward excellent service and correct poor service.

Figure 1 ■ Principal benefits of an effective service-quality information system
Source: L. Berry, *On Great Service: A Framework for Action*, New York: Free Press, 1995, p. 34.

Approaches to service research

A company can choose from many possible research approaches to build a service-quality information system (see Table 1). A firm would not use all approaches in the table in the same system; too much information obscures the most meaningful insights and may intimidate intended users. Conversely, incomplete information injects needless guessing into decision-making or, worse, paints a false picture. The nature of the service, the firm's service strategy, and the needs of the information users determine which service-quality research approaches to use.

An industrial equipment manufacturer might wish to use service reviews to benefit from unfiltered dialogue with multiple users, reach consensus on service

support priorities, and solidify relationships. A restaurant, with a transaction-oriented business, would find service reviews far less efficient that other approaches. Because of the relationship nature of its business, a limousine service should consider new, declining and lost-customer surveys. It should identify any negatives that tarnish new customers' first impressions, or cause other customers to be less loyal or to defect, so it can take corrective measures. A taxi company probably wouldn't use these surveys because of a minimal relationship-marketing potential. A firm whose strategy emphasizes service reliability surely would want to capture and analyze customer service complaints to identify where the service system is breaking down. A company whose strategy depends on point-of-sale service excellence should consider mystery shopping research, which generates feedback on specific service providers.

Four research approaches summarized in the table apply to virtually all organizations and can be considered essential components of a service-quality information system: transactional surveys; customer complaint, comment, and inquiry capture; total market surveys; and employee surveys. These approaches ensure coverage of the three customer types (external customers, competitors' customers, internal customers), document failure-prone parts of the service systems, and provide both transaction-specific and overall service feedback.

Personal involvement in listening

A service-quality information system does not replace the need for managers to interact directly with customers. Becoming well informed about service quality requires more than reading or hearing the results of structured, quantitative studies. It also requires that decision-makers become personally involved in listening to the voices of their customers, which can include participating in or observing qualitative research, such as service reviews and focus groups. And it can include less formal interactions with customers, such as when airline executives query passengers on flights and retailers accompany customers through their stores to ask them what they see, like and dislike.

Table 1 ■ Research approaches for building service-quality information systems

Type	Description	Purpose	Frequency**	Limitations
Transactional surveys*	Service satisfaction survey of customers following a service encounter.	Obtain customer feedback while service experience is still fresh; act on feedback quickly if negative patterns develop.	Continuous	Focuses on customers' most recent experience rather than their overall assessment. Non-customers are excluded
Mystery shopping	Researchers become 'customers' to experience and evaluate the quality of service delivered.	Measure individual employee service behaviours for use in coaching, training, performance evaluation, recognition and rewards; identify systemic strengths and weaknesses in customer-contact service.	Quarterly	Subjective evaluations: researchers may be more 'judgemental' than customers would be; expense limits repetitions; potential to hurt employee morale if improperly used.
New, declining and lost-customer surveys	Surveys to determine why customers select the firm, reduce their buying or leave the firm.	Assess the role service quality and other issues play in customer patronage and loyalty.	Continuous	Firm must be able to identify and monitor service usage on a per customer basis.
Focus group interviews	Directed questioning of a small group, usually eight to twelve people. Questions focus on a specific topic. Can be used with customer, non-customer, or employee groups.	Provide a forum for participants to suggest service improvement ideas; offer fast, informal feedback on service issues.	As needed	Dynamics of group interview may prevent certain issues from surfacing. Focus groups are, in effect, brainstorming sessions; the information generated is not projectable to the population of interest. Focus group research is most valuable when coupled with projectable research.
Customer advisory panels	A group of customers recruited periodically to provide the firm with feedback and advice on service performance and other issues. Data are obtained in meetings, over the telephone, through mail questionnaires or via other means. Employee panels also can be formed.	Obtain in-depth, timely feedback and suggestions about service quality from experienced customers who cooperate because of 'membership' nature of the panel.	Quarterly	May not be projectable to entire customer base. Excludes non-customers. Panelists may assume role of 'expert' and become less representative of customer base.
Service reviews	Periodic visits with customers (or a class of customers) to discuss and assess the service relationship. Should be a formal process with a common set of questions, capture of responses in a database, and follow-up communication with customers.	Identify customer expectations and perceptions of the company's service performance and improvement priorities in a face-to-face conversation. A view of the future, not just a study of the past. Opportunity to include multiple decision-makers and decision-influencers in the discussions.	Annually or semi-annually	Time consuming and expensive. Most appropriate for firms marketing complex services on an ongoing, relationship basis.

Table 1 ■ Research approaches for building service-quality information systems (*continued*)

Type	Description	Purpose	Frequency**	Limitations
Customer complaint, comment, and inquiry capture*	System to retain, categorize, track and distribute customer complaints and other communications with the company.	Identify most common types of service failure for corrective action. Identify through customer communications opportunities to improve service or otherwise strengthen customer relationships.	Continuous	Dissatisfied customers frequently do not complain directly to the company. Analysis of customer complaints and comments offers only a partial picture of the state of service.
Total market surveys	Surveys that measure customers' overall assessment of a company's service. Research includes both external customers and competitors' customers, i.e., the total market.	Assess company's service performance compared to competitors; identify service-improvement priorities; track service improvement over time.	Semi-annually or quarterly	Measures customers' overall service assessments but does not capture assessments of specific service encounters.
Employee field reporting	Formal process for gathering, categorizing and distributing field employee intelligence about service issues.	Capture and share at the management level intelligence about customers' service expectations and perceptions gathered in the field.	Continuous to monthly	Some employees will be more conscientious and efficient reporters than others. Employees may be unwilling to provide negative information to management.
Employee surveys	Surveys concerning the service employees provide and receive, and the quality of their work lives.	Measure internal service quality; identify employee-perceived obstacles to improved service; track employee morale and attitudes. Employee surveys help answer 'why' service performance is what it is.	Quarterly	The strength of employee surveys is also a weakness; employees view service delivery from their own vantage point, subject to their own biases. Employees can offer valuable insights into the root causes of service problems but are not always objective or correct in their interpretations.
Service operating data	A system to retain, categorize, track and distribute key service-performance operating data, such as service-response times, service failure rates and service delivery costs.	Monitor service performance indicators and take corrective action to improve performance as necessary. Relate operating performance data to customer and employee feedback	Continuous	Operating performance data may not be relevant to customers' perceptions of service. Focus is on what is occurring but not why.

* Highlighted approaches normally would be part of any service-quality information system.
** Frequencies of use vary among companies.

In 1993, the cash management division of First National Bank of Chicago changed its customer satisfaction surveys from mail questionnaires to telephone interviews. Then change was prompted by poor response rates to the mail survey and customers' suggestions for improving survey effectiveness: conduct the surveys by phone because they are more efficient and have bank employees who can act on problems make the calls.

First Chicago recruited senior and middle managers to conduct three pre-scheduled twenty-minute phone interviews per month and write reports on each call for the database. Managers were trained to do the interviews and passed a certification test before surveying their first customer. They surveyed each employee of the client firm who had significant contact with the bank. Bank managers were responsible for 'action items' that surfaced in the interviews. The bank's vice president of quality assurance, Aleta Holub, remarked, 'We've really seen a cultural change from getting everyone a little closer to the customer.'[1]

Directly hearing the voices of customers, non-customers and employees adds richness, meaning and perspective to the interpretation of quantitative data. The First Chicago case illustrates the potential impact embedded in literally hearing the customer's voice, rather than hearing only a distilled or numeric representation of it. McQuarrie makes the point: 'Everyone believes his or her own eyes and ears first. Key players hear about problems and needs directly from the most credible source – the customer. Learning is enhanced because of the vivid and compelling quality of first-hand knowledge.'[2]

A well-designed and implemented service-quality information system raises the probability that a company will invest service improvement money in ways that actually improve service. It also continually underscores the need to improve service. Continually capturing and disseminating data reveal not only progress, but problems; not only strengths, but weaknesses. Quality service is never-ending journey. An effective service-quality information system reminds everyone that more work needs to be done.

Developing an effective service-quality information system

The primary test of a service-quality information system is the extent to which it informs and guides service-improvement decision making. Another important test is the extent to which the system motivates both managerial and non-managerial employees to improve service. There are five guidelines for developing a system that can meet these tests:

1. Measure service expectations.
2. Emphasize information quality.
3. Capture customers' words.
4. Link service performance to business results.
5. Reach every employee.

The core success factors embedded are the coverage of external, competitors' and internal customers; the use of multiple measures; and ongoing measurement.

Measure service expectations

Measuring service performance per se is not as meaningful as measuring relative to customers' expectations. Customers' service expectations provide a frame of reference for their assessment of the service. Assume, for example, that a company measures only customers' perceptions of service performance using a 9-point scale. It receives an average perception score of 7.3 on the service attribute 'Performs the service right the first time'. How should managers interpret this score? Is it a good score? Without knowing what customers expect, this is a difficult question. There is no basis for gauging the rating. Managers' interpretation of the 7.3 perception score would likely be far different if customers' average expectation rating for this attribute were 8.2 rather than 7.0. As researchers Goodman et al. ask: 'How satisfied is a satisfied customer? When is good, good enough? Unfortunately, companies that ask their customers how satisfied they are but fail to research customers' expectations cannot answer these questions.'[3]

We collected service quality data from a computer manufacturer's customers (see Figure 2). We measured two levels of expectations: desired service (what the customer believes the service should be and can be) and adequate service (the minimal level of service acceptable to the customer). The top of the tolerance zone represents customers' average desired service-expectation score, the bottom, their average adequate service-expectation score. Service performance is superior if perception scores exceed the zone of tolerance, acceptable if perceptions are within the zone, and unacceptable if perceptions are below the zone.

Comparing the perceptions-only data with the combined perceptions-expectations data demonstrates

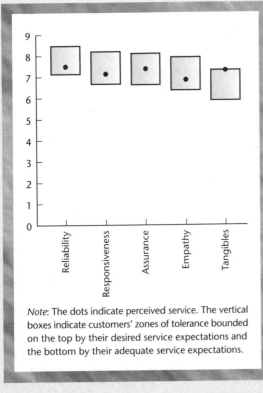

Note: The dots indicate perceived service. The vertical boxes indicate customers' zones of tolerance bounded on the top by their desired service expectations and the bottom by their adequate service expectations.

Figure 2 ■ Service-quality ratings for a computer manufacturer

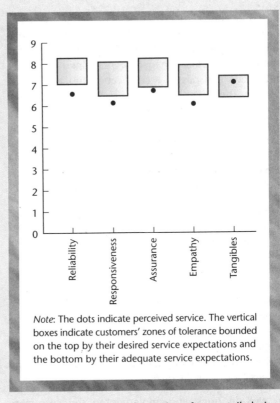

Note: The dots indicate perceived service. The vertical boxes indicate customers' zones of tolerance bounded on the top by their desired service expectations and the bottom by their adequate service expectations.

Figure 3 ■ Service-quality ratings for a retail chain

the diagnostic value of measuring customers' expectations. Were the computer manufacturer to measure only customer perceptions, its management would have little guidance for investing service improvement resources. The perception scores are similar across the service dimensions. However, the inclusion of expectations data clearly shows that improving service reliability should take priority over improving tangibles. Although reliability and tangibles have identical perception scores, customers' expectations for reliable service are much higher. Whereas customers' perceptions barely exceed adequate-level expectations for reliability, they exceed desired-level expectations for tangibles.

We also contrasted perceptions-only and perceptions-expectations data for a retail chain (see Figure 3). Without expectations data, management may con-

clude that the firm's service quality is acceptable because all perception scores are more than a full point above the scale's midpoint of 5. However, the addition of expectations scores suggests a much different conclusion, with service performance on four of the five dimensions not even meeting customers' minimum expectations.[4]

Documenting the value of measuring customer expectations in service quality research is necessary because perceptions-only research is common. Measuring expectations adds complexity and possibly length to the survey process and can be more expensive. Moreover, accurately measuring expectations is not easy. The best way to do it and whether it is even necessary are the subject of debate.[5] Advocates of perceptions-only measurement typically point out that service perception scores explain more variance in an overall service quality measure than a combined expectations-perceptions measure. Perceptions ratings consistently explain more variance, most likely because pieces of the whole (perceptions of specific service attributes) are being regressed against the whole (an overall service perception measure). So why is it so critical to measure customer expectations of service? Because, as Figures 2 and 3 show, managers learn more about improving service when customer expectations provide a frame of reference for interpreting perception ratings.

Emphasize information quality

Quality of information – not quantity – is the objective in building a service-quality information system. The test of information quality is to ask if the information is:

- Relevant?
- Precise?
- Useful?
- In context?
- Credible?
- Understandable?
- Timely?

Relevant service-quality information focuses decision makers' attention on the most important issues to meet and exceed external customer expectations, convert prospects, and enable employees to improve service. The more a service-quality information system focuses on the service priorities of the three customer types, the more likely managers will invest in the most appropriate initiatives that can make a positive difference.

Measuring the importance of service attributes is not the same as measuring customers' service expectations, although they are closely related. Customers' expectations are the comparison standards they use to judge the performance of various service attributes. However, the service attributes are not uniformly important to customers, and it is necessary to specifically measure their relative importance to monitor company and competitor performance on those attributes that drive customers' overall perceptions of service quality.

Information *precision* and *usefulness* go hand in hand. Information that is overly broad or general is not

useful. Researcher Brian Lunde commented: 'One of the worst criticisms that could be made by a line manager about a company's . . . information is that it is "interesting". "Interesting" is code for "useless". The information simply must be specific enough that executives . . . can take action – make decisions, set priorities, launch programs, cancel projects.'[6]

Information on what must be done to improve service is useful. Chase Manhattan Bank has determined empirically that the approval process is the primary driver of customers' quality perceptions for its mortgage loan service. Accordingly, Chase's service information system tracks its performance on the mortgage approval process compared to its principal competitors. However, Chase does not stop with overall perceptions of the mortgage approval process. It also investigates 'sub-drivers' such as quick approval, communication, the appraisal process, amount of paperwork and unchanging loan amount. The information is sufficiently precise so managers know what to do and can assign implementation accountabilities. They review data patterns regularly at management meetings.[7]

An effective service-quality information system presents information dynamically. At any point in time, the system's output tells what is becoming more or less important – the *context*. Fresh data are more valuable when presented in the context of past data. The study of trend data reveals patterns, nuances and insights that one-time data cannot possibly reveal. Is the investment in new telephone technology paying off? Was it a good idea to redesign the account-opening procedures? Is the company's new investment in training reducing error rates? Has competitor advertising about service influenced customer expectations? Has the competitor's new store prototype given its service ratings a boost? Only trend data can answer these and myriad other questions. Ongoing research using common measures across study periods generates trend data that provide context and aid interpretation.

A service-quality information system will not motivate managerial and non-managerial employees unless the information is *credible*. Employees in low rated units may be embarrassed and financially hurt by the system's output and may question the information validity. Companies can improve information credibility by seeking input from operating units on the design of research approaches and the development of specific questions. Information sessions to explain research approaches to employees, with an opportunity for questions and answers, also can be useful. Clear explanations of the research method and sample size should accompany the dissemination of results. Multiple measures – a fundamental tenet of service-quality information systems – enhance information credibility when different measures point to similar conclusions. The use of an outside research firm for data collection can help convey impartiality.

Information quality also is determined by whether the information is *understandable* to intended users. Relevance, usefulness and credibility all are enhanced with easily understood research information. Unfamiliar statistical jargon and symbols confuse, intimidate and discourage users, leading to feigned use of the system and incorrect interpretations of its output. There should be a concerted effort to design a user-friendly system with uniform reports and clear presentation of data.

The *timeliness* of information influences its quality. All the other attributes of information quality are rendered impotent if information is not available when decision-makers need it. Companies should collect data to support their natural decision-making and planning cycles. Monthly transactional survey reports should be ready for the monthly management meeting, total market survey results should feed the annual planning and budgeting process, customer complaint analyses should be ready for the twice-a-month meetings of the service-improvement leadership team. The design of databases should accommodate trend-data retrieval for managers as needed. Companies should continually explore ways to accelerate data collection and dissemination. Firms might fax or e-mail questionnaires to respondents rather than use the postal service. Research results might be distributed internally on a company's intranet.

The information quality tests of relevance, precision, usefulness, context, credibility, understandability and timeliness are not absolutes. Improving information quality is a journey of trial and error, experience curve effects, user feedback and new knowledge. Building an effective system is a never-ending process of refinement. Larry Brandt, associate director of customer service at AMP, a manufacturer of electrical and electronic connectors, points out the necessity of continuous improvement: 'We need to constantly evaluate what it is we're measuring, why we're doing it, and whether the results are worthwhile in the organization's big picture, or we run the risk of wasting time and effort.'[8]

Capture customers' words

The best service-quality information systems are built with qualitative and quantitative databases, rather than strictly the latter. Quantified data are summaries; averages of customers' perceptions of a very specific service issue are still averages. Quantitative data bring many benefits to the service information table, including easy analysis, comparability from one period to the next, and potential projectability. What numbers don't offer are the tone, inflection, feeling, and 'word pictures' from customers' voices. A service quality report showing that 4 per cent of the customer base is very dissatisfied and another 13 per cent is somewhat dissatisfied with the company's service may not get management's attention. However, if the report includes customers' verbatim comments, it may receive a very different reaction.

GTE Supply and Lexus customers illustrate the importance of capturing customers' words. GTE Supply purchases numerous products needed for the telephone operations of its customers, the local telephone companies. By implementing a systematic survey of customers' needs and opinions, GTE has improved service quality. The survey generates both quantitative and qualitative data for each customer. Current numerical quality ratings are compared to previous results to spot problems. In addition, the survey asks two open-ended questions: 'Why do you say that?' (in response to a closed-ended overall quality question) and 'What improvements, if any, could be made by Supply?' The company enters the customers' own words into a database and presents them to its managers along with the numerical data. GTE researchers James Drew and Tye Fussell remarked: 'Tabulations of survey questions can highlight specific transaction characteristics in need of improvement from the customer's viewpoint. In contrast, open-ended comments are especially effective in motivating first-level managers and giving the tabulations substance and a human touch.'[9]

Toyota introduced the Lexus line of luxury cars in the late 1980s, and by the early 1990s, the cars had vaulted to the top of the J.D. Power & Associates ratings in customer satisfaction. Soon after, another luxury carmaker retained Custom Research Inc. (CRI), a marketing research firm, to find out why Lexus owners were so satisfied. CRI conducted a series of focus groups to hear the Lexus story in the owners' words. Most of the Lexus drivers eagerly volunteered stories about the special care and attention they had received from their Lexus dealer. It became clear that although Lexus was manufacturing cars with few mechanical problems, the extra care shown in the sales and service process strongly influenced buyer satisfaction. Owners felt pampered and respected as valued Lexus customers. For example, one female owner mentioned several times during the focus group that she had never had a problem with her Lexus. However, on further probing, she said, 'Well, I suppose you could call the four times they had to replace the windshield a "problem". But frankly, they took care of it so well and always gave me a loaner car, so I never really considered it a "problem" until you mentioned it now.' CRI's research showed that the Lexus policy of always offering service customers a loaner car took almost all the pain out of the service experience. These insights from the focus groups helped explain the reasons behind the high J.D. Power satisfaction scores. And they gave CRI's client a view of the Lexus ownership experience not evident from the scores alone.

When customers express their views on videotape, the effect is even more compelling than printed verbatim comments. For company personnel, nothing beats seeing the intensity of customers' comments. Southwest Airlines shows contact employees videotapes of passengers complaining about service. Colleen Barrett, executive vice president for customers, states: 'When we show the tape, you can hear a pin drop. It's fascinating to see the faces of employees while they're watching. When they realize the customer is talking about them, it's pretty chilling. That has far more impact than anything I can say.'[10]

During the past few years, Levi Strauss & Co., one of the world's most successful companies, has been completely transforming its business processes, systems and facilities. Improving the speed and reliability distribution has been its principal objective. The team leading the transformation used videotaped interviews with customers to help convince the employees in such a successful company that change was essential. One big customer said, 'We trust many of your competitors implicitly. We sample their deliveries. We open all Levi's deliveries.' Another customer stated, 'Your lead times are the worst. If you weren't Levi's, you'd be gone.'[11]

Companies investing in service-quality information systems should consider using what McQuarrie calls 'perennial questions'.[12] A perennial question is open-ended and allows customers to speak directly about what concerns them most. Companies should ask it consistently and save responses in a database to ascertain data patterns. GTE Supply's question, 'What improvements, if any, could be made by Supply?' is a perennial question. McQuarrie offers this example: 'What things do we do particularly well or particularly poorly, relative to our competitors?' Examples of perennial questions directed to employees include:

- What is the biggest problem you face every day trying to deliver high-quality service to your customers?
- If you were president of the company and could make only one change to improve service quality, what change would you make?[13]

Combining customers' words with their numbers has synergy. The combination, when well executed, produces a high level of realism that not only informs but educates, not only guides but motivates.

Link service performance to business results

Intuitively, it makes sense that delivering quality service helps a company at the bottom line. Indeed, accumulating evidence suggests that excellent service enables a firm to strengthen customer loyalty and increase market share.[14] However, companies need not rely on outside evidence on this issue. Firms can develop their own evidence of the profit impact of service quality to make the investment more credible and fact-based for the planning and budgeting process.

A service-quality information system should include the impact of service performance on business results. An important benefit of new, declining, and lost-customer surveys is the measurement of market gains and damage linked to service quality. Surveys can reveal the number and percentage of new customers who selected the company for service-related reasons. Declining and lost-customer surveys can determine why customers are buying less or defecting, allowing estimates of revenue lost due to service. Calculating lost revenue because of service dissatisfaction, categorized by specific types of service dissatisfaction, is a dependable way to focus management attention on service improvement. By computing the average costs for reperforming botched services and multiplying them by frequency of occurrence, companies also can calculate the out-of-pocket costs of poor service. Combining lost revenue and out-of-pocket costs attributable to poor service generally will produce a sum far greater than management would assume without formal estimation.

Firms also can directly estimate the profit impact of effective service recovery by measuring complaining customers' satisfaction with the handling of their complaints and their repurchase intentions. Technical Assistance Research Programs (TARP) has conducted extensive studies documenting the much stronger repurchase intentions of complaining customers who are completely satisfied with the firm's response compared to dissatisfied customers (complainants and non-complainants) who remain dissatisfied. Firms can monitor the relationship between service recovery and business results by measuring dissatisfied customers' propensity to complain (the higher the better

because of the opportunity to resolve the complaint), and by measuring complaining customers' satisfaction with the firm's response and their repurchase intentions. These data can be used to estimate the return on investment in service recovery, i.e., profits attributed to service recovery divided by the costs of service recovery.[15]

Another way to gauge the market impact of service quality is to measure customers' repurchase and other behavioural intentions in transactional and total market surveys. The surveys can ask respondents to rate how likely it is that they will, for example, recommend the firm, do more business with the firm in the next few years, or take some business to a competitor with better prices. Respondents' intentions can then be regressed against their perceptions of service quality to reveal associations between customers' service experiences and their future intentions concerning the firm. We have investigated empirically a battery of thirteen behavioural intention statements. Using factor analysis, the thirteen-item battery reconfigured into five dimensions (see Table 2).[16]

Our research shows strong relationships between service performance and customer loyalty and propensity to switch (see Figure 4). Customers whose service perceptions were below the zone of tolerance were less loyal and more likely to switch to a competitor than customers whose perceptions exceeded the zone. Customers exhibited some willingness to pay more for better service, particularly as service perceptions rose from inadequate to desired. Intentions to complain externally fell slightly across the zone.[17] (The internal response dimension is omitted from our analysis because it is based on a single item from the thirteen-item scale.)

Companies that measure customers' behavioural intentions (or actual behaviours and monitor their sensitivity to changes in service performance gain valuable information on both why and how to invest in service improvement. Assessing the bottom-line impact of service performance will motivate managerial and non-managerial employees to implement needed changes. It will help a company move from just talking about service to improving service.

Table 2 ■ Customers' statements of intention

Behavioural-intentions dimension	Item label	Item wording*
Loyalty to company	1.	Say positive things about XYZ to other people.
	2.	Recommend XYZ to someone who seeks your advice.
	3.	Encourage friends and relatives to do business with XYZ.
	4.	Consider XYZ your first choice to buy ____ services.
	5.	Do more buisiness with XYZ in the next few years.
Propensity to switch	6.	Do less business with XYZ in the next few years.
	7.	Take some of your business to a competitor that offers better prices.
Willingness to pay more	8.	Continue to do business with XYZ if its prices increase somewhat.
	9.	Pay a higher price than competitors charge for the benefits you currently receive from XYZ.
External response to problem	10.	Switch to a competitor if you experience a problem with XYZ's service.
	11.	Complain to other customers if you experience a problem with XYZ's service.
	12.	Complain to external agencies, such as the Better Business Bureau, if you experience a problem with XYZ's service.
Internal response to problem	13.	Complain to XYZ's employees if you experience a problem with XYZ's service.

* Each item was accompanied by a 7-point likelihood scale (1 = 'Not At All Likely' and 7 = 'Extremely Likely')

Reach every employee

A service-quality information system can be beneficial only if decision makers use it. Accordingly, it must be more than a data collection system; it must also be a communications system. Determining who receives what information in what form and when is a principal design challenge. Chase Manhattan Bank vice president John Gregg commented: 'I cannot stress enough the need to systematize the use of survey information, a key learning point for us in the last couple of years. It is not just how actionable the data are, but also the system for regularly reviewing the data and making decisions that determine effectiveness.'[18]

All employees are decision-makers as they regularly make decisions that determine the effectiveness of their actions; therefore, a service-quality information system should disseminate relevant service information to everyone in the organization. Front-line service providers, for example, should receive information about the expectations and perceptions of the external or internal customers they serve. These personnel might receive information different from what executives receive – and in different forms (for example, in training classes, newsletters and videos) – but they should be included in the system. Companies miss an important teaching, reinforcing, culture-building opportunity when they don't share relevant service information with employees lower in the hierarchy.

John Deere shares customer feedback with every employee. Its system is designed so that employees in different functions receive the information in an appropriate form, e.g., via e-mail, a hard copy of customer comments posted on bulletin boards, and specialized monthly reports. Les Teplicky, manager of after-market

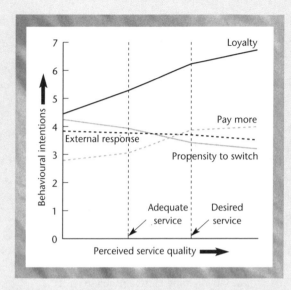

Figure 4 ■ Relationship between service quality and customers' intentions for computer manufacturer

support at John Deere, stated: 'You need senior management buy-in, good data collection, clear analysis – but all that won't matter unless every employee sees something in the information for them.'[19]

Just as in the design of any product, knowing the needs of information users is critical to designing a service-quality information system. The system should revolve around what information different kinds of employees need to help them make good decisions and how and when to communicate the information. (See Table 3 for types of questions to include in both pre-design and post-implementation surveys of targeted information users.) Packaging the right information for each audience and presenting it effectively is key to the success of a service-quality information system. As Peter Drucker stated: 'Knowledge is power. In post-capitalism, power comes from transmitting information to make it productive, not hiding it.'[20]

Table 3 ■ Questions for service-quality information system users

Pre-design	Post-implementation
■ What would you like to know about the customers you serve?	■ Are you receiving the information you need to help the company improve its service? (for managers)
■ What type of information would help you improve service in our company?	■ Are you receiving the information you need to best serve your customers? (for frontline employees)
■ What type of information would you like to have about your own service performance? About your work unit? About the company? About the competition?	■ What information on customer service would you like to receive that you currently do not receive? How would this additional information help you?
■ If you presently receive information on customer service, what type of information is most valuable to you? Why? What is least valuable? Why?	■ What customer service information that you receive is most valuable to you? Why? What is least valuable? Why?
■ What are your preferred ways of receiving customer service information? How often would you like to receive this information?	■ Do you receive customer service information on a timely basis? Please explain.
	■ What could the company do to improve the usefulness of the customer service imformation it provides you?

When listening to customers becomes a habit in a company, when managers find it unthinkable to make service investment decisions unaided by relevant information, when employees eagerly await next month's service performance scores to gauge progress, when virtually all employees understand the service improvement priorities – then it is clear that the organization is systematically using information to improve service.

References

1. Quoted in 'First Chicago Shelves Paper Surveys, Asks Managers to Use the Telephone for Customer Satisfaction Research', *The Service Edge*, Vol. 8, March 1995, p. 4.
2. E.F. McQuarrie, 'Taking a Road Trip', *Marketing Management*, Vol. 3, Spring 1995, p. 11.
3. J.A. Goodman, S.M. Broetzmann and C. Adamson, 'Ineffective – That's the Problem with Customer Satisfaction Surveys', *Quality Progress*, Vol. 25, May 1992, p. 35.
4. For a detailed discussion of this study, see: A. Parasuraman, V.A. Zeithaml and L.L. Berry, 'Alternative Scales for Measuring Service Quality: A Comparative Assessment Based on Psychometric and Diagnostic Criteria', *Journal of Retailing*, Vol. 70, Fall 1994, pp. 201–30.
5. See A. Parasuraman, V.A. Zeithaml and L.L. Berry, 'Reassessment of Expectations as a Comparison Standard in Measuring Service Quality: Implications for Further Research', *Journal of Marketing*, Vol. 58, January 1994, pp. 111–24; J.J. Cronin and S.A. Taylor, 'SERVPERF Versus SERVQUAL: Reconciling Performance-Based and Perceptions-Minus-Expectations Measurement of Service Quality', *Journal of Marketing*, Vol. 58, January 1994, pp. 125–31; and K.R. Teas, 'Expectations as a Comparison Standard in Measuring Service Quality: An Assessment of a Reassessment', *Journal of Marketing*, Vol. 58, January 1994, pp. 132–9.
6. B.S. Lunde, 'When Being Perfect is Not Enough', *Marketing Research*, Vol. 5, Winter 1993, p. 26.
7. J.P. Gregg, 'Listening to the Voice of the Customer', Nashville, Tennessee: Frontiers in Services Conference, Presentation, October 1995.
8. Quoted in 'Changes in Satisfaction Demands and Technology Alter the How's, What's, and Why's of Measurement', *The Service Edge*, Vol. 8, January 1995, p. 2.
9. J.H. Drew and T.R. Fussell, 'Becoming Partners with Internal Customers', *Quality Progress*, Vol. 29, October 1996, p. 52.
10. Quoted in 'Some Ways to Coddle Customers on a Budget', *The Service Edge*, Vol. 6, September 1993, p. 4.
11. D. Sheff, 'Levi's Changes Everything', *Fast Company*, Vol. 2, June–July 1996, p. 67.
12. McQuarrie (1995), p. 12.
13. L.L. Berry, *On Great Service: A Framework for Action*, New York: Free Press, 1995, pp. 51–2.
14. See V.A. Zeithaml, L.L. Berry and A. Parasuraman, 'The Behavioral Consequences of Service Quality', *Journal of Marketing*, Vol. 60, April 1996, pp. 31–46; and R.D. Buzzell and B.T. Gale, *The PIMS Principles*, New York: Free Press, 1987.
15. See *Consumer Complaint Handling in America: An Update Study*, Washington, D.C.: Technical Assistance Research Programs Institute, April 1986.
16. Zeithaml *et al.* (1996).
17. *Ibid.*
18. Personal correspondence.
19. Quoted in 'Rallying the Troops', *On Achieving Excellence*, Vol. 11, February 1996, p. 2.
20. Interview with Peter F. Drucker, *Harvard Business Review*, Vol. 71, May–June 1993, p. 120.

Four customers in search of solutions

Christopher H. Lovelock

Four German telephone subscribers call to complain about a variety of different service problems relating to their home phones.

Among the many customers of Telekom in Frankfurt, Germany, are four individuals living on Lindenstrasse in a middle-class suburb of the city. Each of them has a telephone-related problem and decides to call the company about it.

Heinz Peters

Heinz Peters grumbles constantly about the amount of his home telephone bill (which is, in fact, in the top 2 per cent of all household phone bills in Germany). There are many calls to countries in South America on weekday evenings, almost daily calls to Munich around mid-day, and calls to Berlin most weekends. One day, Mr Peters receives a telephone bill which is even larger than usual. On reviewing the bill, he is convinced that he has been overcharged, so he calls Telekom's customer service department to complain and request an adjustment.

Anna Braun

Anna Braun has missed several important calls recently because the caller received a busy signal. She phones the telephone company to determine possible solutions to this problem. Ms Braun's telephone bill is at the median level for a household subscriber. Most of the calls from her house are local, but there are occasional international calls to Spain or Italy. She does not subscribe to any value-added services.

Marlene von Henneberg

During the past several weeks, Mrs von Henneberg has been distressed to receive a series of obscene telephone calls. It sounds like the same person each time. She calls the telephone company to see if they can put a stop to this harassment. Her phone bill is in the bottom 10 per cent of all household subscriber bills and almost all calls are local.

Richard Rumelt

For more than a week, the phone line at Richard Rumelt's house has been making strange humming and crackling noises, making it difficult to hear what the other person is saying. After two of his friends comment on these distracting noises, Mr Rumelt calls Telekom and reports the problem. His guess is that it is being caused by the answering machine, which is getting old and sometimes loses messages. Mr. Rumelt's phone bill is at the 75th percentile for a household subscriber. Most of the calls are made to locations within Germany, usually at evenings and weekends, although

Mr Mahaleel goes to London

Christopher H. Lovelock

A wealthy Asian businessman is planning to retire. During a trip to London, he visits two international banks seeking estate planning advice and loans to enable his employees to buy the business from him.

It was a Friday in mid-February and Mr Kadir Mahaleel, a wealthy businessman from the southeast Asian nation of Tailesia, was visiting London on a trip that combined business and pleasure. Mr Mahaleel was the founder of Eximsa, a major export company in Tailesia. Business brought him to London every two to three months. These trips provided him with the opportunity to visit his daughter, Leona, the eldest of his four children, who lived in London. Several of his ten grandchildren were attending college in Britain and he was especially proud of his grandson, Anson, who was a student at the Royal College of Music. In fact, he had scheduled this trip to coincide with a violin recital by Anson at 14:00 on this particular Friday.

The primary purpose of Mr Mahaleel's visit was to resolve a delicate matter regarding his company. He had decided that the time had come to retire and wished to make arrangements for the company's future. His son, Victor, was involved in the business and ran Eximsa's trading office in Europe. However, Victor was in poor health and unable to take over the firm. A group of loyal employees had expressed interest to Mahaleel in buying the company from him if the necessary loans could be arranged.

Before leaving Tailesia, Mr Mahaleel had discussed the possibility of a buyout with Li Sieuw Meng, his trusted financial adviser, who recommended that he talk to several banks in London because of the potential complexity of the business deal. Mr Li told him:

> The London banks are experienced in buyouts. What you need is a bank that can provide the necessary credit for the interested buyers in New York and London, as well as Asia. Once the buyout takes place, you'll have significant cash to invest. This would be a good time to review your estate plans as well.

Referring Mahaleel to two competing institutions, The Trust Company and Global Private Bank, Li added:

> I've met an account officer from Global who called on me several times. Here's his business card; his name is Miguel Kim. I've never done any business with him, but he did seem quite competent. Unfortunately, I don't know anyone at the Trust Company, but here's their address in London.

After checking into his hotel in London the following Wednesday, Mr Mahaleel telephoned Mr Kim's office. Since Kim was out, Mr Mahaleel spoke to the account officer's secretary, described himself briefly, and arranged to call at Global's Lombard Street office around mid-morning on Friday.

On Thursday, Mr Mahaleel visited The Trust Company. The two people he met were extremely pleasant and had spent some time in Tailesia. They seemed very knowledgeable about managing estates and gave him some good recommendations about handling his complex family affairs. However, they were clearly less experienced in handling business credit, his most urgent need. Without a substantial loan, his employees would not be able to buy the business from him.

The next morning, Mr Mahaleel had breakfast with Leona. As they parted, she said, 'I'll meet you at half past one in the lobby of the Savoy Hotel, and we'll go to the recital together. We mustn't be late if we want to get front-row seats.'

On his way to Global Private Bank, Mr Mahaleel stopped at Mappin & Webb's, the jewellers, to buy his wife a present for their anniversary. His shopping was pleasant and leisurely; he purchased a beautiful emerald necklace which he knew his wife

---

would like. When he emerged from the shop, the weather had turned much colder and he was caught in an unexpected snow flurry. He had difficulty finding a taxi and his arthritis started troubling him, making walking to the Global office out of the question. At last he caught a taxi and arrived at the Lombard Street location of Global Bancorp about noon. After going into the street-level branch of Global Retail Bank, he was redirected by a security guard to the Private Bank offices on the second floor.

It was 12:15 when he arrived at the well-appointed reception area of the Private Bank. There he was met by Miguel Kim's secretary, who told him:

> Mr Kim was disappointed that he couldn't be here to greet you, but he had a lunch appointment with one of his clients that was scheduled over a month ago. He expects to return about 1:30. In the meantime, he has asked another senior account officer, Sophia Costa, to assist you.

Sophia Costa, 41, was a vice-president of the bank and had worked for Global Bancorp for 14 years (two years longer than Miguel Kim). She had visited Tailesia once, but had not met Mr Mahaleel's financial adviser nor any member of the Mahaleel family. An experienced relationship manager, Costa was knowledgeable about offshore investment management and fiduciary services. Miguel Kim had looked into her office at 11:45 and asked her if she would cover for him in case a prospective client, a Mr Mahaleel, whom he had expected to see earlier, should happen to arrive. He told Costa that Mahaleel was a successful Tailesian businessman planning for his retirement, but that he had never met the prospect personally, then rushed off to lunch.

Singapore Airlines

Sandra Vandermerwe ■ Christopher H. Lovelock

How can a successful international airline continue to increase its passenger volumes against stiff competition? Singapore Airlines is looking at ways to enhance the already high level of in-flight service and is evaluating certain technologically-based improvements.

As Robert Ang[1] left the marketing executives' meeting and walked through the open-air gallery back to his office in Airline House, he remembered what J.Y. Pillay, Singapore Airlines' Chairman, had said four years earlier at the company's 40th anniversary celebrations in 1987. 'At 40 the symptoms of middle age begin and that's when complacency sets in', he had warned. Ang thought to himself, 'And now that we are 44, this risk is even greater if we don't do something to hold onto our customer-oriented image.' The discussion at the meeting on this fine May morning had centred on the role of technology in achieving this goal.

Ang paused to watch a Boeing 747-400 coming in to land. Dubbed the 'Megatop' because of its extended upper deck, the aircraft was the most recent addition to the company's ultra-modern fleet. Singapore Airlines' blue, white and yellow colours shone brightly in the steamy midday heat.

As Ang entered the office complex that housed his marketing systems team, he imagined the passengers starting to disembark after a 12- to 13-hour non-stop trip from Europe. What sort of flight had they had? Had the long journey gone well, reinforcing Singapore Airlines' reputation as one of the world's best airlines? The cabin crew would now be saying goodbye, and the passengers would soon be welcomed into the spacious elegance of Terminal 2 at Changi Airport, one of the largest and most modern in the world.

Ang knew that the company's achievements were already considerable; it had become one of the world's 10 biggest international airlines. But now, on the threshold of a new decade, the question was: could Singapore Airlines continue to attract increasing numbers of international customers?

'We are leaders in service, in comfort and luxury. Our customers tell us they fall in love when they fly with us. Where do we go from here?' were some of the remarks voiced at the meeting. For Robert Ang, there was only one logical answer: they had to satisfy the needs of contemporary travellers, which meant being able to bring the sophisticated technology found in people's homes and offices into the air. 'Very little attention has been given to adapting technology strategically for our business', he had declared to his colleagues that morning. 'For instance, home audio systems are fantastic. But in the air, they're terrible. We have to close this technology gap and provide modern customers with interesting and useful technology-based services.'

Ang's views had been received with interest. His boss, the director of marketing planning, had closed the meeting by asking him to come up with some specific suggestions. 'But,' he had cautioned, 'don't suggest anything that might conflict with the romance and superb personal service we're rightly famous for!'

Background

'How did it all begin?' was a question that people encountering Singapore Airlines for the first time often asked. Many were surprised that a small island republic, measuring only 38 km long by 22 km wide (16 × 24 miles), and with a population of 2.7 million, could have one of the world's largest and most profitable airlines. Even more remarkable were the accolades bestowed by air travel organizations. In 1990, *Air Transport World* magazine named SIA 'airline of the year'; *Conde Nast's Traveler* termed it the 'world's best airline'; and *Business Traveler International* called SIA the 'best international airline'.

Republic of Singapore

Just north of the equator, with a command of the straits between Malaysia and Indonesia, Singapore was ideally located for both shipping and airline routes. Being at the intersection of East and West, it saw itself at the heart of trade and business between the two.

In the 26 years since its independence in 1965, the nation had made what most observers considered to be astonishing economic progress. Per capita national income had reached US$10,450, representing 37 per cent that of Switzerland, which Singaporean planners often cited as their economic model. It boasted not only one of the world's largest and most modern port facilities, but an airport, opened in 1981 and expanded in 1990, of equal calibre. Other accomplishments included a state-of-the-art telecommunications system, well-engineered highways and the new Mass Rapid Transit rail system. Heavy investments in education and a strong work ethic had created a well-trained and motivated workforce. By 1991, Singapore was one of the world's largest shipbuilding and ship-repairing centres, the third largest oil refining and distribution complex, and had also become an important banking and financial centre.

Singapore had made a particular effort to attract high-technology firms, and many international companies had set up offices and plants on the island. Government planners saw technology as a driving force in the economy. As advances in telecommunications proceeded, and Singapore Telecom continued to push towards a fully digitalized system, planners spoke about creating an 'intelligent island'.

History of Singapore Airlines

Who would have believed that a country only one-quarter the size of Rhode Island, the smallest state in the US, would produce one of the most profitable airlines in the world? The story of Singapore Airlines officially started on 1 May 1947, when the first scheduled flight of Malaysian Airlines from Singapore landed in Penang. When both Malaysia and Singapore became independent in the mid-1960s, the name of the carrier was changed to Malaysia-Singapore Airlines. However, it soon became obvious that the two nations had different priorities. Malaysia's main interest was having a flag carrier that would provide domestic and regional routes. But, being a small island, Singapore did not need domestic services; instead, its goal was to have long-distance international routes. It was agreed that the assets should be divided and two separate airlines created.

Singapore Airlines first flew under its own colours in October 1972. When it was announced that Malaysia and Singapore had agreed to establish two separate flag carriers, optimism was tempered by uncertainty and disbelief. Could an airline from such a small country compete in the international big league? Nevertheless, the 1970s seemed to be a good time for an airline to take off and succeed. Not only did the remarkable passenger growth of the 1960s – when traffic was doubling every five years – promise to continue, but ever-increasing numbers of people worldwide were travelling to more places. In addition, exciting new high performance jets were being introduced.

Although Singapore Airlines (SIA) was state-owned, the government's role in policy-making and day-to-day management was minimal; senior executives were told not to expect any subsidy or preferential treatment. What the government did do, however, was to offer foreign carriers the opportunity to operate out of Singapore, under the condition that SIA would receive similar rights, even if they were not exercised immediately. The new airline pushed relentlessly for growth and innovation. Three months before operations began, it signed a contract with Boeing for the delivery of two B747-200s, with an option on two more. It was the first airline in Southeast Asia to order jumbo jets.

Singapore Airlines also concentrated on marketing. The airline's name and its logo – a stylized yellow bird – decorating the aircraft's dark blue tail fin soon became well known on the routes it operated. The goal was to create a distinctly different airline that would be international but retain its Asian personality. Most importantly, top management insisted that it emphasize service to passengers who, they constantly reminded staff, were the unique reason for the airline's existence. In a world where one carrier resembled another, they realized that the cabin crew was the prime link between the passenger and the airline. The idea was to use the island's only real resource – the natural hospitality of its people – as a competitive advantage. In this way, it seemed certain that Singapore's national carrier would be remembered – and remembered favourably.

Research had shown that, when all other things were equal, passengers responded most to the appeal of high quality in-flight services. SIA was the first airline to put 'snoozers' (fully reclining seats) in its aircraft. Since the company did not belong to IATA (International Air Transport Association), SIA's management went against the rules by serving free drinks, offering free movie headsets and other extras. The intent was to firmly establish an image of SIA in customers' minds as *the* airline for fine service.

The 'Singapore Girl' – the personification of charm and friendliness – became a reality after painstaking recruiting, training and retraining. The best-looking and most helpful young women were selected as stewardesses. They were given a maximum of three contract terms of five years each, above average wages and high status in the company. Better staff were given the possibility of promotion to senior jobs within SIA after the five-year period. An extensive and distinctive advertising campaign promoted these stewardesses who dressed in sarong-sebayas, multicoloured, ankle-length dresses made from traditional batik fabric designed by the Paris couturier Balmain. Male flight attendants were more conventionally dressed in light blue blazers and black trousers.

These distinctively uniformed women became the symbol of the airline's mission to deliver high quality, personalized service. Research showed that they had the most lasting impact on passengers. Travellers reported that their beautiful uniform and charm were, in reality, all that the advertising had promised, and that in-flight service was better than anything they had experienced in a long time.

Top management was equally concerned with services on the ground. In 1973, a subsidiary company, Singapore Airport Terminal Services (SATS), was formed to perform ground handling, catering and related tasks. Later, it started offering its services on a contract basis to other carriers that had operations in Singapore. In 1985, SATS was restructured into a holding company with four subsidiaries – SATS Passenger Services, SATS Catering, SATS Cargo and SATS Apron Services.

Singapore Airlines survived the two oil shocks of the 1970s and continued to grow, creating headlines with such innovations as supersonic Concorde service between London and Singapore, operated jointly with British Airways, featuring BA colours on one side of the aircraft and SIA colours on the other. It also expanded its route structure. Huge aircraft orders, including what was then the largest in civil aviation history, were made. Thanks to strong profits, the airline was able to invest in new equipment without incurring significant debt. These enormous purchases were not all incremental additions to the fleet, for the company resold used aircraft after only a few years. Because they had been so well maintained, the 'old' aircraft found ready buyers at good prices in the second-hand market.

The situation in 1991

As one industry observer remarked, '1990 was a year that most airlines would sooner forget!' Battered by recession, a hike in oil prices, high interest rates on heavy debt loads, and the tensions arising from the Iraqi invasion of Kuwait, most major airlines suffered heavy financial losses. The outbreak of hostilities in the Gulf intensified problems – fear of terrorist attacks sharply reduced passenger loads on most international routes. But, at a time when many other airlines were retrenching, Singapore Airlines actually increased its advertising budget.

SIA's consolidated financial results for the fiscal year ending 31 March 1991 showed only a slight decline in revenues, from S$5.09 billion to S$4.95 billion.[2] The number of passengers carried climbed from 6.8 million to 7.1 million, even though the load factor dropped from 78.3 per cent to 75.1 per cent as a result of a jump in fleet size. In 1990, SIA had the highest operating profit of any airline in the world: US$775 million. Apart from its marketing appeal, Singapore Airlines had another point in its favour – the higher margins obtained on airline services in Asia. The Asian carriers did not compete on price among themselves. They preferred non-price forms of competition such as better service, more destinations, more frequent schedules and newer fleets. With the entry of American players into the region, however, price became a more important feature.

The airline's fleet of 29 Boeing 747s and 14 Airbus 310s was the youngest fleet of all international carriers, with an average age of 4.75 years, compared to an industry average of around 10 years. The company had 36 new aircraft on order (of which 28 were the new B747-400s) and another 34 on option. Management was convinced that newer planes were not only more attractive to passengers and helped staff provide better service, but also offered other advantages such as greater reliability and lower fuel consumption. Exhibit 1 compares Singapore Airlines' performance measures with those of other major international airlines.

By 1991 Singapore Airlines was among the ten biggest airlines in the world, as measured in terms of international tonne-kilometres of load carried. Its network linked 63 cities in 37 countries, and soon it would fulfil a long-held ambition to serve the east coast of the United States with transatlantic service from Frankfurt to New York. Singapore Changi Airport had become one of the world's largest and busiest terminals.

Government holdings had been reduced through stock sales to 54 per cent of the company's assets. The airline had joined a trilateral alliance with Swissair and the American carrier, Delta Airlines, to cooperate on customer servicing, interchangeable tour packages, through check-in, joint baggage handling, sharing of airport lounges and joint promotions. It had also become a member of IATA in order to give the airline a voice in key industry forums, and greater access to their technical expertise and accredited sales agents. However, SIA did not want to participate in deliberations on tariff coordination where fare issues were discussed.

Despite the airline's achievements, there were some disquieting signs on the horizon. Competition was

Exhibit 1 ■ Key performance measures, 1990

1990 scheduled passengers carried (international)		1990 scheduled passenger-kilometres performed (international)		1990 operating profits of the top ten of these airlines	
Rank:	Numbers (in thousands)	Rank:	Numbers (in millions)	Rank:	US dollars (millions)
1. British Airways	19,684	1. British Airways	62,834	1. Singapore Airlines	774
2. Lufthansa	13,326	2. Japan Airlines	42,690	2. Cathay Pacific	468
3. Air France	12,417	3. Lufthansa	38,744	3. Japan Airlines	464
4. Pan American	10,096	4. Pan American	38,241	4. British Airways	345
5. Japan Airlines	8,354	5. United	35,334	5. SAS	264
6. American Airlines	8,343	6. Singapore Airlines	31,544	6. American Airlines	67.9
7. SAS	8,335	7. Air France	29,023	7. Lufthansa	0
8. Cathay Pacific	7,378	8. Qantas	27,687	8. KLM	(19.3)
9. Alitalia	7,105	9. KLM	26,382	9. Alitalia	(75.7)
10. Singapore Airlines	7,093	10. American Airlines	24,086	10. Air France	(286)

intensifying and service quality improving among a number of both Western and Asian airlines, including Hong Kong-based Cathay Pacific, Japan Airlines, a new strongly financed Taiwanese start-up called Eva Air and Thai International and Malaysia airlines. The latter two both featured stewardesses in eye-catching uniforms based on traditional costumes.

With rising living standards in Singapore came higher expectations among SIA's more than 13,000 employees, of whom some 4,200 were cabin crew. The company was finding it increasingly difficult to attract younger people, motivate existing employees and maintain its policy of employing the best staff for customer contact roles.

Maintaining the customer service philosophy

Recognizing that the most exciting years were now over, top management continued to stress the importance of SIA's customer philosophy and service culture. The underlying principle that the customer came first was carried through at all levels of the organization. How customers were handled at each point of contact was considered of paramount importance. Company policy stated that if a trade-off had to be made, it should be made in favour of the customer. For example, contrary to the practice at other airlines, no customer was allowed to be downgraded for a Singapore Airlines senior executive who wanted a special seat.

Ground had recently been broken for a new US$50 million training centre, designed to drill all employees in the fine art of serving customers. As reported in the *Straits Times*, Singapore's leading newspaper, everyone – from the floor sweeper to the deputy managing director – would receive this training. The underlying philosophy was to enable staff to place themselves in the customer's position. A lot of the training time was thus experientially based. Key people were sent on special missions to see what other airlines were doing and how customers were handled. Special delay simulation games groomed staff on ways to cope with delay situations, one of the major complaints received from passengers.

One principle remained constant: staff had to be as flexible as possible in their dealings with customers, even if it took more time and effort. Management constantly reiterated that customers could not be told what to do simply because it suited the company. Some passengers wanted to eat as soon as they boarded, others preferred to wait. Customers could not be pigeonholed, they often changed their minds. They might come on board intending to sleep and then decide to watch a movie after all. On long hauls, flexibility was especially important. Most passengers had individual habits that corresponded to their travel agendas, which could include sleeping at the beginning and working later, or vice versa.

Staff had learned that customers were happier when given a choice. Offering more meal variations automatically reduced the number of unhappy people. Menus, typically changed by other airlines no more than four times a year, were altered every week on SIA's high frequency flights. Information technology enabled the chefs to fine-tune meals and immediately withdraw any dishes that were poorly received. Although there were marginal costs associated with such tactics, management firmly believed that these efforts distinguished Singapore Airlines from its competitors. Staff were instructed to find other ways to save money. For instance, the chefs prepared meals only from ingredients in season. Crew members were briefed by the kitchen on how to prepare and serve anything new.

Complaints were encouraged as they provided insight about problems. Once they were received, something could be done to rectify the situation; all complaints were tracked down and followed up. Travellers were invited to submit these complaints in writing. While some customers – typically Americans, Germans and Australians – readily complied, others were less willing to do so in writing. These customers were specifically questioned in follow-up surveys.

A Service Productivity Index (SPI) was computed each quarter in order to assess service quality standards. Multilingual in-flight surveys were used to itemize customers' impressions on key issues; then this information was compiled along with data on punctuality, baggage mishandled/recovered per 1,000 passengers, and the ratio of complaints to compliments addressed to management.

As soon as a complaint relating directly to a specific in-flight experience was received, crew members could be temporarily taken out of the system and given training. Cabin crew members were released from their flight schedules three or four times a year to meet training experts. Senior cabin crew members met every Monday morning for feedback and exchange sessions with service support personnel. One 'ritual' practised was to address the crew from the control centre just before takeoff about topical issues, special promotions and other issues relevant to services.

At the airport in Singapore, staff were encouraged to do everything possible to deal with legitimate customer problems. One story – now part of company folklore – was about a supervisor who found a tailor at midnight and paid a deposit from his own funds to have a suit made for a customer whose luggage had been lost so that the customer could attend an important meeting at noon the next day.

Customer profile and the product line

The product line was divided into three classes of travel – First, Raffles (business) and Economy. First Class accounted for 5 per cent of passengers, Raffles Class for 10 per cent, and Economy Class for 85 per cent. About one million of the seven million seats sold annually were to Singaporeans. Revenues from non-Singaporeans were proportionately higher since they tended to fly longer distances. Of the airline's passengers, 75 per cent were from outside the country and 25 per cent were from home base.

Flights varied in length – from less than one hour to over 13 hours for non-stop flights to Europe. Flights under four hours were all non-smoking, reflecting Singapore's strong national commitment to curtailing tobacco use. Exhibit 2 shows the percentage breakdown of the airline's daily flights by number of hours and amount of overnight travel.

On average, the load factor was somewhat higher in Economy Class (close to 80 per cent) than in Raffles or First. Passengers who flew Raffles Class on a daytime flight might travel First Class on an overnight flight for the extra comfort.

Top management believed that the business passenger market held the future for the airline – both in numbers and yield. At the marketing executives' meeting Robert Ang had just attended, everyone had concurred that technology was the key to improving service to this segment of the market. The expectations of these particular customers, SIA executives knew, were constantly rising and their needs had changed greatly since the previous decade. Research revealed that business travellers:

■ preferred to eat small amounts and less often;
■ wanted more nutrition in their diet;
■ tended to be impatient and resented having to wait;
■ wanted to have the facilities found in airport lounges – such as showers and fax machines – also available in the sky;
■ disliked wasting time on board and wanted to be occupied throughout the flight.

Technological innovation

At the start of the meeting, Robert Ang had pointed out that the only way for the company to genuinely cater to travellers' increasingly sophisticated needs

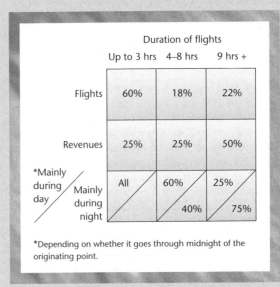

Exhibit 2 ■ Details on duration of flights

was to use technology more strategically for enhancing the quality of service. It was not enough to simply pick easily replicated innovations on an *ad hoc* basis. He had declared:

> Just going out and looking for technology-based solutions will give the market the impression that we are gimmicky and arbitrary in our approach. If we want to protect our competitive position, we've got to find ways to move faster than our competitors and create an enduring advantage for the company. There will be a million problems but, once we agree on the principle of 'technology in the sky' as a competitive tool, we can solve the technical hassles. We have to use technology in the future as we used people in the past to serve customers. If we can match our high-tech services with our soft services, we will be irresistible to customers and will be distinguished from the rest.

Several technological innovations were already planned for introduction later that year. One was the installation of small TV screens at each First and Business Class seat, offering passengers video entertainment. Since other airlines were also doing this, ensuring variety would be pivotal. Another was satellite-linked air-to-ground telephone service which, unlike previously, allowed passengers to make calls even when the aircraft was above the ocean. Although these innovations were important, Ang felt they were not enough. He knew that there would be innumerable possibilities for adding value to the customers' total flying experience – but only if the know-how and technology could be applied correctly.

Almost 80,000 travellers were registered in the Priority Passenger Service (PPS) programme. To become a member, a passenger had to fly at least 60,000 km (37,500 miles) a year in First or Raffles Class. Benefits included extra baggage allowance, automatic flight reconfirmation, priority wait listing, a complimentary magazine subscription and discounts on car rentals, hotels and shopping. Information about each PPS member – such as seat and meal preferences – was stored in a computer and could be automatically implemented when reservations were

made. Ang considered this kind of service to be only the beginning; there was no end to what information technology could do to improve customer service. There was also no compelling technological reason to confine the system to only 80,000 people.

Advertising campaigns

Around 2 per cent of Singapore Airlines' gross income was devoted to advertising and promotion. All expenditures were carefully controlled by the head office, and strategic advertising decisions were all centralized. Tactical advertising that focused on specific routes, schedules or promotions was handled locally, but was strictly monitored in Singapore to guarantee consistency.

The 'Singapore Girl' theme had remained a key element in the company's advertising strategy since day one. Initially, the aim of this strategy was to impart a feeling of romance and luxury service, and so it was dominated by images of sarong-clad women against exotically romantic backdrops. The modern fleet campaign which followed featured aircraft exteriors or interiors with just a small cameo inset of a stewardess at one side.

The purpose of the fleet modernization campaign was to give another strong message to the market: that Singapore Airlines was a leader in aircraft technology. The object was to show that the 'steel' did not overpower the 'silk'. The photographs gave the advertising a deliberately dream-like quality, a theme carried through in the 1990 Raffles campaign – SIA's first attempt to aim specifically at business class travellers.

Research revealed that two out of every three Europeans, Americans and Australians preferred the romantic ads to the technical ones. These passengers were spellbound by the beauty of the stewardesses and impressed by their competence and caring. Japanese and other Asian clients, on the other hand, seemed to prefer the high-tech ads which denoted modernity, reliability and new experiences. The Singapore Girl did not seem so exotic, unusual or appealing to this group.

Sales and distribution system

Like most carriers, Singapore Airlines depended heavily on independent agents to sell its service. In 1973, the airline initiated its own computer reservation and check-in system, KRISCOM. By 1991 this had been replaced by Abacus, a computer reservation system which provided travel agents with an extended array of services including airline and hotel reservations, ground arrangements and regional travel news. Originally created by Singapore Airlines and two other Asian carriers, Abacus was now owned and operated by SIA and nine other carriers, including three American firms. More than 100 carriers, 80 hotel chains and many other travel services had signed up with Abacus to distribute their services through the system.

When reservations were made on Singapore Airlines by travel agents, the recorded preferences of Priority Passenger Service (PPS) travellers would automatically be retrieved from the computer. A wide variety of special meal options, reflecting the travellers' many different health and religious needs, were offered. Special meal requests were forwarded to the catering department which received a print-out of all such requests for each flight. The special meal request was linked to the seat allocated to the passenger. Exhibit 3 shows a simplified flow chart of the linkages between the different databases and the departure control system.

Technology and on-the-ground services

The Ground Services Department was responsible for the ground handling of passengers, baggage, cargo, and mail at all 63 airports in the Singapore Airlines network. At Changi, SATS were in charge, but at other airports the airline had to rely on subcontractors. Even though some Singapore Airlines employees were allocated to these stations, most staff members were host country nationals and frequently had a different way of thinking.

Since what people really wanted was to get in and out of airports as quickly and easily as possible, Ang believed that interventions with staff should be kept to a minimum. Specific problems had to be dealt with and overcome:

It's easier to control the quality of service in the air than on the ground. Key decisions are made at the head office and implemented on board. Airports, on the other hand, are difficult to control. Technology is the key. The airports themselves are too crowded, with too few gates, too few counters and long lines. While in-flight service staff typically *give* customers something – free headsets, free newspapers, free drinks, free meals, free movies – ground service staff *take* – tickets, excess baggage fees, or they say you can't have the seat you want. Thirty percent of all complaints relate to seat assignments, another 20% to aircraft delays. How these delays are handled has a big impact on customer opinion. Passengers become really unhappy when staff can't provide information, find them seats on alternative airlines, or obtain hotel rooms when they are delayed overnight. Lost baggage also accounts for about 20% of total complaints. With better technology and information, not only can we give the same kind of service on the ground as in the air, but we can minimize our risk by providing everyone around the world with a system we know works.

An Outstanding Service On the Ground Programme (OSG) had been started for all passengers and complemented by lounges, equipped with every possible luxury and convenience, instituted earlier for First and Business Class travellers. When Terminal 2 opened at Changi, a new Departure Control System (DCS90) was phased in. A key component was an improved simplified format for the screens used at check-in. It had become increasingly difficult to recruit and retain staff for check-in positions, and the complex software led to delays for passengers. A new user-friendly programme, with menu-driven, on-screen commands was introduced, which simplified both the task and the training.

The benefits for passengers included a simplified and speedier check-in process, with boarding passes and baggage tags being automatically encoded and printed at the check-in. The boarding pass included seat allocation and gate information, and confirmed special requests such as vegetarian meals. At the boarding gate, passengers would simply slip their boarding passes through a reader at the gate and the DCS90 software would verify check-in details against

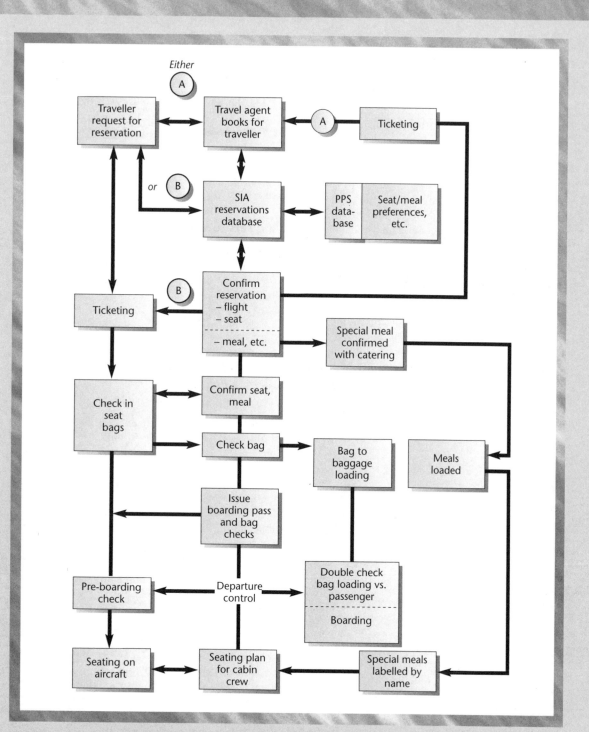

Exhibit 3 ■ Flowchart of databases

boarding passengers. An important security benefit was the automatic matching up of checked baggage with passengers going on board. (Refer to Exhibit 3.)

A Telecar system was introduced to take baggage from one terminal to another within three minutes. It was then manually sorted and handled. If an urgent flight connection had to be made, this fact was communicated to the staff in advance so that baggage could be taken by trolley to the waiting aircraft. Unlike the situation at most other airports, the Skytrain not only took passengers to and from terminals, but staff directed and accompanied passengers to flights with short connecting times, thus minimizing confusion and delays.

Technology and in-flight services

By realizing such innovations as video screens at each seat and better air-to-ground telecommunications, Ang wanted to transform the cabin into an 'office and leisure centre in the sky' which would enhance entertainment as well as business services. Surely almost anything could be possible in the future thanks to technology. But what did the customers value? What was feasible? What would distinguish Singapore Airlines from the competition? What were the real issues? At the meeting, he had told the others:

> We have to be able to provide passengers with as much distraction – be it entertainment or professional – as possible during their flight. It's just the opposite from the situation on the ground. Customers must be able to do whatever they need to do throughout their time with us. And, the choice must be theirs, not ours. They shouldn't have to encounter any problems in dealing with our staff and should, in fact, be encouraged to interact with them as much as possible, since we're very good at that. If technology is used properly and creatively, we can personalize our services still more and make people feel that we really care. For instance, hand-held computers can tell on-board crews everything they need to know about each customer so that services can be customized.

After the meeting, Ang's boss, the director of marketing planning, commented on the suggestions Ang had made. Although the ideas were interesting, he

said, there should be nothing to disturb other passengers, reduce valuable seating space, or adversely affect the company's high level of personal service. Ang, who had anticipated this reaction, responded by saying that the location of the technology on board would be the determining factor. He could think of several options: centring the technology at each passenger's seat; demarcating work and leisure centres at a given spot inside the aircraft; or, alternatively, using crew members to handle the bulk of passenger requests, for instance sending faxes.

Ang sets to work

Back in his office, with a good feeling about the meeting that morning, Robert Ang thought about the three pillars that provided the quality experience the company insisted on for its customers. First was modern aircraft, where Singapore Airlines was already ahead. Second was on-the-ground services, where much remained to be done, despite the accomplishments at Changi Airport. In particular, technology had to be developed so that the company's worldwide network of sales and air staff, agents, and subcontractors could function in unison.

Third was the question of in-flight services. What technology-based services should be developed to improve the customers' experience in the air? Could an 'office in the air' actually work? To what extent could more comfort and entertainment be provided, and how could the first and business class facilities be differentiated from the ones in economy? Most importantly, how could all these ideas be consolidated and effected so that Singapore Airlines would be the technological leader in civil aviation?

Ang knew that the *how* questions needed a lot of thought before a formal presentation could be made to his boss. But it was even more crucial to find a cohesive concept that would be appreciated and bought companywide. Perhaps it would be best to set out the various customer activities in a framework. He began to sketch out a rough flowchart showing the sequence of a typical journey. Before long, he had segmented the chart into three sections: pre-flight activities, in-flight activities and post-flight activities. (Refer to Exhibit 4.) He began to fill in his ideas for using technology at each key point.

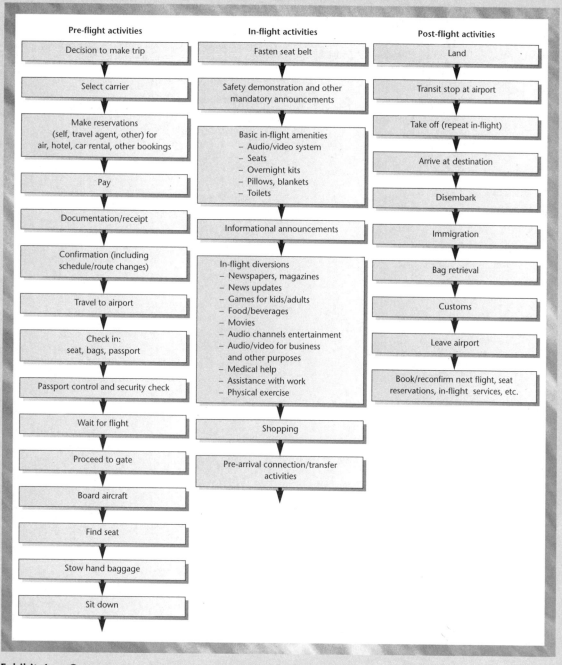

Exhibit 4 ■ Customer experience pre-flight, in-flight and post-flight

When he finally stopped for a coffee break, the sun had already begun to touch the horizon, creating a pale pink haze in the tropical sky. As he rose and stretched, he heard the soft hum of a plane above. 'Must be the flight leaving for Frankfurt', he said aloud.

Notes

1. Disguised name.
2. Representative exchange rates for the Singapore dollar in mid-1991 were: S$1.00 = US$0.60 = £0.33.

Citibank Greece: the Tao of consumer banking

Sandra Vandermerwe ■ Marika Taishoff

As Greece becomes more closely integrated into the European economy, Citibank's retail operations there risk losing their edge to the emerging competition. In response, the bank seeks to introduce what is, for that country, a new philosophy of operating from the customer's point of view.

Looking up at the ancient Acropolis visible from his office window in February 1994, Tom Sisson, Manager for Citibank Consumer Banking in Greece, recalled his initial reluctance to come to Greece in 1989: he had been doing well in Chile where he had set up the first Model Branch, a tangible manifestation of the bank's new process-based philosophy – to provide superior seamless services to customers on their terms rather than the bank's.

Part of Tom's initial reluctance about going to Greece was not knowing the language and having no work experience in Europe. And there was no clearly defined European marketing strategy at the time. Also, Citibank Greece had performed extremely well over the years – which he knew would probably make it even more difficult to persuade the staff – most of whom had been with the bank ten years or more – to change their thinking and behaviour and adopt a new approach to the market. Yet he was convinced that unless the bank, and its branch system, learned to operate from the 'customer's point of view', Citibank's long-standing dominance in the Greek market would soon be eroded.

Citibank in Europe and the Greek banking scene

Citibank had been present in Europe since 1902, and by the 1980s it had consumer operations in nine countries: the UK, France, Spain, Belgium, the Netherlands, Germany, Austria, Italy and Greece. Its widest European retail presence in terms of number of branches was in Germany, where the company had purchased, in 1973, that country's largest and oldest consumer lending bank.

Citibank had been the first foreign bank to set up operations in Greece in 1964. It had focused on the corporate market and quickly acquired the top 20 Greek shipowners as its lead clients. Twenty years later, when Citibank decided to go into the consumer side of the business, many of these shipowners transferred their personal accounts to the bank as well.

There were several interrelated reasons for Citibank's long-standing success in Greece: the banking sector had been heavily regulated by the government, and all the leading Greek banks were nationalized state-run institutions with very strong unions that frequently organized strikes. Liquidity was scarce, and consumer lending was restricted. Typically, any banking experience meant waiting in long queues and dealing with government employees who had a reputation for surliness.

One of Citibank's advantages was that it was not subject to strikes; queues were not as long as in the national banks; the staff was more professional than elsewhere; the ATMs functioned well; and, the bank had an international image. But, on the negative side, the Citibank's branch network was limited; branches were small and overcrowded; and service indicators were deteriorating. Citibank had maintained its average of 90 per cent service levels for some time (compared to the 50 per cent average given to state banks), but other private banks were already at the 80 per cent mark. Also, the staff had been performing a host of new transactions – such as accepting the ever more numerous Visa payments which left insufficient time for customers. And, because they were operations intensive, they had no time to actually sell.

Though the Greek banking system was still government-run, Sisson knew that it was only a question of time before the industry would be entirely deregulated. The year he had arrived (1989), over 10 new private banks had appeared on the local scene. These banks – like Citibank – were not prone to employee strikes and, compared to the state banks, were relatively 'queueless'. In anticipation of deregulation and a spurt in consumer buying habits, more European banks – well-placed to handle international transactions – had moved into the Greek market. As well, there were 11 new Visa issuers and some Greek shipowners who had set up their own banking operations.

Tom believed that all of these new competitors would be after Citibank's target segment – two groups comprised of 825,000 households, or 25 per cent of the Greek population, primarily living in the two major cities of Athens and Thessaloniki. Of the 3.3 million households in Greece, 8 per cent, according to Citibank's research, were in the top segment. These individuals had gone to university, lived in exclusive areas, travelled frequently, and purchased high-quality imported goods. The next bracket, with 17 per cent of the households, were typically high school graduates who lived in more modest neighbourhoods and were not yet buying much imported merchandise.

All of these trends made it clear to Tom that Citibank risked losing its competitive edge to the emerging competition. He knew he had to persuade his staff that merely making a couple of marginal improvements to the existing system would not be enough. What they needed was a new model for growth – a completely different marketing approach.

The Tao of banking as a philosophy

Research had shown that most people considered banking to be a disjointed experience, full of time-consuming activities and hassles. Despite having a certain loyalty to their banks, expectations amongst consumers were low and banking capabilities were generally perceived as poor. This attitude, the top team at Citibank felt, was both a problem and an opportunity.

'Citibanking' would be a new philosophy about a different way to go about marketing services. The 'Citibanking' goal was to create a 'holistic' banking experience – whatever and wherever that might be – rather than expect customers to fit into the activities and operations of the banking fraternity. By providing superior and relevant services for customers – what, when and where they needed them – Citibank hoped to create a full financial relationship with customers, i.e., handle all their banking activities and thereby retain these customers over longer periods of time and go deeper into their wallets.

This concept was soon referred to in-house as the 'Tao of Citibanking'. Like most philosophies, the one at Citibank was conceptually simple. One executive described it this way:

> The fact is, we have to align the bank's activities and processes (what we do and how) to those of the customer, instead of *vice versa*. I've asked myself this question for years: why should a customer change his affairs to suit us? Rather, shouldn't we do what suits him? Yet, this has been going on for decades. Why should customers have to pay their Visa bills when we want them to, making them comply with our operations, when they won't get their salary until two days later? But, the Tao philosophy also means creating a win/win outcome for all. It's about reinventing the way the business works so that everyone gains.

'Tao' was not a new book of rules or commandments or a new product, as some people originally thought. Literally, it meant 'the way' – i.e., the journey or the process – with no beginning or end, an ongoing flow – with continuous progress. The ancient philosophers and mystics in China, where the school of thought originated, applied the Tao concept in a multitude of contexts: the 'way' of the cosmos, the 'way' of the universe, the 'way' of nature, the 'way' of man – and the point they made was that each was important but none could be looked at separately, since they were interrelated and interdependent. Some disciplines in modern science had come to the same conclusion: quantum physics had shown that, on a sub-atomic scale, all particles were inherently interrelated: each shaped by the properties of the particles around them.

In top management's view, Citibank customers would want to have a Tao banking relationship – a total banking experience made up of several interrelated parts – to manage and co-ordinate their financial needs. Although many banking customers were local, they increasingly wanted the same services on a global/pan-European level. For example, there were 2 million Greek families living in the United States, as well as big communities existing elsewhere in the world, e.g. in Australia and Germany. These customers were demanding more global and pan-European capabilities, like foreign currency and other transactions. Already, the number of transactions done by non-local customers using Greek facilities had risen to 2 per cent. And, in a recent survey, 32 per cent of Citibank's Greek customers had asked for services in other countries. Finally, most customers in the upper segments regardless of country were mobile, travelling for business and pleasure, or sending their children to university abroad. There were also local customers who never travelled much, but none the less wanted a bank with a global or pan-European image.

The customer's process as a platform

A common idea of what happened in the 'customer's space' – where they went through the various parts of their banking experiences, in their homes, at the branch or elsewhere – had been formed by Citibank in the US. This process *began* when an account was opened, continued on an *ongoing* basis as customers managed their finances using facilities on a daily basis, and was *extended* when new services were needed – including in other countries.

From the customer's point of view, as Citibank saw it, there were four aspects to this experience that required attention: how the customer gets started; how the relationship works for the customer; how customers use the relationship; and how customers interact with the people they deal with.

To correspond with these four aspects, Citibank then identified a total of nine projects that would encompass all the needs of a new customer's banking relationship. They were:

(1) *One-Step On-Line Relationship Opening*; (2) *CitiCard*; (3) *Integrated Product Package*; (4) *Relationship Pricing and Value*; (5) *CitiStatement*; (6) *Model Branches*; (7) *Citicard Banking Centres*; (8) *CitiPhone Banking*; (9) *Citibanker Difference*.

1 How the customer gets started

Traditionally, the activities in this stage were administrative and time-consuming: customers filled in and signed a host of forms, which were frequently repetitive and redundant, and tended to be irritating. The banker didn't know who the customer was. Phones were always ringing; the tellers were constantly interrupting to ask the banker to countersign another customer's request; and, as the account opening forms could only be printed at a central workstation in the back office, the banker frequently had to abandon the customer to retrieve these documents.

With Citibanking, the *One-Step On-Line Relationship Opening* allowed the banker to ask all the relevant questions and simultaneously type the responses into the computer. This input would create the 'master documentation' about that customer, thus obviating the need to go through the process again whenever a new service or account was needed. Secondly, interruptions in the data gathering flow were minimized, because phones were automatically diverted whenever a banker was with a customer. The banker's workstation was equipped with a printer, thus enabling him to print forms then and there.

As well, the CitiCard bank card – with the customer's name and number – was created on the spot, thus giving the customer instant fulfilment and eliminating any waiting time or the risk of losing the card in the mail.

2 How the relationship works for the customer

This process applied to all the transactions and services related to what the customer 'owned' at the bank, i.e., typically a cheque account, a savings account, money market and investment accounts.

Whenever a customer wanted to make any transaction, he had to go to his branch, fill in a deposit or withdrawal form and wait in line for a teller. Once the customer reached the teller, he had to identify himself and request the needed service. Because some transactions required a dual signature, the teller would have to leave the customer to get the required countersignature from the manager or one of the bankers. Most banks would send out different statements for each one of a customer's accounts, with the various types of services each priced differently.

So as to give the Tao of 'Citibanking' real meaning, everything which comprised what the customer 'owned' at the bank had to be integrated. The four projects within this element of the total banking relationship were: the *CitiCard*; the *Integrated Product Package*; *Relationship Pricing and Value*; and the *CitiStatement*.

a The *CitiCard* was the 'key' to the entire relationship. Not only did it allow the customer to access all his accounts *via* the ATMs, it also instantly identified the customer – after passing his card through the card reader at the teller's desk – to the teller, who could then call the customer by name and have all relevant personal information in front of him, ready and waiting. Because the customer, by using the CitiCard, effectively authorized any transaction being made, having dual control and the manager's countersignature on the transaction was no longer necessary, thus more time was saved.

b The *Integrated Product Package* bundled all the products and services owned by the customer – i.e., cheques, savings, money market, investment, bankcards, etc., – into a single package, simplifying financial transactions and queries.

c Because all CitiOne accounts were linked, *Relationship Pricing and Value* allowed customers to benefit from fee waivers when the total relationship (as opposed to individual activities) reached a minimum size. This tiered pricing system was a flexible rate system, adjusted according to the value of the relationship.

d The *CitiStatement* was the monthly summary – in one consolidated document – of every transaction in all the customer's product and service accounts, showing the total amount of money and/or credit the customer held, and how much he owed.

3 How customers use the relationship

This process defined where, when and how the customer could deal with the bank's distribution facilities. These distribution points generally included the branch itself and two technological distribution points – ATM machines and the phone. Which facility the customer could use mainly depended on the nature of the transaction to be performed or the information required.

With Citibanking, customers could gain access to all distribution facilities, so that any transaction made at a branch could also be done at an ATM or over the phone, i.e., no obstacle should prevent the customer from handling any banking business whenever, wherever and however it was convenient for him. Citibank intended to extend, both functionally and geographically, the use of two technological distribution points, as well as reassess the workings of the branch:

a The automatic teller machines (ATMs) were enhanced so that customers could get cash, make deposits, transfer funds from one account to another, and pay bills. The terminology was changed accordingly: rather than being called ATM centres, these installations became *Citicard Banking Centres*.

 Citibank also did research on the ideal kind of bank interface and adapted what was learned into its CBC technology. The kind of person that customers liked to deal with, research showed, was a woman in her mid-30s who loved her job, was very self-effacing and never embarrassed the customers. These particular features were therefore built into the language and approach presented by the machines, so that it was an 'I–You' relationship. For instance, rather than inform the customer that 'your transaction is being processed', the screen would say 'I'm working on it'.

b The concept of the *CitiPhone Banking* was that whenever a customer phoned – any day of the week, and any time of the day or night – a fully trained Citibanker, not a computer, would respond. No longer just complaint or query centres, these Citibankers were authorized to perform the same transactions as branch bankers.

c The '*Model Branch*' was a project that intended not only to improve the branch premises, but to navigate the customer through all the various transactions performed there – saving time while making the experience as effective and pleasant as possible.

4 How customers interact with the people they deal with

Bank branches were typically run as operations and transaction processing centres. Bankers tended to spend most of their time handling these basic activities, with little time left over to discuss customers' real needs, manage and oversee their accounts, or sell them the kinds of products and services which would have value for individual customers. When the customer could not go to the branch and had to phone in for information, he usually would speak to a different person each time. The people answering the phones were not trained as bankers and could not make any decisions; they were essentially a customer query centre.

If 'Citibanking' really were to work for customers as a total banking relationship, then not only would the roles of the people in the branches and at the remote customer support centres have to change, but a new kind of personality, behaviour, and skills would have to be adopted and encouraged. What 'Citibanking' termed the '*Citibanker Difference*' was meant to convey this change.

Rather than focusing on costs and controls – the underlying activities in an operations and transactions processing unit – Citibankers, whether behind the counter or at the end of a phone line, were expected to identify customers' needs, and sell them the appropriate products and services to meet those requirements. This relationship was not limited to the account advisers, but extended to the customer service representatives as well. Because they were

equipped with card readers that displayed all relevant information about the customer, tellers were encouraged and rewarded for recommending any product which they thought might be of interest or value to that particular customer.

Appraisal and reward schemes were changed accordingly; the account advisers had to set their sales targets with the branch manager, which would be assessed on a regular basis to determine where improvement was needed; those individuals who exceeded their targets were rewarded. Branches also competed with each other in trying to meet or exceed overall branch goals.

The model branch concept

The Model Branch – one of the nine projects initiated in the US and implemented by Sisson in Chile – provided the perfect opportunity to show the 'Citibanking' philosophy in action. But, instead of just telling his staff about it and how it worked in Chile, Sisson decided to take his top team there so that they could see for themselves.

> It was difficult to tell people what I wanted to do, but I knew I could *show* them. That was a breakthrough. Once they saw it in action, they were sold and this created tremendous excitement, accelerating the process dramatically.

The most difficult thing to communicate to the staff was that the Model Branch was not a premises or architectural issue, but rather it was part of the Tao – the way Citibank was to do business with customers, navigating them through *their* experiences inside and outside branches so that they could accomplish *their* banking goals in the quickest and most effective way. It was also about an environment for all customers' sales and services interactions – either face-to-face or remote – with staff that was trained, motivated and rewarded to both sell and support a total customer relationship. Rather than define space in traditional physical, retail and geographic terms, space was to be seen through the Model Branch concept – a total experience for the customer, wherever and whenever that might be.

Small teams were put together by Tom, who intended to convert all 19 Citibank branches into Model Branches over time. These teams were composed of different specialist disciplines – marketing, technology, premises, operations, accounting and human resources – from the selected branches. They all had one goal in mind: how to make the branch more effective from the customer's point of view. By improving the external signage and making it consistent everywhere, and allowing customers to see into the bank through uniformly wide glass windows, this process began before customers even entered the branch; this continued into the vestibule, where customers could easily find and use the CBCs; then to the greeting function and waiting areas equipped with phones, coffee, and product information; in and through to customer service representatives and/or to the private workstations of the account advisers.

Certain guiding 'principles' were to be used. For example, customers could expect to receive the same *consistent* services by phone as in the branch. So, if a customer called from the airport and said, 'I'm on my way to Munich and I forgot to pay my electricity bill', there would be a process in place that could make the payment.

Each of the specialist disciplines followed these standards. For instance, the person at the end of the telephone line had to perform in exactly the same way as the staff would in the branches. Likewise, they had to be equipped with the appropriate technology that provided the customer's profile and real-time information, so that they could make decisions and use judgement when no precedent existed – with the relevant reward and evaluation system in place to ensure this behaviour.

All job descriptions in the model branch were redone, with titles changed to reflect new priorities. For example, tellers became customer service representatives, and customer service representatives became known as account advisers. Supervisory functions were eliminated. The greeter became pivotal to success for two reasons: it was the first person the customer actually dealt with, and it was the greeter's responsibility to screen customers and make sure they were channelled to the correct staff person.

Sisson was adamant that the greeter was not a receptionist. In seniority terms, greeters were second only to the branch manager. Similarly, it was not a customer service job. The greeter had to size up each customer, determine those who might present a sales opportunity and direct them to the staff member responsible for explaining these options.

> If someone walks in to change an address, and is wearing a Hermes tie, a good greeter should instinctively know that there is potential business with this customer. The corollary is that customers who won't buy should not be sent to the account advisers – whose main job is to sell – and so waste everyone's time, including their own. Having the correct person in the correct job improves the relationship with the customers and our efficiency. It leads to a win/win situation all around.

The staff had been allowed to design their own workstations:

> The more we involved them, the more efficiency and commitment we got. Staff had to feel that whatever was done also helped them perform their jobs better. So we let them tell us how to do it.

Each workstation had everything needed to ensure another 'principle', namely *customer non-abandonment*. Whereas, previously, a customer could be left alone as many as five times – because a staff member had to get a needed form, make or receive phone calls, wait to use a photocopier, or take a deposit to the teller, now all workstations interfacing with customers were equipped with everything. As one person explained:

> We choreographed the service process in such a way that customers felt they were getting value, not just because the process was quick, but because they saw the focus was on them; by being the centre of our employee's attention, the relationship concept worked. But, we also wanted the people interfacing with customers to be as efficient as possible, so that the staff could spend more time listening and talking to customers and actually doing the selling.

Although the new marketing 'principles' were made to sound as simple as possible, they involved complex processes. Every single discipline was involved, and staff discovered that they could no longer work in isolation.

Once we had a common idea of what we were trying to do, we knew we had to work together. There was no option. The rest followed quite naturally and the barriers began to fall away. So did the politics – because, at last, we were all after the same thing.

BT: telephone account management

Christopher H. Lovelock ■ *Martin Bless*

To serve its small business customers better, BT has developed an inexpensive account management programme involving telephone contact rather than field visits. The manager of sales development wonders what mix of field and telephone-based channels would be appropriate for managing relationships with larger customers.

'So what would you do in my place, Michael?' asked the regional sales manager.

Michael Tarte-Booth, sales development manager at BT (formerly British Telecom) listened over a pub lunch as his colleague, John Lambert, described the situation. It concerned a small business customer whose telecommunication needs were handled by BT's telephone account management (TAM) programme. Tarte-Booth was very familiar with TAM, having been involved with the programme from its early days.

The customer in question had grown in size, and with the addition of a sixth line, now qualified for personal contact with an account executive. But, when informed of what BT viewed as an upgrade in account handling service, the customer demurred, asking to remain with TAM. Said Lambert:

> They wrote us a letter – I've got it here in my briefcase. It was polite but very firm. They don't want to shift from TAM. But now the field sales people are raising hell, claiming these folks as their own. This situation challenges the whole basis of our account management structure for different sizes of business customer.

British telecommunications

The United Kingdom (UK) was the first European country to depart from the traditional PTT (post, telegraph, telephone) model under which postal and telecommunication services were administered by the same government agency. After being transformed from a government department into a public corporation in 1969, the postal and telecommunications businesses were split apart in 1981. Post Office Telephones became British Telecom. Under the

Conservative government of prime minister Margaret Thatcher, numerous public corporations such as British Airways and British Gas were privatized. Soon the government announced its intention to privatize BT and sell up to 51 per cent of the corporation to the public. In November 1984, more than two million people, including 222,000 BT employees, applied for the one billion shares available. A total of £3.9 billion was raised.[1]

As the sole licensing authority for telecommunication operators, the government took the view that competition and choice between operators would be beneficial to customers. In 1984 it awarded a licence to provide domestic services to Mercury Communications, owned by Cable & Wireless (a recently privatized operator of international telecommunication services).

The government provided breathing space to BT and Mercury by making clear its intention not to licence any further fixed network operators for seven years. Separate licences were awarded to four operators of mobile telecommunication services, including BT and Mercury. To ensure that BT did not abuse its initial virtual monopoly position of fixed network services, an Office of Telecommunications (Oftel) was established to protect the interest of customers. Oftel was widely empowered to oversee and regulate the business conduct and pricing policies of both BT and Mercury. Among other things, it prohibited access by BT marketing personnel to information on customer billing records.

Privatization and the introduction of domestic competition forced a refocusing of BT's activities. Between 1984 and 1991, the company went through two major reorganizations. The second, termed Project Sovereign, was one of the most ambitious attempts to date by a British company to reform its organization, management and culture. These reforms were meant to prepare BT for three challenges. First, the industry's traditional structure – national monopoly operators supplied by national manufacturers – was breaking down throughout the world. Regulatory barriers to international competition were expected to crumble, gradually in some countries, faster in the UK. Second, as companies internationalized, they might prefer to deal with a single telecommunications company worldwide. Providers of telecommunications services would have to tailor their products less to neatly defined geographic markets and more to groups of customers, who could be located globally. And third, more intense international competition and the growing costs of the technology race would lead to concentration of the industry. One manager commented:

> Many people welcomed the changes because of the greater freedom they offered us to respond to evolving market needs and to take advantage of new technologies. But, an equally large group continued to think and act like civil servants, as though we were still a government department. A third group were fence sitters who took a 'wait and see' attitude, but were willing to be converted.

During the 1980s, telecommunications had made tremendous technological strides. For many corporate users, data communications became as important as voice communications. The use of fax machines and electronic mail exploded. BT invested heavily in modernization, unconstrained by the public sector borrowing requirements that the government had imposed before privatization. Coaxial copper cables were replaced by fibre optic cables which offered much greater capacity and better signal quality. New electronic exchanges with digital switches not only operated faster and more accu-

rately but also enabled BT to offer a host of extra services such as automatic call forwarding.

In April 1991, the company changed its trading name from British Telecom to BT and adopted a new motto: 'Putting customers first'. The new organization was structured around three customer-centred divisions: Business Communications, Personal Communications and Special Businesses (including mobile and operator services). Each would deal directly with customers for sales and services, while being supported by other divisions that either managed BT's products and services, operated a worldwide networking capability, or provided development and procurement services. The 31 districts were abolished and only five regions remained of the original geographical structure.

Current situation

With 1990–91 revenues of £13.15 billion, BT was Britain's second largest company (after British Petroleum plc). Reflecting the growth in both domestic and international markets, plus significant cost cutting efforts, BT's pre-tax operating profit in fiscal 1991 rose to £3.08 billion.

BT operated a technologically advanced network, boasting the highest proportion of optical fibre in its system of any major telecommunications operator. The long-distance digital network was complete, while more than three-quarters of all customers in the UK were connected to modern electronic exchanges (a few percentage points behind France, which had the highest share of digitalized exchanges of any major country). Further modernization continued at a rapid pace. Britain and Spain remained the only European nations to have privatized their telecommunication services, but a number of others were expected to follow in 1992–93. BT had also invested heavily in international ventures.

Domestically, BT retained a 94 per cent market share. However, Mercury had adopted a strategy of penetrating the business market, starting with the largest customers – which might have thousands of lines. It was not uncommon for big customers to split their telecommunications business between BT and Mercury. At the consumer level, Mercury's presence was minimal except for pay telephones in busy locations – such as city centres and airports. (Exhibit 1 shows the breakdown of the market by type of subscriber and number of lines.)

Since Mercury had built its network from nothing, it could offer customers state-of-the-art technology and had pioneered a number of service innovations, which BT was seeking to match. But, Mercury's network was still geographically limited, being focused on connecting London to Britain's business centres. Broader penetration required connecting customers to its network via BT's local lines, which often still used conventional technology. Mercury planned to spend £500 million annually during the three years 1992–94 to extend its network and boost its share of the domestic market. It already had 15 per cent of the UK's international traffic and a greater share of private networks. The American telecommunications giant, AT&T (described as the 800 pound gorilla of the industry), was rumoured to be eager to invest in Mercury's future.

Additional network competition was expected to come from British Rail Telecom and from a joint venture between US Sprint and British Waterways (which planned to lay cable along the bottom of its canal network). Local competition was seen as coming from cable television operators, many of whom were affiliated with American regional phone companies, and from operators of mobile (cellular) services.

Creating a pilot telemarketing operation

'You are the most difficult people in the world to buy from!' was how a customer described BT to Anna Thomson soon after she joined the marketing department of the newly created Thameswey district in 1985. Her colleagues quickly came to recognize Thomson's energy, drive and enthusiasm for seeking out innovative approaches. Although recruited as network marketing manager, her responsibilities were soon extended to marketing BT's products and services, and she became district marketing operations manager.

Thomson's prior experience had been in the electricity industry, marketing network usage. In her new

---

Exhibit 1 ■ BT's exchange connections

BT's exchange connections in service in the United Kingdom by type of subscriber 1980–90			
Year (at 31 March)	Total exchange connection (000s)	Residential subscribers (000s)	Business subscribers (000s)
1980	17,353	13,937	3,416
1981	18,174	14,671	3,503
1982	18,727	15,159	3,568
1983	19,186	15,546	3,640
1984	19,812	16,044	3,768
1985	20,528	16,596	3,932
1986	21,261	17,120	4,141
1987	21,908	17,549	4,359
1988	22,857	18,145	4,712
1989	23,946	18,737	5,209
1990	25,013	19,281	5,732

Source: British Telecom.

position, she demonstrated the value of selling customer premises equipment (CPE) as a means of generating network revenues rather than as an end in itself. She adopted an integrated approach to marketing both networks and CPE as complementary products. Thomson remarked that 'inevitably the selling of the one would lead to the selling of the other'. She emphasized that network sales were far more profitable than CPE sales, but traditionally BT had found it difficult to sell the more intangible product.

While analyzing customer relationships at BT, Thomson singled out small business customers as a neglected market.

> The crux of the whole thing is that effective use of modern telecommunications products and services can make a real difference to the development of any small business today. Use of mobile communication tools, the choice of the right fax machine, installation of a switch that can grow easily and cost effectively to cover extra lines, the use of free phone numbers and a wide range of datacoms services – all these things help a small business to be flexible as it reorganizes to meet its own customers' changing needs.

> The right telecom choices at the right time can enable a small business to offer new services (like out-of-hours customer service with call redirect), cut operating costs, and steal a march on their competitors. But, small business owners don't have time to research this all alone and so either miss opportunities altogether or make the wrong choices.

In her view, BT had not devoted enough time and energy to building the type of relationship that created loyalty. The only contact BT generally had with these customers was when they called with a problem or a bill was sent out. Typically, BT sales staff were only talking to small business customers once every three to five years, except when the customer initiated contact. Thomson warned that if nothing changed, BT was liable to lose these customers to competition.

Further analysis revealed that some 750,000 enquiries from customers of all types had not been followed up the previous year. The existing sales process, which was almost entirely focused upon reactive responses

to inbound customer calls, was obviously not working. Large accounts (served by field-based account managers) and those that screamed for attention were catered to at the cost of ignoring a huge market of smaller accounts. What was needed, argued Thomson, were telephone-based representatives to look after smaller business accounts.

Recognizing that the most sophisticated applications of telemarketing strategy were to be found in the USA, Thomson convinced headquarters to retain a leading American consultant, Rudy Oetting, to advise on conducting a pilot test in the Thameswey district. This district extended west and south of London, beyond Heathrow airport, along the M3 and M4 motorway corridors. It contained many vibrant business communities, including a significant number of small high-technology firms. The consultant recommended that BT recruit and train telephone-based sales representatives to sell proactively into exactly that market.

Telephone account management

A variety of terms were used to describe the use of the telephone as a marketing tool. *Telesales* was often used to describe use of the telephone by salespeople as a communication channel through which prospects could be contacted and a single sales transaction consummated. *Telemarketing* was a broader umbrella term for all types of marketing-related telephone usage. *Telephone Account Management* was defined as proactive contact through the telephone channel to customers who required a continuing personal relationship – but not necessarily face-to-face contact – with skilled sales representatives who could function as communication consultants to small businesses.

Rudy Oetting described such people as bright, aggressive account managers who had been trained to listen carefully to customer needs and ask structured, probing questions about each business and its communication activities. The goal was to build a database of information on each customer which would enable managers to farm a territory systematically without ever leaving the office. In some cases, Oetting declared, they would work jointly with field sales;

sometimes they called the shots for the field force, and in other instances, they were the *only* salesforce.

Thomson recognized the potential of such an approach for BT, using its own channel – the telephone – to contact the company's small business customers. She did not accept the traditional view that British business culture would not respond positively to telephone sales contact, being confident it would work well providing the process was oriented towards uncovering and meeting customer needs. But, she saw that the approach would have to be non-threatening and employ well-trained representatives who operated on a much higher level than conventional sales support or customer service personnel. As the concept took shape, Thomson coined the term *telemanaging* which she defined as:

> Managing the customer primarily through the medium of the telephone, using all the sales, marketing systems and management disciplines of account management.

The TAM concept

The term TAM came to be used at BT as an acronym for both telephone account management and a telephone account manager. The latter would be a carefully selected salesperson trained to handle a wide portfolio of products and services, working up to 1,000 assigned accounts entirely by telephone. TAMs would be trained to develop specific objectives for each call. During the call, they were expected to update their knowledge of the customer's situation and needs, check whether any problems needed solving, advise on products and services, take orders, and plan a specific date for the next call. The basic goals would be to ensure that the accounts continued buying from BT rather than the competition, and to develop accounts by selling additional products and services. Said Thomson:

> The job of TAMs is to understand the business objectives and organization of their customers and to help their customers make the right investment decisions at the right time – so that we and they become increasingly successful. It's a partnership based on trust, which has to be earned through proven good advice over time. BT believes that this is the way you become a customer's preferred supplier. The basic goal is to continually build and refresh knowledge of the account base, and be the first to address or even anticipate communications needs. This is true relationship marketing but effected within a volume market because the TAM goes through this process a thousandfold. We use our own core product – the telephone – to do the job, because it allows us to manage and market efficiently to hundreds of thousands of customers. You could say we practise what we preach!

Each TAM would endeavour to develop a relationship based on trust. The customer call would remain the focal point throughout the contact cycle. Whether an order was taken or not, the TAM would establish when the next call was to take place and put it on the calendar. All the information collected would be fed into each customer's electronic file.

Thomson emphasized that the value of an account to BT was much more than just line rental charges and fees for network usage. The company also sold a wide range of telecommunications equipment (ranging from individual handsets to private branch exchanges), installation and maintenance, and an array of value-added services (refer to Exhibit 2 for examples).

When face-to-face contact with the customer was needed, the field sales staff would work together with the TAM. The ultimate responsibility for managing an account, however, would remain with the TAM. Thomson saw teamwork as an essential part of the process. One TAM later described the relationship as follows:

> It works on the basis of whoever can close the sale, should close the sale. This means that we have to work as a team; you cannot have a 'them and us syndrome'. If the TAM is in contact with a customer who wants somebody to pay a visit, it's clear that the sales representative cannot sign the customer up there and then, he or she will pass the case back to the TAM to monitor it. The principle is that if I achieve, we both achieve.

Voice services

CityDirect provides direct connections between London and the USA offering call facilities such as abbreviated dialling and security safeguards.

SpeechLines is a service for intra-company speech connection.

LinkLine is an automatic freephone service which allows business to offer their customers a free enquiry and ordering facility.

CallStream is a service for information providers who sell stored voice or data information via the normal telephone line.

Network services offers call facilities such as call diversion, call barring, call waiting, last number redial, abbreviate dialling and conference call.

Voicecom International provides a 24-hour network of voice mailboxes to send, receive or forward messages from any telephone in the world.

Data services

Datel is a data transmission service available internationally to over 100 countries.

KeyLine provides analog private circuits for data transmission using modems.

Leaseline offers analog circuits that enable subscribers to transport voice, facsimilie, data and telegraph messages nationally and internationally.

KiloStream and MegaStream provide digital, proviate circuits between centres at high operating speeds.

PSS is a nationwide public data network using packet switching techniques.

MultiStream enhances access to the public network at local call rates fo the business community.

Data Direct is a high speed public data service to the USA and Japan.

Prestel is BT's public Videotex service.

SatStream is a satellite service for business communication with North America and Europe.

Telecom Gold is an electronic mail service with over 250,000 mailboxes in 17 countries.

Integrated Services Digital Network (ISDN) allows customers to transmit voice, data, text or image information at high speeds and assured quality without dedicated private circuits.

Exhibit 2 ■ Sample voice and data services offered by BT, 1992

Michael Tarte-Booth

To assist her in implementing the TAM concept, Thomson hired Michael Tarte-Booth, a man with experience in telemarketing on both sides of the Atlantic. Thomson later insisted that, although the vision was hers, nothing would have happened in the field without her colleague's determination to get it right, day after day. His original career had nothing to do with telecommunications. As he observed, 'How I fell into telephone marketing is pure chance.'

After obtaining his undergraduate degree from a British university, Tarte-Booth obtained a masters degree in geography from the University of Minnesota. Then he went to work in Minneapolis for the American Heart Association, a major non-profit organization. They needed someone with demographic expertise to analyze census data and pinpoint those geographic locations (down to specific street blocks) where their best potential lay for recruiting volunteer fund-raisers. Tarte-Booth also inherited responsibility for the association's telemarketing operation. He developed the use of the telephone as a primary contact for volunteer recruitment or direct solicitation of donations. One objective was to ensure that the volunteer callers should use their precious phone hours wisely by contacting only the better prospects. The potential power of this marriage between database marketing and the phone as a delivery channel was demonstrated when revenues increased by over 60 per cent during the first year and 90 per cent in the second.

On returning to Britain, Tarte-Booth was hired by a manufacturer of business systems to set up its telemarketing operation. The company was running a large direct field salesforce, but had neglected its customer base for paper-based products, and had disposed of its customer records for this market. The firm's telephone contact strategy was limited to proactive cold calls by sales representatives to new prospects. Thereafter, the channel strategy was simply inbound, waiting for customers to come back by phone or mail with repeat orders. Tarte-Booth's job was to set up a team that would revitalize the business:

> The goal was to re-create the database by acquisition and integration of lists from numerous different sources so that we knew, after telephone contact, who the customers were and who the prospects were. Our initial objective was to derive sales principally through referrals out to the salesforce. But, we had to start out by qualifying our prospects and calling all the names on our list. The response was impressive.

Other groups within the sales organization recognized the value of this activity. Within two years, the company was also targeting other vertical markets in the hospitality, leisure, and car retail and after-sales industries. Said Tarte-Booth:

> The programme diversified into new markets and more sophisticated applications. We had truly grad-

uated to an account management operation with a primary focus on repeat purchase. Historically, customers had made repeat purchases roughly once every three years, now they were making them every three months! The whole thing about account management is getting to know and anticipate customers' needs by amalgamating the power of the database, the information you glean from customers, and the immediacy of contact by telephone. We found that customers liked the cloak of invisibility provided by the telephone contact. It gives them greater perceived control. Ultimately, they can drop the neutron bomb and hang up.

Inauguration of the TAM pilot

After three months' preparation, the new pilot programme was inaugurated in November 1986. Almost, immediately, BT found that customers demanded a continuing dialogue focused on an understanding of their needs, as opposed to a tactical contact aiming to sell them 'the flavour of the month'. Customers were also motivated by continuity of contact, wanting to deal with a specific person on a regular basis. They would spend up to 20 minutes disclosing information about their business and needs; but having invested that amount of time, they expected the relationship to be perpetuated.

Thomson's primary mission was to tackle the strategic and political issues related to getting TAM accepted within BT and to develop an overall 'Integrated Channel Strategy' to show how all the sales, service and marketing channels (including TAM) should interrelate for BT's objectives to be met. The success of the pilot attracted growing attention. Over the course of the first year, Thameswey achieved a tenfold increase in account coverage and a threefold increase in customer purchasing levels among the pilot customers. These results were achieved at a lower ratio of cost to sales revenues than could have been obtained with face-to-face contact. It also left the field salesforce with more time to talk to larger customers, and enabled them to achieve the high level of consultancy needed in that sector. Tarte-Booth observed:

> The project succeeded strategically because of senior management sponsorship and the interest that

Anna generated in the programme. It was driven through centrally and had very high visibility within the organization.

National implementation

Anna Thomson and Michael Tarte-Booth kept in sight the ultimate aim of national implementation. Achieving that goal required careful documentation of the whole process. Other districts would have to be convinced rather than coerced to adopt TAM. In 1987, Thomson left the district to become national telemarketing manager. She saw her role as selling the concept of telemarketing to senior BT managers. Monthly steering committee meetings were held to discuss the progress of the pilot and make tactical changes. Progress reports, detailing success in achieving evolutionary benchmarks, were widely circulated. As Tarte-Booth recalled, Thomson did not try to convince the corporation that TAM was the 'greatest thing since sliced bread'. Instead, he pointed out:

> We allowed it to prove itself and concentrated on keeping colleagues around the country advised of progress through workshops and seminars. As a result, other districts came of their own accord to enquire about possible implementation. As soon as a district showed serious interest, we followed up with more information in order to gain a commitment. With district autonomy and the fact that TAM was to be implemented on a voluntary basis, the soft sales approach was critical.

In early 1988, Tarte-Booth was appointed national implementation manager. He found that districts whose customer base was dispersed over a wide territory were quick to recognize TAM's value. During 1988, six districts established teams to focus on the small business market. A central development programme was created to train the trainers, build the necessary support structure, and develop the database software for TAM. That programme provided implementation expertise through a 'franchise' package which demanded adherence to the proven methods established in the pilot in exchange for implementation assistance.

By early 1989, districts fell into three distinct categories. In the vanguard were six districts that had already established teams. The second group, described as 'the soft underbelly of resistance', was interested but wanted to wait until TAM had proved itself elsewhere. Some sales managers were reluctant to embrace TAM, which was perceived as threatening since it involved a reappraisal of their approach to customers and a reorganization of field sales responsibilities. Strong resistance came from a third group of districts, principally in London and the South East. This hard core was located in the region that not only had the highest customer density but also faced the greatest competitive threat.

Following the Project Sovereign reorganization, the districts were abolished and field sales territories expanded, thus increasing field reps' travel times. (Exhibit 3 shows the reorganized sales structure, in which first Thomson and later Tarte-Booth held the position of manager of sales development, operating at the same level as the five regional sales managers.)

Training

Tarte-Booth emphasized that 'the TAM programme is not about creaming the market. It's about building loyalty and defending against future competition.' Given the complexity of the task demanded of a TAM, considerable effort was placed on recruiting the right people. The initial interview with candidates was conducted by telephone, followed by written tests and face-to-face interviews, and concluding with psychometric profiling of each candidate prior to final selection. Recruitment was followed by intensive training. BT built three special training schools to develop a consistent approach to customer care.

Training covered attitudes, as well as skills, ranging from how not to sound like a robot when using a call guide (recommended dialogue) to how to gather and enter relevant information about customers. Training also included hands-on experience with the equipment that TAMs would be selling. Over a twelve-month period, a future TAM would follow five training modules interlinked with live frontline experience at his or her home base. The five modules collectively lasted for 13 weeks. Said Tarte-Booth:

> The training programme is designed to be holistic and so embraces the skills, the techniques, the

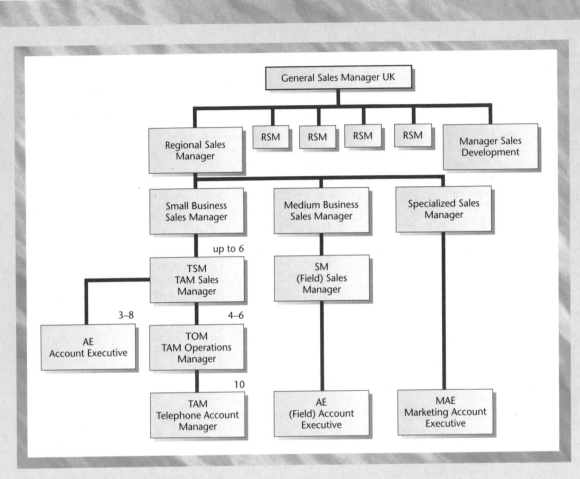

Figure 3 ■ Organization chart

methods, the tools, and the product knowledge integral to the future TAM's job. Their understanding is tested by rigorous role-playing and coaching sessions. The entire account team is trained together, so all members emerge with a clear understanding of how their jobs interrelate. Before returning to their home units, each team converts theory into practice by making live customer calls from the training centre.

Future plans

By early 1992, BT operated 25 TAM call centres around the UK. Total staffing, including TAMs, TOMs (TAM operations managers) and support personnel, exceeded 450 persons. The annual cost of a TAM was around £41,000, of which 50 per cent was salary

(in comparison, field account managers cost £40,000–£60,000 a year, of which about 65 per cent was salary). Anna Thomson had been promoted to a new position, where her task was to develop a global customer service strategy for BT as the company began to expand into a worldwide organization. In this context, TAM was just one part of the jigsaw.

With TAM catering for small business accounts having two to five lines each, Tarte-Booth now turned his attention to other categories of business. His objective was to apply comprehensive account management to the entire customer base, integrating field and phone account management to address the needs of any type of customer. He saw BT's accounts as grouped into slices across a pyramid, with national accounts at the apex and single-line customers at the base. (Exhibit 4 documents the number of accounts in each group and representative average annual revenues per account.)

In three regions, BT was piloting TAM for medium-sized business customers with 6 to 15 lines. Since these customers required an expanded portfolio of products and services, the new programme was more complex than the small business TAM. Bigger customers tended to have a more sophisticated approach to decision making. This process had to be reflected in the call guides, the systems and the training. Tarte-Booth described the new programme as follows:

> It's an evolution of TAM and premised on the same channel structure. As such, it shares much of the methodology established for the small business programmeme, but has evolved to fit the needs of a new market segment.

Further up the pyramid were the key regional accounts, those with more than 15 lines. These customers would continue to be managed on a face-to-face basis through a field salesforce channel. Account managers and specialist executives were in the field to support them, backed by proactive and reactive telephone support. At the top of the pyramid were national accounts – large and lucrative

customers with sophisticated communication needs, often international in nature.

Very small business customers with a single line, such as the consultant who worked from home or the small retail establishment, remained an untapped market. BT had experimentally incorporated the top 10 per cent of this group in TAM but quickly learned that the use of TAMs was not a cost-effective proposition. The cost of TAMs was viewed by some as prohibitively expensive for very small business (VSB) customers. Tarte-Booth contended that 'it's inappropriate to think of TAM in purely cost substitution terms, since BT's objectives are market coverage resulting in account protection and development.'

His proposed solution was to test the use of direct mail, designed to generate inbound calls to a VSB account management team. Catalogues of telephone equipment and services useful to very small businesses would be mailed to large numbers of prospects. The goal would be to stimulate the purchase of upgraded telephone products and services. As these single-line customers grew and acquired second lines, they could migrate up the account management pyramid.

Looking ahead, Tarte-Booth envisaged the desirability of creating a more flexible account management structure:

Exhibit 4 ■ Profile of the account management pyramid at BT

			Representative account data		
Group	No. of accounts	No. of lines per account	Annual revenue per line (range) £	Annual revenue from CPE sales or revenue[1] £	Annual revenue from value added network (range) £
National accounts	300	100+	1,000–3,000	100,000	200,000–500,000,000
Key regional accounts	3,000	15+	1,000–2,000	3,000	25,000–200,000
Medium business accounts	200,000	6–15	900–1,500	500	5,400–22,500
Small business accounts	650,000	2–5	600–900	200	1,200–4,500
Very small business accounts	800,000	1	200–600	100	400

[1] CPE = customer premises equipment.

Developing and implementing account management structures is a fundamentally different task from salesforce management, and the two may well conflict. They also require different skills. What we need is a range of account management options based on different channel configurations. TAM is just one channel within the sales structure at BT. We need a totally integrated and flexible structure for customers, in which their changing needs and preferences will be consistently catered for, whether their need for products and services grows, stabilizes, or shrinks.

The case of Green & Meakin Ltd

Green & Meakin Ltd was a manufacturer of aircraft parts. When the TAM programme was first initiated, the firm had three lines and was assigned to Helen Dewhurst, who had exclusive responsibility for its account. As their TAM, she kept in touch with the company on a regular basis and followed through on all its requests, be it for a single socket, a new piece of telecommunications equipment or an additional line. Feedback from the two partners who owned the firm was very positive. They were pleased, they said, with the prompt and efficient way in which Dewhurst handled their business needs. Their experiences with BT prior to the introduction of TAM had been far from satisfactory: hours had been wasted chasing up requests passed from one person who didn't know or couldn't help to another who often proved to be no better.

As the company grew, so did Green & Meakin's use of telecommunication services. One December day, a sixth line was installed. Unknown to the firm, this additional line automatically set in motion the upgrading process. Dewhurst compiled a file on the company which was handed up to the new team. She then contacted Green & Meakin to inform the company that in future it would be handled by a field account executive, reflecting the growing size and importance of the Green & Meakin account. But, the partners were unhappy. One of them called Dewhurst to state that the firm liked the service she had provided and did not view reassigning their account to a new account group as a useful move. Dewhurst responded that, unfortunately, this was company policy, but added that she was sure they would receive excellent service in the future. When the senior partner still expressed dissatisfaction with the proposed move, she suggested that he call her supervisor, the TAM operations manager. Meeting a similar response from this individual and in turn from her superior, the TAM Sales Manager, the senior partner wrote to John Lambert, the regional sales manager, to complain.

The letter

'Ah, here it is!' exclaimed Lambert, pulling a sheet of paper from his briefcase. 'Read it for yourself, Michael.'

Michael Tarte-Booth unfolded the letter and quickly read it through. It was firm, and to the point (refer to Exhibit 5). 'This is dated ten days ago', he said. 'What's happened in the meantime, John?'

'Well, I simply made copies and sent one each with a covering memo to the relevant TAM operations manager and the sales manager, and told them to sort it out. Neither could agree on a course of action because both claimed Green & Meakin as their own. So they passed the buck back up to their superiors.'

'And then?' queried Tarte-Booth.

'Same problem!' responded Lambert, gloomily. 'Neither of those two folks could agree, either. So yesterday it landed neatly back on my desk like a boomerang. What do you suggest I do?'

The waitress came, cleared away their plates and brought them coffee, which gave Tarte-Booth a moment's breathing space to think. 'This could well happen again in the future,' he said finally, sipping his coffee. 'We can't spend all our time deciding when to make exceptions to the rules. I've been working on a plan to restructure the whole account management function at BT. Let me get back with a draft proposal to you in a few days, and I'll tell you

then what I think we should do about Green &
Meakin, too.'

Tarte-Booth swallowed the rest of his coffee, put
down the cup and stood up. 'Be in touch with you on
Tuesday, John. Thanks for lunch. You did say you
were paying, didn't you?'

Note

1. The value of the pound sterling (£) varied widely against other
currencies during the 1980s. Typical exhange rates in 1991
were: £1.00 = ECU 1.40 = US$1.70 = SFr 2.50. A second sale of
government shares in BT took place in 1991.

Green & Meakin Ltd
582 Thamesview Centre
Reading, Berkshire

Mr John Lambert   7 January 1992
Regional Sales Manager
BT Southwest Region

Dear Mr Lambert

   I am writing to you to express my concern over a proposed change in our account coverage status
with BT. For the past four years, we have received excellent service through our telephone account
manager, Helen Dewhurst. Recently, she informed us that, due to our acquisition of a sixth line, we were
scheduled to be 'upgraded' in the New Year to a field-based account manager who would make personal
visits to us at our offices.

   My partner, Jim Meakin, and I phoned Helen (using the new speakerphone we recently acquired from
BT) to tell her that we were very happy with the service she provided and did not wish to change to a
new account manager. But she told us that the decision was company policy and not hers to change.

   Subsequently, I called her superior, Ms Anderson, and got a similar response. Next, the field sales
manager called to introduce himself and the account manager who would be taking over from Helen. Jim
took the call and said we didn't want to change, but we got the same story about 'company policy'. We
had a similar response when we called the small-business manager and the medium-business sales
manager, respectively. They don't seem to get the point that we are happy being served by Helen over
the telephone.

   So now I'm writing to you and appealing to your common sense rather than to company rule-books.
I know it's your internal policy to reassign customers when they reach a certain size (and we're flattered
that you now consider us a 'medium-sized company'). But the fact is, we don't need someone to keep
coming out to visit us all the time, unless it's to install new equipment or undertake maintenance – which
is a technician's job in any case. We feel strongly that we're better off remaining with Helen.

   We thank you for your consideration and look forward to your response.

                                                                      Yours sincerely,
                                                                      /s/ W.F.F. GREEN, Partner

Exhibit 5 ■ Letter to BT from Green & Meakin Ltd

PART iii

Strategic issues in services marketing

CHAPTER 8

Creating services and adding value

Learning objectives

After reading and reflecting on this chapter, you should be able to:

1. Understand the nature of service products.

2. Describe approaches to new service development.

3. Distinguish between facilitating and enhancing supplementary services.

4. Define the eight petals of the Flower of Service.

5. Show how organizations can use each petal to enhance their core services.

6. Illustrate how technology offers new opportunities to provide value-added supplementary services.

Crossing the English Channel . . . by train[1]

The British were not amused in 1802 when one of Napoleon's generals suggested the idea of digging a tunnel under the English Channel to link Britain and France. They saw it as a military threat and imagined foreign troops using such a tunnel to invade their country. But once raised, the idea never went away again.

In 1987, work finally began on twin rail tunnels and a third, smaller service tunnel between them. The 'Chunnel' as it soon became known, runs over 38 km (23 miles) below the seabed from near Dover to Calais. It took seven years to complete, required the removal of 17 million tonnes of earth, and had cost more than £8 billion (€11 billion) by the time it was opened by Britain's Queen Elizabeth II and France's President François Mitterrand in May 1994.

Until that date, all passengers and freight wishing to cross the English Channel had two options: air or ferry. For passengers, air travel is fast but expensive. It takes slightly more than an hour to fly to Paris from one of London's major airports, but travel from city centre to city centre requires closer to three hours, with the risk of traffic delays. Prior to the Chunnel, the other option on the London–Paris route was to travel by a combination of train, ferry and then train again. Most such trips take six to eight hours. Cars, buses and lorries could drive to one of several ports on the south coast of England and load their vehicles onto car ferries for a sea crossing which takes from 50 minutes to four hours, depending on the route and the type of vessel (conventional ferries compete against faster hovercraft and water-jet catamarans). Rough seas, which are not uncommon, may lead to delays or even cancellation of sailings.

With the advent of the Chunnel, three new passenger travel options became available. Eurostar provides passenger rail service from London to Paris or from London to Brussels (some trains serve intermediate points, too) and Le Shuttle carries cars, buses and trucks on railcars between Folkestone (near Dover) and Calais. International rail freight completes the services offered.

Rather than allowing the new London–Paris passenger service to be operated by British Rail and the SNCF (the existing national railways), a new company was created, named Eurostar. New trains of a striking appearance, designed to cruise at up to 300 km/h (186 mph), were derived from the successful French TGV. These trains cut journey times between central London and central Paris to three hours. (Eventually, completion of a new, high-speed track between London and the Chunnel will reduce the time to two and a half hours.) New station facilities were under construction.

But a host of decisions awaited Eurostar management: Who were the target market segments? What amenities should be offered at the stations and on board the trains? What types of service personnel were needed? How should the service be promoted? What would be the best way to win passengers from the competition? And how should the services be priced?

The most important decision taken was to position Eurostar against the airlines, rather than against existing trains and ferries. The argument was simple: from city centre to city centre, Eurostar was as fast as air travel. Other decisions followed quickly. Prices for the two classes of travel, first and standard, would be set with reference to business and economy air fares (there's no first-class air service between London and Paris). Each stage of the journey, from reservations to arrival at the destination, was carefully examined. Reservations and ticketing must be state of the art. Passenger facilities at the dramatic new Waterloo International station in London would be equal to or better than those in a major air terminal (renovating the existing Gare du Nord in Paris would present more of a problem). Train exteriors and interiors would present a stylish appearance. The passenger cars would be furnished to offer greater comfort and more amenities than a competing airliner, as well as being quieter, smoother and more spacious. In a two-class seating format, an 18-car Eurostar train would be capable of carrying 792 passengers (double the capacity of a Boeing 747).

Personal service by Eurostar employees, at the terminals and in the trains, would equal or exceed that given by airline personnel, requiring careful selection and training. Customer service personnel would have to be multilingual (at a minimum, English and French would be required, as well as Dutch on trains serving Brussels). Their uniforms would be stylish and make them immediately recognizable as Eurostar employees.

Marketers at Eurostar also addressed the needs of different market segments, starting with business travellers. As in business-class air travel, first class Eurostar passengers receive complimentary meals, drinks and newspapers at their seats (those in standard class can purchase food from a roving refreshment cart or visit one of two buffet cars). Unlike air travel, passengers have a choice of smoking or non-smoking cars, and there are no restrictions on use of laptop computers or mobile phones. Public telephones are provided, too. There is also a special Premium First service whose amenities include use of special lounges in the terminals, a fast check-in lane prior to departure, a wider choice of meals and wines on board, and complimentary taxi service on arrival. (Passengers arriving in London can opt for free LimoBike service, which provides chauffeur-driven motorbikes to beat the traffic.)

To promote and reward loyalty, Eurostar has created a Frequent Traveller programme that rewards passengers with free rail and air travel, car rentals and hotel stays. Eurostar's most frequent users can use the executive lounges at the terminal stations. As required by law, special attention has been given to the special needs of disabled travellers, including the design of both the stations and train interiors, as well as staff training. Services for small children and their parents include baby-changing facilities – both on board the trains and in the terminals – and bottle warming. A recently introduced Eurostar service takes travellers directly to the rail station at the entrance to Paris Disneyland. On board the special trains, children will find Disney entertainment and free activity packs, as well as encounter Disney characters waiting at the station to greet them on arrival.

Service products as experiences

In earlier chapters, we noted that a service is a 'performance' rather than a 'thing'. When customers purchase manufactured goods, they take title to physical objects. But service performances, being intangible and ephemeral, are experienced rather than owned. Even when there are physical elements to which the customer does take title – such as a cooked meal (which is promptly consumed), a gold filling in a tooth, a replacement part inside a car – a significant portion of the price paid by customers is for the value added by the accompanying service elements, including labour and expertise and the use of specialized equipment. In the case of the meal, a typical rule of thumb in full-service restaurants is that the cost of purchasing the food ingredients represents about one-fifth of the price of the meal. The balance can be seen as the fees that the customer is willing to pay for renting a table and chairs in a pleasant setting, hiring the services of food preparation experts and their kitchen equipment, and paying serving staff to wait on them.

When customers are required by the nature of the service process to visit the service site – as in people-processing services – or choose to do so in other types of services (such as traditional retail bank branches), they may be asked to participate actively in the process of service creation, delivery and consumption. When they perform self-service, their experiences are often shaped by the nature and user-friendliness (or lack thereof!) of the supporting technology. In both instances, evaluations of the service product are likely to be much more closely interwoven with the nature of delivery in place and time than is the case for manufactured goods.

In Chapter 3, we noted that a service product typically consists of a core product bundled together with a variety of supplementary service elements. The core elements respond to the customer's need for a basic benefit – such as transportation to a specific location, resolution of a specific health problem or repair of malfunctioning equipment. Supplementary services (discussed in depth in the current chapter) are those that facilitate and enhance use of the core service. They range from provision of needed information, advice and documentation, to problem-solving and acts of hospitality.

Designing services for success

Eurostar is a good example of successfully designing a new service to meet customers' needs in the face of long-entrenched competitors. Engineers created a rail transportation system – track, power and vehicles – that is extraordinarily fast, reliable and safe. The train operator, Eurostar, then systematically identified all points of customer contact and used feedback from market research to design delivery processes and a servicescape that would meet or exceed customers' expectations.

Among the many different professional skills employed in creating the Eurostar experience have been those of architects, fashion designers, seating experts, interior designers and artists. The company also recognizes that its customer contact personnel play key roles in creating a satisfying service experience for travellers. Selective recruitment, careful training and ongoing supervision help to ensure superior performance. There is a sense of occasion about travelling Eurostar that is largely missing from air travel today.

As the Eurostar example points out, good service design has elements of both art and science. We'll cover both these aspects in this chapter as we explore some of the methods service providers can use to enhance the effectiveness of service design and execution, including ways of adding value to the core product. In the following chapter, we'll then expand on issues relating to service delivery.

Planning and creating services

All service organizations face choices concerning the types of products to offer and the operational procedures to employ in creating them. Figure 8.1 shows the key steps involved in planning, creating and delivering services; it was inspired by an earlier (but very different) model developed by Sasser, Olsen and Wyckoff, and a subsequent derivative by Maister.[2]

The task begins at the corporate level with a statement of institutional objectives and an appraisal of current or obtainable resources. From market and competitive analysis, marketing opportunities can be identified. We saw in Chapter 5 that a positioning statement can be developed for each service that the firm plans to offer to one or more specific market segments, indicating the characteristics that distinguish it from the competition in meaningful ways.

This positioning strategy must then be related to a statement of the operating assets needed for execution. Can the organization afford to allocate the physical facilities, equipment, information and communication technology, and human resources needed to support a given positioning strategy? Alternatively, could the firm leverage its own resources by using off-balance sheet assets obtained by developing partnerships with intermediaries or even with customers themselves? Does the positioning strategy promise sufficient profits to yield an acceptable return on the assets employed after deducting all relevant costs?

The next step in the process involves establishing a service marketing concept, to clarify the benefits offered to customers and the costs that they will incur in return. This marketing concept considers both core and supplementary services, reliability levels for these services, and where and when customers will be able to have access to them. Costs include money, time, hassle and physical effort.

A parallel step is to establish a service operations concept, which stipulates the geographic scope and scheduling of operations, describes facilities design and layout, and indicates how and when operating assets should be deployed to perform specific tasks. The operations concept also addresses opportunities for leveraging through intermediaries or the customers themselves. Finally, it clarifies which tasks will be assigned to frontstage and which to backstage operations.

These two concepts interact with a set of choices that management must make in configuring the service delivery process – the topic of Chapter 9.

The technological revolution in services

Technological developments during the last 20 years have had a remarkable impact on the way in which services are produced and delivered. Innovations in core services range from new types of medical treatments to high-speed rail service such as Eurostar, and from satellite-based weather forecasting to addressable (that is, inter-active) cable television systems. Developments in telecommunications and computer technology have also led to many innovations in how services are delivered, including the internet. Many of the most significant changes relate to the use of information technology to improve supplementary services – a topic we will discuss in more depth later in this chapter.

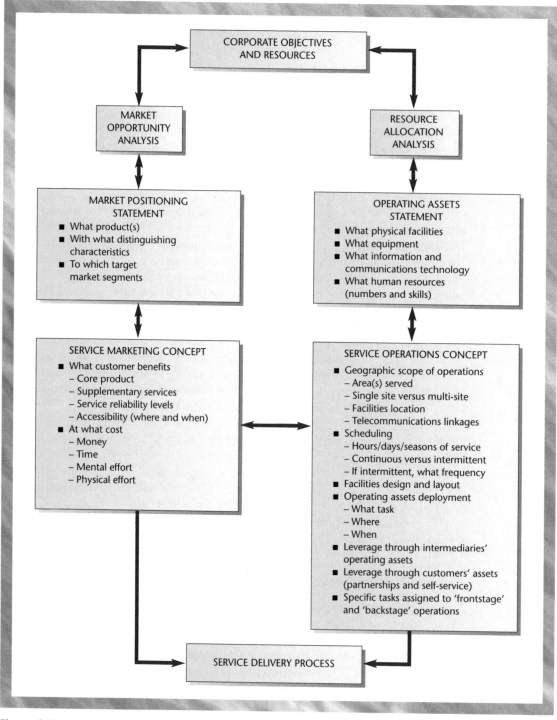

Figure 8.1 ■ Planning, creating and delivering service

Core products and supplementary services

Most manufacturing and service businesses offer their customers a package of benefits, involving delivery of not only the core product but a variety of service-related activities. Increasingly, these services provide the differentiation that separates successful firms from the also-rans. With both services and goods, the core product sooner or later becomes a commodity as competition increases and the industry matures. Although there may still be opportunities to enhance the characteristics of that core product, the search for competitive advantage in a mature industry often emphasizes performance on the supplementary service elements that are bundled with the core. (If a firm can't do a decent job on the core elements, it's eventually going to go out of business!) Our focus in this chapter will be on categorizing the supplementary services that surround core products and demonstrating how useful similarities may exist across industries between these various supplementary services.

The augmented product

Marketing textbook authors have long been writing about the *augmented product* – also referred to as the 'extended product', or the 'product package' – in an effort to describe the supplementary elements that add value to manufactured goods. Several frameworks can be used to describe augmented products in a services context. Lynn Shostack developed a *molecular model* (Figure 8.2), which uses a chemical analogy to help marketers visualize and manage what she termed a 'total market entity'.[3] Her model can be applied to either goods or services. At the centre is the core benefit, addressing the basic customer need, linked to a series of other service characteristics. She argues that as in chemical formulations a change in one element may completely alter the nature of the entity. Surrounding the molecules are a series of bands representing price, distribution and market positioning (communication messages).

The molecular model helps us identify the tangible and intangible elements involved in service delivery. In an airline, for example, the intangible elements include transportation itself, service frequency, and pre-flight, in-flight and post-flight service. But the aircraft and the food and drinks that are served are all tangible. By highlighting tangible elements, marketers can determine whether their services are tangible-dominant or intangible-dominant. The more intangible elements exist, the more necessary it is to provide tangible clues about the features and quality of the service.

Two French researchers, Pierre Eiglier and Eric Langeard, proposed a model based on core and peripheral services. The core service is surrounded by a circle containing a series of peripheral services that are specific to that particular product.[4] Their approach, like Shostack's, emphasizes the interdependence of the various components. They distinguish between peripheral elements needed to facilitate use of the core service (such as the reception desk at a hotel) and those that enhance the appeal of the core service (such as a fitness centre and business services at a hotel).

We will use the term 'supplementary' services (rather than 'peripheral' services), since these elements have the potential to add value to the core service and provide a competitive edge. Both models of the augmented product offer useful insights. Shostack wants us to determine which service elements are tangible and which are

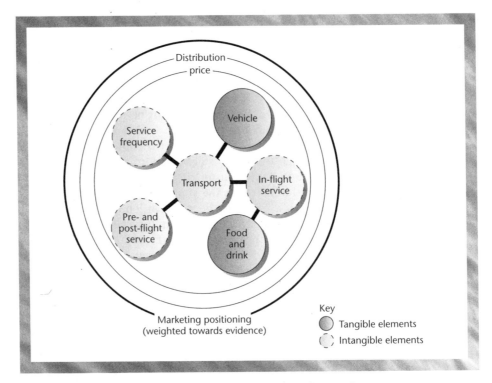

Figure 8.2 ■ Shostack's molecular model: passenger airline service

Source: G. Lynn Shostack, 'Breaking free from product marketing', *Journal of Marketing*, April 1977, published by the American Marketing Association. Reprinted with permission.

intangible in order to help formulate product policy and communication programmes. Eiglier and Langeard ask us to think about two issues: first, whether supplementary services are needed to facilitate use of the core service or simply to add extra appeal; and second, whether customers should be charged separately for each service element, or whether all elements should be bundled under a single price tag. Grönroos clarifies the different roles played by supplementary services by describing them as either facilitating services (or goods) and supporting services (or goods).[5]

Classifying supplementary services[6]

The more we examine different types of services, the more we find that most of them have quite a few supplementary services in common. The first step in identifying existing supplementary services for a product is to develop a flowchart that shows the steps in the service delivery process (see Chapter 4, page 132). In many instances, consumption or use of the core product is sandwiched sequentially between several supplementary services that precede or follow delivery of the core. If you prepare flowcharts for a variety of services, you will soon notice that although core products may differ widely, common supplementary elements – from information to billing and from reservations/order-taking to problem resolution – keep recurring.

There are potentially dozens of different supplementary services, but almost all of them can be classified into one of the following eight clusters. We have listed them as either *facilitating supplementary services* or *enhancing supplementary services* (similar to the model by Eiglier and Langeard that we just discussed and using the term 'Enhancing' rather than Grönroos's 'Supporting').

Facilitating services	**Enhancing services**
Information	Consultation
Order-taking	Hospitality
Billing	Safekeeping
Payment	Exceptions

In Figure 8.3, these eight clusters are displayed as petals surrounding the centre of a flower – which we call the *Flower of Service*. We've shown them clockwise in the sequence in which they are often likely to be encountered by customers (although this sequence may vary widely in practice – for instance, payment may have to be made before service is delivered rather than afterwards). In a well-designed and well-managed service organization, the petals and core are fresh and well-formed. A badly designed or poorly executed service is like a flower with missing, wilted or discoloured petals. Even if the core is perfect, the overall impression of the flower is unattractive. Think about your own experiences as a customer (or when purchasing on behalf of an organization). When you were dissatisfied with a particular purchase, was it the core that was at fault, or was it a problem with one or more of the petals?

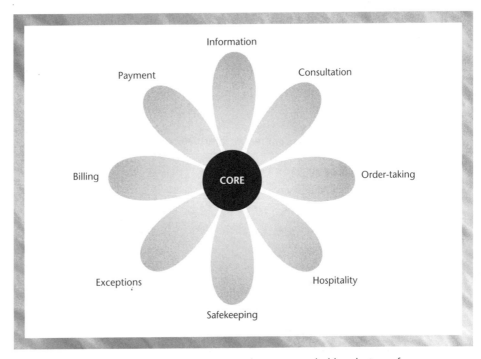

Figure 8.3 ■ The Flower of Service: core product surrounded by clusters of supplementary services

Not every core product is surrounded by supplementary elements from all eight clusters. As we'll see, the nature of the product helps to determine which supplementary services must be offered and which might usefully be added to enhance value and make the organization easy to do business with. In general, people-processing services tend to be accompanied by more supplementary services than do the other three categories; similarly, high-contact services will have more than low-contact services.

A company's market positioning strategy helps to determine which supplementary services should be included (see Chapter 5). A strategy of adding benefits to increase customers' perceptions of quality will probably require more supplementary services (and also a higher level of performance on all such elements) than a strategy of competing on low prices. Firms that offer different levels of service – like First Class, Business Class and Economy Class in an airline context – often differentiate them by adding supplementary services for each upgrade in service level.

Information

To obtain full value from any good or service, customers need relevant *information* (Table 8.1). New customers and prospects are especially information-hungry: they want to know which product will best meet their needs. Other needs may include directions to the site where the product is sold (or details of how to order it), service hours, prices and usage instructions. Further information, sometimes required by law, could include conditions of sale and use, warnings, reminders and notification of changes. Finally, customers may want documentation of what has already taken place, such as confirmation of reservations, receipts and tickets, and monthly summaries of account activity.

Companies should make sure that the information they provide is both timely and accurate, since incorrect information can annoy or inconvenience customers. One firm that automated its information services established a fully upgraded fax

Table 8.1 ■ Examples of information elements

- Directions to service site
- Schedules/service hours
- Prices
- Instructions on using core product/supplementary services
- Reminders
- Warnings
- Conditions of sale/service
- Notification of changes
- Documentation
- Confirmation of reservations
- Summaries of account activity
- Receipts and tickets

request service so that customers could have quicker access to information on forth-coming conferences. However, in some cases the faxes were never sent – even after repeated phone calls from annoyed customers. Other customers received multiple pages of unwanted information.[7] In this case, the company put both itself and the advertised conferences in jeopardy by failing to perform an important supplemen-tary service efficiently and effectively.

Traditional ways of providing information to customers include using front-line employees (who are not always as knowledgeable as customers might like), printed notices, brochures and instruction books. France's telephone-based Minitel video display system was a world leader for many years in delivering a wide array of infor-mation on a small video screen, from train timetables to snow depths at specific Alpine ski resorts. It remains very popular, despite its crude graphics, because it requires only a display attachment for the telephone as opposed to a computer and modem. Other information media include videotapes or software-driven tutorials, touch-screen video displays and menu-driven recorded telephone messages.

The most significant innovation in recent years has been the internet, offering users access to a vast store of information through search engines, bulletin boards and web sites. Examples of useful applications range from train and airline time-tables, details of individual hotels operated by chains across Europe and overseas, assistance in locating specific retail outlets such as restaurants and shops, and estate agencies that list properties for sale or rent on their web sites, complete with photos. As part of a broader public relations effort, the web site of the Italian department store La Rinascente offers information on history, fashion, art and entertainment in Italy. In the field of business logistics, a number of firms offer shippers the opportu-nity to track the movements of their packages – each of which has been assigned a unique identification number – through the relevant company's web site.

Order-taking

Once customers are ready to buy, a key supplementary element comes into play – accepting applications, orders and reservations (Table 8.2). The process of *order-taking* should be polite, fast and accurate so that customers do not waste time and endure unnecessary mental or physical effort. These unwanted costs of service can substan-tially reduce the value of a service to customers by offsetting the benefits they receive (see Chapter 12). Only in rare cases are customers willing to wait great lengths of time to place orders for a service. There's a difference of course between waiting in a queue at a ticket window and putting one's name on a list. People will wait overnight for tickets to a popular concert or sports event.

Technology can be used to make order-taking easier and faster for both customers and suppliers. The key lies in minimizing the time and effort required of both par-ties, while also ensuring completeness and accuracy. For example, many restaurants have incorporated technology into their order-taking systems. Pizza Hut has tested an electronic alternative to the traditional order pad in its Swiss stores. Instead, the server enters orders by number on a handheld device the size of a large calculator, then downloads it to the kitchen via a small receiver in the ceiling. Systems such as these benefit restaurants by placing the responsibility for order accuracy with the customer and providing an instantaneous and accurate record of what has been sold. Some take-out restaurants distribute a fax menu to customers as an alternative to telephone ordering: fill it out, fax it in and then drop by to collect your food!

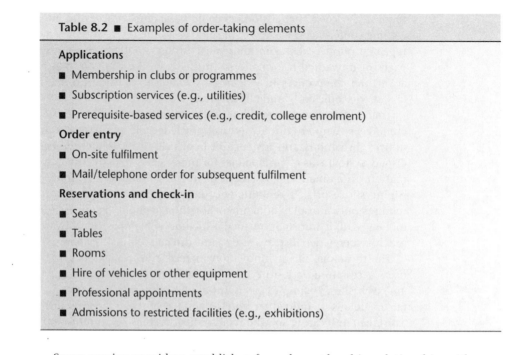

Table 8.2 ■ Examples of order-taking elements

Applications

- Membership in clubs or programmes
- Subscription services (e.g., utilities)
- Prerequisite-based services (e.g., credit, college enrolment)

Order entry

- On-site fulfilment
- Mail/telephone order for subsequent fulfilment

Reservations and check-in

- Seats
- Tables
- Rooms
- Hire of vehicles or other equipment
- Professional appointments
- Admissions to restricted facilities (e.g., exhibitions)

Some service providers establish a formal membership relationship with customers to accomplish order-taking tasks. Banks, insurance companies and utilities, for instance, require prospective customers to go through an application process designed to gather relevant information and to screen out those who do not meet basic enrolment criteria (like a bad credit record or serious health problems). Universities also require prospective students to apply for admission. While most students still complete this process in the traditional way, some are now able to apply through the internet. The London Business School, for instance, allows prospective students to apply to its MBA programme through the medium of its website.

Reservations (including appointments and check-in) represent a special type of order-taking which entitles customers to a specified unit of service – for example, an airline seat, a restaurant table, a hotel room, time with a qualified professional or admission to a facility such as a sports arena which has restricted capacity. The scheduling aspect introduces an extra need for accuracy, since reserving customers seats on the wrong flight is likely to be unpopular with customers. Many reservations include confirmation in the form of a ticket that is exchanged for admission, although some airlines are moving away from this traditional approach.

Ticketless systems, based upon telephone or web site reservations, provide enormous cost savings for airlines, since there is no travel agent commission – customers book directly – and the administrative effort is drastically reduced. A paper ticket at an airline may be handled 15 times while an electronic ticket requires just one step. But some customers are disenchanted by the paperless process. Although they receive a confirmation number by phone when they make the reservations and need only to show identification at the airport to claim their seats, many people feel insecure without tangible proof that they have a seat on a particular flight.[8] And business travellers complain that receipts come days or sometimes weeks after a trip, causing problems for claiming expenses from corporate accounting departments. Some airlines now offer to fax receipts and itineraries on request at the time a flight is booked.

Billing

Billing is common to almost all services (unless the service is provided free of charge). Inaccurate, illegible or incomplete bills offer a splendid opportunity to disappoint customers who may, up to that point, have been quite satisfied with their experience. Of course, such failures add insult to injury if the customer is already dissatisfied. Billing should also be timely, because it will probably result in faster payment – especially if customers are off-site. And if customers are at the service facility, they may be very frustrated if they are forced to endure a lengthy wait for their bill. Business people complain frequently about delays in getting their bills at restaurants when they are ready to return to work after lunch.

Various forms of billing procedures exist, ranging from verbal statements to a machine-displayed price, and from handwritten invoices to elaborate monthly statements of account activity and fees (Table 8.3). Perhaps the simplest type of billing is self-billing, when the customer tallies up the amount of an order and either encloses a cheque or signs a credit card payment authorization. In such instances (which range from pencilled figures on a paper form to sophisticated electronic procedures), billing and payment are combined into a single act. All the seller needs to do is to check that the customer's arithmetic and credit are both good.

More and more, billing is being computerized. Despite its potential for productivity improvements, computerized billing has its dark side, as when an innocent customer tries futilely to contest an inaccurate bill and is met by an escalating sequence of ever larger bills (compounded interest and penalty charges), accompanied by increasingly threatening, computer-generated letters.

Bills and account statements are important documents. Customers like them to be clear and informative, and itemized in ways that make it clear how the total was computed. Unexplained, arcane symbols that have all the meaning of hieroglyphics on an Egyptian monument (and are decipherable only by the high priests of accounting and data processing) do not create a favourable impression. Nor does fuzzy printing or illegible handwriting. With their ability to switch fonts and typefaces, to box and to highlight, laser printers can produce statements that are not only more legible but also organize information in more useful ways.

Table 8.3 ■ Examples of billing elements

- Periodic statements of account activity
- Invoices for individual transactions
- Verbal statements of amount due
- Machine display of amount due
- Self-billing (computer by customer)

Marketing research has a role to play in billing design. The researcher's job is to ask customers what information they want and how they would like it to be organized. BT learned from research that both business and residential customers desired a choice of billing arrangements. Recognizing these differing needs, the telecommunications company segmented its market in terms of *when* customers wanted to pay and *how* they wanted to pay. Customers can now choose between paying monthly or quarterly (every three months). If they opt to pay by cheque, they have 21 days to make the payment if they pay monthly and a month and a half if they pay quarterly. Alternatively, they can pay by direct debit from their bank accounts. Finally, BT offers what it calls its Budget Account billing system which involves quarterly billing but automatic monthly debits of a predetermined amount, thus lowering the sum to be paid at the end of the quarter.

American Express built its Corporate Card business by offering companies detailed documentation of the spending patterns of individual employees and departments on travel and entertainment. Intelligent thinking about customer needs led AmEx to realize that well-organized information has value to a customer, beyond just the basic requirement of knowing how much to pay at the end of each month.

Busy customers hate to be kept waiting for a bill to be prepared in a hotel, restaurant or car rental office. Many hotels and car rental firms have now created express check-out options, taking customers' credit card details in advance and documenting charges later by mail. Companies that do this should be especially certain that their billing is accurate. Since customers use the express check-outs to save time, they are likely to be particularly annoyed if they subsequently have to waste time seeking corrections and refunds. A more reliable express check-out option is now being used by Hertz and several other car rental companies. An agent meets customers as they return their cars, checks the mileage and fuel gauge readings and then prints a bill on the spot using a portable wireless terminal. Many hotels now slip bills under guestroom doors on the morning of departure showing charges to date; others offer customers the option of previewing their bills before check-out on the TV monitors in their rooms.

Payment

In most cases, a bill requires the customer to take action on *payment* (and such action may be very slow in coming!). One exception is bank statements which detail charges that have already been deducted from the customer's account. Increasingly, customers expect ease and convenience of payment, including credit, when they make purchases in their own countries and while travelling abroad.

A variety of options exist to facilitate customer bill-paying (Table 8.4). Self-service payment systems, for instance, require customers to insert coins, notes, tokens or cards in machines. But equipment breakdowns destroy the whole purpose of such a system, so good maintenance and rapid-response trouble shooting are essential. Much payment still takes place through hand-to-hand transfers of cash and cheques, but credit and debit cards are growing in importance as more and more establishments come to accept them. Tokens, vouchers, coupons or other pre-paid tickets represent further alternatives. The highlighted box on page 306 describes the development of the Mondex smart card, described by some as an 'electronic wallet'.

Table 8.4 ■ Examples of paying elements

Self-service

- Exact change in machine
- Cash in machine with change returned
- Insert pre-payment card
- Insert credit/charge/debit card
- Insert token
- Electronic funds transfer
- Send a cheque by post

Direct to payee or intermediary

- Cash-handling and change-giving
- Cheque handling
- Credit/charge/debit card-handling
- Coupon redemption
- Tokens, vouchers, etc.

Automatic deduction from financial deposits (e.g., bank charges)

Control and verification

- Automated systems (e.g., machine-readable tickets operate entry gate)
- Personal systems (e.g., gate controllers, ticket inspectors)

A key aspect of payment is making sure that people actually pay what is due. Ticket collectors (and electronic gate controllers) at points of entry to a service facility, roving inspectors on buses and trains, and security personnel at retail shop exits work to ensure that all users pay the due price. Despite that often-repeated slogan, 'the customer is always right', a small minority of customers are not always well behaved. (Remember those wretched jaycustomers from Chapter 6?) This creates a need for control systems. However, these tasks need to be well organized so that queues do not build up at exit and entry points. Inspectors and security officers must be trained to combine politeness with firmness in performing their jobs, so that honest customers do not feel harassed. But a visible presence often serves as a deterrent.

Consultation

In contrast to information, which suggests a simple response to customers' questions (or printed information that anticipates their needs), *consultation* involves a dialogue to probe customer requirements and then develop a tailored solution. Table 8.5 provides examples of several supplementary services in the consultation category. At its simplest, consultation consists of immediate advice from a knowledgeable service person in response to the request: 'What do you suggest?' (For example, you might ask the person who cuts your hair for advice on different hairstyles and products.) Effective consultation requires an understanding of each customer's current situation, before suggesting a suitable course of action. Comprehensive customer records

The Mondex smart card

The latest technology in card payment systems is what some have called the 'electronic wallet', also known as a stored value card. The best-known version is the Mondex card, developed in the UK but now being commercialized around the world. The card contains a microchip that can store money in electronic form. Each time the Mondex card is used to make a payment, it is run through a reader that automatically deducts the right amount and credits it to the recipient. Using a small portable reader, individuals can transfer money from one person's card to another. Like replenishing a purse with cash after visiting a bank or ATM, the Mondex card can also be reloaded with 'e-cash' from special terminals that can be attached not only to ATMs but also to pay-phones and will eventually be available on home computers.

The card was developed by Britain's National Westminster Bank and underwent an extended market test in the town of Swindon, a city of some 150,000 inhabitants about 130 km (80 miles) west of London. NatWest's partners in the test, which began in June 1995, were Barclay's (another major bank) and British Telecom, which equipped its payphones with the special equipment needed to read Mondex cards. Numerous retailers were also provided with Mondex readers so that customers could use their cards to make purchases in these stores. All 40,000 NatWest and Barclay's customers in Swindon were offered the chance to participate in the test and about 10,000 accepted. The test provided detailed information on the nature and extent of card use, together with an indication of the difficulties and opportunities that might accompany broader commercialization of the concept.

Additional tests followed in other countries. In mid-1996, NatWest established a separate company, called Mondex International, and sold off most of its shares to franchisee banks around the world. Mondex use continued in Swindon and by late 1997 had attracted 13,000 users and 700 retail outlets.

In November 1996, Mondex Canada, owned by ten financial institutions, began the first, community-wide test of the card in North America, selecting Guelph, Ontario, a middle-class city of 95,000 people, located 65 km (40 miles) west of Toronto. City buses, pay telephones, parking meters, vending machines and most restaurants and shops were all equipped to handle electronic cash. Even farmshops selling sweet corn participated. The card's carrying case, similar to a small calculator, doubles as a cash tracker, enabling users to check their cash balances and display the previous ten transactions. After 10 months, Guelph had 7,500 active Mondex card users, who had collectively loaded C$1 million (€540,000) onto their cards, and several major Canadian financial institutions, led by the Royal Bank of Canada, had announced their intention to take Mondex nationwide. The biggest challenge to e-cash, declared the project manager, was the fact that many people still considered cash to be sacred and wouldn't use any form of card!

Using insights from the Canadian experience, New York's two biggest banks began tests in October 1997 in a defined area of Manhattan. Chase Manhattan offered the Mondex card under the MasterCard banner but Citibank offered a different technology called Visa Cash card. Despite differing technologies, however, both cards can be used in the same retail terminal. They can be refilled from local bank ATMs and from special kiosks which have been installed in the area. The Mondex MasterCard, which has a powerful microprocessor for off-line operations, can also be refilled with the aid of a gadget called a Personal-ATM. This small device not only allows individuals to make e-cash transactions between themselves, but can also be connected to a phone line so that users can dial into their banking networks and download cash in the comfort of their homes or offices.

Table 8.5 ■ Examples of consultation elements

- Advice
- Auditing
- Personal counselling
- Tutoring/training in product usage
- Management or technical consultancy

can be a great help in this respect, particularly if relevant data can be retrieved easily from a remote terminal. If you are a college student, your tutors probably rely on electronic access to your student records to provide consultation about what classes you need to complete your degree and graduate.

Counselling represents a more subtle approach to consultation because it involves helping customers better understand their situations and encouraging them to come up with their 'own' solutions and action programmes. This approach can be a particularly valuable supplement to services such as health treatment, when part of the challenge is to get customers to take a long-term view of their personal situation and to adopt more healthful behaviours which may involve some initial sacrifice. For example, slimming clubs like Weight Watchers use counselling to help customers change behaviours so that weight loss can be sustained after the initial diet is completed.

Finally, there are more formalized efforts to provide management and technical consulting. The 'solution selling' associated with marketing expensive industrial equipment and services is a good example: the sales engineer researches the customer's situation and then offers objective advice about what particular package of equipment and systems will yield the best results for the customer. Some consulting services are offered free of charge in the hope of making a sale. However, in other instances the service is 'unbundled' and customers are expected to pay for it. Customers' needs for advice can also be met through one-on-one tutorials or group training programmes to demonstrate use of a particular service or piece of equipment.

Hospitality

Hospitality is potentially a very pretty petal, reflecting pleasure at meeting new customers and greeting old ones when they return. Well-managed businesses try, at least in small ways, to ensure that their employees treat customers as guests. Courtesy and consideration for customers' needs apply to both face-to-face encounters and telephone interactions (Table 8.6).

Hospitality finds its full expression in face-to-face encounters. In some cases, hospitality starts (and ends) with an offer of transport to and from the service site, as with courtesy shuttle buses. If customers must wait outdoors before the service can be delivered, then a thoughtful service provider will offer weather protection; if indoors, then a waiting area with seating and even entertainment (TV, newspapers or magazines) to pass the time. Recruiting employees who are naturally warm, welcoming and considerate for customer-contact jobs helps to create a hospitable atmosphere.

Table 8.6 ■ Examples of hospitality elements

- Greeting
- Food and beverages
- Toilets and washrooms
- Bathroom kits
- Waiting facilities and amenities
  - Lounges, waiting areas, seating
  - Weather protection
  - Magazines, entertainment, newspapers
- Transport
- Security

The Marriott Corporation has made a science of identifying what its hotel guests want in terms of hospitality. In a landmark study, the company's Courtyard by Marriott chain surveyed business travellers about their needs. The study results confirmed that these travellers wanted much more than a friendly greeting at the front desk.[9] They valued trouble-free check-out and meal services, plus in-room access to home and work by voice mail, fax and computer. Marriott provides these things for its business customers in addition to other hospitality services like quiet lounges where guests can relax without being distracted by music or TV noise.

The quality of the hospitality services offered by a firm can increase or decrease satisfaction with the core product. This is especially true for people-processing services where customers cannot easily leave the service facility. For example, both hospitals and airlines provide patients with meals – often accompanied by grumbling from patients or customers about the quantity and quality. Private hospitals often seek to enhance their appeals by providing the level of room service, including meals, that might be expected in a good hotel. Some airlines seek to differentiate themselves from their competitors with better meals; Singapore Airlines is famous for its attentive cabin crew. Despite the importance of these creature comforts to passengers, the airlines still recognize that such amenities do not translate directly into ticket sales. As we noted in Chapter 6, travellers tend to rank attributes such as safety, ticket prices, schedule convenience and frequent flyer programmes as more important than food. However, when these key elements are perceived as broadly similar across competing airlines, hospitality services can provide a competitive advantage.

While in-flight hospitality is important, an airline journey doesn't really end until passengers reach their final destination. Air travellers have come to expect departure lounges, but British Airways (BA) came up with the novel idea of an arrivals lounge for its terminals at London's Heathrow and Gatwick airports. Passengers from the Americas, Asia, Africa and Australia often arrive in London in the early hours of the morning after a long, overnight flight. BA was already using the slogan 'Arrive in better shape' to promote the quality of its in-flight service. A logical extension was to offer holders of first and business class tickets or a BA Executive Club gold card (awarded to the airline's most frequent flyers) the opportunity to use a special lounge where they could take a shower, change, have breakfast and make phone calls or send faxes before continuing to their final destination feeling a lot fresher. It's a nice competitive advantage, which BA has actively promoted.

Safekeeping

While visiting a service site, customers often want assistance with their personal possessions. In fact, unless certain safekeeping services are provided (like safe and convenient parking for their cars), some customers may not come at all. The list of potential on-site safekeeping services is long. It includes: provision of coatrooms; baggage transport, handling and storage; safekeeping of valuables; and even child care and pet care (Table 8.7). Responsible businesses also worry about the safety of their customers. These days, many businesses pay close attention to safety and security issues for customers who are visiting their service facilities. Wells Fargo Bank distributes a brochure with its bank statements with information about using its ATM machines safely. It seeks to educate its customers about how to protect both their ATM cards and themselves from theft and personal injury. And the bank makes sure that its machines are in brightly lit, highly visible locations to reduce any risks to its customers or their possessions. Airlines, too, are struggling to protect the safety of both passengers and their physical possessions as overhead luggage containers become more crowded. Thousands of passengers are hurt each year by falling luggage, ranging from bags and briefcases to vodka bottles and golf umbrellas.

Another set of safekeeping services relate to physical products that customers buy or rent. These services are particularly applicable to products ordered by mail or phone. Supplementary services of this nature may include packaging, pick-up and delivery, assembly, installation, cleaning and inspection. Customers who are purchasing durable goods like cars, cameras or computers may also want to know details of repair and maintenance services, warranties and whether or not they can purchase maintenance contracts as a form of insurance.

Table 8.7 ■ Examples of safekeeping elements

Caring for possessions customers bring with them

■ Child care	■ Coat room
■ Pet care	■ Baggage handling
■ Parking facilities for vehicles	■ Storage space
■ Valet parking	■ Safety deposit/security

Caring for goods purchased (or rented) by customers

■ Packaging	■ Cleaning
■ Pick-up	■ Refuelling
■ Transportation	■ Preventive maintenance
■ Delivery	■ Repairs and renovation
■ Installation	■ Upgrade
■ Inspection and diagnosis	

Exceptions

Exceptions involve a group of supplementary services that fall outside the routine of normal service delivery (Table 8.8). Astute businesses anticipate exceptions and develop contingency plans and guidelines in advance. That way, employees will not appear helpless and surprised when customers ask for special assistance. Well-defined procedures make it easier for employees to respond promptly and effectively.

There are several different types of exceptions:

1. *Special requests.* There are many circumstances when an individual or corporate customer may request some degree of customized treatment that requires a departure from normal operating procedures. In people-processing services, advance requests often relate to personal concerns, including care of children, dietary requirements, medical needs, religious observance and personal disabilities. Special requests are common among customers who are spending many hours (or even days) with a people-processing service, especially when they are far from home. The travel and hotel industries are a good example, with customers' medical and dietary needs presenting commonly encountered reasons for special requests.

Table 8.8 ■ Examples of exceptions elements

Special requests in advance of service delivery

- children's needs
- dietary requirements
- medical or disability needs
- religious observance
- deviations from standard operating procedures

Handling special communications

- complaints
- compliments
- suggestions

Problem-solving

- warranties and guarantees against product malfunction
- resolving difficulties that arise from using the product
- resolving difficulties caused by accidents, service failures, and problems with staff or other customers
- assisting customers who have suffered an accident or medical emergency

Restitution

- refunds
- compensation in kind for unsatisfactory goods and services
- free repair of defective goods

2. *Problem-solving*. Situations arise when normal service delivery (or product performance) fails to run smoothly as a result of accidents, delays, equipment failures, or customers experiencing difficulty in using the product.

3. *Handling of complaints/suggestions/compliments*. This activity requires well-defined procedures. It should be easy for customers to express dissatisfaction, offer suggestions for improvement, or pass on compliments, and service providers should be able to make an appropriate response quickly.

4. *Restitution*. Customers expect to be compensated for serious performance failures. This compensation may take the form of repairs under warranty, legal settlements, refunds, an offer of free service in the future, or other forms of payment in kind.

Managers need to keep an eye on the level of exception requests. Too many exceptions may indicate that standard procedures need revamping. For instance, if a restaurant constantly receives requests for special vegetarian meals since there are none offered, this may indicate that it's time to revise the menu to include at least one vegetarian dish. A flexible approach to exceptions is generally a good idea, because it reflects responsiveness to customer needs. On the other hand, exceptions should be discouraged if they compromise safety, negatively impact other customers or place an unrealistic burden on employees.

Managerial implications

The eight categories of supplementary services forming the Flower of Service collectively provide many options for enhancing the core product, whether it be a good or a service. Most supplementary services do (or should) represent responses to customer needs. As we've mentioned before, some are facilitating services – like information and reservations – that enable customers to use the core product more effectively. Others are 'extras' that enhance the core or even reduce some of its non-financial costs (for example, meals, magazines and entertainment are hospitality elements that help pass the time on what might otherwise be very boring airline flights). Some of these elements – notably billing and payment – are, in effect, imposed by the service provider. But even if not actively desired by the customer, they still form part of the overall service experience. Any badly handled element can have a negative impact on customers' perceptions of service quality. The 'information' and 'consultation' petals serve to illustrate the emphasis we place in this book on the need for education as well as promotion in communicating with service customers.

Not every core product will be surrounded by all eight petals. People-processing services tend to be the most demanding in terms of supplementary elements – especially hospitality – since they involve close (and often extended) interactions with customers. When customers do not need to come to the service factory, the need for hospitality may be limited to simple courtesies in letters and telecommunications. Possession-processing services sometimes place heavy demands on safekeeping elements, but there may be no need for this particular petal when providing information-processing services in which customers and suppliers deal entirely at arm's length. Financial services that are provided electronically are an exception to this, however – companies must ensure that their customers' financial assets are carefully safeguarded in transactions that occur via phone or the Web.

Product policy issues

Managers face many decisions concerning what types of supplementary services to offer their customers. These are primarily product-policy and positioning issues, since companies should make strategic decisions about what supplementary services will help attract and retain customers. A study of Japanese, American and European firms serving business-to-business markets found that most companies simply added layer upon layer of services to their core offerings without knowing what customers really valued.[10] Managers surveyed in the study indicated that they did not understand which services should be offered to customers as a standard package accompanying the core, and which could be offered as options for an extra charge. Without this knowledge, developing effective pricing policies can be tricky. There are no simple rules governing pricing decisions for core products and supplementary services. But managers should continually review their own policies and those of competitors to make sure they are in line with both market practice and customer needs. We'll discuss these and other pricing issues in more detail in Chapter 10.

Tables 8.1–8.8 can serve as a checklist in the continuing search for new ways to augment existing core products and to design new offerings. The lists provided in these eight tables do not claim to be all encompassing, since specialized products may require specialized supplementary elements. In general, firms that choose to compete on a low-cost, no-frills basis will require fewer supplementary elements in each category than they would for an expensive, high-value added product. Different levels of supplementary services around a common core may offer the basis for a product line of differentiated offerings, similar to the various classes of travel offered by airlines for the same flight. Regardless of which supplementary services a firm decides to offer, all of the elements in each petal should receive the care and attention needed to consistently meet defined service standards. That way the resulting flower will always have a fresh and appealing appearance – rather than looking wilted or disfigured by neglect.

Planning and branding service products

In recent years, more and more service businesses have started talking about their *products* – a term previously associated with manufactured goods. Some will even speak of their 'products and services', an expression also used by service-driven manufacturing firms. What is the distinction between these two terms in today's business environment?

A product implies a defined and consistent 'bundle of output' and also the ability to differentiate one bundle of output from another. In a manufacturing context, the concept is easy to understand and visualize. A firm like Hewlett-Packard offers a wide variety of products. Within each category of office machinery that it sells, there is often a product line of several different models. In 1998, for instance, HP's offerings included a line of four 'all-in-one' fax-printer-copier-scanners, under the name OfficeJet. The HP OfficeJet 500 and 570 print in colour and can copy and scan in black and white; they differ from each other primarily in the size of the memory (which is why the 570 costs a little more); the more expensive model 600 not only has more memory and prints faster but also adds colour copying. Finally, the model

Pro 1150Cse, while lacking the fax function, is capable of higher speeds, higher resolution, includes built-in software and can also scan in colour. Services associated with these machines include information, warranty and repair, as well as distribution through a line of authorized dealers. The four models offer purchasers trade-offs between price and performance, but in other respects, customization is found less in the manufactured product than in the supplementary services.

Service firms can also differentiate their products in similar fashion to the 'models' offered by manufacturers. Quick service restaurants are sometimes described as 'quasi-manufacturing' operations since they produce a physical output combined with value-added service. At each site, they display a menu of their products, which are of course highly tangible – burger connoisseurs can easily distinguish Burger King's Whopper from a Whopper with Cheese, as well as a Whopper from a Big Mac. The service comes from speedy delivery of a freshly prepared food item, the ability (in some instances) to order and pick up freshly cooked food from a drive-in location without leaving one's car, the availability within the restaurant of self-service drinks, condiments and napkins, and the opportunity to sit down and eat one's meal at a table.

But providers of more intangible services also offer a 'menu' of products, representing an assembly of carefully prescribed elements that are built around the core product and may bundle in certain value-added supplementary services. Additional supplementary services – often referred to collectively as *customer service* – may be available to facilitate delivery and use of the product, as well as billing and payment. Let's look at some examples from hotels, airlines and retail banking.

Product lines and brands

Most service organizations offer a line of products rather than just a single product. Some of these products are distinctly different from one another – as, for example, when a company operates several lines of business. Within a specific industry, a large firm may choose to offer several, differently positioned entries, each identified by a separate brand name. For instance, the French hotel company Groupe Accor offers seven different brands of hotel in Europe (although not all are available in every country): the 1-star Formule 1, 1- to 2-star Etap, 2-star Ibis, 3-star Mercure, the 4-star Grande Mercure and Novotel brands, and the 4- to 5-star Sofitel. In response to changing market opportunities, companies may revise the mix of products that they offer. Accor's Formule 1, for instance, is a relatively new creation made possible by an inexpensive, prefabricated building design.

Accor is, of course, just one player in the highly competitive hotel industry. Many hotel chains operating in Europe have 'tiered' their offerings to provide alternative service levels and value points to meet the needs of different market segments. Within each offering or brand, the supplier should seek to provide a distinctive and consistent service experience. Visiting a series of Ibis hotels should not result in the traveller's encountering wide variations in quality, style and performance from one unit to another – or even from one room to another.

Another good example comes from British Airways (BA), which offers seven distinct air travel products – sometimes referred to as 'sub-brands' – each targeted at specific market segments. There are four intercontinental offerings – Concorde (supersonic de-luxe service), First (de-luxe subsonic service), Club World (business class), and World Traveller (economy class); two intra-European sub-brands – Club Europe (business class) and Euro-Traveller (economy class); and, within the United Kingdom, Shuttle, offering high-frequency service between London and major British cities. In addition, BA has franchised certain other airlines to operate aircraft in British Airways' colours, providing passengers with a level and style of service that must consistently meet BA-defined specifications.

Each British Airways offering represents a specific service concept and a set of clearly stated product specifications for pre-flight, inflight and on-arrival service elements. To provide additional focus on product, pricing and marketing communications, responsibility for managing and developing each service is assigned to an individual management team. Through internal training and external communications, staff and passengers alike are kept informed of the characteristics of each service. Robert Ayling, BA's chief executive, says of Concorde, 'While it is a part of British Airways, it is seen as a brand in its own right. The Concorde brand stands above all for speed, for getting from London to New York in three hours, twenty minutes. It represents a very exclusive means of travel, and in some ways it is also an exclusive club.'[11]

Except for Concorde, Shuttle and non-jets, most aircraft in BA's fleet are configured in two or three classes. For instance, the airline's intercontinental fleet of 747s is equipped to serve First, Club World and World Traveller passengers. On any given route, all receive the same core product – say a 12-hour flight from London to Kuala Lumpur – but the nature and extent of most of the supplementary elements will differ widely, both on the ground and in the air. Passengers in First, for instance, not only benefit from better tangible elements – such as more comfortable seats that fold into beds, better food and the use of an airport lounge before the flight, but also receive more personalized service from airline employees and benefit from faster service on the ground at check-in, passport control in London (special queues) and baggage retrieval (priority handling). The better the service, of course, the higher the price!

Branding is certainly not limited to airlines and hotels. Indeed, it is particularly useful for clarifying and making tangible distinctive service offerings in fields such as banking and insurance. Across Europe, many financial service firms have created different brands to identify accounts and service packages offering distinctively different features. The objective is to transform a series of service elements and processes into a consistent and recognizable branded service experience, offering a definable output at a specified price. For instance, PPP Healthcare, the second largest provider of healthcare insurance in Britain, offers eight categories of membership at different premiums (prices) under the following brand names: Starter Plan, Key Plan, Key Plan Over 60, Extensive, Extensive Over 60, Comprehensive, Comprehensive Over 60 and Platinum. The core service, referred to by PPP as 'The Heart of Your Membership' includes a personal advisory team, health information line and immediate access to private healthcare treatment. The nature and extent of subscriber coverage varies according to the plan with respect to such factors as in-patient and outpatient treatment, use of private ambulances, home nursing, overseas medical care, psychiatric treatment, dental cover and so forth.

Using research to design new services

When a company is designing a new service from scratch, how can it determine what features and price will create the best value for target customers? It's hard to know without asking these customers – hence the need for research. Let's examine how the Marriott Corporation used market research experts to help with new service development in the hotel industry.

When Marriott was designing a new chain of hotels for business travellers (which eventually became known as Courtyard by Marriott), it hired marketing research experts to help establish an optimal design concept.[12] Since there are limits to how much service and how many amenities can be offered at any given price, Marriott needed to know how customers would make trade-offs in order to arrive at the most satisfactory compromise in terms of value for money. The intent of the research was to get respondents to trade off different hotel service features to see which ones they valued most. Marriott's goal was to determine if a niche existed between full-service hotels and inexpensive motels, especially in locations where demand was not high enough to justify a large full-service hotel. If such a niche existed, executives wanted to develop a product to fill that gap.

A sample of 601 consumers from four metropolitan areas participated in the study. Researchers used a sophisticated technique known as conjoint analysis which asks survey respondents to make trade-offs between different groupings of attributes. The objective is to determine which mix of attributes at specific prices offers them the highest degree of utility. The 50 attributes in the Marriott study were divided into the following seven factors (or sets of attributes), each containing a variety of different features based on detailed studies of competing offerings:

1. *External factors* – building shape, landscaping, swimming pool type and location, hotel size.

2. *Room features* – room size and decor, climate control, location and type of bathroom, entertainment systems, other amenities.

3. *Food-related services* – type and location of restaurants, menus, room service, vending machines, guest shop, in-room kitchen.

4. *Lounge facilities* – location, atmosphere, type of guests.

5. *Services* – reservations, registration, check-out, airport limousine, bell desk (baggage service), message centre, secretarial services, car rental, laundry, valet.

6. *Leisure facilities* – sauna, whirlpool, exercise room, racquetball and tennis courts, games room, children's playground.

7. *Security* – guards, smoke detectors, 24-hour video camera.

For each of these seven factors, respondents were presented with a series of stimulus cards displaying different levels of performance for each attribute. For instance, the 'Rooms' stimulus card displayed nine attributes, each of which had three to five different levels. Thus, amenities ranged from 'small bar of soap' to 'large soap, shampoo packet, shoeshine mitt' to 'large soap, bath gel, shower cap, sewing kit, shampoo, special soap', and then to the highest level, 'large soap, bath gel, shower cap, sewing kit, special soap, toothpaste, etc.'

In the second phase of the analysis, respondents were shown a number of alternative hotel profiles, each featuring different levels of performance on the various attributes contained in the seven factors. They were asked to indicate on a 5-point scale how likely they would be to stay at a hotel with these features, given a specific room price per night (see Figure 8.4).

The research yielded detailed guidelines for the selection of almost 200 features and service elements, representing those attributes that provided the highest utility

Room price per night is $44.85
Building size, bar/lounge
Large (600 rooms) 12-storey hotel with:
- Quiet bar/lounge
- Enclosed central corridors and elevators
- All rooms have very large windows

Landscaping/court
Building forms a spacious outdoor courtyard
- View from rooms of moderately landscaped courtyard with:
  - many trees and shrubs
  - the swimming pool plus a fountain
  - terraced areas for sunning, sitting, eating

Food
Small moderately priced lounge and restaurant for hotel guests/friends
- Limited breakfast with juices, fruit, croissants, cereal, bacon and eggs
- Lunch – soup and sandwiches only
- Evening meal – salad, soup, sandwiches, six hot entrées including steak

Hotel/motel room quality
Quality of room furnishings, carpet, etc. is similar to:
- Hyatt Regencies
- Westin 'Plaza' Hotels

Room size and function
Room 1 foot longer than typical hotel/motel room
- Space for comfortable sofa-bed and 2 chairs
- Large desk
- Coffee table
- Coffeemaker and small refrigerator

Service standards
Full service including:
- Rapid check-in/check-out systems
- Reliable message service
- Valet (laundry pick up/deliver)
- Porter
- Someone (concierge) arranges reservations, tickets and generally at no cost
- Cleanliness, upkeep, management similar to:
  - Hyatts
  - Marriotts

Leisure
- Combination indoor/outdoor pool
- Enclosed whirlpool (jacuzzi)
- Well-equiped playroom/playground for kids

Security
- Night-guard on duty 7 p.m. to 7 a.m.
- Fire/water sprinklers throughout hotel

'X' the ONE box below which best describes how likely you are to stay in this hotel/motel at this price:

Would stay there almost all the time	Would stay there on a regular basis	Would stay there now and then	Would rarely stay there	Would not stay there
☐	☐	☐	☐	☐

*This full profile description of a hotel offering is one of the 50 cards developed by a fractional factorial design of the seven facets each at the five levels (developed by the Marriott's development team). Each respondent received five cards following a blocking design.

Figure 8.4 ■ Sample hotel offering*

Source: Jerry Wind, Paul E. Green, Douglas Shifflet and Marsha Scarbrough, 'Courtyard by Marriott: Designing a Hotel Facility with Consumer-Based Maketing Models', *Interfaces*, January–February 1989, pp. 25–47.

for the customers in the target segments at prices they were willing to pay. An important aspect of the study was that it focused not only on what travellers wanted, but also identified what they liked but weren't prepared to pay for (there's a difference, after all, between wanting something and being willing to pay for it!). Using these inputs, the design team was able to meet the specified price while retaining the features most desired by the target market.

Marriott was sufficiently encouraged by the findings to build three 'Courtyard by Marriott' prototype hotels. After testing the concept under real-world conditions and making some refinements, the company subsequently developed a large chain whose advertising slogan became 'Courtyard by Marriott – the hotel designed by business travellers'. The new hotel concept filled a gap in the market with a product that represented the best balance between the price customers were prepared to pay and the physical and service features they most desired. The success of this project has led Marriott to develop additional customer driven products – Fairfield Inn and Marriott Suites – using the same research methodology.

Achieving success in development of new service products

Most of the research into new product success factors has been confined to industrial or business-to-business markets and has heavily emphasized studies of the development process for new physical goods. Storey and Easingwood argue that in developing new services, 'the product core is of only secondary importance. It is the quality of the total service offering, and also of the marketing support that goes with this, that are of key importance.'[13]

Service firms are not, unfortunately, immune to the high failure rates that plague new manufactured products. A key question is the extent to which rigorously conducted and controlled development processes for new services will enhance their success rate or whether the real challenge lies in market launch. A study by Edgett and Parkinson focused on discriminating between successful and unsuccessful new financial services introduced by 67 British building societies.[14] They found that the three factors contributing most to success were, in order of importance:

1. *Market synergy* – the new product fits well with the existing image of the firm, provides a superior advantage to competing products in terms of meeting customers' known needs, and receives strong support during and after the launch from the firm and its branches; further, the firm had a good understanding of its customers' purchase decision behaviour.

2. *Organizational factors* – there was strong interfunctional cooperation and coordination; development personnel were fully aware of why they were involved and of the importance of new products to the company.

3. *Market research factors* – detailed and scientifically designed market research studies were conducted early in the development process with a clear idea of the type of information to be obtained; a good definition of the product concept was developed before undertaking field surveys.

In a study by Storey and Easingwood, 78 marketing managers in financial services firms were surveyed in an effort to identify factors distinguishing successful from unsuccessful products.[15] The findings were somewhat consistent with those of the study discussed above. In this instance, the key factors underlying success were determined as *synergy* (the fit between the product and the firm in terms of needed expertise and resources being present) and *internal marketing* (the support given to staff prior to launch to help them understand the new product and its underlying systems, plus details about direct competitors, and support).

Courtyard by Marriott's success in a very different industry – a people-processing service with many tangible components – supports the notion that a highly structured development process will increase the chances of success for a complex service innovation. However, it's worth noting that there may be limits to the degree of structure that can and should be imposed. Edwardsson, Haglund and Mattsson reviewed Swedish experience in telecommunications, transport and financial services. They concluded that:

> complex processes like the development of new services cannot be formally planned altogether. Creativity and innovation cannot only rely on planning and control. There must be some elements of improvisation, anarchy, and internal competition in the development of new services . . . We believe that a contingency approach is needed and that creativity on the one hand and formal planning and control on the other can be balanced, with successful new services as the outcome.[16]

The reading, 'Key concepts for new service development', by Bo Edvardsson and Jan Olsson (reproduced on pages 396–412) provides a good review of issues in new service development, based on empirical studies in Sweden; it looks at the topic from a quality perspective, and provides a variety of useful conceptual frameworks.[17]

Conclusion

In mature industries, the core service often becomes a commodity. The search for competitive advantage often centres on the value-creating supplementary services that surround this core. In this chapter, we grouped supplementary services into eight categories, circling the core like the petals of a flower.

A key insight from the Flower of Service concept is that different types of core products often share use of similar supplementary elements. As a result, customers may make comparisons across industries when. For instance, 'If my stockbroker can give me a clear documentation of my account activity, why can't the department store where I shop?' Or 'If my favourite airline can take reservations accurately, why can't the French restaurant up the street?' Questions such as these suggest that managers should be studying businesses outside their own industries in a search for 'best-in-class' performers on specific supplementary services.

Managers should be aware of the importance of selecting the right mix of supplementary service elements – no more and no less than needed – and creating synergy by ensuring that they are all internally consistent. The critical issue is not how many petals the flower has, but ensuring that each petal is perfectly formed and adds lustre to the core product in the eyes of target customers.

Study questions

1. Review the description of Eurostar at the beginning of the chapter and then identify and categorize each of the supplementary services described.

2. How does Eurostar differentiate the different classes of service and justify different pricing levels? (For further, up-to-date information, visit the Eurostar web site at: www.eurostar.com; please note that suffixes to the address will vary by country.)

3. Explain the role of supplementary services. Can they be applied to goods as well as services? If so, how might they relate to marketing strategy?

4. Explain the distinction between enhancing and facilitating supplementary services. Give several examples of each relative to services that you have used recently yourself.

5. How is branding used in services marketing? What is the distinction between a corporate brand like British Airways and the names given to its various classes of service. Why should BA bother to name its business class service 'Club World' instead of just referring to it as business class?

6. Provide some examples of branding from financial services such as retail banking or insurance. Comment on how meaningful these are likely to be to customers.

7. What is the purpose of techniques such as conjoint analysis in designing new services?

Notes

1. Based on information from a variety of sources, including the Eurostar web site, www.eurostar.com, June 1998.
2. W. Earl Sasser, R. Paul Olsen and D. Daryl Wyckoff, *Management of Service Operations: Text, Cases, and Readings*, Boston: Allyn & Bacon, 1978, Table 2.5: 'Operating Characteristics in a Service Environment', p. 21. David H. Maister developed a derivative model titled, 'A Framework for the Analysis of Service Firms', which he used in teaching this course, Management of Service Operations, at the Harvard Business School (unpublished memo, *c.* 1982).
3. G. Lynn Shostack, 'Breaking Free from Product Marketing', *Journal of Marketing*, Vol. 44, April 1977, pp. 73–80.
4. Pierre Eiglier and Eric Langeard, 'Services as Systems: Marketing Implications', in P. Eiglier, E. Langeard, C.H. Lovelock, J.E.G. Bateson and R.F. Young, *Marketing Consumer Services: New Insights*, Cambridge, MA: Marketing Science Institute, 1977, pp. 83–103. Note: An earlier version of this article was published in French in *Révue Française de Gestion*, March–April 1977, pp. 72–84.
5. Christian Grönroos, *Service Management and Marketing*, Lexington, MA: Lexington Books, 1990, p. 74.
6. The 'Flower of Service' concept presented in this section was first introduced in Christopher H. Lovelock, 'Cultivating the Flower of Service: New Ways of Looking at Core and Supplementary Services', in P. Eiglier and E. Langeard (eds), *Marketing, Operations, and Human Resources: Insights into Services*, Aix-en-Provence, France: IAE, Université d'Aix-Marseille III, 1992, pp. 296–316.
7. Stephan A. Butscher, 'Automating Services Can Cause More Problems than It Solves', *Marketing News*, 24 November 1997, p. 4.
8. Calmetta Coleman, 'Fliers Call Electronic Ticketing a Drag', *Wall Street Journal*, 17 January 1997, p. B1.
9. Gail Gaboda, 'For Business Travelers, There's No Place Like Home', *Marketing News*, 15 September 1997, p. 19.
10. James C. Anderson and James A. Narus, 'Capturing the Value of Supplementary Services', *Harvard Business Review*, Vol. 73, January–February 1995, pp. 75–83.
11. Robert Ayling, 'British Airways: Brand Leadership Results from Being True to Our Long-term Vision', in F. Gilmore, *Brand Warriors*, London: HarperCollinsBusiness, 1997, p. 42.

12. Jerry Wind, Paul E. Green, Douglas Shifflet and Marsha Scarbrough, 'Courtyard by Marriott: Designing a Hotel Facility with Consumer-Based Marketing Models', *Interfaces*, January–February 1989, pp. 25–47.

13. Chris D. Storey and Christopher J. Easingwood, 'Determinants of New Product Performance: A Study in the Financial Services Sector', *International Journal of Service Industry Management*, Vol. 7, No. 1, 1996, pp. 32–55 (at p. 48).

14. Scott Edgett and Steven Parkinson, 'The Development of New Financial Services: Identifying Determinants of Success and Failure', *International Journal of Service Industry Management*, Vol. 5, No. 4, 1994, pp. 24–38.

15. Christopher Storey and Christopher Easingwood, 'The Impact of the New Product Development Project on the Success of Financial Services', *Service Industries Journal*, Vol. 13, No. 3, July 1993, pp. 40–54.

16. Bo Edvardsson, Lars Haglund and Jan Mattsson, 'Analysis, Planning, Improvisation and Control in the Development of New Services', *International Journal of Service Industry Management*, Vol. 6, No. 2, 1995, pp. 24–35 (at p. 34).

17. Bo Edvardsson and Jan Olsson, 'Key Concepts for New Service Development', *The Service Industries Journal*, Vol. 16 (April 1996), pp. 14–164.

CHAPTER **9**

Designing service delivery systems

Learning objectives

After reading and reflecting on this chapter, you should be able to:

1. Recognize that successful service delivery systems must address issues of both place and time.

2. Distinguish between physical and electronic channels of delivery.

3. Describe the role of intermediaries in service delivery.

4. Recognize the distinctive challenges to delivery system design posed by high-contact and low-contact service processes.

5. Explain the role of technology in enhancing the speed, convenience and productivity of service delivery systems.

6. Understand the important role of physical evidence in service delivery.

Power and temperature control for rent[1]

You probably think of electricity as a power source coming from a distant power station and of air conditioning and heating in a large structure as fixed installations. So how would you deal with the following challenges? Luciano Pavarotti is giving an open-air concert in Münster, Germany, and the organizers require an uninterruptible source of electrical power for the duration of the concert, independent of the local electricity supply. A tropical cyclone has devastated the small mining town of Pannawonica in Western Australia, destroying everything in its path, including power lines, and it's urgent that electrical power be restored as soon as possible so that the town and its infrastructure can be rebuilt. The French city of Nice requires additional air conditioning for its large convention centre to cool it sufficiently when big meetings are held during the hot summer months. A construction company building tunnels on the new M27 motorway in southern England is having trouble painting the tunnels owing to a combination of low temperatures and condensation. In Amsterdam, organizers of the World Championship Indoor Windsurfing competition need to power 27 wind turbines that will be installed along the length of a huge indoor pool to create winds with a force of 5 to 6 on the Beaufort scale. A US Navy submarine needs a shore-based source of power when it spends time in a remote Norwegian port. Sri Lanka faces an acute shortage of electricity-generating capability when water levels fall dangerously low at the country's major hydroelectric dams as a result of insufficient monsoon rains two years in a row. And Ostend, Belgium wants to operate an ice rink in the city centre during a Christmas fair, regardless of the weather.

These are all challenges faced and met by a company called Aggreko, which describes itself as 'The World's Power Rental Leader'. Aggreko, a provider of power and temperature control rental services, operates from 70 depots in 20 countries around the world. Founded in the Netherlands and now headquartered in Glasgow, the company rents a 'fleet' of mobile electricity generators, oil-free air compressors, and temperature control devices ranging from water chillers and industrial air conditioners to giant heaters and dehumidifiers.

Although much of the firm's business comes from needs that are foreseen far in advance, such as backup operations during planned factory maintenance, cooling for an international exhibition, power for a series of Olympics events or a package of services during the filming of a James Bond film, the firm is also poised to resolve problems arising unexpectedly from emergencies. Its customer base is dominated by large national and multinational companies and government agencies.

Aggreko assembles its own equipment, which is purchased from suppliers who manufacture components to the firm's specifications. Robustness, portability and reliability are essential, given the frequency of transportation and the harsh conditions under which the equipment must sometimes operate. The firm's line of GreenPower generators has been designed for use in environmentally sensitive conditions, requiring tight emission controls, no risk of leaks and avoidance of noise pollution. Much of the equipment rented by the firm is contained in soundproofed, boxlike structures which can be shipped anywhere in the world and coupled together to create the specific type and level of electrical power output or climate-control capability required by the client.

Consultation, installation and ongoing technical support add value to the core service. As a company brochure says 'Emphasis is placed on solving customer problems rather than just renting equipment'. Some customers have a clear idea in advance of their needs, others require advice on how to develop innovative, cost-effective solutions to what may be unique problems, and others are desperate to restore power that has been lost due to an emergency. In the last-mentioned instance, speed is of the essence since downtime can be extremely expensive and in some cases lives may depend on the promptness of Aggreko's response.

Delivering service requires that Aggreko ship its equipment to the customer's site, so that the needed power or temperature control can be available at the right place and time. Following the Pannawonica cyclone, Aggreko's West Australian team swung into action, organizing the despatch of some 30 generators ranging in size from 60 to 750 kVA, plus cabling, refuelling tankers and other equipment. The generators were transported by means of four 'road trains', each comprising a giant tractor unit hauling three 13-metre (40 foot) trailers. A full infrastructure team of technicians and additional equipment were flown in on two Hercules aircraft. The Aggreko technicians remained on site for six weeks, providing 24-hour service while the town was being rebuilt.

Alternative scenarios for service delivery

Of necessity, Aggreko must bring its service-creating facilities to its customers, because the need is location-specific. The same is true of companies such as Rentokil Initial whose work involves servicing customers' offices and factories. In many other instances, involving both people-processing and possession-processing services, customers are expected to come to the provider. But information-based services and some types of retailing and repair services allow customers to deal at arm's length. Some service providers are in a position to offer all three forms of service delivery. Banks serving remote locations sometimes employ a mobile branch housed in a van (or even a boat in the case of the Western Isles of Scotland) in addition to their traditional fixed-location branches and their new website capabilities.

This is both an exciting and challenging time for managers responsible for service delivery. Speed has become an important factor in competitive strategy.[2] Customers are demanding more convenience and expecting services to be delivered rapidly where and when they want them. As the Aggreko example shows, speed of response is vital in the case of emergencies and considerable physical effort and ingenuity may be required to reach the client's location.

New technology is giving service providers the potential to deliver information-based services (and informational processes related to supplementary services) almost anywhere through electronic channels at the speed of light. Customers also save time and effort when they no longer need to visit service factories to obtain the services they need. In addition to transforming information-based services from factory delivery to electronic delivery, forward-looking firms are coming up with new formats to offer face-to-face delivery in new locations, ranging from tiny bank branches occupying booths at the end of supermarket aisles to massage clinics on airport concourses.

Delivering a service to customers involves decisions about where? when? and how? Services marketing strategy must address *place and time*, paying at least as much attention to speed and scheduling issues as to the more traditional notion of physical location. The service product and its means of distribution and delivery are often closely linked; in particular, the nature of the delivery system has a powerful impact on the customer's experience in the case of people-processing services.

Although the organization that creates a service concept is much more likely than a manufacturer to control its own delivery systems, there's also a role for intermediaries, including franchisees. For high-contact services, the design of the physical environment and the way in which tasks are performed by customer-contact personnel jointly play a vital role in creating a particular identity for a service firm, shaping the nature of the customer's experience and enhancing both productivity and quality. Low-contact services are expanding in number, thanks to advances in electronic technology. More and more, these low-contact services, often designed specifically with improved productivity in mind, are being delivered by customers themselves through self-service. The challenge is to make self-service a positive experience.

The nature of the service both influences and is shaped by distribution strategy. Many service firms have a variety of options open to them and the challenge is to select the channel that will best meet the needs of the target segment, so long as price and other costs (including time and effort) remain acceptable. Responding to customer needs for flexibility, some firms offer several alternative choices of delivery channels. Options may include serving a customer at a firm's own retail site, delegating service delivery to an intermediary or franchisee, coming to the customer's house or place of business, and (in certain types of services) serving the customer at a distance through physical or electronic channels.

Options for service delivery

Decisions on where, when and how to deliver service have an important impact on the nature of customers' service experiences by determining the types of encounters (if any) with service personnel, and the price and other costs incurred to obtain service. Several factors serve to shape service delivery strategy. A key question is: Does the nature of the service or the firm's positioning strategy require customers to be in direct physical contact with its personnel, equipment and facilities? (As we saw in Chapter 2, this is inevitable for people-processing services but optional for other categories.) If so, do customers have to visit the facilities of the service organization, or will the latter send personnel and equipment to customers' own sites, as Aggreko does? Alternatively, can transactions between provider and customer be completed at arm's length through use of either telecommunications or modern physical channels of distribution?

A second issue concerns the firm's strategy in terms of distribution sites: should it maintain just a single outlet or offer to serve customers through multiple outlets at different locations? The possible options, combining both type of contact and number of sites, can be seen in Table 9.1, which consists of six different cells.

Customers visit the service site

The convenience of service factory locations and operational schedules may assume great importance when a customer has to be physically present – either throughout

Table 9.1 ■ Method of service delivery

Nature of interaction between customer and service organization	Availability of service outlets	
	Single site	Multiple sites
Customer goes to service organization	Theatre Barbers	Bus service Fast-food chain
Service organization goes to customer	Lawnmowing service Pest control service Taxi	Mail delivery Auto club road service
Customer and service organization transact at arm's length (mail or electronic communications)	Credit card company Local TV station	Broadcast network Telephone company

service delivery or even just to initiate and terminate the transaction. Elaborate retail gravity models are sometimes built in deciding where to locate supermarkets relative to where prospective customers live or work. Traffic counts and pedestrian counts help to establish how many prospective customers a day pass by certain locations. Construction of a motorway or ring-road, or the introduction of a new bus or rail service may have a significant effect on travel patterns and, in turn, determine which sites are now more desirable and which, less so.

Providers come to the customer

For some types of services, the supplier visits the customer. This is, of course, essential when the target of the service is some immovable physical item, such as a tree that needs pruning, a large machine that needs repair, a house that requires pest control treatment or a building that has a temporary need for auxiliary power generation. Since it's more expensive and time-consuming for service personnel and their equipment to travel to the customer than vice versa, the trend has been away from this approach (fewer doctors make home visits nowadays!).

There may still be a profitable niche in serving customers who are willing to pay a premium price for the time savings and convenience of receiving personal visits from service providers. One young veterinary doctor has built her business around house calls to sick pets. She has found that customers are glad to pay extra for a service which not only saves them time but is also less stressful for the pet than waiting in a crowded veterinary clinic, full of other animals and their worried owners. Australia is famous for its Royal Flying Doctor Service, in which physicians fly to visit patients at remote farms and stations. Other more recently established services that are taken to the customer include mobile car-washing, office and in-home catering and made-to-measure tailoring services for business people.

Arm's length transactions

By contrast, dealing with a service organization through arm's length transactions may mean that a customer never sees the service facilities and never meets the service personnel face-to-face. An important consequence is that the number of service encounters tends to be fewer and those encounters that do take place with service personnel are more likely to be made by telephone or, even more remotely, by mail, fax or e-mail. The outcome of the service activity remains very important to the customer, but much of the process of service delivery may be hidden. Credit cards and insurance are examples of services that can be requested and delivered by mail or telecommunications. Repair services for small pieces of equipment sometimes require customers to ship the product to a maintenance facility where it will be serviced and then returned again by parcel service (with the option of paying extra for express shipment).

Any information-based product can be delivered almost instantaneously through telecommunication channels to any point in the globe where a suitable reception terminal exists. As a result, physical logistics services now find themselves competing with telecommunications services. When we were writing this book, for instance, we had a choice of mail or courier services for physical shipments of the chapters in either paper or disk form. We could also fax the materials, feeding in the pages one sheet at a time. But by using e-mail, we were able to transmit chapters electronically from one computer to another, with the option of printing them out at the receiving end. In fact, we used all three methods, depending on the nature of the page (hand-drawn images were faxed) and the compatibility (or lack thereof) of the authors' and publisher's software.

The physical evidence of the servicescape

Physical evidence, one of the 8Ps of integrated service management, relates to the tangible objects encountered by customers in the service delivery environment, as well as to tangible metaphors used in such communications as advertising, symbols and trademarks. The most powerful physical evidence is experienced by customers who come to a service factory and experience employees working in a physical environment. The term servicescape describes the style and appearance of the physical surroundings where customers and service providers interact.[3]

Servicescapes can create positive or negative impressions on each of the five senses. More and more service firms are paying careful attention to the design of the servicescapes that they offer their customers. Consider some of the evidence:

■ Airlines employ corporate design consultants to help them differentiate the appearance of their aircraft and employees from those of competitors. Although many female cabin personnel look interchangeable in their dark blue suits, others have distinctive uniforms that immediately identify them as employees of, say, Singapore Airlines or Emirates or KLM.

■ A significant industry has grown up around theme restaurant design, with furnishings, pictures, real or reproduction antiques, carpeting, lighting and choice of live or background music all trying to reinforce a desired look and style that may or may not be related to the cuisine.

■ The more expensive hotels have become architectural statements. Some occupy classic buildings, lovingly restored at huge expense to a far higher level of luxury than ever known in the past, and using antique furnishings and rugs to reinforce their 'old world' style. Modern hotels often feature dramatic atriums in which wall-mounted elevators splash down in fountains. Resort hotels invest enormous sums to plant and maintain exotic gardens on their grounds.

As in a theatre, scenery, lighting, music and other sounds, special effects and the appearance of the actors (in this case the employees) and audience members (other customers) all serve to create an atmosphere in which the service performance takes place. In certain types of businesses, servicescapes are enhanced by judicious use of sounds, smells and the textures of physical surfaces. Where food and drink are served, of course, taste is also highly relevant. For first-time customers in particular, the servicescape plays an important role in helping to frame expectations about both the style and quality of service to be provided. Because services are intangible performances and it's hard to evaluate them in advance (or even after service delivery), customers seek pre-purchase clues as to service quality. Hence, first impressions are important.

Not all servicescapes are expensive and exotic, of course. Firms that are trying to convey the impression of cut-price service do so by locating in inexpensive neighbourhoods, occupying buildings with a simple – even warehouse-like – appearance, minimizing wasteful use of space, and dressing their employees in practical, inexpensive uniforms.

Servicescapes do not always shape customer perceptions and behaviour in ways intended by their creators. Veronique Aubert-Gamet notes that customers often make creative use of physical spaces and objects for different purposes.[4] Thus diners may appropriate a restaurant table for use as a temporary office desk, with papers spread around and even a laptop computer and mobile phone positioned on its surface.

Role of physical environments

Physical surroundings help to shape appropriate feelings and reactions among customers and employees. Consider how effectively many amusement parks use the servicescape concept to enhance their service offerings. The clean streets of Legoland or Disneyland Paris, plus employees in colourful costumes, all contribute to the sense of fun and excitement that visitors encounter on arrival and throughout their visit. Alternatively, think about the reception area of a successful professional firm – the offices of an investment bank or a consulting firm, where the decor and furnishings tend to be elegant and designed to impress. Physical evidence and accompanying atmosphere impact buyer behaviour in three ways:

1. As an attention-creating medium to make the servicescape stand out from that of competing establishments and to attract customers from target segments.

2. As a message-creating medium, using symbolic cues to communicate with the intended audience about the distinctive nature and quality of the service experience.

3. As an effect-creating medium, employing colours, textures, sounds, scents and spatial design to create or heighten an appetite for certain goods, services or experiences.

Antiques shops provide a nice example of how carefully crafted design can itself become an important marketing tool. As noted by Philip Kotler:

> Many antique dealers also make use of 'organizational chaos' as an atmospheric principle for selling their wares. The buyer enters the store and sees a few nice pieces and a considerable amount of junk. The nice pieces are randomly scattered in different parts of the store. The dealer gives the impression, through his prices and his talk, that he doesn't really know

values. The buyer therefore browses quite systematically, hoping to spot an undiscovered Old Master hidden among the dusty canvases of third rate artists. He ends up buying something that he regards as value. Little does he know that the whole atmosphere has been arranged to create a sense of hidden treasures.[5]

Although retailers primarily sell goods, they tend to compete on service. Traditional shops are finding themselves facing growing competition from non-shop retailers, whose strategy has been to make the selection and ordering process for their customers as simple and time-saving as possible. Customers select goods from printed catalogues, television shopping channels or web sites, and place their orders by mail, phone or e-mail. They have to pay for shipping but can choose between regular or express shipment, with purchases being delivered directly to their homes or offices.

E-commerce begins to reshape the retail landscape

What has been termed 'e-commerce' is growing rapidly. Personal computers and the internet are starting to change the way people shop. From perusing catalogues and shopping by mail or telephone, many people are moving to shop in cyberspace for a wide array of both goods and services.

Forrester Research says that customers are lured into virtual stores by four factors, in the following order of importance: convenience, ease of research (obtaining information and searching for desired items or services), better prices and broad selection.[6] Enjoying 24-hour service with prompt delivery is particularly appealing to customers whose busy lives leave them short of time.

Traditional retailers are having to respond to stiffer competition from internet and telephone-based catalogue retailing. One American company, software and computer retailer, Egghead Inc., has decided to get out of physical retailing altogether. It closed its 80 stores across the US, dismissed 800 of its 1,000 workers, shifted its sales entirely to the internet, and renamed itself Egghead.com.

Other retailers, such as the giant bookstore chain, Barnes and Noble, have developed a strong internet presence to complement their full-service bookstores in an effort to counter competition from 'cybserspace retailers' such as Amazon.com (introduced in Chapter 1), which has no stores. Web sites are becoming increasingly sophisticated but also more user-friendly. They often simulate the services of a well-informed sales assistant in steering customers towards items that are likely to be of interest. Facilitating searches is another useful service on many sites, ranging from looking at what books by a particular author are currently available to finding schedules of flights between two cities on a specific date.

Store-based retailers are responding to this competitive challenge by trying to make the shopping experience more interesting and enjoyable. Shopping centres have become larger, more colourful and more dramatic. Within each centre, individual shops seek to create their own atmosphere, but tenancy agreements often specify certain design criteria in order that each shop may fit comfortably into the overall servicescape. The presence of 'food courts' and other gathering places encourages social interaction among shoppers. Theatrical touches include live entertainment, special lighting effects, fountains, waterfalls and eyecatching interior landscaping, ranging from banks of flowers to surprisingly large trees. Individual stores try to add value by offering product demonstrations and such services as customized advice, gift wrapping, free delivery, installation and warranty services.

Another illustration of giving more attention to the servicescape can be found in resort hotels. Club Med's villages, designed to create a totally carefree atmosphere, may have provided the original inspiration for 'get-away' holiday environments. The new destination resorts are not only far more luxurious than Club Med but also draw for inspiration on theme park approaches to creating fantasy environments, both inside and outside. Perhaps the most extreme examples come from Las Vegas. Facing competition from numerous casinos in other locations, Las Vegas has been trying to reposition itself from an adult destination once described in a London newspaper as 'the electric Sodom and Gomorrah' to a somewhat more wholesome family fun resort. The gambling is still there, of course, but many of the huge hotels recently built (or rebuilt) have been transformed into visually striking entertainment centres that feature such attractions as erupting 'volcanoes' and mock sea-battles.

Place and time decisions

How should service managers make decisions on the places where service is delivered and the times when it is available? The answer is likely to reflect customer needs and expectations, competitive activity and the nature of the service operation. As we noted earlier, different distribution strategies may be appropriate for some of the supplementary service elements (the 'petals' of the Flower of Service that we introduced in Chapter 8) than for the core product itself. For instance, as a customer you are probably willing to go to a particular location at a specific time to attend a sporting or entertainment event. But you probably want greater flexibility and convenience when reserving a seat in advance, so you may expect the reservations service to be open for extended hours, to offer booking and credit card payment by phone or even web, and to deliver tickets by mail.

Where should services be delivered?

Although customer convenience is important, operational requirements set tight constraints for some services. Airports, for instance, are often inconveniently located relative to travellers' homes, offices or destinations. Because of noise and environmental factors, finding suitable sites for construction of new airports (or expansion of existing ones) is a very difficult task. As a result, airport sites are often far from the city centres to which many passengers wish to travel and the only way to make them less inconvenient is to install fast rail links, as has recently been implemented at London-Heathrow.

A different type of location constraint is imposed by the fact that, by definition, ski resorts have to be in the mountains and seaside resorts on the coast. The need for economies of scale is another operational issue that may restrict choice of locations. Major hospitals offer many different healthcare services – even a medical school – at a single location, requiring a very large facility. Customers requiring complex, in-patient treatment must come to this service factory, rather than being treated at home – although an ambulance (or even a helicopter) can be sent to pick them up. This is particularly necessary in cases where specialized medical and nursing care is only available in a limited number of hospitals possessing the necessary equipment and skills.

Some service factories, however, can be created on a very small scale, with numerous individual units being located with reference to where the customers are. The most obvious locations for consumer services are close to where customers live or work. Modern buildings are often designed to be multipurpose, featuring not only office or production space, but also such services as a bank (or at least an ATM), a restaurant, several shops and even a health club. Some companies even include a children's day-care facility on site to make life easier for busy working parents.

Interest is growing in siting retail and other services on transportation routes or even in bus, rail and air terminals. Major oil companies are developing chains of retail stores to complement the fuel pumps at their service stations, thus offering customers the convenience of one-stop shopping for fuel, car supplies, food and household products. Lorry parks on motorways often include launderettes, toilets, ATMs, fax machines, restaurants and inexpensive hotels, in addition to a variety of vehicle maintenance and repair services for both lorries and cars.

In one of the most interesting new retailing developments, airport terminals are being transformed from nondescript areas where passengers and their bags are processed into vibrant shopping malls.[7] By the late 1980s, the operators of major international airports in cities such as London and Singapore were starting to see the opportunities for expanded retail operations. After the British Airports Authority was privatized in 1987 (and changed its name to BAA plc), its management began to look for additional revenues to finance the ever-increasing demands for expansion of the seven airports that it managed in the UK. Property development was one chosen route, another was on-airport retail operations.

Three factors made retailing look very appealing. One was the upmarket demographics of airline passengers, whose numbers continued to grow rapidly. A second was that many passengers had plenty of time to spare while waiting for their flights; one consequence of tighter security requirements was the need to check in earlier for flights; meanwhile, passengers in transit spent time waiting for connections. Finally, many terminal interiors had free space that could be put to profitable use. And as terminals were expanded, new retail sites could be included as an integral part of the design.

BAA recognized that the market for purchases could be divided into several segments, including international premium brand products at tax-free prices, gifts, and both impulse and necessity products for business and holiday use. So the company set to work to broaden the array of shops represented at its terminals, adding branches of prestige department stores such as Harrods, national pharmacy chains such as Boots The Chemist, respected franchises such as Body Shop, and a variety of branded shoe and clothing stores. Food and beverage operations were expanded to offer a broader choice of menus, including well-known chains like McDonald's.

The results have been dramatic. Today, BAA's seven airports in the UK boast more than 550 shops covering a total of over 90,000 m² (1 million square feet) of retail space; more than four-fifths of this space is located at London's Heathrow and Gatwick airports. In the past five years, retail revenues from all sources (including parking and catering, have more than doubled to some £650 million (€910 million) per year. BAA attributes its success in part to rigorous quality control, including a global money-back guarantee on any item purchased from any airport store, plus a guarantee of 'High Street Pricing' (prices charged at the airport are the same as in off-airport locations). The company has since won contracts to manage airport retailing operations in the US and other countries.

When should service be delivered?

In the past, most retail and professional services in industrialized countries followed a traditional and rather restricted schedule that limited service availability to about 40–50 hours a week. In large measure, this routine reflected social norms (and even legal requirements or union agreements) as to what were appropriate hours for people to work and for enterprises to sell things. The situation caused a lot of inconvenience for working people who either had to shop during their lunch break (if the stores themselves didn't close for lunch) or on Saturdays (if management chose to remain open a sixth day). But the idea of Sunday opening was strongly discouraged in most Christian cultures and often prohibited by law, reflecting long tradition based on religious practice. Among commercial services, only those devoted to entertainment and relaxation, such as cinemas, pubs, restaurants and sporting facilities, geared their opening times towards weekends and evening hours when their customers were free. Even so, they often faced restrictions on hours of operation, especially on Sundays. Today, the situation is changing fast. For some highly responsive service operations, the standard has become '24–7' service – 24 hours a day, 7 days a week, around the world.

Factors that encourage extended operating hours

Some services have long operated 24 hours a day, every day of the year. Examples include those services that respond to emergencies, such as fire, police and ambulance, or repairs to vital equipment. Hospitals and first-class hotels provide 24-hour care or room service as a matter of course. Ships and long-distance trains don't stop for the night, they keep on going. Similarly, passenger aircraft operate around the clock, and telephone companies always have operators available on a 24-hour basis.

At least five factors are driving the move towards extended operating hours and seven-day operations. The trend has been most noticeable in the United States and Canada, but it's now spreading rapidly in many European countries.

- *Economic pressure from consumers.* The growing number of two-income families and single wage-earners who live alone need time outside normal working hours to shop and use other services, since they have nobody else to do it for them. Once one shop or firm in any given area extends its hours to meet the needs of these market segments, competitors often feel obliged to follow. Retail chains have often led the way in this respect.

- *Changes in legislation.* A second factor has been the decline, lamented by some, of support for the traditional religious view that a specific day (Sunday in predominantly Christian cultures) should be legislated as a day of rest for one and all, regardless of religious affiliation. In a multicultural society, of course, it's a moot point which day should be designated as special – for observant Jews and Seventh Day Adventists, Saturday is the Sabbath; for Muslims, Friday is the holy day; and agnostics or atheists presumably don't mind. There has been a gradual erosion of such legislation in western nations in recent years, although it's still firmly in place in some countries and locations. Switzerland, for example, still closes down most retail activities on Sundays – except for bread, which people like to buy freshly baked on Sunday mornings.

- *Economic incentives to improve asset utilization.* A great deal of capital is often tied up in service facilities. The incremental cost of extending hours is often relatively modest (especially when part-timers can be hired without paying them either overtime or benefits); if extending hours reduces crowding and increases revenues, then it's economically attractive. There are costs involved in shutting down and reopening a facility like a supermarket, yet climate control and some lighting must be left running all night, and security personnel must be paid to keep an eye on the place. Even if the number of extra customers served is minimal, there are both operational and marketing advantages to remaining open 24 hours.

- *Availability of employees to work during 'unsocial' hours.* Changing lifestyles and a desire for part-time employment have combined to create a growing labour pool of people who are willing to work evenings and nights. Some of these workers are students looking for part-time work outside their classroom hours; some are 'moonlighting', holding a full-time job by day and earning additional income by night; some are parents juggling childcare responsibilities; others simply prefer to work by night and relax or sleep by day; still others are glad to obtain any paid employment, regardless of hours.

- *Automated self-service facilities.* Self-service equipment has become increasingly reliable and user-friendly. Many machines now accept card-based payments in addition to coins and banknotes. Installing unattended machines may be economically feasible in places that couldn't support a staffed facility. Unless a machine requires frequent servicing or is particularly vulnerable to vandalism, the incremental cost of going from limited hours to 24-hour operation is minimal. In fact, it may be much simpler to leave machines running all the time than to turn them on and off, especially if they are placed in widely scattered locations.

Responding to customers' need for convenience

American and Canadian retailing have led the way towards meeting customer needs for greater convenience, but many other countries are now beginning to follow suit. A trend that began in earnest with early morning to late evening service in chemists (pharmacies) and so-called convenience stores has now extended to 24-hour service in a variety of retail outlets, from service stations to restaurants to supermarkets.

The customer's search for convenience has not been confined to convenient times and places, nor to just purchase of core products. People want easy access to supplementary services, too – especially information, reservations and problem-solving. There are now a large number of two-income families. Customers are busy with their personal lives and don't have a lot of time to handle such activities as banking, insurance and even shopping. They expect suppliers to be available to them when it's convenient for customers, not when it's convenient for suppliers; so they want extended hours and easy access. And most of all, they expect one contact to solve their problem, rather than being asked to contact a different office or dial another number.

In many service industries, problem-solving needs were originally met by telephoning a specific shop or company during its regular opening hours. But led by airlines and hotel chains, separate customer service centres have evolved, reached by calling a single number regardless of the caller's location. Some of these centres are operated by the service provider, others are subcontracted to specialist intermediaries (hotel chains, for instance, often delegate the reservations function to independent contractors). Once a firm departs from locally staffed phones and installs a centralized system, most customers will be calling from distant locations.

So, instead of forcing customers to pay the cost of a long-distance call, many firms have installed free-phone numbers. Once one company offers this convenience, competitors often feel obliged to follow the leader.

Moving to 24–7 service

Providing extended-hours customer service is almost mandatory for any organization with a nationwide clientele in countries (or service regions) that cover multiple time zones. Although Europe has fewer time zones than the five found in Canada, there is a three-hour time difference between Moscow and London.

Even having access between 08:30 and 17:00 hours local time is inconvenient for people who want to call a supplier from home before or after work. (If there's a mistake on your bank statement, for instance, you are likely to discover it when you read the mail at home in the evening). So when a pan-European business redefines its customer service goal as offering continent-wide service on a daily basis, from first thing in the morning in St Petersburg to mid-evening in Dublin or Lisbon, then managers don't need a fancy calculator to work out that customer service lines will have to be open at least 17 hours a day. At this point, why not go to 24-hour operation and cater to organizations that themselves operate on a 24-hour schedule as well as to individuals who work odd shifts and get up very early or go to bed very late? It depends on the firm's priorities, the costs involved and the value that customers place on total accessibility.

Most manufactured products create a need for accompanying services, ranging from finance and training to transportation and maintenance. Indeed, the competitiveness of a manufacturer's products in both domestic and global markets is as much a function of the availability and quality of relevant services as the quality of the core product. Increasingly, both manufacturing and service companies rely on computer-based systems to provide the supplementary services that customers need and expect. In turn, servicing these computer systems constitutes a major possession-processing industry.

Powerful computer systems – and the software to run them – have been sold to users all over the world. Although there are many niche players, the market for large computer systems is supplied by a small handful of international firms. Although the applications to which they are put vary enormously, computers are only of value when they are up and running (or ready for service). System failures can have disastrous consequences for their users and also for the users' own customers. Supporting the enormous installed base of equipment and software, as well as helping users to plan for future needs, is a big business, attracting suppliers ranging from worldwide vendors to local service firms.

Historically, maintaining and repairing computers was a task that had to be performed on site. Proximity to the customer can give locally-based 'third-party' vendors a competitive edge over OEMs (original equipment manufacturers), who also tend to be more expensive. Varying educational levels among host-country nationals can also make it difficult for global OEMs such as Hewlett-Packard to ensure consistent standards of service to their customers around the world – a serious problem when dealing with complex equipment where speed and accuracy are of the essence in restoring defective hardware and software to good working order.

If a customer is dependent on a machine or a service 24 hours a day, downtime can be very disruptive. Emergencies don't just involve people. They involve vital equipment and processes, too. If a computer goes down, the consequences can range from personal inconvenience to the shut-down of a major facility; if a transformer blows, electric power may be lost; if a furnace fails in below-freezing conditions, pipes may burst. Sometimes, these types of emergencies are handled by a duty person, reached by a pager or cellular phone, who drives to the site of the problem, makes a physical inspection and undertakes whatever repairs are necessary. But using modern technology, engineers can sometimes fix problems involving high-tech equipment in another location without ever leaving their own offices. And they can even do it from the opposite side of the world.

Hewlett-Packard's global service strategy

In addition to being one of the world's best-known suppliers of computer hardware, with extensive operations in Europe, the Hewlett-Packard Company (HP) is also at the cutting edge of customer support – not only for its own products, but also for customer networks incorporating other vendors' equipment. HP's global service strategy reflects the fact that the company sells its hardware to customers around the world. Many of its largest customers are themselves operating on a global basis and have expectations of consistent, high-quality service wherever the equipment may be located. Competition in this industry is fierce, since HP's major competitors – companies such as IBM, Siemens and NEC – are themselves operating around the world.

In the past, computers had to be serviced locally by an engineer who visited the site in person. This is still true of installation and many mechanical repairs. But today, many problem-solving and repair services can be distributed electronically through telecommunication channels. HP's has created enormous economies of scale through its Customer Support Business Unit (CSBU), which evolved from an earlier phone-in consulting service based in local sales offices.

Facing problems of varying quality, failure to capture needed data and inability to balance workloads across offices, HP developed a centralized North American Response Center in 1984. Subsequently, HP extended the concept outside the United States and created CSBU, which operates some three dozen response centres around the world and delivers support services and tools that extend beyond traditional hardware maintenance.

CSBU maintains a globally standardized set of services that range from site design to systems integration and remote diagnostics. Service can be provided at any hour of the day or night to almost anywhere in the world. In addition to discussing problems with a customer by voice phone, an engineer can run diagnostic tests of faulty hardware or software through telecommunication links, with electronic repairs being transmitted through 'remote fixes'. Standardization also means capability in several languages. For example, a midnight call might originate in Osaka, Japan, from where it goes to the Tokyo Response Center. A bilingual call coordinator then contacts Mountain View, California, where it is 07:00 hours Pacific Time. A Japanese-speaking engineer, based in California, calls the customer back to obtain further information.

To provide this kind of service, HP maintains an integrated global network headed by four major centres: Bracknell (United Kingdom), Atlanta (Georgia) and Mountain View (California) in the United States, and Melbourne (Australia). Each centre is staffed during extended daytime hours, seven days a week, by between 12 and 200 engineers. The size of each centre is a function of the volume of business in the local region. Problems that can't be resolved in a smaller centre may be transferred to one of the major centres; which one actually receives the transfer may depend on the time of day at which the call is made. Because of time-zone differentials, at least one major centre is always in full operation at any time.

The process of service delivery

There's more to the design of new service delivery systems, obviously, than just a description of the physical facilities and equipment and a specification of the service personnel required. These are merely ingredients in a recipe. What we need next are 'mixing' and 'cooking' instructions, so that service staff know what is expected of them and customers understand their own role in service delivery, including how to interact with personnel and facilities. Clarification in advance of the customer's role is vital in the case of self-service. Finally, as in cooking, we need to specify delivery schedules and the time-frames involved for each activity. Increasingly, speed is becoming a vital element in competitive strategy. In many instances, service firms are building their strategies around what are known as fast-cycle operations. It's not only customers who are interested in speedier service. Firms can benefit, too, when faster operation leads to improved productivity and lower costs.

Planning and configuring service delivery

Decisions faced by firms in planning and configuring the service delivery process are summarized in Figure 9.1 and require managers to address the following questions:

- What should be the sequencing of the various steps in the service delivery process? Where (location) and when (scheduling) should these steps take place?

- Should service elements be bundled or unbundled for delivery purposes (for instance, should a service firm take responsibility for all elements or delegate certain supplementary services, such as information and reservations, to an intermediary)?

- What should be the nature of contact between the service provider and its customers? Should customers come to the provider or the other way around? Or for other types of services (e.g., retailing, banking) should the two parties deal at arm's length, using mail and telecommunications (ranging from voice telephone to the Web)?

- What should be the nature of the service process at each step? Should customers be served in batches or individually, or should they serve themselves?

- What should be the serving protocol? Should the firm operate a reservations system or work on a first come, first served basis, with queuing as necessary? Alternatively, should a priority system be established for certain types of customers (such as many firms do for their larger industrial accounts or airlines do for their gold card frequent flyers)?

- What imagery and atmosphere should the service delivery environment (or servicescape) strive to create? For a high-contact service, this concerns decisions on (1) facility design and layout, (2) staff uniforms, appearance and attitudes, (3) the type of furnishings and equipment installed, and (4) the use of music, lighting and decor.

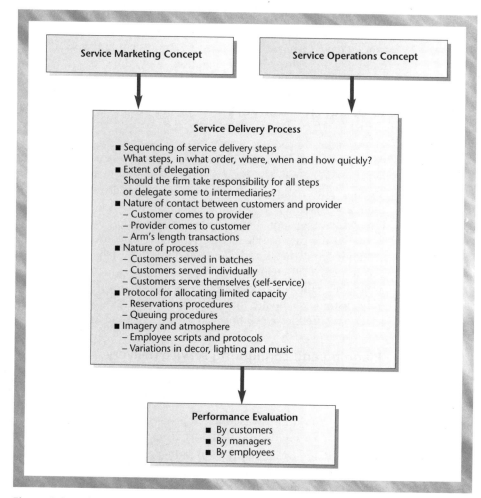

Figure 9.1 ■ Service delivery and evaluation

How technology is revolutionizing service delivery

Technological developments during the last 25 years have had a remarkable impact on the way in which services are produced and delivered. Developments in telecommunications and computer technology in particular continue to result in many innovations in service delivery. An important result is that, more than ever before, customers are now able to serve themselves, rather than requiring the assistance of an employee. Five innovations of particular interest are:

1. Development of 'smart' telephones that allow customers to communicate with a service firm's computer by entering commands on the telephone keypad in response to voice commands. Voice recognition technology is also coming into use.

2. Introduction of broadband telecommunication lines that allow high-speed transmission of large amounts of data (see the boxed description of Kinko's).

3. Creation of freestanding, automated kiosks that enable customers to conduct a variety of simple transactions. Bank ATMs, discussed below, are the best-known example, but many new applications of this technology are coming into use.

4. Development of web sites that can provide information, take orders and even serve as a delivery channel for information-based services.

5. Development of smart cards containing a microchip that can store detailed information about the customer and act as an electronic purse containing digital money.

Local photocopy shop grows into global business service provider[8]

In 1970, 22-year old Paul Orfalea, just out of college, borrowed enough money to open a photocopy shop near the campus of the University of California at Santa Barbara. Covering just 100 square feet (less than 10 square metres), the tiny store contained one copy machine and also sold film processing and felt-tip highlighter pens. Orfalea, the son of Lebanese immigrants, called the store Kinko's after the nickname given to him by his college friends because of his curly reddish hair.

Today, Kinko's operates a copy and printing chain of 24-hour stores from coast to coast in the United States, with branches in the Netherlands, Britain, Canada, Australia and three Asian countries. The company's plan is to expand to 2,000 locations by the year 2000. Kinko's customers can already print in colour in any size, bind their documents as they like, send faxes and work on in-house computers. The objective is to create a global network to take advantage of digital technologies. Many of Kinko's locations have videoconferencing technology and the company even has its own on-line service called Kinkonet.

Soon customers will be able to compose reports in, say, Amsterdam and send them by modem to, say, London where they can be printed and bound for a meeting. The traditional approach of creating text and graphics, printing copies of the report and then distributing these copies to another location (often by expensive courier services) will be replaced by a strategy of creation, electronic distribution to another loca-

tion and printing the reports there. Of course, this arrangement can apply equally well to documents created in one part of Amsterdam and then printed and bound in another store on the other side of the city.

University students are no longer Kinko's only market segment. Its major customer base now lies with small businesses, who often need sophisticated services but can't afford to own the equipment nor take time away from other tasks. The company is also targeting larger corporations.

Kinko's tries to create a partnership with its customers, offering many advisory services, including how to use colour to best advantage and present sales reports more effectively. Several years ago, the company launched a national advertising campaign, positioning the firm to its customers as 'Your Branch Office'. It has also formed partnerships with suppliers in related businesses – such as express package transport – who now sell their own services in certain of its stores.

Just as express package companies like TNT, DHL and FedEx have changed the way firms manage their business logistics, so Kinko's is trying to change the way firms manage their document production and distribution. With the growing trend for professionals and managers to spend more time in the field and to operate through mobile technology in a 'virtual office' far from the corporate base, there is even more need for services available 24 hours a day, 7 days a week, in multiple locations.

One of the most frequently cited service delivery innovations of the past quarter-century has been the automated teller machine (ATM), which has revolutionized the delivery of retail banking services, making them available 24 hours a day every day of the year in a wide variety of convenient locations, often far from traditional retail branches. To expand the geographic area in which service can be delivered to their customers, banks have joined regional, national and even global networks. This means that a bank can also offer service to customers from other banks and collect a fee for doing so. However, a bank's brand identity is weakened when the ATMs used by its customers are branded with the name of other banks or networks. Further, the social bonds between customers and bank staff, which are often responsible for customers' remaining loyal to a particular bank, are now severed.

The creation of global networks means that, once equipped with a valid card and sufficient funds on deposit, customers of a bank in one country can instantly withdraw money in a different currency from another bank's ATM in a foreign country on the other side of the world. These machines can now perform most of the functions of a human bank clerk with a high degree of customization. The machines used by banks in Switzerland even know what language the customer prefers to speak. When opening an account, customers select one of four languages (German, French, Italian and English), and this choice is then encoded onto their ATM cards. These Swiss ATMs greet customers in all four languages, ask them to insert the card, then immediately switch to their preferred language.

Banks in many countries have embarked on programmes of closing bank branches and shifting customers onto cheaper, electronic banking channels, in an effort to boost productivity and remain competitive in an increasingly competitive marketplace. However, not all customers like to use self-service equipment and so migration of customers to new electronic channels may require different strategies for different segments – as well as recognition that some proportion of customers will never voluntarily shift from their preferred high-contact delivery environments. An alternative that appeals to many people, perhaps because it uses a familiar technology, is banking by voice telephone (for a description of First Direct, the world's first, all telephone bank, operating 24 hours a day, every day of the year, please see Chapter 3). The ultimate in self-service banking will be when you can not only use a smart card as an electronic wallet for a wide array of transactions, but can also refill it from a special card reader connected to your computer modem.

Many researchers believe that the advent of the internet is fuelling a radical change in the marketing of both goods and services, but they do not always agree on the ways in which the internet will evolve as a commercial medium and its implications.[9] Adding new delivery channels may complicate life for an established service provider or retailer, who must now choose between a 'no-change' strategy of maintaining traditional physical stores and one of adding web sites that go beyond just an advertising and information presence to offer the alternative channel of virtual stores (complete with virtual displays, on-line catalogues, and secured on-line ordering and payment). Many organizations now see the internet as a way to reach a larger audience (or offer greater convenience to the existing audience). For instance, major auctioneers such as Sotheby's and Christie's advertise their sales on the internet and include all or part of the catalogue on a web site, and provide an e-mail address through which bids may be made.

Most drastic of all is a policy of radical change, similar to that adopted by Egghead.com, under which the firm's physical outlets are closed and replaced by an all-internet strategy. In the latter instance, the challenge for management is to migrate the customers whom the firm wants to keep and attract new ones to replace those who are uncomfortable with arm's length transactions.

In summary, there is a definite trend in the direction of electronic commerce, but experts continue to disagree on what its ultimate impact will be. What is clear is that many customers are choosing to move away from face-to-face contacts with suppliers in fixed locations that only operate during fixed hours to remote contacts 'anywhere, anytime'. As more and more households acquire computers with internet capability, electronic commerce is likely to expand rapidly. In the area of business-to-business marketing, some suppliers now invite corporate customers to participate in access-restricted 'extranets' featuring private web sites that offer specialized catalogues, tailored to the needs and purchasing behaviour of each individual customer. Among other things, such catalogues can present prices that have been pre-negotiated between the two parties and not available to other purchasers.

The underlying goal of modern service delivery systems should be to offer customers more choice; some people opt for face-to-face contact, others like telephone contact with a human being, still others prefer the greater anonymity and control offered by more impersonal contacts, such as mail order or a web site. When purchasing goods and services, some customers like to visit the store to make a physical examination of the items that interest them or discuss the performance characteristics of a service with a knowledgeable seller face-to-face; others are content to watch product demonstrations on TV (sometimes called 'infomercials') and then call a free-phone number to place an order if they have seen something they like; yet another group likes to select its purchases from a nicely printed catalogue and to order by telephone or mail. Finally, a small but fast-growing number of consumers are comfortable examining and purchasing via the World Wide Web. In each instance, although the core product may remain the same, the wide differences in delivery systems mean that the nature of the overall service experience changes sharply as the encounter moves from high contact to low contact.

More and more services now fall into the category of arm's length relationships rather than face-to-face interactions. As Rayport and Sviokla note:

> The traditional *marketplace* interaction between physical seller and physical buyer has been eliminated. In fact, everything about this new type of transaction – what we call a *marketspace* transaction – is different from what happens in the marketplace.[10]

The marketplace

Companies doing business in the marketplace need a physical environment in which customers can get together with suppliers to inspect merchandise or conduct service-related business. We cannot get rid of the marketplace for people-processing services, because these services require customers to enter the physical environment of a service factory. In some instances, customers would not wish to get rid of the marketplace, for it is the physical and social environment that attracts them, as in destination resorts or in shopping malls that create 'total experiences', combining shops with food services, health clubs, entertainment, exhibitions and a chance to socialize.

The marketspace

Companies doing business in the marketspace, by contrast, may be able to replace contact with physical objects by information about those objects (as in a paper or electronic catalogue). Information-based services, of course, don't even require a physical location. Moreover, the context in which the transaction occurs is also different, with on-screen (or on-telephone) contact replacing physical contact; customers may also have the option to replace service from contact personnel by self-service through intelligent interactive systems.

One of the driving forces behind these moves has been time savings, reflecting a desire by customers for ever faster and more convenient service. A second factor has been interest on the part of some customers in obtaining more information about the goods and services that they buy. Paradoxically, electronic contacts may bring customers 'closer' to manufacturers and service suppliers. Managers are beginning to realize that the opportunity to develop increased knowledge of customers may be as important a reason for doing business in the marketspace as seeking cost savings by eliminating physical facilities. Conducting dialogue with customers about their needs and preferences (information which can be stored for future reference) can lead to delivery of better and more customized service – which may create greater value and therefore command higher prices.

In the last analysis, strategy is always a function of what is possible. The internet and other technological developments are changing what organizations are able to do in distribution and delivery of their services. As Shikhar Ghosh notes in his article 'Making business sense of the internet' (reprinted on pages 416–25), determining how to take advantage of the opportunities presented by this fast-developing new channel will not be easy – especially for executives in well-established firms. However, companies that do not want to participate in electronic commerce may still be forced to do so by their competitors or customers.

The role of intermediaries

Many service organizations find it cost-effective to delegate certain tasks. Most frequently, this delegation concerns supplementary service elements. For instance, airlines still rely heavily on travel agents to handle customer interactions like giving out information, taking reservations, accepting payment and ticketing. And, of course, many manufacturers rely on the services of distributors or retailers to stock and sell their products to end-users while also taking on responsibility for such supplementary services as information, advice, order-taking, delivery, installation, billing and payment, and certain types of problem-solving; in some cases, they may also handle certain types of repairs and upgrades. Figure 9.2 uses the Flower of Service framework to illustrate how the firm responsible for a given service concept may work in partnership with one or more intermediaries to deliver a complete service package to its customers.

Even the core product can be outsourced to an intermediary. Delivery firms regularly make use of independent agents instead of locating company-owned branches in each of the different cities they serve; they may also choose to contract with independent 'owner-operators', who drive their own lorries, rather than buying a fleet of lorries and employing full-time drivers. Universities may choose to offer evening or weekend extension courses in local community colleges or other locations, as well as at their main campus, in order to make access more convenient to prospective students. In such instances, the course is designed centrally but delivered locally. And franchising is a popular way of delivering many business service concepts through carefully trained and monitored intermediaries following a standardized format.

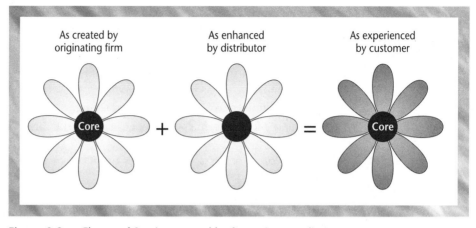

Figure 9.2 ■ Flower of Service created by firm + intermediaries

The challenge of maintaining consistency

A disadvantage of delegating activities is that it entails some loss of control over the delivery system and, thereby, over how customers experience the actual service. Ensuring that an intermediary adopts exactly the same priorities and procedures is difficult, but is vital to effective quality control. Franchisers usually seek to exercise tight control over all aspects of the service performance, including not only output specifications, but also the appearance of the servicescape, employee performance and such elements as service timetables.

But even when the work is done well, there's still a risk that customers will perceive inconsistencies between the intermediary's approach to the task and the overall positioning sought by the primary service organization. Not every franchise operation can design service sites according to a template. In many cases, the chosen intermediary already has its own delivery site, thus affecting the servicescape experienced by customers visiting that location.

Conclusion

'Where? When? and How?' Responses to these three questions form the foundation of service delivery strategy. The customer's service experience is a function of both service performance and delivery characteristics. 'Where?' relates, of course, to the places where customers can obtain service delivery. In this chapter, we presented a categorization scheme for thinking about alternative place-related strategies, including remote delivery from virtual locations.

'When?' is involved with decisions on scheduling of service delivery. Customer demands for greater convenience are now leading many firms to extend their hours and days of service. 'How?' concerns channels and procedures for delivering the core and supplementary service elements to customers. Advances in technology are having a major impact on the alternatives available and on the economics of those alternatives.

Study questions

1. Compare and contrast the strategic and functional roles of servicescape within a service organization.

2. What are the determinants of effective service delivery?

3. What marketing and management challenges are raised by the use of intermediaries in a service setting?

4. In what ways do customers and employees benefit from *productivity* enhancement and improvement in a service setting?

5. Select a service organization with which you are reasonably familiar, and construct what you believe to be a flowchart representative of its service operations system. What appear to you to be 'moments-of-truth', that is critical points within the service delivery process, likely to have a significant bearing on customers' perceptions and sense of satisfaction, and why? How would you go about managing these?

6. Using the same service organization, or another of your choice, examine their use of technology in facilitating service delivery. Might there be other opportunities for technology to be employed beneficially? What are these?

Notes

1. Based on information in Aggreko's 'International Magazine', 1997.

2. See, for example, Regis McKenna, 'Real-Time Marketing', *Harvard Business Review*, July–August 1995, pp. 87–98; Jeffrey F. Rayport and John J. Sviokla, 'Exploiting the Virtual Value Chain', *Harvard Business Review*, November–December 1995; and Regis McKenna, *Real Time*, Boston: Harvard Business School Press, 1997.

3. Mary Jo Bitner, 'Servicescapes: The Impact of Physical Surroundings on Customers and Employees', *Journal of Marketing*, Vol. 56, April 1992, pp. 57–71.

4. Véronique Aubert-Gamet, 'Twisting Servicescapes: Diversion of the Physical Environment in a Reappropriation Process', *International Journal of Service Industry Management*, Vol. 8, No. 1, 1997, pp. 26–41.

5. Philip Kotler, 'Atmospherics as a Marketing Tool', *Journal of Retailing*, Vol. 49, No. 4, 1973, pp. 48–64.

6. Information obtained from Forrester Research's web site: forrester.com, 1998.

7. Based on information supplied by BAA plc, February 1998.

8. Ann Marsh, 'Kinko's Grows Up – Almost', *Forbes*, 1 December 1997, pp. 270–2; and www.kinkos.com, January 1998.

9. See, for instance, Albert Angerhn, 'Designing Mature Internet Business Strategies', *European Management Journal*, Vol. 15, No. 4, 1997, pp. 361–9; Malin Brännack, 'Is the Internet Changing the Dominant Logic of Marketing?', *European Management Journal*, Vol. 15, No. 6, 1997, pp. 698–707; Robert A. Peterson, Sridhar Balasubramanian, and Bart J. Bronnenberg, 'Exploring the Implications of the Internet for Consumer Marketing', *Journal of the Academy of Marketing Science*, Vol. 25, No. 4, 1997, pp. 329–46; Raymond R. Burke, 'Do You See What I See? The Future of Virtual Shopping', *Journal of the Academy of Marketing Science*, Vol. 25, No. 4, 1997, pp. 352–62; John Deighton, 'Commentary on Exploring the Implications of the Internet for Consumer Marketing', *Journal of the Academy of Marketing Science*, Vol. 25, No. 4, 1997, pp. 347–51; and Doug Randall, 'Consumer Strategies for the Internet', *Long Range Planning*, Vol. 30, No. 2, 1997, pp. 147–56.

10. Jeffrey F. Rayport and John J. Sviokla, 'Managing in the Marketspace', *Harvard Business Review*, November–December 1994, pp. 141–50.

CHAPTER 10

Pricing services

Learning objectives

After reading and reflecting on this chapter, you should be able to:

1. Appreciate the factors that shape pricing strategy.
2. Formulate pricing objectives.
3. Define different types of financial costs incurred by companies.
4. Define the different costs of service incurred by customers.
5. Undertake a break-even analysis.
6. Formulate pricing strategies and policies for services.

Low-cost pricing comes to the European airline industry[1]

Beginning in the mid-1990s, a new travel phenomenon emerged across Europe: cheap, no-frills air travel. Although spurred in part by the deregulation and privatization which occurred in many European countries, the real impetus for this new trend was a new breed of European entrepreneur. The early entrants in this new field were Dublin-based Ryanair, UK-based EasyJet (founded by a Greek) and Debonair (created by an Italian), and Brussels-based Virgin Express (a Belgian airline purchased, renamed and transformed by Richard Branson). The model on which many aspects of these three operations were based was the highly successful low-cost US domestic carrier, Southwest Airlines.

Despite prices which, as EasyJet's advertising proclaims, are equal to the 'price of a pair of jeans' – it is possible to fly from London to Amsterdam for as little as £29 (€40) – these airlines have defied the pessimists and are actually making money. In 1997, Ryanair made pre-tax profits of IR£22.3 million (€28.3 million) on turnover of IR£136 million (€173 million), and even the newly created Virgin Express, established in 1996, managed to break even and earn a small profit by 1997, while charging about half the established airfares. These results compare to the mere £6 million (€8.4 million) made by British Airways (BA) – Europe's most profitable established airline – on turnover of £3 billion (€4.2 billion) from its European flights!

What are the costing and pricing secrets of these small, yet financially successful upstarts? Squeezing costs whenever and wherever is obvious. The underlying and shared assumption among these airlines is that for short-haul European travel, the market segment to which they appeal values saving money more than being served food and drink. As EasyJet's founder, Stelios Haji-Ioannou, likes to remind his passengers 'If you want to have a meal, go to a restaurant.' Costs are also shaved on EasyJet by using recycled boarding passes, selling tickets directly rather than through travel agents, offering only economy-class service (there is no first or business class, although 30 per cent of passengers on these low-cost flights are business travellers); and using secondary airports. Although such airports are sometimes difficult for passengers to get to, they have much lower landing charges, which can account for up to 10 per cent of an airline's total expenditures. It's estimated that the costs of these no-frills airlines are 25–50 per cent below those of the established airlines.

But cutting unnecessary costs is just one side of the equation. The other has to do with growing the market by avoiding, whenever possible, direct competition on traditional routes. Analysts say that Ryanair's routes – for instance, from Dublin to Leeds – were previously underdeveloped; rather than taking share away from traditional players, Ryanair has created an entirely new market. Even Virgin Express – whose big sister company Virgin Atlantic pits itself relentlessly against BA on the transatlantic and transpacific routes – has stated that its business strategy is not UK-focused (and therefore not aimed at BA) but rather pan-European in scope. As Branson puts it, Virgin Express will do for the European market what Virgin Atlantic did for transatlantic air travel: revolutionize it. 'For 50 years,' he says, 'Europe had to suffer high air fares. We will make sure those high air fares will come down throughout Europe.' He singles out Germany, Scandinavia and southern France as particularly expensive areas to fly.

Largely as a result of the efforts of this group of service entrepreneurs, who seem to have understood better than the traditional airlines the underlying concepts of corporate costing and pricing, and customer value equations, European air traffic rose by 11 per cent between 1996 and 1997, and promises to grow still further in the years to come. BA's response has been interesting. Rather than dilute the positioning of its existing two-class services (Club Europe and Euro-Traveller), the company has launched an entirely new airline for the low-price, no-frills market. Named GO, this carrier is based at London-Stansted (an airport not served by BA) and is operated independently of BA by a separate management team.

As one industry executive put it, 'After the last recession, there was a change of culture among consumers. They have become far more selective and demanding about choice and price. Airlines have been forced to become ever more cost-conscious and fare-competitive than ever before, and that will not go away. Not all the airlines in the low fare market will necessarily survive, but the concept itself will.'

Paying for service

Have you ever noticed what a wide variety of terms service organizations use to describe the *prices* they set? Universities talk about tuition, professional firms collect fees and banks add service charges. Some bridges, tunnels and motorways impose tolls. Transport operators refer to fares, clubs to subscriptions, brokers to commissions, landlords to rents, museums to admissions charges, utilities to tariffs and hotels to room rates. These diverse terms are a signal that many services take a different approach to pricing than manufacturing firms. So let's take a closer look at what makes pricing a particularly challenging task for service managers. (The discussion that follows assumes a basic understanding of economic costs incurred by companies – fixed, semi-variable and variable costs – contribution and break-even analysis; if you haven't previously been exposed to these concepts, you'll find it useful to review the material in the box on pages 346–7.)

What makes service pricing different?

In Chapter 1, we reviewed some of the key differences between goods and services. Intangible performances are inherently more difficult to price than goods, because it's harder to calculate the financial costs involved in serving a customer than it is to identify the labour, materials, machine time, storage and shipping costs associated with producing a physical good. The variability of both inputs and outputs means that units of service may not cost the same to produce, nor may they be of equal value to customers – especially if the variability extends to greater or lesser quality. Making matters even more complicated, it's not always easy to define a unit of service, raising questions as to what should be the basis of service pricing – a topic we address later in this chapter.

Understanding costs, contribution and break-even analysis

Fixed costs – sometimes referred to as overheads – are those economic costs that a supplier would continue to incur (at least in the short run) even if no services were sold. These costs are likely to include rent, depreciation, utilities, taxes, insurance, salaries and wages for managers and long-term employees, security and interest payments.

Variable costs refer to the economic costs associated with serving an additional customer, such as making a bank transaction, selling a single seat in a train or theatre, serving an extra hotel guest for the night in a hotel, or one more repair job. In many services, such costs are very low; there is, for instance, very little labour or fuel cost involved in transporting an extra bus passenger. In a theatre, the cost of seating an extra patron is probably minimal unless the ticket was sold through an independent agency that takes a fixed percentage of the price as its fee. Selling a hotel room for the night has slightly higher variable costs, since the room will need to be cleaned and the linens sent to the laundry after a guest leaves. More significant variable costs are associated with such activities as serving food and beverages or installing a new part when undertaking repairs, since they include provision of often costly physical products in addition to labour. The fact that a business has sold a service at a price that exceeds its variable cost does not mean that the firm is now profitable, for there are still fixed and semi-variable costs to be recouped.

Semi-variable costs fall in between fixed and variable costs. They represent expenses that rise or fall in stepwise fashion as the volume of business increases/decreases. Examples include adding an extra flight to meet increased demand on a specific air route or hiring a part-time employee to work in a restaurant on busy weekends.

Contribution is the difference between the variable cost of selling an extra unit of service and the money received from the buyer of that service. It goes to cover fixed and semi-variable costs before creating profits.

Determining and allocating economic costs can be a challenging task in some service operations because of the difficulty of deciding how to assign fixed costs in a multi-service facility, such as a hospital. For instance, there are certain fixed costs associated with running the casualty department in a hospital. But beyond that, there are fixed costs for running the hospital of which it is a part. How much of the hospital's fixed costs should be allocated to the casualty department? A hospital manager might use one of several approaches to calculate casualty's share of overheads. These could include (1) the percentage of total floor space that it occupies, (2) the percentage of employee hours or payroll that it accounts for; or (3) the percentage of total patient contact hours involved. Each method is likely to yield a totally different fixed-cost allocation: one method might show the casualty ward to be very profitable, another make it seem a break-even operation, and a third suggest that casualty was making a big loss.

Break-even analysis. Managers need to know at what sales volume a service will become profitable. This is called the break-even point. The necessary analysis involves dividing the total fixed and semi-variable costs by the contribution obtained on each unit of service. For instance, if a 100-room hotel needs to cover fixed and semi-variable costs of €1 million a year and the average contribution per room-night is €50, then the hotel will need to sell 20,000 room-nights per year out of a total annual capacity of 36,500. If prices are cut by an average of €10 per room night (*or* variable costs rise by €10), then the contribution will drop to €40 and the

Understanding costs, contribution and break-even analysis (*continued*)

hotel's break-even volume will rise to 25,000 room nights. The required sales volume needs to be related to *price sensitivity* (will customers be willing to pay this much?), *market size* (is the market large enough to support this level of patronage after taking competition into account?), and *maximum capacity* (the hotel in our example has a capacity of 36,500 room-nights per year, assuming no rooms are taken out of service for maintenance or renovation).

A very important distinction between goods and services is that many services have a much higher ratio of fixed costs to variable costs (see box) than is found in manufacturing firms. Service businesses with high fixed costs include those with an expensive physical facility (such as a hotel, a hospital, a college, or a theatre), or a fleet of vehicles (such as an airline, a bus line or a road haulage company), or a network (such as a telecommunications company, an internet provider, a railway or a North Sea gas pipeline). On the other hand, the variable costs of serving one extra customer may be minimal. Under these conditions, managers may feel that they have tremendous pricing flexibility and it's tempting to price very low in order to make an extra sale. However, there can be no profit at the end of the year unless all fixed costs have been recovered. Many service businesses have gone bankrupt by ignoring this fact (for this reason, low-cost airlines such as Easyjet, Ryanair, Virgin Express and GO need to have a very good understanding of their cost structure and the sales volume needed to break even at particular prices). By contrast, public and nonprofit organizations can use government tax subsidies, donations and income from endowments to cover all or part of the fixed costs.

The intangibility of service performances and the invisibility of the necessary backstage facilities and labour makes it harder for customers to see what they are getting for their money than when they purchase a physical good. Consider the homeowners who call a firm of electricians to request repair of a defective circuit. Two days later (if they are lucky) an electrician arrives. Carrying a small bag of tools, he disappears into the cupboard where the circuit board is located, soon locates the problem, replaces a defective circuit breaker, and presto! Everything works. A mere 20 minutes has elapsed. A few days later, the homeowners are horrified to receive a bill for €65, most of it for labour charges. Just think what the couple could have bought for that amount of money – new clothes, several compact discs, a nice dinner. What they fail to think of are all the fixed costs that the owner of the business needs to recoup: the office, telephone, insurance, vehicles, tools, fuel and office support staff. The variable costs of the visit are also higher than they appear. To the 20 minutes spent at the house must be added 15 minutes of driving back and forth, plus five minutes to unload (and later reload) needed tools and supplies from the van on arrival at the customer's house, thus effectively doubling the labour time devoted to this call. And the firm still has to add a margin in order to make a profit for the owner. But customers are often left feeling that they have been exploited.

Another factor that influences service pricing concerns the importance of the time factor, since it may affect customer perceptions of value. In many instances, customers may be willing to pay more for a service delivered quickly than for one delivered more slowly. Sometimes greater speed increases operating costs, too – reflecting the need to pay overtime wages or use more expensive equipment (a supersonic Concorde costs more to fly per passenger mile than an Airbus A-330). In other instances, achieving faster turnaround is simply a matter of giving priority to one customer's business over another's (clothes requiring express dry-cleaning take the same amount of time to clean; time is saved by moving them to the front of the queue). Finally, the use of different distribution channels – say, electronic banking rather than face-to-face banking – not only has different cost implications for the bank but also affects the nature of the service experience for the customer and the total time required to conduct a transaction. Some people like the convenience of fast, impersonal transactions; others, however, dislike technology and prefer to deal with a real bank clerk. So, a service transaction that has value for one person may not for another.

Ethical concerns

Services in general, and credence services in particular, often invite performance and pricing abuses.[2] When customers don't know what they are getting from the service supplier and lack the technical skills to know if a good job has been done, they are vulnerable to paying for work that wasn't necessary or, if it were, was not well performed. There is an implicit assumption among many customers that a higher priced professional – say a lawyer – must be more skilled than one who charges lower fees. Although price can indeed serve as a surrogate for quality, it's sometimes hard to be sure if the extra value is really there.

Pricing schedules for services are often quite complex. The quoted price may be only the first of several expenditures that customers will incur. Before it went to a flat monthly fee, the internet provider AOL charged a combination of a monthly subscription fee plus an hourly charge beyond a certain minimum. Complexity makes it easy (and perhaps more tempting) for firms to engage in unethical behaviour. In America, the car rental industry has attracted some notoriety for advertising bargain rental prices and then telling customers on arrival that other fees like collision insurance and personal insurance are compulsory; further, the staff sometimes fail to clarify certain 'small print' contract terms such as (say) a high mileage charge that is added once the car exceeds a very low threshold of free miles. The situation in some Florida resort towns got so bad at one point that people were joking: the car is free, the keys are extra! A common practice when the car is returned is to charge fees for refuelling a partially empty tank that are about three times what the driver would pay at the pump. When customers know that they are vulnerable to potential abuse, they become suspicious of both the firm and its employees. It's harder for customer service personnel to deliver friendly service under such conditions.

Assuming that the firm is honest in the first place, the best approach to such situations is a proactive one, spelling out all fees and expenses clearly in advance so that there are no surprises. A related approach is to develop a simple fee structure so that customers can more easily understand the financial implications of a specific usage situation. Nevertheless, pricing scams continue and sometimes lead to government regulations designed to protect customers.

Understanding the costs of service incurred by customers

From a customer's standpoint, the monetary price charged by the supplier may be just the first of many costs associated with purchase and delivery of a service. Let's take a look at what's involved (as you do so, please consider your own experience in different service contexts).

Purchase price plus other financial costs of service

Customers often incur additional financial costs over and above the purchase price. Necessary incidental expenses may include travel to the service site, parking and purchase of other facilitating goods or services ranging from meals to babysitting. We'll call the total of all these expenses (including the price of the service itself) the *financial costs of service*. However, there's more to come, since the costs of service go beyond just financial outlays (see Figure 10.1).

Non-financial costs of service for customers

In most situations, customers are likely to incur a variety of non-financial costs of service, representing the time, effort and discomfort associated with search, purchase and use. Customer involvement in production (which is particularly important in people-processing services and in self-service) means that customers incur such

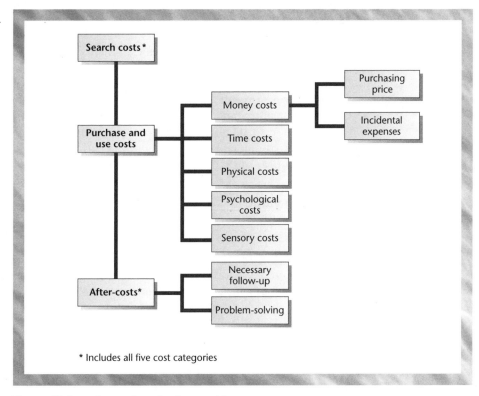

Figure 10.1 ■ Costs of service incurred by customers

burdens as mental and physical effort, and exposure to unwanted sensory experiences – such as noise, heat and smells. Services that are high on experience and credence attributes may also create psychological costs, such as anxiety. Non-financial costs of service can be grouped into four distinct categories.

■ *Time costs of service* are inherent in service delivery. There's an opportunity cost to customers for the time they are involved in the service delivery process, since they could spend that time in other ways. They could even be working to earn additional income. Internet users are often frustrated by the amount of time they waste trying to access a web site (not for nothing do people jest about the World Wide Wait!).

■ *Physical costs of service* (like fatigue, discomfort and occasionally even injury) may be incurred in obtaining services, especially if customers must come to the service factory and if delivery entails self-service.

■ *Psychological costs of service* like mental effort, feelings of inadequacy, or fear are sometimes attached to evaluating service alternatives, making a selection, and then using a particular service.

■ *Sensory costs of service* relate to unpleasant sensations affecting any of the five senses. In a service environment they may include putting up with noise, unpleasant smells, drafts, excessive heat or cold, uncomfortable seating (especially true in high-density aircraft seating configurations), visually unappealing environments and even unpleasant tastes.

In this book, we sometimes refer to physical, psychological and sensory costs collectively as 'effort' or 'hassle'.

As shown in Figure 10.1, the total costs of purchasing and using a service also include those associated with search activities. When you were looking at universities, how much money, time and effort did you spend before deciding where to apply? How much time and effort would you put into comparing alternative barbers or hairdressers if your existing one were to close? And there may be additional costs of service even after the initial service is completed. Thus a doctor may diagnose a medical problem for a patient and then prescribe a course of physical therapy and drugs that must be continued for several months. On the other hand, service failures may force customers to waste time, money and effort trying to resolve the problem.

Understanding value

When customers purchase a specific service, they are weighing the perceived benefits to be obtained from the service against the perceived costs they will incur. Consider your own experience. As a customer, you make judgements about the benefits you expect to receive in return for your anticipated investment of money, time and effort. Although our focus in this chapter is mainly on the monetary aspects of pricing, you have probably noticed that people often pay a premium to save time, minimize unwanted effort and obtain greater comfort. In other words, they are willing to pay higher prices (financial costs of service) to reduce the non-financial costs of service. However, since not all customers are willing (or able) to pay more, service companies sometimes create several different levels of service. For example, airlines and hotels often have different classes of service which offer customers the option of paying more in exchange for additional benefits. The essential trade-off in low-fare airlines is that passengers receive no value-enhancing supplementary services – just the basic core product of air travel plus a minimal level of facilitating supplementary services. By contrast, full-fare airlines compete by adding value to the core service; some companies create special time-saving advantages for their most loyal customers by establishing frequent-user clubs that offer privileges like special phone numbers for reservations or faster check-in desks.

Research findings suggest that customer definitions of value may be highly personal and idiosyncratic. Four broad expressions of value emerged from one study: (1) value is low price, (2) value is whatever I want in a product, (3) value is the quality I get for the price I pay, and (4) value is what I get for what I give.[3] In this book, we base our definition of value on this fourth category and use the term *net value*, which is defined as the sum of all the perceived benefits (gross value) minus the sum of all the perceived costs of service. The greater the positive difference between the two, the greater the net value. Economists use the term *consumer surplus* to define the difference between the price customers pay and the amount they would actually have been willing to pay to obtain the desired benefits (or 'utility') offered by a specific product.

If the perceived costs of service are greater than the perceived benefits, then the service in question will possess negative net value. Customers will probably describe the service as 'poor value' and decide not to purchase it. You can think of calculations that customers make in their minds as being similar to weighing materials on an old-fashioned pair of scales, with product benefits in one tray and the costs associated with obtaining those benefits in the other tray (Figure 10.2). When customers evaluate competing services, they are basically comparing the relative net values. Think about your own decision processes when you go to a restaurant and are trying to select between the different items on the menu.

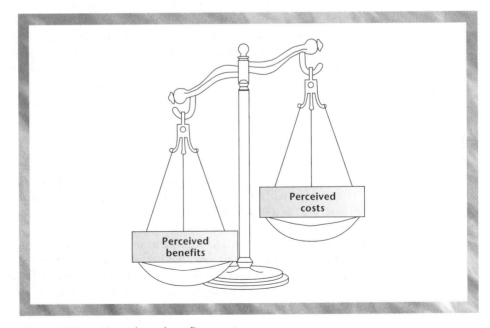

Figure 10.2 ■ Net value = benefits – costs

Increasing net value by reducing non-financial costs of service

A marketer can increase the net value of a service either by adding benefits to the core product, enhancing supplementary services or by reducing the financial costs associated with purchase and use of the product. In many instances, service firms also have the option to improve value by minimizing unwanted non-financial costs of service for customers. Possible approaches include:

■ Reducing the time costs of service involved in service purchase, delivery and consumption.

■ Minimizing unwanted psychological costs of service at each stage.

■ Eliminating unwanted physical costs of service that customers may incur, notably during the search and delivery processes.

■ Decreasing unpleasant sensory costs of service by creating more attractive visual environments, reducing noise, installing more comfortable furniture and equipment, curtailing offensive smells, and ensuring that foods, beverages, or medicines to be consumed taste pleasant.

Cutting these types of costs significantly may even allow service firms to increase the monetary price while still offering what is perceived by customers as 'good value'.

Perceptions of net value may vary widely between customers, and from one situation to another for the same customer. For example, how customers feel about the net value of a service may be sharply different post-use than pre-use, reflecting the experiential qualities of many services. When customers use a service and find that it has cost more and delivered fewer benefits than expected, they are likely to speak angrily of 'poor value'. In extreme cases, when they feel that the supplier misrepresented service features, benefits, costs of service or outcomes, they may seek restitution or even press legal charges on the grounds of fraud. Good managers seek to provide full disclosure of all costs of service associated with search, purchase, use and post-purchase activities; in particular, they carefully scrutinize advertising claims and sales presentations to ensure that customers are not misled.

In the reading, 'Redefining value' (reprinted on pages 393–5), Sandra Vandermerwe emphasizes that companies need to understand that value is not what they put into products and services, but what customers get out of them over a period of time. In other words, understanding the customer's perspective is paramount.

Foundations of pricing strategy

Now let's turn to the issue of how firms should decide on the financial price that they charge for their services. The foundations underlying a firm's pricing strategy can be described as a tripod, with costs to the provider, competition, and value to the customer as the three legs (Figure 10.3).

The costs that a firm needs to recover usually imposes a minimum price – a floor – for a specific service offering, and the perceived value of the offering to customers sets a maximum, or ceiling. The price charged by competitors for similar or substitute services typically determines where, within the floor-to-ceiling range, the price should actually be set. Let's look at each leg of the pricing tripod in more detail.

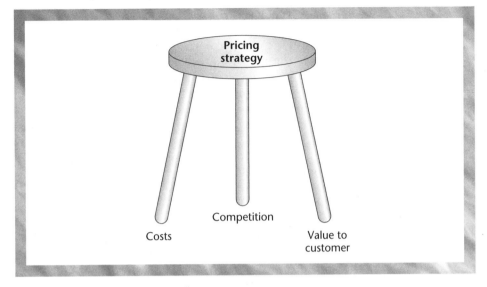

Figure 10.3 ■ The pricing tripod

Cost-based pricing

In this case, prices are set relative to financial costs. Companies seeking to make a profit must recover the full costs – variable, semi-variable and fixed – associated with producing and marketing a service, and then add a sufficient margin to yield a satisfactory profit. When variable costs are low, managers may be tempted to establish unrealistically low selling prices that fail to contribute towards fixed and semi-variable costs. However, some firms make an exception in the case of *loss leaders*, which are products sold at less than full cost to attract customers, who will then be tempted to buy profitable service offerings from the same organization. Managers need to keep track of the actual costs associated with loss leaders so that the amount of promotional subsidy is fully understood.

When industries like electricity and telecommunications were tightly regulated, there was little flexibility for charging substantially different prices to different market segments. In fact, these industries often lacked the information needed to calculate the costs associated with serving different types of user. So managers would determine the total costs incurred during a certain period, divide them by actual unit sales, and thus calculate an average cost per unit of service (defined by such measures as kilowatt-hours or minutes of long-distance calling time). The next step was to add a certain percentage for profit to this average cost and seek permission from the regulatory agency to charge a specific price. As more sophisticated costing analysis came to be used, particularly with the advent of deregulation (or privatization) and increased competition, it became clear that the prices charged to business users had been subsidizing household subscribers who were, in fact, much more expensive to serve.

Competition-based pricing

Firms marketing services that are relatively undifferentiated from competing offerings need to keep an eye on what competitors are charging and should to try to price accordingly. If customers see little or no difference between the services offered in the marketplace, they will be likely to choose the cheapest. In such a situation, the firm with the lowest cost per unit of service enjoys an enviable marketing advantage. It has the option of either competing on price at levels that higher-cost competitors cannot afford to match, or of charging the going market rate and earning larger profits than competing firms.

In some industries, one firm may act as the price leader, with others taking their cue from this company. You can sometimes see this phenomenon at the local level when several petrol stations compete within a short distance of one another or on opposite corners of a crossroads. As soon as one station raises or lowers its prices, each of the others will follow promptly.

During boom times in highly competitive industries such as airlines, hotels and rental cars, other firms are often happy to go along with the leader – particularly if this supplier does not have the lowest costs – since prices are likely to be set at a level which allows good profits. During a downturn in the economy, however, such industries quickly find themselves with surplus productive capacity – unsold seats, empty rooms or unrented cars. In an effort to attract more customers, one firm – often not the original leader – may cut prices. However, pricing is the easiest and quickest marketing variable to change. Sometimes a price war may result overnight as competitors rush to match the other firm's bargain prices.

Value-based pricing

No customer will pay more for a service than he or she thinks it's worth. So marketers may need to do some research to determine how customers perceive the value of their services. In some instances, value may vary according to the situation. For instance, people may be willing to pay more for repair services under emergency conditions (such as a car breakdown on an icy winter night).

Price is sometimes used as a means to communicate the quality and value of a service when customers find it hard to evaluate its capabilities in advance. In the absence of tangible clues, customers may associate higher prices with higher levels of performance on important service attributes.[4] Who is the better lawyer: the one who charges €40 an hour or the one who bills €100 per hour? If nothing else, a high fee suggests past success. Later in this chapter, we examine the opportunities for value-based pricing strategies with greater specificity.

Establishing monetary pricing objectives

Any decision on pricing strategy must be based on a clear understanding of a company's pricing objectives. There are three basic categories of pricing objectives: revenue-oriented; operations-oriented; and patronage-oriented (see Table 10.1).

Revenue-oriented objectives

Within certain limits, profit-seeking firms aim to maximize the surplus of income over expenditure. Managers responsible for public and nonprofit service organizations, by contrast, are more likely to be concerned with breaking even or keeping the operating deficit within acceptable bounds; however, they cannot afford to ignore the revenue implications of pricing strategy. In some organizations, one

Table 10.1 ■ Alternative bases for pricing

(1) Revenue-oriented

Profit-seeking

- Make the largest possible surplus.
- Achieve a specific target level, but do not seek to maximize profits.

Cover costs

- Cover fully allocated costs (including institutional overhead).
- Cover costs of providing one particular service or manufacturing one particular product category (after deducting any specific grants and excluding institutional overhead).
- Cover incremental costs of selling to one extra customer.

(2) Operations-oriented

- Vary prices over time so as to ensure that demand matches available supply at any specific point in time (thus making the best use of productive capacity).

(3) Patronage-oriented

- Maximize patronage (where capacity is not a constraint), subject to achieving a certain minimum level of revenues.
- Recognize differing ability to pay among the various market segments of interest to the organization and price accordingly.
- Offer methods of payment (including credit) that will enhance the likelihood of purchase.

Source: Christopher H. Lovelock and Charles B. Weinberg, *Public and Nonprofit Marketing* (Redwood City, CA: The Scientific Press, 1989), p. 256.

service may be priced to yield a profit that is used to cross-subsidize other services. Such cross-subsidies should be a deliberate choice, not an unplanned outcome of sloppy practice.

Operations-oriented objectives

Capacity-constrained organizations seek to match demand and supply to ensure optimal use of their productive capacity at any given time. Hotels, for instance, seek to fill their rooms, since an empty room is an unproductive asset. Similarly, professional firms want to keep their staff members occupied, railways want to fill empty seats, and repair shops try to keep their facilities, machines and workers busy. When demand exceeds capacity, however, these organizations may try to increase profits and ration demand by raising prices.

Railway operators in Europe, including both state-owned carriers on the continent and private operators in Britain, have been able to increase the number of passengers during off-peak periods through strategies such as discounts for families and pensioners, Apex fares requiring advance purchase, and variations in fare by time-of-day, day-of-the-week and season. These sophisticated pricing strategies are a far cry from the rigid approach followed in years past by Swiss Federal Railways of a fixed price of so many centimes per kilometre.

Similarly, matching hotel demand to the number of rooms available may be achieved by pricing high at peak periods and pricing low in off-peak periods. Repair shops may offer special deals at reduced rates when business is slack. The problem with matching demand to supply through price is that firms may be accused of price gouging (that is, charging extortionate prices) when times are good. And some firms are reluctant to engage in price discounting for fear that customers will equate this with a decline in quality.

Patronage-oriented objectives

New services, in particular, often have trouble attracting customers. Introductory price discounts may be used to stimulate trial, sometimes in combination with promotional activities such as contests and giveaways. Firms wishing to maximize their appeal among specific types of customers may need to adopt pricing strategies that recognize a differential ability to pay among various market segments (as well as variations in preferences among customers for different levels of service).

Price elasticity

The concept of elasticity describes how sensitive demand is to changes in price. When *price elasticity* is at 'unity', sales of a service rise (or fall) by the same percentage that price falls (or rises). When a small change in price has a big impact on sales, demand for that product is said to be price-elastic. But when a change in price has little effect on sales, demand is described as price inelastic. The concept is illustrated in the simple chart presented in Figure 10.4, which shows schedules for highly elastic demand (a small change in price results in a big change in the amount demanded) and highly inelastic demand (even big changes in price have little impact on the amount demanded).

In Chapter 13, we illustrate and discuss demand curves of varying degrees of elasticity, reflecting the differing behaviour of customers in each of several market segments for hotel accommodation.

Most theatres and concert halls do not have a single, fixed admission price for performances. Instead, the price varies according to (1) the location of the seats, (2) the time of the performance, (3) the projected cost of staging the performance, and (4) the anticipated appeal of the performance.

In establishing prices for different blocks of seats (known as scaling the house) it is important to identify what the demand for each price category will be, in order to determine the appropriate number of seats to offer at that price. Poor judgement on this score may result in large numbers of empty seats in some price categories and immediate sellouts (and disappointed customers) in other categories. Management also needs to know theatre-goers' preferences for scheduling of performances – matinées versus evenings, weekends versus weekdays, and possibly even seasonal variations. In each instance, the aim is managing demand over time to maximize either attendance, revenues or a combination of the two (for example, maximizing revenues, subject to a minimum attendance goal per performance of 70 per cent of all seats sold).

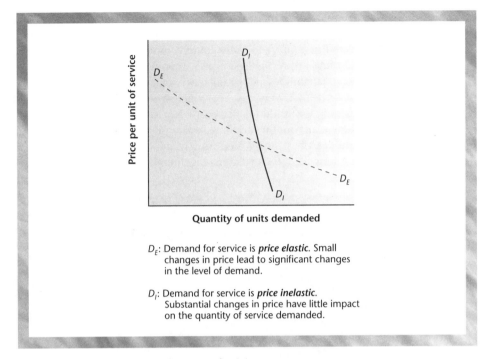

Figure 10.4 ■ Illustrations of pricing elasticity

Yield management

Many service businesses are increasingly concerned with yield management – that is, maximizing the revenue yield that can be derived from available capacity at any given time. Airlines, hotels and car rental firms have become particularly adept at varying their prices for what is (within each industry) essentially the same product, in response to the price sensitivity of different market segments at different times of the day, week or season. The challenge is to capture sufficient customers to fill the organization's perishable capacity without creating consumer surplus for customers who would have been willing to pay more.

In large organizations, such as major airlines or hotel chains, the market is very dynamic, since the situation is changing all the time. For instance, the demand for both business and pleasure travel reflects current or anticipated economic conditions. Although business travellers do not always think of themselves as particularly price-sensitive, many companies employ travel specialists who shop for the best travel bargains they can find within the constraints of an employee's travel needs. Pleasure travellers, by contrast, are often very price-sensitive; a special promotion, involving discounted fares and room-rates, may even encourage people to undertake a trip that they would not otherwise have made.

How does a firm know what level of demand to expect at different prices in a highly dynamic market environment where the factors influencing demand are constantly changing? Advances in software and computing power have made it possible for firms to use very sophisticated mathematical models for use in yield management analysis. In the case of an airline, for example, these models integrate massive historical databases on passenger travel with real-time information on current bookings to help analysts pinpoint how many passengers would want to travel between two cities at a particular fare on a flight leaving at a specified time and date.

Effective use of yield management models can improve an airline's profitability. Some airlines are recognized as more sophisticated than others in their modelling and analytical capabilities (it is said that yield management techniques contribute 5 per cent to British Airways' profits, which would suggest an incremental profit of about £30 million (€42 million) per year). Not surprisingly, the exact nature of the models and their component variables is a closely guarded commercial secret. The boxed example describes how American Airlines, one of the industry leaders in this somewhat esoteric field, uses yield management analysis to set fares for a specific flight.

Pricing seats on Flight AA 2015

Yield management programs require sophisticated software and powerful computers to crunch all the data that are fed into them. Managers, of course, are interested in the output that emerges from the computers rather than in the underlying science. Each flight on a given date is tracked separately. Let's look at American Airlines 2015, a popular flight from Chicago to Phoenix, Arizona, which departs daily at 17:30 on the 2,200 km (1,370 mile) journey – roughly equivalent to the distance between London and Athens.

The 125 seats in coach (economy class) are divided into seven fare categories, referred to by yield management specialists as 'buckets'. There is an enormous variation in ticket prices among these seats: round-trip fares range from $238 (€198) for a bargain excursion ticket (with various restrictions and a cancellation penalty attached) all the way up to an unrestricted fare of $1,404. Seats are also available at an even higher price in the small first-class section. Scott McCartney tells how ongoing analysis by the computer program changes the allocation of seats between each of the seven buckets in economy class:

In the weeks before each Chicago–Phoenix flight, American's yield management computers constantly adjust the number of seats in each bucket, taking into account tickets sold, historical ridership patterns and connecting passengers likely to use the route as one leg of a longer trip.

If advance bookings are slim, American adds seats to low-fare buckets. If business customers buy unrestricted fares earlier than expected, the yield management computer takes seats out of the discount buckets and preserves them for last-minute bookings that the database predicts will still show up.

With 69 of 125 coach seats already sold four weeks before one recent departure of Flight 2015, American's computer began to limit the number of seats in lower-priced buckets. A week later, it totally shut off sales for the bottom three buckets, priced $300 or less. To a Chicago customer looking for a cheap seat, the flight was 'sold out' . . .

One day before departure, with 130 passengers booked for the 125-seat flight, American still offered five seats at full fare because its computer database indicated 10 passengers were likely not to show up or take other flights. Flight 2015 departed full and no one was bumped.[5]

Although AA 2015 for that date is now history, it has not been forgotten. The booking experience for this flight was saved in the memory of the yield management program to help the airline do an even better job of forecasting in the future.

Pricing strategies employing yield management techniques shouldn't necessarily mean blind pursuit of short-term yield maximization. Over-dependence on the output of computer models can easily lead to pricing strategies that are full of rules and regulations designed to prevent less price-sensitive segments from trading down to take advantage of lower-priced offers, penalties for cancelled reservations and cynical overbooking without thought for the consequences to disappointed customers, who thought they had a firm reservation. To maintain goodwill and build relationships, a company should take the long-term perspective. So managers responsible for pricing decisions should build in strategies for retaining valued customer relationships, even to the extent of not charging the maximum feasible amount on a given transaction; after all, customer perceptions of price gouging do not build trust. There should also be thoughtfully planned contingencies for victims of overbooking, with service recovery efforts designed to restore goodwill following disappointment.

Firms should also guard against the risk that pricing policies may become too complex. Jokes abound about travel agents having nervous breakdowns because they get a different quote every time they call the airline for a fare and because there are so many exclusions, conditions and special offers.

Value strategies for service pricing

The key to effective service pricing is to relate the price that customers pay to the value that they receive. Service pricing strategies are often unsuccessful because they lack any clear association between price and value.[6] Berry and Yadav propose three distinct but related strategies for capturing and communicating the value of a service: uncertainty reduction, relationship enhancing, and low-cost leadership.

Pricing strategies to reduce uncertainty

There are three options here, beginning with a service guarantee that entitles customers to a refund if they are not completely satisfied (see the discussion of Hampton Inn's 100 per cent Satisfaction Guarantee in Chapter 7). When well-designed and executed, service guarantees remove much of the risk associated with buying an intangible service – especially for services high in experience qualities, where customers can easily determine after the fact that service was unsatisfactory.

Benefit-driven pricing involves pricing that aspect of the service that directly benefits customers. (This approach forces service marketers to research what aspects of the service the customers do and do not value.) For instance, prices for on-line information services are often based on log-on time, but what customers really value is the information that is browsed and retrieved. In fact, poorly designed web sites often waste customers' time because they make it hard to find what users are looking for. The result is that pricing and value creation are out of sync. When ESA-IRS, a European on-line provider, implemented a new pricing strategy termed 'pricing for information' and based on the information actually extracted, the company found that customers were more willing to use a time-consuming feature called ZOOM which allowed them to search several complex databases simultaneously with increased precision. They started staying on-line longer and the use of ZOOM tripled as customers began to conduct more detailed searches. From then on, the company changed its marketing focus to selling information rather than selling time.

Flat-rate pricing involves quoting a fixed price in advance of service delivery in order to avoid any surprises. In essence, the risk is transferred from the customer to the supplier in the event that the service takes longer to deliver or involves more costs than anticipated. Flat-rate pricing can be an effective strategy in industries where service prices are unpredictable and suppliers are poor at controlling their costs and the speed at which they work. They are also effective in situations where competitors make low estimates to win business but subsequently claim that they were only giving an estimate, not making a firm pricing commitment.

Relationship pricing

When developing and maintaining long-term customer relationships is one of the objectives, pricing strategy has an important role to play. Discounting to win new business is not the best approach if a firm is seeking to attract customers who will remain loyal – research indicates that those who are attracted by cut-price offers can easily be enticed away by another offer from a competitor.[7] More creative pricing strategies focus on giving customers both price and non-price incentives to consolidate their business with a single supplier.

A strategy of *discounting* prices for large purchases can often be profitable for both parties, since the customer benefits from lower prices while the supplier may enjoy lower variable costs resulting from economies of scale. An alternative to volume discounting on a single service is for a firm to offer its customers discounts when two or more services are purchased together. The greater the number of different services a customer purchases from a single supplier, the closer the relationship is likely to be: on the one hand, both parties get to know each other better, and on the other hand, it's more inconvenient for the customer to shift its business.

Low-cost leadership

Low-priced services reduce the monetary burden for customers and are particularly likely to appeal to both corporate and individual customers who are on a tight financial budget. They may also lead purchasers to buy in larger volumes. One challenge when pricing low is to convince customers that they should not equate price with quality. A second challenge is to ensure that economic costs are kept low enough to enable the firm to make a profit when prices are low.

Some service businesses have built their entire strategy around being the low-cost leader. A classic example of a focused pricing strategy in the airline business is that of Southwest Airlines in the United States. Southwest has been studied by airlines all over the world and now has many imitators. In Europe, as we noted earlier in the chapter, these include EasyJet, Ryanair, Virgin Express, Debonair and GO.

Putting service pricing strategy into practice

Although the main decision in pricing is usually seen as how much to charge, there are actually a lot of other decisions to be made, too. Table 10.2 summarizes the questions that service marketers need to ask themselves as they prepare to create and implement a well-thought out pricing strategy. Let's look at each in turn.

Table 10.2 ■ Some pricing issues

1. How much should be charged for this service?

- What costs is the organization attempting to recover? Is the organization trying to achieve a specific profit margin or return on investment by selling this service?
- How sensitive are customers to different prices?
- What prices are charged by competitors?
- What discount(s) should be offered from basic prices?
- Are psychological pricing points (e.g., €4.95 versus €5.00) customarily used?

2. What should be the basis of pricing?

- Execution of a specific task
- Admission to a service facility
- Units of time (hour, week, month, year)
- Percentage commission on the value of the transaction
- Physical resources consumed
- Geographic distance covered
- Weight or size of object serviced
- Should each service element be billed independently?
- Should a single price be charged for a bundled 'package'?

3. Who should collect payment?

- The organization that provides the service
- A specialist intermediary (travel or ticket agent, bank, shopkeeper, etc.)
- How should the intermediary be compensated for this work – flat fee or percentage commission?

4. Where should payment be made?

- The location at which the service is delivered
- A convenient retail outlet or financial intermediary (e.g., bank)
- The purchaser's home (by mail or phone)

Table 10.2 ■ Some pricing issues (*continued*)

5. When should payment be made?

- Before or after delivery of the service
- At which times of day
- On which days of the week

6. How should payment be made?

- Cash (exact change or not?)
- Token (where can these be purchased?)
- Stored value card
- Check (how to verify?)
- Electronic funds transfer
- Charge card (credit or debit)
- Credit account with service provider
- Vouchers
- Third-party payment (e.g., insurance company, government agency)?

7. How should prices be communicated to the target market?

- Through what communication medium? (advertising, signage, electronic display, salespeople, customer service personnel)
- What message content (how much emphasis should be placed on price?)

How much to charge?

Realistic decisions on pricing are critical for financial solvency. The pricing tripod model, discussed earlier (Figure 10.3), provides a useful departure point. Let's just reiterate the three elements involved. The task begins with determining the relevant economic costs and then deciding whether, in a specific situation, the organization should try to cover just variable costs, or whether it should seek to recover a share of the fixed and semi-variable costs, too, as well as include a margin for profit on top. Determining the costs to be recovered at different sales volumes and, as appropriate, the profit margin, sets the relevant floor price.

The second task is to assess market sensitivity to different prices, both the overall value of the service to prospective customers as well as their ability to pay. This step sets a 'ceiling' price for any given market segment. It's very important to be able to make an accurate prediction of what sales volume might be obtained at different price levels.

Competitive prices provide a third input. The greater the number of competing, similar alternatives that appeal to consumers, and the more widely available they are, the greater will be the pressure on the marketing manager to keep prices at or below those of the competition. The situation is particularly challenging when some competitors choose to compete on the basis of low price and have coupled this with an operating strategy designed to achieve low costs.

The wider the gap between the floor and ceiling prices, the more room there is for manoeuvre. If a ceiling price (the maximum that customers are willing to pay) is below the floor price (the lowest price the firm can afford to charge in the light of its costs), the manager must choose between two alternatives: one is to recognize that the service is noncompetitive, in which case it will have to be discontinued. The other is to modify it in ways that differentiate it from the competition and add value for prospective customers, so that it now becomes competitive at a higher price. Public and nonprofit organizations have a third option, which is to seek third-party funding – such as government subsidies or private donations – to cover some of the costs, thus allowing the service to be sold at a lower price. This latter approach is commonly used to make services such as health, education, the arts and urban transport more easily affordable to a broad cross-section of the population.

Finally, a specific figure must be set for the financial price that customers will be asked to pay. This decision raises the question of whether to price in round numbers or try to create the impression that prices are slightly lower than they really are. If competitors promote prices such as €3.95 and €9.95, a strategy of charging €4.00 or €10.00 may convey an image of prices somewhat higher than is really the case. On the other hand, rounded prices offer convenience and simplicity – benefits that may be appreciated by both consumers and salespeople, since they help to speed up cash transactions.

What should be the basis for pricing?

Deciding on the basis for pricing requires defining the unit of service consumption. Should it be based on completing a specific service task, such as cleaning a jacket or cutting a customer's hair? Should it be admission to a service performance, such as an educational programme, or a film, concert or sports event? Should it be time-based, as for using an hour of a solicitor's time, occupying a hotel room for a night, hiring a car for a week, subscribing to a satellite TV service for a month, or paying for a term's tuition at university? Should it be tied to value, as when an insurance company scales its premiums to reflect the amount of coverage provided, or an estate agent takes a percentage commission of the selling price of a house?

Some service prices are tied to consumption of physical resources, such as food, drinks, electricity or gas. For example, rather than charging customers an hourly rate for occupying a table and chairs, restaurants put a sizeable markup on the food and drink items consumed. Transport firms have traditionally charged by distance, with freight companies using a combination of weight or cubic volume and distance to set their rates. Such a policy has the virtue of consistency and reflects calculation of an average cost per kilometre (or mile). However, simplicity may suggest a flat rate, as with postal charges for domestic letters below a certain weight, or a zone rate for parcels that lumps geographic distances into broad bands. Long-distance phone calls reflect a combination of distance and time but, as with transportation, market analysis and competitive practices have largely eliminated strictly distance-based formulae.

Price bundling

As emphasized throughout this book, many services unite a core product with a variety of supplementary services. Meals and bar service on a cruise liner is one example; luggage service on a train or aircraft is another. Should such service packages be priced as a whole (referred to as a 'bundle'), or should each element be priced separately? To the extent that people dislike having to make many small payments, bundled pricing may be preferable – and is certainly simpler to administer. But if customers dislike feeling that they have been charged for product elements they didn't use, itemized pricing may be preferable. Members of a club in Manchester that meets regularly to play bridge have been debating whether the entrance fee for playing in a game should entitle the player to free refreshments.

Some firms offer an array of choices. Telephone subscribers, for instance, can select from among several service options, ranging from paying a small monthly fee for basic service and then extra for each phone call made, or paying a higher flat rate and get a certain number of local, regional or long-distance calls free. At the top of the scale is the option that provides business users with unlimited access to long-distance calls over a prescribed area – even internationally. Bundled prices offer a service firm a certain guaranteed revenue from each customer, while giving the latter a clear idea in advance of how much the bill will be. Unbundled pricing provides customers with flexibility in what they choose to acquire and pay for, but may also cause problems. For instance, customers may be put off by discovering that the ultimate price of what they want, inflated by all the 'extras', is substantially higher than the advertised base price that attracted them in the first place.

Discounting

A strategy of discounting from established prices should be approached cautiously, because it dilutes the average price received, reduces the contribution from each sale, and may attract customers whose only loyalty is to the firm that can offer the lowest price on the next transaction. As noted earlier, there is also a risk that customers who would have been willing to pay more now find themselves enjoying a bargain. Nevertheless, selective price discounting targeted at specific market segments may offer important opportunities to attract new customers and fill capacity that would otherwise go unused. BT's 'Friends & Family' programme (copied from the American carrier MCI) offers customers discounts on calls they make to specific telephone numbers, providing the entire group signs up for service with BT. A key objective is to enlist customers as sales agents and then to cement loyalty – group members have a vested interest in discouraging any member from cancelling BT service and using another supplier. Volume discounts are sometimes used to cement the loyalty of large corporate customers who might otherwise spread their purchases among several different suppliers. Another way to use discounting to build loyalty is by offering existing customers a discount off their next purchase.

The challenge for managers is to understand the price elasticities of different segments and to discourage high-paying segments from taking advantage of discounts designed to lure more price-sensitive consumers. The airlines, in particular, work hard to develop appropriate restrictions on the availability of discount fares (requiring, for instance, that travellers must stay at their destinations over a Saturday night before returning) in order to make it difficult for business travellers (whose fares are often being reimbursed by their employers) to travel cheaply. Discount fares, after all, are designed to attract pleasure travellers taking discretionary trips.

Who should collect payment?

As discussed in Chapter 8, the petals of the Flower of Service include information, order-taking, billing and payment. Customers appreciate it when a firm makes it easy for them to obtain price information and make reservations; they also expect well-presented billing and convenient procedures for making payment. Sometimes managers delegate these tasks to intermediaries. Examples include travel agents who make hotel and transport bookings and collect payment from customers; ticket agents who sell seats for theatres, concert halls and sports stadiums; and retailers who act as intermediaries for repair and maintenance work on physical goods. Although the service organization may have to pay a commission, the intermediary is usually able to offer customers greater convenience in terms of where, when and how payment should be paid. Even after paying commissions, the use of intermediaries often offers a net savings in administrative costs to the primary organization.

Where should payment be made?

Service delivery sites are not always conveniently located. Airports, theatres and stadiums, for instance, are often situated some distance from where potential patrons live or work. When consumers purchase a service before using it, there are obvious benefits to using intermediaries that are more conveniently located, or allowing payment by post. A growing number of organizations now accept telephone bookings and sales by credit card; callers simply give their card numbers and have the charge billed directly to their accounts. Early experiments that allowed customers to use their credit cards to pay through the World Wide Web ran into security problems, but now that these are being resolved through more robust encryption, the Web will doubtless become a popular medium for purchasing a wide array of goods and services.

When should payment be made?

The two basic options are to ask customers to pay in advance of use (as with an admission charge, airline ticket or purchase of postage stamps), or to bill them once service delivery has been completed, as with restaurant bills and repair charges. Occasionally, a service provider may ask for an initial payment in advance of service delivery, with the balance being due later. This approach is quite common with expensive repair and maintenance jobs, when the firm – often a small business with limited working capital – must buy materials up front.

Asking customers to pay for service in advance of use means that the buyer is paying before the benefits are received. But there may be value to the customer as well as to the provider. Sometimes it's inconvenient to pay each time a regularly patronized service – such as the post or public transport – is used; to save time and effort, customers may prefer the convenience of buying a book of stamps or a monthly travel pass. Performing arts organizations with limited funds and heavy up-front financing requirements often offer discounted subscription tickets in order to bring in money before the season begins. For obvious reasons, insurance services always require payment in advance.

How should payment be made?

As shown in Table 10.2, there are a variety of different ways of paying for service. Cash may appear to be the simplest method, but it raises problems of security as well as being inconvenient when exact change is required to operate machines. Tokens with a predefined value are sometimes used to simplify the process of paying road and bridge tolls or bus and metro fares. Accepting payment by cheque for all but the smallest purchases is now fairly widespread and offers customer benefits, although it may require controls to discourage bad cheques.

Credit cards are used for many types of purchases and have gained acceptance around the world. Debit cards – introduced into Europe long before they reached North America – look like credit cards but act more like 'plastic cheques', since the sum charged is debited directly from the holder's account. Electronic point-of-sale terminals are connected directly to banking networks. As acceptance of credit and debit cards has become more universal, businesses that refuse to accept them may find themselves at a competitive disadvantage. Many companies offer customers the convenience of a credit account (which generates a membership relationship between the customer and the firm).

Other payment procedures include directing the bill to a third party for payment and using vouchers as supplements to (or instead of) cash. One example of the former approach involves insurance companies that designate approved garages to inspect and repair customers' vehicles when they are involved in accidents. To make life easier for the customer, the garage invoices the insurance company directly for the work performed, thus saving the customer the effort of paying personally, filing a claim and waiting for reimbursement. Vouchers are sometimes provided by social service agencies to groups such as elderly or low-income people. Such a policy achieves the same benefits as discounting, without the need to publicize an array of different prices and to require those who collect the money to act as police (a role for which they may be unsuited and untrained).

Now coming into broader usage are pre-payment systems based on cards that store value on a magnetic strip or in a microchip embedded within the card. Telephone cards are but one example of this. Service firms that want to accept payment in this form, however, must first install card readers. More sophisticated applications involve partnerships between banks, retailers and telephone companies. Working together, these partners offer a smart card that serves as an 'electronic wallet'; customers can transfer funds to their cards from their bank accounts through the medium of a special telephone attachment. There is also provision to transfer funds from one card to another. For details on the new Mondex smart card, see Chapter 8. A key issue for service marketers to remember in this and other contexts is that the simplicity and speed with which payment is made may influence the customer's perception of overall service quality.

Communicating prices to the target markets

The final task, once each of the other issues has been addressed, is to decide how the organization's pricing policies can best be communicated to the target market(s). People need to know the price for some product offerings well in advance of purchase; they may also need to know how, where and when that price is payable. This information must be presented in ways that are intelligible and unambiguous, so that customers will not be misled and question the ethical standards of the firm.

Managers must decide whether or not to include information on pricing in advertising for the service. It may be appropriate to relate the price to the costs of competing products or to alternative ways of spending one's money. Certainly, salespeople and customer service representatives should be able to give prompt, accurate responses to customer queries about pricing, payment and credit. Good signage at retail points of sale will save staff members from having to answer basic questions on prices.

Conclusion

Customers pay more to use a service than just the purchase price due to the supplier. For them, the costs of service also include related expenditures (such as travel to the service site), plus time, physical effort, psychological costs, and sensory costs. The value of a service reflects the benefits that it delivers to the customer minus all the associated costs. Customers are often willing to pay a higher price when the non-financial costs of service are minimized.

Establishing a pricing strategy for a service business begins with clarification of objectives: is the firm trying to go far beyond just establishing the price itself? Issues such as convenience, security, credit, speed, simplicity, collection procedures and automation may all play a role in improving customer satisfaction with service organizations. Technology has significant potential to facilitate creation of a cashless society, but in practice we are still some distance from that point.

In addition to all these decisions, pricing strategy must address the central issue of what price to charge for selling a given unit of service at a particular point in time (however that unit may be defined). It is essential that the monetary price charged should reflect good knowledge of the service provider's fixed and variable costs, competitor's pricing policies, and the value of the service to the customer.

Study questions

1. Of the various costs of service explained in this chapter, which are likely to be the most significant in different service industries and why?

2. Why is cost-based pricing particularly problematic in service industries?

3. In what ways does competition-based pricing work in favour of many service providers? In what circumstances does it not?

4. Compare and contrast the strategic and functional role of pricing.

5. Explain the concept of yield management in a service setting.

6. From a customer perspective, what serves to define value in the following services:

   (a) a nightclub?

   (b) a hairdressing salon?

   (c) a legal firm specializing in business and taxation law?

7. Select a service organization of your choice and find out what their pricing policies and methods are. In what respects are they similar to or different from what has been discussed in this chapter?

Notes

1. This is based in part on 'Benson Pledges European Sky Wars', by Neil Buckley, *Financial Times*, 30 April 1996; 'Taking a Ticket to Fly Without the Thrills or the Frills: The Growth of a New Breed of Short Haul European Airlines', by Charis Gresser, *Financial Times*, 22 October 1997; 'European Flag Carriers Might be able to Ignore Low Cost Competitors for a While. Eventually, However, Their World Will be Turned Upside Down', *The Economist*, 27 September 1997; 'Do You Want Cheap Fares or Air Miles and Plastic Food?: The Success of Low Cost Airlines', by Joanna Walters, *The Observer*, 17 August 1997.

2. Leonard L. Berry and Manjit S. Yadav, 'Capture and Communicate Value in the Pricing of Services', *Sloan Management Review*, Vol. 37, Summer 1996, pp. 41–51.

3. Valarie A. Zeithaml, 'Consumer Perceptions of Price, Quality and Value: A Means–Ends Model and Synthesis of Evidence', *Journal of Marketing*, Vol. 52, July 1988, pp. 2–21.

4. For a review of the literature in this area and findings from a research study see Injazz J. Chen, Atul Gupta and Walter Rom, 'A Study of Price and Quality in Service Operations', *International Journal of Service Industry Management*, Vol. 5, No. 2, 1994, pp. 23–33.

5. Scott McCartney, 'Ticket Shock: Business Fares Increase Even as Leisure Travel Keeps Getting Cheaper', *Wall Street Journal*, 3 November 1997, pp. A1, A10.

6. Hermann Simon, 'Pricing Opportunities and How to Exploit Them', *Sloan Management Review*, Vol. 33, Winter 1992, pp. 71–84.

7. Frederick F. Reichheld, *The Loyalty Effect*, Boston: Harvard Business School Press, 1996, pp. 82–4.

CHAPTER 11

Communicating to customers: education and promotion

Learning objectives

After reading and reflecting on this chapter, you should be able to:

1. Explain the role of marketing communications in a service setting.

2. Describe how marketing communications differ between services and goods.

3. Discuss the marketing communications mix elements.

4. Understand how the level of customer contact affects communication strategy.

5. Define marketing communication objectives and identify the communication mix elements necessary to reach those objectives.

6. Recognize the potential value of the internet (e-mail and web sites) as a communication channel.

Trying out new spectacle frames on the web[1]

The internet offers creative new opportunities for marketers to communicate with both current and prospective customers. Many web sites simply take advantage of a new medium through which they can distribute the same type of communications that have traditionally appeared in printed form. In other instances, however, marketers have designed web sites that enable current and prospective customers to enter into an interactive dialogue with their organizations.

Dolland & Aitchison (D&A) is a long-established firm which operates a large chain of opticians throughout Britain. Rather appropriately, the company's symbol is an owl with big, round eyes. Recent television advertising by the company humorously recognizes that many people hate getting new glasses. The commercials feature film star Burt Reynolds being dragged reluctantly into one of their outlets to buy a new pair of glasses.

D&A's web site seeks to inform and to educate as well as to sell. For instance, visitors to the site, www.danda.co.uk, will find that it offers pictures and information about the different models of designer sunglasses available from the firm, a rationale for wearing sunglasses to protect one's eyes and the opportunity to place an order directly for postal delivery. There is also a detailed educational section about how to avoid eyestrain when using VDUs (video display units, such as computer screens), including a note about the responsibilities of employers to provide eye tests to employees who use VDUs in their work. For those wishing to visit a D&A store, there is a branch locator which enables prospective customers to enter their postal code (or county) and obtain a list of the company's nearest branches.

However, perhaps the most interesting aspect of the web site is a section titled 'Personal Eyes'. A big issue for many people who wear glasses is what design of spectacle frames will look best on them. If you have poor distance vision, you know how difficult it is to choose a new pair of frames when you can't see what you look like in the mirror without wearing corrective lenses in the first place! (If you don't wear contact lenses, you have to bring a friend with you to help you choose – unless the store offers the services of a video camera to film you wearing different frames.) D&A has come up with a new idea. It invented a concept called 'Personal Eyes' to allow people to try out new frames on the Web, before they even visit a store. Here's how the system works.

First, you need to obtain a passport-sized, full-face photograph of yourself without glasses on. Then you post this to the company, or scan a copy into your computer and e-mail it. On receipt, D&A scan your picture into their own system and send you a user name and password. You are now ready to pull up your face on danda.uk.co, and start scrolling through the firm's large selection of frames, some of which are unique to D&A and others drawn from designer collections. Each time you spot a pair of frames that you think might suit you, you drag the spectacles in question across the screen over the image of your face and see what you might look like when wearing them. You can even put your favourites into a space at the bottom of the screen to make it easy for you to compare and contrast your appearance 'wearing' different frames.

Having selected one or more frames, you then make a note of their reference numbers. By this point, Dolland & Aitchison hopes that you are sufficiently happy with your choice that you will want to visit one of their shops at the first opportunity to try the real frames for comfort and fit (and perhaps have an eye test as well). Other chains may eventually copy this idea, but D&A has gained the competitive advantage (and the publicity) associated with being the innovator.

The role of marketing communication

As the Dolland & Aitchison example shows, marketing communications can take many forms, some of them highly creative. In a competitive environment, effective communications play a vital role in marketing strategy. The advent of the internet has added a potent new medium to the array of media already available. Among the tasks performed by marketing communication are to:

- *Inform and educate* prospective customers about an organization and the relevant features of the goods and services that it offers.
- *Persuade* target customers that a specific service product offers the best solution to their needs, relative to the offerings of competing firms.
- *Remind* customers and prospects of product availability and motivate them to act.
- *Maintain contact* with existing customers, providing updates and further education on how to obtain the best results from the firm's products in the light of each customer's documented usage behaviour.

As we saw in our discussion of the Flower of Service in Chapter 8, information and consultation represent important ways to add value to a product. Prospective customers need information about what service options are available to them, where and when these services are available, how much they cost, specific features and functions, and the particular benefits to be gained. Prospects may also need advice on which of several alternative service packages might best meet their needs. In service businesses, many communication efforts are concerned with educating customers. This is especially true of advertising campaigns for new services or for newly introduced service features.

Persuasion involves developing arguments about why a customer should purchase and use a particular service rather than not purchasing at all or buying a competing brand. Reminders may be needed to make people act on their intentions to buy a particular service, especially when it's offered only at very specific times – like subscribing to concert programmes or purchasing special holiday travel packages.

Communication efforts serve to attract new customers and also to maintain contact with existing users. As emphasized in Chapter 6, reinforcing loyalty and securing repeat sales are usually central to a firm's long-term profitability. Existing customers should not be taken for granted. Techniques for keeping in touch include mailed cards and letters, periodic newsletters by post or e-mail, and contacts by telephone or through other forms of telecommunication, including fax and the internet.

Doctors, dentists and household maintenance services often send annual checkup reminders to their customers. Banks and utility companies that send periodic account statements often include a brief newsletter or print customized information on each statement as a means of keeping in touch with existing customers and promoting new services; companies in both industries also make widespread use of direct mail shots for cross-selling (persuading existing customers to use additional services) and for building customer loyalty. Some hotels, restaurants and insurance companies acknowledge special events such as customers' birthdays and anniversaries. Subscription services send early renewal notices.

Nurturing customer relationships depends on a comprehensive and up-to-date customer database, and the ability to make use of this in a personalized way. Although postal mailings have been the traditional channel of communication, many businesses are now turning to telecommunications to keep in touch with customers – as well as encouraging customers to visit their corporate web sites.

Ethical issues in communication

The tools of communication are very powerful. Few aspects of marketing lend themselves so easily to misuse (and even abuse) as advertising, selling and sales promotion. Communication messages often include promises about the benefits that customers will receive and the quality of service delivery. But if promises are made and then broken, customers are disappointed because their expectations have not been met.[2] Their disappointment, and even anger, will be all the greater if they have wasted money, time and effort, and have either no benefits to show for it or, worse, have actually suffered a negative impact. Employees, too, may feel frustrated.

Sometimes, unrealistic service promises result from poor internal communications. The fact that customers often find it hard to evaluate services makes them more dependent on marketing communication for information and advice. Once a firm gains a reputation for being untrustworthy, that can be hard to shake off.

A different type of ethical issue concerns intrusion into people's personal lives. You can simply turn the page if you don't want to look at an advertisement in a newspaper or magazine. Perhaps you ignore television advertising and talk to friends or family members while the commercials are on (or even leave the room to perform a quick errand during that time). However, the increase in telemarketing in some parts of Europe is a cause of great annoyance among many of those receiving such calls. How do you feel if your evening meal is interrupted by a telephone call from a stranger trying to interest you in buying goods and services in which you have no interest? Many people feel that their privacy has been violated and view the call as an unwanted intrusion.

Internal communications

Marketing communications are used to communicate with service employees as well as with external customers (see Chapter 14). Internal communications are especially critical in maintaining and nurturing a corporate culture founded on specific service values. Such efforts are vital in large service businesses operating in widely dispersed sites, sometimes around the world, where employees may be working far from the head office in the home country. Consider, for instance, the challenge of maintaining a unified sense of corporate purpose at the overseas offices of TNT, Deutsche Bank, Novotel, KLM or McDonalds.

The goals of internal communications include: ensuring efficient and satisfactory service delivery; achieving productive and harmonious working relationships; and building employee trust, respect and loyalty. Progress in reaching each goal depends, in part, on clear communication between management and employees. Commonly used media vehicles include internal newsletters and magazines, private corporate television networks, videotapes, face-to-face briefings and periodic promotional campaigns using displays, prizes and recognition programmes.

Services vs. goods: implications for communication strategy

Several of the differences distinguishing services from goods have important marketing communications implications. The five most relevant differences include:

■ the intangible nature of service performances;

■ customer involvement in production;

■ the need to balance supply and demand;

■ a reduced role for intermediaries;

■ the importance of customer contact personnel.

Let's examine each of these in more detail.

Intangible nature of service performances

Developing a communications strategy for intangible services is quite different from advertising and promoting physical goods. Guidelines should reflect the special characteristics of services.[3] The first is to recognize that service is a performance rather than an object. Advertising should not only encourage customers to buy the service, but should also target employees as a second audience, motivating them to deliver high-quality service. Thus service firms should try to use their own employees – rather than professional models – in their print and broadcast advertisements.

Service providers should also use tangible cues whenever possible in their advertising campaigns. Some companies have successfully incorporated animals and animal motifs as physical symbols for their products. Examples include the Qantas kangaroo, the eagle of Eagle Star Insurance, the black horse of Lloyd's Bank, Merrill Lynch's bull, the lion of Crédit Lyonnais and the Chinese dragon of Hong Kong's Dragonair. The use of easily recognizable symbols takes on special importance when offering services in markets where the local language is not written in Roman script or where a significant proportion of the population is functionally illiterate.

Creating metaphors that are tangible in nature makes intangible claims easier to grasp. Insurance companies, which are faced with marketing a highly intangible product, often use such an approach. Thus one insurance company advertises that 'You're in Good Hands', another presents an umbrella motif to suggest protection, and a third uses the Rock of Gibraltar as a symbol of corporate solidity.

Customer involvement in production

Pressures to improve productivity in service organizations often involve technological innovations in service delivery. If customers will accept technology as a substitute for human effort, or will agree to perform more of the work themselves in the form of self-service, then the service business may stand to cut its costs significantly. But these benefits will not be achieved if customers resist new, technologically-based systems or avoid self-service alternatives. A major challenge for innovative firms is to teach their customers how to use new technologies effectively. When customers are actively involved in service production, they need training to help them perform well – just as employees do.

Even when the technology is not itself new, it may still be new to a particular customer. In many organized outdoor sports and adventure activities, from rock-climbing to white-water rafting, there are inherent risks. The providers of such services have both a legal and a moral responsibility to educate their clients. The better informed customers are of potential dangers, and what to do in the event of, say, a raft tipping its occupants into a stretch of foaming rapids, the more likely they are to remain safe and to have an enjoyable experience. Basic information read earlier in instructional brochures may need to be reinforced and expanded by personal briefings from staff. Educating customers is important for their own self-protection. For instance, Holmes Place, a chain of health and fitness gyms, takes great pains to ensure that its clients use the facilities properly to avoid injury. All new clients are given one-to-one training on how to use different types of equipment in order to obtain the desired physical benefits without hurting themselves. Knowledgeable staff are on hand to offer advice and to check on clients' safety while the latter are working out.

Advertising and publicity can be used to make customers aware of changes in service features and delivery systems that require a different script. Sales promotion also can be used to motivate customers by offering them incentives to make the necessary changes in their behaviour. Promoting price discounts is one way to encourage self-service on an ongoing basis, particularly for retail delivery systems such as self-service petrol pumps (where the difference in price per litre compared with attendant service is often substantial). Premiums, sampling and prize promotions can also be used to encourage customers to adopt a new way of using an existing service. And, of course, well-trained customer contact personnel can provide one-to-one tutoring to help customers adapt to new procedures.

Supply and demand management

Since service performances – such as a seat on the 13:45 flight to Rome or a haircut on Tuesday morning – are time-specific and can't be produced and then stored for resale at a later date, advertising and sales promotions may help marketers shape demand to match the capacity available at any given time. As we discuss in Chapter 13, demand management strategies include reducing usage during peak demand periods and stimulating it during off-peak periods. There are many opportunities for service providers to design, advertise and deliver promotions that communicate an otherwise mundane price reduction in an exciting and attention-grabbing manner. The opportunity is greatest for services when a large gap exists between normal selling price and variable costs (for example, airline seats and hotel rooms).

This permits the firm to offer large discounts (or promotions with a sizeable monetary value) to help fill capacity that would otherwise go unused. Reduced demand outside peak periods poses a serious problem for service industries with high fixed costs, such as hotels. One strategy is to avoid reducing the list price too much and run promotions instead in an attempt to stimulate demand without using price directly as a weapon. When demand increases, the number of promotions can be reduced or eliminated.

It's easier for packaged goods firms to manage manufacturing capacity in the short run than it is for high fixed-cost services such as hotels and airlines to make substantial changes in production capacity. What's more, goods can be stockpiled for sale at a later time, while unused service capacity is often lost forever. So promotional programmes for goods are more likely to be used to encourage trial than to smooth demand – although circumstances do occur when retailers use promotions to dispose of surplus stock.

Reduced role for intermediaries

Intermediaries, such as retailers, often play a significant role in promoting products to customers and educating them in how to use them. But services are less likely than goods to be sold through channel intermediaries. Consumer goods marketers need to decide how to allocate funds between advertising, consumer promotion and trade promotion (that is, promotions designed to reward retailers who agree to stock a particular brand or model). However, service marketers who sell directly to customers – such as banks, restaurants, health clubs and professional firms – have no need for trade promotions at all.

Nevertheless, some service providers do rely on intermediaries for help in selling their products. Firms in the travel and insurance industries, which make extensive use of independent agents and brokers, must compete with other 'brands' not only for physical display space but also for 'top-of-mind' recall in order to obtain adequate push from the intermediary. The presence of intermediaries in a service marketing environment means that internal communication, personal selling, motivational promotions and effective public relations are likely to be critical in maintaining successful working relationships and partnerships between the intermediary and the service firm.

Importance of contact personnel

Because of the critical role played by service employees in enhancing customer satisfaction and building loyalty, it's important for service firms to promote incentives to their customer-contact personnel. Employee incentive programmes are often used as part of an internal marketing effort to ensure quality control in the service facility. Cash bonuses, awards, dinners, recognition programmes and eligibility for prize draws are among the many promotional incentives offered to employees for delivery of outstanding service, success in referrals to sales personnel and achievement of quality targets.

In high-contact services, employees can help implement promotional efforts. For instance, the gift premiums offered by fast-food chains and upgrades to larger or more luxurious vehicles at car rental facilities can both be delivered personally to customers at the point of sale. When customer-contact personnel are actually responsible for sales, they can be motivated and rewarded as part of an overall sales promotion programme.

Setting communication objectives

What role should communication play in helping a service firm achieve its marketing goals? Marketers need to be clear about their goals. Only then can they formulate specific communications objectives and select the most appropriate messages and communication tools to achieve these objectives. For instance, a car hire agency might define as a key objective the need to increase repeat purchase rates among business travellers. To achieve this objective, the firm might decide to implement an automatic upgrade programme and an express delivery and drop-off system. For this to work, communications will be needed to inform customers of this initiative and to educate them on how to take advantage of it. A more specific set of objectives might be: (1) create awareness of the new offering among all existing customers; (2) attract the attention of prospective customers in the business traveller segment, inform them of the new features and teach them how to use the new procedures effectively; (3) stimulate enquiries and increase pre-bookings; and (4) generate an increase in repeat patronage of (say) 20 per cent after six months.

In addition to communicating special offers, reinforcing loyalty, and encouraging repurchase, other common educational and promotional objectives for service marketers are listed in Table 11.1.

The next step is to consider which elements of the marketing communications mix will best convey the desired messages to chosen market segments. Advertising through such media as TV, newspapers, magazines and posters is usually the most visible element in a campaign, while radio is a commonly used sound medium (often too much so!). However, marketers have many other communication tools at

---

Table 11.1 ■ Common educational and promotional objectives in service settings

- Create tangible, memorable images of specific companies and their brands.
- Build awareness and interest to stimulate trial of the service.
- Teach customers how to use a service to their own best advantage.
- Communicate special strengths and benefits of a particular brand.
- Stimulate demand in low-demand periods and discouraging demand during peak periods (including information on the best times to use the service to avoid crowds).
- Counter competitive claims.
- Reduce uncertainty and the sense of risk by providing useful information and advice.
- Provide reassurance (e.g., by promoting service guarantees).
- Recognize and reward valued customers and employees.
- Reposition a service relative to the competing offerings.

their disposal, including personal selling, public relations, sales promotions and corporate design. Perhaps the most exciting new medium available to marketers is the internet, including e-mail and web sites.

Key planning considerations

Planning a marketing communications campaign must also take account of the nature of the service product, and the extent to which it is characterized by *search*, *experience* or *credence* qualities. Also important are the nature, characteristics and behaviour of the target market and audience (see Chapter 4). Managers need to determine the content, structure and style of the message to be communicated, its manner of presentation, and the media most suited to reaching the intended audience. Additional considerations include: the budget available for execution; timeframes, as defined by such factors as seasonality, market opportunities and known or predicted competitive activities; and finally, methods of measuring and evaluating performance.

A useful checklist for marketing communications planning is provided by the '5Ws' model:

- *Wh*o is our target audience?
- *Wh*at do we need to communicate and achieve?
- *Ho*w should we communicate this?
- *Wh*ere should we communicate this?
- *Wh*en do the communications need to take place?

Now let's turn to a review of the different communication tools available to service marketers.

The marketing communications mix

Most service marketers have access to numerous forms of communication, sometimes referred to collectively as the marketing communications mix. Different communication elements have different capabilities relative to the types of messages that they can convey and the market segments most likely to be exposed to them.

Communication experts draw a broad division between *personal communications* (where a representative of the service firm interacts with customers on an individual basis) and *impersonal communications* (where the service firm sends messages to an audience). In the first instance, messages are personalized and move in both directions between the two parties. In the second instance, messages move in only one direction and are generally targeted at a large market segment of customers and prospects rather than at a single individual. However, as you've probably noticed in your own role as a customer, technology has created a grey area between personal and impersonal communications. It's now very easy for a firm to combine word processing technology with information from a database to create an impression of personalization. Think about the direct mailings you receive from time to time that contain a personal salutation and perhaps some references to your specific situation or your past use of a particular product or service.

As shown in Figure 11.1, the communications mix includes a variety of strategic elements, including personal contact, advertising, publicity and public relations, sales promotion, instructional materials and corporate design. This last-mentioned element includes corporate logos, stationery, uniforms, signage and the livery (or colour scheme) used on company vehicles. In its broadest sense, corporate design may extend to many aspects of the physical evidence provided by the servicescape – the physical environment within which service is delivered.

Personal communications

Communications undertaken on a face-to-face basis (or ear-to-ear during telephone calls) embrace not only selling but also training, customer service and word-of-mouth.

Personal selling

This refers to interpersonal encounters on a face-to-face (or in telemarketing, voice-to-voice) basis in which efforts are made to educate customers and promote preference for a particular brand or product. Because face-to-face selling is usually very expensive, it is used more frequently in business-to-business markets – especially when the amounts purchased by each corporate customer are substantial. But as you know from your own experience, there is still widespread use of personal selling in consumer settings. All types of service firms, from department stores to hair salons, use personal selling strategies. For infrequently purchased services like property, insurance and funeral services, the firm's representative often plays a consulting role to help buyers determine their needs and then select from among suitable alternatives.

The direct nature of personal selling allows a sales representative or account manager to tailor the message to fit each customer's particular needs and concerns; effective teaching often benefits from one-to-one 'tutorials'. During a sales call, which may take place in person or by phone, communication flows in both directions between the marketer and the customer. The advantage for the firm is that careful listening by the sales representatives allows them to learn more about their customers. In fact, many sales training programmes place heavy emphasis on developing good listening skills. Through one-to-one dialogue, needs can be identified, questions answered and concerns addressed.

As we saw in Chapter 6, firms are increasingly aware of the importance of developing and maintaining long-term relationships with their customers and are moving away from a transaction mentality that focuses on making a quick sale. Relationship marketing strategies are often based on account management programmes, where customers are assigned to a designated account manager who acts as an intermediary between the customer and the supplier. Account management is most commonly found in industrial and professional firms. In these settings, the services are somewhat complex and customers are likely to have ongoing needs for advice and consultation (we discussed two of the supplementary services in Chapter 8). Examples of account management for individual consumers can be found in insurance, stockbroker and medical services, and even in vehicle maintenance and repair for owners of expensive cars such as Rolls Royce or Mercedes.

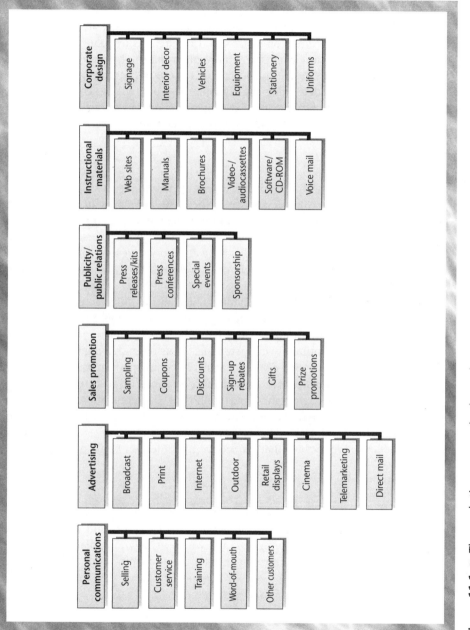

Figure 11.1 ■ The marketing communications mix

Not all service personnel who engage in selling are, in fact, professionally trained salespeople. In addition to a field sales force (which often targets its efforts at institutional customers and intermediaries rather than at individual consumers), many service personnel come into contact with customers face-to-face or by telephone. Professionals in businesses like accounting, engineering and management consulting are required to introduce new clients as well as build lasting relationships with existing ones.

On the other hand, as David Maister points out in his article, 'Why cross-selling hasn't worked' (reprinted on pages 413–15), attempts by professionals to expand relationships with existing clients are, more often than not, unsuccessful. An example of such a failure is illustrated in the case, 'Crosse & Whitewall' (pages 431–5) in which you are invited to determine exactly what has gone wrong. One prerequisite for success in cross-selling is performing at a high level on current assignments, but even that is no guarantee that clients will want to buy additional services from the firm.

Customer service

The primary responsibilities of employees in customer service positions usually entail creating and delivering the service in the customer's presence, as well as providing information, taking reservations and receiving payment, and solving problems. New customers, in particular, often rely on customer service personnel for assistance in learning how to use a service effectively and how to resolve problems. However, it is difficult for employees to provide good service if they themselves are insufficiently informed, trained and supported.

When a customer has the potential to buy several different products from the same supplier, firms often encourage their customer-contact staff to cross-sell additional services. However, these strategies may fail if not properly planned, and some employees who see their jobs primarily in operational terms resent having to act as salespeople. In the banking industry, for example, a highly competitive marketplace and new technologies have forced banks to add more services in an attempt to increase their profitability. Bank clerks, who have traditionally been operations-oriented in providing service, have been asked to promote new services to their customers. Despite training, many feel uncomfortable in this role and are not effective as salespeople. For an in-depth illustration of this situation, see the case 'Menton Bank' on pages 426–30.

Training

Many companies, especially those selling corporate services, offer training courses to managers and employees (and sometimes to customers and suppliers as well). The purpose of customer training sessions (which usually take place post-purchase) is to familiarize users with the product's potential and train them in how to use the service to best advantage.

Word-of-mouth

The comments and recommendations that customers make about their service experiences can have a powerful influence on other people's decisions. So it's realistic to classify what is often called 'word-of-mouth' as a form of marketing communication. Strictly speaking, it is not advertising, because it's not usually paid for – although customers and other influential parties *are* sometimes offered incentives to promote a particular product or company.

Positive word-of-mouth can act as a powerful and highly credible selling agent. Whose recommendations are you most likely to accept: a trusted friend's or a professional salesperson's? At the same time, experienced customers can also be useful in helping inexperienced fellow-customers and teaching them how to use a service. Conversely, negative word-of-mouth can be extremely damaging and can serve to de-market a company and its service offerings. The most appropriate way to think of unpaid word-of-mouth is as a form of publicity that marketers seek to cultivate and shape so that it becomes an effective supplement to other communication activities.

Advertising

Advertising tends to be the most dominant form of communication in consumer marketing and is often the first point of contact between service marketers and their customers. A broad array of paid advertising media is available, including broadcast (TV and radio), print (magazines and newspapers) and many types of outdoor media (posters, hoardings, electronic message boards and the exteriors of vehicles such as buses). The low-cost Irish airline Ryanair has even announced its intention to transform its 20 aircraft into flying billboards, featuring advertisements for products ranging from Kilkenny beer to Jaguar cars.[4]

Some media are more focused than others. Newspapers and television, for instance, tend to reach mass audiences (although research can identify who reads what sections of a newspaper or watches specific programmes). Cinemas, a popular advertising medium, also reach a broad audience. Magazines and radio, by contrast, are usually a more focused medium since most have relatively well-targeted audiences. Advertising in the mass media, such as radio, TV, newspapers and magazines, can be supplemented by brochures delivered through intermediaries or by direct marketing through the post, telephone calls ('telemarketing'), fax or e-mail. As we saw with the opening illustration of Dolland & Aitchison, exciting new opportunities now exist to disseminate information through the internet and World Wide Web. More and more companies are establishing web sites as an information resource for customers and prospects.

Direct marketing, which includes both direct mail and telemarketing, offers the potential to send personalized messages to highly targeted micro-segments, including one-to-one communications. As noted earlier, this form of communication is most likely to be successful when marketers possess detailed information about customers and prospects. E-mail is growing as a direct advertising medium, although many e-mail address lists are still very unfocused. The problem lies with companies that sell inexpensive e-mail address lists containing millions of names. Some advertisers, often promoting very dubious personal services, purchase these lists and then 'spam' millions of prospects with unwanted junk e-mail.

Another form of advertising, often linked to sales promotion, consists of retail displays in store windows. Sophisticated web sites are beginning to replicate retail storefronts with attractive displays in cyberspace, although the time required to download the images often gets in the way of effective communication. Later in this chapter, we'll discuss how service marketers can use the internet most effectively.

In a service setting, advertising is most commonly used to create awareness and stimulate interest in the service offering, to educate customers about service features and applications, to establish or redefine a competitive position, to reduce risk and to help make the intangible tangible. Advertising plays an especially vital role in providing factual information about services and educating customers about product features and capabilities. To demonstrate this role, Grove, Pickett and Laband carried out a study comparing newspaper and television advertising for goods and services.[5] Based on a review of 11,543 television advertisements over a ten-month period and of 30,940 newspaper display adverts that appeared over a twelve-month period, they found that advertisements for services were significantly more likely than those for goods to contain factual information on the following four dimensions: price; guarantees/warranties; documentation of performance; and availability (where, when and how to acquire products). Consumers may rely more on information provided by adverising for services because they lack the ability to use search qualities – and thus their own evaluations based on tangible product attributes – as effectively as they can for goods.

Publicity and public relations

Public relations (PR) involves efforts to stimulate positive interest in an organization and its products and services by sending out news releases, holding press conferences, staging special events and sponsoring newsworthy activities put on by third parties.

A basic element in public relations strategy is the preparation and distribution of press releases (including photos and sometimes videos) featuring stories about the company, specific services and its employees. PR executives also arrange press conferences and distribute press kits when they feel that the story is especially newsworthy. However, unlike paid advertising, there is no guarantee that such stories will appear in the media; and if they do, they may not appear in the positive form desired by the company's PR department (or the outside PR agency retained by the firm). Good relationships with journalists and other media specialists are important in building a receptive climate for press releases. A reputation for openness and honesty is vital when something negative happens – an accident, injuries to customers or employees or market rejection of a new service initiative, for example. Because of this, one of the key tasks that PR specialists perform involves teaching senior managers how to present themselves well at news conferences or in radio and television interviews.

Among other widely used PR techniques are recognition and reward programmes, obtaining testimonials from public figures, community involvement and support, fundraising and obtaining favourable publicity for the organization through special events and *pro bono* work. In this way an organization builds its reputation and credibility, forms strong relationships with its employees, customers and the community of which it is a part, and secures an image conducive to business success. Firms can also win wide exposure through sponsorship of sporting events and other high-profile activities. Sydney, Australia's role in hosting the summer Olympic Games in 2000 has created numerous opportunities for companies to sponsor different activities, not only during the Olympics themselves, but also during the pre-competition period when interest and excitement are building for the event.

Sales promotion

A few years ago, SAS International Hotels devised an interesting promotion targeted at older customers. If a hotel had vacant rooms, guests over 65 years of age could get a discount equivalent to their years – thus, a 75-year-old could save 75 per cent of the standard room price. All went well until a Swedish guest checked into one of the SAS chain's hotels in Vienna, announced his age as 102, and asked to be paid 2 per cent of the room rate in return for staying the night. This request was duly granted, whereupon the spry centenarian challenged the general manager to a game of tennis – and obtained that, too (the results of the game, however, were not disclosed). Events such as these are the stuff of dreams for PR people. In this case, a clever promotion yields a humorous, widely reported story that places the marketing organization in a favourable light.

A useful way of looking at sales promotions is as a communication attached to an incentive. Sales promotions are usually specific to a time period, price or customer group – sometimes all three, as in the SAS example. Typically, the objective is to accelerate the purchasing decision, or to motivate customers to use a specific service sooner, in greater volume with each purchase, or more frequently.

Sales promotions for service firms may take such forms as samples, coupons and other discounts, gifts and competitions with prizes. Used in these forms, sales promotion serves to add value, provide a competitive edge, boost sales during periods when demand would otherwise be weak, speed the introduction and acceptance of new services, and generally get customers to act faster than they would in the absence of any promotional incentive.[6]

Short-term price promotions can offer marketers the following advantages, which are not available through other marketing tools:[7]

- Since promotional costs vary with volume, price promotions are a good weapon for small companies to use in challenging large competitors.

- Promotions reduce the risk of first-time purchase for customers and thus encourage trial.

- Different segments can be charged different prices for the same service when one group receives a promotional discount and the other doesn't.

- Promotions can add excitement to mundane repetitive purchases and appeal to price-conscious consumers.

- Price promotions are particularly useful for adjusting demand and supply fluctuations.

Sales promotions can take many forms. At least six methods are available to service marketers, including samples, coupons, enrolment rebates, entitlement to future discounts, gift premiums and prize promotions.[8] Let's look briefly at each in turn.

Sampling gives customers a chance to learn more about a service by trying it free of charge. For instance, a credit card company may offer cardholders a free one-month trial of a credit card protection service; public transport services offer free rides for a day or two on a newly opened route; or hotels give guests free 15-minute previews of newly released films that are available on its internal pay-TV system. Sampling, however, is used less frequently for services than for consumer package goods. Service marketers usually prefer to offer price discounts or other promotions rather than give away the service for free.

Coupons usually take one of three forms: a straight price cut; a discount or fee waiver for one or more patrons accompanying the original purchaser; or a free or discounted enhancement of the basic service (such as free waxing with each car wash). Traditionally, coupons were printed in newspapers and magazines or sent by direct mail. Today, however, they are often sold in books which provide purchasers with the opportunity to use the services of a wide array of restaurants and cafés, laundry and dry cleaning establishments, garages, cinemas and other suppliers. With the advent of electronic scanning in shops, many of these promotional offers are now implemented electronically.

Short-term discounts are price cuts that are promoted as being available for only a limited time period, such as any form of 'sale' designed to boost business during slack periods. Another example is 'charter memberships' in health and fitness clubs which are sold at decreasing rates of discount prior to opening the club; such strategies help to build a base of customers quickly and improve initial cash flow.

Sign-up rebates may be offered by 'membership' service organizations that charge a preliminary sign-up fee for applying, joining or making connections to a network. Examples include application fees for education institutions, joining fees at many private clubs and installation fees for connections to pay TV systems. To attract new members or subscribers, these fees may be waived or alternatively credited towards payment of future usage fees.

Gift premiums can add a tangible element to services and provide a distinctive image for sponsoring organizations. For instance, some international airlines have used a strategy of providing passengers in first and business classes with a range of free gifts including toiletries, pens, stationery and playing cards. Similarly, to encourage customers (who may hold several credit cards) either to increase their credit purchases or consolidate their charges to a single account, banks and credit card companies have experimented with promotions offering prizes to customers who charged more than specified amounts over a given period. Sometimes, however, gifts are offered simply to amuse customers and create a friendly environment. The Conrad Hotel in Hong Kong places a small teddy bear on each guest's bed and a yellow rubber duck in the bathroom; it reports that many guests take these items home with them.

Prize promotions introduce an element of chance, like a lottery or sweepstakes. They can be used effectively to add involvement and excitement to the service experience and are generally designed to encourage increased use of the service. Fast-food restaurants, video rental outlets and service stations sometimes offer lottery-like promotions tied to special events giving all purchasers tickets with scratch-off award categories. Radio stations may offer listeners the chance to claim instant cash and other prizes if they call within a prescribed time after the announcement is broadcast.

Instructional materials

Promotion and education often go hand in hand. There is little point in promoting a new service – or service feature – if people are unsure of the benefits or don't know how to proceed. Although service personnel are often called on to play teaching roles, they are not always available to help in the locations where customers need them. Traditional approaches use printed materials, ranging from brochures and instruction manuals to step-by-step instructions and diagrams affixed to self-service machines (have a look at a pay-phone, ATM or ticket machine the next time you use one). But in recent years, video and audio instructions have also come to the fore. Supermarkets and department stores sometimes feature a touch-screen store directory. Some banks have video terminals in the lobby where customers can learn about new financial products. Airlines play videos to illustrate aircraft safety procedures and make customers aware of government regulations. The latest instructional media take the form of CD-ROMs and web sites, which are described in the later section on new technologies.

Free telephone calls to specialized information lines are another way in which organizations can help to educate their customers. Consider the 'Health Information Line' offered by PPP Healthcare, the second largest provider of health care insurance in the UK. Members and subscribers can call the company's free 0800 number at any time, 24 hours a day. As stated in the company's advertising literature:

> Whether you need information or just reassurance, there is somebody here to help you. Our Health Information Line. A friendly voice – even in the middle of the night.
>
> You can call our team of registered nurses, midwives, and pharmacists at any time. There's no charge for the call and they're on duty 24 hours a day, 365 days a year. It could be, for example, that your child has woken with a fever on Christmas Day and you're not sure whether or not to call out the doctor. Or perhaps the chemist is shut and you forgot to ask a question about your prescription. Or maybe somebody in your family has been diagnosed with a serious illness and you want to know how to help. No answer is too trivial, too personal or too technical. You can also use our Health Information Line to request free Fact Sheets on a wide variety of topics – all written in plain, clear English.

Corporate design

Many companies have come to appreciate the importance of creating a unified and distinctive visual appearance for all tangible elements that contribute to the corporate image. Corporate design strategies are usually created by external consulting firms and include such features as stationery and promotional literature, retail signage, uniforms and colour schemes for painting vehicles, equipment and building interiors. These elements are created by using distinctive colours, symbols, lettering and layout to provide a unifying and recognizable theme linking all the firm's operations in a branded service experience.

Corporate design is particularly important for companies operating in fiercely competitive markets where the challenge is to stand out from the crowd and to be instantly recognizable in different locations. The highly competitive business of petrol stations provides striking contrasts in corporate designs, from the bright green and yellow stations displaying the BP shield to Esso's red and white.

Many companies use a trademarked symbol, rather than a name, as their primary logo. Shell, for instance, makes a pun of its English name by displaying a yellow scallop shell on a red background, which has the advantage of making its vehicles and petrol stations instantly recognizable even in parts of the world that do not use the roman alphabet. McDonald's 'Golden Arches' is said to be the most widely recognized corporate symbol in the world. Early restaurant designs featured an enormous arch, but today local zoning laws often restrict how this symbol may be displayed on exterior signage. Consistent corporate design for the chain also extends to the style of lettering used, certain aspects of store appearance and the design and colours of employees' uniforms.

International companies need to select their designs with extra care to minimize the risk of conveying a culturally inappropriate message in some countries through an unfortunate choice of colour or images. How easy to recognize are the facilities, vehicles and personnel of your own bank, favourite fast-food restaurant, taxi service and local public transport system? Try the quiz in the boxed insert to see how many internationally used symbols and design elements you recognize.

Can you recognize a service company from these clues?

1. With which three car rental companies are the colours yellow, red and green associated?
2. Which international airline has a flying kanga-roo for its symbol? And which, a maple leaf?
3. Which stockbroker displays a bull as its corporate symbol?

4. How many companies can you name that use a globe-like symbol?
5. Which international bank displays a four-pointed star?

The answers can be found towards the end of the chapter, on page 390.

Servicescape design

As noted in Chapter 9, the term servicescape describes the design of any physical location where customers come to place orders and obtain service delivery.[9] It consists of four dimensions: the physical facility; the location; ambient conditions (temperature or lighting, etc.) and interpersonal conditions. Each of these elements is critical, since the appearance of a firm's service facilities and personnel affect both communication and image building. Corporate design consultants are sometimes asked to advise on servicescape design, especially the visual elements of both interiors and exteriors – such as signage, decor, carpeting and furnishings – in order that they may complement and reinforce the other design elements.

Consider what conclusions you might draw about a car rental firm's service if, on arriving to rent a car, you encountered a smart-looking building with attractive signage, but on entering you noticed in the harsh neon light that the office was small and cramped, the paintwork peeling and clashing in colour with the faded carpet, the signage hand-lettered, the desk and furnishings in contrasting styles, and the agent wearing a smart uniform shirt tucked into dirty jeans? We can think of the servicescape concept in terms of the design of the stage on which the service drama is enacted. A good set and costumes can't save a bad play, but they can greatly enhance the audience's enjoyment of a good one. Conversely, a bad stage-set can create a poor initial impression that is hard to overcome.

Integrated communications for service marketing

In a service setting, marketing communications tools are especially important because they serve to create powerful images and a sense of credibility, confidence and reassurance. Through the use of brand names, unified and recognizable corporate design elements and well-executed servicescapes, companies can give visibility and personality to their intangible service offerings.

Each of the different communication elements described above is a potentially powerful tool that can be used to create and promote a distinctive corporate, brand or product identity, communicate with current and prospective customers, and sell specific products. Marketing communications, in one form or another, are essential to a company's success. Without effective communications, prospects may never learn of a service firm's existence, what it has to offer them or how to use its products to best advantage. Customers might be more easily lured away by competitors and competitive offerings, and there would be no proactive management and control of the firm's identity.

A key task for service marketers is to select the most appropriate mix of communication elements to convey the desired messages efficiently and effectively to the target audience. In well-planned campaigns, several different communication elements may be used in ways that mutually reinforce each other. Sequencing of different communications activities is often important, since one element may pave the way for others. For example, advertising may encourage prospects to request further information by mail, or draw them to a retail site where they may then be exposed to retail displays or interact directly with a salesperson.

Impact of new technologies on marketing communication

As we mentioned earlier in this chapter, the internet and the World Wide Web are becoming increasingly important marketing communications tools. Users of personal computers around the world are spending more and more time online and less time watching TV or reading printed material. By late 1997, internet users in the United States were spending about 13–14 hours online a week – double the amount of time spent just one year previously.[10] Subscriptions and usage in other countries are increasing rapidly.

Marketers have grasped the importance of this development and are rushing to establish a presence on the Web. Advertising expenditures on the internet are expected to grow rapidly, with English-speaking countries leading the way. In many instances, one company's web site may include advertising messages from other marketers with related but non-competing services – take a look, for instance, at Yahoo.com's stock quotes page, which features a sequence of advertisements for a variety of financial service firms. Similarly, many internet pages dealing with specific topics feature a small message from Amazon.com which invites consumers to see what books are available on this very topic by clicking the accompanying hyperlink button to visit the book retailer's site. Forrester Research predicts that spending on internet advertising will reach $15 billion (€12.5 billion) by the year 2003, with 70 per cent of this expenditure taking place in the US. Europe, however, is expected to see the fastest rate of growth, with internet advertising projected to rise from $105 million (€87 million) in 1998 to $2.8 billion (€2.3 billion) by 2003.[11]

Advertisers are using their web sites for a variety of communications tasks, including: promoting consumer awareness and interest; providing information and consultation; stimulating product trial and sales; and facilitating personal communications with customers. Many companies have found that the interactive nature of the internet increases customer involvement dramatically since it is actually a form of 'self-service' marketing where customers are in complete control of the time and extent of contact with the web sites they visit. This can also be useful for self-paced learning, in instances where the site content of interest is educational in nature.

Designing an internet communications strategy

The ability to communicate and establish a rapport with individual customers is one of the Web's greatest strengths. For this reason, the internet is fast becoming almost as common in business-to-business marketing as business cards and fax machines. Marketing through the Web allows companies to supplement conventional communications channels at a very reasonable cost.[12] But like any of the elements of the marketing communications mix, internet advertising should be part of an integrated, well-designed communications strategy. The '5W's' model of communications planning presented earlier in the chapter can provide useful guidelines for marketing on the Web.[13] Let's take a brief look at each element of the model in the context of internet marketing.

Who

Marketers need to consider what target markets they want to reach and whether or not they have access to the Web. A key question for marketing managers is whether or not the demographics of these internet users match those of a firm's target market segment. If so, it should definitely consider maintaining a web site. While most marketers depend on their customers to access web sites from home or work, a few enterprising firms bring the internet to customers, through strategies ranging from so-called 'cyber-cafés' to locating high-tech kiosks in airport frequent-flyer lounges and hotel business centres.[14]

What

A web site should contain information that a company's target market will find useful and interesting. It should also stimulate product purchase and encourage repeat visits. While internet users rank content as the most important factor affecting their decision to return to a web site (they are actually annoyed by sites – and companies – which waste their time with 'frivolous content'), they also want the experience to be 'enjoyable' (either because they found the information they wanted or because the site was unique or entertaining).[15] Companies that do business internationally should be especially careful to investigate the legal, logistical and cultural implications of their web sites in order to avoid damaging their image among global customers. They need to remember that once they establish an internet presence, their site is available world-wide to anyone with web access.[16]

When

A web site is a very dynamic medium, and visitors expect it to be updated regularly or they soon lose interest in returning. Unlike pamphlets and brochures, which may only be redesigned once a year, a web presence must be constantly maintained and upgraded. As internet technology evolves, web sites are becoming increasingly sophisticated. Many companies constantly add new content, attractive graphics and photographs, and interactive capabilities or animation to make their sites attractive to both first-time and repeat visitors.[17] Web sites should probably be updated once every four months, even if it means no more than changing the appearance of the site cosmetically by using a different layout or new illustrations. Remember that it's very easy for customers to compare competitors' offerings on the internet – that information is literally at their fingertips! For example, customers who are shopping for a specific product on-line can browse the web sites of competing retailers in a matter of minutes before making a decision about where to 'shop'.[18]

Where

Firms need to actively promote their web sites to existing and potential customers. Web addresses should be kept simple. They should be displayed everywhere the company name appears including: business cards, brochures, advertisements, trade show entries, catalogues, Yellow Pages and promotional items. Some firms use a direct mail approach by sending out postcards with their web addresses along with an incentive for customers to visit the site. Web addresses are becoming common features of our daily lives. Just think of how many times a day you see them – on television, in newspapers and magazines, and even on the menu of your favourite take-away restaurant!

Why

Companies must provide reasons for people to visit – and revisit – their web sites. They might use their sites to provide valuable information that isn't available anywhere else, like a description of a new technological breakthrough that could save customers time and money, or a comparison of different options for corrective eye surgery.

Transport firms, from airlines to railways, offer interactive sites that enable travellers to evaluate alternative routes and schedules for specific dates, download printed information and make reservations on-line. Some sites offer discounts on hotels and airfare if reservations are made over the internet. Many banks now have interactive sites that allow customers to pay bills electronically, apply for loans and check their account balances. And a web-based business called Home Debut, which allows house buyers to look for a new home online, also provides information about specific neighbourhoods and links to school districts, day care, restaurants and health care providers.[19] Whistler/Blackholm ski resort in British Columbia uses its web site to promote advance on-line purchase of lift tickets at a discount. It then provides instructions on how the on-line ticket window works and where to pick up the tickets, plus responses to frequently asked questions.

Conclusion

Many different communication elements are available to service marketers as they seek to create a distinctive position in the market for both their firm and its products and to reach prospective customers. The options include paid advertising, personal selling and customer service, sales promotions, public relations and corporate design and the evidence offered by the servicescape of the service delivery site. Informational materials, from brochures to web sites, often play an important role in educating customers in how to make good choices and obtain the best use from the services they have purchased.

Some of the distinctive characteristics of services suggest that a different approach is needed to marketing communications strategy than is used to market goods. Advertising, for instance, may provide much needed tangible clues to service quality and performance without raising expectations unrealistically. And internal as well as external public relations management is critical in ensuring sound and enduring relationships, credibility and goodwill. Public relations activities, and the proactive generation of publicity and positive word-of-mouth, should be regarded as a valuable long-term investment necessary to building a service firm's reputation and place within a community.

Marketing communication strategies must, of course, be integrated with strategic decisions related to the other elements of integrated service management (the '8Ps'). To the extent that new technologies enable firms to craft new strategies – especially in areas such as service design, electronic delivery systems, and plans to improve productivity and quality – managers need to consider how to rethink delivery of communication elements, too. The article by Shikhar Ghosh, 'Making business sense of the internet' (reprinted on pages 416–25), is particularly helpful for showing the linkages between electronic communications and electronic delivery of information-based services.

Answers to symbol quiz on page 386

1. Hertz (yellow), Avis (red), Europcar (green).
2. Qantas (kangaroo), Air Canada (maple leaf). Note: some regional Canadian airlines also display a maple leaf.
3. Merrill Lynch (bull).
4. AT&T, Cable & Wireless are both quite well known; aircraft of Continental Airlines have a partial golden globe on their tailfins, while those of the now-defunct airline PanAm featured a complete blue and white globe. (There are others; UPS now paints a golden globe on all its lorries to emphasize its worldwide delivery capabilities.)
5. Citibank (also its parent, Citicorp).

Study questions

1. What roles do personal selling, advertising and public relations play in (a) attracting new customers to a service business, and (b) retaining existing customers?

2. Contrast the relative effectiveness of brochures and web sites for promoting (a) a ski resort, (b) a hotel, (c) the services of a consulting firm, and (d) a full-service stockbroker.

3. In what ways do the physical aspects of a servicescape 'communicate'?

4. Consider each of the following scenarios; determine which elements of the marketing communications mix you would employ and for what purposes. State your reasons.

   (a) A newly established hairdresser's in a suburban shopping centre.

   (b) An established restaurant facing declining patronage due to the arrival of new competitors.

   (c) A large, single-office accounting firm doing business in a major city and serving primarily business clients.

5. For which categories of services are customers at greatest risk when a firm makes advertising claims that it knows to be fraudulent? What types of customers are most likely to be hurt?

6. What are some common educational and promotional objectives in service settings? Provide a specific example for each of the objectives you list.

7. Describe the role of personal selling in service communications. Give an example of a situation where you have encountered this approach.

8. Provide several current examples of public relations efforts made by service companies.

9. Discuss the different types of sales promotions when each might be used. Find examples of several promotional efforts and explain whether or not they are effective communication tools.

10. Locate a web site for a service provider. What do you think the firm's communications objectives for the site are – and are they being achieved? Would you change anything about the site?

Notes

1. Based on information contained in the Dolland & Aitchison web site, www.danda.co.uk, August 1998.
2. Louis Fabien, 'Making Promises: The Power of Engagement', *Journal of Services Marketing*, Vol. 11, No. 3, 1997, pp. 206–14.
3. William R. George and Leonard L. Berry, 'Guidelines for the Advertising of Services', *Business Horizons*, July–August 1981.
4. Kieran Cooke, 'Giant Billboards in the Skies', *Financial Times*, 16 March 1998, p. 14.
5. Stephen J. Grove, Gregory M. Pickett and David N. Laband, 'An Empirical Examination of Factual Information Content among Service Advertisements', *The Service Industries Journal*, Vol. 15, April 1995, pp. 216–33.
6. Ken Peattie and Sue Peattie, 'Sales Promotion – a Missed Opportunity for Service Marketers', *International Journal of Service Industry Management*, Vol. 5, No. 1, 1995, pp. 6–21.
7. Paul W. Farris and John A. Quelch, 'In Defense of Price Promotion', *Sloan Management Review*, Fall 1987, pp. 63–9.
8. Christopher H. Lovelock and John A. Quelch, 'Consumer Promotions in Service Marketing', *Business Horizons*, May–June 1983.
9. Mary Jo Bitner, 'Servicescapes: The Impact of Physical Surrondings on Customers and Employees', *Journal of Marketing*, Vol. 56, April 1992, pp. 57–71.
10. From an online article by Leslie Adler titled 'Internet Becomes Increasingly Important Ad Medium', *Yahoo! Reuters News*, 20 October, 1997.

11. 'Global online ad spending $15 billion by 2003 – report', *Yahoo! Reuters News*, 20 August 1998.
12. Kenneth Leung, 'Keep This in Mind About Internet Marketing', *Marketing News*, 23 June 1997, p. 7.
13. J.D. Mosley-Matchett, 'Include the Internet in Marketing Mix', *Marketing News*, 24 November 1997, p. 6.
14. Cyndee Miller, 'New Services For Consumers Without Home Page at Home', *Marketing News*, 22 April 1996, p. 1.
15. Marshall Rice, 'What Makes Users Revisit a Web Site?', *Marketing News*, 17 March 1997, p. 12.
16. J.D. Mosley-Matchett, 'Remember: It's the *World* Wide Web', *Marketing News*, 20 January 1997, p. 16.
17. Sharon McDonnell, 'For Older Sites, Time for Makeover', *The New York Times Cybertimes*, 12 January 1997.
18. Patrick M. Reilly, 'Booksellers Prepare to Do Battle in Cyberspace', *Wall Street Journal*, 28 January 1997.
19. 'It's Called Shopping for Homes from Home', *Marketing News*, 14 April 1997, p. 12.

Redefining value

Sandra Vandermerwe

Companies need to redefine value in terms which reflect specific improvements for customers. Value is not what goes into products or services, but what customers get out of them over a period of time.

In my book, *From Tin Soldiers to Russian Dolls*, I wrote about tribal folk describing objects in term of what function they serve rather than what they 'are'.[1]

A tree, for example, is described by them as a source of nourishment and protection. A room where people work and live. A bowl holds liquid while the carved rim encircling the bowl decorates.

In other words, each part is described by what it does – i.e. the 'verb' rather than the 'noun'.

Talking verbs not nouns

There is nothing quite so effective as getting people within a corporation to start talking 'verbs' instead of 'nouns', in order to show the difference between what they are selling and what customers are buying.

Thinking and discussion soon go off the 'products', i.e. loans, PCs, insurance policies, copiers, pesticides – and on to the market.

People begin to see the obvious: nouns soon become commodities. Whereas it is the verbs that carry the code for discovering and delivering customer value add.

From this comes the mission.

Table 1 gives some examples.

Ironically one of the most serious drawbacks of sticking to the nouns and defining a corporation in these terms is that it can seriously limit product innovation.

Had the telephone utilities of yesteryear thought in terms of 'mobile communications', 'office liberation', 'mobility' or independence' for say, emerging virtual sales teams, they may not have allowed the now successful Nokia – then an obscure Finnish company – to take hold of the alternative office 'market space' through cellular phone technology.

Had they become masters at connecting people, instead of just lines and cables, they may have asked: Do managers need phones anyway? and thus got themselves into alternative solutions ahead of others in the information networking highway battle.

Of the global appliance industry, David Whitwam of Whirlpool explains that thinking has been so narrowly focused on the machines instead of the fabric care that there has been little radical improvement in appliances in the last 30 years.

He describes their strategy now as:

> Going beyond traditional product definitions we are now studying consumer behaviour from the time people take off their dirty clothes at night until they've been cleaned and ironed and hung in the closet. What are we looking for? The worst part of the process is not the washing or drying. The hard part is when you take your clothes out of the dryer and you have to do something with them – iron, fold, hang them up. Whoever comes up with a product to make this part of the process easier, simpler or quicker is going to create an incredible market.

What the telecommunications and appliance examples show is the growing awareness that new corporations need to redefine value in terms which reflect improvements for customers, instead of only for the products or services.

Reprinted from *The Eleventh Commandment: Transforming to 'own' customers* (Chichester: John Wiley & Sons). Copyright © 1996 by Sandra Vandermerwe.

Table 1 ■ Comparing the 'nouns' to the 'verbs'

The 'nouns'	The 'verbs'
AT&T Lines and phones	Communications/Connectability
Baxter Healthcare (USA) Drugs and medical equipment	Patient healing and comfort
Ciba Geigy Agrochemicals	Safe crop protection
Citiback (Consumer) Loans, credit cards	Total (global) banking experience
Oticon Electronic hearing aids	Lifelong hearing
DuPont Carpet fibre	Enhanced floor covering
Matsushita Home electronics	Human electronics
Nokia Cellular phones	Mobile communications/Freedom/Mobility/Independence
Rank Xerox Photocopiers	Document management
SKF Bearings	Trouble-free operations
Whirlpool Washing machines	Total fabric care
Zurich Insurance Insurance policies	Risk management/Asset protection

Consider these examples.

Matsushita Acoustics and Japanese customers

Matsushita found that a large proportion of its Japanese customers were getting inferior listening performance from their increasingly superior video and TV products.

Why?

They were buying machines that were too big for the size of their rooms; they were not maintaining them well enough; and incompatibility between curtaining and carpet fabrics and acoustic technology adversely affected the sound quality.

Lubricants for utility supplier customers

Despite buying good lubricants, Northumbrian Water was spending lots of money on downtime delays, shortened life of machines and time wasted because its engineers were having difficulty lubricating the pumps needed to move water supply and sewage. (Did you know that 70 per cent of all machine failures in the UK are due to poor lubrication?)

Here were some of the reasons engineers gave: machine suppliers put oil into the pumps, which could not always be mixed with other lubricants in stock; tins were difficult to open with consequent mess and wastage; difficulty was experienced getting oil out of cans into pumps, and dirt in cans led to contamination.

Ciba Geigy's pesticides for US farmer customers

Ciba farmer customers in parts of the US were buying the best chemicals that machines could make for weeds and pest elimination. But while pesticides got rid of the bugs farmers were not necessarily getting a safe crop. Other plants were being affected by the pesticides which killed off the next season's production.

Bally Suisse shoe customers

Bally, the international shoe company, was one of those which had waited until their performance had begun to stagnate before taking the leap.

When Stephano Ferro came to Bally in 1992 he found a company still faithfully following a culture based on making and selling shoes.

What customers had been getting were products that bore testimony to the long-time skill of the shoe craftsman.

What Ferro had to do was radically change the firm so that customers got the look, feel and wear they wanted, to get the results over the lifetime of the shoes – what he called 'total footware performance'.

Hypotheses for customer 'ownership'

What this amounts to is the following.

From a customer's point of view, value is not what goes into products or services.

Value is what customers *get out*.

They get this value out *over a period of time*, rather than at a point in time.

What we should have done in the past to better describe economic value was to look at the proper utilization of products and services.

Productivity would then have been a measure of the improved and increased value customers received, instead of the number and cost of making and selling extra units.

This leads to at least two hypotheses for customer 'ownership':

1. You can put as much *into* a product or service – if customers don't get the value out you will never make them lifelong investments.

And following from that:

2. Increasingly, a firm's ability to 'own' a set of customers depends on its ability get value *out* of products and services for customers, rather than just put and sell more improved versions of them.

Note

1. Sandra Vandermerwe, *From Tin Soldiers to Russian Dolls: Creating Added Value through Services*, Oxford: Butterworth-Heinemann Ltd, 1993.

Key concepts for new service development

Bo Edvardsson ■ *Jan Olsson*

This article presents a new frame of reference for new service development based on empirical studies in Sweden. It argues that the main task of service development is to create the right generic prerequisites for the service. This means an efficient customer process, adapted to the logic of the customer's behaviour and a good customer outcome, i.e., the service is associated with quality. It distinguishes three main types of development: the development of the service concept, the development of the service system (resource structure) and the development of the service process.

Background and aim

Many people see quality as the most important means of competition and a prerequisite for satisfied customers and profitability (Edvardsson and Thomasson, 1991). Although services play a predominant role as regards GDP and employment in the OECD countries, we know very little about quality management of service operations. We know less about quality in service companies than in manufacturing companies (Gummesson, 1991). Our knowledge of quality in services needs to be expanded, both through academic research and through action learning.

Many quality problems are recurrent and may to a great extent be seen as the result of shortcomings in the development of new services (Edvardsson, 1992; Juran, 1992). The service is not designed correctly – quality problems are built in (Gummesson, 1988). Crosby (1989) maintains that 70–90 per cent of all quality problems are recurrent and are built into internal service processes. The corresponding figure for manufacturing companies is 92 per cent, according to Juran (1992).

This article deals with service development strategy from a quality perspective. Our point of departure is that one of the major tasks in developing new services is to build in the right quality from the start.

Our aim is to present a frame of reference for strategic service development with the emphasis on how to build in the right quality from the start. The frame of reference has emerged by degrees from a number of studies within the Service Research Centre (see, for instance, Norling et al. (1992) and from a pilot study in Swedish Telecom's Corporate Quality Group (Edvardsson and Olsson, 1992)). The paper is primarily based on this study. The frame of reference is also being tested in a NUTEK project where we are studying the development of a number of services, such as X2000, Teleguide, 'smart card' services, the job vacancy computer system at AMS offices and Samhall's cleaning concept.

We begin by defining what we mean by customer, quality and service. This leads us on to a discussion of the concept of service development and how to illustrate the results of a service development process. If we can clearly describe the desired results of service development, this will make it easier to ensure that the right quality is built in from the start.

Customer and customer orientation

For us, the customer is the person or organization receiving the outcome of the operation (ISO, 1991). The added value and quality of the service is realized with the customer and is interpreted/perceived by him. Without customers there would be no income and thus no business. The main task of service development is to create the prerequisites for services which the customer perceives have an attractive added value. This presupposes that the company has a thorough understanding of the customer's needs and expectations.

Reprinted from *The Service Industries Journal*, Vol. 16, No. 2, April 1996, pp. 140–64.

Many service markets are being deregulated and competition is increasing. This means that customers are being offered a greater number of options. Customers who are not satisfied with their suppliers – because their needs, wishes and expectations have not been reasonably satisfied – are finding it increasingly easy to change suppliers.

Let us clarify what we mean by needs, wishes and expectations. Needs are basic. Different customers look to satisfy their needs in different ways. Wishes refer to the way in which the customer wants to satisfy a specific need. However, it is not possible for him to satisfy all his wishes since, for instance, he may lack the financial means. In our discussion we use the term demand for those wishes for which the customer has purchasing power.

Expectation is an important concept in connection with service development. Expectation is linked with a phenomenon or object, a specific service or a certain company. Expectation is based on the customer's needs and wishes but it is also influenced, often to a considerable extent, by the company's image or reputation on the market, the customer's previous experience of the service company, the service company's marketing, and so on. In other words, expectation is not linked to the subject, i.e., the customer, or to the object, i.e., the service or service company, but to the interaction between object and subject. Expectation changes over time as a result of changes in customers' wishes. The explanation lies in the fact that object and subject have changed. They are dialectically related.

To understand customers' needs and wishes properly, it is appropriate and often necessary to involve customers in the process of developing new services. Attractive and customer-friendly services emerge from a dialogue with competent and demanding customers. We believe it is very important to have close contact with the customer when developing new services. This requires us to include customers in service development projects, to set up a meaningful dialogue with customers and to make it easier for them to articulate their needs, requirements and wishes. The various value-loaded activities in the service are defined in the dialogue with the customer. We believe that this customer-active paradigm, i.e., working interactively with customers, is to be preferred when formulating and testing the service concept and developing service processes. The direct and active involvement of customers is becoming increasingly common in the development of high technological products but also in the automobile industry, for example at Honda. In our view, a dialogue with customers when developing services is even more natural and urgent.

Services, we maintain, are produced by means of a process, which may be described in various ways, for instance, in the form of internal services to internal customers in a series of steps. The result is an external service to customers on the market. Relations within the company should be seen in the same way as external relations, that is, even within the company there are customers with needs, wishes and expectations, hence the term internal customer. The whole chain of customer relations must be organized; each activity is important if the result is to be a service of the right quality.

Since quality is realized in the service encounter and the customer is the ultimate judge of the service, customer orientation should be a central point of departure for all service development. This means placing the customer in the centre but not being governed in all respects by the customer and what he says. It is important to understand and respect the customer's needs, wishes and requirements but not to follow them slavishly. The customer-oriented service company has insight into the customer's assessment criteria and acts on them. It is also fully aware of the conditions prevailing at the customers' place of business. What is important is that there is a trustful and open dialogue between service company and customer.

Quality

Quality is a multifaceted concept. For us, it is a matter of satisfying the needs and meeting the expectations of three main groups: customers, staff and owners.

Somebody once said that quality, like beauty, is in the eye of the beholder. The quality of a service is very much in the eye of the beholder. This underlines the customer's key role. Therefore, the customer must never be forgotten in service development if we have the ambition of building the right quality into services from the start. It is not easy to define 'quality'. If one were to ask a group of people what they understood quality to mean, one would probably receive as many answers as people asked. Quality is defined in ISO (1991) as 'the totality of features and characteristics of a product that bear on its ability to satisfy stated or implied needs'.

A common definition of service quality is that 'the service should correspond to the customers' expectations and satisfy their needs and requirements'. The definition is customer-oriented but should not be interpreted as meaning that the service provider should always comply with the customer and his wishes. That it is the customer who decides what is good or bad quality does not mean that the customer is always right or that the customer can always fully articulate or verbalize his needs and wishes. We would warn against customer myopia. However, we would also stress how important it is for customers to assist in giving quality a clear and operational content.

In many cases the customer needs assistance in making his needs and quality requirements explicit. One way of helping him is to expose him to new services, the new and better opportunities offered, for instance, by information technology through the simulation of new services. The abstract service is made concrete and it is easier for the customer to make specific comments – even the unspoken needs and wishes are partially revealed.

It is often appropriate to distinguish three groups of people whose expectations, needs and demands should be taken into account; apart from customers, these are staff and owners. One does not want to belittle the importance of customers' perception of quality, on the contrary; but to be able to offer customers the right quality, the other two groups must also be satisfied. Our definition of quality is that it satisfies needs and meets expectations, those of the customers, staff and owners. It is essential to understand fully the various needs and expectations of these groups, how they are formed and how they

change. When developing services, it is crucial to build in the right quality by balancing these partly contradictory demands on the service.

Service – a customer outcome

The International Organization for Standardization (ISO, 1991) defines service as a subset of product. A product is the result of a production process. Producing is a matter of creating added value, that is, the value of what emerges is greater than the sum of the resources consumed during the production process. In a market economy, added value is subjected to continuous assessment. Here the customer plays a key role. The customer's continual decision is to buy or not to buy, his selection of service and service provider. If the customer does not perceive that he receives added value, it is not a matter of production but of destruction, and the customer is obviously disinclined to pay for it.

The customer-perceived outcome can be classified in many ways depending on situation and purpose. For this, suitable variables are used. In connection with service development two sets of variables would seem central: lasting – temporary, tangible – intangible (see Figure 1). A haircut is an example of a tangible,

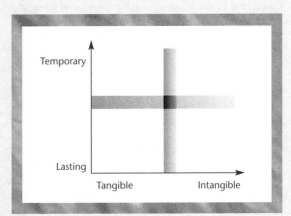

Figure 1 ■ The customer-perceived result classified in terms of the variables: lasting–temporary and tangible–intangible

temporary result; and an insurance policy an intangible lasting one.

Let us illustrate this by consulting services. These services are often 'invisible' and thus difficult for Swedish Telecom to explain and for the customer to assess. This places special demands on marketing to prevent unrealistic, often excessive expectations on the market. The expectations which are created by marketing affect the customer's perception of the outcome. It is the responsibility of the consulting company and the individual consultants to ensure that the customer does not have unrealistic demands and expectations. Not infrequently, however, controlling customer expectations is often forgotten in service development. The design and implementation of marketing – giving the right promises and fulfilling them – should be an integral part of the process of service development.

We believe that the concept of service should be approached from the customer's perspective. It is the customer's total perception of the outcome which 'is the service', which forms the perception of quality and determines whether the customer is satisfied or not. The main task of service development is to create the conditions for the right customer outcome. Customers have different values and different grounds for assessment, they perceive one and the same service in different ways. What the customer does not perceive does not exist – is not a customer outcome.

Service – a customer process

A service is generated by a process. The customer outcome is created in this process. Processes which generate services are different from those in which goods are manufactured. In the latter case, the manufacturing process takes place at one time and in one place, the customer is not present, nor does he participate in the process. In the case of services, however, the customer does take part in the process as co-producer. The customer is present and affects the result in terms of added value and quality. The role, participation and responsibility of the customer in service production must therefore be made clear. This is an important task in service development, as is

the construction of customer-friendly, pedagogical customer processes.

We pointed out earlier that customers have different needs, wishes and expectations. But perhaps it is just as important when discussing service development to take into account the fact that the behaviour of customers varies considerably. The way each customer performs his tasks in the customer process is in some sense unique. This means that the process is customer-unique. The services arise in direct interaction with the customer and the customer is not just the person who receives and assesses the outcome; he/she also creates and produces it.

The customer process must lead to a customer outcome which has sufficient added value for the service to be commercially successful, at least in a long-term perspective. Added value is created in the customer process. The customer receives and actively forms impressions during the process which affect his perception of the outcome.

Seeing the customer as co-producer of services has far-reaching implications for service development. The behaviour of the customer, what is logical and reasonable from the customer's perspective, must be taken into account as the various processes are built up. How should we deal with the fact that the customer has ideas, suggestions, feelings and so on which make it necessary to assume that different customers will behave differently and that one and the same customer may behave very differently on different occasions? How can we create the best prerequisites for a good customer outcome when we cannot control the whole process in which the service is produced?

Service – the prerequisites for the service

In the two previous sections we have highlighted two sides of the concept of service based on the customer perspective: the customer outcome and the customer process. The customer as the recipient and judge of the service in terms of added value and quality – the customer outcome; and the customer as co-producer of the service in his partially unique manner – the customer process. In quality terms we may speak of

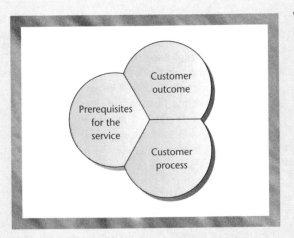

Figure 2 ■ The concept of service as customer outcome, customer process and the prerequisites for service

outcome quality and process quality. In this section we highlight a third aspect of the service concept. Our perspective is now that of the service company.

The customer's total perception of a certain service is thus based on his perception of the outcome and the process. The customer outcome and the customer process are, in their turn, dependent on the prerequisites in the form of resources which have been built up to provide the service or, in other words, to make the service possible.

We maintain that the service company does not provide the service but the prerequisites for various services. The company does not sell services but opportunities for services which are generated in partially unique customer processes with partly different customer outcomes. A logical consequence of our reasoning is that the most central goal of service development is to develop the best and right prerequisites for well-functioning customer processes and attractive customer outcomes. By attractive customer outcomes we mean that, in the eyes of the customer, the service is associated with added value and quality. Naturally, a prerequisite for this is that it may be achieved with some profitability for the company and that the needs and expectations of the staff are reasonably satisfied.

We mean by the prerequisites for the service, for instance, the technical resources, the administrative routines and procedures which customers must understand and apply. We will discuss this in more detail and present a model of the prerequisites for the service in the next section.

If we assume that the customer is co-producer, this means that the customer is either an asset or a 'disruptive factor' in the set of resources providing the prerequisites for the service. This also means that some of the prerequisites are outside the service company, at the customer's or supplier's/partner's and therefore generally cannot be influenced or controlled. Let us exemplify this with Swedish Telecom's services (see Figure 3). The prerequisites might entail the equipment in the form of the telephone exchange and telephones the customer has. Other factors are the knowledge and experience the customer possesses, e.g., in the use of telecommunication equipment.

A strategic issue is how that customer's various resources should and can be utilized. It would seem to be a major strategic task in service development to answer this question. At the same time there would probably be greater risk in that more of the prerequisites for the service were not directly under the control of the company.

Let us relate the discussion in this section with the arguments in the previous ones. A service means

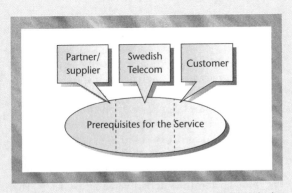

Figure 3 ■ The prerequisites for the service include both what exists within Swedish Telecom and at partners'/suppliers' and customers' premises

creating added value. Added value refers to the customer's perception of the relation between quality and cost. The customer assesses added value on the basis of the outcome he perceives. This outcome is created and interpreted during the customer process. This process does not occur in a vacuum but is dependent on resources. These have been developed and organized by the service company. The company provides the prerequisites for the service. The condition for good services is provided by the prerequisites in the service company, its partners/suppliers and customers. Creating the right prerequisites for a good customer process and a good customer outcome is the main task of service development.

Model of the prerequisites for the service

The prerequisites for the service are the end-result of the service development process. The goal (the right prerequisites) is described by means of a model with three basic components: service concept, service process and service system (Edvardsson, 1991; and Edvardsson and Mattsson, 1992). The term service concept refers to the description of the customer's needs and how they are to be satisfied in the form of the content of the service or the design of the service package. Correspondence or agreement between customer needs and the service offer is essential. The outcome the customer perceives (cf. the discussion in the previous section on service as customer outcome) determines the customer's perception of the quality of the service.

Service process relates to the chain of activities that must function properly if the service is to be produced. Certain activities are more problematic or critical than others. Special attention should be paid to these so that the customer process and the customer outcome achieve the right quality at reasonable cost. The service process is the prototype for every customer process (cf. the discussion in the previous section on service as a customer process). The service process consists of a clear description of the various activities needed to generate the service (Shostack, 1984 and 1987). The service system constitutes the resources that are required by or are available to the service process in order to realize the service concept. It may be described in terms of a number of components. In our model these are the service company's staff, the customers, the physical/technical environment and the organizational structure (Edvardsson and Gustavsson, 1990).

Service concept

Service concept refers to the prototype for the service, i.e., the customer utility and the benefits (value for the user) which the service and its various subservices are intended to provide and convey to the customer. The service concept covers both the description of the customer needs to be satisfied and how they are to be satisfied in the form of the content of the service or the design of the service package, e.g., expressed in terms of core service and supporting services. The service concept is a detailed description of what is to be done for the customer (= what needs and wishes are to be satisfied) and how this is to be achieved (= the service offer).

The service concept specifies the domain of needs with respect to extent and nature (= both primary and secondary customer needs) and the service offer (= both core service and supporting services) to meet this domain. Correspondence between customer needs and service offer is crucial. The service concept forms the point of departure and defines the demand for the prerequisites that must be present for a service with the right quality to be realized.

When discussing customer needs, it is useful to make a distinction between primary and secondary needs (Edvardsson, 1991). Primary needs are those which act as a 'trigger', i.e., the reason why the customer experiences a certain need; for instance, it might be the need to contact a person in the UK. This need can be satisfied in various ways: by phone, telefax, letter, telex or telegram, and so on. Different customers want to satisfy this need in different ways depending on how urgent it is to reach the person quickly and the customer's perception of the advantages and disadvantages of the various alternatives. Let us assume that the customer prefers the telephone. When the customer has decided to make a phone call, further needs arise: how to gain access to a telephone, the telephone number of the person in question, the number for the UK, and so on. These needs are a function or result of the chosen service and are termed secondary needs. Let us call the chosen means of communication the core service. If the customer had chosen to write a letter, other secondary needs would have arisen.

To satisfy these secondary needs, other services are needed, apart from the telephone service, the core service. We have chosen to call these services supporting services. In the case in question, directory enquiries is a supporting service.

Both primary and secondary needs (both explicit and implied) must be dealt with for the customer to be satisfied. Studies show that the customer expects this, and that high customer-perceived quality is based on the fact that, apart from the core service, the service offer also includes a relevant set of supporting services of the right quality, as seen from the customer's perspective. What distinguishes the successful service companies – with respect to customer-perceived quality and profitability – from the less successful ones is often related to the extent and quality of the supporting services. Quality means both that the service represents added value for the customer and that the customer finds it easy to use.

Several of the secondary needs are implied, i.e., the customer assumes that various services are available which will satisfy even secondary customer needs in a reasonable manner. When the service concept is being formulated and the service developed, it is necessary to identify and understand these implied needs, wishes and expectations as well. This requires information on and a thorough understanding of the customers to be served by the service in question. When developing the service concept, attention should be given to the fact that individual services often form part of a system together with other services, existing and/or new. To achieve the right quality and high productivity, these 'system aspects' should also be taken into account.

The service system

The service system includes the resources available to the process for realizing the service concept. The system forms a whole where the sub-systems must function separately but also together with other sub-systems. In our model the various sub-systems of the service system or, put in other terms, the resource structure is made up of the service company's staff, the customers, the physical/technical environment and organization and control. In the following we describe each of these resource categories.

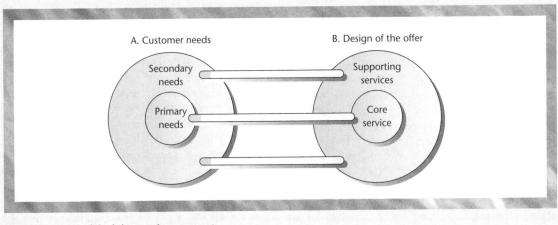

Figure 4 ■ Model of the service concept

The service company's staff

The staff are usually seen as the service company's key resource. We believe it correct to focus on the staff in this way when developing services. There are, namely, studies which show that the customer's perception of the quality of a service depends to a great extent on how he perceives the staff as regards, for instance, their knowledge and commitment (see, e.g., Crane and Clarke, 1988). For many customers, individual staff are by and large synonymous with the service. If we assume this is the case, then we should consider the staff as more than a resource, we should see them as part of the service. The intangible service becomes tangible for the customer in the encounter with individual staff. It is in this interplay between staff and customer, the process of truth, that many services arise and become tangible.

If we see the staff not just as one resource among others but as the critical or decisive factor enabling the customer to perceive that he is receiving a service of the right quality, it is natural to adapt techniques, systems, routines and other resources to human logic, i.e., the customers' and staff's natural way of behaving. Thus, we cannot simply specify the demands on system and processes for a new service on the basis of the service concept. We must also understand how individuals and groups of staff can be encouraged to work in the best manner. We must take their special needs, demands and wishes into account – not just those of the customers. To do a good job, the staff, in the company and the company's partners, must be knowledgeable, motivated and committed.

Knowledge and experience alone have proved to be insufficient for high performance in service companies. Motivation and enjoyment in work are also necessary. Motivation is primarily achieved through work content, relations with fellow workers and one's immediate supervisor, and relations to customers. If we are successful in designing attractive jobs and a stimulating work environment, this will probably be the most important quality-creating factor in service development.

It is a reasonable assumption that the choice of staff (those who are to help provide the service) and their training/education should be an integral part of the development of new services. The staff are often the crucial factor for customer-perceived quality but in some cases they are also the dominant factor on the cost side. Wage costs are on average much higher in service companies than in manufacturing companies. This is a further important reason why staff should be given special status when designing new services. The production system becomes a socio-technical system with the focus on the staff, which should result in the right service and high productivity. The recruitment, training, development and outplacement of staff are often not handled in a systematic and professional fashion in Swedish service companies. Furthermore, the analysis of work content and job design, tasks and reward systems are important but often neglected areas in service development.

The customers

Naturally the customers have a key role. The customer – a company or private individual/household – is part of the service system. It is not just a matter of the customer's knowledge and his ability to assimilate information but also, for instance, the equipment he uses and the administrative routines employed in the customer company. All this is part of the service system and thus influences the prerequisites for the service.

Marketing plays a central role in relations with the customer in establishing quality from the outset. Marketing consists of establishing and developing mutually trustful and profitable customer relations. Marketing is much more than advertising and sales visits. It also includes the design of invoices, dealing with customers on the telephone, information material, the image the media project of the company, but above all the perception of the customer outcome and the customer process.

In order to give the right promises, one must understand customers' needs, wishes and expectations and coordinate one's marketing accordingly. One must not promise more than one's competence or capacity to deliver. The company must have both the will and the ability to provide the services that the customers need and expect.

We believe that an important but often neglected task in marketing – in particular when introducing new services on the market – is to inform the customer and 'train' him in the role of co-producer. This emerges as a major factor in the introduction of new services.

The service system should be so designed that it is easy for the customer not only to take part in but also to actively contribute to the process. When developing new services, it is necessary, we have found, to organize the following: firstly, interaction between customers, e.g., a queue system when the service is overloaded; secondly, the customer's relationship with the company's organization as regards routines; thirdly, the interaction between customers and staff; and fourthly, the interaction with the physical/technical environment.

The exchange, with the customer in the centre, should be organized so that the customer can make the best contribution both by providing information and by performing various parts of the service process.

The physical/technical environment

The physical/technical environment includes premises, computers and other technical systems but also the equipment at partners' and customers' premises. The continuous improvement of the technical environment through the utilization of opportunities offered by technical developments may be absolutely essential for the survival and development of the company. At the same time it is becoming increasingly obvious that technology is not a goal in itself but a means, a means of creating favourable conditions for increasingly better services and increasingly more profitable business deals. Technical developments should be customer-driven and business-driven. Technology-driven developments seldom result in the best added value, the most attractive services and the best customer-perceived quality.

Technical developments alone, even if they are business-driven, are insufficient. Other parts of the service system – the staff, the organizational structure, the administrative regulatory systems and the customers – must interact with the technical environment.

Technology and equipment mean possibilities and limitations. It is a matter of identifying and benefiting from the advantages and possibilities and avoiding the limitations in the service system. Naturally, it may be necessary to change the physical/technical prerequisites to create the right prerequisites for a new service. However, the normal situation is that a new service is, to all intents and purposes, dependent on and must work within the framework of the existing technical environment. The physical/technical resources can have different features and functions, and they can fit more or less well together. It is important, of course, that they do not just work with other physical/technical resources but also suit the organization and are adapted to customer and staff logic.

Organization and control

The fourth component in the system is organization and control. This includes, first of all, the organizational structure, i.e., the division into activity and profit centres. The organizational structure must clearly define responsibility and authority in an appropriate manner. Is the responsibility for the various activities in connection with the introduction of a new service clear? Have responsibility and authority been appropriately delegated? Are profit centres and other activity centres logically and suitably organized with respect to their tasks? Is the company organized to focus on the customer's needs, the service and business?

The second aspect of organization is the administrative support systems. These systems, e.g., planning and information, financial system and wage system, play a key role in controlling the business. The administrative support and control systems require information and supply information about individual services. How the systems for handling administration in service companies are designed is often of much greater importance for the prerequisites for a service than most people realize. In connection with service development even the administrative systems must be adjusted or complemented to produce a workable service.

Thirdly, the interaction, dialogue with customers and other interested parties – in the first place, partners and suppliers – is an important part of the organization and control of the service system. This includes, for instance, how feedback is achieved, how complaints and customer dissatisfaction are handled but also opening hours, telephone times and the possible VIP treatment of major or faithful customers. One aspect is how easy it is for customers to contact the company, a specific department or individual in the company; for example, is it easy to find the person responsible for a certain task, the person or department one wants, or does the company provide parking for visitors?

The fourth aspect we include is the organization of the various activities connected with marketing. There are three important tasks in marketing that need to be organized and controlled. Firstly, using market and customer analyses to understand the competitive situation, customers' needs and demands, and customer logic. Secondly, ensuring that realistic expectations are created. Thirdly, teaching customers how to act/behave in the role of co-producer. Before approaching customers on the market, it is essential to create the right internal conditions and understanding by means of internal marketing to staff and partners. Internal marketing first and then external marketing.

Our model of the service system is presented in Figure 5.

The service process

The service process is the chain or chains of parallel and sequential activities which must function if the service is to be produced. The service process consists partly of activities at partners' and customers' premises. The company thus does not have direct control over all parts of the process but must nevertheless be able to control the process in its entirety.

All parts of the service process are important but some sub-processes or activities are more problematic or critical than others. Special attention should be paid to these to ensure that the customer process and customer outcome have the right quality at reasonable cost. The interfaces between departments within the company and with partners and customers are parts of the process which are often difficult to control.

What is then the difference between service process and customer process? Service process refers to the prototype or model for various customer processes. It must be able to handle several customer-specific processes. The service process consists of a precise description of various standardized and (alternative) activities in the customer process. These activities do

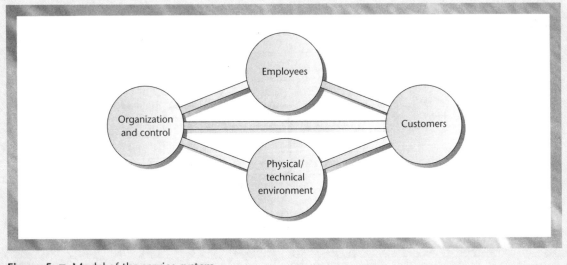

Figure 5 ■ Model of the service system

Source: Edvardsson and Gustavsson (1990: 15)

not take place until the customer activates the service process. The activities to be performed are indicated by the service process, i.e., the prerequisites for the customer process.

> As the complexity of streams of processes increases, so does the probability that a company will lose control of the characteristics that are necessary to meet customer expectations, add value, and hold down costs. The result is the worst of two worlds: as the quality level falls below customer expectations, the cost of producing the product or service increases out of proportion to the value added. (Conti, 1989: 45)

To generate a service which meets the service concept in all respects, it is necessary to determine in detail the process, including microprocesses and individual activities, which will ensure the right service. Quality and productivity must be built in from the beginning by developing the 'right' service process.

We maintain that it is necessary but not sufficient for all departments to participate in the development of the service process. Despite this, there is an obvious risk that each department or function will optimize its 'own' processes and not heed the whole and the inter-functional dependency relations which exist in all organizations. Important managerial tasks in con-

nection with service development include, firstly, creating an understanding of the customer outcome and customer process; secondly, involving the customers in the development process, helping customers articulate their needs, even those that are implicit, and 'attaching importance to the customer's voice'; thirdly, involving strategic partners and suppliers when they are affected.

During the process various parts of the service system are utilized. The system is static, it provides the necessary resources, whilst the process is dynamic, consisting of activities which are linked in microprocesses to form the service process. This process should be designed to utilize the possibilities of the system, not least the service company's staff, and to handle its limitations in the best way. Many new services are more or less dependent on the conditions in the existing system. This means that staff with knowledge and understanding of the possibilities and limitations of the service system, not just at a general level but also in detail, should be involved in service development. Without this contribution it is difficult to see that the service system will support the service process, which is our point of departure.

An important aspect of the service process is the so-called line of visibility, i.e., which parts of the service system the customer should and should not see

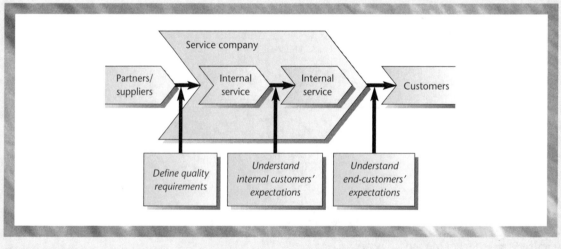

Figure 6 ■ The service process

during the customer process. Seeing the restaurant's kitchen and perhaps the raw materials, and experiencing the smells may influence the customer-perceived quality positively or negatively. Standing in a queue at a bank and, at the same time, seeing the staff behind the counter taking a break is an indication that the line of visibility is poorly drawn.

Studies show that in many instances the service system has in-built recurrent defects, which create more or less serious problems in the service process (see, for instance, Norling, Edvardsson and Gummesson, 1992). In some cases it may be said that the system puts a spoke in the wheel of the service process, which, of course, was not the intention. We must conclude from this that the service process and service system should be developed interactively on the basis of the possibilities and limitations of the latter. The service system may need to be changed and developed but the consequences of these changes for other parts of the system must be simultaneously taken into account.

In Figure 7 we present a model of the prerequisites for the service based on the three components: service concept, service system and service process.

A concept for service development

In this section we first analyze ISO's approach to and description of the process of developing a service.

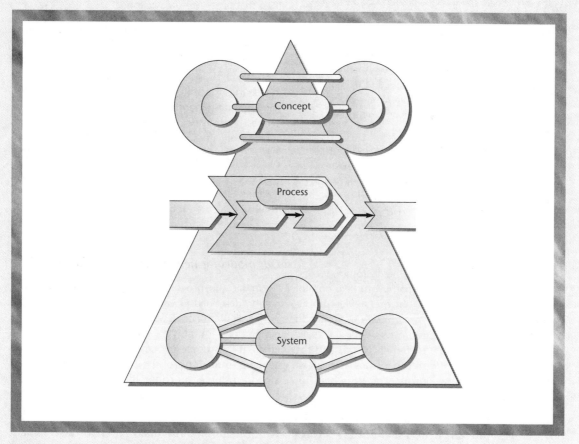

Figure 7 ■ Model of the prerequisites of the service

Then we present a sketch of how we see the process. This is based on the approaches, concepts and arguments presented above.

Service design according to ISO

The ISO standard will probably be very important for certain services. Thus it would seem natural to briefly present and evaluate ISO's description and definition of service design.

ISO, 1991 (E) 'Quality management and quality system elements: Guidelines for services' describes in brief terms what is meant by designing a service.

> The process of designing a service involves converting the service brief into specifications for both the service and its delivery and control, while reflecting the organization's options (i.e., aims, policies and costs).
>
> The service specification defines the service to be provided, whereas the service delivery specification defines the means and methods used to deliver the service. The quality control specification defines the procedures for evaluating and controlling the service delivery characteristics.
>
> Design of the service specification, the service delivery specification and quality control specification are interdependent and interact through the design process. Flow charts are a useful method to depict all activities, relationships and interdependences.
>
> The principles of quality control should be applied to the design process itself. (p. 9)

The term 'service brief' refers to the customer need(s) the service is to satisfy. It is important to take note of the demands that are placed on the service-producing organization and the service to be developed, in order to ensure that the customer's needs are really met. 'This brief defines the customers' needs and the related service organization's capabilities as a set of requirements and instructions that form the basis for the design of a service' (p. 9).

With delimited and specific customer needs as the point of departure, the demands which the service-producing company must take into account when developing and specifying a new service are defined. This description in ISO is very similar to what we have termed the prerequisites for the service. There is a major difference, however, in that ISO does not see the customer as part of the service system but as outside it. The demand for and need of adjustment to the resources and conditions prevailing at the customer's are not taken into account, at least not explicitly. Our view of the service process means that the customer – internal or external – is part of the service-producing organization, and that he contributes actively to the process by performing certain steps or activities. Without this contribution from the customer the service will not be initiated. The wording in ISO is an indication that its approach to reality is still informed by the logic of industrial production rather than that of service production.

However, the ISO standard has adopted a process approach. Developing services is thus a matter of creating conditions for producing added value for the customer. ISO points out that the development of flowcharts is a useful method of specifying activities, relations and dependencies in the service process. The process is termed 'service delivery' which implies 'supplier activities necessary to provide the service'.

ISO defines customer as 'the recipient of a product or service'. They have still not learnt that, apart from being the recipient of the service, the customer (if not in all service production) can be co-producer – to a greater or lesser extent.

Our model for new service development

Naturally, the process of new service development can be described in various ways. We argue that the main task of service development is to create the right generic prerequisites for the service. This means an efficient customer process: the process must be adapted to the logic of the customer's behaviour and a good customer outcome, that is, the service is associated, in the eyes of the customer, with quality and added value.

We distinguish three main types of development within our frame of reference: the development of the

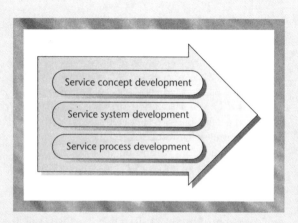

Figure 8 ■ Model of the service development process

service concept, the development of the service system and the development of the service process (see Figure 8). Obviously, the time required for the processes and the dependency relations between them vary from project to project.

Development of the service concept

The idea for the new service is systematically and critically evaluated, taking into account the external and internal, as detailed above. Further, a commercial assessment is made by means of a general cost and income analysis. The concept is developed with the aid of experienced people in the field, both staff from the service company and demanding/knowledgeable customers. The aim is first to decide whether or not to proceed with the idea and then, given a go-ahead decision, to determine the key factors influencing the quality of the service and its value for the customer. This should result in a preliminary concept for the service and details about the customers to whom the service is to be offered – the target market. The new service is compared with existing services and the feasibility of producing it within reasonable technical and economical limits examined. As a basis for the economic assessment, a rough estimate of the cost is made and a preliminary, value-based price set.

With the primary and secondary customer needs as a basis, the service offer, namely the core service and support services, is specified. Further, it is important

to see how well the service offer corresponds to customer needs and how well the projected service fits into the assortment. A crucial point here is to determine the extent to which the existing service system may be used.

Naturally, concept development requires good information. To achieve this, it is most probably necessary to conduct an external analysis of the market conditions and an internal analysis of the strengths and weaknesses of the company. Externally the idea for a new or changed service is evaluated and specified by means of an analysis of customers, competitors and institutions. In the customer analysis the idea is related to the customers' needs, wishes, expectations and behaviour – customer logic. The presumptive clientele's grounds for assessment and links with existing service providers, and the size and development of the market are taken into account.

The competitor analysis identifies the competition both from competitors in the same trade and competitors from 'outside', so-called invaders. Existing services offered by competitors, their strategies and possible new services which may be introduced etc. are studied. The strengths and weaknesses of competitors are identified and assessed. The institutional analysis may, for instance, cover legal demands and conditions, ethical or moral aspects and political conditions. The analyses of customers, competitors and institutions are integrated by specifying and evaluating market conditions in the form of threats and possibilities.

Internal resources are required in order to take advantage of the possibilities offered by the market. These may be technological, financial, knowledge-related and organizational. The internal analysis results in a description and evaluation of the company's strengths and weaknesses in relation to the idea for the new service.

Development of the service system

The service concept places demands on the service system. The resources of the system must be so designed that the concept can be realized, that the right service can be generated. The development of the service system and service process must go hand in hand. The central activities involved in developing the service system include a demand specification on the basis of the service concept, a thorough assessment of the current service system and a detailed description of the design of the system for the new service.

Developing the service system is a matter of selecting and training the staff who are to deal with the new service. They must know exactly what is expected of them, what their responsibilities are, and so on. Their motivation will be increased if they can take part in the development of the system. There are several advantages to be gained here; they will have a better understanding of the service as a whole and their commitment will be greater in that they have been given a chance to influence the process. Developing the service system is also a matter of training and adapting to the customers one has chosen to serve. Training customers is a question of information, education and marketing. According to Harvey et al. (1992) the (detailed) design of the interaction between customers and service company staff is a critical parameter in service development.

A third aspect of the development of the service system concerns the physical/technical environment. The fourth component – organization – must also be improved; this involves administrative support systems, responsibility for the various activities in the service process and a realistic plan for the introduction and marketing of the new service. Harvey et al. (1992) stress the importance of carefully designing the interaction with and demands on suppliers and specifying quality demands to ensure that the process works as intended.

Development of the service process

Developing the service process involves the specification of the activities needed to generated the service. Special attention must be paid to the critical points in the process. The roles and responsibility of customers and partners must be clarified, the control of customers' expectations specified and the procedures for teaching the customer to correctly perform his 'tasks' in the service process decided on. Detailed but comprehensible blueprints of how the service is to be produced can often be of assistance here. Alternative

service processes can be tested with the aid of appropriate computer-based simulation techniques.

Essential activities include the detailed description of the service process with respect to activities and sub-processes, equipment, quality and cost factors, critical points and line of visibility. Costs are calculated in detail and a value-based price determined. Information for the control of customer expectations and marketing communication is produced. Instruments for quality measurement and control are designed.

Figure 9 presents an overview of the development process and its results, i.e., the prerequisites for the service. It should be emphasized that it is the possibilities for the service that are produced, not the service itself. The service is not generated and added value realized until the customer makes use of the possibilities, i.e., the actual service. Not until then does he perceive and assess the service itself.

Conclusion

In this article a new frame of reference for new service development has been presented. The focus is on designed quality. To maintain the viability and profitability of a service company, we argue that it is essential to develop and provide services of the right quality in a resource-effective manner. The quality of the services governs the customer's perception of the company in the market.

The service is produced in a customer process where customer, company and subcontractors are actors. The quality of the process is controlled by the prerequisites each actor takes with him into the customer process. These prerequisites are governed by the company's service concept, service process and service system. The service company must develop and offer a service concept which is appropriate to the customer's needs and which contains attractive added-value and a 'customer-friendly' and generic service process. The service system must provide the necessary resources for the service process.

During the often brief periods of time in which a customer process is activated there is little chance of correcting the quality problems which may arise

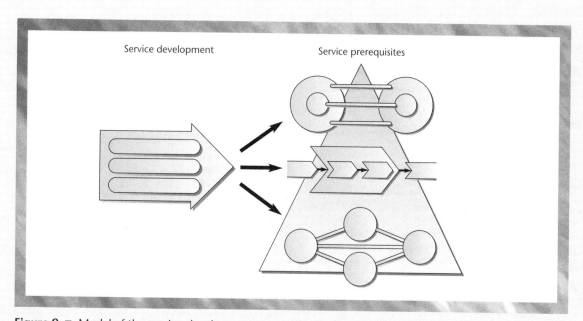

Figure 9 ■ Model of the service development process and the prerequisites for the service

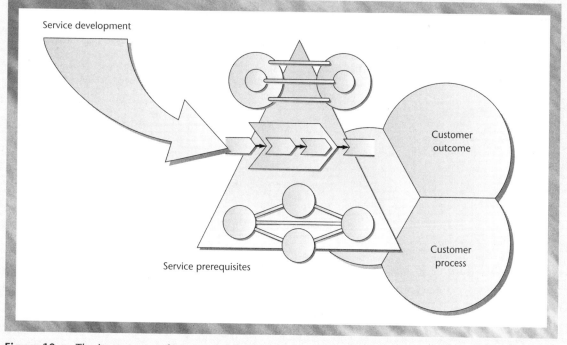

Figure 10 ■ The importance of service development for the service company's internal efficiency and the customer-perceived quality of a service

because of incorrect or poor prerequisites. Thus it is crucial for the quality of the service to develop services which create the best prerequisites. Service development must co-ordinate the development of concept, process and system where each aspect requires special treatment.

References

Conti, T., 1989, 'Process Management and Quality Function Deployment', *Quality Progress*, Vol. 22, No. 12, pp. 45–51.

Crane, F.G. and T.K. Clarke, 1988, 'The Identification of Evaluative Criteria and Cues used in Selecting Services', *Journal of Services Marketing*, Vol. 2, No. 2, pp. 53–9.

Crosby, P.B., 1989, *Let's Talk Quality*, New York: McGraw-Hill.

Edvardsson, B., 1990, 'Management Consulting: Towards a Successful Relationship', *International Journal of Service Industry Management*, Vol. 1, No. 3, pp. 4–19.

Edvardsson, B., 1991, 'Tjänstekonstruktion', Paper presented at the conference 'Kvalitet i kommuner och landsting', Göteborg, 2–3 September (in Swedish).

Edvardsson, B., 1992, 'Service Breakdowns: A Study of Critical Incidents in an Airline', *International Journal of Service Industry Management*, Vol. 3, No. 4, pp. 17–29.

Edvardsson, B. and B.O. Gustavsson, 1990, 'Problem Detection in Service Management Systems – A Consistency Approach in Quality Improvement'. Working paper 90:13, CTF, University of Karlstad.

Edvardsson, B. and J. Olsson, 1992, 'Kvalitet i Tjänsteutveckling inom Televerket', Report from a preliminary study. Televerkets enheten för Koncernkvalitet – MQ, Rapport MQ 69/92 115 (in Swedish).

Edvardsson, B. and B. Thomasson, 1991, Kvalitetsutveckling – ett managementperspektiv. Studentlitteratur, Lund (in Swedish).

Edvardsson, B. and J. Mattsson, 1992, 'Service Design: A TQM Instrument for Service Providers?' Paper for The Service Productivity and Quality Challenge Conference, The Wharton School, University of Pennsylvania, 23–24 October 1992.

Gummesson, B. 1988, 'Att utveckla servicekvalitet eller Varför finns det inga servicekonstruktörer?' in B. Edvardsson and E. Gummesson (eds) 1988, *Management i tjänstesamhället*, Liber. Lund (in Swedish), pp. 67–76.

Gummesson, E., 1991, 'Kvalitetsstyrning i tjänste- och serviceverksamheter – Tolkning av fenomenet tjänstekvalitet och syntes av internationell forskning', Research report 91:4, CTF, Högskolan i Karlstad (in Swedish).

Harvey, J., E. Lefebrve. and L. Lefebrve, 1992, 'Technology and the Creation of Value in Services: a Conceptual Model', Paper presented at The Service Productivity and Quality Challenge Conference, Wharton School, 23–24 October.

ISO 9004-2, 1991, Quality Management and Quality Systems Element – Part 2: Guidelines for Services.

Juran, J.M., 1992, *Juran on Quality by Design – The New Steps for Planning Quality into Goods and Services*. New York: The Free Press.

Norling, P., B. Edvardsson and E. Gummesson, 1992, 'Tjänsteutveckling och tjänstekonstruktion', Research report 92:5, CTF, Högskolan i Karlstad (in Swedish).

Shostack, L., 1984, 'Designing Services that Deliver', *Harvard Business Review*, January–February, pp. 27–43.

Shostack, L., 1987, 'Service Positioning Through Structural Change', *Journal of Marketing*, Vol. 51, January, pp. 34–43.

Why cross-selling hasn't worked

David H. Maister

Attempts by professional firms to expand relationships with existing clients are, more often than not, unsuccessful. There is little chance of making a cross-selling strategy work without first performing at a very high level on current assignments.

Every professional service firm I have ever encountered has had, and still has, the goal of 'cross-selling' – expanding relationships with existing clients in order to increase the range of services delivered. Yet success in this area has been limited. Few firms, if any, have made cross-selling work on a systematic basis. And there is a simple explanation for this apparent failure: firms have been going about it the wrong way.

Who benefits?

Firms have traditionally exhorted their professionals to tell the client about 'the other things we do', and have become frustrated when this produces minimal results. In consequence, they have come to view the barriers to making cross-selling happen as primarily internal: a lack of trust across departments; professionals being protective of their individual client relationships; or incentive systems that cause professionals to worry more about the revenues of their own department than about helping other departments in the firm. These internal barriers are real and deadly. But there is an even more powerful reason why cross-selling efforts have historically failed: cross-selling does little, if anything, for the *client*.

It is obvious what cross-selling will do for the firm: increase revenues and cement client relationships. These are valid and powerful reasons to emphasize this area. But the fact that something is good for the firm is an insufficient test. In any business there is an iron-clad rule which says that if what you are planning to do truly adds value for the clients, you can then benefit from creating that additional value. If it doesn't do anything extra for the clients and just benefits you, then it is almost certainly unsustainable, and will fail.

What does cross-selling do for the client? Usually, nothing. In the traditional approach to cross-selling, firms supplying one service attempt to get their clients to use them for a (distinct) second service, to be performed by a totally distinct group of professionals within the firms. But what does the client get from this that couldn't be obtained by going through a sensible selection process for that second service, independent of the first? If there is little or no overlap in the staffing of the project, why should the client care that the professionals on the second project are in the same firm as the first?

To say that the client benefits because we have terrific skills in the second service area is beside the point. If they're so terrific, your group in that additional area will win the business on their own merits when the client searches for the best firm to handle their need. What is needed is a reason that shows the client that there will be extra benefit from using multiple departments of the *same* firm, above and beyond the individual excellence of each department.

What might this extra benefit be? There are real possibilities, the most obvious of which is this: If the first team serving the client has developed a significant understanding of the client's business, and can share that experience in such a way that it makes the second team more efficient or effective, then the client can *clearly* benefit. Note that to pull this off requires teaming across internal firm boundaries. It requires the original professional serving the client to be actively involved helping the new team in such a way that it benefits the client.

What, therefore, should be pursued is not an engagement for some other professional to work on independently, but some form of joint project. Firms should not be asking their people to sell their partners, but to look for ways for partners in different disciplines to work together. There is thus a critical distinction between traditional cross-selling (where there is no overlap in the delivery of the two distinct services) and integrated selling (of joint, multidisciplinary services), where the client has a chance to receive extra value. 'Pure' cross-selling is hard to justify, but integrated services have a fair shot at working.

It is worth observing that not only does integrated selling do something for the client, but also it helps overcome some of the internal barriers referred to above. If I am asked to sell the services of some other professional on a matter on which I will not be involved, I am subject to all the trust and incentive issues that professionals traditionally worry about. However, if I am looking for follow-on work which will require both the services of another professional *and* my services, then I have less risk and more direct incentive.

Why are you here?

Even if we assume that the firm has figured out a way to make combined – not just additional – services of value to the client, there still remain some barriers to winning client acceptance. Firms must get *organized* in order to market to existing clients. Many firms have appropriately appointed client-relationship partners to oversee the firm's relationship with key accounts. Further, they have correctly assigned specific individuals from other disciplines to be members of the team to market to these specific individual clients. These teams develop *client-service plans* meant to foster the relationship with the target client. However, problems still remain. Too many client-service plans are not really about giving service at all – they're sales plans. Part of the problem is in the very phrase itself, cross-*selling*.

What many professionals fail to realize about selling to existing clients is that clients expect us to *earn* their follow-on business. For example, how many professionals volunteer to attend (at no charge) internal client-management meetings to act as a resource? Or offer to critique, at no charge, a client's internal study, as a gesture of good faith? And how many demonstrate a willingness to earn the next piece of work and not take it for granted? The answer to all of these questions is *very few*.

Unfortunately, the average professional doesn't demonstrate much interest in the client's business. As a litmus test, I frequently take a poll of professionals in order to ask how many regularly read the trade magazines of their top one or two clients. It is the rare firm wherein the proportion of professionals that do this exceeds 10 per cent. It is hard to convince a client that you care about his or her business when it is evident that you don't know what's going on in it.

A truly effective client-service plan will include a set of activities that will help professionals to get to know the client's business better and in a more organized way. (It should be noted that this is not something that can only be done by partners. Smart firms make good use of junior professionals, marketing support staffs and significant others, to ensure that partners have the latest business intelligence on their clients.) A good client service plan will also include activities meant to deepen the business relationship by expanding the amount of client contact, both on and off the current assignment.

As an example of a creative approach to knowing the client's business better, consider the practice of a certain major consulting firm. Every two weeks, all those working on an individual client project get together to discuss what each team member (from the most senior partner to the most junior associate) has learned about what is going on in the client's business since last they met – *two weeks before*! New entrants quickly learn that, when assigned to a client project, they have two responsibilities: to execute their technical tasks, and to learn as much as possible about the client organization. Even the most junior member of the professional staff quickly learns that he or she should be establishing relationships with their counterparts in the client organization, and expressing an interest in the client's business. Not surprisingly, this firm has an outstanding track record of expanding its client relationships. As a not-so-coincidental side benefit, this attention is usually received by the client not as oppressive, but as a welcome, flattering interest in the business.

Unfortunately, examples such as this are all too rare. Too many professionals demonstrate *no* interest in the client, beyond the details of the current matter. They've never discussed the client's strategic plan, they've never sat in on a client's internal meeting, they don't read the client's trade rags – and then they want the client to give them more business!

What clients want

The paradox is that clients *do* want their firms to market to them. In the numerous client panels I have moderated for firms in different professions, I always ask clients how they feel about their outside providers' giving them suggestions for new assignments. The answers are almost uniform: clients tell me that they not only welcome their providers' bringing new ideas – they *expect* that. They do want their outside advisers to keep them apprised of things that they should consider, but what they don't want is a hard sell on every one. 'If there are additional things your firm can help my company with, of course I want to hear about it', one client said. 'We have a mutual interest in doing anything that helps my company. So keep those ideas coming. Just don't expect me to buy every time. Service me, don't sell me!'

Making it happen

There is good news in all of this. Cross-selling *can* be made to work. But firms must recognize that cross-selling is like a PhD programme: there are milestones that must be passed before you are eligible even to try it.

First comes the Bachelor's degree programme of conducting the current assignment in such a way that the client is not only satisfied, but delighted. The client needs to be left thinking, 'Not only did they get me a good result, but it was a pleasure to work with them.' It should be obvious that there's no point in trying to generate more work from existing clients unless you have left them eager to work with you again. This is the familiar 'client service and satisfaction programme' that has been much discussed in recent years.

Next comes the Master's degree programme of investing in the client relationship so that the firm is visibly seen by the client as trying to earn and deserve future work. The emphasis here needs to be on investing, *not* on selling. For example, are we putting on free inside seminars for the client's personnel? Are we performing special studies at our own expense in order to bring to the client information that is customized to the situation at hand?

If we have delighted the client on the current matter, and clearly been seen to be willing to invest in the relationship, then (and only then) can we show up and say for example, 'Our knowledge of your situation suggests that you really ought to look at X. May we bring our specialist partner in to talk to you about this?' Unfortunately, firms historically have neglected delighting or superpleasing the client, and instead have omitted investing in the relationship, just showing up and asking 'Do you want to buy something else?' Of course, the only possible answer is 'No, thanks.' Too many cross-selling programmes start with what we've got and try to push that onto the client.

To be effective, cross-selling must begin with a deep understanding of the client's business, including an educated, up-to-date knowledge about what sort of sticky problems or issues the client faces. And a little bit of sincerity, based on a true desire to help, wouldn't hurt the cause one bit.

Making business sense of the internet

Shikhar Ghosh

To assess the risks and the opportunities associated with doing business on the internet, managers need to know what is possible. Companies that do not want to participate in internet commerce may still be forced to do so by their competitors or customers.

The internet is fast becoming an important new channel for commerce in a range of businesses – much faster than anyone would have predicted two years ago. But determining how to take advantage of the opportunities this new channel is creating will not be easy for most executives, especially those in large, well-established companies.

Three years after emerging into the spotlight, the internet poses a difficult challenge for established businesses. The opportunities presented by the channel seem to be readily apparent: by allowing for direct, ubiquitous links to anyone anywhere, the internet lets companies build interactive relationships with customers and suppliers, and deliver new products and services at very low cost. But the companies that seem to have taken advantage of these opportunities are start-ups like Yahoo! and Amazon.com. Established businesses that over decades have carefully built brands and physical distribution relationships risk damaging all they have created when they pursue commerce in cyberspace. What's more, internet commerce is such a new phenomenon – and so much about it is uncertain and confusing – that it is difficult for executives at most companies, new or old, to decide the best way to use the channel. And it is even more difficult for them to estimate accurately the returns on any internet investment they may make.

None the less, managers can't afford to avoid thinking about the impact of internet commerce on their businesses. At the very least, they need to understand the opportunities available to them and recognize how their companies may be vulnerable if rivals seize those opportunities first. To determine what opportunities and threats the internet poses, managers should focus in a systematic way on what the internet can allow their particular organization to do. Broadly speaking, the internet presents four distinct types of opportunities.

First, through the internet companies can establish a direct link to customers (or to others with whom they have important relationships, such as critical suppliers or distributors) to complete transactions or trade information more easily. Second, the technology lets companies bypass others in the value chain. For instance, a book publisher could bypass retailers or distributors and sell directly to readers. Third, companies can use the internet to develop and deliver new products and services for new customers. And, fourth, a company could conceivably use the internet to become the dominant player in the electronic channel of a specific industry or segment, controlling access to customers and setting new business rules.

By exploring the opportunities and threats they face in each of these four domains, executives can realistically assess what, if any, investments they should begin to make in internet commerce and determine what risks they will need to plan for. A sound internet-commerce strategy begins by articulating what is possible.

Establishing the internet channel

To deliver new services or bypass intermediaries, companies first need to build direct connections to customers. That means more than just designing a web site to market a company's offerings. The behaviour of customers who are already buying goods and services on-line clearly indicates that companies can build momentum in their digital channels by using internet technology to deliver three forms of service to customers.

First, companies are giving customers just about the same level of service through the internet that they can currently get directly from a salesperson. For instance, Marshall Industries, a distributor of electronic components, makes it very convenient for customers to search for and order parts on-line. Visitors to the company's web site can hunt for a part by its number, by a description or by its manufacturer. They can place an order for parts, pay for them electronically, track the status of previous orders and even speed delivery time by connecting directly from Marshall Industries' web site to the shipping company's site.

Second, companies are using new internet technologies to personalize interactions with their customers and build customer loyalty. One way is to tailor the

At what point should you master your internet channel?

Not all companies will want to conduct business over the Web yet. Ask these questions to see if you can reduce costs and increase service levels by establishing an internet channel.

1. How much does it cost me to provide services that customers could get for themselves over the internet?
2. How can I use the information I have about individual customers to make it easier for them to do business with me?
3. What help can I give customers by using the experience of other customers or the expertise of my employees?
4. Will I be at a significant disadvantage if my competitors provide these capabilities to customers before I do?

information and options customers see at a site to just what they want. For example, when visitors arrive at Time Warner's Pathfinder internet site – which contains articles and graphics from more than 25 of the company's publications – they can register, identifying the topics that interest them. Then the Pathfinder site recognizes the visitors whenever they return and tailors the content delivered to their screens.

Similarly, Staples is using personalization to reduce the cost large companies incur when ordering its office supplies electronically. Staples is creating customized supply catalogues that can run on its customers' intranets. These catalogues contain only those items and prices negotiated in contracts with each company. The Staples system can maintain lists of previously ordered items, saving customers time when reordering. By searching and ordering electronically, Staples' customers can reduce their purchase-order processing costs – which through traditional channels can sometimes amount to more than the cost of the goods purchased. And over time, Staples could learn a great deal about its customers' preferences and use that information to offer other customized services that competitors, especially in the physical world, would find difficult to duplicate. For example, Staples could recommend new items to customers to complement what they have previously purchased or offer price discounts for items that customers have looked at in their on-line catalogues but have not yet bought.

Third, companies can provide valuable new services inexpensively. A company could, for example, draw on data from its entire customer base to make available wide-ranging knowledge of some topic. For instance, if a customer has a problem with a product, he or she might consult a site's directory of frequently asked questions to see how others have solved it. Or the customer might benefit from knowing how others have used a particular product. Amazon.com, the on-line bookstore, encourages customers to post reviews of books they have read for other visitors to see, making it possible for customers to scan reviews by peers – in addition to those from publications such as the *New York Times* – before deciding to order a book.

The combination of these three levels of service could make the internet channel very compelling for customers. And because these services are basically just electronic exchanges, they can be delivered at very low cost. Investments in the electronic channel displace traditional sales, marketing, and service costs; moreover, the technology allows companies to offer increasingly higher levels of service without incurring incremental costs for each transaction. For example, Cisco Systems conducts 40 per cent of its sales – $9 million per business day – over the internet. The company expects the volume to increase from its current level of more than $2 billion per year to $5 billion by July. By selling through the internet, the company has reduced its annual operating expenses by nearly $270 million. But Cisco's managers say the real value of the electronic channel is that it allows the company to provide buyers with a range of advantages – convenience, information, personalization, and interactivity – that competitors cannot.

The opportunity for those companies that move first to establish electronic channels is a threat to those that do not. When customers choose to do business through an internet channel, they make an investment of their time and attention. It takes time to figure out how to use a site and become comfortable with it. If a site involves personalization, customers have to fill out profiles and, perhaps, update or otherwise adjust them over time. They may also modify their own systems to make better use of electronic connections: for instance, ten of Cisco's largest customers are installing new software in their own computers to tie their inventory and procurement systems to Cisco's systems. Finally, customers must offer sensitive information, such as credit card numbers, and trust that the seller will manage that information discretely. For these reasons, the average customer, once he or she has established a relationship with one electronic seller, is unlikely to go through the effort again with many suppliers.

This all-too-human reluctance to abandon what works is a formidable obstacle to companies that do not move aggressively enough. Followers in this new channel risk being stuck with the unenviable task of getting customers to abandon investments they have already made in a competitor – and this will be a barrier that increases over time as the relationship between customer and competitor deepens.

The emergence of the direct connection could have another consequence that managers need to anticipate. Companies that currently do not want to participate in internet commerce may be forced to by competitors or customers. Consider how internet commerce could affect Dell and Compaq as potential suppliers of computer equipment to General Electric. Several major divisions of GE are completing plans to put parts and equipment up for bid on the internet. They intend to deal directly with suppliers over the Net and to receive multiple bids for every part. Based on early trials, GE estimates that it will shave $500 million to $700 million off its purchasing costs over three years and cut purchasing cycle times by as much as 50 per cent. The company expects that in five years it will purchase the majority of everything it buys through this Web-based bidding system.

Dell sells computer equipment directly to its customers, sometimes over the internet, but Compaq sells through distributors. That could put Compaq at a disadvantage for GE's business. Its distribution costs are higher, its pricing and information systems are designed for conducting business through distributors, and any move Compaq makes towards accepting orders over the internet could threaten those distributors.

What's worse from Compaq's point of view, Dell could gain internal efficiencies through the internet channel, as Cisco has discovered, and learn a great deal more about customers. Dell is currently selling almost $3 million worth of computers a day through its web site. By the year 2000, the company expects to handle half of all its business – ranging from customer enquiries to orders to follow-up service – through the internet. Such developments are forcing Dell's rivals in the computer industry to develop internet channels of their own. And first movers like Dell, both established companies and start-ups, are already beginning to emerge in other industries, such as auto retailing (General Motors and Auto-By-Tel), financial services (Merrill Lynch and E*Trade), and trade publishing (Cahners and VerticalNet).

As pioneering companies in an industry begin to build electronic channels, rivals will need to reexamine their value chains. New companies have no existing value chains to protect, of course, and so can set up their businesses in ways that take advantage of the internet. But companies that deal through others to reach end-customers (such as Compaq and IBM in the computer industry) will need to weigh the importance of protecting existing relationships with the distributors and partners that account for most of their current revenue against the advantages of establishing future strategic positions and revenue streams. This is one of the most difficult issues that large, established companies face in making decisions about engaging in internet commerce. For instance, although a book publisher might be tempted to use the internet to sell directly to bookstores or even to readers, it runs the risk of damaging long-standing relationships with distributors.

Pirating the value chain

Companies may find they have little choice but to risk damaging relationships in their physical chains to compete in the electronic channel. The ubiquity of the internet – the fact that anyone can link to anyone else – makes it potentially possible for a participant in the value chain to usurp the role of any other participant. Not only could the book publisher bypass the distributor and sell directly to readers, but Barnes & Noble and Amazon.com could decide to publish their own books – after all, they have very good information, gathered and collated electronically, about readers' interests.

Consider how various participants in the personal-computer value chain are already squaring off against one another to reach the end customer. Currently, computer manufacturers like Apple, Compaq and IBM purchase the components that make up the computers from suppliers like Intel (which makes microprocessors) and Seagate Technology (which produces hard-disk drives). Manufacturers supply machines to distributors such as Ingram Micro and MicroAge, which in turn supply retailers like CompUSA. That is the physical value chain for much of the industry (excluding manufacturers that sell through direct

mail, such as Dell and Gateway 2000). But internet commerce is already blurring the boundaries in that chain. Ingram Micro and MicroAge are seeking to bypass the physical retailers by setting up internet-based services that would allow anyone to become an on-line retailer of computers. MicroAge lets physical or virtual resellers choose from a selection of computer systems online whose availability and prices vary daily. Soon, on-line retailers will be able to relay orders directly from customers to Ingram Micro, which will acquire the computers from the manufacturer or if necessary assemble the components, ship the computers directly back to the customer and provide subsequent support services.

At the same time, retailers like CompUSA are establishing their own brands of computers, which they intend to sell both in stores and over the internet. They will order parts electronically from component suppliers. (The internet makes the logistics of such a system easier to manage.) Finally, Apple and other computer makers have made the difficult choice to sell computers over the internet, too.

Should you pirate your value chain?

When companies pirate the value chain of their industry, they are essentially eliminating layers of costs that are built into the current distribution system. Ask these questions to see if the distribution chain in your industry is likely to consolidate and if you should take the initiative to make that happen.

1. Can I realize significant margins by consolidating parts of the value chain to my customer?
2. Can I create significant value for customers by reducing the number of entities they have to deal with in the value chain?
3. What additional skills would I need to develop or acquire to take over the functions of others in my value chain?
4. Will I be at a competitive disadvantage if someone else moves first to consolidate the value chain?

Competition is even coming from outside the value chain. United Parcel Service has announced that it is setting up a service for virtual merchants. Using internet commerce software, a merchant can create a product catalogue and a shopfront on the Web. UPS will then manage the operations. The merchant or its customers will be able to schedule deliveries, track packages, and coordinate complex schedules over the Web. Conceivably, an on-line PC vendor could let consumers create customized machines, made up of components drawn from several different manufacturers. UPS would then gather the parts overnight, deliver them to an assembly facility, pick up the assembled product and deliver it to the customer.

On-line providers of information about computers, such as CNET, are already becoming resellers of software and hardware products. For instance, visitors to the CNET web site can read reviews of software and then order a highly touted product from the CNET store without ever leaving the site. The internet search-service Yahoo! also sells hardware and software through its site by linking seamlessly to partners' sites. Even ancillary players in the industry's value chain – including banks like Barclays and First Union, and telecommunications providers, such as AT&T – have established shopping services on their sites and could sell computers (or anything else) to their customers. In other words, once companies establish an electronic channel, they could choose to become pirates in the value chain, capturing margins from other participants up or down the chain.

Pirates will probably emerge from the ranks of those innovative companies that can recognize where core value will be most effectively delivered to customers over a network. Consider how RoweCom, an electronic subscription agent on the internet, has captured margins from intermediaries in the value chain for periodicals by using the network to change the industry's business model. Publishers traditionally have sold periodicals to libraries through subscription agents. Agents typically consolidate orders from many libraries and forward them to publishers, charging 3 per cent to 5 per cent of the list price for their services. RoweCom allows libraries to order periodicals directly from publishers over the internet and make payments

electronically through Banc One. RoweCom also provides a new level of service. For instance, libraries can place orders at any time and can easily use the site to track their budgets. Most important, however, RoweCom charges $5 per transaction, not the 3 per cent to 5 per cent of the list price. As a result, libraries have been moving their expensive orders to RoweCom. In the past 18 months, more than 75 libraries – including some of the largest in the nation – have subscribed to RoweCom's internet service.

Individual publishers are also linking directly to end users. For example, Academic Press has established an internet channel to deliver content electronically to libraries. Other academic and professional publishers have also done this, but Academic Press has changed the business model for electronic-content delivery. Rather than issuing licences to individual libraries, the company has begun selling site licences for all the libraries in an entire country. For instance, any library in Finland can now access all of Academic Press's publications under a single countrywide licence – eliminating the need for a distributor or an agent. Competing publishers will now need to reconsider their distribution chain in any nation where libraries have signed up for Academic Press's broader licence.

Value chain pirates are in a position to define new business rules and introduce new business models. But pirates will also need to develop new capabilities. Those companies that stand to lose margins to pirates currently provide very real value to customers – such as merchandising skills (which Ingram Micro does not have but CompUSA does), logistics expertise (which CompUSA does not have but UPS does) and information management (which CNET can do better than Apple). To succeed, pirates must be able to provide that value, either by building the skills in house or by allying with others.

IBM discovered this to be the case when in 1996 it launched Infomart, an electronic-content delivery initiative, and World Avenue, a cyberspace mall. IBM had believed that it could use its computer network to become a new intermediary, pirating margins from physical distributors. Infomart would have challenged the physical distribution chain for publications by making it possible for customers to go to a single site to have material from several different publishers delivered to them electronically. World Avenue was to be a single site from which consumers could access a number of different electronic stores. But IBM soon recognized that being a super-publisher required more than just making content available, and on-line merchandising meant more than just being a store-front. IBM lacked the editorial and magazine-circulation skills of publishers and the merchandising and advertising skills of retailers. The computer company had the direct connection to customers, but that was not enough to make the initiatives succeed. IBM halted both initiatives the following year.

Digital value creation

Instead of (or perhaps in addition to) pirating value from others in the value chain, companies that establish internet channels can choose to introduce new products and services. Not only is the internet channel a direct connection to customers or to any participant in the value chain, it is also a platform for innovation. It is a way to produce and distribute new combinations of digital information – or to create new transaction models and services – without incurring the traditional costs of complexity that exist in the physical world. And clearly, innovation will heighten competition if companies choose to create new value through the internet by providing something that had previously been furnished by someone else.

For instance, a broker that has established an internet channel to offer securities transaction services might begin to provide customers with access to research reports for free, which, of course, will harm businesses that offer such reports for a fee. Each time a company, large or small, succeeds in taking away a small piece of someone else's business, it undermines the economics of that business – like termites eating away at the support beams of a house.

The internet presents three opportunities for creating new value by taking away bits of someone else's business. First, a company can use its direct access to customers; each time a customer visits a company's web site is an opportunity to deliver additional ser-

vices or provide a path for other businesses that want to reach that customer. Snap-on Tools Corporation, a manufacturer of professional-grade tools for automobile repair businesses, adds new value for its customers by supplying them with regulatory information about such subjects as waste disposal at no fee. This strengthens Snap-on Tools' relationship with its customers, but it weakens the business of commercial publishers that provide such information for a fee. Netscape Communications Corporation, a company that develops and sells internet software, receives significant additional revenue at very little marginal cost by selling advertising space on its site. Netscape effectively draws revenue away from sites that derive the bulk of their revenue from advertising.

Second, a company can mine its own digital assets to serve new customer segments. Standard & Poor's Corporation, a company that has traditionally provided financial information to institutional customers, is using the information it has stored digitally to pro-

---

Can you create new digital value?

Companies that seek to create digital value using their internet channels could do so in a number of ways. Ask these questions to see how your company could best leverage its existing digital assets or leverage the digital assets of other companies that are on the internet.

1. Can I offer additional information or transaction services to my existing customer base?
2. Can I address the needs of new customer segments by repackaging my current information assets or by creating new business propositions using the internet?
3. Can I use my ability to attract customers to generate new sources of revenue, such as advertising or sales of complementary products?
4. Will my current business be significantly harmed by other companies providing some of the value I currently offer on an *à la carte* basis?

vide financial planning services to individuals over the internet. For a small fee, customers will be able to evaluate the risk of their individual securities portfolios, make portfolio allocation decisions based on the advice of market experts. They can even be alerted electronically to changes in analysts' recommendations that affect their portfolios. Standard & Poor's could never afford to target individuals with this service through a sales force or other traditional sales channels. But by offering the service at low cost over the internet, the company will be able to compete with brokers and financial analysts.

Finally, a company can take advantage of its ability to conduct transactions over the internet to take away value from others. For example, a major bank that has traditionally provided cheque-clearing services is planning to use the internet to offer complete bill-payment services for universities and order-management services for retailers. The new, targeted services should help strengthen the bank's core transaction-processing business, and it will also eat away at the business of companies that currently provide these services, such as those that furnish electronic data interchange (EDI) services.

In all three cases, each addition of digital value by one company weakens the business proposition of another company in a small way. Ultimately, the risk for established businesses is not from digital tornadoes but from digital termites.

Creating a customer magnet

Companies that can establish direct links to their customers, pirate their industry's value chain, and take away bits of value digitally from other companies may put themselves in a position to become powerful new forces in electronic commerce. They may become the on-line versions of today's category-killer stores – such as Toys 'Я' Us and Wal-Mart – and become *category destinations*.

Certainly, there are economies of scale inherent in concentration on the internet. Traditional reasons for having numerous suppliers in an industry are not valid on the internet. First, the internet makes physical distance between consumers and suppliers largely irrelevant: any store is equally accessible to any customer. Second, stores that establish a strong position or dominant brand on the internet can grow rapidly, relatively unhampered by the costs and delays common when expanding in the physical world. Third, single stores can differentiate services for many customer segments, customizing offerings and tailoring the way visitors enter and move around the site to address regional or individual differences. As a result, a small number of companies can meet the diverse needs of large segments of the global market.

But more important, if customers are not willing to learn how to navigate hundreds of different sites, each with its own unique layout, then the Web will turn out to be a naturally concentrating medium. People feel comfortable returning to the stores they know, virtual or physical, because they can easily navigate the familiar aisles and find what they are looking for. They will gravitate towards sites that can meet all their needs in specific categories. And customers will head for the places many other customers frequent if they can interact with one another and derive some value from the interaction.

Consider how this might work. A customer magnet for music compact discs might offer visitors a choice of practically any CD available by connecting to all major distributors. The site might also offer a rich selection of CD reviews from public and specialized sources – everything from the most popular music magazines to the electronic bulletin boards of major music schools. It could enable customers to interact with one another, sharing experiences and opinions. It could also offer several transaction options: customers might choose to participate in for-fee membership programmes or benefit from affinity or loyalty programmes. The site might be structured to appear differently to customers from different countries or to those with varying levels of technical skills. It might also co-opt other sites aimed at the same customer base by offering commissions for every visitor a customer sends along. Finally, the site could create marketing programmes in the physical world to ensure that its brand became synonymous with music CDs. The customer magnet would own the connection, the access and the direct interface to the customer. Industry participants, such as the CD distributors and music magazines, would have to operate through the magnet.

The steps a company could take to become a customer magnet are remarkably similar in very different industries. A solid-waste company, too, could develop the ability to provide its customers with an electronic place for gathering information, for interacting with other customers, and for conducting transactions, and then invest in creating critical mass and momentum. In this instance, industry participants might include government agencies in different countries and various suppliers of pumps and valves.

In any case, it is conceivable that some companies will attempt to control the electronic channel by becoming the site that can provide customers with everything they could want. Customer magnets could organize themselves around a specific type of product or service, a particular segment of customers, an entire industry, or a unique business model. A given industry may have room for only five, or even fewer, such magnets. Being few in number, they will have a tremendous influence on the shape of their industry. They will not own all the assets for delivering service – such as CD distribution or solid-waste pumps – but they could control access to suppliers and subtly sway customers' choices by promoting or ignoring individual brands. Over time, a customer magnet could become the electronic gateway to an entire industry.

Product magnets

Amazon.com has quickly established itself as a product magnet and today is synonymous with book retailing on the Web. Amazon offers customers virtually every book available, provides access to reviews, to book discussion groups, and even to authors themselves. It also offers a number of other services, such as notifying readers by e-mail when a new book is available and recommending books based on patterns perceived in customers' past purchases.

Should I become a customer magnet?

Becoming a customer magnet involves a substantial investment in marketing and infrastructure. Ask these questions to see if you should make the investment to become a magnet or how you should work with other companies to influence the type of customer magnet that develops in your industry.

1. Can my industry be divided into logical product, customer, or business-model segments that could evolve into customer magnets?
2. What services could an industry magnet offer my customers that would make it efficient for them to select and purchase products or services?
3. What partnerships or alliances could I create to establish the critical mass needed to become an industry magnet?
4. Will the emergence of a competing industry magnet hurt my relationships with customers or my margins?

Consider the implications of Amazon's success. Today, only Barnes & Noble rivals Amazon in the electronic channel. Customers will probably need no more than four or five of these companies. As on-line revenues increase for these two electronic merchants, what role will there be in the channel for the thousands of book retailers that have physical operations? Moreover, could Amazon use its infrastructure to move into music or professional periodicals? The tendency toward concentration in the electronic channel, which is unfolding in book sales, is likely to occur in a variety of other product categories as well.

Service magnets

Companies like Yahoo!, Excite and Lycos are becoming magnets in information services about the internet. In less than two years, the field of competitors in this category has been reduced from more than 20 to fewer than five companies, and none of the established Yellow Page companies or other paper-based search providers, such as the *Thomas Register*, is on the list. Today, new search services targeted at ever narrower subsegments – such as those for locating people or telephone numbers – find it more efficient to market themselves under the Yahoo! umbrella rather than go it alone. The cost of attracting a critical mass of customers on the Web is too high for companies that are not magnets. The fact that smaller companies are willing to offer their services through Yahoo! suggests that Yahoo! has already achieved the critical mass it needs to be a service magnet.

Customer segment magnets

New companies are targeting well-defined segments of customers and becoming their premier electronic channel. Tripod, for example, bills itself as an 'electronic community' that targets Generation Xers' – 18 to 35 year olds. The service provides information on such issues as careers, health and money, and facilitates commerce by linking directly to the sites of other companies directed at this segment. Visitors to Tripod's web site can find jobs through Classifieds 2000 for instance, or establish bank accounts through Security First Network Bank. In less than two years, Tripod's community has grown to more than 300,000 members.

Industry magnets

Companies such as Auto-By-Tel and Microsoft CarPoint (which sell cars, trucks, and other vehicles over the internet); Imx Mortgage Exchange; the FastParts Trading Exchange (which distributes electronic components); and InsWeb Corporation (which offers insurance) could become customer magnets for entire industries. These companies bring hundreds of suppliers together under one virtual roof, providing customers with an easy, convenient way to compare and purchase offerings.

InsWeb, for example, allows customers to compare prices for several different products, including health, life, and automobile insurance. The site also contains consumer information about insurance products, lists available agents, gives visitors access to Standard & Poor's ratings of insurance companies, and offers on-line simulation tools to help customers estimate the amount of coverage they may need for certain lines of insurance. If a customer likes a quote for, say, a ten-year term-life insurance policy from a highly rated company, he or she can click on a button to obtain an on-line application form and begin the application process.

The insurance companies that market themselves and sell policies through InsWeb will face challenges similar to those other established companies are likely to encounter when more industry magnets begin to appear in internet channels: How can a company differentiate its products when the rules are determined by other parties? In side-by-side comparisons, how can a company emphasize its unique value? How can it differentiate itself through marketing when the magnet can standardize the information or determine which differentiating features will be emphasized? For a while, insurance providers could refuse to join InsWeb's listings. They might even sell policies through their own individual sites. But customers will prefer the convenience of shopping in one location. If InsWeb can get enough providers and build significant traffic to its site, laggard insurers will have little choice but to participate.

Business model magnets

Companies could become magnets by introducing new business models that take advantage of the interactive capabilities of the internet. For instance, Onsale is an on-line auction house for consumer electronic products, computer equipment, and sporting goods. Customers can visit the site any time, day or night, to learn about various goods and make a bid. Similarly, NECX is establishing a spot market for computer parts. And Altra Energy Technologies is an internet-based marketplace for natural gas that had revenues of more than $1 billion in 1997. Other companies are trying to establish similar marketplaces for advertising space, airline seats, ship-cargo space, and other perishable goods. In each case, an entire industry really only needs one magnet to manage the interactions between suppliers and customers.

Clearly, few companies can justify the investment that will be needed to become a customer magnet. Managers can't yet quantify the financial rewards from such an initiative, and the risks are daunting. It is difficult and expensive for companies to integrate their existing business applications with the internet technologies they will need to conduct commerce on-line. It will also be difficult to integrate electronic processes for commerce with existing physical processes that often involve numerous functions and many business units within an organization. And companies that create customer magnets will likely need to work with competitors – and their systems and processes – to offer customers everything they could want.

But if companies decide that internet commerce is too important to ignore, it may be possible for them to adopt less risky approaches to protect their positions in the electronic channel. For instance, more than ten of the nation's largest banks, including Banc One, Citicorp and First Union, have formed a joint venture with IBM to create a common industry interface for retail banking over the internet. The banks recognize that owning direct access to the customer is critical. They do not want to cede that access to an industry outsider, such as a home-banking software provider like Intuit or Microsoft, or to a single enterprising bank. Instead, the partners in the joint venture are sharing the costs of building a technological base

for electronic banking, and in the process they are attempting to protect their industry's existing relationships with its customers.

Established companies might also stake out competitive positions in the electronic channel by allying with others to create cascading value chains. That is, companies that furnish complementary services to a common customer base could band together to establish an exclusive bundle of services in the electronic channel. For instance, hotels, travel agents, guidebook publishers and car rental agencies could create an exclusive network that would provide customers with everything they need when traveling.

Finally, established companies could find ways to embed their products or services in customer magnets. For instance, Amazon has become a book provider to Yahoo's customers. When someone visits Yahoo's site to search for, say, furniture repair, a button pops up asking the visitor if he or she wants a book on the topic.

For managers in established businesses, the internet is a tough nut to crack. It is very simple to set up a Web presence but quite difficult to create a Web-based business model. One thing is certain: the changes made possible by the internet are strategic and fundamental. However these changes play out in individual industries, they will unquestionably affect every company's relationship with its customers and the value propositions for many companies in the foreseeable future.

Menton Bank

Christopher Lovelock

Problems arise when a large bank, attempting to develop a stronger customer service orientation, enlarges the bank clerks' responsibilities to include selling activities.

'I'm concerned about Karen,' said Margaret Thompson to David Reeves. Thompson was the manager of the Victory Square branch, the third largest in Menton's 292-branch network. Reeves, the branch's customer service manager, was responsible for coordinating the work of the customer service representatives (CSRs, formerly known as bank clerks) and the customer assistance representatives (CARs, formerly known as new accounts assistants).

Thompson and Reeves were discussing Karen Mitchell, a 24-year-old customer service representative, who had applied for the soon to be vacant position of head CSR. Mitchell had been with the bank for three and a half years. She had applied for the position of what had then been called head clerk a year earlier, but the job had been given to a person with more seniority. Now that person was leaving – his wife had been transferred to a new job in another city – and the position was once again available. Two other people had also applied.

Both Thompson and Reeves agreed that, against all criteria used in the past, Karen Mitchell would have been the obvious choice. She was both fast and accurate in her work, presented a smart and professional appearance, and was well liked by customers and her fellow CSRs. However, the nature of the clerk's job had been significantly revised nine months earlier to add a stronger marketing component. They were now required to stimulate customer interest in the broadening array of financial services offered by the bank. 'The problem with Karen,' as Reeves put it, 'is that she simply refuses to sell.'

The new focus on customer service at Menton Bank

Facing aggressive competition for retail business from other financial institutions, Menton Bank had taken a number of steps in recent years to strengthen its position. In particular, it had invested heavily in technology, installing the latest generation of automated teller machines (ATMs) as well as 24-hour automated telephone banking. Customers could also call a central customer service office to speak to a bank representative concerning service questions or problems with their accounts, as well as to request new account applications or new chequebooks, which would be sent by post. Recently, Menton had introduced home banking via the internet. Complementing these new channels was a variety of new retail financial products. Finally, the appearance of the branches was being improved and a recently implemented pilot programme was testing the impact of a radical redesign of the branch interior on the quality of customer service. As more customers switched to electronic banking, the bank planned to close a number of its smaller branches. In the most recent six months, Menton had seen a significant increase in the number of new accounts opened, as compared to the same period of the previous year. And quarterly survey data showed that the bank was steadily increasing its share of new deposits in the region.

Customer service issues

Senior bank personnel had found that existing 'platform' staff – known as new accounts assistants – were ill equipped to sell many of the new products now offered because they lacked product knowledge and skills in selling. As Thompson recalled:

> The problem was that they were so used to sitting at their desks waiting for a customer to approach them with a specific request, such as a mortgage or car loan, that it was hard to get them to take a more positive approach that involved actively probing for

customer needs. Their whole job seemed to revolve around filling out forms.

Internal research showed that the mix of activities performed by clerks was starting to change. More customers were using the ATMs and automated telephone banking for a broad array of transactions, including cash withdrawals and deposits (from the ATMs), transfers of funds between accounts, and requesting account balances. As home banking caught on, this trend was expected to accelerate. But Thompson noted that customers who were older or less well-educated still seemed to prefer 'being served by a real person, rather than a machine'.

Three sites were included in the pilot test of 'new look' branches featuring a redesigned interior. One was the Victory Square branch, located in a busy commercial and retail area, about one mile from the central business district and less than 10 minutes' walk from the campus of a major university. The other test branches were in two different urban areas and were located in a shopping centre and next to a big hospital, respectively.

Each of these three branches had previously been remodelled to include at least five ATMs (Victory Square had seven), which could be closed off from the rest of the branch so that they would remain accessible to customers 24 hours a day. Further remodelling was then undertaken to locate a customer service desk near the entrance; close to each desk were two electronic information terminals, featuring colour touch-screens that customers could activate to obtain information on a variety of bank services. The clerks' positions were redesigned to provide two levels of service: an express counter for simple deposits and cashing of approved cheques, and other counters for the full array of services provided by clerks. The number of positions open at a given time was varied to reflect the volume of anticipated business and staffing arrangements were changed to ensure that more clerks were on hand to serve customers during the busiest periods.

Human resources

With the new environment came new staff training programmes and new job titles. Front-line staff at all Menton branches received new job descriptions and job titles: customer assistance representatives (for the staff at information desks), customer service representatives (for the clerks) and customer service director (instead of assistant branch manager). The head clerk position was renamed head CSR. The training programme for each group began with staff from the three test branches and was being extended to all staff. It included information about both new and existing retail products. (CARs received more extensive training in this area than did CSRs.) The CARs also attended a 15-hour course, offered in three separate sessions, on basic selling skills. This programme covered key steps in the sales process, including building a relationship, exploring customer needs, determining a solution, and overcoming objections.

The sales training programme for CSRs, by contrast, consisted of just two two-hour sessions designed to develop skills in recognizing and probing customer needs, presenting product features and benefits, overcoming objections and referring customers to CARs. All front office staff were taught how to improve their communication skills and professional image: clothing, personal appearance and interactions with customers were all discussed. The trainer said, 'Remember, people's money is too important to entrust to someone who doesn't look and act the part!' CARs were instructed to rise from their seats and shake hands with customers. Both CARs and CSRs were given exercises designed to improve their listening skills and their powers of observation.

Although Menton Bank's management anticipated that most of the increased emphasis on selling would fall to the CARs, they also foresaw a limited selling role for the customer service representatives, who would be expected to mention various products and facilities offered by the bank as they served customers at the customer windows. For instance, if a customer happened to say something about a forthcoming holiday, the CSR was supposed to mention traveller's cheques; if a customer complained about bounced cheques, the CSR should recommend speaking to a CAR about the possibility of having automatic overdraft protection; and if a customer mentioned investments, the CSR was expected to refer him or her to a CAR who could provide information on various savings and investment products. All CSRs were supplied with their own business cards. When making a referral, they were expected to write the customer's name and the product of interest on the back of a card, give it to the customer and send that individual to the customer assistance desks.

To motivate CSRs to sell specific financial products, the bank decided to change the process under which employees at the three test branches were evaluated. All CSRs had traditionally been evaluated half-yearly on a variety of criteria, including accuracy, speed, quality of interactions with customers, punctuality of arrival for work, job attitudes, cooperation with other employees, and professional image. The evaluation process assigned a number of points to each criterion, with accuracy and speed being the most heavily weighted. In addition to appraisals by the customer service director and the branch manager, with input from the head CSR, Menton had recently instituted a programme of anonymous visits by what was popularly known as the 'mystery client'. Each CSR was visited at least once a quarter by a professional evaluator posing as a customer. This individual's appraisal of the CSR's appearance, performance and attitude was included in the overall evaluation. The number of points scored by each CSR had a direct impact on merit pay raises and on selection for promotion to the head CSR position or to customer assistance jobs.

To encourage improved product knowledge and 'consultative selling' by CSRs, the evaluation process was revised to include points assigned for each individual's success in sales referrals. Under the new evaluation scheme, the maximum number of points assigned for effectiveness in making sales – directly or through referrals to CARs – amounted to 30 per cent of the potential total score. Although CSR-initiated sales had risen significantly in the last half-year, Reeves sensed that morale had dropped among this group, in contrast to the CARs, whose enthusiasm and commitment had risen significantly. He had also noticed an increase in CSR errors. One CSR had left, complaining about too much pressure.

Karen Mitchell

Under the old scoring system, Karen Mitchell had been the highest scoring clerk/CSR for four consecutive half-year periods. But after 12 months under the new system, her ranking had dropped to fourth out of the seven full-time clerks. The top-ranking CSR, Mary Bell, had been with Menton Bank for 16 years, but had declined repeated invitations to apply for a head clerk position, saying that she was happy where she was, earning at the top of the CSR scale, and did not want 'the extra worry and responsibility'. Mitchell ranked first on all but one of the operationally related criteria (interactions with customers, where she ranked second), but sixth on selling effectiveness (Exhibit 1).

Thompson and Reeves had spoken to Mitchell about her performance and expressed disappointment. Mitchell had informed them, respectfully, but firmly, that she saw the most important aspect of her job as giving customers fast, accurate and courteous service, telling the two bank officers:

> I did try this selling thing but it just seemed to annoy people. Some said they were in a hurry and couldn't talk now, others looked at me as if I were slightly crazy to bring up the subject of a different bank service than the one they were currently transacting. And then, when you got the odd person who seemed interested, you could hear the other customers in the line grumbling about the slow service.
>
> Really, the last straw was when I noticed on the computer screen that this woman had several thousand in her savings account so I suggested to her, just as the trainer had told us, that she could earn more interest if she opened a money market account. Well, she told me it was none of my business what she did with her money, and stomped off. Don't get me wrong, I love being able to help customers, and if they ask for my advice, I'll gladly tell them about what the bank has to offer.

Selecting a new head CSR

Two weeks after this meeting, it was announced that the head CSR was leaving. The job entailed some

Exhibit 1 ■ Menton Bank: summary of performance evaluation scores for customer service representatives at Victory Square branch for latest two half-year periods

CSR name[3]	Length of full-time bank service	Operational criteria[1] (max.: 70 points)		Selling effectiveness[2] (max.: 30 points)		Total score	
		1st half	2nd half	1st half	2nd half	1st half	2nd half
Mary Bell	16 years, 10 months	65	64	16	20	81	84
Frank Conway	2 years, 3 months	63	61	15	19	78	80
Bruce Greenfield	12 months	48	42	20	26	68	68
Karen Mitchell	3 years, 7 months	67	67	13	12	80	79
Sharon Roberts	1 year, 4 months	53	55	8	9	61	64
Swee Hoon Chen	7 months	–	50	–	22	–	72
Jean Smith	2 years, 1 month	57	55	21	28	79	83

Notes: 1. Totals based on sum of ratings points against various criteria, including accuracy, work production, attendance and punctuality, personal appearance, organization of work, initiative, cooperation with others, problem-solving ability and quality of interaction with customers.
2. Points awarded for both direct sales by CSR (e.g., traveller's cheques) and referral selling by CSR to CAR (e.g., debit card, long-term savings, overdraft facilities).
3. Full-time CSRs only (part-time CSRs were evaluated separately).

supervision of the work of the other CSRs (including allocation of work assignments and scheduling part-time CSRs at busy periods or during employee holidays), consultation on – and, where possible, resolution of – any problems occurring at the clerk positions, and handling of large cash deposits and withdrawals by local retailers. When not engaged on such tasks, the head CSR was expected to man one of the clerk's positions.

When applications for the positions closed, Karen Mitchell was one of three candidates. The other two candidates were Jean Smith, 42, another CSR at the Victory Square branch; and Tony Adams, 24, the head CSR at one of Menton Bank's small suburban branches, who was seeking more responsibility.

Jean Smith was married with two sons at school. She had started working as a part-time clerk at Victory Square some three years previously, switching to full-time work a year later in order, as she said, to save some money for her boys' university education. Jean was a cheerful woman with a jolly laugh. She had a

wonderful memory for people's names and Reeves had often seen her greeting customers on the street or in a sandwich bar during her lunch hour. Reviewing her evaluations over the previous three years, Reeves noted that she had initially performed poorly on accuracy and at one point, when she was still a part-timer, had been put on probation because of frequent inaccuracies in the balance in her cash drawer at the end of the day. Although Reeves considered her much improved on this score, he still saw room for improvement. The customer service director had also had occasion to reprimand her for tardiness during the past year. Smith attributed this to health problems with her elder son who, she said, was now responding to treatment.

Both Reeves and Thompson had observed Jean Smith at work and agreed that her interactions with customers were exceptionally good, although she tended to be too chatty and was not as quick as Karen Mitchell. She seemed to have a natural ability to size up customers and to decide which ones were good prospects for a quick sales pitch on a specific financial product. Although slightly untidy in her personal appearance, she was very well organized in her work and was quick to help her fellow CSRs, especially newcomers. In the most recent six months, Smith had ranked ahead of Karen Mitchell as a result of being very successful in consultative selling (Exhibit 1).

Tony Adams, the third candidate, was not working in one of the three test branches, so had not been exposed to the consultative selling programme and its corresponding evaluation scheme. However, he had received excellent evaluations for his work in Menton's small Longmeadow branch, where he had been employed for three years. Reeves and Thompson had interviewed Tony Adams and considered him intelligent and personable. He had joined the bank after leaving university mid-way through his final year, but had recently started taking evening courses in order to complete his degree. The Longmeadow branch was located in an older part of town, where commercial and retail activity were rather stagnant. This branch (which was rumoured to be under consideration for closure) had not yet been renovated and had no ATMs, although there was an ATM accessible to Menton customers just a few streets away. Adams supervised three CSRs and reported directly to the branch manager, who spoke very highly of him. Since there were no CARs in this branch, Adams and another experienced CSR took turns to handle new accounts and loan or mortgage applications.

Thompson and Reeves were troubled by the decision that faced them. Prior to the bank's shift in focus, Karen Mitchell would have been the natural choice for the head CSR job which, in turn, could be a stepping stone to further promotions, including customer assistance representative, customer service director and, eventually, manager of a small branch or a management position in the regional office. Mitchell had told her superiors that she was interested in making a career in banking and that she was eager to take on further responsibilities.

Compounding the problem was the fact that the three branches testing the improved branch design and new customer service programme had just completed a full year of the test. Thompson knew that sales and profits were up significantly at all three branches, relative to the bank's performance as a whole. She anticipated that top management would want to extend the programme systemwide after making any modifications that seemed desirable.

Crosse & Whitewall: cross-selling professional services

Jacques Bouvard ■ Christopher H. Lovelock

A professional firm specializing in pension fund audits seeks to extend the firm's relationships with existing clients by offering consulting services. But the first attempt at cross-selling is a flop. What has gone wrong and why?

Jean-Baptiste Clement, a new partner and co-director in the Paris office of Crosse & Whitewall, pondered what had gone wrong earlier in the day at his meeting with Française des Métaux, a major metals manufacturer. 'It's as though we were playing in two different ball courts,' he muttered to himself in English, recalling a sports idiom from his time in the United States.

Background on the firm

J.-B. Clement, 42, had joined Crosse & Whitewall three months earlier, in March 1993. C&W was an international professional firm, with headquarters in Chicago, that specialized in pension funds auditing and human resource management. It had been started in 1919 by two young veterans of World War I. Captain William Whitewall had flown as a pilot in the famous 'Lafayette Squadron' and had won a Congressional Medal of Honor for downing seven enemy aircraft in the last months of the Great War. He had also developed a taste for high living and fast cars. On returning to his native Chicago, he had reluctantly gone back to work in the First Illinois Insurance Company (F.I.I. Co.), a large firm owned by his family. Very soon afterward, he met ex-Master Sergeant Crosse at a 'Chicago Welcomes Its Heroes' party. Jeremy Crosse had been badly wounded on the Argonne battlefield and, after losing the use of one leg, had decided to find a rewarding, albeit sedentary, career. He followed the advice of a friend, the head of the Illinois Society of Actuaries, started studying again, and prepared for the first of a long series of examinations to become an actuary. Normally, an actuary would easily find work with an insurance company and, indeed, F.I.I. Co. offered him a position. But, Jeremy Crosse had a better idea.

He had perceived the fact that American corporations were rapidly creating new pension funds for their executives, thus creating a vast new opportunity for a professional firm that could advise them properly and audit their plans every year, as the law required. However, he needed an associate to carry out all the promotional and outside negotiation work. Swashbuckling young socialite 'Wild Bill' Whitewall, with all the right social connections, was the perfect man. Jeremy Crosse soon convinced him that an independent professional career would be much more fun than filing insurance policies or following up damage claims, while waiting for his father to vacate the presidency of F.I.I. Co.

Within ten years, Crosse & Whitewall had become the leader of a new profession. Crosse wrote excellent reports and taught growing numbers of actuaries the essential principles and high ethics of his trade, while the enterprising captain had become the 'darling' of most insurance companies and kept opening new offices around the country. C&W was already well established in the US – in Boston, Hartford, New York, San Francisco and Atlanta – when the depression hit many of its clients. More importantly, the firm had adopted a rolling partnership structure similar to that of leading law firms. The best professionals in the country were attracted to Crosse & Whitewall by a special statute that gave junior partners, upon their election by senior partners, access to shares in the partnership. With its rapid geographic expansion and the excellent economic results of a growing firm, those shares appreciated substantially every year and gave competent professionals an opportunity to become wealthy while working in a congenial environment. On retirement, they had to re-sell their shares to the partnership, typically for a price around 100 times their initial investment.

After weathering the depression more successfully than some of its clients, C&W kept expanding in size and growing in reputation. The number of partners doubled every ten years, reaching 62 in 1958. The real explosion in numbers and revenues happened during the sixties. By 1990, C&W was a worldwide firm with 42 offices, 325 partners and revenues in excess of $750 million. The two founding partners had retired as multi-millionaires, but their basic philosophy had remained. Under a new and somewhat more collegial leadership, C&W still flourished with its combination of high quality professionalism and elegantly aggressive marketing. New divisions had been launched in four areas closely related to pension funds: executive compensation, personnel management, insurance consulting and re-insurance consulting.

Expansion into France

Because of its basic state-run social security retirement payment by 'repartition' rather than by 'capitalization', France had not been an attractive market for C&W. Repartition meant that the retirement premiums levied yearly on the active population and their employers would be used immediately to finance the pensions paid to retired employees. In periods of economic growth and high birthrate, such a system made good sense, even if it did not require the auditing services of C&W.

In the late seventies, however, some corporations started seeing that the combination of a negative growth in the working population, delayed entry into the work force, continued double-digit inflation, early retirement policies and longer life expectancy meant that employees who had contributed all their lives to the retirement of others had a high risk of never receiving, through 'repartition', proper remuneration when they retired.

Having repeatedly been sought by various prestigious clients in France, C&W opened its Paris office in 1979. In 1981 this trickle of demand suddenly

became a torrent with the advent of a Socialist government. Supplementary pension funds became a must for progressive companies which still wanted to attract talented employees.

By 1993, C&W had 11 partners and 120 employees in France, operating from headquarters in Paris and small satellite offices in Lille, Lyons and Toulouse. Total revenues in France were 80 million French francs (about $15 million).

The firm's mission as stated by its director, Peter Williams, was 'to serve large international companies active in France and to develop a national clientele among leading French companies'. In addition, the Paris office had been assigned the task of experimenting with expansion into other types of professional activities that could be adopted worldwide throughout C&W.

Clement changes jobs

Clement had graduated from the prestigious Paris HEC (Hautes Etudes Commerciales) business school. After a two-year stint with Unilever as an assistant brand manager, he had spent two years in California gaining an MBA at the Stanford Business School. On returning to Europe, he had joined the glass division of St-Gobain, holding several jobs in marketing and strategic planning over a four-year period. Through a Stanford classmate, he had then been recruited by the Paris office of International Strategic Consultants (ISC) where he had enjoyed a very successful career for 12 years, the last seven as a partner. He had brought in several large new clients, including two banks and four major companies. But, in time, he had begun to feel restless. His personal interest in the 'soft' side of consulting problems, dealing with people rather than profit and efficiency alone, was not shared by the leadership of ISC.

It was through Peter Williams, one of his neighbours in the plush Paris suburb of Neuilly, that Clement first became familiar with Crosse & Whitewall. Both men served on the board of the private school attended by their children and had come to know each other socially. Over dinner one evening, Williams had suggested that his friend should think seriously about joining C&W. 'Our strategy committee in Chicago is constantly pushing me to develop new lines of professional activity,' he told Clement. 'What you have done with ISC is of real interest to us, and I am sure that you would enjoy working with our personnel management and compensation partners.' Warming to his theme, Williams continued:

We've been hugely successful in our major activity of pension fund auditing: worldwide, we have 350 Fortune International 500 companies as our steady clients. Historically, it's been a very profitable business, enjoying steady growth as the pension funds themselves grow in size. But, this has attracted new competition and the business is becoming more price sensitive than in the past. In addition, it is heavily influenced either positively or negatively by regulatory and national political decisions totally beyond our control.

In France, we're doing reasonably well, but we could certainly use additional revenues, if only to enhance our average revenue per partner and, of course, our bonuses . . . We should enter new professional areas, such as the strategy and general management consulting that you know so well. The synergies with our own main line of activity are obvious. With someone like you on board, and with the team we will help you build up, it should be possible to generate additional cash flow from existing clients, as well as gain new clients for the firm.

During the subsequent months, several conversations took place to explore and confirm their mutual interest further. Both men agreed that a vast potential existed in France among leading French companies as well as with the European affiliates of multinational groups headquartered in Paris.

Peter Williams made several long-distance calls and exchanged confidential faxes with the managing director and most senior partners of the firm about hiring Clement on a quasi-equal basis to himself, in recognition of his extensive experience and in anticipation of expected benefits.

Finally, over lunch at 'Taillevent' one day, Williams offered Clement an immediate directorship – a new departure for C&W – plus a compensation package so generous that it was 'impossible to refuse'. Not only would Jean-Baptiste Clement receive a fixed compensation equal to his present total remuneration, but also included in the package was provision for a large bonus (up to 30 per cent of his salary) on incremental business from existing clients, as well as up to 50 per cent for the successful acquisition of new clients.

Working at C&W

Clement joined the Paris office of C&W in March 1993. His new colleagues welcomed him warmly, but he was surprised to find them somewhat reticent about discussing their own clients. Clement ascribed this to professional respect for confidentiality. He set to work following up several leads of his own and within three months had brought in two new consulting clients. He was also involved in arranging for C&W to audit a supplementary pension fund which one of his former employers was creating for its senior executives.

He had started building up a team of four younger consultants, including one bright young man who, after spending two years in C&W's compensation practice, had decided to move on to strategic work. Jean-Baptiste Clement was already looking forward to the day when he could propose that this enthusiastic consultant become the first junior partner of the new Paris practice . . .

Despite these early successes, Clement was still concerned by the reserved attitude of his colleagues. One day when he was lunching with three of them, he answered their questions about the work he had performed at ISC. Describing a project that he had directed the previous year to reorganize a major oil company, he encountered a mixture of disbelief and incomprehension.

'Do you mean that you and your colleagues actually restructured this enormous company last year?' one of them asked.

'Yes,' Clement replied,

We helped them simplify their structure, reduce the number of levels from eleven to six and even helped them relocate 482 people, saving about 95 million French francs in overhead costs. Then, we streamlined their management information and planning system. Total fees amounted to 12 million French francs for 15 months of continued work by a team that ranged in size from four to seven consultants.

'Hey, what happened to their pension funds?' interjected another of his colleagues.

'Nothing, I believe,' responded Clement, slightly surprised. 'Being nationalized, they only had the usual *retraite des cadres* and social security. Do you want an introduction to their CEO to sell him one of your schemes?'

'No, I was just curious,' the other replied.

'You might try to get the name of the guy who set up their last pension fund,' another actuary partner suggested.

Clement could see that his kind of work was not their 'cup of tea', and he found it just as hard to understand the arcane workings of the assignments in which his actuarial colleagues were involved. He also marvelled at the enormous fees the firm earned for what seemed to him such tedious and repetitive work. He was also deeply impressed by two things: their extensive use of 'pre-cooked' computer programs that seemed to be doing all the work, and the ease of getting repeat business year after year without any need for the costly and time-consuming 'developmental' work required in his own type of consulting. All they did was send a letter of renewal at the end of each year, with a prepared space for the company to sign. It seemed so easy.

One Friday afternoon, just before five o'clock, Clement was beginning to check a 50-page report due at the client's the following Monday, and he still had to write a proposal before going home for the weekend. Two of his partner colleagues poked their heads in at his open doorway. They were carrying raincoats and umbrellas and were evidently leaving for home. Quickly sizing up the situation, one of them, Charles-Henri de Lamenais, remarked cheerily:

'You're obviously in the wrong business, *mon vieux*! You should have got an actuarial degree like us,

instead of wasting your time at Stanford! See you on Monday!'

A presentation at Française des Métaux

Two weeks later, Clement felt he was finally beginning to make progress. After much lobbying, de Lamenais had agreed to open the door to his largest client, Française des Métaux SA (F.M.), a company involved in refining and marketing copper, zinc and high-value alloys. Since Clement had led an ISC consulting team for Amax in Europe several years earlier, he knew the metals business and was certain that he could do something beneficial for de Lamenais's client.

At F.M.'s main administrative offices in La Défense, de Lamenais led Clement along a series of tortuous corridors to the office of Mr Louis Martineau. Expecting to be greeted by an elitist Polytechnicien,[1] typical of the upper echelons of management in such companies in France, Clement was a bit surprised to find that his colleague's principal contact was a harassed-looking little man in a cluttered office. Martineau greeted them politely and cleared several dossiers off the chairs so that the two visitors could sit down.

After the introductions were made and de Lamenais had confirmed that the audit report would be ready on the promised date, Clement launched into his presentation. He delivered a thorough but succinct analysis of five years of published figures, complete with diagrams he had prepared that very morning on his own Macintosh, comparing overall profitability, days of inventory and asset rotation for Française des Métaux and three of its European competitors. Clement concluded what he considered to be a stimulating 15-minute presentation by inviting Martineau to make use of C&W's strategic consulting services in order to help F.M. gain market share and improve profitability.

Expecting an interested response, Clement was amazed to be greeted by complete silence in the room. Not only Martineau but also de Lamenais appeared somewhat bewildered by what they had just heard.

Seeking to regain the initiative, Clement asked Martineau, 'Do you think that your boss would be interested in pursuing these issues further?' Looking slightly ill at ease, the other replied:

> You have to understand that my office reports to the Assistant Finance Director, reflecting the immense amounts of money the company is investing in this pension fund. The fund is also used as collateral for some of the company's borrowings. I don't believe that my boss, Monsieur Lebrun, participates in strategy discussions with our board. Of course, I could ask him to arrange an appointment with our Director-General [CEO]; but I'm told he's a very busy man.

'Thank you, Monsieur Martineau,' de Lamenais said, rising to his feet and holding out his hand. 'My colleague and I really appreciate your willingness to take time out of your busy schedule.' Clement also shook hands with Martineau and thanked him, but was hard put to hide his disappointment. Then, the two partners left the office and retraced their way back to the reception area.

'What happened?' Clement asked as the two of them climbed back into de Lamenais' new Jaguar. 'I thought that I gave him a very convincing line. Wasn't he interested? Or did he simply not understand?'

De Lamenais eased the Jaguar out of the parking lot and smiled wryly. 'I think you scared him rather than impressed him, my friend. And you scared me, too. At one point, when you proposed raising the ante to the level of his superior, I thought that I was going to lose him as a client . . . Never again!'

Jean-Baptiste Clement remained silent for a long time. It was becoming clear to him that the actuarial partners appeared to be more interested in using him and his work to bring in new clients for their own practice rather than the other way around. Yet, he liked what Peter Williams had told him about C&W's combination of professionalism and aggressive marketing. Obviously, a lot still needed to be done before the synergies he and Williams had dreamt about could be achieved.

'Well, I won't give up that easily!' Clement said eventually, as de Lamenais accelerated onto the Champs-Elysées. 'Charles-Henri, let's think this experience through and decide, together with our other partners, what we should do differently if we want to succeed as a team . . . Have you ever heard of cross-selling?'

'No, as a matter of fact, I have not,' de Lamenais answered, 'but Peter has given me the task of setting up the agenda for our yearly Paris Partners Meeting in Chantilly next month. I still have nothing for the morning of the third day. How much time do you need?'

Note

1. A 'Polytechnicien' is a graduate of France's most distinguished engineering school, The École Polytechnique in Paris.

SKF Bearings series: market orientation through services

Restructuring the before and after market

Sandra Vandermerwe ■ *Marika Taishoff*

The world's largest manufacturer of bearings seeks to differentiate its product through enhanced service for customers. Achieving this goal requires restructuring the organization to focus on the needs of different customer segments. The move is met with mixed responses within the company.

In the spring of 1987 Mauritz Sahlin, CEO of SKF, the world's largest bearing company, took a bold step. The time had come to do whatever was necessary to improve profitability and return on assets. He knew that his plan would require a complex reorganization of SKF with far-reaching consequences, but he had no other options.

Production had already been rationalized and was fully automated, leaving little room for real savings. The company could not pull back on R&D expenditures as they were essential to having technological prowess and quality standards. Cutting back on staff would upset the unions and provoke costly stoppages.

He was convinced that the only viable long-term solution was to change the strategic orientation of SKF from the production line to the market. Amidst great uncertainty and speculation, he called together the senior bearing managers from around the world to Saltsjobaden, Sweden, to announce his intention to split the company into three new areas.

> It is essential, he said, that we optimize by structuring around our market relationships instead of our manufacturing capacity. If we want to remain the industry leader in bearings, we must be prepared to give customers what they want rather than merely sell them what we make.

He knew that the traditional, sluggish culture of the company had to be altered. Questions would have to be answered which were not yet part of the existing SKF vocabulary. He expected criticism, resistance and conflict among the divisions. Even confusion for a while. He was prepared to take the risks.

The beginnings and background

As in many industrial success stories, the formation of SKF happened by chance. At the turn of the century Sven Wingquist, a young Swedish maintenance engineer, was fed up with the poor quality of bearings, with frequent stoppages and replacements that not only were expensive but took weeks for suppliers to deliver. The frustrated Wingquist got his employer's blessing to begin work on a new bearing in 1905 and soon perfected a product that was more effective and longer lasting than competitors' models. By 1907 Svenska Kullager Fabriken (SKF), the new company set up to produce and market the technological innovation, was in business.

The ball bearing, a device which allows rotation around a shaft or axle with minimal friction, is an essential part of any motion dependent product, be it car, machine, truck or train. As a result, high-quality bearings soon became an indispensable item for all major industrial sectors, ranging from electrical and heavy industries to transportation. Over the next six decades, SKF grew in tandem with industrial growth and became the world leader in bearing technology and applications.

Up through the mid-1960s, SKF was highly centralized; all aspects of the business such as logistics, global sales, application engineering and public rela-

This case has won a 1997 European Case of the Year prize, awarded by ECCH (the European Case Clearing House), Cranfield, UK.

tions were handled by the parent company in Göteborg. Five European plants produced a wide range of products geared to their own large local customer base. These regional units concentrated exclusively on the manufacturing process, particularly on maintaining cost-effectiveness. Countries did not export to each other or operate internationally except rarely – when the initiative came from Göteborg.

The company's underlying drive was mass production and having high quality standards. In the words of one executive, 'Big was beautiful'. The plants were given significant capital budget allocations. Large economies of scale meant that huge quantities of bearings could be sold at competitive prices on the world market. Operations were integrated as much as possible both horizontally and vertically. A tools division was acquired in order to expand into the manufacture of engineering products and machine tools. Manufacturing machinery was designed in-house so that material flow systems and production techniques could be perfected and capacity increased.

R&D contributed greatly to SKF's strength. Since most bearings had an average life of five years, there was a continuous need to develop new products. About 200 people in the Netherlands were involved in product development and in improving the engineering and performance standards for the product lines. Input was received from the various plants where R&D had a close relationship. As a general rule, SKF preferred to overdesign its products to ensure that the needs and specifications of the plant managers were met.

The 1970s and 1980s: Japanese and European competition

In the early 1970s the Japanese, already strong in Asia, entered the European bearings market. As a result, SKF management was forced to cut costs further 'by whatever means' as well as begin exporting outside their traditional markets. To reach this goal while developing scale economies, production facilities were rationalized along the lines of the Japanese model, i.e., each factory became responsible for making and exporting a specific bearing type for world consumption.

The rise in oil prices in the early 1980s, causing a drop in real wealth and in demand for capital goods and consumer durables, put additional pressure on margins. 'Production Concept 80', aimed at stimulating effective production, at cutting staff and underscoring the manufacturing process in company investment policy, was SKF's response to economic conditions as well as to competitive threats.

This concept, along with the continued emphasis on top quality standards, allowed SKF to remain the number 1 bearings producer. By the late 1980s the company had 20 per cent of the world bearings market share, nearly twice that of its closest competitor, Nippon Seiko of Japan. Another Japanese bearings producer, NTN, had 10 per cent followed by Germany's F.A.G. and Timken of the US with 8.5 per cent each, and the Japanese firm Koyo with 6 per cent of the world market.

Bearings producers were not the only competitors on the world scene. Automobile manufacturers, including Ford, Honda and Mercedes, through their spare parts divisions, were both competitors to and customers of SKF. This was also the case for some specific manufacturers of automobile parts, such as the UK's Quinton Hazel, which would typically purchase SKF bearings and sell them under its own brand name to distributors, thereby cutting into a segment of SKF's traditional customer base.

SKF's position had always been strongest in Europe and Latin America, with 35 per cent and 30 per cent of these markets respectively. In the US, SKF was in third position, with 12 per cent. On average, Europe accounted for 60 per cent of SKF's business, North America for 20 per cent, Sweden 5 per cent and the rest of the world 15 per cent. Despite this comparatively strong market share, worldwide economic and industrial conditions continued to squeeze margins during the first half of the decade. This situation came to a head in 1985 when SKF's volume in the US, susceptible to economic changes and often indicative of what could happen in other regions, plunged 15 per cent. The company was obliged to embark on a substantial restructuring programme in the US.

1986: a financial ebb

By 1986, SKF had 48 factories in 13 countries operating at near or full capacity to produce two million bearings a day. SKF vigorously promoted its products through 35,000 local dealer and distributor (d/d) outlets worldwide, as well as a direct salesforce of 600 throughout 130 countries. Dealers and distributors carried large stocks of limited range, high turnover bearings for SKF, along with competitive bearings and complementary materials and tools.

When Sahlin took the helm as CEO in 1985, SKF was operating at the crest of what amounted to a roller bearing boom. Nevertheless, economic conditions and competitive pressure made it a buyers' market. Bottomline results began to turn flat at SKF that year, when sales slackened and margins narrowed. (The financial profile for the years 1982 through 1986 is shown in Exhibit 1.)

Segmenting the bearings market

With increasing competition, SKF found it more and more difficult to differentiate its product from the others. It had always applied one strategy and organization for all bearing customers. High-quality products were sold in large quantities at competitive prices.

Sahlin questioned this approach and, late in 1986, commissioned research to examine the bearings market in detail. He wanted to establish whether the market could be segmented along any natural split amongst the product lines according to specific customer needs.

Consumers were grouped into three categories:

1. *Automotive OEM* (cars, trucks, electrical), with 32 per cent of SKF bearings sales in Skr.
2. *Machinery OEM* (heavy industry, railway, general machinery), with 27 per cent of SKF bearings sales in Skr.
3. *Aftermarket* (vehicles and industrial), with 41 per cent of SKF bearings sales in Skr.

Whereas bearings were regarded as vital components in the OEM (original equipment manufacturer) market, in the aftermarket they were seen merely as spare parts. Large OEM sales were handled directly by the company's global sales arm. Contracts were substantial and steady. 'Large orders were signed and executed in a routine way.'

The aftermarket sales were made to distributors and dealers, who in turn served end-users. Relationships were entirely different for these markets, as were the services demanded. Delivery requirements, lead-times and quantities, along with type and range of bearings needed, also varied considerably.

Exhibit 1 ■ Financial profile for 1982–86

In Skr (bn)	1982	1983	1984	1985	1986
Consolidated					
Net sales	14.4	16.2	17.8	20.0	20.1
Operating expenses	13.0	14.9	15.9	17.9	18.0
Income after financial income and expenses	.657	.604	1.3	1.4	1.5
Total assets	18.8	18.6	21.8	22.0	22.8
Shareholder equity	5.4	5.2	6.8	6.7	7.3
Return on total assets	8.0	7.4	9.8	9.5	9.3
Price per share	29.2	42.0	43.0	75.0	84.0
Bearings:					
as % of total sales	80	82	80	76	77
as % of total profits	90	95	80	78	75

Source: Annual reports.

There were more than twice as many OEM than aftermarket customers, although fewer in the vehicle business than in machinery. Automotive OEM customers were large and tended to operate centrally on a European, if not global scale. By contrast, machinery OEM users were smaller; their particular strengths tended to be in specific industries and geographic locations. Large OEM customers made up roughly 40 per cent of the total SKF bearings sales in kronor. Lead-times were stable and predictable, making forecasting straightforward. Profit margins were low in the OEM sector. The larger OEM customers, who often set their own prices on substantial, long-term contracts, were particularly cost conscious since 'every cent saved was money in the bank'. SKF was thus under constant competitive pressure to keep price increases at or below the inflation rate.

OEM customers were considered the glamorous end of the business, always given priority by the SKF factories. High volume production and sales standards set for the large OEM customers were applied throughout the rest of the organization. OEMs were not only allocated most of the new product funding, but also attracted SKF's best talent. Some of the reasons for this situation were:

- OEMs would typically deal with big name customers like Volkswagen or Ford, and would be involved in negotiations at a senior managerial level.
- Technical developments for OEMs were more challenging than for the aftermarket because they tended to be more complex and state-of-the-art.
- Orders for the OEMs were larger, steady and more consistent, with lead-times that made well-defined production schedules possible.

By contrast, the aftermarket tended to concentrate on single sale deals for motor dealers and factories. Although price was important, these clients, for whom speed, availability and assistance were essential, were prepared to pay more than the OEM customers. In fact, the higher prices in the aftermarket enabled SKF to do OEM business that otherwise may not have been justified. It had long been suspected that, despite being largely limited to single sales, the aftermarket was the most profitable part of the business. However, since operating results for all the markets were consolidated, this impression was never really confirmed.

The aftermarket was subdivided into two separate categories:

1. *The industrial aftermarket* (factory owners and plant managers), with 66 per cent of SKF aftermarket sales in Skr.
2. *The vehicle aftermarket* (fleet owners and repair shops), with 34 per cent of SKF aftermarket sales in Skr.

In their *industrial* aftermarket business, which contributed two-thirds to the overall aftermarket sales, SKF had concentrated mainly on steel and paper mills. Mines and railways were also a part of this business. These customers had the same basic needs wherever they were geographically situated. The distributor network accounted for 80 per cent of the sales.

For industrial users, the cost of the bearing was 'peanuts compared to the cost of standstill'. They sought to minimize downtime and maximize the recovery speed. Customers spent 75 per cent of downtime locating the proper equipment and people, and only 25 per cent on actually repairing the machine.

The lifetime of a bearing played a fundamental role in the success of these customers' production activities. Longevity was affected by: (1) the quality of the product, (2) how it was installed, (3) protecting the bearing from the environment, and (4) the quality of maintenance management at the factory. The last three factors depended on the users. Most bearings failed because of incorrect installation, inadequate or improper lubrication or environmental contamination.

The *vehicle* aftermarket accounted for one third of total aftermarket sales. Despite the fact that the automobile and truck sectors contributed 24 per cent of SKF's OEM sales, the aftermarket had been relatively ignored. This neglect stemmed from the basic principle, 'if we made it, we sold it'. And since SKF made only a limited range of bearings compared to the great variety of autos, the aftermarket had never been considered a priority.

Dealers for automotive OEMs and independent distributors channelled spare parts through to the car and truck market. Because of the better service they were receiving, garage and fleet owners were increasingly shifting their business to the independents. Bearings comprised only 3–4 per cent of distributor and retailer sales, compared to between 30 per cent and 70 per cent in the industrial aftermarket. The distance from the bearing manufacturer to the final user was much longer in the vehicle aftermarket, with the channel consisting of wholesalers, large retailers and garages. Since cross-referencing of bearing components was not consistent in the industry, it was difficult to ascertain which manufacturer's part was being replaced.

Vehicle dealers and repair shops wanted a bearing quickly because car owners expected vehicles back within a couple of hours. They also needed the right bearing for that particular vehicle. Replacing a bearing presented three problems for the bearing installer: (1) where to find the correct bearing, (2) how to mount and install it, and (3) how to obtain the various accessories to get the job done.

SKF had always regarded distributors as customers rather than as part of the channel to the end-user. Bearings were sold *to* them instead of *through* them. Relationships with end-users were left in the distributors' hands. Sales people loaded up the distributors' shelves and devised all sorts of deals to gain volume, even if items had to be taken back unsold. The distributor network gave Bearing Services the necessary local presence and coverage, and it was often more cost effective than using a direct salesforce to get the bearings to the customer. There was, however, no guaranteed preference for the SKF brand.

Splitting the organization

Research showed that the market for bearings was far from homogeneous. This information confirmed Sahlin's instincts that different target segments had to have their own market strategies and organizations.

No one knew what to expect when Sahlin convened an urgent meeting in Saltsjobaden. As one manager described it, 'Phone calls had been made back and forth to try to find out what was going on and who had been invited. Most of us only found out the next day when it made *The Financial Times*.' At the meeting, Sahlin announced that, as of September 1, the bearings group would be officially reorganized into three new areas:

1. *Bearing Industries* would include all the manufacturing plants producing 'standard' bearings for OEM, both machinery and automotive. The selling would be done by its own salesforce in countries where SKF had factories, such as Germany, France, the UK, the US, Sweden, Brazil, Argentina, Mexico and Italy. In other countries such as Switzerland, Belgium and Holland, Bearing Services would do the selling.

2. *Bearing Services*, carved out of the global sales organization, would handle the entire vehicle and industrial aftermarket as well as some of the smaller OEM's clients with whom the aftermarket distributors did business.

3. *Specialty Bearings* would handle products outside the standard line which needed highly specialized skills. This division would have its own factories and would utilize Bearing Industries' and Bearing Services' salesforce in most countries. Customers included the aerospace industry, medical equipment suppliers, large machine tool producers, and satellite manufacturers which required custom-designed products for highly specialized applications.

Each business area would have its own CEO and separate worldwide profit responsibility. Efforts would be made to keep these autonomous, thus minimizing the need for coordination. Sahlin believed the new structure would allow each business unit to be more flexible, to target and get close to its own customers, thereby commanding better margins. (For the old and new group organization structures, see Exhibit 2.)

The research confirmed Sahlin's earlier instincts that the aftermarket was indeed the profitable end of the business. He had long believed that this market had not been given enough attention but nothing had been done because it was not clear what to do and the financial significance of the aftermarket had never been established. Sahlin was convinced that the key to future profits and customer loyalty was in offering the aftermarket SKF knowhow and expertise. Bearing Services, he decided, would be a major focus for the company in the future.

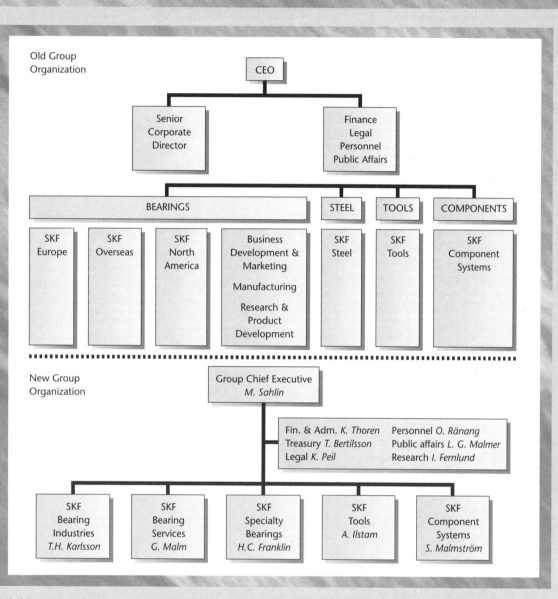

Exhibit 2 ■ Old and new organizational structure

The sales management teams which had been dealing with the aftermarket had previously reported to the manufacturing companies. Now, in the newly formed Bearing Services, they were elevated to the same status as that of their former bosses. Sales and marketing directors in various countries became managing directors (MDs).

Transforming the change process

Previously, all changes at SKF had been very structured. Typically, before any decision could be made, numerous studies were undertaken and proposals scrutinized in order to minimize risk. A kind of 'bible' was then written stating exactly how the change would take place – what had to be done, by when and by whom. As little as possible was left to chance. Sales budgets, production budgets and action plans were put in place before the new process began.

It was clear to Sahlin that SKF not only had to become a market-focused company, but the process of change itself had to be transformed. Although the ultimate goal of improving profits was straightforward, exactly how it would evolve was not 100 per cent clear. The company would have to learn by doing, by feeling out the market and being as flexible as possible.

One thing was obvious: the entire culture of the company needed a jolt. The manufacturing functions had always had the clout, but they would have to give up some of that power. The financial approach to the market would have to change as well. Marketing could no longer be considered an expense or cost centre, but would have to be handled like any other capital investment.

Sahlin knew it would be impossible to move the whole company at once. He expected Bearing Services to be a springboard to a new SKF market culture. Once they began making positive inroads into the market, he was convinced that the rest of the organization would follow. The goal was not to push for sudden and monumental changes but, rather, to let things take shape as they moved along. Small positive steps had to be taken to influence people and convince them about the new SKF way. He drafted a rough outline of how the organization would look and some guidelines for implementation. He wanted that the company's technical expertise be used to serve customers more fully, thus giving SKF a significant competitive edge. A new CEO would be appointed to each of the three areas and left to formulate his own plan.

Göran Malm, a sales and marketing specialist with a financial background, had been the European marketing and sales manager for SKF. He had been Singapore area manager for less than a year when Sahlin called and asked him to head Bearing Services. Malm, who had been pushing for change at SKF for some time, had initiated and set up maintenance support centres in Sweden to provide services for the aftermarket there. He was, Sahlin believed, the ideal candidate for the job. At first Malm was reluctant: he'd only just begun to develop a network in Singapore. Sahlin remained adamant: 'I decide on the priorities, Göran,' came his voice late one night. 'I need you back here. You understand the aftermarket and what the customers want. Let me have your decision soon, Göran.'

Malm had smiled as he put down the phone. He knew the job would be tough, but he also knew he couldn't resist the offer to lead Bearing Services.

Some reactions to the restructuring

■ Most aftermarket sales people liked the idea of the split; they would finally be elevated from the second class status to which they felt they had been relegated. As one marketing director expressed it, 'Suddenly we felt that we were as important as the guys in manufacturing. It was incredible. We knew then that Sahlin was serious about becoming customer-oriented. There had been lots of jokes about the d/d club or, as some called it, the dinner/dance club. That's the way those of us in the aftermarket were seen – wining and dining customers without doing any real work. We were happy that at last someone was listening to us and we could concentrate on customers' needs.'

■ Some of the more traditional administration, engineering and financial executives lacked enthusiasm. They couldn't quite see the point. 'It will simply add extra costs we don't want or need in our business' was the typical remark.

■ Another reservation was whether or not to take the restructuring seriously. 'This is just another reorganization. We've had so many, how long will this one last?' was the refrain.

■ Some thought that too many questions had been left unanswered and that the ultimate objectives were still too vague. It wasn't that they necessarily disagreed with the overall plan: they wanted more data and details so they could 'proceed in an orderly SKF fashion'.

■ Others felt that such a novel approach would simply not be feasible in an institution as bureaucratic as SKF. The stringent reporting requirements to head office and rigid structural barriers were just some of the many obstacles which would have to be overcome. These executives were not convinced that the new structure could fit the managerial techniques and tools that they knew worked.

■ The MDs who had previously controlled both sales and aftermarket did not all react positively when they heard Sahlin's reorganization plan. Some resented the sudden change in status of the people who had previously been working for them and who would be taking away a chunk of their business and their profits. 'Some executives tried to get around it by saying "yes", but then delayed implementation.'

When challenged about these concerns, Sahlin stated repeatedly that he understood the difficulties ahead, but was prepared to take whatever risks were necessary.

Royal Automobile Club: repositioning a service brand

Sandra Vandermerwe ■ *Marika Taishoff*

A venerable British motoring organization has been losing market share in its vehicle breakdown and recovery services to two more vigorous competitors. Research reveals both strengths and weaknesses in perceptions of the RAC. A new strategy is needed to reposition the brand in an evolving environment.

MEMO

TO: David Livermore, CEO
FROM: Jan Smith, Group Strategic Director
DATE: September 1, 1995

David,

After three months in my role, I have had the opportunity to see and discuss most areas of the business, and to understand key issues:

- We lack a long-term cohesive business direction that delivers competitive advantage.
- We do not know what business we should be in for the future.
- We have an internal focus on Divisional issues and lack an appreciation of the wider market place and changes taking place.
- We do not have a clear brand positioning for the RAC, nor do we have a distinct customer proposition.
- We do not know what we spend across the business on marketing/sales by discipline . . .
- We lack 'commercial' bite.

I could continue with this list (it's not all bad) but won't bore you further . . .

The fact that the Royal Automobile Club (RAC) had been steadily losing market share in breakdown and recovery services, its main business, to its rivals the Automobile Association (AA) and Green Flag; that its membership had remained virtually static at 5.8 million since 1992, and that its profitability had been eroding on an annual basis, was one concern to Smith, RAC Group Strategic Director since May of

that year. But even more important was the long-term sustainability of the company: if the RAC were to see it through and prosper into the next millennium, she was convinced that it would have to seriously relook its future business direction and strategic positioning. (See Exhibit 1 for financials.)

By the 1990s motoring was being confronted by two major trends which would have a dramatic impact on the RAC's 'core' breakdown and repair business:

1. *Advanced vehicle technologies*: automobile manufacturers were increasingly embedding engine management and diagnostic electronics into their vehicles – especially in the more expensive models – which could alert automobilists to impending engine or other mechanical failure, and in the process reduced the overall car breakdown rate. Such technological improvements were becoming the norm and, as the cost of chips and other technologies continued to plummet, even the less expensive, standard cars were beginning to have such features built in.

2. *Increasing public and legislative concern about urban traffic congestion and related pollution*: ironically, despite the impressive technological advances in automobiles, traffic speeds in major urban areas in the late twentieth century had returned to late nineteenth-century levels, leaving travellers delayed, frustrated and exhausted. Municipalities everywhere were examining a variety of options to deal with this worsening situation: taxing or even banning automobile use in city centres, and encouraging the development of mass transportation. Notwithstanding these efforts, public transport was also increasingly prone to delays,

---

Exhibit 1 ■ Consolidated financials (in millions £)**

	1992	1993	1994	1995
Subscriptions from members	160.3	175.6	180.4	187.3
Other operating income	51.3	58.0	62.1	64.9
Investment and similar income	8.0	10.2	11.3	10.5
Total income	219.6	244.5	253.8	262.7
Staff costs	79.1	86.3	93.1	100.1
Operating charges*	113.7	126.1	73.7	73.4
Administrative expenses			75.9	83.1
Bank interest payable			0.9	0.7
Share of losses of associate undertakings			–	0.1
Exceptional items	(14.3)	(17.7)	(3.6)	(16.7)
Surplus (deficit) before tax	12.6	14.5	8.2	(11.4)
Taxation	1.8	1.3	(0.4)	(1.0)
Surplus (deficit) for year	10.8	13.2	7.8	(12.4)

* For 1992 and 1993, operating charges, administrative expenses and other expenses combined.
** Consolidated figures representing RAC Motoring Services (including RAC Insurance and other companies), RAC Clubhouse and RAC Woodcote Park Clubhouse.

congestion and cancellations. Because of this situation, which seemed to be worsening, many drivers still preferred the 'private' hassle of driving to the public hassle of mass transportation.

Motoring in Britain and the development of the RAC

The motoring revolution in the UK began in the 1890s, when the first custom-build vehicles began appearing on the roads. Few then would have predicted that, 100 years later, the automobile would have become such an integral and necessary part of life. In its early days, the vehicle was primarily used as a sporting activity and 'motoring', as it was called, was the new sport of kings and others who could afford the luxury of the 'horseless buggy'. The fact that the average motorist in those days drove no more than 13 miles a year did not diminish the fact that motoring was considered an important and significant activity, reserved for the privileged few.

Notwithstanding this prestige however, the early cars were notorious for breaking down. The focus of early drivers was more on the mechanicals of the vehicle – oil, water, maintenance, etc. – than it was on the look, feel or style.

As with most sporting activities, soon a few motoring aficionados began meeting regularly, and it was thus that the Automobile Club was established in 1897. Within a few years practically all British motorists at that time were members of the Club. It encouraged the development of motoring in Great Britain, and strove to manage all the activities of the early motorists' journeying needs. It arranged trials, fostered touring, taught driving, issued road maps, distributed information, approved garages and hotels, organized insurance and legal assistance, and eventually established 'Road Patrols' to help its members when their cars broke down. It was also actively involved in sponsoring and organizing various motor rallies, some of which have continued into the 1990s.

As motoring continued to progress in the UK, so too did the legal efforts designed to ensure that speed limits were respected and that motorists obeyed the 'rules of the road' which were then being put in place. This angered many motorists who felt that the police, in enforcing speed controls and other surveillance methods, were infringing on their rights. In 1905, a group of Club members, unhappy with what they perceived to be the Club's acquiescence to the authorities on this issue, left to form an alternative, more radical organization whose sole purpose was to combat the enactment of traffic and speed controls and to uphold the rights of motorists. This group called itself the Automobile Association (AA) and within the space of five years it would have more members than the Automobile Club, and would maintain its number one market position in the decades to come.

The Club became known as the Royal Automobile Club after King Edward VII bestowed the 'royal' title upon it in 1907, a source, especially in those days, of prestige and a sign of having been admitted into the 'elite' class of organizations and associations.

In 1910, the RAC established its headquarters by building an Edwardian palace on Pall Mall, midway between Buckingham Palace and Trafalgar Square in central London. Its ornate premises, in addition to being an administrative headquarters, also housed a Club with all the amenities of the finest London gentlemen's clubs: restaurant, bar and bedroom suites open to the exclusively male members of the Club. Other RAC clubhouse activities included Pall Mall, bridge, chess, sub-aqua, snooker, squash and rackets and golf. The association of the RAC with the palatial Club premises would henceforth give the group a 'premium' image in the marketplace. The key activity of the RAC however was the providing of emergency repair services to fee paying members whose cars had broken down.

Jan Smith enters as RAC Group Strategic Director

Jan Smith joined the RAC as Group Strategic Director in May 1995; her mandate had been to 'define the RAC for the twenty-first century'. After taking on the job, she told her staff internally that she never stayed in a job longer than two or three years.

> 'Treat me as if I am on loan, and you will get the best out of me.' As Smith recalled, they were astonished at her statement. How could an executive come into an organization with this point of view? 'But I had already learnt that if you stay on any longer than three years, you become "internal" and when that happened you lose the big picture: organizations do things – they don't spend a lot of time thinking.'

Prior to joining the RAC, she had been involved between 1989 and 1991 in setting up and commercializing First Direct, the UK's first, 24-hour phone banking operation. As the marketing director for that brand new initiative which had reshaped the insurance industry, she had taken a new and untested concept and, together with a group of highly creative communications, branding and advertising executives, helped turn it into a huge and unexpected marketplace success. Smith, born 50 years ago in the UK, had also been marketing director of Mazda Cars UK for three years. During her tenure at Mazda she had successfully positioned and built the brand, having increased customer awareness by over 18 per cent. According to press reports written during that time, she had clashed with some dealers who had complained that the advertising she had commissioned was too 'brand-based' and not designed to 'shift the metal'.

Her reputation as an innovative and strategic thinker, combined with her familiarity with the automobile industry, were the key criteria used by the RAC in appointing her to the newly created position at RAC as strategic director. She would sometimes joke that, notwithstanding her title and senior position at the RAC, as a woman she had initially not been allowed membership of the RAC club! (This rule has since been changed after 100 years.)

The breakdown services market in Great Britain

Services for members stranded on the roads when their cars broke down had long been the principal activity of the RAC as well as of its two key competitors, the Automobile Association and Green Flag, and membership fees for the service comprised the main source of income for these firms. In terms of customer base, the AA's customers tended to be slightly older than the RAC's, and Green Flag's tended to be the youngest of all.

The market size for breakdown services for individuals, and the three main players' penetration of the total market for breakdown services, and share of the actual breakdowns which occurred (only 75 per cent of the total market had a breakdown services policy), from 1992 to 1995 are shown below:

Year	1992	1993	1994	1995
Market size	11238	11474	12089	12243
RAC penetration	15.1%	15.4%	15.2%	15.1%
RAC share	24.6%	24.2%	23.5%	23.5%
AA penetration	34.5%	34.8%	34.8%	34.8%
AA share	56%	54.6%	54%	54%
Green Flag penetration	10.3%	11.8%	12.8%	12.9%
Green Flag share	16.7%	18.5%	19.8%	19.9%

Already in the mid-1980s, the fast growing Green Flag (which had changed its name from the National Breakdown Recovery Club in early 1995) was beginning to cut into the customer base of both the RAC and the AA. It had entered the market as a quick and flexible player, priced considerably lower than the AA or the RAC (RAC prices tended to be the highest of the three). Instead of the uniformed patrolmen used by the RAC and the AA, Green Flag relied on a network of garages to perform its services. Green Flag also did less roadside repair work and offered fewer subsidiary services. It relied on sponsorship of the All-England football team to create awareness of its brand name.

Smith recalled that 'Green Flag has always been on our heels, and really began taking our members back in 1990. Market research done then showed that Green Flag was our biggest threat, but no one here seemed to react because they felt it was a niche price market, whereas the RAC differentiated itself on its exclusive image. Also they simply were not in tune with the new marketplace – there was a recession and people were more price sensitive.' Because of its predatory pricing methods, Green Flag also ate into the market share of the AA which, with 8 million members, was the largest and most visible of the three players. The AA responded by massively updating its IT system so as to make its breakdown services more responsive and cost-efficient. It also created a new ad campaign – spending £14.5 million every year; launched a new slogan, 'To our members we are the fourth emergency service' and began investing in insurance and financial services, and in other 'home emergency services' like plumbing and electricity. It also offered insurance services by finding deals for members from a group of 30 leading insurance companies.

In addition to individual customers, another significant market sector for the RAC were contract hire, leasing and fleet management companies. Twenty-five of the top 40 of such customers were RAC clients. The RAC had the highest fleet market share of the three competitors.

The RAC product market

Historically the RAC had marketed a modular range of breakdown products and sub-brands, for example Reflex and Reflex Europe (see Exhibit 2 for descriptions). The communication campaigns for these products focused on price but also presented the RAC as a 'premium' organization. The premium fees were the same for everyone: drivers of expensive, technologically sophisticated vehicles paid the same price as those with older, more standard cars. Typically, this latter group of customers increasingly relied upon the RAC as a substitute for what should have been routine maintenance. The cost of an average breakdown was £60.

As the breakdown industry moved, in the eyes of the market, towards being an insurance provider there was increased pressure from the existing customer base for a no call-out discount. This no call-out discount had been one of the customers' top ten wishes since 1988, although the company had not responded to this request.

Exhibit 2 ■ Examples of key RAC products, their contributions and average fees

Product	Description	1995 contribution (%)	1996 contribution (%)	Average fee to customer over two years
Roadside	RAC comes out to fix the car; if unable, will bring driver to nearest RAC-approved garage	2.8%	12.0%	£42
Roadside Recovery	RAC comes out to fix the car; if unable, will bring driver to the destination of choice	19.7%	36.1%	£75
Roadside Recovery at Home	RAC comes out to fix a breakdown within 1/4 mile of the customer's home; if unable, will bring driver to the destination of choice	2.8%	19.2%	£100
Reflex	If breakdown can't be fixed, same as Recovery but also includes three days' free car hire	17.8%	16.7%	£120
Reflex Europe	Same as Reflex, but valid also across Europe	2.9%	1.8%	£190

Some of the RAC's major products, a brief description of each, the contribution to RAC sales, and the average fee, are shown in Exhibit 2.

The roadside services were performed by the RAC Road Patrols, with their white and blue coloured vans – with the royal insignia – and similarly discreetly attired patrolmen. These patrolmen featured strongly in the company's main advertising theme – the 'New Knights of the Road'. (See Exhibits 3, 4 and 5 for representative advertising; for total RAC advertising expenditures from 1992 to 1996, see Exhibit 6.)

Of its 5.5 million individual customers by 1996, more than 3 million had joined because of a third party, i.e., generally as part of the purchase of a new or used vehicle. The RAC had an information service for potential customers. If someone phoned in for more information on the RAC's products, prices, etc., all the data would be written down manually by RAC staff, and an information pack sent out to the

Exhibit 3 ■ Representative RAC advertisement (1)

Exhibit 4 ■ Representative RAC advertisement (2)   **Exhibit 5** ■ Representative RAC advertisement (3)

prospect. No systematic file or database of these prospective customers existed.

All the breakdown service providers offered a similar set of products. The RAC had believed that a critical differentiator was the speed of response to emergency calls and rate of fix. In 1995 the RAC handled 2.9 million rescue jobs, 85 per cent within one hour, and 82 per cent of these breakdowns were repaired at roadside. Since speed of response depended on the quality and sophistication of the IT linkups between the station headquarters and the

patrol cars, the RAC invested heavily in building the infrastructure for this, and technology was considered a core competence of the company.

In addition to its core breakdown and recovery activities, the RAC also offered a wide range of motoring-related services. These included insurance, holiday and hotel reservations, travel publications, legal services, traffic information and more technically geared services such as 'Battery Assist', designed to help members whose cars wouldn't start because of a flat battery. These incremental businesses were structured

Exhibit 6 ■ Advertising expenditure

RAC Total	TV (£)	Press (£)	Radio (£)	Cinema (£)	Outdoor (£)	Total spend (£)
1992	2,859,788	620,721	1900	0	137,883	3,620,292
1993	441,737	2,089,177	0	0	287,114	2,818,028
1994	1,008,712	5,422,169	130,172	0	1753	6,562,806
1995	1,480,156	4,013,687	8,006	0	0	5,501,849
1996	419,266	1,862,912	63,946	0	0	2,346,124

as profit centres in their own right. By the time Jan Smith had joined, many of these small areas of business had been losing money.

The RAC Insurance group (RACIS) for example, had almost always been a drain on the bottom line. As she put it, 'We understand our core business very well, and for the RAC that core business has always been breakdown services; insurance is seen as an add-on. For the AA, it was different: they see insurance as a key part of their core business, and they're ploughing lots of money into it.' On average, 5 per cent of RAC insurance customers were breakdown customers as well. Smith was concerned that the entry of new players like Direct Line in insurance with their huge critical mass and low operating costs, intensified competition and the continuing drop in premiums, would push RAC's insurance business ever deeper into the red.

The RAC had separate divisions for Marketing, Sales and Customer Service. Marketing's role was to communicate the image of the company, and to oversee memberships renewals. Sales focused on new prospects, whether individual, corporate, fleet or third party, and Customer Service was responsible for responding to customer queries and emergency breakdown calls.

Understanding the present market

In recalling her arrival at the RAC, Jan Smith said:

> I came into a company that was dramatically losing market share. Some of the problems were well

known. For instance, research had been done in the early 90s and the findings should have worried us – our image was weakening, we weren't growing, *and* we weren't keeping our existing customers.

Smith was convinced early in her appointment that the company had to update its market research if it was going to find out why it was losing market share, and in November of 1995, she commissioned a major project.

The market research

Two jump-start groups were commissioned to get a feeling of what people thought about the different breakdown brands. The reason for these jump-start groups was that she and her team wanted to test and structure their methodology. These two groups were asked questions about how they felt about breakdown services, what they thought of the various brands, pricing, insurance, etc. The object was to get feedback on how far brands could stretch, overall direction for the research and some specific questions with which to work.

The methodology was then taken to 16 qualitative groups to assess what people (users and non-users) 'felt' when it came to roadside breakdown services, and how these feelings translated into purchase criteria and decision-making. Increasingly, key consumer motivations were 'about *me*, not my car', for instance:

■ freedom from worry;
■ sense of security;

- vulnerability when stranded;
- need for an ally.

Brands were tested in this research to see how far they could stretch. A brand like Virgin, they found, could be extended into banking and insurance. How far could the RAC brand be stretched? Could the RAC be attached to an airline, or to a cure for AIDS? For example, because the RAC was strongly associated with 'integrity', and financial services generally were not seen as illustrative of 'integrity', the RAC brand did not really stretch into financial services.

Finally, a list of words or phrases, which the participants associated as positive or negative attributes of the main breakdown brands, was generated. (See Exhibits 7, 8 and 9 for the findings from the research.)

Another facet of the research was to compare the 'visibility' of all the players in the breakdown services market. Here, the results were as follows:

- The RAC suffered from poor visibility, especially relative to the AA.
- The AA was visible, out there, unambiguous, 'busy doing it', of and for the people . . . and much more than just breakdown (Roadwatch, high street shops, inspections, road signage, etc.).
- The RAC had much less presence: 'another white liveried van' – could be the police, fire, security firm, mobile plumber . . . not noticed, little sense of beavering away, getting it done.

For Smith, the market research results were clear: the RAC had to play on its positives and get rid of the negatives (see Exhibit 7). With visibility such a strong asset for the AA, the RAC would have to try to take that away from them in their strategy. Achieving both of these imperatives, and quickly, would be her chief concern in the new year.

Moving into a new gear

In November 1995, Neil Johnson, the dynamic General Secretary of the Clubhouse, was appointed CEO of the RAC Motoring Services. Johnson, committed to dramatic change, was a vigorous and energetic person very supportive of the work then undertaken. One month later, almost immediately after the results of the market research study, he asked Smith to take over all of Customer Services, Marketing and Sales. A new Managing Director of Operations was brought in. Previously, Marketing and Operations had been in one section under one person. The objective now was to link the strategic and day-to-day business activities.

Johnson also created and chaired an Executive Committee comprised of Smith, the Group Legal Director, the Group Finance Director, the Managing Director of Operations and the Managing Director of Technical Services.

Once Smith had decided on the actions she would take she needed to communicate to people what was wrong, what she was doing about it and why. She knew that the changes would entail considerable upheaval for people. Videos were put together to

---

Exhibit 7 ■ RAC market research results

+	Integrity	–	Old-fashioned
+	Considerable experience	–	Elitist, stately and aloof
+	Independent and objective	–	Unapproachable
+	An organization of the highest standards	–	Patronizing: an adult/child relationship
+	Premium	–	Expensive
+	Dependable	–	Muddled
+	Traditional values	–	Obsessed with heritage

Exhibit 8 ■ AA market research results

+ Modern	– Voraciously commercial
+ Dynamic	– Short-term expediency
+ Urgent	– Motives often suspect
+ Competitive	– Impersonal
+ Efficient	
+ Visible	
+ Everywhere	

Exhibit 9 ■ Green Flag market research results

+ Cheap (or, arguably, good value)	– Minimum cover – no 'safety net'
+ No frills	– Contractor service experience variable
+ Clarity: what you see is what you get	
+ Good service, exceed expectations	

---

show the reasons for the repositioning and the elements of the strategy. Every member of the Executive Committee appeared in these videos, endorsing the strategy and the commitment to the way forward. Staff were concerned and said, 'We never realized it was like this!' She recalled:

> There had been an element of complacency in the company, people thinking 'we've always been here'. They just did not know what was happening; they didn't know the reason why it was necessary to change. The video was a tangible way of communicating that there was a problem and what would be done about it.

The research results and the video woke people up. Smith went into an accelerated gear. She was adamant that, under these circumstances, the group did not have the luxury of working according to the old rules. It had to radically and quickly rethink what it stood for, what its role was today – and would be in the future – and communicate and demonstrate this

to its customers. Otherwise, she felt, the RAC's centenary year – 1997 – might mark the beginning of the venerable institution's end.

Setting up the virtual team

Smith formed a group to address the RAC's positioning and brand strategy. She wanted some people who had been involved with her in designing the marketing strategy for First Direct as well as key people from key parts of the RAC to be in this team.

Rather than accept a complete team from an established agency, she engaged the skills of certain freelance marketing professionals as well as individuals from major advertising agencies with whom she had worked in the past. As she put it, 'I wanted to capitalize on the brain power of just one or two people in an agency, and not the complete company.' Together, they began brainstorming and approaching the issue of repositioning the RAC and examining options for the way forward.

We sat down to look at everything: the brand, the world in which we were competing, what was happening to consumers and the way in which they were living their lives. In trying to determine how to deal with the competition, how to respond to customer perceptions of the brand, and how to position the RAC as a leader for the future, we recognized we had to redefine the company's business. We also had to redefine what was meant by 'premium', 'leadership' and 'club'.

We had always been a premium brand, leadership had always been central to our positioning. We genuinely were a Club when we started out, but what did all that mean today? How would we not only respond to the changing environment, but help re-create the RAC to become the first-choice service brand of the future?

Hewlett-Packard: distributing services through multi-channels

Sandra Vandermerwe

A major computer manufacturer seeks new ways to sell the firm's services across Europe. Although the firm has historically sold services directly, a marketing manager is convinced that opportunities exist to sell through distribution channels, despite the fact that such intermediaries are used to selling physical products rather than intangibles.

During the early summer months of 1991, Alois Hauk could finally see the light at the end of the tunnel. It had come to him during discussions with the services organization in the UK, experimenting with a new way of selling services. As the Marketing Manager for Hewlett-Packard's (HP) services or organization in Europe it was Hauk's responsibility to ensure continued growth in that end of the business. Service revenues in direct sales of computer services – to multinationals and other large corporations – were up and growing, and he and his team were very proud of that fact. However, in the indirect market – where distribution was through distributors/wholesalers and/or value-added retailers (VARs)/dealers, performance had been miserable. But, that was where the action was and was likely to be in the future. The challenge was to find a better way to penetrate these indirect channels. Hauk knew that, in order to accomplish this task, a new distribution plan would have to be worked out and sold to the rest of the HP organization. He had gathered his team together – away from the office routine – to see how to develop the UK concept further and make it work on a pan-European basis.

'We now have a workable plan,' Hauk remarked to himself as he drove home through the Geneva streets late that warm evening in 1991. Channel members who were buying and selling HP PCs and peripherals or 'boxes' – as they were affectionately referred to – had been reluctant about selling services. This attitude had to be given very careful consideration in planning the implementation of a new distribution approach. Determining what would make them *want* to sell HP services was the real question, Hauk knew.

As far as he was concerned, the week had been a success. In the beginning it had been tough, but finally everyone saw the point and began to offer their ideas. By the end of the week, they had come up with a new service concept. 'With luck,' Hauk said aloud, 'we can have the market test up and running almost immediately.'

The team had met at Au Nice Auberge on Geneva's lake front, where Hauk had spent the first few hours setting the scene. His intention was to generate a sense of urgency quickly, starting with his opening statement:

> Look at our hardware sales. Already, 50 per cent comes from the alternative channels, and we hardly feature there at all. The forecast for 1995 is 80 per cent. Why shouldn't services go the same way? If we don't get into that end of the market, we are not going to grow sufficiently. If we don't grow sufficiently, we're out of business – in the long run anyway.

Not everyone had had the same sense of concern about alternative channels. HP had been successful in services in the direct market where customer relationships were not at all like the ones in the indirect market. Because the channels were fundamentally so different in the way they thought and operated, it was difficult for some people to imagine how HP could be good at both. They felt that it would be better to choose one stream and stick with it. But, Hauk was adamant:

Without indirect channels, we are not only missing 50 per cent of the market, but we are putting ourselves potentially in danger. We can't think about doing well in just one channel or another. Our products are being sold in *both*, and so we need a *multi*-channel approach.

The group had spent the rest of that week analyzing the distribution system, what HP had accomplished to date in computer services, and where they might have gone wrong with the indirect channels. By the end of the week, the basis of a marketing plan had been hashed out.

Hauk went over the details in his head as he turned the car into the driveway of his home. Ultimately, it had seemed clear that success hinged on the idea of selling services like 'boxes'. As he swung into the garage, he thought about the plan they had developed. Was it going to work? It had to . . . at this point there was no alternative.

Background – Hewlett-Packard and its services

At the beginning of the 1990s Hewlett-Packard (HP) was one of the largest international information systems (IS) companies, engaged worldwide in the design, manufacture and service of electronic products and systems. Founded in 1939 by William Hewlett and David Packard, HP started as a manufacturer of electronic testing and measurement instruments, supplying the electronics, telecommunications, aerospace and automotive industries. In the early 1960s, HP extended its electronics technology to the fields of medicine and analytical chemistry. It introduced its first computer in 1966, starting with technical computers and then branching into business computing in the 1970s. In 1993, computers and peripherals represented 71 per cent of the company's worldwide revenues.

With its headquarters in Palo Alto, California (USA), HP operated in over 100 countries. Its European headquarters were in Geneva, Switzerland. With 144 sales and support offices, 21 manufacturing locations, and 15 research and development laboratories throughout Europe, HP had established a significant European presence over the last 30 years.

The European Customer Support Operation reported to the Worldwide Customer Support Operation (WCSO). The European side of this function, at the headquarters in Geneva, was structured into six units, of which Support Marketing was one. (Refer to Exhibit 1 for a list of these six units and their activities.)

The HP Response Centre (RC) was at the hub of HP's Worldwide Customer Support Organization. Its network consisted of 27 electronically linked locations worldwide, serving 97 countries (one in each country) 24 hours a day, 7 days a week. It offered a variety of software and specialized hardware support, including for multi-vendor environments. In each country where HP hardware was sold, there were Support Responsible Offices (SROs) that handled the routine local on-site deliveries. The RCs and SROs worked closely together in virtual teams. When a customer phoned in for a service call, it would go to the RC in that country. They made the diagnosis and decided whether or not someone should be sent to the site. All service findings and experiences were recorded and fed back into the system so as to keep the existing know-how and the database up to date.

In 1991, HP reported total European revenues of $5.4 billion. An independent survey rank HP number six in the world that year in terms of service revenues when 21 per cent of their total revenues went to these intangibles. IBM was number one, Electronic Data Systems number two and Digital, Fujitsu and Xerox numbers three, four and five respectively. From 1990 to 1991 hardware sales at HP increased by 8 per cent while services increased by 15 per cent. The comparable figures for 1991 and 1992 were 12 per cent for equipment and 16.5 per cent for services. HP had 16,200 employees in services in 1991, which made it the 10th largest employer among the top 20 service providers in the world. The company was number 11 in terms of its revenue for each of these service employees. (Refer to Exhibits 2–4 for more detailed statistics.)

Services distribution channels

A multi-channel distribution system for computer hardware, software and services had existed for some time in Europe, although the exact proportions for

Exhibit 1 ■ Structure of European customer support operations – six units

1. **Finance/Administration**
   - Financial planning and reporting
   - Administration

2. **Support materials (based in Grenoble)**
   - Parts logistics
   - Software distribution (on CD-ROM)
   - Board repair

3. **Support marketing**
   - Worldwide PSO and SSO programme development/adaptation
   - Worldwide PSO and SSO programme implementation
   - European marketing initiatives

4. **Systems support organization (SSO)**
   - On-site maintenance
   - Account management
   - Site services
   - Network support

5. **Professional services organization**
   - Educational services
   - Consulting services
   - Systems integration
   - Project management

6. **Response centre operations (RCO)**
   - Call management
   - Usage assistance
   - Remote support
   - Operations support services

direct and indirect – through distributors/wholesalers and VARs/dealers – differed by country. (Refer to Exhibit 5 for visual details on direct labelled (a) channel, and indirect labelled (b) and (c) channels.) Direct (a) meant that vendors went straight to the customers – usually the multinationals and larger domestic corporations – with their goods and services. Those who had internal service facilities either performed their own services or they outsourced them to vendors – a trend that was increasing.

Indirect distribution happened in two ways for computer services: the first (b) was through relatively large VARs/dealers, who typically served medium and small corporations as well as some of the larger accounts. These VARs/dealers provided a substantial number of their customers' service needs, especially software support.

The second alternative channel (c) was through distributors/wholesalers and through thousands of smaller VARs/dealers who covered individual customers (doctors, lawyers, etc.) and very small-sized businesses (of 1–3 employees).

In both cases, the end-users dealt face to face with the VARs/dealers. In other words, the customer went

Exhibit 2 ■ Top 20 service providers ranked by 1991 worldwide service revenues

Company	$ millions	% of total
1 International Business Machines	$14,100	22%
2 Electronic Data Systems	7,028	99%
3 Digital Equipment Corporation	5,612	40%
4 Fujitsu	5,100	27%
5 Xerox	4,550	33%
6 *Hewlett-Packard*	*3,047*	*21%*
7 Unisys	2,808	32%
8 AT&T/NCR	2,700	43%
9 Groupe Bull	2,500	42%
10 Andersen Consulting	2,256	100%
11 Siemens Nixdorf	1,997	27%
12 Ing. C. Olivetti	1,497	21%
13 Cap Gemini Sogeti	1,775	100%
14 Eastman Kodak	1,345	34%
15 Computer Sciences Corporation	1,300	62%
16 AT&T	1,299	42%
17 Hitachi Ltd	1,291	13%
18 Canon	1,105	10%
19 Wang	884	42%
20 Ernst & Young*	861	16%

* Management consulting revenues.   Dataquest/Ledgeway

Exhibit 3 ■ Top 20 service providers ranked by 1991 worldwide service employees

Company	No. of employees	% of change 1990–91
1 International Business Machines	78,500	–3%
2 Electronic Data Systems	70,500	8%
3 Digital Equipment Corporation	42,000	–3%
4 Fujitsu	35,600	4%
5 Xerox	33,100	–1%
6 Andersen Consulting	25,100	6%
7 AT&T/NCR	19,000	–10%
8 Computer Sciences Corporation	18,560	8%
9 Unisys	17,770	–16%
10 *Hewlett-Packard*	*16,200*	*1%*
11 Cap Gemini Sogeti	14,012	–10%
12 Groupe Bull	14,000	–3%
13 Siemens Nixdorf	13,700	–2%
14 Ing. C. Olivetti	10,658	–1%
15 Eastman Kodak	10,500	–5%
16 AT&T	9,600	–14%
17 Price Waterhouse	7,294	N/A
18 Pitney Bowes	7,200	–4%
19 PRC	6,550	–10%
20 Ernst & Young*	6,297	–7%

* Management consulting revenues.   Dataquest/Ledgeway

Exhibit 4 ■ Top 20 service providers ranked by 1991 service revenues per service employee

Company	Revenues per employee ($)	No. of employees
1 Mentor Graphics	361,842	380
2 Stratus Computer	260,968	310
3 Sun Microsystems	243,478	2,300
4 Sequent	233,333	150
5 Convex	223,295	176
6 Prime Computer	213,886	3,039
7 Hitachi Limited	213,388	6,050
8 Amdahl	205,000	2,000
9 Data General	196,500	2,200
10 Apple Computer	196,078	765
11 *Hewlett-Packard*	*188,086*	*16,200*
12 Tandem Computers	185,550	2,000
13 Intel	183,333	600
14 International Business Machines	179,618	78,500
15 Groupe Bull	178,571	14,000
16 Pyramid Technology	176,429	280
17 Harris Adacom	175,000	400
18 Network Equipment Technology	174,444	180
19 Modular Computer	169,014	142
20 Network Systems	168,317	404

Dataquest/Ledgeway

to a store to buy whatever he needed, e.g., a PC. The number of VARs had mushroomed in the 1980s, although some of the larger ones had fallen away in recent years because of diminishing margins. Wholesalers serviced large numbers of VARs/dealers scattered throughout Europe. For example, one wholesaler handled 15,000 dealers – holding their stocks, providing fast delivery and participating in joint marketing efforts with them. This wholesaler also provided its own services.

Looking at relative size, if smaller VARs/dealers were 100 on an index in terms of revenues, the large VARs would typically be 10,000 and the distributors/wholesalers 20,000. The distributors/wholesalers characteristically bought in thousands, VARs in hundreds and end-users in singles.

HP used two different salesforces to serve its direct and indirect customers, both of which sold 'boxes', software and services. The direct salespeople were allocated key accounts and had close contact with their customers. The indirect salesforce, however, had many more customers and their dealings were mostly product based. Hauk and his team had spent a lot of time talking about this issue as they worked through their ideas on how to improve indirect channel penetration. One executive had made the point:

Part of our problem is that the indirect salespeople couldn't care less about selling services. They are not rewarded for it, and the amount of commission they get for services relative to selling 'boxes' is peanuts. On top of that, we tell them they must sell our services to our partners, but then they find these same people are selling their own services. In addition to everything else, the salespeople don't want to upset their clients, which is certainly understandable.

Services discounts and price erosion

Overall, 30 per cent of the services provided to end-users were handled by vendors like HP. The rest came from the VARs/dealers or were taken care of by the customers themselves. The larger VARs (b) did their

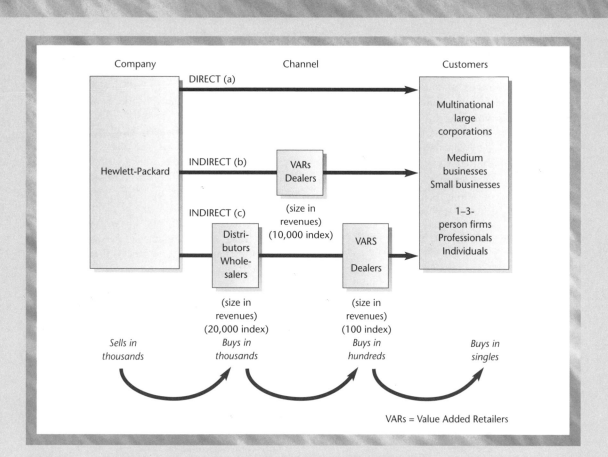

Exhibit 5 ■ Simplified services distribution system – direct (a)/indirect (b/c)

own applications development and customized solutions for their clients. Those who dealt with wholesalers (c) tended more to provide 'shrink-wrapped' services – for example, packaged software such as Lotus.

'Boxes' – PCs, printers and so on, the 'ready-to-use' products – required basic services like maintenance and software support. Workstations and IT systems – 'boxes strung together' – needed to be integrated and required more sophisticated services, including usage support – e.g., help desks, asset management (deciding what to buy and from whom), installation procurement, and planning/consulting. (Refer to Exhibit 6 for the HP services spectrum.)

Street price erosion had gradually plagued indirect distribution, so much so that some of the multinationals

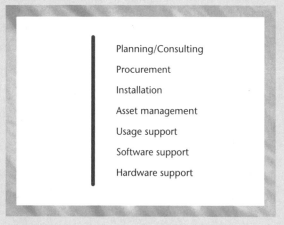

Planning/Consulting

Procurement

Installation

Asset management

Usage support

Software support

Hardware support

Exhibit 6 ■ Service spectrum/indirect channel providers

and larger domestic firms were buying through this channel to get cheaper prices. Price erosion was primarily due to the similarity of the products offered to VARs/dealers, who thus sold on price. What made this situation even more complicated was that discounts were based on volumes for both products and services. With this scheme, HP distributors and wholesalers had only been receiving up to 3 per cent more than some of the larger VARs (b). They, therefore, either had to live on 3 per cent – passing on the rest to their VARs/dealers – or put their VARs/dealers (c) at a disadvantage compared to the larger ones (b).

Also, the margins made by VARs were being eroded due to price wars at the retail level. The irony was that end-users were gaining all the financial benefits of these discounts for products, and yet they still were not really getting the services they needed. As one executive at the Geneva meeting put it:

> It's all very well that our end-users are paying low prices, but not if they can't obtain the commensurate benefits. If HP users don't get the services downstream – for whatever reason – our products can't perform as they should in the marketplace.

Selling direct and indirect services

Early in 1991 when the team met, HP was selling 95 per cent of its services directly and the rest indirectly. Each of these two approaches to selling services was handled differently. The company had made several attempts to do better in the indirect market, offering the wholesalers and VARs margins for selling the HP intangibles . . . but without much success.

In direct selling, HP employees went straight to the customers – the multinationals and large accounts – after hardware had been sold to them, assessed their service needs and prepared a contract which both parties then signed. The salespeople were all experts on HP services; they knew what was available and how prices should be established.

But when it came to selling services to the indirect channel, everything became more vague and complex. Some VARs/dealers wanted to do their own selling and delivery, so HP offered to train them itself (b) or to have the wholesalers (c) for HP products do it. But, by the time these services reached the end-users, they were often not sufficiently HP-specific or were inconsistent from one VAR/dealer to another. Questions about particular HP services would go back and forth, up and down the distribution chain before negotiations could be finalized. The signing of a contract involved many parties, making it even more complicated to complete a deal. Wholesalers and VARs/dealers found the experience unsatisfactory and time-consuming. It was also different from buying and selling 'boxes', the relatively straightforward procedure which they already knew well. So they resisted, thus often missing service opportunities because they had opted for a process that was simpler and more familiar – buying and reselling products.

At the meeting on that spring day, Alois Hauk expressed his opinion:

> We've done all the classic marketing things in the indirect channel, offered good services for our 'boxes' and workstations which the indirect distribution channels can sell at reasonable prices. We've got plenty of pull from our advertising and promotion, and this plus our image and reputation should have attracted end-users.

> But, we've missed the really important point – how the distributors/wholesalers and VARs/dealers work, and what they understand and can do best. The truth is that they know how to buy and sell 'boxes', how to put them on their shelves until their customers come into their warehouses or stores and buy. That's what they are able to do best.

> We've expected them to understand our intangibles and they don't. We've expected them to adapt to our processes and they won't. Even though we've given them margin incentives, they haven't sold our services. There is only one solution: we have to distribute our services like 'boxes'. Make it easy and profitable for them to sell. And if they want to sell their own service as well, we've got to help them deliver it or get them to subcontract the work back to us. Who makes the service delivery is much less important than being sure that end-users with HP machines actually get the services they need.

A new service concept

Selling services like 'boxes' meant somehow making them tangible. This objective, the team agreed, was as important to final consumers and the channel as it was for HP. End-users would be able to 'touch and feel' something solid, intermediaries would be able to stock and store merchandise, to sell and reorder it like any product, and it would complement the software services they sold. HP could use the idea as a promotional and operational vehicle.

A decision was taken to start with hardware maintenance, packaging it literally like a 'box'. It would need a name – 'HP SupportPack' was chosen – and would be presented in a way that was sufficiently attractive to entice customers to buy it. (Refer to Exhibit 7 for the outcome.) Several other principles were agreed upon:

1. It would use 18 European languages, thereby saving on cost.
2. It would be colourful, displaying the HP logo and projecting the feeling of support.
3. It would be designed to sit beside the HP product in the VAR stores so that it could be merchandised and sold simultaneously.
4. It would contain an extension of warranty to 3 years, with a promise that if the hardware broke down, HP would go on site within a day.
5. On the inside, it would explain what customers could expect, and the terms and conditions from HP's point of view.
6. There would be a sticky label inside which could be removed and put directly onto the PC. All the relevant details – like phone number of the support location – would be filled in by the end-user from information included in the Pack.
7. For marketing purposes, a paid reply tear-off card would be inside, which customers would fill in with their details and send off to HP. The company would then register this data in the central and Response Centre bases within the individual countries who had to do the delivery of the services.
8. Whenever a customer called in, there would be a qualifying procedure and a 'recovery routine' made in order to try to solve the problem before HP had to send someone to the site – also to keep costs down.
9. Product salespeople would now receive a commission.
10. Channel partners would receive added margin.

Costing and pricing

The idea was to keep manufacturing costs of the Pack as low as possible. Since delivery costs would remain the same, the only real extra expense for HP would be the investment made to market the new services concept. The plan was to offset these marketing costs by reducing the enormous internal administrative expenses which had been incurred previously on maintenance contracts: for example, keeping up-to-date data, collecting money, reminding customers to pay and renewals.

The new SupportPack would last three years only. After that, the group reasoned, the hardware would probably be obsolete. To Hauk, the ideal situation was to find a concept and an operating system where the administrative expenses would be zero. This goal, he attested, could become a reality if they were clever about the process. As far as delivery costs were concerned, sufficient knowledge from past experience and continuous tracking enabled them to predict failure rates and hence service delivery costs. In any event, the object was to have the portfolio rather than every single deal profitable.

There were two possible ways to handle the pricing of the new service. They could stick to the current volume-based arrangement or find something more suitable. The object was to avoid price wars at the retail level and obviate the animosity which had reigned among retail channel members because of discrepancies in prices.

The team furiously debated various options. A new scheme, based on status, was finally agreed upon – a different approach from what had previously been used in these channels or product arrangements with customers. All wholesalers/distributors and VARs/dealers would receive the same discount, irrespective of the size of their order. Early on, the team had agreed that, first and foremost, they had to find a scheme which would work for the distributor/wholesaler, VAR/dealer channel (c). Then, they could make it fit the larger VARs (b).

Exhibit 7 ■ HP SupportPack

Using a pricing plan based on status rather than volume, the VARs would be on an equal footing, irrespective of their size. Retail prices would therefore be more stable, the group felt. Wholesalers, they reasoned, would also be much happier with the new service concept. They were interested in margins rather than discounts, as every transaction was at a fixed cost. For example, a deskjet printer that retailed at $650 brought the wholesaler $18 with the discount-based scheme. VARs made a similar amount – around $20. With the new SupportPack idea, they not only would be able to draw more income per customer but practically double their margins. Feedback from research done by HP some months earlier revealed that $100 was the threshold for maintenance services for these type of products. If the street price for a SupportPack were set at $100 for example, the wholesaler would make $15.

Outside cover

Inside

Exhibit 8 ■ Direct mail to channel members

Instead of first selling the hardware to customers and then the services – the process being used in the direct channel system – both the hardware and service would be sold together. This new approach, the team felt, would be enormously advantageous for all concerned. HP would receive payment for services from the distributors/wholesalers and large VARs when SupportPacks were bought by these firms.

Then, HP's responsibility would be to deliver these services to end-users when contacted.

Designing the market test

During their meetings in Geneva, Hauk and his team decided that the new service concept had to be tested as soon as possible. But how? They agreed that the *entire* process needed to be tested rather than taking it in bits and pieces. Hauk had suggested:

> Let's first develop the concept in full and then offer it to the channel. Channels are sceptical enough about our services right now. And so are the sales-people. We have to give them something we are pretty sure about and make sure that we avoid creating new problems.

The team also decided to test both channels (b) and (c) simultaneously so as to compare and understand the dynamics between them. Several other decisions were taken as well. They would:

1. Pick only two large well-known wholesalers for this project and one large direct VAR.
2. Make the first test in the UK for five months, then move to another country – probably France. Because the UK tended to be more advanced in this kind of thing, the logic was that the dealers there would be the most receptive, with the French next in line.
3. Send 'taxi drivers' to customers to exchange the broken 'boxes' for new ones – rather than HP engineers – in order to save costs. Customers would not be affected as they could continue working.
4. Use advertising to create pull at the end-user and channel levels (refer to Exhibits 8 and 9 for the

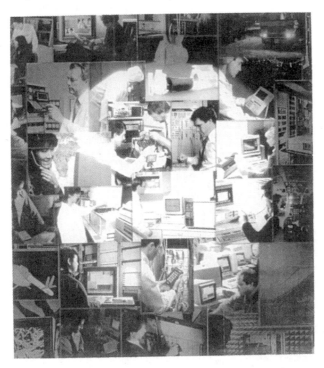

**HP SupportPack.
— A world of computing support, just a call away.**

HEWLETT PACKARD

Your computer product maintenance coverage:

- Three year HP hardware maintenance.
- Affordable.
- Quality support from the original manufacturer.
- Easy problem resolution.
- Peace of mind.
- Prompt service.
- Simple registration.
- Worldwide backing.
- Protection against costly repairs.
- Direct phone number for service.
- Direct service from HP technicians.
- Transferable between customers.
- Covers a range of HP PC products and Printers bought from a dealer.
- No hidden costs.

Exhibit 9 ■ Pull advertising end-users

outcome) and point-of-sale displays to complement training for salespeople in the stores.

5. Keep the concept and marketing strategy pan-European – including the service delivery processes, pricing, packaging, promotion and branding, using icons wherever possible, as well as multi-language packs and promotion. In that way, the company could project one consistent image and keep the costs down.

Alois Hauk closed the garage door and started for the house. On the drive home, he had again reviewed the plan that his team had worked out for increasing sales of HP's services to the alternative channels. Testing would begin soon, and Hauk was counting on the results to prove that this new strategy would be successful.

Lausanne Tourist Office and Convention Bureau

Kimberly A. Bechler ■ Christopher H. Lovelock ■ Dominique Turpin

A medium-sized Swiss city is interested in boosting tourism. Officials are discussing what type of research will provide useful information on why people visit Lausanne and what they think of their experience.

Pierre Schwitzguebel, director of the Lausanne Tourist Office and Convention Bureau, called the meeting of the management committee to order. 'How can we prove that we mean business?' the director asked. 'We need hard data in order to convince the cantonal government of the magnitude of tourism's economic impact on Lausanne and then to win their financial support. Our visitor statistics have been flat for several years. We need assistance if we're to pick up speed in this very competitive field.'

With the anticipated passage of legislation that would grant financial aid to tourism in the mountain communities of the Canton of Vaud (providing a financial aid package that would be funded 40 per cent by the Swiss federal government, 40 per cent by the canton and 20 per cent by the individual communities), there was no time like the present for action. This legislation would mean that a budget of SF 200 million[1] would go toward supporting tourism in the mountain regions to the north and east of Lake Geneva.

'We've got to show them that tourism in Vaud means a lot more than just visits to the mountain villages,' agreed the tourist office's assistant director, Claude Petitpierre, gesturing at the sailboats on Lake Geneva outside the window. 'Why, the cities of Lausanne, Montreux and Vevey alone together account for more than 40 per cent of all tourism in the canton! But just lobbying for money won't do any good. I agree with you, we've got to come up with some solid documentation. We also need better information on why people come to Lausanne and what they think of their experience as a visitor here. That could help us know how we should tailor our services and shape our promotional strategy.'

Switzerland: the 'crossroads of Europe'

From the time the Romans crossed the Alps on their way north, the major land route connecting northern and southern Europe had been through Switzerland. A key route for east–west European travel had also passed through Switzerland between Lakes Constance and Geneva. In more recent years, the country had become connected with cities all over the world via two intercontinental airports – at Zurich and Geneva. Someone had jokingly defined Europe as 'anywhere within two hours of Geneva Airport'.

At the beginning of the 1990s, the Swiss Confederation spanned 41,000 km^2 (16,000 square miles) and included 6.8 million inhabitants, of whom one-sixth were foreigners. In both area and population, the country was roughly the same size as Massachusetts and New Hampshire combined (two states in the US). About one-quarter of Switzerland's land area consisted of lakes, glaciers or high mountains, some of which reached altitudes of over 4,000 metres (13,000 feet). One of the best known was the Matterhorn, 4,478 metres high, dominating the skyline above Zermatt, 169 km (105 miles) southeast of Lausanne.

Switzerland had four official national languages: German, French, Italian and Romansh. Although German was the native language of 65 per cent of all Swiss residents, people at all levels of society spoke one of a variety of local dialects collectively known as *Schwytzertüusch*. Eighteen per cent of the population were native French-speakers, while Italian was the mother tongue of 10 per cent of Swiss residents (more than half were immigrants or migrant workers). One per cent (located in southeastern Switzerland) spoke Romansh, a Romance language said to be closest to the Latin spoken by ordinary people in Roman days.

Government

The Confederation comprised 26 cantons and half-cantons. The Swiss parliament sat in Bern, the national capital. The federal government was responsible for foreign affairs, national defence, customs, communications and monetary controls. Other state functions were the responsibility of the cantons – for example, education, road construction and maintenance, health and police – and were often delegated to the communes (towns and villages).

The Canton of Vaud (officially known as I'Etat de Vaud) was in the western, French-speaking part of Switzerland, often referred to as Suisse Romande. Lausanne was its capital (see Exhibit 1). With 571,973 inhabitants (1989), Vaud was the most populous canton in Suisse Romande, and ranked as one of the largest and fastest growing in the Confederation. However, like many parts of Switzerland, it was currently facing both recession and inflation.

Tourism

The World Tourism Organization estimated that during 1990, there were 390 million tourists worldwide. Tourism provided employment in a wide range of activities with jobs in hotels, restaurants, tourist offices, travel agencies, transport operations and recreational establishments. The revenues generated worldwide were estimated at $194 billion. Industry predictions showed tourism growing at an annual rate of 4 per cent through the year 2000.

The lack of a precise definition of just what constituted a 'tourist' made collection of data difficult. Popular definitions included an individual on vacation, a business traveller, a convention participant, a person staying in a hotel, someone attempting to change housing accommodations, a foreign student, a foreigner receiving medical treatment on an outpatient basis, an individual visiting family or friends for a short time period and someone taking a day trip.

According to the World Tourism Organization, the expenses of the classic tourist (travelling for either vacation or business) could be separated into the following six categories: lodging (34 per cent), food and drink (25 per cent), shopping (15 per cent), recreation (8 per cent), local transportation (5 per cent), and miscellaneous (13 per cent).

Swiss tourism

It was popularly held that the tourist industry started in Switzerland. The first modern tourists, the British, began to come 'on holiday' in the nineteenth century, followed by other Europeans and North Americans. Switzerland soon became known as a 'nation of hotelkeepers', by 1991 hosting more than 20 million visitors annually.

Tourism ranked third among Switzerland's export industries, after machinery and components, and chemicals, and well ahead of the textile and watch-making industries. In 1988, international tourism brought in SF 10.4 billion. Providing 350,000 jobs, Swiss tourism contributed 6 per cent of GNP. However, tourism received little financial support and had no 'lobby' at the federal level. In recent years, industry observers felt that Switzerland was not taking adequate steps to renew its image as a country dedicated to tourism.

The Swiss 'tourism structure' consisted of the Swiss National Office of Tourism with 24 offices worldwide, regional tourist offices (one per canton), as well as local tourist offices. The Swiss National Office, which promoted Switzerland abroad as a tourist destination, was funded 60 per cent by the Confederation and 40 per cent by partners such as Swissair and the Swiss Federal Railways. Budgetary cuts had already forced the closing of the office in Sydney, Australia, and other cutbacks in offices and promotional expenditures were expected. At the local level, tourism officials – such as Lausanne's Mr Petitpierre – were quite worried about this trend, especially since neighbouring Austria was aggressively promoting its own similar offering of lakes, mountains and picturesque alpine villages.

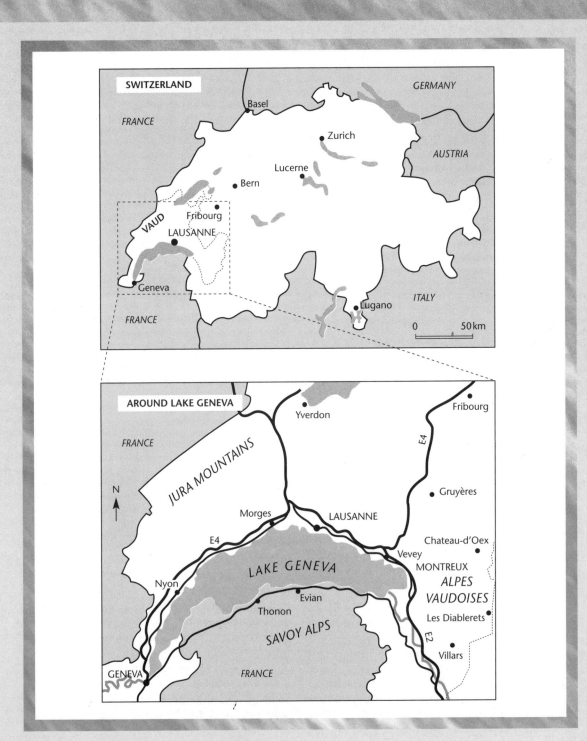

Exhibit 1 ■ Switzerland and the canton of Vaud

The city of Lausanne

Lausanne was located on the shores of Lake Geneva (known in French as Lac Léman), the largest fresh-water lake in Western Europe. The lake was 80 km (50 miles) long and some 13 km across at its widest point. Some described its shape as like a croissant, others more romantically, as like a leaping fish with its tail still in the water. Most of its southern shore was in France, and across the lake from Lausanne stood Evian-les-Bains, famous for its baths and bottled water.

Lausanne, situated 60 km (38 miles) east of Geneva, had a stunning location, built on the side of a steep hill which rose up from the lakeshore. The 30 km stretch of coastline from Lausanne to Montreux, with its combination of manicured flower gardens and terraced vineyards, picturesque villages, harbours and pleasure boats, villas and luxury hotels, was often known as the Swiss Riviera. On a clear day, one could see not only the Savoy Alps across the lake to the south, but east to the upper Rhône Valley and the 3,000 metre (10,000 ft) peaks of the Alpes Vaudoises, and then west to the Jura mountains. Lausanne's elevation ranged from 372 m above sea level at the harbour in Ouchy to 930 m at the top of Mt Jorat. The lake exercised a moderating influence on the local climate; winters were mild and summer temperatures rarely rose much above 30°C (86°F).

The early history of Lausanne dated back to Roman times when Lousonna became the crossroads and staging post on the main lines of communication leading from Italy via the St Bernard Pass to Gaul (modern France), and from the Mediterranean to the Rhine via the Rhône valley.

Remnants of Lausanne's early beginnings provided reminders of its legendary past. The thirteenth-century Gothic cathedral overlooking the city was an important pilgrim destination until it became Protestant during the Reformation, at which time the Calvinists stripped out most of its interior decoration. And in Lausanne's centre was the Tour de l'Ale, an old watchtower which was the only surviving remains of the ramparts which used to surround the city. In 1803, when the Canton of Vaud was carved out of the Canton of Bern, Lausanne became the new canton's capital. During the late eighteenth and early nineteenth centuries, Lausanne welcomed many historic personalities, including Voltaire, Byron, Napoleon, Goethe and Rousseau.

By 1991, with 127,000 inhabitants (250,000 including the surrounding communities), Lausanne was the second largest French-speaking city after Geneva and the fifth largest city in Switzerland.

The city was well known for its institutions of higher education – such as the University of Lausanne, the Swiss Federal Institute of Technology of Lausanne (EPFL), the Lausanne Hotel School (EHL) and the International Institute for Management Development (IMD) – as well as for its many private schools and language institutes. The region boasted many highly regarded hospitals and medical clinics. Lausanne was the headquarters of the International Olympic Committee, and also hosted the main European offices of such multinational companies as Philip Morris, W. R. Grace and Tetra Pak. The international headquarters of Nestlé was located in the neighbouring town of Vevey.

The city provided inhabitants and visitors with a variety of cultural offerings. Performing arts included the Béjart Ballet, the Vidy Theatre, the Lausanne Municipal Theatre and Opera House, the Orchestre de la Suisse Romande and the Lausanne Chamber Orchestra. Museums included the Cantonal Museum of Archaeology and History, the Decorative Arts Museum, the Cantonal Museum of Fine Arts, the Cathedral Museum, the Musée de l'Elysée (photography museum), the Fondation de l'Hermitage (art museum), the Natural History Museum and the Vidy Roman Museum. One especially unusual collection was at the Musé de l'Art Brut (museum of primitive art), where works by non-traditional artists such as recluses, eccentrics, prisoners and inmates of lunatic asylums could be seen. Other distinctive attractions included the Olympic Museum, the Pipe and Tobacco Museum and the Swiss Film Archives. These offerings were further enhanced by Lausanne's Botanical Garden, the Vivarium, and the Servion Zoo.

Tourism

Tourism was often considered to be Lausanne's main economic activity. Unlike the towns of Montreux, Interlaken and Zermatt, Lausanne was not a world renowned tourist centre. Rather, the city was known for the diversity of its 'tourist offer', also serving as a starting point for scenic excursions into the Lavaux vineyards, the surrounding countryside and nearby mountains or for steamer trips on the lake. Tourism was estimated to generate SF 350 million per year for the Lausanne area.

Lausanne depended on five travel segments: vacation stays by individuals or groups; business travel, including seminars, conventions, incentive travel, trade fairs and exhibitions; travel related to teaching or learning; medically related tourism; and event-related tourism such as the Eurovision Song Contest or sports championships such as the European Figure Skating Championship.

Nuitées hôtelières (overnight hotel stays) were the unit of measure used to evaluate tourism trends. Since reaching a peak of 1.1 million in 1970, overnight stays in the Lausanne area had fallen significantly during the following decade, stabilizing during the 1980s at around 850,000 per year (refer to Exhibit 2). This unit of measure considered a night spent in a luxury hotel the same as one in a local campground. But the relative 'economic impact' was in no way comparable. 'We have always wanted to have a system that would enable us to better evaluate the economic impact of tourism,' commented Mr Petitpierre. At present, statistics were mostly descriptive, showing the breakdown of hotel stays by month or by nationality (refer to Exhibits 3 and 4). No attempt had ever been made to examine spending patterns or to obtain information about one-day visitors who were merely passing through the area, perhaps en-route to or from somewhere else in Switzerland or neighbouring France.

The Tourist Office promoted accommodations in small one-star hotels as well as those at the four- and five-star level. 'In order to reach the client looking for a one-star hotel as well as those who prefer the Beau-Rivage, you must promote the qualities of each class of accommodations,' commented the assistant director.

Accommodations

Lausanne had a wide range of lodging establishments catering to meet a variety of needs (refer to Exhibit 5). They included deluxe hotels like the Beau-Rivage Palace and the Lausanne Palace; medium-priced and upper-bracket hotels such as the Hotel Aulac, the Château d'Ouchy, the Hôtel la Résidence and the Royal Savoy; and then several 'budget' to medium-priced hotels, including the Hôtel d'Angleterre (where Lord Byron stayed in 1820) and the Hôtel

Exhibit 2 ■ Hotel overnight stays, 1966–1990: Lausanne vs. all Switzerland

Year	Lausanne (000s)	All Switzerland* (000s)
1966	891	28,400
1967	947	28,800
1968	991	29,100
1969	1,048	30,300
1970	1,101	32,300
1971	1,037	33,100
1972	1,005	33,700
1973	987	33,300
1974	890	31,700
1975	802	30,800
1976	745	29,600
1977	795	33,100
1978	705	32,100
1979	733	29,300
1980	778	33,000
1981	856	34,300
1982	850	32,800
1983	836	32,600
1984	872	33,000
1985	893	33,300
1986	790	32,800
1987	817	32,800
1988	788	32,400
1989	867	34,100
1990	866	34,600

* Excludes permanent guests.
Source: Lausanne Tourist Office.

Exhibit 3 ■ Lausanne overnight stays by month

| | 1990 | | | 1981–90 |
	Swiss	Foreigners	Total	ten-year distribution (%)
January	18	30	48	5.6
February	19	29	48	5.7
March	23	42	65	6.6
April	21	46	67	7.9
May	22	56	78	9.5
June	22	63	85	10.3
July	18	71	89	10.1
August	19	75	95	11.2
September	24	67	91	10.8
October	26	58	84	9.7
November	21	38	59	6.9
December	24	33	57	5.7
Total	258	607	866	100.0

Note: Row and columns totals may not add because of rounding.
Source: Lausanne Tourist Office and Convention Bureau, Annual Report 1990.

Exhibit 4 ■ Lausanne overnight stays by country of origin

| | | | | | | Analysis of 1990 data | |
Country	1981	1985	1988	1989	1990	% of total	Average no. of nights per visitor
France	95	87	87	92	94	10.8	2.0
USA	87	135	66	88	79	9.1	2.1
Germany	85	55	62	64	74	8.6	2.2
Italy	53	46	51	54	57	6.5	1.9
UK and Ireland	46	46	43	53	53	6.2	2.4
Spain	19	19	19	24	30	3.4	1.9
Japan	9	12	19	23	25	2.9	1.5
Greece	11	12	11	15	16	1.8	2.7
Netherlands	20	13	13	17	16	1.8	2.9
Belgium	22	14	15	16	15	1.8	2.4
Other countries	153	174	134	144	148	17.2	3.2
Total foreign visitors	600	613	520	590	607	70.1	2.3
Swiss visitors	256	280	269	277	258	29.9	2.6
Grand total	856	893	788	867	866	100.0	2.4
Percentage change over previous year							
Lausanne	+10.1	+2.4	–3.6	+10.0	–0.1		
All Switzerland	+4.0	+1.1	–1.3	+5.6	+1.4		

Note: Column totals may not add because of rounding.
Source: Lausanne Tourist Office and Convention Bureau.

Exhibit 5 ■ Profile of Lausanne area hotels

Hotels in Lausanne	Date of construction	No. of stars	Double room price	No. of beds	Meeting room(s)	Private garden/ terrace	Within 500m of Lake Geneva	Within 1,000 m of Lausanne railway station
Hôtel du Marché	1820	*	SF90–120	35	Y	Y		
Hôtel d'Angleterre		**	120–160	55			Y	
Hôtel de la Forêt	1960s	**	120–150	30				
Hôtel Régina	1957–58	**/*	130	55				Y
Hôtel AlaGare	1967	***	140–210	92				
Hôtel Aulac	1906	***	150–200	150	Y		Y	
Hôtel le Beau-Lieu	1989	***	140–210	115	Y			
Hôtel Bellerive	1960s	***	140–200	60	Y	Y	Y	Y
Hôtel du Boulevard	1895	***	140–210	46	Y			Y
Hôtel City	1946	***	150–210	110	Y			Y
Hôtel Crystal	1960s	***	140–210	80				Y
Hôtel Elite	1937	***	140–210	57		Y		Y
Hôtel Jan	1957–58	***	150–220	110				
Hôtel de l'Ours		***/***						Y
Hôtel Rex	1960s	**/***	130	46				
Hôtel des Voyageurs	c.1920	***	140–210	52	Y			
Hôtel Agora	1973	****	170–250	180	Y			Y
Hôtel Alpha	1915	****	170–250	240	Y			Y
Hôtel Carlton[2]	c.1910	****	196–266	80	Y	Y	Y	
Le Château d'Ouchy	1893	****	180–250	85	Y	Y	Y	
Hôtel Continental	1964	****	170–1250	180	Y	Y		Y
Hôtel Mirabeau	1904–12	****	180–250	100	Y	Y		Y
Hôtel Moevenpick-Radisson	1988	****	215–260	470	Y	Y	Y	
Hôtel de la Navigation	1954	****	190–240	50	Y		Y	
Hôtel de la Paix	1904/1950	****	220–300	210	Y	Y		
Hôtel la Résidence[1]	1960s	****	220–300	95	Y	Y	Y	
Royal Savoy[1]	c.1910	****	235–295	170	Y	Y		Y
Hôtel Victoria	1904	****	180–250	100	Y			
Beau-Rivage Palace[1,2,3]	1861/1912	****	310–440	320	Y	Y	Y	
Lausanne Palace[2,3]	1915	****	270–400	270	Y	Y		Y

Exhibit 5 ■ Profile of Lausanne area hotels (*continued*)

Hotels on the outskirts of Lausanne	Date of construction	No. of stars	Double room price	No. of beds	Meeting room(s)	Private garden/terrace	Distance to Lake Geneva	Distance to a local train station
Hôtel Beau-Site	1899							
Hôtel de Belmont		***	SF130–160	22	Y	Y		(6.5 km to Lausanne)
Hôtel Bellevue						Y		1 km
Hôtel Cécil[1]		***	130–160	45	Y	Y	2 km	(15 km to Lausanne)
Hôtel du Château								
Hôtel Les Chevreuils	1875	***	140–180	61	Y	Y	8 km	(6.5 km to Lausanne)
Hôtel à la Chotte		***	140–160	28		Y		(7km to Lausanne)
Hôtel du Commerce								
Hôtel le Débarcadère		****	220–300	26	Y	Y		6 km
Hôtel la Fleur-de-Lys								
Hôtel du Galion		***				Y		(9 km to Lausanne)
Hôtel Ibis		**	140–160	230	Y	Y		100 m (10 km to Lausanne)
Hôtel Intereurope		***	140–180	140	Y	Y	100 m	
Novotel Bussigny[1]		***	180	200	Y	Y	4 km	6 km
Hôtel l'Oasis		***						
Hôtel Pré Fleuri[1]		***	150–190	40		Y	600 m	6 km
Hôtel Près-Lac		**	110–130	70			100 m	4 km
Hôtel du Raisin		***	180–220	12	Y			500 m
Auberge de Rivaz		*	100–120	25	Y	Y	100 m	50 m
Motel des Fleurs		**	110	50		Y	15 km	13 km
Motel Vert-Bois[2]	1960s	***	100–150	62	Y	Y	8 km	(8 km to Lausanne)

1 Swimming Pools.
2 Tennis.
3 Sauna/fitness. Y = yes.

Sources: Lausanne Tourist Office and Convention Bureau; *Lausanne – Palace History and Chronicles, 75 Years* (Lausanne: Presses Centrales Lausanne SA, 1991), pp. 147–175; various guides.

Exhibit 6 ■ Available hotel beds in Switzerland

	No. of available beds, 1990
All Switzerland	222,624
Canton of Vaud	19,313
Principal tourist-oriented cities*	
Basel	4,581
Bern	3,219
Geneva	14,826
Lausanne	5,103
Lucerne	5,408
Lugano	7,949
Montreux	3,457
Zurich	15,310

* Figures are for metropolitan areas.
Source: Lausanne Tourist Office and Convention Bureau.

AlaGare. In total, Lausanne had 5,103 beds with an average bed occupancy in 1990 of 46 per cent[2] (for a comparison with other Swiss cities and resorts, refer to Exhibit 6). Collectively, Lausanne's hotels were believed to be less profitable than hotels in most other parts of Switzerland.

A few distinctive hotels, like the Beau-Rivage, were destinations in their own right. But others, like the Hôtel AlaGare, near the railway station, either had to be sold along with the rest of Lausanne's 'tourist offer' or had a loyal clientele composed of tour group operators and business travellers. Lausanne also had a youth hostel (180 beds), a camping site by the lake at Vidy (450 tent sites), furnished rooms (41 beds), apartments, homes and studios (510 beds), special student hostels, and hostels for union members (350 beds). In the hills above the city, there were two campgrounds in Vers-chez-les-Blanc. This wide variety of accommodations reflected Lausanne's strategy of catering to all economic levels from all over the world.

In 1990, the total number of overnight stays in Lausanne had dropped 0.1 per cent over 1989, as compared to a gain of 1.4 per cent for the whole of Switzerland (refer to Exhibit 4).

Restaurants

The attractiveness of Lausanne's 'tourist offer' extended to its restaurant offerings, with cuisine ranging from high gourmet to traditional Swiss, and from classical family fare to fast food.

One of Europe's most renowned restaurants, Girardet, located on the outskirts of Lausanne, was on every serious gourmet's gastronomic tour of Europe. Located in the modest 1929 Crissier town hall, Girardet's nouvelle cuisine included such specialities as ragout of fresh quail with vegetables, baby veal in lemon sauce and hot duck liver in a vinaigrette sauce. Fixed-price menus started from SF 150 ($105) and dinner reservations often needed to be made at least three months in advance.

Local culinary specialities included cheese fondue, *raclette*, Vinzel fritters and cabbage or liver sausage. Fish was popular too; fresh lake fish included *omble chevalier* (char) and trout; fillet of perch was a local favourite. Restaurants featuring Italian, Greek, Chinese or Indian food were also well represented.

Convention facilities

Many conferences and trade fairs were held in Lausanne. One of the largest events, held each September, was the Comptoir Suisse, which provided a good picture of the dynamism and diversity of the Swiss economy, from agriculture to high technology.

Lausanne's prime facility for conventions (congresses/ conferences) was the Palais de Beaulieu. However, there were also convention facilities at academic institutions and at several of Lausanne's hotels (refer to Exhibit 7). Among the events held recently at the Palais de Beaulieu, 9.5 per cent included 1,000–2,000 participants, 4.5 per cent had 2,000–3,000, and 3 per cent attracted 3,000–7,000.

In 1991, the convention/congress schedule was to include the International Conference on Conventional and Nuclear District Heating, the Culinary Institute of America, the Swiss Society of Fertility and Sterility with the Swiss Society of Family Planning, the Swiss Society of Tropical Medicine and Parasitology and the Kiwanis International Europe Twenty-fourth Annual

Exhibit 7 ■ Lausanne conference room capacity

Facility	Largest room (no. of persons)		Total capacity (no. of persons)
Palais de Beaulieu	8,000		12,000
Ecole Polytechnique	520	(Lausanne)	650
Fédérale de Lausanne (EPFL)	500	(Ecublens)	1,500
Université de Lausanne	450	(Palais de Rumine)	450
	300	(Dorigny)	1,500
Hôpital Cantonal Universitaire Vaudois (CHUV)	400		1,000
Hôtel Beau-Rivage Palace	400		1,000
Hôtel Lausanne-Palace	400		850
Hôtel Moevenpick-Radisson	340		750
Hôtel de la Paix	200		350
Hôtel Royal-Savoy	100		250

Source: Lausanne Tourist Office and Convention Bureau.

Convention. Attracting visitors for all hotel categories, conventions also provided the clientele for restaurants, public transport, boat cruises on Lake Geneva, excursion-related services, and admissions to museums and cultural events.

Transportation

Lausanne had an excellent local public transportation network for a city of its size, operated by Transports Lausannois (TL). A dense network of electric trolley buses and diesel buses funnelled through the centre of the town, connecting to two metros (one a cog railway running down to the lakeside at Ouchy), the LEB light rail line operating north of the city, and various stations served by main line and regional CFF (Swiss Federal Railways) trains. A ride on the TL system cost one franc for up to three stops and two francs for longer distances, but visitors could save money by buying multiple-ride tickets and system passes.

Lausanne's central railway station was one of the busiest intercity railway junctions in Europe. Connected to all the big European rail networks, Lausanne was 3.4 hours from Paris by TGV (French high-speed trains) with four services daily, 3.2 hours from Milan, and 5.2 hours from Frankfurt. There were frequent intercity and direct trains between the big Swiss urban centres: Geneva, Bern, Basel, Zurich and St Gallen, as well as connections to towns and villages across the country. Located on the Autoroute du Léman (a limited-access motorway), the city was also easily accessible by road.

Lausanne had no passenger airport of its own, so it was served by Geneva's Cointrin intercontinental airport, only 50 minutes away by highway or train (the airport station was underneath the terminal). Lausanne had a small airfield at La Blécherette, where private aircraft could land and small air taxis could be chartered.

The harbour at Ouchy provided Lausanne with access by water during the warmer months to all the cities on the lakeshore: east to Vevey, where Charlie Chaplin's long residency was commemorated by a statue on the waterfront; to Montreux to attend one of its many festivals; or to the Château de Chillon, a superbly renovated medieval castle in the lake which was made famous by Lord Byron's poem 'The Prisoner of Chillon'. Passengers might find themselves riding a beautifully renovated 80-year-old paddle steamer or a modern motor vessel. Boat trips were also available west to Morges, Nyon and Geneva or south across the lake to Evian, Thonon and Yvoire in France. The Lausanne–Evian/Thonon service operated all year long. Marinas at Ouchy and nearby Vidy were equipped with a total of 1,522 berths for sailing and pleasure boats.

The Lausanne Tourist Office and Convention Bureau

The Office du Tourisme et des Congrès was founded in 1887. Although its services had evolved over time, its mission had remained unchanged: to welcome visitors and to promote Lausanne as a tourist centre. Currently, the Lausanne Tourist Office's main goal was to achieve one million overnight stays a year, up from 865,762 in 1990.

Structure and organization

The Lausanne Tourist Office was a private association, receiving 27 per cent of its SF 4.9 million budget from the city of Lausanne and another 18 per cent from hotel room taxes. The rest of the budget came primarily from other 'partners' such as hotel and restaurant owners who were directly affected by tourism and conventions.

A member of the Association of Les Six Villes Suisses – grouping Lausanne with Geneva, Zurich, Bern, Basel and St Gallen – the tourist office collaborated with these towns to explore common tourist and development issues. But each town was responsible for promoting its own 'tourist offer'. The tourist office did work with Montreux/Vevey (a strong competitor for business and incentive travel as well as for conventions) to develop general promotional campaigns, 'for greater effectiveness and more affordable results,' commented Mr Petitpierre.

In 1987, a new main office and visitor information centre opened in Ouchy. This site, on the lake and close to seven hotels, the steamer terminal and the Ouchy Metro station, was in one of Lausanne's most popular tourist areas. The tourist office employed 40 full-time workers and 30 freelance hostesses who provided reception and information services on an as needed basis. A second, smaller information centre was located 2 kilometres away at the main railway station.

The activities of the tourist office were directly supervised by the director and a seven-member management committee, which included the Mayor of Lausanne and representatives from the society of hotel managers, the society of café and restaurant managers, local businesses, the banking and legal communities, and the Palais de Beaulieu.

Responsibility for day-to-day activities was divided among five departments: Management and Administration oversaw the general management of the office; Information Services managed the two visitor information centres; Publications and Public Relations ensured a liaison with the local press and produced the different office publications; Marketing was responsible for performing market studies and organizing promotion in Switzerland and abroad (an example of recent advertising to promote corporate incentive visits to Lausanne is shown in Exhibit 8) and Reception-Groups-Conferences organized conventions, group stays and incentive trips.

The Information Services department was spread between the tourist office's two visitor centres. At these two locations, the tourist office's employees, each speaking a minimum of three languages (French, German and English) provided visitors with information every day of the year (except Christmas) from 08:00 to 19:00 hours, with office hours extending until 21:00 in the summer.

Each visitor centre had its own information service 'mission'. The smaller office at the station was a one-person operation and focused on Lausanne-related information, providing schedules for the bus, trolley and metro system, youth hostel information and maps. Having a broadly defined 'tourist' service, the main visitor centre provided information not only on the Greater Lausanne area, but also on Switzerland's other major tourist areas. Additionally, this office had an on-line 'Billetel' computer system for ticket sales and reservations, and provided tours of Lausanne as well as summer excursions to the local Lavaux vineyards.

Exhibit 8 ■ Example of incentive advertising

At the main office, multiple copies of some 3,500 different publications (collectively weighing four tons) were stored in an enormous electrically operated filing cabinet which rotated through two floors of the building. 100,000 guidebooks of Lausanne and 80,000 local maps were distributed annually.

Reception and information services at the main office were provided by up to seven people during Lausanne's 'high season' in the summer, when the office received an average of 250 telephone calls, 140 visitors and 20 letters or telefaxes a day. 'We believe in answering written requests as quickly as possible', commented Mr Marko Jankovic, Manager of Information Services. 'But we keep them brief to avoid sending everyone two kilograms of material.' During the rest of the year, there were three people providing these services, with at least one person available during the office's open hours.

The case for new research

After more than two hours of discussion, the management committee had agreed that the idea of tourism as an economic sector was not easily perceived, since tourism functioned as the coordinating 'hub' of a myriad of services. But, committee members were determined to find ways of quantifying – for both the cantonal government and local residents – the significant contribution that tourism made to Lausanne's economy.

At this point in the discussion, Mr Petitpierre had the floor:

> If we look at cities like Nice, Cannes, Paris, Birmingham, The Hague, Amsterdam and Hamburg, it's incredible the financial means they have to promote their cities and their convention centres. At this level, we are absolutely not competitive for the moment. The only way we're going to get the necessary funds is to document the contribution that tourism, in all its forms, makes to the local economy. The statistics we have at present are insufficient. We also need new and more detailed information about our visitors to help us develop strategies for attracting them and then serving them better once they get to Lausanne. And that will require one or more specially commissioned studies.

The director of the tourist office looked around the table. There were murmurs of agreement from other members of the management committee and heads were nodding. As if to emphasize the point, a long blast came from the hooter of one of the lake steamers a few hundred metres away as it prepared to leave for Evian.

It sounds as though both the local economy and this committee are in agreement with you, Claude,' said the director with a smile. 'Why don't you review the possibilities for us and outline a plan of action for some new research?'

Notes

1 The exchange rate for the Swiss franc in 1991 was approximately SF 1.00 = US$0.70 = £0.40.
2 One person staying in a room with two beds would represent a bed occupancy of 50 per cent. Switzerland did not collect room occupancy statistics.

PART iv

Integrating marketing with other management functions

CHAPTER 12

Enhancing value by improving quality and productivity

Learning objectives

After reading and reflecting on this chapter, you should be able to:

1. Define what is meant by both productivity and quality in a service context.

2. Describe the relationship between customer expectations, service quality and customer satisfaction.

3. Explain the gaps model of service quality.

4. Recognize key dimensions of service quality, as described in the SERVQUAL scale.

5. Discuss productivity and quality measurement techniques.

6. Identify the components of a service quality information system.

Nichols Foods: a manufacturing firm competing through service quality[1]

When you purchase food or a soft drink from a vending machine, do you ever pause to wonder about how it got there? The company that owns (or leases) and operates the machine needs a reliable supplier for the items stocked inside. Nichols Foods is a medium-sized manufacturing company that packs and distributes food and beverage products for UK vending machine operators, who in turn sell these products on to the consumers who purchase from their machines. Nichols also sells to retailers and food service businesses.

At first sight, Nichols would seem to face two serious competitive disadvantages in trying to win and keep demanding business customers: it doesn't offer well-known national brands of food and beverage and is one of the most expensive suppliers in the unbranded category. Yet the company has been extremely successful and continues to grow rapidly. Nichols' philosophy is based on providing exceptional customer service in order to generate customer loyalty, which then yields the financial rewards of profits and growth. In this instance, of course, we're looking at business customers rather than individual consumers.

The secrets of the company's success begin internally with careful attention to recruiting PLUs ('People Like Us'). In other words, Nichols hires people who share its culture of customer obsession. Particular emphasis is placed on encouraging employees to provide exceptional service to *internal customers*, thus creating the efficient, timely and high-quality performance internally, which is needed to be able to offer exceptional service externally.

The business strategy of Nichols Foods is to build relationships with its vending-machine operator customers that will lead to long-term partnerships. Armed with a good understanding of the cost savings to be obtained from customer retention (relative to attracting new customers), Nichols devotes substantial resources to the former task. A key area involves investing in educational and training programmes, which are heavily subsidized for external customers. It has identified what their needs are and has run more than 40 programmes covering topics such as sales management, marketing strategy, customer service, law and finance. The company is now recognized as one of the main providers of management, sales and customer care training for the UK vending industry.

To ensure continuous improvement in service quality, Nichols Foods internally measures a wide range of services known to be valued by its customers, including average response time for phone calls, proactive sales calls to customers, promptness of delivery and order accuracy. External measurement is carried out through customer satisfaction surveys and focus groups, with additional feedback encouraged through such channels as a free telephone complaint line and customer feedback questionnaires.

Among its strategies for exceeding customer expectations are surprise service encounters. For instance, when customers arrive at Nichols Foods for a factory visit, they not only have immediate access to priority parking spaces but also find on returning that their cars have been cleaned. In a recent survey conducted by a market research firm, one customer remarked: 'Nichols have something that others do not have – get up and go. They have a way of communicating to their customers that the customer is important. Others are too big for their boots!'

Integrating productivity and quality strategies

Productivity was one of the key managerial imperatives of the 1970s: working faster and more efficiently in order to reduce costs. During the 1980s and early 1990s, improving quality rose to prominence as a major priority; in a service context, this requires efforts to improve customer satisfaction by creating better service processes and outcomes. As we reach the new millennium, we're seeing growing emphasis on linking these two strategies in order to create better value for both customers and the firm. For an exchange to take place between a buyer and a seller, each party must see value in the transaction. As we emphasized in Chapter 10, the perceived benefits must exceed all the perceived costs (including money, time and effort). And for a long-term relationship to be created and survive, both parties must perceive that they are deriving a continuing value from that relationship. Customers evaluate alternative suppliers in a search for greater value; well-managed suppliers continuously seek to improve the value that they derive from each relationship. Nichols Foods competes with other firms wishing to supply packaged food and beverages for the vending machine industry. It's not the cheapest supplier so it has to create value in other ways.

Both quality and productivity were historically seen as issues for operations managers. When the search for improved quality and productivity required better employee selection, training and supervision – or renegotiation of labour agreements relating to job assignments and work rules – then human resource managers were expected to get involved, too. But it was not until service quality was explicitly linked to customer satisfaction that marketers were also seen as having an important role.

The organizational implications are significant, in that enhancing service value requires the marketing, operations and human resources departments to work closely together towards this common goal. Broadly defined, the task of value enhancement requires quality improvement programmes to deliver and continuously enhance the benefits desired by customers; at the same time, productivity improvement programmes must seek to reduce the associated costs. The challenge is to ensure that these two programmes are mutually reinforcing in achieving common goals, rather than operating at loggerheads with one another to achieve conflicting goals. Gummesson notes that although service quality must be viewed in conjunction with service productivity and profitability, quality in the service sector has been widely researched, whereas productivity has not.[2]

In this chapter, we begin with a brief overview of why quality and productivity are important to service marketers. We then examine how to define and measure quality and productivity in a marketing context, paying particular attention to some key findings from the extensive research literature on service quality. The balance of the chapter is devoted to how to improve quality and productivity in different categories of services, with attention being paid to the contribution that information technology can make.

A role for marketing

Creating customer value is widely recognized by theorists as the fundamental basis for marketing.[3] The search for value often begins with market research, seeking to identify the benefits sought by customers or prospects for a given product category and the costs that they are willing to incur to obtain these benefits. But, as Holbrook emphasizes, perceived value is highly personal and may vary widely from one customer to another.[4] In fact, the benefits desired often form the basis for segmentation.

In Part III, we examined some of the key tools available to service marketers for creating services that offer value to target customers. Service design – embracing the core product, supplementary services and the delivery system – is a key element in the value equation and should be directed at enhancing desired benefits and reducing unwanted costs (see Chapters 8 and 9). Re-engineering of existing production and delivery systems may be needed to improve service value, either by adding new benefits or by reducing the associated costs as a result of greater productivity.

Pricing decisions, of course, are intimately related to value for the customer: lowering monetary prices (often a function of improving productivity) while maintaining perceived benefits will serve to increase perceived value. A marketing input is important at this point to advise operations experts on whether or not customers may be willing to make trade-offs, such as paying a higher price to obtain more benefits or avoid unwanted time and effort (Chapter 10). However, unless such a strategy is accompanied by either increased sales volume or lower costs from improved productivity, it may not increase profits. Finally, advertising and other communications efforts may be needed to clarify service benefits (especially when research shows that prospective users misperceive the relevant costs and benefits), encourage trial and educate customers on how to obtain the best value from that service (Chapter 11). Note that Nichols Foods is not the cheapest supplier; instead, it adds value through outstanding service. Its customers are willing to pay a premium for a supplier that is fast, efficient and reliable. They also like the fact that it treats them well and values their business. By offering subsidized training programmes, Nichols helps its customers to run their own businesses more effectively and thus increases productivity for both parties.

Marketing and quality

Marketing's interest in service quality is obvious when one thinks about it: poor quality places a firm at a competitive disadvantage. If customers perceive quality as unsatisfactory, they may be quick to take their business elsewhere. Recent years have witnessed a veritable explosion of discontent with service quality at a time when the quality of many manufactured goods seems to have improved significantly.

Service quality problems are not confined to traditional service industries. Many manufacturing firms are struggling to improve the quality of the supplementary services that support their products – consultation, financing, shipping and delivery, installation, training of operators, repair and maintenance, trouble-shooting and billing, for instance.

From a marketing standpoint, a key issue is whether or not customers notice differences in quality between competing suppliers. Gale puts it succinctly when he says: 'value is simply quality, however the *customer* defines it, offered at the right price'.[5] Improving quality in the eyes of the customers pays off for the companies that provide it: data from the PIMS (Profit Impact of Market Strategy) show that a perceived quality advantage leads to higher profits.[6]

Marketing and productivity

Improving productivity is important to marketers for several reasons. First, it helps to keep costs down. Lower costs mean either higher profits or the ability to hold down prices. The company with the lowest costs in an industry has the option to position itself as the low-price leader – usually a significant advantage among price-sensitive market segments. Firms with lower costs than their competitors also generate higher margins, giving them the option of spending more than the competition on such marketing activities as advertising and promotion, sales efforts, improved customer service and supplementary service extras; they may also be able to offer higher margins to attract and reward the best distributors and intermediaries. Finally, there is the opportunity to secure the organization's long-term future through investments in new service technologies and research to create superior new services, improved features and innovative delivery systems.

Efforts to improve productivity often have an impact on customers, and it's the marketer's responsibility to ensure that negative impacts are avoided or minimized and that new procedures are carefully presented to customers. When the impact is a positive one, then the improvements can be promoted as a new advantage. Finally, as we'll see, there are opportunities for marketers themselves to help improve productivity by involving customers actively in the service production and delivery process.

Definition and measurement

It is commonly said that 'you cannot manage what you do not measure'. Without measurement, managers cannot identify where their firm or products stand now and whether or not desired goals are being achieved. Measurement, in turn, requires careful definition, so that people agree on what they are talking about and what they are measuring. In Chapter 8, we defined the net value of a service to a customer as 'The sum of all the perceived benefits (gross value) minus the sum of all the perceived costs'. Quality and productivity are twin paths to creating value for both customers and companies. In broad terms, quality focuses on the benefits side of the equation and productivity on the cost side.

The primary goal of productivity improvements is to reduce monetary costs, but one route to achieving this goal is to speed up service processes and squeeze out wasted time, which may also benefit customers. Some productivity improvements also yield new service delivery technologies that reduce unwanted physical effort but often place an initial mental burden on customers who are uncomfortable with change.

Defining and measuring quality

The word *quality* means different things to people according to the context. Garvin identifies five perspectives.[7]

- *The transcendent view* of quality is synonymous with innate excellence, a mark of uncompromising standards and high achievement. This viewpoint is often applied to the performing and visual arts. It argues that people learn to recognize quality only through the experience gained from repeated exposure. However, from a practical standpoint, suggesting that managers or customers will know quality when they see it is not very helpful.

- *The product-based approach* sees quality as a precise and measurable variable. Differences in quality, it argues, reflect differences in the amount of some ingredient or attribute possessed by the product. Because this view is totally objective, it fails to account for differences in the tastes, needs and preferences of individual customers (or even entire market segments).

■ *User-based definitions* start with the premise that quality lies in the eye of the beholder; these definitions equate quality with maximum satisfaction. This subjective, demand-oriented perspective recognizes that different customers have different wants and needs.

■ *The manufacturing-based approach*, in contrast, is supply-based, and is primarily concerned with engineering and manufacturing practices. (In services, we would say that quality was operations-driven.) It focuses on conformance to internally developed specifications, which are often driven by productivity and cost containment goals.

■ *Value-based definitions* define quality in terms of value and price. By considering the trade-off between performance (or conformance) and price, quality comes to be defined as 'affordable excellence'.

Garvin suggests that these alternative views of quality help to explain the conflicts that sometimes arise between managers in different functional departments. However, he goes on to argue:

> Despite the potential for conflict, companies can benefit from such multiple perspectives. Reliance on a single definition of quality is a frequent source of problems . . . Because each approach has its predictable blind spots, companies are likely to suffer fewer problems if they employ multiple perspectives on quality, actively shifting the approach they take as products move from design to market . . . Success normally requires close coordination of the activities of each function.[8]

Manufacturing-based components of quality

To incorporate differing perspectives, Garvin developed eight components of quality that could be useful as a framework for analysis and strategic planning. These are: (1) performance (primary operating characteristics), (2) features (bells and whistles), (3) reliability (probability of malfunction or failure), (4) conformance (ability to meet specifications), (5) durability (how long the product continues to provide value to the customer), (6) serviceability (speed, courtesy, competence and ease of having problems fixed), (7) aesthetics (how the product appeals to any or all of the user's five senses), and (8) perceived quality (associations such as the reputation of the company or brand name). Note that these categories were developed from a manufacturing perspective, but they do address the notion of 'serviceability' of a physical good.

Service-based components of quality

Researchers argue that the distinctive nature of services requires a distinctive approach to defining and measuring service quality. Because of the intangible, multi-faceted nature of many services, it may be harder to evaluate the quality of a service than a good. Since customers are often involved in service production – particularly in people-processing services – a distinction needs to be drawn between the *process* of service delivery (what Grönroos calls functional quality) and the actual *output* of the service (what he calls technical quality).[9] Grönroos and others also suggest that the perceived quality of a service will be the result of an evaluation process in which customers compare their perceptions of service delivery and its outcome against what they expected.

The most extensive research into service quality is strongly user-oriented. From focus group research, Zeithaml, Berry and Parasuraman identified ten criteria used by consumers in evaluating service quality (Table 12.1). In subsequent research, they found a high degree of correlation between several of these variables and so consolidated them into five broad dimensions:

- *Tangibles* (appearance of physical elements);
- *Reliability* (dependable, accurate performance);
- *Responsiveness* (promptness and helpfulness);
- *Assurance* (competence, courtesy, credibility and security);
- *Empathy* (easy access, good communications and customer understanding).[10]

Only one of these five dimensions – reliability – has a direct parallel in findings from Garvin's research on manufacturing quality.

Table 12.1 ■ Generic dimensions used by customers to evaluate service quality

Dimension	Definition	Examples of questions that customers might raise
Credibility	Trustworthiness, believability, honesty of the service provider	Does the hospital have a good reputation? Does my stockbroker refrain from pressuring me to buy? Does the repair firm guarantee its work?
Security	Freedom from danger, risk or doubt	Is it safe for me to use the bank's ATMs at night? Is my credit card protected against unauthorized use? Can I be sure that my insurance policy provides complete coverage?
Access	Approachability and ease of contact	How easy is it for me to talk to a supervisor when I have a problem? Does the airline have a 24-hour free phone number? Is the hotel conveniently located?
Communication	Listening to customers and keeping them informed in language they can understand	When I have a complaint, is the manager willing to listen to me? Does my doctor avoid using technical jargon? Does the electrician call when unable to keep a scheduled appointment?
Understanding the customer	Making the effort to know customers and their needs	Does someone in the hotel recognize me as a regular customer? Does my stockbroker try to determine my specific financial objectives? Is the removal company willing to accommodate my schedule?

Table 12.1 ■ Generic dimensions used by customers to evaluate service quality (*continued*)

Dimension	Definition	Examples of questions that customers might raise
Tangibles	Appearance of physical facilities, equipment, personnel and communication materials	Are the hotel's facilities attractive? Is my accountant dressed appropriately? Is my bank statement easy to understand?
Reliability	Ability to perform the promised service dependably and accurately	When a solicitor (lawyer) says she will call me back in 15 minutes, does she do so? Is my telephone bill free of errors? Is my television repaired right the first time?
Responsiveness	Willingness to help customers and provide prompt service	When there's a problem, does the firm resolve it quickly? Is my stockbroker willing to answer my questions? Is the cable TV company willing to give me a specific time when the installer will show up?
Competence	Possession of the skills and knowledge required to perform the service	Can the bank teller process my transaction without fumbling? When I call my travel agent is she able to obtain the information I need? Does the dentist appear to know what he is doing?
Courtesy	Politeness, respect, consideration and friendliness of contact personnel	Does the flight attendant have a pleasant demeanour? Are the telephone operators consistently polite when answering my calls? Does the plumber take off his muddy shoes before stepping on my carpet?

Source: Adapted from Valarie A. Zeithaml, A. Parasuraman and Leonard L. Berry, *Delivering Quality Service: Balancing Customer Perceptions and Expectations*, New York: The Free Press, 1990.

Measuring satisfaction

To measure customer satisfaction with different aspects of service quality, Zeithaml and her colleagues developed a survey research instrument called SERVQUAL.[11] It is based on the premise that customers can evaluate a firm's service quality by comparing their perceptions of its service with their expectations. SERVQUAL is seen as a generic measurement tool that can be applied across a broad spectrum of service industries. In its basic form, the scale contains 22 perception items and a series of expectation items, reflecting the five dimensions of service quality described above. Respondents complete a series of scales which measure their expectations of companies in a particular industry on a wide array of specific service characteristics; subsequently, they are asked to record their perceptions of a specific company whose services they have used, on those same characteristics. When perceived performance ratings are lower than expectations, this is a sign of poor quality; the reverse indicates good quality.

Although SERVQUAL has been widely used by service companies, doubts have been expressed with regard to both its conceptual foundation and methodological limitations.[12] To evaluate the stability of the five underlying dimensions when applied to a variety of different service industries, Mels, Boshoff and Nel analyzed datasets from banks, insurance brokers, vehicle repairs, electrical repairs and life insurance.[13] Their findings suggest that, in reality, SERVQUAL difference scores only measure two factors: intrinsic service quality (resembling what Grönroos termed functional quality) and extrinsic service quality (which refers to the tangible aspects of service delivery and 'resembles to some extent what Grönroos refers to as technical quality'). In another study, Lam and Woo found that the SERVQUAL scale was not stable over time, as revealed by insignificant correlations between test scores and retest scores.[14] Although scores on items in the expectations battery remained fairly stable over time, the performance items were subject to instability even in a one-week test–retest interval.

These findings do not undermine the value of Zeithaml, Berry and Parasuraman's efforts to identify some of the underlying constructs in service quality, but they do highlight the difficulty of measuring customer perceptions of quality. Smith notes that the majority of researchers using SERVQUAL have omitted from, added to or altered the list of statements purporting to measure service quality.[15]

There are some risks, however, to defining service quality primarily in terms of customers' satisfaction with outcomes relative to their prior expectations. If customers' expectations are low and actual service delivery proves to be marginally better than the dismal level that had been expected, we can hardly claim that customers are receiving good quality service!

Satisfaction-based research into quality assumes that customers are dealing with services that are high in search or experience characteristics (see Chapter 1). A problem arises when they are asked to evaluate the quality of those services that are high in credence characteristics, such as complex legal cases or medical treatments, which they find hard to evaluate even after delivery is completed. In short, the customers may not be sure what to expect in advance and they may not know for years – if ever – how good a job the professional actually did. A natural tendency in such situations is for clients or patients to evaluate quality in terms of process factors, such as whether or not they liked the providers' personal style and how satisfied they were with the perceived quality of those supplementary elements that they are competent to evaluate (for example, the tastiness of hospital meals or the clarity of bills for legal services). Consequently, measuring the quality of professional performance may require adding peer reviews of both process and outcomes as these relate to service execution on the core product.

Devlin and Dong offer guidelines on how to measure service quality across every aspect of the business in a real-world setting.[16] To help customers recall and evaluate their service experiences, these authors suggest taking them through each step of their service encounters (this approach is sometimes referred to as a walk-through audit). Stuart and Tax demonstrate the value of the quality function deployment (QFD) process for both strategic service positioning and quality of service delivery; in particular, they illustrate how the 'voice of the customer' can be related to each individual service encounter.[17] Ballantyne, Christopher and Payne argue that service quality improvement must be considered within the context of relationship marketing. In particular, they argue for the need to review service design with respect to the setting of service environment, processes, job design and people.[18]

Vandermerwe describes how a Dutch manufacturer of animal feed sought to add value through consulting services for one of its customer segments, pig farmers.[19] To help breeders get the farmers to achieve the results they wanted, Hendrix Voeders began providing advice at each relevant stage. During the pre-purchase phase, consulting on stock and sow management so that breeding choice and conditions can be optimized. During the purchase phase – when farmers are buying feed for the growing piglets – Hendrix uses a sophisticated artificial intelligence system to customize feed, supplements and medicines to the circumstances of each individual animal. Next, to minimize stress or injury to animals when they are being transported to the abattoir, Hendrix helps select and monitor transport companies. Finally, to ensure good quality in meat processing and distribution, the company sets standards and has established early warning signals.

Defining and measuring productivity

Simply defined, productivity measures the amount of output produced by an organization relative to the amount of inputs required. Hence, improvements in productivity require an increase in the ratio of outputs to inputs. An improvement in this ratio might be achieved by cutting the resources required to create a given volume of output or by increasing the output obtained from a given level of inputs.

What do we mean by 'input' in a service context? Input varies according to the nature of the business, but may include labour (both physical and intellectual), materials, energy and capital (consisting of land, buildings, equipment, information systems and financial assets). The intangible nature of service performances makes it more difficult to measure the productivity of service industries than that of manufacturing. The problem is especially acute for information-based services. A manufacturer's output consists of products like cars, packages of soap powder, transformers or drill bits that can all be counted and readily sorted into different models or categories. Because production and consumption are separated in time, defective items that are caught by quality control inspectors will either be recycled or reworked, thus adding to their respective input costs.

Measuring productivity is difficult in services when the output is hard to define. In a people-processing service, such as a hospital, we can look at the number of patients treated in the course of a year and at the hospital's 'census' or average bed occupancy. But how do we account for the different types of interventions performed – removal of cancerous tumours, treatment of diabetes or setting of broken bones – and the almost inevitable variability between one patient and another? And how do we evaluate the inevitable difference in outcomes? Some patients get better, some develop complications and, sadly, some may die. There are relatively few standardized procedures in medicine that offer highly predictable outcomes.

The measurement task is perhaps simpler in possession-processing services, since many are quasi-manufacturing organizations, performing routine tasks with easily measurable input and output. Examples i,nclude garages that change a car's oil and rotate its tyres or fast-food restaurants that offer limited and simple menus. But the task gets more complicated when the garage mechanic has to find and repair a water leak, or we are dealing with a French restaurant known for its varied and exceptional cuisine. And what about information-based services? How should we define the output of a bank or a consulting firm? And how does the latter's output compare to a law firm's? Lawyers like to boast (or keep quiet) about their billable hours – but what were they actually doing during those hours and how do we measure their output, as opposed to their fees?

A major problem in measuring service productivity concerns variability. As Heskett points out, traditional measures of service output tend to ignore variations in the quality or value of service. In freight transport, for instance, a tonne-kilometre of output for freight that is delivered late is treated the same for productivity purposes as a similar shipment delivered on time.[20]

Another approach, counting the number of customers served per unit of time, suffers from the same shortcoming: what happens when an increase in customer throughput is achieved at the expense of perceived service quality? Suppose a hairdresser serves three customers per hour and finds she can increase her output to one every 15 minutes – giving what is technically just as good a haircut – by using a faster but noisier hairdryer, eliminating all conversation and generally rushing her customers. Even if the haircut itself is just as good, the delivery process may be perceived as functionally inferior, leading customers to rate the overall service experience less positively.

The problem is that classical techniques of productivity measurement focus on outputs rather than *outcomes*; they stress efficiency but neglect *effectiveness*. The need to emphasize effectiveness and outcomes suggests that issues of productivity cannot be divorced from those of quality and value. As noted in Chapter 6, loyal customers who remain with a firm tend to become more profitable over time, an indication of the payback to be obtained from providing quality service. In this vein, Shaw suggests that measures of productivity growth in services should focus on customers as the denominator.[21] He proposes the following units of analysis and comparison:

- Profitability by customer;
- Capital employed per customer;
- Shareholder equity employed per customer.

These measures tell the firm how it is doing. But what managers and employees also need are insights as to how better results may be achieved.

Identifying and correcting service quality shortfalls

If one accepts the view that quality entails consistently meeting customers' expectations, then the manager's task is to balance customer expectations and perceptions and to close any gaps between the two. Zeithaml, Berry and Parasuraman identify four potential shortfalls within the service organization that may lead to a gap between what customers expect and what they receive.[22]

1. Not knowing what customers expect.
2. Specifying service quality standards that do not reflect what management believes to be customers' expectations.
3. Service performance that does not match specifications.
4. Not living up to the levels of service performance that are promoted by marketing communications.

Improving quality, they argue, requires identifying the specific causes of each gap and then developing strategies to close them. Their gaps model is shown in Figure 12.1.

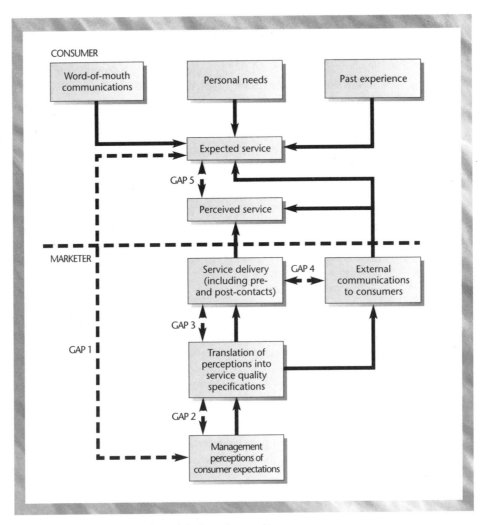

Figure 12.1 ■ Conceptual model of service quality

Source: Valarie A. Zeithaml, Leonard L. Berry and A. Parasuraman, 'Communication and Control Processes in the Delivery of Service Processes', *Journal of Marketing*, Vol. 52, April 1988, pp. 36–58.

Zeithaml *et al.* propose over 40 variables that may explain the magnitude and direction of these four gaps. In a subsequent work, they propose a series of generic steps for closing these gaps (these prescriptions are summarized in Table 12.2).[23]

The strength of the gap methodology is that it offers generic insights and solutions that can be applied across different industries. What it doesn't attempt, of course, is to identify specific quality failures that may occur in particular service businesses. Each firm must develop its own customized approach to ensure that service quality becomes and remains a key objective.

Identifying failure points

A powerful tool for understanding the activities and processes involved in delivering a particular type of service is flowcharting, which we introduced in Chapter 3.

Table 12.2 ■ Prescriptions for closing service gaps

Gap 1 Prescription: Learn what customers expect

- Get a better understanding of customer expectations through research, complaint analysis, customer panels, etc.
- Increase direct interactions between managers and customers to improve understanding
- Improve upward communication from contact personnel to management and reduce the number of levels between the two
- Turn information and insights into action

Gap 2 Prescription: Establish the right service quality standards

- Ensure that top management displays continuing commitment to quality as defined from the customers' point of view
- Get middle management to set, communicate and reinforce customer-oriented service standards for their work units
- Train managers in the skills needed to lead employees to deliver quality service
- Become receptive to new ways of doing business that overcome barriers to delivering quality service
- Standardize repetitive work tasks to ensure consistency and reliability by substituting hard technology for human contact and improving work methods (soft technology)
- Establish clear service quality goals that are challenging, realistic and explicitly designed to meet customer expectations
- Clarify to employees which job tasks have the biggest impact on quality and should receive the highest priority
- Ensure that employees understand and accept goals and priorities
- Measure performance and provide regular feedback
- Reward managers and employees for attaining quality goals

Gap 3 Prescription: Ensure that service performance meets standards

- Clarify employee roles
- Ensure that all employees understand how their jobs contribute to customer satisfaction
- Match employees to jobs by selecting for the abilities and skills needed to perform each job well
- Provide employees with the technical training needed to perform their assigned tasks effectively
- Develop innovative recruitment and retention methods to attract the best people and build loyalty
- Enhance employee performance by selecting the most appropriate and reliable technology and equipment
- Teach employees about customer expectations, perceptions and problems
- Train employees in interpersonal skills, especially for dealing with customers under stressful conditions
- Eliminate role conflict among employees by involving them in the process of setting standards

---

Table 12.2 ■ Prescriptions for closing service gaps (*continued*)

- Train employees in priority setting and time management
- Measure employee performance and tie compensation and recognition to delivery of quality service
- Develop reward systems that are meaningful, timely, simple, accurate and fair
- Empower managers and employees in the field by pushing decision-making power down the organization; allow them greater discretion in the methods they use to reach goals
- Ensure that employees working at internal support jobs provide good service to customer contact personnel
- Build teamwork so that employees work well together, and use team rewards as incentives
- Treat customers as 'partial employees'; clarify their roles in service delivery, train and motivate them to perform well in their roles as coproducers

Gap 4 Prescription: Ensure that delivery matches promises

- Seek inputs from operations personnel when new advertising programmes are being created
- Develop advertising that features real employees performing their jobs
- Allow service providers to preview advertisements before customers are exposed to them
- Get sales staff to involve operations staff in face-to-face meetings with customers
- Develop internal educational, motivational and advertising campaigns to strengthen links between marketing, operations and human resource departments
- Ensure that consistent standards of service are delivered across multiple locations
- Ensure that advertising content accurately reflects those service characteristics that are most important to customers in their encounters with the organization
- Manage customers' expectations by letting them know what is and is not possible – and the reasons why
- Identify and explain uncontrollable reasons for shortcomings in service performance
- Offer customers different levels of service at different prices, explaining the differences between these levels

---

Source: Distilled from Chapters 4, 5, 6 and 7 of Valarie A. Zeithaml, A. Parasuraman and Leonard L. Berry, *Delivering Quality Service: Balancing Customer Perceptions and Expectations*, New York: The Free Press, 1990.

A well-constructed flowchart (or blueprint) enables us to visualize the process of service delivery by depicting the sequence of 'frontstage' interactions that customers experience as they encounter service providers, facilities and equipment. These interactions are supported by backstage activities, which are hidden from the customers and not part of the actual service experience. Each of these frontstage activities can be categorized as part of the core service or a supplementary service element.

But it's important to recognize that backstage problems may well have undesirable frontstage outcomes. As with any map or plan, blueprinting can be undertaken at different levels of detail. A simple blueprint provides a bird's eye view of the overall service delivery process (take another look at the hotel visit flowchart in Figure

4.6 on page 141). Such a diagram displays the major elements of service (both core product and supplementary services), showing the principal interactions with customers and a plausible sequence in which they might take place. This is very helpful for clarifying the elements of the service (is anything missing?), showing the sequence in which these elements are delivered (is this the most appealing sequence for the customer?) and for identifying how failures at one point (such as in over-booking reservations) may have a ripple effect later on in the process (the customer tries to check in and is told no rooms are available).

A more detailed blueprint might focus on a specific activity – such as getting a meal at the hotel restaurant – which can be exploded into a series of sub-activities. For a customer, these actions may include being seated at a table, receiving and reviewing the menu, choosing an aperitif and main course, being served the aperitif, and so forth. Time lines can be attached to each activity to help set standards for speed of service and thus avoid unwanted waits. Managers can then identify the possible types of failures that might occur, take preventive actions to stop failures from happening and develop contingency plans for handling failures that they cannot easily prevent.

Building a service quality information system

Organizations that are known for excellent service are good at listening to both their customers and their customer-contact employees. The fact that everyone was satisfied with this month's performance does not mean that the situation may not change for the worse in the months to come. The larger the organization, the more important it is to create formalized feedback programmes using a variety of professionally designed and implemented research procedures.

Berry and Parasuraman state that companies need to establish ongoing service research processes that provide timely, relevant trend data that managers can use in their decision-making. They argue that:

> companies need to establish ongoing listening systems using multiple methods among different customer groups. A single service quality study is a snapshot taken at a point in time and from a particular angle. Deeper insight and more informed decision making come from a continuing series of snapshots taken from various angles and through different lenses, which form the essence of systematic listening.[24]

They recommend that ongoing research should be conducted through a portfolio of research approaches. Possible techniques include:

■ *Analysis of customers' complaints.*

■ *Post-transaction surveys* (similar to the guest surveys used by hotels).

■ *Ongoing surveys of account holders* by telephone or post, using scientific sampling procedures to determine customers' satisfaction in terms of broader relationship issues.

■ *Customer advisory panels* to offer feedback and advice on service performance.

■ *Employee surveys and panels* to determine perceptions of the quality of service delivered to customers on specific dimensions, barriers to better service, and suggestions for improvement.

■ *Focus group interviews*, conducted separately with both customers and customer-contact employees to study qualitative issues in depth.

- *'Mystery shopping' of service providers* to measure the service behaviour of individual employees (this research is often used by human resource managers as well as marketers).

- *Total market surveys* to compare a firm's performance relative to its competitors, benchmark the leaders, and identify relevant trends.

- *Capture of service operating data*, including service response times, failure rates, and delivery costs.

For more details, see the reading by Leonard Berry and A. Parasuraman, 'Listening to the customer: the concept of a service quality information system' on pages 241–53.

Designing and implementing a large-scale customer survey to measure service across a wide array of attributes is no simple task. Line managers may view the findings as threatening when they involve direct comparisons of the performance of different departments or branches.

A caution on quality improvement programmes

Despite the attention paid to improving service quality, many companies have been disappointed by the results. In some instances, this outcome can be blamed on poor or incomplete execution of the quality programme itself. In other instances, improved measures of service quality do not seem to translate into bigger profits, increased market share or higher sales. Rust *et al.* argue for a 'Return on Quality' approach, based on the assumptions that quality is an investment. Quality efforts – like other investments – must be financially accountable, they say, adding that it's possible to spend too much on quality improvement relative to the likely payoffs, and that not all service quality expenditures are equally valid.[25]

Problem-solving and service recovery

Even businesses that generally perform well on providing quality service still have to deal from time to time with dissatisfied customers. Although the first law of quality might be defined as 'do it right the first time', no quality-minded business can afford to be without contingency plans for how to act when things go wrong. Chapter 7 deals in depth with important issues relating to complaint handling and service recovery. Many problems result from internal failures – faulty merchandise, rude personnel, lengthy delays, defective execution or billing errors. Others are caused by factors outside the firm's immediate control, such as failures in the public infrastructure (phone lines are cut), weather (service facilities are flooded), criminal activities (arson, break-ins, vandalism) or personal troubles for customers (a missing child, a medical emergency, a lost wallet).

How well a firm handles complaints and problem resolution – a key petal on the Flower of Service presented in Chapter 8 – will be a major determinant of whether it retains or loses the customers in question. If a company has thought through all such possibilities, developed contingency plans and then trained its employees accordingly, its people will know what to do and will have the authority to work towards solving the problem.

Solving problems and preventing their recurrence

When a problem is caused by controllable, internal forces, there's no excuse for allowing it to recur. In fact, maintaining customers' goodwill after a service failure depends on keeping promises made to the effect 'we're taking steps to ensure it doesn't happen again!'. With prevention in mind, let's look briefly at some simple, but powerful, quality tools for monitoring service quality and determining the root cause of specific problems that upset customers.

Flowcharting

We've already discussed flowcharts in some depth. Once managers understand the underlying processes behind service delivery, it's easier to identify potential *failure points* which represent weak links in the chain. Knowing what can go wrong (and where) is an important first step in preventing service quality problems.

Control charts

These charts offer a simple method of displaying performance over time against specific quality criteria. Since they are visual, trends are easily identified. Figure 12.2 shows an airline's performance on the important criterion of on-time departures, suggesting that this issue needs to be addressed by management, since performance is erratic and not very satisfactory. Of course, control charts are only as good as the data on which they are based.

The fishbone chart

Cause-and-effect analysis employs a technique first developed by the Japanese quality expert, Kaoru Ishikawa. Groups of managers and staff brainstorm all the possible

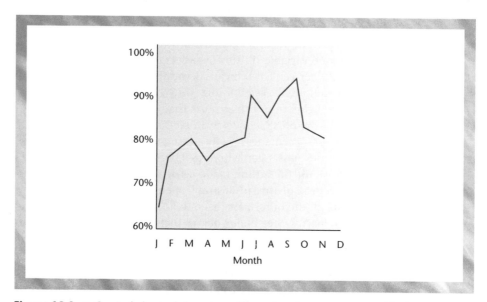

Figure 12.2 ■ Control chart of departure delays showing percentage of flights departing within 15 minutes of schedule

reasons that might cause a specific problem. The resulting factors are then categorized into one of five groupings – Equipment, Manpower (or People), Material, Procedures and Other – on a cause-and-effect chart, popularly known as a fishbone chart because of its shape. This technique has been used for many years in manufacturing and, more recently, in services.

To sharpen the value of the analysis for use in service organizations, Lovelock created an extended framework that comprises eight rather than five groupings.[26] 'People' has been broken into frontstage personnel and backstage personnel, to highlight the fact that frontstage service problems are often experienced directly by customers, whereas backstage failures tend to show up more obliquely through a ripple effect. 'Information' has been separated out from 'Procedures', recognizing that many service problems result from information failures, especially failures by frontstage personnel to tell customers what to do and when. In an airline context, for instance, poor announcement of departures may lead passengers to arrive late at the gate. Finally, the framework adds a new category, 'Customers'.

In manufacturing, customers have little impact on day-to-day operational processes, but in high-contact services, they are involved in frontstage operations. If they don't play their own roles correctly (assuming that they have even been informed of what is expected of them), they may reduce service productivity, causing quality problems for themselves and other customers. For instance, an aircraft can be delayed if a passenger tries to board at the last minute with an oversized suitcase, which then has to be loaded into the cargo hold. An example of the extended fishbone is shown in Figure 12.3, displaying 27 possible reasons for late departures of passenger aircraft.[27] We should recognize, of course, that failures are often sequential, with one problem leading to another.

Pareto analysis

Pareto analysis (named after the Italian economist who first developed it) seeks to identify the principal causes of observed outcomes. This type of analysis underlies the so-called 80/20 rule, because it often reveals that around 80 per cent of the value of one variable (in this instance, number of service failures) is accounted for by only 20 per cent of the causal variable (i.e., number of possible causes). In the airline example above, findings showed that 88 per cent of the company's late departing flights from the airports that it served were caused by only four (15 per cent) of all the possible factors. In fact, more than half the delays were caused by a single factor: acceptance of late passengers (situations when the staff held a flight for one more passenger who was checking in after the official cut-off time). On such occasions, the airline made a friend of that late passenger – possibly encouraging a repeat of this undesirable behaviour on a future occasion – but risked alienating all the other passengers who were already on board, waiting for the aircraft to depart. Other major delays included waiting for pushback (a vehicle must arrive to pull the aircraft away from the gate), waiting for fuelling and delays in signing the weight and balance sheet (a safety requirement relating to the distribution of the aircraft's load which the captain must observe on each flight). Further analysis, however, showed some significant variations in reasons from one airport to another (see Figure 12.4).

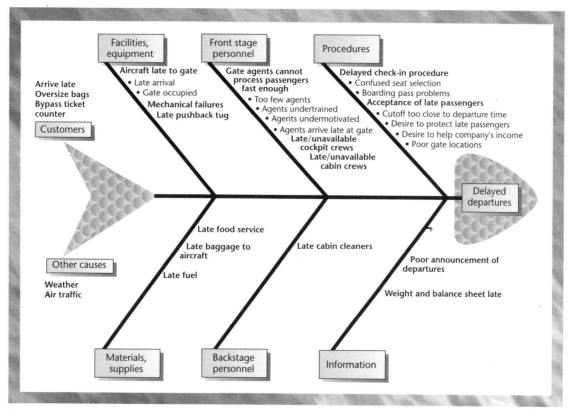

Figure 12.3 ■ Cause-and-effect chart for airline departure delays

Source: Lovelock (based on D.Daryl Wyckoff, 'New Tools for Achieving Service Quality', *Cornell Hotel and Restaurant Administration Quarterly*, November 1984).

A new quality goal: zero defections

Quality failures weaken customers' loyalty to companies and brands. When disappointed customers have a choice of service suppliers, they may decide to abandon the one that has let them down in favour of a competitor. Reichheld and Sasser popularized the term *zero defections*, which they describe as keeping every customer the company can profitably serve. When customers have a membership relationship with an organization, their use of the service can be tracked on an individual account basis. Declining usage – say, less frequent visits to a hotel chain for a business traveller, reduced purchases from a shop, fewer transactions at a bank – are often a good predictor of potential defection. Intervention at this point (with a view to restoring loyalty) is preferable to waiting until the customer ceases all activity or formally closes an account. Not only does a rising defection rate indicate that something is already wrong with quality (or that competitors offer better value), it also signals a probable profit slump ahead.

Reichheld has studied both customer and employee retention in several dozen industries and has worked on retention issues with clients around the world. He says that it's much harder to engineer higher loyalty into a business system than most managers suspect. At the root of the problem, he notes, is that most business people don't recognize the full economic implications of loyalty; they agree intuitively

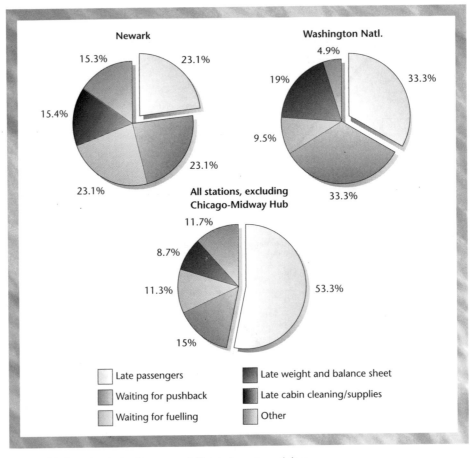

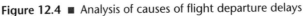

Figure 12.4 ■ Analysis of causes of flight departure delays

Source: Lovelock (based on D.Daryl Wyckoff, 'New Tools for Achieving Service Quality', *Cornell Hotel and Restaurant Administration Quarterly*, November 1984).

with the concept, but haven't made the required investments. The trouble is, they underestimate the value of loyalty but overestimate the ease of creating it. He adds:

> Managers tend to look for ad hoc solutions, such as better recovery efforts, pricing and promotional incentives, and reward programs for regular customers of the 'frequent fliers' variety. But the impact of such efforts is often quite modest, particularly if they're easily copied by competitors.[28]

Top managers must recognize that building and maintaining loyalty is a system-wide challenge, not just a tactical embellishment. Customer loyalty should be seen as standing at the core of sustained competitive success.

Clearly, to the extent that service marketers can uncover customer dissatisfaction and resolve it promptly, the chances of retaining desirable customers are improved. But good complaints handling procedures (see Chapter 7), while highly desirable, can do little more than treat symptoms which, in many cases, have avoidable causes. So it's imperative to work continuously to improve the overall service delivery system and its constituent processes as well. That means getting to the bottom of service problems and making sure they don't recur.

How productivity improvement impacts quality and value

The task of improving service productivity has traditionally been assigned to operations managers, whose approach has typically centred on such actions as:

- Careful control of costs at every step in the process.

- Efforts to reduce wasteful use of materials or labour.

- Matching productive capacity to average levels of demand rather than peak levels, so that workers and equipment are not underemployed for extended periods.

- Replacement of workers by automated machines.

- Providing employees with equipment and data bases that enable them to work faster or to a higher level of quality.

- Teaching employees how to work more productively (faster is not necessarily better if it leads to mistakes or unsatisfactory work that has to be redone).

- Installing expert systems that allow para-professionals to take on work previously performed by more experienced individuals earning higher salaries.

Restructuring or re-engineering the ways in which tasks are performed has significant potential to increase output, especially in many backstage jobs.[29] Also, broadening the array of tasks that a service worker can perform (which may require revised labour agreements) can eliminate bottlenecks and wasteful downtime by allowing managers to deploy workers wherever they are most needed at any given time.

How backstage changes may impact on customers

The marketing implications of backstage changes depend on whether or not they affect or are noticed by customers. If airline mechanics develop a procedure for servicing jet engines more quickly, without incurring increased wage rates or material costs, then the airline has obtained a productivity improvement that has no impact on the customer's service experience.

Other backstage changes, however, may have a ripple effect that extends frontstage and affects customers. Marketers should keep abreast of proposed backstage changes, not only to identify such ripples but also to prepare customers for them. At a bank, for instance, the decision to install new computers and printer peripherals may be driven by plans to improve internal quality controls and reduce the cost of preparing monthly statements. However, this new equipment may change the appearance of bank statements and the time of the month when they are posted. If customers are likely to notice such changes, an explanation may be warranted. If the new statements are easier to read and understand, then the change may be worth promoting as a service enhancement.

Unfortunately, technological changes are often implemented by specialists, such as accountants and systems engineers, who have never been briefed on customer concerns. Instead of a better statement, the net result may be a format that makes the statement difficult to interpret and truncation of the customer's name (CHRISTOPHER H. LOVEL or CHRISTO LOVELOCK) as the data processing department tries to reduce the amount of storage space required. In this example, a backstage productivity gain may appear to customers as a decline in the quality of frontstage output.

Frontstage efforts to improve productivity

In high-contact services, many productivity enhancements are quite visible. Some changes simply require passive acceptance by customers; others require customers to adopt new patterns of behaviour in their dealings with the organization. If substantial changes are proposed, then it makes sense to conduct market research first to determine how customers may respond. Failure to think through impacts on customers may result in loss of business and cancel anticipated productivity gains. Once the nature of the changes has been decided, marketing communication can help prepare customers.

From time to time, a major innovation results in a radical change to some aspect of service delivery. Sometimes, such a change offers significant marketing advantages as well as operational improvements. The advent of the jet airliner was a case in point. When de Havilland Comet 4s and Boeing 707s replaced propeller-driven aircraft on transatlantic routes in 1957, both passengers and airlines benefited. The former enjoyed the comfort of smoother, quieter and much faster flights (for which many were prepared to pay a premium price). The airlines, in turn, found their productivity much increased, since the 707s could carry almost five times as many passengers in a year as the Boeing Stratocruisers or Douglas DC-7s that they replaced – a function of the new airliners' greater speed and capacity, as well as the higher daily utilization that was possible with the more reliable jet engines. Crew members, too, became more productive in terms of the passenger-kilometres of service provided each month.

But radical change is not always understood and appreciated. Consider the case of the Universal Product Code (UPC), designed to simplify both backstage and frontstage activities in supermarkets. By marking packaged goods with UPC bar codes unique to each stock-keeping unit (SKU) and then scanning each item electronically at the checkout, supermarket executives expected to achieve major advantages and efficiencies.[30] They would save the cost of price marking each individual package (and changing those prices whenever the price of an SKU changed); all that would be necessary was to program (or reprogram) the price data for that SKU in the computer. They also expected to reduce clerical time and errors at checkouts (a benefit to customers, too), provide more detailed receipts (also a customer benefit) and generate valuable data from the scanners on product sales.

Unfortunately, things didn't quite work out as planned. UPC symbols began appearing on thousands of consumer products in 1973, but installation of scanners at checkouts took place far more slowly than anticipated. In fact, some large supermarket chains did not make the changeover until the late 1980s. Union resistance and the high cost of the equipment were two factors, but consumer concerns also proved to be a major problem. Consumer groups opposed the new technology on the grounds that removal of individual price marking would allow stores to put through surreptitious price increases. Laws were passed in many US states mandating that packages still had to be individually marked.

Supermarket executives later conceded that they had done a poor job of preparing customers for the change, highlighting the benefits and allaying customer concerns. One firm admitted that it would have been wiser to bring customers into the decision-making process when installation was first planned.

A caution on cost reduction strategies

In the absence of new technology, most attempts to improve service productivity tend to centre on efforts to eliminate waste and reduce labour costs. Skinner sounds a note of caution:

> Resolutely chipping away at waste and inefficiency – the heart of most productivity programs – is not enough to restore competitive health. Indeed, a focus on cost reductions (that is, on raising labor output while holding the amount of labor constant or, better, reducing it) is proving harmful.[31]

Skinner was writing about manufacturing, but he might just as well have been writing about services. Cutbacks in frontstage staffing mean either that the remaining employees have to work harder and faster or that there are insufficient personnel to serve customers promptly at busy times. Although employees may be able to work faster for a brief period of time, few can maintain a rapid pace for extended periods: they become exhausted, make mistakes and treat customers in a cursory manner. Workers who are trying to do two or three things at once – serving a customer face-to-face while simultaneously answering the telephone and sorting papers, for example – may do a poor job of each task. Excessive pressure breeds discontent and frustration among all employees, but especially among customer-contact personnel who are caught between trying to meet customer needs and attempting to achieve management's productivity goals.

Attempts to economize on materials and equipment in the name of 'avoiding wasteful duplication' may similarly backfire. One of the authors once asked a hotel receptionist why it had taken so long to check him out. The employee replied with a tired smile that the four receptionists on the reception desk had to share a single stapler for clipping credit card receipts to the customers' bills, so she had to wait her turn to use it – a perfect example of the old nautical metaphor of 'spoiling the ship for want of a ha'p'orth [half-penny's worth] of tar'.

Customer-driven approaches to improving productivity[32]

In situations where customers are deeply involved in the service production process (typically, people-processing services), operations managers should be examining how customers' inputs can be made more productive. And marketing managers should be thinking about what marketing strategies should be employed to influence customers to behave in more productive ways. We review three strategies: changing the timing of customer demand, involving customers more actively in the production process, and asking customers to use third parties.

Changing the timing of customer demand

Managing demand in capacity-constrained service businesses has been a recurring theme in this book. We introduced it briefly in Chapter 2 and discuss it at greater length in Chapter 13. Customers often complain that the services they use are crowded and congested, reflecting time-of-day, seasonal or other cyclical peaks in demand. During the off-peak periods in those same cycles, managers often worry that there are too few customers and that their facilities and staff are not fully productive. By shifting demand away from peaks, managers can make better use of their productive assets and provide better service. Post Office campaigns to encourage people to 'post early for Christmas' have had some success in getting people to plan ahead, rather than leaving it until a few days before Christmas to post their cards and packages.

However, some demand cannot easily be shifted without the cooperation of third parties such as employers and schools, who control working hours and holiday schedules. To fill idle capacity during off-peak hours, marketers may need to target new market segments with different needs and schedules, rather than focusing exclusively on current segments. If the peaks and valleys of demand can be smoothed, using the tools and strategies we've discussed in earlier chapters, productivity will improve.

Involve customers more in production

Customers who assume a more active role in the service production and delivery process can take over some labour tasks from the service organization. Benefits for both parties may result when customers perform self-service.

Many technological innovations are designed to get customers to perform tasks previously undertaken by service employees. A classic example of such a change, with nationwide implications, was AT&T's automation of the long-distance telephone network (similar to the introduction of subscriber trunk dialling in the UK and other European countries). In the early 1960s, it was said that if the number of long-distance telephone calls continued to grow at the same exponential rate, by the year 2000, every second employee in America would be working as a telephone operator! By 1970, AT&T had installed the direct dialling technology that would allow it to achieve major increases in internal productivity if the number of long-distance operators it employed could be greatly reduced. Yet almost half of all long-distance calls were still being placed with the operator.

So the company launched a major marketing effort to encourage subscribers to dial their own long-distance calls. Substantial price discounts were offered for direct-dial calls and a national advertising campaign was launched to encourage callers to dial direct rather than getting an operator to place the call for them. The adverts said, 'We have two reasons for urging you to dial long-distance calls direct. You save and we save too.' After three years, directly dialled calls accounted for almost 75 per cent of long-distance calls, resulting in productivity savings of about $37 million a year.

Today, many companies are trying to encourage customers with access to the internet to obtain information from the firm's corporate web sites and even to place orders through the Web, rather than telephoning employees at the company's offices. For such changes to succeed, web sites must be made user-friendly and easy to 'navigate' and customers must be convinced that it is safe to provide credit card information over the Web.

Restaurants, which have traditionally had a high labour component and relatively low productivity, represent another service in which customers have been asked to do more of the work. We've become accustomed to self-service salad bars and buffets. But despite the reduction in personal service, this innovation has been positioned as a benefit that lets customers select the foods they want, without delay, in the quantities they desire.

Some customers may be more willing than others to serve themselves. In fact, research suggests that this may be a useful segmentation variable. A large-scale study presented respondents with the choice of a do-it-yourself option versus traditional delivery systems at petrol stations, banks, restaurants, hotels, airports and travel services.[33] For each service, a particular scenario was outlined, since earlier interviews had determined that decisions to choose self-service options were very situation-specific, depending on such factors as time of day, weather conditions, presence or absence of others in the party, and the perceived time and cost involved.

The results showed that in each instance a sizeable proportion of respondents would select the self-service option – even in the absence of time or monetary savings. When these inducements were added, the proportions choosing self-service increased. Further analysis showed some overlap between different services; if respondents didn't serve their own fuel, for instance, they were less likely to use an ATM and more likely to prefer being served by a bank clerk.

Quality and productivity improvements often depend on customers' willingness to learn new procedures, follow instructions and interact cooperatively with employees and other people. Customers who arrive at the service encounter with a set of pre-existing norms, values and role definitions may resist change. Goodwin suggests that insights from research on socialization can help service marketers redesign the nature of the service encounter in ways that increase the chances of gaining customer cooperation.[34] In particular, she argues that customers will need help to learn new skills, form a new self-image ('I can do it myself'), develop new relationships with providers and fellow customers, and acquire new values.

Ask customers to use third parties

In some instances, managers may be able to improve service productivity by delegating one or more marketing support functions to third parties. The purchase process often breaks down into four components: information, reservation, payment and consumption. When consumption of the core product takes place at a location not easily accessible from customers' homes or workplaces (for instance, an airport, theatre, stadium or a hotel in a distant city), it makes sense to delegate delivery of supplementary service elements to intermediary organizations.

Specialist intermediaries may enjoy economies of scale, enabling them to perform the task cheaper than the core service provider, allowing the latter to focus on quality and productivity in its own area of expertise. Some intermediaries are identifiable local organizations, like travel agencies, which customers can visit in person. Others, like hotel reservations centres, often subjugate their own identity to that of the client service company. When intermediaries offer service 24 hours a day nationwide, customer calls can be spread over a broader time base. The peaks and valleys of call demand are further smoothed when the call centre serves an entire continent such as North America, which has multiple time-zones, since busy times in (say) Halifax, Nova Scotia or New York may be quiet periods on the Pacific Coast (and vice versa). The call centre industry is booming in Europe, with Britain, Ireland and the Netherlands hosting the largest number of centres. Pan-European call centres, with provision for different languages, are increasing rapidly in number. Here the Dutch have a particular advantage because of their language skills.[35]

As with any change in procedures, a move to employ intermediaries to provide supplementary services will only succeed if customers know how to use them and are willing to do so. At a minimum, a promotional and educational campaign may be needed to launch such a change.

Sensitivity to customers' reluctance to change

Customer resistance to changes in familiar environments and long-established behaviour patterns can thwart attempts to improve productivity and even quality. All too often, management's failure to look at such changes from the customer's standpoint actually causes resistance. Managers of service operations can, and should, avoid such insensitivity toward their customers. Six possible steps suggest themselves:

1. Develop customer trust

It's harder to introduce productivity-related changes when people are basically distrustful of the initiator, as they often are in the case of large, seemingly impersonal institutions. Customers' willingness to accept change may be closely related to the degree of goodwill they bear towards the organization. If a firm does not have a strong positive relationship with its customers, the latter may be able to block productivity improvements.

2. Understand customers' habits and expectations

People often get into a routine around the use of a particular service, with certain steps being taken in a specific sequence. In effect, they have their own individual flowchart in mind. Innovations that disrupt ingrained routines are likely to face resistance unless consumers are carefully briefed as to what changes to expect. For instance, in introducing the UPC, many retailers seem to have ignored the typical shopper's habit of examining price markings on packages and then watching the cashier punch in the prices on the cash register. Retailers made little effort to prepare consumers for the change and how it would affect them, let alone explain the rationale for this innovation or promote its benefits.

3. Pre-test new procedures and equipment

Before introducing new procedures and equipment, marketers need to determine probable customer response. These efforts may include concept and laboratory testing and/or field testing at one or more sites. When replacing service personnel by automatic equipment, it's particularly important for an organization to develop machines that customers of almost all types and backgrounds will find easy to use. Some self-service equipment looks as if it has been designed by engineers for engineers. Even the phrasing of instructions needs careful thought. Ambiguous, complex or authoritarian instructions may discourage customers with limited command of the language or poor reading skills, as well as people used to personal courtesies from the service personnel whom the machine replaces.

4. Publicize the benefits

Introduction of self-service equipment or procedures requires consumers to perform part of the task themselves. Although this additional 'work' may be associated with such benefits as extended service hours, time savings, and (in some instances) monetary savings, these benefits are not necessarily obvious – they have to be promoted. Useful strategies may include use of mass media advertising, on-site posters and signage, and personal communications to inform people of the innovation, arouse their interest in it, and clarify the specific benefits to customers of changing behaviour and using new delivery systems.

5. Teach customers to use innovations and promote trial

Simply installing self-service machines and supplying printed instructions may not win over many customers, especially those resistant to technology or to change in general. Experience with ATMs shows that assigning service personnel to demonstrate new equipment and answer questions – providing reassurance as well as educational assistance – is a key element in gaining acceptance of new procedures and technology. The costs of such demonstration programmes can be spread more widely in multiple-outlet operations by moving staff members from one site to another as the innovation spreads to new locations. Promotional incentives and price discounts may also serve to stimulate initial trial. Once customers have actually tried a self-service option (particularly an electronically based one) and found that it works well, they will be more likely to use it regularly in the future.

6. Monitor performance and continue to seek improvements

Introducing quality and productivity improvements is an ongoing process. Today's quality advantage may be trumped tomorrow by a competitor's response. And the competitive edge provided by productivity improvements may quickly be erased as other firms adopt similar or better procedures. Service managers have to work hard to keep up the momentum so that programmes achieve their full potential and are not allowed to flag. For instance, managers of firms that have installed pages on the World Wide Web containing information about the company and its services should be checking on whether the number of 'visits' to their Web pages are increasing over time and whether customers who seek information are switching back from the Web to use of the firm's toll-free telephone number.

The important thing is for managers to learn from experience (both good and bad), to take corrective action where needed (whether it involves redesign of facilities and procedures, better communications and educational activities, more dramatic promotional efforts, or more compelling incentives), and to continue searching for new ways to boost quality and productivity.

Conclusion

Enhancing service quality and improving service productivity are often two sides of the same coin, offering powerful potential to improve value for both customers and the firm. A key challenge for any service business is to deliver satisfactory outcomes to its customers in ways that are cost-effective for the company. If customers are dissatisfied with the quality of a service, they won't be willing to pay very much for it – or even to buy it at all if competitors offer better quality. Low sales volumes mean unproductive assets. Needlessly low prices may result in low returns on investment, which also means less productive assets.

The notion that customers are the best judges of the quality of a service process and its outcome is relatively new and replaces (or supplements) other concepts of quality. When the customer is seen as the final arbiter of quality, then marketing managers come to play a key role in defining expectations and in measuring customer satisfaction. However, service marketers need to work closely with other management functions in service design and implementation.

This chapter presented a number of frameworks and tools for defining, measuring and managing quality, including research programmes to identify quality gaps, and blueprinting to identify failure points in service delivery. Peer review may also be an important alternative approach when measuring the core product quality on services that are high in credence characteristics.

Marketing managers should be included in productivity improvement programmes whenever these efforts are likely to have an impact on customers. And because customers are often involved in the service production process, marketers should keep their eyes open for opportunities to reshape customer behaviour in ways that may help the service firm to become more productive. Possibilities for cooperative behaviour include adopting self-service options, changing the timing of customer demand to less busy periods, and making use of third party suppliers of supplementary services.

In summary, value, quality and productivity are all of great concern to senior management, since they relate directly to an organization's survival in the competitive marketplace. Strategies designed to enhance value are dependent in large measure on continuous improvement in service quality (as defined by customers) and productivity improvements that reinforce rather than counteract customer satisfaction. The marketing function has much to offer in reshaping our thinking about these three issues, as well as in helping to achieve significant improvements in all of them.

Study questions

1. How do definitions of service quality differ from those relating to the quality of manufactured products?

2. Why should manufacturers be concerned about service quality?

3. Explain the relationship between service productivity and service quality.

4. Under what circumstances will improvements in service quality and productivity lead to both increased value for customers and higher profits for the firm?

5. Review the five dimensions of service quality. What do 'tangibles' mean in the context of (a) an airline, (b) a retail bank, (c) a hotel, (d) a telephone company?

6. Identify the gaps that can occur in service quality and the steps that service marketers can take to prevent them.

7. Consider your own recent experiences as a service consumer. On which dimensions of service quality have you most often experienced a large gap between your expectations and your perceptions of the actual service performance? What do you think the underlying causes might be? What steps should management take to improve quality?

8. Why is productivity a more difficult issue for service firms than for manufacturers?

9. In what ways can consumers help to improve service productivity? What distinctive characteristics of services make some of these actions possible?

Notes

1. Robert Unsworth, from Nichols Foods, UK.
2 . Evert Gummesson, 'Service Management: An Evaluation and the Future', *International Journal of Service Industry Management*, Vol. 5, No. 1, 1994, pp. 77–96.
3. See, for example, the classic article, Philip Kotler, 'A Generic Concept of Marketing', *Journal of Marketing*, Vol. 36, April 1972, pp. 46–54.
4. Morris Holbrook, 'The Nature of Customer Value: An Anthology of Services in the Consumption Experience', in R.T. Rust and R.L. Oliver, *Service Quality: New Directions in Theory and Practice*, Thousand Oaks, Calif.: Sage Publications, 1994, pp. 21–71.
5. Bradley T. Gale, *Managing Customer Value*, New York: The Free Press, 1994.
6. Robert D. Buzzell and Bradley T. Gale, *The PIMS Principles – Linking Strategy to Performance*, New York: The Free Press, 1987.
7. David A. Garvin, *Managing Quality*, New York: The Free Press, 1988, especially Chapter 3.
8. *Ibid.*, pp. 48–9.
9. Christian Grönroos, *Service Management and Marketing*, Lexington, MA: Lexington Books, 1990, Chapter 2.
10. Valarie A. Zeithaml, A. Parasuraman and Leonard L. Berry, *Delivering Quality Service*, New York: The Free Press, 1990.
11. A. Parasuraman, Valarie A. Zeithaml and Leonard Berry, 'SERVQUAL: A Multiple Item Scale for Measuring Consumer Perceptions of Service Quality', *Journal of Retailing*, Vol. 64, 1988, pp. 12–40.
12. Simon S.K. Lam and Ka Shing Woo, 'Measuring Service Quality: A Test-Retest Reliability Investigation of SERVQUAL', *Journal of the Market Research Society*, Vol. 39, April 1997, pp. 381–93.
13. Gerhard Mels, Christo Boshoff and Denon Nel, 'The Dimensions of Service Quality: The Original European Perspective Revisited', *The Service Industries Journal*, Vol. 17, January 1997, pp. 173–89.
14. Lam and Woo, *op. cit.*
15. Anne M. Smith, 'Measuring Service Quality: Is SERVQUAL Now Redundant?', *Journal of Marketing Management*, Vol. 11, Jan/Feb/April 1995, pp. 257–76.
16. Susan J. Devlin and H.K. Dong, 'Service Quality from the Customers' Perspective', *Marketing Research*, Vol. 6, No. 1, 1994, pp. 5–13.
17. F. Ian Stuart and Stephen S. Tax, 'Planning for Service Quality: An Integrative Approach', *International Journal of Service Industry Management*, Vol. 7, No. 4, 1996, pp. 58–77.
18. David Ballantyne, Martin Christopher and Adrian Payne, 'Improving the Quality of Services Marketing: Service Re(design) is the Critical Link', *Journal of Marketing Management*, Vol. 11, Jan/Feb/April 1995, pp. 7–24.
19. Sandra Vandermerwe, 'Quality in Services: The "Softer" Side is "Harder" (and Smarter)', *Long-Range Planning*, Vol. 27, No. 2, 1994, pp. 45–56.
20. James L. Heskett, *Managing in the Service Economy*, New York: The Free Press, 1986.
21. John C. Shaw, *The Service Focus*, Homewood, IL: Dow Jones-Irwin, 1990, pp. 152–3.
22. Valarie A. Zeithaml, Leonard L. Berry and A. Parasuraman, 'Communication and Control Processes in the Delivery of Service Processes', *Journal of Marketing*, Vol. 52, April 1988, pp. 36–58.
23. Zeithaml *et al.*, *Delivering Quality Service*.
24. Leonard L. Berry and A. Parasuraman, 'Listening to the Customer – The Concept of a Service Quality Information System', *Sloan Management Review*, Spring 1997, pp. 65–76.
25. Roland T. Rust, Anthony J. Zahonik and Timothy L. Keiningham, 'Return on Quality (ROQ): Making Service Quality Financially Accountable', *Journal of Marketing*, Vol. 59, April 1995, pp. 58–70.

26. Christopher Lovelock, *Product Plus: How Product + Service = Competitive Advantage*, New York: McGraw-Hill, 1994, p. 218.

27. These categories and the research data that follow have been adapted from information in D. Daryl Wyckoff, 'New Tools for Achieving Service Quality', *Cornell Hotel and Restaurant Administration Quarterly*, November 1984.

28. Quoted in Lovelock, *op. cit.*, p. 221.

29. See, for example, Michael Hammer and James Champy, *Reengineering the Corporation*, New York: Harper Business, 1993.

30. A stock-keeping unit (SKU) represents a specific brand of a product category in a given package size or format. Thus, 100g, 250g and 500g jars of Maxwell House instant coffee represent three different SKUs; the same three package sizes of Maxwell House decaffeinated instant coffee represent another three SKUs; and other brands, in turn, would represent other SKUs.

31. Wickham Skinner, 'The Productivity Paradox', *McKinsey Quarterly*, Winter 1987, pp. 36–45.

32. This discussion is based in part on Christopher H. Lovelock and Robert F. Young: 'Look to Consumers to Increase Productivity', *Harvard Business Review*, May–June 1979, pp. 168–78.

33. Eric Langeard, John E.G. Bateson, Christopher H. Lovelock and Pierre Eiglier, *Services Marketing: New Insights from Consumers and Managers*, Cambridge, MA: Marketing Science Institute, 1981, especially chapter 2. A good summary of this research is provided in J.E.G. Bateson, 'Self-Service Consumer: An Exploratory Study', *Journal of Retailing,* Vol. 51, Fall 1985, pp. 49–76.

34. Cathy Goodwin, 'I Can Do It Myself: Training the Service Consumer to Contribute to Service Productivity', *Journal of Services Marketing,* Vol. 2, Fall 1988, pp. 71–8.

35. Stephen Hoare, 'Your Call Will Be Answered Soon by One of Our Operators', *Director,* November 1997, pp. 76–80.

Balancing demand and capacity

Learning objectives

After reading and reflecting on this chapter, you should be able to:

1. Understand the elements that comprise productive capacity for a service organization.

2. Explain how to use capacity management techniques to meet variations in demand.

3. Understand the concept of demand cycles and their underlying causes.

4. Formulate demand management strategies appropriate to specific situations.

5. Understand how well-designed waiting environments can reduce the perceived burden for customers of waiting for service.

6. Know the basics of designing an effective reservation system.

7. Understand the principle of asset revenue generating efficiency and the use of segmented reservations strategies to improve profitability.

Cape Cod: a seasonal tourist destination

Cape Cod is a remarkable peninsula of narrow land in the northeastern United States, about 90km south of Boston. Jutting out into the Atlantic off the Massachusetts coast its shape resembles a long arm, bent at the elbow. Native Americans have lived there for thousands of years. The Pilgrims landed there in 1619 but continued across Cape Cod Bay to found Plymouth; however, not long afterwards, more immigrants from England settled on the Cape itself. Fishing, whaling, agriculture and salt works were among the principal industries in the nineteenth century. By the mid-twentieth century, all but fishing – itself in decline – had virtually disappeared and tourism was beginning to assume some significance.

Events in the early 1960s put the Cape firmly in the public eye. John F. Kennedy became president of the United States and was regularly photographed at his family's vacation home in Hyannisport; while in office he signed legislation creating the Cape Cod National Seashore, preserving large areas of the Outer Cape as a national park. And the song, 'Old Cape Cod', commissioned by tourism promoters and sung by the popular Patti Page, unexpectedly climbed to the top of the charts and was heard around the world. With its beaches and saltmarshes, sand dunes and fishing harbours, picturesque towns and lobster dinners, the Cape rapidly became a destination resort. Today, it draws millions of visitors each year from eastern North America and is increasingly attracting European tourists.

In summer, the Cape is a busy place. Colourful umbrellas sprout like giant flowers along the miles of sandy beaches. The car parks are full. There are queues outside most restaurants and managers complain about the difficulty of hiring and retaining sufficient staff. (In fact, hundreds of young people are recruited from Europe each summer to work on the Cape; the largest single group are students from Ireland, looking for an enjoyable working holiday.) Shops and cinemas are busy, especially when it rains. The Mid-Cape Highway is clogged. Hotels display 'no vacancy' signs. Fishing trips have to be booked well in advance. Holiday cottages are fully rented, it's hard to get a car reservation on the ferries to the islands of Nantucket or Martha's Vineyard, and the visitor centres at the National Seashore are crowded with tourists.

Return for a weekend in mid-winter, and what do you find? A few walkers brave the chill winds on the otherwise empty beaches. You can park in almost any legal space you wish. Many restaurants have closed (their owners are wintering in Florida) and only the most popular of the remaining establishments even bother to suggest reservations. Student workers have gone back to college and the shops have laid off seasonal workers and, in some cases, cut the hours of remaining employees. As a result, there is seasonal unemployment among some of the full-time residents.

It's rare in winter to be unable to see the film of your choice at your preferred time. The main problem on the Mid-Cape Highway is being stopped for speeding. If a motel sports a 'no vacancy' sign, that means it's closed for the season; others offer bargain rates. Recreational fishing? You must be crazy – there may even be ice on Cape Cod Bay! Owners of holiday cottages have drained their water systems and boarded up the windows. You can probably drive your vehicle straight onto one of the car ferries to the islands (although the sailing schedules are more limited), and the rangers at the visitor centres are happy to talk with the few visitors who drop by during the limited opening hours.

Faced with such a sharply peaked season, economic development agencies are working to extend the Cape's tourism season beyond the peak months of July and August, seeking to build demand in spring and autumn. Among their targets are tourists from Europe, who appreciate the old world charm of the Cape and tend to spend more money than visitors from Boston or New York.

The ups and downs of demand

Fluctuating demand for service – like that experienced by retailers, cinemas, motels, restaurants, ferries and other establishments on Cape Cod – is not just found in holiday resorts. It's a problem that besets a huge cross-section of businesses serving both individual and corporate customers. These demand fluctuations, which may range in frequency from as long as a season of the year to as short as hourly, play havoc with efficient use of productive assets.

Solving – or at least, minimizing – this problem is an important goal for many service organizations, since it can make the difference between financial success and failure. Strategies for balancing demand and capacity typically require close cooperation between marketing, operations and human resource managers. Teamwork is vital, since there are real limits as to what managers from any one of these functions can achieve alone.

Unlike manufacturing, service operations create a perishable *inventory* which cannot be stockpiled for sale at a later date. That's a problem for any capacity-constrained service that faces wide swings in demand. The problem is most commonly found among services that process people or physical possessions – such as transportation, lodging, food service, repair and maintenance, entertainment and health care. It also affects labour-intensive, information-processing services that face cyclical shifts in demand. Accounting and tax preparation are cases in point.

Responding to shifts in demand

The situation is a familiar one around the world – not just on Cape Cod. 'It's either feast or famine for us!' sighs the manager. 'In peak periods, we're turning customers away. In low periods, our facilities are idle and our employees are standing around looking bored.'

Most services are unable to store their finished output. This lack of stock doesn't matter when demand levels are relatively stable and predictable. However, it raises problems for organizations that face wide swings in demand, especially when their capacity is relatively fixed. The factors of production may be in place and ready to serve, but an empty seat on a flight loses its chance to earn money for the airline on a specific flight once the aircraft takes off. The same is true of hotels that sell room nights, professionals who sell their time, service garages and holiday cottages on Cape Cod. Readiness to serve is wasted if there are no customers to purchase the service at that time.

Services involving tangible actions to customers or their possessions are more likely to be subject to capacity constraints than are information-based services. In the latter instance, however, similar capacity problems may occur when customers are obliged to come to a service site for delivery, as in live entertainment or traditional retail banking.

Financial success in these capacity-constrained industries is, in large measure, a function of management's ability to use productive capacity – staff, labour, equipment and facilities – as efficiently and as profitably as possible. However, the goal shouldn't be to utilize staff, labour, equipment and facilities as much as possible, but rather to use them as productively as possible. As you will see, this chapter is relevant to issues of productivity and quality, which we introduced in Chapter 1 and discussed in more depth in Chapter 12. Successful service managers recognize that managing demand and managing capacity are essential not only to productive use of the firm's assets, but also for giving customers the quality service experiences that they are looking for.

From excess demand to excess capacity

At any given moment, a fixed-capacity service may face one of four conditions (Figure 13.1):

- *Excess demand* – the level of demand exceeds maximum available capacity with the result that some customers are denied service and business is lost.

- *Demand exceeds optimum capacity* – no one is actually turned away, but conditions are crowded and all customers are likely to perceive a deterioration in the quality of service delivered.

- *Demand and supply are well balanced* at the level of optimum capacity. Staff and facilities are busy without being overworked and customers receive good service without delays.

- *Excess capacity* – demand is below optimum capacity and productive resources are underutilized, resulting in low productivity. Those customers who do come may find the experience disappointing or have doubts about the viability of the service.

You'll notice that we've drawn a distinction between *maximum capacity* and *optimum capacity*. When demand exceeds maximum available capacity, some potential customers may be turned away and their business lost for ever. But when demand is operating between optimum and maximum capacity, there's a risk that all customers being served at that time may start to receive inferior service. In such conditions, Armistead and Clark argue that service managers need to employ what they call a coping strategy to control the fall in service standards and thus prevent customer dissatisfaction.[1]

Sometimes optimum and maximum capacities are one and the same. At a live theatre or sports performance, a full house is desirable, since it stimulates the players and creates a sense of excitement and audience participation. The net result? A more satisfying experience for all. But with most other services, you probably feel that you get better service if the facility is not operating at full capacity. The quality of restaurant service, for instance, often deteriorates when every table is occupied, because the staff are rushed and there's a greater likelihood of errors or delays. And if you're

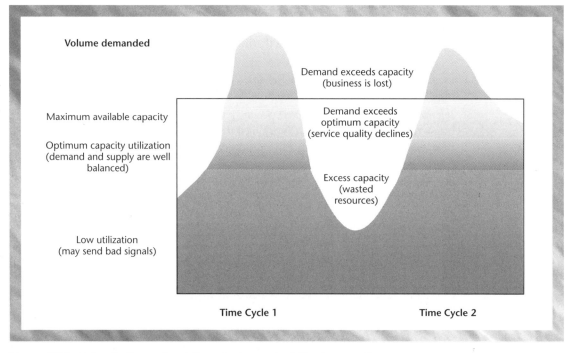

Figure 13.1 ■ Implications of variations in demand relative to capacity

travelling alone in an aircraft with high-density seating, you tend to feel more comfortable if the seat next to you is empty. When repair and maintenance operations are fully scheduled, delays may result if there is no slack in the system to allow for unexpected problems in completing particular jobs.

There are two basic solutions to the problem of fluctuating demand. One is to adjust the level of capacity to meet variations in demand. This approach, which entails cooperation between operations and human resource management, requires an understanding of what constitutes productive capacity and how it may be increased or decreased on an incremental basis. The second approach is to manage the level of demand, using marketing strategies to smooth out the peaks and fill in the valleys so as to generate a more consistent flow of requests for service. Many firms use both approaches.

Measuring and managing capacity

What do we mean by productive capacity? The term refers to the resources or assets that a firm can employ to create goods and services. In a service context, productive capacity can take at least five potential forms.

1. *Physical facilities designed to contain customers* and used for delivering people-processing services or mental stimulus processing services. Examples include hospital clinics, hotels, passenger aircraft, buses, restaurants, swimming pools, cinemas, concert halls and college classrooms. In these situations, the primary capacity

constraint is likely to be defined in terms of such furnishings as beds, rooms, seats, tables or desks. In some cases, local regulations may set an upper limit to the number of people allowed in the interest of health or fire safety.

2. *Physical facilities designed for storing or processing goods* that either belong to customers or are being offered to them for sale. Examples include supermarket shelves, pipelines, warehouses, car parks, freight containers or railway freight cars.

3. *Physical equipment used to process people, possessions or information* may embrace a huge range of items and be very situation-specific – machinery, telephones, hairdryers, computers, diagnostic equipment, airport security detectors, toll gates on roads and bridges, cooking ovens, bank ATMs, repair tools and cash registers are among the many items whose absence in sufficient numbers for a given level of demand can bring service to a crawl (or a complete stop).

4. *Labour*, a key element of productive capacity in all high-contact services and many low-contact ones, may be used for both physical and mental work. Staffing levels for personnel, from restaurant waiters and waitresses to nurses to telephone operators, must be sufficient to meet anticipated demand – otherwise customers will be kept waiting or service rushed. Professional services are especially dependent on highly skilled staff to create high value-added, information-based output. Abraham Lincoln captured it well when he remarked that 'A lawyer's time and expertise are his stock in trade'.

5. *Infrastructure*. Many organizations are dependent on access to sufficient capacity in the public or private infrastructure to be able to deliver quality service to their own customers. Capacity problems of this nature may include busy telephone circuits, electrical power failures (or 'brown-outs' caused by reduced voltage), congested airways that lead to air traffic restrictions, and traffic jams on major roads.

Measuring capacity

Measures of capacity utilization include: the number of hours (or percentage of total available time) that facilities, labour and equipment are productively employed in revenue operation, and the percentage of available space (e.g., seats, cubic freight capacity, telecommunications bandwidth) that is actually utilized in revenue operations. Human beings tend to be far more variable than equipment in their ability to sustain consistent levels of output over time. One tired or poorly trained employee staffing a single station in an assembly-line operation like a cafeteria restaurant can slow the entire service to a crawl. In a well-planned, well-managed service operation, the capacity of the facility, supporting equipment and service personnel will be in balance. Similarly, sequential operations will be designed to minimize the likelihood of bottlenecks at any point in the process. In practice, however, it's difficult to achieve this ideal all the time.

Stretching and shrinking the level of capacity

Some capacity is elastic in its ability to absorb extra demand. A carriage on the Underground or Metro, for instance, may offer 40 seats and allow standing room for another 60 passengers with adequate handrail and floor space for all. Yet at rush hours, when there have been delays on the line, perhaps 200 'standees' can be accommodated under sardine-like conditions. Service personnel may be able to work at high levels of efficiency for short periods of time, but would quickly tire and begin providing inferior service if they had to work at such a pace all day long.

Even where capacity appears fixed, as when it's based on the number of seats, there may still be opportunities to accept extra business at busy times. Some airlines, for instance, increase the capacity of their aircraft by slightly reducing legroom throughout the cabin and cramming in another couple of rows. Similarly a restaurant may add extra tables and chairs. Upper limits to such practices are often set by safety standards or by the capacity of supporting services, such as the kitchen.

Another strategy for stretching capacity is to use the facilities for longer periods. Examples of this include restaurants that open for early dinners and late suppers, universities that offer evening classes and summer programmes, and airlines that extend their schedules from, say, 14 to 18 hours a day. Alternatively, the average amount of time that customers (or their possessions) spend in process may be reduced. Sometimes this is achieved by minimizing slack time, as when the bill is presented promptly to a group of diners relaxing at the table after a meal. In other instances, it may be achieved by cutting back the level of service – say, offering a simpler menu at busy times of day.

Chasing demand

Another strategy, known as 'chase demand', involves tailoring capacity to match variations in demand. Possible ways to adjust capacity as needed include:[2]

- *Schedule downtime during periods of low demand.* To ensure that 100 per cent of capacity is available during peak periods, repairs and renovations should be conducted when demand is expected to be low, and employee holidays should be taken then.

- *Use part-time employees.* Many organizations hire extra workers during their busiest periods. Examples include postal workers and retail shop assistants at Christmas time, extra staff within tax preparation service firms at the end of the financial year, and additional hotel employees during holiday periods and major conferences.

- *Rent or share extra facilities and equipment.* To limit investment in fixed assets, a service business may be able to rent extra space or machines at peak times. Firms with complementary demand patterns may enter into formal sharing agreements.

- *Cross-train employees.* Even when the service delivery system appears to be operating at full capacity, certain physical elements – and their attendant employees – may be underutilized. If employees can be cross-trained to perform a variety of tasks, they can be shifted to bottleneck points as needed, thereby increasing total system capacity. In supermarkets, for instance, the manager may call on stockers to operate cash registers when checkout queues start to get too long. Likewise, during slow periods, the cashiers may be asked to help stock shelves.

Creating flexible capacity

Sometimes, the problem lies not in the overall capacity but in the mix that's available to serve the needs of different market segments. For instance, on a given flight, an airline may have too few seats in economy even though there are empty places in the business class cabin; or a hotel may find itself short of suites one day when there are standard rooms still available. One solution lies in designing physical facilities to be flexible. Some hotels build rooms with connecting doors. With the door between two rooms locked, the hotel can sell two bedrooms; with the door unlocked and one of the bedrooms converted into a sitting room, the hotel can now offer a suite.

Facing stiff competition from Airbus Industrie, the Boeing Co. received what were described, tongue-in-cheek, as 'outrageous demands' from prospective customers when it was designing its new 777 airliner. The airlines wanted an aircraft in which galleys and lavatories could be relocated, plumbing and all, almost anywhere in the cabin within a matter of hours. Boeing gulped but solved this challenging problem. Airlines can rearrange the passenger cabin of the 'Triple Seven' within hours, reconfiguring it with varying numbers of seats allocated among one, two or three classes.

One nice example of highly flexible capacity comes from an eco-tourism operator in the South Island of New Zealand. During the spring, summer and early autumn months the firm provides guided walks and treks, and during the snow season it offers cross-country skiing lessons and trips. Bookings all year round are processed through a contracted telephone-answering service; guides and instructors are employed on a part-time basis as required; the firm has negotiated agreements to use national parks huts and cabins; and it has an exclusive arrangement with a local sports goods store whereby equipment can be hired or purchased by clients at preferential rates. As needed, they can arrange charter bus service for groups. Yet despite this capacity to provide a range of services, the owners' capital investment in the business is remarkably low.

Understanding the patterns and determinants of demand

Now let's look at the other side of the equation. To control variations in demand for a particular service, managers need to determine what factors govern that demand. Research should begin by getting some answers to a series of important questions.

Questions about demand

1. *Do demand levels follow a predictable cycle?* If so, is the duration of the cycle:

- one day (varies by hour);
- one week (varies by day);
- one month (varies by day or by week);
- one year (varies by month or by season; or reflects annually occurring public holidays);
- some other period?

Often, multiple cycles operate simultaneously. Thus, demand for passenger transport may vary by time of day, day of the week, and season all at once.

2. *What are the underlying causes of these cyclical variations?*

- Employment timetables
- Billing and tax payment/refund cycles
- Wage and salary payment dates
- School hours and holidays
- Seasonal changes in climate
- Occurrence of public or religious holidays
- Natural cycles, such as coastal tides

3. *Do demand levels seem to change randomly?* If so, could the underlying causes be:

- Day-to-day changes in the weather (consider how rain and cold affect the use of indoor and outdoor recreational or entertainment services);
- Health events whose occurrence cannot be pinpointed exactly (heart attacks and births affect the demand for hospital services);
- Accidents, natural disasters (such as earthquakes) and certain criminal activities (these require fast response from fire, police and ambulance, and also from disaster recovery specialists and insurance firms)?

4. *Can demand for a particular service over time be disaggregated by market segment* to reflect such components as:

- use patterns by a particular type of customer or for a particular purpose;
- variations in the net profitability of each completed transaction?

Multiple influences on demand

Most periodic cycles influencing demand for a particular service vary in length from one day to twelve months. In many instances, multiple cycles may operate simultaneously. For example, demand levels for public transport may vary by time of day (highest during commuter hours), day of week (less travel to work on weekends but more leisure travel) and season of year (more travel by tourists in summer). The demand for service during the peak period on a Monday in summer may be different from the level during the peak period on a Saturday in winter, reflecting day of week and seasonal variations jointly.

Figure 13.2 shows how the combination of four time-of-day periods (morning peak, midday, afternoon peak, evening/night), two day-of-week periods (weekday, weekend) and three seasonal periods (peak, shoulder, off-peak) can be combined to create 24 different demand periods. In theory, each of these might have its own distinct demand level (at a given price) and customer profiles (with resulting differences in needs and expectations). But in practice, analysis might show close similarities between many of the periods. Such a finding would make it possible to collapse the framework into a total of perhaps 3–6 cells, each requiring a distinct marketing treatment to optimize the use of available capacity and obtain the most desirable customer mix.

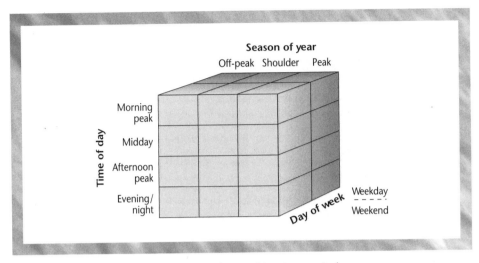

Figure 13.2 ■ Identifying variations in demand by time period

Analyzing demand

Keeping good records of each transaction helps enormously when it comes to analyzing demand patterns based on past experience. Computer-based services, such as telecommunications, can automatically track customer consumption patterns by date and time of day. Where relevant, it's also useful to record weather conditions and other special factors (a strike, an accident, a big conference in town, a price change, launch of a competing service, etc.) that might have influenced demand.

Random fluctuations are usually caused by factors beyond management's control. But analysis will sometimes reveal that a predictable demand cycle for one segment is concealed within a broader, seemingly random pattern. This fact illustrates the importance of breaking down demand on a segment-by-segment basis. For instance, a repair and maintenance shop that services industrial electrical equipment may already know that a certain proportion of its work consists of regularly scheduled contracts to perform preventive maintenance. The balance may come from 'walk-in' business and emergency repairs. While it might seem hard to predict or control the timing and volume of such work, further analysis could show that walk-in business was more prevalent on some days of the week than others and that emergency repairs were frequently requested following damage sustained during thunderstorms (which tend to be seasonal in nature and can often be forecast a day or two in advance).

Not all demand is desirable. In fact, some requests for service are inappropriate and make it difficult for the organization to respond to the legitimate needs of its target customers. Have you ever wondered what it's like to be a controller for an emergency service (such as 999 in Britain)? People differ widely in what they consider to be an emergency. Imagine yourself in the huge communications room at police headquarters. A grey-haired sergeant is talking patiently on the phone to a woman who has dialled 999 because her cat has run up a tree and she's afraid it's stuck there. 'Ma'am, have you ever seen a cat skeleton in a tree?' the sergeant asks her. 'All those cats get down somehow, don't they?' After the woman has hung up, the sergeant turns to a visitor and shrugs. 'These kinds of calls keep pouring in,' he says. 'What can you do?' The trouble is, when people call the emergency number with complaints about noisy parties next door or pleas to rescue cats, they may be slowing response times to fires, heart attacks or violent crimes. Discouraging *undesirable demand* through marketing campaigns or screening procedures will not, of course, eliminate random fluctuations in the remaining demand. But it may help to keep peak demand levels within the organization's capacity to serve.

No strategy for smoothing demand is likely to succeed unless it's based on an understanding of why customers from a specific market segment choose to use the service when they do. It's difficult for hotels to convince business travellers to remain on Saturday nights since few executives do business over the weekend. Instead, hotel managers may do better to promote weekend use of their facilities for conferences or pleasure travel. Attempts to get commuters to shift their travel to off-peak periods will probably fail, since such travel is determined by people's employment hours. Instead, efforts should be directed at employers to persuade them to adopt flexitime or staggered working hours. These firms recognize that no amount of price discounting is likely to develop business out of season. However, resort areas, such as towns along the coast, may have good opportunities to build business during the 'shoulder seasons' of spring and autumn by promoting different attractions – such as hiking, birdwatching, bicycling, visiting ancient monuments and looking for bargains in antique stores – and then altering the mix and focus of services to target a different type of clientele.

Strategies for managing demand

In a well-designed, well-managed service operation, the capacity of the facility, supporting equipment and service personnel will be in balance with each other and with demand. Similarly, sequential operations will be designed to minimize the risk of bottlenecks at any point in the process. This ideal, however, may prove difficult to achieve. Not only does the level of demand vary over time, often randomly, but the time and effort required to process each person or thing may vary widely at any point in the process. In general, processing times for people are more variable than for objects or things, reflecting varying levels of preparedness ('I've lost my credit card'), argumentative versus cooperative personalities ('If you won't give me a table with a view, I'll have to ask to see your supervisor'), and so forth. In both professional services and repair jobs, diagnosis and treatment times vary according to the nature of the customers' problems.

Disaggregating demand by market segment

Can marketing efforts smooth out random fluctuations in demand? The answer is generally no, since these fluctuations are usually caused by factors beyond the management's control. But detailed market analysis may sometimes reveal that a predictable demand cycle for one segment is concealed within a broader, seemingly random pattern. For example, a retail store might experience wide swings in daily patronage, but note that a core group of customers visited every weekday to buy staple items such as newspapers and sweets.

The ease with which total demand can be broken down into smaller components depends on the nature of the records kept by management. If each customer transaction is recorded separately, and backed up by detailed notes (as in a medical or dental visit, or an accountant's audit) then the task of understanding demand is greatly simplified. In subscription and charge account services, when each customer's identity is known and itemized monthly bills are sent, managers can gain some immediate insights into usage patterns. Some services, such as telephone and electrical, even have the ability to track subscriber consumption patterns by time of day. Although these data may not always yield specific information on the purpose for which the service is being used, it is often possible to make informed judgements about the volume of sales generated by different user groups.

Managing demand under different conditions

There are five basic approaches to managing demand. The first, which has the virtue of simplicity but little else, involves *taking no action and leaving demand to find its own levels*. Eventually customers learn from experience or word-of-mouth when they can expect to queue to use the service and when it will be available without delay. The trouble is, they may also learn to find a competitor who is more responsive! More interventionist approaches involve influencing the level of demand at any given time, by taking active steps to *reduce demand in peak periods* and to *increase demand when there is excess capacity*.

Two more approaches both involve *storing demand until capacity becomes available*. A firm can accomplish this, either by introducing a booking or *reservations system* that promises customers access to capacity at specified times, or by *creating formalized queuing systems* (or by a combination of the two).

Table 13.1 links these five approaches to the three basic situations of excess demand, sufficient capacity and excess capacity and provides a brief strategic commentary on each. Many service businesses face all three situations at different points in the cycle of demand, and so should consider use of the interventionist strategies described.

Using marketing strategies to shape demand patterns

Four of the elements of integrated service management introduced in Chapter 1 have a role to play in stimulating demand during periods of excess capacity, and in decreasing it (de-marketing) during periods of insufficient capacity. Manipulating price and other costs of service is often the first strategy adopted for bringing demand and supply into balance, but changes in product elements, variations in the place and time of service delivery, and the use of promotional and educational efforts can also play important roles. Although each element is discussed separately, effective demand management efforts often require changes in two or more elements jointly.

Price and other costs of service

One of the most direct ways of reducing excess demand at peak periods is to charge customers more money to use the service during those periods. Other costs, too, may have a similar effect. For instance, if customers learn that they are likely to face increased time and effort costs during peak periods, this information may lead those who dislike spending time waiting in crowded and unpleasant conditions to try later. Similarly, the lure of cheaper prices and an expectation of no waiting may encourage at least some people to change the timing of their behaviour, whether it be shopping, travel or visiting a museum.

Table 13.1 ■ Alternative demand management strategies for different capacity situations

Approach used to manage demand	Capacity situation relative to demand		
	Insufficient capacity (excess demand)	Sufficient capacity* (satisfactory demand)	Excess capacity (insufficient demand)
Take no action	Unorganized queuing results. (May irritate customers and discourage future use.)	Capacity is fully utilized. (But is this the most profitable mix of business?)	Capacity is wasted. (Customers may have a disappointing experience for service like theatre.)
Reduce demand	Pricing higher will increase profits. Communication can be employed to encourage usage in other time slots. (Can this effort be focused on less profitable/ desirable segments?)	Take no action (but see above).	Take no action (but see above).
Increase demand	Take no action, unless opportunities exist to stimulate (and give priority to) more profitable segments.	Take no action, unless opportunities exist to stimulate (and give priority to) more profitable segments.	Lower price selectively (try to avoid cannibalizing existing business; ensure all relevant costs are covered). Use communications and variation in products/ distribution (but recognize extra costs, if any, and make sure appropriate trade-offs are made between profitability and usage levels).
Store demand by reservation system	Consider priority system for most desirable segments. Make other customers shift (a) to outside peak period or (b) to future peak.	Try to ensure most profitable mix of business.	Communicate that space is available and that no reservations are needed.
Store demand by formalized queuing	Consider priority for most desirable segments. Seek to keep waiting customers occupied and comfortable. Try to predict waiting period accurately.	Try to avoid bottleneck delays.	Not applicable.

* 'Sufficient capacity' may be defined as *maximum available capacity* or *optimum capacity*, depending on the situation.

Some firms use pricing strategy in sophisticated ways in order to balance supply and demand. For the monetary price of a service to be effective as a demand management tool, managers must have some sense of the shape and slope of a product's demand curve – that is, how the quantity of service demanded responds to increases or decreases in the price per unit at a particular point in time (see Figure 13.3). It's important to determine whether the demand curve for a specific service varies sharply from one time period to another (will the same person be willing to pay more for a weekend stay in a hotel in Brittany in summer than in winter? The answer is probably yes.). If so, significantly different pricing schemes may be needed to fill capacity in each time period. To complicate matters further, there may be separate demand curves for different segments within each time period; for instance, business travellers are usually less price sensitive than tourists (see Figure 13.4).

One of the most difficult tasks facing service marketers is to determine the nature of all these different demand curves. Research, trial and error, and analysis of parallel situations in other locations or in comparable services, are all ways of obtaining an understanding of the situation. Many service businesses explicitly recognize the existence of different demand curves by establishing distinct classes of service, each priced at levels appropriate to the demand curve of a particular segment. In essence, each segment receives a variation of the basic product, with value being added to the core service through supplementary services to appeal to higher-paying segments.

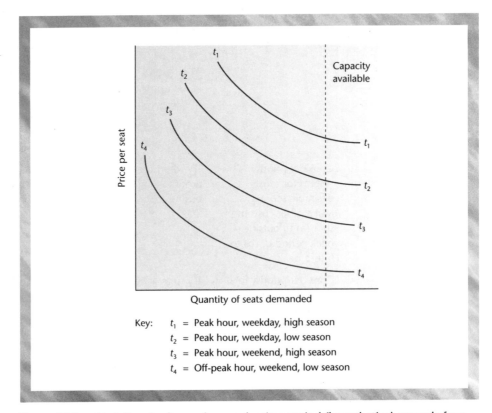

Figure 13.3 ■ Variations in demand curves by time period (hypothetical example for a transport service)

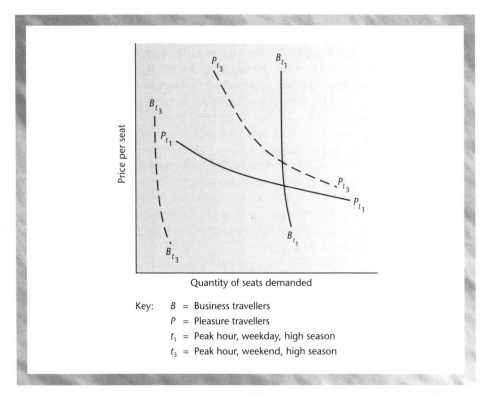

Figure 13.4 ■ Differing demand curves for different segments in two time periods (hypothetical transport example)

For instance, first-class service on airlines offers travellers wider seats, free drinks and better food; in computer and printing service firms, product enhancement takes the form of consultation, faster turnaround and more specialized services; and in hotels, a distinction is made between rooms of different size and amenities, and with different views.

In each case, the objective is to maximize the revenues received from each segment. When capacity is constrained, however, the goal in a profit-seeking business should be to ensure that as much capacity as possible is assigned to the most profitable segments available at any given time. For instance, airlines will hold a certain number of seats for business passengers paying full fare and place restrictive conditions on excursion fares for tourists (such as requiring advance purchase and a Saturday night stay) in order to prevent business travellers from taking advantage of cheap fares designed to attract tourists who can help fill the aircraft. As we saw in Chapter 10, pricing strategies of this nature are known as *yield management*.

Changing product elements

Although pricing is often a commonly advocated method of balancing supply and demand, it is not quite as universally feasible for services as for goods. A rather obvious example is provided by the respective problems of a ski manufacturer and a ski slope operator during the summer. The former can either produce for stock or try to sell skis in the summer at a bargain price. If the skis are sufficiently discounted, some customers will buy before the ski season in order to save money.

However, in the absence of skiing opportunities, no skiers would buy lift tickets for use on a midsummer day at any price. So, to encourage summer use of the lifts, the operator has to change the service product offering. For instance, resorts in the Alps – such as Grindelwald in Switzerland – encourage summer visitors to take lifts high up the mountain, see the view, go hiking and eat at the restaurant on the mountain. Ski resorts have always tried to attract summer hikers. Now some are taking advantage of the mountain biking craze. At a growing number of resorts, mountain bikers can rent bikes from the lodge at the base, take them up to the summit on specially equipped lift-chairs, and ride their bikes down the trails. Ski resorts also look for a variety of additional ways to attract guests to their hotels and rental homes in the summer. Possibilities include offering such activities as a championship golf course, tennis, water sports, roller-blading and a children's daycamp.

Similar thinking prevails at a variety of other seasonal businesses, Thus, tax preparation firms offer bookkeeping and consulting services to small businesses in slack months, educational institutions offer weekend and summer programmes for adults and senior citizens, and small pleasure boats offer cruises in the summer and a dockside venue for private functions in winter months. These firms recognize that no amount of price discounting is likely to develop business out of season.

Many service offerings remain unchanged throughout the year, but others undergo significant modifications according to the season. Hospitals, for example, usually offer the same array of services throughout the year. By contrast, resort hotels sharply alter the mix and focus of their peripheral services such as dining, entertainment and sports to reflect customer preferences in different seasons.

There can be variations in the product offering even during the course of a 24-hour period. Some restaurants provide a good example of this, marking the passage of the hours with changing menus and levels of service, variations in lighting and decor, opening and closing of the bar, and the presence or absence of entertainment. The goal is to appeal to different needs within the same group of customers, to reach out to different customer segments, or to do both, according to the time of day.

Modifying the place and time of delivery

Rather than seeking to modify demand for a service that continues to be offered at the same time in the same place, some firms respond to market needs by modifying the time and place of delivery. Three basic options are available. The first represents a strategy of *no change*: regardless of the level of demand, the service continues to be offered in the same location at the same times. By contrast, a second strategy involves *varying the times when the service is available* to reflect changes in customer preference by day of week, by season, and so forth. Theatres and cinema complexes often offer matinées at weekends when people have more leisure time throughout the day. During the summer, cafés and restaurants may stay open later because of extended daylight hours and the general inclination of people to enjoy the longer, balmier evenings outdoors. In the lead-up to Christmas, many shops extend their opening hours.

A third strategy involves *offering the service to customers at a new location*. One approach is to operate mobile units that take the service to customers, rather than requiring them to visit fixed-site service locations. Mobile libraries and car wash services, in-office tailoring services, home-delivered meals and catering services, and vans equipped with primary care medical facilities are examples of this. A cleaning and repair firm that wishes to generate business during low-demand periods might offer free collection and delivery of portable items that need servicing. Alternatively, service firms whose productive assets are mobile may choose to follow the market when that, too, is mobile. For instance, some car rental firms establish seasonal branch offices in popular holiday locations. They transport large numbers of cars to these towns so that holidaymakers arriving by air, train or cruise ship will be able to have a car available.

Promotion and education

Even if the other marketing variables remain unchanged, communication efforts alone may be able to help smooth demand. Signage, advertising, publicity and sales messages can be used to educate customers about the timing of peak periods and encourage them to avail themselves of the service at off-peak times when there will be fewer delays. Examples include Post Office requests to 'Mail Early for Christmas', public transport messages urging non-commuters, such as shoppers or tourists, to avoid the crush conditions of the commuter hours, and communications from sales representatives for industrial maintenance firms advising customers of periods when preventive maintenance work can be done quickly. In addition, management can ask service personnel (or intermediaries such as travel agents) to encourage customers with discretionary time to favour off-peak periods.

Changes in pricing, product characteristics and distribution must be communicated clearly. If a firm wants to obtain a specific response to variations in marketing mix elements it must, of course, inform customers fully about their options. As discussed in Chapter 11, short-term promotions, combining both pricing and communication elements as well as other incentives, may provide customers with attractive incentives to shift the timing of service usage.

Storing demand through queuing and reservations

What can a manager do when the possibilities for shaping demand and adjusting capacity have been exhausted and yet supply and demand are still out of balance? Not taking any action and leaving customers to sort things out is no recipe for service quality or customer satisfaction. Rather than allowing matters to degenerate into a random free-for-all, customer-oriented firms try to develop strategies for ensuring order, predictability and fairness. In businesses where demand regularly exceeds supply, managers can often take steps to store demand. This task can be achieved in one of two ways: (1) by asking customers to queue, usually on a first-come, first-served basis, or (2) by offering them the opportunity of reserving or booking space in advance. Let's look at each in turn.

Managing customer behaviour through queuing systems

Richard Larson suggests that, when everything is added up, the average person may spend as much as half-an-hour a day waiting in a queue. This translates to 20 months of waiting in an 80-year lifetime![3] Some countries are worse than others

– the former Soviet Union was notorious for the incredibly long queues in which people had to wait to buy food and other products.

Nobody likes to be kept waiting. It's boring, time-wasting and sometimes physically uncomfortable, especially if there is nowhere to sit or you are out-of-doors. And yet waiting for a service process is an almost universal phenomenon: virtually every organization has queues somewhere in its operation. People are kept waiting on the phone, they queue to pay for their grocery purchases, and they wait for their bills after a restaurant meal. Then they either wait for a bus or sit in their cars waiting for traffic lights to change.

Physical and inanimate objects wait for processing, too. Letters pile up on an executive's desk, shoes sit on racks waiting to be repaired at the cobblers, cheques wait to be cleared at a bank, an incoming phone call waits to be switched to a customer service agent. In each instance, a customer may be waiting for the outcome of that work – an answer to a letter, a pair of shoes ready to be picked up, a cheque credited to the customer's balance or a useful contact with the service person (instead of being kept on hold listening to a recorded message that keeps repeating, 'your call is important to us').

The nature of queues

Queues occur whenever the arrivals at a facility exceed the capacity of the system to process them. Any type of queue is a symptom of unresolved capacity management problems. Analysis and modelling of queues is a well-established branch of operations management. Queuing theory has been traced back to 1917, when a Danish telephone engineer was charged with determining how large the switching unit in a telephone system had to be to keep the number of engaged signals within reason.[4]

As the telephone example suggests, not all queues take the form of a physical line in a single location. When customers deal with a service supplier at arm's length, as in information-processing services, they call from home, office or college using telecommunication channels such as voice telephone or the internet. Typically, calls are answered in the order received, often requiring customers to wait in a virtual line. Some physical queues are geographically dispersed. Travellers wait at many different locations for the taxis they have ordered by phone to arrive and pick them up.

Increasing capacity by adding more service personnel is one way to reduce customers' wait times. But taking in additional employees is not always the best solution in situations where customer satisfaction must be balanced against cost considerations. So, managers should consider a variety of alternatives, such as:

■ rethinking the design of the queuing system;
■ redesigning processes to shorten the time of each transaction;
■ managing customers' behaviour and their perceptions of the wait;
■ installing a reservations system.

Let's begin by looking at what is involved in designing a queuing system.

Elements of a queuing system[5]

We can divide queuing systems into six elements before the customer receives service:

1. The *customer population* from which demands for service originate (sometimes known to operations researchers as the calling population).

2. The *arrival process* – times and volumes of customer requests for service.

3. *Baulking* – decision by an arriving customer not to join the queue (usually because the wait appears too long).

4. *Queue configuration* – design of the system in terms of the number, location and configuration of queues.

5. *Reneging* – decision by a customer already in the queue who has not yet been served to leave rather than wait any longer (usually because the queue is moving too slowly).

6. *Customer selection policies* – formal or *ad hoc* policies on whom to serve next (also known as queue discipline).

Customer population

When planning queuing systems, *operations managers* need to know who their customers are and something about their needs and expectations. There is, obviously, a big difference between a critically injured patient arriving by ambulance at a hospital casualty ward and a sports fan arriving at a stadium ticket office. Although neither is an inanimate object, such as shoes needing repair which could, in theory, be left to wait for several weeks, the hospital needs to be more geared for speed than the stadium.

Arrival process

The rate at which customers arrive over time – relative to the capacity of the serving process – and the extent to which they arrive individually or in clusters, will determine whether or not a queue starts to form. We need to draw a distinction between the *average* arrival rate (e.g., 60 customers an hour = one customer every minute) and the *distribution* of those arrivals during any given minute of that hour. In some instances, arrival times are largely random (for instance, individuals entering a store in a shopping centre). In other instances, some degree of clustering can be predicted, such as arrivals of many students in a cafeteria within a few minutes of classes ending. Managers who anticipate surges of activity at specific times can plan their staff allocations around such events (for instance, opening an additional cash register).

Baulking

If you're like most people, you tend to be put off by a long queue at a service facility and may often decide to come back later (or go somewhere else) rather than waiting. Sometimes this is a mistake, as the queue may be moving faster than you realize. Managers can disguise the length of queues by making them wind around corners, as often happens at theme parks. Alternatively, they may indicate the expected wait time from specific locations in the queuing area by installing information signs.

Queue configuration

There is a variety of different types of queues. Here are some common ones that you may have experienced yourself in people-processing services (see also Figure 13.5 for diagrams of each type).

■ *Single queue, single stage.* Customers wait to conduct a single-service transaction. Waiting for a lift or a bus is an example.

■ *Single queue, sequential stages.* Customers proceed through several serving operations, as in a cafeteria queue. In such systems, bottlenecks will occur at any stage where the process takes longer to execute than at previous stages. Many cafeterias often have queues at the cash register because the cashier takes longer to calculate how much you owe and to give change than the servers take to put food on your plate.

■ *Parallel queues to multiple servers (single or sequential stages).* This system offers more than one serving station, allowing customers to select one of several queues in which to wait. Fast-food restaurants usually have several serving queues in operation at busy times of day, with each offering the full menu. A parallel system can have either a single stage or multiple stages. The disadvantage of this design is that queues may not move at equal speed. How many times have you chosen what looked like the shortest only to watch in frustration as the queues either side of you move at twice the speed because someone in your queue has a complicated transaction?

■ *Designated queues.* Different lines can be assigned to specific categories of customer. Examples include express lines (for instance, six items or less) and regular lines at supermarket checkouts, and different check-in lines for first class, business class and economy class airline passengers.

■ *Single queue to multiple servers ('snake').* Customers wait in a single queue, often winding sinuously back and forth between rope barriers (hence the name). As each person reaches the head of the queue, he or she is directed to the next available serving position. This approach is encountered frequently in banks, post offices and at airport check-ins. Its advantages are fairness and reduced anxiety. The presence of ropes or other barriers makes it difficult for inconsiderate people to queue-jump. At the margin, it may also discourage reneging.

■ *Take a number.* In this variation of the single queue, arriving customers take a number and are then called in sequence, thus saving the need to stand in a queue. This procedure allows them to sit down and relax (if seating is available) or to guess how long the wait will be and do something else in the meantime – but risk losing their place. Users of this approach include travel organizations and supermarket departments such as the butcher or delicatessen.

Hybrid approaches to queue configuration also exist. For instance, a cafeteria with a single serving queue might offer two cash register stations at the final stage. Similarly, patients at a small medical clinic might visit a single receptionist for registration, proceed sequentially through multiple channels for testing, diagnosis and treatment, and conclude by returning to a single queue at the receptionist's desk to book a follow-up appointment.

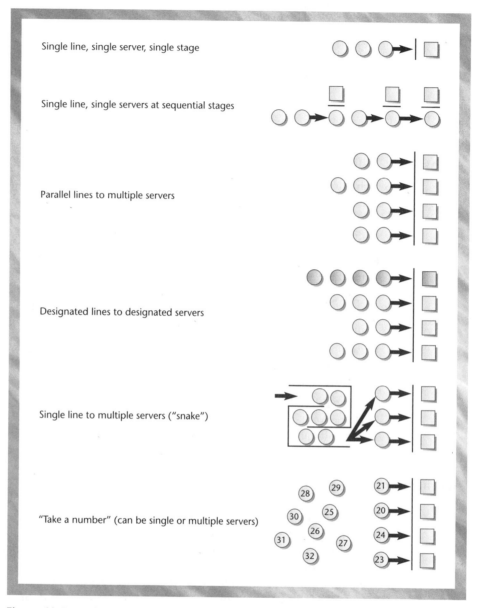

Figure 13.5 ■ Alternative queue configurations

Reneging

You know the situation (perhaps all too well!). The queue is not that long, but it's moving at a snail's pace. The person at the front of the queue has been there for at least five minutes and his problem seems nowhere near solution. There are two other people ahead of you and you have an uneasy feeling that their transactions are not going to be brief either. Looking at your watch for the third time, you realize that you only have a few minutes until your next appointment. Frustrated, you turn and leave. In the language of queue management, you have reneged. One of the things planners need to determine is how long a wait can be before customers start reneging, since some may never return.

Customer selection policies

Most waiting lines work on the principle of first come, first served. Customers tend to expect this – it's only fair, after all. In many cultures (but not all), people get very resentful if they see later arrivals being served ahead of them for no good reason. There are, however, some valid exceptions. Medical services will give priority to emergency cases and airline personnel will allow passengers whose flights are soon due to leave to check in ahead of passengers taking later flights.

Matching queuing systems to market segments

Although the basic rule in most queuing systems is first come, first served, not all queuing systems are organized on this basis. Market segmentation is sometimes used to design queuing strategies that set different priorities for different types of customers. Allocation to separate queuing areas may be based on:

- *Urgency of the job* – at many hospital casualty wards, a triage nurse is assigned to greet incoming patients and decide which ones require priority medical treatment and which can safely be asked to register and then sit down while they wait to be treated.

- *Duration of service transaction* – banks, supermarkets and other retail services often institute 'express lanes' for shorter, less complicated tasks.

- *Payment of a premium price* – airlines usually offer separate check-in lines for first class and economy class passengers, with a higher ratio of personnel to passengers in the first class queue, resulting in reduced waits for those who have paid more.

- *Importance of the customer* – special areas may be reserved for members of frequent user clubs. Airlines often provide lounges, offering newspapers and free refreshments, where frequent flyers can wait for their flights in greater comfort.

Minimizing the perceived length of the wait

Operations managers should know better than to treat people who are waiting for service as if they were inanimate objects (although that doesn't stop some organizations from doing so!). As we saw in Chapter 12, customers may view the time and effort spent on consuming services as a cost. People don't like wasting their time on unproductive activities any more than they like wasting money. They also prefer to avoid unwanted mental or physical effort, including anxiety or discomfort.

People often think they have waited longer for a service than they actually did. Studies of public transportation use, for instance, have shown that travellers perceive time spent waiting for a bus or train as passing $1\frac{1}{2}$–7 times more slowly than the time actually spent travelling in the vehicle.[6] Tolerance for waiting may also be related to the nature of the institution providing service. A study conducted in Switzerland among customers of the Swiss PTT and those of the country's leading retailer, Migros, found that what customers defined as a tolerable waiting time for service was 30 per cent higher for the retailer than for the post office. Kostecki hypothesized that this was because shopping at Migros was seen as a more pleasant experience than going to the post office.[7]

The psychology of waiting time

The noted philosopher William James observed: 'Boredom results from being attentive to the passage of time itself.' Based on this observation, David Maister formulated eight principles about waiting time.[8] Adding two additional principles gives us a total of ten, summarized in Table 13.2. Let's examine each proposition in turn and review some appropriate actions.

Table 13.2 ■ Ten propositions on the psychology of waiting lines

1. Unoccupied time feels longer than occupied time.
2. Pre-process and post-process waits feel longer than in-process waits.
3. Anxiety makes waits seem longer.
4. Uncertain waits are longer than known, finite waits.
5. Unexplained waits are longer than explained waits.
6. Unfair waits are longer than equitable waits.
7. The more valuable the service, the longer people will wait.
8. Solo waits feel longer than group waits.
9. Physically uncomfortable waits feel longer than comfortable waits.[9]
10. Waits seem longer to new or occasional users than to frequent users.[10]

Unoccupied time feels longer than occupied time

When you're sitting around with nothing to do, time seems to crawl. The challenge for service organizations is to give customers something to do or to distract them while waiting. Doctors and dentists stock their waiting rooms with piles of magazines (all too often, many months old and irrelevant to patients' interests) for people to read while waiting. Car repair facilities may have a television for customers to watch. Theme parks supply roving bands of entertainers to amuse customers queuing for the most popular attractions.

Pre- and post-process waits feel longer than in-process waits

There's a difference between waiting to buy a ticket to enter a theme park as opposed to waiting to ride on a roller coaster once you're in the park. There's also a difference between waiting for coffee to arrive towards the end of a restaurant meal and waiting for a waitress to bring you the bill once you're ready to leave. Rental car firms sometimes get the process started early by assigning an agent to obtain information on customers' needs while they wait; in that way, service delivery – namely assigning a specific car – can begin as soon as each person reaches the front of the queue. These firms also try to minimize customer waiting when the car is returned, employing agents with hand-held terminals to meet customers in the parking area, enter fuel and mileage, and then compute and print bills on the spot.

Anxiety makes waits seem longer

Can you remember waiting for someone to arrive at a rendezvous and worrying about whether you had got the time or the location correct? While waiting in unfamiliar locations, especially out-of-doors and after dark, people often worry about their personal safety.

Uncertain waits are longer than known, finite waits

Although any wait may be frustrating, we can usually adjust mentally to a wait of known length. It's the unknown that keeps us on edge. Imagine waiting for a delayed flight and not being told how long the delay is going to be. You don't know whether you have the time to get up and walk around the terminal or whether you need to stay at the gate.

Unexplained waits are longer than explained waits

Have you ever been in an underground train or lift which has stopped for no apparent reason without anyone telling you what is going on? Not only is there uncertainty about the length of the wait, there's added worry about what is going to happen. Has there been an accident on the line? Will you have to leave the train in the tunnel? Is the lift broken? Will you be stuck for hours in close proximity with dubious-looking strangers?

Unfair waits are longer than equitable waits

Expectations about what is fair or unfair sometimes vary from one culture or country to another. In some countries, people expect everybody to wait their turn and are likely to get irritated if they see others jumping the queue or being given priority for no apparent good reason.

The more valuable the service, the longer people will wait

People will queue overnight under uncomfortable conditions to get good seats at a major concert or sports event which is expected to sell out.

Solo waits feel longer than group waits

Waiting with one or more people you know is reassuring. Conversation with friends can help to pass the time, but not everyone is comfortable talking to a stranger.

Physically uncomfortable waits feel longer than comfortable waits

'My feet are killing me!' is one of the most frequently heard comments when people are forced to stand for a long time. And whether seated or unseated, a wait seems more burdensome if the temperature is too hot or too cold, if it's drafty or windy, and if there is no protection from rain or snow.

Unfamiliar waits seem longer than familiar ones

Frequent users of a service know what to expect and are less likely to worry while waiting. New or occasional users of a service, by contrast, are often nervous, wondering not only about the probable length of the wait but also about what happens next. They may also be concerned about such issues as personal safety.

What are the implications of these insights? When increasing capacity is simply not feasible, you should try to be creative and look for ways to make waiting more palatable for customers. An experiment at a large bank in Boston found that installing an electronic news display in the lobby didn't reduce the perceived time spent waiting for teller service but it did lead to greater customer satisfaction.[11] Heated shelters equipped with seats make it more pleasant to wait for a bus or train in cold weather. Restaurants solve the waiting problem by inviting dinner guests to have a drink in the bar until their table is ready (that approach makes money for the house as well as keeping the customer occupied). In similar fashion, guests waiting for a show at a casino may find themselves queuing in a corridor lined with slot-machines.

Reservations

Ask someone what services come to mind when you talk about reservations and most likely they will cite airlines, hotels, restaurants, car rentals and theatre seats. Suggest synonyms like 'bookings' or 'appointments' and they may add haircuts, visits to professionals such as doctors and consultants, holiday cottages, and service calls to fix anything from a broken refrigerator to a neurotic computer.

Reservations are supposed to guarantee that the service will be available when the customer wants it. Systems vary from a simple appointments book for a doctor's surgery, using handwritten entries, to a central, computerized data bank for an airline's worldwide operations. When goods require servicing, their owners may not wish to be parted from them for long. Households with only one car, for example, or factories with a vital piece of equipment, often cannot afford to be without such items for more than a day or two. So a reservations system may be necessary for service businesses in fields such as repair and maintenance. By requiring reservations for routine maintenance, management can ensure that some time will be kept free for handling emergency jobs which, because they carry a premium price, generate a much higher margin.

Designing a reservations system

Reservations systems are commonly used by many people-processing services including restaurants, hotels, airlines, hairdressing salons and doctors. Such systems allow demand to be controlled and smoothed in a manageable way. By capturing data, reservation systems also help organizations to prepare financial projections. Taking bookings also serves to pre-sell a service, to inform customers and to educate them about what to expect. Customers who hold reservations should be able to count on avoiding a queue, since they have been guaranteed service at a specific time. A well-designed reservations system allows the organization to deflect demand for service from a first-choice time to earlier or later times, from one class of service to another ('upgrades' and 'downgrades'), and even from first-choice locations to alternative locations.

However, problems arise when customers fail to arrive or when service firms overbook. Marketing strategies for dealing with these operational problems include:

■ requiring a deposit;

■ cancelling non-paid bookings after a certain time;

■ providing compensation to victims of overbooking.

The challenge in designing reservations systems is to make them fast and user-friendly for both reservations staff and customers. Many organizations now give customers the option of making their own reservations on the company's web site – a trend that seems certain to grow. Whether customers talk with a reservations agent or make their own bookings, they want quick answers to queries about service availability at a preferred time.

Linking reservations to yield management strategies

Private sector services are in business to make a profit. Many capacity-constrained service businesses have expensive physical facilities and equipment plus a pool of full-time personnel. In effect customers pay 'rent' for the use of facilities and personnel. Assuming for the moment that the costs associated with serving different segments remain constant, then the higher the price and the greater the volume of usage, the greater the profits. However, different customer segments vary in their ability and willingness to pay.

Organizations often use percentage of capacity sold as a measure of operational efficiency. For instance, transport services talk of the 'load factor' achieved, hotels of their 'occupancy rate' and hospitals of their 'census'. Similarly, professional firms calculate what proportion of a partner's or an employee's time can be classified as billable hours, and repair shops look at utilization of both equipment and labour. By themselves, however, these percentage figures tell us little of the relative profitability of the business attracted, since high utilization rates may be obtained at the expense of heavy discounting – or even outright giveaways.

As shown in Chapter 10, yield management strategies are concerned with obtaining the best possible revenue yield over time from each available unit of capacity. At the same time, they seek, wherever possible, to obtain even a minimal return from perishable capacity units rather than nothing at all. Success in this endeavour requires knowing the mix of customers at any given time and then developing strategies that avoid selling each unit at prices below what existing customers would be willing to pay.

Understanding and measuring the yield forces explicit recognition of the opportunity cost of accepting business from one segment when another might subsequently yield a higher rate. Consider the following problems facing sales managers for different types of capacity-constrained service organizations:

■ Should a hotel accept an advance booking from a tour group of 200 room nights at €100 each when these same room nights might possibly be sold later at short notice to business travellers at the full rack rate of €150?

■ Should a railway with 30 empty freight cars at its disposal accept an immediate request for a shipment worth €300 per car or hold the cars idle for a few more days in the hope of getting a priority shipment that would be twice as valuable?

- How many seats on a particular flight should an airline sell in advance to tour groups and passengers travelling at special excursion rates?

- Should an industrial repair and maintenance shop reserve a certain proportion of productive capacity each day for emergency repair jobs that offer a high contribution margin and the potential to build long-term customer loyalty, or should it simply follow a strategy of making sure that there are sufficient jobs, mostly involving routine maintenance, to keep its employees fully occupied?

- Should a printshop process all jobs on a first-come, first-served basis, with a guaranteed delivery time for each job, or should it charge a premium rate for 'rush' work, and tell customers with 'standard' jobs to expect some variability in completion dates?

Good market information supported by good marketing sense is the key to making appropriate decisions in such instances. The decision to accept or reject business should represent a realistic estimate of the probabilities of obtaining higher-rated business, together with a recognition of any damage to customer relations that might result from rejecting low-rated business. Based on past experience and an understanding of current market conditions, prices can be set that reflect the demand curves of different market segments.

Few service businesses have the resources to develop the sophisticated yield management models found in major airlines, which today are changing capacity allocation from hour to hour in the light of dynamic market information. However, guidelines are still needed in other businesses for sales personnel and reservations staff. A simple approach is to segment the market in ways that are relevant to both profitability and relationship management, and then create projections for future dates of the mix of customers that can be anticipated based on past experience. In this way, targets can be assigned to advertising and sales personnel, reflecting how management expects to allocate available capacity among different market segments at a specific point in time. (See Figure 13.6 for an example from a hotel that sets different sales targets both by day of the week and by season.)

These allocation decisions also constitute vital information for reservations personnel, indicating when to stop accepting reservations from certain segments. To simplify the process for booking clerks, the firm's best customers can be assigned personal account numbers as well as being invited to reserve through telephone numbers or web sites that are not publicly advertised.

Marketing's role in yield management

Clearly, the adoption of customer mix sales targets that may vary from day to day – or even from hour to hour – puts a premium on accurate market analysis and forecasting. But the economic and strategic benefits are likely to outweigh the planning and research costs involved. Setting specific sales targets by segments, with recommended prices for each segment, reduces the risk that business will be booked in advance at a discount when there is a high probability of later obtaining business for the rate in question from a higher-paying segment. Sales targets also reduce the risk that potential business from lower-rated segments will be turned away in the hope of obtaining a higher-priced sale when the chances of obtaining the latter are actually very small. Similarly, operations personnel will be better able to plan service levels, staffing and availability of special features if they have a good idea of the business mix that is likely to be obtained on specific dates.

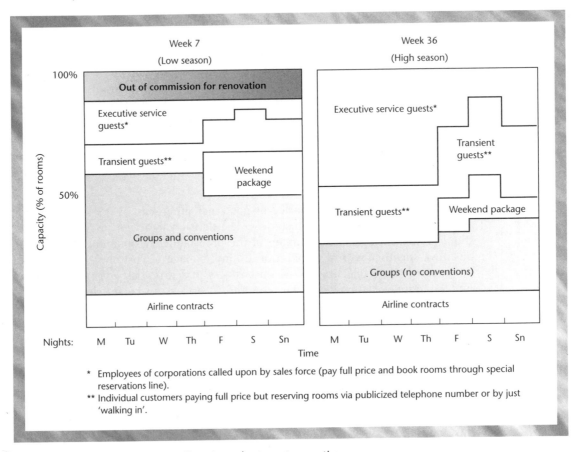

Figure 13.6 ■ Setting capacity allocation sales targets over time

One possible constraint on management's desire to maximize yield in the short term is the need to maintain good customer relations, especially with customers that provide extensive repeat business or use substantial capacity during periods of low demand. In the former instance, perceived price gouging (charging extortionate prices) during peak periods may alienate customers and result in negative word-of-mouth publicity. In the second instance, it may sometimes be necessary to take low-rated business in the peak period in order to ensure continued patronage during off-peak periods. Each case should be taken on its own merits, with careful assessment being made of who needs whom the most – the buyer or the seller.

Information needs

Managers require substantial information to help them develop effective demand management strategies and then monitor marketplace performance. Needs include:

- *Historical data* on the level and composition of demand over time, including responses to changes in price or other marketing variables.
- *Forecasts* of the level of demand for each major segment under specified conditions.

- *Segment-by-segment data* to help management evaluate the impact of periodic cycles and random demand fluctuations.

- *Sound cost data* to enable the organization to distinguish between fixed and variable costs and to determine the relative profitability of incremental unit sales to different segments and at different prices.

- In multi-site organizations, *identification of meaningful variations in the levels and composition of demand* on a site-by-site basis.

- *Customer attitudes* towards queuing under varying conditions.

- *Customer opinions* on whether the quality of service delivered varies with different levels of capacity utilization.

Where might all this information come from? Although some new studies may be required, much of the needed data are probably already being collected within the organization – although not necessarily by marketers. A stream of information comes into most service businesses, especially from transaction data. Sales receipts alone often contain vast detail. Most service businesses collect detailed information for operational and accounting purposes. Although some do not record details of individual transactions, a majority have the potential to associate specific customers with specific transactions. Unfortunately, the marketing value of these data is often overlooked and they are not always stored in ways that permit easy retrieval and analysis for marketing purposes. Nevertheless, collection and storage of customer transaction data can often be reformatted to provide marketers with some of the information they require, including how existing segments have responded to past changes in marketing variables.

Other information may have to be collected through special studies, such as customer surveys or reviews of analogous situations. It may also be necessary to collect information on competitive performance, because changes in the capacity or strategy of competitors may require corrective action.

Conclusion

Fluctuating demand for service is a problem for numerous service businesses, especially those with expensive fixed capacity. Since service output can rarely be produced and then stocked for future sale, strategies must be developed to balance demand against available capacity. Designing and implementing such strategies typically require close cooperation between marketing, operations and human resource managers.

Options range from using marketing efforts to smooth the peaks and valleys of demand to managing the level of available capacity to match the level of demand. When demand exceeds supply, queues may develop and lead to customer frustration unless carefully organized. Reservations systems can be used to guarantee customers access to the desired service at a specified time and thus save them from having to wait in a queue.

The time-bound nature of services is a critical management issue today, especially with customers becoming more time-sensitive and more conscious of their personal time constraints and availability. People-processing services are particularly likely to impose the burden of unwanted waiting on their customers, since the latter cannot avoid coming to the 'factory' for service. Reservations can shape the timing of arrivals, but sometimes queuing is inevitable. Managers who can act to save customers' time (or at least make time pass more pleasantly) may be able to create a competitive advantage for their organizations. Use of yield management techniques, meanwhile, can help firms in certain capacity-constrained industries to develop sophisticated pricing strategies designed to improve profitability by selling to different segments at different prices.

Several of the 8Ps of integrated service management underlie the discussion in this chapter. The first is *productivity*. Since many capacity-constrained service quality organizations have heavy fixed costs, even modest improvements in capacity utilization can have a significant effect on the bottom line. However, managers must be careful not to degrade the quality of customers' service experiences by packing them into a service facility beyond the level of optimum capacity. In this chapter we have also shown how managers can transform fixed costs into variable costs through such strategies as using rented facilities or part-time labour. Creating a more flexible approach to productive capacity allows a firm to adopt a 'chase demand' strategy, thereby improving productivity.

Decisions on *place and time* are closely associated with balancing demand and capacity. Demand is often a function of where the service is located and when it is offered. As we saw with the discussion of alpine resorts, the appeal of many destinations varies with the seasons. Marketing strategies involving use of product elements, price and other costs services, and promotion and education are often useful in managing the level of demand for a service at a particular place and time.

Study questions

1. Why is capacity management particularly significant in a service setting?

2. What is meant by 'chasing demand'?

3. What does stock mean for service firms and why is it perishable?

4. Select a service organization of your choice and identify their particular patterns of demand with reference to Figure 13.1.

    (a) What is the nature of this service organization's approach to capacity and demand management?

    (b) What changes would you recommend in relation to its management of capacity and demand, and why?

5. Distinguish between optimum and maximum capacity. What are their respective implications for customers, employees and managers?

6. Define capacity in relation to all the service elements offered to customers by (a) an airline, (b) a hotel, (c) a management consulting firm, (d) a full-service restaurant.

7. List at least two implications of each of the cyclical events outlined on pages 518–19 for different types of services available on Cape Cod.

8. Review the five approaches to managing demand. Give examples of their applicability to different types of business-to-business services.

9. Make a list of the queuing systems in place at five or more service organizations in the town where you live or are going to college. In your view, how satisfactory are they for customers and how might they be improved?

Notes

1. Colin G. Armistead and Graham Clark, 'The "Coping" Capacity Management Strategy in Services and the Influence on Quality Performance', *International Journal of Service Industry Management*, Vol. 5, No. 2, 1994, pp. 5–22.

2. Based on material in James A. Fitzsimmons and M.J. Fitzsimmons, *Service Management for Competitive Advantage*, New York: McGraw-Hill, 1994; and W. Earl Sasser, Jr., 'Match Supply and Demand in Service Industries', *Harvard Business Review*, November–December 1976.

3. Dave Wielenga, 'Not So Fine Lines', *Los Angeles Times*, 28 November 1997, p. E1.

4. Richard Saltus, 'Lines, Lines, Lines, Lines … The Experts Are Trying to Ease the Wait', *The Boston Globe*, 5 October 1992, pp. 39, 42.

5. This section is based in part on James A. Fitzsimmons and Mona J. Fitzsimmons, *Service Management for Competitive Advantage*, New York: McGraw-Hill, 1994, pp. 264–90; and David H. Maister, 'Note on the Management of Queues', 9-680-053, Harvard Business School Case Services, 1979, rev. 2/84.

6. Jay R. Chernow, 'Measuring the Values of Travel Time Savings', *Journal of Consumer Research*, Vol. 7, March 1981, pp. 360–71. (Note: this entire issue was devoted to the consumption of time.)

7. Michel Kostecki, 'Waiting Lines as a Marketing Issue', *European Management Journal*, Vol. 14, No. 3, 1996, pp. 295–303.

8. David H. Maister, 'The Psychology of Waiting Lines', in J.A. Czepiel, M.R. Solomon and C.F. Surprenant, *The Service Encounter*, Lexington, MA: Lexington Books/D.C. Heath and Co., 1986, pp. 113–23.

9. M.M. Davis and J. Heineke, 'Understanding the Roles of the Customer and the Operation for Better Queue Management', *International Journal of Operations & Production Management*, Vol. 14, No. 5, 1994, pp. 21–34.

10. Peter Jones and Emma Peppiatt, 'Managing Perceptions of Waiting Times in Service Queues', *International Journal of Service Industry Management*, Vol. 7, No. 5, 1996, pp. 47–61.

11. Karen L. Katz, Blaire M. Larson and Richard C. Larson, 'Prescription for the Waiting-in-Line Blues: Entertain, Enlighten, and Engage', *Sloan Management Review*, Winter 1991, pp. 44–53.

Managing customer-contact personnel

Learning objectives

After reading and reflecting on this chapter, you should be able to:

1. Appreciate that expenditures on human resources should be seen as an investment that will pay dividends, rather than a cost to be minimized.

2. Understand the strategic importance of recruitment, selection, training, motivation and retention of employees.

3. Define what is meant by the control and involvement models of management.

4. Understand the benefits and implications of employee empowerment.

5. Recognize how different approaches to human resource management affect customer satisfaction and retention.

Empowering public employees to deliver excellent service[1]

Public employees have not traditionally been known for their responsiveness to customers, nor their eagerness to deliver quality service (although, in fairness, many fine exceptions to this negative stereotype have always existed). Historically, working in the public sector offered long-term job security in a very regimented environment. Today, the situation is evolving away from this model, reflecting a changing political environment, financial pressures and rising customer expectations. Many public sector jobs, such as refuse collection in numerous cities, have been privatized or subcontracted. In other instances, services continue to be offered by public agencies in different branches of government, but efforts are being made to manage them in more creative ways that allow employees to be more responsive to customer needs. Even the use of the term 'customers' represents a significant break with the traditional use of such terms as 'the public', 'citizens' or 'taxpayers'.

Employees working for the London Borough of Bromley serve a resident customer base of 300,000 residents, including many immigrant families from a wide array of different backgrounds. They also serve people who visit or work in the borough, which is located in the south-eastern area of Greater London. Among the many services offered by the borough council are those of its Environmental Health & Trading Standards (EH&TS) department. Meeting the varied expectations of a broad cross-section of people in matters of public health, fair standards of trading and the environment may seem an almost impossible task, but the 90 employees of Bromley's EH&TS service meet extraordinary demands on a daily basis.

The aim of the EH&TS service is to promote and protect the public health of the people who live in, work in and visit Bromley, to ensure fair standards of trading and to enhance the quality of the environment – all at an acceptable cost and quality level. Food safety, public health services, housing services, pollution monitoring, safety in the workplace, animal welfare, and weights and measures are among EH&TS's responsibilities. Complaints concerning public nuisance or consumer problems such as noise, housing conditions, rubbish, pollution, drainage, smells, pests, food, incorrect pricing, faulty goods and services all fall directly into the lap of EH&TS.

At a time when the demand for town services is increasing but resources are diminishing, the challenge is to provide high-quality service and ensure its availability to everyone living and working in the borough. In response, the chief environmental health officer, Richard Foulger, and his colleagues have developed a model of total quality service. The department has prepared a written charter of the services on offer and the standards of service that customers can expect. This includes a pledge to respond to all complaints or requests for service within three working days, or within 24 hours if the problem poses a serious threat to public health. Performance against targets is regularly communicated to staff and reviewed by the elected members of the borough council. Customers are surveyed regularly to establish their most important service areas and to determine the quality of service they are actually receiving.

Among its staff members, EH&TS has set up several quality improvement teams. One of these teams has special responsibility for developing new customer care initiatives, such as training for staff to sensitize them to the needs of people who are deaf or hard of hearing or redesign of leaflets for different ethnic communities. Seminars have been conducted to educate customers on recent changes in the law that may affect them and informational brochures have been distributed in immigrant languages that include Farsi, Hindi, Chinese and Bengali.

One novel customer service initiative involves a safety equipment loan scheme (for example, gates that can be installed on staircases), which aims to reduce the number of accidents in the home among children under five, especially those from disadvantaged families which might not be able to afford to purchase such equipment.

The management team at EH&TS has paid particular attention to employees in terms of identifying the necessary skills and competencies they will require to carry out the department's different functions and then ensuring that they receive the necessary training. Employees now drive many aspects of the improvement process themselves. Devolved decision-making ensures that staff members are in a position to resolve complaints as soon as they arise. Staff suggestions and the work of quality improvement teams are providing a steady stream of customer-focused innovations. EH&TS employees are encouraged to 'communicate freely, not defensively; listen; follow up swiftly; and care'.

'Although our customers don't have a lot of choice, because we are the only provider of most of the services we offer, we aim to treat each customer as if they did,' says Foulger. The service philosophy that now permeates Bromley's Environmental Health & Trading Standards department highlights both the need and possibilities for change in many other areas of the public sector.

Human resources: an asset worth investing in

Many organizations have used the phrase, 'People are our most important asset', but all too few act as though top management really believes it. However, behind most of today's successful service organizations stands a commitment to effective management of human resources. Management styles and corporate cultures may differ widely, but in high-contact service organizations especially there is a recognition that the quality of personal service encounters plays an important role in creating customer satisfaction and, in the private sector, competitive advantage. In the public sector and many nonprofit organizations, too, as our example from the London Borough of Bromley suggests, creative new approaches to service delivery and non-traditional ways of managing employees go hand in hand when the goal is to provide better service to customers.

Key elements in human resource management (HRM) include recruitment, selection, training and retention of employees. Successful service firms are characterized by a distinctive culture of service, leadership and role modelling by members of top management and active involvement of HR managers in strategic decisions.

Employees are seen as a resource to be nurtured, rather than a cost to be minimized, and are empowered to make decisions on their own, rather than having to go continually to their supervisors to ask for permission.

Hal Rosenbluth, owner of a chain of successful travel agencies, argues in his book, *The Customer Comes Second*, that a company's first focus should be on its employees: 'Only when people know what it feels like to be first in someone else's eyes', he writes, 'can they sincerely share that feeling with others.'[2] Within a service organization, other employees may serve internal suppliers and internal customers, as they work 'backstage' to support the efforts of frontstage colleagues who are serving end-customers directly.

High-contact service encounters

Almost everybody can recount some horror story of a dreadful experience they have had with a service business – and usually, they *love* to talk about it! If pressed, many of these same people can also recount a really good service experience. Service personnel usually feature prominently in such dramas – in roles either as uncaring, incompetent, mean-spirited villains or as heroes who went out of their way to help, anticipating customer needs for resolving problems in a helpful and empathetic manner. Think about your own recent service experiences. In what ways have you been treated particularly well or badly lately by service personnel?

In high-contact service encounters, we tend to remember the role played by frontstage personnel better than any other aspect of the operation. In many respects, these employees *are* the service. A single employee may play many roles: part of the product and part of the delivery system, adviser and teacher, marketer, and even – if the customers get unruly – police officer (like a 'bouncer' in a nightclub). Service people may also play a vital role in lower-contact jobs where customers interact with the firm by telephone and an agent's voice is the only form of human contact.

Customer-contact personnel must attend to both operational and marketing goals. On the one hand, they help to 'manufacture' the service output. At the same time, they may also be responsible for marketing it (for instance, 'We've got some nice desserts to follow your main course' or 'We could clean your machine at the same time that we repair the electric motor' or 'Now would be a good time to open a separate account to save for your children's education'). In the eyes of their customers, service personnel may also be seen as an integral part of the service experience. In short, the service person may perform a triple role as operations specialist, marketer and part of the service product itself.

This multiplicity of roles – known as boundary spanning – may lead to role conflict among employees, especially when they feel as physically and psychologically close to customers as they do to managers and other employees.[3] In their article 'Intra-organizational aspects of service quality management: the employees' perspective' (reprinted on pages 616–34), Barbara Lewis and Gard Gabrielsen report findings from a survey of more than 300 front-line employees in Norwegian financial service firms to determine their perspective on recent service quality initiatives. Among the problems uncovered by this research was the absence of a service quality culture within the organizations and employee frustration with recent policy changes designed to improve productivity that made it more difficult for them to be both efficient and helpful to customers.

In general, organizations whose services involve extensive service encounters tend to be harder to manage than those without such encounters. Because of the human element, consistent service delivery becomes that much harder to achieve, thereby complicating the task of those responsible for productivity and quality improvement efforts.

Several special characteristics may be important in recruiting and training high-contact employees. These include interpersonal skills, personal appearance and grooming, knowledge of the product and the operation, selling capabilities and skills in co-production (that is, working jointly with customers to create the desired service). Additional characteristics, particularly valuable in selling situations, include monitoring nonverbal clues (such as the customer's body language) and adjusting one's behaviour in the context of social situations. Both technical and interpersonal skills are *necessary* but neither alone is *sufficient* for optimal job performance.[4]

Emotional labour

Service encounters entail more than just correct technical execution of a task. They also involve such human elements as personal demeanour, courtesy and empathy. This brings us to the notion of *emotional labour*, defined as the act of expressing socially appropriate (but sometimes false) emotions during service transactions.[5] For instance, some jobs require service workers to act in a friendly fashion towards customers, others to appear compassionate, sincere or even self-effacing. Trying to conform to customer expectations on such dimensions can prove to be a psychological burden for some service workers when they perceive themselves as having to act out emotions they do not feel.

Think for a moment of the following different service jobs and ask yourself what type of emotions you expect each of them to display to customers in the course of doing their job: emergency ward nurse, bill collector, computer repair technician, supermarket cashier, dentist, flight attendant, kindergarten teacher, prosecuting barrister, minister officiating at a baptism, police officer on motor patrol, waitress in a family restaurant, head waiter in an expensive French restaurant, stockbroker, funeral director. Now ask yourself: what is driving your own expectations as a prospective customer of such employees?

Customer-contact employees comply with so-called 'display rules' through both acting and the expression of spontaneous and genuine emotion.[6] Display rules generally reflect the norms imposed both by society – which may vary from one culture to another – and by specific occupations and organizations. For instance, consider your responses to the questions posed in the previous paragraph; we'd be surprised if your expectations for nurses weren't rather different from what you would expect of bill collectors. Expectations may also reflect the nature of a particular encounter (what emotions would you expect a waiter to display if you discovered a cockroach in your glass?). Acting requires employees to simulate emotions that they do not actually feel, accomplished by careful presentation of verbal and nonverbal cues, such as facial expression, gestures and voice tone. Within limits, such acting skills can be taught; some people are natural actors. Under certain conditions, service providers may spontaneously experience the expected emotion without any need for acting, as when a firefighter feels sympathy for an injured child taken from a burning building.

Human resource (HR) managers need to be aware that performing emotional labour, day after day, can be stressful for employees as they strive to show feelings that may be false. From a marketing standpoint, however, failure to display the emotions that customers expect can be damaging and may lead to complaints that 'employees don't seem to care'. The challenge for HR managers is to determine what customers expect, recruit the most suitable employees and train them well. Grayson concludes that investment in such human resource strategies – which can be quite expensive – is most worthwhile for service situations in which exchanges between employees and customers take place in the context of long-term relationships, but less important when exchanges are simply discrete transactions in which the two parties are unlikely to encounter each other again.[7]

When service personnel have been exposed to traumatic events, such as injuries or death involving customers or co-workers, professional counselling may be needed to allow the workers to express their feelings and share them with others. Special training on how to handle such emotions is often offered to workers in such fields as policing, firefighting and emergency medical care, because of the frequency with which they are likely to be exposed to traumatic situations in the normal course of their jobs.

Job design and recruitment

The goal of job design is to study the requirements of the operation, the nature of customer desires, the needs and capabilities of employees, and the characteristics of operational equipment in order to develop job descriptions that strike the best balance between these sometimes conflicting demands. Many of the most demanding jobs in service businesses are so-called boundary-spanning positions, where employees are expected to be fast and efficient at executing operational tasks as well as courteous and helpful in dealing with customers. Many service encounters are potentially 'a three-cornered fight' between the needs of semi-conflicting parties: the customer, the server and the service firm. If the job is not designed carefully, or the wrong people picked to fill it, there's a real risk that employees may become burnt-out and unproductive.

Empowerment of employees[8]

How important is the much advocated practice of empowering employees to use their discretion to serve customers better? Job designs should reflect the fact that service personnel may encounter customer requests for assistance in remote sites at any hour of the day and night. For instance, employees of Bromley's EH&TS department spend most of their time out in the community, often entering people's homes or workplaces. Under the right conditions, providing employees with greater discretion (and training in how to exercise their judgement) may enable them to provide superior service on the spot without referring to rule books or taking time to seek permission from higher authority. From a humanistic standpoint, the notion of encouraging employees to exercise initiative and discretion is an appealing one. Empowerment looks to the performer of the task to find solutions to service problems and to make appropriate decisions about customizing service delivery. It depends for its success on what is sometimes called *enablement* – giving workers the tools and resources they need to take on these new responsibilities.

Advocates claim that the empowerment approach is more likely to yield motivated employees and satisfied customers than the 'production-line' alternative, in which management designs a relatively standardized system and expects workers to execute tasks within narrow guidelines. But is the choice between these two approaches really so obvious? The truth is, different situations may require different solutions. The payoffs from greater empowerment must be set against increased costs for selection and training, higher labour costs, slower service as customer-contact personnel devote more time to individual customers, and less consistency in service delivery.

Control vs. involvement

The production-line approach to managing people is based upon the well-established 'control' model of organization design and management, with its clearly defined roles, top-down control systems, hierarchical pyramid structure and assumption that management knows best. Empowerment, by contrast, is based on the 'involvement' (or 'commitment') model, which assumes that most employees can make good decisions – and produce good ideas for operating the business – if they are properly socialized, trained and informed. It also assumes that employees can be internally motivated to perform effectively and that they are capable of self-control and self-direction. Although broad use of the term 'empowerment' is relatively new, the underlying philosophy of employee involvement is not.

In the control model, four key features are concentrated at the top of the organization, while in the involvement model these features are cascaded down through the organization:

1. Information about organizational performance (e.g., operating results and measures of competitive performance).
2. Rewards based on organizational performance (e.g., profit-sharing and stock ownership).
3. Knowledge that enables employees to understand and contribute to organizational performance (e.g., problem-solving skills).
4. Power to make decisions that influence work procedures and organizational direction (e.g., through quality circles and self-managing teams).

Levels of employee involvement

The empowerment and production-line approaches are at opposite ends of a spectrum that reflects increasing levels of employee involvement as additional knowledge, information, power and rewards are pushed down to the front line. Empowerment can take place at several levels:

■ *Suggestion involvement* empowers employees to make recommendations through formalized programmes, but their day-to-day work activities do not really change. McDonald's, often portrayed as an archetype of the production-line approach, listens closely to its front line; innovations ranging from Egg McMuffin to methods of wrapping burgers without leaving a thumbprint on the bun were invented by employees.

■ *Job involvement* represents a dramatic opening up of job content. Jobs are redesigned to allow employees to use a wider array of skills. In complex service organizations such as airlines and hospitals, where individual employees cannot offer all facets of a service, job involvement is often accomplished through the use of teams. To cope with the added demands accompanying this form of empowerment, employees require training, and supervisors need to be reoriented from directing the group to facilitating its performance in supportive ways.

■ *High involvement* gives even the lowest-level employees a sense of involvement in the total organization's performance. Information is shared. Employees develop skills in teamwork, problem-solving and business operations, and they participate in work-unit management decisions. There is profit-sharing and employee ownership of shares in the business.

As shown in Table 14.1, a strategy of empowerment is most likely to be appropriate when certain factors are present within the organization and its environment. It's important to emphasize that not all employees are necessarily eager to be empowered. Many employees do not seek personal growth within their jobs and would prefer to work to specific directions rather than having to use their own initiative.

Table 14.1 ■ Factors favouring a strategy of employee empowerment

- Business strategy is based on competitive differentiation and on offering personalized, customized service.

- The approach to customers is based on extended relationships rather than on short-term transactions.

- The organization uses technologies that are complex and non-routine in nature.

- The business environment is unpredictable and surprises are to be expected.

- Existing managers are comfortable with letting employees work independently for the benefit of both the organization and its customers.

- Employees have a strong need to grow and deepen their skills in the work environment, are interested in working with others, and have good interpersonal and group process skills.

Source: David E. Bowen and Edward E. Lawler, III, 'The Empowerment of Service Workers: What, Why, How and When', *Sloan Management Review*, Spring 1992, pp. 32–9.

Recruiting the right people for the job

There's no such thing as the perfect, universal employee. First, some service jobs require prior qualifications, as opposed to giving employees the necessary training after they are recruited. A nurse can apply for a job as a hotel receptionist, but the reverse is not true unless the applicant has nursing qualifications. Second, different positions – even within the same firm – are best filled by people with different styles and personalities. It helps to have an outgoing personality in many frontstage jobs which involve constantly meeting new customers; a shy, retiring person, by contrast, might be more comfortable working backstage and always dealing with the same people. Someone who loves to be physically on the go might do better as a restaurant waiter/waitress or courier than in a more sedentary job as a booking clerk or bank cashier. Finally, as Levering and Moskowitz stress:

> No company is perfect for everyone. This may be especially true in good places to work since these firms tend to have real character . . . their own culture. Companies with distinctive personalities tend to attract – and repel – certain types of individuals.[9]

Recruiting criteria should reflect the human dimensions of the job as well as the technical requirements. This brings us back to the notions of emotional labour and service as theatre. The Walt Disney Company, which is in the entertainment business, actually uses the term *casting* and assesses prospective employees in terms of their potential for on-stage or backstage work. On-stage workers, known as *cast members*, are assigned to those roles for which their appearance, personality and skills provide the best match.

Who must be hired vs. what can be taught

As part of its turnaround efforts in the early 1980s, British Airways started paying more attention to its passengers' concerns and opinions. When research findings showed that travellers desired warmer, friendlier service from cabin crew, the airline first tried to develop these characteristics through training. But human resource managers soon concluded that while good manners and the need to smile could be taught, warmth itself could not. So the airline changed its recruitment criteria to favour candidates with naturally warm personalities. It also changed its recruitment advertising to capture the challenges of the work instead of emphasizing the glamour of travel. For instance, one advert showed a drawing of a small child sitting in an airline seat and clutching a teddy bear. The headline read: 'His mum told him not to talk to strangers. So what's he having for lunch?'

What makes outstanding service performers so special? Often it's things that *cannot* be taught, qualities that are intrinsic to the people, qualities they would bring with them to any employer. As one study of high performers observed:

> Energy . . . cannot be taught, it has to be hired. The same is true for charm, for detail orientation, for work ethic, for neatness. Some of these things can be enhanced with on-the-job training . . . or incentives . . . . But by and large, such qualities are instilled early on.[10]

The logical conclusion is that service businesses that are dependent on the human qualities of their frontstage service personnel should devote great care to attracting and hiring the right candidates.

A number of progressive companies have come to the conclusion that the selection process should start not with the candidate, but with the individuals responsible for recruiting. In a sense, it is the recruiters who must ensure that hiring decisions reflect and reinforce the company's distinctive culture. For instance, at Southwest Airlines, recently rated the best company to work for in America, everyone hired to work in the airline's People Department – Southwest doesn't use the terms 'human resources' or 'personnel' – comes from a marketing or customer-contact background.[11] This marketing orientation is displayed in internal research on job descriptions and selection criteria, whereby each department is asked: 'What are you looking for?' rather than told: 'This is what we think you need!' Southwest invites supervisors and peers (with whom future candidates will be working) to participate in the in-depth interviewing and selection process. More unusually, it invites its own frequent flyers to participate in the initial interviews for cabin crew and to tell candidates what they, the passengers, value. The People Department admits to being amazed at the enthusiasm with which these busy customers have greeted this invitation and at their willingness to devote time to this task.

Challenges and opportunities in recruiting workers for technology-based jobs

It used to be thought that only manufacturing jobs could be exported. Today, however, technology allows both backstage and frontstage service jobs to be located around the world. American insurance companies, for instance, have recruited workers in Ireland to process claims. Paperwork is flown in daily from the United States and digitized information transmitted back to mainframe computers on the other side of the Atlantic (because of the five-hour time difference, the Irish are using those mainframes at times when they would normally be underutilized).

Barbados, Jamaica, Singapore, India and the Philippines are emerging as other potential English-speaking locations for telecommunicated services, not only for backstage work but also for such frontstage supplementary services as airline reservations and technical helplines. Customers may be quite unaware of where the service person they are talking to is located. The key issue is that they deal with people who have the personal and technical skills – plus the enabling technological support – to provide high-quality service.

Expert systems can be used to leverage employees' skills to perform work that previously required higher qualifications, more extensive training or simply years of experience. Some systems are designed to train novices by gradually enabling them to perform at higher levels. Many expert systems capture and make available to all the scarce expertise of outstanding performers. American Express uses a well-known expert system called Authorizer's Assistant (originally called Laura's Brain, after a star authorizer), which contains the expertise of its best credit authorizers. It has improved the quality and speed of credit decisions dramatically and contributed enormously to corporate profitability.[12] An expert system contains three elements: a knowledge base about a particular subject; an inference engine that mimics a human expert's reasoning in order to draw conclusions from facts and figures, solve problems and answer questions; and a user interface that gathers information from – and gives it to – the person using the system. Like human experts, such systems can give customized advice and may accept and handle incomplete and uncertain data.

Rapid developments in information technology are permitting service businesses to make radical improvements in business processes and even completely re-engineer their operations.[13] These developments sometimes result in drastic changes for existing employees. In other instances, firms have redefined jobs, created new employee profiles for recruiting purposes and sought to hire employees with a different set of qualifications.

In the early 1990s, Singapore Airlines (SIA) was having trouble in recruiting and retaining check-in agents for its home base at Changi Airport. It was getting harder to recruit people with the necessary skills at the wages SIA was willing to offer. And once they were on the job, many agents found it rather unchallenging. The predictable result: relatively high turnover and constant repetition of the expensive recruitment and training process. As part of a major programme to update its departure control systems, SIA computer specialists worked to create new software for check-in procedures, featuring screen formats with pull-down windows, menu-driven commands and other innovations on the video terminal displays – all designed to speed and simplify usage. The net result is that SIA has been able to lower the educational criteria for the check-in position. The job is now open to people who would not previously have qualified and who view the work and the wages as fairly attractive. Because the new system is so much easier to use, only one week's training is needed – a significant saving to SIA. Employee satisfaction with this job is up and turnover is down. Finally, agents are able to process passengers faster, making the former more productive and the latter happier.

A growing number of customer-contact employees work by telephone, never meeting customers face-to-face. As with other types of service work, these jobs can be very rewarding or they can place employees in an electronic equivalent of the old-fashioned sweatshop. As discussed in the BT example below, recruiting people with the right skills and personalities, training them well and giving them a decent working environment are some of the keys to success in this area.

Recruiting employees who work by phone at BT

BT (formerly British Telecom) is not only a major supplier of telecommunication services, but also an active user of its own medium, the telephone, for managing relationships with its business accounts. Like a growing number of firms that do business by phone, it is very dependent for its success on recruiting and retaining employees who are good at telephone-based transactions with customers whom they never see. Executives responsible for BT's telephone account management (TAM) operation, serving small business customers, are highly selective in their recruitment efforts. They look for bright, self-confident people who can be trained to listen to customers' needs and use structured, probing questions to build a database of information on each of the 1,000 accounts for which an account manager is responsible.

BT begins its recruitment process with a telephone interview to see if candidates have the poise, maturity and good speaking voice to project themselves well and inspire trust in a telephone-based job. (Curiously, most recruiters of telephone-based employees leave this all-important telephone test until much later in the process.) Those who pass this screen proceed to written tests and personal interviews.

Successful candidates receive intensive training. BT has built special training schools to create a consistent approach to customer care. Would-be account managers receive 13 weeks' training over a 12-month period, interspersed with live front-line experience at their home bases. They must develop in-depth knowledge of all the services and customer premises equipment that BT sells, as well as the skills needed to build relationships with customers and to understand their business needs. Modern telecommunications technology is bewildering, for so much is changing so rapidly. Customers need a trusted adviser to act as consultant and problem-solver. And it is this role that BT's TAM programme has succeeded in filling. For all the impressive supporting technology, the programme would fail without good people at the other end of the phone.

Service jobs as relationships

Marketing theory argues that successful relationships are built on mutually satisfying exchanges from which both customers and suppliers gain value. This same notion of value can be applied to any employee who has a choice of whether or not to work for a particular organization; the best employees usually do have opportunities to move on if dissatisfied. The net value of a job is the extent to which its benefits exceed its associated costs. The most obvious benefits are pay, health insurance and pension funding. However, most jobs also generate other benefits. Some offer learning or experience-building opportunities; some positions provide deep satisfaction because they are inherently interesting or provide a sense of accomplishment; still others provide companionship, a valued chance to meet other people, a sense of dignity and self-worth, opportunities to travel and the chance to make a social contribution.

But working in any job has its costs, too, beginning with the time spent on the job and travelling to and from work. Most jobs also entail some monetary costs, ranging from special clothes to commuting and childcare. Stress can be a psychological and physical cost in a demanding job. Unpleasant working conditions may involve exposure to noise, smells and temperature extremes. And, of course, some jobs require intense physical or mental effort. It can be helpful for HR managers to view employees as customers who may leave if dissatisfied. Measuring employee satisfaction can help to identify what workers see as the benefits of their job and what as drawbacks.[14] Decisions to change the nature of the service operation frequently affect employees, too. The perceived value of their jobs may go up or down as a result. But not everybody has the same priorities and concerns – there is segmentation among employees as well as among customers. Part of the HR challenge is to match round pegs to round holes of the right diameter.

Frontstage service jobs add another dimension: frequent customer contact – sometimes but not always involving extended relationships with the same customers. Depending on the employee's personality, such encounters may be seen in the abstract as a benefit to enjoy or a cost to be borne. In reality, good training, good support and satisfied customers should increase the pleasure (or diminish the pain), while the reverse will also be true.

Job design cannot be restricted to ensuring that the firm gets its money's worth out of employees. It must also consider the design of the working environment, and whether or not employees have the tools and facilities they need to deliver excellent service. Smart human resource managers know that if a job is changed through redesign, it will become more or less attractive to certain types of employees – and they can usually predict which ones. To an increasing degree, health and safety legislation is requiring changes in the workplace to eliminate physical and even psychological hazards, but only management can create a positive working climate – and that takes a long time. Reducing the negative aspects of the job and improving its positive ones may make it easier for firms to recruit and retain the best available employees, without having to pay premium salaries and increase the emphasis on conventional 'benefits'. Employees who enjoy their work are more likely than unhappy ones to give good service to customers.

In Europe, as in many parts of the world, significant changes are taking place in the context of employment (including sustained high unemployment in some countries), relationships between employers and employees, and in the nature of jobs themselves.[15] Technology is radically changing the nature of some jobs, eliminating others and creating new ones. Backstage service jobs and those based on telecommunication links, such as customer service centres, are being shifted to new geographic locations – sometimes even to a different country or a different continent. In the absence of full employment, a shift in the balance of power has taken place between employers and labour, with the former the beneficiaries. Under such circumstances, it is relatively easier for senior managers to take decisions that favour shareholders rather than employees, often in ways that should raise ethical concerns.

For many workers and managers, these broad environmental changes can lead to insecurity. Others, by contrast, may come to the conclusion that they are responsible for their own career paths and owe no loyalty to their present employers. The latter, it should be noted, are often the very employees whom firms should be trying to retain, either because they are ambitious and high-performing, or because their skills are in short supply.

Employee retention and customer retention

Researchers have found strong correlations between employees' attitudes and perceptions of service quality among customers of the same organization.[16] One retail banking study showed that when employees reported a strong service orientation imperative in the branch where they worked, customers reported that they received higher quality service. A follow-up study determined that customer intentions to switch to a competitor could be predicted, based on employee perceptions of the quality of service delivered. It also found that employee turnover probabilities were predictable, based on customer perceptions of service quality. Simply put, where customers reported high service quality, employees were less likely to leave. A reasonable inference is that it is not very rewarding to work in an environment where service is poor and customers dissatisfied. A study of a van rental business found that higher levels of employee satisfaction were related to both lower turnover and fewer worker compensation claims.[17]

When jobs are badly paid, boring and repetitive, with minimal training, service is poor and turnover high. Poor service generates high customer turnover, too, making the working environment even less rewarding. As a result, the firm spends all its resources trying to recruit both new customers and new employees. Loyal employees, by contrast, know the job and, in many cases, the customers too. To the extent that long-term employees are customer-oriented, knowledgeable and remain motivated, better service and higher customer retention should result.

Researchers have been able to document the economic value of both customer retention (see Chapter 6) and employee retention.[18] Many companies restrict their economic potential through human resource strategies that are practically guaranteed to ensure high turnover of their personnel.

Cycles of failure, mediocrity and success

All too often, bad working environments translate into dreadful service, with employees treating customers the way their managers treat them. Businesses with high employee turnover are frequently stuck in what has been termed the 'Cycle of Failure'. Others, which offer job security but little scope for personal initiative, may suffer from an equally undesirable 'Cycle of Mediocrity'. However, there is potential for both vicious and virtuous cycles in service employment, with the latter being termed the 'Cycle of Success'.[19]

The cycle of failure

In many service industries the search for productivity is pursued with a vengeance. One solution takes the form of simplifying work routines and hiring workers as cheaply as possible to perform repetitive work tasks that require little or no training. The cycle of failure captures the implications of such a strategy, with its two concentric but interactive cycles: one involving failures with employees; the second, with customers (Figure 14.1).

The *employee cycle of failure* begins with a narrow design of jobs to accommodate low skill levels, emphasis on rules rather than service and the use of technology to control quality. A strategy of low wages is accompanied by minimal effort on selection or training. The consequences include bored employees who lack the ability to respond to customer problems, become dissatisfied and develop a poor service attitude. The outcomes for the firm are low service quality and high employee turnover. Because of weak profit margins, the cycle repeats itself with hiring of more low-paid employees to work in this unrewarding atmosphere.

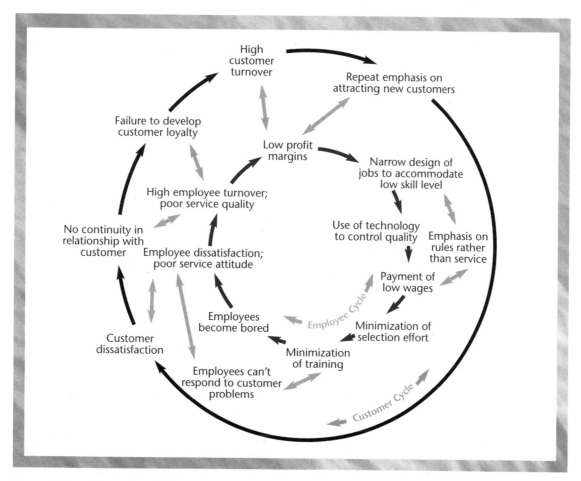

Figure 14.1 ■ The cycle of failure

Source: Leonard A. Schlesinger and James L. Heskett, 'Breaking the Cycle of Failure in Services', *Sloan Management Review*, Spring 1991, pp. 17–28.

The *customer cycle of failure* begins with repeated emphasis on attracting new customers who become dissatisfied with employee performance and the lack of continuity implicit in continually changing faces. These customers fail to develop any loyalty to the supplier and turn over as rapidly as the staff, thus requiring an endless search for new customers to maintain sales volume. The departure of discontented customers is especially worrying in light of what we now know about the greater profitability of a loyal customer base. For conscientious managers, it should be deeply disturbing to contemplate the social implications of an enormous pool of nomadic service employees moving from one low-paying employer to the next and experiencing a stream of personal failures in part because of the unwillingness of these employers to invest in efforts to break the cycle.

Managers have offered a veritable litany of excuses and justifications for perpetuating this cycle:

- 'You just can't get good people nowadays.'
- 'People just don't want to work today.'
- 'To get good people would cost too much and you can't pass on these cost increases to customers.'
- 'It's not worth training our front-line people when they leave you so quickly.'
- 'High turnover is simply an inevitable part of our business. You've got to learn to live with it.'[20]

Too many managers make short-sighted assumptions about the financial implications of low pay/high turnover human resource strategies. Part of the problem is failure to measure all relevant costs. Often omitted are three key cost variables: the cost of constant recruiting, hiring and training (which is as much a time cost for managers as a financial cost), the lower productivity of inexperienced new workers, and the costs of constantly attracting new customers (requiring extensive advertising and promotional discounts). Also ignored are two revenue variables: future revenue streams that might have continued for years but are lost when unhappy customers take their business elsewhere; and potential income from prospective customers who are deterred by negative word-of-mouth. Finally, there are less easily quantifiable costs such as disruptions to service while a job remains unfilled, and loss of the departing employee's knowledge of the business (and its customers).

The cycle of mediocrity

Another vicious employment cycle is the 'Cycle of Mediocrity' (Figure 14.2). It's most likely to be found in large, bureaucratic organizations – often typified by state monopolies, industrial cartels or regulated oligopolies – where there is little incentive to improve performance and where fear of entrenched unions may discourage management from adopting more innovative labour practices.

In such environments (which today are in decline), service delivery standards tend to be prescribed by rigid rule-books, oriented towards standardized service, operational efficiencies and prevention of both employee fraud and favouritism towards specific customers. Employees often expect to spend their entire working lives with the organization. Job responsibilities tend to be narrowly and unimaginatively defined, tightly categorized by grade and scope of responsibilities, and further rigidified by union rules. Salary increases and promotions are based on longevity, with

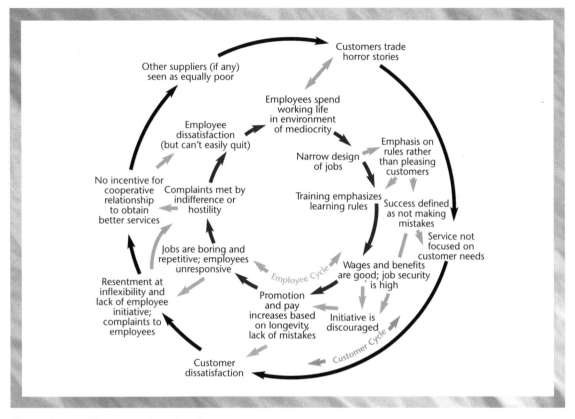

Figure 14.2 ■ The cycle of mediocrity

Source: Christopher H. Lovelock, 'Managing Services: The Human Factor', in W.J. Glynn and J.G. Barnes (eds), *Understanding Services Management*, Chichester: John Wiley & Sons, 1995, p. 228.

successful performance in a job being measured by absence of mistakes, rather than by high productivity or outstanding customer service. Training, such as it is, focuses on learning the rules and the technical aspects of the job, not on improving human interactions with customers and fellow-workers. Since there are minimal allowances for flexibility or employee initiative, jobs tend to be boring and repetitive. However, in contrast to *cycle of failure* jobs, most positions provide adequate pay and often good benefits, combined with high security – thus making employees reluctant to leave. This lack of mobility is compounded by an absence of marketable skills that would be valued by organizations in other fields of endeavour.

Customers find such organizations frustrating to deal with. Faced with bureaucratic hassles, lack of service flexibility and unwillingness of employees to make an effort to serve them better on grounds such as 'That's not my job', users of the service may become resentful. What happens when there is nowhere else for customers to go – either because the service provider holds a monopoly or because all other available players are perceived as being as bad or worse? We shouldn't be surprised if dissatisfied customers display hostility towards service employees who, feeling trapped in their jobs and powerless to improve the situation, protect themselves through such mechanisms as withdrawal into indifference, playing overtly by the rule-book or countering rudeness with rudeness. The net result? A vicious cycle of mediocrity in which unhappy customers continually complain to sullen employees (and also to other customers) about poor service and bad attitudes, generating ever greater defensiveness and lack of caring on the part of the staff. Under such circumstances, there is little incentive for customers to cooperate with the organization to achieve better service.

The cycle of success

Some firms reject the assumptions underlying the cycles of failure or mediocrity. Instead, they take a long-term view of financial performance, seeking to prosper by investing in their people in order to create a 'cycle of success' (Figure 14.3). As with failure or mediocrity, success applies to both employees and customers. Broadened job designs are accompanied by training and empowerment practices that allow frontstage personnel to control quality. With more focused recruitment, more intensive training and better wages, employees are likely to be happier in their work and to provide higher quality, customer-pleasing service. Regular customers also appreciate the continuity in service relationships resulting from lower turnover, and so are more likely to remain loyal. Profit margins tend to be higher and the organization is free to focus its marketing efforts on reinforcing customer loyalty through customer retention strategies, which are usually much less costly to implement than strategies for attracting new customers.

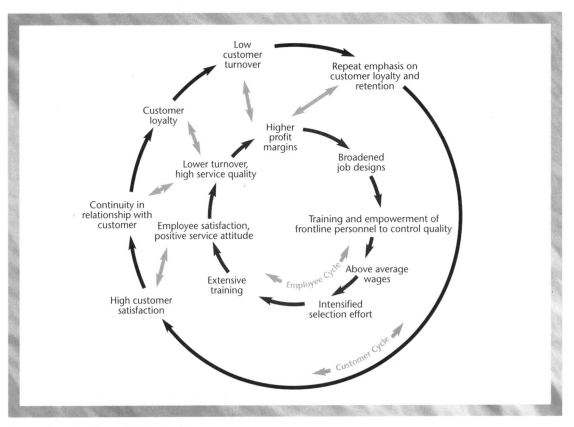

Figure 14.3 ■ The cycle of success

Source: Leonard A. Schlesinger and James L. Heskett, 'Breaking the Cycle of Failure in Services', *Sloan Management Review*, Spring 1991, pp. 17–28.

Deregulation of many service industries and privatization of government corporations have often been instrumental in rescuing organizations from the cycle of mediocrity. In both the US and Canada, formerly monopolistic regional telephone companies have been forced to adopt a more competitive stance. In many countries, once-mediocre public corporations – such as BT and Lufthansa – have undergone radical culture changes in the wake of privatization and exposure to a more competitive environment. A slimming down of the ranks (usually resulting in retention of the more dynamic and service-oriented employees), redefinition of performance criteria, intensive training and major reorganizations have created service firms that are much better placed to offer customers good service. In many parts of Europe, such changes are currently in full swing.

The role of unions

If HRM innovations are to achieve their full potential, employee cooperation is essential. The power of organized labour is widely cited as an excuse for not adopting new approaches in both service and manufacturing businesses. 'We'd never get it past the unions', managers say, wringing their hands and muttering darkly about restrictive work practices. Unions are often portrayed in the press as villains, especially when high-profile strikes inconvenience millions; past examples of particularly disruptive industrial disputes range from British railway workers to Air France employees, and from Irish bank personnel to Canadian postal workers.

Many managers seem to be rather antagonistic towards unions. Jeffrey Pfeffer has observed wryly that 'the subject of unions and collective bargaining is . . . one that causes otherwise sensible people to lose their objectivity'.[21] He urges a pragmatic approach to this issue, emphasizing that 'the effects of unions depend very much on what *management* does'. The higher wages, lower turnover, clearly established grievance procedures and improved working conditions often found in highly unionized organizations may yield positive benefits in a well-managed service organization where there is mutual respect between management and other employees. From a marketing perspective, greater experience on the job and long-term familiarity with customers may help to boost productivity and quality, as well as cementing customer loyalty. We need to be careful to avoid stereotyping unions in the outdated mould of militantly antagonistic environments where extreme demarcation of job responsibilities leads to slow, surly and unresponsive service for customers, punctuated by frequent work stoppages. That's an outdated and unhelpful perspective in most European countries today.

Many of Europe's most successful service businesses are, in fact, highly unionized. The inescapable conclusion is that the presence of unions in a service company is not an automatic barrier to high performance and innovation, unless there is a long history of mistrust, acrimonious relationships and confrontation. However, management cannot rule by fiat: consultation and negotiation with union representatives are essential if employees are to accept new ideas (conditions that are equally valid in non-unionized firms, too).

Human resource management in a multicultural context

The trend towards a global economy means that more and more service firms are operating across national frontiers. Other important trends are increased tourism and business travel, plus substantial immigration of people from different cultural backgrounds into developed economies, as is now true of a majority of European countries. The net result is pressure on service organizations to serve a more diverse array of customers – with different cultural expectations and speaking a variety of languages – and to recruit a more diverse workforce.

Striking a balance between diversity and conformity to common standards is not a simple task, since societal norms vary across cultures. When McDonald's opened a fast-food restaurant in Moscow, management trained staff members to smile at customers. However, this particular norm did not exist in Russia and some patrons concluded that staff members were making fun of them! Another example of how transferring American standards to European operations may run into cultural conflicts comes from the troubled early history of Euro Disney (see box below).

Part of the HRM challenge as it relates to culture is to determine which performance standards are central and which should be treated more flexibly. For instance, some public service agencies in Britain (and elsewhere) which require employees to wear uniforms have been willing to allow Sikh employees to wear a matching colour turban with badge. But others have generated conflict by insisting on use of traditional uniform caps. Multiculturalism may also require new HRM procedures. Thus, the decision to be more responsive to customers (and even employees) whose first language is not English may require changes in recruiting criteria, use of role playing exercises and language training.[22]

Euro Disney and the challenges of multiculturalism

Few service ventures of recent years have attracted as much media comment and coverage as the Walt Disney Co.'s latest venture, Disneyland Paris. Although most of the reported financial losses stem from real estate problems and low occupancy in the hotels, the cultural difficulties of creating and running an American-style theme park in the heart of Europe have been widely publicized. Since Disneyland Paris replicates three successful Disney theme parks, top management's objective has been to ensure that the park adapts itself to European conditions without losing the American feel that has always been seen as one of its main draws. For officials of the European company, Euro Disney, the new park just outside Paris has proved even more of a challenge than Disney's first foreign theme park, Tokyo Disneyland, which opened in Japan in 1983. Unlike the California, Florida or Tokyo parks, no one nationality dominates the Paris park. So

handling languages and cultures has required careful planning, not least in terms of employee recruitment, training and motivation.

Knowledge of two or more languages has been an important criterion in hiring 'cast members' (front-line employees). Months before opening day, recruitment centres were set up in Paris, London, Amsterdam and Frankfurt. During the park's first season (1992), approximately two-thirds of those hired were French nationals; the balance included another 75 nationalities, principally British, Dutch, German and Irish. Some knowledge of French is required of all employees; about 75 per cent of employees spoke this language fluently, another 75 per cent spoke English, roughly 25 per cent spoke Spanish and 25 per cent, German.

The reservations centre caters to people of many tongues, with special phone lines for each of 12 different languages. The main information centre in the park, City Hall, is staffed by cast

Euro Disney and the challenges of multiculturalism (*continued*)

members speaking a broad cross-section of tongues. Special procedures have been instituted at the park's medical centre to handle medical emergencies involving speakers of less commonly encountered languages. With over 70 nationalities represented among its employees, there is a high probability that a cast member can be found somewhere on site to interpret in such a situation. The company has noted the language capabilities of every employee, can access them by computer (who do we have on duty who speaks Turkish?), and can page them immediately by beeper or walkie-talkie.

However, Euro Disney has encountered many cultural problems in training and motivation. The company's 1990 Annual Report announced that 'a leading priority was to indoctrinate all employees in the Disney service philosophy, in addition to training them in operational policies and procedures'. The apparent goal was to transform all employees, 60 per cent of whom were French, into clean-cut, user-friendly, American-style service providers. Since the founding of Disneyland in 1958, Disney has been known for its strict professional guidelines. 'The Look Book', for example, dictated that female employees should wear only clear nail polish, very little, if any, make-up, and, until recent years, only flesh-coloured stockings. Men could not wear beards or moustaches and had to keep their

hair short and tapered. Guests should be greeted within 60 seconds of entering a facility and helped as needed.

According to media reports, a key challenge has been to train French employees to adopt Disney standards. The park's manager of training and development for Disney University was quoted as saying: 'The French are not known for their hospitality. But Disney is.' During the first four months of operations, more than 1,000 employees left the park. According to management, half resigned, and the rest were asked to leave. Subsequently, the women's grooming guidelines were modified because 'what is considered a classic beauty in Europe is not considered a classic beauty in America'. Female cast members can now wear pink or red nail polish, red lipstick and different coloured stockings as long as they 'complement [the] outfit and are in dark, subdued colours'.

Another Disney trademark is to smile a lot. Yet as one observer commented, 'If the French are asked to smile, they will answer "I'll smile if I want to. Convince me."' The training had to be adapted in order to suit the European workforce. Although Disney stressed total customer satisfaction, in the eyes of some employees the company had imposed controls that had made that goal impossible to deliver.

Source: Based on information in *Management Today*, October 1997, pp. 80–1.

Conclusion

It's probably harder to duplicate high-performance human assets than any other corporate resource. To the extent that employees understand and support the goals of an organization, have the skills needed to succeed in performing their jobs, work well together in teams, recognize the importance of ensuring customer satisfaction and have the authority and self-confidence to use their own initiative in problem-solving, the marketing and operational functions should actually be easier to manage.

Study questions

1. List five ways in which investment in recruiting and selection, training and ongoing motivation of employees will pay dividends in customer satisfaction for such organizations as (a) an airline, (b) a hospital, (c) a restaurant.

2. Define what is meant by the control and involvement models of management.

3. What is emotional labour? Explain the ways in which it may cause stress for employees in specific jobs. Illustrate with suitable examples.

4. Identify the factors favouring a strategy of employee empowerment.

5. What is the distinction between empowerment and enablement? Can you have one without the other?

6. Highlight specific ways in which technology – particularly information technology – is changing the nature of service jobs. Provide examples of situations in which use of IT is likely to (a) enhance and (b) detract from employee job satisfaction.

7. What can a marketing perspective bring to the practice of human resource management?

8. What important ethical issues do you see facing human resource managers in high contact service organizations?

Notes

1. From *Management Today*, October 1997, pp. 80–1.
2. Hal E. Rosenbluth, *The Customer Comes Second*, New York: William Morrow, 1992, p. 25.
3. David E. Bowen and Benjamin Schneider, 'Boundary-Spanning Role Employees and the Service Encounter: Some Guidelines for Management and Research', in J.A. Czepiel, M.R. Solomon and C.F. Surprenant, *The Service Encounter,* Lexington MA: Lexington Books, 1985, pp. 127–48.
4. David A. Tansik, 'Managing Human Resource Issues for High Contact Service Personnel', in D.E. Bowen, R.B. Chase, T.G. Cummings and Associates, *Service Management Effectiveness*, San Francisco: Jossey-Bass, 1990, pp. 152–76.
5. Arlie R. Hochschild, *The Managed Heart: Commercialization of Human Feeling*, Berkeley: University of California Press, 1983.
6. Blake E. Ashforth and Ronald W. Humphrey, 'Emotional Labor in Service Roles: The Influence of Identity', *Academy of Management Review*, Vol. 18, No. 1, 1993, pp. 88–115.
7. Kent Grayson, 'Customer Responses to Emotional Labour in Discrete and Relational Service Exchange', *International Journal of Service Industry Management*, Vol. 9, No. 2, 1998, pp. 126–54.
8. This section is closely based on David E. Bowen and Edward E. Lawler, III, 'The Empowerment of Service Workers: What, Why, How and When', *Sloan Management Review*, Spring 1992, pp. 32–9.
9. Robert Levering and Milton Moskowitz, *The 100 Best Companies to Work for in America*, New York: Currency/Doubleday, 1993.
10. Bill Fromm and Len Schlesinger, *The Real Heroes of Business*, New York: Currency Doubleday, 1994, pp. 315–16.
11. Robert Levering and Milton Moskowitz, 'The 100 Best Companies to Work for in America', *Fortune*, 12 January 1998, pp. 84–95.

12. Rajendra Sisodia, 'Expert Marketing with Expert Systems', *Marketing Management*, Spring 1992, pp. 32–47.

13. Thomas H. Davenport, *Process Innovation: Reengineering Work through Information Technology*, Boston: Harvard Business School Press, 1993.

14. Roland T. Rust, Greg L. Stewart, Heather Miller and Debbie Pielack, 'The Satisfaction and Retention of Frontline Employees: A Customer Satisfaction Measurement Approach', *International Journal of Service Industry Management*, Vol. 7, No. 5, 1996, pp. 62–80.

15. Joel Bonamy and Nicole May, 'Service and Employment Relations', *The Service Industries Journal*, Vol. 17, No. 4, 1997, pp. 544–63.

16. This research is summarized in Benjamin Schneider and David E. Bowen, *Winning the Service Game*, Boston: Harvard Business School Press, 1995; and Benjamin Schneider, Susan S. White and Michelle C. Paul, 'Linking Service Climate and Customer Perceptions of Service Quality: Test of a Causal Model', *Journal of Applied Psychology*, Vol. 83, No. 2, 1998, pp. 150–63.

17. Benjamin Schneider, 'HRM – A Service Perspective: Towards a Customer-focused HRM?', *International Journal of Service Industry Management*, Vol. 5, No. 1, 1994, pp. 64–76.

18. James L. Heskett, W. Earl Sasser and Leonard A. Schlesinger, *The Service Profit Chain*, New York: The Free Press, 1997.

19. The terms 'cycle of failure' and 'cycle of success' were coined by Leonard A. Schlesinger and James L. Heskett, 'Breaking the Cycle of Failure in Services', *Sloan Management Review*, Spring 1991, pp. 17–28. The term 'cycle of mediocrity' comes from Christopher H. Lovelock, 'Managing Services: The Human Factor', in W.J. Glynn and J.G. Barnes (eds), *Understanding Services Management*, Chichester: John Wiley & Sons, 1995, p. 228.

20. Schlesinger and Heskett, *op. cit.*

21. Jeffrey Pfeffer, *Competitive Advantage Through People*, Boston: Harvard Business School Press, 1994, pp. 160–3.

22. Christopher Lovelock, *Product Plus: How Product + Service = Competitive Advantage*, New York: McGraw-Hill, 1994, chapter 19.

CHAPTER 15

Organizing for service leadership

Learning objectives

After reading and reflecting on this chapter, you should be able to:

1. Understand that marketing activities in a service organization extend beyond the responsibilities assigned to a traditional marketing department.

2. Recognize the interdependence in service organizations of the marketing, operations and human management functions.

3. Discuss the causes of interfunctional tensions and how to avoid them.

4. Be familiar with new organizational forms for service businesses beyond the traditional pyramid-shaped hierarchy.

5. Appreciate the nature of leadership in a service organization.

Building marketing competence in a ferry company[1]

When Stena Line purchased Sealink British Ferries, the Scandinavian company more than doubled in size to become one of the world's largest car-ferry operators. Stena was known for its commitment to service quality and its organization included a department dedicated to monitoring quality improvements. By contrast, this philosophy was described as 'alien' to Sealink's culture, which reflected a top-down, military-style management structure. Throughout the history of Sealink, which had once been a subsidiary of state-owned British Railways, management's priorities had focused on the operational aspects of ship movements. The quality of customers' experiences received only secondary consideration.

The Stena executives charged with integrating Sealink into their company recognized Sealink's managerial weaknesses, which included a lack of attention to strategic development in a rapidly evolving industry. Not only was there significant competition from other ferry companies, but many of the ferry routes across the English Channel now faced competition from the new Channel Tunnel. Innovative ferry designs, such as the water-jet propelled catamarans built by shipyards in Finland and Australia, offered customers a faster and more comfortable ride than traditional ships, and the opportunity to include many more amenities than the fast but noisy hovercraft.

Sealink had been organized into a number of divisions, based on different ports and routes, with all decision-making being tightly controlled by top management at headquarters. Not only were decisions at the divisional level subject to review at HQ, but divisional managers themselves were separated by two levels of management from the functional teams close to the actual operation. This organizational structure led to conflicts, slow decision-making and an inability to respond quickly to market changes. Basically, HQ managed the company by issuing directives to their middle managers in each division. Sealink's general approach was to create company-wide standards that could be applied across all divisions, rather than customizing policies to the needs of individual routes.

Stena's philosophy was very different. The parent company operated a decentralized structure in Sweden, believing that it was important for each management function to take responsibility for its own activities and to be accountable for the results. Recognizing the diversity of the different UK ferry routes, Stena quickly introduced decentralized decision-making at its British subsidiary. It wanted management decisions to be taken by people who were close to the market and who understood the local variations in competition and in demand for ferry travel. Some HQ functions were moved out to the divisions, including much of the responsibility for marketing activities.

Prior to the merger, no priority had been given to punctual or reliable operations. On one of the British routes, for instance, ferries were often late, but standard excuses were used on the weekly reports, customer complaints were ignored and there was little pressure from customer service managers to improve the situation. After the takeover, however, the situation started to change. The operational problem of late departures and arrivals was gradually solved through concentration on individual problem areas. On one route, for instance, the port manager involved all operational staff and gave each person 'ownership' of a specific aspect of the improvement process. They kept detailed records of each sailing, together with reasons for late departures, as well as monitoring competitors to see how their ferries were performing. Apart from helping solve problems, this participative approach created close liaison between staff members in different job positions; it also helped members of the customer service staff to become more knowledgeable and to learn from experience. Within two years, the Stena ferries on this route were operating at close to 100 per cent punctuality.

On-board service was another area singled out for improvement. Historically, customer service managers offered passengers a very basic level of service, doing what was convenient for staff rather than for customers. For instance, staff members would take their meal breaks at times when customer demand for the service was greatest. As one observer noted, 'Customers were ignored during the first and last half hour on board, when facilities were closed . . . Customers were left to find their own way around [the ferry] . . . Staff only responded to customers when [they] initiated a direct request and made some effort to attract their attention.' So it was agreed that personnel from each on-board functional area should choose a specific area for improvement and work in small groups to achieve this. In the short run, some teams were more successful than others, resulting in inconsistent levels of service and customer orientation from one ship to another. In time, customer service managers shared ideas and reviewed their experiences, making adaptations where needed to suit the interior layout of individual ships. This approach contributed to eventual success in achieving consistent service levels throughout all sailings and all ferries.

Service leadership

What comes to mind when you hear the term 'service leadership'? Do you think of the role of the chief executive in leading the organization? Or of positions of leadership at different levels in a service business, right down to that of an individual leading a team and motivating its members to provide good service to customers? Alternatively, perhaps you may think in terms of market leadership, focusing on those companies that are viewed as leaders in a particular service industry – setting the standards for service quality, recognized for initiating important innovations, and defining the terms on which other companies seek to compete.

In practice, service leadership embraces all three perspectives. Realistically, it's very difficult for a firm to achieve and maintain leadership in an industry if it lacks human leaders. Much has been written on the topic of leadership. It has even been described as a service in its own right.[2] Bennis and Nanus distinguish between *leaders* who emphasize the emotional and even spiritual resources of an organization and *managers* who stress its physical resources, such as raw materials, technology and capital.[3]

The qualities that are often ascribed to leaders in general include vision, charisma, persistence, high expectations, expertise, empathy, persuasiveness and integrity. Typical prescriptions for leader behaviour stress the importance of such activities as establishing (or preserving) a culture that is relevant to corporate success, putting in place an effective strategic planning process, instilling a sense of cohesion in the organization, and providing continuing examples of desired behaviours. For instance, the late Sam Walton, the legendary American founder of the Wal-Mart retail chain, proclaimed the importance of managers as 'servant leaders'.[4]

There are important distinctions between leading a successful organization which is functioning well and trying to turn around a disfunctional one. In Walton's case, he created the company and the culture, so his task was to preserve that culture as the company grew and select a successor who would maintain an appropriate culture as the company continued to grow. Another example of a leader, who has created a very effective service culture and works hard to maintain it, was introduced in Chapter 6; he's Feargal Quinn, managing director of the Irish supermarket chain, Superquinn.

In contrast, Jan Carlzon, the former chief executive of SAS, sought to transform the inappropriate culture he found at the airline, moving it from an operations focus to a customer focus (highlighting 'moments of truth'), with a particular emphasis on serving the needs of the business traveller.[5] Central to achieving these goals were his efforts to 'flatten the pyramid' by delegating authority downwards towards those employees who dealt directly with customers. In addition to internal leadership, Walton, Carlzon and Quinn assumed external leadership roles, serving as ambassadors for their companies in the public arena and promoting the quality and value of their firms' services. Transformational roles similar to Carlzon's were adopted by many of the chief executives who led large, formerly government-owned corporations through the privatization process. Well-known British examples include Sir Iain Vallance of BT and the team of Lord King and Sir Colin Marshall at British Airways.

There is a risk, of course, that prominent leaders may become too externally focused at the risk of their external effectiveness. The predominantly American model of CEOs who enjoy enormous incomes (often through exercise of stock options), maintain princely lifestyles and bask in widespread publicity may even turn off low-paid service workers at the bottom of the organization. Another risk is that a leadership style and focus which has served the company well in the past may become inappropriate for a changing environment. Jan Carlzon eventually left SAS during an economic turndown. And family dynasties may come to an end, too, if the successors to the founder prove ineffectual. As noted in the discussion of Club Med in Chapter 4, although Gilbert Trigano and then his son Serge were effective leaders for many years, the family was ousted after it proved unable to lead the company in the new directions required by the changing social and economic environment of the 1990s.

Berry argues that service leadership requires a special perspective: 'Regardless of the target markets, the specific services, or the pricing strategy, service leaders visualize quality of service as the foundation for competing'.[6] Recognizing the key role of employees in delivering service, he emphasizes that service leaders need to believe in the people who work for them and make communicating with employees a priority. Love of the business is another service leadership characteristic he highlights, to the extent that it combines natural enthusiasm with the right setting in which to express it. Such enthusiasm motivates individuals to teach the business to others and to pass on to them the nuances, secrets and craft of operating it. Berry stresses the importance for leaders of being driven by a set of core values which they infuse into the organization, arguing that 'A critical role of values-driven leaders is cultivating the leadership qualities of others in the organization'. He also notes that 'values-driven leaders rely on their values to navigate their companies through difficult periods'.[7]

In hierarchical organizations, structured on a military model, it's often assumed that leadership at the top is sufficient. However, as Vandermerwe points out, forward-looking service businesses need to be more flexible. Today's greater emphasis on using teams within service businesses means that

> leaders are everywhere, disseminated throughout the teams. They are found especially in the customer facing and interfacing jobs in order that decision-making will lead to long-lasting relationships with customers . . . leaders are customer and project champions who energize the group by virtue of their enthusiasm, interest, and know-how.[8]

Integrating marketing with other management functions

What are the keys to success in service businesses, especially for those operating in highly competitive environments? A number of themes run through this book, including:

- The notion of service as a time-bound performance comprising both a core product and an array of supplementary services.
- The importance of understanding and managing the operational processes including the creation and delivery of different types of services.
- The roles that customers play in participating in these service processes (roles that vary according to the degree of contact involved); the need for firms to seek distinctive positions in the market that will enable them to play to their competitive strengths.
- The competitive advantage of offering what target customers perceive as superior value – and ways of creating this value in a service context.
- The challenges involved in managing contact between employees and customers.
- The burgeoning role of technology as a factor in reshaping both the nature of services and the ways in which they are delivered.
- The challenges associated with operating in international markets.

The Stena example illustrates some of the challenges facing managers who seek to turn round a service business which has historically lacked a customer focus. Stena Line was fortunate to have a tried-and-tested framework for delivering a high level of service to its customers and was able to reorganize the management structure in its newly acquired British subsidiary to achieve similar results. However, these improvements did take time.

In this chapter, we present some of the issues facing service managers who want their businesses to be customer-focused and more effective at designing and implementing marketing programmes. As we have demonstrated throughout this book, the marketing function in services cannot be viewed in isolation from other management activities. Evert Gummesson has long emphasized that the work of the traditional marketing department embraces only a small portion of the overall marketing function in a service business – a point also stressed by Christian Grönroos.[9] More recently, Gummesson notes the move to *network organizations* and what is sometimes called the *virtual corporation*, in which boundaries are fuzzy around a core competence and relationships are highly flexible.[10]

Changing relationships between marketing, operations and human resources

Compartmentalizing management functions or subjugating one function to another is not an appropriate way to organize a service firm. In the reading 'Putting the service-profit chain to work' (reproduced on pages 638–48), Heskett *et al.* set out a series of causal links in achieving success in service businesses.[11] These links are summarized in Table 15.1. As you can see, the eighth link in the chain is that top management leadership underlies the chain's success.

In a subsequent book, Heskett, Sasser and Schlesinger cite several leadership behaviours that are critical to managing the different links in the service profit chain.[12] Some behaviours relate to employees (links 4–7) and include spending time on the front line, investing in the development of promising managers, and supporting the design of jobs that offer greater latitude for employees; also included in this category is promoting the notion that paying higher wages actually reduces labour costs after reduced turnover, higher productivity and higher quality are taken into account. Another set of service leadership behaviours focuses on customers (links 1–3) and include an emphasis on identifying and understanding customer needs, investments to ensure customer retention, and a commitment to adopting new performance measures that track such variables as satisfaction and loyalty among both customers and employees.

These themes and relationships illustrate the mutual dependency that exists between marketing, operations and human resources, initially illustrated in Chapter 1 (see Figure 1.3). Although managers within each function may have specific responsibilities, strategic planning and the execution of specific tasks must be well coordinated. Responsibility for the tasks assigned to each function may be present entirely within one firm or distributed between the originating service organization and its subcontractors, who must work in close partnership if the desired results are to be achieved. Let's review the role of each of these three key functions and how each relates to broader strategic concerns.

Table 15.1 ■ Causal links in the service profit chain

1. Customer loyalty drives profitability and growth.
2. Customer satisfaction drives customer loyalty.
3. Value drives customer satisfaction.
4. Employee productivity drives value.
5. Employee loyalty drives productivity.
6. Employee satisfaction drives loyalty.
7. Internal quality drives employee satisfaction.
8. Top management leadership underlies the chain's success.

The marketing function

Production and consumption are usually clearly separated in manufacturing firms. In most instances, a physical good is produced in a factory in one geographic location, shipped to a retailer or other intermediary for sale in a different location, and consumed or used by the customer in a third location. As a result, it's not normally necessary for production personnel to have direct involvement with customers, especially for consumer goods. In such firms, marketing acts to link producers and consumers, providing the manufacturing division with guidelines for product specifications that reflect consumer needs, as well as projections of market demand, information on competitive activity and feedback on performance in the marketplace. In this linking role, marketing also works with logistics and transportation specialists to develop strategies for distributing the product to prospective purchasers.

In service firms, as we've seen throughout this book, things are different. Many service operations – especially those involved in delivering people-processing services – are literally 'factories in the field', which customers enter at the specific time that they need the service. Ferries like those operated by Stena Line could even be described as floating factories! In a large chain (such as hotels, fast-food restaurants or car rental agencies), the company's service delivery sites may be located across a country, a continent or even the entire world. When customers are actively involved in production and the service output is consumed as it is produced, there has to be direct contact between production (operations) and consumers. This can take place in either a physical location or through telecommunications. In some instances, there's no contact with personnel, since customers are expected to serve themselves independently or communicate through more impersonal media such as mail, fax or web sites.

How should marketing relate to operations and human resources when production and consumption take place simultaneously? In manufacturing firms, marketers assume full responsibility for the product once it leaves the production line. But in services, contact between operations personnel and customers is the rule rather than the exception – although the extent of this contact varies according to the nature of the service. In many instances, operations management is responsible for running service distribution systems including retail outlets. Yet none of this reduces the need for a strong, efficient marketing organization to perform the following tasks:

■ Evaluate and select the market segments to serve.

■ Research customer needs and preferences within each segment.

■ Monitor competitive offerings, identifying their principal characteristics, quality levels and the strategies used to bring them to market.

■ Design the core product, tailoring its characteristics to the needs of chosen market segments and ensuring that they match or exceed those of competitive offerings.

■ Select and establish service levels for supplementary elements needed to enhance the value and appeal of the core product or to facilitate its purchase and use.

■ Set prices that reflect costs, competitive strategies and consumer sensitivity to different price levels.

■ Tailor location and scheduling of service availability to customers' needs and preferences.

- Develop communications strategies, using appropriate media to transmit messages informing prospective customers about the service and promoting its advantages.
- Develop performance standards for establishing and measuring service quality levels.
- Create programmes for rewarding and reinforcing customer loyalty.

The net result is that the marketing function in service businesses is closely interrelated with, and dependent on, the procedures, personnel and facilities managed by the operations function. To a greater degree than in manufacturing, marketing, operations and human resources must work together day-to-day. Although initially seen as a poor relation by many operations managers, marketing has now acquired significant management clout in many service businesses, with important implications for organizational design and assignment of responsibilities.

Marketing's influence within the organization can be enhanced by demonstrating its effectiveness, specifically the way in which marketing strategies add value to the business. In the article, 'Measuring your marketing success' (reprinted on pages 611–15), David Maister looks in particular at the marketing statistics that are relevant to the success of a professional firm.

The operations function

Although marketing's profile has risen, the operations function still dominates line management in most service businesses. This is hardly surprising, because operations – typically the largest department – creates and delivers the service product. Operations managers are responsible not only for equipment and backstage procedures, but also for company-owned retail outlets and other customer facilities. In high-contact services, operations managers may direct the work of large numbers of employees, including many who serve customers directly. In technology-driven firms, operations managers take primary responsibility for the technological infrastructure, and interface with research and development specialists to design and introduce innovative delivery systems.

In many firms, most operations managers have been with the organization longer than their marketing colleagues and believe that they understand it better. Yet there's a growing recognition of the contributions that marketers can make, not least in understanding customer motivations and habits, identifying opportunities for new product development and entry into new markets, telling customers and prospects about the product, and creating strategies to build customer loyalty in highly competitive environments. Even operations managers who feel that marketing should not become directly involved in line management, recognize that marketing specialists can provide useful inputs to service design. This perspective is illustrated by the following comment from a senior operations manager in a quick-service restaurant chain:

> The customer evaluates your total product – the store, the product, the price, the courtesy and service of the employees, and the convenience. So you can turn off the customer very easily by falling down on any one of those variables. That's not so true in packaged goods. Marketing doesn't have any direct line authority at the store level [in our firm]. That's operations. But the rules have to be followed so that service standards are adhered to, and marketing has an input to these standards.[13]

The human resources function

Few service organizations are so technologically advanced that they can be operated without employees. Indeed, many service industries remain highly labour-intensive. People are needed for operational tasks (either front- or backstage), to perform a wide array of marketing tasks and for administrative support.

Human resources emerged as a coherent management function during the 1980s. Historically, responsibility for matters relating to employees was often divided among a number of different departments, such as personnel, compensation, industrial relations and organization development (or training). In their daily work, many employees report to operations departments. As defined by academic specialists, 'Human resource management (HRM) involves all managerial decisions and actions that affect the nature of the relationship between the organization and its employees – its human resources'.[14]

Just as some forward-looking service businesses have developed an expanded vision of marketing, viewing it from a strategic perspective rather than a narrow functional and tactical one, so is HRM coming to be seen as a key element in business strategy. Personnel-related activities in a modern service corporation can be subsumed under four broad policy areas.[15]

1. *Human resource flow* is concerned with ensuring that the right number of people and mix of competencies are available to meet the firm's long-term strategic requirements. Issues include recruitment, training, career development and promotions.

2. *Work systems* involve all tasks associated with arranging people, information, facilities and technology to create (or support) the services produced by the organization.

3. *Reward systems* send powerful messages to all employees as to what kind of organization management seeks to create and maintain, especially as to desired attitudes and behaviour. Not all rewards are financial in nature; recognition may be a powerful motivator.

4. *Employee influence* relates to employee inputs concerning business goals, pay, working conditions, career progression, employment security and the design and implementation of work tasks. The movement towards greater empowerment of employees represents a shift in the nature and extent of employee influence.[16]

In many service businesses, the calibre and commitment of the labour force have become a major source of competitive advantage,[17] especially in high-contact services where customers can discern differences between the employees of competing firms. A strong commitment by top management to human resources is a feature of many successful service firms.[18] To the extent that employees understand and support the goals of their organization, have the skills and training needed to succeed in their jobs, and recognize the importance of creating and maintaining customer satisfaction, marketing and operations should both be easier to manage.

Danish firm cleans up around the world

As a business region, Scandinavia is usually associated with finance, shipping, high-tech machinery and cars. Yet a Copenhagen-based firm, ISS (International Service System), has established itself as the world leader in cleaning services. The Danish Cleaning Company was founded in 1934 with two customers and a staff of 43; it was an independent subsidiary of a security company. Ten years later, it had 2,000 employees. By 1973, ISS had grown into a large scale, international group. The company's rapid international expansion began with Sweden, then moved to Norway, Germany, Switzerland, the UK, the Netherlands, Austria, Spain, Finland and Brazil.

The experience of growing internationally – primarily through acquisition – impressed on ISS's senior executives the importance of people management and, in particular, of developing skills in what many people view as the archetypal low-skill activity. Accordingly, ISS set up the Centre for Service Management near Copenhagen in 1976, well before most other 'know-how intensive' service companies recognized the strategic importance of such a cultural, behavioural and managerial initiative. Perhaps more than in any other industry, the front-line workers in a cleaning business are the real representatives of the company and their work directly incorporates the basic determinants of customer satisfaction. The skills taught to the cleaners at the centre include not only how to conserve time and cleaning supplies, improve quality and minimize accidents and

injuries, but also how to interpret each client's contract so as to assess its profitability for ISS and its unique needs as a customer.

In addition to training, the company emphasizes employee motivation, seeking to create a sense of teamwork by organizing workers into teams who work and travel together from site to site. It also offers career planning, giving workers the opportunity to move into management. ISS has successfully differentiated itself from competitors by the quality of its service employees, their relationship with customers and their higher rates of productivity.

The result is much higher levels of both employee retention (in an industry renowned for low employee morale and high turnover) and customer retention than are typically found in this industry. Profits have been growing at 15 per cent annually. By 1997, revenues topped €1.5 billion and the company had operations in more than 30 countries, employing over 100,000 people.

ISS has launched an 'Aim 2002' programme to accelerate and systematize the transformation of the company from what is predominantly a general cleaning group into a customer-driven service enterprise providing general and specialized of cleaning services; the latter include integration of cleaning, catering and laundry service solutions, and the outsourcing of all cleaning operations. Targeted customers and customer segments include Euro Disney, hospitals and other health-related organizations, factories and hotels.

Interfunctional conflict[19]

As service firms place more emphasis on marketing, there's increased potential for conflict among the three functions, especially between marketing and operations. Marketing managers are likely to see the operations perspective as narrow and one-sided. Similarly, they get frustrated by employee resistance to change or labour agreements that constrain the firm's ability to introduce new services and innovative delivery systems. How comfortably can the three functions coexist in a service business, and how are their relative roles perceived? Sometimes marketing and operations appear to be at loggerheads, as exemplified by the following comment from one senior executive:

> Marketing's role is typically seen as constantly adding superiority to the product offering so as to enhance its appeal to customers and thereby increase sales. Operations sees its role as paring these elements back to reflect the reality of service constraints – staff, equipment, and so forth – and the accompanying need for cost containment.

Revenue vs. cost orientation

Operations managers tend to focus on improving efficiency and keeping down costs, whereas marketers look for opportunities to increase sales and build customer loyalty. Although a proposed marketing innovation may have the potential to attract customers and offer the likelihood of increased sales, the financial and opportunity costs may sometimes be too high to permit its profitable introduction. Marketers who take the trouble to understand the nature and limitations of the existing operation are less likely to fall into the trap of pushing a new service that represents a poor fit with existing facilities, skills and procedures. However, marketers who have earned credibility with their colleagues in operations and human resources may be able to make the case for investment in new facilities and equipment, changes in labour agreements and retraining of current personnel in new procedures (or even new recruits).

Different time horizons

Marketing and operations often have different viewpoints concerning the need to expedite a new service. Marketers may be oriented to current customer concerns and eager to achieve an early competitive advantage (or to regain competitive parity) by introducing a new product. The operations division may prefer to adopt a longer time horizon in order to develop a new technology or to refine new operating procedures. Similarly, human resource managers may caution against rushing to change the nature of employees' jobs, especially in situations where it may take time to obtain acceptance and commitment from employee associations or union leaders.

Perceived fit of new products with existing operations

Another problem relates to compatibility. How well does a new product, which may be very appealing to existing and prospective customers, fit into the operation? An executive in a fast-food restaurant chain related the operational problems attending the introduction of a new menu item:

> It was a big mistake. Our stores are small. They didn't have space for the new equipment that was needed. It really didn't fit with our existing business and was just a square peg in a round hole. Of course, just because it wasn't right for us doesn't mean it wouldn't have been a great success in another quick-service restaurant company. It was really popular with our customers, but it started to mess up the rest of our operation.

If a new product is incompatible with existing production facilities, expertise and employee skills, it follows that good quality execution may be infeasible. There is, of course, a difference between a permanently bad fit and short-term start-up problems. Resistance by operating personnel is one such start-up problem. There's often a natural tendency to want to make the job as easy as possible and first-line supervisors may be reluctant to disturb existing patterns by imposing new procedures on employees.

The three imperatives

Changing traditional organizational perspectives doesn't come readily to managers who have been comfortable with established approaches. It's easy for them to become obsessed with their own function, forgetting that all areas of the company must pull together to create a customer-driven organization. Achieving the necessary coordination and synergy requires that top management establish clear imperatives for each function (Figure 15.1).

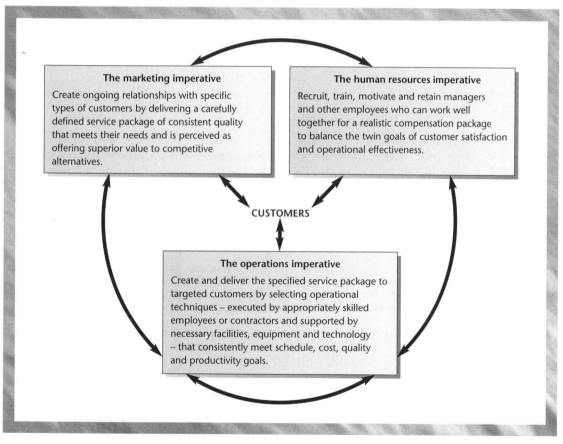

Figure 15.1 ■ Integrating three functional imperatives

Each imperative should relate to customers and define how the function in question contributes to the overall mission. Although a firm will need to phrase each imperative in ways that are specific to its own business, we can express them generically as follows:

The marketing imperative

The firm will target specific types of customers whom it is well equipped to serve, and then create ongoing relationships with them by delivering a carefully defined product package of 'all actions and reactions' that they desire to purchase. Customers will recognize this package as being one of consistent quality that delivers solutions to their needs and offers superior value to competing alternatives.

The operations imperative

To create and deliver the specified service package to targeted customers, the firm will select those operational techniques that allow it to consistently meet customer-driven cost, schedule and quality goals, and also enable the business to reduce its costs through continuing improvements in productivity. The chosen operational methods will match skills that employees or contractors currently possess or can be trained to develop. The firm will have the resources not only to support these operations with the necessary facilities, equipment and technology, but also to avoid negative impacts on employees and the broader community.

The human resources imperative

The firm will recruit, train and motivate managers, supervisors and employees who can work well together for a realistic compensation package to balance the twin goals of customer satisfaction and operational effectiveness. People will want to stay with the firm and to enhance their own skills because they value the working environment, appreciate the opportunities that it presents, and take pride in the services they help to create and deliver.

Part of the challenge of service management is to ensure that each of these three functional imperatives is compatible with the others, and that all are mutually reinforcing.

Reducing intra-organizational tension

Top management's responsibility is to develop structures and procedures that harness the energy of managers in different departments, rather than allowing it to be dissipated in interfunctional disputes or permitting one department to dominate (and thereby frustrate) the others. There are a number of ways in which service firms seek to reduce interfunctional tension.

Transfers and cross-training

One approach is to transfer managers from one functional department to another to ensure better understanding of differing perspectives. By working in another department, the transferred manager learns the language and concepts of the other function, understands its opportunities and constraints, and recognizes how its priorities are established. A related approach is to cross-train managers and employees to perform a broader variety of tasks, rather than remaining narrow specialists.

Creating cross-functional taskforces

Another approach is to create a taskforce for a specific project, such as planning the introduction of a new service, improving quality or enhancing productivity. As at Stena Lines, such groups are normally formed on a temporary basis with a defined deadline for completing a specific task. Ideally, groups should be composed of individuals from each functional area who are well attuned to the others' viewpoints. In operations, this means looking for what one manager has termed 'field hands' – personnel who are practical and understand how to deal with people, rather than being totally systems and technology-oriented. For marketers, taskforce membership requires an orientation towards operating systems and what is involved in making them work from both a staffing and technical perspective; it doesn't necessarily require detailed technical training or an understanding of the inner workings of technology.

Taskforce participants should represent a microcosm of the organization yet be insulated from the pressures and distractions of day-to-day management activities. Properly planned and managed, the team environment provides a forum for discussion and resolution of many of the problems likely to occur during, say, the development and commercialization of an innovative service. There needs to be an external mechanism for settling any disputes which taskforce members cannot resolve among themselves. When a marketing manager is assigned the leadership role, top management's commitment to this individual must be explicit, because it flies in the face of the traditional seniority of operations.

New tasks and new people

Organizational change requires that new relationships be developed, jobs redefined, priorities restructured and existing patterns of thought and behaviour modified – often sharply. There are two schools of thought here. One involves taking the existing players and redirecting them. The other calls for replacing these people with new ones. The extent to which replacement is feasible depends not only on organizational policies and procedures, but also on the availability of suitable new people – either outside or inside the firm. Larger firms obviously have a bigger pool of people on whom to draw; they have managers and specialists in other divisions or regions who have not been 'contaminated' by close exposure to the activity in question, yet are sufficiently knowledgeable about the organization that they can quickly be productive in a new project.

Process management teams

A more permanent form of team is that which is organized around a specific process. In a marketing context, this approach may include brand management organizations created to plan and coordinate the design and delivery of all frontstage elements for a particular product. One example is found in the brand management teams that are responsible for planning and managing each of the different classes of service offered by an international airline.[20] Another example is found in the executive operating committees that manage individual hotel units in a chain.

Instituting gain-sharing programmes

These programmes allow employees to share in improved profits (or in the cost savings achieved at a nonprofit organization). The most significant form of sharing in the fortunes of a business comes through employee stock ownership programmes (ESOPs), especially when participation is broadly based and employees own a substantial share of the equity.

Marketing activities at different levels in the organization

Large, dispersed service businesses are usually divided into operating regions, and sometimes subdivided into territories or divisions. In international markets, four different levels may exist: headquarters, countries, regions and units. An important issue is what marketing tasks should be undertaken at what levels. Much depends on the degree of autonomy assigned to each level of operating management: is the product standardized or do unit (or territory or regional) managers have authority to customize? Even if the product is standardized, are country, regional or unit variations in pricing, delivery and communications appropriate? In an international context, a key strategic issue underlying such decisions is whether the firm wishes to operate on a truly transnational basis or whether it is content to preside over a loose confederation of largely independent national subsidiaries. We address some of these issues, as they relate to pan-European or global marketing, in Chapter 16.

Staff marketing functions are most commonly associated with the head office. But in large service businesses where marketing strategies and markets must necessarily vary widely from unit to unit, certain staff functions may be performed at the country, regional or even unit level. The trade-off is one of responsiveness to local conditions versus the operating efficiencies and depth of expertise that can be obtained from centralization. At Stena Line, the goal was to decentralize and push decision-making down to the field level – in this instance, specific ports and the ships that sailed from those ports – on the grounds that the nature of demand and competition for ferry service varied considerably from one route to another.

Where line marketing functions are concerned, another important issue is whether it makes sense to focus on geographic market segments served from the closest operating unit as opposed to segmenting customers in other ways and serving them across a broader geographic area. One of the great benefits of international expansion for a firm that targets a narrow niche in the market is that it can increase its market potential without departing from its niche focus. For information-based services, which can be delivered electronically, geographic segmentation may become irrelevant when there is little need for face-to-face contacts between customers and service personnel. Instead, segmentation may be based on other, more relevant criteria, such as language, national laws, level of benefits desired and willingness to pay for them, usage frequency, and so forth.

Ensuring that service encounters are customer-oriented

One reason why a customer orientation has to extend well beyond the marketing function in a service business relates to service encounters between customers and service employees. As we noted in Chapter 3, a fundamental aspect of service operations is the distinction between the 'frontstage' and the 'backstage'. Frontstage procedures are those experienced by the consumer. In the case of low-contact services, such procedures represent a very small proportion of the service firm's total activities. For instance, the extent of personal contact between customers and credit card companies is limited to receiving and paying a monthly statement, and an occasional letter or telephone call if problems arise. Tasks such as review of credit card applications, credit checks and processing of credit card slips all take place behind the scenes.

By contrast, in a high-contact service such as a hotel the customer is exposed to the physical facilities and is likely to have service encounters with numerous hotel personnel, ranging from telephone reservation agent to doorman, from porter to receptionist, and from waiter/waitress to housekeeper. Whatever the nature of service encounters, they should be designed and executed with customer needs in mind. One of the most revealing weaknesses of Sealink at the time of its takeover by Stena Line was the fact that service personnel on board the ferries actively ignored passengers and organized their jobs for their own convenience, not the customers'.

Improving customer service in response to competitive pressures

As business in general – and the service sector in particular – becomes more competitive, the need for meaningful competitive differentiation is sharpened. Increasingly, this differentiation includes a search for superior performance not only on the core product but also on each of the supplementary service elements that we discussed in Chapter 8. Achieving such differentiation requires a commitment to formalize standards for all service encounters that might reasonably be anticipated, in ways that reflect the nature of the industry, the culture of the organization and its desired position in the market. The necessary management tasks will require coordination between managers from different functional backgrounds. These tasks will include:

1. Conducting ongoing research to determine customer needs, wants and satisfaction levels concerning each of their service encounters.
2. Identifying the key sources of customer satisfaction (or dissatisfaction) and relating them to current service elements.
3. Setting service-level standards for different tasks.
4. Designing jobs and technological systems to meet these standards.
5. Periodically revising standards and delivery systems in the light of changing customer preferences, technological innovation and competitive activities.

As emphasized in our discussion of quality issues in Chapter 12, the human side of quality is also important. Poor performance may include bad manners as well as substandard operational execution. In this instance, the responsibility of an expanded human resources function includes training in human relations skills as part of developing a stronger customer perspective on the part of all contact personnel.

Creating the petals of the flower of service

If you have already read Chapter 8, you will recognize that the widely used term 'customer service' is basically an umbrella term for delivering the various types of supplementary services that surround the core product like the petals of a flower.

The array of jobs that fall under the customer service umbrella is quite broad. Figure 15.2 highlights some of the jobs that go with specific petals of the flower of service. What other ones can you suggest?

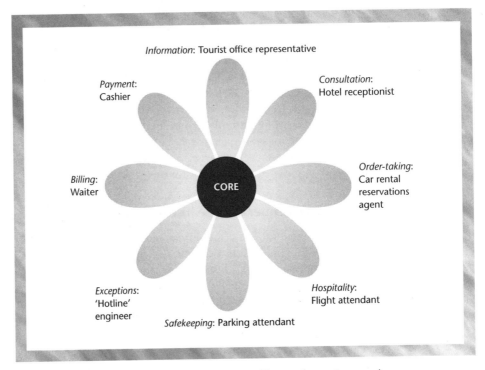

Information: Tourist office representative

Payment: Cashier

Consultation: Hotel receptionist

Billing: Waiter

CORE

Order-taking: Car rental reservations agent

Exceptions: 'Hotline' engineer

Hospitality: Flight attendant

Safekeeping: Parking attendant

Figure 15.2 ■ Examples of jobs providing specific supplementary services

In terms of job assignments, customer service may involve people who:

■ provide information and technical advice in their capacity as members of the sales support staff;

■ take orders and reservations over the phone and pass them along to those individuals responsible for order fulfilment;

■ communicate with customers following receipt of orders or reservations to provide information on availability, advise on shipping dates or reservation details, confirm shipment or trace missing orders;

■ greet customers on arrival at a service facility, offer refreshments and attend to other needs;

■ take responsibility for customers' cars, bags, coats or other possessions while they are at a service facility;

■ maintain contact with customers while supervising assembly or completion of special or customized orders;

■ schedule transportation and expedite deliveries to customers;

■ handle installation and repairs;

- attend to special requests, resolve problems, handle complaints;
- compile billing information, send out bills, accept payment, pursue delinquent payers, make refunds.

The management challenge is to coordinate every aspect of customer service in a broader function that is, itself, integrated with marketing and operations strategies. At all times, the need to take a customer perspective is paramount. In small businesses, a single person may undertake numerous different customer service tasks and see only a small slice of each customer's overall service experience.

How technology changes organizations and control systems

One of the driving forces for organizational change is technology, with its dramatic potential for rearranging traditional notions of space and time. First Direct, the 24-hour all-telephone bank introduced in Chapter 3, has no branches and never sees its customers. In contrast to traditional banks, with their rigid hierarchical structures – often comprising multiple layers of management, both functional and geographic divisions, and a strong need for control procedures to oversee widely scattered branches – First Direct has a very flat organization, with minimal social or physical distance between the chief executive and the teams of telephone-based banking representatives who serve the bank's customers.

Technology's role in integrating management functions

Another example of technology's power to reshape service organizations comes from Singapore's World of Sports (WOS) retail chain. The firm's stores are, of necessity, dispersed geographically, separated from each other and from the head office and its adjoining warehouse. The firm's goals of 'Speed, Simplicity and Service' are achieved not only through a carefully selected, well-trained and enthusiastic staff, but also through information technology. The latter consists of systems for monitoring all sales and all stocks in real time.

Intelligent terminals at the point of sale capture every sales transaction. Instant information is available on each transaction as it occurs, categorized by the specific item of merchandise – technically known as a stock-keeping unit (SKU) – time of sale, store and identity of salesperson. Store managers have more time available for coaching and customer relations instead of exercising control. Computerization has revolutionized physical logistics, enabling WOS to create a 'virtual warehouse', which consolidates the firm's entire stock and can be searched for individual SKUs with great speed. If one shop does not have a desired item in stock, a sales assistant can immediately search the warehouse stock and that of other shops. This facility allows the firm to supply a broader range of items without the expense of large in-store stocks: information about merchandise and where it is located has become as important as the merchandise itself.

Like WOS, many retailers have moved to install intelligent terminals that can communicate directly with a central computer. Traditional cash registers are out. The data collected by these terminals can be consolidated and analyzed in many ways to meet the needs of different management functions. Figure 15.3 offers a generic representation of how the IT revolution in logistics impacts other management functions. Data collected at

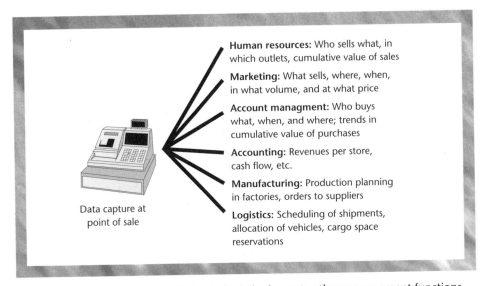

Figure 15.3 ■ How the IT revolution in logistics impacts other management functions

point of sale not only provide a control tool to managers in many different functions but can also serve to integrate their activities in ways that enhance mutual cooperation.

How technology is leveraging customer service

Regis McKenna, a consultant to numerous hi-tech firms, has declared: 'I believe that technology is creating a marketplace where everything is going to become service-like'.[21] As service firms grow larger and extend their operations across broader geographic areas, corporate managers may become far removed from the day-to-day operations of the business – and thus from their customers. This development requires new efforts to achieve service consistency across time and geography. Information technology can often help provide the solution.

Service firms with multi-site operations are trying to develop programmes for building closer ties with customers by centralizing certain functions that don't require face-to-face contact. Computer technology and telecommunications make it possible to provide national (or even global) on-line service from a central location to serve customers who require information, wish to place orders or seek to resolve problems. At the same time, technology is creating opportunities for real-time feedback from the marketplace.

McKenna makes the point that marketing's traditional, research-based connections to customers are no longer sufficient in a real-time world:

> More continuous connections with customers can provide information that focus groups and surveys cannot . . . The knowledge of individual customer needs that companies can capture through technology harkens back to the days when the butcher, baker, and candlestick maker knew their clientele personally. In that setting, customer service relationships were built in face-to-face transactions . . . Today's technology can recreate the conversation between the shopkeeper and the customer.[22]

Among the procedures that companies are adopting to obtain information from their customers are freephone numbers to ring with questions and complaints, corporate web sites that offer information and the opportunity to communicate with the organization by e-mail, and electronic self-service systems (as in electronic banking) that enable the firm to monitor customers' use of its services on a real-time basis.

Many customer service activities involve information-dependent petals of the flower of service. As such, execution can easily be undertaken by telecommunications. Increasingly, firms are centralizing their efforts to provide faster, more consistent, higher quality service.

Conclusion

Within any given service organization, marketing has to coexist with operations – traditionally the dominant function – whose concerns are cost- and efficiency-centred rather than customer-centred. Marketing must also coexist with human resource management, which usually recruits and trains service personnel, including those who have direct contact with the customers. An ongoing challenge is to balance the concerns of each function, not only at head office but also in the field. To a growing degree, information technology is serving to knit together units that were once geographically separated.

To grow and remain competitive, service firms often expand beyond national frontiers. So, in the following chapter, we address issues relating to internationalization.

Study questions

1. Explain the significance of Gummesson's statement that the work of the traditional marketing department embraces only a small portion of the overall marketing function in a service business.

2. Identify the nature of the tasks that are traditionally assigned to the marketing, operations and human resource functions. Identify which of the tasks in one function have an impact on one or both of the others.

3. What do you see as the causes of tension between the marketing, operations and human resource functions? How might they vary from one industry to another?

4. In your view, which marketing tasks should be centralized in an international airline and which should be delegated to local managers in a large city served by that airline? How might the situation change for a chain of fast-food restaurants?

5. Identify ways in which technology has been used to improve customer service in two industries with which you are familiar. In what ways has it made service inferior?

Notes

1. Based, in part, on information in Audrey Gilmore, 'Services Marketing Management Competencies', *International Journal of Service Industry Management*, Vol. 9, No. 1, 1998, pp. 74–92.
2. See, for instance, the special issue on 'Leadership as a Service' (Celeste Wilderom, guest editor), *International Journal of Service Industry Management*, Vol. 3, No. 2, 1992.
3. Warren Bennis and Burt Nanus, *Leaders: The Strategies for Taking Charge*, New York: Harper and Row, 1985, p. 92.

4. James L. Heskett, W. Earl Sasser, Jr. and Leonard A. Schlesinger, *The Service Profit Chain*, New York: The Free Press, 1997, p. 236.
5. For an interesting discussion of Carlzon's philosophy of leadership, see K.J. Blois, 'Carlzon's *Moments of Truth* – A Critical Appraisal', *International Journal of Service Industry Management*, Vol. 3, No. 3, 1992, pp. 5–17.
6. Leonard L. Berry, *On Great Service*, New York: The Free Press, 1995, p. 9.
7. Leonard L. Berry, *Discovering the Soul of Service*, New York: The Free Press, 1999, pp. 44, 47.
8. Sandra Vandermerwe, *From Tin Soldiers to Russian Dolls*, Oxford: Butterworth-Heinemann, 1993, p. 129.
9. Evert Gummesson, 'The Marketing of Professional Services: An Organizational Dilemma', *European Journal of Marketing*, Vol. 13, No. 5, 1979, pp. 308–18; and Christian Grönroos, *Service Management and Marketing*, Lexington, MA: Lexington Books, 1990, pp. 175–8.
10. Evert Gummesson, 'Service Management: An Evaluation and the Future', *International Journal of Service Industry Management*, Vol. 5, No. 1, 1994, pp. 77–96.
11. James L. Heskett *et al.*, 'Putting the Service Profit Chain to Work', *Harvard Business Review*, March–April 1994.
12. Heskett, Sasser and Schlesinger, *op. cit.*, pp. 236–51.
13. Quoted in Eric Langeard, John E.G. Bateson, Christopher H. Lovelock and Pierre Eiglier, *Services Marketing: New Insights from Customers and Managers*, Cambridge, MA: Marketing Science Institute, 1981.
14. M. Beer, B. Spector, P.R. Lawrence, D.Q. Mills and R.E. Walton, *Human Resource Management: A General Manager's Perspective*, New York: The Free Press, 1985.
15. *Ibid.*
16. David E. Bowen and Edward T. Lawler, III, 'The Empowerment of Service Workers: What, Why, How and When', *Sloan Management Review*, Spring 1992, pp. 31–9.
17. See, for example, Jeffrey Pfeffer, *Competitive Advantage through People,* Boston: Harvard Business School Press, 1994.
18. See, for example, Benjamin Schneider and David E. Bowen, *Winning the Service Game*, Boston: Harvard Business School Press, 1995; and Leonard L. Berry, *On Great Service: A Framework for Action*, New York: The Free Press, 1995, chapters 8–10.
19. This discussion is based, in part, on E. Langeard, J.E.G. Bateson, C.H. Lovelock and P. Eiglier, *New Insights from Customers and Managers*, Cambridge, MA: Marketing Science Institute, 1981. Unless otherwise indicated, all quotations in this section are taken from this study.
20. Torin Douglas, 'The Power of Branding', *Business Life*, April–May 1988.
21. Regis McKenna, 'Everything Will Become a Service and How to Be Successful When It Does', *ITSMA Insight* (newsletter published by Information Technology Services Marketing Association, Lexington, MA), Spring 1995, p. 1.
22. Regis McKenna, 'Real-Time Marketing', *Harvard Business Review*, July–August 1995, pp. 87–98.

Developing strategies for transnational operations

Learning objectives

After reading and reflecting on this chapter, you should be able to:

1. Understand the forces that are stimulating internationalization.

2. Appreciate the cultural challenges and economic opportunities presented for service firms as the European Union evolves towards a single market.

3. Compare and contrast the pan-European market with that of the United States.

4. Recognize the distinction between a transnational strategy versus a multilocal one.

5. Demonstrate how information technology can help to integrate previously independent service units.

Groupe Accor: innovation and internationalization[1]

Paris-based Groupe Accor is one of the world's leaders in several complementary and integrated services: hotels, travel agencies and car rentals. According to industry experts, Accor is one of only three truly global hotel companies, each represented in more than 60 countries (the other two are Sheraton and Holiday Inn). Over the years, the group, whose sales were over FFr 100 billion (€15 billion) in 1997, has also proved itself to be a highly innovative service provider, be it in terms of its profound market opportunity analysis, its integrated offerings or its international growth strategies.

Accor, the first truly European hotel chain, has become the largest such chain in the world. It operates several distinct categories of hotel, such as the four/five-star Sofitel, three/four-star Novotel, three/four-star Mercure and three/two-star Ibis. Accor also pioneered the budget hotel concept typified by its Formule 1 chain. In the United States, Accor operates the Motel 6 chain of budget motels.

Accor's Chairman and Chief Executive Jean-Marc Espalioux believes that Accor has to be a global company and has launched an initiative named Accor 2000, which is designed to give Accor the integrated structure needed to operate and compete on a global basis. Hotel activities have been restructured into three strategic segments – Motel 6; budget hotels; and mid-scale/upscale hotels comprising Mercure, Novotel, Sofitel, and leisure and resort hotels. There are also two functional divisions. The first, a global services division, is being created to spearhead the major functions common to all hotel activities: information systems, reservation systems, maintenance and technical assistance, purchasing, key accounts, and partnerships and synergy between hotel and other activities. The second, the hotel development division, is structured by brand and by region and is responsible for working with the management of each hotel to develop marketing, service development and growth strategies. According to Mr Espalioux:

> In view of the revolution in the service sector which is now taking place, I do not see any future for purely national hotel chains – except for very specific niche markets with special architecture and locations, such as Raffles in Singapore or the Ritz in Paris. National chains can't invest enough money.

Throughout the 1990s Groupe Accor expanded across Europe, and introduced their Novotel and Sofitel brands into the US market. But in the 4-star and 5-star markets, where several very large chains compete for the same customers, achieving a critical mass in those sectors has proved difficult. On the other hand, Accor's budget hotel concept, known as Formula 1 in the US, has done well after recovering from some initial setbacks, and is now the world leader in the budget hotel category. All told, Accor hotels are present in 140 countries, with more than 60 per cent of hotel sales and 75 per cent of income coming from outside France.

Accor is continuing its internationalization drive, focusing on further consolidating and integrating its European network. The identity of each of its hotel brands is strictly maintained. Across Europe, Sofitel consistently delivers similar room and hotel facilities, plus the same pricing strategies, while a different set of strategies is employed by Novotel. For example, Sofitel has inaugurated what it calls multimedia 'on-line' rooms, where guests can have access to internet and e-mail, CD-ROMs, and so forth. Novotel, meantime, has launched a customer loyalty card, WorldWide Express, which facilitates the check-in procedures for frequent Novotel customers across Europe.

The group is also intent on building a presence in such emerging markets as Poland, Hungary and other ex-Soviet bloc countries. Mr Espalioux is also very aware that the underlying obstacle to successful globalization in services is people:

> Globalization brings considerable challenges which are often underestimated. The principal difficulty is getting our local management to adhere to the values of the group. [They] must understand our market and culture, for example, and we have to learn about theirs.

Because international cooperation, communication and teamwork are integral to achieving global consistency, Accor has eliminated, as much as possible, hierarchy, rigid job descriptions and titles, and even organizational charts. Employees are encouraged to interact as much as possible with their colleagues and with guests. They define the limits of their jobs within the context of the overall 'customer experience', and are recognized and rewarded on how well they meet these definitions. In addition to these structural and organizational initiatives, video conferencing and other technologies are used extensively to create and reinforce a common, global culture among Accor employees around the world. As part of the Accor 2000 strategy introduced in March 1998, there are plans to link all of the group's European hotels together through a sophisticated IT network. But even this, Espalioux admits, may not be enough: 'Every morning when I wake I think about the challenges of coordinating our operations in many different countries'.

Moving from domestic to transnational marketing

Throughout this book, we've sought to provide an international perspective on services marketing, presenting examples, cases and research findings not only from within Europe but also from countries on other continents. With only a few exceptions, however, most of our discussion of strategy and execution has emphasized activities taking place within a specific national market – what can be termed local or domestic marketing. In this chapter, we will place services marketing in the broader context of developing an international strategy for service businesses and examine the forces that drive pan-Europeanization in particular and, more broadly, globalization.

Some services were international in scope long before the term 'scientific management' was invented or the first marketing course taught. International services such as shipping, banking and insurance, for example, followed and facilitated early trade routes. With the advent of international air travel and telecommunications, both the opportunity and the need for international delivery of a wide array of services have grown dramatically, either displacing or complementing parallel delivery of similar services by purely domestic operations. Some firms – such as hotel chains

– follow their customers into new markets, others extend their geographic reach in search of new opportunities to increase their sales and expertise.

As more and more firms offer services in foreign markets – often around the world – and as international trade in services increases, important questions are being raised concerning the design and implementation of international service marketing strategies. What do we mean by international strategy? How do the distinctive characteristics of service businesses affect development of a pan-European or even global strategy? What should be the basis of competition against other players in the pan-European service sector? These are questions for government policy-makers as well as corporate managers.

Many firms in Europe are now operating across national frontiers, but not all have gone as far as Groupe Accor in developing a coherent international strategy. At this point, we need to draw the distinction between domestic, multi-domestic and transnational strategies.

What is a transnational strategy?

From a strategic perspective, planning and execution of the different management functions need to be integrated across national frontiers, rather than just taking place independently on a domestic basis within each of a variety of different nations. *Transnational* strategy involves the integration of strategy formulation and implementation across all the countries in which the company elects to do business, in contrast to a *multi-domestic* (or 'multi-local') approach which provides for the independent development and implementation of strategy by management units within each country.[2] In its broadest form, transnational strategy becomes global in form and we speak of globalization.

Although we can see a growing number of well-known service brand names popping up all over Europe, this does not mean that the companies behind the brands have a truly pan-European strategy. Many allegedly European strategies today are basically multi-domestic in nature. For instance, even though a number of European retail banks now have offices and even networks outside their countries of origin, in most instances, there is little transnational integration. One reason for this is that few retail customers need to conduct business in several different countries; when people travel within Europe, their main financial need is usually to have a debit or credit card that can be used to make retail purchases and ATM withdrawals across the Continent. To achieve this, all that is needed is that the bank that issues the card should be affiliated with a global network such as Visa or MasterCard. However, the situation is predictably different in corporate and investment banking, since pan-European corporations increasingly demand pan-European financial services.

Although research into global strategy for service businesses is still in an evolutionary stage, we can apply its insights to examination of the challenges of pan-Europeanization. One key research theme is that globalization potential depends on industry characteristics[3] – and particularly on specific industry drivers – such as market forces, cost factors, technology, government policies and competitive factors.[4] A second key theme is that the use of global strategy should differ by dimension of strategy and for different elements of the value-adding chain.

How should different types of service firms move from *multi-local* strategies – that is, purely domestic marketing strategies within a variety of countries – to creation of truly *transnational* strategies? In the balance of this chapter, we discuss the elements of transnational strategy and examine five drivers that stimulate the internationalization of an industry: market factors, costs, technology, favourable government policies and competition.[5] We then link the five industry globalization drivers to the different types of service processes introduced earlier in the book. Further insights come from examining how the flower of service concept of core and supplementary services can be applied to both standardization and customization of services in a global setting.

Insights for Europe from studying service strategies in the United States

As we consider issues in transnational marketing, it's useful to recognize that some of the challenges facing managers are an extension of those already found in large, domestic economies, but taking place on a much larger stage that presents sharper economic, cultural and political distinctions. A significant dimension of international services marketing concerns questions of scale and diversity. There are already, of course, important differences between marketing within a relatively compact domestic economy – such as (say) Ireland, Denmark, Slovenia or Portugal – and marketing in the larger European countries, such as France or Germany. In the former instances, the populations in question are small to medium-sized, government is relatively centralized and the geographic areas to be served are smaller than one of the larger US states. But the American market is so much larger that it can serve to provide insights for domestic marketers from a single European country seeking to expand across the Continent.

Visitors from Europe who tour the United States are often overwhelmed by the immense size of the country, surprised by the diversity of its people, astonished by the climatic and topographic variety of the landscape, and impressed by the scale and scope of some of its business undertakings. Consider some of the statistics. Marketing at a national level in the 'lower 48' states involves dealing with a population of some 265 million people and transcontinental distances that exceed 2,500 miles (4,000 km). If Hawaii and Alaska are included, the nation embraces even greater distances, covering six time zones, incredible topographic variety and all climatic zones from Arctic to tropical. From a logistical standpoint, serving customers in all 50 states might seem at least as complex as serving customers throughout Europe, North Africa and the Middle East – were it not for the fact that the United States has an exceptionally well-developed communications, transportation and distribution infrastructure. The United States is far less homogeneous than national stereotypes might suggest. As a federal nation, the US has a diverse patchwork of government practices. In addition to observing federal laws and paying federal taxes, service businesses operating nationwide may also need to conform to relevant state and municipal laws and must plan for variations in tax policies from one state to another. Changes in both state and federal regulations are opening up new opportunities for many service businesses and encouraging consolidation. A particular case in point is retail banking, previously constrained to operate in limited geographic areas such as statewide or even, within a state, just countywide. Today, the move is towards national banking and many banks are expanding rapidly to take advantage of economies of scale. The preferred method of expansion appears to be merger or acquisition, rather than organic growth.

As the US population becomes increasingly more mobile and multicultural, market segmentation issues have become more complex for American service marketers operating on a national scale. In addition to the varied accents and even dialects of American English, marketers encounter growing populations of immigrants (as well as visiting tourists) who speak many other languages. Although Spanish heads the list, the list itself is incredibly long. A recent study of students attending schools in Cambridge, Massachusetts, a city of some 90,000 inhabitants within the Greater Boston conurbation, revealed that they spoke no fewer than 56 languages! American economic statistics show a wider range of household incomes and personal wealth (or lack thereof) than is found almost anywhere else on earth. Corporate customers, too, often present considerable diversity, although the relevant variables may be different.

Faced with such an enormous and diverse domestic marketplace, most large American service companies simplify their marketing and management tasks by targeting specific segments. Some firms do so on a geographic basis (sometimes because of government regulations, as in local telecommunications). Others target certain groups based on demographics, lifestyle, needs or (in a corporate context) industry type and company size. Smaller firms wishing to operate nationally usually choose to seek out narrow market niches, a task made easier today by the growing use of the internet (and web sites, in particular). Yet the largest national service operations face tremendous challenges as they seek to serve multiple segments across a vast geographic area. They must strike a balance between standardization of marketing-mix strategies and adaptation to local market conditions – decisions that are especially challenging when they concern high-contact services where customers visit the delivery site in person.

To obtain the cost efficiencies needed for competitive pricing, a growing number of American service firms are electing to place their backstage operations in areas of the United States that offer either low-cost operations or geographical advantages (some are even moving certain operations outside the country). When Citicorp relocated its back-office credit card processing operations from New York to South Dakota many years ago, the move caused a sensation. Today, it would be much less noteworthy. Memphis was a logical choice of national hub location for Federal Express, because the city is close to the centre of gravity for package movements within the US and has a good airport that is rarely affected by weather problems. Similarly, lower costs in Texas and hubbing opportunities at the then new Dallas-Fort Worth airport were compelling reasons in the 1970s for American Airlines to relocate its head office and other backstage activities from New York. Turner Broadcasting Systems' choice of Atlanta for CNN operations demonstrated that a successful national (and now global) news and entertainment business need not be headquartered in the traditional media centres of Los Angeles or New York.

What can managers of growing European service firms learn from studying the United States? An important insight is that many of the challenging strategic decisions facing service marketers who now operate (or wish to operate) in pan-European markets are extensions of decisions already faced by firms operating on a national basis in the United States. Although geographically more compact than the United States, the 15-nation European Union (EU) has an even larger population (375 million versus 265 million) and is culturally and politically more diverse, with more distinct variations in tastes and lifestyles, plus the added complication of 11 official national languages and a variety of regional tongues, from Catalan to

Welsh. As new countries join the EU, the 'single market' will become even larger. The anticipated admission of several countries in Eastern Europe early in the twenty-first century will add further cultural diversity and bring the EU market closer to Russia and the countries of Central Asia.

Within the EU, the European Commission has made huge progress in harmonizing standards and government regulations and in opening up competition, but the task remains incomplete and there is a variety of subtle ways in which national governments can drag their feet on compliance. An important economic step towards freer and simpler trade is European monetary union, creating a single currency, the euro (€), out of 11 of the 15 existing currencies.

However, although the potential for freer trade in services within the EU is increasing at a rapid rate, we need to recognize that 'Greater Europe', ranging from Iceland to Russia west of the Ural Mountains, includes many countries which are likely to remain outside the Union for some years to come. Some of these countries, such as Switzerland and Norway, tend to enjoy much closer trading relations with EU nations than others.

Euro-consumer clusters within the pan-European market

American marketers often divide the United States into broad geographic clusters – such as New England, Mid-Atlantic, South, Midwest, Southwest and Northwest – reflecting climatic and other regional distinctions in lifestyles and purchasing patterns. Instead of national markets, one homogeneous mass market, or a collection of small specialized markets, the most likely outcome is that new Euro-consumer clusters will emerge, formed by consumers living close to each other (but not necessarily in the same country).

Within each cluster, there are likely to be some similarities in needs and purchasing behaviour which may cut across traditional cultural and national boundaries. There are several ways to cluster Euro-consumers, depending on the market or product. Each company will have to take its own circumstances into consideration, including the type of services that it offers.

A starting point for discussion of such clustering is suggested by research undertaken in 1989 by Vandermerwe and L'Huillier, whose findings argued for dividing Europe into six Euro-consumer clusters based on factors that included geography, per capita income levels, and age distribution of the population.[6] In several instances, one region of a country is located in one cluster and another in a second. We have modified and updated their conclusions to apply to the 15 countries forming the EU in 1999 – Austria, Belgium, Denmark, Finland, France, Germany, Greece, Ireland, Italy, Luxembourg, The Netherlands, Portugal, Spain, Sweden and the UK.

Table 16.1 presents brief profiles of each Euro-consumer cluster, describing income levels relative to the EU average, age distribution relative to the EU as a whole, and principal languages spoken (in many cases, of course, there are also regional and immigrant languages). Note that non-EU countries (e.g. Switzerland and Norway) and the still-depressed former East Germany have been excluded from the clusters. These clusters apply, of course, to individual consumers and households. If one were to develop a cluster map for certain types of business-to-business services, the results might look distinctively different, reflecting such issues as industry specialization, exploitation of different natural resources, climate and infrastructure.

Table 16.1 ■ Six clusters of Euro-consumers

Cluster 1: Northwestern Europe

■ United Kingdom and Ireland

■ Income levels near European average

■ Average EU age profile

■ Principal language: English

Cluster 2: Northeastern Europe

■ Northern Belgium (Flanders + Brussels), The Netherlands, Northern Germany (excluding former East Germany), Denmark, Sweden and Finland

■ Above average income

■ High proportion of middle-aged people

■ Principal languages: German, Dutch, Danish, Swedish and Finnish

Cluster 3: West Central Europe

■ Northern and Central France, Southern Belgium (Wallonia), Central Germany and Luxembourg

■ Average income level

■ Low proportion of middle-aged people, high proportion of older people

■ Principal languages: French and German

Cluster 4: East Central Europe

■ Southern Germany, Austria, Northern and Central Italy, and Southeastern France

■ High proportion of middle-aged people

■ Above average income level

■ Principal languages: German, French and Italian

Cluster 5: Southwestern Europe

■ Spain and Portugal

■ Relatively young population

■ Below average income level

■ Principal languages: Spanish and Portuguese

Cluster 6: Southeastern Europe

■ Southern Italy and Greece

■ Relatively young population

■ Below average income level

■ Principal languages: Italian and Greek

Forces for internationalization of service businesses

What drives internationalization of service businesses? Research by Yip identified several forces or *industry drivers* that influence the globalization of manufacturing firms.[7] We will now apply a modification of his framework to services in a pan-European context. Five categories of industry drivers favour pan-Europeanization and transnationally integrated strategy. They are market drivers, competition drivers, technology drivers, cost drivers and government drivers. The relative significance of each driver varies by service category. In some instances, there may even be variations by industry. Let's look at each category in turn.

Market drivers comprise the following elements: common customer needs, pan-European customers, pan-European channels, transferable marketing and lead countries. One factor of particular significance to many service industries is the presence of pan-European (or global) customers who demand consistent service from suppliers across Europe (or around the world) and the availability of international channels in the form of fast-developing physical supply chains or electronic networks. As large corporate customers themselves become pan-European, they often seek to standardize and simplify the suppliers they use in different countries for a wide array of business-to-business services.

This trend has been particularly noteworthy in recent years among information-based services. For instance, companies that operate globally often seek to minimize the number of auditors they use around the world, expressing a preference for using 'Big Five' accounting firms that can apply a consistent approach (within the context of the national rules prevailing within each country of operation). A second example comes from the move to global management of telecommunications, as evidenced by the coordinated service offered by Deutsche Telekom, France Telecom and their American partner Sprint which allows multinational corporations to outsource management of their international telecommunications needs. Corporate banking, insurance and management consulting are further examples. In each instance, there are real advantages in consistency, ease of access, consolidation of information and accountability.

A related trend can be found among some of the people-processing services used by international business travellers and tourists, who often feel more comfortable with predictable international standards of performance for such travel-related services as airlines and hotels. In possession-processing services, the development of international logistics capabilities (among European suppliers, Dutch firms have been particularly active in this sphere) has encouraged many manufacturers to outsource responsibility for their logistics function to a single firm, which then coordinates transportation and warehousing operations across Europe or even further afield.

Competition drivers are composed of high levels of exports and imports in a specific industry, the presence of competitors from different countries, interdependence of countries and the transnational policies of competitors themselves. Competition drivers exercise a powerful force in many service industries. To the extent that customers, who themselves operate across Europe, are known to value pan-European provision of services, a firm may be obliged to follow its competitors into new markets in order to protect its position in existing ones. Similarly, once a major player moves into a new foreign market, a scramble for territory among competing firms may ensue, particularly if the preferred mode of expansion involves purchasing or licensing the most successful local firms in each market.

Technology drivers are composed of advances in the performance and capabilities of telecommunications, computerization and software, miniaturization of equipment and the digitization of voice, video and text so that all can be stored and transmitted in the digital language of computers. For information-based services, the growing availability of broad-band telecommunication channels, capable of moving vast amounts of data at great speed, is playing a major role in opening up new markets. Access to the internet or World Wide Web is accelerating around the world. But there may be no need to duplicate all informational elements in each new location. Significant economies may be gained by centralizing 'information hubs' on a continent-wide or even global basis. It may also be advantageous to take advantage of favourable labour costs and exchange rates by consolidating operations of supplementary services (such as reservations) or back-office functions (such as accounting) in just one or a few selected countries.

Cost drivers include pan-European (or global) economies of scale, steep experience curve effects, sourcing efficiencies, favourable logistics, differences in country costs (including exchange rates), the need to recoup high product development costs and a rapid decline in the costs of key communication and transportation technologies relative to their performance. The effect of these drivers varies according to the level of fixed costs required to enter an industry and the potential for cost efficiencies. Lower operating costs for telecommunications and transportation, accompanied by improved performance, serve to facilitate entry into international markets. Barriers to entry caused by the upfront costs of equipment and facilities may be reduced by such strategies as equipment leasing (as in airlines), seeking investor-owned facilities such as hotels and then selling them on management contracts, or awarding franchises to local entrepreneurs. However, cost drivers may be less applicable for services that are primarily people-based and so require re-creating most elements of the 'service factory' in multiple locations. Under such circumstances, scale economies tend to be lower and experience curves relatively flatter. In service businesses in which new product development costs are low, cost drivers are also likely to be less significant.

Government drivers comprise favourable trade policies, compatible technical standards, common marketing regulations, government-owned competitors and customers, and host government policies. The actions taken by the European Commission to create and enhance the single market are of great significance for pan-European service strategies in numerous industries. Looking at a broader global picture, we can expect government drivers to be more favourable for people-processing and possession-processing services that require a significant local presence, because these services can create local employment opportunities. In contrast, governments often impose regulations to protect home-based services, such as passenger and freight transportation, from attacks by foreign carriers operating on the same routes (although such restrictive practices are increasingly under attack). A typical action involves restricting foreign airlines' landing rights or their ability to pick up passengers at an intermediate stop on a scheduled flight between two other countries.

If transportation services are easily exported, information-based services are even more so. Data, after all, can move around the world almost instantaneously through electronic channels. Governments can play an important role in requiring adoption of internationally compatible technical standards. However, unrestricted imports of services in categories ranging from entertainment to finance are often seen as both an economic and cultural threat. Hence such government actions as regulating international banking (widely practised), banning private ownership of satellite dishes (already implemented in China, Iran, Singapore and Saudi Arabia) or seeking to limit access to services on the internet.[8]

Modes of internationalization

Few firms are in a position to move swiftly from a purely domestic posture to a broad international presence. Typically, the move takes place over many years, beginning with expansion into selected markets. As with domestic expansion, several options are available. Vandermerwe and Chadwick[9] suggest three broad modes of internationalization, highlighted in Figure 16.1. The first, which is restricted to information-based

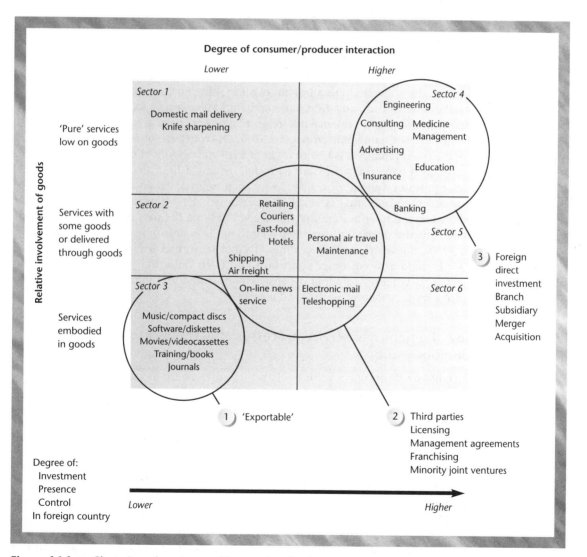

Figure 16.1 ■ Clustering of services and internationalization modes

Source: Sandra Vandermerwe and Michael Chadwick, 'The Internationalization of Service', *The Services Industries Journal*, January 1989, pp. 79–93.

services, involves capturing a service performance in some storage medium – a video cassette, diskette or CD-ROM, and then exporting what is now a physical good by mail order or local distributors. Customers obtain the value they are seeking by self-service through playback devices or computers. Entertainment, software and databases are all examples of such an approach. Alternatively, the service can be delivered through such channels as satellites, the internet, cinemas or broadcast stations.

The second approach involves reliance on third parties, through such arrangements as licensing agents, brokers, franchising and minority joint ventures. The extent of their responsibilities may vary from handling just a few supplementary services, such as provision of information and reservations, to delivering the entire service package and being responsible for all domestic marketing activities. Some intermediaries operate under their own names and simply identify themselves as agents or distributors, some link their name to that of the originating service organization (a common practice in international professional firms), while others (as in many franchises) completely assume the marketing identity of the original service organization and implement a global marketing strategy.

The third approach involves full control, achieved either through direct investment in a new operation or a buyout of an existing business which is then absorbed into the original company. International banks and express package firms have used both routes to gain a presence in foreign markets, as have accounting firms (see the case, Peters & Champlain, on pages 651–5). Buyouts are often favoured when the goal is to gain rapid access to a new client base and personnel who are already experienced in serving them, in contrast to following existing clients into new markets. The acquisition route is, of course, faster than internal expansion and allows immediate access to operating systems and personnel. The drawback is that substantial redirection and re-education may be needed to bring the new acquisition into alignment with the purchaser's existing operation. This task may result in a disruptive period during which quality declines, valued personnel leave and others are dismissed, leading to customer confusion and even defection to competitors. A big question is whether to adopt a consistent transnational marketing strategy or to create a strategy tailored to the local market.

How the nature of service processes affects opportunities for globalization

As emphasized throughout this book, not all services are the same. Let's explore the effects of international drivers on three categories of services which were discussed at length in Chapter 2: (1) people-processing services which involve each customer directly in delivery of services targeted at the customer's physical person; (2) possession-processing services targeted at physical objects belonging to the customer; and (3) information-based services targeted either at customers' minds or at their intangible assets.

People-processing services involve physical interactions with customers and necessarily require either that these people travel to the service 'factory' or that service providers and equipment come to the customer. In both instances, the service provider needs to maintain a local geographic presence, stationing the necessary personnel, buildings, equipment, vehicles and supplies within reasonably easy access of target customers. If the customers are themselves mobile – as in the case of business travellers and tourists, then the same customers are likely to be patronizing a company's offerings in many different locations, and making comparisons between them.

Possession-processing services may also be geographically constrained in many instances. A local presence is still required when the supplier must come to service objects in a fixed location; in the case of smaller, transportable items, certain services can be provided at more remote service centres – although transportation costs, customs duties and government regulations may constrain shipment across large distances or national frontiers. On the other hand, modern technology now allows certain types of service processes to be administered from a distance through electronic diagnostics and transmission of so-called 'remote fixes'.

Information-based services are, perhaps, the most interesting category of services from the standpoint of global strategy development, because they depend upon the transmission or manipulation of data in order to create value. The advent of modern global telecommunications, linking intelligent machines to powerful databases, makes it increasingly easy to deliver information-based services around the world. Local presence requirements may be limited to a terminal – ranging from a simple telephone or fax machine to a computer or more specialized equipment like a bank ATM – connected to a reliable telecommunications infrastructure. If the local infrastructure is not of sufficiently high quality, then use of mobile or satellite communications may solve the problem in some instances.

Overall assessment of drivers

Are some types of services more easily driven to internationalize than others? Our analysis suggests that this is, indeed, the case. Looking at the summary in Table 16.2, we can see important variations in the impact of each of the five groups of drivers. However, government drivers, expressed in terms of economic policy, regulation and protectionism, are often specific to individual industries (as evidenced by recent Directives from the European Commission concerning liberalization of air transport and telecommunication services within the EU). On an intercontinental or global scale, we can note bilateral British–American negotiations on commercial air travel and trade agreements within specific industries hammered out through the World Trade Organization. What this means is that we may need to examine drivers for internationalization at the level of individual industries, as well as in terms of broader service categories.

At the same time, it's useful to note that many of the factors driving internationalization also promote the trend to nationwide operations among service industries that previously operated only at a regional or local level. The market, cost, technological and competitive forces that encourage creation of nationwide service businesses or franchise chains are often the same as those that subsequently drive some of the same firms to operate transnationally. Yet many types of services, from plumbers to landscaping, still remain purely local in scope, as a review of business categories in the Yellow Pages reveals.

National and regional government drivers, too, can be influential in shaping service industry growth within federal nations such as Germany, the United States or Canada. Contrast, for instance, the sharply different ways in which retail banking has evolved in Canada as compared to the United States. The former has long had banks that served customers from coast to coast. In the United States, by contrast, the federal government banned interstate banking in the 1930s (a policy that is now beginning to be reversed), but state governments imposed their own tough regulations. Until recently, banking regulations varied widely between different states. For instance, the huge state of California permitted banks to operate branches statewide,

Table 16.2 ■ Impact of globalization drivers on different service categories

Globalization drivers	Service category		
	People processing	**Possession processing**	**Information-based**
Competition	Simultaneity of production and consumption limits leverage of foreign-based competitive advantage in frontstage of service factory, but advantage in management *systems* can be basis for globalization.	Lead role of technology creates driver for globalization of competitors with technical edge (e.g., Singapore Airlines technical servicing for other carriers' aircraft).	Highly vulnerable to global dominance by competitors with monopoly or competitive advantage in information (e.g., BBC, Hollywood, CNN), unless restricted by governments.
Market	People differ economically, and culturally, so needs for service and ability to pay may vary. Culture and education may affect willingness to do self-service.	Less variation for service to corporate possessions, but level of economic development impacts demand for services to individually owned goods.	Demand for many services is derived to a significant degree from economic and educational levels. Cultural issues may affect demand for entertainment.
Technology	Use of IT for delivery of supplementary services may be a function of ownership and familiarity with technology, including telecommunications and intelligent terminals.	Need for technology-based service delivery systems is a function of the types of possessions requiring service and the cost trade-offs in labour substitution.	Ability to deliver core services through remote terminals may be a function of investments in computerization, quality of telecommunications infrastructure and education levels.
Cost	Variable labour rates may impact on pricing in labour-intensive services (consider self-service in high-cost locations).	Variable labour rates may favour low-cost locations if not offset by shipment costs. Consider substituting equipment for labour.	Major cost elements can be centralized and minor cost elements localized.
Government	Social policies (e.g., health) vary widely and may affect labour costs, role of women in frontstage jobs and hours/days on which work can be performed.	Tax laws, environmental regulations and technical standards may decrease/ increase costs and encourage/discourage certain types of activity.	Policies on education, censorship, public ownership of communications and infrastructure standards may impact on demand and supply, and distort pricing.

but for many years Massachusetts, a much smaller state, restricted each bank's operations to only one of the state's 14 counties, whereas in Illinois, one of the larger states, each bank was limited to just a single office. These branching restrictions have now fallen, in most states, before the twin forces of bank holding companies and electronic ATM networks.

In Europe, aggressive economic development efforts by regional government agencies, such as those in Wales or Catalonia, have succeeded in attracting foreign investment. Targets of particular interest are customer call centres and the back offices of large international service businesses. In certain parts of Europe, traditional political boundaries make little economic sense. For example, the Rhône Alps area of south-eastern France, with Lyon at its core, is aggressively promoting itself as a multi-country region (embracing portions of France, Switzerland and Italy). Lyon, in particular, argues that the city offers excellent infrastructure proximity to many of the great economic centres of Europe and is a logical site for corporate headquarters.

Transnational strategy for supplementary services

So far, we've focused on describing global strategy as it relates to different categories of core services. However, as we saw in Chapter 8, the core product – a bed for the night, restoring a defective computer to good working order, or a bank account – is typically accompanied by a variety of supplementary elements. Many manufacturing businesses, too, offer their customers a package that includes a variety of service-related activities. These supplementary elements not only add value and provide the differentiation that separates successful firms from the also-rans; they also offer opportunities for firms to develop effective transnational strategies.

The Flower of Service model (see Figure 8.3 on page 299 and Tables 8.1–8.8) groups supplementary services into eight categories (information, consultation, order-taking, hospitality, safekeeping, exceptions, billing and payment). Not every core product – whether a good or a service – is surrounded by supplementary elements from all eight clusters, of course. In practice, the nature of the product, customer requirements and competitive practices help managers to determine which supplementary services must be offered and which might usefully be added to enhance value and make it easy to do business with the organization.

One determinant of what supplementary services to include is market positioning. A strategy of adding benefits to gain a competitive edge probably requires more supplementary services (and also a higher level of performance on all such elements) than one of offering a basic service with minimum frills. In developing a transnational strategy, management must decide which, if any, supplementary elements should be consistent across all markets and which might be tailored to meet local needs, expectations and competitive dynamics. Such decisions lie at the heart of standardization vs. customization, but services offer much more flexibility in this respect than do physical goods. Let's look at the implications of creating a transnational strategy for each of the eight groups of supplementary services.

Information

To obtain full value from any good or service, customers need relevant information about it. New customers and prospects are especially information-hungry. Transnationalization affects both the location of information access and the nature of that information (including the languages and format in which it is provided).

Consultation and advice

In contrast to information, consultation and advice involve a dialogue to probe customer requirements and then develop a tailored solution. Customers' need for advice may vary widely across Europe (or around the world), reflecting such factors as level of economic development, nature of the local infrastructure, topography and climate, technical standards and educational levels.

Order-taking (including reservations)

Once customers are ready to buy, a key supplementary element should come into play: accepting applications, orders and reservations. Transnationalization affects both the nature and location of order-taking access, such as the potential for instituting global reservation systems.

Hospitality: taking care of the customer

A well-managed business should try, at least in small ways, to treat customers as guests when they have to visit the supplier's facilities (especially when, as is true for many people-processing operations, the period extends over several hours or more). Cultural definitions of appropriate hospitality may differ widely from one country to another, such as the tolerable length of waiting time (much longer in Russia than in Germany) and the degree of personal service expected (higher in France, for instance, than in the Scandinavian countries).

Safekeeping: looking after the customer's possessions

When visiting a service site, customers often want assistance with their personal possessions. Expectations often vary by country, reflecting culture and levels of affluence. For example, most restaurants in the United States bar dogs, but in France most will tolerate them, and in China some restaurants may even cook them for you!

Exceptions

Exceptions fall outside the routine of normal service delivery. They include special requests, problem-solving, handling of complaints/suggestions/compliments, and restitution (compensating customers for performance failures). Special requests are particularly common in people-processing services, as in the travel and hotel industries. International airlines, for example, find it necessary to respond to an array of medical and dietary needs, sometimes reflecting religious and cultural values. Problem-solving is often more difficult for people who are travelling abroad than it would be in the familiar environment of their native country. For many Europeans, simply crossing a national frontier still means a change of currency and language – and even a change of script from Roman to Cyrillic. It's easier to be a victim of crime (or just fearful of it) in an unfamiliar setting and the consequences are likely to be more unsettling. Despite improvements in public health across Europe, many northern Europeans still worry about water quality and the risk of disease when travelling in parts of Southern and Eastern Europe. And sadly, travelling in the Balkans remains fraught with danger. Travel service firms such as American Express and Thomas Cook often capitalize on their ability to help cardholders facing medical or other emergencies far from home.

Billing

Customers need clear, timely bills that explain how charges are computed. With abolition of currency exchange restrictions in many countries, travellers from many nations now expect to be able to make purchases on their credit cards almost anywhere and to have bills converted to their home currencies. In a pan-European setting, therefore, currencies and conversion rates need to be clarified on billing statements. Even after the first stage of monetary union, euros will still have to be converted into pounds and certain other currencies. In some instances, prices can be displayed in several currencies, although this policy may require frequent adjustments in the light of currency fluctuations.

Payment

Ease and convenience of payment (including credit) are increasingly expected by customers when purchasing a broad array of goods and services. Acceptance of major credit cards and travellers' cheques solves the problem of paying in foreign funds for many retail purchases, but some shops go even further to accommodate customers. At London's Heathrow Airport, travellers can pay bills for restaurants and other stores with banknotes from several major currencies. The advent of the euro will greatly simplify payment procedures across Europe once the initial hurdles of its introduction are overcome. Firms with operations outside the euro bloc may find themselves obliged to accept payment in both euros and the local currency as a service to their customers.

Why information-based supplementary services lend themselves to transnationalization

As we saw in Chapter 8, most supplementary services are information-based and can potentially be delivered from remote locations. In theory, a global company could centralize its billing on a global basis, using postal or telecommunication distribution channels to deliver the bills to customers, suitably converted to the relevant currency. (The same approach, on a geographically smaller scale, could be applied to pan-European billing.) Similarly, information, consultation, order-taking/reservations, problem-solving and payment can all be handled through telecommunications. As long as the appropriate languages are available, many such service elements could be delivered from almost anywhere. By contrast, hospitality and safekeeping will always have to be provided locally, because they are responsive to the physical presence of customers and their possessions.

Elements of global transnational strategy

How do we determine whether a firm's international strategy can realistically be described as *transnational* rather than *multi-local*? And how might the distinctive characteristics of service businesses affect the ability or necessity to adopt and implement specific aspects of a transnational approach?

Five 'transnational strategy levers' serve to determine whether international strategy is primarily multi-local (re-created independently in each location) or primarily transnational.[10] Within each dimension, strategic options cover a spectrum that ranges from a strictly multi-local orientation to a completely global one. Let's look at the *global* end of the spectrum for each of these five dimensions (recognizing that if taking a purely European view we could substitute the word 'pan-European' for 'global'). Judicious use of these global strategy levers can enable a firm to obtain one or more important benefits: cost reductions, improved quality of products and processes, greater customer preference and increased competitive leverage.

Global market participation

Management selects countries in which to market its services not just on the basis of stand-alone attractiveness; it also considers the potential of each market to contribute to broader globalization benefits.

Delivering global products

The firm offers a standardized core product (either a good or a service) that requires a minimum of local adaptation.

Global location of value-adding supplementary services

The value chain is broken up across different countries; with management adopting a strategy of creating supplementary services in one country (or a limited number of countries) for worldwide delivery, rather than duplicating each activity in many different countries. Looking at this another way, we could say that in a given location, the flower of service is pieced together with individual petals imported electronically from around the world. Technology allows information-based petals to be delivered in real time to the service site from anywhere with good telecommunication links.

Global marketing

Management employs a consistent marketing approach around the world, although not all elements of the marketing mix need be identical. Typically, corporate design is identical (except for language variations) and advertising themes and execution are recognizably similar. Market positioning, however, may vary somewhat in the light of local competitive offerings.

Global competitive moves

These are integrated across countries. The same type of move is made in different countries at the same time or in some systematic sequence. In highly competitive industries, a competitor may be targeted in one country in order to drain the resources that it was planning to apply in another country, or an assault by a competitor on the company's position in one country may be countered by a vigorous marketing campaign against that same competitor in a different country.

Services and transnational market participation

Certain types of services seem very easy to spread around Europe (or the world), and others very difficult. In the 'easy' category fall simple service concepts that are easily replicable and therefore franchisable. Some 'essential' services, such as banking, telecommunications, hospitals and airlines, operate in heavily regulated environments, making it difficult to gain rapid penetration of foreign markets. But progress is being made in establishing global reputations for service businesses that are closely associated with a specific country (consider, for instance, American Express, BT, Crédit Suisse, Lufthansa, Mandarin-Oriental Hotels, Qantas, Royal Bank of Canada, Singapore Telecom and Zurich Insurance). Similarly, many formerly national brands are becoming well known throughout Europe, even though their sphere of operations does not extend outside this continent.

Historically, businesses that rely on trust and the reputation of their personnel – such as law firms and other professional service providers – have found it difficult to demonstrate quality to potential foreign customers and to adopt a professional style that fits the local culture. Ways to overcome such hurdles include not only extensive advertising and public relations, but also hiring host country nationals who have obtained education and work experience in other countries. Another approach is through mergers and alliances. Five of Europe's leading commercial law firms recently joined forces to create Europe's largest legal practice (the second largest in the world). The new firm allies Linklaters of the UK to the German, Dutch, Belgian and Swedish members of the Alliance of European Lawyers.[11]

A pan-European strategic approach to market participation involves building significant share in strategically key markets. Some countries have strategic importance beyond their stand-alone attractiveness, such as adding sufficient volume to achieve broader economies of scale, or being the home market of major international customers and competitors, or else a key centre of industry innovation. Failure to participate in these strategic markets can undermine international competitiveness. However, the criteria for identifying such countries vary between manufacturing and service industries, as illustrated by the following global example.

In the case of manufacturing, it's now widely recognized that many American and European manufacturing companies have suffered from not building significant positions in Japan, thus limiting potential economies of scale in manufacturing, failing to gain exposure to Japanese innovation and high customer standards, and being unable to create in that market a hostage for good behaviour on the part of Japanese rivals operating in Europe and North America.

On the other hand, except for network organizations (notably airlines, logistics firms, travel services and financial services), it's hard to see how a service firm's presence or absence in Japan (or any other individual country) significantly affects its global strategic position, other than contributing revenues and profits. A few Western service companies have built successful businesses in Japan, either because their Western orientation (such as American-style fast food) appealed to Japanese consumers or because they were creating an international network that could not afford to be absent from such a major market.

For network firms, highly specific geographic locations may be seen as essential. No financial service firm with global ambitions, for instance, can afford not to have a presence in New York, London or Tokyo. Similarly, a financial firm with pan-European ambitions would probably feel obliged to have a presence in London, Frankfurt, Paris and Zurich – and possibly Amsterdam and Milan, as well. Even in this electronic age, birds of a feather still find value in flocking together! Similarly, there is intense competition among airlines for landing rights and gates at key global hub airports such as London-Heathrow, New York-JFK and Los Angeles International. For intra-European travel, many other airports would join Heathrow as key geographic locations, including London-Gatwick, Frankfurt, Paris Charles-de-Gaulle, Amsterdam-Schipol and Zurich.

In the case of travel-related services, wider global market participation makes a brand more valuable to customers. Thus, American Express traveller's cheques and credit cards are useful precisely because they are widely accepted in most countries. Similarly, international airlines enhance their appeal as they fly to more destinations and provide more connections at their hubs. There is a growing trend for airlines to form global partnerships with carriers that have complementary routes and then to coordinate their schedules so as to feed passengers to each other's services. One example is Northwest Airlines and KLM; a second is the Star network which includes United Airlines, Lufthansa, SAS, Thai, Varig and Air Canada; and a third is British Airways, which has taken equity stakes in a German subsidiary, two French airlines and the Australian airline, Qantas. In 1998, BA announced formation of the Oneworld network in partnership with American Airlines, Canadian Airlines, Cathay Pacific and Qantas.

Delivering global goods and services

Turning to the second transnational strategy lever, it may be easier to create a globally standardized service than a globally standardized physical product. One great dilemma for manufacturing businesses is how to balance global standardization with local customization. Designing, then manufacturing, a global product with a degree of local customization may require major trade-offs. It has proved hard to achieve in fields ranging from cars to refrigerators. In contrast, the nature of service delivery, which often takes place at the point of consumption, makes both standardization and customization equally feasible. Local elements (e.g., cuisine) can be easily added to a pan-European formula for a business such as a hotel chain. Further, employing local nationals as customer-contact personnel may overcome the foreignness of a standardized service (e.g., use of local cabin crews by international airlines). As we shall see later, it is relatively easy to provide a globally standardized core service, augmented and differentiated by nationally customized supplementary service elements.

Location of value-adding service activities

Some service businesses have not achieved the same level of success abroad as in their home country. One reason for failure may lie in not being able to transfer home-based sources of advantage. Euro Disney cannot duplicate at Disneyland Paris in northern France the sunny weather of Florida and southern California, nor (so far) has it been able to re-create within the ranks of its French 'cast' the friendliness of its American staffers (see the 'Euro Disney' case on pages 103–18). By contrast, Club Med has succeeded in duplicating almost all of its value chain in each of its warm weather locations, meticulously reproducing its successful core formula, which includes a unique staff (the famous Club Med GOs – Gentils Organisateurs – who enjoy a lot more flexibility than do Disney staffers), a village near the water, fun and games, and a high probability of pleasant weather. (However, as noted in Chapter 5, the company has had more difficulty in adjusting to changing market trends about what is desired in a holiday.) With the exception of advance information and reservations – usually delivered by travel agents – most supplementary services are duplicated at each site. Similarly, there is a different core product but a high degree of consistency at Club Med ski locations, where the company also duplicates most supplementary services on site, from food and après-ski entertainment to ski rentals and instruction.

Service firms can exploit differences in national comparative advantages as they seek to build more efficient value chains. A growing number of service-based businesses have identified key backstage activities that can be conducted more cheaply but without loss of quality in a different country from where their customers are located. For example, some US banks and insurance companies now send cheques and claims to be processed in East Asia or in Ireland. Meanwhile, Swissair has transferred part of its accounting operations to India. American Express Europe processes all its continent-wide billing activities in Brighton, on the south coast of England. This strategy is being adopted for frontstage service elements, too, as companies build global reservation and customer service systems that are networked around Europe or even around the world.

Transnational marketing of services

In general, services seem to make more use of international branding than do manufacturing firms, especially in consumer markets. The uncertainty created by intangibility can be offset by strong branding, so the primary task of the brand name or trademark for a service is to offer recognition and reassurance, rather than performing other functions such as positioning or local adaptation. McDonald's operates under the same name and 'golden arches' trademark around the world, so that both locals and travellers know that they will get the genuine McDonald's experience. Travel-related services virtually require the same brand name globally. How much value would an American Express card lose if the local brand were Russian Express in Moscow?

International branding is supported by transnational advertising and consistent corporate design, featuring recognizable colour schemes (yellow for Hertz, bright green for BP service stations) and an easily identified logo and trademark. Transnational or global advertising campaigns – sometimes termed 'strategic advertising' as distinct from local or 'tactical' promotions – often employ the same video sequences with voice-over in the local language. One of the challenges when creating global campaigns – even more than pan-European campaigns – is to create visual themes that will travel well across different cultures. In recent years, for instance, British Airways' TV advertising has featured dramatic opening scenes followed by people of many races coming together in visually stunning locations. The need to be able to create and implement such campaigns for global clients has been an important factor in globalization of the advertising industry.[12]

In contrast, simultaneity of production and consumption in many service businesses means that firms have less need to worry about consistent pricing across national frontiers. Except for those information-based services that can be captured in printed or electronic hard copies, it's still relatively difficult to buy a service created in one country and then sell it in another. On the other hand, there are sometimes wide disparities between prices for international telephone calls, depending on the country in which it originates. For instance a call from Rome to London is more expensive than London to Rome. This anomaly has been exploited by companies such as BT, which offers customers travelling abroad the opportunity to use their BT Charge Card service, which involves dialling a local number to reach an English-speaking BT operator who will then place the call and charge it at British rates to the customer's home account. In the case of multinational customers, many service businesses try to avoid charging the same customer different prices in different countries without good justification. Increasingly, the purchasing departments of multinational companies are beginning to behave as transnational rather than multi-local customers. Recognizing this development, Hewlett-Packard offers worldwide contracts to its major global accounts for both manufactured products and services.

Transnational competitive moves

Service-based businesses need to make integrated competitive moves as much as do manufacturing-based businesses. But the key feature of such moves, cross-country coordination, can be both easier and more difficult. Coordination is likely to be simpler for service firms that reproduce a strong core formula across Europe or around the world. In such businesses, corporate headquarters plays a continuing role in monitoring the strategies of overseas units, such as restaurant chains and hotels. But the prevalence of franchising in services, and its resulting dispersion of ownership, complicates the task of transnational coordination. Most accounting firms, for example, still manage their international operations mostly on a quasi-franchise basis, with little sharing of ownership or profits across countries. (Arthur Andersen is an exception and some other big professional firms are looking to follow suit.) Coordination may also be less necessary when both production and consumption occur locally and central support plays a minor role.

Pan-European strategies in business logistics[13]

Four of the most significant European trends of the 1990s – European integration, the privatization and deregulation of former government monopolies in the utilities sector, intensified international competition and ever more demanding business customers – have had profound repercussions across most European service sector companies. Perhaps nowhere more so however than amongst the variety of companies involved in logistics – ranging from the express delivery of mail and documents, to the warehousing and transportation of parcels, spare parts and completed products.

Differentiation and positioning

For the leading international logistics companies in the field of express delivery – who now call themselves, and act as, 'integrators' – DHL, FedEx, UPS and TNT – the challenge is multiple: how to differentiate and position themselves while at the same time developing and entrenching long-term partnerships with their ever more demanding multinational clients. As the UK marketing director for UPS puts it, the 'relationship between multinational clients and logistics suppliers is close to a true partnership, with the logistics company having to find impossible solutions to apparent intractable problems'.

Increasingly, positioning such a firm effectively in the €110 billion European logistics market means stretching the boundaries of traditional logistics and finding ways to differentiate beyond the speed and price of delivery.

The search for value-added services

The stakes are high, as more and more European multinationals see logistics not just as a cost, but as a means of giving themselves a competitive edge. For example, some client companies prefer to have their delivery vehicles painted to display the livery (colours and logo) of the logistics company's brand, rather than their own, since they want their customers to see that they are entrusting delivery to an 'integrator', and not just traditional, old-fashioned distribution. In turn, good financial margins for the logistics firms are increasingly to be found not in basic delivery but in the value-added services they can provide and be known for.

Even the largest of these companies – DHL, with 38 per cent market share – is not immune to the radical shift in its business, and it too is devising ways to make itself integral to a broad spectrum of its clients' operations. For instance, one of its clients – a European multinational – has hundreds of salespeople, all of whom are highly dependent on their laptops both to record sales information and download it to the mainframe at headquarters. Given the importance of the laptop to the salesperson, dropping, breaking or losing it would be catastrophic. In order to deal with such an eventuality, DHL not only maintains a supply of spare laptops in its warehouses, but also configures keyboards in the needed language (i.e., adding umlauts for German salespeople, acute and grave accents for the French, etc.), and keeps copies of each salesperson's sales records which can be downloaded onto the spare laptop. The idea is that the spare laptop should perform in exactly the same way, and with the same data, as the broken or stolen one. For DHL, this is a far cry from its traditional role as just an on-time deliverer, and more akin to its desired positioning as an integral partner to its corporate clients.

Other logistic firms feel that the future lies in information and electronic technology. Companies like UPS and FedEx, for example, are focusing on these activities and positioning themselves accordingly. As part of its two-pronged strategy to strengthen intra-European as well as global services, UPS is using IT to position itself solidly as both 'international' and 'local' across Europe. Not only has it launched web sites in French, German, Italian, Spanish and English, which provide information on products and services, but it has also created pages for customers in Switzerland, Belgium, Holland, Denmark, Austria, Portugal, Ireland and even Catalonia (the Catalan-speaking region of Spain anchored by Barcelona), to allow them to track their packages practically on a minute-by-minute basis.

In addition to investments in IT, a big effort is being put into vehicles and infrastructure, and one strength of its European operations is the ability to link with its specialist subsidiary, UPS Worldwide Logistics, to offer added value services. For instance, when orders come into the European operations of US computer manufacturer Gateway in Dublin, Gateway staff pick and pack the goods for sale directly to the customer. However, on-site UPS staff arrange the shipping. Using ferry and road services, consignments move through UPS's European road network via hubs in the UK, France and Germany for delivery in about three days to the customer. According to UPS sources, four months after this new European strategy, UPS volumes rose by 9 per cent.

Another positioning tack is being applied by TNT – since 1996, part of KPN, the Dutch privatized post and telecom utility active in bulk business mail. Following the merger between these two firms, it has become Europe's largest player in express mail delivery, with the most extensive network on the Continent, and the undisputed leader in global mail services to business, an area in which the former Dutch utility had already firmly positioned itself. In fact, KPN's postal subsidiary, PTT Post, had long been the most internationally minded of Europe's mail services, and had aggressively bid for and acquired the business of the region's bulk mailers. By the time of the merger with TNT, its international business – as a proportion of revenues – was twice as high as that of other European post offices.[14]

While the established companies continue to battle to capture the European corporate market, newcomers are also entering the scene. In fact, such is the anticipated growth potential of this sector for those firms which can position themselves as real partners and integrators, that even the US manufacturer GE, through its service arm GE Capital, has decided to enter the market. UK-based Penske Logistics Europe, 79 per cent owned by GE Capital, plans to revolutionize European logistics by becoming the single service provider in logistics for all of Europe.

Like the four major players (although it is not focusing on speedy, time-based delivery of small packages), Penske also plans to steer clear of purely 'physical logistics' by getting involved in other parts of its clients' production processes and value chains, such as taking over ownership of clients' stocks, sub-assembling components and scheduling in-bound material. And, through its 'fulfilment centre', it will offer services such as debt collection, tax representation and product testing for MNCs headquartered outside Europe.[15] The overriding objective for Penske is to build the first seamless, pan-European delivery network, designed to provide truly integrated European solutions with a single commercial interface.

As all of the players – the well established and newcomers alike – concur, the future of the industry is all about added value. Being able to position themselves accordingly is the strategic challenge now facing these service companies, and will ultimately determine whether or not they succeed.

Conclusion

More and more service businesses are now marketing across national borders. However, an international strategy needs to be more than just a collection of domestic (or 'multi-local') strategies. A truly transnational strategy – whether it be pan-European in scope or even global – requires selecting countries on more than just stand-alone attractiveness; it must also consider the potential of each market to contribute to the broader benefits associated with a large international business. Delivering global products requires that the firm offer a standardized core product (either a good or a service) that requires a minimum of local adaptation. Supplementary services, however, offer flexibility in that many can be either standardized or tailored to meet the needs of customs in local markets. Transnational marketing requires that management should use a consistent marketing approach in every country where it does business, although not all elements of the marketing mix need be identical. Market positioning, however, may vary somewhat in the light of local competitive offerings. Finally, competitive moves should be integrated across countries, with the same type of move being made in different countries at the same time or in some systematic sequence.

Stimulating (or constraining) the move to transnational strategies are such industry drivers as market factors, costs, technology, government policies and competitive forces. However, significant differences exist in the extent to which the various drivers apply to people-processing, possession-processing and information-based services. Within each broad service category, it's important to analyze each industry systematically to determine not only how specific drivers currently affect that particular industry, but also to project how they might change over time. Similarly, managers need to evaluate alternative strategies for their own company, in the light of its size and market position, as well as corporate objectives, values and investment criteria.

Managers should also consider the opportunities that exist to standardize each supplementary service element as well as the core product. Continuing advances in information technology make even global strategies feasible for many information-based elements. As a result, certain supplementary services can be delivered from a central location, using conventional telecommunications or the internet. Others, however, require localized delivery systems, including local personnel and facilities. The combination of a globally standardized core product and customized supplementary services may offer service firms the opportunity to achieve the benefits of both system-wide efficiency and local market appeal.

Study questions

1. Explain the distinction between 'multi-local' and 'transnational' marketing strategies as they relate to (a) the EU, and (b) the world.

2. What can service marketers who are planning pan-European strategies learn from studying the United States?

3. Review the six 'Euro-clusters' proposed on pages 591–2. What alternative ways of clustering the population of Greater Europe (including countries currently outside the EU) might be particularly useful to service firms that offer information-based services?

4. Select three different service industries. In each instance, which do you see as the most significant of the five industry drivers as forces for pan-Europeanization, and why?

5. To what extent should service businesses attempt to standardize both core and supplementary service elements when marketing throughout the EU? Suggest specific instances where you believe that a strategy of mass customization would be more appropriate for some of the supplementary services.

6. Review the five transnational strategy levers. Define the *local* (that is, country-specific) end of the spectrum for each of these five dimensions. What actions might be required to move a service firm towards the *global* end of the spectrum on each dimension?

Notes

1. Information on Groupe Accor is derived from Andrew Jack, 'The Global Company: Why There is No Future for National Hotel Chains', *Financial Times*, 10 October 1997; W. Chan Kim and Renee Mauborgne, 'Value Innovation: The Strategic Logic of High Growth', *Harvard Business Review*, January–February 1997; and Ken Irons, *The World of Superservice: Creating Profit through a Passion for Customer Service*, London: Addison-Wesley, 1997, pp. 121–3.

2. See Thomas Hout, Michael E. Porter and Eileen Rudden, 'How Global Companies Win Out', *Harvard Business Review*, September–October 1982, pp. 98–108; C.K. Pralahad and Yves L. Doz, *The Multinational Mission: Balancing Local Demands and Global Vision*, New York: The Free Press, 1987; and George S. Yip, 'Global Strategy . . . in a World of Nations?', *Sloan Management Review*, Vol. 31, Fall 1989, pp. 29–41.

3. Michael E. Porter, 'Changing Patterns of International Competition', *California Management Review*, Vol. 28, Winter 1986, pp. 9–40.

4. George S. Yip, *Total Global Strategy: Managing for Worldwide Competitive Advantage*, Englewood Cliffs, NJ: Prentice Hall, 1992.

5. Christopher H. Lovelock and George S. Yip, 'Developing Global Strategies for Service Businesses', *California Management Review*, Winter 1996, pp. 64–86.

6. Sandra Vandermerwe and Marc-André L'Huillier, 'Euro Consumers in 1992', *Business Horizons*, January–February 1989.

7. Yip, *op. cit.*; Johnny K. Johansson and George S. Yip, 'Exploiting Globalization Potential: US and Japanese Strategies', *Strategic Management Journal*, October 1994, pp. 579–601. (Note: the original framework embraced four drivers; we have broken out technology as a fifth and separate driver.)

8. See, for example, 'An Intruder in the Kingdom: Saudi Officials Try to Police Taboo Subjects on the Internet', *Business Week*, 21 August 1995, p. 40; 'Chat Rooms and Chadors. Iran: Will the Internet Open a Closed Society?', *Newsweek*, 21 August 1995, p. 36.

9. Sandra Vandermerwe and Michael Chadwick, 'The Internationalization of Service', *The Services Industries Journal*, January 1989, pp. 79–93.

10. See Yip, *op. cit.*, especially pp. 15–23.

11. Robert Rice and William Lewis, 'Five Firms Link to Create Biggest Legal Practice in Europe', *Financial Times*, 24 July 1998, p. 1.

12. P.W. Daniels, 'The Internationalization of Advertising Services in a Changing Regulatory Environment', *The Service Industries Journal,* Vol. 15, No. 3, July 1995, pp. 276–94.

13. Information in the section is based on: Peter Martin, 'The Resurgence of Privately Owned Postal Services is Creating New Global Giants Capable of Handling All Aspects of Distribution for Business', *Financial Times*, 3 October 1996; Michael Terry, 'Tough result to Deliver – Observers Doubt UPS's Chances of Overtaking the World Market Leader, DHL', *Financial Times*, 13 June 1997; Charles Gresser, 'GE to Set up Europe-Wide Logistics Venture', *Financial Times*, 26 August 1997; Charles Batchelor, 'Specialists are Increasing their Share of Europe's $130 Billion Logistics Market, But they Must Make Allies of IT and the Environment to Progress', *Financial Times*, 7 October 1997; Jonathan Prynn, 'Logistics: The Age of Integration Dawns', *Financial Times*, 9 October 1997; and 'Penske Logistics Europe Expands its Network', *Transport News*, 18 March 1998.

14. Peter Martin, 'The Resurgence of Privately Owned Postal Services is Creating New Global Giants Capable of Handling All Aspects of Distribution for Business', *Financial Times,* 3 October 1996.

15. Charles Gresser, 'GE to Set up Europe-Wide Logistics Venture', *Financial Times*, 26 August 1997; 'Penske Logistics Europe Expands its Network', *Transport News*, 18 March 1998.

Measuring your marketing success

David H. Maister

Marketing is about getting better business not just more business. Firms should monitor the calibre of their practice, not just its volume.

When I ask those who work in professional service firms what formal measures they use to monitor the success of their marketing efforts, the most common response is 'Well, if revenues go up, we feel we've succeeded'. Similarly, when I have sat in on practice-group marketing meetings, it is invariably gross revenues that they discuss. This all seems reasonable – but, as we shall see, revenues are an insufficient (and potentially misleading) indicator of marketing success.

What the revenue measure fails to reflect is that marketing in a professional firm is (or should be) about getting *better* business, not just *more* business. Firms should spend more time tracking and formally monitoring the calibre of business they bring in, not just its volume. Yet few firms have such mechanisms in place.

What do I mean by 'better' business? There are two tests that new business must meet to be classified as better business: the income-statement test and the balance-sheet test.

The income-statement test

The income-statement test is simplicity itself: work is better business if it is more profitable than work the firm traditionally obtains. This should seem so obvious as not to merit much discussion. In principle, most firms would claim that they take profitability considerations into account when deciding where to place their marketing efforts. The reality, however, is often different. I have observed more than a few firms whose approach to practice development is 'If it moves, shoot it'. Or, to phrase it another way, 'We've never seen a piece of new business we didn't like'.

Profitability considerations, in practice, end up being ignored in marketing. Individuals pursue every opportunity presented to them, and a few that aren't. Above all else, generating *volume* is the underlying marketing philosophy. Yet there are many firms who were so successful in their marketing that they ended up with lower profits per partner than when they started. Taking in every piece of low-profit business you can get is a fine way to grow, but I wouldn't call it great marketing.

Firms do this for a number of reasons, one being insecurity. If you are not confident in your marketing ability to attract and win the best business, then it's easy to justify that you have to go after any business you can. Of course, this can be (and is in many firms I have observed) a self-fulfilling prophecy. Practice groups get so busy proposing on every request for proposal they see that they have no *time* to go after better business. If it is suggested that they should propose on fewer low-profit, low-probability opportunities and spend the extra time more productively on some other part of the marketing effort, one gets the reaction: 'We couldn't do that! You mean actually decline to respond to a proposal opportunity? We *never* do that!'

A second cause of this behaviour is that firms tend to overemphasize 'business origination' (i.e. marketing success) in their performance criteria for senior professionals. The more business you generate, the better you look. Rarely do firms have the systems in place equipped or inclined to ask 'Was the business that this person generated profitable?' When performing statistical analyses on compensation systems, I almost always discover that, although

Reprinted from *True Professionalism*, New York: The Free Press, 1997. © 1997 by David H. Maister.

there usually is a correlation between the volume of revenues generated and compensation, there either is no measure of engagement profitability or else it exists but is not correlated with compensation awards. Quite simply, the firm's professionals believe that they'll be rewarded for bringing in business – period. Profitability is nice, but secondary.

In many firms this is not an unintended side-effect – they truly do believe that all new business is good business (especially in a recession). They argue that they must keep their people busy, and that even less than fully profitable work is economical if their staff would otherwise be idle. This argument is an irrefutable example of short-term thinking. *Of course*, low-profit work is better than no work – *this* year. But again we must point out that this can hardly be called 'marketing success': taking any work you can get is no way to build a business. To be successful, a firm must win more than its fair share of the profitable work, and marketing-success measures must be established to track this.

There is an additional problem here. Many firms that do measure profitability at the engagement or project level use proxy measures for profitability such as *realization rate* (the percentage of standard fees that the project will command). But this is an insufficient measure. Profits do indeed come from high fees and high margins but firm owners or partners can also make good profits by taking in lower-fee work which allows good leverage (i.e., a high ratio of employees to owners or partners). To properly track their marketing success, firms need to have a costing system which reveals the true (fully costed) profitability of each job. Only then can they tell whether their marketing efforts are helping them to improve.

The balance-sheet test

If we're bringing in profitable work, then our marketing must be working – yes? Unfortunately – no! There's another hurdle to jump over. We must ask ourselves whether or not we are bringing in work that will help us improve our skills and stay competitive. The jobs that professionals work on can be either asset-*milking* (taking advantage of and exploiting existing skills, relationships and reputation) or asset-*building* (offering the opportunity to develop new skills by working on frontier innovative projects, building new and stronger client relationships that will pay dividends in future years and creating a reputation in new fields or market segments).

Which of the two types of work are generated by a firm's marketing efforts is critical to its success. In any given year, either asset-milking *or* asset-building work can generate good current profits. But too much asset-milking work will leave the firm exposed strategically. Skills and reputations depreciate over time, and only by building new skills, relationships and reputations can a firm thrive over time.

Most firms would agree with this reasoning, and even accept it intellectually. However, it is the rare firm that has found a way to build this reasoning into its management practices. How many firms have a functioning formal screen to evaluate new business opportunities based upon their asset value? How many firms regularly review their mix of new business, and assess not only the quantity of the practice but also its calibre? The answer is: relatively few.

Doing these things is not complicated. Here's one effective way to build it into your management process: every three months or so, each of your practice groups (discipline groups, offices, industry teams, etc.) should get together and pull out the list of every new engagement they have worked on in the previous quarter. Someone from outside the practice group (a managing partner or a group head from a different group) should attend, to play the role of 'friendly sceptic'.

At the meeting, each new engagement is assigned a set of scores, using the criteria shown in Figure 1. In essence, you will be probing to ask 'What did this piece of business do for us?'. The answer 'It provided revenue and kept us busy' is nice enough, but should never be accepted as sufficient. There truly is good revenue and less good revenue, and firms must be honest with themselves about what they have.

Naturally, no firm will want to be idealistic with this review; not all engagements provide skill-building opportunities. (After all, the baby *does* have to be fed.)

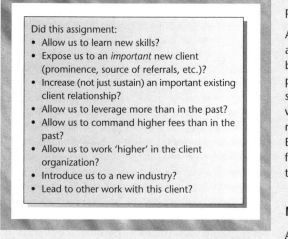

Did this assignment:
- Allow us to learn new skills?
- Expose us to an *important* new client (prominence, source of referrals, etc.)?
- Increase (not just sustain) an important existing client relationship?
- Allow us to leverage more than in the past?
- Allow us to command higher fees than in the past?
- Allow us to work 'higher' in the client organization?
- Introduce us to a new industry?
- Lead to other work with this client?

Figure 1 ■ Assessing the calibre of the practice

However, if a majority of the assignments fall at the low end, it will be obvious that whatever the revenue growth has been, there is still marketing to be done.

Specific guidance on marketing will also be generated quarter-by-quarter. Perhaps in one period you are doing well on generating important new clients, but have done nothing to deepen your relationships with important key accounts. This review will highlight that, and suggest where your marketing efforts next period need to be placed.

The presence of a 'third party' friendly sceptic is important in making this review process a practical management tool. If the team is asked to rate itself, it is very easy to rationalize any piece of new business. A case can always be made that a given new client is 'important', and that a new project 'offers us the opportunity to learn something new'. It is healthy to have someone play the 'challenging' role to expose these rationalizations.

It should be stressed that this qualitative review of the calibre of the practice does *not* imply more meetings associated with running the practice. Most firms already get together regularly to discuss marketing efforts and results. All that is being proposed here is that the group begin with its traditional discussions,

and then add this balance-sheet review as a regular part of all marketing meetings.

After some practice with this system, the questions asked here can be used not just as a look-back device; but can become part of a *prospective* screening process set up to determine where marketing efforts should go, and which opportunities are (or are not) worth pursuing. My strong advice is to begin with the regular look-back process, which is easier to enforce. Experience has shown that in all but the smallest of firms, effective prospect screening is a difficult process to administer, indeed.

Marketing statistics

An additional way to monitor and track the calibre of your practice is to pay attention to certain key marketing ratios. Consider the following examples, each of which is introduced by a pertinent question.

What percentage of your revenues will recur next year without any effort? Naturally, some professions (say audit or actuarial) have an easier time estimating this than others, but the exercise is a useful one for every professional firm. Go down the list of your existing clients, and estimate how much revenue that client is going to provide you next year.

Yes, it will be an estimate, but forcing your lead professionals on each account to answer this question will inveigle them into productive reflections on the strength of the relationship, where the client's business is going, and (not coincidentally) what you and your firm have to do to ensure that continued revenue stream.

What is your total marketing capacity, measured in person-hours? This simple question, unanswered in many firms, requires only that each person involved in business development either declares or is assigned a fixed (or at least a minimum) amount of non-billable time that he or she has agreed to contribute to the marketing effort.

Many firms can readily tell you their marketing expenditures (after all, *that's cash!*) but not the hours spent thereon. Yet it is the hours invested, and not the cash spent, that is determinative of marketing success. If you don't know your aggregate marketing-hours capacity, how can you manage your marketing efforts? And if you can't manage your marketing efforts, how can you hope for marketing success?

How many person-hours do you spend on a typical proposal? I am always surprised at how few firms have a ready answer to this question. Only *some* firms – the exceptions – can tell you precisely the time, as well as cost, of each and every professional and support person invested in pursuing each specific opportunity as relentlessly as necessary.

The reasons for keeping track of this are obvious: it is exceedingly helpful to know how much it costs you to acquire each piece of business, so that you can both track your return on selling investment and continue to learn about where to place your marketing resources. Obvious – but not always observed.

What percentage of assignments that you pursue do you win? Again, I am amazed at how many firms can answer only with impressionistic guesses. In the *best* firms, a detailed analysis of these statistics shows not only the number of assignments won and lost, but also patterns in which kinds of jobs the firm tends to win.

For example, what is the average monetary size of the proposals you win, versus the average size of the ones you lose? Do you tend to win the bigger ones or the smaller ones, or is there no difference? Do you tend to win more with bigger clients than with smaller ones? Are there industry trends in which jobs you win or lose? Questions such as these will tell you as much about your market image and your market's perception of you as will any market-research study.

What is the size of your average assignment? Since small jobs often take as much marketing effort as large ones, there are obvious economies of scale in marketing. For most professional firms, it will also tend to be true that, on average, your larger jobs will be more profitable. Hence 'average size of job' is a key measure of marketing success.

Naturally, one must avoid fooling oneself here. If your work tends to be divided into phases, then care must be exercised in defining this measure. Some firms

finesse the issue by examining total revenue per client, rather than per assignment. While this is sometimes necessary, it is unfortunate because it says very different things about your marketing if you have lots of small jobs for a client, or a lesser number of larger jobs. Hence it is worth trying to calculate (and pay attention to) average job size.

What percentage of all fees spent by clients on services in your area do they pay to you? Total revenues per client is an interesting statistic. But far more interesting is the percentage penetration. Are you one of a number of vendors to them, or are you their dominant (or at least preferred) supplier? Quantifying this can of course be tricky, since you need to ask the clients how much they might spend – but you would be surprised how many clients will cooperate by giving you a ballpark figure.

Even if you have to estimate heroically, it's worth asking yourself how many of your clients demonstrate by their actions that they view you as their dominant or lead supplier. Client relationships that will predictably and reliably produce future revenue should be treated as being among your most valued assets – and you ought to keep close tabs on your assets. Don't finish reviewing your marketing efforts until you've got a good handle on this one!

What percentage of your business is won on a noncompetitive, sole-source basis? (This interesting marketing statistic is related to the first statistic discussed above.) This ratio is probably the best measure of quality that you have. If the percentage is low, it means that you don't have a market niche that thinks of you as either differentiated or the quality leader in your practice area. Or, stated another way: the quality of your referrals is not good enough. Note that there's a world of difference between referrals such as 'Yes, they are competent; you should consider them' and those that say 'They are the only people to use!'.

What percentage of this year's revenues are from clients you had never worked for prior to this year? (This is the obverse of the repeat-business ratio, the percentage of revenues from existing clients.) Let this new client ratio get too high, and you'll find yourself working harder at marketing than is necessary.

What percentage of your top 10 clients were top 10 clients three or five years ago? This is yet one more way to examine your client-retention rate (and hence your need for new client marketing). The topic is sufficiently important to examine in multiple ways.

What percentage of your revenues come from services you didn't offer three or five years ago? This new service ratio is becoming increasingly important as the professions continue to experience rapidly changing client needs.

I am sure there are other ratios used to monitor marketing efforts that would shed light on the calibre of your practice. Figure one out that would help you to learn something about your practice! Meanwhile, check out the summary list shown in Figure 2: how many of the questions can you answer about *your* practice?

Summary

In discussing these concepts with professional firms around the world, I frequently hear the following objection: 'David, aren't you being unrealistic? After all, times are tough and we have to be grateful for *any* business we can get. Yet you're telling us to worry about the "asset value" of our work. Isn't this an unreasonable standard?

My answer is 'No'. While readily acknowledging that in tough times a firm may need to accept work that scores low on the criteria in my questionnaire, it is nevertheless a reality of professional life that the firm's future depends on bringing in asset-building work.

If a firm is not building new skills, strengthening existing relationships and creating new ones, then its future

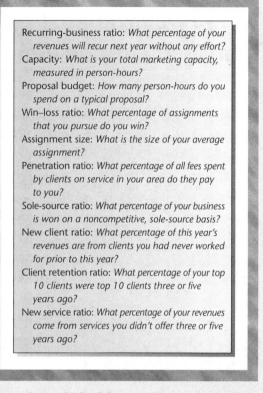

Recurring-business ratio: *What percentage of your revenues will recur next year without any effort?*

Capacity: *What is your total marketing capacity, measured in person-hours?*

Proposal budget: *How many person-hours do you spend on a typical proposal?*

Win–loss ratio: *What percentage of assignments that you pursue do you win?*

Assignment size: *What is the size of your average assignment?*

Penetration ratio: *What percentage of all fees spent by clients on service in your area do they pay to you?*

Sole-source ratio: *What percentage of your business is won on a noncompetitive, sole-source basis?*

New client ratio: *What percentage of this year's revenues are from clients you had never worked for prior to this year?*

Client retention ratio: *What percentage of your top 10 clients were top 10 clients three or five years ago?*

New service ratio: *What percentage of your revenues come from services you didn't offer three or five years ago?*

Figure 2 ■ Which of these marketing statistics do you monitor?

is truly at risk. And the responsibility for ensuring that future lies with wise management of marketing efforts, incorporating balance-sheet thinking into the basic-volume orientation that most marketing efforts are built on today. Yes, marketing is even more complicated – and important – than you thought it was.

Intra-organizational aspects of service quality management: the employees' perspective

Barbara R. Lewis ■ Gard O.S. Gabrielsen

The article concentrates on intra-organizational aspects in the implementation of service quality management. Literature review is followed by presentation of an empirical investigation in financial services in Norway, in which the perspective of front-line employees, regarding recent service quality initiatives, is measured.

Service quality management is now of concern in all organizations, in particular in the people-intensive service industries which are also characterized by increasing competition, rapid product imitation and sophisticated consumers. In this environment, service quality is often proposed as a differentiation strategy, designed to enhance customer relationships and, in turn, long-term profitability.

The authors have researched the implementation of service quality initiatives in financial services in Norway, where service quality management is a relatively new concept. The overall research objectives were to: determine the extent to which Norwegian banks emphasize service quality as a strategic variable; examine how the service quality process is organized and managed in the banks; identify organizational and environmental variables which affect the service quality process; and compare the perspectives of management and front-line employees.

In this article they review literature which relates to the implementation process of service quality with an emphasis on intra-organizational aspects, especially the human element of the initiatives. This is followed by a brief introduction to the financial services industry in Norway at the time of the research, and a description of the empirical investigation carried out. The data presented and discussed in the article are from a survey of front-line employees focused on their opinions about aspects of service quality management which influence their ability and motivation to provide quality service. The management perspective is considered in detail elsewhere: see Gabrielsen (1993), and Lewis and Gabrielsen (1995). Data analysis and discus-

sion are related back to the relevant literature, and the conclusions offer suggestions for continuing research in the area of service quality management.

Literature review

The research literature relevant to the research is wide-ranging. Firstly, it is necessary to comment on corporate strategy and service quality, and the critical nature of service encounters in developing service strategies. This leads into a discussion of the need for customer-oriented organizations and, in turn, the development of appropriate organizational policies with respect to internal marketing. Integral to internal marketing are the human resource management activities of organizations to include empowerment for service quality, and issues relating to employee satisfaction and retention. Finally, consideration is given to research focused on systems and infrastructure which are vital in the delivery of quality service, and to service recovery.

Service quality and strategy

Coyne (1986: 54) defined competitive strategy to be 'an integrated set of actions that produce a sustainable competitive advantage over competitors', and Porter (1980) had previously proposed three generic competitive strategies namely: cost leadership, focus and differentiation – which is relevant in the current service quality focus.

Reprinted from *The Service Industries Journal*, Vol. 18, No. 2, April 1998, pp. 64–89.

In financial services, the traditional marketing mix has become insufficient as a basis for developing competitive strategies and service quality is increasingly providing scope for differentiation as suggested and discussed by a number of writers (Wong and Perry, 1991; Coscun and Frohlich, 1992; Thwaites and Glaiser, 1992; and Coyne, 1993). In particular, Raynor (1992) stresses that strategic quality necessitates a continuous process of improvement which is culture based and institutionalized within an organization, and Easingwood and Storey (1991) identified quality as one of four factors highly correlated with success in financial services.

Further, implicit in the arguments in favour of strategic quality is the concept of relationship marketing, where the emphasis is focused on close relationships with customers rather than on individual transactions (Christopher et al., 1991). In this context, it is now well documented that long-term customer relationships are more profitable than individual transactions (e.g., Reichheld and Sasser, 1990; Heskett et al., 1990), and Thamara (1991) proposed that service quality is a major determinant in developing lasting customer relationships.

Moments of truth

Moments of truth (or service encounters) are critical in the development and maintenance of relationships and, thus, service quality. Albrecht (1988: 26) defined a moment of truth to be 'any episode in which a customer comes into contact with any aspect of the organisation and gets an impression of the quality of its service', i.e., a customer's perceptions of service quality are determined during service encounters. Zeithaml (1991) highlights the significance of service encounters due to the experience aspects of services; and Lewis and Entwistle (1989) and Bitner (1990) discuss the need to manage encounters. In addition, Albrecht and Bradford (1990) and Heskett et al. (1990) refer to the value adding (to the core service) activity of service encounters which makes them central to the heart of any service strategy.

Further, Albrecht (1988) proposes the 'cycle of service', i.e., the chain of events a customer goes through

as he/she experiences the service, which identifies the key moments of truth. Integral to this is the role of employees in service encounters (to be discussed).

The outcome of service encounters is determined by the interactions between service providers and customers and is influenced by: the personal characteristics and social and cultural characteristics of both customers and employees; systems and procedures, structure and technology; and organizational culture (see Solomon et al., 1985; Edvardsson et al., 1989; Albrecht and Bradford, 1990; Grove and Fisk, 1991; and Morgan and Chadha 1993). This relates to Lehtinen and Lehtinen's (1991) concept of interactive quality, i.e., that service delivery and, thus, perceived service quality are functions of interactive processes. This, in turn, requires organizations to manage and control their service encounters via technical control systems and procedures, management of human aspects and development of a service-oriented culture.

The customer-oriented organization

Service quality is subjective and is experienced and judged by customers during service encounters. Thus, the need for creating customer-oriented cultures where every employee feels a personal responsibility for delivering excellent service quality is essential. Key writings in this area are those of Schein (1985) and Morgan (1986), and Kotter and Heskett (1992), who distinguish between two levels of corporate culture: at a deeper level, basic assumptions and values which are difficult to change and, at a more superficial level, behaviour patterns which may be manipulated more easily. The challenge for any service quality initiative is to implement a 'high performance' culture whereby the service quality philosophy is institutionalized in a set of basic assumptions and beliefs (Long, 1988).

It could be proposed that the ultimate goal of any service quality initiative is to create an organizational climate similar to Mintzberg's (1991: 353) 'missionary organization' – where all parts of the organization strive towards a goal, in this case service quality. Gummesson (1991) describes this as 'the love factor', and he contends that service quality is often more dependent on the power of personal involvement and staff commitment than on systems, structure and standards.

Various researchers have discussed how such a culture may be developed. A starting point may well be explicitly articulated mission statements (see Albrecht, 1988; Payne, 1988; and Kotter and Heskett, 1992) focused on customer satisfaction and encouraging every employee to feel a personal responsibility for satisfying the customer in the best possible manner. However, Campell and Yeung (1991) and Peters and Waterman (1982) highlight that it takes time for mission statements to become accepted and institutionalized.

Further, leadership has a vital impact on developing and sustaining an organization's service-orientation. The leader's role has been the focus of research by Carlzon (1987: 426) who describes a leader as a 'visionary, a strategist, an informer, a teacher and an inspirer'. Howcroft (1991) concentrates on the leader's role in developing and communicating a vision of the business. A crucial aspect of modern leadership is the leaders' responsibility to motivate the organization and demonstrate through action what they consider to be important (see Peters and Austin, 1985; Albrecht, 1988; and Bennett and Brown, 1992).

An aspect clearly related to this is the executive's ability to communicate and create close relationships with subordinates (Coulson-Thomas, 1991); employees must feel that the leader genuinely believes in the service quality concept. Thus, the culture-oriented, customer and employee concerned leader with excellent communication skills has been described by Nadler and Tushman (1990) as a charismatic leader; they stress, quite rightly, that leaders must also exhibit the necessary administrative and managerial skills.

Internal marketing and organizational policies

Integral to any service quality strategy is the need for internal marketing, the marketing of the service quality philosophy to employees (Flipo, 1986). Organizations need to develop programmes aimed at internal markets in parallel to those for their external markets (see Lovelock, 1991; and Piercy and Morgan, 1991).

At a strategic level, the purpose of internal marketing is to create an internal environment which supports customer consciousness and sales-mindedness amongst personnel and, at a tactical level, internal marketing focuses on internal personal selling and internal information systems in order to sell services and marketing efforts to employees (Grönroos, 1981 and 1985).

Further, Piercy and Morgan (1991) propose an internal marketing mix containing: product – the strategy to be sold; price – efforts to be required from employees; communication – media to inform and persuade; and distribution – venues at which the product and communication are delivered.

A central element in internal marketing theory is the recognition of internal processes which influence the ultimate service delivery – which involve both customer-contact (front-line) personnel and supporting personnel (Ahmed and Simintiras, 1991). Varey and Brooks (1992) suggest the term 'internal customer' to apply to both managers and employees, and they discuss the concept of internal markets.

Human resource management and service quality

Aspects of human resource management which are especially relevant with respect to internal marketing and the delivery of quality service are recruitment and selection, training, empowerment and employee satisfaction and retention.

Recruitment and selection includes appropriate allocation of people to positions to ensure employee–job fit in both front-line and support personnel positions (Zeithaml et al., 1988). Indeed, selection procedures may take service quality-related variables into account (Lewis and Entwistle, 1989; and Zeithaml et al., 1988), and Schelsinger and Heskett (1991) refer to the need to look for 'customer responsiveness and communication skills'.

With respect to training, employees need skills and product knowledge (i.e., technical qualifications) to provide technical quality (Grönroos, 1984), and also expertise to allow them to perform reliably and consistently (Parasuraman *et al.*, 1991). Training programmes need to minimize role ambiguity (Zeithaml *et al.*, 1988), recognize teamwork (Berry *et al.*, 1990), and teach group dynamics and communication skills (Ballantyne, 1990). Cespedes (1992) also stresses the need for internal coordination of employees in different areas with varying skill resources.

Further, a number of researchers (Albrecht and Bradford, 1990; Edwards and Clutterbuck, 1991; and Coyne, 1993) talk about the need for educating rather than training employees. Their suggestion is that education is more concerned with the total development of an employee – the objectives being to teach initiative, flexibility and motivation – to maximize service quality. Cornish (1991) illustrates this when describing Citibank's training programmes.

Companies need to invest time, money and effort in appropriate training activities (Albrecht and Bradford, 1990; Schelsinger and Heskett, 1991; and Berry and Parasuraman, 1991), and Davidow and Uttal (1989) stress that training – as an element of personnel policy – is linked to overall company strategy and, therefore, is multi-functional involving corporate planners, marketing and human resource management. In addition, Lovelock (1991) and Daniel (1992) stress that training is a continuous process of improvement, and Sherden (1988) comments that it is an investment in future competitive strength.

Empowerment for service quality

The extent to which an employee's level of perceived control contributes to his or her ability to deliver service quality has been highlighted by Zeithaml *et al.* (1988) and Shreeve (1991). Organizational rules, procedures and culture need to provide customer-contact employees with flexibility and authority in serving customers. Organizations have to be careful that quality control programmes take into account the complexity of service encounters and the significance of speed, flexibility and interaction (Heskett, 1987) and do not reduce service providers' full potential (Ballantyne, 1990).

Empowerment has two dimensions. The technical dimension emphasizes the benefits of speed and organizational efficiency (see Clutterbuck, 1989; and Firnstahl, 1989 – who emphasize that employees need responsibility and authority to act quickly, without a long chain of command). The second dimension emphasizes psychological aspects such as motivation and job satisfaction, and assumes that most people are willing to perform at their best if given the opportunity, i.e., more autonomy (see Peters and Waterman, 1982; and Bailyn, 1993).

One problem with respect to increased empowerment of front-line personnel is middle manager resistance, discussed by Carlzon (1987) and Albrecht (1988). They suggest that middle managers need advice and information with respect to their changing roles, which is a further aspect of communicating a service quality vision convincingly throughout an organization.

The link between increased empowerment, motivation and job satisfaction, and in turn customer satisfaction and service quality, is discussed by several researchers including Heskett (1987) in his concept of the 'quality wheel'. Motivated and satisfied employees will impact on external customer satisfaction, and lead to increased employee retention rates. Overall, employee motivation, satisfaction and retention are influenced by several factors to include training, corporate culture and service quality strategies, and evaluation and rewards criteria.

Evaluation criteria tend to be based on accounting data such as sales and profit figures, but they also need to include an employee's ability to deliver quality service (Zeithaml *et al.*, 1988; Cespedes, 1992). Managers can also be evaluated on the basis of their branches' levels of customer service – to ensure their commitment (Beatty and Gup, 1989).

Rewards include both monetary incentives (Heskett *et al.*, 1990) and more symbolic rewards (Peters and Waterman, 1982; Peters and Austin, 1985; and Peters, 1987) examined celebration and recognition to 'improve the quality of work life and keep the work place fun' (Bennett and Brown, 1992). This is of particular importance in culture building where such aspects may enhance a positive customer-oriented culture.

Systems and infrastructure

To achieve service quality, organizations also need appropriate infrastructures with respect to customer research ability, technology and service standards and control.

Customer research ability

This enables identification of customers' expectations/requirements of service quality, and their evaluations and opinions about service quality (Coyne, 1989; Crosby, 1991). Formal and informal methods may be used (Albrecht and Bradford, 1990), utilizing qualitative and quantitative methods (Ohmae, 1989; Miller, 1992) and may include employee involvement (Peters, 1987).

Technology vs. human resources

In the quest for productivity in the services sector companies need to strike a balance between efficiency and service quality (Drucker, 1991). Efficiency may be achieved by increased emphasis on technology, and standardized and decustomized service (Coscun and Frolich, 1992), but this may lead to a trade-off with service quality (Schlesinger and Heskett, 1991) – if customers prefer personalized service (Beatty and Gup, 1989). Further, the costs and benefits of different staffing levels need to be considered (Peters, 1987; Schlesinger and Heskett, 1991). In addition, Coyne (1993) proposes that sustainable competitive advantage in high-contact organizations must be based on maximizing front-line decision competence and flexibility, through greater investment in people.

Therefore, technology should be seen as an aid for delivering quality service, e.g., with respect to information technology (Olaisen and Revang, 1991), to free staff from routine tasks to give them more time to deal with customers and service (Pirrie, 1990) and to assist in production and delivery (Drucker, 1991).

Service standards and control systems

Setting standards and designing service processes may be aided by: 'service blueprinting', to identify potential failure points (Shostack, 1984); Hauser and Clausing's (1988) House of Quality technique; work-shops (Armistead and Clark, 1991); and distinctions between internal and external standards (Collier, 1987). Further, the 'tools' of Total Quality Management are increasingly being applied in the services sector with respect to developing standards and quality control procedures (see Haynes and Duvall, 1992; Yasin et al., 1992; and Boaden and Dale, 1993).

However, in accepting the importance/value of quality control techniques, one also has to take account of the functional dimensions of service, experienced by the customer at the service encounter, e.g., social interaction, flexibility and initiative (Leonard and Sasser, 1982; Berry et al., 1990), emphasizing yet again the need to invest in human resources and to develop customer-oriented corporate cultures.

Service recovery

The final element of this literature review deals with service recovery, which is integral to a service quality programme and has been the focus of several pieces of research. Mistakes do happen in service delivery and customers do complain about inferior service, albeit only a minority (Peters, 1987; Hart et al., 1990), although service guarantees do encourage customer feedback with respect to unsatisfactory service quality (Hart, 1988; Heskett et al., 1990). As a result, customers may stop doing business/defect, thus impacting on profits (Reichheld and Sasser, 1990).

Consequently, service recovery becomes a strategic tool in the pursuit of service excellence and customer loyalty (Firnstahl, 1989; Berry and Parasuraman, 1991). Recovery systems and procedures should not be too rigid, and recovery efforts typically relate to the speed and creativity with which employees respond to service flaws – which is dependent on empowerment, flexibility and authority (Firnstahl, 1989; Berry et al., 1990; Hart et al., 1990; and Reichheld and Sasser, 1990).

Further, managers need to know what customers expect from service recovery (Singh and Wilding, 1991). In addition, Berry and Parasuraman (1991) recommend that companies analyze service failure in order to be prepared for future situations, and

Reichheld and Sasser (1990) emphasize the need to approach, if possible, defecting customers to get feedback.

Empirical investigation

Financial services and the Norwegian banking industry

The financial services industry, worldwide, has been subject to major changes in the last two to three decades. It has, typically, been a period of growth in response to factors such as deregulation and intensifying competition within the industry, and trends towards financial conglomeration and the globalization of business; spurred on by increasingly sophisticated technology and consumer – both retail and corporate – awareness. However, the recent climate of recession has presented various economic difficulties which have increased the need for financial services organizations to be not only customer-oriented but also efficient in their business management, which has increased the search for new competitive strategies including a focus on service quality initiatives.

The opportunity arose in 1993 to investigate service quality initiatives in banks in Norway. During the period 1988–92 the Norwegian banking industry had experienced a crisis. Their environment had been characterized by various macroeconomic activities to include: postwar credit and monetary policies; deregulation; a credit boom; competition; a rocketing stockmarket; and an explosive consumption of imports. The banks' response had been a market growth strategy, including lending, with an emphasis on size rather than profitability – which led to bad debts and decentralization – but with a lack of training, communication and control.

The downturn/recession in the economy in the late 1980s led to high levels of unemployment (Hellestol and Nygaard, 1993) and increasing bad debts for the banks in both corporate and retail markets and consequent losses recorded by the larger institutions. The banking crisis peaked in 1991, but was stalled by government intervention. The government injected money such that by the end of 1992, 70 per cent of the banking industry was state-owned. This has led to various transformations in the industry.

The banks have cut costs through a policy of rationalization and employee lay-offs on a large scale (approximately 20 per cent in a four-year period), and branch closures. There has also been centralization (and automation) of 'back-room' operations and expertise, with branches concentrating on service and sales-oriented activities. This presents various problems with regard to customer orientation, e.g., with respect to service recovery when materials are held centrally. These changes have impacted negatively on organizational culture. Employee morale has been weakened, the working environment is less pleasant and customers (may) criticize front-line personnel for the banks' rationalization. If a destructive or negative culture has been created this could undermine efficiency and customer orientation, and relations between management and employees (who are traditionally loyal) may be soured. Further, the banks have been criticized for cutting training and development costs, although management are aware of the need for increased competence among staff and the importance of training.

Despite this scenario of internal improvement with respect to cost control and staff reduction, the major banks have appreciated the need to develop, with the resources available, customer-focused activities, a 'sales culture', and the concomitant attention to internal customers, i.e. employees. Successful service quality management represents a huge challenge to these organizations; the problems they face have been extreme and even though commitment is genuine, the necessary resources are still lacking.

Research methodology

Following an analysis of the Norwegian banking market and the service quality literature, in-depth interviews were carried out with top management in three of the four major banks which dominate the retail financial services market. Their participation in the study led to structured interviews with a number of managers at headquarters, regional and branch level which aimed to: reveal the importance attached to service quality management; examine the service quality process; and identify organizational and environmental variables which affect this process. The findings from these interviews are discussed by Gabrielsen (1993) and Lewis and Gabrielsen (1995).

The second part of the investigation, the focus of this article, comprised a survey of front-line employees, to assess their opinions about aspects of service quality management relevant to their ability and motivation to provide quality service. A structured survey questionnaire was developed using data from the interviews, observations and company documentation (annual reports, strategy documents, customer surveys, organizational charts), together with knowledge of the service quality literature. Attitude and opinion statements were developed using Likert-type scales (1 = strongly agree to 6 = strongly disagree), and the questionnaire (in Norwegian) developed through several stages of piloting and revision. It was distributed through the banks' internal systems to a systematic probability sample of 600 line employees working in positions which involve customer contact, in the Oslo/Akershus region where the heavy concentration of financial institutions has enhanced their appreciation of customer awareness and the need for quality service.

Three hundred people replied, a response rate of 52 per cent, of whom 54.7 per cent were male and 45.3 per cent female. Respondents were relatively old and experienced, largely as a result of the recent lay-offs based on a last-in first-out principle. The age distribution was: 18–25 yrs, 1.7 per cent; 26–35 yrs, 25.9 per cent; 36–45 yrs, 37.2 per cent; 46–60 yrs, 31.2 per cent; 60+ yrs, 4.0 per cent. Only 4 per cent had been with the bank for less than five years, other lengths of service were: 6–10 yrs, 15.5 per cent; 11–15 yrs, 22.4 per cent; 16–20 yrs, 22.0 per cent; 20+ yrs, 36.2 per cent. With respect to education levels reached, 16.3 per cent had not completed secondary education, a further 66.7 per cent had stopped after secondary education, and 23 per cent had university qualifications.

Results and discussion

The survey questionnaire completed by the front-line employees comprised 83 attitude and opinion state-

ments grouped under eight headings: organizational culture and working environment; individual attitudes; the role of management; role perception and training; infrastructure and organizational systems; evaluation and rewards; service recovery; and improvements. The findings presented in the following sections focus only on the mean scores for each statement; and for those statements worded negatively the scores were inverted prior to calculation. Subsequent analysis investigated differences between the participating banks using one-way variance analysis, and variations between demographic groups (i.e. sex, age, education level and experience with the bank) using t-tests. Few differences in responses were found between the sexes and age groups, but a number of differences were evident in relation to education and length of service (see Gabrielsen, 1993).

Organizational culture and internal (working) environment

To establish to what extent the present banking (corporate) culture is aligned/compatible with the prevailing service quality initiatives, two cultural characteristics were explored: the degree of unity (i.e. organizational wide shared vision/aim) and the extent of customer orientation (see Table 1, statements 1 to 5).

The degree of unity seems high, with most respondents having a fairly strong perception that all parts of their bank strive towards a commonly shared ambition (91 per cent expressed at least some agreement with statement 1). This may indicate that the banks have developed aims which are well communicated and understood. The employees feel little confusion about the current ambitions of their banks and consider management and themselves as pulling together in the same direction. With respect to customer orientation, the high scores for statements 2–5 indicated the development of a customer aware culture, with over 80 per cent of the respondents showing some level of agreement.

Respondents were positive and optimistic about the internal working environment (statements 6, 9, 10, 11), despite recent developments, although it was

Table 1 ■ Cultural and internal working environment

Statement	Mean score	Deviation
1 In our bank management and employees work together towards a common goal.	4.76	0.95
2 Our bank focuses on the customer.	4.39	1.14
3 Our bank is concerned with service quality.	4.63	1.10
4 Our bank's service quality has improved during the last two years.	3.91	1.41
5 Employees encourage each other regularly to serve the customers.	4.27	1.11
6 The internal working environment in the bank is good.	4.66	1.09
7 Co-operation is good between internal units.	4.01	1.15
8 Communication is good between internal units.	3.87	1.15
9 The internal working environment in the bank is positive and optimistic.	4.05	1.11
10 The working environment has improved during the last two years.	3.31	1.28
11 Employees talk often about quitting or finding a new job.	3.10	1.49
12 In our branch, we are all closely welded together.	4.83	1.13
13 The branch manager attempts to create a good social environment in our branch.	4.57	1.25

generally felt that it had not improved in the last two years. This optimism may well be a reflection of the improving financial situation at the time of the survey – with layoffs seemingly finalized and internal environments becoming more predictable.

Further, most employees identify strongly with their branch (statements 12, 13), in particular 88 per cent had agreement with the statement 'we are all closely welded together', which implies that interpersonal relations and climate are good. It may well be the case that feelings towards branches are of a more loyal and positive nature than towards the organization – indeed, there was some expression that cooperation and communication between internal units was not good (statements 7 and 8).

Individual attitudes

This section of the questionnaire focused on the extent to which individual employees understood service quality, are customer oriented and are motivated to participate in the service quality initiatives. There were some very high levels of agreement with the statements offered (see Table 2).

Perceptions of service quality

For any service quality initiative to succeed, employees must have favourable perceptions, e.g., Seddon (1992: 81) writes 'it is primarily attitude which determines success; people with the right attitude will make changes to any system, structure, or procedure as necessary'. Thirty-one per cent of respondents had some agreement with the statement 'the strong focus on service quality is exaggerated'. However, the consumer orientation was high, with 98 per cent agreeing that 'my most important task is to help the customers in meeting their needs', and 99 per cent with 'I try to show initiative when customers need help'. Further, 94 per cent agreed that 'I feel it as a personal defeat if I serve a customer poorly'. In addition, the majority (90 per cent) disagreed that 'it is important to sell even though the customers do not

Table 2 ■ Individual attitudes

Statement	Mean score	Deviation
14 My most important task is to help the customers in meeting their needs.	5.48	0.81
15 I feel a personal responsibility for creating good impressions of the bank.	5.62	0.61
16 The strong focus on service quality is exaggerated.	2.75	1.43
17 It is important to sell, even though the customers do not strictly need the products.	1.95	1.19
18 I try to show initiative when customers need help.	5.41	0.66
19 Customers should not expect me to help them with problems which are not related to my areas of responsibility.	2.46	1.25
20 I enjoy my job.	5.08	0.92
21 I feel part of a team in my branch.	5.10	1.00
22 I am motivated to do my best for the bank.	5.09	0.93
23 I feel it as a personal defeat if I serve a customer poorly.	5.11	1.02

strictly need the products'; thus distinguishing between sales and service.

Individual motivation (statements 15, 20, 21, 22)

This consumer orientation may be viewed as a prerequisite in the service quality process. In addition, employees need to feel responsible for meeting and exceeding customer expectations and creating lasting impressions of the bank, i.e. individual motivations need to be high. This was clearly evident in so far as 99 per cent of respondents agreed that 'I feel a personal responsibility for creating good impressions of the bank'; 95 per cent with 'I am motivated to do my best for the bank'; 94 per cent with 'I feel part of a team in my branch'; and 94 per cent with 'I enjoy my job'. This high level of motivation may be due to good local working environments and augurs well for commitment to the banks' service quality initiatives.

The role of management

It was evident from the earlier stages of the project that top management was perceived to be distant from the branches, with an emphasis placed on the role of regional management. This section focused on regional management, to see if these managers have established a more visible profile. Questions dealt with relations between managers and employees, and employees' perceptions of the management's role in the service quality process. The mean scores (see Table 3) were lower than for other sections of the questionnaire.

Perceptions of regional management

Eighty-four per cent of employees expressed at least some confidence in the regional managers (statement 25), and 88 per cent perceived them to be competent (statement 24). Ninety-two per cent agreed that their closest supervisor (i.e., their branch manager) is concerned with the customers' needs, and emphasizes the importance of service quality (94 per cent), but only 67 per cent with the statement 'the regional management understands the customers' needs'. One explanation for the regional management's apparent lack of sensitivity for customer needs may be related to their interest in the line employees' situation – the majority of employees felt that regional managers do not understand, or are interested in, their situation; nor listen to signals from customer-contact positions. Only 41 per cent agreed that 'the

Table 3 ■ The role of management

Statement	Mean score	Deviation
24 The regional management is competent.	4.67	1.04
25 I have confidence in the regional management.	4.55	1.10
26 The regional management understands the customers' needs.	3.88	1.19
27 The distance between my branch and the regional management is wide.	3.93	1.32
28 The regional management emphasises the importance of service quality.	4.55	1.16
29 The regional management devotes a lot of time to motivating the bank's employees.	3.00	1.19
30 The regional management is interested in and understands my job.	3.17	1.30
31 The regional management is visible to the bank's employees.	2.88	1.30
32 The regional management should be more visible to the bank's employees.	4.88	1.07
33 The regional management is interested in my opinions about the bank.	3.25	1.43
34 The regional management attaches much importance to my opinions.	2.92	1.32
35 My closest supervisor is concerned with the customer's needs.	4.86	1.07
36 My closest supervisor emphasises the importance of service quality.	5.07	0.93
37 I have enough formal authority and control of my work to perform my duties satisfactorily.	4.66	1.25

regional management is interested in and understands my job'; 44 per cent that 'the regional management is interested in my opinions about the bank'; and as few as 33 per cent agreed that 'the regional management attaches much importance to my opinions'.

Regional management as culture shapers

Given the importance of culture management in service quality strategy, questions were included to assess the extent to which the bank employees perceived the regional management to actively engage in such activities. Responses indicate that the regional managers were perceived to be distant and anonymous and, therefore, not involved in culture management. Only 35 per cent agreed (slight agreement only) that 'the regional management devotes a lot of time to motivating the bank's employees'; 33 per cent that 'the regional management is visible to the bank's employees'; and 92 per cent felt that the

'regional management should be more visible'. These responses provide evidence of the low profile of regional managers, which mitigates against leadership, and, thus, culture is more or less left to be developed by chance where other organizational elements closer to the individual employee, such as colleagues and branch managers, will influence this process the most.

Role perception and training

The questions now moved from 'softer aspects' such as culture and attitude to more technically related aspects, including the role of training. Customer contact – employees' key role in determining external customers' perceptions of an organization's service quality – depends on their knowledge, skills and behaviour. The extent to which these develop is influenced by each employee's perception of his or her role, and by the quantity and quality of training.

Role perceptions

Zeithaml *et al.* (1988: 45) emphasized the significance of avoiding role ambiguity – 'role ambiguity may occur because employees are uncertain about what managers or supervisors expect from them and how to satisfy those expectations'. Thus, employees' understanding of their roles is a major determinant of their ability to serve the customers. Ninety-four per cent of respondents agreed that they were fully aware of what was expected from them, and 94 per cent felt that they are normally well informed about the bank's aims and strategies and, thus, the various organizational areas relevant for their jobs; and so, role ambiguity was not a problem (see Table 4).

This result is, perhaps, surprising given the changing role of customer-contact staff and the expectation that they engage in active sales and perform customer service in a more proactive and dynamic manner. One possible explanation may be clear and explicitly designed job specifications, extensive information policies and training. In addition, the age profile and experience in the banks of respondents may have led to high perceptions of their abilities and understanding. Alternatively, the perception may be based on previous banking practice, whereas recent changes have altered the requirements put upon them (see Antil, 1992: 46 for discussion of this survey problem).

Training

Eighty-four per cent of employees agreed that they had received enough training to perform their duties as expected, relating primarily to the technical dimensions of quality – and possibly attributable to their relatively long experience with the bank. With respect to abilities related to functional service dimensions, only 66 per cent agreed that they are encouraged to learn new ways to serve the customer, and only 43 per cent said they often participated in training programmes to learn new ways to serve the customer; although 70 per cent agreed that such training programmes are valuable and helpful. Overall, 92 per cent agreed that training should take place more often, suggesting a need for increased investment in training – in order to achieve high levels of service quality.

Infrastructure and organizational systems

The banks had been restructuring in response to the banking crisis, in terms of lay-offs, centralization and standardization, and this section of the questionnaire was concerned with employees' perceptions of the present infrastructure and organization and its impact on levels of service. Levels of agreement with the statements presented were, in general, relatively low (see Table 5).

Table 4 ■ Role perception and training

Statement	Mean score	Deviation
38 I am fully aware of what is expected from me in the bank.	5.21	0.92
39 I am normally well informed about the bank's aims and strategies.	4.89	0.87
40 I have received enough training to perform my duties as expected.	4.64	1.08
41 I am encouraged to learn new ways to serve the customer.	3.90	1.23
42 I often participate in training programmes to learn new ways to serve the customer.	3.23	1.43
43 These programmes are valuable and helpful.	3.94	1.30
44 Training should take place more often.	4.80	0.96

Table 5 ■ Infrastructure and organizational systems

Statement	Mean score	Deviation
45 Technology and routines are designed to meet my requirements.	3.73	1.31
46 The increased centralization of operational functions has improved service quality.	2.99	1.32
47 I would serve the customers better in a more decentralized organization.	4.02	1.34
48 Lack of formal authority prevents me from serving the customers satisfactorily.	3.15	1.42
49 I have normally enough time to perform my duties as expected.	3.22	1.35
50 The internal communication in the bank is good.	3.89	1.17
51 Under-capacity is a problem in our branch.	4.25	1.47
52 Our bank is concerned with enhancing cooperation and communication across functional lines.	3.54	1.21
53 The internal units understand and are concerned with the customer's needs.	3.38	1.23
54 Our bank has developed clear and explicit service targets.	4.14	1.23
55 These targets are accepted all over the bank.	3.77	1.18
56 The bank's targets are important and useful.	5.02	0.92

Organizational restructuring

As many as 37 per cent of employees felt that technology and routines were not designed to meet their requirements (statement 45); and 60 per cent felt that increased centralization of operational functions had not improved service quality (statement 46). Conversely, 68 per cent agreed that they would serve the customers better in a more decentralized organization, and 42 per cent felt that lack of formal authority prevents them from serving the customers satisfactorily. A possible explanation for such negative reaction related to internal communication and cooperation: as many as 34 per cent of respondents felt that internal communication in their bank was not good; 43 per cent disagreed that their bank is concerned with enhancing cooperation and communication across functional lines; and 53 per cent disagreed that the internal units understand and are concerned with the customers' needs – thus creating frustration for front-line employees in relation to the support, or lack of it, they receive from the internal back-up units. Therefore, it appears that employees feel that the increased centralization has created barriers to communication and so limited their ability to serve the customers rapidly and effectively.

The effect of redundancies

It was hypothesized that the substantial reduction in staff numbers, to cut costs, would cause customer satisfaction to suffer; and, indeed, respondents perceived their working environment to have become more stressful and that time pressure prevents them from performing adequately. Only 39 per cent agreed that they normally have enough time to perform their duties as expected; and 72 per cent agreed that under-capacity is a problem in their branch. The solution to this problem might be, partially, via training activities rather than staff numbers *per se*.

Service standards

Respondents were also questioned as to whether or not they felt their bank has developed standards for service and if these are accepted all over the bank. Seventy-four per cent were aware/agreed that their bank has developed clear and explicit service targets. Further, most employees perceived these standards positively with 93 per cent agreeing that the banks' targets are important and useful. This consensus reflects the relatively strong customer orientation previously identified. Even so, not all respondents agreed that the targets are accepted all over the bank (only 61 per cent, with 39 per cent disagreeing), i.e., these line employees are possibly perceiving that internally located units are neglecting the standards set for service. This ties in with any internal communications gaps whereby back-room personnel have limited awareness of the requirements of front-line personnel, i.e., their 'internal customers'.

Evaluation and rewards

Employee evaluation and rewards impact on levels of motivation and hence on service quality delivered. Respondents' limited agreement with the attitude statements pertaining to both organizational philosophies about rewards and recognition, and the present policies and systems, indicated scope for change/improvement (see Table 6).

Some respondents (26 per cent) did not feel appreciated by their bank and a number (18 per cent) did not agree that their job is perceived as important by the management. Further, there was limited evidence

of 'celebration' of good performance, possibly a function of both the recent banking crisis and the traditional, passive, culture of the banks. Forty-one per cent of respondents said they did not often receive feedback from supervisors; and 38 per cent did not agree that 'my closest supervisor usually praises good performance'. With respect to rewards systems, several statements were designed to consider whether or not the employees felt that the present systems encourage them to deliver service excellence. Only 28 per cent agreed (72 per cent disagreed) that 'the bank rewards me when I deliver good service'; and only 22 per cent agreed with the statement 'the evaluation and reward systems motivate me to deliver good service'. Further, two-thirds of respondents felt that 'more individualized reward schemes would be beneficial'. At the time of the survey, the banks were emphasizing sales and so it was not surprising that half the respondents agreed that 'the evaluation criteria encourage sales at the expense of service'. If this is evidence of transaction marketing rather than relationship marketing then the long-term consequences are potentially serious.

Service recovery

This was investigated in terms of employees' understanding and acceptance of the concept, and the present role of service recovery management in the

---

Table 6 ■ Evaluation and rewards

Statement	Mean score	Deviation
57 I feel appreciated by our bank.	4.12	1.29
58 I feel that my job is perceived as important by the management.	4.39	1.23
59 The bank rewards me when I deliver good service.	2.71	1.34
60 I often receive feedback from my superiors.	3.63	1.45
61 My closest superior usually praises good performance.	3.82	1.46
62 The evaluation and reward systems motivate me to deliver good service.	2.64	1.26
63 The evaluation criteria encourage sales at the expense of service.	3.31	1.46
64 More individualized reward schemes would be beneficial.	3.85	1.63

Table 7 ■ Service recovery

Statement	Mean score	Deviation
65 Our bank has developed clear routines about how to deal with dissatisfied customers.	3.04	1.30
66 Our bank encourages customers to complain if anything goes wrong.	3.43	1.28
67 The bank normally compensates customers for inconvenience caused by our mistakes.	4.32	1.22
68 I feel a personal responsibility to help customers who complain, even though another person has made the mistake.	5.16	0.90
69 I feel enough formal authority to handle complaining customers rapidly and satisfactorily.	3.90	1.35
70 It is important to compensate customers for the inconvenience our mistakes cause.	5.27	0.94
71 The training programmes emphasize how to deal with service recovery situations.	2.84	1.14

banks – which showed evidence of scope for major improvement (see Table 7). Almost all of the employees (97 per cent) agreed that 'it is important to compensate customers for the inconvenience our mistakes cause', and that they 'feel a personal responsibility to help customers who complain even though another person has made the mistake'. Thus, there was evid-ence of a high awareness of, and willingness to help, customers with problems, again confirming the previously observed customer orientation.

The responding employees were, however, rather critical of the banks' management of service recovery. Only half (53 per cent) agreed that their bank encourages their customers to complain if anything goes wrong, and as few as 36 per cent agreed that their bank has developed clear routines for dealing with dissatisfied customers. Further, as few as 27 per cent agreed that their training programmes emphasize how to deal with service recovery situations. Even so, nearly two-thirds of them (65 per cent) did agree that they had enough formal authority to handle complaining customers rapidly and satisfactorily; and 79 per cent believed that the bank normally compensates customers for inconvenience caused by

mistakes. Overall, a need for changes in both strategy and tactics (e.g. training programmes and empowerment) was evident.

Improvements

The final section of the questionnaire invited employees' opinions with respect to the possibilities for service quality improvements in their bank. The scores were high for all the items offered (see Table 8) with over 90 per cent of respondents agreeing, at least to some extent, that there is room for improvement with respect to: service quality (in general); internal working environment; customer orientation; training; the evaluation and reward systems; internal communication; and systems to deal with dissatisfied customers. The employees were only slightly less critical of: the competence of top management and of their closest superior; relations between management and employees; and task specifications. However, one needs to bear in mind the style of questioning, in effect inviting respondents to be critical; other styles, e.g., open-ended questions, are likely to generate less 'negative' answers.

Table 8 ■ Improvements

There is room for improvement in our bank when it comes to . . .	Mean score	Deviation
72 Service quality	5.04	0.95
73 Internal working environment	4.81	0.99
74 Customer orientation	4.82	0.89
75 The top management's competence	4.42	1.22
76 My closest superior's competence	3.98	1.37
77 Relations between management and employees	4.42	1.21
78 Training	4.73	0.97
79 Task specifications	4.10	1.19
80 Evaluation and reward systems	4.70	1.14
81 Internal communication	4.63	0.96
82 Systems to deal with dissatisfied customers	4.77	0.99

Conclusions

This study of service quality management has focused on functional dimensions of service quality, in particular people and culture-related variables. An empirical investigation took place in Norwegian banks following a banking crisis which resulted in: a number of short-term, cost-cutting, rationalization policies including staff cuts – which impact on motivation and create uncertainty; and a lack of financial resources to invest in the necessary infrastructure and organizational development. The other side of the coin was that the crisis had awakened the banks to increasing competition and the fact that total commitment from ALL organizational groups is required, including a focus on service quality management. Thus, the crisis may have enhanced a team spirit and welded personnel together – especially at the branch level.

The participating banks each had a service quality strategy designed to create a competitive advantage, customer relationships and, hence, long-term profit. However, there was still a focus on technical rather than functional aspects of service quality, and no real service quality culture within the organizations: thus, there was a need for development of personnel policies and internal marketing to maximize human potential.

An important dimension of cultural development is pro-active and visible leadership to include showing real commitment to, and ownership of, the service quality process, and personal involvement/execution. The findings from the employees' survey indicated that visible leadership with respect to service quality was lacking. Top management was perceived to be distant and regional managers were perceived to be anonymous by employees. Overall it would appear that the banks' management need to be concerned with the organizational culture and acknowledge that human resources are an intrinsic part of the service and quality delivered, and the potential of employees (to be customer aware, innovative and to use initiative) needs to be enhanced/maximized with appropriate leadership.

The role of employees

The role of employees in service encounters cannot be overstated, as the quality of interaction between employees and customers is a prime determinant of the customers' perceptions of service quality. For routine transactions, speed and efficiency are major contributors to customer satisfaction, but in other situations, e.g., dealing with customer requests and problems, loan and credit arrangements and service recovery, a more personalized response is needed – which necessitates the empowerment of front-line employees. Empowerment requires being given authority and responsibility to act and react – having the skills/ability to demonstrate initiative and flexibility.

The structure in the participating banks at the time of the survey, however, appears not to encourage these qualities and mitigates against empowerment and employee responsiveness. The banks' recent policies towards centralization of operations, responsibility and decision-making, and standardization, are aimed to increase productivity and supposedly, simultaneously, enable front-line employees to devote their attention to sales and customers. However, the front-line employees who responded felt somewhat frustrated by these changes and policy: for example, when they are responsible for communicating outcomes (e.g., with respect to credit and loans) and delivering service packages to external customers, but cannot influence the quality of the 'product'. They felt they were not empowered, for more complex service encounters, to be sufficiently helpful and efficient – thus, risking the dissatisfaction of external customers. So, although management perceived the changes as pre-requisites for successful quality strategies, front-line employees felt that recent developments, in fact, undermine service quality.

The leaking bucket

Further evidence from the research related to 'defection management'. The banks were giving little attention to service recovery and customer defection: they appeared to be lacking an aware and pro-active attitude to these areas. For example, there was no training for front-line employees on how to handle dissatisfied and complaining customers, and limited authority when dealing with such situations: and it was evident that customers are not encouraged to complain about problems and mistakes. This may be due, partly, to a limited understanding of the economics of long-term customer relationships (Reichheld and Sasser, 1990). Thus, it would appear that the banks need to incorporate service recovery and defection management as integral to service quality programmes if these initiatives are to have real value; crucial to which is the training and empowerment of front-line personnel. If a fundamental principle of service quality is customer retention, then service recovery performance is vital and could be the differentiating factor with respect to service quality strategy.

Future research

This study has been an exploratory one concerned with intra-organizational aspects related to the implementation of service quality initiatives. Aspects which affect service encounters, and which influence line employees' behaviour and ability to serve, have been highlighted. The fieldwork was particular to the recent situation in Norwegian financial services and identified a number of areas relevant for service quality management, especially those concerned with the cultural aspects of service quality. The relationship between service-oriented organizational cultures and effective service quality strategies was highlighted and, hence, a need for culture management.

Further research should pursue cultural aspects in more detail, and in other service industries, and include longitudinal studies – to investigate intra-organizational forces on cultural change and the impact on service quality and customer relationships and retention.

Continuing investigations might also focus on primary customer research in the context of varying service cultures, to include the benefits and limitations of centralization vs. decentralization, standardization vs. customization, and automation vs. personalized service.

Finally, the relationships between productivity, service and profitability provide continuing opportunities for service quality management researchers in financial services and in other service sector industries. For example, in financial services, should the same or differing 'levels of service' be provided to customer segments with varying demand for, and use of, specific services and, hence, their profitability to the supplying organization?

References

Ahmed, P.K and A.C. Simintiras, 1991, 'Facilitators and Distributors of Service Quality: a Guide for Survival and Growth', European Business Management School, Working paper No. 15, Swansea, Wales: University of Swansea.

Albrecht, K., 1988, *At America's Service*, Homewood, Illinois: Dow Jones-Irwin.

Albrecht, K. and L.J. Bradford, 1990, *The Service Advantage*, Homewood, Illinois: Dow Jones-Irwin.

Antil, J.H., 1992, 'Are you Committing Marketcide?', *The Journal of Services Marketing*, Vol. 6, No. 2, Spring, pp. 45–53.

Armistead, C. and G. Clark, 1991, 'Improving Service Delivery', *Managing Service Quality*, July, pp. 281–7.

Bailyn, L., 1993, 'Patterned Chaos in Human Resource Management', *Sloan Management Review*, Vol. 34, Winter, pp. 77–83.

Ballantyne, D., 1990, 'Turning the Wheel of Quality Improvement – Continuously', *International Journal of Bank Marketing*, Vol. 8, No. 22, pp. 3–11.

Beatty, S.E. and B.E. Gup, 1989, 'A Guide to Building a Customer Service Orientation', *Journal of Retail Banking*, Vol. 11, No. 2 (Summer).

Bennett, D.R. and C.W. Brown, 1992, 'Managing Sales and Service to Achieve a Culture Change', *The Bankers Magazine*, September/October, pp. 30–5.

Berry, L.L., V. Zeithaml and A. Parasuraman, 1990, 'Five Imperatives for Improving Service Quality', *Sloan Management Review*, Vol. 31, No. 4, Summer, pp. 29–38.

Berry, L.L. and A. Parasuraman, 1991, *Marketing Services: Competing through Quality*, New York: The Free Press.

Bitner, M.J., 1990, 'Evaluating Service Encounters: the Effects of Physical Surroundings and Employee Responses', *Journal of Marketing*, Vol. 54, April, pp. 69–82.

Boaden, R.J. and B.G. Dale, 1993, 'Managing Quality Improvement in Financial Services: A Framework and Case Study', *The Service Industries Journal*, Vol. 13, No. 1, January, pp. 17–39.

Campell, A. and S. Yeung, 1991, 'Creating a Sense of Mission', *Long Range Planning*, Vol. 24, No. 4, pp. 10–20.

Carlzon, J., 1987, *Moments of Truth*, New York: Ballinger Publishing Company.

Cespedes, F.V., 1992, 'Once More: How do you Improve Customer Service', *Business Horizons*, Vol. 35, No. 2, March–April, pp. 58–66.

Christopher, M., A. Payne and D. Ballantyne, 1991, *Relationship Marketing*, Oxford: Butterworth-Heinemann Ltd.

Clutterbuck, D., 1989, 'Developing Customer Care Training Programmes', *Marketing Intelligence and Planning*, Vol. 7, No. 1/2, pp. 34–7.

Collier, D., 1987, 'The Customer Service and Quality Challenge', *The Service Industries Journal*, Vol. 7, No.1, January, pp. 77–90.

Cornish, F., 1991, 'Building a Customer Oriented Organization', in *Services Marketing*, C.H. Lovelock (ed.), London: Prentice Hall Int., pp. 394–7.

Coscun, A. and C. Frohlich, 1992, 'Service: the Competitive Edge in Banking', *The Journal of Services Marketing*, Vol. 6, No. 1, pp. 15–21.

Coulson-Thomas, C.J., 1991, 'Managing Culture Change', *Managing Service Quality*, May, pp. 187–92.

Coyne, K., 1986, 'Sustainable Competitive Advantage: What it is, What it isn't', *Business Horizons*, Vol. 29, No. 1, January–February, pp. 54–61.

Coyne, K., 1989, 'Beyond Fads: Meaningful Strategies for the Real World', *Sloan Management Review*, Vol. 32, Summer, pp. 69–76.

Coyne, K., 1993, 'Achieving a Sustainable Service Advantage', *Journal of Business Strategy*, Vol. 14, No. 1, January–February, pp. 3–10.

Crosby, L.A., 1991, 'Expanding the Role of CSM in Total Quality', *International Journal of Service Industry Management*, Vol. 2, No. 2, pp. 5–19.

Daniel, A.L., 1992, 'Overcome the Barriers to Superior Customer Service', *Journal of Business Strategy*, Vol. 13, No. 1, January–February, pp. 18–24.

Davidow, W.H. and B. Uttal, 1989, *Total Customer Service: The Ultimate Weapon*, New York: HarperCollins.

Drucker, P.E., 1991, 'The New Productivity Challenge', *Harvard Business Review*, Vol. 69, No. 6, November–December, pp. 69–79.

Easingwood, C.J. and C. Storey, 1991, 'Success Factors for New Consumer Financial Services', *International Journal of Bank Marketing*, Vol. 9, No. 1, pp. 3–10.

Edvardsson, B., B.O. Gustavsson and D.I. Riddle, 1989, 'An Expanded Model of the Service Encounter with Emphasis on Cultural Context', Service Research Center – CFT, Research Report No. 4, Karlstad, Sweden: University of Karlstad.

Edwards, D. and D. Clutterbuck, 1991, 'Motivation and Problem-Solving', *Managing Service Quality*, July, pp. 275–80.

Firnstahl, T.W., 1989, 'My Employees are My Service Guarantee', *Harvard Business Review*, Vol. 67, No. 4, July–August, pp. 28–34.

Flipo, J.P., 1986, 'Service Firms: Interdependence of External and Internal Marketing Strategies', *European Journal of Marketing*, Vol. 20, No. 8, pp. 5–13.

Gabrielsen, G.O.S., 1993, 'An Intra-Organisational Approach Towards the Implementation of Service Quality Management in Norwegian Banking', MSc Thesis, Manchester School of Management.

Grönroos, C., 1981, 'Internal Marketing: an Integral Part of Marketing Theory', in J.H. Donnelly and W.R. George (eds), *Marketing of Services*, Chicago: American Marketing Association, pp. 236–8.

Grönroos, C., 1984, 'A Service Quality Model and its Implications', *European Journal of Marketing*, Vol. 18, No. 4, pp. 36–44.

Grönroos, C., 1985, 'Internal Marketing: Theory and Practice', in T.M. Bloch, G.D. Upah and V.A. Zeithaml (eds), *Services Marketing in a Changing Environment*, Chicago: American Marketing Association, pp. 41–7.

Grove, S.J. and R.P. Fisk, 1991, 'The Dramaturgy of Service Exchange: an Analytical Framework for Services Marketing', in *Services Marketing*, C.H. Lovelock (ed.), London, Prentice Hall Int., pp. 59–68.

Gummesson, E., 1991, 'Truths and Myths in Service Quality', *International Journal of Service Industry Management*, Vol. 2, No. 3, pp. 7–15.

Hart, C.W.L., 1988, 'The Power of Unconditional Service Guarantees', *Harvard Business Review*, Vol. 66, No. 4, July–August, pp. 54–62.

Hart, C.W.L., J.L. Heskett and W.E. Sasser, 1990, 'The Profitable Art of Service Recovery', *Harvard Business Review*, Vol. 68, No. 4, July–August, pp. 148–56.

Hauser, J.R. and D. Clausing, 1988, 'The House of Quality', *Harvard Business Review*, Vol. 66, No. 3, May–June, pp. 63–73.

Haynes, R.M. and P.K. Duvall, 1992, 'Service Quality Management: A Process Control Approach', *International Journal of Service Industry Management*, Vol. 3, No. 1, pp. 14–23.

Hellestol, Y. and O. Nygaard, 1993, 'Nytt Ar med Ledighetsrekord', *Aftenposten*, Vol. 21, No. 1, p. 28.

Heskett, J.L., 1987, 'Lessons in the Service Sector', *Harvard Business Review*, Vol. 65, No. 2, March–April, pp. 118–26.

Heskett, J.L., W.E. Sasser and C.W.L. Hart, 1990, *Service Breakthroughs – Changing the Rules of the Game*, New York: The Free Press.

Howcroft, J.B., 1991, 'Customer Satisfaction in Retail Banking', *The Service Industries Journal*, Vol. 11, No. 1, January, pp. 11–17.

Kotter, J.P. and J.L. Heskett, 1992, *Corporate Culture and Performance*, New York: The Free Press.

Lehtinen, U. and J.R. Lehtinen, 1991, 'Two Approaches to Service Quality Dimensions', *The Service Industries Journal*, Vol. 11, No. 3, July, pp. 287–303.

Leonard, F.S. and W.E. Sasser, 1982, 'The Incline of Quality', *Harvard Business Review*, Vol. 60, No. 5, September–October, pp. 163–71.

Lewis, B.R. and T.W. Entwistle, 1989, 'Managing the Service Encounter: A Focus on the Employee', *International Journal of Service Industry Management*, Vol. 1, No. 3, pp. 41–52.

Lewis, B.R. and G.O.S. Gabrielsen, 1995, *An Intra-Organisational Approach Towards The Implementation of Service Quality Management*, Manchester School of Management.

Long, R.H., 1988, 'High-Performance Bank Culture', *Journal of Retail Banking*, Vol. 10, No. 3, Fall.

Lovelock, C.H., 1991, *Services Marketing*, London: Prentice Hall.

Miller, T.O., 1992, 'A Customer's Definition of Quality', *Journal of Business Strategy*, Vol. 13, No. 1, January–February, pp. 4–7.

Mintzberg, H., 1991, 'Crafting Strategy', in Mintzberg and J.B. Quinn (eds), *The Strategy Process*, Prentice Hall.

Morgan, G., 1986, *Images of Organisation*, Sage Publications Inc.

Morgan, R.E. and S. Chadha, 1993, 'Relationship Marketing at the Service Encounter: the Case of Life Assurance', *The Service Industries Journal*, Vol. 24, No. 1, January, pp. 12–25.

Nadler, D.A. and M.L. Tushman, 1990, 'Beyond the Charismatic Leader: Leadership and Organisational Change', *California Management Review*, Winter.

Ohmae, K., 1988, 'Getting Back to Strategy', *Harvard Business Review*, Vol. 66, No. 6, November–December, pp. 149–56.

Olaisen, J. and O. Revang, 1991, 'The Significance of Information Technology for Service Quality: from Market Segmentation to Individual Service', *International Journal of Service Industry Management*, Vol. 2, No. 3, pp. 26–46.

Parasuraman, A., L.L. Berry and V. Zeithaml, 1991, 'Understanding Customer Expectations of Service', *Sloan Management Review*, Vol. 32, No. 3, Spring, pp. 39–48.

Payne, A.F., 1988, 'Developing a Marketing Orientated Organisation', *Business Horizons*, May–June, pp. 46–53.

Peters, T., 1987, *Thriving on Chaos*, Pan Books.

Peters, T.J. and N. Austin, 1985, *A Passion for Excellence*, New York: Fontana/Collins.

Peters, T.J. and R.H. Waterman, 1982, *In Search of Excellence*, New York: Harper Collins Publishers.

Piercy, N. and N. Morgan, 1991, 'Internal Marketing: the Missing Half of the Marketing Programme', *Long Range Planning*, Vol. 24, No. 2, pp. 82–93.

Pirrie, D., 1990, 'Service and Costs', *Banking World*, December, 19–20.

Porter, M.E., 1980, *Competitive Strategy: Techniques for Analysing Industries and Competitors*, New York: The Free Press.

Raynor, M.E., 1992, 'Quality as a Strategic Weapon', *Journal of Business Strategy*, Vol. 13, No. 5, September–October, pp. 3–9.

Reichheld, F.F. and W.E. Sasser, 1990, 'Zero Defections: Quality Comes to Service', *Harvard Business Review*, Vol. 68, No. 5, September–October, pp. 105–11.

Schein, E., 1985, *Organizational Culture and Leadership*, San Francisco: Jossey-Bass.

Schlesinger, L.A. and J.L. Heskett, 1991, 'Breaking the Cycle of Failures in Services', *Sloan Management Review*, Vol. 32, No. 3, Spring, pp. 17–28.

Schlesinger, L.A. and J.L. Heskett, 1991, 'The Service Driven Company', *Harvard Business Review*, Vol. 69, No. 5, September–October, pp. 71–81.

Seddon, J., 1992, 'A Successful Attitude', *Managing Service Quality*, January, pp. 81–4.

Sherden, W.A., 1988, 'Gaining the Service Quality Advantage', *The Journal of Business Strategy*, Vol. 9, No. 2, March–April, pp. 45–8.

Shostack, L., 1984, 'Designing Services that Deliver', *Harvard Business Review*, Vol. 62, No. 1, January–February, pp. 133–9.

Shreeve, G., 1991, 'Re-Inventing the Wheel', *The Banker*, May, pp. 10–14.

Singh, J. and R.E. Wilding, 1991, 'What Occurs Once Customers Complain', *European Journal of Marketing*, Vol. 25, No. 5, pp. 30–46.

Solomon, M.R., C. Surprenant, J.A. Czepiel and E.G. Gutman, 1985, 'A Role Theory Perspective on Dyadic Interactions: the Service Encounter', *Journal of Marketing*, Vol. 49, Winter, pp. 99–111.

Thamara, T., 1991, 'Quality Converts Customers into Long-Term Partners', *The Bankers Magazine*, September/October, pp. 52–7.

Thwaites, D. and K. Glaiser, 1992, 'Strategic Response to Environmental Turbulence', *International Journal of Bank Marketing*, Vol. 10, No. 3, pp. 33–40.

Varey, R. J. and R. Brooks, 1992, 'Superior Customer Service Quality Through Internal Marketing?', *5th Services Marketing Workshop*, Manchester School of Management, November.

Wong, S.M. and C. Perry, 1991, 'Customer Service Strategies in Financial Retailing', *International Journal of Bank Marketing*, Vol. 9, No. 3, pp. 11–16.

Yasin, M.M., R.F. Green and M. Wafa, 1992, 'Statistical Quality Control in Banking', *International Journal of Bank Marketing*, Vol. 9, No. 2, pp. 12–16.

Zeithaml, V., 1991, 'How Consumer Evaluation Processes Differ Between Goods and Services', in *Services Marketing*, C.H. Lovelock (ed.), London: Prentice Hall, pp. 39–47.

Zeithaml, V.A., L.L. Berry and A. Parasuraman, 1988, 'Communication and Control Processes in the Delivery of Service Quality', *Journal of Marketing*, Vol. 52, April, pp. 35–48.

Altering the way the company really works

Sandra Vandermerwe

Building new processes designed to create more value for customers requires helping employees decide what they need to do differently and to set new goals for themselves.

In transforming to 'own' customers it's more important to create new 'competitive spaces' in which skills, resources and know-how can come together and behave as one customer value-creating and delivery system, than it is to restructure corporations into new neat categories.

With a customer logic seriously under way, people quickly begin to think about new roles and ways of working and the skills, behaviour and know-how needed to deliver value add at critical points in the customer activity cycle.

No amount of traditional restructuring will lead to the kind of fundamental deep changes in mindset and working patterns we are talking about here.

As Paul Allaire, CEO of Rank Xerox, who has personally spent a good deal of time and energy focusing on processes to achieve his new vision for the company, said:

> There is a formal structure and then there's the way the company really works. You have to change the way it really works.

As I mentioned before, several executives who have been through or are in the process of driving their corporations to the market place, warn against restructuring, especially at the start of a customer transformation process: they say it can take energy and resources off the real issues at a very crucial time.

Given an alternate view of the world – that people understand and accept – new structures are likely to succeed.

Whereas restructuring without a solid customer base and grounding methodology makes the ₁radical change in desired behaviour unlikely, if not impossible.

Redesigning processes as enablers

People like Allaire and others say that it's through a number of core processes that the way a company works ultimately gets changed.

Provided, they add, you know what it is you have to change to.

From emphasis in the past to doing things better–faster–cheaper, the attention during the educational phase of the transformation is to enable people to achieve the dual goal of putting value in while taking non-value out.

It's about putting the tools, technology, training infrastructure and incentives in place so that people can get on and do what's necessary, acknowledging that 'the best way' can change, depending on the individual customer and circumstances.

Processes become a key enabler.

They become the connecting device for pulling the parts together, tying and uniting the various delivery entities within a 'solution-based community'.

And the customer activity cycles of the internal entities supporting the delivery units are linked by these new processes – all of which form the new corporate architecture.

What's a good process?

A good process is not just a new detailed statement of how things are now done.

In fact, the better the new processes the less need for control.

Good processes release energy, time and creative talents during a transformation, rather than inhibit or box people in.

The best processes are self-correcting and self-improving, and as such they are constantly evolving.

How to build new processes is a process in and of itself, and learning how to do that, on an ongoing basis, is part of the transformation agenda.

Building new processes at Sun Life Assurance

New corporations involve their people early on in building new processes, to get momentum flowing.

According to Les Owen this was a critical part of moving people from the initial feelings of fear to involvement, excitement and personal commitment at Sun Life Assurance.

It's about comparing what people have been recruited and trained for, and how they must now spend their time. (At Sun Life they discovered that over 70 per cent of what people had learned in the first and second years was about internal systems – nothing to do with customer value add.)

Building new processes is also about helping people decide what it is they must do differently and set themselves fresh goals.

A 'straw poll' was taken of the staff – a person stationed outside the Sun Life cafeteria with a clipboard asked employees: 'If you were a Sun Life customer, how long would you expect to wait to get your policy processed?' The general response given was 10 days.

The results of the poll were published and circulated throughout the company. The goal of 10 days that people came up with was far higher than management say they would have set.

Defining the 'as is'

Before processes are redesigned, corporations go through a period of finding out how things are currently done.

During this exercise, a lot will surface of great value if the information is creatively extracted, and the process well managed.

It's important to involve the people who do the doing in the exercise, and make sure that what comes out as 'as is', is indeed representative of what goes on.

In addition to the normal process mapping techniques, involving and discussing with the people who do the doing increases the probability of getting commitment and speeding up the changes.

Northumbrian Water embarked on an interesting exercise called 'A Day in the Life of . . . '. On a voluntary and confidential basis, close to 100 people across the business – from engineering to sewage operators – were closely observed.

Having all gone through customer activity cycles in previous workshops, they understood the customer mindset and gave input on what they needed to make changes – some of which they had already begun to initiate – happen; what barriers were still blocking them; and how they could best accomplish new customer performance.

Some dos and don'ts on process

Here are the main dos and don'ts in building new processes:

Don't:
Graft incremental improvements onto existing processes.
Do:
Let people go about doing things, as if they could start from scratch, based on a shared interpretation of customer value.

Don't:
Redesign processes to simply cut costs.
Do:
Make both putting value in *and* taking non-value out, the twin objectives and processes, one of the enablers.

Don't:
Get experts in who form special teams isolated from the people who do the work, and have to make the transformation happen.

Do:
Involve as many people as you can who are in customer contact, and let them make the assessments and recommend the changes – in other words, let them tell you how they want to do it differently.

Don't:
Try to force the new organization into boxes and arrows – some of the best decisions and actions can't be 'boxed in'.

Do:
Start from the customer activity cycle and work back to find gaps and needed connections.

Don't:
Allow processes to be redesigned as an exercise separate from the vision, mission and new world view.

Do:
Make the new mental model, set of tools and terminology an integral part of reworking the processes.

Putting the service-profit chain to work

James L. Heskett ■ *Thomas O. Jones* ■ *Gary W. Loveman* ■
W. Earl Sasser, Jr ■ *Leonard A. Schlesinger*

When service companies put employees and customers first, a radical shift occurs in the way they manage and measure success. The service-profit chain puts 'hard' values on 'soft' measures, relating profitability, customer loyalty and customer satisfaction to the value of services created by satisfied, loyal and productive employees.

Top-level executives of outstanding service organizations spend little time setting profit goals or focusing on market share, the management mantra of the 1970s and 1980s. Instead, they understand that in the new economics of service, front-line workers and customers need to be the centre of management concern. Successful service managers pay attention to the factors that drive profitability in this new service paradigm: investment in people, technology that supports front-line workers, revamped recruiting and training practices, and compensation linked to performance for employees at every level. And they express a vision of leadership in terms rarely heard in corporate America: an organization's 'patina of spirituality', the 'importance of the mundane'.

A growing number of companies that includes Banc One, Intuit Corporation, Southwest Airlines, ServiceMaster, USAA, Taco Bell and MCI know that when they make employees and customers paramount, a radical shift occurs in the way they manage and measure success. The new economics of service requires innovative measurement techniques. These techniques calibrate the impact of employee satisfaction, loyalty and productivity on the value of products and services delivered so that managers can build customer satisfaction and loyalty and assess the corresponding impact on profitability and growth. In fact, the lifetime value of a loyal customer can be astronomical, especially when referrals are added to the economics of customer retention and repeat purchases of related products. For example, the lifetime revenue stream from a loyal pizza eater can be $8,000, a Cadillac owner $332,000,

and a corporate purchaser of commercial aircraft literally billions of dollars.

The service-profit chain, developed from analyses of successful service organizations, puts 'hard' values on 'soft' measures. It helps managers target new investments to develop service and satisfaction levels for maximum competitive impact, widening the gap between service leaders and their merely good competitors.

The service-profit chain

The service-profit chain establishes relationships between profitability, customer loyalty and employee satisfaction, loyalty and productivity. The links in the chain (which should be regarded as propositions) are as follows: profit and growth are stimulated primarily by customer loyalty. Loyalty is a direct result of customer satisfaction. Satisfaction is largely influenced by the value of services provided to customers. Value is created by satisfied, loyal and productive employees. Employee satisfaction, in turn, results primarily from high-quality support services and policies that enable employees to deliver results to customers. (See the figure, 'The links in the service-profit chain'.)

The service-profit chain is also defined by a special kind of leadership. CEOs of exemplary service companies emphasize the importance of each employee and customer. For these CEOs, the focus on

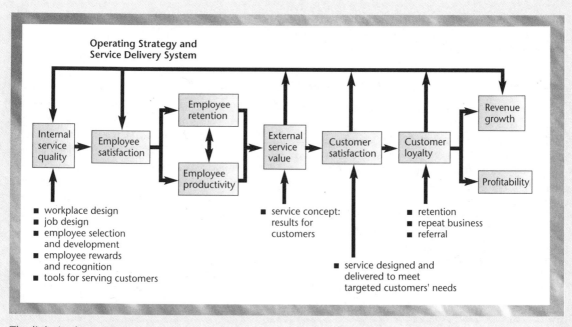

The links in the service-profit chain

customers and employees is no empty slogan tailored to an annual management meeting. For example, Herbert Kelleher, CEO of Southwest Airlines, can be found aboard airplanes, on tarmacs and in terminals, interacting with employees and customers. Kelleher believes that hiring employees that have the right attitude is so important that the hiring process takes on a 'patina of spirituality'. In addition, he believes that 'anyone who looks at things solely in terms of factors that can easily be quantified is missing the heart of business, which is people'. William Pollard, the chairman of ServiceMaster, continually underscores the importance of 'teacher-learner' managers, who have what he calls 'a servant's heart'. And John McCoy, CEO of Banc One, stresses the 'uncommon partnership', a system of support that provides maximum latitude to individual bank presidents while supplying information systems and common measurements of customer satisfaction and financial measures.

A closer look at each link reveals how the service-profit chain functions as a whole.

Customer loyalty drives profitability and growth

To maximize profit, managers have pursued the Holy Grail of becoming number one or two in their industries for nearly two decades. Recently, however, new measures of service industries like software and banking suggest that customer loyalty is a more important determinant of profit. (See Frederick F. Reichheld and W. Earl Sasser, Jr, 'Zero Defections: Quality Comes to Services', HBR, September–October 1990.) Reichheld and Sasser estimate that a 5 per cent increase in customer loyalty can produce profit increases from 25 per cent to 85 per cent. They conclude that *quality* of market share, measured in terms of customer loyalty, deserves as much attention as *quantity* of share.

Banc One, based in Columbus, Ohio, has developed a sophisticated system to track several factors involved in customer loyalty and satisfaction. Once driven strictly by financial measures, Banc One now conducts quarterly measures of customer retention; the number of services used by each customer, or *depth of relationship*; and the level of customer satisfaction. The strategies derived from this information help explain why Banc One has achieved a return on assets more than double that of its competitors in recent years.

Customer satisfaction drives customer loyalty

Leading service companies are currently trying to quantify customer satisfaction. For example, for several years, Xerox has polled 480,000 customers per year regarding product and service satisfaction using a five-point scale from 5 (high) to 1 (low). Until two years ago, Xerox's goal was to achieve 100 per cent 4s (satisfied) and 5s (very satisfied) by the end of 1993. But in 1991, an analysis of customers who gave Xerox 4s and 5s on satisfaction found that the relationships between the scores and actual loyalty differed greatly depending on whether the customers were very satisfied or satisfied. Customers giving

Xerox 5s were six times more likely to repurchase Xerox equipment than those giving 4s.

This analysis led Xerox to extend its efforts to create *apostles* – a term coined by Scott D. Cook, CEO of software producer and distributor, Intuit Corporation, describing customers so satisfied that they convert the uninitiated to a product or service. Xerox's management currently wants to achieve 100 per cent apostles, or 5s, by the end of 1996 by upgrading service levels and guaranteeing customer satisfaction. But just as important for Xerox's profitability is to avoid creating *terrorists*: customers so unhappy that they speak out against a poorly delivered service at every opportunity. Terrorists can reach hundreds of potential customers. In some instances, they can even discourage acquaintances from trying a service or product. (See the graph, 'A satisfied customer is loyal'.)

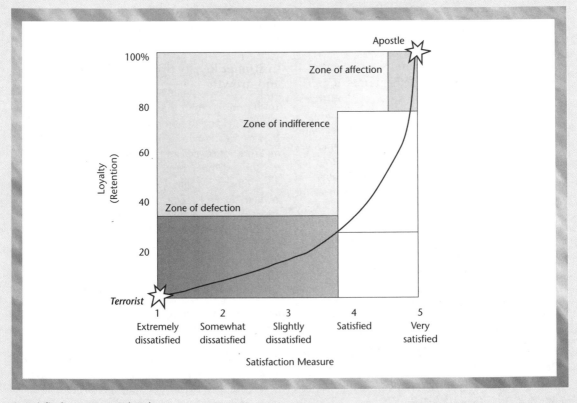

A satisfied customer is loyal

Value drives customer satisfaction

Customers today are strongly value oriented. But just what does that mean? Customers tell us that value means the results they receive in relation to the total costs (both the price and other costs to customers incurred in acquiring the service). The insurance company, Progressive Corporation, is creating just this kind of value for its customers by processing and paying claims quickly and with little policyholder effort. Members of the company's CAT (catastrophe) team fly to the scene of major accidents, providing support services like transportation and housing and handling claims rapidly. By reducing legal costs and actually placing more money in the hands of the injured parties, the CAT team more than makes up for the added expenses the organization incurs by maintaining the team. In addition, the CAT team delivers value to customers, which helps explain why Progressive has one of the highest margins in the property-and-casualty insurance industry.

Employee productivity drives value

At Southwest Airlines, the seventh largest US domestic carrier, an astonishing story of employee productivity occurs daily. Eighty-six per cent of the company's 14,000 employees are unionized. Positions are designed so that employees can perform several jobs if necessary. Schedules, routes and company practices – such as open seating and the use of simple, colour-coded, re-usable boarding passes – enable the boarding of three and four times more passengers per day than competing airlines. In fact, Southwest deplanes and reloads two-thirds of its flights in 15 minutes or less. Because of aircraft availability and short-haul routes that don't require long layovers for flight crews, Southwest has roughly 40 per cent more pilot and aircraft utilization than its major competitors: its pilots fly on average 70 hours per month versus 50 hours at other airlines. These factors explain how the company can charge fares from 60 per cent to 70 per cent lower than existing fares in markets it enters.

At Southwest, customer perceptions of value are very high, even though the airline does not assign seats, offer meals, or integrate its reservation system with other airlines. Customers place high value on Southwest's frequent departures, on-time service, friendly employees, and very low fares. Southwest's management knows this because its major marketing research unit – its 14,000 employees – is in daily contact with customers and reports its findings back to management. In addition, the Federal Aviation Administration's performance measures show that Southwest, of all the major airlines, regularly achieves the highest level of on-time arrivals, the lowest number of complaints, and the fewest lost baggage claims per 1,000 passengers. When combined with Southwest's low fares per seat-mile, these indicators show the higher value delivered by Southwest's employees compared with most domestic competitors. Southwest has been profitable for 21 consecutive years and was the only major airline to realize a profit in 1992. (See the figure, 'How Southwest compares with its competitors'.)

Employee loyalty drives productivity

Traditional measures of the losses incurred by employee turnover concentrate only on the cost of recruiting, hiring and training replacements. In most service jobs, the real cost of turnover is the loss of productivity and decreased customer satisfaction. One recent study of an automobile dealer's sales personnel by Abt Associates concluded that the average monthly cost of replacing a sales representative who had five to eight years of experience with an employee who had less than one year of experience was as much as $36,000 in sales. And the costs of losing a valued broker at a securities firm can be still more dire. Conservatively estimated, it takes nearly five years for a broker to rebuild relationships with customers that can return $1 million per year in commissions to the brokerage house – a cumulative loss of at least $2.5 million in commissions.

Employee satisfaction drives loyalty

In one 1991 proprietary study of a property-and-casualty insurance company's employees, 30 per cent of all dissatisfied employees registered an intention to leave the company, a potential turnover rate three times higher than that for satisfied employees. In this same case, low employee turnover was found to be linked closely to high customer satisfaction. In contrast, Southwest Airlines, recently named one of the country's ten best places to work, experiences the highest rate of employee retention in the airline industry. Satisfaction levels are so high that at some of its operating locations, employee turnover rates are less than 5 per cent per year. USAA, a major provider of insurance and other financial services by direct mail and phone, also achieves low levels of employee turnover by ensuring that its employees are highly satisfied. But what drives employee satisfaction? Is it compensation, perks or plush workplaces?

Internal quality drives employee satisfaction

What we call the *internal quality* of a working environment contributes most to employee satisfaction. Internal quality is measured by the feelings that employees have toward their jobs, colleagues and companies. What do service employees value most on the job? Although our data are preliminary at best, they point increasingly to the ability and authority of service workers to achieve results for customers. At USAA, for example, telephone sales and service representatives are backed by a sophisticated information system that puts complete customer information files at their fingertips the instant they receive a customer's call. In addition, state-of-the-art, job-related training is made available to USAA employees. And the curriculum goes still further, with 200 courses in 75 classrooms in a wide range of subjects.

Internal quality is also characterized by the attitudes that people have toward one another and the way people serve each other inside the organization. For example, ServiceMaster, a provider of a range of cleaning and maintenance services, aims to maximize the dignity of the individual service worker. Each year, it analyzes in depth a part of the maintenance process, such as cleaning a floor, in order to reduce the time and effort needed to complete the task. The 'importance of the mundane' is stressed repeatedly in ServiceMaster's management training – for example, in the seven-step process devised for cleaning a hospital room: from the first step, greeting the patient, to the last step, asking patients whether or not they need anything else done. Using this process, service workers develop communication skills and learn to interact with patients in ways that add depth and dimension to their jobs.

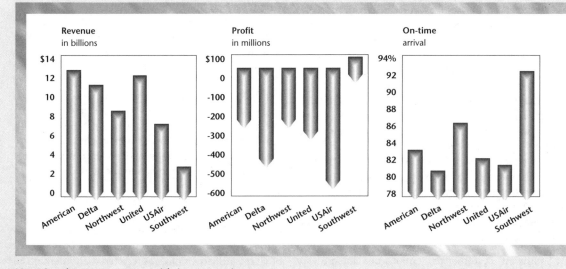

How Southwest compares with its competitors

Leadership underlies the chain's success

Leaders who understand the service-profit chain develop and maintain a corporate culture centred around service to customers and fellow employees. They display a willingness and ability to listen. Successful CEOs like John Martin of Taco Bell, John McCoy of Banc One, Herb Kelleher of Southwest and Bill Pollard of ServiceMaster spend a great deal of time with customers and employees, experiencing their companies' service processes while listening to employees for suggestions for improvement. They care about their employees and spend a great deal of time selecting, tracking and recognizing them.

For example, Brigadier General Robert McDermott, until recently chairman and CEO of USAA, reflected, 'Public recognition of outstanding employees flows naturally from our corporate culture. That culture is talked about all the time, and we live it.' According to Scott Cook at Intuit, 'Most people take culture as a given. It is around you, the thinking goes, and you can't do anything about it. However, when you run a company, you have the opportunity to determine the culture. I find that when you champion the most noble values – including service, analysis, and database deci-sion making – employees rise to the challenge, and you forever change their lives.'

Relating links in the chain for management action

While many organizations are beginning to measure relationships between individual links in the service-profit chain, only a few have related the links in mean-ingful ways – ways that can lead to comprehensive strategies for achieving lasting competitive advantage.

The 1991 proprietary study of a property-and-casualty insurance company, cited earlier, not only identified the links between employee satisfaction and loyalty but also established that a primary source of job satisfac-tion was the service workers' perceptions of their ability to meet customer needs. Those who felt they did meet customer needs registered job satisfaction levels more than twice as high as those who felt they didn't. But even more important, the same study found that when a service worker left the company, customer satisfac-tion levels dropped sharply from 75 per cent to 55 per cent. As a result of this analysis, management is trying to reduce turnover among customer-contact employ-ees and to enhance their job skills.

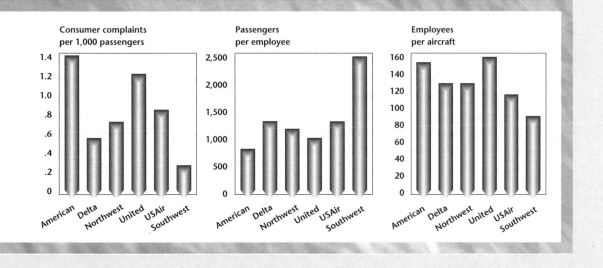

Similarly, in a study of its seven telephone customer service centres, MCI found clear relationships between employees' perceptions of the quality of MCI service and employee satisfaction. The study also linked employee satisfaction directly to customer satisfaction and intentions to continue to use MCI services. Identifying these relationships motivated MCI's management to probe deeper and determine what affected job satisfaction at the service centres. The factors they uncovered, in order of importance, were satisfaction with the job itself, training, pay, advancement fairness, treatment with respect and dignity, teamwork and the company's interest in employees' well-being. Armed with this information, MCI's management began examining its policies concerning those items valued most by employees at its service centres. MCI has incorporated information about its service capabilities into training and communications efforts and television advertising.

No organization has made a more comprehensive effort to measure relationships in the service-profit chain and fashion a strategy around those relationships than the fast-food company, Taco Bell, a subsidiary of PepsiCo. Taco Bell's management tracks profits daily by unit, market manager, zone and country. By integrating this information with the results of exit interviews that Taco Bell conducts with 800,000 customers annually, management has found that stores in the top quadrant of customer satisfaction ratings outperform the other stores by all measures. As a result, Taco Bell has linked operations managers' compensation in company-owned stores to customer satisfaction, realizing a subsequent increase in both customer satisfaction ratings and profits.

However, Taco Bell's efforts don't stop there. By examining employee turnover records for individual stores, Taco Bell has discovered that the 20 per cent of the stores with the lowest turnover rates enjoy double the sales and 55 per cent higher profits than the 20 per cent of stores with the highest employee turnover rates. As a result of this self-examination, Taco Bell has instituted financial and other incentives in order to reverse the cycle of failure that is associated with poor employee selection, subpar training, low pay and high turnover.

In addition, Taco Bell monitors internal quality through a network of 800 numbers created to answer employees' questions, field their complaints, remedy situations, and alert top-level management to potential trouble spots. It also conducts periodic employee roundtable meetings, interviews, as well as a comprehensive companywide survey every two or three years in order to measure satisfaction. As a result of all this work, Taco Bell's focus on employee satisfaction involves a new selection process, improved skill building, increased latitude for decision making on the job, and further automation of unpleasant 'back-room' labour.

Relating all the links in the service-profit chain may seem to be a tall order. But profitability depends not only on placing hard values on soft measures but also on linking those individual measures together into a comprehensive service picture. Service organizations need to quantify their investments in people – both customers and employees. The service-profit chain provides the framework for this critical task.

Service-profit chain audit

A service-profit chain audit helps companies determine what drives their profit and suggests actions that can lead to long-term profitability. As they review the audit, managers should ask themselves what efforts are underway to obtain answers to the following questions and what those answers reveal about their companies.

Profit and growth

1. How do we define loyal customers?

Customers often become more profitable over time. And loyal customers account for an unusually high proportion of the sales and profit growth of successful service providers. In some organizations, loyalty is measured in terms of whether or not a customer is on the company rolls. But several companies have found that their most loyal customers – the top 20% of total customers – not only provide all the profit but also cover losses incurred in dealing with less loyal customers.

Because of the link between loyal customers and profit, Banc One measures *depth of relationship* – the number of available related financial services, such as checking, lending and safe deposit, actually used by customers. Recognizing the same relationship, Taco Bell drives its desire to increase 'share of stomach' by broadening the selection of food purchases a customer can potentially make. As a result, the fast-food chain is trying to reach consumers through kiosks, carts, trucks and the shelves of supermarkets.

2. Do measurements of customer profitability include profits from referrals?

Companies that measure the stream of revenue and profits from loyal customers (retention) and repeat sales often overlook what can be the most important of the three Rs of loyalty: referrals. For example, Intuit provides high-quality, free lifetime service for a personal finance software package that sells for as little as $30. The strategy makes sense when the value of a loyal customer is considered – a revenue stream of several thousands of dollars from software updates, supplies and new customer referrals. With this strategy in place, Intuit increased its sales to more than $30 million with just two U.S. field sales representatives.

3. What proportion of business development expenditures and incentives are directed to the retention of existing customers?

Too many companies concentrate nearly all their efforts on attracting new customers. But in businesses like life insurance, a new policyholder doesn't become profitable for at least three years. In the credit-card finance business, the break-even point for a new customer is often six or more years because of high-marketing and bad-debt costs in the first year of a relationship with cardholders. These costs must be defrayed by profits from loyal customers, suggesting the need for a careful division of organizational effort between customer retention and development.

4. Why do our customers defect?

It's important to find out not only where defectors go but also why they defect. Was it because of poor service, price, or value? Answers to these questions provide information about whether or not existing strategies are working. In addition, exit interviews of customers can have real sales impact. For example, at one credit-card service organization, a phone call to question cardholders who had stopped using their cards led to the immediate reinstatement of one-third of the defectors.

Customer satisfaction

5. Are customer satisfaction data gathered in an objective, consistent and periodic fashion?

Currently, the weakest measurements being used by companies we have studied concern customer satisfaction. At some companies, high levels of reported customer satisfaction are contradicted by continuing declines in sales and profits. Upon closer observation, we discovered that the service providers were 'gaming' the data, using manipulative methods for collecting customer satisfaction data. In one extreme case, an automobile dealer sent a questionnaire to recent buyers with the highest marks already filled in, requiring owners to alter the marks only if they disagreed. Companies can, however, obtain more objective results using 'third party' interviews; 'mystery shopping' by unidentified, paid observers; or technologies like touch-screen television.

Consistency is at least as important as the actual questions asked of customers. Some of Banc One's operating units formerly conducted their own customer satisfaction surveys. Today the surveys have been centralized, made mandatory, and are administered by mail on a quarterly basis to around 125,000 customers. When combined with periodic measurement, the surveys provide highly relevant trend information that informs the managerial decision-making process. Similarly, Xerox's measures of satisfaction obtained from 10,000 customers per month – a product of an unchanging set of survey questions and very large samples – make possible period-to-period comparisons that are important in measuring and rewarding performance.

6. What are the listening posts for obtaining customer feedback in your organization?

Listening posts are tools for collecting data from customers and systematically translating those data into information in order to improve service and products. Common examples are letters of complaint. Still more important listening posts are reports from field sales and service personnel or the logs of telephone service representatives. Intuit's content analysis of customer service enquiries fielded by service representatives produced over 50 software improvements and 100 software documentation improvements in a single year. USAA has gone one step further by automating the feedback process to enter data online, enabling its analysis and plans departments to develop corrective actions.

7. How is information concerning customer satisfaction used to solve customer problems?

In order to handle customer problems, service providers must have the latitude to resolve any situation promptly. In addition, information regarding a customer concern must be transmitted to the service provider quickly. Customers and employees must be encouraged to report rather than suppress concerns. For example, one Boston-area Lexus dealer notified its customers, 'If you are experiencing a problem with your car or our service department and you can't answer "100% satisfied" when you receive your survey directly from Lexus, please give us the opportunity to correct the problem before you fill out the survey. Lexus takes its customer surveys very seriously.'

External service value

8. How do you measure service value?

Value is a function not only of costs to the customer but also of the results achieved for the customer. Value is always relative because it is based both on perceptions of the way a service is delivered and on initial customer expectations. Typically, a company measures value using the reasons expressed by customers for high or low satisfaction. Because value varies with individual expectations, efforts to improve value inevitably require service organizations to move all levels of management closer to the customer and give frontline service employees the latitude to customize a standard service to individual needs.

9. How is information concerning customers' perceptions of value shared with those responsible for designing a product or service?

Relaying information concerning customer expectations to those responsible for design often requires the formation of teams of people responsible for sales, operations and service or product design, as well as the frequent assignment of service designers to tasks requiring field contact with customers. Intuit has created this kind of capability in product development teams. And all Intuit employees, including the CEO, must periodically work on the customer service phones. Similarly, at Southwest, those responsible for flight scheduling periodically work shifts in the company's terminals to get a feel for the impact of schedules on customer and employee satisfaction.

10. To what extent are measures taken of differences between customers' perceptions of quality delivered and their expectations before delivery?

Ultimately, service quality is a function of the gap between perceptions of the actual service experienced and what a customer expected before receiving that service. Actual service includes both final results and the process through which those results were obtained. Differences between experiences and expectations can be measured in generic dimensions such as the reliability and timeliness of service, the empathy and authority with which the service was delivered, and the extent to which the customer is left with tangible evidence (like a calling card) that the service has been performed.

11. Do our organization's efforts to improve external service quality emphasize effective recovery from service errors in addition to providing a service right the first time?

A popular concept of quality in manufacturing is the importance of 'doing things right the first time'. But customers of service organizations often allow one mistake. Some organizations are very good at delivering service as long as nothing goes wrong. Others organize for and thrive on service emergencies. Outstanding service organizations do both by giving front-line employees the latitude to effect recovery. Southwest Airlines maintains a policy of allowing front-line employees to do whatever they feel comfortable doing in order to satisfy customers. Xerox authorizes front-line service employees to replace up to $250,000 worth of equipment if customers are not getting results.

Employee productivity

12. How do you measure employee productivity?

13. To what extent do measures of productivity identify changes in the quality as well as the quantity of service produced per unit of input?

In many services, the ultimate measure of quality may be customer satisfaction. That measure should be combined with measures of quantity to determine the total output of the service organization. At ServiceMaster, for example, measures of output in the schools and hospitals cleaned under the company's supervision include both numbers of work orders performed per employee hour and the quality of the work done, as determined by periodic inspections performed by ServiceMaster and client personnel. Similarly, Southwest Airlines delivers relatively high levels of productivity in terms of both quality and quantity. In fact, outstanding service competitors are replacing the typical 'either/or' trade-off between quality and quantity with an 'and/also' imperative.

Employee loyalty

14. How do you create employee loyalty?

Employee loyalty goes hand in hand with productivity, contradicting the assumption that successful service providers should be promoted to larger supervisory responsibilities or moved to a similar job in a larger business unit. ServiceMaster and Taco Bell have expanded jobs without promoting good service workers. At ServiceMaster, effective single-unit managers are given supervisory responsibilities for custodial, maintenance, or other workers at more than one hospital or school. Taco Bell gives restaurant general managers a 'hunting license' to help identify and operate new satellite feeding locations in the neighbourhoods served by their restaurants and rewards them for doing it.

15. Have we made an effort to determine the right level of employee retention?

Rarely is the right level of retention 100%. Dynamic service organizations require a certain level of turnover. However, in calibrating desired turnover levels, it is important to take into account the full cost of the loss of key service providers, including those of lost sales and productivity and added recruiting, selection and training.

Employee satisfaction

16. Is employee satisfaction measured in ways that can be linked to similar measures of customer satisfaction with sufficient frequency and consistency to establish trends for management use?

Taco Bell studies employee satisfaction through surveys, frequent interviews and roundtable meetings. Customer satisfaction is measured by interviews with customers conducted biannually and includes questions about satisfaction with employee friendliness and hustle. Both the employee and customer satisfaction rankings are comprehensive and conducted on a regular basis. With these data, the company can better understand overall trends and the links between employee and customer satisfaction.

17. Are employee selection criteria and methods geared to what customers, as well as managers, believe are important?

At Southwest Airlines, for example, frequent fliers are regularly invited to participate in the auditioning and selection of cabin attendants. And many take time off from work to join Southwest's employee selection team as it carries out its work. As one customer commented, 'Why not do it? It's my airline.'

18. To what extent are measures of customer satisfaction, customer loyalty, or the quality and quantity of service output used in recognizing and rewarding employees?

Employee recognition may often involve little more than informing individual employees or employees as a group about service improvements and individual successes. Banc One goes one step further, including customer satisfaction measures for each banking unit in its periodic report of other performance measures, mostly financial, to all units.

Internal service quality

19. Do employees know who their customers are?

It is particularly difficult for employees to identify their customers when those customers are internal to the company. These employees often do not know what impact their work has on other departments. Identifying internal customers requires mapping and communicating characteristics of work flow, organizing periodic cross-departmental meetings between 'customers' and 'servers', and recognizing good internal service performance.

In 1990, USAA organized a PRIDE (Professionalism Results in Dedication to Excellence) team of 100 employees and managers to examine and improve on a function-by-function basis all processes associated with property-and-casualty insurance administration, which included analyzing customer needs and expectations. The PRIDE effort was so successful that it led to a cross-functional review of USAA's service processing. Service processing time has been reduced, as have handoffs of customers from one server to another.

20. Are employees satisfied with the technological and personal support they receive on the job?

The cornerstone of success at Taco Bell is the provision of the latest in information technology, food service equipment, simple work-scheduling techniques and effective team training. This practice led to the establishment of self-managing teams of service providers. Also, the quality of work life involves selecting the right workers. Better employees tend to refer people who, like themselves, are motivated by ownership and responsibility to create customer satisfaction. Internal service quality can also be thought of as the quality of work life. It is a visible expression of an organization's culture, one influenced in important ways by leadership.

Leadership

21. To what extent is the company's leadership:
  (a) energetic, creative vs. stately, conservative?
  (b) participatory, caring vs. removed, elitist?
  (c) listening, coaching, and teaching vs. supervising and managing?
  (d) motivating by mission vs. motivating by fear?
  (e) leading by means of personally demonstrated values vs. institutionalized policies?

22. How much time is spent by the organization's leadership personally developing and maintaining a corporate culture centred around service to customers and fellow employees?

Leaders naturally have individual traits and styles. But the CEOs of companies that are successfully using the service-profit chain possess all or most of a set of traits that separate them from their merely good competitors. Of course, different styles of leadership are appropriate for various stages in an organization's development. But the messages sent by the successful leaders we have observed stress the importance of careful attention to the needs of customers and employees. These leaders create a culture capable of adapting to the needs of both.

Relating the measures

23. What are the most important relationships in your company's service-profit chain?

24. To what extent does each measure correlate with profit and growth at the front-line level?

25. Is the importance of these relationships reflected in rewards and incentives offered to employees?

Measures drive action when they are related in ways that provide managers with direction. To enjoy the kind of success that service organizations like Southwest Airlines, ServiceMaster and Taco Bell have enjoyed, looking at individual measures is not enough. Only if the individual measures are tied together into a comprehensive picture will the service-profit chain provide a foundation for unprecedented profit and growth.

Red Lobster

Christopher H. Lovelock

A peer review panel of managers and service workers from a restaurant chain must decide whether or not a waitress has been unfairly fired from her job.

'It felt like a knife going through me!' declared Mary Campbell, 53, after she was fired from her waitressing job at a restaurant in the Red Lobster chain. But instead of suing for what she considered unfair dismissal after 19 years of service, Campbell called for a peer review, seeking to recover her job and three weeks' lost wages.

Three weeks after the firing, a panel of employees from different Red Lobster restaurants were reviewing the evidence and trying to determine whether Mary had, in fact, been unjustly fired for allegedly stealing a guest comment card completed by a couple of customers whom she had served.

Peer review at Darden Industries

Red Lobster was owned by Darden Industries, which also owned a second large restaurant chain known as Olive Garden. The company, which had a total of 110,000 employees, had adopted a policy of encouraging peer review of disputed employee firings and disciplinary actions several years earlier. The company's key objectives were to limit industrial tribunal cases and ease workplace tensions. Advocates of the peer review approach, which had been adopted at several other companies, believed that it was a very effective way of channelling constructively the pain and anger that employees felt after being fired or disciplined by their managers. By reducing the incidence of litigation, a company could also save on legal expenses.

A Darden spokesperson stated that the peer review programme had been 'tremendously successful' in keeping valuable employees from unfair dismissal. Each year, about 100 disputes ended up in peer review, with only ten subsequently resulting in litigation. Red Lobster managers and many employees also credited peer review with reducing racial ten-

sions. Ms Campbell, who said she had received dozens of calls of support, chose peer review rather than take the case to court not only because it was much cheaper, but 'I also liked the idea of being judged by people who know how things work in a little restaurant'.

The evidence

The review panel included a general manager, an assistant manager, a server, a hostess and a bartender, who had all volunteered to review the circumstances of Mary Campbell's dismissal. Each panellist had received peer review training and was receiving regular wages plus travel expenses. The instructions to panellists were simply to do what they felt was fair.

Campbell had been fired by Jean Larimer, the general manager of the Red Lobster in Marston, where the former worked as a waitress. The reason given was that Campbell had asked the restaurant's hostess, Eve Taunton, for the key to the guest comment box and stolen a card from it. The card had been completed by a couple of guests whom Campbell had served and who seemed dissatisfied with their experience at the restaurant. Subsequently, the guests learned that their comment card, which complained that their prime rib of beef was too rare and their waitress was 'uncooperative', had been removed from the box.

Ms Larimer's testimony

Larimer, who supervised 100 full- and part-time employees, testified that she had dismissed Ms Campbell after one of the two customers complained angrily to her and her supervisor. 'She [the guest] felt

This case is based on information in a story by Margaret A. Jacobs, in the *Wall Street Journal*. Personal names have been changed.
© 1999 by Christopher H. Lovelock.

violated', declared the manager, 'because her card was taken from the box and her complaint about the food was ignored.' Larimer drew the panel's attention to the company rule book, pointing out that Campbell had violated the policy that forbade removal of company property.

Ms Campbell's testimony

Campbell testified that the female customer had requested that her prime rib be cooked 'well done' and then subsequently complained that it was fatty and undercooked. The waitress told the panel that she had politely suggested that 'prime rib always has fat on it', but arranged to have the meat cooked some more. However, the woman still seemed unhappy; she poured some steak sauce over the meat, but then pushed away her plate without eating all the food. When the customer remained displeased, Campbell offered her a free dessert. But the guests decided to leave, paid the bill, filled out the guest comment card and dropped it in the guest comment box. Admitting that she was consumed by curiosity, Campbell asked Eve Taunton, the restaurant's hostess, for the key to the box. After removing and reading the card she pocketed it. Her intent, she declared, was to show the card to Ms Larimer, who had been concerned earlier that the prime rib served at the restaurant was over-cooked, not undercooked. However, she forgot about the card and later, accidentally, threw it out.

Ms Taunton's testimony

At the time of the dismissal, Taunton, a 17-year-old student, was working at Red Lobster for the summer. 'I didn't think it was a big deal to give her [Campbell] the key,' she said. 'A lot of people would come up to me to get it.'

The panel deliberates

Having heard the testimony, the members of the review panel had to decide whether Ms Larimer had been justified in firing Ms Campbell. The panellists' initial reactions to the situation were split by rank, with the hourly workers supporting Campbell and the managers supporting Larimer. But then the debate began in earnest in an effort to reach consensus.

Peters & Champlain

Christopher H. Lovelock

An international accounting firm is invited by a large client, whose audits it undertakes in seven countries, to submit a competitive proposal for auditing the client's accounts in 53 countries around the world.

Piet de Lesseps studied the fax he had just received from Robert Poirot, audit director of Montini Van Buren (MVB), a major engineering and construction company. De Lesseps, based in Belgium, was a highly regarded client service partner of Peters & Champlain (P&C), one of the Big Six international accounting firms. He was eager to cement the relationship that had united his old firm, Peters & Heinz, with one of its former rivals, ABNZ Stone Champlain. Poirot's company was also the product of a recent merger and was now seeking to consolidate its auditing relationships around the world. De Lesseps scented a great opportunity to raise Peters & Champlain's profile worldwide.

In his fax, Poirot stated that his board wished to cut the number of accounting firms serving MVB worldwide from the current 34 to just one. Proposals were being sought from all Big Six firms, and MVB intended to select a shortlist of three from which, after further discussions, a single winner would then be chosen.

Later in the day, de Lesseps met with Jacques van Krabbe, managing partner of the Brussels office, to discuss MVB's request. The two recognized that such an engagement would be of great interest to their firm on an international basis. As de Lesseps declared, 'We've had their Belgian business for years. This new request makes them more than just another large national client and potentially a worldwide gain for P&C.' The partners concluded that it would be appropriate to turn to P&C/Europe in Paris for support in developing a suitable proposal.

Van Krabbe took one more look at the fax. 'You'd better get cracking, Piet!' he said. 'It's already early December and Poirot says here that he wants proposals by January 31.'

Montini Van Buren

MVB was an international engineering and construction company. It had been formed in 1990 by the merger of an Italian company, Ing. Umberto Montini SpA of Milan, and a Franco-Belgian firm, Van Buren, Walschaerts, Lesage SA, whose headquarters were in Brussels. Van Buren's traditional expertise had been in tunnelling, hydroelectric and irrigation projects, and port construction. Montini was best known for its innovative work in bridge design and construction; the firm had also been active in building airports, and both firms had had a number of large highway construction contracts. Although Van Buren had been profitable in recent years, Montini had lost money in two of the three preceding fiscal years. The merged company consolidated its headquarters activity in Luxembourg, while also retaining major administrative functions in Brussels, Milan and Paris.

Montini Van Buren planned and executed major construction projects around the world, sometimes as the consulting engineers, sometimes as the primary contractor, and sometimes as a subcontractor. For really large projects, MVB might enter into consortium agreements with other firms. Significant current activities included work on the Channel Tunnel, preliminary engineering studies for a new transalpine rail tunnel, a deep-water port in Indonesia, building hydroelectric dams in Canada, India and Argentina, a new subway line in Mexico City, several large bridges on three continents, airport expansion projects in Nigeria, Australia and several European countries, and highway construction around the world, notably in Asian and African countries. Most projects on which MVB worked ran for three to five years or more, although it would sometimes bid on smaller projects that would provide high visibility, entrée to new markets, or exposure to significant engineering challenges. Many projects were commissioned by government agencies and some, such as bridges and dams, extended across national frontiers.

MVB operated in 53 countries, some of which were sales offices working to obtain future contracts. Its accounts were audited on a country-by-country basis by no less than 34 different accounting firms. Local firms held more than 50 per cent of these engagements, with the balance being held by the Big Six – notably P&C, Jones Pittman, and Coulson & Stuart, which also audited the consolidated accounts in Luxembourg. Peters & Champlain were MVB's auditors in seven countries, including Belgium. Many of these relationships extended back a decade or more. In Belgium, for example, Piet de Lesseps had landed the Van Buren, Walschaerts, Lesage engagement as a junior partner 12 years earlier.

Client concerns

Two days later, de Lesseps travelled to Luxembourg to meet Robert Poirot. He had learned before the meeting that Poirot, who was French, had been recruited by MVB just four months earlier. It was he who had persuaded the board to consolidate the company's auditing relationships. However, de Lesseps had also learned from phone conversations with several P&C partners in different countries that a number of MVB offices were unhappy with the plan, having only recently gone through a similar change due to the merger of formerly separate Montini and Van Buren offices in many countries where both predecessor firms were operating. In fact, P&C had lost the audit engagement for MVB's merged Caracas office to another Big Six firm, Jones Pittman. In three other locations, however, P&C had been the winner, merging with a local firm in two cases and beating out Martin Amundsen, another Big Six firm, in the third instance.

Poirot impressed de Lesseps with his intellect, professionalism, and ambition for both himself and his new company. He came straight to the point, acknowledging his recent arrival at MVB and prefacing his remarks with the comment, 'You know more about this organization than I do!' He told de Lesseps that the decision on selection of worldwide auditors for MVB would involve inputs from a number of other senior executives, including the managing director, Mr Garelli (former chief executive of Montini), the deputy MD, Mr Brecht (former CEO of Van Buren, Walschaerts, Lesage), the finance director, Mr D'Amato, and his deputy, Mr Brugge, and would have to be ratified by the board of directors. Poirot told de Lesseps that he had had some contact with P&C in his previous position with a large chemicals company and had not been overly impressed. 'However, I'm approaching this proposals process with an open mind,' he declared. 'All existing relationships are up for change in the interests of selecting a single firm to conduct our audit engagements worldwide.' Poirot also emphasized that MVB had no interest in follow-on services and was seeking proposals that were strictly limited to audit services.

De Lesseps left Luxembourg impressed by Poirot, but wondering whether other individuals involved in the selection process at MVB would share the audit director's specific expectations for the outcome. From his own experience in serving MVB's Belgian operations, he knew that the firm perceived relatively little difference between competing Big Six auditors and tended to drive a hard bargain on fees. However, he was not sure how firmly this view was held by former Montini executives, such as the managing director, Mario Garelli, or the finance director, Carlo D'Amato (who reported to Garelli).

A few days later, de Lesseps managed to arrange a meeting in Paris between Garelli, who was in town to visit MVB's French office, and Christopher Diebold, P&C's executive partner from the New York office. The meeting at Garelli's hotel was brief but cordial. Garelli told the other two that he had personally commissioned Poirot to organize the process of selecting new auditors worldwide and had been pleased with his presentation to the board. He also emphasized the matrix structure of the firm which was organized both geographically and by major activity groups, such as tunnelling, bridge construction, marine facilities, and so forth.

De Lesseps had known Michel Brugge, the deputy finance director, for several years, since he had formerly been with Van Buren. D'Amato was approaching retirement age, and it seemed likely that his deputy might succeed him within the next two years – or possibly sooner. Brugge had told de Lesseps in the past that he could not envisage replacing Coulson & Stuart as the auditors on the consolidation accounts. Since Brugge appeared to be the strongest person with respect to appointment of new auditors, it was felt unlikely that Garelli would attempt to overrule him.

The proposal team gets together

Following his meetings with Poirot and Garelli, de Lesseps moved quickly to create a proposal team in Brussels. The European office in Paris provided him with a writer/researcher, Marie-Laure Cot. A partner from the Milan office, Ugo Bianchi, who knew the construction business well, agreed to participate in the team's initial strategy session.

The team's first meeting was held two days before the Christmas holidays. Ms Cot had prepared a dossier summarizing key information about MVB's operations around the world. This included a table listing MVB's 53 country offices and its current auditors in each one (refer to Exhibit 1).

Opening the meeting, de Lesseps declared:

> Winning this proposal would be very significant for Peters & Champlain. It's not just the revenues from the worldwide engagement that we're interested in, but also the opportunity for P&C to put into place the 'One Firm, Worldwide' concept that we've talked about so often since the merger. To get this type of business, it's not sufficient to demonstrate that we have a worldwide network of strong local firms – we have to be perceived as truly international in outlook.
>
> We're dealing here with some very distinct differences in culture. On the one hand, there's Van Buren, which is Belgian and where most of top management is Flemish; however, they have given considerable autonomy to their French minority interests, especially in view of all the work they brought in on the Channel Tunnel. The French would never allow themselves to be run by the guys in Brussels! Then there's the old Montini operation based in Italy, but also very strong in

Switzerland and Germany, where Van Buren was never able to make much headway. The merger has greatly strengthened the company around the world. Separately, each firm was active in about 35 countries, jointly MVB now operates in 53. And they have a broader array of expertise now; Montini had an outstanding reputation on bridges, highways and airport construction, while Van Buren was big in dams, tunnelling and seaports.

> From my conversations with MVB it's clear that they see audit work as a commodity – a low price commodity. This was particularly true of Van Buren. Their head office in Brussels would make a short list for their office in each country to choose from. They always claimed that industry knowledge was less important than price.

> Poirot told me that he saw all Big Six firms as fairly equal in quality, but that MVB would be concentrating on global reach, and how each firm would approach the audit and deliver the feedback – the product that they would like to get out of the audit. He said they would concentrate much more on that than on the industry focus itself. What he is interested in knowing is how we propose to approach the audit, how we will manage the audit – how we would organize ourselves, set up our reporting procedures, and so on. He kept emphasizing the end product. He downplayed the opinion on the consolidated financial statements and focused more on the feedback we might be able to offer.

Examining the audit process

De Lesseps rose from his chair, walked to the board, picked up a blue marker, and sketched out a rectangle which he divided into four columns. At the top of the first column, he wrote 'Planning'. The second was headed 'Execution', the third, 'Reporting', and the fourth 'Follow Up'. Turning to the group, he remarked:

> You could describe the audit process like this. You do your planning based on significant areas that you identify. You can apply this to various things, such as the budget, which is the precalculation of the profitability of an engagement. In the follow up, you can determine whether it was actually profitable or not. My point is that for each stage there

Exhibit 1 ■ Countries with MVB operations and names of auditors as of December 1991

Region/Country	Current auditors[1]	Region/Country	Current auditors[1]
Europe/Near East		*Central & South America*	
Austria	Local firm	Chile	Local firm
Belgium	P&C	Costa Rica	Local firm
	(Peters & Champlain)	Ecuador	Local firm
Cyprus	FBG-WB	Guyana	Local firm
	(FBG-Wills Boswell)	Panama	JP
Denmark	JP (Jones Pittman)	Venezuela	JP
Finland	Local firm		
France	Local firm	*North Africa/Arabia*	
Germany	C&S (Coulson & Stuart)	Egypt	Local firm
Greece	Local firm	Iraq	Local firm (office closed)
Hungary	unaudited	Kuwait	Local firm
Italy	C&S	Morocco	Local firm
Netherlands	P&C	Saudi Arabia	DMC
Norway	Local firm		
Portugal	Local firm	*Central & Southern Africa*	
Spain	Local firm	Ivory Coast	Local firm
Sweden	JP	Kenya	C&S
Switzerland	DMC	Nigeria	FBG-WB
	(Davis, Miller & Campbell)	South Africa	Local firm
Turkey	Local firm	Zimbabwe	Local firm
United Kingdom	Local firm		
		Asia-Pacific	
North America & Caribbean		Australia	P&C
Bahamas	Local firm	Hong Kong	P&C
Canada	P&C	India	Local firm
Dominican Republic	JP	Indonesia	Local firm
Jamaica	Local firm	Japan	Local firm
Mexico	Local firm	Malaysia	C&S
Trinidad	P&C	New Zealand	Local firm
United States	C&S	Singapore	P&C
		Taiwan	DMC
Central & South America		Thailand	Local firm
Argentina	JP		
Brazil	MA (Martin Amundsen)	*CONSOLIDATION*	
		(Luxembourg)	C&S

[1] Only Big Six firms are named.

are products. The products for the planning stage are the audit plan and the approach plan. For the execution stage, there are audit programs and working papers. Under reporting we have the audit report and management letter. Finally, under follow up, there's the invoice.

With his marker, de Lesseps circled the entire group of products at the bottom of the four columns (refer to Exhibit 2). 'Some clients consider the whole thing to be a commodity,' he declared. 'But my point is that a commodity consists of a number of detailed products. And you can differentiate your service by adding value to some of these products.' He then underlined 'management letter', 'audit plan' and 'approach plan', adding:

> Here's where the big opportunity to add value takes place – the management letter. And the contents and value of that letter are dependent on what you do in the audit plan and approach plan, such as identifying weak spots. You don't start working until you understand what you need to do, you know what the significant areas are and document them to management. You can increase your likelihood of coming up with comments that are likely to be of value to management in terms of how they are running their company.

> An audit is much more than adding or taking away numbers. We're talking about understanding the business, risk analysis, and so forth. When you're dealing with multinational clients, it becomes much more important to understand the business in a global sense. With a local client, you can deal with a local environment and focus on local issues, local tax laws, and so forth. In companies like MVB, your primary contacts on the top level are often a small group of managers who have a huge multinational company and feel a little bit uncomfortable in terms of their ability to control the whole system. They look to the auditors to give them additional comfort with respect to the quality of the international operation – are the numbers reliable, do they have control over their operations, do they know what kinds of assets they have, and do they collect cash on their assets? This is what should be reflected in the management letter.

De Lesseps opened the floor to discussion. One of the senior managers present, Caroline O'Brien, raised an, issue:

> Mr Poirot says he doesn't want us to do anything that isn't material to the consolidation. But legal reporting requirements in many countries still have to be observed. He wants us to bring down fees, but I'm not sure he understands that MVB's legal structure requires substantially more audit work than might be necessary for purely business reasons.

'That's a good point,' de Lesseps admitted. 'I think Poirot still has quite a lot to learn about MVB. But it doesn't alter the fact that the market for audit services is changing from a cost plus basis to a price-led situation.'

Stages	Planning	Execution	Reporting	Follow-up
	Significant issues	Significant issues	Significant issues	Significant issues
Products	Audit plan Approach plan	Audit programme Working papers	Audit report Management letter	Invoice

Exhibit 2 ■ Framework sketched by Piet de Lesseps

The Russian Foundation for Social and Health Assistance: society as customer

Sandra Vandermerwe ■ *André Vandermerwe* ■ *Marika Taishoff*

The director of a nonprofit organization specializing in services involving disaster relief, social care and the promotion of healthy lifestyles for Russia's most disadvantaged citizens seeks to win financial support for its work among European corporations and individuals.

Andrei Kisselev had been back in Russia only two and a half years, but it seemed to him – as he hurried across the square past the former Communist Party headquarters – like for ever. This feeling was substantiated by what he had accomplished. His organization now had close to 81 million roubles in contributions, 230,000 volunteers and nearly three-quarters of a million cases completed (refer to Exhibit 1 for results from mid-1990 to mid-1992).

Within five minutes, Kisselev was in the hallway of the building which housed the Russian Foundation for Social and Health Assistance. Although it was not yet 8 a.m., the corridors were already crowded with people – as they had been every morning since the bureau had opened in January 1990. There were pregnant mothers, old war veterans on crutches, young scrawny children and unshaven, unkempt men who had probably spent the past couple of nights sleeping on the street.

Kisselev had created a service centre for them, but they always wanted to see him, the Executive Director. These people were the down-and-out portion of the Russian population – the 2 per cent who were really desperate. 'My customers,' he said aloud. He threaded his way through the crowd and climbed the stairs to his cramped office. It was the month of June, nearly the hottest one on record. In the background, he could glimpse the multi-coloured and gold-leafed cupolas of the Kremlin church. After almost three years of this venture, he was only still barely eking out a living. 'On the other hand,' Kisselev thought, 'considering that I was lured back to Russia by a job that never materialized and then was given the grand total of $850 to run this organization, maybe I'm not doing so badly after all.'

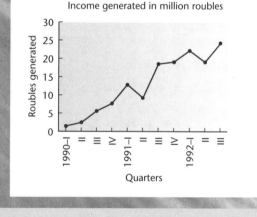

Number of volunteers:

Mid-91:	75,000
End 91:	190,000
Mid-92:	220,000

Amount of contributions:

Mid-90:	3.5 million roubles
Mid-90 – mid-91:	33.1 million roubles
Mid-91 – mid-92:	80.9 million roubles

Number of cases handled:

Disaster/Refugee Cases:	137,000
Social Welfare & Primary Health Care:	517,000

Income generated in million roubles

Exhibit 1 ■ Results from mid-1990 to mid-1992

Kisselev returns to Russia

Kisselev would not forget his return to Russia:

> I got back to Moscow, my home town, where I had expected to see a whole new world, so different from the Moscow I had left almost 10 years earlier. And what did I find? Empty stores, prices high and getting higher every day, people begging on every street corner, and, not surprisingly, a resistance to the reforms. People were suffering: only about 5 per cent of the 150 million people in Russia lived well. They were the ones who could buy whatever they wanted – it only took money, and for foreigners it was cheap. Despite all the new buildings, shops and restaurants, the remainder of the Russian people were struggling. At least 20 per cent definitely needed help, and 2–5 per cent were desperate.

Although his options were few, Kisselev had remained uncertain about taking up the offer to direct the Russian branch of the Soviet Charity and Health Fund. He had decided to speak to some of the people running the Fund in other Soviet republics; they were all Communist Party members. Kisselev mentioned his ideas about long-term preventative health and social programmes, where the needs of individual communities and localities would be determined, and programmes would cater to their needs; where the information and decision-making flow would be bottom-up, not top-down, and where progress could actually be tracked and measured. They had no idea what he was talking about.

The use of the word 'charity' in the organization's name – with its old-fashioned and derogatory connotations – also disconcerted Kisselev, and he discovered that the Fund had no statutes: it existed without any formal documentation.

None the less, he was convinced that there was an opportunity to make his ideas a reality, and an enormous potential to apply the concepts he had learned in the West. But, at the very first meeting with the Chairman of the Central Committee, it was obvious that the man was not the least bit interested in the Russian Fund, and certainly was not prepared to help beyond the allocation that had already been made. Kisselev saw this fact as both good and bad. On the one hand, there was no strong ally to help him; but, on the other hand, the chairman was part of a bygone era that no longer held the views of the new Soviet power elite. Kisselev would try to work this situation to his advantage.

Kisselev spent a month preparing statutes for the organization, something that lawyers usually did – funds permitting, and then he held a conference in March 1990 to have them adopted. He also used that occasion to officially rename the Fund: henceforth, it would be known as 'The Russian Foundation for Social and Health Assistance'. Then, Kisselev began thinking about the best way to spend the $850 …

Forming a new corporation

Through the statutes, Kisselev formalized the three activities that he felt the fund should specialize in: disaster relief, social care and the promotion of healthy lifestyles. The foundation's customers were also formally defined: the lonely, the handicapped – including children, the elderly and the homeless, i.e., all categories of social rehabilitation which no other agency in Russia properly handled.

Raising more money was his most immediate concern. Although charitable institutions – such as the Soviet Red Cross – had long existed in the USSR, the 'contributions' had been mandatory rather than voluntary. Run by the Communist Party, all Russians had had to pay 30 kopecks a year to the Red Cross – just another form of tax. Where the money had been sent or how it had been used was never divulged.

Individual contributions were also obligatory for the Soviet Veterans' Association, as well as for the more recent charitable organizations which had begun to emerge in the mid-1980s, as a result of the combination of the Afghan war, the Chernobyl incident and a generally more relaxed attitude towards the creation of the new organizations under perestroika. These agencies, including most notably the Afghan Veterans' Association and the Lenin Children's Fund, were all government funded. The Lenin Children's Fund had received an upfront starting grant from the government of 152 million roubles.

The newly formed Russian Foundation for Social and Health Assistance had no recourse to government funding; it had to raise funds and spend them well if it wanted to survive. And there was only one way to get this money: from donors. How to find them, reach them and convince them was Kisselev's most pressing concern in that early summer of 1990.

The fact that he was starting a new organization – one unburdened by past history and associations – would, he reckoned, make his task easier. He campaigned widely on television and radio to broadcast his message. One of his first moves was to target the top 600 corporations and invite them to join the foundation by contributing 100,000 roubles – about $14,300 – each.

> I showed them why we would be different and how we ran it in the West. I was careful to demonstrate that this was not in conflict with the government. I talked about social responsibility and that they had the power to decide whether a better Russia could be built. I explained why it was important. I promised them that we wouldn't engage in any buying and selling, and that they would know what was happening to their contributions. I talked and talked and talked, and tried to get the right kinds of people involved. The media gave me support and, before long, people had heard about us. I knew that once the large, high-profile companies started giving, the others would follow – and I was right.

He appealed to individuals in a different way as well. He set up money collection centres throughout Russia, including airports. Within the space of just a few months, over 50,000 roubles – in all kinds of currencies – were coming in every week. By the end of the first six months, the Foundation had collected 3.5 million roubles from the Russian people.

Three months following his initial campaigns, a poll of Russian urban and rural populations was taken. The Foundation was cited in it as one of the top three charitable organizations known to the public at large. The two others were the Soviet Red Cross and the Lenin Children's Fund.

Building up the workforce and creating a network of branches

Enlarging the Foundation was his second objective. In this business, Kisselev knew, if money were to be raised, it would have to be spent. But spent well. Both sides of the equation had to work. They had to manage their funds so that they could get the best performance from each unit generated.

He saw the potential source of volunteers coming from an area greater than the USA or Africa, since there was no reason to be constrained in his search for volunteers to the Russian republic alone: there were 25 million Russians living in other republics as well. He again rallied the mass media to his cause, whose coverage of the Foundation gave it wide exposure in all the republics. He appealed to the public at large and urged individuals to give their know-how and free time to the Foundation. Again it worked.

By mid-1991, 75,000 volunteers had been enlisted. They came from all the provinces of Russia. The average age was 50; retired people predominated because they had the time. Younger university students also participated.

In addition to volunteers, Kisselev wanted the best professional staff – people with the right kind of technical, medical and managerial expertise – so that the institution could be run by the same principles as an enterprise anywhere in the world. He hired several people of this calibre but, after the first year, he had to let them go because the Foundation was unable to pay what the commercial market was offering. The economic situation was rapidly deteriorating throughout the provinces, and people now had no choice but to work for the money. To attract the kind of professionals Kisselev considered so vital to the organization's success, fund-raising efforts would have to be intensified.

By mid-1991, Kisselev and the 75,000 volunteers had raised over 30 million roubles. Now, he was in a position to begin looking for the right kind of staff. Although the salaries he offered were still comparatively low, he was able to add certain fringe benefits – such as petrol costs. Additionally, efficient fund-raisers would get a 50 per cent bonus at the end of the year, and consistently high performers received 13th-month salaries. But, Kisselev stipulated in his work contracts – still new in Russia – those employees who did not perform would have to leave. Performance would be gauged by both how much money they raised and how efficiently they distributed it.

By then, the Russian Foundation had also opened a network of 77 branches in each Russian province. To head these branches, Kisselev selected people with high social profiles, especially in the cities that were Russian power bases. In St Petersburg, for instance, he chose the wife of a well-known admiral to head that area's operations. Shortly afterwards, that branch had over 2,000 volunteers. Each branch had 3–5 people who were paid centrally and whose base salaries were covered by their budgets. All other branch activities were paid for by their fund-raising efforts. Although he wanted as much decentralization as possible, Kisselev did insist that the branches abide by certain policies:

■ The branches had to follow national fund-raising procedures; all monies were to be collected centrally and dispensed locally.
■ Branches had full autonomy to decide what projects they wanted to work on, and what was necessary to get the job done. Decisions on hiring, firing, bonuses and other such issues remained local. The only decision-making prerogative held by Kisselev was the choice of chairperson nominated by the branch, although he had never gone against a branch's wishes.
■ All the branches were expected to work to the same standards and were to be measured accordingly. Non-performance would not be tolerated.
■ All projects had to be evaluated, so that the donors could know where the money was going, and what benefits were realized.
■ All branches had to use the same colour schemes, size and style of image – so as to give them a consistent image amongst donors, beneficiaries, volunteers and the public at large.

There were ten people in the Moscow head office in addition to Kisselev: three in finance, two in branch relations, two in mass media, two in health and one in social welfare. Besides overseeing all operations, Kisselev also handled disaster relief. There were no secretaries since everyone had a PC. Kisselev also concentrated on building the image of the Foundation, training the various branch managers to use media and work with the press. A communications network was also created, so that the branches could easily and rapidly communicate, coordinate and upgrade their professional capacity by working together.

One of his most pressing challenges was finding ways to retain volunteers. Initially, Kisselev designed a bonus scheme for them. He then went further, trying to make a tangible form of recognition – using medals, etc. – for the contributions made by certain individuals and teams. A sense of belonging to the Foundation was something else that Kisselev felt was essential for employee morale, satisfaction and motivation. He thought about uniforms for the volunteers, for instance, so that they would feel they were all part of the same family, as well as be identifiable to the public at large. He also wanted some recognizable symbol for the Foundation as a whole, so that the people working for the institution would know and agree on what they stood for. An emblem was designed and adopted. (Refer to Exhibit 2 for an illustration of this emblem.) Kisselev had asked the branches for their feedback; 35 of them disapproved – saying it resembled a jail cell, but the agency assured Kisselev that it would succeed in the long term if he persisted.

It was essential for Kisselev that the branches learn to work together and share goals, information and objectives. He arranged a reunion in Moscow three times a year for all the branch people to talk to each other and exchange experiences. For Kisselev, the object of these meetings was not just to get his people to think about how to raise more money but, more importantly, about why and how they had to be different from the other organizations. He was personally convinced that about half of the branches were top class, motivated by doing exciting work, seeing the results, and getting visibility and coverage locally. A quarter needed to be improved and, to accomplish this, he intended to set up a system of benchmarking and job rotation. The other quarter were weak and seriously needed to have some people in those branches replaced.

Exhibit 2 ■ Foundation emblem

Expansion at home and abroad

The coup of August 1991, which disgraced Gorbachev and put Yeltsin in power, further darkened the economic picture in Russia. The ranks of the unemployed continued to climb. For Kisselev, the Foundation had become an even more critical institution: there was an even greater vacuum to be filled in Russia, as more people fell into the 'deprived' and 'desperate' categories, and would need assistance of all sorts – medical, nutritional and housing being the most urgent. The August coup also spurred on the creation of new, free-market type enterprises.

He continued to court the support of high-profile and influential opinion makers for both money and goods, as well as soliciting the over 100,000 foreigners living in Moscow who had funds and would, Kisselev was convinced, want to make a contribution. He was especially interested in moving to the next step – accelerating fund-raising outside the country. Twelve branches participated in a trial charity bazaar in the Arctic. The local inhabitants made souvenirs, put them in boxes and then trekked along the route from Murmansk to Norway, selling them in small villages and on cruise ships. Revenues were coming in,

and the Foundation itself became better known. Plans were designed to expand this kind of operation into Germany and other parts of Europe.

Relief and support efforts were also stepped up, both inside Russia and in other countries. For example, children from five Russian provinces who had been affected by Chernobyl were sent to Germany for holidays. Everything was provided for them: buses were hired, and German families gave them board and lodging. Next, the Foundation began building a network in Germany, France, Switzerland, Italy, Norway and the US, both to raise funds and to create a string of experts worldwide who could be called upon when needed.

Kisselev ascribed the Foundation's success to several factors:

1. *Its reputation as being a 'doer', not just a 'taker'.* Individuals and localities which needed funds for humanitarian causes addressed the Foundation directly. For instance, the Mayor of Nizhni Novgorod had long been trying to raise funds to send a child to London for open heart surgery. He finally approached Kisselev: the money was raised within a few days, the child sent to London and the operation successfully performed.

2. *Its adoption of an open-book policy.* Donors could earmark the projects they wanted their money allocated to, and could see how that donation was being used, and the actual and future benefits received. Kisselev had been adamant that even more important than raising money was proving to large donors that their contributions were being put to the uses intended. In this way, the donors themselves had a stake in the successful operation of the Foundation's services. (Refer to Exhibit 3 for a list of these services.)

3. *Its image of being honest, 'clean'.* The fact that it was seen as actually 'doing' things, and did not buy and sell goods for a profit, put the Foundation in a completely different league from its competitors. So much so that President Yeltsin referred to the Foundation as having a 'noble image', and Mrs Yeltsin, who had been lobbied by 300 agencies asking for her support, accepted Kisselev's invitation to join the Foundation's Board.

1. Transportation of patients for medical treatment.

2. Medical consultations for the very poor and needy.

3. Maintenance costs for the medical staff in orphanages and in homes for the aged and disabled.

4. Purchase and distribution of drugs and medication.

5. Home medical attendance for the disabled, patients and elderly; provision for such services as the delivery of food and fuel, home laundry, house cleaning.

6. Organization of employment opportunities for disabled through businesses which meet the Foundation's criteria.

7. Financial aid to the poor, families with many children, orphans, disabled persons and patients.

8. Developing and financially supporting programmes in the field of health protection and social security.

9. Provision of food stuffs and clothes for the poor.

10. Assistance in the reconstruction, equipment and improvement of health and welfare institutions.

11. Medical and financial assistance to children suffering from infantile cerebral palsy.

12. Assistance to AIDS sufferers.

13. Joint participation with municipalities in the distribution of humanitarian aid and the organization of charity canteens for the poor and homeless.

Exhibit 3 ■ The main types of aid and services provided

By mid-1992, the Moscow headquarters was receiving hundreds of messages a day – both thank you letters and complaints. Whenever there were dissatisfied customers, Kisselev himself took action by sending out quality teams, assessing the causes and what had to be done, and trying to fix the grievances.

The human side of business

The changes Kisselev could discern in Russia in the first year following the coup were not limited to economic ones. There was a deeper, more subtle shift happening, the consequences of which promised to be even more profound. He had expected it, but not quite as quickly or as dramatically. Organizations that had been created or operated prior to the August coup were beginning to be associated – both by the new power structure and by the public at large – with the old values and traditions, which no longer had a

place in the new Russia. No matter what their intentions, political leanings or visions, such institutions ran the risk of being discredited. And, even the new Russian organizations and enterprises were not generally trusted, and were perceived as having their own political agendas as well.

He also saw a resurgence of the long-suppressed sense of European identity amongst Russians. They no longer wanted to be isolated, separated culturally and socially from the continent at large, nor did they see any reason for it. While this feeling was the most pronounced in the big cities, Kisselev could also observe it when he spoke with the people in small towns and communities. Corporate donors were even more forthright: they wanted to know whether the Foundation was known in Europe or not.

Kisselev was soon convinced that the only way to establish and maintain local credibility was by building a 'Euro-presence'. And equally, the only way he could pursue his ideas locally was by building European support for his initiatives – some of which were simply too expensive to depend on national contributions alone. He began to contact his former colleagues and partners abroad, seeking their ideas and suggestions.

Kisselev had plans to make the Russian Foundation a force abroad. If he wanted to continue to grow and attract donors – especially those with hard currencies – then he just might not have, he knew, any other option. In the autumn of 1992, he signed an agreement with the oldest, non-governmental humanitarian agency in the world: the Italian 'Misericordia'. Created about 750 years ago, the Misericordia was more powerful than the Red Cross in Italy: it had over 620,000 volunteers, close to 1,200 ambulances, and ran hospices, canteens and other facilities for the sick and needy in Italy. It had never before extended its services outside of that country. Unlike the Russian Foundation, all its volunteers remained anonymous, following a tradition dating back to the Middle Ages when they actually wore hoods.

The agreement between the Russian Foundation and the Misericordia was intended to foster the exchange of experiences, promote joint fund-raising efforts, and create a Florence-based, Euro-wide organization comprised of a variety of similar institutions around the world.

Kisselev was convinced that he could persuade corporations both inside and outside Russia to give some of their short-term profits for the benefit of others. There was a wave, he believed, of 'social conscience' within business circles which was as powerful as any

of the traditional motives and objectives. He maintained that he was offering corporations – and the individuals who ran them – the opportunity to participate in the well-being of the society within which they functioned. On a more practical level, he was selling them a way to eradicate some of the negative feelings about business which had been welling up in communities everywhere.

No government in the world, no matter how enlightened or generous, could solve all social problems, he kept repeating to the press. Such governments could only create the favourable conditions for organizations such as his to undertake worthy causes. And these organizations could not take the required steps without the support of business.

> I'm selling corporations and individuals a chance to feel better about themselves. It's a kind of moral satisfaction, a broader view of the world and their role in it. Also, the results we get for them are tangible ones, and what we do will certainly be profitable. Businesses make a very real investment – in the well-being of society, in hope for improvement, decreased social tension, and the prevention of social unrest and disease. This creates a better environment for them to make more profits.

Kisselev saw his organization as a pressure group for change: 'We are the humanitarian side of business. This is not socialism: it is social consciousness. It's a mechanism for societies to grow and become healthy. It's a self cure. Russians aren't the only ones concerned about this need: the whole world is aware of it. Values are changing, and organizations such as ours represent that change, and give business an opportunity to make a contribution to society at large . . .'

First Direct: branchless banking

Jean-Claude Larreché ■ Christopher H. Lovelock ■ Delphine Parmenter

In October 1996, seven years after it first opened outside Leeds, England, First Direct was still attracting attention as an innovator that operated a bank with no branches. Intrigued by its success, financial service providers wanted to understand how unseen customers conducted business around the clock over the telephone. An article in the *New York Times* reported:

> Representatives from banks around the world are making the pilgrimage to this industrial city in the north of England for a glimpse of what might be their stagnant industry's equivalent of a miraculous cure. For not only is First Direct the world's leading telephone-only bank, it is the fastest growing bank in Britain. In just six years, it has signed up 2% of Britain's notoriously set-in-their-ways banking subjects, who call its rows of bankers 24 hours a day, seven days a week, to pay bills, buy stock, and arrange mortgages. (3 September 1996)

Success not only put First Direct in the media limelight but it also helped to maintain high levels of enthusiasm, pride and motivation internally. Fearful that complacency might hinder the bank's ability to uphold growth and success, CEO Kevin Newman never lost sight of the bank's challenges in an increasingly competitive and deregulated environment:

> I believe that in going forward three things need to be developed. We have to be utterly low cost. We must be able to individualize the manufacturing process and recognize that all our customers are individuals. Thirdly, we must build a strong brand as people need to identify with institutions they can trust.

'Kevin', as everyone called the chief executive, sat among the telephone sales staff in First Direct's headquarters on the outskirts of Leeds, 190 miles (300 km) north of London. Newman had installed the information systems that were instrumental in getting the new bank off the ground in 1989.

Subsequently, he was promoted to operations director in 1990 and CEO in October 1991. Newman came to the bank from the mass-market retailer, Woolworth's, after having worked at Mars, the candy and consumer goods manufacturer. Although Kevin Newman did not start his career as a banker he was, at 35 years of age, undoubtedly the youngest banking CEO in Britain.

The birth of the First Direct concept

In the mid-1980s, Midland Bank, the fourth largest bank in the UK with 2,000 branches, began looking at ways of attracting more affluent and up-market customers. As Peter Simpson, subsequently First Direct's commercial director, remarked:

> If you are losing market share you can do two things: you can grow organically or inorganically. Midland Bank had limited capital, so there was nowhere to go inorganically; its reserves had been spent on the over-priced Crocker National Bank acquisition in North America and with Latin American debt. Organically, the retail banks in the United Kingdom were giving away current accounts for free, and sacrificing their profits in terms of customer value.

Consequently, in June 1988 Midland drafted a team of executives on a project code-named 'Raincloud'. Mike Harris, a former Midland executive, returned as a consultant to lead the top-secret investigation. An examination of consumers' banking habits highlighted that there was a substantial niche of people whose banking transactions were not branch-based. According to a national market research study of British bank customers by MORI in 1988:

This case is intended to be used as a basis for class discussion rather than to illustrate either effective or ineffective handling of an administrative situation.

Copyright © 1997 INSEAD, Fontainebleau, France.

- 20 per cent of account holders had not visited their branch in the last month
- 51 per cent said they would rather visit their branch as little as possible
- 48 per cent had never met their branch manager
- 38 per cent said banking hours were inconvenient
- 27 per cent wished they were able to conduct more business with the bank over the phone.

This was the beginning of an idea. Rather than reposition the branch network, the taskforce wondered what it would be like to have a bank with no branches. The team discovered that as early as 1981 a Dutch bank, Nederlanse Credietbank, had set up Direktbank with a small telephone staff to cater to the needs of an upscale segment. Since 1986, Bank of America offered an additional service that enabled branch customers to process transactions by pressing buttons on touch tone telephones in response to a voice-activated computer. And in France, several banks allowed customers to make account enquiries via the videotext Minitel screens linked to their home phones.

The Midland team envisioned an entirely new type of bank that would operate from one centre, 24 hours a day, 365 days a year. Employing the UK's 47 million telephones as a low-cost delivery system, it would use human operators rather than a machine to perform all the functions of a traditional bank. Next, Harris's team faced the difficult task of presenting to the Midland board of directors a proposal for a new concept that might compete with its own branch network. Although Midland Bank had successfully retained its customer base with a long list of innovative banking products, it had to acquire additional business to stay afloat. Working with experts in marketing, operations, human resources and technology, Harris was named chief executive of the proposed stand-alone telephone bank. He was given one year to design and launch it.

Developing operational systems and initial job design

Rather than incur the delay and expense of obtaining its own bank charter, First Direct was set up as a division of Midland Bank. Short on time – Midland anticipated another bank would introduce a similar telephone service – the team proceeded secretly, working 18-hour days. After much brainstorming, the team baptized the new bank 'First Direct' to reflect its pioneering concept of working directly with customers. As far as Midland was concerned, First Direct was a completely new brand and a completely new business. A black and white corporate identity symbolized the simple, economical nature of the new bank.

The start-up staff of about 50 worked initially out of London while the operations team evaluated a variety of potential sites for First Direct's one and only office. They were attracted to Leeds as the city offered moderate rental rates and a regional labour pool accustomed to lower salaries than in southern England. Additionally, the Yorkshire accent was recognized as easy to understand, warm and friendly. First Direct leased a modern building in an industrial park outside Leeds that could be modified to suit the bank's needs.

Procedures had to be built from scratch so that any traditional branch transaction could be handled in one telephone call. The planners decided that customers could obtain cash through the Midland automatic teller machines (ATM) network and make deposits electronically, while transactions would be cleared and statements processed at one of Midland's regional processing centres. First Direct would benefit from its parent's massive technology investments of the late 1980s; otherwise Midland played no managerial role.

Next, the team turned to new technology to deliver a portfolio of payment, savings and lending instruments over the phone. A survey of the best call centres in the United States and Canada provided guidance in setting up the systems. First Direct improved upon existing technology to make all customer information accessible by any telephone operator. Furthermore, they integrated the screen and telephone systems so a call could be passed along without the customer having to repeat the entire conversation.

Another group designed job descriptions to meet service standards and the use of high-tech work tools. It was obvious that the new bank's telephone-based staff would have an assignment very different from a traditional bank teller who counted cash, filled out deposit slips, and looked for forged signatures. A visit to Federal Express's Memphis hub provided insight as to how to recruit, train and motivate staff. Kevin Gavaghan, then marketing director of Midland Bank, remembered how the hiring criteria were determined:

> In hiring, First Direct were looking for people that were fast and efficient but more importantly people with warm and engaging personalities. The first flood of applicants showed the way; the first six months proved it. The qualities required were more often than not found in the social professions – teachers, nurses, even firefighters – frequently people working difficult hours under difficult circumstances. Empathy and responsiveness under pressure marked these types out from the traditional bank clerk whose reserve and process-orientation proved at times impossible to reverse.

Initial recruitment advertising gave only sketchy details of employment opportunities in the financial services sector; there was no mention of Midland Bank. As early as May of 1989, First Direct began hiring telephone advisers who were called Banking Representatives (BRs). Training sought to improve the candidate's communication and listening skills so that they sounded friendly, mature and well informed over the phone. By the time of launch, 200 BRs were prepared to answer enquiries and process customer transactions.

Getting off to a slow start

First Direct inaugurated its service at midnight on Sunday, 1 October 1989, in a pointed reference to its seven days a week, 24-hour operation. Although for legal reasons its advertising had to mention that First Direct was a division of Midland Bank, it sought to distance itself from Midland to bring in new customers. First Direct selected a British agency known as a creative 'hot shop', Howell Henry Chaldecott Lury (HHCL), to orchestrate an aggressive £6 million advertising campaign that kicked off one hour before the bank opened for business.

Traditional banks did not see First Direct as a threat. Sceptics doubted that the concept of telephone banking would ever catch on, or that it would ever be profitable. The competitive spirit within Midland was such that no one anticipated a great deal of cannibalization. Furthermore, as First Direct targeted individuals with relatively high disposable incomes, existing banks never feared it would gain significant market share. Although First Direct was from the outset overwhelmed with telephone enquiries, acquiring new customers proved difficult. Soon the media reported it to be a flop.

Despite its slow start, First Direct began winning a growing number of customers after its first full year of business. By December of 1992, it had almost 250,000 account holders, about 70 per cent of whom had reportedly been attracted from competitors. A year later, Gene Lockhart, CEO of UK Banking at Midland, declared that First Direct had acquired over 350,000 customers, only 20 per cent of whom were formerly Midland customers. The bank lost very few customers, approximately 2 to 3 per cent per year, the majority as a result of 'natural causes'. In 1996, the bank had 640,000 customers and was acquiring about 125,000 new customers a year – the equivalent of opening one new branch each week (Exhibit 1).

During the first six years of operations, First Direct's offices adapted to accommodate this phenomenal growth. With the 75,000 square foot (7,000m²) building in the Arlington Business Centre fully utilized, First Direct unveiled a second purpose-built facility three miles away at Stourton in November 1994. The Arlington location accommodated both back-office operations (foreign investments section, lending services and mortgage underwriters) and the front-office call centre (customer service and new customer department) on a single floor without walls. Besides a second call centre, the 150,000 square foot (14,000m²) Stourton site housed credit and risk services, investments, new mortgage enquiries, the insurance division, and customer enquiries (Visa, direct debits, standing orders, customer relations). The operations and information technology (IT) staff occupied part of the same trading floor at the centre of the business. The different teams mapped their areas by the signs that hung from the ceiling (Exhibit 2).

Exhibit 1 ■ First Direct: estimated account data

Date	Total number of customers	Total number of accounts	Calls/day	Staff
April 1996	641,000	1,100,000	32,000	2,400
December 1995	586,000	800,000	26,000	2,300
December 1994	476,000	700,000	21,000	1,900
December 1993	361,000	500,000	16,000	1,500
December 1992	241,000	350,000	11,000	1,000
December 1991	136,000	200,000	7,000	500
December 1990	66,000	105,000	3,000	300
December 1989	11,000	N/A	N/A	250

Source: Estimates based on Midland Bank Annual Reports and Internal Sources First Direct, 1996

Telephone advisers did not have their own desks but transferred mobile units containing stationery and personal belongings to any desk available during their shift. This 'hot desking' approach enabled full capacity utilization over the non-stop work shift. Kevin Newman was based in Arlington and all the directors sat with their departments at their respective sites – no one had a private office. Richard Rushton, customer services director, had a desk at each site. A mini-van made the ten-minute connection between the two sites every hour.

By early 1996, it was estimated that First Direct served a customer base equivalent to 200 branches. However, the telephone bank employed only 2,400 individuals where a branch network would require a staff of almost 4,000. Its staffing costs were about half those of a typical retail-oriented commercial branch. The construction of a third building adjacent to Stourton was scheduled for completion by June 1997.

Efficient information systems were instrumental in keeping costs down. The business required non-stop processing power to perform on-line transactions and to access the bank's mainframe computers. The hub of First Direct's operations, the on-line customer database, used two Sequoia UNIX-based computers at Arlington and Stourton. It also supported and interfaced with the 1,800 personal computers that ran various applications across the two sites. Third parties provided IT support for transaction clearing, card service processing, and credit scoring. First Direct used an automatic call distribution (ACD) system to manage one of the largest call centres in the UK. It routed calls to unoccupied operators and bounced calls back and forth between the two centres to balance work loads.

First Direct achieved break-even by the end of the 1994 financial year and in 1995 reported its first full year of profitability. In 1996, Kevin Newman commented on the bank's financial performance:

> As you know, we have been circumspect about releasing this information for commercial competitive reasons and I do not wish to change this policy. I can, however, indicate that our return on equity is extremely attractive (i.e., 25% plus). Our return on investment is equally attractive, at least as good as that currently being achieved by the UK clearing banks.

Retail banking in the United Kingdom

Until the 1970s, the so-called Big Four British clearing banks, namely Lloyds, Midland, Barclays and National Westminster, dominated retail banking in the United Kingdom while building societies

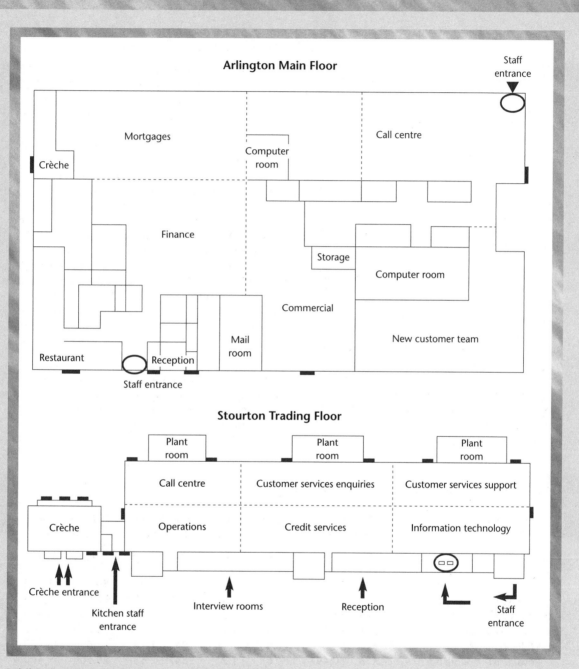

Exhibit 2 ■ Simplified floor plan Arlington and Stourton

controlled the mortgage market. Much like the US savings and loan institutions, building societies provided funds for the purchase of homes from a pool of members' savings. No new bank charters had been issued by Britain's central bank, the Bank of England, since the end of the nineteenth century.

However, in the 1970s the Bank of England allowed banks to provide a more complete range of personal financial services, from share dealing and insurance broking to the provision of financial advice. Additionally, the 1979 Banking Act opened up the mortgage market to institutions other than building societies by formally dissolving the interest rate cartel. In turn, the building societies obtained the right to offer checking accounts and unsecured loans. Abbey National was one of the first institutions to take advantage of this shake-up, becoming a bank in 1989. The early 1980s saw further deregulation, tax incentives and an economic boom in the UK that greatly enhanced personal wealth for many individuals.

By 1993, four of the top ten building societies had obtained bank charters and were competing directly with the Big Four banks in the provision of a broad range of consumer banking services. Consequently, by the early 1990s Britain had an excessive number of banks and branches, difficult to sustain in the face of economic recession and increased automation. Inevitably, several much-publicized mergers followed. The Hongkong & Shanghai Banking Corporation (HSBC) bought Midland Bank in July 1992. Three years later, Britain's biggest building society, Halifax, planned a merger with Leeds Permanent, the coun-try's fifth biggest. The consolidation process accelerated markedly in 1995 (Exhibit 3).

Parallel to this industry-wide reshaping, individual banks and building societies embarked on their own downsizing programmes by closing branches and centralizing transaction processing. The total number of branches fell by 15 per cent between 1980 and 1992, with a loss of over 100,000 jobs. More qualified or senior staff were often replaced by lower-paid, less-qualified workers. The banks and building societies soon attracted unfavourable media attention and criticism for their long queues, high level of errors and exorbitant customer charges. In response to these attacks, Midland Bank was the first to introduce charge-free banking and personal loans. In the late 1980s, the Henley Centre for Forecasting found that customer dissatisfaction remained higher in banking than in any other retail sector in Britain. However, only one in 30 British consumers switched banks in a given year. Despite increased competition, only one person in five could distinguish between the services offered by the various banks.

Many financial institutions saw automation and new technology as ways to replace some expensive branch transactions. Customers responded enthusiastically and automated teller machines proliferated. Banks made ATM network share agreements and also

---

Exhibit 3 ■ UK retail banks – statistics 1989 & 1995

Retail Banks	Assets (£ millions)		Pre-tax profits (% of total assets)		Number of branches		Number of employees	
	1989	1995	1989	1995	1989	1995	1989	1995
National Westminster Bank	116,189	166,347	0.3	1.1	2,997	2,215	86,600	61,000
Barclays Bank	127,616	164,184	0.5	1.3	2,645	2,050	85,900	61,200
Lloyds Bank TSB[1]	83,023	131,750	−0.7	1.3	3,722	2,858	87,500	66,400
Abbey National[2]	37,201	97,614	1.3	1.1	678	678	13,600	16,300
Midland Bank[3]	62,619	92,093	−0.4	1.1	2,042	1,701	47,500	43,400
Royal Bank of Scotland	27,436	50,497	0.8	1.2	842	687	20,500	19,500
Bank of Scotland	14,073	34,104	1.3	1.3	527	411	12,100	11,300

Notes: 1. Lloyds Bank merged with TSB in October 1995 and acquired Cheltenham & Gloucester in 1995.
2. Abbey National acquired National & Provincial in 1995.
3. Midland Bank was acquired by HSBC Holdings plc in July 1992.
Souce: Annual Abstract of Banking Statistics, British Bankers Association, 1996, Vol. 13.

installed cash machines in non-branch locations like supermarkets. With new technology, telephone-based banking now offered person-to-person, person-to-computer or even computer-to-computer based transactions at an estimated cost as low as one-sixth that of conventional branch-based transactions (Exhibit 4).

As early as 1983, the Nottingham Building Society offered Britain's first subscription telephone banking service, known as Homelink. However, the service attracted only 5,000 subscribers. Another pioneer, The Royal Bank of Scotland launched its Home and Office Banking System in 1984 and Direct Line insurance in 1985. By 1996, the use of telephone banking in one form or another was widespread throughout the industry (Exhibit 5).

The introduction of debit cards and smart cards also favoured the advent of electronic banking. As an alternative to cash, NatWest and Midland Bank piloted the Mondex smart card in July 1995. Positioned as an electronic wallet, it allowed customers to store cash, debit purchases electronically and replenish the card from their accounts at an ATM or through specially equipped telephones. In 1995, Barclays, the largest retail bank in the UK, launched a home banking service accessed through the customer's personal computer.

- **Automatic Call Distribution – ACD**
  Systems that manage a high volume of incoming calls by routeing and placing each call in a queue to the next available operator so that the caller never hears a busy signal.

- **Computer Integrated Telephony – CIT**
  Computer databases are linked to the incoming call, allowing call handlers to quickly access customer files.

- **Calling Line Identification**
  An additional CIT service which shows the number at the source of the call.

- **Interactive Voice Recognition and Response**
  CIT systems can react to the tones entered by telephone, or even recognize certain predetermined voice inputs.

- **Teletext and Videotext-based Access**
  Videotext terminals, with screens and keyboards, provide an interactive access to a bank's computer. The national French Minitel system is the most developed network in Europe; British Telecom offers a similar Prestel network.

- **Multi-Media Kiosks**
  Stand-alone multi-media kiosks may communicate with the customer using powerful interactive digital text, audio, video and animation.

- **PC-based Access**
  A personal computer may access a bank's computer via a modem and telephone network.

- **Internet World Wide Web Site**
  Home banking customers may connect to their bank's proprietary web site via private dial-up networks and tap into their personal accounts.

Source: Data gathered from various publications.

Exhibit 4 ■ Banking technology

Exhibit 5 ■ Sample of direct financial services in the United Kingdom

Institution	Service	Launched	Description
Bank of Scotland	CardCall	October 1993	Add-on telephone enquiry service using interactive voice response
	HOBS	1985	Add-on teletext banking service
	Phoneline		Add-on operator-based home banking
Royal Bank of Scotland	Direct Line	1985	Direct insurance services via telephone operators
	Direct Banking	April 1994	Full service 24-hr telephone banking by touch-tone phone or operator
TSB	Speedlink	1987	Add-on mass-market telephone banking service via voice recognition
	PhoneBank	October 1994	Operator-based home banking
National Westminster Bank	Actionline	September 1988	Add-on automated 24-hr touch-tone enquiry service; later with operators
	Primeline	September 1991	Up-market fee-based telephone service via personal account managers
with Thomas Cook	Touch	1995	Add-on banking and travel services via stand-alone videotext kiosks
Nottingham Building Society	Homelink	1983	Add-on home banking service offered via BT Prestel videotext network
Midland Bank	Customer Service Centre	May 1993	Add-on customer service enquiry via operators
Co-operative Bank	Armchair Banking	1992	Add-on telephone banking service with operator
Barclays Bank	Barclaycall	July 1993	Add-on mass-market telephone banking service via operators
		1995	Electronic computer-to-computer banking
Alliance & Leicester Giro	Telecare	1995	Integrated telephone banking via operator
	Swiftcheck		Automated telephone enquiry
Nationwide	Home Banking	1995	Computer-based home banking
Clydesdale	Telebank	1995	Computer-based home banking
Lloyds Bank	Lloydsline	1994	Add-on up-market telephone banking service manned by operators
Marks & Spencer		April 1995	Insurance services by telephone
Virgin Group	Virgin Direct	March 1995	Financial services via telephone

Source: Data gathered from various publications.

Acquiring new customers at First Direct

The majority of First Direct's new prospects called the bank on a toll-free line. Direct mail activity produced high call volume and brought in nearly one half of new customers. More importantly, word-of-mouth recommendations generated about one-third of customer acquisitions. Customer polls showed that 87 per cent of the customer base was either extremely or very satisfied with First Direct, compared with an average of 51 per cent for conventional banks; 85 per cent of its consumers actively recommended the bank to friends, relatives or colleagues (Exhibit 6). In both 1994 and 1995, First Direct achieved the largest net gain of all UK banks and building societies in customers transferring their checking account.

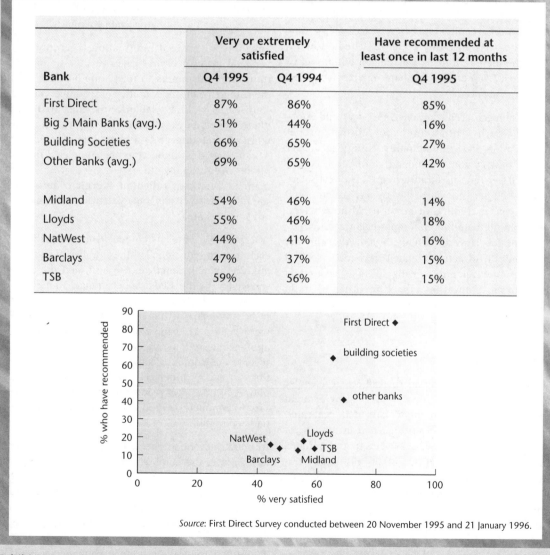

Bank	Very or extremely satisfied		Have recommended at least once in last 12 months
	Q4 1995	Q4 1994	Q4 1995
First Direct	87%	86%	85%
Big 5 Main Banks (avg.)	51%	44%	16%
Building Societies	66%	65%	27%
Other Banks (avg.)	69%	65%	42%
Midland	54%	46%	14%
Lloyds	55%	46%	18%
NatWest	44%	41%	16%
Barclays	47%	37%	15%
TSB	59%	56%	15%

Source: First Direct Survey conducted between 20 November 1995 and 21 January 1996.

Exhibit 6 ■ Customer satisfaction for UK retail bank customers, year-end 1995

The new customer team answered enquiries, opened accounts, explained the mechanics of telephone banking and carried out the initial processing and assessing of the 17,000 prospects that applied every month. They obtained basic customer details (name, address, date of birth) before taking the caller through the application process over the telephone. Then, the computer system automatically generated a preprinted application form for customers to sign and return. Next, First Direct formally processed the application and made various fraud and credit checks. Credit scoring requirements were strict because new customers were instantly issued 25 cheques and a £100 cheque guarantee card that potentially gave access to £2,500 credit. The bank rejected about 50 per cent of applicants.

New customers received a 'Welcome' pack and established security procedures to ensure proper identification and confidentiality. Ninety-seven per cent of new customers opened a cheque account; about 70 per cent also transferred their direct salary deposits, 60 per cent opened a savings account, and 40 per cent a credit card account. Although First Direct did not require a minimum balance, the average account balance was about £1,000. After the first three months of activity, First Direct made several mailings and telephone calls to take customers through the 'Education' phase in order to build awareness of the range of investment and lending services provided.

Customer service

The heart of First Direct was the call centre. Regular customers could call at any time of the day or night on a special telephone number charged at local rates, regardless of where the call originated in the UK, or contact the bank from overseas via a special number. First Direct received over half of all calls outside traditional banking hours, many on public holidays. The average customer called First Direct once a month. During peak hours, from 10 a.m. to 12 noon and 6 p.m. to 9 p.m., nearly 800 people worked the phones. That number dropped in the middle of the night to about 40 operators.

Banking reps verified the customer's identity and retrieved the account information on the computer screen. The Customer Information System recorded each customer contact and gave BRs access to all the customer's accounts and business history. Day-to-day transactions such as balance enquiries, electronic payment of bills, or a transfer of funds between accounts could all be completed by the same representative, without the customer being transferred. In fact, BRs could handle 85 per cent of the enquiries. Some BRs were accredited to deal with more complicated Visa card or foreign currency requests.

For more specialized information regarding loans, personal insurance, mortgages or investments, BRs transferred customers to telephone advisers within the respective business units. For example, mortgage counsellors were available from 7 a.m. to 12 midnight, seven days a week, for advice on a new mortgage, remortgage or a home improvement loan. A mortgage application could be completed over the phone. Additionally, an experienced group of BRs manned what was called an overnight 'mushroom squad' to answer any type of customer enquiry in any business area.

Telecaster screens suspended from the ceilings in each department signalled the number of calls waiting, the average length of the wait, and the current service level expressed as a percentage. To meet minimum service objectives, 75 per cent of all calls had to be answered within 20 seconds or less. If callers were put on hold for more than two minutes, BRs apologized and arranged a call-back. The bank recorded customer calls to safeguard against transaction errors. As much as possible was done via the phone, but for legal reasons it was sometimes necessary to complete written documents after the phone had been put down.

Although no one at First Direct dealt with customers face-to-face, the employees elected to wear business dress to convey a sense of professionalism. The 1,200 banking representatives (50 per cent of the total staff) formed the customer's overall impression of the company. Bringing with them their own experience as bank customers, BRs strove to be flexible enough to accommodate those customers who complained that the bank's rigid systems did not always meet their needs. When things went wrong, BRs tried to go overboard to recover customers.

At First Direct there was no such thing as a normal workday. Workweeks varied between 16 and 36 hours and there was no premium paid for night or weekend shifts. Full-time BRs worked a 36-hour week with a 10-minute break every two hours and a half-hour lunch break. The 1996 television advertising campaign put pressure on the call centre not only from increased enquiries but also by increasing the average call length of existing customers from three to three and a half minutes. Some telephone advisers were more than willing to work overtime, often putting in 14-hour shifts and taking over 200 calls in a day. (Overtime was paid at one and a quarter times the hourly rate.) Although the staffing was based on sophisticated forecasts, an additional 30 seconds spent with each of First Direct's 32,000 daily callers was likely to jam the call centre. Newman recognized that working in the call centre was a tough job:

> Calls come in incessantly, one after another. So, after having answered 150 calls it is difficult to keep the momentum going and to be sincerely friendly on the phone especially when handling tedious transactions. But our business is built on how the next call is answered. The biggest part of my leadership role is to enable a culture which allows people to feel very positive about their contribution to our business so that they may deliver genuine smiles over the phone. This cannot be obtained by *telling* people to do so; they can only do it because they believe it.

The commercial department's principal function was data management geared at building a one-to-one customer relationship. Database specialists fed information to the new product development team and the communications team to jointly determine and optimize marketing strategies. The Management Information Database (MIND) software combined transactional information with behavioural data to predict the next product a customer was likely to purchase. This database prompted BRs to cross-sell other financial services when clients called with routine requests and also helped personalize their conversations with customers:

Sylvia (BR):	Hello, First Direct. How may I help you?
Mr Scott (Customer):	Good evening, I would like to order some US dollars please.
Sylvia:	Your account number please?
Mr Scott:	58-395-123.
Sylvia:	Thank you. Please bear with me while I verify some information for security reasons. Could you please give me the third digit of your password?
Mr Scott:	Five.
Sylvia:	And the date of your wedding anniversary?
Mr Scott:	February 14th.
Sylvia:	Thank you, Mr Scott. How many US dollars would you like to order?
Mr Scott:	It depends, I'm going skiing in the States. Can you tell me if there is a cash machine in Vail, Colorado please?
Sylvia:	I'll need to ask you to hold the line for a minute while I find that information for you sir.
Mr Scott:	Thank you.
Sylvia:	Hello, yes in fact there is a Cirrus ATM machine at the First Interstate Bank at 38 Redbird Drive in Vail.
Mr Scott:	In that case, I'll only take $500 in cash with me and use the cash machine at the resort.
Sylvia:	Right. I'll put in an order for $500. Shall I debit your cheque account and have the currency delivered by registered mail to your home address?
Mr Scott:	Yes, please.
Sylvia:	Thank you sir. You should receive it within three days. We'll include a confirmation of the amount deducted. Have a nice trip!

A few weeks later:

Peter (BR):	Hello, First Direct. How may I help you?
Mr Scott:	Good evening, I would like to make a payment to British Gas please. My account number with First Direct is 58-395-123.
Peter:	Thank you. Please bear with me while I verify some information for security reasons. Could you please give me the first digit of your password please?

Mr Scott: Three.

Peter: And your mother's maiden name?

Mr Scott: Bradford.

Peter: Thank you Mr Scott. I'll be glad to arrange your payment to British Gas. By the way, were you able to find the First Interstate cash machine in Vail when you were on your skiing holiday in Colorado? I hope everything went well.

People and development

First Direct was the largest private employer in Leeds with over 2,400 employees by early 1996; it projected to add an extra 550 by year-end. On average the staff were between 20 and 40 years of age; nearly 69 per cent were women and 24 per cent part-timers (Exhibit 7). Recruitment was carried out continually via a 24-hour phone answering service that provided application information. Two meeting rooms adjacent to the lobby in Arlington were reserved exclusively for interviewing. It was becoming more difficult to recruit telephone advisers because Leeds had become a hub for call centres. (By 1996, there were over 350 24-hour call centres within the United Kingdom in the retailing, banking and utility sectors.) The team leaders who interviewed the 60 BRs hired each month looked for people with a positive attitude who were enthusiastic about joining a first-class organiza-

tion. First Direct also had a reputation for providing comprehensive training and a benefits package that included a mortgage subsidy, a pension scheme and 27 vacation days (Exhibit 8).

Recruited from a non-banking background, BRs did not come into contact with customers until they had successfully completed a seven-week training course conducted by 20 in-house trainers. Four weeks were devoted to understanding the bank's products and communication systems. They also practised telephone techniques such as voice projection skills to regulate the pitch and volume vital to create trust and confidence. The last three weeks concentrated on role-playing to build excellent listening skills and the ability to access and input data accurately and efficiently. Only a small part of the customer interaction was scripted for the beginning and end of conversations. Banking representatives were encouraged to use what they thought were the right phrases, given the nature of the rapport. To become a full-fledged BR required passing a total of 54 internal accreditation tests over the first nine months of employment (Exhibit 9).

All the BRs were assigned to teams of individuals working the same shift pattern. A team leader acted as a coach and watched the customer service screens to make sure that everything ran smoothly and to identify any members who might need assistance. A

Exhibit 7 ■ First Direct workforce profile

Sex	%	Status	%	Age	%	Service length	%
Male	31	Full-time	76	<20	1	<1 yr	22
Female	69	Part-time	24	20–25	29	1 yr	22
				26–30	26	2 yr	16
				31–35	20	3 yr	14
				36–40	14	4 yr	7
				41–45	6	>5 yr	19
				46–50	3		
				>50	1		

Source: First Direct Workforce Profile, May 1996.

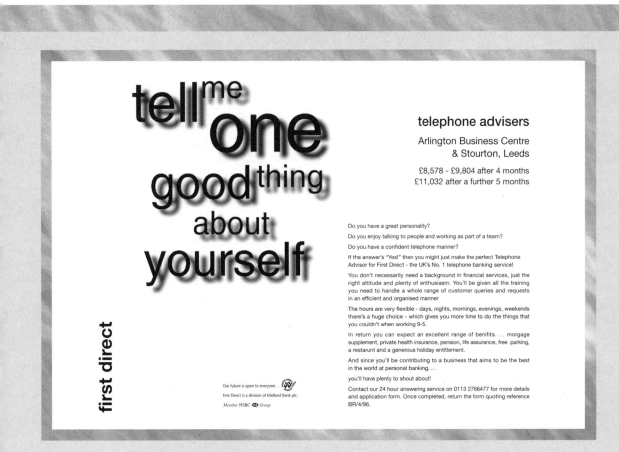

Exhibit 8 ■ Banking representative recruitment advertising

lengthy call was a clear signal of a customer problem or complaint. There were over 100 teams in the two call centres with names like 'Vernon's Vikings', 'JJ and the Dinos', and 'Hard Time Lovers'. Sales competitions, product awareness sessions and theme days were organized regularly between the teams to bond people together.

The level of basic pay related to the market and to individual acquisition and development of skills rather than to the pay and grading structures of traditional banks. Annual appraisal ratings determined the level of performance bonuses that could go as high as 5 per cent of annual salary. Each year, nearly 30 per cent of the BR staff moved to other departments such as lending services or mortgages. It took about 18 months to learn the job and to get to know the company before applying for other jobs. Such career opportunities helped keep turnover low at 11 per cent. In 1996, 40 per cent of the employees had been with the firm for at least three years.

First Direct's facilities reflected the needs of a 24-hour workforce. A private security firm manned the entrance to the car parks and reception areas throughout the night. The company restaurant served breakfast, lunch and dinner from 7 a.m. to 9 p.m. seven days a week while vending machines made hot and cold drinks available free of charge around the clock. Daycare centres at both Arlington and Stourton looked after 150 small children.

Marketing strategy

Management did not foresee telephone-only banking as having universal appeal. In fact, First Direct

Exhibit 9 ■ First Direct training programmes

Customer service	Duration
Account operating	7 weeks
Back office	1 day
Customer development	1 day

Team leader development programme	Duration
Coaching & feedback	2 days
Motivation	2 days
Effective team leading	3 days
Time and priority management	2 days

Formal training for managers	Duration
Counselling skills	2 days
Developing your team	2 days
Influencing & assertion	2 days

Miscellaneous formal training courses	Duration
Presentation skills	1 day
Written communication skills	1 day
Interview skills	2 days
Appraisal skills	2 days

Source: First Direct, Training & Development Guide, May 1996.

estimated that telephone banking would ultimately attract up to 10 million of the UK's 36 million bank customers. Most First Direct customers were between 25 and 44 years of age, living in metropolitan areas and working as professionals, managers or in high-grade clerical positions. Research also showed that about 50 per cent of its customers owned personal computers – twice the market average (Exhibit 10). These busy professionals were attracted by the offer of speed and convenience; their extensive use of the bank's services also generated higher profitability. A *New York Times* journalist estimated:

> The average balance is ten times higher at First Direct than at Midland, while the overall costs are 61% less. Overall, First Direct makes money on 60% of its customers, compared to 40% at the average British bank. (3 September 1995)

First Direct rated several times among the 'Best Buys' of *Which?* magazine's consumer reports on retail banking (Exhibit 11). It also won the 1995 *Unisys/Sunday Times* 'Customer Champion Awards' for outstanding customer service in financial services and as overall winner. The First Direct brand seemed to create a service halo; research showed that First Direct customers had a satisfaction level with the ATM system double that of Midland Bank customers, even though they shared the identical network.

Among its full range of traditional banking services (Exhibit 12), First Direct featured its interest-bearing cheque account that offered an automatic fee-free overdraft facility of £250 and cash withdrawals of £500 a day subject to sufficient funds. However, fees accumulated rapidly if customers exceeded the agreed overdraft. First Direct encouraged customers

Exhibit 10 ■ Comparative customer profiles: First Direct vs. all British banks

	First Direct customers	British bank customers
Age		
15–19	1%	9%
20–24	3%	6%
25–34	33%	20%
35–44	32%	17%
45–54	22%	16%
55–64	9%	13%
65+	0%	19%
Sex		
Male	50%	49%
Female	50%	51%
Socio-economic group		
AB	46%	19%
C1	36%	29%
C2	12%	23%
DE	6%	29%

British socio-economic group definitions

Grade	Social status	Occupation
A	Upper middle class	Higher managerial, administrative or professional
B	Middle class	Intermediate managerial, administrative or professional
C1	Lower middle class	Supervisory or clerical, and junior managerial, administrative or professional
C2	Skilled working class	Skilled manual workers
D	Working class	Semi- and unskilled manual workers
E	Lowest level of subsistence	State pensioners or widows, casual or lowest-grade workers

Sources: (1) First Direct NOP Survey, January 1996; Fieldwork November 1995–January 1996.
(2) The Financial Research Survey NOP, April–September 1996.

to maximize short-term returns by frequently transferring money between their cheque accounts and multiple savings accounts. There were no transaction charges for any of First Direct's basic services. Advertising claimed that the lack of branches enabled it to pass on savings to customers. Even the Visa card was free of annual charges, offering up to 56 days' interest-free credit as well as free travel accident insurance. First Direct was also known to offer better interest rates on mortgages, personal loans and Visa cards (Exhibit 13).

While most UK banks marketed mortgages in the spring or car loans in July, First Direct's approach was to mail customers information only when they needed it. When First Direct added car insurance in March 1995 to complement the life and household insurance products already offered, it adopted a soft-sell approach. BRs were prompted to collect car insurance renewal dates from customers and to record this information on the customer database. As renewal dates approached, customers received a quotation either in the mail or by phone.

Communications strategy

The First Direct brand tried to communicate a no-frills, hassle-free approach to banking more in tune with customers' lifestyles. Matthew Higgins, market planning manager, explained:

> People do not see banks as a fundamental part of their lives. We are trying to market First Direct as a background activity. No bank should be at the top of customers' minds. The whole idea with First Direct is that it is efficient, easy, and available when you want it. You simply tap into it and then you go away and do something more interesting.

		Service avaliabile	Name of service	Cleared balance	Recent transactions	Standing orders	Bill payment	Customer transfer	Transfer to third party
Home-banking systems	**Tone-based and voice-based**								
	Abbey National			✓			13	✓	✓
	Alliance & Leicester Giro		Swiftcheck	✓	12				
	Bank of Cyprus		Cytel	✓					
	Clydesdale		TeleBank Telephone Service	✓			11	✓	✓
	Co-operative		Routine Information Line	✓	see[3]				
	NatWest		Actionline		25	✓	44	✓	✓
	National & Provincial		Tele Banking[4]	✓	5		10	✓	
	Nationwide		Home Banking	✓	6		21		
	Northern Rock		Telephone Banking	✓	5				
	The Royal Bank of Scotland		Direct Banking 'Push Button'	✓	see[5]		No limit	✓	
	Save & Prosper		Serviceline[6]		5				
Home-banking systems	**Operator-based**								
	Abbey National		Telephone Banking	✓	No Limit	see[7]	13	✓	✓
	Alliance & Leicester Giro		Telecare	✓	3 months[8]	✓	No limit	✓	✓
	Alliance & Leicester			✓	3 months[8]	✓	No limit	✓	✓
	Bank of Scotland Centrebank		Banking Direct	✓	3 months	✓	No limit	✓	✓
	Bank of Scotland		Phoneline	✓	3 months	✓	No limit	✓	✓
	Barclays		Barclaycall	✓	3 months	✓	No limit	✓	✓
	Clydesdale		Telephone Centre	✓	4 months	✓		✓	
	Co-operative		Armchair Banking	✓	No limit	✓	No limit	✓	
	First Direct			✓	No limit	✓	No limit	✓	✓
	Lloyds		LloydsLine	✓	see[9]	✓	No limit	✓	✓
	NatWest		Primeline[10]	✓	No limit	✓	No limit	✓	✓
	The Royal Bank of Scotland		Direct Banking	✓	6 months	✓	No limit	✓	
	Save & Prosper		Premier 24 Hour Banking Service[5]	✓	2 years	✓	No limit	✓	
	TSB		PhoneBank	✓	see[11]	✓	99	✓	✓
Systems	**Computer-based**								
	Bank of Scotland and Bank of Scotland Centrebank		HOBS		3 months	✓	No limit	✓	✓
	Clydesdale		TeleBank	✓	250/6 mths	see[7]	No limit	✓	✓
	Nationwide		PC Home Banking	✓	12		21		

1 Calls are on a free-phone number until September 1996, the number after that is not yet established   2 There is also a one-off set-up charge of £10
5 Last six debits or credits, during last six months   6 Minimum opening balance is £2,500 for Premier acc; £1,000 for Classic delay
9 That day's entries and those on the current and previous statements   10 Available only to those earning over £20k pa

Exhibit 11 ■ Home banking systems compared by *Which?* (Consumers' Association)

Source: Which? (May 1996, p. 53), an independent monthly consumer magazine published by Consumers' Association, 2 Marylebone Road, London NW1 4DF

Order statement	Order cheque book	Operating hours		Charges and costs					Other details
		Availability	Service charge	Scenario costs: low user (£)	Scenario costs: medium user (£)	Scenario costs: frequent user (£)	Scenario costs: heavy user (£)		Other information
✓		24 hours		0.59	5.17	14.13	20.33		
✓	✓	24 hours		see[1]	see[1]	see[1]	see[1]		
		24 hours	£10 a year[2]	11.58	21.37	40.64	56.59		Tone only
✓	✓	24 hours		1.58	13.75	36.89	59.22		Tonepad £12
✓		24 hours		0.59	5.17	14.13	20.33		Tone only
✓	✓	24 hours		0.59	5.17	14.13	20.33		
✓		24 hours		1.58	13.75	36.89	59.22		Tonepad £5
✓		24 hours		1.58	13.75	36.89	59.22		Tone only
✓		24 hours		1.58	13.75	36.89	59.22		Tone only, Tonepad £7.99
✓	✓	24 hours		0.59	5.17	14.13	20.33		Tone only
		24 hours							Tone only
✓	✓	Mon-Fri 8am to 9pm Saturday 8am to 4pm		0.59	5.17	14.13	20.33		
✓	✓	24 hours		0.59	5.17	14.13	20.33		
✓	✓	24 hours		0.59	5.17	14.13	20.33		
✓	✓	24 hours		0.59	5.17	14.13	20.33		
✓	✓	24 hours		0.59	5.17	14.13	20.33		
✓	✓	Mon-Fri 7am to 11pm Sat-Sun 9am to 5pm		0.59	5.17	14.13	20.33		
✓	✓	Mon-Fri 8am to 8pm		0.59	5.17	14.13	20.33		
✓	✓	6am to 12am		0.59	5.17	14.13	20.33		
✓	✓	24 hours		0.59	5.17	14.13	20.33		
✓	✓	8am to 10pm		0.59	5.17	14.13	20.33		
✓	✓	24 hours		0.59	5.17	14.13	20.33		
✓	✓	24 hours		0.59	5.17	14.13	20.33		
✓	✓	24 hours		1.58	13.75	36.89	59.22		
✓		24 hours		0.59	5.17	14.13	20.33		
✓	✓	Mon-Fri 6am to 1am Sat-Sun 6am to 12pm	£4 per month	48.59	53.17	62.13	68.33		Screenphone £99 or use your own PC
✓	✓	24 hours	£4 per month[12]	48.59	57.97	76.53	80.33		
✓		24 hours		0.59	5.17	14.13	20.33		

3 The last six debits, three credits   4 The MAX account does not have an overdraft facility
7 You can check standing orders but not change them   8 You can request the last 30 months of transactions, but this will entail a short delay
11 Entries on current statement only   12 There is a charge of 5p per minute, Monday to Friday 8am to 6pm, Saturday 8am to 1pm

Exhibit 12 ■ First Direct products and services

Type	Product	Features
Cheque	Interest-bearing cheque account	Interest-bearing, no fees £250 automatic fee-free overdraft Automatic bill payment
Debit/Credit cards	First Direct Debit Card	£100 cheque guarantee card £500 daily cash withdrawals from 7,000 ATMs Access to Switch* network Access to Cirrus and Maestro ATM network
	VISA Card	No annual fee 56-day interest-free credit £500 daily cash withdrawals Membership Visa points programme
Savings & Investments	High Interest Savings Account (HISA) 60-day accounts	Unlimited withdrawals Minimum deposit £2,500 60-day notice for withdrawals
	Fixed Interest Savings Account Money Market Account Tax Exempt Savings Account (TESSA) Personal Equity Plan (PEP) Share dealing Direct Interest Savings Account Financial planning	– £5,000 minimum deposit – Medium- to long-term tax-free investment Buying or selling on London stock exchange High interest rates paid on balances over £1,000 One free withdrawal or transfer per quarter Personal financial planning advice
Mortgages	Variable rate mortgages Home improvement loans Equity release loan	25-year financing of 80 per cent of purchase price – Financing from £3,000 of 95 per cent of home value
Loans	Flexiloan Personal loan	Rolling loan plan between £500 and £10,000 Variable interest rate –
Insurance	Car insurance Life insurance Home insurance	– – –
Travel services	Foreign currency/Traveller's cheques Travel insurance	Home delivery within 24 hours 12-month individual coverage

* Switch electronic debit card was launched in October 1988 by a consortium of three banks: Midland Bank, National Westminster Bank and Royal Bank of Scotland. It enabled purchases to be paid in supermarkets, petrol stations and shops using the Switch network in the UK.
Source: First Direct brochures, March 1996.

Exhibit 13 ■ Comparative interest rates: First Direct and other British banks

	NatWest	Lloyds	VISA Card Royal Bank of Scotland	Barclays	First Direct
Card	Access/Visa	Access	Visa	Barclaycard	Visa
APR*	22.9%	22%	21.7%	21.6%	19.5%
Annual fee	£12	£12	£10	£10	none

*APR = Annual percentage rate.
Source: First Direct, February 1996.

	NatWest	Alliance & Leicester	Variable Rate Mortgages Halifax	Abbey National	Barclays	First Direct
Interest rate	6.99%	6.99%	6.99%	7.04%	6.99%	6.69%
APR*	7.20%	7.20%	7.20%	7.30%	7.20%	6.90%

*APR = Annual percentage rate.
Source: First Direct, March 1996.

The purpose of First Direct's initial offbeat ad campaign was to break into a sluggish market by getting people to switch banks. This was a challenging task as it was an industry joke that the British were more likely to change their partners than their bankers. The launch advertising helped First Direct stand out in the crowded financial services market. In 1991, First Direct entrusted Chiat Day, a creative American agency, to invest £3 million in television commercials underlining its customers' extraordinary satisfaction with the new telephone bank. Unfortunately, the resulting campaign did not build the brand and First Direct stayed off the air for three years in search of new solutions. The 1995 television campaign also failed to develop the theme of banking and living in harmony.

Between 1991 and 1995, the press was used almost continuously to attract new customers through offers of high-quality service and no fees. As competition intensified, Chiat Day came out in 1993 with a press campaign to differentiate the pioneer from the new players. Simultaneously, First Direct mailed out brochures explaining the mechanics of telephone banking to a broad upscale audience. The mailing combined with the press ads generated an overwhelming number of customer enquiries. Unable to keep up with the demand, First Direct cut short the campaign so as not to compromise service quality.

Finally, in 1996, First Direct turned to WCRS, a major international advertising network, part of the EURO-RSCG group. Their brief revolved around the necessity of developing a more disciplined approach to building the First Direct brand. WCRS had a solid reputation for image development with clients like BMW cars and Orange mobile phones. Not until 1996 did television advertising demonstrate what it meant to bank with First Direct. Back on the air with two six-week bursts between January and April of 1996, the 'Tell me one good thing about your bank' campaign underlined the advantages of First Direct to attract dissatisfied customers from competitors. The £7 million television, radio, press and direct mail campaign raised meaningful brand awareness among the target audience from 30 per cent to 45 per cent (Exhibit 14).

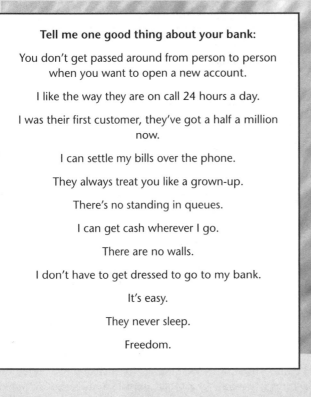

Tell me one good thing about your bank:

You don't get passed around from person to person when you want to open a new account.

I like the way they are on call 24 hours a day.

I was their first customer, they've got a half a million now.

I can settle my bills over the phone.

They always treat you like a grown-up.

There's no standing in queues.

I can get cash wherever I go.

There are no walls.

I don't have to get dressed to go to my bank.

It's easy.

They never sleep.

Freedom.

Exhibit 14 ■ First Direct television advertising slogans, 1996 campaign

Source: First Direct 1996 television campaign – each spot (from 10 to 20 seconds) featured one of the above slogans as a response to 'Tell me one good thing about your bank'.

Management style, organization and culture

In February 1996, Newman restructured the business into five units that operated as profit centres: banking, savings and investments, lending, insurance and mortgages. Product management moved out of the commercial department into integrated operational units at the heart of the business. With this structure each business could eventually acquire customers directly. All the business unit heads reported to Richard Rushton who also managed the banking unit directly – including the call centre, the new customer team, customer service relations and enquiries, customer service support and business planning. All the central support functions such as IT, finance, operations, commercial, credit services and personnel and training were outside this structure.

Known for its leading edge management practices, First Direct attracted top quality managers. Only 50

per cent came from a banking background. Six directors reported to Newman: commercial, customer and financial services, information technology, personnel, finance, and credit services (Exhibit 15). Their principal task was to develop strategy and people through coaching, while Newman dealt directly with their subordinates on business issues. Thirty distinct roles were key within the organization, where individual accountability and competence were far more important than titles or functions. Although First Direct ran a business around the clock, most managers kept traditional 8 a.m. to 6 p.m. schedules, spending a great deal of time on the floor where they could get first-hand feedback from employees and a feel for service levels. Unlike traditional British banks, everyone was on a first name basis and ate in the same cafeteria. Newman firmly believed in leading by example; the only perk he enjoyed was a company car.

The corporate mission statement greeted all employees as they entered the lobby at each site:

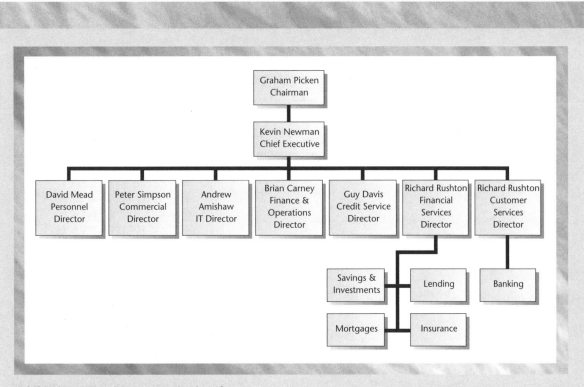

```
                          ┌─────────────────┐
                          │  Graham Picken  │
                          │    Chairman     │
                          └─────────────────┘
                                   │
                          ┌─────────────────┐
                          │  Kevin Newman   │
                          │ Chief Executive │
                          └─────────────────┘
```

Exhibit 15 ■ First Direct organization chart

Source: First Direct, May 1996.

Our mission:	to be the best in the world of personal banking
Pioneering:	the first 24-hour person-to-person telephone bank
Successful:	UK's fastest growing bank with 640,000 customers
Responsive:	the most satisfied bank customers in the UK

First Direct had earlier identified five core business values – responsiveness, openness, right first time, respect and contribution – which were a fundamental part of the training programme and widely shared by employees. This mindset made employees feel part of something special and it was reflected in the image projected to customers over the phone. In 1996 a sixth core value, '*kaizen*', or continuous improvement, was added following the suggestion of a new management hire. To get the entire organization focused on continuous innovation, the internal communications specialist launched a theme day during which the building was decorated in '*kaizen* yellow' and everyone wore T-shirts that they had decorated with coloured pens to express their own creativity.

The challenges ahead

In only seven years, First Direct had made a significant impact on the industry and had become a worldwide reference for telephone banking. By 1996, most banks and building societies offered their customers some form of direct access. Direct Line insurance had broadened its offering to include lending, mortgages and savings products to its two million policy-holders. Furthermore, competition was now by no means restricted to banks, building societies or insurance companies. Richard Branson's Virgin Direct, launched in March 1995, subsequently introduced savings plans and low-cost life insurance via the telephone. Even the retailing chain Marks & Spencer offered life insurance from early 1995 (Exhibit 16).

Exhibit 16 ■ Sample of direct financial services across the globe

Country	Bank	Service	Launched	Description
France	Paribas	Banque Directe	March 1994	Full service telephone banking with 30 operators
	Credit Commercial de France	Videocompte	1983	Originally add-on videotext service, eventually offered phone-based vocal access, customer advisers and PCs
	Compagnie Bancaire	Cortal	1984	Stand-alone home banking offering videotext access, phone-based vocal system and customer advisers
	Credit Mutuel Bretagne	Citelis	1995	Web site home banking
Germany	Commerzbank	Comdirect	February 1995	Add-on full service telephone banking via operators and inter-active voice response
	Citibank	CitiDirect	September 1995	Add-on full service telephone banking via 100 operators
Netherlands	Nederlanse Credietbank	DirektBank	1981	Stand-alone telephone bank with small telemarketing staff
Portugal	Banco Commercial Portugues	Banco 7	1994	Stand-alone full service telephone banking via telephone operators
Spain	Banco Santander	Open Bank	April 1995	Spain's first stand-alone telephone bank
	Argenteria Group	Bex Banco Directo		
Sweden	Skandia	Skandia Bank	October 1994	Stand-alone telephone bank using an interactive voice recognition system and a few agents
Middle East	National Bank of Kuwait	Watani National Phone Bank	August 1990	Add-on telephone service via interactive voice response system
Brazil	Banco 1	Unibanco		Stand-alone full service telephone banking service answered by managers
USA	Wells Fargo	Person-to-Person	1988	Add-on 24-hour customer service with operators
	Chase Manhattan	Chase Direct		Add-on service
	First Chicago Bank	First Direct		Add-on service
	Huntington Bancshares	Huntington Direct		Stand-alone full service telephone banking via operators and interactive video kiosks

Source: Data gathered from various publications.

First Direct was constantly faced with the predicament of not compromising on service and price so as not to lose those customers who complained that it had grown too quickly. Yet to meet the objective of one million customers by the year 2000, First Direct needed to sign on another 400,000 people. Furthermore, First Direct recognized that its management methods might not necessarily be appropriate in the future. Management wondered how to keep all the strengths of the business and its innovative culture as, over the next five years, it grew to 10,000 employees located at four or five sites.

Critics charged that First Direct had not kept up with banking technology as it did not offer an on-line home banking service. This additional channel would provide increased convenience to customers while further reducing transaction costs. A significant minority of First Direct customers had spontaneously requested PC access to their accounts. Although the HSBC Group signed a deal with Microsoft in late 1995, First Direct did not expect to offer an on-line banking service until 1997. Newman explained his perspective:

> The mode of distribution is changing – at the moment we definitely see it as person-to-person over the telephone. Do we believe that people will bank electronically over the next ten years? We are not fussed about how quickly or by which means our customers choose to access all or part of their banking electronically. The elements for us are: when they do so what is the role of a bank, and how do we deliver competitive advantage in this environment? We must always remember that our 'moments of truth' are the telephone contacts with the Banking Representatives. With PC access this disappears, thus limiting our opportunities. Creating value in an electronic world will be a key issue for First Direct. We like to think that we are not really in banking but distribution. We just happen to supply financial products.

Federal Express: quality improvement programme

Creating value and building barriers to competition

Christopher H. Lovelock

The most innovative company in express shipments faces a very competitive marketplace. To maintain its lead, Federal Express has developed an intensive quality improvement programme, involving active participation of employees. But this is expensive to implement and, with profits declining, a senior vice president wonders how to maintain future investment in the programme.

'The first year of our quality improvement programme was really a great success. But the last six months have been tough,' said Thomas R. Oliver, shaking his head ruefully. Oliver, senior vice president, sales and customer service, was talking about some of the challenges facing Federal Express as it sought to maintain momentum on quality improvement efforts in early 1990.

> Last August, we merged with Flying Tigers, which has proved to be more difficult than anyone anticipated in terms of impacting service. In September, Hurricane Hugo, perhaps the most powerful storm of the century, disrupted our operations in the south-eastern United States. Then there was the San Francisco earthquake in October. In December, the Mount Redoubt volcano in Alaska began erupting a huge ash cloud, which totally dislocated our international flights through Anchorage. That volcano's still erupting on and off. The Friday before Christmas, the coldest weather seen in Memphis in the past 50 years caused burst water pipes and a computer foul-up that shut down our Superhub sorting operation. And now we're facing a profit crunch. Our revenues are way up, but we've incurred very heavy costs from the Tiger purchase and the continued expansion of our international operations.

Oliver pushed the company newspaper *Update* across the table. 'Earnings drop; costs to be controlled,' read the headline. He explained that Federal's third quarter profits for fiscal year (FY) 1990 were down by 79 per cent to $5.2 million on revenues of $1.7 billion (up 35 per cent over last year). Then he added:

> A going concern that is doing reasonably well but not making the desired level of profit can experience a big courage gap on the quality issue. People know what it costs to train management, to train employees, to continuously train new hires, to give people 'time around the clock' to work quality issues, and to organize the implementation of the various ideas that emerge. Yet, they aren't clear about the benefits. I want to ensure that last year's interest in quality doesn't get pre-empted by this year's interest in cutting costs.

The evolution of a legend

Few companies had achieved legendary status as quickly as Federal Express. People loved to tell stories about the firm, incorporated in 1971 by Frederick W. Smith, Jr., then aged 27. The earliest story told how Smith had sketched out the concept of a national hub-and-spoke airfreight network in a paper written while an undergraduate at Yale. The professor told Smith that his concept was interesting but unfeasible because of competition and regulation, and gave the young man a 'C' grade. But after service in Vietnam, Smith went on to turn his dream into reality, basing the hub in his home town of Memphis, Tennessee.

Development of this material was supported by the Alfred P. Sloan Fellows Program at the Sloan School of Management, Massachusetts Institute of Technology. This case has won a 1993 European Case of the Year prize, awarded by ECCH (European Case Clearing House, Cranfield, UK).

The concept was simple. Federal Express couriers, based in cities around the country, would pick up packages and take them to a local station, from where they would be flown by air to a central hub. Memphis was selected since it was centrally located in the US and airport operations were rarely disrupted by bad weather. At the hub, packages would be unloaded, sorted, reloaded and flown to their destinations, where they would be delivered by couriers driving Federal Express vans. Because of federal regulations, the new airline had to be chartered as an air taxi operator and was restricted to aircraft with a carrying capacity of 7,200 pounds (3.3 tonnes). Initially, Federal flew Dassault Falcons, French-built executive jets converted into mini-freighters.

On an April night in 1973, 14 Falcons took off from cities around the US and flew to Memphis. In total, they carried 186 packages. Not surprisingly, the company lost money heavily in its early years. But aided by aggressive sales and clever advertising, package volume built steadily and by 1976 the firm was profitable. Thereafter, growth in revenues, profits and package volume was rapid (see table below).

With the 1978 deregulation of the airfreight industry (for which Smith had lobbied heavily), Federal went public and bought larger aircraft. Having redefined service as 'all actions and reactions that customers perceive they have purchased', management began a major investment in information technology, creating an online order-entry system known as COSMOS. This was designed to provide superior customer service in the face of increasing competition from UPS, Emery, the US Postal Service and other express delivery firms.

Federal's early advertising slogan 'When it absolutely, positively has to be there overnight' became almost a national byword. By FY 1985, Federal's sales exceeded $2 billion and its advertising jabbed fun at the competition, asking provocatively, 'Why fool around with anybody else?'. Later, to emphasize its role as a tool for JIT (just-in-time) inventory management procedures, the company began using the slogan, 'It's not just a package, it's your business'.

Following the purchase of Flying Tigers in August 1989, analysts forecast that Federal's total revenues for FY 1990 could exceed $7 billion. By now the company was an American institution. Its vans with their distinctive purple, orange and white colours were everywhere; its aircraft could be seen at most airports; and the verb 'to Fedex' (meaning to ship a package overnight) had become as much a generic expression for office workers as the term 'to Xerox'.

For 19 years, Federal Express had had a single leader, its chairman, Fred Smith, who was still only 46 years old. Outside management experts noted that it was unusual for an entrepreneur whose company had grown so large, so fast, to continue to lead the firm. Smith appeared to have a remarkable ability to supply vision, inspire loyalty and create a climate in which innovation and risk taking were encouraged and rewarded. Although the Federal Express Manager's Guide ran to 186 pages, Smith's core philosophy for the corporation was simple:

	Fiscal year ending 31 May					
	1976	1981	1986	1988	1989[1]	1990[2]
Annual revenues ($m)	75	589	2,573	3,883	5,167	7,000
Annual net income ($m)	4	58	132	188	185	110
Average daily express packages (000s)	15	87	550	878	1,059	1,250
Average daily heavyweight vol. (000lbs)[3]	–	–	–	–	4,019	3,300

[1] Includes Tiger International operations for the last four months.
[2] Projections.
[3] 1,000lbs = 0.455 metric tonnes.

Federal Express, from its inception, has put its people first, both because it is right to do so and because it is good business as well. Our corporate philosophy is succinctly stated: People – Service – Profits (P-S-P).

Line haul operations

Federal's operating concept of a hub in Memphis, served by aircraft flying spoke-like routes from cities all around the US, had been only slightly modified over the years. But the technology and scale of the operation had changed dramatically. The sorting facility at Memphis International Airport had been enormously expanded. The Superhub, as it was known, now covered some 23 acres (100,000 m³), consisting of a matrix of 83 conveyor belts moving at right angles to one another. Aircraft arrived at Memphis almost continuously between 11:00 p.m. and 1:15 a.m. Using specially designed equipment, a crew of 14 workers could unload 44,000 pounds (20 tonnes) of freight from a Boeing 727 in 12 minutes.

The freight began its journey through the Superhub on a wide belt, known as the Primary Matrix, moving at 10 mph (16 km/h). Watching the packages rush by on this belt and then be diverted by guide arms into specific sort areas reminded one visitor of seeing a mountain torrent in full flood. Although the sort was assisted by computers, much of the process was labour-intensive and expected to remain so. Once reloaded, the aircraft left Memphis between 2:15 and 3:45 a.m.

Regional domestic sorting facilities had been established; packages travelling between two East coast cities were sorted in Newark, New Jersey, rather than being sent to Memphis, while packages travelling between West coast destinations were sorted in Oakland, California. A second national hub had been opened in Indianapolis, south-east of Chicago. These facilities were served by large trucks as well as by aircraft; packages travelling shorter distances were frequently transported entirely by truck.

Since 1979, Federal had offered service to and within Canada. In 1985, the company inaugurated international service and began to build up a network of routes around the world. A European hub was established in Brussels, the capital of Belgium (and administrative centre of the twelve-nation European Community). Federal planned to build up significant intra-European business as well as transatlantic volume. Overseas expansion was aided by the purchase of existing courier firms in each national market (nine were purchased in FY 1989).

In December 1988, Smith announced what the press described as 'an ambitious and highly risky plan' to pay $895 million for Tiger International, Inc., the world's largest heavy cargo airline, best known for its Flying Tiger airfreight service. Although Tiger had some domestic business, most of its revenues came from international services. The merger was a key step towards realizing Smith's goal of making Federal 'the world's premier priority logistics company'. Six 'Freight Movement Centres' – located in Anchorage, Memphis, Chicago, New York, Brussels and Tokyo – now coordinated Federal's international traffic, which was expected to generate 30 per cent of the firm's revenues in FY 1990.

A major benefit was Tiger's overseas operating rights, including landing rights in Japan. The merger allowed Federal to operate its own aircraft on routes where transportation had formerly been contracted out to other carriers. It also catapulted Federal into the heavy cargo business; previously, the firm had limited most packages to 150 pounds (68 kg) maximum weight, as well as imposing length and girth restrictions. Another important asset was Tiger's fleet of aircraft, including 21 Boeing 747s. However, these benefits came at the cost of taking on significant debt at a time when margins were being squeezed by price competition and heavy upfront costs were being incurred due to overseas expansion. There was also the challenge of merging two sharply different corporate cultures.

The scope of the operation in 1990

By 1990, Federal Express was one of the world's largest airlines, with a fleet of some 350 aircraft. This fleet comprised 170 trunk line aircraft (21 Boeing 747s, 25 McDonnell-Douglas DC-10s, 118 Boeing 727s, and 6 DC-8s) and another 180 feeder aircraft used for shorter-distance operations. The firm served 119 countries and had 1,530 staffed facilities worldwide. Some four-fifths of its 86,000 employees were based in the United States, including 17,300 employees in Memphis. Federal operated over 20,000 vans and almost 2,000 large trucks in the US, plus another 6,300 vehicles in international locations.

A visitor to Memphis might be surprised to see a large fleet of snowploughs and other snow-removal vehicles sporting Federal Express colours. The company had purchased this equipment in 1988 after a heavy snowstorm – unusual for Memphis which had almost no snow removal equipment – had badly disrupted operations one night. 'We only need this equipment about one night every two years,' explained a company official. 'But when we need it, we really need it!'

The average daily volume for express packages (up to 150 pounds in the US) was around 1.25 million. Federal's average package weighed 5.4 pounds (2.5 kg) and yielded a revenue of over $16; a significant price increase would take effect on 1 April 1990. Document shipments weighing just a few ounces (100–200g) had a declining share of package volume; the Fedex Overnight Letter represented 37 per cent of all express packages in FY 1989, down from 40 per cent two years earlier. The company offered three levels of delivery speed in the United States: Priority Overnight (next business morning by 10:30 a.m. in most locations); Standard Overnight (next business day for shipments of five pounds or less, with delivery before 3:00 p.m. in most locations); and Standard Air (second business day). Federal's rates tended to be more expensive than most of its US competitors.

For heavyweight shipments, the average daily volume was around 5,000 units. These shipments weighed an average of almost 800 pounds (360 kg) each – some were so large that they required an entire aircraft – so they were handled separately from the normal hub sorting operations. The revenue for each shipment ranged widely but the average was around $850.

The express package industry was consolidating and the company's chief operating officer, James L. Barksdale, described the challenge facing its 1,300 sales professionals: 'We're in a tough business. Our competitors are tough, mean, go-getting folks. They are not a bunch of idiots. I wish they were.' Within the US, the key players were Federal Express (with about 45–50 per cent of the market), UPS (15 per cent), Airborne (10–15 per cent), Emery/Purolator (5 per cent), US Postal Service (10 per cent) and others (5 per cent). Federal had purchased Purolator's Indianapolis hub. Overseas, Federal faced UPS, Emery, DHL and Australian-owned TNT, plus the express divisions of national postal services and airline freight and package services.

Information technology

For Federal Express, information about each package was seen as just as important as the package itself. Information also played a key role in achieving the most effective utilization of the entire physical operation. Dr Ron J. Ponder, senior vice president for information and telecommunications, described the line-haul operations (package sorting and transportation) as one of several parallel fibres running through the entire business. The others included a series of major information networks. 'We run three data processing houses at Federal,' explained Ponder, a former business school professor. 'There are the traditional, commercial revenue systems that every company has; a line-haul flight operations system that is unique to airlines; and COSMOS, our customer service house.'

To me, quality is everything we do. Our goal for availability – communication and systems – is 99.8 per cent. We've cranked that up during the last ten years from about 88 per cent. Each year, we keep raising the bar. We're running some of the highest systems availability numbers in North America. Most companies are happy at 95 per cent or 96 per cent.

Our computer centre is now one of the largest in the world under one roof, and we have the highest transaction rates of any shop in North America on a daily basis. Last month, we had 320 million transactions from all over the world go through our computer systems. We measure each one of them. Less than 86,000 exceeded our standard internal compute time of one second, which you have to have to run these massive parallel systems. Each morning at 8:30, we have a conference call in this division with perhaps 50 people in on it. We start off with any problems we've had in the last 24 hours.

In addition to overseeing the systems, I do the strategic architectural planning that lets this company use technology to the greatest possible advantage for customer satisfaction and competitive superiority, and for reducing operational costs to improve productivity.

Ponder believed that Federal Express had a sharply different view of technology from most companies.

Technology transfer – or being able to absorb new technology – is a cultural thing that we've built in here. One of the keys to our success is that we constantly embrace new technology. For most companies, that's very painful and they don't like it. It's painful to leave what works and is cheap for new, expensive, unknown approaches. So they don't do it. At Federal, we would rather get an innovation a year earlier and develop back-up systems to counter a relatively high failure rate than to wait until the failure rate – and the price – have been reduced to more 'acceptable' levels. Most folks prefer to wait until a technology matures.

You can view technology as a wave in the ocean, washing in debris. Most people concentrate on the debris that floats in. 'Oh, isn't this neat!' they'll say of some device. 'Where can I use it?' And that's where I think they mess up. I view technology as the wave itself, not the individual things that are brought to shore. We knew what we wanted to do ten years ago but the technology wasn't there. So we were waiting for the wave and constantly prodding manufacturers to create what we needed as that wave rolled in.

Asked what new waves Federal Express was watching, Ponder listed battery technology, continued miniaturization, the maturing of relational databases (essential to maintaining detailed customer files) and, most importantly, a new generation of computer hardware and software using RISC (Reduced Instruction Set Computing) architecture. The net effect would be more computing power and faster access to information for less money.

COSMOS and DADS

Federal prided itself on having one of the most sophisticated customer service systems in the world.

COSMOS (Customer, Operations, Service, Master On-line System) was first installed in 1979 and had been constantly upgraded to cope with the more than 260,000 calls now received, on average, each working day. COSMOS had evolved into a worldwide electronic network that transmitted critical package information to Memphis. Its major components were an order-entry system for customers to request package pickups, a continuously updated record of each package's progress through the Fedex system that could be used to trace a missing package, financial records for billing purposes, and a huge relational database that could also be used for marketing analysis and planning.

The system worked in much the same way around the world. In the US, customers had a choice between requesting a pickup or, for a reduced fee, of dropping off a package at a drop-box or at one of Federal's business service centres. To request a pickup, customers telephoned a toll-free number that connected to a customer service agent (CSA) at one of 17 call centres around the nation. Calls could be diverted from one centre to another to maintain the company's response-time standards. Since most calls were received in the mid to late afternoon, peak volumes could be shifted to centres in other time zones. The CSA requested the shipper's account number which was entered on an electronic order blank on the video screen. (Refer to Exhibit 1.) Armed with this information, the system automatically provided the CSA with the account name, address, phone number, pickup location, contact name and other relevant data.

An alternative method was to call a special Automatic Pickup number. In response to the promptings of a recorded voice, callers used the buttons on their touch-tone telephones to enter their account numbers and then, as a cross-check, their postal zip code, followed by the number of packages being shipped. The voice would then provide a confirmation number and latest pickup time. These service requests were transmitted automatically to the nearest origin station.

Federal was also testing a custom-designed desktop unit, smaller than a telephone, called 'Hello Federal'.

Customer Information

Location ID _____ Zip Code _____ Pickup Time _____ Cut off _____

Account # _____ Company Name _____

Address _____

City _____ State _____ Type of Account _____

Contact person _____ Phone # _____ Extension _____ Close time _____

Remarks to Courier _____

Local Area Promotions _____

Package Information

Pickup Day _____ Total Packages _____ Total Weight _____ Rate _____

Time Package ready _____ Supplies Requested _____ Commodity Shipped _____

Remarks by CSA _____

Dispatcher's Remarks _____

Dispatcher's # _____ Exceptions _____ Credit Approved _____

Courier's # _____ Time _____ Date _____

Note: The screen display has been clarified and simplified for purposes of case presentation, with abbreviations written out in full.

When a customer called Federal Express, the customer service agent first asked the caller for a Federal Express account number. When this was typed in, most other customer information (other than details of the caller's request , e.g., pickup) was automatically retrieved from the computer's memory and displayed on the screen, from where it could then be verified with the caller.

Exhibit 1 ■ Contents of Federal Express dispatch request screen

This device had a full alpha-numeric keypad, an adjustable LCD screen, and buttons to press for pickup, package tracing information, and requests for airbills and packaging. The requested information was displayed on the screen; no voice communication was needed. Since each unit was programmed with the shipper's account number, it was not necessary to provide account identification when calling. If the tests proved successful, the company planned to offer a 'Hello Federal' unit free to any customer shipping a predefined volume of packages three or more days per week.

Once a pickup request was received, the CSA entered shipping information through COSMOS to alert the dispatch centre nearest to the pickup location. The message was received by the dispatch centre's DADS (Digitally Assisted Dispatch System) computer which, in turn, sent the information to a courier. The request was displayed on a small DADS video screen in the courier's van or on a portable unit the size of a slim briefcase used by walking couriers.

One customer, a management consultant working out of a home office, testified to the efficiency of the system:

> It was only the second time that I had used the Automatic Pickup service and I still didn't have 100% confidence in it, but I knew that it was a little faster than talking to a CSA in a call centre and I was in a hurry. I had just finished a report for one client and was about to leave for the airport on a visit to another client. So I sealed up the report, phoned for a cab, and then called the Automatic Pickup number to place my order. The taxi arrived in five minutes, which was pretty good. As I was getting into the cab, what should roll up but the Federal Express van to pick up my package. I was so astonished that I got out of the cab and asked the courier how he had arrived so quickly. 'I was driving on the next street,' he said, 'when your request came up on my screen.'

Tracking the package through the Federal Express system

Each airbill contained a unique 10-digit bar code label which was scanned by an infrared light pen every time the package changed hands. The first scan, known as PUPS (Pick Up Package Scan), took place at the pickup location. Using a hand-held terminal called a COSMOS IIB SuperTracker (a little bigger than the remote control for a TV set), the courier scanned the bar code and then entered on a key pad the type of service, handling code and destination zip code. The SuperTracker recorded this information, added the time of pickup, and responded on its LCD display with a routeing and sorting code which the courier then handwrote on the package. Dr Ponder noted, 'Miniaturization has

enabled us to stretch the communications system right to the customer's doorstep.'

On returning to the van, the courier plugged the SuperTracker into a shoe within the dispatch computer, which transmitted its information to COSMOS. In many overseas countries, this data transfer took place when the van returned to its station. Once unloaded, each package received a Station Outbound Package Scan (SOPS) before being reloaded into a container for transport to a sorting hub. Any exceptions, such as packages that were damaged or missed the aircraft, received a P.M. eXception (PMX) scan. These data were then transmitted to COSMOS. Similar scans were made at several other points. (Refer to Exhibit 2.)

Finally, at the delivery point, the package received a Proof Of Delivery Scan (PODS). The courier entered the recipient's first initial and last name, as well as a code for delivery location, and the SuperTracker automatically recorded the time. If the package were delivered to an alternative location (for instance, a neighbouring building) or no one was available to accept delivery, it received instead a Delivery EXception (DEX) scan and full details were entered.

The records provided by these scans enabled Federal to offer full custodial care of all packages. A trace of a missing package would reveal in seconds the time and location of the latest scan. No competitor could match this level of tracing capability. Said Ponder, 'The notion of picking up and delivering a package without being able to offer the customer total information on it is totally unacceptable to us.'

Automated systems for high-volume customers

Federal had formed a team called Customer Automation to assist customers in managing their shipments more effectively. The result was a family of automated shipping and invoicing systems designed to reduce paperwork and tie the company more closely to its large volume customers.

Tape Invoice offered customers a weekly invoice on magnetic tape, instead of paper. By running the invoice tape on the computer, customers could

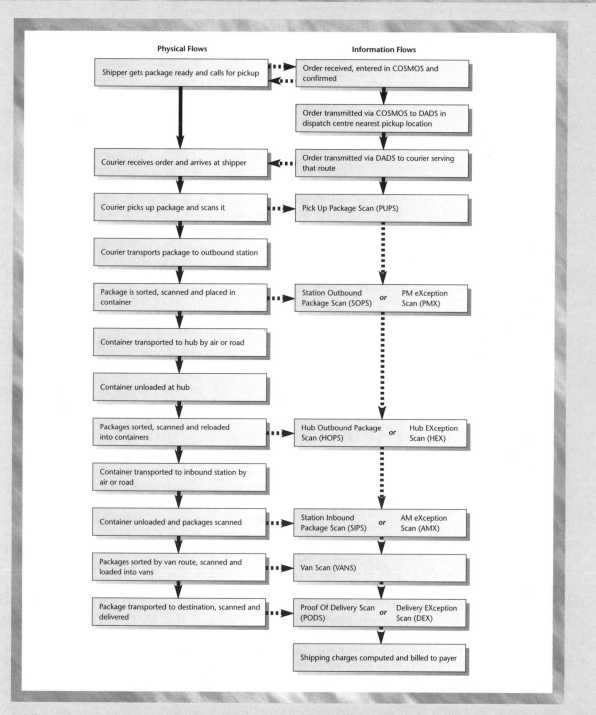

Exhibit 2 ■ Physical flows and information flows for Federal Express packages

analyze Federal Express shipping information any way they wished. Such data could be fed directly into the firm's accounting system.

Powership 2 was a shipment management system that streamlined package preparation and billing. Federal provided customers with an electronic weighing scale, microcomputer terminal, bar code scanner and printer at no charge; all the customer paid was telephone charges. The system eliminated the need for airbills and express manifests, and could be programmed to store up to 32,000 recipient names and addresses. The printer could generate barcoded address labels. Powership 2 rated packages with the right charges, automatically combining package weights by destination to provide volume discounts. Daily invoices could be prepared automatically, as could customized management reports. Customers could trace their own packages through COSMOS.

Powership Plus allowed customers to link their computers with Federal Express's tracking and invoicing systems. If the package weight were known (which was true for many mail order items) users could quote shipping rates, delivery schedules and tracking numbers to their own customers at the very time they entered purchase order. Next, they transmitted information directly to the warehouse, where the barcoded address label could be printed and applied. When each night's shipping was complete, users would transmit their shipping data to Federal. At the end of the week, they would send Federal Express a computer tape containing the week's shipping data, plus a cheque for the total shipping charges.

New quality initiatives

Quality had been implicit in Federal's efforts from the beginning. In 1975, its advertising claimed 'Federal Express. Twice as Good as the Best in the Business' (a slogan comparing Federal's performance against its then leading competitor, Emery Air Freight). The firm's emphasis on reliability was captured in its classic slogan, 'Absolutely, Positively Overnight'. Management had long recognized the connection between doing things right the first time and improving productivity: 'Q = P' (quality equals productivity) was the internal rallying cry.

Employee orientation

As chairman, Fred Smith constantly set goals of improving reliability, productivity and financial performance to promote the corporate imperative of People – Service – Profits. Particular attention was paid to leading and motivating employees. Regular communication with employees had always been a corporate priority. As the company grew in numbers and geographic scope, increasing reliance came to be placed on the use of videotaped messages for both communication and training. In 1987, Federal launched FXTV, a real-time business television network broadcasting daily by satellite to over 700 locations in the US and Canada from studios in Memphis. Satellite hook-ups with overseas locations were arranged for special occasions. Each month, FXTV produced about 20 hours of broadcast TV, plus 10–15 hours of videotape.

Since 1985, a confidential employee survey had been conducted annually called Survey Feedback Action (SFA). It consisted of 26 statements with which the employee was asked to agree or disagree on a five-point scale ranging from 'strongly agree' to 'strongly disagree'. Scores were reported for employee work groups not for individuals. The first ten questions (refer to Exhibit 3) related to employees' views of their managers. The percentage of favourable responses on these items constituted what was known as the SFA Leadership Index.

The full SFA Index represented the percentage of positive responses on all 26 items, including questions on pay, working conditions, views on senior management, and feelings about the company. Other companies administered the same survey, so scores could be compared with those from employees in other firms. Federal had consistently obtained above-average ratings.

In 1983, Smith initiated 'Bravo Zulu' awards (from the US Navy signal flags for BZ, meaning 'Well done!'), which allowed managers to provide instant recognition to employees for excellent service within the company. Stickers bearing the signal flags could be placed on paperwork or a memo; managers also had authority to issue a Bravo Zulu voucher worth up to $100.

1. I can tell my manager what I think.

2. My manager tells what's expected.

3. Favouritism is not a problem in my work group.

4. My manager helps us do our job better.

5. My manager listens to my concerns.

6. My manager asks for my ideas about work.

7. My manager tells me when I do a good job.

8. My manager treats me with respect.

9. My manager keeps me informed.

10. My manager does not interfere.

Note: The above sentences paraphrase the actual wording used in compiling the Leadership Index. Employees were asked to review each statement carefully and then to express their agreement or disagreement with that statement on a five-point scale.

Exhibit 3 ■ Survey Feedback Action programme: components of Leadership Index

Outstanding examples of customer service were celebrated with Golden Falcon awards, consisting of a gold pin and ten shares of Federal Express stock (worth about $500 in early 1990). About 20 such awards were made each year. Nominees were often identified by customer calls or letters; a typical example might concern extraordinary effort in tracking down and delivering a missing package. Golden Falcon and Bravo Zulu awards, and the stories behind them, were publicized to motivate employees and create corporate legends.

An unsuccessful first look at quality training

It was not until 1985, when Smith and senior officers became concerned about a possible slowdown in the business and decline in profitability, that the company first addressed quality improvement techniques at the corporate level. Smith hired a consultant to conduct an off-site meeting with top management, but it was not a success. As Tom Oliver recalled, 'Everyone walked away with a calculator and a statistics book, but our interest had not been captured.' Some improvements were made, but the idea lost momentum. Smith was soon preoccupied with the problems of ZapMail, the company's same-day facsimile service, which was discontinued in 1986 with a write-off of some $360 million – the company's first major setback since its start-up days.

Two and a half years passed, during which the feared slowdown was replaced by a period of explosive growth. By mid-1987, the sales and customer service division was struggling with service problems that were becoming increasingly serious as the company continued to expand. As senior vice president of the division, Oliver decided it was high time to re-explore the quality issue.

Working with ODI

Disappointed with the previous statistically based approach to quality improvement, Oliver selected Organizational Dynamics, Inc. (ODI), an international consulting firm headquartered in Burlington, Massachusetts. ODI's great advantage, from Oliver's perspective, was that it paid little attention to statistical techniques but a lot more to the thought processes and involvement of people within the company in developing quality programmes.

ODI began by designing and leading quality planning workshops for senior executives from all divisions. The product of each workshop was a series of action plans, setting priorities for problems needing resolution. Next, ODI focused on the sales and customer service division. Under the leadership of ODI vice president Rob Evans, the consultants trained all managers in the division to understand the quality process, then began training employees and creating quality action teams. ODI also trained facilitators from other divisions, including ground operations. A key goal was to get people to analyze what were often complex problems, rather than shooting from the hip with instant solutions. Different versions of the programmes were developed for managers and employees.

The Quality Advantage Program began with a module on 'The Meaning of Quality', introducing five pillars on which a quality organization must be built:

- Customer focus – a commitment to meeting customer needs;
- Total involvement– 'improving quality is everyone's job';
- Measurement – where and when to take action; documenting progress;
- Systematic support – applying strategic planning, budgeting and performance management to quality improvement efforts;
- Continuous improvement – always reaching for new and better ways to perform one's job.

'The Cost of Quality' module identified the costs of not doing quality work – rework, waste, unnecessary overtime and job dissatisfaction. The goal was to help participants estimate their own cost of quality, break this down into avoidable and necessary costs, and then plan ways to reduce avoidable costs. The third module, 'You and Your Customer', described the customer–supplier chain and helped participants to see that everyone in Federal Express was both a customer and a supplier. Participants learned to identify their own key customers and suppliers within the company, as well as how they were linked, and then to align customer needs and supplier capabilities in order to meet agreed requirements.

The 'Continuous Improvement' module emphasized that it was everyone's responsibility to fix and prevent problems, showed how to identify early warning signals, and required that everyone strive to meet customer needs in innovative ways. The fifth module, 'Making Quality Happen', was directed at managers, supervisors and professionals; it described how to take a leadership role to implement quality programmes.

A separate programme, Quality Action Teams (QATs), focused on how to implement quality improvement. ODI taught a problem-solving process consisting of four phases: focusing on a particular problem or opportunity, analyzing data, developing solutions and action plans, and executing plans for implementing

solutions. To help the QATs perform each of these tasks, ODI taught participants how to apply 20 problem-solving tools, including fishbone analysis, flowcharting and cost–benefit analysis.

Setting goals for people – service – profits

By June 1988 (the beginning of fiscal year 1989), Oliver had concluded that to make quality improvement work for customer service, it was critical to involve domestic ground operations. Most problems at Federal were cross-divisional in nature, in the sense that one division created a certain output and passed it on to the next one. That next division's problems were often directly related to what had happened earlier up the line. Commenting on this, Oliver noted:

> We were able to put across the idea that one of the big difficulties in getting cross-divisional cooperation was the multiplicity of different goals. These goals might individually maximize the performance of each division, but collectively resulted in a deterioration of performance for the system. We realized that the more each unit tried to maximize its own performance, the more it tended to send difficult problems downstream. So we concluded that what we needed for Federal Express were three very simple goals.

First, we took the existing SFA Leadership Index. The leadership a manager provides has a tremendous impact on the positive attitudes of the employees. We determined to use this index as the single goal in our people management process and established a goal of 72 for FY 1989, up from 71 the previous year.

People – Service – Profits implied a profit goal, so we set a goal of a 10 per cent operating margin on the domestic business. That goal was irrespective of individual department performance. Service had historically been defined in terms of couriers' on-time delivery efforts, what percentage of packages were delivered by 10:30 a.m. There were a lot of problems with that service level measure: specifically, we could get that package delivered by 10:30 a.m. on the wrong date! It was also a limited measure, suggesting that Federal could be successful simply by delivering packages on time. That was no longer true!

We found that the information associated with packages had as much to do with customer satisfaction as did delivery. For instance, 'don't know' answers to questions upset customers. As we reviewed customer correspondence, we found that the angriest of all the letters we got were those where our information processes failed us as opposed to those where we didn't deliver on time. What was needed was a broader measure that also addressed other shortcomings that upset customers, such as failure to answer the phone quickly, damaged packages, etc.

ODI stressed the danger of using percentage as targets. In an organization as large as Federal Express, delivering 99 per cent of packages on time or having 99.9 per cent of all flights land safely would still lead to horrendous problems. Instead, they approached quality from the standpoint of zero failures. Oliver emphasized:

It's only when you examine the types of failures, the number that occur of each type, and the reasons why, that you begin to improve the quality of your service. For us, the trick was to express quality failures in absolute numbers. That led us to develop the Service Quality Index or SQI, which takes each of 12 different events that occur every day, takes the numbers of those events and multiplies them by a weight from one to ten points, based on the amount of aggravation caused to customers – as evidenced by their tendency to write to Federal Express and complain about them. Fred Smith calls it our 'hierarchy of horrors'.

The SQI, pronounced 'sky', was computed as a daily average. (Exhibit 4 shows its 12 components.) Like a golf score, the lower the index, the better the performance. Based on internal records, it was calculated that the average score during FY 1988 (which ended on 31 May 1988) would have been 152,000 points per day – out of a potential maximum of 40 million per day if everything possible had gone wrong. The goal set for FY 1989 was the same – 152,000 points – but since package volumes were expected to rise by 20 per cent, this goal actually represented a 20 per cent improvement. Employees were urged to 'Reach for the SQI!'.

To reinforce the significance of these three corporate-wide goals, senior management tied the entire management bonus process to achievement of the three goals. Simply put, there would be no bonus for any manager at the end of FY 1989 unless the company achieved all three goals. 'Needless to say, that caught everyone's imagination.' Oliver smiled wryly and continued:

It was very different from our previous approach of having managers' bonuses based on their ability to meet individual management-by-objective goals without regard to whether that did or didn't help the corporate process. In the actual unfolding, fiscal year 1989 turned out to be the best year we had had in a long, long time. We achieved the profit goal despite some difficult circumstances, and the SQI came in at 133,000 points. The Leadership Index reached 76. It was the largest single jump in the history of the SFA process, in terms of managers' relationships with employees.

ODI's Evans believed that one reason for the SQI successes was that Federal had set up 12 QATs, each of which focused on a specific SQI category. As CEO, Fred Smith provided active support and encouragement. Most teams were headed by a vice president. Results were posted weekly, and every three months each QAT reported out to Smith, Barksdale and other senior executives. Quarterly awards were given in four categories: (1) greatest impact on SQI results; (2) best use of the quality process (using tools that had been taught); (3) best understanding of root causes (identifying and working on underlying problems rather than superficial effects); and (4) best use of line employees (gathering information from the people closest to the process who knew it best).

Activities during FY 1990

While training continued, efforts were made to facilitate a bottom-up movement in quality improvement. John West, manager of quality improvement, saw his job as a catalyst to bring about shared approaches to problem solving. West coordinated training efforts with ODI and had established a network of quality

Exhibit 4 ■ Service Quality Index (SQI): FY 1990 goals vs. actual for first nine months

Beginning in FY 1989, the overall quality of service was measured by the Service Quality Index (SQI). This index, which was based on the findings of extensive customer research, weighted service failures from the customers' perspective and comprised the twelve components shown below.

Failure type	Weighting factor	FY 1990 goals (June 89–May 90) Goal for average daily occurrences	Weighted daily failure points	June 89–Feb 90 Actual average daily failure points
Right day late service failures	1	22,000	22,000	33,561*
Wrong day late service failures	5	11,522	57,606	74,674*
Traces (not answered by COSMOS)	1	4,170	4,170	5,165
Complaints reopened by customers	5	851	4,255	2,330
Missing proofs of delivery (PODs)	1	4,959	4,959	6,260
Invoice adjustments requested	1	12,852	12,852	11,921
Missed pickups	10	152	1,526	1,548
Lost packages	10	72	725	1,102
Damaged packages	10	181	1,815	2,868
Delay minutes/aircraft ('0' based)	5	327	1,635	16,821
Overgoods (no labels)	5	327	1,635	1,788
Abandoned calls	1	4,782	4,782	8,073
Total average daily failure points (SQI)			125,000	166,111

* Estimated
Note: SQI points were reported on a daily basis, as well as on a weekly, monthly or year-to-date daily average.

professionals in each of Federal's ten divisions. These people formed a quality advisory board which met bi-weekly to discuss failures and successes.

One of these professionals was Linda Griffin, senior quality administrator for domestic ground operations, which had 40,000 employees working out of 600 stations. Griffin felt that while the quality programme had enjoyed many 'surface' successes, the challenge was to coordinate the replication of these successes by getting people to describe what they had actually done and how they did it, as opposed to simply talking about the results. Forms and electronic mail systems had been created to make it easy to record this information, while a reward system encouraged people to turn in details of their successes. Said Griffin:

Recognition programmes have a mutual benefit. They motivate and reward employees and create some peer pressure. At the same time, management gets to see the value of the training programmes, which reinforces the belief that training is the right thing to do.

One replicated success concerned a sorting table designed by employees in the Phoenix station to prevent missorts caused by envelopes sliding into the wrong destination pile. They sent a videotape of the table design to the company's industrial engineers, who developed several versions of the sort table for different-sized stations. Couriers in a QAT at another station were frustrated with the problems (such as missed pickups) caused when the regular courier on a route had to be replaced by a substitute unfamiliar with obscure addresses, building entrances, location of freight elevators, and pickup or delivery locations on different floors, etc. So they designed an informational booklet describing each route. The result was a sharp increase in on-time delivery and productivity. This idea had now been incorporated in the 'Policy and Procedures' manual for all stations.

Sharing success stories was seen as a way to get more people involved in QATs and to improve working relations within the company through customer–supplier alignments. West commented:

> People tend to gravitate toward QATS, which are more fun. We really have to push the notion of customer–supplier alignment. People and departments don't always work well together. W. Edwards Deming, the American quality pioneer, claims that about 95 per cent of quality problems are management problems, because of the way the system was designed.

Federal's satellite broadcast network, FXTV, was employed in both a sharing and training role. Rob Evans participated in a programme entitled 'Customer/Supplier Alignment: The First Step in Quality', designed to reinforce earlier quality training. Evans began his segment of the live broadcast by reminding viewers of the 'Right Things Right' grid, a simple four cell matrix developed by ODI.

> That grid is a simple way to look at the work we do from two different angles. The first angle is *how* we do the work we do. We either do things wrong or we do things right. The second angle has to do with *what* work we actually do, doing the right things or the wrong things. When we put these two together, we have four possibilities. We could be doing the right things wrong; that's the old way of looking at quality problems and, of course, that happens. We could be doing the wrong things wrong, really wasting our time. Or we could be doing the wrong things right, things that don't matter to our customers, internal or external, but doing a very good job of them. The fourth possibility is doing right things right. This is the only one that adds value to our customers and our company.

In a quality organization, people spend the great majority of their time doing the right things right. What we've found at ODI is that most managers spend 45–60 per cent of their time doing the right things right, but the rest is wasted – time, effort, money. Of that wasted time, about half seems to fall into the wrong things right category.

Pressures and distractions

Top management was delighted by improvements in SQI and other measures during FY 1989, but then the picture changed dramatically. The average daily SQI goal of 125,000 points for FY 1990 (on a higher package volume) was ravaged by the dislocations of the Tiger merger and a series of natural disasters during the autumn and winter. Mount Redoubt's volcanic ash cloud grounded five of Federal's 747s at the Anchorage hub in Alaska for two days and forced subsequent Far East flights to operate through Seattle, using more fuel and carrying less freight. The computer shutdown at the Memphis Superhub on 22 December resulted in manual sorting, delayed deliveries, and an average daily SQI for that week of 613,842. At the end of February, the year-to-date daily average stood at 166,111.

Meantime, a sharp earnings decline had led to company-wide cost-reduction efforts, including some impacting quality facilitation. Some outside financial analysts had suggested that the company's financial situation made it vulnerable to a takeover. Tom Oliver was very concerned that the momentum of the quality improvement efforts not be lost.

> Most companies need four to five years of continuous effort before employees and managers alike really understand that this is *the* way to approach problems. The fact that we had some initial successes was certainly positive, but by no means have we gotten it to the point where if you scratch an employee, you're going to get a quality-related response. And that's especially true of first-level management who feel tremendous pressure to achieve budget-related financial results.

We've found that the SQI process works really well for the corporation as a whole, but Federal Express doesn't have the ability to develop a precise tracking of these events down to individual locations, so our station-level goals tend to stay related to the service-level measurement (on-time deliveries) instead of the broader SQI perspective. We're trying to work aggressively on measurement systems so that Federal can use that information more precisely in measuring and managing the performance of first-line managers. Feedback is critical in any quality process.

Much remains to be done. But it always comes back to these questions: Is it financially feasible to spend the dollars and take the time to train the people? Will we spend the time and money to let them work the issues after they are trained? Are investments in quality high enough in the corporation's competing priorities? In the sales and customer service division's case, feedback systems require substantial investments in data systems resources. We want to make them, but we're always fighting the allocation process.

Right now, everyone is trying to minimize their own costs and efficiency; in the process, they're sending enormous costs downstream. The tendency in corporate management is to seek good budgets and financial controls for every individual unit in operation. A well-managed corporation has a very strong financial system – but a strong, department-oriented financial system is precisely what you're trying to get around when you're attempting to approach things from a systemic quality and cost viewpoint. You must expend money at the source of the problem to eliminate the waste expenses later in the process. But people won't do it, because they don't get the benefits; some other department and the customers do.

Almost every change we've made in Federal's services has no measurable ROI (return on investment). You cannot, in effect, prove the reductions in cost because they're systemic reductions, as opposed to individual area reductions. In any case, changes in the quality of service impact customer revenues as much as or more than they impact costs. In the final event, one needs to make these decisions based on the impact on customers and on the system, as opposed to precisely measured return-on-investment calculations.

Oliver glanced at the clock. It was almost time for another senior executive meeting on cutting costs. ODI had submitted a proposal for the next phase of the quality training programme, and there were numerous internal projects as well. His best estimate was that future training and other key quality initiatives would, if properly funded, cost as much as $200 per employee in the first year and half of that in subsequent years. 'It all comes down to that courage gap,' he said to himself as he gathered up his papers and strode out of the office.

Index

•••